COME TOGETHER

Come Together

JOHN LENNON IN HIS TIME

Jon Wiener

Random House New York

Library of Congress Cataloging in Publication Data
Wiener, Jon.
Come together.
Bibliography: p.
Includes index.
1. Lennon, John, 1940–   . 2. Rock musicians—
Biography. I. Title.
ML420.L38W5   1984   784.5'4'00924   83-43194
ISBN 0-394-53570-7
ISBN 0-394-72097-0 (pbk.)

Manufactured in the United States of America
Typography and binding design by J.K. Lambert
24689753
First Edition

=====

Grateful acknowledgment is made to the following for permission to reprint previously published material:

ATV Music Group: lyrics from the following John Lennon and Paul McCartney songs: "A Day in the Life," Copyright © 1967; "Cold Turkey," Copyright © 1969; "Come Together," Copyright © 1969; "Don't Let Me Down," Copyright © 1969; "Gimme Some Truth," Copyright © 1971; "God," Copyright © 1971; "Good Morning, Good Morning," Copyright © 1967; "Happiness Is a Warm Gun," Copyright © 1968; "How Do You Sleep?," Copyright © 1971; "Instant Karma!," Copyright © 1970; "Isolation," Copyright © 1971; "It Won't Be Long," Copyright © 1964; "It's So Hard," Copyright © 1971; "Julia," Copyright © 1968; "Mother," Copyright © 1971; "New York City," Copyright © 1972; "Power to the People," Copyright © 1971; "Revolution," Copyright © 1968; "Lucy in the Sky with Diamonds," Copyright © 1967; "The Ballad of John and Yoko," Copyright © 1969; "Tomorrow Never Knows," Copyright © 1966; "Well Well Well," Copyright © 1971; "Working Class Hero," Copyright © 1971; and "Yer Blues," Copyright © 1968. All songs © Northern Songs, Ltd. All rights in the U.S. and Mexico controlled by Maclen Music, Inc., c/o ATV Music Corp., 6255 Sunset Blvd., Hollywood, CA 90028. Used by permission. All Rights Reserved.

The British Broadcasting Corporation: excerpts from *The Lennon Tapes,* an interview with John Lennon, published by BBC Publications 1981. Used with permission.

Capital Radio: excerpts from "An Evening with John Lennon." Audio, 1975. Used with permission of Capital Radio, London, England.

Circus Magazine: excerpts from "Crippled Inside: An Interview with John Lennon," by Ray

to Judy

Contents

I know you, you know me
One thing I can tell you is you got to be free
Come together, right now
Stop the war!

John Lennon in concert,
Madison Square Garden, August 1972

Introduction: FBI Rock Criticism

Buried deep in the twenty-six pounds of files the Federal Bureau of Investigation and the Immigration and Naturalization Service gathered on John Lennon, there is a report to FBI director J. Edgar Hoover describing John's 1971 appearance in Ann Arbor, Michigan, at an antiwar rally.* The FBI informers who watched him knew what no one else in the audience did: John considered his appearance at the rally a trial run for a national anti-Nixon tour, on which he would bring rock and roll together with radical politics in a dozen cities. He had been talking about ending the tour in August 1972 at a giant protest rally and counterculture festival outside the Republican national convention, where Richard Nixon would be renominated.

The undercover source began his report by explaining, "Lennon [was] formerly with group known as the Beatles." You had to begin at the beginning with Mr. Hoover. "Source advised [that] Lennon prior to rally composed song entitled, 'John Sinclair,' which song Lennon sang at the rally. Source advised this song was composed by Lennon especially for this event." Informers typically exaggerate their own value to their employers. "Source" here was "advised" the same way fifteen thousand other people in the audience were, by Lennon's announcement onstage.

*Notes keyed to pages begin on page 343. A chronology appears on pages 325–28.

The Reagan administration refused to release the rest of this report in April 1981. The FBI cited its authority under the Freedom of Information Act to withhold "information which is currently and properly classified . . . in the interest of the national defense or foreign policy." I filed an administrative appeal. In January 1983 the Justice Department Review Committee declassified the FBI report on the John Sinclair concert, and the assistant attorney general for legal policy released eight more pages of it.

The portion that had been withheld "in the interest of the national defense or foreign policy" began with a complete set of the lyrics to the song "John Sinclair." They had been classified "confidential" by the FBI since 1971, even though they were printed on the back cover of John's 1972 album, *Some Time in New York City:* "Was he jailed for what he done / Or representing everyone?" (Sinclair had been jailed on a marijuana charge.) Copies had been forwarded to the FBI offices in Boston, New York, Chicago, Milwaukee, San Francisco, and Washington, D.C. Perhaps the FBI thought that John planned to bring the tour to these cities. Along with the lyrics sheet, the FBI sent a report from its files on the performance itself: John's wife Yoko Ono "can't even remain on key"; John's "John Sinclair" "probably will become a million seller . . . but it is lacking Lennon's usual standards."

Here was FBI rock criticism: J. Edgar Hoover's middle-aged men in dark suits trying to figure out whether John Lennon would succeed in bringing rock and revolution together. No other rock star aroused the government's fears this way. No other rock star was ordered deported, as John was, in a government effort to prevent a concert tour.

Was the FBI justified in regarding John Lennon as a significant political force? Or was it only acting out Nixon's paranoia, his desire to remove every obstacle to his own reelection, no matter how insignificant?

The experiences of anger and exaltation that rock music provided for countless young people were not in themselves political experiences. Lennon knew that. He also knew that rock could become a potent political force when it was linked to real political organizing—when, for example, it brought young people together to protest the Vietnam war. In 1971 and 1972 he made a commitment to test this political power. The twenty-six pounds of files reveal the government's commitment to stop him.

John's appearance in Ann Arbor was his first concert in the United States since the Beatles' 1966 tour. He shared the stage with the most prominent members of the "Chicago Seven," who had led the antiwar protests outside the Democratic national convention in 1968: Jerry Rubin, founder of the Yippies; Bobby Seale, chairman of the Black Panther Party; Dave Dellinger, the veteran pacifist; and Rennie Davis, the New Left's best organizer. Stevie Wonder made a surprise appearance. All of them called for the release from prison of John Sinclair, a Michigan activist. Sinclair had led the effort to make rock music the bridge between the antiwar movement and the counterculture, and between black and white youth. He had already served two years of a ten-year sentence for selling two joints of marijuana to an undercover agent.

On the proposed tour Lennon and his friends planned to raise money to revive local New Left organizing projects and to urge young people to come to the "political Woodstock" outside the Republican national convention in August. John had been talking to Bob Dylan, trying to get him to join the tour. None of these plans had been made public.

Fifteen thousand people cheered in Ann Arbor's Crisler Arena as John and Yoko finally took the stage at three A.M. "We came here to show and to say to all of you that apathy isn't it, that we *can* do something," John said. "Okay, so flower power didn't work. So what. We start again." More cheering. Then he sang his song: "John Sinclair."

John's appearance at the Free John Sinclair rally marked the culmination of a personal, political, and artistic transformation that had begun much earlier. He had taken his first steps toward radical politics in 1966, when he defied Beatles manager Brian Epstein and publicly denounced the Vietnam war. After that, he went through several phases in an effort to link pop and politics:

Rock against revolution: In 1968 John argued that the path to liberation lay through psychedelic drugs and meditation rather than through radical politics—that genuine liberation was personal rather than political. He expressed himself in rock and roll, in the song that began "You say you want a revolution."

Avant-garde peacenik: After John got together with Yoko in 1968, he realized that to transform himself he needed to join in transforming the world. With this discovery he took on the project of sixties radicalism as his own: a simultaneous struggle for personal and political liberation. With the 1969 "bed-ins for peace" John and Yoko launched a bold campaign of New Left media politics. They staged pop events, seeking to convey a radical message through the establishment media, to use them to undermine the system of which they were a part.

Personal/political artist: Moving to the left in 1970, John began working as an artist to discover and expose the social roots of his personal suffering, to make music that revealed the painful and bitter truth about his life as a "working-class hero."

Songwriter for the movement: In New York in 1971 and 1972 John eagerly joined the struggles against war, racism, and sexism, and wrote what he called "front-page songs" to spread the word. He was taking up the topical songwriting that Bob Dylan and even Phil Ochs had given up. The album he recorded during this period, *Some Time in New York City*, was denounced by critics and ignored by fans.

Defeated radical: The Nixon administration tried to deport John because of his political activities. In the ensuing three-year legal battle he lost his artistic vision and energy, his relationship with Yoko disintegrated, and he gave up his radical politics. In this period Lennon became a defeated activist, an artist in decline, an aging superstar.

Feminist father: John could not rest with this betrayal of the most active and creative period of his life. He worked his way back to Yoko and to feminism, a strand of sixties radicalism that had grown in the seventies. With *Double Fantasy* John linked pop and politics once again, now as the feminist househusband and exemplary father.

Those who find satisfaction in squalid "revelations" about Lennon's life face a problem: John revealed his own weaknesses and failings ruthlessly. He spoke publicly about his heroin use and his drunkenness, and about the feelings of envy and bitterness that intermittently overwhelmed him. He also spoke publicly about his dream of peace and love. But it wasn't his dream that made him a hero; it was his struggle to expose and overcome his anger, misery, and pain.

John's growing self-consciousness in the late sixties was part of a wider cultural phenomenon in which rock critics and antiwar writers began to think seriously about the relationship between the counterculture and the antiwar movement, began to examine the political status of rock music and the cultural dimension of New Left politics. When John Lennon released a new record, it wasn't simply consumed by a passive audience; when he announced a new political project, it wasn't simply observed. People argued about his projects.

His openness to new ideas, his eagerness to try new things and take risks, his willingness to appear foolish, made him an appealing person, especially in contrast to most superstars, who never strayed from their media images. But John also posed a problem for his fans. Often it was hard to decide whether to be embarrassed by him or proud of him. He won both enthusiasm and ridicule. Writers filled the underground and alternative press and the rock magazines with these arguments. This growing self-consciousness of a new generation must also be examined and understood in order to understand Lennon's significance.

John was not the only figure to receive this scrutiny, and he knew it. The counterculture and the antiwar movement constantly measured him against two others: Bob Dylan and Mick Jagger. John regularly glanced over his shoulder at their projects. Sometimes he tried to top them, sometimes he challenged one or the other with a radical change in direction. They did the same to him. At a few rare moments the work of all three converged. To understand Lennon one must also understand the achievements and limitations of Dylan and Jagger.

The phases of Lennon's development that earned the most publicity, and the most ridicule, were his involvement with LSD and then with the Maharishi Mahesh Yogi. In fact, each of these phases lasted approximately eight months. John started taking a lot of LSD in the fall of 1966 and stopped in August 1967; he met the Maharishi that same month and broke with him the following April. The period of his most intense political activism lasted almost five times as long, beginning with the bed-in in March 1969 and ending with his last antiwar demonstration in May 1972. This accounting ignores the fact that his withdrawal from activist politics was forced on him by the Nixon administration's deportation proceedings. The three-year deportation battle was also political. John's defense went beyond legal technicalities, as he challenged and sought to expose the Nixon administration's abuse of power.

But in a larger sense, political and social questions were central to John's work as a musician and his thinking about himself in every phase of his life —from his inchoate teenage rebellion against respectability, and his identification through music with the oppressed, to his repeated posing of questions of personal liberation and its relation to political and social issues. He changed his mind more than once, but he never gave up his commitment to face the questions.

As John's efforts to link pop and politics developed, he worked on a series of problems, which he summarized as "becoming real": how to understand the oppressiveness of rock stardom; how to bring together the struggles for personal and political liberation; how to create art that is both radical and popular, how to tell the truth with rock and roll; how to survive political persecution; how to renew commitments; how to return to music. To understand John Lennon is to understand this struggle to be real.

Part I

PROLOGUE

1

"The Dream Is Over"

 Is rock revolutionary? A burning issue not so long ago, today this question sounds absurd. But it was not so clear in the late sixties that rock was compatible with the status quo. Rock was the music of young people who opposed injustice and oppression. The war in Vietnam and the antidrug laws stood for the injustices of America, and the rock world rallied against them. Rock as a whole was at least antiestablishment, and much of the rock world openly defied and ridiculed the nation's political and corporate leaders.

Time magazine's claims for the political significance of rock were as strong as those made in the underground press. After half a million young people turned up at the Woodstock festival, *Time* explained rock was "not just a particular form of pop, but . . . one long symphony of protest . . . basically moral . . . the proclamation of a new set of values . . . the anthem of revolution." The FBI files on John Lennon indicate that the Nixon administration held the same view.

The clearest sign that something was wrong with this picture came in 1969, a year when antiwar demonstrators in many cities were being arrested and beaten by police. That year Columbia Records ran a series of ads in underground newspapers headlined "The Man can't bust our music." *Ramparts*, the New Left's glossy muckraking magazine, explored the issues in an article titled "Rock for Sale." It pointed out that Columbia, among others, was finding the youth "revolution" a source of impressive profits. Rock's proportion of Columbia's sales had increased from 15 percent in 1965 to 60 percent four years later.

The New York *Times* reported that "several large establishment-oriented corporations are interested in cashing in on the youth market that Woodstock proved exists. These firms are hiring highly paid youth consultants to advise them on forthcoming trends." The most important intermediary between the counterculture and the corporations was *Rolling Stone*, founded by Jann Wenner in 1967 (with John Lennon in *How I Won the War* on the first cover), which reached a circulation of a quarter of a million by 1970 and bought the back page of the New York *Times* to advertise, "If you are a corporate executive trying to understand what is happening to youth, you cannot afford to be without *Rolling Stone.*"

Despite this evidence, those who concluded that rock was nothing more than a capitalist commodity were wrong. The corporate world found that it could not shape youth culture the way it was used to shaping consumer society. In 1967 the record companies had been taken by surprise by the triumph of Janis Joplin's "Piece of My Heart" and Grace Slick's "White Rabbit." Scrambling to regain control of pop music, they set out to find a successor to this "San Francisco sound," as they dubbed it. San Francisco: lots of colleges, students, bands, something like . . . Boston! Thus MGM Records launched an expensive promotion of the "Boss-town sound."

The effort met with disaster. Young people ignored MGM's claim that Ultimate Spinach was 1968's successor to Big Brother and the Holding Company. Jon Landau led the campaign of refusal, writing a series of scathing reviews in *Rolling Stone* and demonstrating the self-consciousness and confidence of the counterculture.

Hearst Publications launched a magazine in 1968 aimed at the youth audience. *Eye* ran John Lennon on the cover, Bob Dylan inside, and an article titled "10 Student Rebels Explain Their Cause." Nevertheless the magazine quickly failed. Hearst learned the same lesson that MGM Records had: the counterculture had partial autonomy from corporate domination.

The record companies concluded that they had to advertise in the underground press. Some radicals feared that the undergrounds were being co-opted by the ads, but they needn't have worried. Underground papers did not change their editorial content to get ads, and readers demonstrated an impressive ability to resist being manipulated by the companies. (This situation also precipitated the papers' downfall a couple of years later, when the FBI orchestrated the withdrawal of corporate advertising from the radical newspapers.)

During the sixties black music reached its largest white audience in history. This simple fact marks one of the most significant political dimensions of the counterculture. Fifties rock had led in breaking down some of the racial barriers in America. But not until the sixties did white youth celebrate a black superstar—Jimi Hendrix. Never before had so many whites danced to black music, like the Supremes' "You Keep Me Hangin' On" and Martha and the Vandellas' "Nowhere to Run."

The contrast to the Reagan years could not be more striking. In 1981 and 1982 there were virtually no black musicians played on America's rock stations, and in 1983 there were two—Michael Jackson and Prince. Many stations that had once been leaders of counterculture rock found that on the rare occasions when they played black artists, irate listeners called demanding that the "nigger music" be taken off the air. The stations too often complied.

All this suggests that no simple equation can be drawn between rock and radicalism; that rock is a medium capable of carrying contradictory politics; that the corporations have tried to dominate it, but have not consistently succeeded.

Rock could become a real political force, however, when it was linked to real political organizing. The 1972 anti-Nixon tour John Lennon planned with Jerry Rubin and Rennie Davis was intended to forge that link. Many others worked on similar projects, including radio stations like Boston's WBCN, which mixed music that challenged the status quo with news about protest movements.

In this undertaking, making music posed a problem: what could politically radical rock sound like? What could it be as music? Elephant's Memory was a movement bar band, playing Chuck Berry riffs and singing left-wing lyrics. That was good for raising people's spirits, and for the party after the demonstration. The MC5, which John Sinclair managed, wanted more: they wanted their music to be radical in form. They developed an early version of punk, anticipating by several years the elemental rage of the Clash. The 1970 album *John Lennon/Plastic Ono Band* represented another possibility.

=====

As a politically committed artist, John fought a destructive as well as a creative battle. Beginning in December 1970 with the release of *Plastic Ono Band* and his historic *Rolling Stone* interview *Lennon Remembers*, he worked to destroy his own status as a celebrity, to attack the Beatles as a cultural ideal of joy and fun. He described them as commodities created by a capitalist industry, he exposed their alienation as artists, he portrayed them as "a contradictory and doomed social institution within an exploiting culture," as New Left activist Todd Gitlin wrote at the time. Along with this work of destruction came a struggle to create new music, music that would bring his experience together with the larger issues of the day. With *Plastic Ono Band* John took rock music across a threshold, beyond the themes of youth rebellion, beyond the established forms of protest music, toward a radical new synthesis of the personal and the political.

The album contains the song titled "God," in which John declares that he doesn't believe in Jesus, in Kennedy, in Buddha, in Elvis; the litany goes on, until he sings "I don't believe in Beatles," when the music suddenly ceases —but only for an instant. It ends

> I was the Walrus
> But now I'm John
> And so dear friends
> You'll just have to carry on
> The dream is over

In the song John takes the chord changes of the classic rock and roll slow dance, plays them more slowly than they had ever been played before, and builds on them some of the most moving music in all of rock. "God" rejects political, religious, and cultural false consciousness. John undertakes a deliberate shattering of the illusions of the sixties, starting with the dream of the Beatles as the representation of a genuine community, a harmonious group of equals, filled with creative energy. This is a false dream, John says, and it is finished now. He can't and won't serve as our god any more; he declares that he is a person, like we are—he's just "John." For us to carry on, we need to find a way to shatter these gods outside of us, to transfer power from our mythical heroes to ourselves, to each other. In this project we are no longer his fans, but in a much more human way his "dear friends." This suggests a profound and radical truth. In one stroke it brings together the personal and the political.

This view was challenged after John's death by radical journalist Andrew Kopkind in New York's *Soho News.* "Long before Tom Wolfe, Lennon announced the advent of the Me Generation, declaring his disbelief in every cause, cult hero and movement . . . 'I just believe in me,' he sang." But the litany John recites does not reject "every movement." It was carefully written to include pop heroes, liberal heroes, and the varieties of Eastern mysticism that had captured large parts of the counterculture. Political radicalism is not on the list.

In fact, the same Andrew Kopkind wrote nine years earlier one of the most thoughtful articles on the song's achievement: "What's so startling and so wrenching about the Lennon documents . . . is that they suggest a radical way out; a way to deal with dreams. Lennon's way, it seems to me, is a revival of honesty, a commitment to authenticity of feeling that overcomes real fears of self-contradiction, failure, and pain. In that sense, the value of his personal depositions . . . is not in the promulgation of a 'correct line,' but in the presentation of a real personal and public struggle to be free." Others recognized the song's significance for the New Left: Todd Gitlin, who was putting together an anthology of movement poetry, wrote, "To make private pains and struggles public, as Lennon has done, is to say, 'you can do it too.' Lennon revives the idea of leader as exemplar."

The second song on *Plastic Ono Band* was "Working Class Hero." In his 1970 interview *Lennon Remembers,* John called it "a song for the revolution. . . . It's for the people like me who are working class, . . . who are supposed to be processed into the middle class. . . . It's my experience, and I hope it's a warning to people."

> Keep you doped with religion and sex and TV
> And you think you're so clever and classless and free
> But you're still fucking peasants as far as I can see
> A working class hero is something to be . . .
> If you want to be a hero, well, just follow me

In "Revolution" John had insisted on the separation of the personal from the political: "free your mind instead" of changing institutions. Here he abandons that separation and takes on the project of bringing the personal together with the political, by locating the social origins of his own personal misery. In attempting to "free his mind," he suggests, he remained a "fucking peasant."

Many people took the title "Working Class Hero" as John's affirmation of his roots. In fact, it was profoundly ironic. To be this kind of "hero," he declared, was to be destroyed as a person. John was working to escape that fate, to become a different kind of hero. John wanted to "be real," he often said. But he knew he couldn't achieve that just by being himself. His self was precisely the problem. His Beatle identity was obviously unreal. But the song declared that his pre-Beatle self, his working-class self, was also a creation of oppressive social and cultural forces. To be himself he couldn't simply rediscover his identity in his roots. He had to create his identity. To become real was to take the self as problematic, as a vast field of possibility. John was setting an example for young people who claimed the freedom to "become real" in their own ways. He was undertaking what New Left political theorist Marshall Berman identified as the politics of authenticity.

John was also undertaking a second project: exposing the social origins of suffering that people thought was purely personal and private. Through self-disclosure he hoped to achieve a critical distance from his feelings. He was seeking insight into the historical forces, reproduced in psychological form, that had shaped those feelings of suffering. Although his own experience as a superstar was unique, he was playing an exemplary role for a New Left that was just beginning to examine the personal dimension of social crisis.

John was suggesting that the personal crisis experienced by youth in the late sixties had become a political issue in its own right. He was suggesting that a radical movement had to explain how the isolation people experienced in bourgeois society could be overcome, and what "liberation" meant for personal relationships. *John Lennon/Plastic Ono Band* sought to illuminate the intersection of history and private experience. That project, bringing together the personal and the political, lay at the heart of New Left radicalism.

John could claim "Working Class Hero" as a "revolutionary" song because it confronted the obstacles facing revolutionary movements. John explained, "The workers are dreaming someone else's dream . . . As soon as they start being aware of all that, we can really begin to do something. . . . The idea is not to comfort people, not to make them feel better, but . . . to constantly put before them the degradations and humiliations they go through to get what they call a living wage."

And in his interview *Lennon Remembers,* conducted just after the album was released, he expanded on his portrayal of the workers as "fucking peasants," powerless despite the appearance of change in the sixties: "The people who are in control and in power, and the class system and the whole bullshit bourgeois scene is exactly the same except that there are a lot of middle-class kids with long hair walking around in trendy clothes . . . The same bastards are in control, the same people are runnin' everything. . . . They're doing exactly the same things, selling arms to South Africa, killing blacks on the street, people are living in fucking poverty with rats crawling all over them, it's the same. It just makes you puke. And I woke up to that, too. The dream is over."

The blackness of John's political mood in that winter of 1970–71 in some ways matched that of the New Left, which had gone through the Chicago Seven trial, the invasion of Cambodia, and the Kent State killings. Despite the most massive protest in the history of American colleges and universities, the Nixon administration continued to destroy the people and countryside of Southeast Asia. Many radicals felt the same sense of powerlessness John expressed in the *Rolling Stone* interview. The seriousness of their commitments, and the depth of their despair, gave them a growing sense of isolation.

John expressed a similar feeling in "Isolation," a song of intense sadness. He and Yoko, "Just a boy and a little girl," were "trying to change the whole wide world." And in a strange echo of the growing terrorist element in New Left politics, John's song "Remember," with its remorseless beat, told listeners that, when the world was driving them "mad," they should "remember the fifth of November." Then it ended abruptly with the sound of a massive explosion. Americans didn't understand it, but every British person knows that November 5 is Guy Fawkes Day, the day an English radical tried to blow up the Houses of Parliament in 1605. The year *Plastic Ono Band* was released, the number of guerrilla-styled bombings and acts of arson in the United States was around forty per week, according to the government. John was thousands of miles away from these mainly symbolic acts of protest, but his songs captured the emotional tone of that year of rage and despair.

Plastic Ono Band also contained his first moves toward feminism. On the tumultuous and savage "Well Well Well," John describes sitting with Yoko and talking about revolution

> Just like two liberals in the sun
> We talked of women's liberation
> And how the hell we could get things done

The frustration with too much "talk," the use of "liberal" as an epithet, the insistence on "getting things done," all expressed the frustrated spirit of the New Left.

Even in his most personal music, John tried to link larger social questions to his own experience. The album opened with "Mother," expressing the feelings John uncovered in his work with primal therapist Arthur Janov: "Mother, you had me / But I never had you." John's singing had the inflections and nuances of soul music, but he ended the song by screaming over and over, "Mama, don't go / Daddy, come home." The story of John's family background had been known to everyone who was interested, at least since 1968, when Hunter Davies' official biography was published. "I lost her twice," John later explained, "once as a five-year-old when I moved in with my auntie. And once again at fifteen when she actually, physically died." No one had ever sung a song like "Mother," with its almost unbearable screams of childhood terror.

Later John explained that he had been drawing on the sound of Jerry Lee Lewis at the recording session for "Mother." "I put 'Whole Lotta Shakin'' on . . . I was playing 'Whole Lotta Shakin',' then playing 'Mother,' then playing 'Whole Lotta Shakin',' then playing 'Mother,' to get that guts and feeling."

Was it Janov who taught him to scream? He pointed to his pre-Janov screams on "Cold Turkey" and "Twist and Shout," and to Little Richard screaming "Wop bop pa loo ma, ba lop bam boom." "Don't get therapy confused with the music," he said in *Lennon Remembers*.

The song seems a completely personal statement, arising from John's unique experience. But he claimed that it had a more general significance. At his 1972 Madison Square Garden concert John introduced the song by saying, "People think it's just about *my* parents, but it's about everyone's, alive and half dead."

"Mother" was followed by "Hold On John": "we're gonna win the fight." Ringo Starr's drumming was nervous and jittery. Because the pain expressed in the stretched and broken phrases hurt so much, the beauty of the music was especially soothing. John explained the song: "It's all right now, this moment, so hold on now. . . . We might get a moment's happiness any minute now, that's what it's all about. . . . That's how we're living, cherishing each day and dreading it too. It might be your last day."

The music on *Plastic Ono Band* seemed radically spare and elemental, almost crude at times. John played piano or guitar, with only two backup musicians, his old friend from the Hamburg days, Klaus Voormann, on bass, and Ringo playing drums with tremendous intensity (especially fierce on the primitive-sounding "I Found Out"). John explained he was "trying to shave off all imagery, pretensions of poetry, illusions of grandeur, what I call à la Dylan. . . . Just say what it is, simple English, make it rhyme and put a backbeat on it."

"It's terribly uncommercial, it's so miserable," he said about the album in *Lennon Remembers*. "But it's reality, and I'm not going to veer away from it for anything." He knew he had succeeded: "It's the best thing I've ever done."

Plastic Ono Band seemed like a complete break with John's previous work. In fact, it marked the culmination of a long process of personal and political change. John took his first steps away from the Beatles in 1966, in the city where Elvis lived, the city that Chuck Berry sang about: Memphis, Tennessee.

2

First Steps toward Radical Politics:
The 1966 Tour

 When the Beatles arrived in Memphis on their 1966 summer tour, they discovered that a massive Christian rally, organized by a hundred fundamentalist ministers, had been scheduled to protest their appearance. The problem was John. He had recently said the Beatles were "more popular than Jesus." The English, in their matter-of-fact way, had concluded he was correct. But in the God-fearing United States, the religious right accused him of "blasphemy" and took after him like a pack of wolves while the media watched and chuckled. The "more popular than Jesus" controversy pushed John to take his first steps away from the Beatles and toward the antiwar activism that would become central to his life and work.

The leader of the Memphis ministers had a name that could have come out of a B movie: the Reverend Jimmy Stroad. He issued a grim challenge, declaring that the Christian rally would "give the youth of the mid-South an opportunity to show Jesus Christ is more popular than the Beatles." And he offered as competition against the Beatles not only Jesus but also Jay North, the child actor who had played Dennis the Menace on TV.

Until John's "Jesus" comment the Beatles had been the good boys of rock, in contrast to the nasty and sexually aggressive Rolling Stones. Parents considered the Beatles playful and harmless. Ed Sullivan liked them. But America's fundamentalist ministers saw them in a completely different light. "What have the Beatles said or done to so ingratiate themselves with those who eat, drink and think revolution?" asked David Noebel, author of a series of anti-Beatle tracts beginning in 1965. "The major value of the Beatles to the left in general . . . has been their usefulness in destroying youth's faith in God." He carefully combed through all of John's work and came up with strong evidence that the "Jesus" remark was part of a larger and more sinister pattern. In John's book *A Spaniard in the Works* he had written about "Father, Sock, and Mickey Most." (Mickey Most produced records by Herman's Hermits.) That phrase, Noebel felt, did a lot to destroy youth's faith in God and his only begotten sock.

In Memphis the city commission agreed with the fundamentalists. An official statement declared, "The Beatles are not welcome in Memphis." Memphis, where Elvis Presley had recorded his first songs, awakening John Lennon from his teenage torpor; Memphis, the subject of a Chuck Berry classic the Beatles had played over and over in their early days; Memphis, where Jerry Lee Lewis had sung about the shaking that was going on; Memphis, a center of black music, where that very summer of 1966 Carla Thomas recorded the rocking "Let Me Be Good to You" and Sam and Dave recorded the stirring "Hold On, I'm Comin' "—how could the Beatles not be welcome in Memphis?

The day after the city fathers issued their statement, Beatles manager Brian Epstein revealed his strategy: apologize for everything. He released a telegram to the press declaring that he "wished to assure the people of Memphis and the mid-South that the Beatles will not, by word, action, or otherwise, in any way offend or ridicule the religious beliefs of anyone throughout their forth-coming concert tour. . . . Furthermore, John Lennon deeply and sincerely regrets any offense that he might have caused."

The week before the concert, the local newspaper was filled with debate, including statements from several ministers attacking the fundamentalist counterrally. The rector of Holy Trinity Episcopal Church wrote, "I do not care for the Beatles. I would not go to their concert. I do not even think that the noise which they produce falls in the category of what we call music. Nevertheless, the truth of John Lennon's statement cannot be denied."

A Methodist pastor quoted part of John's statement and declared that it contained a correct description of the anti-Beatle ministers in Memphis: "Jesus was all right but his disciples are thick and ordinary. It's them twisting it that ruins it for me." A Memphis youth attending Louisiana State University wrote that the city fathers should "for once in their lives overcome the idea that everything that enters Memphis not carrying a cross is evil. . . . Is your religion so weak that four rock-and-roll players can shake it?"

The Beatles and their entourage had been frightened as the Memphis date approached. When they left London, fans had screamed, "John, please don't go; they'll kill you!" John had the same fear. Later he explained, "I didn't want to tour because I thought they'd kill me—'cause they take things so seriously there. They shoot you, and then they realize it wasn't that important. So I didn't want to go. But Brian, and Paul, and the other Beatles persuaded me to come. I was scared stiff." He wasn't the only one. Paul McCartney had "a horror of being shot onstage," according to Peter Brown, the Beatles' personal assistant. As the Beatles got off their plane in Memphis, Paul remarked ironically, "We should be wearing targets here." Because of the fear of a sniper in the audience, police at the concert were asked to "keep a lookout for firearms."

Subsequent accounts of what actually happened at the Beatles concert and the counterrally were confused. A best-selling history of the Beatles reported that while the Beatles were getting ready to go onstage, "outside the Ku Klux Klan were holding an 8,000-strong counter demonstration." In fact, the number of demonstrators outside the concert hall was closer to eight than eight thousand, but they were indeed Klansmen, wearing full white-sheet regalia. That never happened to Mick Jagger, despite his efforts to be outrageous. It was an honor of sorts for John to be the only white rock-and-roller to provoke a Klan picket line.

In the middle of their performance a sound like a gunshot rang out. A wave of fear crossed the Beatles' faces. "Every one of us looked at each other," John later explained, "'cause each thought it was the other that had been shot. It was that bad. I don't know how I did it." Each quickly saw the others were okay, and they continued playing without missing a beat. Later they learned that what they had heard was only a cherry bomb.

While twenty thousand heard the Beatles, only eight thousand showed up across town for the counterrally, half of whom were adults. They didn't really count in the battle for the hearts of the mid-South's youth. Reverend Stroad implicitly conceded that Christ did not seem to be as popular as the Beatles, even in Memphis. He issued a new statement: the rally had "shown the whole world that Christianity will not vanish," so at least John had been disproven on that point.

Poor attendance was not the counterrally's only problem. Dennis the Menace did not appear. Some of the fundamentalists objected to the program, and a group of thirty walked out of the rally in protest. Their spokesman declared that young people had been "decoyed" by promises of a "Christian testimonial service," but instead they had been given music inspired by Satan.

They objected in particular to a vocal group that sang Christian songs "to a modified 'twist' while an accompanying combo maintained a throbbing beat," the newspaper reported. It quoted the protesters: "We might as well have gone to the Beatles."

======

From the beginning of rock and roll, fundamentalist churches and white racists had organized against it. In 1956 the New York *Times* had reported that Southern white church groups were attempting to suppress "Negro style" rock music because it corrupted white youth. The Alabama White Citizens Council, which had been organized to combat the civil rights movement, also took a stand on rock and roll, calling it "a means of pulling the white man down to the level of the Negro. It is part of a plot to undermine the morals of the youth of our nation." Members of the White Citizens Council attacked and beat Nat "King" Cole during a concert in Birmingham in 1956. Ten years later John's "Jesus" remark brought the same social forces back into the limelight.

Memphis was not the first American city to witness right-wing protests against Lennon's remark. The first demonstrations had been organized in Birmingham, the city which in 1966 symbolized the violent repression of civil rights. Three years earlier the Birmingham police had attacked civil rights demonstrators with high-pressure fire hoses and arrested 2,543 of them in a single week. Later the same year a black church in Birmingham was bombed, killing four girls. Now, at the end of July 1966, two weeks before the Beatles were to begin their fourth American tour, Birmingham was back in the news, as a local disc jockey named Tommy Charles organized a rally at which "protesters" tossed their Beatles albums into a giant tree-grinding machine, turning them into dust. Mr. Charles told visiting reporters that he was thirty-six years old "but I think like a teenager."

Within a few days, thirty other radio stations announced that they were banning Beatles records. Most were in the South, but stations in Boston and New York joined the ban. They included the one that had first promoted Beatlemania, calling itself "W-A-Beatle-C." Newspapers across the country published striking photos of kids in crew cuts grinning at Beatles record–burnings. The TV news showed a girl gleefully ripping the pages out of John's book *In His Own Write* and tossing them into the flames. The Grand Dragon of the South Carolina Ku Klux Klan held a ceremony in which he attached a Beatles record to a large wooden cross and set the cross on fire. The symbolism of the Beatles' music on the cross apparently escaped his notice.

The most striking event took place in Longview, Texas, where a record-burning was held on Friday the thirteenth of August, organized by radio station KLUE. The next day its transmitter was hit by lightning, knocking its news director unconscious and blasting the station off the air. The anti-Beatle organizers failed to draw the obvious conclusion.

The American demonstrations gained international support as the right-wing governments of Franco Spain and South Africa banned all Beatles music. South Africa lifted its ban on the Beatles when the group split in 1970, but continued to prohibit the broadcast of John's records. The Vatican's official newspaper *L'Osservatore Romano* announced that "some subjects must not be dealt with profanely, not even in the world of beatniks." Beatniks?

John's "Jesus" remark had been at the top of the agenda at the first press conference when the Beatles began their tour on August 12 in Chicago. That city had just been the site of organized attacks on black people. The previous month Martin Luther King, Jr., had led a demonstration of forty thousand people in Chicago, seeking to end discrimination in jobs and housing there. The campaign was his first attempt to confront institutional racism in the North. A week before the Beatles arrived in the city, a mob of four thousand whites, led by members of the American Nazi Party and the Ku Klux Klan, attacked and beat seven hundred black marchers, including King. He stated afterward, "I have seen many demonstrations in the South, but I have never seen anything so hostile and so hateful as I've seen here today."

For the media, however, the big news in Chicago on August 12 was not racist violence, but rather John's apology to Christians: "If I said television was more popular than Jesus, I might have gotten away with it. . . . I just said what I said and it was wrong, or it was taken wrong, and now there's all this."

The reporters were unsatisfied. The next question was "But are you prepared to apologize?"

John tried again. "I'm not anti-God, anti-Christ or antireligion. I am not saying we are greater or better. I believe in God, but not as one thing, not as an old man in the sky. I believe that what people call God is something in all of us. I believe that what Jesus and Mohammed and Buddha and all the rest said was right. It's just that the translations have gone wrong. I wasn't saying that Beatles are better than God or Jesus. I used 'Beatles' because it's easy for me to talk about Beatles."

Reporters continued to press him: "Are you sorry about your statement concerning Christ?"

"I wasn't saying whatever they're saying I was saying. . . . I'm sorry I said it, really. I never meant it to be a lousy antireligious thing. . . . I apologize, if that will make you happy. I still don't know quite what I've done. I've tried to tell you what I did do, but if you want me to apologize, if that will make you happy, then okay, I'm sorry."

"Would you say you are being crucified?"

John was no fool. "No," he said emphatically and with great bitterness, "I would not say that *at all.*"

For John to have to apologize, and to submit to reporters' questions about his religious beliefs, was humiliating. He looked like a good boy who didn't want to offend anyone. But that was not the way John wanted his "apology" understood. He tried to preserve some integrity by speaking truthfully. He had read *The Passover Plot* by Hugh J. Schonfield, the premise of which, he explained, was that "Jesus' message . . . had been twisted by his disciples for a variety of self-serving reasons." The book had convinced him that the disciples were "thick and ordinary," as he told Maureen Cleave, who covered the Beatles for the London *Evening Standard.* When reporters asked about his belief in Christ, he replied by referring to "Jesus," a man rather than the savior. And his equation of Jesus with Buddha and Mohammed was a not-so-subtle act of defiance of the fundamentalists.

John could have shouted that he'd never tour again. He certainly didn't need the money. But the record-burning really bothered him. Something as simple as people listening to records had turned into a bitter dispute. That's why, he said, he felt he had to do something to defuse the conflict.

Finally, he talked at the Chicago press conference about "the trouble with being truthful." "You hope sometimes that if you're truthful with somebody, they'll stop all the plastic reaction and be truthful back and it'll be worth it. But everybody is playing the game and sometimes I'm left naked and truthful with everyone biting me."

This remarkable image anticipates the central theme of John's work after the Beatles' breakup. The nude photos on the *Two Virgins* cover, and the *Plastic Ono Band* album of 1970, expressed John's desire to tell the naked truth about himself. The appearance of this theme as early as 1966 suggests that John did not learn it from Yoko, as many would suggest in 1970. In fact, it had been a preoccupation of his for at least two years before he met her. His relationship with Yoko, however, made it possible for him to move the project of self-revelation to the center of his work as an artist.

John's "apology" was accepted by the Vatican, and by the New York *Times.* The latter ran a pretentious editorial under the headline "What He Meant Was . . ." It concluded, "The wonder is that such an articulate young man could have expressed himself imprecisely in the first place."

Although the Jesus remark captured the public's attention that summer, the Beatles involved themselves in another political controversy that would become much more important for John: the war in Vietnam. Two months before the "Jesus" controversy, American disc jockeys had received the new Beatles album, *"Yesterday" . . . and Today.* Its cover showed the Beatles surrounded by slabs of raw, red meat and decapitated dolls. *Time* announced that the cover was "a serious lapse in taste," and frightened Capitol Records executives issued an apology for what they called an "attempt at pop satire."

John, asked to explain, told reporters the butcher cover was "as relevant as Vietnam." He intended to be neither witty nor irreverent. He spoke seriously. The Beatles may not have intended the butcher cover to be a comment on American butchery in Vietnam, but once it was suppressed, John cast it in that light. His statement showed for the first time that John perceived the "relevance" of Vietnam—that the war was on his mind.

During the Beatles' American tour that summer of 1966, the Johnson administration escalated its war. In June the United States bombed Hanoi for the first time and announced a policy of systematic bombing of North Vietnam. The antiwar movement was growing. The previous year Students for a Democratic Society had sponsored the first march on Washington protesting the war, and twenty-five thousand people came. Shortly afterward students at Berkeley held a thirty-six-hour teach-in against the war, and twelve thousand came to listen. In 1966 antiwar activity was spreading to campuses not usually considered centers of radicalism. When Johnson went to Princeton that spring to defend his Vietnam escalation, he was met with a large demonstration. LBJ questioned the manhood of opponents of the war: he called them "nervous Nellies."

John followed the news closely. Maureen Cleave wrote during that summer that he "reads all the daily newspapers. . . . He watches all TV news coverage." The air war filled the front pages. As the Beatles left Memphis, the local newspaper reported, "Reds gun down U.S.' hottest pilot as Communist gunners score their heaviest toll of the war in bringing down U.S. planes. U.S. warplanes struck back, smashing North Vietnam with a record 139 bombing missions. U.S. fliers streaking from Guam bagged their 18th MIG and hammered Communist targets in the South."

When the Beatles held their ritual New York press conference later in the same week, the first questioner asked them to comment on any aspect of the Vietnam conflict. They answered in unison, "We don't like war, war is wrong," several times in a row. John later gave his own brief and trenchant answer to the question, what did they think about the war? "We think of it every day. We don't like it. We don't agree with it. We think it's wrong."

It was a bold and risky move, which Brian Epstein had urged them to avoid. John was aligning himself with antiwar students. He knew that only 10 percent of the public agreed with them at this time, according to opinion polls. And it was unprecedented for a leading rock group to take a political stand of any kind. That was only for Bob Dylan and Phil Ochs. John's 1966 statement deserves scrutiny. British historian Eric Hobsbawm commented, "Most British people at the time would have said they thought the war in

Vietnam was wrong, but very few would have said, 'We think about it every day.' That's remarkable."

The contrast with their earlier New York press conferences was striking: no more playful banter, no more smiling faces. The Fab Four looked "tired and pale," the New York *Times* reported. They were becoming part of the growing political conflict in America. On August 24, the same day the Beatles played their second Shea Stadium concert, newspapers reported that the House Un-American Activities Committee (HUAC) had proposed legislation to set criminal penalties for "obstruction of the Vietnam war effort." HUAC had investigated a Berkeley plan, led by Jerry Rubin, among others, to send medical supplies to North Vietnam and block troop trains.

That same day Stokely Carmichael announced a new political strategy for the Student Nonviolent Coordinating Committee, "Black Power." "We must form our own institutions, credit unions, co-ops, political parties, write our own histories," he declared, calling on white radicals in SNCC to leave the organization and instead work among whites to fight racism. Newspapers that day also reported that Mao's "Red Guards for the cultural revolution" held their first major demonstration in Peking.

The antiwar movement, black power, Maoism—each of these would become increasingly important in John's life and music over the next few years, first when he denounced radicals "carrying pictures of Chairman Mao" in his 1968 song "Revolution" and then when he returned to New York in 1971 wearing a Mao badge, joining Jerry Rubin and sharing the stage with Black Power spokesmen.

John expected the mass media to trumpet the news that the Beatles had joined the antiwar camp. Everything about the Beatles sold newspapers. In fact, Epstein shouldn't have worried. The antiwar statement was published only in local New York newspapers, and even they did not feature it. The *Daily News* devoted six pages to Beatles coverage but only one sentence to the antiwar declaration. *Time* and *Newsweek* ran long stories on the Beatles' tour, focusing on the storm over John's "Jesus" remark and ignoring the antiwar statement completely. John was portrayed as an arrogant egomaniac who had finally been slapped down by an outraged public. "Lennon forgiven," *Newsweek* chuckled, failing to see a crucial event in his life: his first step out of the role of the "lad from Liverpool" toward radical politics. In the future, John would make sure that his political statements could not be ignored.

———

The Beatles' coming out against the war in 1966 did not surprise writers on the left, several of whom had already written about them. *Sing Out!*, the leading magazine linking folk and protest songs with the civil rights and antiwar movements, might have been expected to oppose the Beatles, as it opposed virtually all Top Ten pop. But a report from England in the January 1964 issue found a radical current in the Beatles' music. "Their enjoyment of life now is a strong protest and alternative to world preparation for war and the strong bureaucratic governments that surround us all," the magazine declared. The Beatles were saying " 'We have the right to a chance,' and that is why they are popular."

The American Communist Party went much further, claiming the Beatles as part of the left. At the fortieth anniversary celebration of the *Daily Worker* in Carnegie Hall in March 1964, a speaker noted that it was "on the same Carnegie Hall stage . . . [that] the Beatles made their American debut several weeks ago," the UPI reported. "He said the Beatles marched in the ban-the-bomb protest march two years ago and lauded them as 'one of us.' Everybody cheered the Beatles." The speaker must have been referring to the Campaign for Nuclear Disarmament's Aldermaston March, which ended on April 23, 1962, with a rally of 150,000 people in London's Hyde Park, the largest antiwar demonstration in recent British history. The Beatles could not have been present; they were playing in Hamburg. Nevertheless Robin Blackburn of the *New Left Review* had a similar recollection in 1981: "It was widely believed in the movement in 1963 and 1964 that John had worn a CND badge."

Terry Eagleton wrote one of the most thoughtful of the early New Left appraisals of the Beatles. A student at Oxford at the time, he would later become a leading Marxist literary critic and an authority on Walter Benjamin. In 1964 he found the Beatles significant because "more than most pop-singers, they have bridged the class-gaps within youth between student and worker, massing them against the largely unresponsive adult world." But unlike the American Communist Party speaker, he refused to claim them as part of the left. Their "Liverpool scepticism, the slow realism, can no longer be channeled politically," he wrote. "Their humor is irresponsible, often merely verbal, always involved with fantasy. . . . On stage, their intelligence comes through as a quality of sceptical, self-aware detachment: they enjoy singing, but refuse to commit themselves fully to the conventions, retaining selfhood, unwilling to take themselves wholly seriously."

Eagleton's serious appraisal stood in sharp contrast to the condescending treatment the Beatles received in the mass media. They wore their hair trimmed above the ear and brushed down across the forehead. The press regarded this as feminine and thus a subject for endless mirth. Disc jockeys referred to the Beatles as "the guys—with hair in their eyes." TV comedians put on Beatle wigs and won big laughs. Ed Sullivan did it. Billy Graham told reporters, "I hope when they get older they get a haircut." Even President Lyndon Johnson tried to be a comedian. Greeting the British prime minister, he quipped, "Don't you feel they need haircuts?"

Their music was ridiculed along with their haircuts. "The Beatles apparently could not carry a tune across the Atlantic," the New York *Herald Tribune* wrote after their appearance on the *Ed Sullivan Show* in 1964. The New York *Times* found their music "a fine mass placebo." New York disc jockey William B. Williams would play "I Want to Hold Your Hand" on WNEW and comment, "A lot of people want to hold their noses."

Even the favorable press coverage was condescending. The London *Daily Mirror* wrote, "They wear their hair like a mop—but it's WASHED, it's super clean." And some of the British reporters barely concealed their resentment and hostility. Michael Braun, a writer who traveled with the Beatles in 1964, overheard a *Daily Mirror* reporter talking with a colleague after the Ed Sullivan appearance: "It's about time to start bursting these boys' balloons. Their heads are getting too big." That is exactly what the press set out to do to John beginning in 1968.

"Serious" analysis of Beatlemania as a social phenomenon usually pondered the sexual implications of the haircuts. "The Beatles display a few mannerisms which almost seem a shade on the feminine side, such as the tossing of their long manes of hair," Dr. Joyce Brothers wrote in the New York *Journal-American.* Not to be outdone, the New York *Times* turned to Dr. Renee Fox, who declared in a front-page story, "They are male and yet have many female characteristics, especially their floppy hair-dos."

At the time the Beatles responded with their famous good humor. What do you call that haircut? "Arthur." Are you part of a social rebellion against the older generation? "It's a dirty lie." John's responses showed more hostility, especially when asked "Which one are you?" At an embassy reception in Washington, the British ambassador said, "Hello, John." "I'm not John, I'm Charlie," he replied, ". . . that's John," pointing to George Harrison. "Hello, John," the ambassador said to George. A CBS reporter dragged John in front of a camera and told him, "You are looking in the face of forty million people. How do you feel?" He replied, "Do you really want to know?"

No one knew it in 1964, not even John, but that exchange would become a central theme of his life and work: How do you feel? / Do you really want to know? When Jann Wenner of *Rolling Stone* asked him "How do you feel?" in 1970, John's answer took up forty thousand words. In 1964 his response, "Do you really want to know?," indicated only that he had something he was concealing. It would be a few years before John could overcome that need to repress his real feelings.

The Beatles' summer tour of America in 1966 marked the point at which John began to answer the question honestly. He started by saying how he felt about the war in Vietnam. Later he looked back with justifiable pride on the decision to speak out. He called it "a pretty radical thing to do, especially for the Fab Four. . . . The continual awareness of what was going on made me feel ashamed I wasn't saying anything. I burst out because I could no longer play that game any more."

He had begun expressing radical ideas about politics before the tour began. "The trouble with government as it is is that it doesn't represent the people. It controls them," he told *Disc Weekly,* a magazine which was not known for political radicalism, in April 1966. "All they seem to want to do—the people who run the country—is keep themselves in power and stop us knowing what's going on. . . . I'm not saying politicians are all terrible men. It's just the system of government that I don't like. It'll be hard to change."

The banning of the butcher cover, the humiliating apology he was forced to make for his "Jesus" remark, the Ku Klux Klan picket line and right-wing counterrally, his fear of being shot in Memphis—these crucial events were "just too much" for John, as he said in a subsequent interview, especially in a country that was pouring devastation on the Vietnamese. As a result of their experiences on the 1966 American tour, the Beatles decided it would be their last.

Once John had broken the taboo on telling what he really felt and thought, there was no turning back. The extent of the transformation he had undergone that summer became clear in the fall of 1966, when John gave *Look* magazine an interview. His comments on class, politics, and youth culture were virtually identical to what he would say in the famous interview *Lennon Remembers* more than four years later. What effect did the Beatles have on British society? In 1966 he answered, "Everybody can go around in England with long hair a bit, and boys can wear flowered trousers, but there's still the same old nonsense going on. The class thing is just as snobby as it ever was." In 1970 he said, "The class system and the whole bullshit bourgeois scene is exactly the same except that there is a lot of middle-class kids with long hair walking around London in trendy clothes." Asked about the early Beatles in 1966, he said, "We weren't as open and as truthful when we didn't have the power to be. . . . We had to wear suits to get on TV. We had to compromise." In 1970 he said, "Brian put us in suits . . . But we sold out, you know."

Since 1966 John had been expressing ideas that still seemed striking and radical at the end of 1970: an insistence that the counterculture had not brought real social change, a class-conscious hostility to the British elite, a mixture of resentment and shame over the Beatles' abandonment of their early rebellious stance, and a deep desire to be truthful. The American summer tour of 1966 marked the first step in John's development as a self-conscious radical. What he needed now was a form for these feelings, a way to express these ideas in his work.

Part II

ROCK AGAINST REVOLUTION

3

Private Gripweed and Yoko Ono

"We can't go on holding hands forever," John declared in July 1966. "We have been Beatles as best we will ever be." That fall he went to work on *How I Won the War*. In the conventional interpretation, John did the film in an effort to find something to do after the Beatles stopped touring; his acting was good enough, but the work bored him, so he decided not to do any more films. This view fails to grasp the real significance the film had in his development. *How I Won the War* was John's first big step toward becoming a "real person" engaged with the peace movement and the avant-garde. The film is his earliest major statement as a serious artist of an antiwar position which would become the central theme of his public life.

John's development in these directions has typically been attributed to the influence of Yoko. Of course it's impossible to exaggerate her significance in his transformation, but *How I Won the War* was an artistic collaboration with film director Richard Lester, two years before John teamed up with Yoko. In his earlier work with Lester on *A Hard Day's Night* John had done a beautiful job of being a Beatle, and perhaps because of that collaboration he was able to work with Lester toward creating a new identity for himself.

In *How I Won the War* a detachment of British soldiers in World War II is sent out on a mission to build an "advanced cricket pitch" a hundred miles behind enemy lines in the North African desert. The leader, Lieutenant Ernest Goodbody, is a typical upper-class officer, spouting patriotic clichés. His men all have working-class backgrounds, and are familiar types: the hero, the coward, the fat man, the bully, and the loner, Private Gripweed, played by John with his marvelous Liverpool accent. The commanding officer, Colonel Grapple, is a complete idiot. He comes across one of his tanks which has been hit by a shell and shoots it to put it out of its misery. The squad moves from the desert to the European front, where Goodbody finds his first real friend: a captured Nazi officer who prefers to know nothing about Dachau and Buchenwald and spends his time painting watercolors of a bridge over the Rhine. Goodbody buys the bridge from the German with a check he knows will bounce. Virtually all his men have been horribly slaughtered, but he couldn't care less. The war was great, and he won it—with a bad check.

How I Won the War had only a superficial resemblance to black comedy or satire like *Dr. Strangelove.* It was a radically new kind of film, which drew upon elements of avant-garde theater. Lester repeatedly broke the narrative we expect in a movie: actors stepped out of their roles to address the audience, or appeared suddenly in strange costumes; death scenes were interrupted by the appearance of parents on the battlefields, giving fatuous comfort and advice.

How I Won the War was above all a critique of war movies. Everyone carries war movies in their heads, Lester suggested, especially soldiers. He showed a brave but tiny band of British marching into the camp of a much larger Nazi contingent, energetically whistling the theme from *Bridge on the River Kwai.* The Germans, overwhelmed by this stirring spectacle, surrendered. This reflexive element—film about film—linked *How I Won the War* to the currents of modernist art.

The film systematically and self-consciously exploded the ways movies had portrayed war. Hollywood has made war a special kind of entertainment: an uplifting spectacle, filled with lessons about heroism, sacrifice, and comradeship, concealing its true monstrosity. Lester started with the familiar dramatic device of the buddies on the battlefield, and then brutally interrupted it by inserting newsreel footage of real World War II battles, showing sickening scenes of anonymous mass slaughter. Virtually all the fictional soldiers died too, and none died Hollywood deaths, heroes in the eyes of their buddies and thus the audience. Their deaths were lonely, miserable, and absurd. Lester showed heroism to be a pathetic, deadly illusion in modern war. He linked Hollywood's glorification of past wars with contemporary issues toward the end of the film, when one ghostly soldier said to another, "There's a new war shaping up in Vietnam; do you think you'll be in it?" "No," the other replied, "I don't like the director."

John submerged himself in the role of Gripweed, putting on glasses and cutting his hair—a potent symbol of his changing identity. After *How I Won the War* was finished, John did not take off the wire-rimmed National Health Service glasses that had been part of the character he played. Keeping the glasses was a sign that he was creating a new identity for himself, in which the antiwar Private Gripweed was a part. The glasses became a symbol of this new John Lennon, the owlish hippie, more serious and intellectual, no longer looking like a teen idol.

Time, *Life*, and *Newsweek* all panned the film for its politics. *Time*'s critic barked that it was "tasteless" and objected particularly to the film's satirical treatment of Winston Churchill. Richard Schickel used his review in *Life* to criticize the antiwar movement. The film "reminds one of nothing so much as an ill-organized peace parade with its coalition of pediatricians, housewives, students, flower children and Black Power advocates shambling along the street. . . . If war is too important a matter to be left to the generals, then peace is too important a matter to be left to those who cannot coherently organize a parade or a movie."

The hostile critics failed to see the film's real problems. It ridiculed officers, portraying them as blithering idiots. But would war be any better if military officers were intelligent, competent professionals? Lester failed to distinguish between just and unjust wars. He did not seem to see that the war against fascism had a higher moral status than the Vietnam war.

———

How I Won the War represented a giant step for John, especially in comparison to the two Beatles movies Lester had directed. Back in 1963, the head of United Artists in London told producer Walter Shenson, "We want a low-budget comedy with the Beatles." Shenson wasn't enthusiastic, but Lester was, in spite of the terms UA proposed. It was to be "an exploitation film," he recalled. "Their principle was to make it as quickly as possible and get it out before the Beatles' popularity faded. It was to be made as a local picture for the English market, because at that point they had not gone on American tour."

A Hard Day's Night did not resemble earlier rock and roll films, most of which had basically the same plot: "Let's-put-on-a-prom-and-invite-the-Teen-Chords." Lester's film told the story of a day in the life of the Fab Four, and did so with *cinéma-vérité* energy and style. The lads traveled by train to a concert performance, dodging screaming fans, meeting reporters and promoters, and escaping when they could to romp by themselves. The film dramatized the conflict between the freedom and exuberance of the Beatles, with their working-class accents, and the calculation of the businessmen seeking to exploit or oppress them.

In an early scene, the Beatles get into a dispute on a train with an upper-class businessman reading the *Financial Times.* John says, "Y' can't win with this sort. After all, it's his train, isn't it, Mister?"

"Don't take that tone with me, young man!"

"Give us a kiss," John replies, puckering up.

A manufacturer of trendy clothes wants George's endorsement. "You'll like these," he says. "You really 'dig' them. They're 'fab' and all the other pimply hyperbole."

"I wouldn't be seen dead in them. They're grotty."

"Of course they're grotty, you wretched nit! That's why they were designed, but that's what you'll want."

"I don't care."

"And that pose is out too, Sunny Jim. The new thing is to care passionately and be right-wing."

John mocks the TV director, who protests, "I've won an award."

"A likely story," John tells him. The director wants them to rehearse. When Ringo agrees, John says, "He's betrayed his class."

And in a scene from the script, cut from the film, the Beatles' car "overtakes a company director's Rolls. JOHN lowers his window and the BOYS let out an imaginary hail of bullets at the executive in the back. He reacts violently and starts to shout at them. . . . What we hear is unpleasant."

The film showed the Beatles resisting the businessmen of the entertainment world with playfulness and a self-deprecating wit. Of course, this wasn't John's idea. The script was written by Alun Owen, picked by John and the others because he was a fellow Liverpudlian and because they liked his work. He spent several days observing the Beatles on tour, where he developed the ideas that went into the script. Visually, the oppressiveness faced by the Beatles is represented by claustrophobic interiors. The most exhilarating moments of the film come when the Beatles finally break out, escaping into an open field. While the soundtrack plays "Can't Buy Me Love," the boys play a vigorous game of soccer with an imaginary ball, take a series of jumps shot in slow motion so that they look like they're flying, and, in a glorious helicopter shot, cross and recross the field in perfect time to the music. The scene ends with a strange man saying, "I suppose you know this is private property."

Lester also succeeded in working music into a film more smoothly than anyone had done before. We see some of the songs played in rehearsal; some are heard over a jukebox in a dance club; some we watch over a bank of TV monitors in the control booth as the Beatles perform. Throughout the film the lads are moving closer to a live concert. When it finally comes, at the end of the film, they sing "Tell Me Why," "If I Fell," "I Should Have Known Better," and "She Loves You." The Beatles glow with passionate energy, the songs are driving and joyous, and the audience, in a series of close-ups and fast pans, greets them with wave after wave of screaming, cheering, and sobbing.

The songs in *A Hard Day's Night* showed that Lennon and McCartney were growing as writers. On the title cut, John sang the verses and Paul the choruses. The song had more complicated chord changes than anything in rock music, eleven chords in all; the opening chord gained fame as the most complex and baffling one. John sang "Tell Me Why" and "I Should Have Known Better," strong dance numbers, and "I'll Cry Instead," one of the first songs in which he told the truth: "I've got a chip on my shoulder that's bigger than my feet."

Paul sang "Money can't buy me love," in a driving song whose sentimental message challenged John's version of the rock classic "Money—that's what I want," which he had been singing since the Beatles' Hamburg days in 1960–1962, before Beatlemania. After *A Hard Day's Night* they replaced John's "Money" with Paul's "Can't Buy Me Love" in their concert repertoire. John didn't sing his song again until he left the Beatles.

John's character in the film was not distinct from Paul's or George's. They all played more or less the same part, playful, witty, and irreverent. Only Ringo was established in a distinctive role. Lester explained subsequently that Ringo had been chosen arbitrarily to be the sad one who would go on a long walk by himself. "We were trying to separate their characters officially, because they were—especially at this time—more like each other than was safe," Lester said. Groucho Marx felt the problem had not been solved. He went to see *A Hard Day's Night* because people said it was reminiscent of the Marx Brothers' films. But, Groucho complained, "the Marx Brothers' characters were different. The Beatles are all the same."

The film cost United Artists a mere $600,000. It opened three months after the first day of shooting. Just as UA had planned, the advance album sales put the film in profit before it opened. UA did not realize how big the film's gross would be: $5.6 million, which set a record for a rock movie, outstripping Elvis' *Viva Las Vegas* by half a million. (That figure would be dwarfed by the rock films of the seventies: *Woodstock* made $16 million in 1970, *American Graffiti* made $56 million in 1973, and *Saturday Night Fever* made $74 million in 1977.) But *A Hard Day's Night* was not even nominated for the Academy Awards for best film or best musical score. They went respectively to *My Fair Lady* and *Mary Poppins*.

A Hard Day's Night won praise for its political stance from the American Communist Party's youth magazine, which devoted part of its first issue to an assessment of the film. The magazine praised the Beatles as "the true and unique voice of Liverpool's working class," who despite their success had "managed to keep their Merseyside modesty and their working class wit." The film showed their "refreshing, light-hearted contempt for the very society that has made them what they are," and their "irreverent, witty attacks . . . on the hallowed idols in our world of conformity and complacency."

Lennon's second film with Lester, *Help!*, opened in August 1966. *A Hard Day's Night* had been whimsical and fanciful, but its plot dealt with the social reality of the Beatles' careers. It worked because it hit home. Its humor mattered. *Help!* in contrast had a plot that was stupid and irrelevant: the sinister Orientals of old Hollywood B movies, trying to get back a sacred jewel. The film's other flaws were attempts to overcome this basic one—the "witless orgy of expensive production that strangles the Beatles," as critic Dwight MacDonald put it, the extravagant locations in the Alps, in the Caribbean, and at Stonehenge, the dizzy pace and constant effort to be wildly comic. When John sang "Help!," he could have been singing about their problems in the film itself.

Lester later explained the problem he faced in making *Help!* It couldn't be about their work; they had already done that in *A Hard Day's Night.* It couldn't be about their real lives; drugs, marijuana, and sex on the road were taboo. It couldn't be a real fiction film; the Beatles lacked the discipline to learn lines. "They had to be passive," Lester concluded. "We had to create this huge baroque fantasy through which they passed." John later complained that they felt like extras in their own film. Lester's comments indicate just how right John was.

———

After John finished *How I Won the War,* he returned to London and started following the avant-garde art scene. In November 1966 he went to the Indica Gallery, run by Marianne Faithfull's husband, John Dunbar. Yoko Ono was finishing the installation of her show for its opening the next night. She was married and living with her husband, Tony Cox. "The first thing that crossed my mind," she later recalled about meeting John, "was that I wouldn't mind having an affair with a man like that. It was so nice and pleasant and he seemed so sensitive and imaginative. I remembered every bit of our conversation afterwards, although I didn't realize that he was John Lennon. I was an underground person, and such an artistic snob. I knew about the Beatles, of course, . . . but I wasn't interested in them."

If Yoko was attracted to John as a person, he was fascinated by her as an artist. She had been part of the New York avant-garde for fifteen years. Born in Japan in 1933, daughter of a prominent banker, she had moved to New York with her family when she was nineteen, and went to Sarah Lawrence in the mid-fifties. She left before graduating, and started sponsoring loft concerts in lower Manhattan in 1959. Among those who attended were John Cage, Max Ernst, Robert Rauschenberg, and Jasper Johns.

She performed in Japan with Cage in 1960, learning from him about musical composition based on random choices and silence and about the use of unconventional sources for music, such as his piece for twelve radios tuned to different stations. Kate Millett was also in Japan, and remembered that "Yoko was utterly fearless in the face of Japan's tedious Victorian conventions. Women were not allowed to go out at night. But she went everywhere she wanted to, did whatever she wanted to. By herself, she was doing a daring art form in a country that hardly permitted women to participate in the art world at all. She seemed to have an enormous amount of strength and unconventionality and scintillating mental power."

She gave a concert of conceptual music at Carnegie Hall in 1961 in which the audience heard sounds made as performers moved around a dark stage. The New York *Times* reviewer spelled her name "Yoke One." She had a one-woman show at a Madison Avenue gallery the same year, showing her "instruction paintings." In one, viewers were told to light a match in front of a blank canvas and watch the smoke. The book *Grapefruit* was a collection of these instructions. She had five hundred copies printed in Japan in 1964, after spending two years there giving concerts and readings.

She returned to New York and in 1964 joined Fluxus, an international group developing conceptual art. Her work appeared in the 1965 Fluxorchestra concert at Carnegie Hall. In her "Sky Piece," the "orchestra is bandaged together and dragged off the stage." The February 1966 edition of the Fluxus newspaper announced "Yoko Ono & Dance Co." and their "Do It Yourself Fluxfest." It gave *Grapefruit*-styled instructions for a thirteen-day performance, beginning with "breathe" for the first day, and including for subsequent days "watch the sky" and "carry a stone until you forget about it."

She came to London in 1966 to show her work and during that time met John. In 1967 she moved to the center of public controversy with her *Film No. 4, Bottoms,* in which 365 notable people appeared one at a time for ten seconds each. Their bare bottoms filled the frame. When the film censors banned it, she said, "It's quite harmless. There's no murder or violence in it. Why shouldn't it be given a certificate?" She explained that she wanted to break down the "aristocratic professionalism" of the film world and to use humor to challenge the pretensions of art films. The same year she wrapped the lions in Trafalgar Square, a year before Christo wrapped his first piece, the fountain at the Spoleto festival.

"Our minds met before our bodies did," John later explained. At first "we weren't going to be lovers." Instead, he wanted to become her patron, sponsoring her shows and producing her music on Apple Records. He underwrote her "Half-Wind Show" at London's Lisson Gallery in 1967. Yoko's work exemplified the art of the sixties. The avant-garde artists of the fifties had created permanent objects; Yoko created ideas and performances. Her work was ephemeral. The fifties artists had worked with the traditional media of painting and music. She rejected these in favor of everyday or unconventional materials. The fifties avant-garde had left its audience contemplating its work. Yoko worked to draw the audience into the art in a more active way. The fifties artists had been weighty and serious; Yoko's work was humorous, playful, and modest in comparison, but at the same time thoroughly uncompromising in its radicalism.

"Yoko's art was like a big open door for John, like stepping into a sunny field," Dan Richter said. He had been Yoko's assistant in London before she met John and worked for the two of them afterward. "She offered John a legitimacy for things he really didn't have form for yet." And Yoko was not only an esthetic radical. She was a woman in a man's world, and a Japanese person in an Anglo-American world. Passionately dedicated to her work and to challenging the barriers of the white male New York art scene, she had to be courageous and strong. John had never met such a woman.

John had made a start at moving out of the Fab Four, toward telling the truth, toward using his power as a superstar to present radical ideas in experimental forms. But he didn't want to do all this by himself. "I just didn't have the guts to do it," he explained in 1980. "Because I didn't know where to go." He always worked with a partner, in an artistic collective. *How I Won the War* was not enough of a success to make Lester his new partner, and acting in feature films was too slow for John. And at this point, in 1967, it had never occurred to him that a woman could be his creative partner. He admired Yoko, but wasn't ready to leave his wife Cynthia to join her. So his partner was still Paul.

4

Sgt. Pepper and Flower Power

Songs about childhood: that was the first project John and Paul undertook in 1966. Each did one, and the Beatles put more effort into recording them than they had given to most of their albums. The songs came out as opposite sides of the same single, with Paul's "Penny Lane" on the A side. He sang sweetly and affectionately about the "blue suburban skies" of his childhood shopping center.

John's feelings about his childhood were not sweet. His childhood experiences hurt him. How badly he would not be able to say until the *Plastic Ono Band* album in 1970. But the song he recorded at the end of 1966 represented a step in that direction: "Strawberry Fields Forever."

The song was part of his first attempt to move beyond the Beatles. He wrote it in Spain, during the shooting of *How I Won the War*. He worked on the song for six full weeks—"time to think," he called it.

When he sang "I'm going to Strawberry Fields," he was singing about a real place in Liverpool: a grim orphanage. It was not far from his Aunt Mimi's, with whom he lived from the age of five, after his father abandoned him and his mother decided to have his aunt raise him. His sense of loss over these childhood traumas was expressed for the first time in the song. He was taking his first steps toward the awful screams "Mama, don't go / Daddy, come home" on the opening track of the *Plastic Ono Band* album.

When he sang "Nothing is real," he was doing something he had never done before: naming the childhood feeling that had intensified during his life as a Beatle. The line anticipated the project of "becoming real," which he declared in 1970. But in 1966 he couldn't imagine overcoming that sense of unreality. He could barely express his feelings of isolation—"No one I think is in my tree"—and hopelessness—"it doesn't matter much to me."

Few understood what John was doing. He wanted it that way. He had carefully concealed his ideas in a dizzy, dreamy *tour de force* of sound that saturated the listener with music. But the Beatles had ceased to exist as a band on that song; John was alone, his music coming from electronic devices in the recording studio, not from the Fab Four. The promotional video for the song helped conceal John's real purpose, opening with the Beatles romping in a big field on a beautiful sunny day. He knew what people wanted from the Beatles: their playful optimism, not the terrifying truth about his feelings of abandonment, isolation, and hopelessness.

After the Beatles released "Strawberry Fields Forever," Paul got an idea for a new album: bring the songs together around a single concept. The Beatles would assume the identities of another band, old-time music-hall entertainers, and the music on the album would take rock on a tour of popular styles of the century: marching bands, circus music, folk songs, jazz hits, the new psychedelic sounds. They would create dazzling effects in the studio, effects that had never been put on a pop album before.

Sgt. Pepper's Lonely Hearts Club Band, with its rich variety of sounds and feelings, seemed to show that rock had become broad enough and free enough to express anything. Greil Marcus, writing on rock for the San Francisco underground *Express Times,* recalled listening to an advance copy with friends: "You mean this thing is going to be in the stores, we can buy it, listen to it ourselves?" The album made history in a dozen ways: it brought art to pop; it mixed good-time rock and roll with thoughtful ballads; its cover—a collage of the Beatles surrounded by heroes and celebrities—was amazing; its budget—$75,000—and sales—2.7 million in the United States—were unprecedented. But John's work on the album pulled him off the road leading from *How I Won the War* to the radical art of the *Plastic Ono Band* album. For him *Sgt. Pepper* was a step backward.

The album was mostly Paul's. He was the principal composer of seven of the twelve songs. "She's Leaving Home" was a gem of realism, and his whimsy was never more delightful than on "Lovely Rita" and "When I'm Sixty-four."

After the reprise of the "Sgt. Pepper" theme, after the end of the music-hall performance, John sings about real life, right now, with its loneliness and horrors. "A Day in the Life" presents a vivid contrast to the playful optimism of the rest of the album.

The opening line took on a terrible new meaning after John was killed: "I read the news today oh boy." The "oh boy" seems too real: sad, vulnerable, and puzzled. The lyrics represent a kind of dream journalism in which the facts of an ordinary day do not connect. John tells how terrible events are presented by the media as a form of entertainment, leaving the viewer feeling confused, isolated, anxious, and filled with dread. The images are concise and chilling: a suicide in a car, crowds that stand and stare and then turn away. John sings with a controlled intensity. His voice is at first subdued; soon it almost cracks with despair. The insistent beat disintegrates. The music reaches a crescendo of dissonance.

Paul's bridge interrupts: the narrator awakens, and with a routinized, nervous energy, gets ready to go to work, where he falls back into his "dream." John returns with more of the day's news: "four thousand holes in Blackburn, Lancashire." Later he explained this image as coming from a newspaper article on potholes in the street, near the article describing the man who committed suicide. The newspaper regards the terrible suicide and the insignificant potholes equally as "news." Sgt. Pepper's band ended its concert complimenting its "lovely audience." John then describes the audience in the Albert Hall as "holes," lifeless and empty.

His response to these terrifying images is to propose to turn us on. But this trip will not be fun, it will not be getting high with a little help from our friends. This is turning on in pain and defeat, to escape the misery of "a day in the life." At the end John's terror and despair have turned into an irrevocable hopelessness. The music culminates in a dissonant, formless, nightmarish orchestral crescendo, ending with a forty-three-second chord of utter finality.

John's other songs included "Good Morning, Good Morning," which hinted at his dark feelings, and then denied them: "I've got nothing to say but it's okay." He contributed the weakest song on the album, "Being for the Benefit of Mr. Kite." Its elaborate circus sound effects only emphasized that it lacked something. The song of John's that caused the most excitement was "Lucy in the Sky with Diamonds." It was psychedelic.

John had fun telling straight reporters the song's title came not from the initials LSD, but from something his four-year-old son Julian had written. The reporters didn't really need to ask. If they had read the words on the jacket sleeve, they would have seen that the song described an acid trip. If they had actually listened, they would have heard John's effort to simulate a trip with sounds. The music captured some of the swooning euphoria of the acid experience, but the lyrics were cloying, even in 1967: "rocking horse people eat marshmallow pies."

The line about "flowers that grow so in-cred-ibly high" ·did provide a nice image for a central chapter in the history of youth culture: flower power and psychedelia. LSD, its advocates promised, brought a new kind of experience and knowledge. It broke down the barriers that separated people from the rich, hidden utopia within themselves. It gave people an immediate, sensuous experience of colors and sounds, and promised a direct, authentic knowledge of the self and others. It revealed the extent to which bourgeois culture locked people into drab routines, cutting them off from their true feelings and perceptions. It exposed the isolation and repression of daily life in straight society. It brought emotional experiences so intense you would never be the same afterward.

There was also the possibility that this experience would be too intense, this self-knowledge too frightening, unbearable: the "bad trip." People had killed themselves on bad trips, people had gone into mental hospitals when they came down. For John, with his feelings of isolation and hopelessness, taking LSD required either recklessness or courage.

When John took it, and thereby joined the counterculture elite, he wanted to make music out of his experiences. Bob Dylan had shown it could be done in "Mr. Tambourine Man," which conveyed the dreamy quality of one kind of marijuana high. John set out to do the same for LSD. His song "Tomorrow Never Knows" on *Revolver* described the psychedelic quest for knowledge with strange, distorted sounds that had nothing to do with rock music: violin snatches, barrelhouse piano, tapes running backward. The lyrics were paradoxical and stirring: "Play the game existence to the end / Of the beginning." "Lucy in the Sky" emphasized simply the visual weirdness induced by LSD—the marmalade skies. This was the acid trip at its most trivial.

The way to self-knowledge through LSD was to dissolve the ego, to let go of desire and ambition, John explained in "Tomorrow Never Knows." You found yourself by losing yourself. This approach combined a life-affirming optimism with a profound passivity. For some, LSD provided an intense form of recreation; for John it was the basis of a completely serious search for himself. As critics Robert Christgau and John Piccarella put it recently, he "went with the flow down into the flood."

Although this search for self-knowledge through LSD was an honorable one, it didn't work for John. Three years later in *Lennon Remembers* he explained, "I got the wrong . . . message on acid—that you should destroy your ego. And I did, you know." It nearly brought him to disaster. But at the end of his LSD experience, isolated from the Beatles, with his defenses broken down, he would be compelled to return to basics, to start over.

During the summer of 1967, however, none of this was clear. The Beatles as a group stood not only for the quest for self-knowledge through LSD but for "flower power." Flower power seemed hopelessly apolitical to New Left activists, but it represented a profound cultural revolution. The hippies rejected virtually all of bourgeois society: its sexual repression, private property, individualism and competition, authoritarian family, definitions of masculinity and femininity, linear logic, and compulsive cleanliness. Flower power asserted a utopian politics. Its communes brought to life an alternative community and culture on the fringes of the straight world. This community valued play over work, spontaneity over order, shared poverty over individual acquisitiveness.

Flower power opposed the politics not only of the mainstream but also of the left. Hippies saw the confrontation tactics and mass demonstrations of the antiwar movement as a mirror of the status quo: they addressed the same issues, sought the same kind of power, reproduced the straight world's forms of domination and repressive work routines.

Despite this explicit rejection of political activism, the hippies contributed to the development of the New Left—perhaps in spite of themselves, and typically without any conscious intention. They expanded the arena of the political. The government's foreign and domestic policies were not the only, or even the most important, forms of oppression that had to be challenged. Domination in the family, the oppressive organization of work and play, sexual repression—the hippies insisted that a radical movement had to address these issues of personal life, had to pursue a politics of liberation.

They insisted also that the challenge to bourgeois society had to go beyond criticism and protest. The values of the counterculture had to be put into practice every day. The radical project was not just for some distant future; the work of creating a new society had to begin immediately, in the interstices of the old one.

The forms of protest with which the hippies confronted straight society were playful, imaginative, and improvised. When buses brought tourists to stare at Haight-Ashbury in 1967, hippies ran alongside holding up mirrors. Hippie street life emphasized the put-on; hippies were happy to shock straight people. This style made its mark on the movement's tactics. It demonstrated how new forms of protest and resistance could be created. It expanded the definition of the political act.

Hippies understood that revolutions require a transformation not only of social and political organization but also of consciousness. They understood better than the early New Left that society exercised domination not just over the organization of daily life but also over forms of thought. Thus they sought to create new kinds of subjectivity, to liberate the imagination. Over the next several years John would embrace each of these central themes of the counterculture and work to bring them into New Left politics.

During the summer of *Sgt. Pepper*, however, these links between the counterculture and the New Left remained murky for John and for everyone else. The underground press began to express the values and concerns of both movements, but was not yet making any sustained effort to examine the areas of antagonism and alliance. The first underground papers—the Los Angeles *Free Press*, the Berkeley *Barb*, New York's *East Village Other*—were satisfied to mix articles about the drug culture, sexual freedom, police brutality, macrobiotics, and protest demonstrations with record reviews. A serious debate about sixties music and politics would not begin for another year, and it would be provoked by John and his song "Revolution." In the meantime, virtually everyone loved *Sgt. Pepper.*

Robert Christgau, who would lead in developing the self-consciousness of the New Left and the counterculture about music and politics, was writing in a music magazine called *Cheetah* at the time. He called *Sgt. Pepper* "the best rock album ever made" because of its "exploration of the formal possibilities" of "aboriginal rock and roll," and because it served as a "catalyst for the entire youth movement." The youth movement, he wrote, "sadly, perhaps, is not about overthrowing society. It is about living with it, coping. . . . While part of me feels ashamed every day for my own society, another part of me is very much of that society."

The Beatles' right-wing critics argued that *Sgt. Pepper* was communistic. The proof, they said, was on the album cover, where among the figures standing behind the Liverpool lads they found Karl Marx. The critics failed to note that Marx stood next to Oliver Hardy and behind an Indian guru who has never been identified. And Marx was the only political figure. The other radical heroes of the decade—Fidel, Che, Mao, Ho Chi Minh—were absent. But the immediate predecessors of the counterculture were there, those antagonists of bourgeois respectability, Lenny Bruce and William Burroughs.

Sgt. Pepper found listeners in the most unlikely places. A writer for *Christian Century* recalled that "With a Little Help from My Friends" was played at "an underground Eucharist service" held by a group planning a Lutheran conference on war and racism. The worship leader explained that "while many people thought 'friends' were drugs, Beatles lyrics usually had more than one meaning, and people who were sticking their necks out on the Vietnam issue would indeed need 'a little help from their friends.' "

Time magazine devoted a cover story to *Sgt. Pepper.* The Beatles' early music had "blended monotonously into the parched badlands of rock," the magazine declared with breathtaking ignorance. But *Sgt. Pepper* had changed all that. It turned pop music into "an art form." "A guaranteed package of psychic shivers," the record made "parents, professors, even business executives" into Beatle fans. This was supposed to be a compliment.

The *Time* story made Richard Goldstein's penetrating review seem particularly impressive. "For the first time, the Beatles have given us a package of special effects, dazzling but ultimately fraudulent," he wrote in the New York

Times. The Beatles had turned away from their achievements on *Revolver* and *Rubber Soul,* "the forging of rock into what is real. It made them artists, it made us fans. . . . We still need the Beatles, not as cloistered composers, but as companions. And they still need us, to teach them how to be real again."

=====

Sgt. Pepper contained no hint of the social and political conflicts that intensified through 1967. That spring, while the Beatles worked on the album, the antiwar movement in America took some big steps. Martin Luther King, Jr., finally declared, "We must combine the fervor of the civil rights movement with the peace movement." Women Strike for Peace demonstrated at the Pentagon; five thousand scientists petitioned for a bombing halt; and University of Wisconsin students forced Dow Chemical recruiters off campus. Dow manufactured napalm, the jelly dropped from American planes which clung to the skin of the Vietnamese as it burned.

Ramparts magazine revealed in March that the National Student Association had received more than $3 million from the CIA through dummy foundations. The magazine subsequently revealed that thirty other organizations and publications which claimed to be independent had been secretly funded by the CIA. On April 15 the largest antiwar demonstration to date was held in New York City, as 250,000 people marched down Fifth Avenue in a "peace parade," while 50,000 more marched in San Francisco. Heavyweight boxing champion Muhammad Ali was arrested after refusing induction into the Army. He had been denied conscientious-objector status. Boxing authorities immediately stripped him of his title as sports became politicized around the issues of war and race.

The summer of *Sgt. Pepper* was also the summer of ghetto rebellions in the United States. In mid-July Newark exploded: blacks battled police over a ten-square-mile area. After five nights, 24 blacks had been killed, more than 1,500 were injured, and 1,397 were arrested. A commission set up by the governor criticized the "excessive and unjustified force" used by National Guardsmen and police, who shot at black people indiscriminately and vandalized black businesses. A week later the Detroit ghetto exploded. Snipers held off National Guardsmen, and for the first time in twenty-five years officials summoned federal troops to quell a civil disturbance. The toll in Detroit was thirty-six blacks killed along with seven whites, over two thousand injured, five thousand arrested, and five thousand left homeless from 1,442 fires. Smaller riots broke out in Harlem, Milwaukee, Cambridge, Maryland, Minneapolis, and Chicago.

The ghetto uprisings revealed to white America the rage of the black underclass. They demonstrated the indiscriminately brutal response of white authority and suggested the tremendous gulf that separated white youth in the summer of *Sgt. Pepper*, flower power, and the peace movement from ghetto youth shouting "Burn, baby, burn." Census statistics released later in the year showed the material basis for black rage: 41 percent of nonwhite families earned less than $3,000 a year, compared to 12 percent of white families; the unemployment rate for blacks was double that for whites; most black young people attended segregated schools.

The Six-Day War in the Mideast took place that same summer. Israel launched a surprise attack on Egypt in June, responding to Egypt's military buildup, expulsion of the UN emergency force from the Sinai, and alliance with Syria, Jordan, and Iraq. Peter Brown described how the war touched the Beatles: "There was enormous pressure from the Jewish establishment in London during the war to get the Beatles to appear in a benefit concert for Israel. Brian said, 'Absolutely not.' He would never do benefits. He argued that you can't select these things wisely, so it's better not to do them at all. Our aim is to sell records, he said, so we should keep out of anything controversial. The pressures Jewish leaders applied were really pretty nasty ones. People like Lew Grade and Co. really put the old screws on Brian. It wasn't that he didn't sympathize with the cause. It was that he'd made this rule and he wasn't going to bend it, even if it affected something so close to him."

In the middle of that summer of conflict, the Beatles played a new song, written and sung by John: "All You Need Is Love." Seven hundred million people heard it in a worldwide TV satellite broadcast. It became the anthem of flower power that summer. Radicals continued to denounce John for it for the rest of his life.

The song expressed the highest value of the counterculture. In retrospect, "love" seems an absurdly naïve slogan. For the hippies, however, it represented a call for liberation from Protestant culture, with its repressive sexual taboos and its insistence on emotional restraint. John's song seemed to say that to find happiness, you didn't "need" the traditional bourgeois virtues— individualism, aggressiveness, competition, acquisitiveness. All you needed was love.

Neither the song's fans nor its critics had listened to it closely. John did not say that love would solve the world's problems. He suggested that the world's problems would take care of themselves; thus life could be devoted to love instead of to solving problems and achieving distant goals. The song presented the flower-power critique of movement politics: there was nothing you could do that couldn't be done by others; thus you didn't need to do anything about the killing in Vietnam or the oppression of America's blacks.

Everyone should relax and enjoy this place and this moment. John was arguing not only against bourgeois self-denial and future-mindedness but also against the activists' sense of urgency and their strong personal commitments to fighting injustice and oppression.

As usual, New Left writers were not unanimous about "All You Need Is Love." Most objected to John's message of acquiescence in the status quo, but some found things to like in the song. The SDS paper at Cornell University argued that it conveyed a "gentleness combined with strength" that distinguished it from most of rock, which was "an assault." The movement needed more of this nonviolence, and John was pointing the way.

On the flip side was a sweet self-satire, "Baby You're a Rich Man," in which Paul asks John questions in a soprano voice: What music is he going to play in the new key he's found? They were thinking about psychedelia at the time, but that question—what to do with his new ideas—was one John would start asking himself more and more seriously.

John followed that with "I Am the Walrus," released at the end of November 1967, the wildest music the Beatles ever recorded. Later he said he understood the Walrus in the Lewis Carroll poem to be a symbol of socialism, resisting the capitalist Carpenter. He was wrong about that. The Walrus and the Carpenter were both villains, eating the poor oysters they lured to take a walk with them. That isn't what made the Walrus important to John. He remembered the lines " 'The time has come,' the Walrus said, 'to talk of many things: of shoes and ships and sealing-wax, of cabbages and kings.' " When John sang "I Am the Walrus," he was identifying with this articulate symbol of the imagination.

The first line referred to the LSD-inspired project of destroying his ego— "I am he as you are he"—and asserted the sixties communal ideal: "we are all together." In each verse, John poured out a torrent of disjointed images, ending with "I'm crying." He sang that line without expression, with a blankness that was frightening. He was hinting that LSD wasn't working for him, but he was also disguising his bad feelings in a dizzying spectacle of sounds and words, as he had done with "Strawberry Fields Forever." He was not yet able to tell the truth simply and directly.

―――

The triumph of *Sgt. Pepper* served as a challenge to the Rolling Stones, Bob Dylan, and the rest of pop music in the summer of 1967. The Stones had started recording new material when *Sgt. Pepper* came out; they stayed in the studio another three months, working on the album that would be measured against the Beatles' masterpiece. Their work was interrupted by Mick Jagger's and Keith Richards' trials on drug charges. Two days before

Sgt. Pepper's release, Jagger was found guilty of possessing four ampheta-mine pills and sentenced to six months in prison; Richards, found guilty of permitting his house to be used for the smoking of hashish, was sentenced to one year. Even the ruling-class *Times* of London had to object, publish-ing an editorial titled "Who Breaks a Butterfly on a Wheel?" The Beatles jointly made a political statement, signing a full-page ad in the the *Times* three weeks after the release of *Sgt. Pepper* calling for the legalization of marijuana.

Jagger's drug bust and draconian sentence drove him to the left. "The way things are run in Britain and the States is rotten and it is up to the young to change everything," he declared after his trial. "The time is right now, revolution is valid. The kids are ready to burn down the high-rise blocks and those stinking factories where they are forced to sweat their lives away. I'm going to do anything, anything that has to be done, to be a part of what is about to go down."

Their Satanic Majesties Request, recorded between June and September and released in November 1967, had none of this anger. It was the Stones' attempt to be more psychedelic than *Sgt. Pepper,* and it was a failure. Jagger had pushed to do it, and Brian Jones had opposed it, arguing the Stones should stay true to their roots in rhythm and blues. Americans missed the pun in the title: British passports read, "Her Britannic Majesty . . . requests and requires . . ." The Stones were referring to their recent drug busts, which made it impossible for them to travel freely. They tried to hide the weakness of the music by putting a 3-D cover on the album. At least the Beatles couldn't top that.

Sgt. Pepper was loved by the counterculture and imitated by the Stones, but it was challenged by Bob Dylan. In January 1968, six months after the Beatles' album appeared, he released his first album since his motorcycle accident a year and a half earlier: *John Wesley Harding.* The Beatles' music sounded extravagant; Dylan simply strummed his acoustic guitar. The Beatles were playful; Dylan was serious. The Beatles' sources ranged from the British music hall to the Indian raga; Dylan drew strictly on American music. Even the cover of *John Wesley Harding,* a plain black and white photo of Dylan surrounded by two Native American musicians and one woodsman, was a reply to the cover of *Sgt. Pepper.* Dylan's response to the Beatles, Robert Christgau wrote in May 1968, was "salutary" and "mature."

John Wesley Harding offered not only an artistic alternative to *Sgt. Pepper* but also a political one. While none of the songs spoke directly about the war, the entire album expressed a subtle awareness of it and showed how it was affecting Dylan. The Beatles' playfulness and fantasy ignored the war's exis-tence, while Dylan's new songs acknowledged it by trying to be real, and by playing fewer games than ever before. The best song on Dylan's album, "All along the Watchtower," expressed a new commitment to truthfulness and seriousness. The song opened with the old Dylan, "the joker," looking for a way out. But he had learned that life is too short for joking. New Left critics were less happy with "Dear Landlord," which seemed like his coming to terms with authority in society. But it was hard not to like the tender "I'll Be Your Baby Tonight."

Dylan himself was talking about John. "The last time I went to London I stayed at John Lennon's house," he told an interviewer. "You should see all the stuff that Lennon bought: big cars and a stuffed gorilla and thousands of things in every room in his house, cost a fortune. When I got back home I wondered what it would be like to have all those material things. I figured I had the money and I could do it, and I wondered if it would feel like anything real. So I bought all this stuff and filled my house with it and sat around in the middle of it all. And I felt nothing." He wasn't a working-class lad from Liverpool.

Meanwhile, in a different realm of popular music which for a while seemed untouched by artistic or political ambitions, the Beach Boys had been perfecting their sound, a celebration of complacent white middle-class suburban youth. Jim Miller has written sensitively about the contradictions faced by their brilliant leader Brian Wilson: "His business was the revitalization of myths he wished were true and knew were false." "California Girls" peaked at Number Two that summer. A masterpiece of white pop harmony, it later became a shampoo commercial. The Beach Boys' most ambitious album, *Pet Sounds*, somehow became obsolete when the new Beatles album appeared. After *Sgt. Pepper* the Beach Boys never got one of their songs into the Top Ten. Suddenly their records had become oldies.

During the summer of *Sgt. Pepper* the alternatives posed by soul music and soft rock became clearer than ever before. When *Sgt. Pepper* was released in June, the Number One song was Aretha Franklin's "Respect." Her album *I Never Loved a Man (The Way I Love You)* followed. More than anyone else, she brought the apocalypse of gospel to the white rock audience, singing with desperation and urgency. "Respect" was a powerfully rocking statement of feminist, black pride.

"Respect" was replaced in the Number One spot by the Fifth Dimension's "Up Up and Away," which realized its potential later when it became a TWA commercial. Smokey Robinson's greatest song, "The Tracks of My Tears," didn't get any higher than Number Nine. This was also the season of the shlock flower-power anthem that told people going to San Francisco to be sure to wear a flower in their ear.

At the end of the summer of *Sgt. Pepper* the Beatles seemed to have everything: they were a critical and popular triumph, they had the power to do anything they wanted. Then manager Brian Epstein died of an accidental overdose of sleeping pills. He was thirty-two years old and a millionaire. "I knew we were in trouble then," John said later in *Lennon Remembers*. "I thought, 'We've fucking had it.'"

5

From Brian Epstein to the Maharishi

John feared the future after Brian Epstein's death because he knew how important Epstein had been in taking those Liverpool tough guys and turning them into the Fab Four. Epstein came from a prosperous family of provincial Jewish merchants. The family store sold furniture and lamps, pianos and sheet music. As a child in local private schools, Brian was the victim of anti-Semitism. As an adult, Epstein had the misfortune to be gay in a social world where that was taboo. Forced to lead a double life, respectable businessman by day and homosexual by night, he was intermittently attacked by "queer-bashing" gangs of tough youths and occasionally subjected to blackmail and extortion.

Epstein, an energetic young businessman, persuaded the family to open a big record store and make him manager. When Beatle fans started asking for their records, Brian decided to find out what the excitement was about. He went to see them downstairs at the Cavern Club in November 1961; he was twenty-seven years old at the time. He called his book describing how he discovered them *A Cellarful of Noise;* Eric Idle of Monty Python parodied it as *A Cellarful of Goys.* Epstein signed a formal contract to manage the Beatles in December 1961.

The Beatles before Brian had been shaped by the material conditions of music-making in the rock clubs of Hamburg, West Germany. They spent a good part of the years from 1960 to 1962 working on Hamburg's Reeperbahn, with its strip clubs, prostitutes, and brawling sailors. Playing eight hours a night, the Beatles developed a loud, hard, exuberant style and a raw, desperate look. They had to play loud to drown out the drunks, they had to keep playing during the fights, and the crowds demanded a wild stage show. The Beatles could "make show," as the Germans put it—especially John, who screamed and leaped around the stage. "We'd been meek and mild musicians at first," drummer Pete Best said later. "Now we became a powerhouse."

The live recording made at the Star Club in Hamburg in 1962, released in 1977, suggests the energy with which the Beatles made show. Its twenty-six songs also indicate that the Beatles began as rock and roll purists. John's songs included Chuck Berry's "Sweet Little Sixteen," the Isley Brothers' "Twist and Shout," and Gene Vincent's "Be-Bop-A-Lula." Paul did Little Richard's "Long Tall Sally" and his "Kansas City" medley. John and Paul covered Phil Spector's first hit, "To Know Him Is to Love Him," and sang a Lennon-McCartney original, "I Saw Her Standing There." Paul also displayed a taste for sentimental shlock: he sang "A Taste of Honey," "Bésame Mucho," and "Falling in Love Again" for the Hamburg drunks.

The Beatles regarded their audience as adversaries. John recalled later that he "used to shout in English at the Germans, call them Nazis and tell them to fuck off." The louts just clamored for more. British sailors sometimes stopped by; they weren't much better. "After a few drinks," John recalled, "they'd start shouting 'Up Liverpool!' "

John and the other Beatles returned to Liverpool from Hamburg, as Eric Idle said in his parody *The Rutles*, "full of experience and pills." In March 1961 they made their first appearance at the Cavern Club, which would serve as their base as they became Liverpool's top group. The audience consisted of local teenagers instead of drunken sailors, but the working conditions there resembled Hamburg's: the music had to be hard and loud, the beat had to be strong.

Already the Beatles were distinguishing themselves from other local groups. "When we got back from Hamburg," John later said, "every group had a lead singer in a pink jacket. We were the only group that didn't have that one guy out front. . . . That was how we broke through: by being different." A group without a leader, they created their music collectively— a rare phenomenon that explained part of their magic and contributed to their appeal. The communal aspect of their artistic work, which would become so significant a symbol of the sixties, was already part of the Beatles before Brian.

Before Brian Epstein appeared on the scene, the Beatles had taken some important steps. They developed their collective identity and their loud and hard style, they practiced on the classics, they lived the life of drugs, sex, and rock and roll. But the most important steps in their musical and cultural development lay ahead. The Hamburg tapes contain none of Lennon and McCartney's musical inventiveness or lyrical brilliance and little of the originality with which they would soon transform pop music. Their character as individuals in a group had not yet developed. The Beatles before Brian remained old-fashioned working-class tough guys.

Epstein got them an audition at Decca Records, at which they sang the Coasters' "Searchin'." A man named Dick Rowe turned them down. A year later Paul said, "Rowe must be kicking himself now." John replied, "I hope he kicks himself to death."

In July 1962 Epstein convinced George Martin of EMI to sign the Beatles to its Parlophone subsidiary. Martin, who would play a major role in creating the sound of their later albums, had worked on the *Goon Show,* one of John's favorites. In his first move he got rid of the Beatles' mediocre drummer, Pete Best. The Beatles replaced him with Ringo, whose identity as the sad and lovable one masked a genuine musical talent.

Epstein now insisted the Beatles give up their leather outfits and their tough-guy appearance. When their first album, *Please Please Me,* appeared in March 1963, the cover showed them smiling in cheap new suits, looking clean, eager to please, and distinctly working-class. Eight months later *With the Beatles* came out, and Epstein had transformed them again. The Beatles wore black turtleneck sweaters, looked serious, and appeared in an arty shot with dramatic lighting and a grainy print. They looked like bohemian students, thoroughly middle-class.

They gave up their macho image, not because they were drawn to a less sexist conception of themselves, but because they wanted to win middle-class fans, to make money; as John said in *Lennon Remembers,* to "make it very, very big." If their motives were less than noble, the cultural consequences of their transformation were nevertheless positive: they helped loosen the straitjacket of conventional sex roles. The definitions of masculine and feminine that prevail in our society do not come directly from nature. Young people have to be taught what they mean, and rock plays a central role in this cultural process. Pop music provides a way for young people to express their sexuality, but it also tends to reinforce sexual stereotypes, and to deny the existence of alternative sexual identities. In this way rock operates also as a form of sexual control.

The Beatles challenged the way rock constructed male and female sexuality. Before the Beatles, rock organized sexuality around two poles: "cock rock" and "teenybop." Cock rock was (and remains today as "heavy metal") an explicit, crude expression of male sexual domination. The performers constantly reminded the audience of their prowess. Plunging shirts and tight pants prominently displayed male bodies. Microphone stands and guitars served as phallic symbols. The music itself was structured to suggest arousal and climax; the lyrics, and especially the vocal style, were assertive and arrogant. Women were portrayed as sex objects, or as possessive, endangering the freedom of men. The sexual meanings of cock rock were especially clear at live concerts.

Teenybop was consumed almost exclusively by girls. The male teenybop idol—Paul Anka provided the best example in the pre-Beatles era—was vulnerable, needy, and full of self-pity. He was young, soft, pretty and puppy-like, romantic, and easily hurt. Most important, he was anxious to find true love. He sang about feeling lonely. He was often let down or stood up. He needed a sensitive and sympathetic soulmate. For teenybop fans, pinups, posters, and TV appearances had almost as much significance as live performances.

The Beatles challenged the cock rock/teenybop division. They were something new: as rock theorists Simon Frith and Angela McRobbie wrote, "neither boys-together aggression nor boy-next-door pathos." Their personae suggested that the ideal male was no longer the tough, crude, and emotionally distant person, nor was he the lonely, pretty boy next door. He didn't take himself completely seriously, the way the traditional male did, and he was smarter, more energetic, and warmer.

Guardians of traditional sex roles objected to the Beatles' departure from the stereotyped male identity. Within the traditional framework, this could only be interpreted one way; thus the Beatles were denounced for being "feminine." That was wrong: they never acted like women.

Undoubtedly the Beatles remained deeply sexist in their own relationships with women at this time. And undoubtedly the Beatles' new sexual identities were part of a larger cultural change. But the Beatles helped construct a new, nonmacho male sexuality when other rock stars didn't.

The construction of this new ideal male figure was not John's project. The idea seems to have come from Epstein, who was gay, and whose only conscious purpose was to make the Beatles more popular. He was not shaping them into his own ideal of male sexuality; he was drawn to the exaggerated macho style, and, in any case, he kept his work and his sex life completely separate. Other groups had gay managers whose sexual preferences did not affect the way their music was presented. Nevertheless something about Brian's own break with conventional sexuality may have contributed to the way he shaped the Beatles' new sexual identity.

The Beatles' challenge to rock's organization of sexuality was less than relentless, especially in their early songs. Lennon and McCartney's lyrics often respected teenybop romantic conventions. Boys and girls held hands and fell in love, and John often promised not to be too sexually aggressive: "I'll be good like I know I should," he sang, and "I'm happy just to dance with you."

However, John also wrote a series of songs making obvious sexual demands, a theme from cock rock. In his very first song, he told his girl, "Please please me." His next song pleaded, "Love me do." John's raucous and passionate "I Want to Hold Your Hand" was a masterpiece of sexual frustration: when he touches her, he can't hide his "love," she's got "that something," and when he "feels that something," he wants to—hold her *hand,* sung with a head-shaking falsetto cry. Another of John's early songs triumphantly announced that he had discovered how to get girls to give in: All he had to do, he declared, was tell them the words they wanted to hear.

In John's early songs he concealed his bad feelings beneath teenybop conventions. He repressed his fears, his anger, and his depression, along with the vague wishes for peace and freedom that he would express in the next few years. The bad feelings he sang about were limited to the misery of the teenybop idol who had lost his girl. The one exception to these clichés was "There's a Place," in which he confessed that, when he felt "low," he went to a place where "there's no time and I'm alone." "It's my mind," he declared, a line whose awkwardness testified to its truthfulness. This idea would grow in significance in his music and his life over the next decade.

The Beatles' challenge to the conventions of cock rock and teenybop triumphed not just because of their personae but also because of their music. They broke out of three-chord cock rock and four-chord teenybop. Their songs brought in minor chords and unexpected sevenths, and had many more changes than guitar-players were used to. "All My Loving" had six chords; the next year "A Hard Day's Night" had eleven. Bob Dylan recognized Lennon and McCartney's creativity: "Their chords were outrageous," he said, "just outrageous." And they played their outrageous chords over a rough R&B beat. The Beatles sounded new and exciting because their songs had a structure that really was new and exciting.

The Beatles' musical triumph over cock rock and teenybop also depended on John's and Paul's singing. They sounded exhilarating, joyous, exuberant. Their singing style was not, however, as original as their music-writing; they had learned the screams, shouts, and falsetto cries of gospel-rooted R&B, and practiced the sweet, close harmonies introduced by early Motown and girl groups. The escalating cries of "Come on!" in "Please Please Me" and the call-and-response shouts of "Yeah!" in "It Won't Be Long" were pure R&B. Their vocal style thrilled a white audience that had not yet discovered the new black music, with its total release and wild expression of feeling.

Little Richard, who played on the same bill with the Beatles in Liverpool in 1962, was quoted in the newspaper *Mersey Beat* as saying, "Man, those Beatles are fabulous. If I hadn't seen them I'd never have dreamed they were white. They have a real authentic Negro sound." That was almost exactly what Sam Phillips said he found in Elvis: "Someone with the Negro sound and the Negro feel." There is no reason to believe Little Richard actually said the words attributed to him by *Mersey Beat*, or that, if he said them, he meant them, but still the parallels are striking. The Little Richard quote wouldn't have been published unless it expressed the way the Beatles wanted to be seen and heard. But the Beatles didn't simply cover black hits; they incorporated the black vocal-group style into their own distinctive songs. John never tried to "sound black"; he was proud to sing with his Liverpool accent.

The Beatles' music was created under conditions that gave them a degree of artistic autonomy rare in the world of pop music. Because they wrote their own songs, they were free from the grip of the hack songwriters and A&R men of the music-publishing industry. Because they accompanied themselves, producers had less power over how they sounded. Because they had served a long apprenticeship, and because they tried out their songs in front of live audiences before recording them, they knew what made their music work better than producers and executives did. As a result, under Epstein's management their music was really theirs; its passion and exhilaration were authentic.

Finally, the Beatles' triumph was part of a larger cultural change. In the last week of August 1963, the pop charts blossomed. The Beatles released "She Loves You," with John singing lead. In the United States new black music was gaining a white audience; that same week the Number One song was Little Stevie Wonder's "Fingertips, Pt. 2." And Number Two was Bob Dylan's "Blowin' in the Wind," sung by Peter, Paul and Mary. The same week, 200,000 people joined the march on Washington and heard Martin Luther King's "I have a dream" speech. The sixties were beginning.

In his most candid interviews, John repeatedly said that the Beatles under Epstein "sold out." That seems a harsh judgment, influenced perhaps by a facile contrast with Mick Jagger. But when Jagger played the part of rock's bad boy, he wasn't doing it to uphold a principle; he was reproducing a cock-rock stereotype. When the Beatles moved from being leather-clad tough guys to gentler and smarter people, they weren't selling out; they were constructing an alternative to the macho stereotype, and their music was expressing a wider range of feelings than rock and roll had ever expressed before.

However, when Epstein reshaped the Beatles' identities, he did force John to give up one important part of himself: his anger. That does not seem to have been true of any of the other Beatles. It's not clear that they gave up anything. But John was a genuinely angry young man. His anger may have been inchoate, expressed through the stereotypes of working-class macho, but it was real. When he played the cheerful wit, he had to repress a vital part of himself. And he couldn't do it for very long. It made him depressed. When he finally went into therapy, he learned to draw on his anger to create his greatest music.

John never had a close relationship with Brian, except during one brief period in 1963. In April John's wife Cynthia gave birth to their son Julian. Cynthia wrote in her memoirs, "It was a week before I saw my husband." John had been on tour; the Beatles had just that week achieved their first British Number One song, "Please Please Me," on which John sang lead. Cynthia remembered John's arrival as "a wonderful moment."

" 'He's bloody marvelous, Cyn. . . . Who's going to be a famous little rocker like his Dad then?' " But a crowd began to gather, and "very quickly . . . John was beginning to feel trapped."

"Before he left he told me that Brian had asked him to go on holiday to Spain with him and he wanted to know if I objected. I must admit that the request hit me like a bolt out of the blue. . . . I was well aware that John deserved a holiday. He had just completed a tour and recording sessions. I concealed my hurt and envy and gave him my blessings. He was delighted and left me a happy man."

In 1980 an interviewer asked John about this trip with Brian. "It was almost a love affair, but not quite," he said. "It was never consummated. But we did have a pretty intense relationship. And it was my first experience with someone I knew was a homosexual. . . . We used to sit in cafés and Brian would look at all the boys and I would ask, 'Do you like that one? Do you like this one?' "

John was touchy about homosexuality when he returned. Several weeks later, at Paul's twenty-first birthday party, John picked a fight with a local disc jockey who had helped them get several bookings. Later he explained to Hunter Davies, his official biographer, "I smashed him up. I broke his bloody ribs for him. I was pissed at the time. He'd called me a queer."

The spring of 1963 was filled with significant events for John: his first child was born the same week that he had his first nationwide hit song. It must have given him an intense sense of his own potency. The excitement of life on the road with the boys, a male adolescent fantasy come true, stood in sharp contrast, however, to the utter conventionality of Cynthia and the life she promised him. Her memoir conveys this clearly if inadvertently: John felt trapped by the crowded room, she says, but also he felt trapped by the prospect of his new role as father in a traditional household.

To escape this fate, at least briefly, John eagerly went off with Brian. If Brian found John attractive, John wasn't necessarily interested in a sexual relationship with him. Brian was twenty-nine, six years older than John. That six years separated two generations. Brian grew up before Elvis, before rock and roll. He dressed in business suits. He was in charge of the Beatles' business. He took care of them while they played music. John, faced with the prospect of being a father to Julian, preferred to go away with Brian, who had been a good father to him. For John, Brian's homosexuality may not have been as important as his status as an adult, one who didn't need John to grow up, who liked him as a youth.

After the Beatles gave up touring in 1966, a year before Epstein's death, they hardly ever saw him. Part of Brian's misery that year arose from his sense of uselessness in his work as the Beatles' manager, and part arose from despair over his doomed love affairs. "I'm no good with women," he once told his assistant, "and I'm no good with men."

By the early seventies John learned through Yoko how traditional sex roles oppressed women, and how the same ideology and power structure that oppressed women also oppressed homosexuals. In 1973 he contributed a poem and a drawing to *The Gay Liberation Book.* That took courage; virtually all of the other celebrity contributors—Gore Vidal, Allen Ginsberg, Paul Goodman—were themselves gay. John's knowledge of Epstein's suffering must have been in his mind when he decided to support gay liberation.

John and the others learned of Epstein's death while they were beginning another major step away from the conventional life of rock superstars: receiving instruction from the Maharishi Mahesh Yogi. John hoped meditation would do what LSD hadn't, bring him closer to truth and reality. Meditation also promised to provide some relief from his depression. "Through meditation I've learned how to tap energy that I've had in me all the time," he told talk-show host David Frost. "Before I could only reach this extra energy on good days when things were going well." With the enthusiasm of a convert, he recommended it to everyone: "Not just a special few, or brainy people or cranks, but everyone." John's song "Across the Universe" sought to convey the experience of meditation, admitting its fatalism and pessimism—"Nothing's gonna change my world." Years later he explained that meditation had offered a much-needed escape from life as a Beatle. "Somebody had a place in which I could withdraw," he said.

Going to India was George's idea. John and George had consistently been the radicals among the Beatles. They had insisted on denouncing the war in Vietnam; they took LSD first. John never drew back from new experiences the way Paul did. He wanted to find answers to the questions that troubled him, and he wanted relief from the unhappiness of Beatle life. He went to India, with the rest of the group.

Ringo left first, discreetly claiming the "food" didn't agree with him. John didn't change his mind about the value of meditation until the Maharishi was accused of sexual misconduct. In *Lennon Remembers* John explained what happened when they told him they were leaving. He asked, " 'Why?' I said, 'If you're so cosmic, you know why.' . . . And he gave me a look like 'I'll kill you, you bastard.' "

Mick Jagger had from the beginning called the Maharishi a "bloody old con man." Jagger told Keith Richards, "I can understand George falling for all that peace, love, and pay-the-bill crap, but not John. I'd always thought John was a bright lad."

John had spent less than eight months as a follower of the Maharishi—from August 1967 until April 1968—a brief period, especially in light of the media attention that relationship received. John never said the climactic trip to India had been a mistake. "I did write some of my best songs while I was there," he said, pointing to "Yer Blues" and "I'm So Tired." "The experience was worth it if only for the songs that came out."

During the time he spent meditating with the Maharishi, John's political interests continued to develop. In October 1967, two weeks after John appeared with the Maharishi on the *David Frost Show, How I Won the War* opened in London. At the premiere John explained his reasons for making the film: "I hate war. If there is another war I won't fight and I'll try to tell all the youngsters not to fight either. I hate all the sham." That political statement was the strongest he'd ever made.

Two days after the premiere, 100,000 people marched on the Pentagon. The Sunday newspapers reported both events. It was a fortuitous coincidence: the new kind of antiwar film that Lennon made with Lester found a counterpart of sorts in a new kind of political action. Both consciously sought to break the barriers of conventional definitions, to find new ways of declaring an antiwar position, to seek a transformation not only of government policy but also of the forms of political expression.

=====

In 1968 sustained debates began to appear in print that explored the Beatles' meaning and significance for the New Left and the counterculture. Two years before, discussions of the Beatles had been confined to mainstream magazines like *Time* and *Look;* the teen and fan magazines also wrote about them. The mass media had defined the audience for articles about the Beatles as puzzled parents and dumb fans; no self-conscious youth culture existed in print. That began to change in 1967, as the growing underground press wrote about *Sgt. Pepper,* but those articles mainly celebrated the Beatles' music.

The English took the lead early in 1968, when the *New Left Review* ran a debate about the alternative forms of personal and political engagement offered by the Beatles and the Rolling Stones. The prevailing view of the Beatles as "original, mature, serious, and thoughtful" was challenged by Alan Beckett. He argued that their music had "a dangerous tendency towards denial that there is anything difficult in relationships."

The Stones' music, in contrast, with its "arrogance, brutality and narcissism," constituted "a completely justifiable and welcome attack on the amorous clichés of popular music" and especially on the Beatles' kind of "facile intimacy." The Stones' music could have a "constructive, liberating effect on the individual," because it is "only when such feelings have been isolated, recognized and incorporated into the self, that they can be transmuted." The Stones' *Satanic Majesties,* however, which had been released a few months earlier, he judged a failure. Its attempt at psychedelic music resulted in "hackneyed imagery" that stood in sharp contrast to John's authentic accounts of the psychedelic experience, "Strawberry Fields" and "I Am the Walrus."

In a second *New Left Review* piece Richard Merton argued that the Beatles "have never strayed much beyond the strict limits of romantic convention. . . . Central moments of their *oeuvre* are nostalgia and whimsey, both eminently consecrated traditions of middle-class England. Lukacs's pejorative category of the 'pleasant' which dulls and pacifies fits much of their work with deadly accuracy." Here Merton was pointing to Paul's special contribution.

As for the Stones, their music is "about sexual exploitation, not narcissism," he argued. "The enormous merit—and audacity—of the Stones is to have repeatedly and consistently defied what is a central taboo of the social system: mention of sexual inequality. They have done so in the most radical and unacceptable way possible: by celebrating it. The light this black beam throws on the society is too bright for it. Nakedly proclaimed, inequality is *de facto* denounced."

Yet another *New Left Review* writer challenged this conclusion. "Who does the denouncing?" Michael Parsons asked. "Merton seems to mean that the Stones, by presenting us with a blatant and undisguised statement of male domination and exploitation," enable us to recognize and denounce it. But, he argued, we should not assume that the Stones adopt the same critical attitude that we do. Merton responded that "an artist's private purpose is not determinant of the objective meaning of his work. . . . Celebration of inequality is incompatible with it, because it taunts the oppressed to liberate themselves. The insistently jeering note of so many Jagger/Richards compositions is a form of solidarity."

The debate on sixties music and politics thus portrayed the Stones and the

Beatles as representing antagonistic social and cultural stances: "The Beatles want to hold your hand, the Stones want to burn your house" was the way one rock writer summed it up. But this argument overlooked the way those differences had been created by the media. The musical origins of the two groups were virtually identical. "Both of us came out of the same Chuck Berry, Little Richard, Elvis Presley school of music," Keith Richards admitted in 1981. "I think a lot of the difference between us was imaginary," the creation of Brian Epstein and Stones manager Andrew Oldham, both geniuses of public relations.

Jagger and Lennon did many of the same songs in 1963 and 1964: both sang Chuck Berry's "Carol," both sang Barrett Strong's "Money," both covered Arthur Alexander (Jagger did "You Better Move On," Lennon did "Anna" and "Soldier of Love"); both did Jerry Leiber and Mike Stoller songs (Jagger did "Poison Ivy," Lennon did "Some Other Guy"); both covered Motown men—Jagger sang Marvin Gaye's "Hitch Hike" and Lennon sang Smokey Robinson's "You've Really Got a Hold on Me." And Jagger sang a Lennon-McCartney composition: "I Wanna Be Your Man."

There were differences in the musical taste of the two groups. The Stones played Chicago blues—Jimmy Reed, Muddy Waters, and Little Walter—while the Beatles did more recent R&B: Little Richard, Larry Williams, and the Isley Brothers. The Beatles concentrated on cover versions of established black hits, while the Stones became connoisseurs of obscure black music; their cover of Slim Harpo's "King Bee" was emblematic. And the Stones never would have done "Till There Was You" or "A Taste of Honey." Public relations did not explain that. The difference between Brian Jones and Paul McCartney did.

Because the early Stones' similarities to the Beatles seemed stronger than these differences, because they too covered American black hits and had "long" hair, the Stones feared they would be cast as "Beatle look-alikes." It was a sensitive point. When a reporter asked if the Stones' hairstyle owed anything to the Beatles, Jagger replied defensively, "Art students have had this sort of haircut for years, even when the Beatles were using hair cream."

Stones manager Andrew Oldham saw the way out of the "Beatle look-alike" dilemma. He would cast the Stones as the antithesis of the Beatles. Jagger, Richards, Jones, Bill Wyman, and Charlie Watts would be turned into a tough, defiant working-class group. If even Mum liked the Beatles, the Stones would become the group parents loved to hate. The media went for it. The London *Daily Mirror* ran a headline in March, "Would You Let Your Daughter Go with a Rolling Stone?" The first Associated Press report in the United States called them "dirtier, streakier and more disheveled than the Beatles."

The irony was that the tough, defiant, proletarian-looking Stones came from bourgeois families. Jagger's father had been a teacher. The Jagger home had "an atmosphere of middle class 'gentility,' " their 1965 official biography stated. While John had flunked every subject in his O-level examinations at age sixteen, Jagger passed seven of his, and did even better on his A-levels two years later. "Mick seemed destined for a steady office job," his mother recalled. "That was why he went to the London School of Economics to study accountancy."

Brian Jones did even better in school, passing his O-levels in nine subjects a year early and doing well on his A-levels. "He sometimes talked of becoming a dentist," his mother said. Keith Richards came from a background closer to John's: son of an electrical engineer, he was a "problem" student and a Teddy boy. He went to art college dreaming of becoming a rock musician. While the Beatles worked their way from Liverpool to London, Jagger attended LSE and his band played in suburban Richmond.

At the same time that Jagger was assuming his working-class tough-guy role, another identity for the Stones was being shaped. *Vogue* magazine featured Jagger in 1964 in a portrait by David Bailey, the hippest high-fashion photographer. Jagger's group, the accompanying article said, was "quite different from the Beatles, and more terrifying. 'The effect is sex,' wrote one observer, 'that isn't sex, which is the end of the road.' " Before the Stones had their first Number One single, Jagger was being portrayed as fashionable and hip, mysteriously androgynous, and on his way to becoming one of high society's "beautiful people." In 1964 such a portrayal of John Lennon or any of the other Beatles was unimaginable.

That July the Stones' "It's All Over Now" became their first Number One British single, replacing the Animals' "The House of the Rising Sun" on the charts. At concerts in England their fans rioted regularly. In Blackpool, not far from Liverpool, the biggest rock riot in British history broke out at a Stones concert: fifty were injured, seventy police were called to fight fans, who ripped out the theater's chandeliers and tossed a Steinway grand piano off the stage. Riots also broke out in Paris following the Stones' concert. Police arrested 150. John must have been envious.

Thus, while the Beatles' manager insisted that John Lennon give up his anger to become "really big," the Stones' manager insisted that they act angry. This left John with the sense that he had sold out and that the Stones were more authentic rock and roll rebels. In retrospect, the Stones seem to have been playing the stereotyped cock rock role while the Beatles took more risks in challenging sexual conventions. But this difference became clear only in the seventies with the development of feminism.

As the New Left and the counterculture became more self-conscious and articulate in the late sixties, the Beatles and the Stones came to represent the real alternatives young people faced: they could sell out and accommodate themselves to adult, bourgeois society, or they could defy it, seeking to change both society and themselves. In 1968 John Lennon himself could no longer escape that choice.

6

May '68: Rock against Revolution

In the spring of 1968 Europe's radical youth took to the streets
with new energy. It would also be a season of revolutionary
transformation in John's personal life. Those who visited
John at home with Cynthia early that spring found him
deeply depressed. Cynthia thought "it had something to do
with student riots."

Thousands of students demonstrated in February in West Berlin, supporting the Vietnamese National Liberation Front and protesting the attempted
assassination of New Left leader Rudi Dutschke. The next month in London,
a huge march on the American embassy in Grosvenor Square was dispersed
by riot police on horseback, a shocking display of official violence. And on
May 6 students began their historic uprising in Paris. These waves of revolutionary politics washed into John's life, at home in Weybridge. May '68
brought his personal liberation: he spent his first night with Yoko Ono.

Since he had met her in 1966, he had wanted to collaborate with her on
art projects. In May '68, while students were fighting in the streets of Paris
and Cynthia was out of town, John invited Yoko to his home. "We were very
shy together at first," she recalled. They spent the night making electronic
music on John's bank of tape recorders. Everyone else thought his absorption
with abstract sound was weird. "Then," he said, "we just made love right
there in that little studio."

"She's me in drag," he answered when interviewers asked what attracted him to her. The Liverpool rock-and-roller thought he was the same person as the Japanese avant-garde artist; it was a breathtaking statement. It revealed how alienated he had become from his identity as a Beatle. John and Yoko were inseparable beginning in May '68.

Before May '68, liberal social theorists had proclaimed that bureaucratic capitalism and the consumer society had resolved the fundamental social conflicts and made radical politics obsolete. The students of Paris challenged that. They began by rebelling against bureaucracy in the university, fighting massive street battles with the police. As students overturned state authority in the universities, workers overturned capitalist power in the factories. Two weeks after the student rebellion began, ten million workers had joined a general strike; they occupied their factories, just as students had occupied the universities. What had seemed a stable and prosperous capitalist society had been brought to the brink of revolution. Historian Mark Poster wrote, "The monstrous spectacle of meaningless toil and passive consumption gave way to an exhilarating, joyous festival." The slogans of May included "It is forbidden to forbid," "A cop lives in each of us; we must kill him," and "Power to the imagination," an idea John would later turn into the song "Imagine."

John followed the May events closely in the papers and on television. In a great failure of intellect and imagination, he accepted the view that the most important feature of the May events was the violence of the students. He opposed it as a matter of principle. He knew the violence of the American war in Vietnam remained the most important political issue, and he went on American television on May 22 to denounce it as "insanity." But he also decided to declare his separation from the revolutionaries in the streets of Paris and elsewhere. He wrote a song in India when he "had this, you know, 'God will save us' feeling about it," he said later in *Lennon Remembers*. The first version of "Revolution" was recorded on May 30 at Abbey Road studios.

The events John was thinking about had begun earlier that year, when radicals and reactionaries alike had been stunned by the unprecedented victory of the Vietnamese National Liberation Front. The Tet offensive had coordinated surprise attacks on every major Vietnamese city. NLF troops penetrated the compound of the American embassy in Saigon, shattering whatever hope the American public still held that the United States could win its war. Grassroots antiwar sentiment, mobilized around the candidacy of Senator Eugene McCarthy in the Democratic presidential primaries, forced LBJ to declare he would not seek reelection.

In New York City, students at Columbia University seized campus buildings, protesting the university's expansion into neighboring Harlem; a thousand club-swinging policemen drove them out. Martin Luther King was assassinated in Memphis; ghetto riots broke out in a dozen cities. Students held antiwar demonstrations at two hundred colleges and universities.

The Yippies called on all young people opposed to the war to gather in Chicago in August at the Democratic national convention. Most movement leaders opposed that demonstration, arguing that the plan was irresponsible and provocative. None of the rock stars who had been invited attended except Phil Ochs and Country Joe and the Fish. Most potential demonstrators stayed away. Fewer than ten thousand showed up, while hundreds of thousands had attended mobilizations in New York and Washington, D.C. On the eve of the convention it looked like the demonstrations would be a failure.

A police riot made the demonstrations historic. Mayor Richard Daley put twelve thousand police on twelve-hour shifts, had twelve thousand more National Guardsmen and Army troops called up, armed them with rifles, bazookas, and flame throwers, and ordered them to shoot to kill. Theodore White later wrote that Hubert Humphrey was "nominated in a sea of blood." The Rolling Stones released "Street Fighting Man," in which Jagger sang about the time being right for revolution; it was immediately banned from the airwaves in Chicago and Berkeley. And the new Beatles single came out, addressing the New Left directly, written and sung by John: "You say you want a revolution. . . ."

The New Left and counterculture press responded immediately. The Berkeley *Barb* wrote with typical excess, " 'Revolution' sounds like the hawk plank adopted in the Chicago convention of the Democratic Death Party." "Hubert Humphrey couldn't have said it better," Jon Landau agreed. *Ramparts* called the song a "betrayal"; the *New Left Review* called it "a lamentable petty bourgeois cry of fear." Robert Christgau wrote in the *Village Voice*, "It is puritanical to expect musicians, or anyone else, to hew to the proper line. But it is reasonable to request that they not go out of their way to oppose it. Lennon has, and it takes much of the pleasure out of their music for me."

Ramparts objected to two lines in particular. It quoted from the chorus, where John said he knew it was going to be "all right," and commented, "Well, it isn't. You *know* it's *not* gonna be all right." It also criticized John's lines "You say you want a contribution," where he states he won't give "money for people with minds that hate." "They've gotten so far from thinking of 'contribution' to a political cause as meaning what they can do as artists that they conceive of their role essentially as that of millionaires," *Ramparts* declared. The magazine had a point, with which John would soon agree when he began to contribute to the peace movement as an artist.

John's song suggested he wouldn't support a revolution until he could see "the plan." His radical critics objected to that. The movement did not have a plan, in the sense that political parties with central committees did. The movement did have a project: liberation, self-emancipation, participatory democracy. The plan was that people should take part in making the decisions that affect their lives. The plan was to break out of the system that required official plans, and instead to liberate the imagination. At the time John couldn't see this project, but he would within the year.

"Revolution" was a message song, and "the words of a message song just lie on the floor," Greil Marcus wrote at the time. But there was "a message in the music which is ultimately more powerful than anyone's words"—something the political critics of John's "Revolution" had missed. "There is freedom and movement in the music, even as there is sterility and repression in the lyrics," Marcus wrote. "The music doesn't say 'cool it' or 'don't fight the cops.' . . . The music dodges the message and comes out in front."

Time devoted an entire article to the song, something it had never done before. It reported to its readers that the Beatles had criticized "radical activists the world over," and that the whole thing was "exhilarating."

John hinted that his position was not so firmly antagonistic to the left in the second version of the song, released on the "White Album" (officially titled *The Beatles*) two months after the single. In subsequent interviews he explained that the single version had been produced the way Paul wanted it, while the album version was done John's way—slower, so that the words could be understood better. And John's way had one significant change in the words: after he sang "When you talk about destruction / Don't you know that you can count me out," he added "in." The "in" was omitted from the lyrics printed on the sleeve but was perfectly clear on the record, sung with equal emphasis to the "out." "I put in both because I wasn't sure," he said. Already John was revealing some ambivalence about his relationship to the New Left—and on precisely the issue that separated the radicals most sharply from the "all you need is love" world view the Beatles had done so much to promote.

The song marked John's decision that he had political responsibilities, and that he ought to fulfill them in his music. That was a momentous decision, much more significant than the lyrics of the song. Some of the issues he raised in the song were, in any case, legitimate. He was concerned about the nature and extent of the destruction advocated by revolutionaries, he wanted to know how they envisioned future society, and he seemed to say that the politics of Maoist students were self-defeating: they weren't "gonna make it with anyone, anyhow." But he took these genuine problems of revolutionary morality and strategy as an excuse for abandoning politics altogether and substituting in its place a quest for personal liberation: "free your mind instead." More than anything else, this argument aroused the radicals' anger.

Some on the left defended "Revolution." The SDS newspaper at Cornell

University said John was right to reject radicals with "minds that hate," and praised the Beatles for consistently advocating "pacifist idealism" in the face of increasing violence both in the world and among leftists. "You can argue about the effectiveness of non-violence as a tactic, but it would be absurd to claim that it is a conservative notion. . . . The Beatles want to change the world, and they are doing what they can."

Then there was the issue of the "shoo-be-do-wahs" with which Paul and George answered John's "You know it's gonna be—." The Beatles are not fools, Michael Wood argued in *Commonweal.* They know it's absurd to say "it's gonna be all right." The "shoo-be-do-wahs" suggest "they mean that statements about whether it is or it isn't are all part of that political crap they dislike so much"—a cogent interpretation.

Jonathan Cott pushed John on the same question in a *Rolling Stone* interview later that year. He asked what John would say to a black person who tried to "free his mind" but found that racist institutions still oppressed him. "That's why I did the 'out and in' bit," John answered. "I don't know what I'd be doing if I was in his position. I don't think I'd be so meek and mild. I just don't know."

John revealed more about his political thinking in the electronic collage "Revolution 9," also recorded in May '68. He later explained that he thought he was "painting in sound a picture of revolution": no melody, no words, no chords, no singing, nobody playing instruments—and, as Christgau and Piccarella point out, "for eight minutes of an album officially titled *The Beatles,* there were no Beatles." The whole thing sounded frightening, chaotic, inhuman. John had no sense that a revolution could liberate people's creative energy, free them from old forms of oppression, forge a new community. No wonder he wanted to "see the plan."

At least nineteen cover versions of "Revolution" have been released in the United States, including one by the Columbia Musical Treasury Orchestra, a Hawaiian guitar version by Santo and Johnny (whose "Sleep Walk" spent three weeks in the Number One slot in September 1959), and one by the Chords (could they be the same Chords who sang the original "Sh-Boom"?).

More interesting than any of these was Nina Simone's musical answer to John's song. A black jazz singer, she had worked hard for the civil rights movement and had written her own personal protest song, "Mississippi—Goddamn!" She had R&B hits in the mid-sixties with "I Put a Spell on You," "Don't Let Me Be Misunderstood," and "Young, Gifted, and Black." Her reply to John, also titled "Revolution," had a similar musical and lyrical structure to his song. She told him that if he wanted to sing about revolution, he would have to "clean" his "brain." John had told revolutionaries to count him out of any destruction; she sang about destroying oppression and injustice, and declared that the Constitution, which John had defended, would have to be changed. A year later in *Lennon Remembers* John said he thought Nina Simone's answer was "very good," that he "enjoyed somebody who reacted immediately to what I had said."

Despite its significance for the New Left, "Revolution" never was a great hit. Paul had worried from the beginning that it needed to be made more commercial to succeed. His pop instincts were correct. The song does not appear on the official list of Beatles' million sellers. It peaked in the charts at Number Twelve. Part of the problem was that it was the B side of Paul's "Hey Jude," which became the biggest Beatles hit in history and drowned out "Revolution" in the fall of 1968. The masses of Beatles fans were not terribly interested in "Revolution." Many must have ignored the words and danced to the beat. Others misunderstood it: one Cleveland disc jockey introduced it by remarking that the song "calls for a reevaluation of our entire society." For the left, however, the song confirmed their worst suspicions: the Fab Four were the good boys of rock, rock's liberals.

John's "Revolution" aroused the interest not only of the left but also of the far right. William Buckley paid mocking tribute to its message in his syndicated column, and was promptly attacked by the John Birch Society—from the right. According to the Birch Society's magazine, "The Beatles are simply telling the Maoists that Fabian gradualism is working, and that the Maoists might blow it all by getting the public excited before things are ready for 'revolution'—'it's gonna be all right.' In short, 'Revolution' takes the Moscow line against Trotskyites and the Progressive Labor Party, based on Lenin's *Leftwing Extremism:* [sic] *An Infantile Disorder.*" As final evidence for this interpretation, the Birchers were urged to listen to the other key pro-Soviet statement on the White Album, "Back in the U.S.S.R."

———

"Revolution" cast the personal and the political as antagonistic forms of liberation, but it was not the first rock song to do that. Four years earlier *Another Side of Bob Dylan* had appeared, and stunned his fans. "My Back Pages" dismissed his engagement with social issues. It was the first and greatest of his betrayals. After betraying protest for personal songs, he would betray folk for rock, then rock for country. Then, from 1979 to 1982, the Jew from Hibbing, Minnesota, declared himself a born-again Christian. He told topical songwriter Phil Ochs in 1964, "The stuff you're writing is bullshit, because politics is bullshit. It's all unreal. The only thing that's real is inside you. Your feelings. Just look at the world you're writing about and you'll see you're wasting your time. The world is, well—it's just absurd."

Another Side marks the point for the counterculture at which personal and political liberation were first set in opposition. When Dylan opened the battle with "My Back Pages," many in the New Left took the bait, arguing against him that the political should take precedence over the personal. Dylan insisted that his nightmares were more important than any political issues, and showed what that meant with his new music; that "struck a responsive chord with millions of kids who were living a similar nightmare," John Landau wrote at the time, "who felt more deeply about that than they ever could about protest politics." Dylan was more a leader now than before. This phase of his work helped create a cultural climate in which John, and other rock songwriters, could break out of the pop format to express their own dreams and nightmares.

Dylan's shift away from political and social commitment in his music might have been motivated, as some on the left charged, by his desire to conquer the media and make millions. It's more likely that he had been uncertain, confused, and fearful during the previous two years. He had been forced to create virtually in public. His fans made him too important a symbol and he didn't like it.

Until 1964 he had thought of himself as a folk poet in the mold of Woody Guthrie. That year he was gaining a new sense of himself as an artist, reaching deep into his imagination and finding wild and disturbing images. He was seeking a completely different kind of meaning, one that seemed much more important to him. Hostile to organized left politics but deeply anti-authoritarian, committed to personal liberation from bourgeois conventions, Dylan pointed the way to the apolitical side of the counterculture. John's "Revolution" represented another step down the same path.

=====

John's songs on the White Album, released in the summer of 1968, had been written after he gave up on LSD—after he nearly disappeared into the nightmare sound collages it inspired—after he was forced to start over, to rebuild his music from the ground up. In his LSD days he had tried to destroy his ego; on the White Album he returned to assert himself with new and thrilling passion. He sang about the misery of the Beatles' impending breakup, with the hardest rock they had played in years—"I'm So Tired," and again in the terrifying "Yer Blues": "Feel so suicidal / Even hate my rock and roll."

"Happiness Is a Warm Gun" ridiculed the American obsession with weapons. Some interpreted it as an antiwar song. John had never sounded better. "Oh, I love it," he said later in *Lennon Remembers*. "I think it's a beautiful song." "Sexy Sadie" told about his break with the Maharishi.

Most of all John sang about Yoko, about his wild love for her: when he holds her, he sings in "Happiness Is a Warm Gun," he knows "no one can do me no harm." He conveyed their passion and their belief they had nothing to hide—a sentiment soon to be dramatized on the cover of their *Two Virgins* album. And he sang more tenderly than anything he had sung before: "Julia, Julia, Oceanchild calls me." Julia was his mother, and "Oceanchild" was a translation of "Yoko."

In the late summer and fall of 1968, the White Album was being compared with the Stones' new *Beggar's Banquet*. The verdict on the left was unanimous: the Stones had moved further into the vanguard. "The Beatles were always nice kids, a little weird maybe," *Ramparts* argued; "the Stones are still freaks and outlaws." "The Beatles satirize and parody the fringes of contemporary life," Jon Landau wrote for Liberation News Service; "the Stones deal with the themes that lie at its center."

The main complaint against the White Album was that its playfulness and gentle satire had become at best irrelevant and at worst reactionary. Landau pointed especially to Paul's "Rocky Raccoon" and George's "Piggies": "The Beatles have used parody on this album precisely because they were afraid of confronting reality. It becomes a mask behind which they can hide from the urgencies of the moment."

Beggar's Banquet and the White Album represented the opposing elements of the counterculture at the major turning point in its history. Millions of young people enjoyed active sex lives, took drugs, and rejected the traditional family. Rock music more than anything else had expressed their ideology, and the Beatles' music celebrated their triumph.

The problem was what came next. The *New Left Review* analyzed the situation in 1970 from a Marxist perspective: bourgeois society had retreated at the level of ideology, the ideology of family and decency, but had "recuperated" at the level of property and work relations, which had not been explicitly challenged by the counterculture. "The radicalism of the initial revolt thus spent itself swiftly, because of the very attainability of its ostensible targets," Richard Merton wrote. "Banally triumphant," rock music "ceased to have any esthetic charge." That was the problem with the White Album. The Beatles continued to express the old themes of the counterculture. They represented the "weak solution" to the problem of what to do next.

Beggar's Banquet represented the "strong solution," a musical turning outward, toward the political and social battles of the day. Although *Beggar's Banquet* was a response to politics, its songs were nothing like protest music. They were more personal and they expressed more complex and ambivalent feelings.

No song better captured the feeling of 1968 than "Street Fighting Man."

Jagger's song echoed Martha and the Vandellas' masterpiece, "Dancing in the Streets," which had blasted out of thousands of radios after blacks battled police and National Guardsmen in New York City, Philadelphia, and Chicago in 1964. In "Street Fighting Man" Jagger took it as a given that he was part of the radical movement or at least sympathetic to it. The song told the truth about how it felt to be taking to the streets. "The first flush of mastery and self-confidence dissolves into a confusion of very real doubts," Greil Marcus wrote at the time. Jagger expressed anger, but also wondered whether he could in fact do anything: this is life on the left, a reality too often denied by more doctrinaire voices. "The Stones strike for realism in contrast to the Beatles' fantasies," Jon Landau agreed. "They want to transcend the escapist and the self-congratulatory," which figured so prominently in the White Album. Jagger's "Street Fighting Man" gave voice to real uncertainties which the New Left often denied. John himself would soon begin his own struggle with these political and artistic problems.

The doubts expressed in Jagger's lyrics were erased by the music, Landau wrote, with its "violence, certainty, and repetition." Geoffrey Cannon made the same point in *Partisan Review:* the music was not hesitant, but "relentless, inescapable." "The Stones may not be sure where their heads are," Landau concluded, "but their hearts are out in the streets."

The true story about how Jagger came to write the song was later told by Tony Sanchez, who said that, early in 1968, Jagger became "a committed revolutionary." He had been a student at the London School of Economics in the early sixties, where he had been immersed in a Marxist subculture. "Although he disagreed with their doctrines," Sanchez wrote, "he understood the fundamental wrongness of capitalism." The absurd drug trials that he, Keith Richards, and Brian Jones had undergone, and the radicalism of much of their audience, led Jagger to adopt a New Left position.

Jagger explained his political views in the London *Sunday Mirror:* "Nobody would get me in uniform to kill a lot of people I've never met and have nothing against anyway. I know people say they're against wars, and yet they go on fighting them. Millions of marvelous young men are killed, and in five minutes everybody seems to have forgotten all about it. War stems from power-mad politicians and patriots. . . . Anarchy is the only slight glimmer of hope. Not the popular conception of it—men in black cloaks lurking around with hidden bombs—but a freedom of every man being personally responsible himself. There should be no such thing as private property."

Jagger "leaped at the chance of joining the revolution," Sanchez recalled, when tens of thousands of angry young people stormed into Grosvenor Square in March 1968 to demonstrate against American imperialism and the Vietnam war outside the huge, modern American embassy. At first the other demonstrators did not notice Jagger, and he linked arms with a young man on one side and a young woman on the other. The demonstrators came close to breaking through the police lines and storming the embassy. "But then he was recognized; fans demanded autographs, newspapermen scuffled with one another to interview him. He fled, realizing bitterly that his fame and wealth precluded him from the revolution—he was a distraction, not a leader. He suddenly felt impotent—his power seemed trivial, meaningless, beside that of a revolutionary student leader like Tariq Ali." He wrote the song to express these feelings: what could he do, except sing in a band?

"Salt of the Earth," also on *Beggar's Banquet,* has two parts. Keith Richards sings the first, and seems to declare his solidarity with the "hard-working people" and their "back-breaking work." Jagger sings the second part, describing his real feelings about workers: they didn't seem real to him; they seemed "strange." Americans writing about the song praised its truthful ambivalence. Jagger and Richards expressed respect and admiration for the oppressed, but also recognized the gulf that separated "us" from "them," and refused to idealize them. This honesty stood in sharp contrast to a recitation of leftist clichés.

English radicals heard the song differently. They recognized the first part as the "emptily patronizing phrases the ruling class has mouthed through the ages." Richard Merton wrote in the *New Left Review* about the "odiously anachronistic tradition of the 'toast' to patronize (insult) the 'poor,' celebrate (humiliate) the 'humble,' salute (scorn) the 'uncounted millions.' " In the song, the working class is concealed by ruling-class clichés, which share certain elements with Marxist clichés. When the clichés were broken down, what Jagger found was not the workers themselves, but only his own feelings of distance and isolation from them. The *New Left Review* called it "an extraordinary construct, one of the boldest and yet most delicate that British rock has ever achieved."

For the New Left, the events of May '68 had raised the question of its relation to the working class in a direct and compelling way. Jagger faced the question and truthfully expressed his feelings. He admitted that what he knew about workers consisted of ruling-class clichés and his own sense of estrangement. That task was different and more difficult for John in 1969. His knowledge was much more personal and painful: he knew the working class's own clichés about itself, he knew he had lived them in his own life and been crippled by them. These truths he would discover and reveal two years later, when he wrote "Working Class Hero."

Beggar's Banquet had one other notable song, "Sympathy for the Devil," which posed far greater problems than "Street Fighting Man" or "Salt of the Earth." It claimed to be about real politics and to have a historical sense.

Jagger asks who assassinated the Kennedys and answers, "You and me." These assassinations, the Bolshevik revolution, and the Nazi *Blitzkrieg* were the work of the same diabolical forces, he declared. The conviction with which Jagger sang was all the more disturbing.

Marshall Berman, writing in the *New American Review,* found a profound truth in "Sympathy for the Devil": it's not easy to separate "good" violence from "bad" violence. The counterculture tended to deny that good intentions can lead to terrible consequences. The New Left tended to think they could "change the world without dirtying their hands or their hearts." But the song suggested that "every one of us who wants to overcome the power of the Pentagon must come to terms with the Pentagon within himself." The song was "annoyingly vague" in that it didn't offer any advice about how to do this. But it contributed "a deeper awareness of the ambiguities of radical will and action, a tragic self-knowledge."

To others it also sounded as if Jagger was suggesting simply that all violence was bad—the flower-power cliché—at the same time that he found it groovy. His song was a seductive invitation to join in a diabolical game. Jagger was trying to have it both ways. He provoked an aura of glamorous danger, and then claimed he couldn't understand why "there's always trouble when we sing this song." Berman admitted that "on one level we have to be angry with this man," but still, "we cannot deny him our sympathy," because the wisdom in his own song eluded him when he came face to face with its consequences at Altamont.

When they tried to release *Beggar's Banquet,* the Stones found their route blocked by Decca, which objected to the cover photo of a toilet wall covered with graffiti. When the Beatles' "butcher cover" was banned, John had said it was "as relevant as Vietnam." Jagger four years later made a similar statement, objecting to "Decca's involvement with the manufacture of weapons of war." The Stones had no more success than the Beatles did. The album came out with a plain white cover.

In the wake of May '68, while the underground press debated the political and social significance of the Beatles and the Stones, the *New York Times Magazine,* with surprising ingenuity, portrayed John as the opponent of Herbert Marcuse. The magazine ran an interview with Marcuse, describing him as "the most important philosopher alive. For countless young people . . . this 70-year-old scholar is the angel of the apocalypse." In the interview Marcuse was far from apocalyptic. "Revolution postulates first of all the emergence of a new type of man with needs and aspirations that are qualitatively different from the aggressive and repressive needs and aspirations of established societies. . . . The working class today shares in large measure the needs and aspirations of the dominant classes; without a break with the present content of needs, revolution is inconceivable." Against this, John's words are quoted in larger and bolder type: "You say you want a revolution." Photos of each of them appeared as well, Marcuse frowning and John smiling.

However, over the next three years John came to share many of Marcuse's views. Marcuse told his interviewers that "the most interesting aspect of the events of May" was the idea that "imagination is power: that is truly revolutionary. It is new and revolutionary to try to translate into reality the most advanced ideas and values of the imagination. . . . truth is not only in rationality, but just as much and perhaps more in the imaginary." That was the theme John would present in "Imagine."

Part III

AVANT-GARDE PEACENIK

7

Two Virgins

 In May '68 the Beatles launched their own record company, Apple. They called it "Western communism," an effort to free themselves from the heavy hand of corporate domination, to gain autonomy for themselves as artists. They also hoped to bring other promising artists into Apple and to make experimental music. At the beginning it seemed as if the Beatles might succeed. It also seemed as if Apple could easily deteriorate into the biggest institution of hip capitalism, in which the Beatles gained nothing except the profits from the sale of their records, profits that Capitol had previously held.

Apple as business-as-usual was the ominous theme of a day John and Paul spent giving interviews at the St. Regis Hotel in New York City. No underground papers, fan magazines, or rock monthlies were invited. Instead, John and Paul talked with *Fortune, Business Week,* and the financial writers for *Time* and *Newsweek.* An even more ominous sign appeared when *Rolling Stone* featured a full-page photo of Beatle wives modeling clothes from the Apple boutique. Using the wives to sell Beatle stuff was more crass and sexist than anything Capitol had done.

While they were in New York in April to announce the formation of Apple, John and Paul did an interview for WNET radio, in which John expressed at length his vague political ideas. He was asked about his views of the war. "It's another piece of insanity," he replied. "It's another part of the insane scene. It's just insane. It shouldn't be going on. There's no reason for it—just insanity." If John didn't have an analysis of the war, he did take a strong position, and the media picked it up: "Lennon calls war insane."

The interviewer continued, "The whole idea of whether you get involved, or stay out of it, whether you're turned on, or turned off—how do you feel about that?"

"We believe you should turn on, stay in, and change it," John said, acting as the official Beatles spokesman.

"You mean getting involved in the establishment?"

"Change it, because unless you change it, it's gonna be there forever. Change it, and not replace it with another set of Harris tweed suits. Change it completely. But how you do that, we don't know."

Paul was getting uneasy about this radicalism. "What we've decided at the moment," he said, "is to try to get into—ah—business. So when we go to those big companies, we talk to them as though we're—one of them," he said with an apologetic laugh.

"But of course we're not," John snapped.

"People don't communicate with hippies because they don't like the look of them," Paul said.

"We're gonna package peace in a new box," John said, ignoring Paul, and using Yoko's political rhetoric for the first time.

"We're trying to get to the people who are in control," Paul continued, "and say, come on, straighten it out."

"Money talks," John muttered. Then he chuckled; " 'It bites,' as Bob Dylan says." John and Paul were clearly headed in different directions.

The interviewer asked, "Do you think the press distorts a great deal of what you do?"

"Yes," John answered. "I don't think there is anywhere any truth coming over about what is happening, at all. There is no truth coming out at all." The interviewer laughed nervously. "I'm not saying the newspapers are intentionally evil," John explained. "It's just that the system won't allow truth to come out. So there's something wrong with the system."

They went on to discuss the racial situation in Britain. John and Paul criticized the rise of racist politics there and speculated about whether British racism was more severe than American. John declared he thought it would be soon.

And what about the future of the Beatles? John called the Beatles "a machine" which he wanted to use "for good." That summed up his vague desires to become engaged in the world outside pop music.

John held an exhibition of his own artwork, which he called "You Are

Here." It opened at London's Robert Fraser Gallery in July 1968 and consisted of Yoko's kind of conceptual art. Viewers first went through a large collection of charity boxes, soliciting funds for causes ranging from the Sons of the Divine Providence to the National Canine Defense League. Downstairs, a large white circle of canvas stood; in the center, viewers found the words "you are here" in John's handwriting—the familiar phrase from London Underground maps, now endowed with a playfully metaphysical significance.

At the opening, John released 365 helium-filled balloons, each with a message asking whoever found it to reply to John at the gallery. "Replies came in by the hundreds," his art assistant Anthony Fawcett recalled, "objecting to John's upcoming divorce from Cynthia, his association with Yoko, his wealth, his long hair, and his presumption at stepping into the preserve of art." The man on the street wanted John to stay a Beatle.

"The idea of John Lennon being an artist just didn't make sense to people," Dan Richter recalled. "They couldn't understand it. They thought maybe it was a joke. But John above all was a serious artist." In fact, earlier in his life John had wanted to be an artist, and had attended the Liverpool Art College from the time he was seventeen until the Beatles began to have some success.

===

Art colleges like Liverpool's were neither snobbish nor upper-class. Many of their students came from working-class families. At Liverpool Art College in 1957, the dominant subculture was Bohemian. Students wore floppy sweaters, read the Beat poets, and listened to jazz. John, however, held on to his working-class tough guy identity, wearing Teddy boy clothes and listening to rock and roll.

John felt alienated from art college, but in 1959 he gained a friend, Stu Sutcliffe, whose passionate engagement with art infected him. Sutcliffe taught him about the French Impressionists' rebellion against bourgeois conventions, and John for the first time understood the liberating potential of art. Sutcliffe won a prize at the biggest art exhibition in Liverpool. John's Aunt Mimi told a story about John dragging her to see Sutcliffe's painting. "It seemed to be all khaki and yellow triangles. I looked at it and I said, 'What *is* it?' Well! John got hold of my arm and hustled me outside. . . . 'How could you *say* a thing like that, Mimi?' He gave his chest a big thump, and bellowed, 'Art comes from in here!' " Stu Sutcliffe had given eighteen-year-old John ideas that would attract him ten years later to Yoko Ono.

John was not the only English rock star to go to art college in his youth. Keith Richards, Pete Townshend, David Bowie, Eric Clapton, Ray Davies, co-founder of the Kinks, and Jimmy Page, founder of Led Zeppelin, were all art college students, as Simon Frith has pointed out. Art colleges are places for working-class teenagers who reject a working-class future and lack the energy or desire to climb the ladder of success. Keith Richards explained: "In England, if you're lucky you get into art school. It's somewhere they put you if they can't put you anywhere else."

Although John rejected both the professional training and the student subculture of the Liverpool Art College in 1957–59, art school provided him with psychological resources he would need to succeed as a rock musician. Art college emphasizes the value of the expressive life. It gives its students the sense that they belong to an elite: they see things differently and have creative powers that distinguish them from the rest of society. It fosters an intense individualism and self-obsession, traits that help students hold on to their ambition and their senses of themselves, and thereby survive the inevitable disappointments and failures of their early careers.

His drawing teacher remembered John in class. The students would put their work up, and the class would discuss it. "John's effort was always hopeless—or he'd put up nothing at all. . . . Then one day in the lecture room, I found this notebook." It contained caricatures, stories, verse, "the wittiest thing I'd ever seen in my life." A fellow student asked to see John's "poetry." Everybody else's was imitation Ginsberg or Ferlinghetti. John's was different, the student recalled: "A piece of pure rustic wackiness concerning a farmer, it had freshness and originality in its sheer lunacy."

John had begun these notebooks long before art college, as an adolescent at Quarry Bank Grammar School. He filled exercise books with his stories, poems, drawings, and cartoons, and titled them "The Daily Howl." John's weather report was typical: "Tomorrow will be muggy, followed by Tuggy, Wuggy, and Thuggy."

John's style of humor was not completely original. In 1973, writing in the *New York Times Book Review,* he recalled "The Daily Howl": "Looking at it now, it seems strangely similar to the *Goon Show,*" he remarked. The *Goon Show* was broadcast over the BBC from the time John was twelve until he was sixteen. Written by Spike Milligan with Peter Sellers, it featured a uniquely English kind of humor, which resembled that of the Marx brothers in some ways. The *Goon Show* gained an almost cultlike status. It was not odd for John to have been an enthusiastic fan; it was unusual that he was inspired by the show to begin his own writing and drawing, which tapped a different part of his imagination than rock and roll did, mixing outrageous fantasies and pure wordplay, wilder and more anarchic. "The Daily Howl" was not, however, a private world for John. He read it aloud at school to his friends. He needed an audience for this side of his imagination too.

John didn't stop writing his *Goon Show*–Lewis Carroll prose even after the Beatles became popular. In 1961 he wrote an occasional column for *Mersey Beat*. A typical effort was a "guide" to the local clubs. One was "strictly no members only," another "the Bohernia of Liddypool," and the third was for "membrains only." He even spent his own money running classified ads: "Wanted urgently by ex-rock group: five portable D.D.T. guns."

John the literary artist launched one project at the height of Beatlemania: the book *In His Own Write*, published in March 1964. It rapidly became the best-selling book in England, displacing James Bond. The *Times Literary Supplement* declared the book was "worth the attention of anyone who fears for the impoverishment of the English language and the British imagination." The *Sunday Times* called it "a rich plumcake of verbal cross-references, sophisticated punning, and semi-poetic wisdom. . . . The voice is young, skeptical, and northern." The stories in this collection had been compiled from John's writings in *Mersey Beat*, some of which in turn had come from his earlier "Daily Howl" and others of which he had written during the 1963 and 1964 tours. All the stories were filled with puns, jokes, and satire. Within a year he wrote a second volume: *A Spaniard in the Works*.

Critics delighted in quoting their favorite passages. Michael Wood liked "Father Cradock turns round slowly from the book he is eating and explains that it is just a face she is going through"; he also liked "people dance with wild abdomen," and the sending of "stabbed, undressed envelopes." Others quoted John's brilliant report on Harold Wilson's defeat of Sir Alec Douglas-Home: "Harassed Wilsod won the General Erection with a very small marjorie over the Torchies. Thus pudding the Laboring Partly back into powell after a large abscess. . . . Sir Alice Doubtless-Whom was—quote—'bitherly dithappointed' but managed to keep smirking on his 500,000 acre estate in Scotland with a bit of fishing and that. . . . The Torchies, now in apperition, have still the capable qualities of such disable men as Rabbit Bunloaf and the very late Harrods McMillion." John could be viciously clever about conventional politics.

"The first thing any literate person will notice on reading through Mr. Lennon's book is that it all comes out of one source, namely the later work of James Joyce," critic John Wain wrote in the *New Republic*. "Not only the determination to communicate almost exclusively in puns, but the equally determined smutty, blasphemous and subversive tone, are Joycean. . . . Mr. Lennon has, at one stroke, put the young nonreader in touch with a central strand in the literary tradition of the last thirty years in every English-speaking country."

Joyce had broken with the traditional narrative novel of the nineteenth century, in which one voice or character unified the text. In *Ulysses* the voices of many storytellers intertwine and finally language takes on a life of its own, playing with possibilities of meaning not found in everyday life. Marshall McLuhan has observed that Joyce, along with several other major modernists —Dylan Thomas and William Faulkner—came out of a "backward oral area" where storytelling was a living part of popular culture.

Lennon came from the same background. He grew up in an Irish subculture that valued verbal play over novel-reading. So even if John never studied or even read Joyce, he could still be part of the same undertaking, rejecting "the formal controlled use of language that resulted from the 19th century's drive towards logic, systematization and the shading out of ambiguities." The writer who led this literary attack on the classic bourgeois world view "considered himself a man of the people, a life-long socialist and iconoclast," Wain wrote of Joyce. John regarded himself in much the same way.

But Lennon's writings had a significant weakness, Wain argued. John had "nothing personal to communicate, . . . nothing in the way of content except his automatically youthful irreverence . . . his ability to thumb a lift from the *Zeitgeist.*" The significance of the work was that "the language is doing the talking, delightedly revealing its own potentialities."

In many ways it was absurd to compare Lennon with Joyce. Joyce's punning in *Finnegans Wake* was systematic, John's was haphazard. The source of Lennon's style, Michael Wood argued, was not Joyce, but grammar school: "The place for this intelligent, informed and infantile humor. . . . Grammar school pupils are alert, disciplined, and frightened. Their pleasures are psychological—torturing a nervous teacher—and fairly secret. . . . All this is in Lennon. The adult world makes him larf, and his books are a vengeance."

John's wild and playful stories presented a sharp contrast to his much more conventional song lyrics. The people in the stories are violent and deformed. Terrible things happen to them. Mr. Boris Morris, "the jew with a view," gets shot in the face at the Hunt Ball, and everybody says "what a clever mask that man has on." Eric Hearble wakes up with "an abnorman fat growth" on his head, which cries out for help. Frank clubs his wife to death so she won't see him "all fat on her thirtysecond birthday." John wrote these at the same time he was writing "Love, love me do, you know I love you." His verbal imagination was going into his stories rather than his song lyrics.

=====

By late 1968 the political significance of pop groups had become a central issue for the New Left. Almost without exception the Rolling Stones were held up as the revolutionaries, in contrast to the accommodationist Beatles —much to John's chagrin. At first he was simply defensive, but gradually he articulated his own position, differentiating himself more and more clearly from the rest of the Beatles.

Jean-Luc Godard, the most important radical filmmaker of the sixties, made a film with the Rolling Stones in the wake of May '68. He called it *One Plus One*. In the U.S. it was distributed under the title *Sympathy for the Devil*. The best parts of the film document the Stones working on that song, and show the amazing transformation it underwent. Godard also shows the weirdness of the recording studio, where musicians play in compartments separated by partitions. He shows the patience, good humor, and inventiveness of the Stones.

These scenes are interrupted by others which are hard to understand: black militants in a junkyard read powerful passages from LeRoi Jones and Eldridge Cleaver, and act out attacks on white women. A woman named Eve Democracy is pursued through the woods by aggressive interviewers. A man reads *Mein Kampf* to the camera in a porno shop. Clever graffiti-writers do their work on London streets, and a voice-over reads random pages of a sex thriller in which the characters are leading political figures.

In interviews, Godard claimed these juxtapositions as part of a revolutionary cinema. He didn't think a revolutionary movie could tell a story about characters the way Hollywood movies did. It had to make the viewers ask questions and think. And they did. Did Godard accept the Jagger-Richards view of history expressed in the song "Sympathy for the Devil"—that the same diabolical force was present in the Russian Revolution, the Nazi *Blitzkrieg,* and the Kennedy assassination? He replied, "We don't know what kind of song it is. It's just words, the beginning of words. It never goes to the end." That was naïve. Nearly every young person in the Western world knew the song, because they had bought the album. And the producer reversed the meaning of Godard's ending. Godard had left the Stones' song unfinished, like the revolution itself; the released version ended with the Stones singing the song from beginning to end.

Newsweek thought the Stones' work on the song symbolized the work of the revolution, developing slowly but inexorably. Godard denied that. He regarded the black militants more positively than the Stones. The blacks were also practicing, but they were practicing for real political struggle, while the Stones were only making a record. However, in Godard's film the Stones were the only figures who made progress, who got anywhere, who got things together. What did that say about his view of radical politics?

Godard joined the radical critics of the Beatles just after he finished the film in September 1968. The underground newspaper *I.T.* asked for his assessment of the opportunities for the left in Britain. "It's good here," he answered, "because there are plenty of people with money and open minds. But alas, they don't use their minds, and they are usually corrupted by money. People could do things but won't. Look at the Beatles for instance."

John was incensed. "That's sour grapes from a man who couldn't get us to be in his film *One Plus One,*" he told Jonathan Cott in his first *Rolling Stone* interview.

Cott, to his credit, pushed John, pointing out that Godard had criticized them for rejecting activist politics, for not "trying to blow up the establishment."

"What's he think we're doing?" John replied. "He wants to stop looking at his own films and look around."

The same month—August 1968—that John released "Revolution," Soviet tanks rolled into Prague and crushed the Czechs' efforts to create "socialism with a human face." Both communist and capitalist states had resorted to force to preserve the status quo. In Prague as well as Paris, people fought for new freedoms in 1968.

Eldridge Cleaver emerged as a powerful black writer in 1968 with the publication of *Soul on Ice.* In it he recounted his career as a rapist and later a prison inmate, and he also wrote about the Beatles. Black rhythm and blues were "the basic ingredient, the core, of the gaudy cacophonous hymns with which the Beatles of Liverpool drive their hordes of Ultrafeminine fans into catatonia and hysteria," he said. "For Beatle fans, having been alienated from their own Bodies so long and so deeply, the effect of these potent, erotic rhythms is electric. Into this music, the Negro projected—as it were, drained off—a powerful sensuality, his pain and lust, his love and his hate, his ambition and his despair. The Negro projected into his music his very Body."

John discussed the passage in a subsequent interview. "It's something like that, it gets through, to me it got through, it was the only thing to get through to me after all the things that were happening when I was 15."

Cleaver went on to make the connections explicit: "The Beatles, the four long-haired lads from Liverpool, are offering up as their gift the Negro's Body. . . . the Beatles—soul by proxy." The Beatles had already suggested the same thing when they titled an earlier album *Rubber Soul.* The New York *Times* named *Soul on Ice* "one of the ten outstanding books of the year," and Cleaver became an editor of *Ramparts* and a leader of the Black Panthers, advocating armed self-defense for black people.

In October 1968 John and Yoko were arrested after an early-morning raid on Ringo's London apartment, where they were staying. Police charged them with possession of cannabis. "The thing was set up," John later declared. Two weeks before, a friend in the press had warned him that the police were preparing to arrest him because "you're the loudmouth." From the very beginning, then, his drug arrest had been politically motivated. "So believe me," he said, "I'd cleaned the house out." The same "headhunting cop," Detective Sergeant Norman Pilcher, who arrested John "went around and busted every pop star he could get his hands on," including Jagger and

Richards. John said, "Some of the pop stars had dope in their houses, and some didn't. It didn't matter to him. He planted it. That's what he did to me. He said, 'If you cop a plea, I won't get you for obstruction, and I'll let your missus go.' I thought, 'It's a hundred dollars, it's no skin off my nose.' "

It was John's first real confrontation with the power of the state, and it contributed to his radicalization. The dope bust was a small battle compared to the three-year war he would fight with the U.S. Immigration and Naturalization Service beginning in 1972. But the personal cost to John and Yoko was terrible. Yoko was pregnant at the time of the arrest, almost suffered a miscarriage that day, and was hospitalized, given blood transfusions, and confined to bed. John insisted on staying with her in Queen Charlotte's Maternity Hospital, and the newspapers ran photos of him sleeping on the floor at her bedside: "No bed for Beatle John." The fact that they were not married caused a scandal. A month after the arrest, on November 21, doctors declared that Yoko would lose the baby. John had a tape recorder brought to their room; with a stethoscopic microphone, he recorded the unborn baby's heartbeats before it died.

Under English law the fetus was mature enough to require a death certificate, which in turn required a name. John named the child John Ono Lennon II and had a tiny coffin made, and the baby was buried at a secret location.

A week later John and Yoko appeared as required in Marylebone Magistrates Court, Yoko still weak, both feeling utterly defeated. In exchange for dropping the charges against Yoko, John pleaded guilty. Because of government harassment, they felt, they had lost their first child.

═══

In October 1968 the *Black Dwarf,* the leading Marxist underground newspaper in the London New Left, published its first attack on the Beatles. That issue was headlined "Workers and Students: Don't Demand; Occupy Your Schools, Your Factories." The issue contained reports on student protests in England as well as at Columbia University, in Frankfurt, Germany, and in Japan; an article on Herbert Marcuse; and one by Rudi Dutschke. A column on music argued the prevailing New Left position: the Stones' "Satisfaction" and "Play with Fire" are "classics of our time, . . . the seed of the new cultural revolution. . . . Soon, we hope, the young workers and students are going to be so united and strong that even in this old cess-pit of decaying capitalists the banner of libertarian socialism will be seen as the only hope. But as we grow more conscious of the struggle to come, so, of course, does our enemy. And this is where the Beatles come in." John's "Revolution" showed the Beatles were "deliberately safeguarding their capitalist investment." The author concluded, "Although I've liked the Beatles in the past I hope that they get so fucked up with their money-making that they become as obscure as Cliff Richard."

The next issue of the *Black Dwarf* drew on the Stones' status as radicals. Published just before a new march on the American embassy, it ran the headline "Marx/Engels/Mick Jagger." The editors ran an essay by Engels under the headline "On Street Fighting." Originally published in 1849, it read, "Let us have no illusions about it: a real victory of an insurrection over the military in street fighting is one of the rarest exceptions. . . . Even in the classic time of street fighting, the barricade produced more of a moral than a material effect." Next to that appeared the words to "Street Fighting Man" in Jagger's own handwriting, which he had sent to show his support for the march.

On another page readers found "An open letter to John Lennon," by John Hoyland. He gave the familiar New Left response to "Revolution," focusing on John's line "change your mind instead." "What we're up against is not nasty people, not neurosis, not spiritual undernourishment. What we're confronted with is a repressive, vicious, authoritarian system. A system which is inhuman and immoral . . . It must be destroyed, ruthlessly. This is not cruelty or madness. It is one of the most passionate forms of love. . . . Love which does not pit itself against suffering, oppression and humiliation is sloppy and irrelevant." He added that the Stones "have understood this, and in their music refuse to accept the system that's fucking up our lives." The letter told John that the ruling class "still hates you . . . because you act funny and because you're working class, in origin at least, and you're undisciplined, and above all you've been going out with a foreigner." It concluded, "Come and join us."

This criticism brought a written response from John, which led to an important relationship with the *Dwarf*'s editor, Tariq Ali, during a crucial year of John's growing engagement with New Left politics. Ali headed the Vietnam Solidarity Committee, which had organized impressive marches on the American embassy. Tariq Ali recalled a telephone call he received shortly after the Hoyland letter appeared. "It's John Lennon here. You're publishing these attacks on me."

"These aren't attacks. They're just friendly criticisms, John, and you're very welcome to reply."

He said, "Oh, well, I will."

The January 1969 issue of the *Black Dwarf* contained his reply. The theme of that issue was "Women, sex and the abolition of the family." The editorial, written by Sheila Rowbotham, argued that the Marxian concept of revolution must be expanded to include a qualitative transformation of personal and sexual relations between men and women. An important essay in its own right, the editorial has special significance. In 1980 John asked the BBC, "Where's the women in Tariq Ali's revolution?" Tariq Ali's reply was to point to the *Black Dwarf* issue in which John's own letter appeared. And indeed Sheila Rowbotham's editorial is a more thorough feminist statement than John and Yoko ever produced.

The editors opposed the puritanism and sexism of communist societies, and also the exploitative sexual "freedom" represented by the *Playboy* philosophy. They argued that "the loosening of traditional ties has far too often replaced one form of sexual oppression by another. . . . The frenetic pursuit of quantity in sex is also a crude psychological response to the quantification and competitiveness of private enterprise," which has nothing to do with a socialist conception of freedom. "The answer is not to abolish the family, but to abolish repression and mystification within the family, and to stress that the family is only one possible form of personal and sexual relationship." The point is to provide people with choice.

John's "very open letter" replying to the radical critics of "Revolution" followed the feminist editorial. He was angry and hurt. "I don't worry about what you, the left, the middle, the right or any fucking boys club think. I'm not that *bourgeois,*" he wrote bitterly. "I'm not only up against the establishment but you too." He reiterated the position he had taken in "Revolution": "I'll tell you what's wrong with the world: people—so do you want to destroy them? Until you/we change our heads—there's no chance. Tell me of one successful revolution. Who fucked up communism, christianity, capitalism, buddhism, etc.? Sick heads, and nothing else."

He defended Apple on socialist grounds: "We set up Apple with the money we as workers earned, so that we could control what we did productionwise." In response to the argument that the Stones were radicals and the Beatles liberals, John wrote, "Instead of splitting hairs about the Beatles and the Stones—think a little bigger. Look at the world we're living in, and ask yourself: why?" That was a good point. He concluded, "You smash it—and I'll build around it."

The rejoinder, signed by John Hoyland, had in fact been written collectively by the editorial committee. In response to John's argument that what's wrong with the world was "narrow minds—sick heads—people," the editors wrote, "We don't blame people, and we wouldn't want to shoot all the capitalists because we think it's natural for them to behave the way they do. What we blame is the form of society which produces them—which *by its nature* is competitive, puts profits before principle, places power and privilege in the hands of the few at the expense of the many. Given such a society a lot of people rich and poor are necessarily selfish, narrow-minded, unscrupulous. They have to be. That's the way the system works. Build a better form of society—one based on cooperation and participating and sharing—and people will respond accordingly."

Admitting that some of the arguments in the original John Hoyland letter had been patronizing and trivial, the editors struck home in a critique of John's distance from the mass movements of the day and his writing about "sick heads." "What do you think about a person who claims to be concerned about people and their values, but remains silent when confronted by the actual struggles and sufferings of most of the human race? Are they sick too?"

John's line "free your minds instead" received an equally powerful critique. "What makes you so sure that a lot of us haven't changed our heads in something like the way you recommend—and then found out *it wasn't enough,* because you simply cannot be completely turned on and happy when you know that kids are being roasted to death in Vietnam, when all around you you see people's individuality being stunted by the system. Why couldn't you have said—'as well'—which is what I would say?"

Finally, the Hoyland rejoinder appealed for John to join the New Left. "The feeling I've got from songs like 'A Day in the Life' is part of what has made me into the kind of socialist I am. But then you suddenly went and kicked all that in the face with 'Revolution.' That was why I wrote to you —to answer an attack you made on us, knowing that what you said would be listened to and respected by millions, whereas whatever reply we make here is read by only a few thousand. . . . I just wish you were a bit more on our side. We could do with a few good songs." Three months later John and Yoko became antiwar activists and released "Give Peace a Chance."

In November 1968 the *Two Virgins* album was released the same day that John's marijuana conviction was announced. The cover photo showed John and Yoko in the pose the newspapers called "full frontal nudity." The album's electronic music had been made during the first night they spent together in May. The media responded with predictable outrage. "It just seemed natural for us," John explained mildly. "We're all naked really." This was the same man who as a youth had sung, "You've got to hide your love away." Now he wanted to tell the naked truth; they had nothing to hide. For centuries nakedness had signified becoming real. Rousseau and Marx had both used nakedness as a metaphor for the absence of lies and illusions. John and Yoko were joining a distinguished radical tradition. John explained that the cover said, "Look, it's two people—what have we done?" He added, "Of course I've never seen me prick on an album or in a photo before: 'Watnearth, there's a fellow with his prick out.' "

When the nude photo appeared a week after Yoko's miscarriage, the press reminded everyone that John and Yoko were each married to other people. The coincidence of these events in the same week as John's drug conviction marked him as a depraved person in the eyes not only of the establishment but also of many conventional Beatle fans. This season marked the lowest point yet in his public standing, when the London press was heaping scorn and abuse on him relentlessly. They blamed Yoko for the changes in John, and she took the brunt of the hostility, some of it brutal. Beatle groupies outside the Apple offices and the Abbey Road studios would hurl racist insults at her, yelling "Hey, Chink," a term which refers, of course, not to Japanese, but to Chinese. Her tormentors were stupid as well as racist.

The FBI took an interest in John and Yoko's *Two Virgins* cover, as shown in the files released under the Freedom of Information Act. Throughout his career J. Edgar Hoover had been obsessed with sexual radicalism. In May 1968, as part of the FBI campaign against the New Left, Hoover had instructed agents to gather information on the "scurrilous and depraved nature of many of the characters' activities, habits, and living conditions." In October he sent an angry follow-up memo criticizing agents for ignoring the "mounting evidence of moral depravity" and the "obscene display" of radical youth. In January 1969 the special agent in charge of the FBI in New Haven, Connecticut, reported to J. Edgar Hoover on a campus demonstration at the University of Hartford. Two hundred students protested the administration's suspension of the campus newspaper for publishing "nude photographs, front and back, of Beatle JOHN LENNON holding hands with his girlfriend YOKO ONO." Copies of the FBI report were also sent to the Army, to military intelligence, and to the Secret Service. Hoover hoped that the publication of lurid reports of the depravity of young radicals would help "neutralize" the New Left.

FBI representatives met with the assistant attorney general to examine the *Two Virgins* cover. Hoover wrote to an interested congressman that the FBI and the Justice Department concluded that it "does not meet the existing criteria of obscenity from a legal standpoint." When a Florida congressman requested information from Hoover showing that "a substantial number of criminals have been exposed to pornography," the FBI filed the request with the *Two Virgins* material, in keeping with Hoover's peculiar ideas about sex.

Before John could marry Yoko he had to divorce Cynthia. They had married six years earlier, when he got her pregnant, before the Beatles had their first hit. John did not have the courage to tell her of his divorce plans. He sent an associate to do it. Then he had divorce papers served on her, accusing her of adultery.

Peter Brown, the Beatles' personal assistant who arranged the divorce, said in an interview, "I think he wanted to believe it. It was very circumstantial, but it sounded convincing to us all. We all knew that John had not been a particularly good husband. Who could blame her if she went off and was discreet about a little love affair?"

John would soon tell *Rolling Stone* that the Beatles' life on tour was like Fellini's *Satyricon,* one long orgy. He made his love for Yoko into headlines all over the world. Yet he told Cynthia he was divorcing her because of her adultery. She wrote in her memoir, "All I could think of was how cruel and cowardly was the act." She was right.

———

At the end of 1968 it seemed as if a decade's worth of significant events had been packed into one year. Then, from out of the past, the original king of rock and roll reappeared, and the sudden juxtaposition of past and present made the history of youth culture especially vivid for a moment. In December 1968 Elvis appeared on TV for the first time in eight years. He had inspired John's love of rock and roll in 1957. "Been a long time, baby," Elvis ruefully told the audience. He looked and sounded gorgeous, backed up only by a small group and singing in front of a live audience.

"After the huge orchestras and fantastic sound effects and multi-tracking of *Sgt. Pepper,* it is a revelation to see Elvis alone," Boston's *Old Mole* said. Elvis' performance reminded the *Mole* of the origins of the counterculture. "Before the civil rights movement, Elvis was the only rebellion we had," the *Mole* argued. "He was the beginning of our critical youth culture, the great antagonist of the stultifying, repressive, empty world of middle-class American adults. He stood for energy, exuberance, and sexuality, for the community and solidarity of young people against their elders. Youth culture has grown, while Elvis deteriorated into a purely commercial product. . . . But whatever he has become, Elvis was absolutely crucial to our development, and that is his real significance for us today."

At the beginning of March 1969, Yoko was invited to give an avant-garde jazz concert in Cambridge. "They didn't realize that we were together," she explained. "They were saying, 'Well, are you going to bring a band?' So John said, 'I'm the band, but don't tell them.' So I said, 'Yes, I'll bring a band with me.'" John continued the story. "We arrived in Cambridge. . . . The people were looking and saying, 'Is it? Is it?' I just had a guitar and an amp, and that was the first time I'd played just pure feedback. The audience was very weird, they were all these sort of intellectual artsy-fartsies from Cambridge, and they were uptight because the rock and roll guy was there. . . . The reaction I got from the quote, unquote, avant-garde group was the same reaction that she got from the rock and roll people: . . . 'What the hell—who the hell is he?'" It was "the first time I appeared un-Beatled," he said, explaining that he played "Ike Turner to her Tina."

Three months after the concert, Yoko described her screams and John's earsplitting feedback as "a very strong sound but filled with sadness." John insisted that "there's as much of my effort and energy, and much of my experience and being . . . in my guitar" in their Cambridge music "as there is on 'Strawberry Fields.' "

In the spring of 1969 the Beatles released John's "Don't Let Me Down." He had already sung about Yoko on the White Album, on "Happiness Is a Warm Gun" and "Everybody's Got Something to Hide Except Me and My Monkey" and "Julia"—but he had never been this passionate before: "Ooh, she done me, she done me good." He was in love for the first time, he declared, singing as if his life depended on it. The chorus of the song, "Don't let me down," had the most gorgeous, tormented harmony the Beatles had ever recorded. John seemed to be singing not only to Yoko but also to his fans, appealing to them to understand his new life with Yoko that was drawing him away from the Beatles, into the world of radical politics and art.

8

Avant-Garde Peacenik

John and Yoko married in March 1969, moved into the Amsterdam Hilton for their honeymoon, and announced that a happening was about to take place in their bed. Holland was permissive, but the chief of Amsterdam's vice squad issued a stern warning: "If people are invited to such a 'happening,' the police would certainly act." Fifty newspeople crowded outside their hotel room. "These guys were sweating to fight to get in first because they thought we were going to be making love in bed. That's where their minds were at," John later recalled. "How could they think that?" Yoko asked. "Because we'd been naked: naked, bed, John and Yoko, sex." When the newsmen entered, John and Yoko were sitting in bed, wearing pajamas. "I hope it's not a let-down," John said. "We wouldn't make love in public—that's an emotionally personal thing."

He announced that they would stay in bed for a week, "our protest against all the suffering and violence in the world." The idea was to make use of the amazing image John and Yoko had. While people were looking, they would say something about what they thought, to get people talking about it. So they conducted interviews ten hours a day, starting at ten in the morning.

"We're sending out a message, mainly to youth, or to anybody interested in protesting against any form of violence," John explained later. "Things like the Grosvenor Square marches in London, the end product of it all was just newspaper stories about riots and fighting. We did the bed-in in Amsterdam . . . just to give people the idea that there are many ways of protest. . . . Protest for peace in any way, but peacefully, 'cause we think that peace is only got by peaceful methods, and that to fight the establishment with their own weapons is no good because they always win, and they've been winning for thousands of years. They know how to play the game of violence. But they don't know how to handle humor, and peaceful humor—and that's our message really."

John's pacifism seemed stupid to the left. Robert Christgau's response in the *Village Voice* contained some striking insights: "All revolutions are unpleasant, but the ones you lose are really for shit," he wrote. "But if it happens, it happens, and everybody chooses sides. All of John Lennon's rationalizations are correct. Violence does lead to more violence . . . But Lennon would never have achieved enlightenment if thousands of his forebears hadn't suffered drudgery far worse than protest marches and cared enough about certain ideals—and realities—to risk death for them."

If the left was hostile, the establishment press was outraged by the bed-in. Particularly in the London press, John and Yoko received a torrent of abuse. "This must rank as the most self-indulgent demonstration of all time," one columnist wrote. Another commented that John "seems to have come perilously near to having gone off his rocker."

Yoko defended the bed-ins on the grounds of the impracticality of other forms of protest for them. "We can't go out in Trafalgar Square because it would create a riot," she said. "We can't lead a parade or a march because of all the autograph hunters. We had to find our own way of doing it, and for now Bed-Ins seem the most logical way."

If the bed-ins seemed to combine a whimsical pacifism with a necessary practicality, in fact they had a much more serious and radical basis. Yoko in particular was drawing on her background as an artist to bring performance art together with radical politics. She and John were seeking to overcome the apolitical and antipolitical aspects of the avant-garde in a way that would also liberate radical political activity from its traditional forms, especially the protest march.

The bed-in also represented an early exercise in New Left media politics. John and Yoko rejected the view, held by many in the antiwar movement, that the newspapers and TV were necessarily and exclusively instruments of corporate domination of popular consciousness. The two of them sought to work within the mass media, to undermine their basis, to use them, briefly and sporadically, against the system in which they functioned. This strategy had obvious dangers, but it represented a bold effort to break out of the insularity of the older peace movement. It was based on a commitment to reach a new audience with radical politics, and it expressed a seriousness in grappling with new cultural forms which powerfully affected popular thinking.

As a media event the bed-in certainly conquered the front pages and TV news, but did that help the antiwar movement? Did John and Yoko's nonviolent message reach politically apathetic Beatle fans? The link between mass-media rock and radical politics remained uneasy in 1982, when Joe Strummer of the Clash talked about his own angry efforts to shake the rock audience out of its apathy, to attack corporate power and racism. "Every night we play, I wonder who our audience is," he said. "Maybe we're only entertaining most of them, but that's not really so bad when you think about it—look what it *is* that we entertain them with. You have to think you're making a difference to some of them—it's like fighting a big war with a few victories, but you might never know when one of those victories might be a big one. . . . I'd rather talk to a naïve person than a cynic. Sure, there are a lot of young naïve people out there, but at least they can be moved."

In the weeks after the bed-in, John barely concealed his irritation with the question "How successful was it?" He told Radio Luxembourg, "Successful enough for everyone who's interviewed us to ask how successful it was. The reaction to our action was successful." In any case, those who questioned the "effectiveness" of the bed-in missed part of its significance. Liberals consistently criticized the radical antiwar movement for being "ineffective," asserting that effective leaders worked for changes within the system. John and Yoko, along with the counterculture and the New Left, rejected that conception. They considered respectable, routine politics to be part of the problem. To attack the conventions of ordinary politics, to undermine its forms, itself had radical significance. By staying in bed for a week to protest the war, by "doing their own thing," John and Yoko were consciously rejecting the liberal conception of political effectiveness.

Yoko explained how they felt after the bed-in. "Because people kept saying we were crazy, we went into a very, very deep depression. We thought, 'Oh well, they were right. We didn't do very much. And it didn't help the world.' We were very sad, because there was no response. But then we started to get a tremendous, beautiful response around the end of the year. And that gave us hope."

John gave an example: "Some guy wrote, 'Now, because of your event in Amsterdam, I'm not joining the RAF, I'm growing my hair.'" A skeptical interviewer asked whether staying in bed meant anything, even as a symbol. "Imagine if the American army stayed in bed for a week," John replied.

But, the interviewer persisted, wouldn't it be better if people "went out and did something?"

"If you say you can do better than that, do it," John said. "Go ahead and top us!"

"A lot of people are jeering, aren't they? Not taking you seriously."

"It's part of our policy not to be taken seriously," John replied. "Our opposition, whoever they may be, in all their manifest forms, don't know how to handle humor. And we are humorous. We're Laurel and Hardy. And we stand a better chance under that guise, because all the serious people like Martin Luther King and Kennedy and Gandhi got shot." Today this flawed political logic has become tragically ironic.

The interviewer went on to ask, "If anything happened to you, how would you like to be remembered?"

John replied, taking the question as referring to both of them: "As the great peaceniks."

"That before your music?"

Without hesitation: "Oh sure."

John and Yoko launched "acorns for peace" when they returned to England after the bed event. They sent acorns to all the heads of state in the world, urging them to plant the acorns as a symbol of peace. Politically the project was objectionable. A gesture toward popular antiwar forces would have been infinitely more democratic than symbolic diplomacy between John and Yoko on the one hand and the world's dictators, tyrants, and politicians on the other. Only two world leaders planted their acorns: Pierre Trudeau and Golda Meir.

In April John wrote "The Ballad of John and Yoko," a new kind of song for him: a chronicle of events. The lyrics told about their real lives that spring —their problems finding a place to get married, the Amsterdam bed-in, the press reports about them. John was so excited he insisted on recording the song immediately, even though George and Ringo weren't available. On April 22 he and Paul recorded it alone, overdubbing the parts the other two would have played. The music was the most direct he'd ever written, based on the simplest rock and roll structure and rhythm. John's singing was wonderfully expressive. The lyrics were filled with jokes and puns, and the chorus told the truth about his frustration with the media and the officials who stood in their way: "Christ you know it ain't easy."

How hard was it for John and Yoko at this point? "Very hard," Peter Brown explained in an interview later. "A lot of it was because they took such controversial positions, like the bed events. They were setting themselves up to a certain extent. But the English press is really awful. They loathe success. If you are eccentric, they hate that. So they went after John and Yoko. It was terrible."

"The Ballad of John and Yoko" became the Number One song in Great Britain, Germany, Austria, Holland, Norway, Spain, Belgium, Denmark, and

Malaysia, and reached Number Eight in the United States. The line about how he was going to be crucified aroused John's old enemies among the fundamentalists, who had never forgotten his "more popular than Jesus" remark. Over half the Top Forty stations in the United States banned the record. John was thrilled by his discovery of a new form for rock lyrics. Its success encouraged him to continue to work with the form. This effort would reach a disastrous conclusion on the *Some Time in New York City* album.

In May 1969 John and Yoko decided to bring their peace campaign to the United States, where it really belonged. But Nixon's immigration officials refused John's request for an entry visa—the first blow in what would become a protracted war lasting from 1972 to 1975. John and Yoko announced plans for a bed-in in the Soviet Union; "It's easier to get into Russia than the U.S.," John complained. They settled on Montreal as the city closest to the U.S. media to stage their second bed-in for peace, arrived in May 1969, and did more than sixty radio interviews.

In the preceding weeks, Harvard students had gone on strike against university complicity in the war, and in Berkeley people challenged private property rights, creating a communal park in a vacant lot owned by the University of California. During John and Yoko's Montreal bed-in, university officials called the police to clear and destroy the park. A force of almost eight hundred police moved on six thousand demonstrators, killing one, blinding another, and injuring over a hundred. Subsequently twenty thousand people marched in protest against police violence and in support of the park.

John followed the struggle closely from Montreal, speaking with Pacifica radio station KPFA in Berkeley twice on the day of the first big confrontation. In the calls, which were broadcast, John declared his support for People's Park, but urged demonstrators to avoid a confrontation with the police. "I don't believe there's any park worth getting shot for," he declared. "You can do better by moving on to another city or going to Canada. . . . Then they've got nothing to attack and nobody to point the finger at."

The KPFA announcer couldn't believe John was serious. "What would you do right now if you had twenty thousand people or so outside, sitting there —would you tell them to leave, or should they like have a festival, or what?"

"A festival is more like it, man," John replied. At least he wasn't going to tell everybody at People's Park to drive to Canada that afternoon. "Sing— 'Hare Krishna' or something. But don't move about if it aggravates the pigs, don't get hassled by the cops, don't play their games. I know it's hard. Christ, you know it ain't easy, you know how hard it can be," he said. "But every- thing's hard—it's better to have it hard than not have it at all." What could the demonstrators do about the police? "Entice them! Calm them! You can make it, man! *We* can make it—together!"

After the first confrontations John declared, "The students are being conned! It's like the school bully: he aggravates you and aggravates you until you hit him. And then they kill you, like in Berkeley. Establishment, it's just a name for—evil. The monster doesn't care—the blue meanie is insane. We really care about life. Destruction is good enough for the Establishment. The only thing they can't control is the mind, and we have to fight for sanity and peace on that level. But the students have gotten conned into thinking they can change it with violence and they can't, you know, they can only make it uglier and worse."

John's statements urging demonstrators to avoid a clash with police were not consistent with the theory and practice of nonviolent resistance. From Gandhi to Martin Luther King to the early SNCC protests, nonviolent movements had refused to use violence themselves but had practiced confrontation politics, directly challenging the repressive force of the established order with their own bodies. "Direct action against injustice" was often politically necessary when other appeals had been exhausted. "We will not obey unjust laws or submit to unjust practices," Martin Luther King often said. "We will meet your physical force with soul force." This was the doctrine of nonviolence. John claimed to support nonviolence, but in 1969 he didn't understand it.

John's spirited but vague and confused remarks angered some. "Lennon's call firmed up his newfound status as a pompous shit," Robert Christgau wrote. But why did People's Park demonstrators listen to John in the first place—given his lack of political experience in (not to mention his opposition to) confrontation politics? Christgau explained it well: They "recognized that John Lennon knew something about commitment even if his politics were fatuous. In the worst of times, music is a promise that times are meant to be better. Ultimately, its most important political purpose is to keep us human under fire. John Lennon . . . is often better at keeping us human than trusty propagandists like Phil Ochs."

In subsequent days, John seemed to be reconsidering his position on confrontation politics. A reporter in Montreal asked whether he condemned student violence or campus building takeovers. "Sit-ins are okay," John replied. "I don't see why they have to destroy the building to take it over."

"Are you condemning the methods used at Harvard and Berkeley recently?"

"We're not condemning anything. We're just saying, 'How about thinking of something else?' "

In their most radical act in the Montreal bed-in, John and Yoko welcomed an American Army deserter to their bedside in Montreal. Introduced as a twenty-two-year-old from "Boston and the Fort Dix stockade," he brought his wife and six-month-old daughter. He came as a member of the American Deserters Committee, one of fifty deserters whom Canada legally admitted. The deserter explained to John and the assembled media, "We were told by the system to go and kill."

"I'm sympathetic," John replied. "The only way we can change the system is to do it nonviolently. . . . Gandhi's way," he said.

A reporter picked up on that point: "Should the U.S. have come to Britain's aid in 1941, when Hitler threatened?"

"What happened then was right for that moment," John replied.

One hostile interviewer came to John and Yoko's bedside in Montreal: cartoonist Al Capp, who drew the "Li'l Abner" comic strip. He expressed the views of those who supported the war and were enraged by the countercul-ture. "You would say," he began, ". . . 'Let's be kind to Hitler.' " Of course that wasn't what John had said, but Yoko took the bait.

"Loving Hitler doesn't mean allowing him to do whatever he wants," Yoko replied.

"Tell me how you stop him," Capp said.

"If I was a Jewish girl in Hitler's day," Yoko said, "I would approach him and would become his girlfriend. After ten days in bed, he would come to my way of thinking. This world needs communication. And making love is a great way of communicating." It was a terrible answer.

"Why didn't the Jewish girls think of that?" Capp commented, his voice filled with contempt. "They were so smart, you know; yet they never thought of that. . . . If Jewish girls would have gotten into the sack with Hitler, we would have spared six million Jews being burned, and thirty million people killed. Oh, why weren't you there then to advise us. . . . I think it's stark raving madness."

"What's mad about it?" John asked quietly.

"Because actually the Jewish girls didn't even have to offer," Capp replied, his voice rising in anger. "They were commanded, from the age of puberty on, to become prostitutes, for every one of the storm troopers. Don't you know your history?"

"What do you think the Americans have been doing in Vietnam?" John replied.

"What young men do everyplace," Capp shot back. "And why do you deny them the right to behave exactly as your friends in Berkeley do?"

"I keep answering this question," John said emphatically. "I'm not for destruction, whether it's a table, a chair—"

Capp broke in: "Simmer down for me, would you? Just—just rest."

Yoko tried to make peace. "Let's have a conversation, instead of behaving—"

Capp wouldn't let her talk either. "I'd be delighted with any conversation. . . . I read that you said you were very shy people. Yet these—" He pointed to the nude photos on the *Two Virgins* cover and chuckled.

John said, "Does that prove we're not shy?"

"Certainly not," Capp said. "If that isn't a picture of two shy people, I'd like to know what shyness is. Ah, what *filth!* . . . I think everybody owes it to the world to prove they have pubic hair. And you've done it. I applaud you for it. . . . And I tell you that's one of the greatest contributions to enlightenment and culture of our time."

"I hadn't noticed," John said.

Capp tried to return to his notes. "In the lyrics you said you were going to be crucified."

"Don't take it literally," John said. "They're gonna crucify me, and you, and everyone else."

"I will not permit you to speak for me," Capp barked.

"Well I took the liberty, Mr. Capp, of speaking on behalf of people in general. And if it upsets you—"

"It does upset me," Capp answered. "If I'm going to choose a spokesman, I'll choose—Vaughn Monroe. I'll choose Madame Nhu. . . . You're not my spokesman."

"I'm everyone's spokesman," John said calmly.

"You're not mine," Capp insisted.

John shouted, "I'm a representative of the human race. I'm speaking for us all."

"Whatever race you're the representative of, I ain't part of it," Capp said, his voice full of scorn. ". . . You belong to a race all your own. You don't represent me, and you don't write songs for me."

"I do it *especially* for you," John announced.

"I'll let Kate Smith sing my songs."

"Who do you write your cartoons for?" John asked.

"I write my cartoons for money. Just as you sing your songs for exactly the same reason. It's exactly the same reason much of this is happening, if the truth be told."

That made John mad. "Don't you think I could make money in some other way than sitting in bed for seven days, taking shit from people like you?"

"Look here, now, don't say this," Capp said in a complaining tone. "You got into bed so people like me would come and see you."

John shouted, "Not for money!" Then, more quietly, "For your sake."

"What you've just done is"—Capp's voice filled with rage and contempt —"you've said you're taking *shit* from people like me. Now, I was *invited* here. You *knew* I was coming."

"Yes, sure," John said calmly. "But we're not doing it for money. You indicated I was doing it for money. Don't you have manners?"

Capp was taken aback. "Why, I'm your guest," he said.

"I'm yours," John replied.

"No you're not," Capp said in his complaining voice. "This is your bedroom."

Yoko spoke: "This is everyone's bedroom."

Capp went back to his notes. "This business about 'they're gonna crucify me': what indications have you had that you're about to be crucified?"

John answered quietly, "I say we're all about to be crucified if we don't do something about war."

Capp paused and murmured, "Well, that isn't anything new. People have been saying that for a long time."

John's voice rose: "Who's saying it's something new?"

The exchange dramatized the gulf that separated the counterculture from the mainstream. What drove the mainstream into a frenzy, even more than political radicalism, was cultural radicalism—the music and the symbols of sexual freedom.

═══

The last night of the Montreal bed-in John taught everyone in the room the new song he had written, and recorded it on an eight-track portable tape recorder he had installed. On John's first non-Beatles recording, the backup singers were Yoko, Dick Gregory, Timothy Leary, Tommy Smothers, Murray the K, Petula Clark, a rabbi, a priest, and the Canadian chapter of the Radha Krishna Temple. The song, the musical product of the bed-ins, was "Give Peace a Chance."

Released as a single in the United States in July 1969, the song reached Number Fourteen on the American charts in September and Number Two on the British charts. It received Top Forty radio play for nine weeks, and became a million-seller worldwide.

On October 1, 1969, demonstrators held the first of a new series of protests, Vietnam Moratorium Day. Millions of people demonstrated in cities and towns across America. Organizers explained that these local protests were a prelude to a gigantic demonstration to be held in Washington, D.C., the next month. Nixon sent Spiro Agnew to respond as he had in the past. The Vice President said antiwar demonstrators were "encouraged by an effete corps of impudent snobs who characterize themselves as intellectuals."

Impudent snobs picketing the White House and on the steps of St. Patrick's Cathedral in New York sang the new song, "Give Peace a Chance." "The organizers of the marches did not promote the song," one observer commented. "It just happened."

On November 15 Vietnam Moratorium Day was declared in Washington, D.C. Pete Seeger led nearly half a million demonstrators singing John's song at the Washington Monument—while Richard Nixon sat in the White House with Bebe Rebozo, watching football on TV. Seeger later described that day. "I guess I faced the biggest audience I've ever faced in my entire life," he said. "Hundreds of thousands, how many I don't know. They stretched as far as the eye could see up the hillside and over the hill. I'd only heard the song myself a few days before, and I confess when I first heard it I didn't think much of it. I thought, 'That's kind of a nothing of a song, it doesn't go anyplace.' I heard a young woman sing it at a peace rally. I never heard his record. I didn't know if the people there had ever heard it before. But I decided to try singing it over and over again, until they did know it.

"Well, we started singing, and after a minute or so I realized it was still growing. Peter, Paul and Mary jumped up and started joining in. A couple of more minutes, and Mitch Miller hops up on the stage and starts waving his arms. I realized it was getting better and better. The people started swaying their bodies and banners and flags in time, several hundred thousand people, parents with their small children on their shoulders. It was a tremendously moving thing."

Later an interviewer asked John what he had thought about that day. "I saw pictures of that Washington demonstration on British TV, with all those people singing it, forever and not stopping," he said. "It was one of the biggest moments of my life."

In *Lennon Remembers* he explained, "I'm shy and aggressive, so I have great hopes for what I do with my work and I also have great despair that it's all shit. . . . I go through all that, and in me secret heart I wanted to write something that would take over 'We Shall Overcome.' . . . I thought, why doesn't somebody write one for the people now. That's what my job is, our job is."

John succeeded, as *Newsweek* recognized in an article on the song. "Now it will serve as the centerpiece for sing-ins at shopping centers planned in Washington and will join the list of carols to be sung in projected nationwide Christmas eve demonstrations. . . . The peace movement has found an anthem."

When antiwar demonstrators took the song into the streets, they made it a chant with a melody, a single line repeated monotonously over and over.

Often they sang it with a pleading tone. Movement radicals considered the song vague and apolitical.

But the original recording made at the Montreal bed-in was neither monotonous, nor pleading, nor vague. The hotel room was packed with people, most of whom were singing along, following the words that John had pasted on the wall across from their bed. He was full of energy, laughing, shouting, "Come on, come on—yeah!" Tommy Smothers sat next to the bed on a folding chair, right next to John; Timothy Leary sat cross-legged on the floor, shirtless and ecstatic; sick-looking Krishnas kept their eyes closed and wagged their heads in time to the music.

John sang with a cheerful enthusiasm. The song bounced along over a simple rhythm. And he sang verses filled with words, apparently whimsical nonsense lyrics about madism, bagism, shagism, and dragism. Closer examination reveals that the song had clear politics. John's verses called on people within the antiwar movement to put aside political differences and factionalism and to unite around the simple demand for "peace." John treated political positions as "isms," and he contrasted ideologically-minded activists talking about "this-ism, that-ism," about revolution versus evolution, with those asking only to give peace a chance.

On the White Album he had explicitly opposed those who took a revolutionary position. Here he simply called on them to put aside their political differences with liberals. If the apolitical character of the song aroused opposition from the left, it also contributed to the song's success in a peace movement that itself tended to avoid deeper political questions. As Pete Seeger said in 1981, "Undoubtedly some people wanted to say a lot more than 'give peace a chance.' On the other hand, history gets made when people come to the same conclusion from many different directions. And this song did hit a common denominator. There's no doubt about it."

At least twelve cover versions of "Give Peace a Chance" have been released in the United States, the performers ranging from the Everly Brothers to the Jazz Crusaders to Louis Armstrong to Mitch Miller. It had a separate life on gospel records, sung by groups like the Wondrous Joy Clouds. The most surprising of these is the cover version by the Mike Curb Congregation. Curb represented the political right wing in pop music, provided the music for the 1972 Republican national convention, and later got himself elected lieutenant governor of California as a Ronald Reagan protégé. Asked in 1982 why he had been singing "Give Peace a Chance," he did not answer.

The credits on the Apple single of "Give Peace a Chance" are strange. For the first time in his life John wrote and sang on a record without the Beatles. But he did not take credit as performer. He gave that to "Plastic Ono Band." His name appears twice: as co-producer, with Yoko; and as co-author, with

Paul. Paul did not co-author the song, but John was sticking with the agreement, made almost a decade earlier, that any song written by either would be credited to "Lennon-McCartney." That credit on "Give Peace a Chance" suggested that John was not quite ready to break up the Fab Four. But the record made a significant statement: as John left the Beatles, he joined the antiwar movement.

The "Renunciation of What the Beatles Had Stood For"

 In July 1969 John purchased Tittenhurst Park, an eighteenth-century Georgian mansion with seventy acres of grounds, located in Ascot. It didn't seem appropriate for a budding cultural and political radical. But John didn't intend to live like an aristocrat. He transformed the estate into a self-sufficient center for music and art, with a complete recording studio and extensive production facilities, including graphics and print shops. In August he and Yoko moved in. They used the facilities for the *Plastic Ono Band* and *Imagine* albums.

One of their first guests was Bob Dylan, who helicoptered over after his performance on the Isle of Wight. "We were both on fucking junk," John said in *Lennon Remembers,* which made "Cold Turkey" particularly relevant. A film shot during this visit shows him feeling sick and worrying he's going to throw up. He later remarked, "I've never seen it but I'd love to."

While John was taking his first steps toward an engagement with radical politics, Dylan's music was deteriorating in both its quality and its social significance. In 1969 he brought out *Nashville Skyline,* a dismaying series of pop clichés recorded in the country-music capital with Johnny Cash. Jon Landau called it "Dylan's *McCartney.*" To Anthony Scaduto it seemed like Dylan had undergone "some sort of Kafkaesque brain-washing by a crew of mind doctors from desolation row." Dylan's songs spoke of "an America that was very sure of God, country, flag and white supremacy." Scaduto was going too far, but Johnny Cash was a favorite of war supporters. Nixon would soon invite him to play "Okie from Muskogee" and "Welfare Cadillac" at a White House concert. Whom would Dylan sing with next? Kate Smith, one disillusioned fan predicted.

Not everyone was dismayed. SDS activist Carl Oglesby defended *Nashville Skyline,* arguing that "Dylan was becoming interested in the white working class at the same time the Movement did. As the Movement was getting turned on to the alienated, displaced white hillbillies in Northern cities and more and more convinced that if we didn't reach the white working kids there would be no future, he comes along with *Nashville Skyline,* which says in so many words that the problem from now on is to talk to America. It's a move to working class language. . . . Dylan as strategist, Dylan making a decision to reach another constituency."

Dylan himself taunted his critics on the left. He asked an interviewer for the magazine *Sing Out!,* "How do you know I'm not, as you say, for the war?" He sounded like a person without real commitments. The contrast between him and John couldn't have been sharper.

In September 1969 the founder of the Hare Krishna movement, Swami Bhaktivedanta, arrived as a houseguest of John and Yoko's at Tittenhurst Park; he was George's guru. John had broken with the Maharishi more than a year earlier, but several Hare Krishna people had joined him in Montreal at the bed-in. The Swami worked to convince them that "peace and prosperity will be the immediate worldwide result" of the adoption of Krishna consciousness and the chanting of the mantra "Hare Krishna." However, the Swami firmly insisted, "if you don't receive the mantra through the proper channel, it may not really be spiritual." He warned them against the Maharishi, Paramahansa Yogananda, and three or four other rivals of his, attacking their credentials to dispense mantras.

John, always the antiauthoritarian, challenged the Swami: "How would you know anyway?"

The Swami explained that his own mantras worked, while those of his rivals didn't, because he was "a member of an authorized line of disciplic succession."

"Who says who's actually in the line of descent?" John protested. "I mean, it's just like royalty."

The Swami saw he had a problem. "Try to understand the principle of authority," he said—definitely a mistake in dealing with John. "You say that you want to know how to find out who's an authority. The answer to this question is that Krishna is the real authority." He told John about a "great spiritual authority in the bona fide disciplic succession" who told questioners, "You intellectual fools, just worship Krishna."

Yoko replied, "But every sect says that."

The Swami's last statement in the published transcript is "You should accept only those who are directly attached to Krsna [sic] as His authorized representatives." Shortly thereafter John and Yoko asked the Hare Krishnas to leave Tittenhurst. John had come back to his 1967 opinion of the group, when he ridiculed them in "I Am the Walrus" as "elementary penguins."

Late in the summer of 1969 Paul persuaded the other Beatles to go back into the studio to make an album the way they used to do it. John interrupted his peace campaign, George stopped recording Krishna chants, Ringo set aside his film career. For the last time, the four Beatles met at Abbey Road.

The album by that name, released in October, opened with John's "Come Together." He had begun it as a political song for the counterculture and the movement when Timothy Leary had been thinking about running for governor of California. The song mixed political and sexual metaphors nicely, and was as clever as anything John wrote in his Lewis Carroll/"Daily Howl" mode. It would take on new significance for him during the summer of 1972, when he did it at Madison Square Garden as a rocking antiwar song addressed to all opponents of Nixon's policy in Southeast Asia. Looking back on the song in 1980, John commented, " 'Come Together' is *me.* "

The rest of John's work was not his best: two love songs to Yoko, "I Want You" and "Because," and two Liverpool sketches, "Mean Mr. Mustard" and "Polythene Pam," which together were slightly more than two minutes long. The nadir of the album was "Maxwell's Silver Hammer," by Paul. John called it "a nice little song for grannies to dig." The album ended, appropriately enough, with Paul singing alone. Robert Christgau wrote from Berkeley, "Opinion has shifted against the Beatles. Everyone is putting down *Abbey Road* . . . One evening I put it on. It gives me a headache."

Some listeners found political relevance even on *Abbey Road.* An Episcopal priest working with the antiwar organization Clergy and Laity Concerned wrote in *Christian Century* that Paul's "Carry That Weight" was the favorite song of draft resisters who had taken refuge in Sweden. Living with the weight of their decision to go into exile rather than fight an unjust war, "they would gather in pubs and play the song over and over," singing that there was no way to go home.

——

The rock festivals held during the summer of 1969 expressed the energy and complexity of youth culture. John played at one in Toronto. He liked it so much he decided to hold his own, a more political and nonprofit version of Woodstock.

The original inspiration for rock festivals was the Monterey International Pop Festival of 1967, which made Jimi Hendrix, Otis Redding, Janis Joplin, and the Who superstars in America. The performers received only payment for expenses; the profits were supposed to go to free clinics and ghetto music programs. The film of the festival shot by D. A. Pennebaker showed millions what they had missed.

By 1969 rock festivals expressed the counterculture's contradictions. The first was between hip capitalists, who saw a new way of making money off youth culture, and New Leftists, who saw rock festivals as an expression of youth culture's challenge to capitalist America. The second was between the ideology of flower power and the violence growing out of the drug subculture as some young people switched from psychedelic drugs to barbiturates combined with alcohol.

The Southern California festivals were the most violent: at the Palm Springs festival in April 1969, 250 were arrested after extensive rioting, and at the Newport '69 festival in Orange County, not far from Nixon's Western White House, there were 300 injuries and $50,000 in property damage.

The promoters of the Woodstock festival hoped fifty thousand people would come. Half a million showed up on August 15, 1969, "the largest, most peaceful gathering of teen-agers ever to come to pass in modern times," its historian declared. Rock critic Greil Marcus was there. "The limits have changed now," he wrote, "they've been pushed out, the priorities have been rearranged. . . . All over the nation, kids are moving to rock and roll. It's the most important thing in their lives."

The New York *Times* didn't like it. Noting that it rained, and that there weren't enough toilets, the paper ran an editorial titled "Nightmare in the Catskills," declaring with shaky syntax that the "hippies . . . had little more sanity than the impulses that drive the lemmings to march to their deaths in the sea."

"Remember Woodstock?" Liberation News Service asked its readers. "Remember how the radical press attacked this biggest rock festival in the history of the world because it was a business that was going to make a profit of $1 million by selling us our own music? Remember how so many kids came they couldn't collect tickets, and a quarter of a million people got in for free? And remember how the promoters announced that they *lost* $1 million, and how everyone called that a victory for the people?" It turned out that the promoters made plenty of money, probably a million off the festival and many millions from the movie. LNS called the festival "a victory for the businessmen who make a profit by exploiting youth culture." A decade later, rock impresario Bill Graham indicated that he saw it the same way: "The real thing that Woodstock accomplished," he said, "was that it told people that rock was big business."

Woodstock showed the political radicals how weak they were in the counterculture. The Yippies had been unable to get twenty thousand people to come to Chicago to demonstrate against the Democrats the previous summer. The Woodstock promoters drew more than twenty times that. At Woodstock the political radicals had printing presses running in their tents. They distributed a pamphlet, urging a political perspective, that began with quotes from Eldridge Cleaver and Bob Dylan: "You're either part of the solution or part of the problem" and "He not busy being born, is busy dying." The high point for the politicos came when Country Joe, singing solo, did his antiwar anthem "Feel Like I'm Fixin' to Die Rag," and most of the audience joined in enthusiastically.

The low point, the moment when the contradiction between political and cultural radicals became unmistakable, occurred when Abbie Hoffman appeared on stage. He started to make a pitch for John Sinclair, the Michigan activist jailed on a marijuana conviction, and was driven off the stage by Pete Townshend. Hoffman made the best of the situation, rushing into print with a book, *Woodstock Nation,* claiming the festival for the struggle against "Pig Nation." He said his battle in the streets of Chicago with the police the previous summer resembled his battle onstage at Woodstock with the Who, "aristocrats of the rock empire."

Townshend was still thinking about Woodstock thirteen years later. "All those hippies wandering about, thinking the world was going to be different," he told an interviewer. "As a cynical English arsehole I walked through it all and felt like spitting on the lot of them. . . . Nothing was going to change. Not only that, what they thought was an alternative society was basically a field full of six-foot-deep mud laced with LSD. If that was the world they wanted to live in, then fuck the lot of them."

Ellen Willis, a leading radical feminist and rock writer, perceived the possibilities of a different kind of Woodstock. Rock, she wrote that summer, "can be—and has been—criminal and Fascistic . . . as well as revolutionary." That was an uncanny forecast of the forces that four months later would shatter the Altamont festival.

The Woodstock promoters had written to John Lennon, promising any sum of money if the Beatles would appear. John replied that he couldn't deliver the Beatles, but could come himself with the Plastic Ono Band. Michael Lang, producer of the festival, decided that wasn't good enough. John stayed home.

John and Yoko agreed to play at the Toronto Rock and Roll Revival in

September. It was his first live concert appearance since the Beatles had stopped touring in 1966, and the first time he had played a concert without the other Beatles since 1957. The band he put together consisted of Eric Clapton on lead guitar, Klaus Voormann from the Hamburg days on bass, and Andy White on drums. Chuck Berry, Gene Vincent, Jerry Lee Lewis, and Bo Diddley also appeared; an audience of twenty thousand turned up.

John was so nervous, he said later, "I just threw up for hours until I went on." He sang "Money" for the first time at a live performance since the Beatles took it out of their tour repertoire six years earlier. It represented the raw, uninhibited energy of John's rock and roll youth. He sang "Blue Suede Shoes" and "Dizzy Miss Lizzie" from the same period. He sang a new song, "Cold Turkey," a studio version of which would be released as his second non-Beatles single. And he ended with a long, raucous version of "Give Peace a Chance."

If "Money" and "Dizzy Miss Lizzie" represented John's musical origins, "Cold Turkey" represented a significant step forward, away from the Beatles toward a new kind of music. The song was a brutal exercise in truth-telling, without any of the nightmare surrealism of his psychedelic period. He wanted everyone to know his experience of withdrawal from heroin. John's screams of pain were almost too realistic; he had learned that from Yoko, not from Arthur Janov, the founder of primal therapy, who had not yet appeared in their lives. The song expressed a frenzied despair and a desperate, childlike appeal for help—"Oh I'll be a good boy, please make me well / I'll promise you anything, get me out of this hell." Musically it was stripped down to the most elemental chord structure; its relentless rhythm sizzled and burned. Again John sang as if his life depended on it. With the stark, painful truth-telling of "Cold Turkey" he was on the way to his *Plastic Ono Band* album.

Yoko sang "Don't Worry Kyoko," addressed to her six-year-old daughter from a previous marriage, whose father had refused to allow mother and daughter to see each other. John began the song with oddly familiar guitar chords, which turned out to be the same ones that began the Everly Brothers' "Wake Up Little Susie." And Yoko sang "John, John, Let's Hope for Peace." Over an electronic drone, she whimpered, shuddered, groaned, and then screamed his name. The piece was powerful and disturbing.

John was delighted when he heard the tapes of their performance; he had them released as an album two months later: *Live Peace in Toronto,* by the Plastic Ono Band. "I don't care who I have to play with, but I'm going back to playing on stage," he said. "I can't remember when I've had such a good time."

The Stones released *Let It Bleed* in November, demonstrating once again their impressive historical sense. The album began with the magnificent

"Gimme Shelter," which expressed the feeling that would soon prevail in the counterculture; it ended with Jagger's version of wisdom, anticipating the end of the sixties: "You Can't Always Get What You Want."

===

"Give Peace a Chance" was John's contribution to the peace movement in America, but he was still British—not only a British citizen and resident, but also, since 1965, a Member of the British Empire (MBE). The Beatles' investiture by the queen had been unequivocal testimony to the establishment's recognition of their triumph. John, a class-conscious young man, had never liked the accolade. When he first received word of the honor in a personal letter from a representative of the queen, according to Peter Brown, "he was so disgusted he threw it in a pile of fan mail and never answered it." Buckingham Palace had had to ask a second time, and Brian Epstein dictated the appropriate response.

On November 26, 1969, John decided to return his MBE as an act of political protest. Anthony Fawcett, an assistant to John and Yoko at the time, recalled the day: "After breakfast . . . John rushed downstairs and told Les, the chauffeur, to leave right away for his Aunt Mimi's house in Bournemouth to bring the medal back off the top of her TV set." John drafted a statement. "Your Majesty, I am returning this MBE in protest against Britain's involvement in the Nigeria-Biafra thing, against our support of America in Vietnam, and against 'Cold Turkey' slipping down the charts. With Love, John Lennon of Bag." John and Yoko delivered the letter and medal in person to the tradesmen's entrance to Buckingham Palace—an affirmation of his working-class roots—and then John met the press. "Whenever I remember it I used to flinch," he explained, "because basically I'm a socialist."

The newspapers blasted John, focusing on his reference to "Cold Turkey." He explained, "A few snobs and hypocrites got very upset . . . but that saved it from being too serious. . . . You have to try and do everything with humor, and keep smiling." The MBE itself was "mostly hypocritical snobbery and part of the class system," John said. "I only took it to help the Beatles make the big time. I know I sold my soul when I received it, but now I have helped to redeem it in the cause of peace." He added, "Of course my action was a publicity gimmick for peace."

Bertrand Russell wrote John, "Whatever abuse you have suffered in the press as a result of this, I am confident that your remarks will have caused a very large number of people to think again about these wars."

Americans did not appreciate the significance of the event, but it had a stunning impact in Britain. Eleven years later, in John's London *Times* obituary, the MBE event loomed large. The early Beatles had been "at the spearhead of the formation of a new role for Britain in the world." In the *Times*'s view, the Beatles had suggested that England was not "a country suffering economic, political and foreign policy problems," but rather "a dynamic, creative, forward looking" nation that had "plucked the lead in progressive music from America's grasp." John's returning his MBE "signaled his final renunciation of what the Beatles had stood for."

Late in 1969 John and Yoko joined a campaign against famine in Biafra, the province of Nigeria that had been waging a secessionist war for a year. A week of events were scheduled for Trafalgar Square in late October. John and Yoko announced they would show two of their avant-garde films on a gigantic screen outdoors. The *Times* was disturbed about "the bizarre treat of being able to watch the face of John Lennon smiling interminably on a monstrous cinema screen." The Ministry of Public Works tried to ban the showings, but St.-Martin's-in-the-Fields provided church property for the erection of the screen.

In December John and Yoko joined the Christmas fast organized by the Save Biafra Campaign at Rochester Cathedral. John may have been moved to support this campaign by a one-man demonstration against him a year earlier, at the underground "Alchemical Wedding" at the Royal Albert Hall. John and Yoko had appeared in a bag there to the accompaniment of flute music. Their performance was interrupted by a man who paraded in front of the stage with a banner about famine in Biafra. He shouted, "Do you care, John Lennon? Do you care?"

For John and Yoko to call attention to the suffering of Biafrans was to criticize the British government, which was providing arms for the Nigerians. But "the left in Britain had no position on Biafra," activist Tariq Ali said. "It tended to regard both sides with equal disdain, except that no one supported the British government. We said Britain shouldn't be interfering at all." Many conservatives opposed British support for the Nigerians simply because the Soviets also supported them. John and Yoko's campaign against famine in Biafra was a purely humanitarian one that had no special leftist content.

By the end of 1969 John and Yoko were contributing to a wide variety of groups and projects. Besides the Biafra campaign, they gave a thousand pounds to establish a school for gypsy children in England, and they offered an Irish island he owned to the London Street Commune as a haven for street people and squatters.

In December John and Yoko launched their "War Is Over" campaign, buying billboard space in London, New York, Hollywood, Toronto, Paris, Rome, Berlin, Athens, and Tokyo. The billboards read, "War Is Over—If You Want It—Happy Christmas, John and Yoko." To open the campaign,

John and Yoko played a "War Is Over" benefit concert for UNICEF at the Lyceum Theatre in London, John's first live concert in England in four years. George Harrison, Eric Clapton, Billy Preston, and Keith Moon joined him onstage, probably the greatest Plastic Ono Band ever assembled. They played a screaming fifteen-minute version of "Cold Turkey." *Rolling Stone* wrote that John "showed the crowd that his fervor for peace and Yoko hadn't dimmed his talent or displaced his sense of humor. . . . The locals still loved him." Second and last they played a screaming half-hour version of "Don't Worry Kyoko." Yoko was greeted with "malicious snickers and twisted grins . . . embarrassed looks and hip scorn," *Rolling Stone* said. "Without John's strong backing, she'd be crucified."

Black activist Dick Gregory commented later, "We're not used to seeing an Asian that ain't bent over, smiling, apologetic. She never was that. When was the last time people in the press interviewed any Asian, much less an Asian woman, that looked you right in the eye, and answered your question, and could be as belligerent with her answer as you are with your question?

"I've never seen a relationship that was as equal. They came together, they moved together. It would have been very easy for him to be just John Lennon —the press didn't want this Asian to be part of it. But he said, 'It's me and her. We are one.' He demanded that you not overlook her—that takes a very special animal."

Not everyone understood John and Yoko's "War Is Over" campaign. John Sinclair wrote, "You are going to sound awfully fucking stupid trying to tell the heroic Vietnamese people that 'the war is over if you want it' while they are being burned and bombed and blown out of their pitiful little huts and fields." This was unfair: whatever the weaknesses of John and Yoko's 1969 campaign, it was directed at the American people. The billboards went up in Times Square and on Sunset Strip, not in Hanoi.

"You've got the power," John told young people in a July 1970 interview. "All we have to do is remember that: we've all got the power. That's why we said, 'War is over if you want it.' . . . Don't believe that jazz that there's nothing you can do, 'just turn on and drop out, man.' You've got to turn on and drop *in.* Or they're going to drop all over you. . . . And if you're hip to that, you've got to make your parents hip to that. Instead of despising them, use some compassion."

John did not know that a similar "War Is Over" campaign had been launched by Phil Ochs and the Los Angeles *Free Press* more than two years earlier. Ochs wrote an article for the paper in June 1967 calling for a "War Is Over" rally in Los Angeles, across from the Century Plaza Hotel, where Lyndon Johnson was scheduled to speak at a five-hundred-dollar-a-plate dinner and the Supremes were to entertain. Ochs wrote a song for the occasion:

"I Declare the War Is Over." Lots of people came, marched down the Avenue of the Stars to the hotel, and chanted, "The war is over!" Ochs started to sing his song; the police ordered the crowd to disperse and then attacked, beating the marchers while TV cameras, on hand for the President, whirred. Delighted by the extensive TV coverage, Ochs staged a second "War Is Over" demonstration in New York's Washington Square Park in November 1967. Paul Krassner and the Diggers commune helped organize it. This time the police did not attack, but again the press coverage was extensive. The *Village Voice* ran a front-page story on the event.

Ochs had demonstrated that clever and novel forms of protest could win much more media coverage than traditional antiwar demonstrations. Jerry Rubin and Abbie Hoffman grasped the implications of Ochs's "War Is Over" events. Shortly after the Washington Square demonstration, they began to plan an even bigger festival at which their "Youth International Party" would nominate a pig for President outside the Democratic national convention in Chicago the following August.

Although the similarities between John and Yoko's "War Is Over" campaign and the proto-Yippie ones which preceded it are striking, the differences are equally significant. John and Yoko put up billboards; Ochs organized demonstrations which thousands of people attended. John and Yoko were a long way from real mass politics.

BBC-TV featured John as a "Man of the Decade" in a special broadcast on December 31, 1969. In a long interview, John reflected on the sixties. "Not many people are noticing all the *good* that came out of the last ten years," he said. "The moratorium and the vast gathering of people in Woodstock—the biggest mass of people ever gathered together for anything other than war. . . . The good thing that came out of the sixties was this vast, peaceful movement."

And with his sweet optimism, he said, "The sixties were just waking up in the morning. We haven't even got to dinnertime yet. And I can't wait! I can't wait, I'm so glad to be around."

10

Hanratty and Michael X

 Injustice in Britain was the focus of John and Yoko's next political campaign. It centered on the case of James Hanratty, executed for murder in 1962. In December 1969 John was in the headlines again, announcing, "I am taking up the case in the hope of forcing a public inquiry into this man's hanging."

The next day John and Yoko attended the premiere of Ringo's film *The Magic Christian*. They stepped out of their white Rolls-Royce and unfurled a banner reading "Britain murdered Hanratty." On hand were the film's star, Peter Sellers, and Princess Margaret, among others. Later the same week John and Yoko held a bag event to further publicize the Hanratty case. While James Hanratty, Sr., father of the executed man, gave a speech at Speaker's Corner in Hyde Park, John's white Rolls appeared and two men carried a large white bag out of it. The bag displayed a sign reading "A silent protest for James Hanratty." The wriggling bag in the Rolls joined a procession of marchers to No. 10 Downing Street to present a petition demanding an official inquiry into the hanging. When John and Yoko performed at the Lyceum in London on December 15, Yoko began "Don't Worry Kyoko" by screaming "Britain! You killed Hanratty—you murderer!"

The murder for which Hanratty had been executed had been committed in 1961, when Michael Gregson and his lover Valerie Storie parked, as they often did, in a wheat field, after dark, outside London. A man with a gun appeared and forced them to drive down the A6 highway to a rest area, where he shot Gregson, raped Storie, then shot her. Gregson died, Storie recovered.

The case filled the front pages of Britain's newspapers. The police soon found the man they considered the perpetrator: Peter Alphon. They had evidence that, on the murder night, he had stayed in a hotel room where cartridge cases from the murder gun had been found. Alphon matched almost perfectly the Identikit picture Storie put together. He had behaved oddly after the murder. His alibi was proven to be a lie. He was a loner, known to be a fascist. Storie, however, failed to pick Alphon out of a lineup. Nevertheless, at the same lineup another woman identified him as the man who had tried to rape her, shouting "I am the A6 killer," two weeks after the murder. Despite this the police released Alphon and arrested the man who had occupied the hotel room the night before the murder: James Hanratty.

Hanratty and twelve other men appeared in a lineup before Storie. She picked Hanratty. Two of the four other people who saw the killer shortly after the crime also picked him. Hanratty was a twenty-five-year-old with a working-class background who had spent most of the previous seven years in prison for stealing cars and burglarizing houses. At the time he was wanted for burglary. He had never owned or used a gun, and he had never committed any sex crimes. It was the longest murder trial of a single defendant in British history. The jury found Hanratty guilty, the judge sentenced him to death, and in April 1963, only six weeks after the trial ended, he was hanged.

But the case remained in the public eye. During the first three years after the hanging, a new book was published annually arguing that Hanratty was innocent. The case for Hanratty was presented on an hour-long BBC program in 1966 and on the *David Frost Show* in 1967. Hanratty's defenders worked to show that he could not have been at the murder site. Hanratty told the police and his lawyers he had been in Liverpool at the time of the murder. But when he took the witness stand in his own defense, he changed his story and said he had been forty miles away from Liverpool in a town called Rhyl. It was late in the trial, and his lawyers were unable to find supporting witnesses before it ended. By 1968, five years after his execution, Hanratty's supporters had found seven reliable witnesses to corroborate his statement.

The second argument of Hanratty's defenders was that the real murderer was Peter Alphon, the man the police had first accused. Alphon himself supplied the strongest evidence. He began, after the trial but before the execution, telling the newspapers he believed Hanratty innocent and calling for a reprieve. A month after the execution, Alphon handed a friend notes for a confession to the A6 murder. On the first anniversary of the murder, Alphon visited Hanratty's parents and offered them money in compensation for the death of their son. Later he called them and confessed to the murder. The police did nothing about it.

In May 1967 Alphon walked into the London offices of *Life* magazine and offered to confess to the A6 killing for payment. The magazine refused to pay. Nevertheless Alphon held a press conference in Paris at which he confessed publicly for the first time, making headlines in London. He said he had been hired to frighten the couple, but not to murder them, by a fellow fascist who knew them and was enraged by their adulterous affair. Alphon called this person "Mr. X." The gun, he said, was provided by a mutual friend of Alphon's and Hanratty's, who cooperated in framing Hanratty. This person had served as the chief prosecution witness against Hanratty and had committed suicide just before the execution. Nine days later Alphon announced that his confession was a lie. Then he retracted his retraction. In the fall of 1968 he wrote to the Home Secretary, "I killed Gregson, the Establishment murdered Hanratty." A year later he named Mr. X in an effort to provoke a criminal libel charge and trial, but there was no response from the authorities or Mr. X.

In November 1969 Hanratty's parents stayed at the house of a wealthy nephew, John Cunningham, who lived in Ascot. He introduced his aunt and uncle to his neighbor John Lennon. John told an interviewer that he had "spent many hours with the parents and with the witnesses and lawyers. They convinced us there was a miscarriage of justice without a shadow of a doubt." Mr. Hanratty, Sr., had done the most to convince John. He had worked for twenty-five years and was foreman of a housing project cleaning crew—an ordinary working-class person of the older generation. It was at this point that John and Yoko launched their campaign.

The Hanratty case provided the basis for a powerful indictment of the British system of justice. It showed a young working-class man ruthlessly persecuted by a state that had little concern for finding the real criminal, but wanted to convict someone and claim to be doing its job; a state that hurried to execute the convicted man despite the existence of reasonable doubts about his guilt; a state that refused to consider evidence that an injustice had been committed even as that evidence became more and more compelling.

The Hanratty defense had never organized any real political activity, and was never taken up by any political groups. A few members of Parliament spoke in favor of an inquiry. The only prominent figure to become active in the case was Paul Foot, the leading left-wing journalist in Britain, who published an article in September 1966 naming Peter Alphon as the murderer and then published an outstanding book on the case in 1971.

John and Yoko's campaign seemed like a quixotic one, personal and apolitical, focusing on a single case of injustice. In fact, their involvement in the

Hanratty case coincided with a major campaign to abolish the death penalty in Britain. The same newspapers that reported John's statements that an innocent man had been executed also reported the progress of the Labour Party's fight in the House of Commons to end hanging. The opposition was powerful. The Tories presented a petition favoring the death penalty with one million signatures. Nevertheless the House of Commons voted to end capital punishment in December 1969, and the Lords concurred two days later.

John had been engaged with serious issues, but, he complained, "The Beatles are treated like Britain's children. . . . It's depressing when the whole family is picking on you." The press continued to treat John with undisguised hostility. The *Times* objected, in its ruling-class fashion, to the "unfortunate image of hippy earnestness directing liberal causes from the deep upholstery of a Beatle's income."

The *Daily Mirror*'s abuse was more flamboyant. It ran a headline naming John "Clown of the Year" at the end of 1969. "John Lennon means well," the tabloid began. "But it is not what goes on in the mind, rather what comes out of the mouth, that sets Mr. Lennon slightly apart from his fellow human beings. And out of that particular mouth this year has emerged the most sustained twaddle and tosh since Zsa Zsa gave way to Cassius Clay." Reviewing the period that began with the nude *Two Virgins* cover and ended with the Hanratty campaign, the *Mirror* found the bed-in the most outrageous. "That fatuous affair" had been based on "the notion that the contentious forces of mankind would pause in awe of this nut-nibbling couple in old Amsterdam." The article concluded, "Mr. Lennon's cry is 'Peace!' How about giving us some, chum?" With that, the *Mirror* ceased its coverage of John's political activities for more than a year.

In an interview in *Jazz and Pop* magazine early in 1970, John spoke about political responsibilities. The interviewer said, "The Establishment reminds me of a mule: to get their attention, you have to knock them over the head first."

John disagreed: "They know what's going on."

"No they don't. They close their eyes to whatever they want to."

John began to get angry. "They know damn well what the game is. And until people realize that the Establishment do know what's going on, and then take their responsibility of doing something about it, we're stuck."

When the other Beatles were reluctant to record John's "Instant Karma!" he recorded it on his own in January 1970 and released it two weeks later—his first official non-Beatles record. John's rich, deep voice, the strong beat, and the stark sound were irresistible. His words seemed to mean something, but friends disagreed about exactly what it was. For some, it sounded like a promise of enlightenment as easy as instant coffee. Others liked the part about recognizing your brother "in everyone you meet" and the democratic affirmation in the lines "Who do you think you are, a superstar? Well, right you are!"

John began the record with the same three notes as Richie Barrett's "Some Other Guy," tying his song to a classic of fifties rock and a staple of the Beatles' repertoire in their Hamburg days. The record was the first solo recording by a Beatle to go gold. It seemed to show that John could be as successful a solo artist as he had been with the Beatles. But no subsequent single of his would do as well until "Whatever Gets You thru the Night" four and a half years later.

At the beginning of January 1970, the *Times* for some reason put John on the front page with a statement that all future proceeds from his songs and records would go toward "promoting peace"—whatever that meant. In February he paid fines of 2,344 pounds imposed on ninety-six people involved in protests against the South African rugby team in Aberdeen, Scotland. The campaign to ban teams representing that racist government had gone on for more than a decade. John was a latecomer, but a welcome supporter. In March the Campaign for Nuclear Disarmament held a "Festival for Life" at Victoria Park, Bethnal Green. Eight thousand people heard rock music, poetry and drama, and a telephone speech from John. He announced that Yoko was expecting a baby, "and if we are going to have a baby, we must have peace for it to survive."

Meanwhile back in the U.S.A., the Vietnam Moratorium Committee held a "Winter Carnival for Peace" in Madison Square Garden. Pulled together in one week, the show drew a capacity crowd and had the largest gate for a nonsports event in Garden history. All the performers on the seven-hour program donated their time. Blood, Sweat and Tears, the Rascals, and the Voices of East Harlem won standing ovations. Peter, Paul and Mary, Judy Collins, and Richie Havens sang. Jimi Hendrix walked off the stage after announcing that "it just wasn't coming together" for his group. Harry Belafonte commented on the absence of blacks from the audience, arguing, "You do not find many blacks, not because the blacks are not committed to peace, but most of them are busy trying to get the same foot off their necks"—the foot on the necks of the Vietnamese. "There can never be peace as long as there's racism," he said.

Folk singer Tom Paxton released a single, "Crazy John," criticizing the bed events and the "War Is Over" campaign. John had not identified himself closely enough with the people: "They never come near you, John / So how can you teach them?" Robert Christgau commented, "In an ass-backwards way, Paxton is right, for if John were capable of such easy formulas, he might be almost as boring as Paxton himself."

===

In February 1970 John and Yoko staged another striking media event: they had their heads shaved and their hair auctioned, with the money going to a leading black-power spokesman in London, who called himself Michael X. John's appearance with Michael X "destroyed his last shred of credibility with the press," Peter Brown wrote; "the next morning, for the first time in Beatles history, not one photograph of the event appeared in any of the London papers."

For four years Michael had presented himself as a kind of British Malcolm X. He had risen from a career as a hustler and pimp to become a critic of British racism who was quoted often in the London underground press. A controversial figure, he was distrusted by many on the left, black as well as white. Two years after John and Yoko began supporting him, he was accused of murdering an associate in Trinidad and found guilty. In 1975 he was hanged. John and Yoko insisted that Michael was a legitimate political figure, innocent of the murder charge against him. They supported his legal appeals to the end.

V. S. Naipaul's hundred-page essay on Michael X, serialized in London's *Sunday Times Magazine* in 1973, painted a devastating picture of him: a grotesque political fraud, a rip-off artist who manipulated John and Yoko, a militant who was only an entertainer, a leader who had no followers, and also a murderer. Naipaul was a literary celebrity, and the publication of his powerful essay was a media event. But Naipaul was hardly an unbiased source. Born in Trinidad himself, he made a career out of portraying Third World radical movements as hopelessly deluded, irrational, corrupt, and brutal.

Nevertheless Naipaul's assessment of Michael is shared, at least in part, by leading figures in the New Left. Robin Blackburn, a student leader at the London School of Economics at the time and an editor of the *New Left Review*, recalled in 1981, "I didn't have much confidence in Michael. Our attitude was a rather polite lack of interest. He presented himself as simply the English equivalent of Malcolm X. . . . Michael didn't develop organically out of the English black community. But if you didn't know the black community very well, you could easily think he was a legitimate leader. In fact, Michael was a rather shallow and derivative figure."

Tariq Ali, who led in organizing the Vietnam Solidarity Campaign in London during the late sixties, went further. "Michael X was a hustler pure and simple," he said in 1981. "I knew him. I never clashed with him, and he never clashed with me. He read Malcolm X's autobiography and started acting it out. The Blackhouse [Michael's cultural center] was a fraud. It was just making money for himself." If Naipaul and others are right about Michael X, John and Yoko's support for him was the biggest mistake in their engagement with radical politics.

Their support for Michael was a response to the racial situation in Britain in the late sixties. In 1968 Enoch Powell, a member of Parliament representing Northern Ireland, and a Protestant, galvanized racist sentiment by predicting race war in Britain. His message was that Britain's immigrant blacks presented a mortal threat to the English and had to be forced to go back where they came from. Otherwise, he thundered, "in this country in 15 or 20 years' time the black man will have the whip hand over the white man."

Powell immediately became the country's most controversial figure in decades. He moved racism to the center of British politics and was bitterly denounced by everyone on the left. Tom Nairn wrote in the *New Left Review* that Powell was not a simple-minded racist, but "a much more conscious and ambitious reactionary" who was successfully reshaping the political system. "Besides his directly intoxicating impact on the petty bourgeoisie and sections of the working class, Powell indirectly has shifted the bourgeois parliamentary system itself, including the Labour Party, in his direction," Nairn argued.

Michael X sought out John and Yoko and presented himself as an advocate of nonviolence, a black leader committed to avoiding the racial bloodbath Enoch Powell seemed to be seeking. John told an interviewer, "We spent hours with Michael. . . . I talked and talked and talked with him, and he told me . . . how he has as many enemies in the black movement as the white because of his peaceful stand."

Michael had in fact advocated peaceful solutions to Britain's race conflict. In an interview in the Manchester *Guardian* in 1968 he was asked how full-scale race riots could be avoided. "Direct communication between the ghetto community and the Government" was his suggestion. "This would have to be on the highest possible level. The many ramifications of this are impossible to go into here, but it entails the use of interpreters and the recognition of the ghettoes as a colonial people."

The *Guardian* correctly described this proposal as "arrogant and confused" and Michael as "strong on rhetoric, short on argument." Colin MacInnes was the only white person to join Michael's Racial Adjustment Action Society. Writing in the *New Statesman* in 1968, he praised Michael's autobiography as "essential reading for everyone who wants to understand the black version of the racial dispute in England." But, he noted, Michael "tells us little or nothing of his ultimate intentions" and is "weak on theory for constructive action."

Given that John and Yoko wanted to support nonviolent activism among British blacks, in the face of Enoch Powell's diatribes, what were their alternatives to Michael X? Stuart Hall, a Jamaican who emigrated to England in the early fifties as a teenager, was the founding editor of the *New Left Review* and a central figure in London sixties politics. "Aside from Michael, there was very little else," he said in 1983. "He had visibility, he had an organization, he had a space, he had influence in the community. I don't think that a great deal politically could ever have been organized around him. But Michael for a time was what was going on. If you asked, in the late sixties, 'Who is the voice of Britain's blacks?,' most people would answer, 'He is.' "

In fact, Michael's relationship with London's New Left began much earlier than most activists realized. Stuart Hall is one of the few who knew him before his transformation into a militant. "In 1960, after race riots broke out in London's Notting Hill, the London New Left club helped organize black community tenants' associations. The worst landlord was a guy named Rachman. He had black hustlers and enforcers working for him. We discovered that Rachman's hardest runners were organized by this guy called Michael de Freitas—who several years later took the name Michael X. Michael started coming to the tenants' association meetings. He was in God knows how many rackets—housing, drugs, prostitution. But he as also genuinely into trying to set up the tenants' association.

"From the very beginning he was like Malcolm: he came off the street, he knew that street thing, how to hustle and survive. That was what life was like. In England at the time there was no black politics. So he connected to what there was: rackets. A number of us thought, 'This guy could be fantastic, if only we could clarify his mind.' If you converted him politically, or if you gave him a different apparatus to run, he would run it with the same efficiency.

"He used to come into the *New Left Review* office and just sit and talk to me about whatever was in his head. One of the things that was in his head was that his mother was white, and he felt a tremendous ambiguity because of that. Although this was well before black power, the struggle was increasingly being defined as a black struggle. And he knew that I came from a rather similar situation—my mother much lighter than my father, et cetera.

"It wasn't until Michael saw Malcolm that he recognized himself. I've always thought that, at that stage [1965], if there had been a developed political movement, he could have been another Malcolm. But although the black community became politicized at that point, it never generated permanent political structures. Even now, in the eighties, there are a lot of local things but nothing national. So there wasn't the opportunity for him to go into an existing political movement and use his skills.

"So instead he set out to create a black movement through his own personal force—which I'm afraid brought to the surface his megalomania, and the ambiguities in him that he had to deny. He claimed to be blacker than anybody else, he said he'd always been heavily political.

"In the late sixties the media had a desperate need for a figure exactly like him. They had no other outstanding black figure to quote. They couldn't get anybody else to make statements about the blacks of Britain; nobody else was sophisticated enough and articulate enough. Michael knew that."

Michael's Blackhouse, which John and Yoko supported financially, was "more a symbolic rallying point than an actual organizing base," Hall said. "He wasn't into serious organizing. He didn't have well-worked-out positions. He knew how to talk fairly convincingly, to the media and to celebrities like John and Yoko. But he never became anything like an organic spokesman of the black community. Nobody was, but he certainly was not."

Michael had served a year in jail in 1968 for having violated the Race Relations Act. The act, which made it a crime to make racially provocative statements, had originally been passed to protect blacks from attacks by white racists. (In the United States the act would be an unconstitutional denial of freedom of speech.) In 1971 Michael was charged with extortion. Rather than return to prison, he fled to Trinidad and established a commune. John made a public demonstration of his support by visiting Michael as his house-guest in April 1971, which helped Michael establish himself as a legitimate political figure there.

Within a year, however, police announced they had found the bodies of two of Michael's associates and charged him with murder. One of the victims, buried in Michael's lettuce patch, was a distant relative of his, Joseph Skerritt. The other, found in the garden next door, was Gale Benson, a white woman, the daughter of a wealthy Tory member of Parliament who was rumored to be a British secret service officer. Gale Benson had joined Michael's commune after falling in love with his associate Hakim Jamal. The British papers played up the sensational story of the ruling-class white girl murdered by black radicals and pretty much ignored the poor black man Skerritt. Probably most people believed Michael was hanged for killing Gale Benson. In fact, he was never tried for her murder.

The jury found Michael guilty and sentenced him to death. John told radical artist and activist Jon Hendricks, "We have to do something about this." "So we started the old route," Hendricks said; "forming a group, organizing a committee, finding lawyers." One of the first people they asked to join them was Yoko's old friend, the feminist and radical Kate Millett.

In a 1982 interview she recalled asking Hendricks, " 'Do you think the guy's innocent?' He said, 'It doesn't matter if he is or not, because we're against capital punishment.' And I said, 'Yes, but I'm interested to know whether he's innocent.' So he gave me all the materials. I spent a week or ten days doing nothing but reading them and taking notes. It was like a detective novel, but it was real. There seemed every chance that the whole thing was the most outrageous frameup there could be."

=====

No one knows what actually happened at the murder site. Hendricks suggested in 1982 that Michael was framed because he was "a threat to the Eric Williams government. Michael had an agrarian reform plan to make Trinidad self-sufficient. Trinidad is an oil country, and Williams had made the country dependent on oil income. Michael argued that this was wrong. Trinidad should concentrate not on developing its oil, but on its agriculture. It was a naturally rich agricultural country. Michael's farm, Christina Gardens, was an experiment in self-sufficiency. And Michael, though partly a creation of the press, was certainly an eloquent spokesperson for black rights."

The Eric Williams government may have perceived Michael himself as a potential threat, or may have hastened to execute him simply as an example to other black power spokesmen. Trinidad had been moving toward revolution, and "Black power" was the rallying cry of Williams' opponents. In 1970 they held antigovernment marches daily in Port of Spain, and "revolutionary pamphlets appeared everywhere, even in schools," Naipaul reported; "sections of the regiment declared for the marchers." Michael was in London at this point, but he was already preparing the ground for his return to the island several months later. He hoped to lead the black power movement in Trinidad.

Black activist Dick Gregory visited Michael there. "He was a fantastic human being," Gregory said later in an interview. "He understood suffering. We'd go through the little shanty towns and people would just come out like he was God. Cops were scared of him. I said, 'Michael, you're leaving yourself open. You can't do this, man. You cannot come into a country and start feeding people and doin' right without watching your back. They'll just wipe you out.'" Eric Williams by this time was notorious for his paranoia and hatred of opposition of any kind. Thus the defense committee's claim that Michael was framed and executed because he threatened Eric Williams' government is plausible.

The facts surrounding Michael's trial supported this claim. Michael's conviction had been based on "flimsy, questionable evidence," the *New Statesman* argued. The only evidence was the word of two presumed accessories to the crime. One was already serving a twenty-year term at the time of the trial, and the other, originally charged with the crime, was released after testifying against Michael.

The strangest aspect of the trial was the tactics of Michael's lawyer. The only direct evidence against Michael was offered by the man who had by his own admission killed Gale Benson. His credibility as a witness should have been destroyed on those grounds. Surprisingly, Michael's lawyer never took up that issue in his cross-examination.

With the star prosecution witness unchallenged, Michael's only hope was to take the stand himself and try to convince the jury of his innocence. Hostile lawyers feared his rhetoric would be effective in outwitting the prosecutors and persuading at least one member of the jury to vote for acquittal—which would have saved his life.

To everyone's amazement, Michael "elected" not to take the stand, after being persuaded by his attorney not to. His conviction and sentencing followed quickly. This attorney, a politician from St. Lucia, had sent Michael a telegram after his arrest, offering to represent him and boasting that he had never lost a murder trial. The *New Statesman* revealed that he had never appeared in any murder trial before Michael's. Finally, one juror who favored Michael became mysteriously ill during the trial, and "recovered just as mysteriously as soon as he was discharged."

Although the trial did not establish Michael's guilt, many on the left were not convinced of his innocence. "I think it's possible Michael committed the murder," Stuart Hall said in 1983. "I don't think it's possible that he planned it. But I think that, by then, Michael was deeply caught up with his own power and charisma in ways that couldn't be expressed. It was the sense that that was possible that made a lot of people in London unwilling to argue for his innocence."

In 1971 Kate Millett wanted to know about that. She later recalled, "John and Yoko [who had moved to New York City in 1971] came up here to my farm [outside Poughkeepsie, New York], in a funny rented car, after I'd read all the stuff. They stayed for a couple of days. We went through it all. I asked them point-blank, 'What about this guy? How much of what he's accused of would he ever be capable of doing?'

"They said he had a lot of imperfect sides, he was a hot talker, he could be jazzy on the super-militant side. But he wasn't up to any of these things: 'See what you can do to help him.' We were all nervous and very scared. John and I were both Irish—I think each of us had a kind of Irish horror of hanging. We felt we had never had anything this important do to: save somebody's life.

"We had a long wonderful crazy dinner. But the real moment the whole time had built up to was calling Trinidad and talking to Michael's wife, telling her of our plans to form an international defense committee. When that was done, John and Yoko got into their little car and headed back to the city. I went out and bought some cigarettes. And when I came back, there was somebody here in a car. And they left in the biggest hurry you ever saw. And I thought, 'Oh Jesus.' From the time I'd spent in Ireland, I knew more than I wanted about British agents and how they work—the ones who very quietly rifle through all your stuff, the hit-people. I thought, 'I could be taking on all this crap too.' "

After Michael's conviction, Dick Gregory decided to return to Trinidad. "I met with the lawyer Kunstler and Lennon. They gave me the name of Michael's lawyer and said he would meet me at the Trinidad airport. When I got there, nobody met me except the police. 'What are you here for?'— like they didn't know. I told them, 'I'm here to protest for my friend.'

"I went to the hotel and still the lawyer didn't come. Then a sympathetic newspaperwoman came by and told me the government had the lawyer scared. So I picketed the jail, all alone. I was nervous. I had no doubt that the British government and the CIA were behind the plans to execute Michael. I said to myself, 'At least I don't feel like a punk. And as soon as I'm done with my picketing, I'm going to run and get the next plane out.' And I did.

"When I got back to New York, John and Yoko and Kunstler and I met. I told them the case was bigger than just somebody being executed: 'They are out to kill a political force. . . . It is gonna be very difficult to save Michael.' "

In 1973 Trinidad and Tobago were still British colonies. Michael had a right to appeal to the British privy council to have his death sentence over-turned. John himself wrote a statement in July 1973: "Do you realize that any day now a man—Michael Malik—Michael X—will be hung in Trinidad after a suspicious trial through a system inherited from the *British.* He was born a member of the British empire. Legalized murder—capital punishment —is no way to deal with political prisoners, or anyone else for that matter. We urge you to do what you can for this human being. Every time we turn our backs on someone who needs help we take a step backwards in time. Please help save a life."

He sent copies to Her Majesty the Queen, the Duke of Edinburgh, Prince Charles, Princess Anne, Princess Margaret, and Lord Snowdon—the royal family. He sent copies to Prime Minister Edward Heath, the Hon. Harold Wilson, the Archbishop of Canterbury, Bernadette Devlin, M.P., Michael Foot, M.P., and Sir Lew Grade. He sent copies to Paul and Linda McCart-ney, George and Patti Harrison, Ringo and Maureen Starkey, David Frost, Cliff Richard, Malcolm Muggeridge, and the presidents of the Oxford and Cambridge student unions. He sent copies to all the London newspapers plus the editors of *Private Eye,* the Liverpool *Echo,* and the underground *Red*

Mole and *I.T.* Because Michael was a Muslim, John sent copies to the heads of all the Muslim nations.

Kate Millett toured England, trying to arouse support for Michael. Speaking at the Oxford Union (she had an Oxford literary degree), she argued that Michael "appears to have been framed and railroaded by a government deliberately persecuting him as a promising and charismatic political and social leader of his people." Michael, she said, was "an organizer. A liberator. A mover and an agitator for greater dignity and opportunity for all the many blacks and coloreds of Britain, a symbol—however detested or ambiguous—for the many colonials flooding into England in the sixties." The *New States-man* was the only newspaper or magazine to join the campaign, running a front-page editorial, "The Case for Michael X," that summer.

John and Yoko did get several prominent American organizations and individuals to join their campaign. Amnesty International asked Eric Williams to halt the execution. The PEN American Center petitioned Queen Elizabeth to prevent the execution. Its president at the time was Jerzy Kosinski, and its board included Hannah Arendt, I. B. Singer, Leon Edel, and Eliot Janeway.

The names of several more familiar radicals appeared on the defense committee. William Burroughs issued a statement: "I have known Michael X since 1964 and have always found him to be a gentle and moderate person and a writer of considerable distinction. . . . Nothing could be less conducive to improved race relations in Britian and elsewhere than the execution of Michael X on such shaky evidence and in the presence of such clearly motivated political prejudice on the part of the Trinidadian authorities." William Kunstler wrote that the prosecution had established no motive for the crimes. Dick Gregory praised Michael as "a fellow traveller in a common struggle." Gloria Steinem, Judy Collins, and Leonard Cohen joined the committee.

When the British campaign failed to bear fruit, the committee turned with desperation to the Eric Williams government, pleading for mercy. John and Yoko sent a telegram to Williams' daughter Erica in December 1973: "Michael Abdul Malik, free spirit and visionary, down on hard times, is scheduled to be hung any day now. It is too late to weigh the merits of his innocence or to deny his guilt. We know him as a friend and brother. We ask you to do whatever you can to save this man and any other men among you. Whether done by state or citizen, killing is not the solution. All life is sacred, there is no room for hatred. Give peace another chance."

In February 1974 John auctioned the piano on which he had composed many Beatles songs, with the proceeds to go to Michael's legal defense. John hoped Michael's lawyers would win a plea to the Trinidad Supreme Court arguing that the death penalty was cruel and unusual punishment. "If the plea succeeds it could spell the end of capital punishment throughout Britain's former colonies," the London *Sunday Times* explained. The solicitor-general secretly persuaded a judge to hear the motion during Christmas vacation, when, he knew, Michael's attorney would be unable to attend. The hearing was held on December 28, and the judge used the nonattendance of the defense counsel as grounds to dismiss the motion as "frivolous and vexatious."

"We got the word at six P.M. that Michael was to be executed the next morning," Jon Hendricks recalled. "We spent all night on the phone. Judy Collins was trying to reach Prime Minister Wilson, I was trying to reach Julius Nyerere, president of Tanzania, who had been friendly to Michael. As dawn approached, we knew we had failed."

The hanging was barbaric. "The dead man must remain suspended a full hour, during which the officials are served breakfast in the death cell," the *New Statesman* reported. "At the end of the hour the body is cut down and taken to the prison hospital and its final degradation: a slashing of the wrists and the tendons of the feet." The execution was carried out "In the name of Queen Elizabeth the Second, by the Grace of God Queen of Great Britain, Northern Ireland and the British Dominions beyond the seas, defender of the faith." Kate Millett said, "The execution of Michael X was a bitter, draining, terrible experience."

John's critics often accused him of trendiness, of an inability to maintain a commitment to any project or point of view for long. His support for Michael X provides the strongest counterexample. Long after Michael had lost the limelight, long after his claims to leadership had evaporated, John and Yoko stuck by him.

11

Altamont and Toronto

 On December 9, 1969, the Rolling Stones played a free concert at the Altamont Speedway, near San Francisco, which two summers earlier had been the city of "peace and love." Here a black man was killed by whites while the Stones played. Mick Jagger refused to accept any responsibility for the disaster, and didn't challenge the interpretation that Altamont marked the end of the sixties. Lennon, without directly attacking Jagger, insisted that superstars had political responsibilities, and that he himself would take the responsibility for demonstrating that Altamont did not mark the end.

The Maysles brothers' film *Gimme Shelter* told some of the story of what happened at Altamont and who was responsible. Twenty-four hours before the concert the site was moved, and the parking, sanitation, and stage were totally inadequate. Hell's Angels were enlisted to provide "security" for the Stones, to keep people off the stage. The Angels got more aggressive as the day went on, beating people. The Stones came on as night fell. During their third song, "Sympathy for the Devil," they stopped in the middle.

Twenty feet from where Jagger pranced and sang, Hell's Angels attacked an eighteen-year-old black man with a white girlfriend, who apparently were trying to join the two hundred people onstage. The man was Meredith Hunter. "An Angel grabbed Hunter's head, then punched him, then chased him back into the crowd," *Rolling Stone* reported after interviewing witnesses. He may have been stabbed the first time at this point.

Jagger told the audience, "Brothers and sisters, come on now! That means everybody, just cool out! Everybody be cool, now. Come on." He turned toward the side of the stage where Hunter had been. "How are we doing over there?" he asked. "Can we still collect ourselves? I don't know what happened. I couldn't see, I hope you're all right. Are you all right? Okay, let's just give ourselves another half a minute before we get our breath back. Everyone just cool down. Is there anyone there who's hurt? Okay, I think we're cool, we can groove. We always have something very funny happen when we start that number."

They started to play "Under My Thumb." The Angels had chased Hunter in front of one of the camera crews, twenty rows back from the stage. Hunter grimaced, perhaps because he had already been stabbed once. His eyes looked glazed; he pulled a gun; his girlfriend desperately tried to pull him away from the Angels; they surrounded him; they grabbed his gun; one stabbed him in the back; he fell as the Angels gathered tightly around him.

Jagger stopped the song again. "Why are we fighting? Why are we fighting? We don't want to fight at all. Who wants to fight, who is it? Every other scene has been cool. We gotta stop right now. You know, if we can't there's no point." The Angels did not stop beating Hunter. Keith Richards stepped up to the mike, and said, "Either those cats cool it, man, or we don't play." Jagger almost sobbed, "If he doesn't stop it, man . . ." Richards said, "Keep it cool! Hey, if you don't cool it, you ain't gonna hear no music!" An Angel grabbed the mike and shouted "Fuck you!" at Richards.

The Angels moved away from Hunter. He had been stabbed five times in the body, nine times in the head, and twice in the neck. He had nine head abrasions, presumably from kicks. People went to help him. They held up their own bloodied hands to show Jagger how bad it was. Jagger said into the mike, "We need a doctor here now! Look, can you let the doctor get through, please. We're trying to get to someone who's hurt." A doctor appeared, and Hunter was carried away. The Stones continued the concert, ending with "Satisfaction" and "Street Fighting Man."

Rolling Stone published a series of remarkable investigative articles about the events. The Stones had hired the Angels, paying them with five hundred dollars' worth of beer. The Stones' representative had the gall to defend the Angels, saying, "The Hell's Angels were as helpful as they could be in a situation which most people found very confusing." At Woodstock, "security" had been provided by a brilliantly discreet sheriff and a nonviolent commune, the Hog Farm. Its leader, "Wavy Gravy," had been at Altamont. Afterward he said there had been no need for the Angels in the first place, and that the Angels should have been asked to leave once they started fighting. The audience "could have taken up a collection and laid another five hundred dollars on them to split, which they would have done, man." Jagger himself could have taken the responsibility for asking them to leave.

The Stones had wanted a free concert, it turned out, to provide the background for a movie which they hoped to get out before the Woodstock film. They hired the Maysleses to shoot it. The Maysleses used seventeen film crews, each with security provided by Hell's Angels. The concert was free, but the Stones planned to make several million dolars from the film. Hunter's mother and sister said they had never received any message of condolence from the Stones or their representatives. Reporting this news, *Rolling Stone* ran a front-page headline, " 'The Stones Have Not Acted Honorably.' "

The district attorney charged one Hell's Angel, Alan Passaro, with murder. The jury found him innocent. The police investigation had turned up only one witness to the killing, even though hundreds of people had seen it. *Rolling Stone* rightly criticized this "lassitude" of the authorities. The judge let the defense exclude all prospective black jurors from serving. The defense then played on the racial theme to the all-white jury, emphasizing that Passaro had been confronted by a tall black man with a gun. Aside from the one witness, the only other evidence the D.A. presented was the film, showing Passaro knifing Hunter in the back twice. But Hunter had been stabbed in the back five times, only one of which killed him, severing his pulmonary artery. The defense emphasized the film didn't prove Passaro struck the death blow.

Rolling Stone concluded that "the state of California had accused only one of many who should be defendants. How could one Hell's Angel be held more accountable than Mick Jagger, for his incitement to Satanism?" But the Hell's Angels committed the murder. The magazine also suggested that the responsibility for Hunter's death was shared with the Stones' representative who hired the Angels, with the sheriff and the Highway Patrol for failing to "assure the public safety," and with the county health department, which might have been able to save Hunter's life if emergency facilities had been present. That made sense.

Keith Richards pleaded ignorance. The Stones had given a free concert once before, in London at Hyde Park. English Hell's Angels had guarded the stage, and the concert had been peaceful. "I didn't know what kind of people the Angels were here," he said. "The [Grateful] Dead told us, 'It's cool. We've used them for the last two or three years, [Ken] Kesey cooled them out.' . . . The Angels shouldn't have been asked to do the job. I didn't know that. . . . Someone else should have known." "It could only happen to the Stones, man," he concluded, claiming that Altamont made them victims, that they didn't share responsibility for the crime committed there.

Jerry Garcia of the Grateful Dead took some of the responsibility. "When the fighting was going on and the Rolling Stones were playing 'Sympathy for the Devil,' then I knew that I should have known," he said. But in his view the Stones, especially Jagger and his Satanic routine, shared the responsibility: "You know, you can't put that out without it turning up on you somewhere."

Only one person tried to stop the Angels: Marty Balin, singer in the Jefferson Airplane. During their set early in the afternoon, the Angels started beating a black man, and Balin jumped off the stage in the middle of a song to stop them. He was beaten unconscious. Grace Slick and the rest of the Airplane continued the set.

Ralph J. Gleason, who had been covering the San Francisco music scene for the *Chronicle* for twenty years, did some of the most serious and thoughtful writing about Altamont. "People are responsible—not only for themselves but for their brothers and their actions," he argued. "To put Hell's Angels on that stage and tell them they were in charge and give them free beer so they'd get swacked out of their minds is a criminally irresponsible action." But hadn't the Angels provided "security" at the first Human Be-In at Golden Gate Park? "At the Be-In they were in charge of the generator and the cable," Gleason explained. "Altamont was the first time the Angels have been on stage as a security force." And they had beaten someone badly at the Be-In. "I didn't write about that . . . I was wrong," he said. Gleason quoted doctors from the Medical Committee for Human Rights, who said the Stones had been "totally irresponsible" and "reprehensible" in failing to arrange for adequate medical facilities at Altamont. And he quoted Timothy Leary, who criticized Jagger for drinking from a bottle of Jack Daniel's onstage, setting an example for the Angels' own drinking and for those mixing alcohol and speed.

When *Gimme Shelter* opened, the debate over Jagger's responsibilities intensified. "It was pitiful to see the reactions of Mick to the violence," Gleason wrote. "His human inadequacy was revealed." Albert Goldman wrote in the New York *Times* that the film was "a whitewash of Jagger," concealing his responsibility in three ways. By spending the first half of the film on the Stones' concert at Madison Square Garden, the Maysles suggested that Jagger had been right when he cried, "All the other scenes were cool!" What the film failed to show was the careful security precautions (and high ticket prices) that prevented violence at the other big concerts.

Second, the film failed to explain the Stones' responsibility for the presence of the Angels. It suggested this was the way concerts were usually policed in the Bay Area, which was false. Finally, the film emphasized Meredith Hunter's gun, suggesting that he might have been aiming it at Jagger, and that the Angels may have saved Jagger's life. The film did not explain that Hunter was trying to escape from the Angels' blows when he drew his gun;

it concealed the fact that the Angels continued to stab and beat Hunter to death after they had his gun; it failed to report that Hunter had no criminal record and no history of violence, and that Passaro had a long record.

Peter Schjeldahl, a counterculture poet and critic, challenged Goldman in the New York *Times.* He found the film "thrilling, disturbing, shocking and moving," and ultimately "a humanizing experience." He accepted the film's depiction of the facts: "One witnesses the gun, the knife, the struggle. It is horrible but, one suddenly senses, it is past. Somehow it is bearable. . . . The film ends with life bestirring itself, emerging from the shock and going on." Thus the film "presents a full-bodied image of life in our times, an image unforgettable in its richness and passion." It's disturbing that the counterculture's representative in this debate would shrug off this murder of a black man so easily.

═══

While the Stones had been planning a free concert that would provide the backdrop for a big money-making film, John and Yoko had also been planning their own free concert—but with a different purpose. In September they had agreed to take part in a festival that would bring together music and antiwar politics. Altamont did not deter them. On the contrary, it increased their eagerness to demonstrate the positive side of the counterculture. One week after Altamont, John and Yoko flew to Canada to announce that the Toronto Peace Festival would be held over the July 4 weekend. "We aim to make it the biggest music festival in history," John said.

Reporters asked, what about Altamont? How would John and Yoko's festival avoid the problems the Stones had? Altamont had resulted from "the image and the mood the Stones create," John argued. "I think if you create a peaceful scene, you stand a better chance."

After the Toronto festival, "we would like to take the whole package on tour, especially to Russia and Czechoslovakia," John said at the press conference. The FBI noted that, and the quote from the *Village Voice* appeared in John's file when it was released twelve years later.

John also announced an "International Peace Vote." "We're asking everyone to vote for either peace or war and to send in a coupon with their name and address." As soon as 20 million people responded, the results would be announced. It seemed like a boring idea, uncharacteristic of the avant-garde peaceniks. What was the point of the peace vote? "We are the power, the people are the power," John explained. "As soon as the people are aware they have the power, then they can do what they want."

Reporters objected, won't people say you are being naïve? John gave a decent response: "That's their opinion and that's okay. Let them do something else and if we like their ideas, we'll join in with them." He concluded, "Until then, we'll do it the way we are. We're artists, not politicians. . . . We do it in the way that suits us best. . . . Publicity is my trade, and I'm using it to the best of my ability." Artists whose trade was publicity: that seemed confused. Of course nobody wants to be a "politician," but John, in seeking to mobilize people against Nixon, was certainly doing politics.

The week after the press conference, John and Yoko met with Canadian Prime Minister Pierre Trudeau. "John enthusiastically outlined the plans for the peace festival, explaining why he felt Canada was the best place for such an event," Anthony Fawcett recalled. "Trudeau seemed genuinely interested in the idea." He even offered official government endorsement and assistance. John left in an elated mood, telling reporters outside, "If there were more leaders like Mr. Trudeau, the world would have peace." Back in London, John told Fawcett, "It was the best trip we've ever had. We got more done for peace this week than in our whole lives."

Jann Wenner took John's enthusiasm about the Trudeau meeting to its logical, if ridiculous, conclusion: "A five-hour private meeting between John Lennon and Richard Nixon would be a more significant summit than any Geneva Summit Conference between the USA and Russia," he wrote. John's idea for the peace festival was a better one: mobilize the masses against Nixon with music.

The peace festival preparations went into high gear. The organizers set up a "Peace Network" consisting of almost four hundred radio stations in the United States and Canada. *Billboard* magazine donated a page to announce it. The network promised subscriber stations a steady flow of "John and Yoko Peace Messages" and "Peace Network Reports." Stations were to ask their listeners to send in news of peace activities in their local communities: demonstrations, draft resistance, benefit concerts, film showings, poster contests. The reports would then be sent out over the network. And of course the biggest news would be the plans for the Toronto Peace Festival. Among the four hundred that subscribed were New York City's two biggest rock stations. The FBI, noting that the Peace Network was announced in Canada, classified it under "New Left—Foreign Influence."

Rolling Stone, to Wenner's credit, publicized the festival plans. One correspondent wrote that, even in Mexico that winter, "everywhere we went we met somebody who was planning to make the Toronto scene. We met people from Oregon, California, Kentucky, Nevada, Colorado, New York and Washington. They all had Toronto down for July. Their conversations were filled with 'festival facts': the Beatles would be there and it'd be their last appearance together. Peter Fonda was doing the film. It was going to be free. The Stones were coming. Dylan would be there."

At the end of 1969 John and Yoko issued a statement which expressed their sense of the radical transformation taking place. They declared that 1970 would be "Year One. Because we believe the last decade was the end of the old machine crumblin' to pieces. And we think we can get it together, with your help. . . . We have great hopes for new year. . . . We know we'll all be there, at least in July, for the Peace Festival. And we want to set the atmosphere way ahead of July so that we don't have anything like the Rolling Stones concert. We don't want any of that jazz."

But the principal organizers of the Toronto festival lost their grip on reality. At a press conference they announced they had invented an "air car" which flew on psychic energy, and promised John and Yoko would fly one into the festival site. John broke with them ostensibly over the issue of ticket pricing, insisting that the festival be free of charge.

John wrote an article himself for *Rolling Stone* in April, explaining the situation. "Do we still need a Festival?" he asked. "Yoko and I still think we need it, not just to show that we can gather peacefully and groove to rock bands, but to change the balance of energy power. . . . Have we all forgotten what vibes are?"

John's political naïvete and earnestness may have been cloying, but after Jagger's performance at Altamont, John suddenly looked a lot better. He didn't want Altamont to mark the end. He wanted the sixties to go on, spurred by his own antiwar music festival. "We've got to keep hope alive," he said, "because without it we'll sink."

But despite his immense resources, he couldn't get it organized. During the key weeks when the festival went off the tracks, John and Yoko were immersed in the problems of their personal lives. They spent the time at a remote Danish farmhouse where Tony Cox, Yoko's ex-husband, let them see Kyoko. Even if he hadn't had these preoccupations, John had never had anything to do with the business side of the Beatles, with organizing performances or tours. That was a job people did for them. Now he had Allen Klein keeping track of the Toronto festival organizers, but Klein wasn't a concert promoter either. He was basically an accountant whose specialty was auditing record company sales statements and getting big advances on records. The problem was with the people John let organize the festival. And when he broke with them, he failed to get anybody to start over. The collapse of the Toronto Peace Festival plans made Altamont all the more important: it marks one of John's most significant political failures.

Part IV

PERSONAL/POLITICAL ARTIST

12

Primal Therapy and the Breakup

The film *Let It Be* appeared in the spring of 1970, a month after the official breakup. It showed everyone how the Fab Four had reached the end of the line. George resented Paul, Ringo was ineffectual, John seemed deeply depressed. But when they went up on the roof and played "Get Back," suddenly their old spark glowed again one last time. In their first "concert appearance" outside the recording studio since San Francisco almost four years earlier, they couldn't have been more distant and removed from their fans. And, like the Rolling Stones at Altamont, they appeared only because the sequence was supposed to be the center of a film.

The sessions had been Paul's idea, based on what could be called the myth of rock and roll renewal. The conflicts and paralysis of the present, he argued, could be overcome by returning to their musical roots, playing rock and roll together without embellishment, without additional musicians, without over-dubbing. Bob Dylan had pointed the way with *John Wesley Harding*. "Get Back" was the theme of this project. It failed.

Getting back to Liverpool, John sang "One after 909," a rocker he wrote as a schoolboy, and he and Paul did "Maggie May," a traditional Liverpool sing-along. John had one good new song, "Across the Universe," describing meditation in a string of poetic images. In another of his songs, "Dig It," he ad-libbed lyrics that showed that the FBI and CIA were on his mind.

The responsibility for turning the tape into an album was eventually given to Phil Spector, who abandoned the original conception of the quest for simplicity and authenticity. He took the hundreds of hours of tapes the Beatles had recorded and did just what they had tried to avoid: added layers of overdubbing and massive backup sound. "Across the Universe" was the only song to benefit from this effort. It had never been rock and roll anyway. The rest of the album was correctly judged a disappointment by most critics, and by Paul, who disassociated himself from it. John didn't seem to care.

The Chicago Seven were convicted early in 1970 of conspiring to cross state lines to incite a riot at the Democratic national convention in 1968. The trial had made them media celebrities. Abbie Hoffman and Jerry Rubin would enlist John in their political projects when he arrived in New York a year and a half later, and Bobby Seale, who had been bound and gagged in the courtroom on the judge's orders, would also do some political work with John. The defendants appealed the verdicts, arguing that the judge's conduct had been an outrage. The appeals court agreed, and eventually all charges and contempt citations were dropped.

The same month New York *Times* reporter Seymour Hersh exposed the My Lai massacre. Two years earlier, American troops had entered a small Vietnamese hamlet, lined up hundreds of unarmed women, children, and old men in a ditch, and killed them all. The murders had been covered up by higher officials. Dozens of soldiers and veterans came forward to testify that My Lai had not been an isolated incident, that they had participated in similar massacres of helpless civilians. Officials refused to hear the testimony. Only one man was found guilty of a crime at My Lai, and Nixon pardoned him. More and more people were coming to see the American war as an atrocity and Nixon, Henry Kissinger, and other high policy-makers as war criminals. My Lai made the task of ending the war more urgent.

On April 30, 1970, Nixon went on TV and announced a new escalation of the war: the United States was invading Cambodia to "clean out" communists. That country's neutralist government had been overthrown a month earlier by a right-wing military coup. Campuses across the nation went on strike.

At Yale University a May Day rally was held in support of New Haven Black Panthers. Jerry Rubin and Abbie Hoffman led thousands of students singing "All we are saying is smash the state," a savage satire of John and Yoko's simple pacifism. Elephant's Memory Band provided the music; John would pick them as his backup band a year and a half later.

Four days later, at Kent State University in Ohio, deep in Middle America, the campus ROTC building was burned. Governor James Rhodes declared that radical students were "the worst type of people we harbor in America" and sent 750 National Guardsmen to the campus, telling them to "eradicate the problem." California governor Ronald Reagan had already pointed the way, calling for a "bloodbath" if necessary to deal with student radicals. On May 4, in the early afternoon, students held what the President's Commission on Campus Unrest later called "a peaceful assembly on the university commons," the "traditional site of student assemblies." Nevertheless, the Guardsmen ordered them to disperse, and then opened fire with M-1 rifles, firing at least sixty-one shots into the crowd of students. They killed four and wounded nine.

The first sustained national student strike in U.S. history followed. It shut down a total of 450 colleges and universities. ROTC buildings were burned at the University of Iowa, Colorado College, the University of Nevada, the University of Alabama, and Ohio University. More than half of the demonstrations took place at schools where there had been no previous antiwar protests. The movement was spreading especially into state universities in the Midwest, the South, and the Southwest. The authorities often responded with violence: twelve students at the State University of New York at Buffalo were wounded by shotgun blasts, nine students at the University of New Mexico were bayonetted.

Nixon called antiwar students "these bums, you know, blowing up campuses." The father of one of the women killed at Kent State replied, "My child was not a bum." Vice President Spiro Agnew called the Kent State killings "predictable," given the "traitors and thieves and perverts . . . in our midst." A hundred thousand demonstrators headed for Washington the night after the killings. Nixon couldn't sleep. In the middle of the night he wandered over to the protest assembly gathering at the Washington Monument and tried to talk football with antiwar students. Nixon's telephone log shows he made fifty-one phone calls in the middle of that night, eight of them to Kissinger, who later wrote that the President was "on the edge of a nervous breakdown."

Two weeks after the campus protests began, white policemen and highway patrolmen went on campus at the all-black Jackson State University in Mississippi, responding to reports of "student disorder." They fired 150 rounds of ammunition into a girls' dormitory, killing two and wounding twelve black young people. The President's Commission later concluded their action was "completely unwarranted and unjustified." America's campuses were swept by a new wave of rage and dismay.

The FBI had a lot to do that spring, but it took time out to worry about John and Yoko. The two of them went to Los Angeles in April, and J. Edgar Hoover cabled the Los Angeles FBI office: "While Lennon has shown no propensity to become involved in violent anti-war demonstrations, remain alert for any information of such activity on his part." The suggestion was absurd. John's political activities during the last year had included meeting with Prime Minister Trudeau and sponsoring "War Is Over" billboards. He went to Los Angeles preoccupied not with the political but rather with the personal. John and Yoko had gone into therapy with Arthur Janov.

═══

John learned about Arthur Janov and primal therapy in March 1970, when the book *The Primal Scream* arrived in the mail at Tittenhurst. Janov hadn't sent it; "somebody at the publishing house was into Lennon and sent it for a literary review," Janov explained.

The book explained that "the suppression of feeling" is the basic cause of emotional suffering, tension, and fear, and that it had deep roots in childhood experience. "The single most shattering event in the child's life," Janov wrote, "is that moment of icy, cosmic loneliness . . . when he begins to discover that he is not loved for what he is and will not be." This discovery is too overwhelming for the child; "he cannot live knowing that [his parents] are not really interested in him . . . that there is no way to make his father less critical or his mother kind." This "terrible hopelessness of never being loved" has to be denied and buried. Thus neurosis is born.

"That's me, that's me!" John declared after reading Janov's book. His father, Freddie, abandoned him and his mother, Julia, shortly after he was born. When John was five, Julia decided not to raise him and "gave" him to her sister Mimi and brother-in-law George. Mimi explained in 1968 why Julia did it: She "met another man whom she wanted to marry. It would have been difficult to take John along as well, so I took John." Thus he had ample reason to feel that neither of his parents wanted or loved him.

Janov's book offered a dramatic cure for these repressed feelings: reexperiencing the original childhood Pain, which Janov spelled with a capital P. This required crying and screaming the way children do—the "primal scream." In 1980 John recalled, "I would never have gone into it if there hadn't been the promise of this scream, this liberating scream." The goal of primal therapy was indeed a liberation, not "improved functioning in socially acceptable ways," Janov wrote, not even "a more thorough understanding of one's motivations." The liberation Janov promised consisted of recovering the full experience of feelings. "Feeling is the antithesis of Pain," Janov wrote. "The more Pain one feels, the less pain one suffers."

The book also explained Janov's understanding of LSD and heroin. LSD "stimulates intense real feelings," but also a "wild flight of ideas . . . that is often a race away from feeling." These feelings and ideas remained fragmented and disconnected; they could not be held on to or organized into a meaningful pattern. Janov described heroin as one of the most effective means of deadening feelings, necessary when the individual has run out of internal defenses against emotional pain. Primal therapy made both unnecessary.

For John, then, *The Primal Scream* vividly described his own childhood experience of parental abandonment, and did so with a profound empathy for the child's feelings. It described his recent involvement with LSD and heroin, and explained why they had not brought him lasting relief. And it promised not a better adjustment to society but something much more valuable to him: greater access to the feelings that were the heart of his work as an artist.

John and Yoko asked Arthur and Vivian Janov to come to Tittenhurst to begin primal therapy. The Janovs spent March 1970 there. "When we arrived, John was simply not functioning," Arthur Janov recalled in an interview. "He really needed help." Dick Gregory had been another recent visitor at Tittenhurst. "Lennon had a lot of problems after he came out of the drug thing," he said later in an interview. "He asked me to come and help. I came in to rebuild the body. My main concern was cleansing out the body and not doing it too fast. I was able to put him on the type of vitamin regimen that would replenish what the drugs had wiped out, and also fast him on a small scale. I explained to John: you have to take out the physical source of the pain. Then you can work on the mental source."

John and Yoko went to Los Angeles for five months beginning in April to continue working with the Janovs at their Primal Institute. A year later John explained the experience to the London underground paper *Red Mole:* "It's excruciating, you are forced to realize that your pain, the kind that makes you wake up afraid with your heart pounding, is really yours. . . . All of us growing up have to come to terms with too much pain. Although we repress it, it's still there. The worst pain is that of not being wanted, of realizing your parents do not need you in the way you need them. When I was a child . . . this lack of love went into my eyes and into my mind. Janov doesn't just talk to you about this but makes you feel it. . . . For me at any rate it was . . . facing up to reality."

"John was really taken with primal therapy," Arthur Janov recalled. "He wanted to rent the *QE2* and have us sail around the world doing primal therapy; he wanted to buy an island and found a primal nation. He was pretty serious. I put the kibosh on it."

John's own comments on his work with Janov are revealing. In earlier years, when he discovered psychedelic drugs and then Eastern mysticism, he had fervently declared their powers to solve the world's problems. But when asked about Janov in the media, he refused to say "this is it." His claims were modest. At the end of 1970 he said primal therapy might not work for other people, but nothing else would work as well for him. He explained as concisely as he could: before primal therapy, he wasn't feeling things. The therapy allowed him to experience his feelings continually, which often made him cry. What he found out about himself left him astounded. That was all he wanted to say.

Janov argued that Lennon's primal therapy was incomplete, interrupted by the Immigration Service. "The government really got him out of this therapy. The therapy takes at least thirteen–fourteen–fifteen months. What happens is that first you break down your defenses. John had tremendous access to his feelings; but he needed a lot of help. I worked with him from March through July—five months. That was when he was forced to leave. It really botched the whole process." The INS files released under the Freedom of Information Act tend to confirm Janov's account: the INS required that John and Yoko leave the United States on August 1, 1970, despite their numerous appeals for more time in Los Angeles.

Just after John left primal therapy, he released his first real post-Beatles album, *John Lennon/Plastic Ono Band.* He wrote most of the songs in Los Angeles, while he was seeing Janov, and recorded them when he got back to Tittenhurst. The evidence the album presents is absolutely clear: even if John did not properly complete primal therapy, his work with Janov enabled him to unlock his greatest creative powers, to transform himself from a depressed and suffering superstar into a serious and committed artist. After his work with Janov, John was able to take on the project of uniting the personal and the political in his art and in his life. Primal therapy helped John free himself from the expectations of superstardom, to gain real autonomy for himself, to work creatively as an artist with his feelings of misery, rage, and love. John's work with Janov enabled him to achieve many of the personal goals of sixties radicalism.

———

While John moved to the left in 1970, Bob Dylan went in the other direction. Princeton University granted him an honorary degree in June for "having conferred the greatest benefits either upon the country or upon mankind as a whole." The counterculture regarded this as another despicable sell-out. One underground newspaper declared that Princeton was the "home of Amerika's wealthy, alcoholic post-adolescents." The trustees had "taken time off from their war contracts" to honor Dylan, who "has slipped back into the slime."

If the indictment of his honorary degree seemed excessive, the indictment of his new album, *Self-Portrait,* was not. Released in June 1970, it confirmed everything his radical critics had been saying. *Rolling Stone* printed an essay by Greil Marcus that began, "What is this shit?" Jon Landau wrote, "It speaks to us in the blighted language of a dying culture, a culture Dylan now seeks to take refuge in." Ralph J. Gleason called for a boycott of Dylan.

Dylan defended himself seven months later, telling an interviewer, "I told them not to follow leaders. . . . Because I wanted out, they all started to rap me . . . It's all bullshit. . . . They only want somebody to lead them out of their troubles. . . . I got enough to keep me busy without looking for other people's problems." It was fine for Dylan to refuse to tell people what to do with their lives. The question people asked was, what was he doing with his? He had renounced his old commitments to music engaged with social justice; now it seemed that he had no values or goals to replace it.

Just when the critics were finished with Dylan, he won them all back. *New Morning*, released late in 1970, was "a love song to life," Anthony Scaduto wrote. Robert Christgau gave it an A, and Ralph Gleason called off his boycott, declaring, "We've got Dylan back again." In "Day of the Locusts" Dylan sings about his Princeton honorary degree. The university is society's tomb, a dark chamber. Professors are judges, students are machines. Dylan escapes, driving with his sweetheart to North Dakota. The song was a fake, but it said what the underground press wanted him to say about the university. John's assessment was more accurate: when asked in *Lennon Remembers* about *New Morning*, he said it "wasn't much." He added that he had not been a Dylan fan since Bob "stopped rocking."

But Dylan did not seem to be satisfied with his new identity as the man of love. He wanted more. He spent some time with Rabbi Meir Kahane and the Jewish Defense League in the fall of 1970, hoping they could provide the values to replace those he had renounced. He lost his enthusiasm for the JDL after they made a number of attacks on Soviet diplomatic personnel.

The difference between black and white antiwar feeling was illustrated that fall, when Jimmy Cliff released a single, "Vietnam"; it was nothing like "Give Peace a Chance." Cliff's song told a strong and simple story of parents and friends learning that a soldier has died in Vietnam. Few people listened to it. Jimi Hendrix died in 1970. His "Star-Spangled Banner," heard on the Woodstock album and movie, released the same year, turned the national anthem into a bombing attack—a powerful image at the height of the Vietnam war.

Vice President Agnew attacked the Beatles in a campaign speech in Reno in September 1970. American youth were being "brainwashed" by rock music into a "drug culture," he charged. "We may be accused of advocating song censorship for pointing this out, but have you really heard the words of some of these songs? The Beatles have a song which includes the words, 'I get by with a little help from my friends, I get high with a little help from my friends.' . . . Until it was pointed out to me, I never realized that the 'friends' were assorted drugs." He urged Nevadans to reject "creeping permissiveness" and vote for "square" Republicans. Better late than never: the Beatles song he quoted had been out for more than three years.

John obviously had not been thinking of himself as a Beatle for some time, but it was Paul who began legal proceedings to dissolve the Beatles' partnership in November 1970. "It's only a rock group that split up," John said in an interview at the time. "It's nothing important. You have all the old records. . . . But even young people refused to accept change. The underground is the same as the overground. I told people long ago, 'I'm not going to be singing "She Loves You" when I'm thirty.' I was thirty last year, and it was then when I broke the band up." John pointed to the Stones to illustrate the problem. "When I listen to the Stones' music, nothing's ever happened. The same old stuff goes on and on and on. So I think it would be good if they broke up and made some individual music. Nothing personal, Mick, you know I love you. And Keith. But I think it would do them good to split up."

The individual Beatles were making "far better music" as solo artists than as a group, John went on. "Because we're not suppressed. When the Beatles were at their peak, we were limiting each other's capacity to write and perform—by having to fit it into some kind of format. That's what caused the trouble."

A decade later, it's impossible to sustain John's judgment. The sum of the solo work of the four ex-Beatles never equaled their collective work. John had to get out for his own reasons, and in this statement he was being generous to the others. At the time the charts provided some justification: *McCartney* and "My Sweet Lord" were doing well. They weren't "far better" than Beatles music at all, but they did give Paul and George a chance to work and to succeed without the limits set by the Beatles as a collective. And John had "Give Peace a Chance" and "Instant Karma!"—a good start, but by no means "far better" than his own Beatle work.

John refused to see how the limits that the Beatles set for each other had really worked in their music. They checked and cancelled out each other's weaknesses. The Beatles at their peak were a community whose members fulfilled themselves best by working with one another. Their work as collective artistic producers made them legitimate heroes of the communal counterculture of the sixties.

When the Beatles' collective broke up, the other three became solo artists. John didn't. He left to join a new artistic collaboration, a new creative partnership—the Two Virgins, the avant-garde peaceniks. This partnership was in fact much more provocative and challenging because it included a woman who was also nonwhite. Of course Yoko was more than an artistic collaborator for John, but she was also precisely that. In giving up the Beatles, John was not turning his back on collaborative artistic production. He was making a deeper and more intense commitment to the sixties dream of overcoming the isolation of individualism.

13

Working-Class Hero

 "It's no game," John said about working on the *Plastic Ono Band* album. "It's bloody tough. At first I'm dying to do it and get in there and do one track, and then I think, 'Oh Christ I wish I'd never started. It's so hard.'" Dan Richter worked as John and Yoko's personal assistant while they did *Plastic Ono Band*. "John was always writing music," he said. "He would sit down at any piano and work on things, even in hallways. He'd play things over and over for months. A couple of months later he would change them. A couple of months later he'd record them. And it would turn out to be a magnificent song. But recording *Plastic Ono Band* was very painful."

The album posed a challenge to rock as an idiom. It was a difficult work. Listening to it was not fun. It offered only an artist's revelations of his life. Thus the response to John's album was as much a measure of the rock audience as it was of the music itself.

The critics recognized John's achievement on *Plastic Ono Band*. Stephen Holden wrote in *Rolling Stone* that the album was "a new kind of populist art song—eloquent in its careful simplicity and radically honest . . . a painful and profound self-exorcism and self-renewal."

Jon Landau wrote about "the crushing, exhilarating emotive quality" of the album. "For every expression of despair over his past, he had one of optimism for the future." The listener was "inevitably pulled in," in a way that made the album the "prototype for confessional work" against which others would henceforth be measured.

Robin Blackburn had special praise for "Working Class Hero" in the *Red Mole*. "Lennon refuses to make any equation between his music and politics or to imply that rock equals revolution. . . . Indeed, 'Working Class Hero' explicitly asserts the opposite: that the proletarian superstar is a convenient safety valve for bourgeois society, not an index of social liberation."

Robert Christgau wrote the most insightful review of the album. "Even when he is fervidly shedding personas and eschewing metaphor, John knows, perhaps instinctively, that he communicates most effectively through techno-logical masks and prisms. Separating himself from the homemade pretensions of, say, McCartney . . . he wants to reach us with a message that is also a medium and really equals himself." Thus "John's greatest vocal performance, . . . from scream to whine, is modulated electronically. John's voice is echoed, filtered, and double tracked. . . . The guitar and even the drumming is distorted." Critics had complained that many of John's lyrics were crude clichés. "Of course they are," Christgau retorted. "That's just the point, because they are also true, and John wants to make clear that right now truth is far more important than subtlety, taste, art, or anything else."

John knew that some of the most enthusiastic reviews were written by critics who didn't understand what he was doing on the album. An inter-viewer quoted one: " 'Like all seminal rock, it's timeless in its concept,' " and asked, "Is that the sort of quote you appreciate?" "Well," John replied, "it's better than 'shit-head.' "

The response of the rock audience was not as strong as that of the critics. *Plastic Ono Band* became a certified million-seller six weeks after it was released. But it never reached Number One in the charts, peaked at Number Six, and spent a modest four weeks in the Top Ten. Everyone noticed that, in comparison, *McCartney* had been Number One for three weeks. George's *All Things Must Pass* was even more successful, spending seven weeks at Number One.

John pointed to four earlier songs that anticipated the truth-telling of the *Plastic Ono Band* album: "I'm a Loser," "Help!," "In My Life," and "Straw-berry Fields Forever." He called them his best and most truthful Beatles songs. John recorded "I'm a Loser" in October 1964 and released it on the *Beatles '65* album. The song had the simple boy-girl theme of other early Lennon-McCartney compositions, and a series of embarrassing rhymes: clown/frown, sky/cry, fate/too late. In live concerts he sang it with an inappropriate pop-star grin. But the chorus of "I'm a Loser" hinted at John's real feelings, his bad feelings, for the first time.

He wrote "Help!" in April 1965, during the shooting of the movie. The lad from Liverpool, brilliant and wealthy and powerful, had said a few months earlier, "We love every minute of it, Beatle people!" But here he sang about feeling "down" and "insecure" and appreciating help. It wasn't teen schmaltz, like Rick Nelson's "Teenage Idol"; it was real. No white rock singer had ever sung a song like it before. Bob Dylan's songs were profoundly personal, but they expressed defiance, mockery, bitterness. He never asked for anybody's help.

The lyrics to "Help!" had the emotional authenticity of soul music, the kind of feeling Otis Redding and Aretha Franklin expressed. But musically the song was pure Beatles, with its striking changes between major and minor chords, its exhilarating falsetto cries, and its driving mid-tempo beat. "The real feeling of the song was lost because it was a single and it had to be fast," John said in a 1971 interview. "I've thought of doing it again sometime and slowing it down." He never did, but Tina Turner did, singing it as a tribute to him after his death. She sang it as an intense soul song, sobbing out the line "Please, please, help—me."

When he wrote it, he said later, he was in his "fat Elvis period." The Beatles were on location for the film in the Caribbean, visiting the governor of the Bahamas, being put down by "junked-up middle-class bitches and bastards" who made disparaging remarks about their working-class manners. He couldn't stand it, he said in *Lennon Remembers;* it was mortifying, it made him feel terrible. He came home and wrote "Help!"

In retrospect, what made "Help!" such an achievement for John was that he did it without the example and encouragement of Yoko. In subsequent interviews, he expressed a justifiable pride in "Help!," in knowing he had been that sensible, that aware of himself.

"In My Life," released on *Rubber Soul* in 1965, John described as his first major piece of work, "the first song I wrote that was really, consciously about my life." It was also a favorite of writers on the left, from the London underground *Black Dwarf* in 1969 to Bruce Dancis in *In These Times* in 1980. In the song, John left behind his identities as a teenage rebel and a Liverpool lad. He sang as a grownup, tenderly and honestly, about his past, about places and lovers and friends. A gorgeous baroque piano played the melody on one verse.

When rock stars released new albums, they did publicity interviews, but there had never been anything like John's interview *Lennon Remembers,* published in *Rolling Stone* in two parts beginning on January 7, 1971. For starters he talked about the Fab Four: "Fuckin' big bastards," he called them. You had to be a bastard to make it, he said, and the Beatles were "the biggest bastards on earth." That was a shocker.

Then he discussed his experience with heroin. He'd already sung "Cold Turkey," but somehow its meaning had eluded his detractors. Taking heroin, he said, was "just not too much fun." He denied that he ever injected it, and explained that he and Yoko turned to it only when they were "in real pain" because of the "shit thrown at us." They got into heroin, he concluded, because of what the Beatles and others were doing to them. But they also got out of it, he insisted. Blaming the Beatles was refusing to take responsibility himself; he would later return to hard drugs, especially methadone; but his satisfaction in having gotten out of heroin addiction in 1970 was well earned.

Yoko took a more favorable attitude toward drugs. "There isn't a person in the world who doesn't take drugs," she told *Crawdaddy*. "After all, anything you need after you've fulfilled the requirements for minimum survival can be regarded as a drug. Cigarettes, candy, the second steak, the second glass of water. . . . These are all drugs." That was absurd, but she didn't stop there. "Excessive talking can also be a drug, as can laughing and telephone calling and letter writing and buying too many clothes. Life would be boring if you had only one thing to wear. . . . Drugs make life less boring." That was an exaggerated version of the sixties' defense of drugs—"you drink martinis, we smoke grass"—but it didn't distinguish between recreational drugs like marijuana and addictive drugs like heroin.

John raged against the Beatles' audience in *Lennon Remembers*. When the Beatles arrived in the United States in 1964, he said, Americans were wearing Bermuda shorts, crew cuts, and braces on their teeth; they were an "ugly race." Being a Beatle was "torture" because of the fans, who were "just sucking us to death," making him feel like a circus animal. He resented performing for "fucking idiots" who lived vicariously through him.

Critics especially drove him into a frenzy. When they criticized him, he said, he wanted to scream, "Look at me, a genius, for fuck's sake!" What would it take to prove it to them? "Don't dare, don't you dare fuckin' dare criticize my work like that. You, who don't know anything about it. Fuckin' bullshit!" John was violating the most fundamental taboos of the music business.

Editor Jann Wenner asked about the contrast everyone had been drawing between the politically engaged Stones and the Beatles. John said he resented the implication that the Stones were the revolutionaries and the Beatles weren't. If the Stones were, he said, so were the Beatles—not much of an argument. But what about his criticism of people carrying pictures of Chairman Mao in "Revolution"? He had really believed that love was all you needed, he replied. "But now I'm wearing a Chairman Mao badge, that's where it's at." That sounded only slightly less vacuous.

Wenner said that a violent revolution would be the end of the world. "Not necessarily," John shot back. Lots of people said that, but he didn't agree. He recalled that when he was seventeen, he wished for a revolution so that he could "do what the blacks are doing now" (rioting in the streets). John was identifying with the oppressed, viewing revolution as a violent settling of scores. That was an accurate view of one part of past revolutions, but a limited view. He didn't argue that revolutionary politics could be a creative process, seeking to meet social needs that were now neglected or ignored.

John spoke with enthusiasm about revolutions in art as well as in politics. He said that in retrospect he despised his art school teachers because they never taught him about Marcel Duchamp. He had to learn from Yoko, who taught him that "fuckin' Duchamp was spot on." John explained that Duchamp put everyday objects, like a bike wheel, on display and said, "This is art, you cunts."

Duchamp didn't put it quite that way, but it's not hard to understand why John would be drawn to his work. Beginning in 1910 Duchamp had worked to break down the barriers between art and daily life. He mocked the pretensions of artists who claimed to be creating beautiful objects. He introduced elements of play and humor at the same time that he expressed contempt for the art world. He worked, art historian Calvin Tomkins wrote, with "a cool and seemingly effortless confidence," neglected through the thirties and forties until his work was recognized in the fifties. John regarded avant-garde art with genuine respect and admiration.

===

"Working Class Hero" was the first song John sang about his social origins, but from the beginning of Beatlemania he had always said he came from the working class. And from the beginning, writers on the left, old and new, had considered the significance of that claim. The British *Daily Worker* was the first. In September 1963, at the beginning of Beatlemania, it sent a reporter to Liverpool to see the Beatles. "Working class?" he wrote. "Yes, like all of today's pop singers." The Beatles' Liverpool was "a sprawling area of murky slums and muddy seas, . . . 80,000 crumbling houses and 30,000 on the dole." The Beatles "may be the pride of Merseyside, but it's too easy for talent scouts to exploit job-hunting youngsters, being fed dreams of instant fame and money." The Cavern was packed at mid-day: "Who wants to leave when the thud-thud-thud batters job hunting from your mind? . . . Who wants to swap a cosy thought-free cellar for a worried outside, where me dad may be out of work and the telly is the only comfort in an unsanitary house?"

John's Aunt Mimi, who raised him from the time he was five, challenged all this. "I get terribly annoyed when he is billed as a street-corner boy," she told the *Daily Express.* "We had a very comfortable home in a good area."

What were his social origins and cultural roots? John's father, Freddie, came from the lower ranks of the Liverpool proletariat, working as a ship's waiter when he wasn't unemployed. After he abandoned John and his mother, they lived with her parents, who were also part of working-class Liverpool. Her father worked for a company that salvaged sunken ships. When Julia gave five-year-old John to her sister, Mimi Smith, he moved up the social scale a notch. Mimi's husband, George, owned a dairy. They lived in a semidetached house in a respectable suburb, even though it was only three miles from the grimy industrial center of the Liverpool docks. Uncle George died when John was twelve, which made Mimi's lower-middle-class respectability more precarious during John's teenage years.

Although John's uncle had been self-employed rather than a wage-earner, and they lived in a decent suburb instead of an industrial slum, the line separating small proprietors like George Smith from the respectable working class was a fine one. In any case, all of Liverpool had a deeply working-class aspect, especially from the perspective of middle-class London. "Before the Beatles, Liverpool was a place you never admitted coming from," Peter Brown said in an interview. "It's a very poor town." It's also a town known for its strong labor movement, and had been a militant center of the general strike of 1926.

John Lennon may not have been raised in a real proletarian family, but he was part of a distinctly working-class youth culture: the world of Teddy boys and rock and roll. It all hit John at Quarry Bank Grammar School, itself a place of some significance in working-class culture. It was called "the Eton of the Labour Party" because its alumni included two socialist cabinet ministers. John at Quarry Bank seemed to be becoming a different kind of working-class hero—a rebel. His rebellion was tied to the new music coming from America.

In 1956, when John was sixteen, he heard "Heartbreak Hotel." "That was the end," he said. "My whole life changed. I was completely shaken by it. Nothing really affected me until Elvis." Shortly afterward a friend played him Little Richard's "Long Tall Sally." "When I heard it, it was so great I couldn't speak."

Rock and roll had the same meaning for John Lennon that it had for millions of other young people. It was the sound of rebellion, an anti-authoritarian music which accompanied struggles against teachers and parents, struggles against the pressures to get good grades, to pick a career, to be respectable. John was not only a rock-and-roller, he also made himself a Teddy boy, with clothes and a haircut that outraged adults and decent society. The headmaster of Quarry Bank Grammar School considered John to be "the worst Teddy boy among the pupils in his charge," especially after John's Uncle George died unexpectedly. He was the tough guy, defiant at school, and obsessed with rock and roll, a teenage working-class rebel.

John held on to his working-class consciousness as the Beatles had their first great triumphs. On tour in 1963 he told an interviewer, "People say we're loaded with money, but by comparison with those who are supposed to talk the Queen's English, that's ridiculous. We're only earning. They've got capital behind them and they're earning on top of that. The more people you meet, the more you realize it's all a class thing."

When the Beatles were invited to play for the Queen at the Royal Variety Performance in October 1963, John's class consciousness burst out again. Before they went on, Brian Epstein asked John how he could get that kind of upper-class audience to join in. "I'll just ask them to rattle their fucking jewelry," John said. On stage he used the line without the "fucking" and it became the most widely quoted evidence of his wit.

When the Beatles left Liverpool and moved to London in 1964, the local working-class community took pride in their triumph. They were regarded the way Liverpool's successful variety-hall performers had been: "still warmly 'alright' because they remain of them in spirit and have conquered the 'moneyed classes' with their working class wit," cultural historian Richard Hoggart wrote. "They have stormed the posh citadels; 'good luck to 'em!' ''

In London "the first thing we did was to proclaim our Liverpool-ness to the world, to say 'It's all right to come from Liverpool and talk like this,' '' John said in a 1970 interview. Retaining their working-class accents was a significant act in England. Peter Brown explained: "In London, the Liverpool accent was a sign that you were poor and badly educated. It was important if you were going to be successful that you get rid of it."

Working-class Liverpool saw things the other way around. It was a serious offense if community members "gave themselves airs," "got above themselves," "were lah-de-lah," or "were stuck up." "The Liverpool fans would have become very angry indeed if the Beatles had suddenly started speaking posh," Peter Brown said. Thus when the Beatles retained their accents, they demonstrated to working-class Liverpool that, despite their sudden wealth and fame, they hadn't joined "them"; they were still part of "us."

The working-class Liverpool that John left behind had profoundly shaped his experience, as he said in a 1980 interview, making him an "instinctive socialist." The "instinctive socialism" of England's northern working-class cities was not always explicitly political. It rested on a strong sense that the world was divided between "them" and "us." "The world of 'them' was the world of the bosses," Richard Hoggart wrote. " 'They' were 'the people at the top,' 'the higher-ups,' the people who 'aren't really to be trusted,' 'talk posh,' and 'treat y' like muck.' " "Us" consisted not so much of the working class of the nation but rather the local working-class community, the neighborhood, with its traditions of mutual support. "Us" was a sense that arose from "a knowledge born of living close together, that one is inescapably part of a group, from the warmth and security that knowledge can give, from the lack of change in the group and from the frequent need to 'turn to a neighbor.' "

The hostility toward "them" included the military. Antimilitarist feeling was strong in English working-class culture, and went with a cynical attitude toward nationalism. "Them" included the politicians who sent you off to war and the officers who made the soldier's life miserable. These aspects of working-class culture contributed to John's pacifism. His song "I Don't Wanna Be a Soldier Mama," on the *Imagine* album, had the same title as a favorite working-class song from World War I. The film *How I Won the War* expressed the working-class sense that officers were ludicrous idiots who posed a deadly threat to their men. This antimilitarist attitude, endemic in the English working class, found a new audience among American youth during the Vietnam war.

The antagonism of "us" against "them" is expressed typically with humor that debunks the pretenses of wealth and power. "The real working-class hero," Hoggart wrote, was "the cheerful man, the wit." Liverpool's variety comedians were especially famous. Compared to the Protestant north of England, Liverpool's Irish Catholic subculture and its comedians were more expressive, and had a distinctive verbal flair. They could "talk the hind legs off a donkey." The distinctive feature of Liverpool comedians was their deadpan humor—the ironic remark made with an absolutely straight face. Liverpool working-class culture was the primary source of John's clever wordplay and his "irreverent wit" that American writers found so surprising and new.

John pointed to other ways his Liverpool origins shaped his development. Because Liverpool is a major port, sailors would come home with blues records from America. Peter Brown described his own Liverpool days: "When I worked in the record store, we had a big country music following and also a following for blues music—all the seamen who'd been to the United States. We had a very big record business in some kinds of black music that hardly sold anywhere else in the country. And that was what the Liverpool groups got into—country and black music."

Thus John turned to working-class youth culture to define himself as a rebel against middle-class aspirations and conventions. Working-class culture made him an "instinctive socialist," giving him a deep hostility to Britain's ruling class, a hatred of war, and a special kind of verbal humor. He drew on all these traditions in his music.

However, working-class culture also established significant obstacles John had to struggle to overcome. The most important of these, he later realized, was its deep sexism. During John's childhood and adolescence the patriarchal family served as the unquestioned bedrock of working-class society and personal identity. The father was "master of his own house" while the mother's world was sharply limited. "Her own menfolk may appear careless for her much of the time," Hoggart wrote, "but like to buy ornaments inscribed 'What is home without a mother.' " In this world young men were supposed to be tough. Although John's lower-middle-class aunt objected to his Teddy boy identity, it was easy for him to become the rebellious working-class hero. It was impossible for him to become a feminist without rejecting the most fundamental values of the culture from which he came.

14

The Red Mole

 John called Tariq Ali, one of the leading figures in the British New Left, in the fall of 1969 to say he'd like to get together. Ali had published the exchange of letters with John in the *Black Dwarf* and now edited a newspaper called the *Red Mole* (after the same Marx quote as Boston's *Old Mole:* the mole represents the underground revolution).

"Once a month, twice a month, he would ring up to talk to me," Tariq Ali said. "We'd just rap. Then we would have a meal together. He'd ask me questions. He was sincerely interested." There were several reasons for this. At the Amsterdam bed-in John had explained that the 1968 march on the American embassy convinced him to speak out against what he saw as the violence within the antiwar movement and launch his own personal peace campaign. Tariq had been a leader of that march. In a sense, John had been debating with him at a distance for more than a year.

Tariq Ali as leader of the Vietnam Solidarity Committee had been violently denounced in the establishment press, and had been denied permission to enter the United States because of his radical politics. John may well have identified with him on these counts. He too had been abused and ridiculed by the press for his peace campaign; he too was denied permission to enter the United States to engage in antiwar politics.

Tariq invited Robin Blackburn to join the discussions. Blackburn was a leader of the student movement at the London School of Economics and an editor of the *Red Mole*. Dan Richter, John and Yoko's personal assistant during this period, summed up the situation. "John was anti-establishment. There was this revolution going on. Tariq and Robin worked hard on it. They had ideas; they were intellectuals; they expressed their ideas clearly and succinctly." So John wanted to get to know them.

One of the first topics in their conversations was the Vietnam Solidarity Committee marches. Tariq recalled, "I said I wished he had come with us, and marched, and sung at the end. He said, 'But you know I didn't like the violence.' And I said, 'But you know we weren't the cause of that violence, John.' I explained to him that on the first big demonstration, in October 1967, we almost got into the American embassy—the police weren't prepared. On the second occasion, in March '68, there were lots of hippies and pacifists demonstrating. Mounted police charged like cossacks wielding batons, and the hippies threw flowers at them and said things like 'Peace, man.'

"I told John, 'Those hippies were trampled into the ground. So what's your choice? Either you're trampled or you try to defend yourself.' He then said, 'You're right.' I said, 'Obviously the press portrays us as the ones who initiate it.' He knew from his own experience how the press had distorted his peace efforts." (Tariq Ali did not tell John that Mick Jagger "marched just behind me in the March '68 demonstration; we exchanged greetings. Mick Jagger was far more radical than John that year.")

Robin Blackburn remembered that "John was absolutely undogmatic. This was refreshing. And all his judgments on areas he knew were very perceptive. I think he had in him a far more intransigent hostility to the established order than people realized. He saw English society dominated by a conservative and repressive ruling class, a very narrow-minded ruling class, which he'd already clashed with as an artist. And he saw English society as being fairly racist."

Finally John and Yoko invited Ali and Blackburn to Tittenhurst for an interview that would be published in the *Red Mole*. "I still remember this absolutely massive custom-made car drove up to the *Red Mole* offices," Ali said. "John had sent his chauffeur to pick Robin and me up." Halfway through the interview, they stopped for a break. "Robin went to the toilet, and John brought out a very beautiful box with about six different kinds of hash in it. He said, 'Which would you like?' I said, 'I don't really smoke.' He said, 'Why?' I said, 'I don't in any case, but secondly the International Marxist Group, of which I am a member, has a code which says that comrades shouldn't because they can be busted for it.' He was very appreciative of that."

The interview appeared in March 1971. "I've always been politically minded," John began, "and against the status quo. It's pretty basic when you're brought up, like I was, to hate and fear the police as a natural enemy and to despise the army as something that takes everybody away and leaves them dead somewhere. . . . I've been satirizing the system since my childhood. . . . I was very conscious of class, they would say with a chip on my shoulder."

John explained his sense of the tasks facing the New Left: "We should be trying to reach the young workers because that's when you're the most idealistic and have least fear. Somehow the revolutionaries must approach the workers because the workers won't approach them. But it's difficult to know where to start. . . . The problem for me is that as I have become more real, I've grown away from most working-class people—you know, what they like is Engelbert Humperdinck. It's the students who are buying us now, and that's the problem. . . . Working-class people also reacted against our openness about sex. . . . Also, when Yoko and I got married, we got terrible racialist letters. . . . It seems to me that students are now half-awake enough to try and wake up their brother workers. If you don't pass on your own awareness then it closes down again. . . . I'd like to incite people to break the framework, to be disobedient in school, to insult authority."

Lennon perceived the strategic problem facing the New Left, he saw the obstacles, and he tried to imagine ways of overcoming them. His political thinking did not go beyond the prevailing New Left ideas, but he had undergone a major transformation. One year earlier the *Black Dwarf* editors, Tariq Ali included, had suggested to John that he was making a mistake in separating himself from "the actual struggles" of the day. In the *Red Mole* interview he declared that he shared the New Left project.

"We can't have a revolution that doesn't involve and liberate women," he insisted—a perspective that put him in the vanguard of male radicals in 1971. "It's so subtle the way you're taught male superiority. It took me quite a long time to realize. . . . Yoko was quick to know how people who claim to be radical treat women. . . . Of course, Yoko was well into liberation before I met her. She'd had to fight her way through a man's world—the art world is completely dominated by men—so she was full of revolutionary zeal when we met. There was never any question about it: we had to have a 50-50 relationship, or there was no relationship, I was quick to learn."

John used the interview more to pose problems than to make pronouncements. Blackburn and Ali mentioned workers' control, and John asked, "Haven't they tried out something like that in Yugoslavia? . . . I'd like to go there and see how it works." They said that French workers took over factories in May '68, and John asked, "But the Communist Party wasn't up to that, was it?" They mentioned Mao, and John commented, "It seems that all revolutions end up with a personality cult—even the Chinese seem to need a father figure. . . . In Western-styled Communism, we would have to create an almost imaginary workers' image of *themselves* as the father figure."

John also recognized the sense of frustration and exhaustion that had gripped the entire left by this time. "We all have bourgeois instincts within us, we all get tired," he said. "How do you keep everything going, keep up revolutionary fervor?" And he talked about the dilemma of strategy. "What can you do? You can't take power without a struggle. Because when it comes to the nitty gritty they won't let the people have any power. They'll give us all the rights to perform and dance for them, but no real power. I don't know what the answer is."

These were precisely the questions the New Left had in 1970: cultural revolution, workers' control, relations with the old left. John was not, as many critics complained, simply repeating radical clichés in a mindless way. On the contrary, one gets a sense of him as a thoughtful and intelligent but genuinely modest person working to develop his own understanding of radical politics. Blackburn later commented, "In retrospect, he gave a better account of himself than we did of ourselves."

The publication of the interview made headlines in London, where excerpts appeared in the *Observer*, along with a photo of John and Yoko wearing *Red Mole* T-shirts. John's move from drugs and mysticism to New Left politics was summed up by his statement "The acid dream is over," which became the title of the interview as it was reprinted throughout the underground press in the United States in June 1971. *Ramparts* magazine, which had previously captured headlines by exposing the CIA's clandestine funding of the National Student Association and by publishing Che Guevara's secret Bolivian diaries, ran John and Yoko on the cover of its July 1971 issue and reprinted the *Red Mole* interview under a banner headline, "The Working Class Hero Turns Red."

"The song 'Power to the People' was the direct musical consequence of our interview with them in *Red Mole*, " Tariq Ali explained. "John rang me up the day after the interview and said, 'Look, I was so excited by the things we talked about that I've written this song for the movement, so you can sing it when you march.' I said, 'This is great!' He said, 'Well, do you want to hear it?' I said, 'What do you mean, over the phone?' He said, 'Well, I won't sing it, I'll just read you the words.' So he did, and said, 'What do you think?' I said, 'I think it's fine and I'm sure lots of people will be singing it on demonstrations.' "

"Power to the People" was released as the antiwar movement intensified its efforts in its 1971 spring offensive. On April 30 two thousand Vietnam veterans, organized by Vietnam Veterans against the War, rallied in Washington, D.C. Nothing like it had ever occurred in American history. One by one these men, many of them missing limbs and in wheelchairs, gave their names, ranks, military units, and decorations, some shouting defiantly, some sobbing; then each hurled his combat medals on the steps of the Capitol. It was stunning and heartbreaking.

On May 3 mass civil disobedience took place in Washington with the slogan "Stop the war or we'll stop the government." Young people filled the streets of the capital, singing, "All we are saying is get Nixon's ass." The civil disobedience was met with massive repression. Twelve thousand demonstrators were arrested in a single day. (In 1975 the U.S. district court in Washington in a landmark decision awarded them a total of $12 million in damages for false arrest and imprisonment.)

The demonstrators enraged Richard Nixon. According to a White House transcript released in the fall of 1981, he told H. R. Haldeman he should "hire Teamsters to go in and knock their heads off." Haldeman replied, "Sure. Murderers. Guys that really, you know, that's what they really do. . . . They're gonna beat the shit out of these people. And uh, and hope they really hurt 'em." One of those who was really hurt was Abbie Hoffman, beaten by unidentified thugs.

The same week as the demonstrations, "Power to the People" reached Number Eleven on the Billboard Hot 100. (In England it peaked even higher, at Number Six.) John sang it as a street song, a marching song, a fighting song. This was a new world for him. In his earlier political song, "we" had asked our leaders to give peace "a chance." Now Lennon asserted that decisions should be made, not by those in power but rather by the people as a whole. "Power to the People" is of course only a slogan, but it is a supremely democratic slogan, and moreover one that has the virtue of recognizing political reality—that politics is above all a struggle for power. The finest image was in the lines "When we come into town, singing / Power—to the people!"

The verses laid out John's new political position. First he put forward a revolutionary perspective, self-consciously reversing the statement he made in the 1968 single "Revolution," which had begun "You say you want a revolution," and concluded "count me out." Now he began "We say we want a revolution / Better get it on right away." The second verse offered a socialist perspective, declaring that the workers should get "what they really own." And the third put forward a feminist perspective, bringing together the personal and the political:

> I'm gonna ask you comrade and brother
> How do you treat your own woman back home
> She got to *be* herself
> So she can *free* herself

This indeed was precisely the demand the women in the New Left were addressing to movement men. They were insisting that the struggle for equality in personal relations within the movement was inseparable from the struggle to create a more just and democratic society. John had adopted that position as his own.

The song, amazingly enough, became a great popular success. The authoritative *Book of Golden Discs* lists it as a million-seller worldwide. It almost cracked the American Top Ten, and did better than "Give Peace a Chance" and better than "Revolution." It received Top Forty airplay for nine weeks in the spring of 1971, a striking achievement for a revolutionary socialist and feminist marching song. (Equally remarkable is the fact that ten years later, when "Give Peace a Chance" had long since been deleted from the Capitol catalogue, "Power to the People" was still available and stocked in record stores.)

"Power to the People" alarmed critics. Roy Carr of *Melody Maker* wrote that the song displayed "the dreadful curse of the brainless militant." Beatles historian Nicholas Schaffner described John "parroting the well-worn clichés of 'the movement.' " On the other hand, Atlanta's *Great Speckled Bird* called it "the best movement song since 'Blowin' in the Wind.' " Greil Marcus, who disliked most of John's political songs, called this one "a nervy 45." Liberal critics argued that one part of society should not hold all the power. "Rubbish," John replied. "The people aren't a section. . . . I think that everyone should own everything equally and that the people should own part of the factories and they should have some say in who is boss and who does what."

Even at this peak of political commitment, however, John did not try to work outside the capitalist media. On the contrary, he continued to work through the recording industry and toward the AM radio market, two of the more corrupt and debased institutions of the capitalist marketplace. He continued to produce records as commodities, to be sold in record stores and played on the radio between commercials for other products. His effort to make commercial hits out of songs like "Power to the People" was more risky and adventurous than the work of ostensibly successful political songwriters like Tom Paxton or Phil Ochs. There was a kind of closure around their work and their audience that was absent from John's. Far from expecting radical political songs from him, many of his fans felt betrayed by his new advocacy of socialism and feminism. John wanted to use his celebrity to reach an audience as yet unmoved by radical politics.

———

As part of his growing activist commitments in the spring of 1971, John joined in the defense of a London underground magazine called *OZ*. The magazine, Robin Blackburn explained, "was at the Yippie end of the spectrum. The left as such didn't have much to do with it, except that *OZ* published a lot of left-wing writers," notably Tom Nairn, who wrote *The*

Break-Up of Britain a decade later. The magazine featured a kind of anarchic satire. Its editor, Richard Neville, later admitted that "in London, not only did satirical intention seem redundant—other people were doing it better— but as a critical reaction to society it seemed inadequate and ultimately reactionary."

The issue that aroused the wrath of the authorities appeared in 1970. The editors had invited teenagers to submit and edit material. This "schoolkids' issue" of *OZ* included a lesbian drawing on the cover. Another drawing showed rats disappearing up vaginas—"sexist and raunchy, some sort of adolescent boy's anti-female fantasy," Robin Blackburn said. The adult editors were arrested and charged with contributing to the delinquency of minors. "The trial was a sort of Victorian farce conducted in a British courtroom," Tariq Ali recalled. "It was a big joke. We all became involved in supporting *OZ* whether we agreed with them or not."

The prosecution told the jury that *OZ* advocated "lust without love," a concept that was "loathsome, repulsive, and depraved." The defense presented an expert medical witness, who testified that the lesbian drawing on the cover "would not convert people to lesbianism unless such a tendency was there already." The magazine had printed a shocking cartoon of Rupert Bear, beloved by every British child, shown with a huge erect penis, raping an elderly woman. During the trial the prosecution emphasized the cartoon's depravity.

The schoolkids' issue included an excellent article by an eighteen-year-old from Reading, which was ignored during the trial. It objected to the commercialization of the counterculture. "The media's tactic is 'take it over, package it, sell it back to itself.' We haven't infiltrated them, they've infiltrated us. . . . Now the revolution is a groovy way to sell things." The schoolkids' issue also included a tribute to the four Kent State students killed by National Guard gunfire the previous May. John's name came up during the trial: he was a subscriber to *OZ*, it turned out. Other subscribers included prominent reporters and a former cabinet minister. The defense hoped the list would impress the jurors.

The obscenity trial lasted longer than any other in British history, twenty-six days. The jury announced a verdict of guilty. The judge sentenced the editors to fifteen months in prison, a shocking punishment; the previous obscenity verdict had led to a fine of 100 pounds. The London *Daily Mirror* headlined its story, "Why the Ferocious Sentences?" The Manchester *Guardian* headline read, "MPs Condemn OZ Gaolings." And the London *Daily Express* quoted John denouncing the trial and verdict as "disgusting fascism." Mick Jagger was also quoted: "If there has been a moral crime committed, it is by the police and the judge." Only the *Times*, the pillar of the establishment, supported the verdict and sentence, on the grounds that young people must be protected.

This argument enraged Claud Cockburn, the distinguished left-wing columnist for *Private Eye.* "It is obvious enough now that the *Times*'s editors ought to have been sent to prison for prominently publishing the My Lai affair. One can think of few things more likely to give any sensitive young person a deep trauma than the news of the grisly massacre itself, the 'explanations' and self-justifications produced by the uniformed murderers, and the subsequent defense of the chief murderer by the President of the United States."

The *Red Mole* wrote that the *OZ* trial and verdict helped "unmask the realities of class rule. It forces our rulers to undermine their ideological power by using nakedly their material power. But legal repression too has its cargo of ideology: judicial impartiality, 'the rule of law.' . . . In general the liberal outcry that follows legal repression does not challenge this ideology. . . . The simple truth is that the great majority of judges are and have to be deeply reactionary custodians of the interests of the ruling class. Similarly, juries are overwhelmingly middle class and middle-aged in composition. It is as urgent to attack and unmask this pillar of bourgeois power as it is to expose the workings of the capitalist economy."

The *OZ* defense committee announced it would appeal, and John and Yoko joined the fundraising effort. They wrote the songs "God Save Us" and "Do the Oz," released as a single by Apple in July 1971. John played on both and sang lead on "Do the Oz," calling the group "the Elastic Oz Band." Full-page ads appeared in all the British underground and radical newspapers: "Every major country has a screw in its side, in England it's *OZ. OZ* is on trial for its life. John and Yoko have written and helped produce this record —the proceeds of which are going to *OZ* to help pay their legal fees. The entire British underground is in trouble, it needs our help. Please listen— 'God Save Oz.' "

The song is a mid-tempo rocker, filled with puns, asking God to save *OZ* from destruction and us from "de queen." The record is John's most obscure, and the songs have never been included on any album. Greil Marcus put "Do the Oz" on his list of "the best of rock and roll," classifying it as a record that "would leave an essential gap in that story if it were passed over."

John's support for *OZ* made him the object of some *Private Eye* humor. The magazine in the past had referred to him as "Spiggy Topes." Now they ran a story quoting "Len Trott, member of the Acting Editorial Board of Wozz: 'I would like to say a word about Comrade Topes, who is supplying the bread to pay for the legal expenses incurred at the trial. A lot of people have put Spiggy down in the past as being nothing but a half-witted pop singer with too much money, which frankly may be true, in part, but since yesterday, when his cheque came in, you have to hand it to him, to my mind, that he is prepared to stand up and be counted on behalf of international socialism.' " The story seemed elitist and hostile. But when Tariq Ali asked John whether he had seen the piece, he replied, "Yes, it's hilarious."

In August John and Yoko joined 1,500 marchers in a demonstration supporting *OZ* and opposing British policy in Northern Ireland. John told reporters that the state's repression of the counterculture and of Ulster's Catholics "are integral matters and cannot be divided." Marching up crowded Oxford Street, wearing a *Red Mole* T-shirt, carrying a placard reading "For the IRA, Against British Imperialism," shouting through a bullhorn, John led demonstrators chanting "Power to the people!" For the first time he had joined the young radicals who were taking to the streets.

15

"We Hope Some Day You'll Join Us"

Six months after "Power to the People" John released "Imagine," which easily became the most popular and widely covered song of his post-Beatles period. In the fall of 1971, however, the single failed to reach Number One or sell a million copies. It peaked in the charts at Number Three and spent only nine weeks on the Top Hundred, the same amount of time "Power to the People" had. "Instant Karma!" had done considerably better back in 1970. (Particularly galling to John and his fans was the success of Paul's relentlessly cheerful "Uncle Albert/Admiral Halsey," released just before "Imagine"; it easily reached Number One, went gold, and won a Grammy.)

Given the great simplicity and clarity of "Imagine," it's remarkable how many critics misunderstood it. The *Rolling Stone* memorial issue after John's death said the song portrayed a world that was "irrational yet beautiful." Why "irrational"? Is our world of greed and hunger more rational? *Beatlemania* author Ron Schaumburg called it an "altruistic" song. Altruism means "unselfish concern for the welfare of others." But John was not saying he wanted to give up something to benefit others. He wanted that world for himself too. The New York *Times* reviewer called it a song of "optimism." It was, but since when did that great encyclopedia of advertisements consider a call to "imagine no possessions" to be "optimistic"? The World Church asked John if it could use the song and change the lyrics to "Imagine *one* religion." John told them they "didn't understand it at all."

Even Paul didn't understand the song very well. He told *Melody Maker*, "I like . . . 'Imagine' which is what John is really like, but there was too much political stuff on the other albums." John retorted in a published letter, "So you think 'Imagine' ain't political, it's 'Working Class Hero' with sugar on it for conservatives like yourself! Join the Rock Liberation Front before it gets you."

Of course the song is utopian, and the utopian imagination was always a keystone of New Left thought, distinguishing it from the bread-and-butter politics of traditional socialism. "Imagine," together with "Working Class Hero" from the *Plastic Ono Band* album, expressed the New Left position for which Herbert Marcuse was the spokesman: the potential power of the working class is undermined by a repressive culture; restoring the utopian imagination is a key step toward social transformation.

At least twenty-three cover versions of "Imagine" have been released in the United States, including a reggae version by Ella Boothe, a jazz version by Hank Crawford, and a great doo-wop version by the Capris. Several black singers have covered the song, including Diana Ross, Ben E. King, and Sarah Vaughan. Of course Joan Baez recorded it. The song has a separate life in the easy-listening world, with Ray Conniff leading a list of soothing choral and orchestral versions heard intermittently in elevators and dentists' waiting rooms.

The song has its critics, on both the left and the right. The Philadelphia Workers' Organizing Committee argued that the song "carries the presumption that Lennon, and some other chosen few, are already 'there,' and it remains only for the rest of us to join them. Beyond offering the invitation, Lennon sees nothing more to do." It's too bad they hadn't heard "Power to the People." *Rolling Stone* called "Imagine" "undistinguished" and "methodical" when it was released, and criticized its "technical sloppiness and self-absorption." And John's fundamentalist critics were still preoccupied with his "more popular than Jesus" remark from five years earlier. They scrutinized the lyrics of "Imagine" and triumphantly reported that "imagine there's no heaven" was the very first line. The song made the destruction of religion its number one priority, taking precedence over the destruction of property and the state. Lennon hadn't changed a bit.

In the context of that year's politics, however, "Imagine" seemed to many movement people a hymn to the New Left in defeat. The movement was completely exhausted and in ruins by the fall and winter of 1971. Some of its leaders were dead, some underground. Despite the largest peaceful protests in the nation's history and the most militant and widespread civil disobedience, Nixon was riding high in the saddle and headed for an easy reelection. In that cold winter of 1971–72, as radicals sat together in front of their stereo systems, smoking dope and listening to "Imagine," they thought about how little they had accomplished. The song was a reminder of the ultimate goals which made the efforts of the past worthwhile despite their apparent lack of success. "Imagine" was a song that would help to keep those goals alive for the next season of struggle.

On the *Imagine* album, the title song was followed by "Crippled Inside," a stupid song which made ironic use of a ragtime piano and infectious ricky-ticky percussion. It told Paul he could "live a lie" until he died. Phil Ochs had already exploited the same ironic possibilities more than once. The difference was that while Ochs sang about Johnson or Nixon, John sang about Paul. The most striking thing about "Crippled Inside" was that it was followed by John singing "Jealous Guy." Written to Yoko, it was placed on the record in a way that suggested it might apply to Paul as well. "It's So Hard" was a big, strong blues with heavy bass and drums, twanging guitar and raucous alto sax, sung in a deep echo chamber. The lyrics expressed "blue" feelings, but in John's truth-telling mode: "To be somebody, you got to shove / But it's so hard."

"I Don't Wanna Be a Soldier Mama I Don't Wanna Die" was a Spector sound extravaganza. *How I Won the War* in 1967 had expressed a similar sentiment. The "Mama" to whom John expressed these fears was the same one at whom he screamed "Mama, don't go" on *Plastic Ono Band.* This was an antiwar song with the most elemental politics. Phil Ochs's "I Ain't a'Marchin' Anymore" had some analysis, Country Joe's "Feel Like I'm Fixin' to Die Rag" had been clever and bitter. John's song, in contrast, was a primitive chant about his fears, sustained, intensified, remorseless, until the final cries of "Oh no" moved from fear to defiance.

Side two opened with "Gimme Some Truth," a thrilling torrent of angry words, harnessing the "Joycean" gobbledegook of John's youth, of the "Daily Howl," to express political outrage. He denounced the politicians responsible for the war in Vietnam as "short-haired yellow-bellied sons of Tricky Dicky"; he ridiculed sexists as "tight-lipped condescending mommies' little chauvinists." His commitments couldn't be bought off; he wasn't going to sell out —not again. Dylan, the master of rock and roll venom, had never quite managed anything like this. Musically the song was hard-driving rock with a striking chord progression and a fine solo by George. In the next decade only one record would equal it, musically and politically: Stevie Wonder's irresistibly rocking "You Haven't Done Nothin'."

"Gimme Some Truth," together with "Imagine," summed up the radical vision John had developed over the preceding two years: anger about the present balanced by hope for the future; hard energy balanced by gentle lyricism; complexity and bitterness balanced by simple beauty: a genuine achievement.

Not everybody saw it that way at the time. *Rolling Stone* called "Gimme Some Truth" "simplistic ranting." Others denounced it as another of Lennon's clichés. On the other hand, one underground paper declared, " 'Imagine' is Lennon's vision but 'Gimme Some Truth' gives that vision its real power. . . . It's the best song on the album."

"Oh My Love," a simple love song, followed. It set listeners up to be knocked out by the next one, "How Do You Sleep?" "The only thing you done was yesterday," John sang to Paul, turning his best-loved song into a symbol of his musical deterioration. The brilliant viciousness of the lyrics, aimed at an old friend, resembled the best of Bob Dylan, the master of the genre. (Dylan's viciousness, however, was always aimed at the women in his life. He never sang to a man the way John sang to Paul.)

In the *Red Mole* interview conducted earlier the same year, John had spoken of his own pain and fear, "the kind that makes you wake up afraid with your heart pounding." The song "How Do You Sleep?" asked how Paul had managed to escape the self-doubt and depression and anxiety that made John suffer so much. John overcame his nightmares and sleeplessness only through intensive work with Janov; how come Paul got off so easily?

Some couldn't take the song. *Rolling Stone* called it "horrifying and indefensible, . . . a song so spiteful and self-indulgent that it sanctified the victim and demeaned the accuser." But when John informed Paul that the sound he made was Muzak, he was simply telling the truth about Paul's album *Ram*, which had come out four months earlier. Within a year and a half Paul would deteriorate even further with *Red Rose Speedway*, which may be the worst album ever made by a major rock figure.

On "How Do You Sleep?" John stated that Paul had no talent. He would make a different statement in *Lennon Remembers* a few months later. He declared that Paul did not realize how much talent he really had: "I think he's capable of great work. . . . I wish he wouldn't do it. . . . In my heart of hearts I wish I was the only one." That was an incredibly honest revelation.

The bitter certainties of "How Do You Sleep?" were followed by the phony self-doubt of the next song, "How?," in which John seemed proud of feeling insecure. The violins didn't help.

The last song on the album was "Oh Yoko!"—playful, loving, passionate. He called her name in the middle of the night, in the middle of a shave, in the middle of a dream. Everything worked to perfection: the acoustic rhythm guitar, the shifts between major and minor chords, and John's Dylanesque harmonica, which he hadn't played on a record since *A Hard Day's Night.*

John's previous album had ended with the horrifying "My Mummy's Dead"; to end now with "Oh Yoko!," with such unambiguous happiness, suggested how far he had come in his personal life since the Beatles broke up. It would not be easy for him to hold on to this happiness.

=====

Imagine was John's first Number One album since the breakup, and his most successful post-Beatles album by far. In Britain *Plastic Ono Band* had peaked at Number Eight. *Imagine* spent three weeks at Number One and was still in the Top Thirty in the spring of 1973, sixteen months after it was released.

In the United States the story was similar. *Plastic Ono Band* had been in the Top Ten for four weeks; *Imagine* was there for twelve. It inspired people to go back and listen to *Plastic Ono Band*, which returned to the charts for five weeks after *Imagine* hit Number One. No other album of John's would do as well as *Imagine* until *Double Fantasy*.

These chart facts meant that John had achieved his objective. He had taken the personal and political insights of *Plastic Ono Band* and made music out of them that a mass audience wanted to hear. Dan Richter, who worked as John and Yoko's personal assistant on the album, commented, "John succeeded in using his power to walk the tightrope between pop and art. He accomplished something he had never previously done. It was a watershed."

The New Left critics agreed. Robert Christgau had some criticisms: "He needs continual reminders of his pop heritage, to balance his oedipal heritage and his class heritage." But as a whole the album represented "an invigorating development for those of us who have been straining to link rock and politics. . . . At its best it is richer and more exciting than *Plastic Ono Band.*" The Underground Press Syndicate was unqualified in its judgment: "John Lennon has really grown. He's a poet and a prophet and a radical and a man."

In an interview after finishing the *Imagine* album, John called it "uncompromisingly commercial," a fine phrase, and talked about what making it had been like. "It isn't easy, it's torture. Well, mainly torture. Oh, Yoko says the writing is easy compared with the recording. That's when I go through hell. When I've finished an album I think 'screw it!' for a bit, and I think I won't write any more songs because I don't have to be panicked into it. Then when I haven't done any for a few months, I get all paranoiac thinking 'Oh, Christ, I can't write. I'll have to do some more.' "

He had a Janovian interpretation of his career. "It's like always putting yourself on trial in front of the world . . . to see if you're good enough for mummy and daddy—you know, 'Now will you love me if I stand on my head and play guitar and dance and blow balloons *and* get an award from the Queen *and* sing "She Loves You," now will you love me?' "

In another interview at this time he spoke about feelings of worthlessness. "Everybody has this guilt complex that they're no good, that they're not talented, that they're useless, that there's something wrong with them. It's not true. There's nothing wrong with any of you out there, there's nothing *wrong* with you. You shouldn't feel guilty about wanting. People will repress themselves from even allowing themselves to want. . . . At least allow yourselves to want."

And he told about "this guy called Claudio," who "thought the whole *Plastic Ono Band* album was about him. . . . He sent telegrams for nine months saying, 'I'm coming, I'm coming, and I'll only have to look in your eyes and then I'll know.' So last week he turned up at the house. He looked in my eyes, and he didn't get any answer. . . . I said, 'The album might strike a corresponding chord in your experience, but it's basically about me. You better get on and live your own life. You're really wasting your time." John didn't realize how dangerous the Claudios could be.

John and Yoko appeared onstage at New York's Fillmore East in June 1971 to jam with Frank Zappa and the Mothers of Invention. It was a promising idea. An early advocate of cultural revolution, Zappa had used his music to satirize fifties popular culture and to lampoon conventional politics. He and the Mothers of Invention stood for outrageousness, a stance that was not alien to John and Yoko. "We appreciate Zappa's intellectual struggle to get through to people," John said. Musically Zappa had been adventurous, pioneering the tape editing process as a creative element in rock, and bringing jazz influences to his music. He was completely at home with Yoko's screams. The Beatles had been the target of his satire, first with *We're Only in It for the Money*, a parody of *Sgt. Pepper*, and then with "Oh No" on *Weasels Ripped My Flesh*, a devastating reply to "All You Need Is Love." Increasingly, however, his work was marred by a puerile sexism. John and Yoko liked their "live jam" with Zappa enough to include it as side four of *Some Time in New York City*, but their brand of cultural revolution didn't mix with his. They never played together again.

The same day they played with Zappa, John appeared on Howard Smith's radio talk show on WPLJ. In a German accent he announced, "This is WFBI, playing all your favorite toons; this is Edgar Hoover here, and I'd like to do your room."

A caller said, "You'd like to do my room? What color would you like to paint it?"

John: "No, no. I'm gonna *Hoover* it, haw, haw, haw!" Within six months J. Edgar Hoover would begin surveillance of John; within a year John would claim his "room" had been bugged. That would end his joking about the FBI and its director.

It was George Harrison, not John Lennon, who organized the political concert of 1971: the Concert for Bangla Desh, held in Madison Square Garden on August 1. It promised to help ease famine in the new nation which had seceded from Pakistan. Civil war there had left a million people dead from starvation, disease, and near-genocidal massacres. John had been invited to appear, and he was planning to until George told him that Yoko was explicitly not invited. He refused to appear without her. The highlight of the concert, of course, was Bob Dylan, who sang "Blowin' in the Wind" and "A Hard Rain's A-Gonna Fall" and played acoustic guitar, just like the old days. *Rolling Stone* praised the concert as evidence that the social conscience of sixties rock had not yet died.

The concert made a quarter of a million dollars for UNICEF. The live album and the film were to be the real moneymakers, raising close to $10 million. But the release of the album was delayed, and *New York* magazine charged that Allen Klein, John's financial guru as well as George's, was allegedly pocketing some of the receipts. Klein sued the magazine for $100 million, then dropped the suit. The taxman tied up the rest of the concert proceeds. As a demonstration of George Harrison's social conscience, the concert was a moving success; as a source of real aid for Bangla Desh, it was a serious failure.

"Happy Xmas (War Is Over)," recorded three months after the *Imagine* album, had none of the forced jolliness or phony sentimentality of most Christmas rock. Instead, it conveyed John's sense that the year had been a hard one: the road was so long, he sang. It had the old Lennon self-scrutiny: "another year over . . . and what have you done?" It had the Lennon antiwar message. With Yoko and the kids of the Harlem Community Choir in the background, John sang passionately about the year to come, "Let's hope it's a good one, without any fear." In the new year that hope would be destroyed.

=====

After John finished *Imagine,* he and Yoko continued meeting with Robin Blackburn and Tariq Ali. Ali recalled that, one time when John invited them over, Régis Debray was in the *Red Mole* office, having just been freed from a Bolivian prison. "We asked Debray if he wanted to come along. He said, 'Oh yes! I'm amazed you people have such contacts.' When we arrived, we told John we'd brought Régis Debray. He didn't know who Debray was. Fortunately, John didn't make a gaffe. I took him to one side and said, 'Look, this poor comrade has been locked up in a horrible Bolivian prison and tortured and he's just come out.' I told him who he was and how he'd known Che Guevara. John was then very warm towards Debray. It was a somewhat bizarre meeting." Blackburn summed up the situation: "Debray had heard all about the Beatles but wasn't sure which one John was; John had heard all about Che but didn't know who Debray was." The Lennon-Debray meeting was filmed: John was enthusiastic about the footage and wanted to include it in the film they were making, the soundtrack of which would be John's *Imagine* album and Yoko's *Fly*. Debray, however, was uneasy about the whole thing and asked that it not be included. John and Yoko complied.

Blackburn explained that their discussions with John and Yoko explored the possibilities of "political collaboration." "He was setting up a project with a not-very-well-assorted group of people who were into alternative technology, alternative media, alternative politics and lifestyles, and he was going to provide the facilities. And he asked what he could do to help the *Red Mole*. He said he would give us the money to buy a new printing press." Tariq Ali recalled, "I said, 'Look, that would be very nice, but that's not the central problem. The central problem is to set up a tax-exempt foundation for you to carry out both political and cultural work which helps the left.' He thought that was a very good idea. We had some meetings with him to try and get it off the ground: the foundation would make films, issue pamphlets, sponsor tours. He was quite keen on it. We developed a name for it—the Red Grapefruit Foundation, after Yoko's book *Grapefruit*. We drew up the papers. Then Lennon left for New York. The plan fell through. We hadn't accepted any money for the *Red Mole* at all, which made the comrades on the editorial board furious."

John's ties with the *Red Mole* led him to his first engagement with a classical struggle of industrial workers in August 1971. Eight thousand workers at the Upper Clydeside Shipbuilders (UCS) in Scotland refused to stop work after the Tory government declared them "redundant" (laid off). Instead, they occupied the factories in a direct challenge to the government. The left, old and new, joined in a nationwide campaign of support. The *Red Mole* devoted a special issue to the struggle, which John read and talked about. The cover showed an old poster of a fat, ugly capitalist confronted by a militant worker. Tariq Ali remembered John saying, "That's an amazing cover. Where did you get it? They look just like that, the capitalists!"

The shipyards had been the center of Scottish working-class radicalism and militance throughout the twentieth century. "A factory occupation is, *de facto*, workers' control," the *Red Mole* editors argued. "The continued working of the yards would transform the demand for keeping the yards open into a demand for nationalization under workers' control." The Clydeside workers had massive support for their campaign; forty thousand people had demonstrated in Glasgow in June, and seventy thousand demonstrated in August. The occupation had the potential to capture the imaginations of workers in other regions of Britain, in industries facing layoffs. They too could be spurred to occupy their factories. But, the *Red Mole* explained, "because no wages would be paid for work done in occupied Clydeside factories, enormous financial support has to be prepared all over the country."

John declared himself an eager supporter of the UCS workers. The *Times* reported that he and Yoko were sending a thousand pounds one week to the "shop stewards' fighting fund," and that they were also sending roses—a fine touch. But John's engagement with the British left was cut short a week later. "He suddenly packed and went to New York," Tariq Ali recalled. "I had been talking to him two weeks before and not a word of it. And then one day when I rang he said, 'We're leaving, we're going off to New York, I'm fed up.' "

In fact John and Yoko were moving to the United States to search for Yoko's seven-year-old daughter, Kyoko. The girl's father, Tony Cox, had taken her, although their 1969 divorce decree had not granted him custody. During the previous year Cox had occasionally called Yoko to tell her he needed money to pay his bills. When she sent the money, he would let her spend a few days with her daughter. Then Yoko would lose contact until Cox's next call from someplace else. By the middle of 1971 he had completely disappeared. John and Yoko had private investigators tracking Cox as he moved from continent to continent. First they learned that Kyoko was being guarded by disciples of the Maharishi in a communal children's camp on the Spanish island of Majorca, while Cox meditated with the guru.

In July Yoko and John had appeared in court in the U.S. Virgin Islands, where Yoko's divorce had been granted, and asked for custody of Kyoko. Cox, anticipating that Yoko would win, challenged the proceedings in a Houston, Texas, court the same month. Since the American courts would resolve the custody issue, and since Cox and Kyoko were in Texas, John and Yoko decided to move to the United States.

John left England for personal reasons, but in so doing he was walking away from people and projects to which he had made commitments. Most of those obligations were tentative, but they had a special significance for him. They represented the biggest commitments he had made to a real political movement.

Had John remained in England at this point, Robin Blackburn suggests, instead of going to New York and Jerry Rubin and Abbie Hoffman, his contribution to radical politics would have been far more significant as well as more satisfying to him personally. The New Left in the United States faced growing isolation and self-destruction. In Britain in the early seventies, radical politics continued to develop and broaden, as the New Left joined with working-class struggles.

In 1972, after the Clydeside strike, a historic miners' strike challenged the Tory government. "The miners would have radicalized John even further,"

Blackburn said, "and would have drawn a direct link between his own class origins and the class struggle in Britain—the first glimpse of which you got with his solidarity with the Clydeside strikers."

John could have done a lot in British movement politics. Many musicians started with benefit concerts; John started doing benefits when he got to New York. At one of the Clydeside benefit concerts a strike leader said, "We're really grateful to you young Londoners here tonight for helping us in our fight to raise the dignity of working people and I think it's appropriate that music was the means of raising money tonight, because music expresses the longing of the soul. If you don't let us down, we won't let you down." It's not hard to understand the suggestion that John belonged at benefits like that one, more than at the John Sinclair concert in Ann Arbor.

If John had stayed in Britain, he would have found others working on the same project of bringing together rock music and radical politics. The development of punk rock had a strongly political dimension, especially the Sex Pistols' "God Save the Queen," written in 1977 for the silver jubilee of Queen Elizabeth II, and the music of the Clash. Many of these musicians joined to put on the "Rock against Racism" campaign of the late seventies. John would have been more politically effective, and could have found it more personally rewarding to join this effort than to sing about Angela Davis on the *David Frost Show* in New York.

Blackburn admitted his analysis was highly speculative. "I don't want to say he would have fitted in here smoothly," he said. "Lennon had this radically disconcerting quality, even to people on the left. He would have been upsetting all sorts of received ideas and shibboleths. Who knows how he could have developed? There was a more soundly established and more diverse left wing and labor movement here. We had a stronger link between the New Left and the working class. But a lot of the struggles in Britain in the seventies were pretty elemental. We did not have a coherent socialist movement and a cultural dimension that went along with it. Still, I think the chances of John's political development continuing would have been far greater in Britain than in the U.S."

While John was engaged with British New Left politics, he produced the *Imagine* album and "Power to the People"; after moving to the United States he produced the disastrous *Some Time in New York City.* His work declined, not when he moved from Beatles music to political music, as many have argued, but rather when he moved from British politics to American politics. As a person, he wanted to live in New York City; as a political artist, he had great achievements in London.

But could John have continued to develop as a political artist in Britain in a personally satisfying way? The British political world in the late seventies was probably too structured for him. A classic political battle between capital and labor raged through the decade. And social lifestyles were more rigid in Britain in the seventies. The lines separating classes were inflexible, with few spaces in between. Being a multimillionaire socialist, let alone a socialist activist, would have been extremely difficult. For John the contradictions might well have been unendurable. New York in contrast offered a society that was much more open, with a Bohemian enclave in which a working-class superstar could flourish.

"The Beatles are treated like Britain's children," John said. So he left his own society, forced out by its closure, drawn to America's openness. In America he found room to develop as an artist and a person. In America he would be worn down by a relentless campaign of Nixonian harassment. In America he would be killed.

Part V

MOVEMENT SONGWRITER

16

Life on Bank Street

 The seventeenth floor of the St. Regis Hotel, on New York's Fifth Avenue, became John and Yoko's new American home in August 1971. Shortly after their arrival Hendrik Hertzberg interviewed them for *The New Yorker.* They explained that they were drawn to the city's racial and ethnic diversity. "It has more Jews than Tel Aviv," Yoko said. "And more Irish than Dublin," John said. "And blacks, and Chinese, and Japanese," Yoko added. John perceived his journey from Liverpool to New York as part of an historic pattern: "Liverpool is the port where the Irish got on the boat to come over here, and the same for the Jews and the blacks. The slaves were brought to Liverpool and then shipped out to America. . . . We got the records—the blues and the rock—right off the boats. . . . and we knew the next place was America."

The first time they walked down the street in New York, John said, a woman came up to him and wished him good luck with his "peace thing." "It's really inspiring to be here," he said, "it's the hippest place on earth, . . . and it just makes you wanna rock like crazy."

Although he did not know it, John fit in only too well with the celebrity world of New York's antiwar movement in 1971. Organizationally the city's left was weak. The antiwar movement was based on the Mobilization, which consisted of famous leaders and tens of thousands of otherwise unorganized people who turned out for its marches and rallies. It was Jerry Rubin who saw the opportunity to recruit John.

He explained how it happened. "I was a very depressed and confused Jerry Rubin. Everyone around me was depressed and confused. Everyone in the Movement was condemning everything, condemning the Chicago Conspiracy Trial, condemning our whole history." Then a friend sat him down and played "Working Class Hero." Rubin realized that "on a mini scale I had many of the same problems, and had been going through much of the same suffering as John Lennon." The song "was really a psychiatrist for me, . . . a means for finding out who I was."

When the New York *Daily News* announced that John and Yoko had come to New York, Rubin called Apple and arranged to meet them the next Saturday afternoon in Washington Square Park. On Saturday Rubin waited under the arch with Abbie and Anita Hoffman. "Then we see them walking toward us. He's wearing American flag sneakers and she's dressed all in black. We run up to meet them. It's love at first sight. . . . We dug his sense of humor, we were knocked out by her sincerity."

"John was very playful," Rubin said. "As we passed cops he would lie down on the floor of his limo, wave his red, white, and blue sneakers out the window, and shout, 'Look, I'm a patriot!' . . . At one time we're all talking in the back of their car and John says, 'I want to go to China.' But then he stops and he wonders if the Chinese know about the Beatles song 'Revolution.' So he says, 'That's all right, I'll just tell them that Paul wrote it.' "

They talked for five hours, Rubin said, in Abbie Hoffman's Lower East Side apartment: "How the Yippies had been applying Beatle tactics to politics, trying to merge music and life. We talked about their bed-in as a Yippie action. All five of us were amazed at how we had been into the same kinds of things all these years."

Abbie had developed a strategy of media politics similar to John and Yoko's. "All we can do is create certain kinds of images and get people to react to those images, to make ourselves visible," he had said. "On *Meet the Press* every fifteen minutes there comes an ad for Brillo. They say, 'You want Brillo, man, Brillo will get you laid. You can brush your teeth with Brillo, you can do anything you want, it's the greatest thing in the twentieth century.' And it's totally irrational, it's a fuckin' lie, it's bullshit; but at the end of the fuckin' show, nobody's bought any of the political views that people are putting forth on *Meet the Press*—they're buyin' fuckin' Brillo!" The political lesson was to communicate with novel, striking events rather than in the routinized language and forms of traditional politics.

John and Yoko's first American demonstration took place near Syracuse, where Yoko was installing a show at the Everson Museum. They joined

Onondaga Indians protesting the takeover of part of their lands by the government for a freeway. In a statement for the media, John told the Indians, "Everybody knows your people have been robbed and slaughtered since the Europeans moved in here. I'm very surprised that, in an area like Syracuse with so many universities and so many students, so many of them talking about love and peace and radicalization and 'get the soldiers out of Vietnam,' that there doesn't seem to be very many of them helping you around here." This statement showed how far John had come since the bed events. The advocacy of "peace and love" had proved inadequate. Now he was suggesting the antiwar movement engage in local political struggles, that radical students move off campus to support protests in surrounding communities.

After Yoko's opening at the Everson Museum in Syracuse, they returned to the city and told Jerry Rubin they'd made a decision: "Yoko says that they want to be part of the movement for change in America. John says he wants to put together a new band, he wants to play and he wants to give all the money back to the people. I was so ecstatic I embarrassed them." This decision led to the plan for a national anti-Nixon concert tour, of which the John Sinclair concert was the test run.

Jerry Rubin had sought out John and Yoko; they sought out Robert Christgau, after reading his article "Now That We Can't Be Beatle Fans Anymore" in the *Village Voice* at the end of September. It was a brilliant piece on the breakup, the music and the politics in the *Plastic Ono Band* and *Imagine* albums, and John and Yoko's relationship. John and Yoko wrote a letter to the editor: "We have never read anything about us that was as observant as your article." Then they invited Christgau to Syracuse for Yoko's Everson show and John's thirty-first birthday party; and when they returned to the city, they went over to his East Village apartment.

"On Avenue B the limo attracted more attention than the star—one of the local youngsters thought *I* was the Beatle, while another didn't know what a Beatle was," Christgau recalled. "After sitting around awkwardly in my dingy living room for a few minutes we repaired to the Cookery for discussions of Chuck Berry's jail years and celebrity as a depletable resource—John wondered whether he should lay low for a while. He seemed astonishingly quick and intense—partly, no doubt, because he was."

=====

John and Yoko visited John Cage, with whom Yoko had worked a decade earlier, and who lived in the West Village on Bank Street. They ran into Cage's next-door neighbor, Joe Butler of the Lovin' Spoonful. He was looking for someone to sublet his apartment. "I said, 'You guys must be sick of the hotel by now, I have a place,' " he recalled. "So they came down. John just said, 'This is such a nice place.' " It had two big rooms; Tittenhurst had a hundred. Even though Butler was still there, they insisted on moving in immediately.

So John and Yoko left the luxurious St. Regis in November and moved to Butler's two-room apartment at 105 Bank Street. The three of them lived there together for two weeks while Butler found a new place. "They were always taking their clothes off," he recalled. "But then I was too. I was into nude therapy, I was in *Hair.* John was amazingly flabby. Even though he wasn't heavy, he didn't seem to have any muscle tissue. She was trying to turn him around, get him into good food and healthy snacks." While they all lived together, "John was learning how to type," Butler remembered. "At a certain time every day he would go to his typewriter, sit up very straight, and practice his typing. The only thing is that he would type the most obscene things, like 'I'm sucking Yoko's pussy.' "

Sometimes John and Yoko "got into spats. Just like anybody else. She would push it and finally back off. He really still did dominate the relationship." Butler summed up: "They were two people who really loved each other. They were a nice couple. When they could get away from all the bullshit, they really had a good time with each other."

Settled on Bank Street, John and Yoko invited movement leaders from New York to come over: Yippies, Panthers, New Left leaders, East Village underground poets, feminists. Kate Millett recalled the scene at their apartment: "It was pretty frantic because there were all these secretaries running around and the telephones were always ringing. But it was nice to get through the front room into the bedroom and just sit. The TV would be going—thank God they didn't have the sound on—and everybody would smoke dope and talk.

"The first couple of times I met John, I was terribly charmed and impressed. He was lovely. Delightful. So intelligent and so funny and so busy. He'd be playing nine different crazy instruments, odd African whatchies. And you always wanted to say how much you admired him and had enjoyed his music these many years. But you said it in a way that made you feel particularly stupid.

"Yoko loved it if you'd be there to see her. It must have been a little bit overwhelming to have so much attention focused on John Lennon. She held her ground. She was tough. So I would spend as much time with her as I could. We'd talk about what we ought to do, and what needs to be done— delightful pie-in-the-sky stuff. But a lot of it was serious, too."

Allen Ginsberg, poet, activist, and Zen enthusiast, was invited to Bank Street. He had been introduced to John in 1965 in London by Bob Dylan;

at the time he and John had discussed Blake. "The use of dope laws for political repression was one of my special interests," he recalled in 1983. "We talked about his bust in England, and I sang him a song of mine, 'The CIA Dope Calypso.' John had a little broken ukelele and I had a harmonium and we jammed together a little bit.

"I was involved with meditation. I had a broken leg, so I lay down on the floor and showed him how I meditated noncrosslegged, in a corpse posture. We got into a discussion about whether meditation was worthwhile. He had been disillusioned by the Maharishi.

"At the time, I was a little suspicious of the Maharishi. He'd been given red-carpet treatment by the government, and he was telling people to be neutral on the Vietnam war. I met the Maharishi at a press conference at the Plaza Hotel and reminded him that many people thought the CIA was enabling his journey. He gave me a satisfactory answer: no matter whether people fought or didn't fight, as long as they meditated he thought that would be an improvement. So I talked that over with John.

"I told him I thought that meditation practice was a good idea. John asked me if I believed in God. I said yes. He challenged me on that. My meditation at that time was, alas, somewhat theistic—schmaltzy, sentimental. He was nontheistic, which was pretty smart; he was ahead of me there. So it was hard for me to defend meditation practice itself, when my own idea of it was based on a theistic premise that John had rightly seen as baseless." (In 1978 Ginsberg visited John and Yoko at their apartment in the Dakota. "He said he'd been lying in bed listening to WBAI," Ginsberg recalled, "and he heard this voice reciting language and he thought it was really fine. He said he wondered who it was. At the end they said it was a recording of Allen Ginsberg reciting 'Howl.' He said to me, 'All these years I've wondered what you did!' ")

John and Yoko got a taste of another side of New York life when a previous tenant of Butler's reappeared, "a guy I had evicted for not paying the rent," Butler remembered. "He came back with a henchman. John came to the door and they pushed their way in with guns in their hands. The guy proceeds to take the two things in the place that are worth something: my color television and my Dali lithograph. John says to him, 'Don't take the telly, I want to watch it.'

"The guy also takes John's wallet and address book. The guy just wanted his money, but in the address book there was stuff that nobody was supposed to know, stuff that Bobby Seale had told him—Eldridge's number and Tim Leary's number. So John and Yoko's chauffeur put the word out through the Mafia that the guy better return it: 'I don't want to have to tell Bobby Seale's people that you have the book.' And the book was returned. We were all very upset that this was their introduction to the Village. But John seemed to like it. For once he had been treated like everybody else!"

Ten years later Bobby Seale, co-founder and chairman of the Black Panther Party, said he recalled talking with John about the incident. "We heard that some dudes were threatening to hurt John. I said, 'Threat? On John here?' I said, 'Oh, no, baby,' 'cause we were armed, you know. We discussed it. We didn't think John's bodyguard, an ex–New York cop, was handling it right in terms of John's best interests. I said, 'John, you need to get rid of that dude. That dude is not the kind of dude you need.' And then John says, 'Well, what if I get two or three Panthers?' I said, 'No, John, we're not a bodyguard organization. We're a political organization. But you need to get you some-body better than this, man.' I told our New York people to keep an eye out for John down there, and told John that if he needed any help, call these guys and they'll be right down."

Rubin was John and Yoko's closest friend in the New York radical world. He spent more time at their Bank Street apartment than any of the others. "This was John's 'Imagine' period," he recalled. "He used to sing it at home a lot. I heard 'Imagine' so many times I thought my ears would fall off.

"John was more radical than I was in this period," Rubin said. "He would joke about their earlier projects, saying, *'She's* the one who's into peace and love.' He was angry, really angry. He ranted and raved about the police. Yoko would tell him, 'You should have love for the pigs. All pigs are victims.' He wasn't political in the sense of being a planner—but emotionally, in his gut reaction, he was very radical: 'It's them versus us.' " In sum, "They wanted to be radicals. It was as simple as that."

They were interested in the black community. "John and Yoko used to say to me, 'We want to go to Harlem. We want to go to Harlem and shake hands with the people.' I said, 'You're rich white celebrities, you're going to go up there in a limousine, you're naïve!' "

Rubin saw a side of Lennon that he concealed from many others. "This was a bitter period for John," Rubin said. "Bitter, bitter, bitter. He was bitter about Paul McCartney. He ranted and raved about Paul. Ranted and raved about Allen Klein. Ranted and raved about being a celebrity. He hated it."

Rubin also talked about John's drug use. "I liked John when he would get stoned on grass. He'd get real mellow and nice. On coke he would get very aggressive. On heroin: very sad. I saw John and Yoko in their house, shaking for five hours straight in a cold sweat, getting off heroin."

Stew Albert, Rubin's closest associate, said, "I saw them go cold turkey that time, but my best recollection is that they were trying to kick methadone. They were miserable. Jerry and I brought a skilled chiropractor in to help them relax their bodies. It helped a little. But they weren't able to kick methadone that time.

"I remember them discussing heroin," Albert said. "They hadn't taken it for a while, and were having a casual conversation about whether to do it some more. They had somebody who could score some. But they decided not to. I did some massage work on them myself at that time, and I know I didn't see any tracks. So if they were taking heroin, they weren't shooting it. I'm sure about that.

"Jerry saw much more of them than I did; he may have known they were taking drugs that I was not aware of," Albert said. "But whatever drugs they may have been doing, it didn't affect the quality of their actions. They were always lucid."

David Peel, the best-known street musician of the Lower East Side, played to large crowds in Washington Square Park every weekend. Howard Smith of the *Village Voice* brought John and Yoko to see his show shortly after they arrived. "I was shook up," Peel said. "No famous people ever come to see me play. No normal people ever come to see me play. I'm a Beatle freak, I had been brainwashed, I was into that 'All You Need Is Love,' peace no matter which way you get it. I gave my speech, 'No rock and roll singer ever paid to see an audience, so why should an audience pay to see a rock and roll singer?' That was street logic." John recalled the speech: "I'm standing in back of the crowd feeling all embarrassed." Then Peel sang his song "The Pope Smokes Dope," "because I knew something about his marijuana bust. Howard Smith told me later that John said, 'I gotta meet that man who sings "The Pope Smokes Dope."' "

"A week or so later Jerry Rubin called me up and said, 'John and Yoko want to go to the East Village to hang out with the kids, the people.' So I brought my guitar. We met by the Fillmore East. I said, 'How you doin',' and started singing 'The Pope Smokes Dope.' He starts singing along with me, Yoko starts singing, everyone else starts singing, then the cops come and of course they have to stop what's happening. I was so happy. The fact that he was on the streets—that really turned me on."

John recalled, "We got moved on by the police. It was all very wonderful." Later he sang about the afternoon in his song "New York City." Peel also wrote a song about the day, "The Ballad of John and Yoko." "I told Jerry, he told them, and they had me come over to Bank Street to sing it for them! I was extremely nervous. 'John Lennon Yoko Ono New York City are your people / John Lennon Yoko Ono New York City is your friend.' It's very simple but catchy. They got very turned on and asked me to make a record with them."

Peel was now signed to Apple (he had already released *Have a Marijuana* on the Elektra label). John and Yoko produced his new album, *The Pope Smokes Dope,* and Apple released it in April 1972, the same week as the single "Woman Is the Nigger of the World." Peel remembered, "At Apple the secretaries called me 'a fate worse than death.' There was no way the album was gonna sell, you know. And Paul really got peeved about it. But I didn't care. Because we have freedom of expression, and freedom of selection, and he also has the freedom of depression." More street logic. John later explained, "We loved his music, and his spirit, and his philosophy of the street. That's why we decided to make a record with him. People say, 'Oh, Peel, he can't sing, and he can't play.' But David Peel is a natural, and some of his melodies are good."

David Peel was the opposite of everything John Lennon had been as a Beatle. John was a superstar and a multimillionaire, but he felt oppressed as a person and stifled as an artist. He couldn't go out in the streets of London. He was besieged by lawyers and accountants. Peel rejected the business of rock music, immersed himself in the local radical community, and played for free in the park. He was flourishing and happy. If his music wasn't great, his life had what looked like a radical freedom.

===

Stew Albert, Rubin's fellow Yippie, remembered the political discussions at Bank Street. "Lennon always said he was more comfortable with us than with Tariq and Robin because our style of politics was similar to show business, which he was used to and could understand. It was an environment he felt comfortable in. And he viewed America as the big time. If you could change America, you were changing the world. But I can see one part of him being attracted to us, and another part being attracted to a more classical Marxist left."

Bobby Seale visited John and Yoko a year after the Chicago conspiracy trial, in which he had shown impressive strength and determination when the judge had him bound and gagged in the courtroom. In 1982 he recalled visiting John and Yoko. "I went to Bank Street twice. You know, John's the type of dude who would sit up in the bed with his legs all folded up. Yoko, she's an energetic person, always moving. We told them about our People for Medical Research health clinic, and our Free Breakfast for Children program—we were feeding close to two hundred thousand kids at one point in 1969. John wanted to know how he could support our community survival programs. We rapped a very long time.

"He had political consciousness. It's just that he had it on another level. When I finally got to know John Lennon, I realized we could have been very close, much closer than I've been with other celebrities. I was pretty close at one time with Marlon Brando. And we got to know Jane Fonda pretty well. See, John went out for us. He wanted to really do something."

John told Elliot Mintz, a leading figure on Los Angeles' counterculture radio, about the Free Breakfast for Children program of the Black Panther Party when they met a few months later. "He agreed that proper nutrition in the morning was necessary for kids to learn," Mintz recalled. "They made a contribution."

Albert remembered that Huey Newton also came to Bank Street to meet John and Yoko. "They hit it off," he said. "They got along nicely. Afterward, Huey sent John a letter saying he had listened very closely to 'Imagine,' and that the ideas it put forward were similar to his own theory, which he called 'intercommunalism.' John was very proud of that letter. He showed it to Jerry and me."

John and Yoko also got together with A. J. Weberman, the man who invented garbology, the study of people's garbage to gain information and insights into their private lives. Through garbology and the practice of "analytic analysis," Weberman concluded that Dylan had become a heroin addict in 1970 or 1971. He launched the "Dylan Liberation Front" to "get Bob off drugs and politically active again." John for a time wore one of Weberman's buttons that said "Free Bob Dylan."

Weberman led a demonstration outside Capitol Records at the beginning of December to protest its failure to release the Bangla Desh concert album. "Pakistanis starve because of Capitol's greed," one sign read. During the demonstration two people wearing bags appeared. One carried a sign reading "Capitol-ist stop trying to split up John and Yoko. He is no longer a Beatle." Weberman explained that "Capitol is trying to include Yoko as a Beatle under an old contract with the Beatles, made before they were superstars. That way Capitol can get away with paying her less than if she were considered on her own merit. Capitol is holding up her album because of the dispute. Yoko plans to give all the money she would get through a more lucrative contract to various political groups."

At the demonstration, Weberman announced, "John and Yoko are the newest members of the Rock Liberation Front, a group dedicated to exposing hip capitalist counterculture ripoffs and politicizing rock music and rock artists." Many believed that the people in the bags were John and Yoko. They had assigned their filmmaker Steve Gebhardt to cover the demonstration.

During the same week the Rock Liberation Front split, as leftist groups had been doing intermittently throughout the twentieth century. John and Yoko joined Jerry Rubin and David Peel in declaring themselves the legitimate Rock Liberation Front and denouncing Weberman. The *Village Voice* published their open letter to Weberman, asking him to "publicly apologize to Bob Dylan for leading a public campaign of lies and malicious slander against Dylan in the past year." Weberman had charged Dylan with "deserting the movement," but Dylan "was there before the movement and helped create it." Weberman's campaign against Dylan was part of a destructive tendency in the movement, "everyone attacking each other and spreading false rumors. . . . It's time we defended and loved each other, and saved our anger for the true enemy, whose ignorance and greed destroys our planet."

The *Village Voice* letter aroused the interest of the FBI, which copied and filed it. Perhaps this Rock Liberation Front posed a new revolutionary threat to America. The FBI files contain the instructions to search their indexes for other reports on the "organization."

Weberman relented, citing Dylan's new record "George Jackson" as evidence that Dylan had changed his ways. Weberman continued to work on the demonstrations planned for the Republican national convention in Miami. John contributed "thousands" for the demonstration, he said.

Another of Weberman's targets was Allen Klein, John's manager, who took 20 percent of everything John made. Klein was accused in a *New York* magazine article of pocketing some of the receipts from George's *Bangla Desh* album. Weberman led the Rock Liberation Front in a demonstration titled "Klein the Swine." They occupied Klein's office as if it were a campus administration building and got the anti-Klein charges into *Variety, Rolling Stone,* and the *Village Voice.* Weberman said the demonstration "convinced John and Yoko they were being ripped off by Klein." A year later John fired Klein, who sued him, George, and Ringo for $19 million. (In 1977 Klein settled for $4.2 million, after negotiations with Yoko. In 1979 he served a prison sentence for tax evasion.)

===

John and Yoko strengthened their ties with the New Left by agreeing to write a regular column for a new political and cultural magazine, *SunDance.* First word of the magazine came in December 1971, when a benefit auction was held to raise money. John was among the "artist-auctioneers," along with Jasper Johns, Robert Rauschenberg, Larry Rivers, and Andy Warhol. Among the items to be auctioned off was the original manuscript for Abbie Hoffman's *Steal This Book.* The FBI noted John's participation.

Craig Pyes, editor of the new magazine, recalled how John and Yoko had been persuaded to become columnists. "Jerry took me to Bank Street to meet them. They were on their bed. John was working on the songs for *Some Time in New York City;* Yoko was working on the artwork for the cover. He played us an acoustic version of 'Attica State' and 'Luck of the Irish' and asked me what I thought of them. I told him they were fantastic. Then he began talking about *Rolling Stone* and picked up a copy of *Lennon Remembers: The Rolling Stone Interviews.* He handed it to Jerry. 'Here,' he said, 'here's a copy of "Lennon Regrets." '

"In it was a little card from Wenner, on the occasion of the second printing, saying, 'This book is more yours than mine.' Lennon said, 'Who does he think he is? "More yours than mine." He just ripped me off with this. He didn't have my permission to reprint it. He asked me to help him out, so we gave him the interview. Then without telling us he prints it up as a book.' We talked a little about *SunDance*. He said, 'If you get something started, let me know.' And he asked some questions about John Sinclair, who he was just learning about.

"It was time to go. On the way out I said, 'How would you like to write a column for *SunDance?*' He said, 'Well, *Esquire* asked us. Why should I write for *SunDance?* Doesn't *Esquire* have ten million circulation?' I said, 'Yes, but *Esquire* is completely owned by pigs. We've got to build up our own media. How are you going to break *Rolling Stone* without cooperation?' He said, 'Yeah. Well, okay.'

"Afterwards Jerry said, 'He's going to write a column for you, isn't that great?' I said I was against it, it would just be some elitist trip. That was the spirit of the times. Then as my understanding of the commercial venture grew, I changed completely, and I had to spend an hour convincing my co-editor it was a good idea.

"We didn't ask John and Yoko for money. The fact that they were identified with the magazine was great for us, it was like money in the bank. But by the third issue we were so broke I had to go to them. I said, 'Look, we're desperate, our cover story on Nixon and the Mafia just has to come out. Can you give us anything?' They didn't like the idea. They felt put upon. But they gave us five thousand dollars."

Issue number one of *SunDance* appeared in April 1972, with a banner headline on the cover, "John and Yoko on Women—Robert Scheer on China." Editors Craig Pyes and Ken Kelley promised the magazine would provide "an alternative to what is too often the rhetorical shallowness of the underground papers, the academic aloofness of the leftist journals, and the camouflaged news management of the 'straight' press." The masthead listed John and Yoko as regular contributors of a column titled "Imagine." In that issue Scheer, until recently an editor of *Ramparts,* argued that the American left should not attack Mao for meeting with Nixon, but rather should welcome the meeting as a blow against domestic anticommunism. Another article presented an eyewitness description of a mutiny of a platoon of American troops in Vietnam, refusing to go on a night ambush patrol near the Cambodian border.

John and Yoko called their first column "It's Never Too Late to Start from the Start." "Contemporary men are too steeped in the game of competition and following social rituals," they said. The women's movement needed to respond to the needs of ordinary women, for whom child care was the leading issue. If the women's movement ignored them, "the average woman will go back to producing babies again, or perhaps settle for less time-consuming affairs . . . all in the age-old attempt to solve her frustration with diversions." And the women's liberation movement could "end up with men making another token gesture such as allow a few comely Smith graduates on TV news." Line drawings by John surrounded the three-page article.

SunDance number two, published later in 1972, featured a fifteen-thousand-word essay by Robert Scheer on the Pentagon Papers, and John and Yoko's discussion of their new political music: "To us, it is a direct descendant of Yoko's early peace events and *Grapefruit* (pre-John), and also John's satire in *Spaniard in the Works.*" Issue number three contained a set of *Grapefruit*-styled instructions of Yoko's to encourage couples to get along better. Then the magazine ran out of money and ceased publication.

John reflected on his life in a New York radio interview late in 1971, linking the personal, political, and artistic sides of his experience, and discussing superstardom, women's liberation, and Vietnam. First he talked about how he grew up. "One has oneself in the beginning and there's a constant process of society and parents and family trying to make you lose yourself. Like 'Don't cry, don't show any emotion,' that kind of jazz. And that goes on all your life.

"I remember that at sixteen I still had myself"—an intriguing statement. "From sixteen to twenty-eight or twenty-nine, that's when it got lost. The struggle to mature, to be a man, to take responsibility—although we were in a cocoon of superlife, in those hotels on tour, we still had to go through the basic maturing that every teenager has to go through, whether it's with or without drugs, in a room somewhere, or alone in a big office building, working their scene out. Probably thirty is about the age you should be waking up and realizing that you're in control of yourself."

How did he do it? "Yoko really woke me up to myself. She didn't fall in love with the Beatles, she didn't fall in love with my fame, she fell in love with *me,* for myself. And through that she brought out the best in me—by encouraging me in my artwork, my films, and my writing, which are all things I did almost like a hobby. She woke me up."

She also woke him up to women's liberation. "Only when a woman's there with you, pointing out the prejudice, did I notice it," he explained, describing a recent recording session that Yoko had been part of. "We all said, 'God almighty!' It was going on all the time: pure prejudice! Continuous prejudice, night and day, I don't know how they survive. And then all the other boys were saying, 'You're goddam right! We never noticed it! Look at it! We'll have to ask our wives if this is going on with them.' "

Yoko felt it might be wise to describe the situation a little more fully. "I'm not saying that, just because I'm a female, people should address me. I was a filmmaker who was there working. And after we finished the work, the engineer came to John and said, 'Nice working with you, John; nice *meeting* you, Yoko.' A complete difference. But he was *working* with both of us."

John commented, "I used to say, 'You must be paranoiac, saying everyone's ignoring you and treating you badly.' . . . But it's so blatant! . . . If I treated Paul and George or Ringo or any man friend that way, expected from them what I expected from a woman, they'd walk off. They'd say, 'Sod you, I'm leaving.' I started thinking, how am I treating her? How *dare* I ask these things or expect this from her? . . . And then I learned to have a friendship with her, it was the first woman I've ever had a relationship with that wasn't a purely chauvinist pig with his lay. I had never met any woman with any kind of mind before, they'd all been dummies. Then I found out she thought all men were dummies."

"I despised men before I met John," she said.

"It's incredible," he said with undiminished excitement.

He announced the Plastic Ono Band had been stabilized around a nucleus: Klaus Voormann, Jim Keltner, Nicky Hopkins, Phil Spector, "who wants to go on the road as rhythm guitarist for some unknown reason," Yoko, and "possibly Eric Clapton." The band would break out of the way rock stars presented themselves in concerts. "We don't want to have this concept of us, gods and superstars, on stage, blessing the audience with our vast talents. I want to somehow involve the audience, whether it's through theater or happenings going on in the audience, some way the audience expresses themselves at least as much as we do. Because we go up there almost for a kind of therapy."

He praised Chuck Berry, whose lyrics expressed "that grasping, capitalist necessity" in American culture. And "the meter of his lyrics was unbelievable. If you listen to Dylan's *Highway 61* album, you hear Chuck Berry's meter throughout." (John was thinking especially of "Nadine.")

The inevitable question about drugs was asked. "Blaming the kids for taking drugs is a lot of rubbish," John said. "This society we have built for ourselves makes it such that none of us can live without one form of drug or another. What kind of society is that? Instead of just having adverts saying 'We're gonna talk straight about dope and it ain't no good, says Art Linkletter,' I think they ought to get down to deciding why everybody, from Art Linkletter and his beer, to us with our cigarettes, or whatever it is—why are we doing this?" Linkletter had recently testified before Congress on youth and drugs, after his daughter died on an acid trip. In his testimony he denounced the Beatles as "leading missionaries of the acid society." John concluded, "What kind of society is it that makes us have to take drugs to protect ourselves against society?" If John didn't have an answer, he was posing the radical question. But he wasn't distinguishing between relatively harmless drugs like marijuana, and heroin. He also wasn't taking responsibility for his own use of methadone.

The interviewer played a word-association game with John. To "Vietnam" he responded "racism." That was a major change. Two years earlier he had said "insanity." Now he had a terse analysis: "That's all I have to say about Vietnam. I just know one thing: they've never dropped atom bombs or napalm on any whites anywhere." As he perceived the social context in which American policy was made, his understanding of the war was becoming more genuinely political.

"Celebrities feel a void," black activist Dick Gregory said. "They go to drugs, they try to buy up everything they can find. I met Lennon when he was coming out of that. The movement did him a favor. I don't know where he would have gone had it not been for the movement."

"You wonder, when a person gets so rich and famous, where their motivation comes from," Stew Albert said. "You're not hungry any more. Politics was a new hunger for John. It was a new world to learn."

17

"It Ain't Fair, John Sinclair"

John and Yoko read Ed Sanders' poem, "The Entrapment of John Sinclair," and Jerry Rubin convinced them to play at the "Free John Sinclair" rally in Ann Arbor in December 1971, as the first stop of a national anti-Nixon tour. Sinclair had long worked in the vanguard of cultural radicalism—first as a beat poet, then as a central figure in the Detroit radical arts scene, in a big commune, in the local underground press; finally as a political organizer of the White Panther Party and as the manager of an important band, the MC5. He had been in prison for more than two years, serving a ten-year sentence for selling two joints to an undercover agent.

Sinclair was first of all a radical writer. In 1967 he had started a magazine he called *Guerrilla: A Monthly Newspaper of Contemporary Kulchur.* The first issue printed the 1938 manifesto "Towards a Free Revolutionary Art" by André Breton and Diego Rivera, opposing all censorship of art, from the left as well as the right. The classified section of Sinclair's magazine included an ad which read, "Guerrillas wanted! with certain skills—medical, electronic, chemical, mechanical. Applicants should understand that in addition to the use of their skills, they will also be engaged in combat." Applications were to be sent to a post office box in New York's East Village. Another ad read, "LSD guidelines: famous secret of 10,000 trips without a mishap. Send

$1" to Laguna Beach, California. Sinclair resigned from his own magazine when the other editors declared as editorial policy that "hippies will not be, finally, the decisive factor in the coming social, cultural and spiritual revolution on the American continent." The editors were moving in a more orthodox Marxist direction; Sinclair was sticking with the hippies.

Sinclair's band, the MC5, released *Kick Out the Jams* in 1969. Its raw proto-punk energy propelled it into the pages of *Time*, *Newsweek*, the *Village Voice*, and *Rolling Stone*. Sinclair wrote wild manifestos to go with the album: "With our music and our economic genius we plunder the unsuspecting straight world for money and the means to revolutionize its children at the same time. And with our entrance into the straight media we have demonstrated to the honkies that anything they do to fuck with us will be exposed to their children. . . . We don't have guns because we have more powerful weapons—direct access to millions of teenagers is one of our most potent, and their belief in us is another. But we will use guns if we have to. We have no illusions." Sinclair published a book in 1971, *Music and Politics*, which declared, "Music means nothing unless it poses itself as a threat to class hegemony, by, for example, persuasively advocating the destruction of Western thought and the capitalist economic system." Sinclair was not a man for political compromises.

Along with Sinclair's strident argument that rock could mobilize youth to overthrow capitalism, he proclaimed a vile sexism. "We will fuck their daughters in dressing rooms / while their mothers whimper in front of the television set," he wrote in one of his poems. An MC5 sex photo published in the Berkeley *Barb* was particularly offensive. As Ellen Willis wrote at the time, Sinclair "espouses a version of utopia in which women are reduced to faceless instruments of his sexual fantasies."

In October 1968 the White Panther Party was formed, with John Sinclair as Minister of Information. He issued a bloated manifesto declaring that their purpose was to "put the cultural revolution into an explicitly political context by merging the total assault of the culture program of rock and roll and dope and fucking in the streets with armed self-defense and what Eldridge Cleaver and Huey P. Newton called 'the mother country radical movement.' " *Rolling Stone* writer Stu Werbin added, "The White Panthers considered the MC5 their strongest weapon."

The New Left's strategy in trying to bring youth culture together with radical politics was examined by New Left organizer Mark Naison in the magazine *Radical America* in 1970. He named the questions a project like Sinclair's had to face: "What drugs should it encourage people to use and what drugs it must fight; what music and dress and sexuality can it tie in to its politics without sacrificing women's liberation; what programs can it create to link the spontaneity of street culture with a collective spirit and respect for work."

Based on his own experiences as an organizer in the Bronx, Naison concluded, "the movement must build upon youth culture rather than imitate it. Revolutionaries must probe beyond the primitive thrill of seeing working-class kids with long hair and militant rhetoric; they must look beyond a sense of frustration and hatred for the pigs. In every contact with the street culture, they should try to create institutions which bring out a collective spirit, which enable people to be revolutionary between demonstrations, which provide more satisfying ways of meeting basic human needs."

One measure of the political success Sinclair had with his commune and rock groups can be found in the determination of the local authorities to stop him. Lieutenant Warner Stringfellow of the Detroit police told him in 1966, "I know who you are; we'll get you this time and drown you, you worthless prick." They got him in 1969, when Sinclair was arrested for selling two joints to an undercover cop and sentenced in July to ten years.

He continued to work from prison with his commune and bands. An official of the intelligence section of the Michigan state police testified in 1970 before the U.S. Senate Internal Security Subcommittee, the same body whose staff would propose deporting Lennon two years later: "I would like to say at this time that it is the opinion of myself and that of my department that the White Panther Party is working toward obtaining control of large masses of young people for the primary purpose of causing revolution in this country." So they had noticed. "The method used to recruit these people is based on a complete dropout of our society and the adoption of a system involving rock music and the free use of drugs and sex in a setting of commune living. . . . Gentlemen, we would have to consider the White Panther Party as an organization bent on total destruction of the present government of the U.S."

In the meantime, after Sinclair went to prison, the MC5 had split with him and the White Panther Party. "Our political ideas were different from John's," one of them explained in 1972. "His philosophy was rock and roll and dope and fucking in the streets. Fine. But our point of view was much more flippant, crazy, light-hearted." They got a new manager, rock critic Jon Landau, who didn't seem flippant and crazy. Together they turned out *Back in the USA*, a key sixties rock album. (When the group disbanded, Landau went on to manage Bruce Springsteen.)

In prison Sinclair's writing became more eloquent: "Young people know that the only purpose of these [marijuana] laws is to intimidate, harass, and repress young sisters and brothers who have embraced a life style or a culture which you have declared illegal, who don't share your dinosaur's eye view of the world. We know that the laws are designed to stifle cultural and political freedom, to stigmatize young people as felons and criminals, and perhaps worst of all, to cover up for the inability or the unwillingness of the police and prosecutors to stop the traffic of heroin and other narcotics which are slowly killing off the spirit of our people. We know we aren't criminals much less felons, and we know that it is the state itself which must be rehabilitated." John Sinclair had been in the state prison for two and a half years when John and Yoko joined a large group of New Left leaders to hold a giant rally calling for his release.

The rally was the culmination of a long political campaign, which Sinclair himself had directed from inside prison. "When we planned this event," he explained in 1983, "long before we had any idea that John and Yoko would take part in it, we had it timed to put maximum pressure on the legislature to change the marijuana laws before their 1971 session ended. The year before, we had watched them take the bill down to the end and then refuse to vote on it on the last day. I was personally determined not to let this happen again, because I was the one doin' the time, which got to be very gruesome.

"November first my appeal was heard by the Michigan supreme court, and we made a big event out of that. It was videotaped for the first time in Michigan history, and had a lot of media coverage. As the end of the legislative session approached, we took out a full-page ad in the Detroit *Free Press*, calling on the legislature to change the law, with a lot of prominent people as signatories. We called in favors from everybody we knew around the country to come and play or speak at the rally."

John and Yoko had not been part of the original rally plans. The organizers had advertised a series of speeches by movement heavies including Jerry Rubin, Rennie Davis, Dave Dellinger, and Bobby Seale, all fresh from the Chicago Seven trial, with music by Phil Ochs. They worried about filling the hall, so Rubin went to John and Yoko and then announced the good news. Many people refused to believe an ex-Beatle was going to make his first U.S. concert appearance at the rally; John and Yoko agreed to make a tape for radio broadcast saying they really were coming to Ann Arbor.

Concert organizer Peter Andrews said he then got another call: "Stevie Wonder on the line." He'd heard about John's plans to appear. Although he opposed drugs, he supported John Sinclair and wondered if he could appear too. The concert had already sold out hours after John and Yoko's tape was broadcast. The organizers decided to keep Wonder's presence a secret and make it a surprise.

The day before the rally, the legislature voted on the bill. They lowered the penalty for possession of marijuana drastically, from four years to one. The penalty for sale had been twenty years to life; they lowered that to four years.

The concert-rally began with Allen Ginsberg. "I was thrilled to be part of that combination of popular culture and political action," he recalled in 1983. He spent half an hour chanting a long mantra, improvising a song about John Sinclair and the culture that had imprisoned him. Up, Sinclair's new band, played "Jailhouse Rock" for the man behind bars, and a version of Chuck Berry's "Nadine," with new words about a member of the Weather Underground:

> Ber-nadine, sister is that you
> Your picture's in the post office
> But the people are protecting you

Poet and underground rock musician Ed Sanders spoke. Bob Seger played.

Bobby Seale compared Sinclair's imprisonment with the Angela Davis case. In an interview ten years later, he recalled that the audience at the Ann Arbor rally showed a lot of enthusiasm for environmental issues. "I got to speaking and riled the crowd up; I said, 'The greatest form of pollution on the face of this earth is the bullets and bombs falling on the bodies of the Vietnamese!' Fifteen thousand people roared, 'Yeah!' Some girl threw her blouse off. I said, 'The only solution—to pollution—is a people's humane revolution!' More roaring. Now she's buck naked. I said, 'I don't believe this stuff, honestly,' this was that wild hippie stuff. That's what I really remember."

Phil Ochs sang a Phil Ochs song about Nixon. Rennie Davis talked about Vietnam. Dave Dellinger said, "We've got to get John Sinclair out so he can start organizing the music for the people's convention at San Diego next summer," to coincide with the Republican national convention (which was later moved to Miami).

Archie Shepp played avant-garde jazz, followed by Commander Cody playing country rock—testimony to Sinclair's diverse musical tastes and connections. John Sinclair's mother appeared, a spirited woman with a strong midwestern accent. "You can teach more to your parents than your parents taught you," she told the fifteen thousand kids in the arena. "I'm speaking of course from personal experience."

An ecstatic Jerry Rubin yelled, "What we are doing here is uniting music and revolutionary politics to build a revolution around the country! . . . A lot of events like this one will take place between now and San Diego," he said, referring to the plans he had been making with John and Yoko. The Michigan audience may not have appreciated the significance of that statement, but the FBI agents in the audience certainly did, especially when Rubin called for "a million of you to turn up at the Republican national convention to humiliate and defeat Richard Nixon." Thousands yelled, "Right on!"

A telephone hookup was established over the public address system with John Sinclair in jail. His sobs filled the arena as he spoke with his wife and young daughter.

Then surprise guest Stevie Wonder took the stage. He was at the peak of his musical power. "Superstition" would soon be a Number One hit, hard rock the Stones couldn't match. He had been making politically significant music since 1963; at the same time the Beatles released John's "She Loves You," Stevie Wonder's passionate, rolling version of "Blowin' in the Wind" topped the rhythm and blues charts. That night in Ann Arbor Wonder rocked and stomped through "For Once in My Life," bringing the crowd cheering to its feet, then gave a brief speech attacking Nixon and Agnew.

At two A.M. a one-hour wait began. At three o'clock the man who came out was not John Lennon but David Peel. The audience voiced their displeasure. The *Village Voice* reported that Peel, "a fresh breath of 8th Street, obviously didn't give a shit that thousands were trying to boo him off the stage." Peel himself later recalled, "The place is screaming mad. And I'm enjoying every bit of it, because being on the streets, we're conditioned to the boos. It's all the same to me." He sang, "John Lennon Yoko Ono New York City are your people," not exactly the song for Ann Arbor, and another one, the words to which were mainly "Bob Dylan Robert Zimmerman."

———

Finally, seven hours after the concert began, John and Yoko came on: his first concert appearance in the United States since the Beatles waved goodbye at San Francisco's Candlestick Park five years earlier. "The room was so high you felt like laughing or crying with happiness or pinching yourself to see if it was really happening," Jerry Rubin recalled. "John was terrified going onstage," Stu Werbin said. "He was following Stevie Wonder, with a makeshift band, trying out new material. He worried that people might start yelling for 'Hey Jude.' "

John opened with "John Sinclair," followed by Yoko's "Sisters, O Sisters" and John's "Attica State." None had ever been heard before. The basic tracks for these songs on the album *Some Time in New York City* were recorded that night. The song "John Sinclair" is stronger and more intriguing than critics have realized, especially when one sees John singing it in the (unreleased) film *Ten for Two*. John ended each verse with the phrase "gotta set him free," repeating "gotta" no less than fifteen times over a dissonant guitar chord. The lyrics referred to recent revelations that the CIA was involved in heroin trafficking in Southeast Asia on a massive scale while Sinclair rotted in jail for selling two joints.

The song worked on another level as well. The song asked fans to "free John now." Which John? Both had been busted for marijuana and subsequently persecuted, and John seemed to be singing as much about himself as about Sinclair in that line. He made the connection between Sinclair and himself explicit in the next line, "Let him be like . . . me," that is, a "free" man. What seems to have moved John was not the difference between his freedom and Sinclair's imprisonment but rather the similarity between Sinclair's physical imprisonment and his own emotional status as a prisoner in the role of ex-Beatle.

Writers described the Sinclair concert as a kind of left-wing concert for Bangla Desh. Instead of George Harrison and Bob Dylan, Ann Arbor had John Lennon and Stevie Wonder; instead of easing starvation in Asia, they sought to rebuild the movement in the United States. Others measured Ann Arbor against the greatest festival: "What went down here was beyond Woodstock," the *East Village Other* declared. "Woodstock was muddy. That's where what's his name, Peter Townshend, tried to bully Abbie Hoffman off the people's stage for being directly political." Jerry Rubin also saw Ann Arbor as an advance over Woodstock. "We were there not just to get high or go crazy with music, but to free a brother from the Man's jail and to pool our energy to focus attention on political prisoners throughout America." The *Michigan Daily* agreed that the organizers had achieved their goal: "One couldn't distinguish where the songs left off and the politics began."

The alternative press was not unanimous. The editors of the *Outlaw* in St. Louis wrote that, in Ann Arbor, "a cavalcade of stars raised tens of thousands of dollars toward the legal expenses of another movement star. We hope it can start to happen for non-stars too." Leslie Bacon, the young activist who had played backup guitar on stage with John and Yoko, afterward said that they were "the least offensive of the heavies. And that's saying a lot." The *Village Voice* critique was sharper. John and Yoko had "urged political activism and support for John Sinclair, but during the entire evening no one had offered or even hinted at new strategies. It was depressing."

Jerry Rubin provided his answer, explaining the significance of the Sinclair rally in the *East Village Other*. What had happened in Ann Arbor, Rubin wrote, was "not a rock concert; it was not a teach-in. It was some beautiful new combination of rock and political event, some new form of mass celebration and affirmation."

Although music had been the drawing card, it had not been a rock festival. During the previous three years, Rubin wrote, "rock festivals turned into mass freakouts, with ugly rapes and mad pushing and shoving. The sweet pot high turned into a heroin disaster area. Rock music became a new capitalist product and rock stars became movie stars. Our streets turned into Desolation Row. Finally, individually and collectively, we said Stop! . . . We knew we had to root out of our own family the evils of male chauvinism, bad drugs, capitalist rip-offs, and movie stardom.

"Somehow the arrival of John and Yoko in New York has had a mystical and practical effect that is bringing people together again. . . . We need more public events, even a huge political Woodstock at the Republican National Convention next August in San Diego. . . . One, two, three, four, many more Ann Arbors!" That was exactly what the Nixon White House feared.

The concert had an amazing aftermath: Sinclair was set free fifty-five hours after John and Yoko left the stage. "I had already served twice as much time as the maximum sentence under the new law," Sinclair later explained. "The court had refused to give me appeal bond for two and a half years. That to me was the heaviest part of the case. The fact that the constitutionality of the law was being challenged should have made for an automatic release on bond. But a judge ruled that I was a danger to society and therefore shouldn't be granted bond. It was an unprecedented legal maneuver. I would have perhaps taken a different course of action had we anticipated that. They wanted to keep me in there pretty bad. But after the legislature had passed this law, the court didn't have a leg to stand on. So they let me out." Jerry Rubin called the release "an incredible tribute to the power of the people. . . . We won! We freed John! Fifteen thousand people freed John!"

John Sinclair came to Bank Street with his wife Leni, Ed Sanders, and David Peel. "Jerry was in ecstasy handling the introductions," Stu Werbin wrote. "He glowed a burnt pink: 'Is this far out? Did I tell you it was going to be fantastic? Look at this group! Would you look at this group!' " A decade later, Sinclair recalled that "Lennon was very groovy—if that term means anything today. A real sweet, warm, nice, outgoing type of guy."

Werbin transcribed the conversation: "Sinclair talks about juke box music, Lennon talks about his guitar; Leni and Yoko talk about food co-ops and traveling kitchens; Rubin and Sanders talk about New York City; Peel is talking about himself." Then John began explaining his ideas to the Sinclairs. " 'We've been planning to do a tour for some time. Your needs got us out earlier than we anticipated. . . . Now we have a taste of playing again and we can't wait to do more. We want to go around from town to town, doing a concert every other night for a month, at least. We'll pick up local bands along the way in each town.

" 'If some of the bands have enough bread, they can tag along to the next town. We also want to have bands playing outside of the arenas on the streets, on the nights of the concerts. There will be people to take care of all these arrangements. I just want to be a musician and transmit some love back to the people. That's what attracts me most, getting to play with a band again. It will be the regular scene, but without the capitalism. We'll play for the halls and the people will pay to get in but we'll leave our share of the money in the town where it can do the most good. We want it to be the regular scene except we also want to raise some consciousness.' "

The key to John and Yoko's decision, Sinclair later commented, was that they had seen "how the Ann Arbor event was professionally produced and promoted. That was a revelation to them: people on the left could do something properly. The idea was that everybody going out would be committed to the concept, that you wouldn't have just a bunch of technicians and union guys. The tour would be a good time with like-minded people. The idea was to do it on your own terms, with some content, beyond just entertainment. Man, it was very thrilling."

" 'This is gonna be a motherfucker to organize,' Sinclair told Lennon. 'But if it works, we'll be developing strong relationships with youth cadres all over America.' 'It'll work! It's gonna happen!' " Rubin said.

The concert organizers thus considered the Ann Arbor rally to have been a successful test of a new tactic and a new strategy. Jerry Rubin had referred to it as a "political Woodstock"; Dave Dellinger had spoken of a "people's convention"; Yoko had said they did not regard this as a "one-shot affair." For years the New Left had been deeply divided between the media activists and the community organizers. Rubin and Hoffman knew how to grab headlines and TV coverage to denounce the war and attack the warmongers; they favored dramatic confrontations. The community organizers believed the only lasting change would come out of a sustained grassroots mobilization directed not only at the war but at local issues.

The Ann Arbor rally suggested that the two strands of New Left politics could be brought together: put the powers of the media activists at the service of community groups and issues, connect different local struggles within a larger antiwar movement. John Sinclair had been in jail for two and a half years of a ten-year term when the Ann Arbor concert was held; two days later he was released. What else might a newly mobilized local movement accomplish?

"It seemed to me like the great breakthrough that everybody had been waiting for," Allen Ginsberg recalled. "To redo Chicago '68, but in a much wiser way—as a real festival of life, instead of an aggressive contest. I thought that an enormously important social and political and artistic union was taking place. And Lennon seemed to be taking the responsibility."

"The main thing Yoko and I are doing is to change the apathy that all the youth have, especially in America," John explained in an interview at the time. "They think there's nothing to do and it's all over and they want to be on speed and junk and just kill themselves. Our job now is to tell them that there is still hope and we still have things to do. . . . It's only the beginning, we're just in the inception of revolution. . . . We must get them excited about what we can do again.

"That's why we're going to go on the road. But all the shows we'll do are free, or all the money will go to prisoners or poor people. We hope to start touring in America, and eventually go 'round the world, possibly go to China, too."

"And spotlighting the local problems wherever we go," Yoko added.

"So possibly when the Stones are touring America for money, we'll be touring for free. What are you gonna do about that, Mick? *Viva la revolución!*"

"John and Yoko talked to Dylan about coming on the tour," Rubin said. Dylan had written a song with Allen Ginsberg, urging people to attend the concert-rally planned for the Republican national convention. They called it "Come to San Diego." "We talked to Lennon about it," Ginsberg remembered, "and he said we could put it out on Apple. So we went into the Record Plant and put it together. But John split with Allen Klein, and the record never came out." (It was finally released in 1983 on an Allen Ginsberg album, *First Blues.*)

"Dylan came to my house and complained about A. J. Weberman," Rubin recalled. "He said he had been in Israel on his thirtieth birthday and A.J. was picketing his house in New York and it was written up in the papers there so he had to cut his Israel trip short. So I forced A.J. to apologize publicly to Dylan. Yoko actually got him to write the letter in the *Voice.* I thought that when Dylan saw he was free of A.J., he'd be so appreciative that he would agree to tour the country with John and Yoko, raising money for political causes and rallying people to go to San Diego. We'd make musical history as well as political history. The whole thing was going to revive the sixties. That was my plan."

Stew Albert described how he tried to get Dylan to come on the tour. "There was this guy named One-Legged Terry, an Israeli who had lost his leg in an industrial accident on a kibbutz, and sued the kibbutz. He may have been the only person ever to do that. And he won. Dylan was getting into the Jewish thing, and Terry was teaching him Hebrew. The idea was you could maybe get Dylan to do something by selling it to Terry. It made Terry a very popular guy. Terry said he had noticed his charisma was growing.

"Lennon was trying to get Dylan into the tour. We couldn't ever get a commitment from Dylan. But Lennon said he was sure that if the tour started getting big headlines, Dylan would jump into it." John Lennon and Bob Dylan on the road together, working to revive the movement, organizing against Nixon and his henchmen: it would have been amazing! "Yeah," Albert said. "That's why they didn't let it happen."

18

The Apollo Theatre
and the *Mike Douglas Show*

 John and Yoko played the Apollo Theatre in Harlem the weekend of December 17, 1971, in a benefit concert for the families of prisoners shot in the Attica prison uprising. A few months before, 1,200 inmates at the Attica Correctional Facility in upstate New York, most of them black, had seized fifty hostages and taken over D yard. An "observers committee" had been formed, which included attorney William Kunstler and columnist Tom Wicker. They met with the inmates and drafted thirty far-reaching demands: minimum wages for prisoners' work, religious freedom (demanded by Black Muslims), competent medical care, uncensored reading material, more fresh fruit and less pork, and the establishment of a mechanism to respond to prisoners' grievances. The state corrections commissioner agreed to all the demands except two: amnesty for inmates accused of injuring guards during the uprising, and appointment of a new warden. The demands he accepted would have constituted a model for prison reform if they had been implemented. The observers committee pleaded with Governor Nelson Rockefeller to come to Attica and break the stalemate. He refused.

Seventeen hundred state troopers, National Guard soldiers, and sheriff's deputies charged D yard the morning of September 13, shooting from the walls, from underground tunnels, and from helicopters. Many fired dum-dum bullets that had been outlawed by the Geneva Convention. Some inmates were shot more than ten times. Initially, only injured guards received medical treatment. Some prisoners were allowed to bleed to death. Thirty-two prisoners and ten guards were killed and eighty-five were wounded.

The New York *Times* reported that "prisoners slashed the throats of utterly helpless, unarmed guards," and declared in an editorial that "the deaths of these persons reflect a barbarianism wholly alien to civilized society." But the next day a courageous county medical examiner revealed the identity of the real barbarians: all ten hostages had been killed by National Guard gunfire.

At the benefit concert for the families, 1,500 people filled the theater to capacity. Master of ceremonies Livingston Wingate, executive director of the New York Urban League, told them, "The Black community will never forget that valiant brothers, who refused to remain ignored, brutalized and hopeless men, were murdered." Aretha Franklin sang.

Then Wingate announced that "John and Yoko Lennon" had "written a new song so that the world will never forget what happened." They sang "Attica State." The chorus, declaring that everyone lives in Attica State, was typical of the rhetorical excess of the period: society is a prison. But John seemed to identify with the prisoners. "All they want is the truth," he sang, echoing a line from "Gimme Some Truth," on the recently released *Imagine* album. Although the song had awkward lines, it also had some strong ones, expressing how people felt after Attica: "Fear and hatred cloud our judgment / free us all from endless night." At the end John said in a quiet voice, "It's an honor—and a pleasure—to be here at the Apollo, and for the reasons we're all here."

Yoko sang "Sisters, O Sisters" and received polite applause. John returned to the mike and said, "Some of you might wonder what I'm doing here with no drummers, nothing like that. Well, you might know I lost my old band, or I left it. I'm putting an electric band together, but it's not ready yet. Things like this keep coming up, so I'll have to just busk it. So I'm gonna sing a song you might know: it's called 'Imagine.' " He sang, beautifully, playing his own acoustic guitar with no other accompaniment—a unique performance.

It was the ex-Beatle's second concert appearance in the United States in five years, in the media capital of America, but the straight press ignored it. The only news or reviews appeared in Harlem's *Amsterdam News* and in Liberation News Service. John quietly contributed a large sum to the Attica Defense Fund, perhaps $10,000.

In subsequent days John did his best with the announcer's suggestion that the song should keep the memory of Attica alive. He wore a button reading "Indict Rockefeller for Murder—Attica" and sang the song at virtually all his subsequent concerts and TV appearances in 1972: the *David Frost Show,* the *Mike Douglas Show,* and the One-to-One concert in Madison Square Garden.

He got a taste of middle America's politics in January 1972, when he sang the song on the *David Frost Show* and invited the audience to discuss it. "You're making it sound like the only worthwhile people in this world are people who committed crimes and were put away," a woman said, her voice breaking with emotion.

John rushed to reply: "When we say 'poor widowed wives,' we're not just talking about prisoners' wives, we're talking about policemen's wives, anyone that was there—"

"They must have done something wrong in the first place, or they wouldn't have been there!" a man shouted, ignoring John's explanation.

John disregarded him and continued making his point. "We're like newspapermen, only we sing about what's going on instead of writing about it."

"Wait till they kill your son or daughter or your mother or father!" the angry man shouted. More people started yelling: "You talk about what society's done to them—"

John shouted over the din, "*We* are society. . . . We are *all* responsible for *each other!* We have to be."

"Well then, why don't you become policemen—" the first woman asked rhetorically.

"Because we're *not* policemen. We're singers. You have to tell people what's going on. In England you have to tell people what's going on in Ireland. It's the same." He announced that he and Yoko had attended the benefit for families of Attica victims, "to show we care and that we don't just live in ivory towers in Hollywood watching movies about ourselves. We care about what's going on—in New York, in Harlem, in Ireland, in Vietnam, in China."

A man in the audience told John, "Walk through one of those neighborhoods at two in the morning. You wouldn't be singin' about the people who ended up in jail for muggin' ya."

"I'm not singing only about the people who are locked up in jail. This song says forty-three people were killed, forty-three on *both sides.*"

The man insisted on his point: "Fine, but if they hadn't of done something wrong they wouldn't have been there."

John decided to respond to that argument. "Why did they do something wrong? Because they never had a chance in life."

Yoko asked, "Can you say you've never done anything wrong in your life?"

"There are degrees of wrong," another member of the audience argued cogently.

John replied, "I understand that society hasn't worked out what to do with people who kill and violent people. But there are a lot of people in jail who aren't violent, who don't kill, and they're in there for no reason at all, and then they go mad in jail." The audience divided, some booing and some cheering. "Only a small minority are actually barmy enough to have to be restrained," John argued. "Let's make it human for them while they're in there."

"But this song glorifies them!" a woman shouted.

"We're not glorifying them," John insisted. He spoke emphatically: "This song will come and go. But there will be another Attica tomorrow." That was a forceful conclusion. Frost broke for a commercial.

The same month, John appeared at the trial of the Harlem Six, black members of a religious group who had been charged with murder six years earlier and held in jail without a trial and without bail the entire time. Stew Albert recalled that, in the courtroom, "there was a guy seated a few rows ahead of us who turned around and started looking at Lennon. He was wearing a Marine belt buckle, had short hair, a severe face, and was tall and lean and muscular. Then he got up and walked over to our row and stood in front of Lennon and went through some karate motions. Then he went back to his seat, without saying a word. It was scary. I went and told the bailiffs, and they got rid of the guy. John was shook up, but he was a gutsy guy, and he didn't let it get to him."

At the end of the day John went outside and made a statement about the issues in the trial. "Racism is a hard thing for whites to understand. It takes a lot to open your eyes, but I see it now because I'm married to a Japanese."

=

In mid-February John and Yoko co-hosted the *Mike Douglas Show* for an entire week in one of the more remarkable programs in the history of daytime TV. At the time, Douglas had one of the highest-rated talk shows in the country. John and Yoko picked half the guests, and Douglas the other half. Guests included Bobby Seale, Jerry Rubin, Ralph Nader, and Chuck Berry, who appeared the same day as the Nixon appointee who supervised the Peace Corps.

The studio audience faced a warmup man before the show opened. "Okay, group, you already know that John and Yoko are here, they've had a couple of hit records and everything, but this is the *Mike Douglas Show,* you know, and Mike will be coming out first to do a song and I know he'd appreciate it if you give him a really big hand too. He doesn't know I'm out here, so when you give him a big hand it will be a big surprise to him."

Ten seconds later Douglas came on stage to enthusiastic applause and burst into a Paul McCartney hit, "Michelle." When he finished, the audience applauded enthusiastically again. Introducing John, Douglas said, "The song I just sang is written by this gentleman." Still more applause.

John was on his best behavior. "You sang it very well. I wrote the middle-eight."

Douglas: "That's usually the toughest part. . . . What would you like to talk about this week?"

"Love, peace, communication, women's lib—"

"Racism," Yoko injected.

John continued, "—racism, war, prisons." Douglas announced that Ralph Nader would be a guest. John said, "He's the kind of guy that sets an example. He *does* something. I asked him today, 'When you gonna run for President?' She can be minister of peace and I'll be minister of music." The audience laughed excited TV laughter and applauded.

Elephant's Memory appeared for the first time with John and Yoko, and played "It's So Hard" from the *Imagine* album. Stew Albert later explained, "He wanted them because they had a brass sound, which distinguished them from the Beatles. John thought that McCartney with Wings had gone too much into repeating the Beatles sound."

Then Yoko explained a project: "Call a stranger every day and say 'I love you—pass this message along.' By the end of the year everybody in the world will have gotten your love. There are so many lonely people in this world, and we have to tell them we're connected." Douglas agreed to give it a try. Yoko dialed a number at random. When a woman answered, she heard, "This is Yoko. I love you. Please pass this message along."

The audience giggled with nervous sympathy for the woman. She paused, said, "Yes, all right," in a singsong voice, and hung up—a generous response to an inane call.

Yoko explained her "mending piece," which was more imaginative. She would start with a broken teacup. Each day on the show she and Mike would put some pieces back together. At the end of the week, the cup would be mended. Douglas said he didn't get the point. The first day's show ended.

The Tuesday show opened up with Douglas singing Ringo's "A Little Help from My Friends." Yoko asked everyone in the audience to simultaneously shout out the first thing that came to mind. They did it. "That clears the air," John said.

Yoko read from Douglas' cue card, "Would you say, John, that you've become very political and even radical in your thinking?"

Douglas, a bit miffed, said, "How do you expect me to remember all that? I've got to write it down." They showed a clip from the *Imagine* film, John singing "Oh My Love." Yoko brought out her guest, filmmaker Barbara

Loden, whose husband was Elia Kazan. They discussed the problems of women artists who have famous spouses.

Then came the Jerry Rubin segment. Douglas introduced him: "Quite honestly, my feelings are quite negative about this young man, but John wanted him on the show."

"And Yoko," Yoko interjected.

"John and Yoko—I'm curious to know why you want him on the show."

John explained, "When we first met Abbie and Jerry, we were both nervous. I thought, 'Be careful, bomb-throwing freaks.' But we were both pleasantly surprised. They weren't anything like their media images." But Rubin claimed to be a virtuoso at manipulating his media image with outrageous and irresistible stunts. "We thought we should give him a chance to show what he's actually doing and actually thinking about and what his hopes are for the future. . . . Because he's a movement hero."

The audience applauded dutifully as Rubin joined them. He said, "Nixon has automated the war in Vietnam so that it's machines killing people; created a situation where forty-three people can be murdered at Attica; created a situation where four kids can be killed at Kent State."

John started interviewing him. "A) What is the movement? B) Did it die, and what are the differences in it now, compared to four years ago?"

Rubin talked quickly and nervously. "The movement is—I hope—everybody watching television. It doesn't have any narrow definition." He was getting off to a shaky start.

For encouragement, Yoko murmured, "Very beautiful."

"It's all black people right now in jail, who I know watch this show, because when I was in jail the show was on. It's all the students, it's all the people who believe that this country, since it's capitalist, is inherently oppressive, and also tries to dominate the world. I was in Chile in summer and saw how this country dominates the economy of Chile. The way the movement has changed is that the rhetoric has grown calmer, because the repression is so heavy that anyone who does anything gets arrested, jailed, killed."

Douglas could not contain his anger. "This is the only country in the world where a man can say something like this on television," he announced.

Rubin replied, "I've got five years in jail facing me for saying things like this. So it's just not true."

Douglas returned to the cue cards. "I hear that you're against drugs. Do you want to elaborate on that?"

John prompted Rubin: "Heroin."

Rubin picked it up: "No, I'm not against drugs, just heroin." The audience laughed and applauded. "As the Knapp Commission showed, the police are protectors of the heroin trade. And heroin is used against black people and against young white people right now."

John declared, "Heroin's a killer."

Rubin continued, "Too many young kids are taking downers and heroin because they see no future for themselves in this country, because they have no hope for change in this country, they see no decent communal life in which they can be creative and help themselves. As a revolutionary movement, we have to build an alternative to that despair"—a fine statement.

John asked his next question. "A few years ago you said, 'Let's not vote, voting's irrelevant.' I had that feeling too, and I never did vote in my life. But now you're saying, 'Register to vote.' That doesn't seem very radical to me. What's the change from two years ago?"

"There's an eighteen-year-old vote this time. We think that all young people should vote as a bloc, just like we think women should vote as a bloc. We've got to get Nixon out of the White House. We've got to end the automated warfare in Vietnam. We've got to end the despair—" Suddenly Douglas' theme song swelled up and drowned Rubin out, indicating that the director had called for a hasty commercial break. "Wait a minute!" Rubin shouted. "We'll be right back!" Douglas shouted.

When they returned, Rubin had won permission to finish his point, but not to criticize Nixon by name. He did a good job: "Everybody should register to vote—that's power, if we all vote together. We shouldn't vote for any candidate who doesn't withdraw everything from Vietnam. We ought to go to both conventions, in Miami and San Diego, and nonviolently make our presence felt."

John emphasized, "Nonviolently."

Rubin continued, "Because if we do anything any other way, we'll be killed. That's the kind of country we live in." The audience booed.

Douglas seized the initiative: "You don't really believe that," he said with parental disapproval.

Rubin replied, "Kent State. Kent State." But he realized he had gone too far.

John tried to rescue him: "Look, everybody's entitled to their opinion. . . . Whatever is going on, we're all responsible for."

Douglas pulled out a moth-eaten cliché. "You talk about everything that is wrong. What do you think is right about this country?"

Rubin: "What's right is that there are people in this country who want to change it."

Douglas: "That's all?"

"The system is corrupt. But the children of America want to change the country. That's what's beautiful."

John said, "Right on!" The audience took its cue from him and burst into applause. They were easily swayed.

Douglas kept pushing Rubin. "Why are you so bitter about a country that affords you the opportunity to get on national television and say these things?" He had a distinctly self-congratulatory tone.

"Because I know what it does to Indians, blacks, and Vietnamese, and I know what it's doing to me for saying these things."

John felt Rubin was becoming too negative. "The reason for you to go on a show whose audience is not geared to you," he prompted, "is that you have trust in enough of those people."

John was smart, and Rubin picked up on it immediately. "Yes, we have tremendous faith in the people in this country."

"Speaking of trust," Douglas said, "didn't you say in your book *We Are Everywhere* that you wouldn't trust anyone who hadn't ever done time? Do you trust John and Yoko? They haven't done time." Douglas spoke as if he had completely demolished Rubin.

"Oh, yes they have," Rubin said confidently. Douglas was stunned to hear this.

"He means symbolically!" John shouted with frustration.

Rubin saw Douglas' problem. "They've suffered, they've experienced oppression. He's Irish, she's Japanese."

John added, "And every woman is included—they've all suffered, 'done time.' You can't take it literally." The second show ended.

═══

That segment was scrutinized by the FBI, whose Section 14 recorded and transcribed it. Their report classified Rubin as an "extremist" and John as "SM-NL" (Security Matter–New Left). Their transcript emphasized that Rubin had said, "I'm working very hard with people all over the country to defeat Nixon." The FBI seemed to think its tasks included helping Nixon's reelection campaign. It distributed ten copies to field offices throughout the country, as well as the Secret Service, the Alcohol, Tobacco and Firearms Division, and the U.S. naval investigative services.

Wednesday's show began with Douglas singing "I Whistle a Happy Tune," which came not from Lennon and McCartney but from Rodgers and Hammerstein. Yoko announced that she would sing "Sisters, O Sisters." John quipped, "It's not about nuns."

This was Chuck Berry day. John said, "When I hear good rock, the caliber of Chuck Berry, I just fall apart, I have no other interest in life, the world could be ending and I wouldn't care. Rock and roll—it's a disease of mine."

Douglas said, "In those days, songs didn't have messages"—a swipe at John's recent efforts at topical music.

John corrected him gently: "Chuck Berry's lyrics were intelligent. In the fifties, when people were singing about virtually nothing, he was writing social

Beatles album–burning, Waycross, Georgia, August 1966

After auctioning their hair at Sotheby's for Michael X
and his Blackhouse in London, February 1970

With Jerry Rubin and Abbie Hoffman,
New York City, fall 1971

"The Working-Class Hero Turns Red,"
July 1971

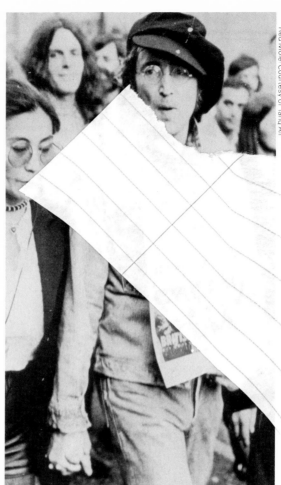

The *OZ*/IRA demonstration, London, August 1971

**Demonstrating
with Onondaga Indians,
Syracuse, New York,
October 1971**

Courtesy of Danny Schechter

**"Interviewed" by Danny
Schechter at the International
Feminist Planning Conference,
Harvard University, Cambridge,
Massachusetts, June 1973**

**Peace rally, New York City,
May 1972**

UPI

John and Yoko's first U.S.
concert, Ann Arbor, Michigan,
December 1971

Outside U.S. District Court,
New York City, August 1974

FREE JOHN SINCLAIR AND ALL POLITICAL PRISONERS!

JOHN SINCLAIR FREEDOM RALLY

NATION

FRIDAY
DEC
10
1971

FRIDAY
DEC
10
1971

SPEAKERS
RENNIE DAVIS · ALLEN GINSBERG · FR. JAMES GROPPI · SHEILA
MURPHY LABOR DEFENSE COALITION · JERRY RUBIN · ED SANDERS · BOBBY SEALE BLACK PANTHER PARTY
LENI SINCLAIR RAINBOW PEOPLE'S PARTY · MARGE TABANKIN NSA · JONNIE LEE TILLMON N.W.R.O.
MUSIC
JOHN LENNON & **YOKO ONO** & FRIENDS
ARCHIE SHEPP & ROSWELL RUDD WITH CJQ · PHIL OCHS
UP · COMMANDER CODY AND HIS LOST PLANET AIRMEN · JOY OF COOKING · DAVID PEEL ·
MCs BOB RUDNICK & ANNE LeVASSEUR
SOUND BY VULCAN

CRISLER ARENA
ANN ARBOR

**John gets his green card,
New York City, July 1976**

**Yoko's photo of John and
Sean, 1975**

comment, songs with incredible meter to the lyrics, which influenced Dylan, me, and many other people."

Yoko felt he'd gone too far. "Chuck Berry's songs have a beautiful spirit. They don't have to say something directly political."

John read from a cue card, "If you tried to give rock and roll another name, you might call it Chuck Berry. In the fifties, a whole generation worshipped his music. Today, past and present came together. And the message is, 'Hail, hail rock and roll.' " Together they sang a ragged "Memphis," chatted, and then sang a strong "Johnny B. Goode," about the boy named Johnny whose mother told him some day he would lead a band.

Yoko brought out a macrobiotic chef, who taught John and Douglas to make his kind of pizza. John introduced a biofeedback expert: "It used to be only yogis and people in the East could do things like lower their own blood pressure." Things were getting a little flaky. The third day ended.

Thursday began with Douglas singing "Don't Worry about Me." John sang "Imagine." Douglas asked John about his father, presumably because John wanted to talk about him on TV. "He knew where I was all my life— I lived in the same house with my auntie up till twenty-four or twenty-five. . . . He put a lot of pressure on me in the press. I opened the paper and it said, 'John's dad is washing dishes and why isn't John looking after him?' I said, 'Because he never looked after me.' So I looked after him for the same period he looked after me, about four years. Then I said, 'Now you can go out and find your own way too.' "

Yoko wanted to change the tone: "Also they look alike."

John: "He looks a little like one of me. He's only five foot tall."

Douglas: "What is he doing now?"

"I guess he's retired. He just married a twenty-three-year-old girl. He's had another son. So he's getting along fine. . . . When I was sixteen I reestablished a relationship with my mother for about four years. She taught me music. . . . Unfortunately, she was run over by an off-duty policeman who was drunk at the time. In spite of all that, I still don't have a hate-the-pigs attitude." That movement term—"pigs"—was a shock on TV. "I think everybody's human. But it was very hard for me, and it still comes out from time to time."

It was also the day Bobby Seale was scheduled. He had brought two young blacks, a student leader from Oakland who talked about a national conference of black students, and a medical student who talked about sickle-cell anemia, a hereditary disease of black people. John interviewed him, asking why there hadn't been more research seeking a cure. Then John introduced Seale, chairman of the Black Panther Party. A Gallup poll that month showed that 60 percent of black people considered the Panthers a source of pride for their community. Seale described the Panthers' "survival programs." They ran twelve community health clinics, at which thirty thousand people had been tested for sickle-cell anemia. They had their Angela Davis free food program, a free shoe factory, a clothing factory, a program to provide transportation so that families could visit prisoners, and a program to provide money for indigent prisoners to spend at prison commissaries.

John asked, "What is the philosophy of the Black Panther Party? A lot of people don't know."

"Our philosophy is what we call intercommunalism," Seale explained. "We're not nationalists. We don't believe in nationalism. Nationhood has always been hooked up to superiority. It's akin to racism."

"That's why I said in my song, 'Imagine no countries,' " John commented.

Seale continued, "Our understanding of the economics of intercommunalism is based on a redistribution of the wealth—that's where our survival programs have become significant. Three quarters of the world is born oppressed. We practice intercommunalism in the black community so that others can learn. If the poor and oppressed people start uniting around basic programs that serve their basic interests, they won't have to be poor."

Yoko played straight man: "How can individuals help you?"

"We'd like for as many people as possible to come and check us out and realize that we're not people to be scared of. . . . The press done one of the dirtiest things five years ago when the Black Panther Party got started. They said the Black Panther Party picked up guns to go into the white community to kill white people. We've been here five years, we've never done that, that was never our intention. Our intention was to defend ourselves against unjust, brutalizing, racist attacks on black people in the black community—attacks by police and other racists. But you defend yourself not only with guns, but also with these basic programs. Because violence is also manifest in hunger, in rats and roaches, in dilapidated living conditions. People can send donations, but we'd like for black people to actually come in and work for these programs, because they're actually their programs." They showed film of Yoko singing "Mrs. Lennon" from the *Imagine* film. The show ended.

Friday began with Douglas singing "Day In, Day Out" in his best Frank Sinatra style. The audience asked questions of John and Yoko. The first was from a young woman, who wondered whether demonstrations helped: "I want to know what I can do—me, just personally, to help people get better and, like, help the peace thing."

John said, "People tend to think somebody's going to save them—a President, or whoever your hero might be. But it's only us all deciding to do something. Just making that decision—'I want to do something'—is a start." Yoko said, "You can start with the people around you." They didn't have any real answer for the woman's straightforward question.

John sang "Luck of the Irish," repeating that the proceeds from the song went to the civil rights movement in Northern Ireland. Yoko sang a Japanese folk song. Douglas closed by singing, "To John and Yoko, all my thanks for being my co-hosts / I'd like to say this week with you was really the most." The week was over.

During the week conflicts had broken out with Douglas behind the scenes. Bobby Seale described one: "The central committee of the Party voted that on my day I had to go on last. When we got there, Mike Douglas said, 'No, he's going on first, where we've got him slotted.' And I told Yoko, 'No, I'm not going on at that time, and that's all there is to it.' They could show my films of the breakfast program. And Yoko got on my side, outright. And went and bawled out Mike, called him a racist bastard or something. John and Yoko told Mike, 'These guys are revolutionaries, you shouldn't push them around. If you don't let Bobby go on when he wants to, we'll leave the show right now.' Shocked Mike Douglas. So I went on last."

Most of John and Yoko's political guests had been defendants in the Chicago conspiracy trial. Obviously this was Rubin's idea. Seale and Rubin had become movement celebrities because of the news coverage of the Chicago conspiracy trial. They were picked for those roles not by the movement, but first of all by the government prosecutors and then by the media. Rubin in particular had been sharply criticized by many sections of the New Left. But if they were not legitimate movement representatives, that wasn't John's fault. That was the responsibility of the American left itself, disorganized and represented by superstars almost by default. John was working with the movement as it existed, for better or for worse. On this occasion it is especially clear that he shared in its limitations as well as its achievements.

Stu Werbin recalled leaving the studio after finishing the show. "The limousine's at the curb, and there were a couple of thousand people waiting and screaming for the *Beatles.* John blanched and started to shake. Yoko, Jerry, and I sort of pushed him in. For five minutes he was white and couldn't talk. Finally he said, 'Don't they know the Beatles are over?' "

19

Front-Page Songs

John wrote "Luck of the Irish" after civil rights demonstrators in Northern Ireland were fired on by British troops in January 1972; thirteen demonstrators were killed. "Bloody Sunday" provoked massive Irish protests against the British. Six days later John and Yoko eagerly joined a demonstration in New York organized by the Transport Workers Union and sang their new Irish song. When they got back to Bank Street, John dictated a press release, speaking energetically and referring to himself in the third person.

"Today at Forty-fourth and Fifth Avenue, outside the BOAC building, there was a demonstration in protest against the internment and killing of Irish people in the civil rights movement. Present amongst many people—five or six thousand—were senators and congressmen, also John and Yoko, Jerry Rubin and Stew Albert. John and Yoko sang 'Luck of the Irish,' the proceeds of which they announced would be donated to the Irish civil rights movement.

"The police were particularly cooperative as most of them were Irish. The meeting was a great meeting and it got lots of media coverage. The weather was freezing cold." Yoko shouted from the background, "With a beautiful blue sky." John continued, "The Lennons looked like refugees—John hadn't shaved for a few days, and Yoko was wrapped up like an Eskimo. At first they went 'round unrecognized, but finally they were announced.

"The people joined in singing with the Lennons and great applause and shouting was heard, especially on such lines as 'Why are the English there anyway?' and 'The bastards commit genocide.'" John was delighted to report that his protest song had gone over so well. "The whole thing was a success, there was no violence, and if you hear otherwise it's a lie." He was having a hard time maintaining his radio-announcer demeanor. "The mood of the crowd was a happy one under the circumstances, considering we were all there to show our sympathy for the thirteen people who were mercilessly shot down by the British imperialists." He uttered that term with the confidence of a political veteran.

"The purpose of the meeting was to show solidarity with the people who are going to march tomorrow in Northern Ireland. Representatives of the IRA spoke, including some secret leaders who had flown in especially for the meeting, considering its importance to try to awaken the American Irish who are rather middle-class." Here he broke off for a moment to review the statement, and he returned to make a correction.

"We wish to stress that the song by the pop stars was not the important part of the meeting, but the gathering of the people and the sincerity with which they gathered, and their friendly spirit, was." He had to be reminded, but he wanted to emphasize the element of democratic participation.

"The speeches were mainly a denunciation of the British in Ireland, telling them to get out because they had no right there. Also there were lots of words spoken about the fact that the Protestant Northerners had been shipped over by the English in the nineteenth century to colonize the North. It was decided that a referendum by the whole of Ireland, including Eire, should decide what country they belong to." John was delighted to be explaining the political issues. Yoko injected a different note: "The crisp clean air represented and symbolized the atmosphere of the people there."

John continued his statement, still in the third person. "Before John and Yoko sang, Lennon made a short speech about his Irish ancestry, and the main thing he said was 'My name is Lennon and you can guess the rest,' which got a great round of applause from the people." He wanted everyone to know about his success as a political speaker. "And he stressed the fact of his Liverpool upbringing, an area eighty percent dominated by Irish descent. Lennon reminded the crowd that in England, Liverpool is called 'the capital of Ireland.'" He said that was everything he could think of.

Then he gave instructions to transcribe the statement and divide it into paragraphs with grammatically correct sentences. His first priority was to get it out to the English music papers. People were assigned to call UPI and Reuters, and John called a friendly reporter at the *Daily News,* asking, "Do you think you can make sure it's a nice one in your paper?" Not many people could put it so directly. This was why John had said, "Publicity is my trade."

John, Yoko, and Jerry Rubin picked photos to be released, and watched the first TV news report, an extremely brief one. John asked, "Is that all?" Rubin replied, "That's all." "Oh fuck," John muttered.

He spoke on the phone with someone who conveyed a report that had just come over the radio news. John said with excitement, "They had me saying, 'Any government that doesn't allow demonstrations like this should be put away,' and Yoko saying, 'There should be demonstrations like this all over the world.'" Their publicity efforts were successful; the story made page one of the *Times* in London.

The next day in Northern Ireland, twenty-five thousand people defied a government ban to march in protest against the killings. The leaders of the march included Bernadette Devlin and Vanessa Redgrave.

Subsequently an interviewer asked John whether his support for the IRA was compatible with his opposition to violence. "I don't know how I feel about them, because I understand why they're doing it and if it's a choice between the IRA and the British army, I'm with the IRA. But if it's a choice between violence and nonviolence, I'm with nonviolence. So it's a very delicate line." So far he had only restated the question. "Our backing of the Irish people is done really through the Irish Civil Rights, which is not the IRA." That was more consistent with his position. He had another point he wanted to emphasize: "I'm always getting accused of hopping from subject to subject—'one minute he's on meditation, the next he's on peace.' . . . Well, the Irish thing isn't new for me. I was always on the Irish thing."

Later John and Yoko issued a statement responding to British critics. "Of course we sympathize with soldiers who are killed or wounded, anywhere, as we feel for the American soldiers forced to fight in Vietnam. But our deepest sympathies must surely go to the victims of British and American imperialism." They reviewed the history by which the English made Ireland a colony, settling English people there in the nineteenth century. "If the Northern Protestants so desperately want to be British, let them be repatriated to Britain. . . . We ask for the American Irish to wake up to their responsibility in the same way the Jewish people respond to the problems of Israel."

This political cause proved to be the only one John shared with Paul McCartney, who released his own song, "Give Ireland Back to the Irish," shortly before John's record of "Luck of the Irish" came out. Paul's song was immediately banned from British radio and TV. EMI protested that the song was not anti-British because it contained no incitement to violence. Despite the ban on airplay, Paul's song reached Number Twenty on the English charts, remaining for six weeks (and eight weeks on the American charts). John wanted to release his "Luck of the Irish" as a single, with a photo of him singing it at the New York demonstration on the cover. A few copies were sent out to disc jockeys, but the response was so negative the single was cancelled.

John's lyrics made even the most sympathetic fans wince. "God on their side" rhymed with "genocide." Killing thirteen people was not genocide. That kind of rhetorical excess, characteristic of the movement in this period of disintegration, destroyed whatever credibility the song had. Moreover, this song about genocide had a wildly inappropriate tune in the style of an Irish folk song. The verse before "genocide" suggested that people "walk over rainbows like leprechauns." That must have been Yoko's advice to the IRA. Finally, the basic concept of the song offended the Irish. John said if you had their luck, "you'd wish you were dead . . . you'd wish you were English instead." When an American Lennon fan sang the song in a pub in Belfast that year, he was nearly beaten up and forced to take it back.

The struggle against British imperialism in Northern Ireland was an obvious cause for Lennon, but all he did was write the song and participate in one demonstration. Kate Millett commented, "It takes being there a while —and with political people—before you really can claim this cause which has been creeping up on you forever. He must have felt a certain foolishness: Liverpool Irish, what's that?" Still, he loved his one demonstration for Ireland. He should have done more.

Early in 1972 John wrote "Angela," about Angela Davis, a black radical and intellectual. At the same time Mick Jagger wrote "Sweet Black Angel" and Dylan wrote "George Jackson." It was a unique moment in the history of rock's relation to radical politics, as each of rock's three greatest artists was moved to sing about the same events.

Angela Davis had been a student of Herbert Marcuse's, and was fired from the faculty of the UCLA philosophy department by the university's Board of Regents after an undercover agent named her as a member of the Communist Party. She had become a leader of the campaign to free Black Panther George Jackson and two others from Soledad Prison, where Jackson had been serving a one-year-to-life sentence for a seventy-dollar gas station robbery. In August 1970 George's younger brother Jonathan Jackson entered the Marin County Courthouse and drew a carbine. Joined by two prisoners, including Soledad Brother Ruchell Magee, he took the judge, the district attorney, and several jurors hostage, apparently seeking to exchange them for the Soledad Brothers, three black men whose imprisonment had become a *cause célèbre* for the New Left. Their van was attacked by prison guards, leaving the judge and three black men dead, including Jonathan; the D.A. and the jurors were seriously wounded.

Angela had bought the guns, so the D.A. charged her with kidnapping, conspiracy, and murder. She went underground and was captured at the end of December. In August 1971, a year after the Marin shootout, George Jackson was shot in the back and killed by San Quentin guards who claimed he was attempting to escape. While John and Yoko sang their new song "Angela" on the *David Frost Show* in January 1972, Angela herself was awaiting trial in the county jail in San Jose, California.

"We got a request 'Will you please write a song about Angela?' from the Angela Davis people," John later explained. "So there, how do you write a song about somebody you don't really know?" John and Yoko's song declared their solidarity with her. It may be the worst song John ever wrote. But his political commitments were clear: he wanted to put his music and his status as a rock star to use in defending her. The song "Angela" suggested the difficulties John faced in trying to create music that would directly address particular issues.

Dylan's song "George Jackson," released as a single in 1971, was decent, moving in parts, and much better than John and Yoko's "Angela"—especially where Dylan sang about the prison guards who watched and cursed Jackson, who feared both his power and his love. The song immediately became the object of controversy. For months A. J. Weberman had been denouncing Dylan for abandoning radical politics. Now Weberman told Liberation News Service that the song showed Dylan was at last "coming around." As a result, "I'm never going to harass him or his family again." The L.A. *Free Press* had a similar interpretation. They ran a picture of Dylan on the cover, with the headline "He's Back." Anthony Scaduto, just finishing his Dylan book, asked eleven "experts" to listen to the new song. Eight "felt strongly that Dylan was not being honest in the song, that he had written it to get all the Webermans of this world off his back." Scaduto published this finding in a Dylan profile in the *New York Times Magazine. Rolling Stone* agreed with the conclusion.

Robert Christgau dissented. "This is ugly nonsense," he wrote, arguing that both sides were equally wrong. "George Jackson" was neither phony protest nor real protest. It was Dylan's "responding with real human sympathy to a hideous assassination." Scaduto eventually came around to the same position. "It works, as music, and as an effective verbalization of the anguish so many felt over the killing." He changed his mind about Dylan's motives after learning from several mutual friends that Dylan wrote the song after he finished reading Jackson's book *Soledad Brother.*

"George Jackson" got some airplay and would have gotten more if the lyrics had not included the word "shit." It peaked at Number Thirty-three in the charts. Dylan apparently cooled to the song. He never put it on an album, even though he released more than a dozen in the next decade. Today it is virtually impossible to obtain.

Mick Jagger's "Sweet Black Angel," on *Exile on Main Street,* was a completely different kind of song. The lyrics made no explicit reference to Angela and were extremely hard to hear. But the song was good enough to play over and over, and repeated playings revealed that Mick was alluding to the Marin Courthouse escape attempt, the injustice of Angela's trial, and her own heroism: she was in chains, but she continued her struggle. Jagger also hinted that he was turned on by her heroism. John and Yoko had gone on national TV to declare their support for Angela; Dylan had released a single pointing out the injustice of George Jackson's prison death. Jagger, in contrast, avoided making any kind of public statement with his music. He did sing discreetly about his admiration for her. Although "Sweet Black Angel" was the best song of the three, it had no political intentions.

=====

John recorded "Woman Is the Nigger of the World" in March 1972 and performed it for the first time on the *Dick Cavett Show* in May. The song declared John's commitment to feminism. The refrain was a great cry that rolled along, sung with intense feeling. The words described many of the ways men oppressed women: they tell them not to be so smart, then put them down for being dumb, then put them on a pedestal. They made them "paint their face and dance." John had come a long way since his 1965 song, telling a "little girl" that, if he caught her with another man, she should "Run for Your Life."

Kate Millett defended "Woman Is the Nigger of the World." "It was endlessly argued that women have nothing to complain about, blacks are more oppressed," she recalled in 1982. "But even if you said this was only a metaphor, it provoked a great deal of male chauvinist feeling. It was a shocking thing to say. And it made John instantly unpopular. I think a man takes a considerable risk in putting his neck out for a woman. Because women won't always understand him, and men sure as hell understand what smacked of betraying them."

Nevertheless, "Woman Is the Nigger of the World" had a didactic element that weakened it. And there was something disturbing in the song's emphasis on the total victimization of women by men. It assumed that all women lack "guts and confidence"—John sings, "If you don't believe me, just take a look at the one you're with."

This was both condescending and erroneous. The women's liberation movement was begun by women in the civil rights movement and the New Left who had the guts and confidence to test the myths and assumptions about female nature against their own experience. They were able to do this because, as historian Sara Evans has argued in her book *Personal Politics,* within the movement they had learned to know their own strength. The New Left provided them with an egalitarian ideology which emphasized the personal nature of political action, the value of community and cooperation, and the necessity of freedom for the oppressed. They had to do it because the same movement that gave them so much also placed them in subservient roles —as secretaries, housekeepers, and sex objects. Despite the weaknesses in this song's ideas, no other male superstar even attempted to address other men this way, raising the issue of their oppression of women.

The song, released as a single, peaked at Number Fifty-seven in June 1972, and did the worst of all John's post-Beatles singles. Many stations banned it for using the derogatory term "nigger." *Broadcasting* magazine reported that only five AM stations added the record to their playlists. "I think it will offend people," the program director of New York City's WOR-FM said. "I tried it out on a couple of girls in the office, and they thought it was offensive." John tried to reverse the ban. "Dick Gregory helped us by getting us in *Ebony* . . . posing with pictures of us with a lot of black guys and women, who stood up and said, 'We understand what he's saying, we're not offended.' "

ABC-TV wanted to ban "Woman Is the Nigger" when John and Yoko said they would sing it on the *Dick Cavett Show.* Cavett recalled the controversy in a 1983 interview. "Every show is run before something called Network Standards and Practices before it's broadcast," he explained. "I never could find out what their standards were, but I was all too familiar with their practices." Why did they try to ban the song? "Maybe the network was getting pressure from Washington—it wouldn't suprise me—because I had John and Yoko on, and they felt they had to show they had done something."

Cavett persuaded Standards and Practices to let him air the song, "but I had to tape this mealy-mouthed disclaimer." The broadcast of the show was interrupted by an insertion, in which Cavett read a statement: "At this point in the show, which was taped a week ago, John and Yoko got into something which ABC feels may develop into, in their words, 'a highly controversial issue.' It revolves around the song 'Woman Is the Nigger of the World,' and the obvious fact that some members of our black audience will, or may, be offended by the use of that word. In the next segment, John Lennon gives his reasons for writing the song, and for using the word. I permitted this insertion into the show as the only alternative to full deletion by ABC of the segment. Watch it; let us know what you think." He recalled in 1983, "As I predicted, there was a great deal of protest—about the mealy-mouthed apology. I don't think there was any about the song."

John got Ron Dellums, chairman of the Congressional black caucus, to issue a statement defending John's use of "nigger" in the song. John proudly read the statement on the Cavett show: "If you define 'nigger' as someone whose lifestyle is defined by others, whose opportunities are defined by others, whose role in society is defined by others, the good news is you don't have to be black to be a nigger in this society. Most of the people in America are niggers."

John gave Yoko credit for the title of the song. It was part of a statement she made in an interview published in March 1969 in *Nova*, a glossy English magazine something like *Vogue*. The jacket for the single of "Woman Is the Nigger" reproduced the *Nova* cover that showed John and Yoko and quoted Yoko's statement. In fact, the statement had been part of a strange and fascinating exchange with John: "I believe in reincarnation," John said. "I believe that I have been black, been a Jew, been a woman." At this point Yoko said, "Woman is the nigger of the world." That became a song, and "I've been a Jew" didn't.

Yoko later explained that her statement had been "directly inspired by life with John." "When I met John he was a typical male chauvinist. He had been in an all-male group and had come from a background where the men were all-important. They were always having man-to-man talks and going to the pub together. Women were kept in the background, serving tea, keeping out of the men's talk. John never expected to meet a woman who would talk back, who would expect to share everything on an equal basis." When they first started living together, "he was used to looking at the paper first in the morning."

John parodied himself: "You'll not touch papers till Dad's read it, you know . . . slippers and pipe."

"What is this I am not supposed to read the papers first?" Yoko shouted. "I couldn't believe it. . . . It's on a trivial level, but all these things accumulate, you know, and that's why I was inspired to say 'Woman Is the Nigger of the World.' But, you see, John is very quick to adapt to new situations. He comprehends things quickly and he understood that I was right. All the men and women around him were yes-men and he was getting tired of it and he was lonely. So from the beginning he did not want me to be another yes-man."

A male reviewer in *Rolling Stone* blasted "Woman Is the Nigger" as "simply a list of injustices clumsily set" and "almost unintelligible. . . . shouted at us in the tone of a newsboy." Others had been "more coherent and persuasive than the Lennons."

Later John disputed this criticism. He argued that "Woman Is the Nigger" was the first women's liberation song, pointing out that it came before Helen Reddy's "I Am Woman." What really makes John's song significant is that it is by a man and sung to men. The task John took on was difficult. Few subsequently attempted it. Donovan tried in "Liberation Rag" on his 1976 album *Slow Down World;* Robert Palmer tried the same year with the old Jamaican song "Men Smart, Women Smarter" on *Some People Can Do What They Like;* Tom Robinson tried with "Right On Sisters," on the 1978 album *Power in the Darkness.* None had any more success than John had.

John and Yoko pulled together their political songs of the season and released them in June as an album, *Some Time in New York City.* To emphasize the political topicality of the music, the cover looked like the New York *Times,* with song titles as headlines and lyrics as articles. The motto "Ono news that's fit to print" appeared. In the "Weather" box, they reprinted the First Amendment: "Congress shall make no law . . . abridging the freedom of speech." They had a photo of Angela Davis, and another one Yoko designed, Nixon dancing nude with Chairman Mao. The album contained a postcard of the Statue of Liberty; but instead of holding the torch, her right arm was raised in a clenched fist and she wore the black glove of the black power movement. John's own handwriting appeared at the bottom: "Some Time in New York City, 1972."

The album contained the songs they had written for and performed at the Attica benefit at the Apollo, the John Sinclair benefit in Ann Arbor, "Angela" from the *David Frost Show,* "Woman Is the Nigger of the World," recently released as a single and played on the *Dick Cavett Show,* "Luck of the Irish," played at the IRA demonstration, plus two songs of Yoko's. (A second record was included, *Live Jam,* with performances recorded at the London Lyceum in 1969 with Eric Clapton and at the New York Fillmore in 1971 with Frank Zappa.)

Some Time in New York City had one great new song that had never been heard before: "New York City." It was a political-biographical chronicle like "The Ballad of John and Yoko," recounting recent events in their lives. In the song John declared his love for the city's life, especially its political scene; he described meeting David Peel; he sang about the benefit concert at the Apollo, and about the films he and Yoko were making. Elephant's Memory played behind John. "New York City" featured the great honking tenor sax of Stan Bronstein. John concluded the song with a reference to his immigration case: "If the man wants to push us out / We're going to jump and shout!"—a statement of cheerful defiance, phrased in the classic language of rock and roll.

White sixties rock had few celebrations of city life, street life. The only songs by white rockers that can compare to John's "New York City" are "Summer in the City" by the Lovin' Spoonful and Bruce Springsteen's "Out in the Streets." White sixties rock more often expressed a wish for the beach —"Surfin' U.S.A."—or for a different kind of city life: When you go to San Francisco . . .

When the album was ready to be released, John and Yoko invited Phil Ochs over. "They wanted Phil to hear it before it came out, because he was the world's greatest writer of topical songs," Stew Albert said. "Phil singled out a number of songs for praise. All of them had been written by John alone. He hadn't praised any of Yoko's. They never invited him back."

Albert remembered that, when the *New York City* album was released, "Lennon was optimistic that it would be very successful. It was considered quite a plus to have gotten Spector to produce it, and the recording sessions had been fun. Spector was really into it, jamming along. He was doing what he liked."

Critics hated the album. Greil Marcus raged against its "horrendous . . . protest epics" and "witless" politics. "It was hard to take his new political commitments seriously; here, the question of taking his music seriously never came up," he wrote. *New Musical Express* denounced its "glib politicizing and overdependence on clichés." *Melody Maker* attacked its "mindless over-kill, cheap rhetoric, and appallingly bad lyrics." Stephen Holden wrote in *Rolling Stone* that the album was "so embarrassingly puerile as to constitute an advertisement against itself. . . . Only a monumental smugness could allow the Lennons to think that this witless doggerel wouldn't insult the intelligence and feelings of *any* audience." Craig Pyes wrote virtually the only positive review of the album, declaring in *SunDance* that he liked the album's politics: "It's good that some people are still harboring a nostalgia for liberation."

Only Robert Christgau appreciated the significance of the effort John was making to create a new kind of political music. "The time is right for such a move," he wrote in *Newsday,* in an article headlined "The Political Power of Rock and Roll." "It's true that what used to be called protest music accomplished less with words than rock and roll did with nothing but sound —inflections that shook teen-agers out of their white-skin gentility; rhythms that aroused their sexuality and aggressiveness—but now things are more complicated. It's no accomplishment to boogie adolescents into youth rebellion any more. The hip young are rapidly turning into another interest group, like labor unions. If rock and roll is to continue to function politically, it must continue to liberate its audience—to broaden fellow-feeling, direct energy, and focus analysis."

Christgau evaluated the music on this basis and concluded that "John appears to have plunged too fast. . . . The lyrics exhibit a fatal movement and avant-gardist flaw: while seeking to enlighten, they condescend." But he held out the hope that this effort might be more successful in the future. "*Imagine* was a successful popularization of *Plastic Ono Band*'s experiments. Who is to say John can't do it again?"

"Front-page songs" was John's term for his new work. He and Yoko explained the album in their *SunDance* column. "The songs we wrote and sang are subjects we and most people talk about, and it was done in the tradition of minstrels—singing reporters—who sang about their times and what was happening." In retrospect, John said, "I don't think they are the best songs I've ever written, because I was trying too hard—but the *concept* I was trying to get over was writing about what the people are saying now. And that's what I lost myself in—by not writing about what *I* was thinking and saying. It worked in 'Give Peace a Chance,' but it didn't work in other songs."

The concept of the front-page song had a history, which John learned after the album's release. John recalled, "Yoko said, 'Well, you know what we did there,' and I said, 'No. We got into a lot of trouble, that's all I know.' So she took me to see Richard Foreman's production of *The Threepenny Opera*, by Bertolt Brecht, which I didn't know. I said, 'Ah, I see, so we're not alone.'"

The front-page song had also been the program of American protest music in the early sixties, picking up where Woody Guthrie had left off. Phil Ochs wrote an article for *Broadside* in 1962, titled "The Need for Topical Music." "Every newspaper headline is a potential song, and it is the role of an effective songwriter to pick out the material that has the interest, significance and sometimes humor adaptable to music," he declared. In 1964 Ochs had released an album, *All the News That's Fit to Sing*, which he conceived as "a musical newspaper." The songs included "Talking Vietnam," "Talking Cuban Crisis," and "Too Many Martyrs." And he did a concert tour that year: "From New York's Greenwich Village, Phil Ochs sings Songs from the Headlines!"

===

To understand the failure of John's efforts on the *New York City* album, it is helpful to examine Bob Dylan's success a decade earlier. In 1962 and 1963 Bob Dylan's engagement with the civil rights movement led him to write protest and topical songs that also succeeded as art. "I used to love his protest things," John said in 1970 in *Lennon Remembers*.

Dylan's political songs grew out of his ties to the civil rights movement. The link was Susan Rotolo, the woman Dylan was living with in late 1962 —and who appeared at his side on the cover of *The Freewheelin' Bob Dylan*, hurrying through the winter slush of Greenwich Village. Suze, as she is called in the Dylan literature, had a strong commitment to the movement and worked full time as a secretary for the Congress of Racial Equality (CORE), the civil rights group that had sponsored the freedom rides in May 1961. At that time a bus full of brave activists, black and white, challenged the segregated waiting rooms, restaurants, and restrooms in the South's bus stations. They were repeatedly beaten by mobs of white thugs and jailed by racist police. From her desk at the New York CORE office, Suze took calls from field workers describing the day-to-day struggle in the deep South.

When Suze and Bob started living together, the front lines of the civil rights struggle were in Albany, Georgia, where Martin Luther King and seven hundred other activists had been arrested in their campaign to desegregate the downtown business district. During the Albany campaign, Dylan wrote his first political song, "The Ballad of Emmett Till"—about a fourteen-year-old black from Chicago who, while visiting relatives in the Mississippi delta in 1955, made the mistake of whistling at a white woman. Till was beaten, shot to death, and thrown into a river. The murderers went free. Dylan's song was a traditional ballad. He told friends at the time, "I think it's the best thing I've ever written."

The next month, in April 1962, he wrote "Blowin' in the Wind," after talking all night in a Village coffeehouse about "civil rights, and the failure of America to fulfill its promises." Dylan told Anthony Scaduto, "It means a lot to me, that song, it means a whole lot to me." The song was as clear and sharp as the best of Woody Guthrie or Pete Seeger, but also richly allusive and not at all simplistic or dogmatic. Soon Peter, Paul and Mary released it as a single, which within two weeks had become the fastest-selling single in Warner Brothers history. It was even played by black stations in the South that had never touched white folk music. "Blowin' in the Wind" became an anthem of the civil rights struggle, and it made Dylan the movement's best poet-songwriter.

Now his protest and topical songs poured forth. When James Meredith was denied admission to the University of Mississippi, and two people were killed in rioting, Dylan wrote "Oxford Town." When civil rights leader Medgar Evers was murdered, he wrote "Only a Pawn in Their Game." When Kennedy talked tough to Khrushchev, he wrote "Masters of War." And during the Cuban missile crisis of October 1962, he wrote "A Hard Rain's A-Gonna Fall." It conveyed a sense of terror with a series of chilling images, none of which were typical of folk music or protest songs. He explained, "During the Cuban thing, I wanted to get the most down that I knew about into one song, the most I possibly could." Dylan had drawn on his own imagination to create a masterpiece.

All these songs appeared on the same album, *The Freewheelin' Bob Dylan*, released in May 1963, just after the Beatles' "Please Please Me" hit Number One on the British charts. Bob Dylan, twenty-two years old, had brought his personal vision and his political commitments together with a power and a beauty that neither he nor anyone else would later equal. John, who was also twenty-two at the time, was a child in comparison.

In July 1963 Dylan traveled to Greenwood, Mississippi, to demonstrate his support for the SNCC voter-registration drive there and to give a concert with Pete Seeger, Josh White, and Theodore Bikel. The New York *Times* reported on the concert, explaining that "Bobby Dillon [sic], like Mr. Seeger, is white."

The Greenwood project was the most dangerous and heroic one the civil rights movement had yet undertaken. SNCC strategist Bob Moses had argued that, if the system of segregation could be broken in rural Mississippi, where the racists' grip was tightest, it would break throughout the South. But the sheer physical dangers made the Greenwood project seem to many a suicidal one. The situation became even more threatening when the Kennedy administration made it clear that it was not going to live up to its promises to provide federal protection for voter-registration workers in the deep South.

The appeal of Greenwood for Dylan was in part a romantic one: to be in deepest enemy territory, at the side of real heroes, was something Woody would have done. Nat Hentoff interviewed Dylan for a *New Yorker* profile, and he talked about the SNCC "freedom fighters." "I've been in Mississippi, man. I know those people as friends. Like Jim Foreman, one of the heads of SNCC. I'll stand on his side any time." Dylan was justifiably proud of his trip. It took courage and demonstrated that his commitments were real.

In August Dylan joined 200,000 people at the march on Washington, calling for new civil rights legislation. He sang "Pawn in Their Game" at the concluding rally, while Peter, Paul and Mary sang his "Blowin' in the Wind," which stood at Number Two on the charts. From the same podium, Martin Luther King shouted out, "No, we are not satisfied, and we will not be satisfied, until justice rolls down like water and righteousness like a mighty stream." Finally, in January 1964, Dylan released what would be the last of his "protest" albums, whose title song spoke for all young people drawn to the movement: "The Times They Are A-Changin'."

Carl Oglesby, who helped create SDS in 1962, recalled the significance of Dylan and his music for the New Left. "He wasn't a song writer who came into an established political mood, he seemed to be part of it. . . . This cross-fertilization was absolutely critical in Dylan's relationship to the movement and the movement's relationship to Dylan. He gave character to the sensibilities of the movement."

John's engagement with radical politics obviously did not lead him to the same kind of artistic success on *Some Time in New York City*. That album demonstrated that John wasn't very good at writing topical songs. Perhaps he was too British to write good music about American politics; perhaps the topical song was passé; Dylan and Ochs had both given up a decade earlier. John seemed to have forgotten that he could take a political position without declaring it in a song. He didn't need to write "Attica State." Singing "Imagine" at the Apollo Theatre benefit for the Attica families said enough. (Bruce Springsteen played "The River" for the first time in the "No Nukes" concert and film, showing one way of bringing music and political commitments together.)

Critics placed the blame for the *New York City* album on John's engagement with movement politics. They missed the more immediate problem: John's decision to collaborate with Yoko in writing and performing pop songs. Before this they had done separate parallel albums, each in their own style: separate *Plastic Ono Band* albums, *Imagine* and *Fly*, and singles with John on the A side and Yoko on the B side: "Power to the People"/"Open Your Box." Yoko's efforts had been "experimental" and avant-garde rather than pop.

If John's topical songs weren't great, Yoko's were even less successful. John was the sole author of two songs, the best on the album: "New York City" and "John Sinclair." Yoko was the sole author of "We're All Water," which didn't belong in this context; of the painfully weak "Born in a Prison," and the stronger "Sisters, O Sisters" with its reggae beat. John and Yoko took credit as co-authors for "Angela," "Luck of the Irish," "Attica State," and "Sunday Bloody Sunday," all of which were failures. The only exception to this pattern was "Woman Is the Nigger," which listed them as co-authors. But John gave the impression that Yoko's contribution was limited to authorship of the line in the title.

John wanted not only to live with Yoko but also to work with her. But on their first collaborative pop album, John had more responsibility. He was the great pop songwriter. He should have found a way to strengthen the album's songs. The failure of *Some Time in New York City* seriously undermined their project of collaboration. They would not try it again until *Double Fantasy*, eight years later.

Part VI

DEPORTATION AND THE EX-RADICAL

20

Deportation:
"A Strategic Counter-Measure"

 The archsegregationist and reactionary Strom Thurmond, Republican senator from South Carolina and member of the Senate Internal Security Subcommittee of the Judiciary Committee, received a secret memorandum in February 1972 titled "John Lennon." It had been drafted by the committee staff. The memo noted that John had appeared at the John Sinclair rally along with members of the Chicago Seven. "This group has been strong advocates of the program to 'dump Nixon,' " the memo reported. "They have devised a plan to hold rock concerts in various primary election states for the following purposes: to obtain access to college campuses; to press for legislation legalizing marijuana; to recruit persons to come to San Diego during the Republican National Convention in August 1972. These individuals are the same persons who were instrumental in disrupting the Democratic National Convention in Chicago in 1968. . . .

"[Rennie] Davis and his cohorts intend to use John Lennon as a drawing card to promote their success. . . . This can only inevitably lead to a clash between a controlled mob organized by this group and law enforcement officials in San Diego. . . . If Lennon's visa is terminated it would be a strategic counter-measure."

Thurmond endorsed the memo and passed it on to Attorney General John Mitchell. It was precisely the sort of thing recommended by the counsel to the president, John Dean, in his August 1971 memo, "Dealing with Our Political Enemies." He suggested, "We can use the available political machinery to screw our political enemies." On February 14 Mitchell's deputy, Richard Kleindienst, sent a note to Immigration and Naturalization Service (INS) Commissioner Raymond Farrell about Lennon: "Ray, . . . When is he coming? Do we have any basis to deny his admittance?" The heart of the problem eluded Kleindienst: Lennon had already been admitted to the country six months earlier. If Kleindienst had turned on his TV that day, he could have seen John beginning his week-long stint on the *Mike Douglas Show.* But the INS knew what to do when Attorney General Mitchell passed on Thurmond's suggestion: on March 6 it revoked John's visa and began deportation proceedings.

John thus faced the same treatment that the federal government had given to other radicals: Wobblies, anarchists, communists, Emma Goldman, Charlie Chaplin, Bertolt Brecht—and now John Lennon. Who would have thought in 1967 that the man who wrote and sang "All You Need Is Love" would join this historic company?

John was not the only one of Nixon's "enemies" to feel the power of the White House in February and March 1972. Nixon's program of political sabotage, run by Donald Segretti, undermined the primary campaign of Democratic front-runner Edmund Muskie by sending embarrassing letters on his campaign letterhead. In the resulting furor, Muskie dropped out of the race. Political contributions made before April 7 did not have to be publicly reported under the new campaign financing law. Nixon fund-raisers worked feverishly through February and March, inviting the multinationals to make secret illegal contributions of corporate funds of $100,000 each. The oil industry came up with $4.9 million, and the grand total of secret corporate contributions was $20 million.

Some of these campaign funds paid for activities planned by G. Gordon Liddy and E. Howard Hunt. They proposed in January that the Committee to Re-Elect the President (CREEP) spend a million dollars on covert operations, including mugging demonstrators at the Republican national convention in San Diego and abducting the leaders to Mexico. Rubin and Hoffman were selected for abduction; John was not. When the plan was presented to Attorney General Mitchell, he said it was "not quite what I had in mind" and cost too much. Liddy came back with a plan to break into Democratic national headquarters in Washington to plant bugs and photograph documents. Mitchell liked that better. The operation was carried out on June 17 at the Watergate offices of the Democrats; Washington police caught the perpetrators in the act. A cover-up directed by H. R. Haldeman and John

Ehrlichman successfully kept the press from developing the story until after Nixon's reelection. Thus the Nixon administration's persecution of John Lennon was one small part of a massive illegal effort to assure Nixon's reelection, one example of an abuse of power that eventually led Congress to move toward Nixon's impeachment.

John, who was in the studio recording *Some Time in New York City* when the deportation order was issued, brought his legal problems to New York immigration attorney Leon Wildes. "When they first came to me, I told John he could ruin my reputation," Wildes said in 1983. "In fifteen years I had never lost a residence case. But nobody had won his kind of case previously. His case was a real loser."

How had the government found out about John's plans to tour with Davis and Rubin? Jerry Rubin had asked Rennie Davis, the movement's greatest organizer, to move his operation from Washington into John's basement on Bank Street to set up the tour. Davis' "tribe," Stew Albert said, had been infiltrated by a Washington police officer named Annie Collegio. Her movement name was "Crazy Annie." She was later exposed by a government security officer who defected to the left.

John's main file in the FBI Central Records System in Washington, D.C., was a "100 case file," the classification number for "domestic security" investigations. The New York FBI was the "Originating Office" with primary responsibility for the Lennon investigation. It began intensive surveillance of him after the December 1971 John Sinclair concert. Hoover sent special instructions regarding the Lennon investigation to the agents in charge of the FBI offices in New York, Los Angeles, San Diego, and Washington, D.C., on February 15: "Recipients are reminded that investigative instructions relating to possible disruptions during RNC [Republican national convention] must be handled on expedite basis and by mature, experienced Agents. Recipients carefully note dissemination instructions"—instructions about which agencies and offices were to receive reports on Lennon. Three paragraphs of this memo have been withheld on the grounds that they concern the CIA.

In January and February 1972, the months immediately preceding the deportation order, the FBI filled John's file with reports on the "Election Year Strategy Information Committee (EYSIC)," Rennie Davis' effort to set up the concert tour. The FBI's first mention of EYSIC is dated January 28: "The public will soon become aware of its existence [*sic*] and purpose—anti-Calrep activities" (i.e., demonstrations outside the California Republican national convention). Hoover declared in a February 11 cable, classified "Secret," that EYSIC was "obviously being heavily influenced by John Lennon."

After dozens of memos and reports, the special agent in charge of the FBI in New York City sent a confidential "airtel"—FBI jargon for a communication sent by air mail—to J. Edgar Hoover on March 29 reporting the latest on EYSIC: "The organization ceased to exist approximately the first of March," one month after its founding. The INS ordered Lennon deported on March 6; thus EYSIC's dissolution did not come in response to the deportation order. Nor did the deportation proceedings change Lennon's plans, as J. Edgar Hoover himself noted in a memo dated April 10: "Subject continues to plan activities directed towards RNC and will soon initiate series of 'rock concerts' to develop financial support."

The FBI also tied John to Stew Albert. Its files showed that Albert had been arrested at a Progressive Labor Party (PL) demonstration at the Berkeley City Hall six years earlier. The next paragraph explained that PL "was founded in 1962 by individuals expelled from the Communist Party, USA, for following the Chinese Communist line." The conclusion in regard to John was obvious: associating with communists! For the FBI, that alone was enough to justify an undercover investigation. Associating with communists happened to be a right protected by the First Amendment, but the implication that Albert was a member or sympathizer of PL wasn't true. He was known to the press as Jerry Rubin's "Yippie Lieutenant," a bitter antagonist of the humorless PL. In a 1982 interview Albert dismissed his 1966 arrest at a PL demonstration as "a youthful indiscretion."

The FBI memo on John dated March 16, 1972, reports that his "temporary residence" was "the Saint Regis Hotel, 150 Bank Street, New York City." Bank Street is in Greenwich Village; but every New York cop and cab driver knows the St. Regis is on Fifth Avenue in midtown. At the time, John and Yoko were living at 105 Bank Street, having checked out of the St. Regis four months earlier. Three weeks after this memo, Hoover cabled the head of the New York office, ordering him to "promptly initiate discreet efforts to locate subject." The elusive Lennon seemed to have given the slip to the agents who looked for him at the Bank Street St. Regis.

———

John and Yoko announced a press conference at which they would make their first public statement on the deportation order. Wildes recalled the preparations: "We reviewed carefully beforehand how we were going to present it and who was going to cover what territory. At the conference, all of a sudden, out of nowhere, they both take tissues out of their pockets, wave them, and issue the 'Declaration of Nutopia' ": "We announce the birth of a conceptual country, NUTOPIA. Citizenship of the country can be obtained by declaration of your awareness of NUTOPIA. NUTOPIA has no land, no boundaries, no passports, only people. NUTOPIA has no laws other than cosmic. All people of

NUTOPIA are ambassadors of the country. As two ambassadors of NUTOPIA, we ask for diplomatic immunity and recognition in the United Nations of our country and its people."

"Yoko apologized later," Wildes said. "She said, 'Leon, you have to understand. We are artists. We have a message.' It was nice of her to take the time to explain it to me."

John took the stand briefly on March 16. "They were very nervous about attending hearings," Leon Wildes remembered. "It was a nerve-wracking thing for them. I used to go to their apartment early in the morning before hearings to dress them, believe it or not. The government was moving to separate their cases and assign them to different judges, because Yoko didn't have this criminal conviction. I remember dressing them that day in identical black suits, white shirts, black ties. They looked exactly alike. I told them to hold hands throughout the hearing and not let go. I wanted to show that they were a matched set and shouldn't be separated."

John's testimony concerned Yoko's eight-year-old daughter, Kyoko. Yoko had recently been granted temporary custody of Kyoko by a second American court, which stipulated that Kyoko be raised in the United States. Tony Cox, however, had the girl and still could not be found. Yoko wanted to stay in the United States to try to find her. John argued that if he was deported, Yoko would have to choose between abandoning her daughter or her husband.

The FBI and the INS came to the conclusion that the battle between John and Yoko and Tony Cox for Kyoko was a fraud, that all three were cooperating "to keep child hidden as tool of delaying deportation hearings." Because John claimed he didn't know where Kyoko was, they proposed charging him with perjury.

John reported that he was being followed. "I'd open the door, there'd be guys standing on the other side of the street," he told Capital Radio. "I'd get in the car, and they'd be following me in a car. Not hiding. They *wanted* me to see I was being followed." He nervously described this surveillance on the *Dick Cavett Show* on May 11.

John didn't know it, but he was being subjected to a standard form of harassment the FBI called "tailgating." They used it to intimidate uncooperative or defiant subjects of surveillance. One FBI document specifically recommended that the tactic be used against the New Left: "It will enhance the paranoia endemic in these circles and will further serve to get the point across that there is an FBI agent behind every mailbox."

John later told *Hit Parader* magazine, "We knew we were being wiretapped on Bank Street, there was a helluva lot of guys coming in to fix the phones." He told Capital Radio, "I was so paranoid from them tappin' the phone and followin' me; how could I prove they were tappin' me phone?

There was no way. . . . Reporters said, 'Who's gonna chase you? You're not that important.' And I wish I wasn't. I wish they didn't find it such an important thing."

The FBI subjected John to other "dirty tricks." A few months earlier, the St. Louis *Globe-Democrat* had run a report that John and Yoko were seen with Abbie Hoffman and Jerry Rubin at Max's Kansas City in New York the previous July. "Over drinks Lennon gave Hoffman and Rubin an envelope containing fifty $100 bills—$5,000—for 'the cause.' According to my sources, Lennon, the most radical Beatle, said he hoped some of the money would assist members of the SDS who are being sought for several bomb outrages." The article was not true. John never supported terrorists, and didn't carry around bundles of hundred-dollar bills.

Almost certainly this story was planted by the FBI. Hoover's effort to "neutralize" the New Left included distribution of damaging or derogatory stories to "cooperative news media." Hoover recommended stories about money items second only to sex stories, and wasn't concerned about the truth of the stories in question: "Money is such a sensitive issue that disruption can be accomplished without facts to back it up," the director stated in one memo. The *Globe-Democrat* was, according to internal FBI documents, "especially cooperative with the Bureau. . . . Its publisher is on the Special Correspondents list."

John and Yoko were subject to still other dirty tricks. One of the most offensive appears to have been an effort to brand their friend Jerry Rubin as an undercover agent. Attorney Wildes recalled in 1983, "I received information from someone who claimed that Jerry Rubin was a CIA plant, that his task was to bait Lennon and get information about him for the CIA. This source sent me all kinds of what they claimed was documentation. I showed it to John and Yoko." Rubin himself said that John "considered the possibility that I was a CIA agent."

Wildes appears to have been the target of a notorious FBI tactic, called "putting a snitch jacket on a subject" in Bureau circles. The tactic was especially recommended in the FBI's secret, illegal campaign to disrupt the New Left, which they called "COINTELPRO." On COINTELPRO's twelve-point master plan, item number three proposed "the creating of impressions that certain New Left leaders are informants for the Bureau or other law enforcement agencies." Tom Hayden was one activist to whom the FBI sought to "attach the stigma of informant or Government 'fink,'" according to FBI files. Rubin, like Hayden, had been a defendant in the Chicago conspiracy trial and was an equally important target for FBI dirty tricks.

On April 10 J. Edgar Hoover wrote a memo on the status of the case. "Lennon is allegedly in U.S. to assist in organizing disruption of RNC,"

Hoover declared—a ridiculous statement about why John and Yoko left England. Because of his legal appeals in the deportation proceedings, "strong possibility looms that subject will not be deported any time soon and will probably be in U.S. at least until RNC." Hoover instructed the New York office to "remain aware of his activities and movements. . . . Careful attention should be given to reports that subject is heavy narcotics user and any information developed in this regard should be furnished to narcotics authorities and immediately furnished to Bureau in form suitable for dissemination." In other words, the FBI wanted to set John up for a drug bust that could provide further ammunition in the Nixon administration's attempt to deport him before the Republican national convention.

The first full hearing in the deportation proceedings against John took place on April 18. Wildes argued that John and Yoko were of good character, telling the hearing officer that "yesterday they were appointed to the faculty of New York's University." It was an amazing announcement: Lennon a professor! Students could get academic credit for taking his course! The announcement somehow escaped the attention of the media, but the FBI agents in the room rushed the news to Hoover. He ordered it checked out —and got the reply, "New York Office confirmed that Lennon has been offered teaching position at New York University for summer of 1972 and school officials presume that subject will accept."

In the same hearing Wildes also announced that John and Yoko had just been "appointed by an executive assistant to President Nixon to participate in a national anti-drug media effort." Hoover received an erroneous version of this statement, indicating that John had been appointed to Nixon's National Commission on Marijuana and Drug Abuse. A long internal FBI memo stated, "Observations: Irony of subject being appointed, if true, is overwhelming since subject is currently reported heavy user of narcotics and frequently avoided by even Rennie Davis and Jerry Rubin, due to his excessive use of narcotics." That was ridiculous—Davis and Rubin never avoided John.

Agents sent out to corroborate the report of Lennon's presidential appointment replied to the director, again under an "urgent" label: "Inquiry developed no information indicating Lennon has been appointed." In their effort to avoid deportation, Hoover apparently concluded, John and his lawyers were lying, and the lies were about President Nixon. The FBI went to work on a memo informing the Oval Office about Lennon and his efforts to avoid deportation.

Nixon's chief of staff, H. R. Haldeman, was kept informed of the progress of the FBI's campaign to "neutralize" Lennon. A full report on John was sent to "Honorable H. R. Haldeman," dated April 25, 1972. The released portion begins, "Dear Mr. Haldeman: John Winston Lennon is a British citizen and former member of the Beatles singing group," and explains that "INS has been attempting to deport him . . . since February 29." Haldeman was informed that John's attorney "read into the court record that Lennon had been appointed to the President's Council for Drug Abuse," that this claim of Lennon's was false, and that "this information is also being furnished to the Acting Attorney General," presumably for a possible indictment of Lennon for perjury. Six paragraphs of the letter remain classified by the Reagan administration "in the interest of national defense or foreign policy."

None of the documents that have been released was sent to or from Richard Nixon himself. But this does not mean Nixon was not involved. "It seems to me that Haldeman did not need a report on this if he wasn't reporting to Nixon," Leon Wildes said in 1983. "Nixon took such an intimate interest in the smallest of details. Remember that was the first year they gave eighteen-year-olds the right to vote in a presidential election. Lennon was the guy who could have influenced the eighteen-year-old vote the most. In my mind there is a moral certainty that Mr. Nixon had discussions about Mr. Lennon."

The Haldeman letter referred him to a fuller FBI internal report sent by E. L. Shackelford to E. S. Miller. Those agents' names appeared in the news subsequently in a different connection. Miller (along with agent Mark Felt) was found guilty of breaking and entering in the FBI investigation of the Weather Underground. He and Felt are the only FBI agents ever to be convicted of crimes committed on the job. (Ronald Reagan pardoned them when he took office in 1981.) Their supervisor on that case was E. L. Shackelford. These facts suggest that the FBI may have committed the same kinds of illegal acts against Lennon that their agents were convicted of having committed in the Weather Underground case.

John, meanwhile, released his new single, "Woman Is the Nigger of the World," backed by Yoko's "Sisters, O Sisters," on April 24. They had taken a crucial step in the immigration case on April 18, when they charged for the first time that the deportation proceedings against them had been based on their antiwar stand. In fact, that was only part of the real reason. At this point no one outside Nixon's inner circle knew the full story of Nixon's effort to block demonstrations planned for the Republican national convention. That would not come out for another year.

Hoover received an eyewitness report on the press conference. "Lennon was observed by a representative of the FBI to make a press release in which he inferred [sic] INS was attempting to deport him due to his political ideas," Hoover was informed in a teletype marked "urgent." He could have read it in the paper.

The same day a headline on the front page of section two of the New York *Times* declared, "Mayor Lindsay Deplores Action to Deport Lennon as a 'Grave Injustice.' " Three days later the *Times* declared its support for John and Yoko in an editorial, which argued that the INS was persecuting them for their "unconventional views and radical statements." The "National Committee for John and Yoko" announced its formation, declaring the "real reason" for the deportation order was "their antiwar stand, their ability to affect the thinking of youth, and their support for unpopular beliefs."

A week later John and Yoko took a trip to Washington to lobby for relief from the INS. Doing their best to look like liberals, they attended a party where they spoke with Senators Charles Percy, Illinois Republican, and Alan Cranston, California Democrat. New York Republican Jacob Javits was supposed to come but cancelled at the last minute, probably bowing to White House pressure. Various columnists and reporters were present. The Washington *Post* wrote up John and Yoko's "very sedate behavior," John's "coat and tie," Yoko's "long black dress with a sequined front," and their "soft-spoken and pleasant and earnest . . . appeal for help."

"Why are you being deported?" Geraldo Rivera asked in one of his first major TV interviews.

"The real reason is that I'm a peacenik," John replied simply.

"Will you give up your opposition to the war because of the deportation order?"

"No. Nothing will stop me." Defying the U.S. government took real courage when the penalty was deportation.

And at the beginning of May John's FBI file received a new classification, upgraded from "Security Matter–New Left" to "Revolutionary Activities." No explanation of the change appears in the file.

===

On May 9 Nixon announced he was mining North Vietnamese ports and ordering massive new bombing raids. Instead of ending the war, as he had promised, he was continuing to escalate it, trying to bomb the Vietnamese into submission—although it had been proven time and time again over the previous six years that, while the bombing did cause terrible destruction, it only increased the Vietnamese determination to resist.

The antiwar movement responded with a new wave of demonstrations, more frenzied and despairing than ever before. College students massed on streets and highways, blocked entrances to military installations, and fought the police who came to dislodge them. In Minneapolis the governor activated 715 National Guardsmen after police failed to control thousands of demonstrators. At the University of New Mexico in Albuquerque, police gunfire wounded at least nine people. In Madison, Wisconsin, and Berkeley, police battled antiwar demonstrators through the night. A thousand students from the University of Florida at Gainesville blocked U.S. Highway 441; another thousand blocked intersections in Boulder, Colorado, with burning automobiles and logs; students from the University of Chicago and Northwestern University blocked expressways in Chicago and Evanston; students from Santa Cruz and Santa Barbara blocked the Pacific Coast Highway. In Washington, D.C., five hundred high school students marched on the Capitol. Federal buildings and military bases were blocked in Binghamton, New York, Burlington, Vermont, and western Massachusetts (where President John William Ward of Amherst College was arrested). At Princeton 350 students seized the Woodrow Wilson School.

In Congress four Democratic representatives filed a resolution to impeach Nixon for "high crimes and misdemeanors" in waging illegal war in Southeast Asia. John Conyers of Michigan, Bella Abzug of New York, William F. Ryan of New York, and Ron Dellums of California argued convincingly that Nixon's worst crimes had been committed not at the Watergate headquarters of the Democratic National Committee but in Southeast Asia.

The second major hearing in the deportation proceedings against John took place on May 12 in the midst of these massive demonstrations. Despite the threat of imminent deportation, he worked to remain active in the movement. John spoke at a New York antiwar rally at Fifth Avenue and Forty-second Street. Thousands of demonstrators chanted, "Out! Now! Out! Now!" John told them, "We ain't used to speakin', but we all know why we're here. I read somewhere that the antiwar movement was over—ha ha!" The demonstrators laughed and cheered. "We're here to bring the boys home. But let's not forget the machines. Bring the machines home, and then we'll really get somewhere." Then he led the crowd in singing "Give Peace a Chance."

Yoko also spoke. According to the FBI files, she "told the 30,000, maybe 40,000, maybe 50,000 gathered there that the time had come for North Vietnam to invade America." The FBI was alarmed, apparently assuming she was speaking literally.

And John announced his support for a demonstration on May 20 in Manhattan demanding complete U.S. withdrawal from Indochina, and a second march in Washington, D.C., the following Sunday. The announcement received wide publicity and was carefully noted by the FBI.

J. Edgar Hoover died in mid-May, and Nixon appointed L. Patrick Gray to take over as the FBI's acting director. In addition to overseeing the case against John, Gray was also enlisted in the Watergate coverup, burning incriminating materials from Howard Hunt's safe and later providing the

Nixon White House with FBI reports on its investigation of the Watergate break-in. On the Lennon case, Gray tried to insulate the FBI from any public role. In one of his first memos on the case, he wrote the special agent in charge in New York City, "FBI agents testifying would not be in Bureau's best interest and could result in considerable adverse publicity." Anything the FBI found would be given to the INS; they would absorb the public's hostility to the administration's persecution of Lennon.

The night before John and Yoko's big deportation hearing, they appeared on the *Dick Cavett Show* to explain their case. Cavett recalled in 1983, "I was sharing the same kind of feelings he was, because of other heavy-handed things I knew the government had done. I learned that the White House was keeping a check on the guests I had on, and that they were very unhappy about it. They had called my staff and said, 'We happen to know that you've had the following five people appear, who spoke against the SST' [the supersonic transport plane Nixon regarded as a high priority]—that's when I became aware of an ominous scorekeeper in Washington. That startled me a bit—to learn there was a man cutting notches in a stick."

When John explained his case to the TV audience, "there was a kind of sweetness about him," Cavett continued. "I did not get the feeling that they were fearful about harassment. Later on they may have been. He found it almost impossible to believe that so much effort was being expended against him, that there was so much paranoia on the part of the government. He was a songwriter and had some sincere beliefs. I'm sure he couldn't comprehend the amount of power he had."

The hearing opened with a bombshell: Yoko found that she had been issued a green card, granting her permanent residency, when she was married to Tony Cox. That made the grounds for deporting her dubious at best.

The INS case against John was stronger. The law under which the government was attempting to deport John declared that no alien could be granted residence in the United States who had been convicted of possession of marijuana ("no matter how small, at any time in his lifetime and under any circumstances," Wildes was fond of adding). "The issue resolves itself into whether or not what happened in England amounts to possession under our law, and whether what he possessed in England was actually marijuana under our law," Wildes explained. In fact John had been convicted of possessing "cannabis resin." Wildes called an expert witness on marijuana, a Harvard Medical School professor. He testified that cannabis resin is a generic term and not the same thing as marijuana.

Wildes then called a series of character witnesses. The first was Thomas P. F. Hoving, who explained that he was director of the Metropolitan Museum, a member of the New York State Council on the Arts, a Princeton

Ph.D. in art history, and a member of the board of "a number of major corporations. . . . There are few people in the last period of this decade in all of the arts, whether it's painting or sculpture, or architecture, who have contributed so much and in extremely deep and essential manner as Mr. Lennon," he declared. "And I would say my basic business in life, sir, as a person, is to recognize, exhibit, and teach about artistic qualities. . . . I would say that if he were a painting, he would be hanging in the Metropolitan Museum." The special hearing officer seemed impressed by Hoving. "I am a member of the museum," he declared.

Dick Cavett was called as a character witness. In 1983 he described attending the deportation hearing. "When I arrived and Lennon greeted me, we both sort of grinned in a way that seemed to say there's something unreal and silly about this—dressing up in jackets and ties and trying to appear respectable. It seemed unlikely that this was happening in anything but a play."

On the stand, he gave his statement: "By their constant restless activity, testing themselves, fulfilling themselves in challenging artistic ways, they are an inspiration. Young people who are in danger of falling into apathy seem to be impressed by the example of the Lennons, as people who are concerned with what is valuable and true and the best way of expressing it."

The mystery of Lennon's presidential appointment was solved by the next witness, Eric Schnapper of the American Bar Association (ABA). He explained that he was an assistant to the president of the ABA (not of the USA) and that Lennon was going to be working with the Committee on Drug Abuse of the Young Lawyers' Section of the ABA, making antidrug ads. It wasn't President Nixon's committee on drug abuse, which in fact had a different name: the National Commission on Marijuana and Drug Abuse, a name Wildes had never mentioned. Wildes had referred to "a national anti-drug media effort."

There had never been any public confusion about Wildes's brief statement the previous month; the only people to have gotten mixed up were J. Edgar Hoover, then H. R. Haldeman and various Justice Department officials. Despite the furious activity of the FBI three weeks earlier, giving Haldeman (and Nixon, presumably) the erroneous information that Lennon claimed Nixon had appointed him to the National Commission, there is nothing in the FBI files to indicate it informed the White House of the correct information.

The only character witness to get involved in a direct dispute with the INS lawyer was the pugnacious Allen Klein. Klein said John and Yoko should not be deported because of their extensive activities for charitable causes and for peace. INS attorney Vincent Schiano asked, "Do I understand you to say that

if they . . . were not famous and did not do anything [for peace], it would
be all right to deport them?"

"No," Klein replied. "I said you wouldn't deport them."

"That is your opinion," Schiano fired back.

"That is my opinion, RIGHT."

"However erroneous."

"And, I am sure, shared by millions of people."

"Not by the Immigration Service."

The head of the National Committee for John and Yoko asked to present
to the hearing officer almost two hundred letters it had gathered, but Schiano
tried to prevent it: "The documentation is immaterial, irrelevant, and in-
competent in the cause of this case." Besides, he said, "it would be easy for
the government to produce an equal number of letters from people who have
the opposite opinion." The hearing officer accepted them anyway. (Schiano
got his revenge; he got the FBI to write a memo on the International
Committee for John and Yoko, and distribute it to the Internal Security
Division of the Justice Department, the State Department, and the American embassy in London.)

The letters, testifying about the couple's contributions to America as
artists, had been written by artists and celebrities. The committee included
people who didn't usually support the same causes. The alphabetical list
included Clive Barnes and Joan Baez, Tony Curtis and Ornette Coleman,
Mitch Miller and Kate Millett, Meyer Shapiro and Phil Spector, Edmund
Wilson and Stevie Wonder. Virtually the entire New York art world signed
the petition—Jasper Johns, Roy Lichtenstein, Claes Oldenburg, Robert
Rauschenberg, and Larry Rivers—as did most of the New York literary
establishment, including Norman Mailer, Saul Bellow, Joseph Heller, John
Updike, and Kurt Vonnegut. The actors who signed included Fred Astaire,
Ben Gazzara, and Jack Lemmon.

The official committee statement declared that "this proceeding consti-
tutes a violation of constitutionally guaranteed freedoms of speech and expression, and, as an abrogation of civil rights, must be viewed as a disguised
attempt to silence opposition to the Government's policies and actions."
Most of the letters, however, made a different, weaker protest, arguing that
the deportation proceedings were an attack on artistic freedom.

Most were carefully composed and professionally typed, but Bob Dylan's
was scrawled in large handwriting: "John and Yoko add a great voice and
drive to this country's so called ART INSTITUTION. They inspire and transcend
and stimulate and by doing so, only help others to see pure light and in doing
that, put an end to this mild dull taste of petty commercialism which is being

passed off as artist art by the overpowering mass media. Hurray for John & Yoko. Let them stay and live here and breathe."

Novelist John Updike wrote two lines: "They cannot do this great country any harm, and might do it some good." Poet Gregory Corso was even more brief: "Artisans and universal megagalactic entities—Ergo, let my people go —stay—etc." That must have helped a lot. New York *Times* drama critic Clive Barnes took a different tack, describing John as "a major influence in the development of current popular music"—a statement as self-evident as it was lukewarm. Leonard Woodcock, president of the United Auto Workers, sent one of the strongest statements, a telegram declaring that "it would be an outrage and a tragedy for this country if John Lennon and Yoko Ono are deported." The entire music department of Brown University signed a statement of support. Cal Arts, one of the country's top art schools, promised to appoint John and Yoko as visiting artists if the INS let them stay in the U.S.A.

Feminist Kate Millett wrote one of the few letters to make the political issues explicit. "What makes Yoko Ono and John Lennon so crucial to our contemporary culture is their refusal to live only in the world of art," she wrote. "Instead, they have reintegrated art with the social and political facets of life and offered us something like moral leadership through their committed pacifism. Using all the resources of their prestige and popularity, they have unceasingly protested the crimes of humanity upon itself."

Two distinguished supporters explicitly rejected John and Yoko's politics. Art critic Clement Greenberg wrote, "I most definitely want to dissociate myself from the Committee's rhetoric . . . in imputing political motives to the Department of Justice in its attempt to deport them." And novelist Joyce Carol Oates wrote, "I certainly don't endorse many of their publicly-expressed opinions, but I believe that they, and anyone else, have the right to these opinions."

——

The administration, however, remained convinced that Nixon's reelection required that Lennon be deported. On May 24 Acting Director Gray received a report from his New York office indicating that INS attorney Schiano "has received information that the LENNONS are planning a large rock concert in Miami during the Conventions and that the rock concert was to be held in front of the convention hall." Schiano had developed a plan to prevent John from appearing at the Miami concert-rally: the INS, he reported, could try to "restrict their travel."

Reports of the plans John had been making with Jerry Rubin and Rennie Davis had begun to appear in the press. "Lennon is reportedly planning a

'people's tour' by the new Lennon-Memory band, to play benefit concerts,"
one such report read. "But whom the tour will benefit has not been revealed."
The underground press went further. "The pigs probably REALLY freak when
they think about how the people's movement will be strengthened as John
and Yoko feed more and more money to causes by playing benefits across the
country, as they hope to do," the Ann Arbor *Sun* said.

"I think in his subconscious mind the Beatle part of him still lived," Dick
Gregory said in a 1984 interview. "Right up to 1972, America to him was
the response they got to the *Ed Sullivan Show* back in 1964. Then to see
how vicious this government was—that caught him by surprise. I said to him,
'You're findin' that you can smoke all the pot you want as long as you don't
break out of that superstar mold, as long as you're in the business of shake,
rattle, and roll. If you start meddling in real business, they'll reduce you down
to a nigger. They'll make you act the way niggers are supposed to act—very
quiet, behaving themselves.' "

Soon John was declaring in public and in private that he was cancelling
his tour plans. In May he went back to the *Dick Cavett Show* and said, "They
think we're going to San Diego, or Miami, or wherever it is. We've never said
we're going, there'll be no big jam with Dylan, because there's too much
going on." He told another interviewer, "The only thing we ever intended"
was "to do some concerts," not "have a riot" or "finance revolution." And
he emphasized it to his political friends. Stew Albert remembers John telling
him, "We're not going, and we're telling everybody we're not going."

John was acting on the advice of his attorney. "I constantly advised them
not to involve themselves in any of these associations" with Jerry Rubin and
his friends, or with the convention demonstration plans, Wildes said in 1983.
"John and Yoko were coming to the government and asking for a favor. They
were in the position of supplicants. What they were asking for is given to you,
not because you have a right to it, but because the government in its discre-
tion determines that it is appropriate to give it to you. I let them know that
I thought it was counterproductive to be in the presence of these people or
do anything that would upset the Immigration Service and give them further
reason to be nasty."

None of those involved in planning the anti-Nixon tour seem to have urged
John to defy the government and risk deportation; none accused John of
selling out. John Sinclair's 1983 statement was representative: John and Yoko
were "headed for trouble. Cancelling the tour plan was wise. I know how
much it meant to them to stay here—partially because of the thing with the
kid. I understood perfectly."

Still, for John to give up the tour plans that had seemed so promising, so
thrilling, for him to admit that Nixon had defeated him, must have left him

feeling humiliated, weak, and powerless. He had always feared and hated selling out; could he have avoided accusing himself of it now? Even his capitulation didn't stop the relentless Immigration Service: it continued to seek his deportation anyway—which must have made John feel even more frightened and humiliated. In May 1972, however, no one, not even John, understood how much he would be damaged by these psychological wounds.

21

From Madison Square Garden
to Election Night

Some Time in New York City was released in mid-June; the jacket included a petition addressed to the White House, "Let Them Stay in the U.S.A." Fans wrote in by the thousands. The letters ordinary people sent to the President or their congressmen constitute a significant portion of the Immigration and Naturalization Service documents about John's case released under the FOIA. The letters are the voice of people who left no other record of their thoughts and feelings.

The grammar and spelling of these letters testify to the unsophisticated character of many of their authors. Some protested John's "deportment," others his "exportation," and one said he shouldn't be "exspelled." Many writers declared this was their first such effort. "Dear Mr. Nixon, I am a 14 year old, concerned girl who at the moment lives in Canton, Ohio. I've always wanted to write to the president and have a 'voice' in something maybe that would make up his mind. So now for the first time I'm going to say what I think is right." Another declared, "I was complaining to my father that they should not kick John Lennon out of the country so he said write to your senator so here I am writing to you."

At the other end of the emotional spectrum was the letter that read "I am a Vietnam veteran and I think it's absurd to deport John & Yoko Lennon. I demand you deport Nixon and his gang of goons and psychos."

Many of the letters made simple appeals: "My dear Mister Mitchell, Whatever the bans are on John & Yoko how about dropping them." "If he leaves millions of his fans will be very unhappy. Especially me! Good luck in office God Bless you and your family A 13 year old." "If the Lennons are deported, it will be just cause to feel very low about being American."

Other letters had a note of hysteria. "You're trying to kick a man out of this, so called, 'Great Country of ours' because of something in the PAST! If that's your idea of a Great Country, man, I think you should be exiled to an insane asylum!" Many referred to John's artistic contributions, but only one declared that "if it weren't for John, Paul, George, and Ringo, we'd still be living in the '50s with slicked back hair and plain clothes, white socks, and penny loafers."

Some letter-writers did their best to make arguments they thought would convince Nixon: "Lennon's charitable activities in this country have only been surpassed by those of Bob Hope," one declared, and another wrote, "I was appathetic about this country. . . . But then I heard John speak of how young people can make it better. . . . Sir, I'm a registered voter now, and I'm active in our school's Ecology Club. So you see? John has taught me to be a better American." That wasn't exactly what John was after when he sang about "yellow-bellied sons of Tricky Dicky."

Most writers dwelled on John's contributions as an artist and the value of his advocacy of peace, but some were more directly political. "He is the symbol of an entire generation," one politico wrote with eloquence, "and to treat him so shamefully and to hound him so unmercifully is a slap in the face to that 'entire generation.'" "This is their crime," a writer in Lafayette, Indiana, declared: "in the land of free speech they have spoken freely."

A few suggested the possibility of more militant opposition: "I'm sure we could hold demonstrations even use violence, but would anything we did change the situation? I doubt it. You and the rest of the government, want him out, real bad."

While the INS received thousands of letters supporting John and Yoko, it also received dozens demanding their deportation. Their supporters wrote respectful, reasoned letters for the most part, but opponents often wrote violent denunciations. And what enraged opponents most was not their antiwar activities but rather their nude album cover and their earlier advocacy of psychedelic drugs. Cultural radicalism, more than political radicalism, drove opponents into a frenzy.

"John Lennon and his Japanese mistress are displaying their nude bodies in public and on his records, should be stopped, then punished and run out of the country," one opponent wrote. "The U.S. is not a cesspool for every trash that wants to live here," another declared. Still another denounced "the filthy art show of theirs in Syracuse" as "out and out pornography." Another protested that the *New York City* album cover, which showed Nixon and Mao dancing in the nude, was "obscene and grossly slanderous to the President." "Time has not lessened my position on deporting John Lennon & 'wife' Yoko Ono," an opponent declared. "There new interest is 'Primol Therapy' a supposed new cult originated by 'Dr.' Arthur Jono in Los Angeles. Lennon & wife are English and Indian problems not ours."

Some of the letters were genuinely crazy. The head of the "anti-Degradation League" wrote that John had "proved himself a major Sodomite. . . . He's responsible for much of the degradation which has been heaped on millions of young Christian Americans. He has exhibited the morals of an alley cat with his nude posing for photograph record albums . . . and his open bedroom sex sideshow interviews."

These letters were filled with false information. John was not a "convicted drug addict," as one writer claimed; Yoko was his wife, not his mistress; they never appeared in public in the nude; the bed-ins were not sex shows. And even if these statements had been true, they did not provide legal grounds for deportation anyway.

Other opponents argued that John should be deported for his politics. John "is a traitor he affiliated himself with Anti-war demonstrators stood by Vietcong flag and denaunced US," one letter complained. Another wrote, "I don't approve of them staying here they are, and have been, very subversive to this nation which they are in all demonstrations anti-Americans." A would-be informer wrote, "To my knowledge, Lennon and his wife have participated in meetings at which at least one known and documented communist was present."

Occasionally opponents offered information of some interest. "I was born and educated in Liverpool England," one letter began. "John Lennon as I recall was always a radical and because of his anti-social beliefs was considered to be sort of a naïve nut."

The INS also received letters from genuine psychotics who had become obsessed with John and Yoko. "I can no longer remain silent," one letter read. "I know the where abouts of Kyoko Cox." INS officials ordered agents to "establish contact" and "send investigators." Ten days later the agents reported that the writer "turned out to be a 'flower child' who says she had a 'vision' that Kyoko was being held someplace 7/? miles from Monterey."

Another psychotic complained to the INS about "Yoko Ono and the bugging of my apartment and the harassment she continues to pursue at me. . . . She has harmful machines in her apartment . . . some sort of spying device.

. . . She is the sole operator, & destroying my personal life; career, family life etc. . . . It's gone on for too long and I feel Yoko Ono should be put in her place." He said he'd already complained to their attorney Leon Wildes. At the time few realized how serious such threats could be.

John's fight against deportation won support from many sources. The Black Panther Party was one. "Ex-Beatle Told to 'Love It or Leave It'; U.S. to Deport John Lennon for Singing for the People," a headline in the Panther Party newspaper declared. The article denounced "the fascist U.S. government," which "saw its chance to 'get even' with John Lennon, who had previously, on many occasions, used his talents as a song writer and singer to criticize American aggression in Vietnam and oppression of the masses of people in the U.S. itself."

The Panthers drew the parallel between John and Yoko's experience and that of American blacks. "John has been no stranger to oppression and poverty, having been born of working class parents in one of the most miserable sections of England, the ghetto of Liverpool"—this was the kind of exaggeration John's Aunt Mimi had been objecting to for a decade. "John Lennon was able to escape his poverty, just as a few Blacks in America have been able to, by becoming an entertainer." "If Yoko had been a white woman, instead of Japanese, she would have automatically been awarded her child by the U.S. courts; but judicial racism and preference for her former white husband drove the case on a ridiculously long period of time." The Panther paper pointed to John's recent songs, "Luck of the Irish" and "Attica State," as well as the older "Gimme Some Truth." The article concluded, "With the people's support, they can beat the pigs. All Power to the People!"

The rhetoric seems exaggerated today, but there was a fascist aspect to the Nixon administration's persecution of John, if fascism is defined as the use of state power to eliminate political opposition, without regard for civil rights or liberties. And Yoko doubtless had been the target of racism. The remarkable thing was that America's leading black revolutionary organization would declare its solidarity with John and Yoko. Their ties to the black movement were now much stronger, compared to their earlier relationship in London with Michael X.

Rolling Stone also supported John. In June Ralph J. Gleason wrote an article summoning allies into action. "Where the hell is everybody? Why aren't the telegraph wires humming and the post office clogged and the court room filled with the people who owe . . . such an immeasurable amount of pleasure and illumination and experience to him for his music?"

While John and Yoko won support in the media, they also received denunciations. Syndicated right-wing columnist Victor Lasky described Yoko as John's "dirty-mouthed wife" and wrote that "their services to the cause of furthering Communist aggression in Indochina and weakening this country's will to resist will undoubtedly win for them Hanoi's highest honors."

═════

In the spring of 1972 John and Yoko decided they wanted to see the U.S.A. They set out driving across the country, with their assistant Peter at the wheel of an old Rambler. They ended up renting a house in Ojai, California, where Elliot Mintz met them on June 9. He had already interviewed them several times on the telephone for his show on a leading Los Angeles FM radio station. "The day we met," he recalled, "we talked politics for five or six hours. We talked about the issues they raised in the songs on *Some Time in New York City*, and about their immigration situation, among other things.

"Most of the conversation took place outside around the swimming pool. When we went inside the house, I was ushered into the bathroom. John and Yoko sat down on the edge of the tub and closed the door. I stood watching, having no idea why I should find myself in this unique circumstance. Yoko turned on the hot and cold water in the bathtub. As the water hit the tiled tub, they whispered to me that they believed the house might be bugged. Perhaps we were not alone. Then she turned the water off and we walked to the den. I was petrified.

"They were very enthusiastic about their new album, and played me an acetate. Their attitude was, 'How about this! It's brand new!' Listening to 'Woman Is the Nigger of the World' and 'Attica State' for the first time that day, I thought about how much the political climate had changed since the sixties; I thought, 'They are taking a real chance this time. And they are not afraid.' I was overwhelmed by their dedication to the issues they believed in."

Mintz had been doing successful interview and call-in shows for six years over many L.A. radio and TV stations. His guests had included many of the heroes of the sixties: Mick Jagger, Timothy Leary, R. D. Laing, Jack Nicholson, Donovan, Salvador Dali, Joan Baez, and John and Yoko. "Then I played *Some Time in New York City*," he recalled. "Shortly thereafter the program director and general manager called me in for a meeting about 'the overall future direction of the station.' When they finished, I said, 'Just let me say goodbye on the air.' They let me. The last song I played was 'Power to the People.'"

John and Yoko traveled from Ojai to San Francisco and called Craig Pyes at the *SunDance* office to say they wanted to get together. "'By the way,' Yoko said, 'do you know anybody doing acupuncture?' I told her I knew one with an illicit practice," Pyes recalled; it was all illegal at the time. She asked him to bring him to their hotel.

"I called Dr. Hong, a sixty-five-year-old Chinese acupuncturist in San

Mateo. He had never heard of John and Yoko or the Beatles. I told him, 'They're very famous singers.' He didn't understand English too well; he agreed to come and see them because he thought I had said 'senators.'

"After they saw Dr. Hong I sat down with them. We talked for five hours straight. John told me they wanted to see an acupuncturist because they were addicted to methadone. John said they had tried heroin, but 'it's the methadone that's terrible; you should do an article on it.' He said, 'We got off of heroin cold turkey in three days, but we've been trying to shake methadone for five months.' I tried to get *him* to write the article, but he wouldn't." In fact, the black market in methadone had already been recognized as a problem by the New York *Times*.

"Later I learned they also wanted help from an acupuncturist in conceiving. They wanted to have children, and had been having trouble. A student of Dr. Hong asked him what John and Yoko's problem was; he answered, 'Sex and drugs.'

"After we talked about methadone, we talked about the movement. John was doing most of the talking. He was real agitated and very political, but it wasn't the kind of politics that I was used to in the Bay Area, with fine distinctions between Marxist positions. He said, 'What I'd like to do is get Nixon and Kissinger and all them in a room and just blow it up.' He wasn't plotting to blow them up, but he was very angry. This was the easiest and quickest way he could think of to save the world. I said, 'An act of terrorism like that is elitist and denies the people their own political process.'

"He wanted to discuss whether Jerry and Abbie were CIA agents. I said, 'I know them, and I'm positive they aren't.' I said, 'Why do you ask?' He said a guy in Chicago had linked everything together. John wasn't convinced, but he at least entertained the idea.

"He talked about the two versions of 'Revolution,' 'count me out' and 'count me in.' I said, 'Well, are you out, or are you in?' He said, 'I don't know.' I thought that was a cop-out.

"He was concerned about the new album, *Some Time in New York City*. The vibes they were getting were bad. The album wasn't getting airplay. The record company wasn't pushing it."

John and Yoko left their hotel and, seeking more acupuncture, moved to the Chinese section of San Mateo, into Dr. Hong's tiny pink stucco house. The superstars spent a week there, sleeping on the living-room couch. John told Pyes it reminded him of his own Liverpool working-class childhood.

Dr. Hong had a little Chinese doctor's office set up in his living room, with an herb cabinet and a magazine stand displaying copies of *Black Belt, Judo,* and *Peking Review,* the official theoretical journal of the Chinese communists. When Hong was not treating patients, he practiced kung fu, which, he claimed, he taught at the San Mateo police department. John watched him practice and was impressed. "The most amazing thing," Pyes recalled, "was Mrs. Hong. Dr. Hong had worked in Liverpool during the early forties, unloading Liberty ships; Mrs. Hong thought that John was her husband's illegitimate son, because they looked alike."

In San Francisco John and Yoko also got together with Paul Krassner, a friend of Yoko's from the early sixties. He had been one of the first Yippies, and since 1958 had been publishing *The Realist*, a wild magazine of radical politics and obscene humor. The Watergate break-in had taken place six weeks before John and Yoko arrived in San Francisco, and the Nixon cover-up at that point was functioning perfectly. But Krassner had immediately understood the significance of Watergate and planned to devote the next issue of *The Realist* to it. He had a long Watergate article by conspiracy theorist Mae Brussell set in type, "but I didn't have the money to print the magazine— they wanted five thousand dollars cash in advance—and I didn't know how I was going to get it.

"I got home from the printer, and Yoko was on the phone," Krassner recalled in 1983. "She and John were in town and wanted to have lunch. I gave them the galleys of Mae Brussell's article. Apparently her account of the government's techniques and motivations fit right in with what was happening to them. I told them I didn't have the money to print it. There wasn't much persuasion necessary. We went to the Bank of Tokyo and they withdrew five thousand dollars cash. I remember as the issue came off the press I got melodramatic and called John in New York and said, 'I can die happy now.' He just said, 'Tut tut.' He was humble; he knew his power but he didn't take himself as seriously as his causes."

Mae Brussell's article in the August 1972 issue of *The Realist* penetrated the cover-up of the Watergate burglary, at a time when the news media accepted Nixon's statement that "no one in the White House staff, no one in this Administration presently employed, was involved in this very bizarre incident." *The Realist* article appeared two months before Woodward and Bernstein made headlines with their story in the Washington *Post*. Brussell correctly identified the break-in as one element of a much larger illegal campaign aimed at Nixon's enemies. She linked information about the Watergate burglars' CIA connections, remarks made by John Mitchell's wife, Martha, about administration "dirty tricks," and reports that Nixon's reelection strategy included plans to use provocateurs to make it appear radicals were disrupting the Republican national convention. John must have realized that Nixon's effort to deport him was part of this larger effort.

But how large was it? Brussell did not view Watergate simply as one element in Nixon's reelection campaign; it had been planned, she declared, as part of a "political coup d'état" by the same people who "put Hitler in power" and "killed President Kennedy and Robert Kennedy." They had now made "provisions . . . to eliminate the outdated Constitution" and were prepared to cancel the 1972 elections and create "a Fascist dictatorship" in the United States. This crackpot conspiracy theorizing had been inspired in part by recent statements by Louis Tackwood, who claimed to reveal information he had learned as a police undercover agent.

To be sure, understanding the real dimensions of the Watergate conspiracy was not easy that summer. Even when Woodward and Bernstein later presented their evidence, Nixon's spokesmen convinced many that the *Post* stories were a "collection of absurdities," "a senseless pack of lies," "the shoddiest type of journalism." Nevertheless, for John to sponsor the publication of Mae Brussell's crazy views, he must have been deeply frightened about his own case. "We were all in a very paranoid state," Krassner recalled in 1983. "Everybody called me paranoid, and I thought maybe I was paranoid —a lot of paranoia is just ego fulfillment. You think you're so important that they will persecute you. It was a tricky area."

Krassner's speculations about conspiracies went beyond linking the Kennedy assassination and Watergate. He told John about his "theory that, with all the political assassinations, there were also cultural assassinations. I was wondering what he thought about the possibility that the deaths of Janis Joplin, Jim Morrison, Jimi Hendrix, and maybe Otis Redding may have been made to look like suicides, because they were rebels and role models on the crest of the wave. John said, 'No, no, they were just going in a self-destructive direction.' A few months after that, when things must have gotten really heavy with him, he reminded me of that conversation and said, 'Listen, if anything happens to Yoko and me, it was not an accident.' " That remark, made late in 1972, showed how the deportation order had aroused some of John's deepest fears.

———

In an effort to demonstrate his good citizenship, John accepted an invitation from Geraldo Rivera to headline a benefit concert at Madison Square Garden in August 1972 for Rivera's One to One foundation. The foundation promoted individual treatment for mentally retarded children, which today seems uncontroversial. In 1972, however, a national scandal had erupted after Rivera exposed the nightmarish conditions under which retarded people lived at New York State's Willowbrook home. On his TV news show Rivera showed film revealing that Willowbrook residents were physically abused, denied adequate clothing, and left in filthy conditions.

"The whole idea of the event was to take mentally retarded people out of the closet," Rivera explained. "Aside from being warehoused in horrible, wretched, filthy places, they were also being kept out of public view. The fund-raising concert sought to deinstitutionalize them. We also wanted to bring them into a great public space so people could see them and relate to them on a one-to-one basis—that's where we got the title.

"We planned a big festival for one afternoon in Central Park, and 'Imagine' was the theme. Each retarded person from an institution would be paired with one able-bodied volunteer—twenty-five thousand people in the park. The issue arose whether the retarded should come to the matinee concert at Madison Square Garden. Obviously it would be a huge revenue loss. So Allen Klein and John just bought fifty thousand dollars' worth of tickets and gave them to the retarded kids and volunteers."

Suddenly John got cold feet, after the concert had been sold out for weeks. "John said he didn't want to do it," Rivera recalled. "He said he hadn't played in public for years, he hadn't rehearsed with a band, he was just too nervous. . . . When they had that rush of insecurity, Yoko told me that she and John called Paul and Linda. They said, 'Let's bury the hatchet and appear together at the concert.' Why Paul said 'No' I'll never know." Rivera and others managed to calm John's fears and get him to start rehearsing with Elephant's Memory.

The next problem came from ABC, which planned to run the concert as a TV special. "They became very skittish about how much Yoko would be musically involved in the hour broadcast," Rivera remembered. "It was a very, very sensitive issue. Because Yoko was very much a factor in getting John to say yes in the first place. It would never have happened but for Yoko, and John was committed to her having almost equal billing." ABC won that round. The TV special had virtually none of Yoko's singing.

The concert bill included Stevie Wonder, who had played the John Sinclair concert with John and Yoko. His "Superstition" had just reached Number One on the charts. Roberta Flack and Sha Na Na also appeared, recruited by Rivera. John had appeared at big concerts only twice before without the Beatles: at the 1969 Toronto Rock and Roll Revival, which he agreed to do on one day's notice and rehearsed with his pickup band on the plane; and in Ann Arbor, which also was a performance without a real band. The One to One benefit was the only fully rehearsed public concert John gave between the 1966 American tour and his death.

The show was a triumph. Despite pressure to play down his politics, John's radicalism lay at the heart of his performance. He sang his Beatles song "Come Together," emphatically pointing his finger at the audience on the line "One thing I can tell you is you got to be free!" He changed the words, to "Come together / Stop the war / Right now!" A great cheer arose from the thousands of people in the Garden, while he repeated the phrase "Come together" over and over, giving an old song an urgent new political meaning. Nixon had been right to fear this power.

In this context "Instant Karma!" also took on a new political significance, when John sang "You better recognize your brothers / In everyone you meet," and asked, "Why in the world are we here? Surely not to live in pain and fear." He sang "Imagine," with another subtle but meaningful change: "Imagine no possessions / I wonder if *we* can" instead of "if *you* can." Instead of addressing his audience as an outsider, he placed himself among them. And he sang "Cold Turkey" with a frightening intensity. What had him "on the run" this time was the government, and his screams of pain and rage were too realistic, too genuine. Most in the audience were blind to his obvious pain; they cheered and applauded, having a great time. At the end of the song, John said softly but with unmistakable irony, "You enjoyed that, didn't you?" Then he recovered his good spirits with an exuberant "Hound Dog." He may not have believed in Elvis, but he still loved his early music.

For the finale John and Stevie Wonder led the entire cast and audience in a sizzling reggae version of "Give Peace a Chance," more angry and defiant, the hottest he had ever done. Twenty thousand people in Madison Square Garden sang the refrain over and over, while John shouted, "No more war!" and Stevie Wonder moaned, "Oh baby, say it again!" It was a triumphant political moment for John, and one of the great moments of political music of the decade.

═══

As the Republican convention approached, the Miami FBI office was brought into action. Acting Director Gray sent a memo: "Miami should note that LENNON is reportedly a heavy user of narcotics known as 'downers.' This information should be emphasized to local Law Enforcement Agencies, with regards to subject being arrested if at all possible on possession of narcotics charge." FBI agents do not enforce the laws making possession of narcotics a crime. They had to get the local cops to try: this memo sounds like a concrete proposal from the FBI that local police set John up for a drug bust. "INS has stressed to Bureau that if LENNON were to be arrested in US for possession of narcotics he would become more likely to be immediately deportable," the memo explained to agents too dumb to get the point.

In July the FBI prepared a new information sheet on John and his links to radicals and communists. This time they attached "descriptive data and photograph of Lennon," perhaps the single most amazing item in his entire file. First, it's surprising that the FBI believed its agents needed a photo of John to be able to identify him. His face was one of the best known in the world. But the truly astonishing fact is that the photo in the FBI file is not of John. It's David Peel.

Peel actually did look something like John at the time. He wore the same wire-rimmed glasses and had the same haircut. *Rolling Stone* had run a photo of John at the John Sinclair concert, which they captioned "Does he look like David Peel?"

On August 1 the San Francisco FBI informed the acting director that John was going to come out for McGovern in the 1972 elections. The source of this information was a newsletter of a small socialist group, dutifully quoted in the FBI memo: "the only mass-based, independent political party calling for Socialism: the People's Party!" John and Yoko did urge people to vote, not to sit the election out, and to vote against Nixon and for McGovern. The *New York City* album cover had included the slogan "Remember to Vote." John and Yoko wrote in their *SunDance* column, "To the hard-hats who think that they don't have the power to free themselves from the tyranny and suppression of the capitalists: it's not their power or money that is controlling you. Their power depends on your fear and apathy. . . . REMEMBER TO VOTE."

Many radicals took the same position in support of McGovern, arguing that the political choices in 1972 were fundamentally different from 1968. In 1968 Humphrey had defended Johnson's war policy; but McGovern was not Humphrey, and Nixon was as bad as his opponents had predicted. John and Yoko, of course, had additional reasons for wanting Nixon defeated: his attorney general had initiated the deportation proceedings. Some musicians actually worked for McGovern: Warren Beatty organized benefit concerts at which Simon and Garfunkel, the Grateful Dead, and Peter, Paul and Mary appeared. They raised $1.5 million.

The Republicans met in Miami from August 21 to 24, 1972, to renominate Nixon. The FBI's attempt to locate John among the demonstrators provides a ludicrous conclusion to its Keystone Kops effort to keep track of his activities. An FBI agent working "as a member of the Weatherman Task Group" traveled from New York to Miami. He reported to the acting director that John "was not observed by the case agent" in Miami and "it is believed that the subject did not travel to Miami for the Republican National Convention as he had previously planned."

A month later the FBI was still trying to prove that John had been there. The Miami FBI reported to the acting director that they were examining the records of all 1,200 people arrested during demonstrations at the convention to see if John was among them. The idea that John could have been arrested at the Republican convention without the media finding out was particularly absurd. The investigation in Miami continued for two more months, until October 24, when the head of the Miami FBI reported to the acting director his firm conclusion: the records "failed to reflect that the subject was one of those arrested."

John hit the low point of his performing career when he and Yoko appeared with Elephant's Memory on the Jerry Lewis Telethon on Labor Day in September 1972. "John and I love this country very much, and we're very happy that we're still here," Yoko said. "At this time last year we had it a little easier," John said—they hadn't received a deportation order. "Jerry is one of our favorite comedians," he added.

Then they played good music—"Imagine" and their reggae "Give Peace a Chance"—for a bad cause. The problem was not with helping victims of muscular dystrophy; the problem was the way Jerry Lewis did it. The case was made succinctly in 1982 by two groups representing eight million handicapped Americans. The American Coalition for Citizens with Disabilities and the Disability Rights Center attacked the Jerry Lewis Telethon for portraying disabled people as pitiful and doomed. They do need help, the groups declared, but they also are asking for a little respect.

Before and after John and Yoko appeared, Jerry Lewis went through his telethon shtick, making maudlin appeals for cash, alternately mugging and weeping, parading victims of muscular dystrophy across the Las Vegas stage, and generally claiming to be the friend to the sick. Most offensive of all was his cuddling up to corporate America. Public-relations men from United Airlines, McDonald's, Anheuser-Busch, and others appeared to hand Jerry checks. He responded by pontificating about what wonderful friends we all have in the corporations.

John and Yoko permitted themselves to be exploited this way because they were trying to clean up their act, to impress the immigration authorities that they were good citizens. And, to be fair, many big stars went on the telethon; Paul and Ringo did in subsequent years. However, there were other points where John and Yoko could have stopped on their way from Jerry Rubin to Jerry Lewis. The One to One benefit provides the best example. An impeccable cause from the perspective of the INS, it was also politically preferable to Jerry's telethon. The One to One benefit arose out of a political scandal. It was associated with a demand that the state of New York provide better and more humane treatment for retarded people. And the benefit itself was a straight concert, with a minimum of sentimentalizing the victims or claiming credit for the performers.

During the presidential campaign that fall, Nixon raised and spent more money than any candidate in history—much of it illegal corporate contributions laundered through Mexican banks. A massive campaign of sabotage and espionage effectively divided and embarrassed Democratic candidates. The war in Vietnam, of course, was the central issue. Two weeks before election day Secretary of State Henry Kissinger announced, "Peace is at hand" in the negotiations. (Six weeks after the election the United States mounted the most terrible bombing raids of the entire war, destroying Bach Mai hospital, the largest in Southeast Asia.)

On November 7, 1972, Nixon won 60.7 percent of the popular vote, more than any Republican candidate in history, and the largest plurality since LBJ defeated Goldwater in 1964. Nixon got more electoral votes than LBJ had, carrying every state except Massachusetts and the District of Columbia.

John had thought McGovern could win, even though the polls had consistently reported that he didn't have a chance. McGovern's defeat meant that the INS would remain in Nixon's hands and that John's deportation was much more likely. But the full impact of that fact didn't hit John until election night, when he went to Jerry Rubin's to watch the returns.

John and Yoko didn't arrive until McGovern's crushing defeat had become clear. "He came into the house screaming," Rubin said, "crazy with rage."

"This is it?" he shouted. "This is *it?* I can't believe this is fuckin' *it!* I mean, here we are—*this* is the fuckin' revolution: Jerry Rubin, John and Yoko, and accessories. This is the fuckin' middle-class bunch that's gonna protect *us* from *them!*"

"How can you call us bourgeois?" someone shouted. "You're a fuckin' capitalist!"

"I know I'm a fuckin' bourgeois capitalist. That doesn't mean I can't—"

Stan Bronstein of Elephant's Memory interrupted him. "You, John, *you* are gonna protect you from them. You and your friends. Organize your friends, organize your block, organize your neighborhood!" Somebody else shouted, "Yeah, organize people. They'll listen to *you.*"

"Listen to me? Man, where've you been? They haven't been listening to me!" Then he went around the room, shoving and pushing people, telling them, "You're not strong, you can't even beat Nixon!"

"There were about six people left," Rubin later recalled. "John walked over to a woman—nobody famous—and started fondling her in front of everybody. Then he took her into my bedroom. It was a humiliation for Yoko—total humiliation. I'd never seen him do anything like it before. He was totally out of it on drugs. Their relationship ended right there—even if they did live together for a few more months. That's what broke John and Yoko up."

Ordinary rock stars were expected to sleep with women they met at parties. John himself had spoken of the Beatles' *Satyricon* on tour. John's actions on election night at Rubin's apartment shocked his friends because he had grown away from the life of ordinary rock stars. But when he saw the political triumph of his tormentors, he fell into a self-destructive rage, turning first on his friends, then on Yoko. As his political hopes were destroyed, he struck destructive blows at his personal life. Thus, in an unintended way, the link John had forged in his own life between the personal and the political held firm.

═══

The radical leaders with whom John had been involved ended their political careers at about the same time. Rennie Davis went first: he lost his mind to a boy guru. Rubin, hounded and ridiculed by the new generation of Yippies (who called themselves Zippies), withdrew from politics and disappeared into a smorgasbord of therapies and health fads. Abbie Hoffman, trapped selling cocaine, went underground.

Some critics and fans maintained that John's involvement with them had been a mistake from the beginning. Certainly the Yippies' weaknesses were more significant than their strengths. If they had the boldness to try to work with the mass media, they made themselves celebrities rather than leaders responsible to an organized movement. If their outrageous stunts exposed the pretensions and boredom of routine politics, they lacked a real analysis or strategy. If they spoke to counterculture youth outside the universities, they encouraged a mindless militance.

Not all of this was the Yippies' fault. The participatory and anti-elitist values of SDS worked against the development of New Left leaders and organizations. The political inexperience and the emphasis on personal commitment which characterized the student movement led to a belief that the solution to every political problem was increased militance. The reliance on Third World revolutions for ideological models isolated the New Left from mainstream America. All of these problems existed independently of the Yippies.

John shared some but not all of the Yippie flaws. His easy access to the media spotlight increased his distance from the kind of political work necessary for building a real movement. And Yippie media tactics did not help John's personal goals. Abbie Hoffman and Jerry Rubin were people who became celebrities; John was a celebrity who wanted to become a person. Yippie politics were not a good way to accomplish that.

John parted company from the Yippies, and from the New Left as a whole, on one key political point: the escalation of militance. To his credit, John never argued that increasing militance was the test of revolutionary commitment. As a pop star, he had been trained to think about reaching the masses of ordinary young people. Perhaps that helped him see how the cult of militance isolated the left. And his pacifism also helped him avoid the excesses of militant tactics.

In spite of their flaws, the Yippies had brought John into the real world of sixties politics, a reality that had been almost completely absent from Beatle life, and which was not Yoko's forte either. With the Yippies, John campaigned against the British in Northern Ireland, politics which expressed his own class and ethnic roots. He spoke out against the repression of black radicals in the United States. And of course he worked long and hard to end the war in Vietnam.

His feminism also developed during this period of activism, independently of his Yippie connections. "They could have been lots more on center for feminism," Yoko's friend Kate Millett said in 1983. "When they arrived in New York, the antiwar movement was in a state of disintegration. But we feminists were doing pretty well. They could have used their prestige to do something big—big concerts—there were umpteen ways to move."

John's movement friends often thought about what he could have done that wouldn't have aroused the Nixon administration. Maybe Nixon wouldn't have gone after John if he hadn't considered the reckless Yippie plan for demonstrations at the Republican national convention; or if he hadn't agreed to the ambitious Yippie plan for a concert tour mixing rock and radical politics; or if he hadn't gone along with the frenzied Yippie engagement with so many issues; or if he'd joined the movement in America earlier, when it was growing instead of disintegrating; or if he hadn't teamed up with Jerry Rubin, who reflected and magnified some of his own weaknesses; if instead of Rubin he had found someone who could have provided balance for his politics the way McCartney had balanced his music. Maybe if he hadn't been so enthusiastic, so committed, so extreme, maybe then the Nixon administration would have left him alone.

But that wouldn't have been John. He could no longer be a moderate man. He wasn't alone; especially after the May 1972 mining of Haiphong Harbor, few in the movement could remain moderate. And John's passionate commitments lay at the heart of his best work. They were among his most appealing qualities.

It has often been argued that the movement destroyed itself through its own stupidity. That was not the case with the anti-Nixon tour John had been planning. It didn't destroy itself; it was destroyed, by government repression. The strategy and tactics of the tour made it extremely promising—so much so that the Nixon administration felt it had to act. John's problem was not the stupidity of his political plans, but rather their potential effectiveness.

22

"Lennon Forgets"

 With the reelection of Nixon, the FBI realized it had accomplished its task in the Lennon case. "In view of subject's inactivity in Revolutionary Activities and his seemingly [*sic*] rejection by NY radicals, his case is being closed," the head of the New York office reported to the acting director.

The INS, however, refused to follow suit. One week after election day its attorneys filed a new brief, indicating they had no intention of letting up on Lennon. That was a grim development. Nixon had what he wanted: four more years, plus the humiliation of his opponents, including Lennon, who had been driven from activist politics. But that wasn't enough for the administration. John's worst fears were coming true.

One bright spot appeared on this otherwise dark landscape. London Detective Sergeant Norman Pilcher, who had arrested John in 1968, was himself charged with "conspiracy to pervert the course of justice" on November 8, 1972. John had been saying the marijuana Pilcher found in his London apartment had been planted before his arrest. If Pilcher was found guilty, John's conviction might be reversed, and the INS would have no basis for deporting him. Wildes requested a delay in John's hearings until Pilcher's verdict was in, but the INS refused to wait.

On December 19 another glimmer of hope appeared for John when a bill was introduced in the British Parliament that would expunge minor marijuana convictions like his own. Wildes immediately requested a delay from the INS, which it denied. On March 23, 1973, INS hearing officer Ira Fieldsteel issued a forty-seven-page opinion: Yoko's application for permanent residency was granted, John's was denied. He had sixty days to leave the country.

Wildes appealed to an INS board on April 2. On April 13 he filed a request under the Freedom of Information Act for INS documents, hoping to prove that other aliens with minor marijuana convictions like John's had not been deported. On April 26 he requested a delay in the appeal proceedings until the documents were provided. The appeals board scheduled oral arguments for September 10.

John's defense team had a second strategy: change the immigration law. On April 30 a bill was introduced in Congress giving the attorney general the power to grant residency to aliens with minor marijuana convictions. The bill was sponsored in the House by Edward Koch of New York (later mayor) and in the Senate by Alan Cranston of California. Neither of New York's senators —Conservative James Buckley and Republican Jacob Javits—had been willing to sponsor the bill, but twelve other representatives co-sponsored it. Congress didn't pass it that year, but ten years later essentially the same bill became law.

Around this time John and Yoko bought an apartment in the Dakota, a historic building on Central Park West inhabited by celebrities, including Lauren Bacall, Leonard Bernstein, and Rex Reed. Over the next few years John and Yoko bought additional apartments in the building as they became vacant. Some first-floor apartments were turned into their offices, and they lived on the sixth floor, with a glorious view of Central Park. The move out of their two-room apartment in Greenwich Village and into the celebrity-filled Dakota symbolized their withdrawal from political activism.

In June John went to Cambridge, Massachusetts, with Yoko, where she gave a performance for the 350 delegates attending the International Feminist Planning Conference convened by the National Organization for Women at the Harvard Divinity School. John and Yoko were drawing closer to the feminist movement "as they began to see the antiwar movement from the feminist perspective as male-dominated," their assistant Jon Hendricks later explained.

Danny Schechter, the "news dissector" at Boston's WBCN-FM, interviewed them. No radio station had done more to link the counterculture with New Left politics. Schechter asked Yoko how John had changed as a result of his engagement with women's issues. "You might think it's trivial," she said. "He's learning what it is to cook. . . . He's starting to open up that side."

Schechter asked John, "You a good cook?"

John answered in falsetto, "A man's work is never done, my dear." Then in his own voice: "No, I just wanted to do it. Actually I've only cooked one meal." That did sound trivial. "Most males are brought up not knowing how to cook or look after themselves. If nobody was around I'd probably starve to death. It's been a process of four or five years. It was like having one eye shut. Once you start acknowledging that women are oppressed, you can never go back. We're not a quote completely liberated couple, and we still go through a lot of struggle. It's usually for space." John was using the movement terminology: "struggle."

"How do you deal with monogamy as a couple?" Schechter asked, one of the central questions of the day.

"Very well," John said in a mock-deadpan voice.

Yoko answered, "Many women fool around because they're deprived of expressing themselves in any other way. I have so much work to do. Between my work and John there's very little time left. Because I give so much attention to my work, I'm concerned about are we giving enough to each other."

John gave his answer. "Both of us before were sexually pretty free individuals. . . . It's like when you're a kid and have some money and go to the candy shop and fill yourself full of everything. You can do that for your whole life if you want. But what the hell, you have to spend your whole time at it. And we prefer to spend our whole time together, or working on our relationship. We don't get enough time together."

Schechter brought up the delicate question of John's recent distance from radical politics. "Politically you seem to have not been visibly connected with what little has been happening."

"Exactly," John replied, "what little has been happening." But he knew that wasn't the reason. "When it gets into the media, it's the same as the Beatles. People say, 'Oh, that's what you're doing. Please keep doing that forever so we can get it adjusted in our heads as to what you are doing.' Well, we're just living and moving on."

John did not have a coherent explanation of why he was "moving on," away from movement politics, although there were plenty of reasons for him to make such a move, some better than others. His immigration fight precluded it. He had gotten discouraged and disillusioned by McGovern's defeat. Lots of others had too.

Schechter tried a different tack: "Are you working on any musical projects?"

"I don't work on musical projects," John said emphatically. "I either write songs or I don't. It's getting to be work. It's ruining the music. It's like after you leave school and you don't want to read a book. Every time I strap the guitar on, it's the same old jazz. I just feel like breathing a bit." He was not admitting that the failure of the *New York City* album had undermined his artistic energy. He went on to comment that on "the first album I put out on my own—George was on that. Or was it Ringo? George was on *Imagine.*" He was having trouble remembering even his greatest work.

Yoko tried to help, pointing out that John wasn't the typical musician churning out one album after another, unable to imagine anything else to do. "It's really sad that people have such set minds. But John just dives into things —boom, like that—and sees what happens. People say, 'Why are you at this conference? What's your intention?' We just dived in, and a lot of things happened as a result." She was right; that was one of John's strengths. But it also caused him a lot of pain when the projects he dived into dried up.

Finally Schechter asked the inevitable question about the possibility of a Beatles reunion. "Just imagine the Beatles getting together again," John replied. "Whatever they did would not be good enough." Already the Beatles were "they" instead of "we." "Because everybody has this incredible dream about how it was in the sixties. But it could never be the same. It's just a dream—"

Schechter interrupted: "—which, I think someone once said, is over."

"Yeah," John shot back, "but we haven't woken up yet."

Yoko had recently released an album of feminist songs, *Approximately Infinite Universe,* her best album of the seventies. It's so much better than her work on *Some Time in New York City,* recorded only seven months earlier, that it's hard to believe the same person did both. The album gained a following among feminists: Ellen Willis and Kate Millett each list it as one of their favorite feminist albums. "Catman," a song with a driving dance beat, spoke for some feminist troublemakers, "the rosies." They hurled sexual taunts at the uptight Catman: "Hey dumbballs," Yoko sang, telling him to stop "shining" his "tools." "Don't be a prune . . . give us all you've got."

"What a Mess" ridiculed men who argue that fetuses have a right of life. She did it in her staccato singing style, with a heavy Latin blues accompaniment. "What a Bastard the World Is" powerfully expressed female rage and fear. "What a bastard you are," she sang, "leaving me all night missing you." She called him a jerk, a pig, the scum of the earth; then her fear of loneliness overcame her anger, and she cried, "Please don't go, I didn't mean it." She said that women's liberation was "nice for Joan of Arc," but was a "long way for Terry and Jill."

"I Want My Love to Rest Tonight" was a unique feminist love song, expressing forgiveness for a man: "Sisters don't blame my man too much," she sang, and told them also not to blame their men too much. Men were all raised by women, who encouraged their competitiveness and taught them to repress tender feelings. The lyrics were too didactic, but still it was a surprising and impressive song. "What Did I Do!" was pure funkadelic rhythm. Yoko's shrieks and cries fit in nicely with the raucous band. "Move on Fast" had a furious rock beat. Yoko sang in a nervous, blank voice that qualifies as proto–New Wave.

Several of the songs expressed strong, even violent, feelings: "feeling cold from fear of needing you, feeling faint from fear of wanting you" in "Shirana-katta (I Didn't Know)," and "Feel Like Smashing My Face in a Clear Glass Window." The best of these songs about feeling bad was the last one, "Looking Over from My Hotel Window" at "age thirty-nine . . . ninety-five-pound bundle but it's trouble when there's nowhere to leave." Accompanied only by Yoko herself on piano, with an echo on her voice, the song was haunting.

Approximately Infinite Universe spent twice as long on the *Billboard* charts as her two previous albums, *Yoko Ono/Plastic Ono Band* and *Fly*. It was on the charts a total of six weeks—a modest success. It should have had a much bigger audience. John was credited as producer, and the album was dedicated to him, "my best friend of the second sex."

It's easy to read these songs for signs of her impending separation from John. But *Approximately Infinite Universe* had a larger significance: its successful bringing together of the personal and the political. Yoko's commitment to honesty in her music, her ability to face contradictory feelings, and most important, her willingness to make private fears public, allowed others to see that they were not alone. These steps toward overcoming isolation have been fundamental to the feminist movement.

═══

In the misery of the deportation struggle, the Watergate crisis provided some pleasure for John and Yoko. At the end of June 1973 they attended the Senate Watergate Committee hearings in Washington to see in person the men who had disrupted their lives, to watch them twist slowly, slowly in the wind. "I thought it was better on TV," he said, "because you could see more. When it first came on I watched it live all day, so I just had the urge to actually go. . . . Every time there was a break in the proceedings I had to sign autographs. I was looking like a Buddhist monk at the time with all my hair chopped off, and I thought nobody would spot me. But they spotted Yoko, and assumed—rightly—that I must be with her."

While in Washington, John took part in his first demonstration since the Haiphong Harbor bombing protests a year earlier. He and Yoko joined twenty people picketing the South Vietnamese embassy in June, demanding freedom for a political prisoner held by the Saigon government. They explained that the prisoner was a woman, a Buddhist, and a neutralist who opposed the war, and that she had been imprisoned for almost two years. The Washington *Post* ran a photo of John and Yoko at the demonstration, wearing coolie hats. John could still practice his old trade, publicity, when he wanted to.

John's best chance of winning his immigration case was for the Watergate crisis to deepen, which of course it did. In October Nixon ordered his new attorney general, Elliot Richardson, to fire the Watergate special prosecutor, Archibald Cox, for seeking the White House tapes. Richardson refused and resigned. The White House chief of staff, General Alexander Haig, told William Ruckelshaus, the next official in line, "You have received an order from your Commander-in-Chief." He too refused and was fired.

Five days after this "Saturday Night Massacre" outraged public opinion, John seized the time and struck back at the crippled President with a lawsuit. The suit demanded that the INS affirm or deny that it had violated the law by wiretapping or surveillance of John and/or Wildes. John made public an INS memo that appeared to order wiretapping and surveillance. Titled "The Supervision of the Activities of Both John and Yoko Lennon," sent from "Supervisor, Intelligence Division, Unit 2" to "Regional Director, Group 8," the memo read, "Their relations with one (6521) Jerry Rubin, and one John Sinclair (4536), also their many commitments which are judged to be political and unfavorable to the present administration. This was set forth to your office in a previous report. Because of this and their controversial behavior, they are to be judged as both undesirable and dangerous aliens.

"Because of the delicate and explosive nature of this matter the whole affair has been handed over to the I&N Service to handle. Your office is to maintain a constant surveillance of their residence and a periodic report is to be sent to this office. All cooperation is to be given to the I&N Service and all reports are to be digested by this office."

In the suit John requested that a hearing be held to determine whether the government prejudged his case, and whether his rights had been violated by the surveillance. A second suit filed the same day demanded that the INS supply the documents Wildes had requested under the FOIA. John's suit made headlines; for the first time the connection between Nixon's abuse of power in the Watergate break-in and his effort to deport Lennon was becoming clear to the public. News of John's suit appeared in the New York *Times* next to an ad calling for Nixon's impeachment.

The government responded to John's wiretapping charges on October 31. The FBI file shows that, in response to a court order, one part of the Bureau asked another whether there was any truth in John's allegations. "Review failed to indicate that Lennon or premises in which he had proprietary interest have been subjected to any lawful electronic surveillance," the FBI report concluded.

The FBI statement provided a perfect example of the "nondenial denial," which was becoming a familiar part of the Watergate defense presented by Nixon and his associates. These were strongly worded statements which on close examination were found to contain carefully constructed loopholes. The FBI response to John's suit contained at least three. It said he had not been subject to any "lawful" FBI surveillance; but he claimed their surveillance had been unlawful. The FBI said its "review failed to indicate" surveillance, which left open the possibility that its review had been incomplete. And the FBI denied that it had surveyed John, which left open the possibility that he had been bugged and followed by other government agencies, such as the INS or the New York police.

=====

The sixties were over, but living parts of the New Left could still be found in feminist, Third World, and environmental groups; the left in some places organized around local issues such as housing, rent control, and food co-ops. Even if John had remained a political activist, it would have been hard for a person in his position—English superstar—to find a way to join these activities after the war was over. In this political context, what is remarkable about John is not that he became inactive. What is remarkable is that he maintained a radical position at all. At a time when many good radicals completely burned themselves out or fell silent, John continued to work on and put out new political songs, as was evident on his next album, recorded in September and released the next month: *Mind Games*.

"It was originally called *Make Love Not War*," John said in 1980. "But that was such a cliché that you couldn't say it any more, so I wrote it obscurely, but it's all the same story." When the album came out, he recalled, "everybody was starting to say the Sixties was a joke, it didn't mean anything, those love-and-peaceniks were idiots. . . . I was trying to say, 'No, just keep doin' it.'"

Critics didn't hear the album's political music. Roy Carr of *Melody Maker* praised it as a "rejection of the mindless militancy" of *Some Time in New York City*. *Beatlemania* author Ron Schaumburg, who hated all of John's political music, picked out "Bring on the Lucie" as one he especially liked, as did other critics of John's politics, including Beatles historian Nicholas Schaffner. That song, however, is as political as anything John wrote. The first verse explained John's response to his immigration struggle: paranoia is every-where, he said, but it helped to shout "Free the people, now!," which in fact was the chorus of the song. The next verse addressed Nixon and his henchmen: as their Watergate crimes were exposed, John reminded them of Vietnam and the blood of the people they killed. Musically, the song was reminiscent of "Power to the People" but was more personal, expressing John's own fears aroused by the threat of deportation.

The liner notes indicated that the song following "Bring on the Lucie" was the "Nutopian International Anthem." The jacket included the "Declaration of Nutopia," John's whimsical retort to the deportation order, issued back before the case had become so oppressive. When listeners looked for the "Nutopian International Anthem" on the record, they found nothing. Many concluded that the song consisted of three seconds of silence between cuts on the album—an old John Cage trick.

On the whole, *Mind Games* revealed the extent of the damage the deportation fight was doing to John as an artist. The new album marked a return to the rich sound of *Imagine*, which was a good sound, but at this point in John's work it indicated he was drawing back from risk-taking. His best work had always been risky: the stark and intensely personal *Plastic Ono Band*, the simple and lyrical "Imagine." Along with the feelings of powerlessness and fear instilled by the government came a loss of artistic energy and confidence.

Critic Lester Bangs did hear the political songs on *Mind Games*, and he didn't like them. "This ain't Frantz Fanon, it's the same fat limey who sang 'Twist and Shout,' " he wrote in *Creem* at the time. "Through his successive solo albums John's always incredibly gauche topical toons have been undergoing a purgative loosening-up which has now reached its final stages and the pinnacle of eloquence here, where he throws all those trite slogans around like dice." Bangs thought this "obviously can only be healthy for all concerned," since the ideas John expressed on the album were "meaningless gibberish."

The politics of *Mind Games* were considered by other rock writers. *Crawdaddy* praised John for "managing to submerge his politics, in deference to the Immigration Man, while keeping a subversive edge." Jon Landau considered the album worse than *Some Time in New York City*, as John was "lost in the changing social and musical environment of the seventies."

John did an interview in *Crawdaddy* in which he summed up his year. Recalling that his historic *Rolling Stone* interview had been titled "Lennon Remembers," he suggested this one be called "Lennon Forgets."

Had he forgotten about the failure of the *New York City* album? "I can't remember what I felt," he said. "I must not have been happy about it because who likes to get crapped on, but I was still glad and proud of 'Woman Is the Nigger of the World.' I believe it and it was a good record. It sounds good and just too bad nobody wanted to hear it or play it. . . . What else was there? Oh yeah, it was alright but it wasn't what they wanted, whoever 'they' are."

That wasn't what he was supposed to be saying. The publicity campaign for *Mind Games* was handled by Tony King, who told John, "You're not angry, you're not a radical. . . . You're a musician, not a crusader. That's the message the press should give the public. When people like you, John, they want to buy your albums. When they don't like you, . . . they don't want your records in their homes. It's as simple as that."

John wasn't successful at following these instructions, as his promo interview in *Melody Maker* revealed. "Tell me about the new album," he was asked. "The album's called *Mind Games,*" he said, "and it's, well, just an album. It's rock and roll at different speeds. It's not a political album, or an introspective album. . . . There's no very deep message about it. . . . The only reason I make albums is because you're supposed to."

Mind Games had modest success. It peaked in the charts at Number Nine. The *New York City* album had peaked at Forty-eight, *Imagine* at Number One. It remained on the charts for eighteen weeks, not much longer than *New York City.* During the same period the *Ringo* album reached Number Three, and Paul's *Band on the Run* reached Number One for four weeks and spent an awesome seventy-four weeks on the charts. The "Mind Games" single did poorly, getting no higher than Number Eighteen. In 1980 John claimed credit for his having been one of the first to incorporate reggae. The "Mind Games" single has "basically a reggae middle-eight if you listen to it," he said. "It ain't bad."

In the year and a half since the first deportation order, John and his lawyers had appeared at six hearings or decisions; they had made motions, made requests, or filed briefs on fourteen different occasions; they had gone to U.S. district court and the Board of Immigration Appeals; they had gotten bills introduced in Parliament and in Congress. Despite this herculean effort John was still under order to depart in sixty days, temporarily suspended during appeal. Under this relentless pressure, John's work and his personal life were deteriorating.

John and Yoko reached the point where they decided a separation was necessary. Yoko told John to go to Los Angeles. Elliot Mintz explained, "It was as if she was saying, 'Go to Disneyland. Go to Hefner heaven. Get your hit of all that stuff. Just get it out of your system.' " He finished *Mind Games* in September and left in October with their assistant May Pang.

From the perspective of his immigration battle, John's breakup with Yoko was a dangerously self-destructive act. For a year and a half John had been arguing that deporting him would split up a couple searching for their daughter. Just six months before, Yoko had pleaded with immigration hearing officer Fieldsteel not to compel her to choose between her child and her husband. After the most recent deportation order, John and Yoko had issued a joint statement: "Having just celebrated our fourth anniversary, we are not prepared to sleep in separate beds. Peace and love." Their defense committee had gotten hundreds of their celebrity friends and thousands of their supporters to argue that deporting John would be cruel and heartless to Yoko. By going to California with May Pang "he was affecting his eligibility," Leon Wildes said later. "His case was being threatened. The government was interested. I would get an occasional call from the government: 'I understand your clients aren't living together, Leon.' I had to tread very carefully."

John and Yoko had come together in May '68, taken LSD, appeared naked, given peace a chance, and generally done their own thing; they had exemplified the spirit of the decade. The sixties finally expired in 1973, when the United States withdrew its troops from Vietnam, when Nixon's presidency collapsed, and when the oil embargo and the ensuing recession destroyed the economic boom which had enabled youth culture to flourish. Just as John and Yoko together had represented the high point of the sixties, their breakup in 1973 seemed to symbolize its end.

23

"No More '74"

 "Whoopee! Bachelor life!"—that was John's initial response to their decision to separate. "I picked them up at the airport in L.A.," Elliot Mintz recalled. "He was pretty excited. He was free, on his way to Hollywood. He had a pile of traveler's checks and said he didn't know how to turn them into money. I took him to my bank, where he signed a hundred hundred-dollar checks and the bank gave him ten thousand dollars in cash. He'd had a couple of drinks on the plane, and insisted on putting the ten thousand dollars in his pocket. John told me he'd never been in a bank before. I said, 'Would you like to see what a supermarket looks like?'

"He was really happy for about a week. I took him for a tour of the stars' homes. He pointed out the house where he and Yoko had lived when they were in therapy with Janov. He wanted to show me the house where the Beatles met Elvis, but we couldn't find it. We went out almost every night. He was most excited about a restaurant called the House of Pancakes. We went there at four A.M. because it was the only place open at that hour and we were both hungry. He loved the vinyl and Formica booths and the plastic menus. I don't think he'd been in that kind of unpretentious restaurant in many years. What he really loved was the six little jars of different kinds of syrup on the table—all you wanted, for free. The syrup reminded him of

English treacle—a kind of gooey marmalade, he said, which had been a special treat when he was a kid in Liverpool."

One night Jerry Lee Lewis was playing the Roxy. John had never seen him live; Elliot Mintz took him, and "after the show I introduced John to him backstage. John fell down on his knees and kissed his shoes. Jerry Lee reached out his hand and said, 'That's all right, son, that's all right.'"

There were other moments when John did things that excited him: visiting Elton John, meeting Elizabeth Taylor at a party, going to Las Vegas. But "the excitement of being on his own in L.A. seemed to me to last about a week," Mintz said. "After that a sadness set in, and it never got better. It got progressively worse. His main ambition was getting back to Yoko.

"One sad, sleazy afternoon," Mintz recalled, "we went to a topless bar called the Losers' Club. It was three in the afternoon. Only serious drinkers were in there at that hour. He had a few and I had a few. He kept asking what Yoko was saying to me. John knew Yoko and I spoke almost every evening on the phone. He wanted to know whether it looked like he'd be able to come back yet. We watched one of the topless dancers, finished our drinks, and walked out of the bar. A light rain was falling; it looked like a storm was beginning in L.A. He started singing softly, 'We make them paint their face and dance. . . .' That day he just wanted to go home."

John's "lost weekend," as he later called this period of separation from Yoko, consisted of "eighteen months when the feminist side of me died slightly." It's significant that he would explain it in reference to feminist values. In fact he did revert to the drunken, macho style of his angry Liverpool youth. Living with May Pang, sharing a beach house with Ringo, Keith Moon, and Klaus Voormann, and hanging around with Harry Nilsson, he alternated between ordinary misery and intermittent explosions of blind, self-destructive rage.

May was the negation of Yoko. Whatever else Yoko was, she could be a difficult and demanding person—especially when she and John weren't getting along. May made no demands on John at all. Yoko was six years older than John; May was eleven or twelve years younger. Yoko came out of the New York avant-garde art scene; May had been a secretary for a rock music company. She had none of Yoko's intellectual background; it's hard to imagine that John had much to talk to May about. But she could sing oldies with him, which Yoko couldn't.

In May's book she portrays herself as a powerless person, grateful for his attention, terrified of his violent outbursts, meekly submitting to his abuse. "With John, *any* moment could be the end," she wrote. "How could I stay with someone who was so dangerous? I was heartbroken. I was so much in love. . . . I must have been crazy."

The incident that symbolized the entire eighteen-month period occurred at the Troubadour club in Los Angeles in March 1974, when John, drunk, was thrown out for heckling the Smothers Brothers. The next day, when a photographer accused John of having hit her during the fracas, the incident got wide press coverage, which included the New York *Times* and the Washington *Post.* The incident didn't help John as a supplicant before the INS; their vigilant clerks clipped and filed the articles, potential evidence against him.

Heckling the Smothers Brothers may have seemed like drunken fun to some observers, but for John it had a darker significance. Tommy Smothers had joined John and Yoko at the Montreal bed-in and sang with them at the recording of "Give Peace a Chance." The Troubadour incident humiliated him, on the opening night of his attempt at a comeback, in a club full of industry people and his friends. John's cruelty that night in Los Angeles was helping to erase the memory of an energetic, optimistic day in Montreal.

Reflecting on this period in 1980, John said he had been "suicidal" on a subconscious level. "I didn't want to see or feel anything." The song "I'm Losing You," on *Double Fantasy,* probably is a recollection of his lost weekend with May: "Here in some stranger's room . . . what am I doin' here at all?"

═══

John did make some music in Los Angeles. He went to work with producer Phil Spector on an oldies album that would eventually be released as *Rock 'n' Roll. Mind Games* had been a step backward, to the sound of the *Imagine* album. John decided that if he wasn't going to forge ahead into uncharted territory, as Yoko would, if he was going into a musical retreat, he might as well go all the way, back before Yoko, to the earliest music that inspired the Beatles.

The project was based on the myth of rock and roll renewal—that John could restore himself as a musician by returning to the roots of rock and thereby regain its pristine energy. "I thought, what can I do to break the regime of writing the songs John Lennon writes about feelings," he explained. "The old rock and roll songs are my favorite songs. I admired the originals so much I wouldn't dare touch them. But by now people were ruining everything"—that was a sad remark—"so I thought, 'What the hell.' "

The songs John decided to cover on *Rock 'n' Roll* were not just any old oldies. They represented his own personal musical history. John sang Buddy Holly's "Peggy Sue" on *Rock 'n' Roll.* The name "Beatles" had been inspired by Buddy Holly's Crickets, and "That'll Be the Day" was the first song John learned to play on the guitar in 1957. He had sung other Buddy Holly songs:

"It's So Easy" as Johnny and the Moondogs in his first TV appearance in 1959, and "Words of Love," which the Beatles recorded in 1964.

The oldest oldies on *Rock 'n' Roll* were Fats Domino's "Ain't That a Shame" and Gene Vincent's "Be-Bop-A-Lula," which John had sung with the Quarrymen in 1957, when he was seventeen. Gene Vincent had appeared with the Beatles at the Cavern in 1962. On *Rock 'n' Roll* John sang more songs by Little Richard than anyone else: "Slippin' and Slidin'" and "Reddy Teddy" from 1956, and "Rip It Up" from 1958. In 1962 the Beatles had appeared on the same bill with Little Richard in Liverpool. Paul had always done the Little Richard songs; now John was getting his chance at last.

John did two Chuck Berry songs on *Rock 'n' Roll:* "You Can't Catch Me," which he admitted he copied in the opening lines of "Come Together," and "Sweet Little Sixteen." That song had been part of the Beatles' Hamburg repertoire. John's version of "Bony Maronie" on *Rock 'n' Roll* was the fourth Larry Williams song on which he had sung lead, including "Dizzy Miss Lizzie" on *Beatles '65.*

Between October and December 1973 John worked in the studio. Then Spector disappeared with the master tapes and left cryptic messages suggesting parallels to John Dean's knowledge of the contents of the Watergate tapes. John couldn't get the INS to let him stay, he couldn't get along with Yoko, and he couldn't get Spector to let him finish the tracks they had recorded. Nothing was working for him.

An interviewer who visited John in 1974 found him lying on his bed, eating take-out Chinese beef and vegetables, and watching himself on TV. He was coming out of court after the latest round of immigration hearings. "Now that seems a sane young man to me," he said. "Should definitely be allowed to stay." John's legal fight against deportation continued to take his time and attention throughout his separation from Yoko. In March 1974 Wildes went to U.S. district court seeking a temporary restraining order to delay the Immigration Appeals Board ruling; the suit was titled *John Winston Ono Lennon v. the United States of America.* The court denied his request on May 1. On July 18 the board rejected John's appeal and once again ordered him to leave the country within sixty days or be forcibly deported.

John won some respectable editorial support from the *Wall Street Journal* and the New York *Post.* The former called the INS treatment of him "intolerable"; the latter contrasted the Immigration Service's relentless prosecution of him with their "less than zealous" pursuit of suspected Nazi war criminals hiding in the United States. The newspapers should have made that argument two years earlier, when the first deportation order was issued. This was the time for investigative journalism, for an exposé of Nixon's abuse of power in pursuing Lennon. No newspaper took on that task.

Meanwhile Nixon continued to sink. On November 17 at Walt Disney World in Florida he had uttered the famous words "I am not a crook." On December 8 he revealed he had paid less than $1,000 in taxes in 1970 and 1971, which aroused more anger among the men on the street than the news that he had bugged the Democratic National Committee. In April 1974 the IRS stated that Nixon owed $432,787 in back taxes and $33,000 in interest penalties. On May 9 the House Judiciary Committee began formal impeachment hearings.

On July 24 the Supreme Court unanimously ordered Nixon to release sixty-four Watergate tapes to the special prosecutor. On July 27 the Judiciary Committee voted 27 to 11 to recommend to the full House that Nixon be impeached for criminal acts committed in covering up the Watergate break-in and for obstruction of justice in the subsequent investigation. On August 8 Nixon resigned; on September 8 Gerald Ford granted him a pardon, leading many to conclude that Nixon's representatives had struck a deal with Ford before he was appointed Agnew's successor. John's congressional supporters reintroduced the amendment to the immigration laws in August, and the press reported that "Lennon now has political lobbyists working overtime in Washington trying to influence members of both the Senate and the House Immigration Committees."

Wildes's efforts to demonstrate the political motivation behind the deportation order were running into a stone wall: the Senate Internal Security Subcommittee (SISS), whose staff had first suggested deporting John. "It was kind of odd that this whole thing should come from a Senate committee," Wildes said in 1983. "They were getting around the Freedom of Information Act by fronting for the FBI. The key is that Senate committees are not covered by the Freedom of Information Act. When you write in and ask for a copy of anything, they don't even bother to respond. I had a suit against the Senate Internal Security Subcommittee lined up, but never filed it."

John didn't know it, but SISS had a twenty-year history of extralegal harassment of radicals. A month after the first deportation order, the Washington *Post* called SISS "one of the Senate's most secretive, expensive and insulated institutions." Civil libertarian Frank Donner wrote that SISS, along with its counterpart in the House, the Un-American Activities Committee (HUAC), "more effectively handicapped movements for change in this country than any other component of the American intelligence apparatus."

The SISS staff, which came up with the deportation idea, had twenty-six members, described in the Washington *Post* as "a lot of ex-McCarthyites who sit around thinking evil thoughts and talking about the Communist conspiracy." The subcommittee's annual budget was half a million dollars. J. Edgar Hoover frequently testified before the committee, as did numerous undercover agents and ex-radicals.

The man who "ran the show," according to the *Post,* was not subcommittee chairman James O. Eastland, but rather chief counsel J. G. Sourwine, a sixty-three-year old former Nevada newsman who gained notoriety in the fifties for his obsession with hunting Reds. His power on Capitol Hill was so great during that decade that some called him "the ninety-seventh senator." His trademarks were abusive treatment of witnesses called before the subcommittee and a "scorn for legal niceties" in committee investigations. Sourwine had extensive contacts with FBI and CIA sources, which he reportedly used to obtain materials he published as the work of his own staff. Wildes was almost certainly correct in suspecting that the committee's information on Lennon's political plans had originated with the FBI.

At the time the SISS staff suggested deporting Lennon, they were coming under increasing criticism from Congress for their high budget and lack of "productivity" in legislative matters. Their principal contribution to the American people that year was the completion of parts 8 and 9 of their hearings on "extent of subversion in the New Left." These consisted of testimony by police officers and undercover agents on John Sinclair and the White Panther Party and the SDS Radical Education Project. In the subcommittee's annual report for 1972, Sourwine failed to list the memo on deporting Lennon as evidence of the staff's productivity.

While Wildes couldn't get anything out of SISS, the INS responded in August to his suit demanding records of deportation proceedings similar to John's. He discovered that more than a hundred aliens with drug convictions had been allowed to stay in the country by being granted "non-priority status" for "humanitarian" reasons. That disproved the INS claim that John's deportation was required by law. Many of those allowed to stay had been convicted of much more serious crimes than had John—heroin possession, rape, even murder. Wildes passed his research on to columnist Jack Anderson, who featured it at the end of August. Anderson understood the situation: he himself had recently been the target of a campaign of Nixon dirty tricks.

John filed a new lawsuit in November, requesting that a federal judge allow him to question immigration officials and examine documents to determine whether he was a victim of a political vendetta by former Attorney General John Mitchell. On January 1, 1975, Mitchell was found guilty in the Watergate coverup trial, along with Haldeman and Ehrlichman. The next day a U.S. district court judge granted John's request: his first real victory.

=====

Over that summer John returned to New York City with May Pang and recorded what turned out to be his first Number One single since the Beatles' breakup, "Whatever Gets You thru the Night," and a Number One album, *Walls and Bridges.* Each hit the top of the charts in November. The single marked the abandonment of everything John had stood for since the Beatles' breakup. "Whatever gets you through the night," he sang, "it's all right, it's all right." What had been getting him through the night was his boozing buddies.

The song marked a disturbing reversal of a theme that had appeared repeatedly in his earlier work. On the *Imagine* album, the most devastating question he could pose to Paul was "How do you sleep?" In his *Red Mole* interview in 1970 he had spoken of his own sleeplessness, of waking up in the middle of the night "afraid with your heart pounding." The lesson he had learned then was that the fear and pain "are really yours, you can't repress them or avoid them."

The last verse of his new song, "Whatever gets you to the light," seemed admirably ecumenical, but has to be heard against the shattering litany on *Plastic Ono Band*, where he stated that he didn't believe in Buddha or mantra. John's new song sounded happy, but its implications were ominous: he was throwing away self-knowledge he had acquired only after a profoundly painful struggle. It seemed like John was turning himself into Paul, the person without political values, who put out Number One songs and who managed to sleep soundly. Maybe that's why John told Elton John that "Whatever Gets You thru the Night" was "one of my least favorites."

"You don't know what you got / Until you lose it" on *Walls and Bridges* was first of all about Yoko, but it also spoke of John's loss of radical commitment and energy. The best song on the album was "Steel and Glass": "There you stand with your L. A. tan." Some critics interpreted it as an attack on Allen Klein, in the same spirit as John's earlier anti-Paul songs. In fact, it expressed a profound self-hatred: "Your mother left when you were small / But you're gonna wish you wasn't born at all." "Bless You," which John sang to Yoko in someone else's arms, demonstrated emotional strength, and "Going Down on Love" had some of the harsh realism of *Plastic Ono Band*.

The album closed with "Sittin' on My Ya Ya," "Starring Julian Lennon on Drums and Dad on Piano and Vocals," the lyrics sheet says. It probably would have been better for their relationship just to make music together and not put it on the album. But the cut did provide a hint that fatherhood could provide an alternative to the unhappiness of John's life in 1974, a hint that John wanted to make a statement in his music about being a "Dad."

If the music was disturbing in many ways, *Walls and Bridges* had a wonderful cover, cut into three strips showing childhood paintings on one side which flipped over to make different funny faces of John's. The paintings, which his Aunt Mimi had saved since he was eleven, had been the first hint of John's artistic aspirations. The lyrics sheet was filled with Lennon whimsy. It bore the motto "Possession is nine-tenths of the problem—Dr.

Winston O'Boogie," which echoed "Imagine no possessions." (Winston was John's middle name.) Credits were distributed on different cuts to Dr. Winston O'Ghurkin and the Rev. Thumbs Ghurkin (in subsequent years John and Yoko frequently traveled under the names "The Rev. Fred and Ida Ghurkin," Elliot Mintz reported). Other credits were listed for the Hon. John St. John Johnson, Kaptain Kundalini, Dr. Dream, Booker Table and the Maitre d's, Dwarf McDougal, and his cleverest and most truthful persona of this period, Mel Torment.

On the back cover John printed a long entry from a book on Irish family names, which concluded about "Lennon," "no person of this name has distinguished himself in the political, military or cultural life of Ireland, or for that matter in England either." Underneath John had written "Oh yeh?"

The cover also contained a cryptic line of small print, "I saw a UFO." He interviewed himself about it in Andy Warhol's *Interview* magazine.

"Q. Were you drunk? High? Having a primal?

"A. No, actually I was very straight. . . . I went to the window, just dreaming around in my usual poetic frame of mind. . . . What the Nixon is that! I says to myself (for no one else was there.) Is it a helicopter? No! It makes no noise. Ah, then, it must be a balloon! (Frantically trying to rationalize it, in my all too human way.)

"Q. Aren't you afraid people won't believe you—crazy Lennon/Maharishi/etc.

"A. That's just one of the many burdens I will have to bear in this day of waterbabies, inflation, generation crap, highly influential, but not untidy."

Walls and Bridges sold a million copies in a month after its release. It sold twice as many copies as *Mind Games* and *Plastic Ono Band,* and stayed on the American charts almost as long as *Imagine.* A second single off the record also penetrated the Top Ten: "#9 Dream," which stayed on the charts for twelve weeks. But the album didn't have any point, except to demonstrate that Lennon still could make hit records. In a promo interview about the album, John admitted as much: "The only thing new about it is, it's new." His PR people must have been dismayed by this truth-telling.

"I'm not ashamed of the album," John said in 1980. "There's craftsmanship on *Walls and Bridges.* There's some good. And there's the semi-sick craftsman who put the thing together. There's no inspiration and there's misery. . . . It gives off an aura of misery. Because I was miserable."

"Yoko and I were apart, I had been through the immigration stuff and there was all the pressure of the music business. Making music was no longer a joy. . . . I was trapped and saw no way out."

John expressed his alienation from radical politics in an interview in the *Observer* at the end of 1974. "Politics? Well, let's just say I'm still as political as I ever was, which was never that much. Jerry Rubin and Abbie Hoffman were almost the first people to contact me when I came to New York. Now I prefer to meet people like Tennessee Williams," he stated. "I have to admit that some of my early political activities with Yoko were pretty naïve. But Yoko was always political in an avant-garde kind of way. She had this idea that you must always make use of the newspaper publicity to get across the idea of peace." To be separated from Yoko was to be separated from politics.

As for his old comrades, "the trouble with Rubin and Hoffman was that they never wanted laughter—they wanted violence." John had forgotten that the people he was talking about had been notorious for their clowning. "I've never been into violence myself. . . . All you need is love, like the song says. That's really my ultimate political belief. We all need more love." John had fallen back on the vapid flower-power sentiments of 1967. He concluded, "I found that being political interfered with my music. I'm still a musician first, not a politician."

Of course no one wants to be a "politician," with its implications of corruption. But John had been a political artist, an artist engaged with political issues. "Being political" in this sense had not interfered with his music; on the contrary, it had been the basis of "Imagine" and "Gimme Some Truth" and "Working Class Hero." John's willingness to obliterate this work was disturbing. It suggested that his separation from Yoko was also a separation from the achievements they had shared.

As for Yoko, "I still love her, but we're two artists and we found it hard living together. We talk on the phone every day. . . . Yoko and I are still very good friends." John, whose verbal genius was legendary, was speaking in Hollywood clichés.

"I was always a little political," he explained in another interview around the same time. "But I got to be hanging around with political people. . . . I become whoever I'm with. If I'm with a madman, I become mad. And if I'm with somebody I love, I become lovely. I'm like a cloud in the wind." Clouds, however, don't have responsibilities, and they don't become miserable and self-destructive.

———

After releasing *Walls and Bridges* John went back to work on the *Rock 'n' Roll* album, without Spector, and recorded nine of the thirteen songs on the final album in four days. He released it in February 1975.

Rock 'n' Roll represented an effort to recapture the energy of John's pre-Yoko youth. The effort failed. Nothing on it equaled the early Beatles versions of the same songs, and most didn't equal the *Let It Be* outtakes. There were a few strong tracks: John's "Stand by Me" was memorable, sung with real passion—obviously for Yoko. "Slippin' and Slidin' " had a lot of the old exuberance. "Just Because" was powerful and sad. But as a whole, as Jon Landau wrote, John's search for his past had left him sounding like a man without a past. That must have made him feel even more lost.

John had worried that the album was not good enough to release. When he finally got the Spector tapes, "I couldn't stand to listen to 'em," he said. He did, and found that only four tracks could be salvaged. "I didn't know what to do with it. . . . Either just throw this away or finish it off, make enough tracks to finish the album." He tried the latter. "I thought, 'If it works, it works.' Stuck 'em all together. . . . Now what? I thought, 'It's not good enough for what they've been waiting for.' So I thought, 'I won't put it out.' Then I played it for some people, and they said, 'It's all right.' It's all right? It's not bad at all! I quite like some of it! So I put it out." He should have followed his own initial judgment and not listened to his friends.

As with *Walls and Bridges,* the best thing about *Rock 'n' Roll* was the album cover: a gorgeous black and white photo of John in Hamburg when he was twenty-two, lounging in a doorway in a leather jacket, with his name in beautiful neon lights, just like Chuck Berry promised in "Johnny B. Goode." The album didn't do badly on the charts, peaking at Number Six, higher than *Mind Games* but not as high as *Walls and Bridges.* He tried "Stand by Me" as a single, which stalled at Number Twenty.

With *Mind Games* and *Walls and Bridges,* John had failed to re-create the sound of his best post-Beatles work; now with *Rock 'n' Roll* he had failed to re-create the sound of the best of the early Beatles. Goofing around on the last track of *Rock 'n' Roll,* John said in a jolly announcer's voice, "And so we say farewell from Record Plant West." "Something flashed through me mind as I said it," he recalled in 1980: "Am I really saying farewell to the business?" He remembered that the day he met Paul he was singing "Be-Bop-A-Lula" at the church fair, and now on his oldies album he was singing it again. "I'm saying farewell from the Record Plant, and I'm ending as I started." He had run out of ideas.

On Thanksgiving Day, 1974, Elton John appeared at Madison Square Garden. Toward the end of his concert John joined Elton onstage, and together they did "Whatever Gets You thru the Night," "Lucy in the Sky with Diamonds," and "I Saw Her Standing There," singing energetically and in perfect harmony. "It was a great high night, a really high night," John later recalled. It turned out to be the last concert appearance in his life. Yoko was in the audience, they met backstage after the show, and he moved back into the Dakota six weeks later. "The separation didn't work out," he explained.

John described the separation and the reunion a little more fully in a conversation at the Dakota recorded by Elliot Mintz for one of his syndicated radio programs a year later. "A friend called me yesterday. He's just split with his woman. When Yoko and I were apart, she did a spiritual trip. His girlfriend is doing the same. He's liable to hit the bottle, like I did. I said, if you can possibly be strong enough, the spiritual trip is better, because when we got back together, Yoko was in far better condition than me. You come to the same conclusion; all roads lead to Rome. But it's a hell of a way to get there, crawling around on your hands and knees in the middle of the night. That's the advice I gave him. I hope he takes it, but he probably won't. He'll probably have to go the hard way, because he's male and we express ourselves in those ways. I've been through it. That's unimportant. It's over."

In April John went on Tom Snyder's *Tomorrow* show to talk about his immigration case. He looked pale and tired. Six years after the bed-in, he was still having to deal with interviewers asking cute questions: "There was a time you and Yoko invited everybody to come into the bedroom, while you were there," Snyder said.

"We held a bed-in for peace," John replied with great patience.

"Exactly. Why do you do these things?"

Snyder gave him a chance to explain his immigration case from the beginning. He brought along his attorney, Leon Wildes, who summed up the situation with remarkably concise prose: "We have some information that the deportation proceedings against John were not normally brought. . . . We understand that a series of memoranda led from the attorney general all the way down to the district director for New York, and that the action he took was not as a result of John's immigration status, but rather with the intention of preventing John from exercising constitutionally protected rights." (Wildes later recalled that, before the show, John told him, "If you want to be quoted, don't say anything more than five words long.")

Snyder then asked a reasonable question: "You could live almost anywhere you wanted in this world. Why put up with this hassle?"

"Because I'd like to live in the land of the free, Tom," John said with an ironic smile. "And if it was up to Joe Doe on the street, he either doesn't care about it, or would be glad to have an old Beatle living here. I like to be here, because this is where the music came from, which is my whole life and got me where I am today." He smiled again, realizing the irony of the remark. "I love the place. I'd like to be here."

A few months later another interviewer asked John what he now thought about the sixties. "I am not in the group of people who think that, because all our dreams didn't come true in the Sixties, everything we said was invalid." John still claimed to have been part of the movement: "our dreams." He went on, "There isn't any peace in the world despite our efforts, but I still believe the hippie peace-and-love thing was worthwhile." Then he spoke about his own recent life. "If somebody stands up and smiles and then gets smacked in the face, that smack doesn't invalidate the smile. It existed." He didn't want to "invalidate" the "smile" that got him in trouble: his antiwar activities.

"The actual peace events we staged came directly from Yoko. . . . The bed sit-in in Canada was one of the nicest ones, and I participated almost like a spectator because it was Yoko's way of demonstrating." John was denying how active and enthusiastic his participation had been. And he was completely neglecting their engagement with the movement in London and New York in 1971 and 1972. John was minimizing the extent of his political activities, but he wasn't disavowing them.

Pete Hamill interviewed John for *Rolling Stone* in June and asked what had happened to his radical commitments. John said the INS had him so "jumpy" that he was "nervous" even "commenting on politics." He didn't like the fact that his taxes paid for weapons of destruction, but he didn't think he could "do a Joan Baez"—lead a tax resistance movement—he didn't have "that kind of gut." He was "sick of being in crusades," he said, because every time he got "nailed up before I'm even *in* the crusade." He was right about that. He never got to go on the anti-Nixon tour he had planned.

Hamill asked how John's political commitments had affected his music. "It almost ruined it," John replied, arguing that politics had turned his poetry into journalism. It's true that John's "front-page songs" on the *New York City* album did not succeed for the most part. But he no longer recalled the ideas that had made *Plastic Ono Band* and *Imagine* so brilliant. Instead he took the disappointment of *Some Time in New York City* as a pretext for abandoning all the forms of political art.

When he was engaged with social issues, he said, it seemed like the most important thing in his life. But in retrospect it looked to him like "clutching at straws" which were "always blowin' out of your hands." Now he felt it had all been "a waste of time. . . . Just keep moving around and changing clothes is the best. That's all that goes on: change." This statement was one of the most damaging John ever made about himself. It fit the accusation made by his most hostile critics, that John's cultural and political radicalism was simply another fad for him, as fleeting and dubious as meditation with the Maharishi, that he was unable to make a serious commitment or sustain an interest in any project for very long.

But if John no longer considered himself a radical artist, what was he? He came close to accusing himself of having sold out again, having abandoned his radicalism in exchange for a career as a superstar in America. He seemed to realize that his self-destructiveness was a punishment for abandoning real commitments. He said he had "this great fear" that he had "settled for the *deal.* . . . I seem to do all the things I despise most."

At the same time he was minimizing the importance of his activist period in New York, he could not help recalling that it had been a great time. After the benefit at the Apollo Theatre for the Attica families and the John Sinclair rally, "I felt like going on the road and playing *music.* . . . I was ready to go on the road for pure *fun.* . . . They kept pullin' me back into court! . . . Now, the last thing I want to do is perform. That's a direct result of the immigration thing. In '72, I wanted to go out and rock me balls off onstage and I just stopped."

Finally Hamill asked him what he saw himself doing at sixty. He said he could see himself writing children's books, that he wanted to give others what he had gotten as a child from *The Wind in the Willows* and *Alice in Wonderland* and *Treasure Island*—books that had "opened my whole being." He didn't know why he was thinking about children's books, he said. "It'd be a strange thing for a person who doesn't really have much to do with children." He didn't tell the press, but Yoko was five months pregnant.

He did one other long interview at this point, with Capital Radio in Britain. "We were part of the peace movement, believe it or not," he said with a mixture of irony and sadness. "Nobody else hung out with them baddies like I did." He was talking about Jerry Rubin and Abbie Hoffman and Bobby Seale. "Maybe I was dumb. But I was interested. They were interesting people and I wanted to hear what they had to say about everything."

The interviewer asked what he thought about critics who said *Imagine* was his best work. "Up them. . . . As far as I'm concerned, the best piece of work I ever put out is still the 'Mother'/'Working Class Hero' album." His critical judgment was still intact. "Always remember this: when 'From Me to You' came out, the *NME* [*New Musical Express*] said 'Below Par Beatles.' That was our third or fourth single, and we were already finished, we were already not good enough. We couldn't top 'She Loves You.'" He was hoping that someday he would top the *Plastic Ono Band* album.

And what were his plans for the future? He declared his determination not to return to the life of his year-long "lost weekend." "I don't want to do that again," he said. "No more '74."

＝＝＝

On October 7, 1975, Judge Kaufman of the U.S. court of appeals overturned the deportation order. Ruling on the narrowest of legal points, he accepted Wildes's argument that John's 1968 British conviction should be ignored because the law in Britain at that time did not require that the accused know the illegal nature of the substance he possessed. Kaufman did not rule on John's contention that the deportation order had been based on his political activities and beliefs. He ordered the INS to reconsider John's application for permanent residence.

Two days later Yoko gave birth to a boy, eight pounds, ten ounces. It was John's thirty-fifth birthday. John recalled that day in a conversation Elliot Mintz recorded on January 1, 1976, when Sean was not quite three months old. "We'd done Leboyer and Lamaze natural childbirth, but at the last minute they don't let me in, because it was cesarean. So I was stuck on the other side of the wall. Then I hear this crying. I'm paralyzed, thinking, 'Maybe it's another one next door.' But it was ours. And I was jumping around and swearing at the top of my voice and kicking the wall with joy, shouting 'F-ing great!'

"Then I was just all eyes for the baby. I just sat all night looking at it, saying, 'Wow! It's incredible!' She'd been knocked out after the cesarean; when she woke up I told her he was fine, and we cried."

They named him Sean Ono Lennon. "Sean" is "John" in Irish. Later John explained that being Irish is "not too good in England." When he told his Aunt Mimi his newborn son's name, she cried, "Oh my God, John, don't *brand* him!" Telling the story, John collapsed in laughter.

He remained a political thinker, even about the details of the baby's life. "The baby things you can buy are very crummy-looking and badly made," he told Mintz in the same recorded conversation. "I know why that is. It's obvious. You don't hand down the baby clothes or baby bed to the next generation. The first six months' stuff now is all disposable. So the first things you give the little human being as it joins the world are the cheapest, lousiest bits of crap he's ever liable to touch. And they're at their most sensitive. I'm sure we're never more sensitive than the first few years. It's almost a symbol of our society."

But what to do about producing hit records? John told Los Angeles *Times* rock writer Robert Hilburn in 1980, "Wasn't I the greatest pop seer? Hadn't I written 'The Dream Is Over'? Was I not the great John Lennon who could see through all the world's hypocrisy? The truth is I couldn't see through my own."

He took an important step toward truth in the song "Fame," which he wrote that year with David Bowie. Bowie put it at the end of his *Young Americans* album, with John singing and playing backup. The song described the hollowness of the life symbolized by limousines.

He recalled in 1980 that Yoko had told him he didn't have to make records. That had never occurred to him. The idea was both terrifying and liberating. "Walking away is much harder than carrying on." "It was more important to face myself and face reality than to continue a life of rock 'n' roll. . . . Could the world get along without another John Lennon album? Could I get along without it? I finally realized the answer to both questions was yes." John pulled together an album of his greatest hits since the breakup and announced his withdrawal from the music business and from public life. He declared he would become a househusband.

Part VII

FEMINIST FATHER

24

Watching the Wheels

 In his 1980 interviews John delighted in describing his typical day as a househusband. "My life was built around Sean's meals ... like Mrs. Higgins in Wisconsin." He got up about six, went to the kitchen, got a cup of coffee, "coughed a little." He had a cigarette; the papers arrived at seven. Sean got up at 7:20. John supervised his breakfast. He no longer cooked it: "got fed up with that one." But he made sure he knew what Sean was eating.

Sometimes when he woke up, Yoko would already be in the office on the first floor of the Dakota—they lived on the sixth. If she passed through the kitchen on her way, he would make her a cup of espresso. Then he would hang around until about nine to make sure Sean watched *Sesame Street* and not the cartoons with the commercials. The nanny would take Sean out to do something, and John would go back to his room, the bedroom were he did "everything." He might call over the intercom to see what Yoko was doing downstairs.

The time between breakfast and lunch, he found, went quickly. "You hardly have time to read the paper, that's presuming it ain't raining and the nanny can take Sean out, so you get a break from the constant 'Daddy, look at this, Daddy look at that.' . . . Then it's bloody lunchtime."

He would go back at twelve to see that Sean got a good lunch, and be with him while he ate. If the day was not too hectic, he would meet Yoko for lunch. Then he would have from one until five for himself, to "stay in, go out, read, write, whatever." At five he would find Sean. Dinner was at six, "usually Yoko's still down in the office." At seven Sean had his bath, and John always watched the news. At 7:30 he and Sean would watch "kids' stuff" on TV. He was still careful to protect Sean from commercials, turning off their sound with his remote switch. At eight he took Sean to his bedroom and kissed him goodnight. "The nanny probably reads him a story, whatever they get up to in there."

Finally he would call Yoko, who would still be at work in her office: "What the hell you doin' down there? You still down there?" Sometimes he could persuade her to stop and do something with him. Often she would work until ten, take two hours off, then go back to work at midnight—" 'cause she's always calling the West Coast or England or Tokyo or some god-forsaken place that is on a different time zone from us." And that, he concluded, was "a regular day" at the Dakota.

John described this typical day in virtually every interview he did promoting *Double Fantasy.* He loved the sheer ordinariness of daily life with Sean. He'd never had that kind of life before. He was giving Sean what he felt he lacked in his own childhood, when he got "no time instead of it all," as he said in "Working Class Hero." Also, he was fulfilling real needs of his own. He seemed more contented than ever before, as several people noted. John's Aunt Mimi told the Liverpool *Echo* in 1979, "He really seems much more settled and happy now than he used to be. When he phones he wants to talk about Sean and about when he was a little boy himself." Patric Walker, a friend from Liverpool, saw him at Christmas in 1978. "He was fantastic, very relaxed and joking that he was the highest-paid househusband in the world. . . . He doesn't need concerts and he doesn't need adulation and he doesn't need applause. I think he's the one Beatle that is really happy the way he is."

John never intended to remain a househusband indefinitely. He always intended to go back to work when Sean was five, when Sean would go to school (or get a tutor). Perhaps part of the satisfaction that he was expressing in 1980 came from a sense of having achieved what he wanted to with Sean in his first five years, a sense of completion that meant he could move on to do some of his own work.

At times his old depression returned, John admitted. When an interviewer asked him in 1980, "Where's the friction in your life?," he replied, "The friction is in living. In waking up every day. And getting through another day." He knew what it was like to be deeply depressed. But the responsibilities of parenting forced him to control it. "If I'm feeling depressed, he starts getting that way. . . . So I'm sort of obliged to keep up. But sometimes I can't because something will make me depressed and there's no way I can deal with it. And then he, sure as hell, he'll get a cold or trap his finger in a door or something will happen, you know, and so now I have a sort of more reason to stay healthy and bright. I can no longer wallow in it and say this is how artists are supposed to be."

The mundane routine was broken when John started recording *Double Fantasy*. For the first time in Sean's life, John went to work, became preoccupied with his work, and went on the rock musicians' schedule, staying up all night and sleeping in the daytime. John would arrive home in time for Sean's breakfast. "He'd see me where I was so different, sort of shredded. . . . Then one day when we were sort of lyin' down on the bed together, maybe watching some cartoons or whatever. And he just sat up and said, 'You know what I want to be when I grow up?'

"And I said, 'No, what is that?'

"He looked me right in the eye and said, 'Just a daddy.' [Telling the story, John laughed.]

"And I said, 'You don't like it that I'm working now, right, and going out a lot.'

"He says, 'Right.' [John laughed again.]

"I says, 'Well, I'll tell you something, Sean. It makes me happy to do the music. And I might have more fun with you if I'm happier, right?'

"He says, 'Uh huh.' And that was the end of that."

But John worried that he hadn't handled it well, and said he went through periods of terrible guilt making *Double Fantasy*. "I needn't feel guilty. I'm entitled to have my own space too. But still, God, it racks you. . . . But he needs to have space too. . . . When I'm not around he relaxes more. . . . He does need a break from me. . . . You see, if I knew all the secrets of right and wrong—well, I wish we all knew the secrets. Nobody really knows; that's the point." This was the "real life" John had been seeking for so long.

———

In his withdrawal from public activism into family life, John was also moving along with part of the generation of the sixties. Some radicals criticized this turn of his. Andrew Kopkind wrote after John's death that he "idealized the nuclear family ideal [*sic*] with a pluperfect marriage, a quiet life in the Dakota and a new record of unrelenting sentimentality. He could be inducted into the moral majority." Kopkind is wrong here. When John chose private life, he made it clear that it was not out of a commitment to the traditional family. On the contrary, he said it was out of a commitment to the personal politics of feminism. In a radical reversal of conventional patterns of child care, John took responsibility for the tasks of the "mother" and Yoko took responsibility for the family's business affairs.

In 1980, in his first major interview in five years, John once again sought to link his own private experience with larger social issues. "I'll say to all housewives, I now understand what they're screaming about. Because when I try to describe it [life as a househusband], I'm describing most women's lives. That's just what I've been doing for five years. It just so happens that this thing called John Lennon was doing it, who was supposed to be doing something else.

"But what I'm telling you is that I was being just like a hundred million people who are mainly female. I just went from meal to meal. Is he well? Has he eaten enough vegetables? Is he over-eating?" "You feed them, you don't get a gold record, they just swallow it. If they swallow it," he said in another interview, "that means you were a hit." Meanwhile Yoko has been working. "How is *she* when she comes back from the office? Is she going to talk to me, or is she just going to talk about business?" Thus John identified with the oppressed housewife, and suggested in an exemplary way that men could take care of babies—not just changing a diaper, but taking responsibility for the baby's day.

John's reversal of sex roles was a radical departure from bourgeois conventions, but it had some important limitations. It preserved the distinction between the worldly person and the domestic person, the distinction between "work" and "family." Moreover, John's becoming a househusband was limited as an exemplary act because most families could not survive on the wife's earnings alone. Most important, withdrawal from the world necessarily reinforces the isolation individuals face in bourgeois society, which has been a key obstacle to radical social movements—and which John exposed in a song on the *Plastic Ono Band* album, "Isolation."

John considered himself a feminist, but many feminists objected to this definition of the family because the public/private split on which it rests has always been associated with the subordination of women. John's immersion in his family was criticized by some because it expressed the prevailing view that the family is the only social institution that can foster love, support, respect, and cooperation. Socialists have refused to confine these qualities to the family and have analyzed it as an arena of conflict, of struggles for power and autonomy. John worked as a househusband to make his family a haven in a heartless world. The radical project is to make the world less heartless.

John's early life suggests why he did not join the socialist feminists' critique of the nuclear family and their demand for sexual freedom. John hadn't felt oppressed by the nuclear family. He felt he had missed out on its haven in a heartless world. He regretted that as a father he had largely ignored his first son, Julian, while he was living the life of Beatle *Satyricon.* His experiences as a child and as a Beatle made family life a goal to be achieved rather than a familiar source of oppression.

Superstardom doesn't die easily. John sometimes wanted to be a superstar househusband. Yoko tried not to let him get away with it. "I've learned to make bread, which I was thrilled with," John said. "I took a Polaroid of my first bread."

Yoko interjected, "In a good old macho tradition, he had to record it in history."

"I was thrilled, it's not macho anybody," John said. "It was the first bread. It looked great, and it tasted good. . . . I was so excited that I could do it, that I would bring all the staff in to each lunch."

"He makes the bread, and if they don't eat it, it's a personal insult," Yoko said. "We went through that one."

John had a cook and a nanny for Sean. He knew his life wasn't ordinary. "I'm a rich housewife," he said. "But it still involves caring, and making sure the sheets are being looked after by whomever I employ, and the staff all come to me with their problems. They don't go bothering Yoko, because she's dealing with the money."

He admitted it had been a struggle in the beginning. "In the first 18 months it was hard to stop jumping onto a piano. . . . Then I got to a point where I can live without music." The idea that Lennon would want to live without music brings dismay if not disbelief at first. But he had made four albums that failed in various ways in the four years before he withdrew: *Some Time in New York City, Mind Games, Walls and Bridges,* and *Rock 'n' Roll.* What he could live without was the music business—the pressure to turn out albums, to make hits, to match his greatest work.

Had he learned to live without music? Elliot Mintz commented, "John was prone to exaggeration to make a point. The fact is that during the years in question there was always music being played. He would play the piano. Elton [John] sent him an electric Yamaha for his thirty-eighth birthday that we set up in the room we later called the Club Dakota. When he wanted to listen to music, he went into the old bedroom. He had huge speakers on either end of the headboard of their bed. He had his stereo components at his right, his old Sony amp, and a tape-to-tape duplicator with headphones.

"For one of his birthdays Yoko got him a beautiful Wurlitzer jukebox, a classic one with bubbles. It only took 78s, so we went out to old record stores and filled it with songs we both loved, Johnnie Ray, Frankie Laine. We sat in that room for hours watching the old Wurlitzer whirl and listening to the records. He became an enormous fan of forties music. He loved Bing Crosby, and Willie Nelson's album of forties songs. He loved the old songs on the

Nilsson Schmilsson album, by Harry Nilsson, and an English singer called Gracie Field—their Judy Garland. He listened to WBAI all the time, and to lots of classical music as well. Occasionally we would listen to some vintage Carl Perkins, Jerry Lee Lewis, Lonnie Donegan, and some of the classic old rockers." But he was staying as far as he could from seventies rock.

When John gave up his public career to raise Sean, he didn't give up his imagination or his creative life. He continued to create imaginative works, but he kept them private, sharing them only with his closest friends. He wrote a novel called *Skywriting by Word of Mouth,* which he showed to Elliot Mintz in 1976. "It was a hundred-and-fifty-page draft," Mintz recalled, "done in a kind of stream-of-conscious, *Spaniard in the Works* style of writing, but much funnier, with incredible wordplay."

He also wrote a play, Mintz reported, and "he must have written a dozen or two songs or poems. He created at least a hundred drawings or sketches, and twenty or thirty collages, real time-consuming collages, using figures and shapes he cut out of magazines. They were exquisite. John and I traded sound collages, mini–radio plays on tape. He would take some Alistair Cooke, a WBAI lecture, something from Billy Graham off the TV, mix it with music, talk over it, sing over it; he would create a cast of characters speaking in different voices—he had a holy person from the East called 'the great Wok.' It must have taken him five or ten hours to compose a brilliant one-hour sound collage. Then he'd put it in the mail and send it to me as a gift. I would do the same."

John told one interviewer, "I'm interested in history, but I'm particularly fond of ancient history." He wanted to write a history book, Mintz reported, under a pseudonym—"where he could do all the research himself and write it in a way that would be exciting, without anyone knowing it was him. Had he lived, I have no doubt that he would have tackled that. He was interested in the history of the Celts. He was fascinated by Thor Heyerdahl's book of scholarly papers, *Early Man and the Ocean: A Search for the Beginnings of Navigation and Seaborne Civilizations.* He was interested in the British slave trade, how some of the great British mansions were built by black slaves who arrived from Africa in the port of Liverpool."

John told another interviewer, "I'm an avid reader. . . . I read everything from *Scientific American* to *East-West Journal.*" He read his airmail edition of the Manchester *Guardian* every week. He sent Elliot Mintz books to read, with notes in the margins about what to look for. "One of the books John sent me was *The Lazy Man's Guide to Enlightenment.* He inscribed it, 'This is positively the last book I will send you on achieving enlightenment through reading.' "

"He loved talking politics," Mintz reported. "I always knew that at four

P.M. the phone would ring, because the six o'clock news had just ended in New York. If it didn't ring at four, it would ring at four-thirty; that meant he had watched Walter Cronkite too. He wanted to brief me on what I should look for in the news that would be broadcast in L.A. three hours later. Sometimes he would go on for so long I would miss the news."

======

The Beatles' assets were freed in 1977, following the resolution of their lawsuits concerning the breakup. John must have received several million dollars in back record royalties. In addition, songwriting royalties from the performance of Lennon-McCartney tunes by others must have earned him at least ten or twelve million dollars a year. He didn't disagree when his wealth was estimated at $150 million. What did John and Yoko do with all this money?

First of all they spent a lot, in the same ways ordinary rich people do. They had a house full of servants. They bought jewelry and furs. They traveled all over the world. When they flew someplace, they would buy not only their own first-class seats but all the seats on either side of them and in front of them and behind them, to protect themselves from fans and admirers. That doesn't seem out of line for a multimillionaire superstar. Many rich people buy their own planes. When John decided to go to Bermuda with Sean in 1980, he got a sixty-foot yacht. That too made him like many boring rich people. Yoko spent lots of money collecting Egyptian art and antiques, including a real mummy. (When it was delivered, could John resist singing "My Mummy's Dead"?)

They spent money, and they also invested it—Yoko's department. John had never handled his own money; that had been Brian Epstein's job, and then Allen Klein's. John had concluded that Epstein got ripped off by others, and that Klein was ripping him off. Putting Yoko in charge was an excellent solution, especially since she seemed to be good at it. He also claimed the decision had significance as a feminist act. How many other millionaires put all their financial affairs in the hands of their wives? How many other women in the world had complete control of $150 million?

Yoko's most famous investment was in cows. She bought 250 Holsteins, the Cadillac of dairy cows, and 1,600 acres of pasture in upstate New York to graze them on. She sold one cow at the New York State Fair in Syracuse in 1980 for a record price, $265,000. John was delighted. And she still had 249 left.

She also bought real estate, announcing that "property is the best thing to have during times of inflation." The farms in the Catskills were probably worth around $700,000 at the time, during the late seventies. She bought two historic mansions, one on Long Island Sound at Cold Spring Harbor, which cost $450,000, and one in Palm Beach, Florida, which cost $700,000. It had been built by the Vanderbilts and then owned by the same people who had owned the Hope diamond. It had seven bedrooms, five servants' rooms, an indoor pool, an outdoor pool, and fifty yards of private beach. John and Yoko's idea was to spend the summer on Long Island and the winter in Florida, something New Yorkers had been doing for almost a century. But some old fans expressed a sense of betrayal about these houses: what was the Walrus doing out there in debutante country? Palm Beach in particular hurt. It was a place where elderly people wore tuxedos to charity balls and went to bed early. To picture John in this world was grotesque.

Those who charged him with selling out had forgotten about his earlier residences. As soon as the Beatles hit it really big, John went out and bought a mock Tudor castle in Weybridge, London's stockbroker belt. Then he moved to a huge Georgian estate in Ascot, Tittenhurst Park. The only time in his adult life he didn't live in an extravagant place was on Bank Street in Greenwich Village. And if the working-class lad from Liverpool wanted to own mansions, he never really lived in them. "I found that I spent most of the time on the bed with the TV," he said.

Yoko's investing was the object of a lot of carping. What was she supposed to do, lose money? John had already done that, with Apple. Or maybe John should have let some WASP investment banker put his money into stocks and bonds? None of the people who said rude things about Yoko handling John's money ever said much about Mick Jagger or Bob Dylan or Pete Townshend and their investments. It was good for John that for the first time in his life he had somebody taking care of his money whom he trusted and who did a good job.

She did a lot of negotiating with lawyers: "They're all male," he explained, "big and fat, vodka lunch, shouting males, like trained dogs, trained to attack." But Yoko could handle them. John was proud of her.

John talked about his money when interviewers were smart enough to ask. "I enjoy the security of knowing I've got money. I've still got that lower-class fear. Philosophically, I can see that worrying or caring about money is a load of shit. But it isn't a load of shit, either. . . . Wealth per se doesn't make me happy. But like my Aunt Mimi always said, I'd sooner be miserable in luxury."

John and Yoko were doing the right thing in taking care of their money, but they were also supposed to give some away. Even the most reactionary and selfish rich people give lip service to that principle. And the groups working for peace and for feminism desperately needed financial support.

John and Yoko declared a policy of tithing themselves. That meant they should have been giving away at least several hundred thousand dollars a year.

John and Yoko's Spirit Foundation was not the vehicle for these contributions. According to the foundation's tax returns, obtained from the IRS, it was not founded until December 1978, its original assets were only $100,000, and the only contribution it made in 1979 was $10,000 to the Salvation Army.

Shortly after John's death the Spirit Foundation distributed $285,000, but that was not John and Yoko's money. It came from contributions made by thousands of people in memory of John, as Yoko had requested. Nevertheless, the way that money was divided up gives some idea at least of Yoko's priorities. The largest contribution, $50,000, she gave to "various disarmament groups, anonymously, so we would not be pressed to become politically involved with them." Giving the money was laudable; not wanting to be "involved" showed how far she had moved away from an engagement with the peace movement since the early seventies.

The bulk of the rest of the contributions went for programs providing health care, drug rehabilitation, and child-abuse counseling in New York City, including $20,000 each to the Harlem Interfaith Counseling Service and the East Harlem Family Health Service. These sound like deserving and noncontroversial projects with a progressive aspect. Two groups with a more active left-liberal political orientation received smaller contributions—Amnesty International and the ACLU, $10,000 each. But these two seemed to have been balanced by gifts of equal size to groups supported by people on the right, the Police Athletic League and the Salvation Army.

Assuming John and Yoko's private contributions before John's death were organized along similar lines, the support for disarmament groups, Amnesty International, and the ACLU represents a continuation of some of their earlier commitments. The absence of support for feminist groups, programs, or health centers is equally notable.

Although they kept secret whatever contributions they made to peace groups, they held a media event in 1979 to make public a contribution of a thousand dollars to buy bulletproof vests for New York City policemen. The amount was insignificant, but the cause and especially the carefully orchestrated publicity were not. Of course cops shouldn't be killed while enforcing the law. But it was a question of priorities: were police deaths the most significant social problem in New York City in 1979? In fact police work is not one of the most dangerous occupations. Proportionately more firemen and miners are injured on the job than cops. The contrast between secret contributions to peace groups—if in fact they made any in the late seventies—and public contributions to support the local police revealed a disturbing shift in John and Yoko's priorities.

During this period Yoko's old weakness for tarot card readers, numerologists, and psychics grew. She became more dependent on them to "advise" her on running both her personal life and her business affairs. Once these practitioners of the metaphysical arts and sciences learned to manipulate her, she seemed afraid to make decisions without them, unwilling to face her fear of life's uncertainties.

John went along with her. Elliot Mintz recalled that John told him, "She will say things you will not understand. Go with it. She's always right." Mintz said she would send John off on "direction trips." Once she told him to head southeast, and he ended up in South Africa; once he went around the world when she "advised" him to. Did he go along just to placate her, or did he really give up his own judgment? What happened to his 1971 statement that he didn't believe in I Ching or tarot?

After John was killed, Yoko's tarot card reader went to the tabloid *Star*, promising to tell "shocking secrets" about John and Yoko's sex life, and did his best to write a book. Yoko should have sent them all packing after they failed to tell her about the events that were in the cards for December 8, 1980.

=

After his withdrawal from politics and music, John missed the great political concerts. He missed the "Evening with Salvador Allende" at Madison Square Garden in 1974, after the United States supported a coup that destroyed Latin America's oldest democracy. Bob Dylan sang "Blowin' in the Wind" with Phil Ochs and Dave Van Ronk; Dennis Hopper read Allende's last speech and cried; the Living Theater did a piece on the torture of political prisoners; Dave Van Ronk dedicated "He was a Friend of Mine" to Allende.

Most important, John missed the "War Is Over" rally on Mother's Day, 1975, in New York's Central Park. In April, during the final battle for Vietnam, the Saigon army had refused to fight, and on April 30 the last Americans had left Vietnam in helicopters departing from the roof of the American embassy in Saigon. The official toll was 56,555 Americans killed, 303,654 wounded, in fourteen years of fighting, which cost American taxpayers $141 billion. The number of Vietnamese casualties is unknown but probably over one million. The "War Is Over" rally was a time for rejoicing and reflection. The Vietnamese had defeated the Americans on the ground, but they never had the power to stop American bombing and thus end the war. Only the American people had that power. And they did stop the bombing and end the war.

The antiwar movement, despite all its limitations, won one of the few great political victories in the history of American radicalism. No European left movement could match its success in bringing such a massive imperialist war to an end. John, by writing the song that became the anthem of the peace movement, and by committing himself to the struggle, made a significant contribution. He shared in the achievement. It's sad that he didn't go to the "War Is Over" rally to sing "Give Peace a Chance" one last time.

John missed the 1976 Democratic presidential primary campaign with its unprecedented fundraising by rock musicians. Jerry Brown had Linda Ronstadt, Jackson Browne, the Eagles, and Chicago. Sargent Shriver had Neil Diamond and Tony Orlando and Dawn. Birch Bayh had Stephen Stills. Hubert Humphrey had James Brown. The old New Leftists, Arlo Guthrie and Harry Chapin, worked for Fred Harris. The winner was Jimmy Carter and the Allman Brothers.

Most significant in terms of his own roots, John missed the "Rock against Racism" festivals in London in 1978, the most politically significant rock events of the decade. "For eighteen months in 1977 and '78 it was touch-and-go whether English working-class youth would fall into the hands of the neo-Nazi National Front," activist Stuart Hall explained. "A group of radicals set out to win leading rock groups to an antiracist activism. They organized concerts and let those groups express the theme in their own idiom." Eighty thousand people turned out to hear the Clash, Elvis Costello, and the Tom Robinson Band, among others. "Rock against Racism was one of the few successful efforts by the left to consciously contend for cultural leadership," Hall said. "It was a critical moment, a turning point in the development of the practice of cultural politics. Rock against Racism stopped the move by working-class youth toward the National Front dead in its tracks." John had defended Michael X, he had denounced the war in Vietnam as "racist," he had supported the Black Panthers; he belonged at "Rock against Racism."

And John missed the Hurricane Carter benefits organized by Bob Dylan in 1976. Carter, a former boxing champion, had been imprisoned ten years earlier, found guilty of murdering three people in a Jersey City, New Jersey, bar. Dylan's song "Hurricane" opened his *Desire* album, which became the biggest seller of his career. "Hurricane" told the story of the murders and argued that Carter was innocent. The song evoked the hot New Jersey night and the viciousness of the cops. Dylan's voice never sounded more expressive, and he sang with urgency and anger.

In December 1976 Dylan launched his "Rolling Thunder Revue" tour and scheduled two dates as benefits for Carter's defense. The "Night of the Hurricane" benefit filled Madison Square Garden to capacity with twenty thousand people. Dylan sang "The Times They Are A-Changin' " with Joan Baez. He attracted impressive political support for the benefit: two congressmen (Edward Koch and Herman Badillo), Mayor Kenneth Gibson of Newark, and Coretta King. Candice Bergen and Dyan Cannon also came, as did Walt Frazier of the New York Knicks. The Houston Astrodome benefit presented an amazing array of music stars: Stevie Wonder and his nineteen-piece band, who brought the crowd to its feet chanting "Free the Hurricane"; Stephen Stills, Carlos Santana, Richie Havens, and Isaac Hayes; playing drums behind Dylan on "Maggie's Farm" was Ringo Starr.

Nine months after Dylan's song came out, the New Jersey supreme court unanimously ordered a new trial for Carter, ruling that the prosecutor had "substantially prejudiced" a fair trial by concealing evidence of Carter's innocence. Carter went free on bail posted by Muhammad Ali.

In June the New York *Times* ran a front-page story exposing massive waste and internal dissension in the Carter defense committee. The benefit concerts at Madison Square Garden and the Houston Astrodome had been among the most successful in history, taking in $600,000, but only $38,000 of that went to the law firms defending Carter, and another $15,000 went for his bail. Although the performers had appeared without pay, $547,000 had been reported as "expenses."

Dylan bore at least some of the responsibility for the fundraising fiasco, as the headliner at the benefit concerts and the defense committee's most prominent supporter. The limousines, parties, and hotel charges that were listed as "expenses" suggested that Dylan and his party were living it up at the expense of the man who had been sitting in his ten-foot cell.

More damaging to Carter's case were the charges by the woman who chaired his defense committee that he had assaulted her in a motel room. The prosecution gleefully used her charges to ask the court to revoke Carter's bail and put him back in jail. She made it clear that she considered him capable of murder. The *Times* insinuated that all these problems arose when the blacks on the defense committee pushed whites out of leadership positions.

The new jury heard six weeks of testimony and affirmed the original guilty verdict. Carter received a life sentence for murder for a second time. The only voices that continued to maintain his innocence were left-wing sectarian newspapers: the *Militant,* the *Guardian,* and *Workers' Power.* If Dylan commented on the verdict, it didn't make the papers.

————

John's final hearing before the Immigration Service was held in July 1976. The case had been sent back after Judge Kaufman ruled that John's British marijuana conviction did not provide a legitimate basis for denying his application for permanent residency in the United States. John answered the questions of the hearing officer: had he ever been a member of any organization that attempted to overthrow the United States government? "No." Would he like to make a statement? "I'd like to publicly thank Yoko, my wife, for looking after me and pulling me together for four years, and giving birth to our son at the same time. There were many times that I wanted to quit, but she stopped me. I'd also like to thank a cast of thousands, famous and unknown, who have been helping me publicly and privately for the last four years. . . . I hope this is the end of it."

Attorney Leon Wildes presented character witnesses. Norman Mailer took the stand. He called John "one of the greatest artists in the Western world," and added, "I've always thought it was a terrible shame that we had to lose T. S. Eliot and Henry James to England." Geraldo Rivera testified that the money John raised at the 1972 One to One concert "liberated at least sixty retarded children from the pits of hell." Sculptor Isamu Noguchi said that for a child of a biracial couple, like Sean, the United States was "the only place where he has an even chance to live normally." The hearing officer told Noguchi, "I've enjoyed your coffee table for years." Actress Gloria Swanson praised John for his opposition to junk food for children. Then hearing officer Ira Fieldsteel read his decision: "I find him statutorily eligible for permanent residence." The courtroom filled with applause, and John and Yoko went outside for their last immigration press conference.

In 1979 Kurt Waldheim, secretary-general of the UN, tried to organize a Beatles reunion as a benefit for the Boat People fleeing Vietnam. He called Peter Brown, the Beatles' personal assistant from the Apple days. Brown recalled, "I said to him I thought it was a waste of time, it wouldn't work, it would be embarrassing to all concerned, it was very unlikely they would do it under any conditions, even for this well-deserving cause. The artistic considerations were boundless: what would they play? Apart from the personal differences. I said, 'What I would suggest to you, Mr. Secretary-General, is that you have a concert at which each of them would appear, but they didn't have to play together.' I said I would help him do that.

"So we framed a letter, which he wrote, saying in the first paragraph, 'Your friend Peter Brown suggested the concert be constructed this way.' They gave me the letters, and I made sure they got to each of them directly. Yoko said, 'Peter, you're naïve.' I've been called many things in my life, but never naïve. She said, 'You don't understand the subtleties of this international situation, especially where you're dealing with the Orient.' She absolutely blocked the whole thing. She wouldn't let me speak to John." Nevertheless, John found the proposal intriguing and wrote a postcard to a friend, "Looks like the boys and I will be playing for those sailing enthusiasts, the Boat People." The concert never came off.

In May 1979 John and Yoko ran a "love letter" to their fans as a paid advertisement in newspapers in New York, London, and Tokyo. They wanted everyone to know they were feeling great: "Sean is beautiful. The plants are growing. The cats are purring." That was nice. They reported that "More and more we are starting to wish and pray. . . . Wishing is . . . effective. It works"—especially when you've got a hundred million bucks. They continued in this vein, remorselessly: "Magic is real. The secret of it is to know that it is simple, and not kill it with an elaborate ritual which is a sign of insecurity." They paid $18,000 to convey this helpful hint to readers of the New York *Times*. The ending was something like an old Beatles song: "We love you." Almost everybody shrugged. Those who still cared about John were appalled.

In the interviews John did publicizing *Double Fantasy*, he was asked the same inevitable question. John never said "When I hear the words 'Beatles reunion,' I reach for my gun," but occasionally he came close. "Why should the Beatles give more?" he shouted at *Playboy*'s David Sheff. "Didn't they give everything on God's earth for ten years? Didn't they give *themselves?* Didn't they give all?"

One other question drove John into a rage.

Playboy: "What about the charge that John Lennon is under Yoko's spell?"

Lennon: "If you think I'm being controlled like a dog on a leash because I do some things with her, then screw you. Because—fuck you, brother and sister, you don't know what's happening. I'm not here for you. I'm here for me and her and the baby. . . . If they can't see that, they don't see anything. . . . Let them jack off to Mick Jagger, okay? . . . Don't bother me. Go play with the Rolling Wings."

The interviewer tried to escape John's wrath by changing the subject.

Playboy: "Do you—"

Lennon: "No, wait a minute. Let's stay with this a second. Sometimes I can't let go of it. . . . Nobody ever said anything about Paul having a spell on me! . . . Why didn't they ever say, 'What is this John and Paul business?'

"You know, they're still congratulating the Stones on being together a hundred and twelve years. Whoopee! At least Charlie and Bill still got their families. In the eighties they'll be asking, 'Why are those guys still together? Can't they hack it on their own?' . . . They will be showing pictures of the guy with lipstick wriggling his ass, and the four guys with the evil black makeup on their eyes trying to look raunchy. That's gonna be the joke in the future, not a couple singing together or living and working together."

$$25$$

Starting Over

John wouldn't listen to any new music during his years as a househusband. But if he had been looking for music with something to say, he would have listened to reggae, the music from the slums of Jamaica, whose elusive, unrushed lyrics and rhythms proclaimed the possibility of revolution. He knew it. "In the last ten years, the thing I missed most about England was reggae," he said in 1980. He would have listened to Bob Marley's *Natty Dread* in 1975, fiery and lyrical songs about oppression and resistance. He would have listened to Peter Tosh's "Equal Rights" in 1977, which seemed to be speaking straight to the author of "Give Peace a Chance": "Everyone is crying out for peace / None is crying out for justice." He would have listened to punk—to the Sex Pistols' "God Save the Queen" and to *The Clash* in 1977. They expressed the rage of working-class youth more powerfully than ever before, they challenged capitalist control of mass music, and they raised questions about musical meaning, suggesting "new sounds, new forms, new texts," as critic Simon Frith said.

John identified with British punks. He said he had seen some of their music on video in 1980. "I thought, oh, that's how we used to behave at the Cavern before Brian told us to stop throwing up and sleeping on stage and swearing. . . . Yeah, I think it's great. I absolutely do." He recalled the time he and

Yoko and a Plastic Ono Band played the Lyceum in London in 1969. "That was a heavy show, and a lot of the audience walked out. But the ones that stayed, they were in a trance, man. There were about two hundred kids at the front there, somewhere about 13, 14, 15. . . . You know, I hear touches of our early stuff in a lot of the punk/new wave stuff. I hear licks and flicks coming out. And—it pleases me. I think—I bet—I'd love to know, were they in that audience?"

He also would have listened to Bruce Springsteen's *Darkness on the Edge of Town* in 1978. Springsteen did something John couldn't: he rooted his identity and his music in the working-class community where he had grown up. Springsteen himself explained in 1982, "The whole time I was growing up, I couldn't wait to get away from my neighborhood. Now, when I can go anywhere in the world, I keep coming back to it." John had the opposite feeling; he had to escape his roots to become himself. Springsteen drew on his experience and knowledge to make himself a genuine working-class hero. He sang about the reality of working-class life, especially about its pain and defeats. He did it without cynicism, with a passionate honesty, and with a love for rock and roll. John heard "Hungry Heart" in 1980: "I think it's a great record," he said. "To me it's got the same kind of period sound as 'Starting Over.' "

If John had checked up on the Rolling Stones, he would have found that Mick Jagger didn't have anything new to say, but that the Stones brought their moth-eaten riffs and themes back to life in 1978 with *Some Girls.* He would have found that Bob Dylan had a lot to say in 1979: he was saved and everybody else wasn't. Dylan earned grudging admiration for having found something else to betray; on the other hand, the Jews had enough problems already.

Elvis died in August 1977, fat, miserable, and full of drugs. John knew that he had once been headed in the same direction. "The king is always killed by his courtiers," he said. "The king is overfed, overdrugged, overindulged, anything to keep the king tied to his throne. Most people in that position never wake up." But he found out. "What Yoko did for me . . . was to liberate me from that situation. . . . She showed me what it was to *be* Elvis Beatle and to be surrounded by sycophants and slaves who were only interested in keeping the situation as it was."

John knew his rise with the Beatles had parallels with Elvis' six years earlier: in each case working-class youth conquered the world with the thrilling energy of their music. Each bought fancy cars and big houses. But while John grew and transformed himself, Elvis had become impoverished as an artist and a person. John had a restlessness and ambition; Elvis seemed satisfied. John wanted to be more than a Beatle: he wanted to be a writer, an artist, part of the great social movement of the times; then he wanted to be a loving father and husband. John survived superstardom while Elvis didn't.

Greil Marcus' unforgettable essay on Elvis emphasized that "the culture he came out of was a set of forces that could have held him back and worn him down as easily as they gave him life." In fact Elvis' cultural origins may well have held him back. Compared to the psychological resources that Elvis found in Tupelo and Memphis, British working-class culture gave its young men more. The British working class is proportionately a lot bigger than its American counterpart, and more unified. As a result its culture is more cohesive and confident. The American working class is divided racially, regionally, and ethnically. In England the lower middle class is drawn into proletarian culture, as John was in his youth, while in the United States the pull is in the opposite direction, with the working class drawn toward middle-class culture. Lennon came from the British working class, but Elvis did not come from the "American working class." He came from the white working-class South. To the mainstream, the culture Elvis came out of was dumb and degraded, and Elvis was a stupid hillbilly, a redneck who came from white trash.

The disaster for Elvis was that he played the part he was assigned. He made dumb movies and had dumb fun. John drew on the strength of British working-class culture to join the sixties project of liberation and self-transformation, while Elvis couldn't get out of the stereotype of the rich redneck. In public he wasn't angry or resentful; he stayed humble and respectful. But he went home and got loaded and one day it killed him.

═══

John and Sean went on vacation to Bermuda in 1980. For five years John hadn't written any songs, hadn't even listened to any contemporary rock. Now in Bermuda he walked into a disco where the B-52's' "Rock Lobster" was playing. It sounded like the music Yoko had been making a decade earlier. John was thrilled. "Get the axe and call Mother," he told the guy with him. ("The axe" was his guitar; "Mother" was Yoko.) On the phone he told her, "They're ready for you this time, kid." Immediately songs started pouring out of him, "like diarrhea," he said. He would call Yoko and sing them on the telephone. She'd write a reply song. Within two weeks they had twenty-two.

With *Double Fantasy* John returned to the risk-taking that had been at the heart of his best music. He sang a beautiful song about rejecting the role of macho rock star: "Watching the Wheels." It is a gentle manifesto. In the song John breaks deep cultural taboos, rejecting everything a man is supposed to be in our culture—aggressive, ambitious, success-oriented, striving to dominate. "People say I'm crazy, doing what I'm doing," he sings—giving up his career as a superstar to become a househusband. That echoed the line in "Imagine": "You may say I'm a dreamer." "When I say that I'm okay, they look at me kind of strange / Surely you're not happy now you no longer play the game." He declares he has turned his back on "the merry-go-round," that he "just had to let it go."

What John revealed on "Watching the Wheels" was that he had simply walked away from the swagger and sneer of the classic rock and roll male tradition, a tradition kept alive *ad nauseam* by a hundred macho rock stars. John said it ten years earlier, but *Double Fantasy* gave it new meaning: he didn't believe in Elvis. "Watching the Wheels" showed the extent to which John had drawn on his feminist commitments to declare his independence of the macho ideal. The result was a song considerably more radical than "Woman Is the Nigger of the World" in that it expressed his own self-transformation.

Double Fantasy could have been subtitled " 'I Found Out,' Part Two." On other songs John sings about his new feelings of gratitude and tenderness for Yoko, and his great love for his "beautiful boy" Sean. In all these songs John turned his back on the traditional male themes in rock music. No one should have been surprised by this; John had broken other taboos for male superstars a decade earlier, when he released *Plastic Ono Band*. The critics for the most part understood that earlier album and recognized its achievement. But when *Double Fantasy* appeared, the responses of many critics ranged from discomfort to dismay to contempt: this gentle man was not the one they wanted. They could appreciate John's 1970 screams of rage and despair over his mother, but his new songs of gratitude toward his wife they found much harder to take. With breathtaking perversity, Beatles historian Geoffrey Stokes called the album "basically misogynist," while Robert Christgau, in an otherwise beautiful and brilliant essay, called *Double Fantasy* "basically sexist."

When the Four Tops sang "Can't Live without You," the *Village Voice* critics did not present a diagnosis of separation anxiety. When James and Bobby Purify sang "I'm Your Puppet," no one suggested that therapy would be a more appropriate forum to air these feelings. But when John sang "Woman, you understand / The little child inside the man," a cry of dismay arose: this was "infantilization," and it was not acceptable, at least not from this white man with whom the critics identified. For them, a man who is not a strong, mature adult at every moment, a man who acknowledges feelings of need and dependency, is in real danger of becoming weak and helpless. It was precisely this deeply held belief that John challenged on *Double Fantasy*. That his challenge was neither strident nor dogmatic, that he simply suggested another direction, made it even harder to deal with.

The proponents of the "infantilization" interpretation have not heard the rich variety of songs and feelings which are right there on the vinyl. Stokes wrote for the *Voice* that the album celebrated a love "so all-fired powerful it exists without pain, without conflict." To Simon Frith it all sounded "comfortable and happy." Andrew Kopkind heard only "unrelenting sentimentality." Stephen Holden called the album a "pop fairy tale of perfect heterosexual union." But this is the album on which Yoko sings to John, "Give me something that's not cold / Come on come on." John replies, in one of the strongest songs he has ever written, "You say you're not gettin' enough / But what about all that bad bad bad stuff?" Yoko's next song says, "I'm moving on; it's getting phony." Is this really a picture of perfect domestic bliss?

Even if we confine our attention to John's songs, we need to ask whether together they paint a picture of baby John and mother Yoko. In "Cleanup Time" he's the king and she's the queen. In "Beautiful Boy" he's the loving father singing to his son, and mother is not mentioned. In "Watching the Wheels" he's the former superstar who has walked away from that macho world. In "Starting Over" he's the deep-voiced suitor proposing a week of love-making. In "I'm Losing You" he's angry and despairing over their "bad bad stuff." Which leaves "Woman": "I can hardly express / My mixed emotions at my thoughtlessness." Ask any mother the last time she heard this sentiment expressed by one of her children.

Many of these themes were familiar in pop music. Smokey Robinson sang a dozen songs apologizing for his thoughtlessness. Stevie Wonder sang "Isn't She Lovely" about his newborn daughter. John himself sang "When I'm home, everything seems to be right" in "A Hard Day's Night," expressing some of the feelings that led him to become a househusband twelve years before he did it.

"I'm Losing You" is the strongest song on the album, and John knew it. He wanted to make it the single, but feared it would be bad karma at a time when he was trying to make a comeback on a collaborative album. Yoko had him believing in magic. His low-down, snarling singing had never been better, as he describes himself in "some stranger's room—what am I doing here at all?" It sounds like he woke up in another woman's bed. "I know I hurt you then / But hell, that was way back when . . . don't want to hear about it." He's angry, he knows she's angry, but his fear overpowers his anger. Over and over he comes back to the refrain, "I'm losing you."

In "Dear Yoko" John has fun with his separation anxiety. He rhymes "sea" with "TV" and says that when all was said and done, the two of them are really one. Yes, this was a neurotic merger fantasy, but he made irresistible music out of it. His passion was as playful as it was intense. It was his best song in this vein since "Oh Yoko!" on the *Imagine* album a decade earlier.

John insisted that the *Double Fantasy* album was not a hymn to private life, but rather was a continuation of his longstanding project to link the personal and the political. In his last *Rolling Stone* interview he argued that there was a direct connection between the political issues raised in his old songs and the personal ones on *Double Fantasy*. "We're not the first to say, 'Imagine no countries' or 'Give peace a chance,' but we're carrying that torch, . . . passing it from hand to hand, . . . that's our job." And he told the RKO Radio Network, "This album doesn't say imagine the whole world like that, because I've said that. What I'm saying now is, now let's put the spotlight on the two of us and show how we're trying to imagine there's no wars, to *live* that."

"When I was singing and writing this," John explained, "I was visualizing all the people of my age group for the sixties being in the thirties and forties now, just like me, and having wives and children and having gone through everything together. I'm singing to them. . . .

"I'm saying, 'Here I am now, how are you? How's your relationship going? Did you get through it all? Wasn't the seventies a drag, you know? Here we are. Well, let's try to make the eighties good, you know, 'cause it's still up to us to make what we can of it.' . . .

"We survived. You have to give thanks to God or whatever it is up there. The fact that we all survived. We all survived Vietnam and Watergate and the tremendous upheaval of the whole world.

"We were the hip ones in the sixties, but the world is not like the sixties. The whole world's changed and we're going into an unknown future, but we're still all here."

John thus maintained the sense of responsibility that had made him a genuine leader. He maintained a commitment to his audience to use his musical skills and his power as a superstar to tell the truth and to illuminate what was happening. *Double Fantasy* expressed this commitment as strongly as "Give Peace a Chance" had twelve years earlier.

Neither Mick Jagger nor Bob Dylan maintained the commitments that made them heroes of the sixties. Ever since Altamont, Jagger had evaded his responsibilities, content to be a survivor, a man who at least sometimes made good, strong music. And Bob Dylan's entire career since 1964, his repeated "betrayals" of his fans, has been an effort to escape the responsibilities of superstardom.

In the long interviews he did in 1980 to publicize *Double Fantasy*, John was often asked how he regarded his activist years a decade earlier. He gave two different sorts of answers. Back in *Lennon Remembers* in 1970, he had said, "I have great hopes for what I do with my work, and I also have great despair that it's all shit." A decade later he had the same hopes and the same despair. His first interview in five years appeared in *Newsweek*, where he told Barbara Graustark it had all been shit: "That radicalism was phony, really," he was quoted as saying. "What the hell was I doing fighting the American government just because Jerry Rubin couldn't get what he always wanted— a nice, cushy job?" (Rubin had recently gone to work on Wall Street, bringing joy to reactionaries everywhere.)

John had forgotten what he had been fighting for: not for Jerry Rubin, but for an end to the war in Vietnam and for women's rights. John may have been thinking, "I sold out, but Jerry Rubin sold out more"—cold comfort. Whatever he was thinking, the statement was a bad one for what it said about John, and a sour note on which to begin his comeback.

He had more bitter words when he talked to Lisa Robinson shortly afterward. "All the rock critics are age 38, 40, the same age as me, and they're all the ones wishing for the 1960s to come back. . . . They probably even want a war so that we can have an anti-war movement, . . . so we can grow our hair again and say peace and love, you know. But we don't need the sixties." John's old friend from the East Village, David Peel, had an excellent response: "The only thing that would have been bigger than 'Bring back the Beatles' would have been 'Bring back the people.' "

When *Playboy* asked John what he thought about his song "Power to the People," he thought it was "all shit": "It didn't really come off. I was not thinking clearly about it. It was written in the state of being asleep and wanting to be loved by Tariq Ali and his ilk, you see. . . . I couldn't write that today." But when Sheff showed him the album jacket for *Some Time in New York City,* he gazed at it and said, "Man, it's nice to see this!" He went on to reiterate his commitment to socialism: "In England, there are only two things to be, basically: you are either for the labor movement or for the capitalist movement. Either you become a right-wing Archie Bunker . . . or you become an instinctive socialist." And when *Newsweek* asked if he was a Buddhist, he replied in a playful spirit that he could be called a "Zen Marxist."

======

Late in November John and Yoko made plans to take part in a demonstration in San Francisco. Japanese workers in Los Angeles and San Francisco had struck against three companies that imported and distributed Japanese food products in the United States. The biggest of the three, Japan Foods Corporation (JFC), was a subsidiary of the Japanese multinational Kikkoman, best known for its soy sauce. The three firms together accounted for 90 percent of the Japanese food imported and sold in the United States. Their workers in the U.S. were primarily Japanese, and their management was almost exclusively Japanese. The workers, members of the Teamsters Union, rejected a company offer of wage increases of 3 percent annually for three years. That was well below the inflation rate and also well below the rate at which white warehousemen and drivers were paid for similar work. In Los Angeles and San Francisco, workers went on strike November 13.

The strike and associated boycott quickly became a major test of the power of Japanese firms in the United States to resist Japanese-American workers' demands for equal pay. The struck companies received substantial support from the Japanese businessmen's association of Southern California and from Japanese-American multinationals like Mitsubishi and Sumitomo.

Striking workers knew they had to win during December, the biggest month for sales of imported Japanese food. The shop steward of the Los Angeles local said he would ask for a public statement of support from John Lennon and Yoko Ono, who was his cousin. The shop steward, Shinya Ono, was an employee at JFC and a well-known labor activist in Los Angeles' Little Tokyo. Forty-two years old, he had spent years organizing immigrant workers in low-wage industries and tenants threatened by redevelopment. He was regarded in Little Tokyo as "a kind of Japanese-American Woody Guthrie." Shinya Ono had been a student activist in New York City during the sixties. He had been an editor of *Studies on the Left,* the first magazine of the New Left, and had become a prominent figure in the Weatherman faction of SDS in 1969 and 1970.

Shinya Ono persuaded John and Yoko to make a public statement. Yoko supported them, he explained to the striking workers, because she was Japanese; John supported them even though he was a superstar. He understood their situation, he knew how they felt, because before he became a star he had come from the working class. "She had sympathy, he had empathy."

John and Yoko sent their statement to the L.A. strikers, who rushed it to the media:

"We are with you in spirit. Both of us are subjected to prejudice and abuse as an Oriental family in the Western world.

"In this beautiful country where democracy is the very foundation of its constitution, it is sad that we have to still fight for equal rights and equal pay for the citizens.

"Boycott it must be, if it is the only way to bring justice and restore the dignity of the constitution for the sake of all citizens of the U.S. and their children.

"Peace and love, John Lennon and Yoko Ono. New York City, December, 1980." That was John's last written political statement.

John and Yoko asked Shinya whether there were any plans for a big rally or march. "If so," they told him, "we'll come out to help, and bring the kid." The plans were made for a march and rally in San Francisco the week of December 8, and John, Yoko, and Sean got their plane tickets. "John was very happy to do this," Yoko explained later, "because John had a son who was half Oriental. So he was envisioning carrying Sean" at the march and rally.

The last time John and Yoko had taken to the streets was in 1973, at a demonstration in midtown Manhattan protesting Nixon's mining of Haiphong Harbor. Now he was planning to return to the streets, marching for racial equality with his five-year-old son on his shoulders.

The Los Angeles strikers planned a rally to coincide with the one in San Francisco and asked for a statement addressed to them that they could read at theirs. John and Yoko made arrangements to call Nobu Kurasako, one of the strikers, with their new statement on December 8. He waited at home all day.

=====

While Nobu waited in Los Angeles for the call, John in New York did another interview promoting *Double Fantasy*, this one with the RKO Radio Network. The interviewers asked him about "Power to the People." Now he was filled with great hopes, and he spoke of the way he had sustained and developed his radical commitments over the decade since "Power to the People." "In retrospect," he said, "if I were trying to say that same thing again, I would say the people have the power. I don't mean the power of the gun; [but] they have the power to make and create the society they want."

He reiterated his commitment to feminism, the strand of New Left politics he had adopted most completely. "I'm more feminist now than I was when I sang 'Woman Is the Nigger of the World.' I was intellectually feminist then, but now I feel as though . . . I've tried to really live up to my own preaching. . . . Isn't it time we destroyed the macho ethic? . . . Where has it gotten us all of these thousands of years? Are we still going to have to be clubbing each other to death? Do I have to arm-wrestle you to have a relationship with you as another male? Do I have to seduce her . . . because she's a female? Can we not have a relationship on some other level? . . . I don't want to go through life pretending to be James Dean or Marlon Brando."

He also spoke of "the opening up of the sixties. . . . Maybe in the sixties we were naïve and like children and later everyone went back to their rooms and said, 'We didn't get a wonderful world of flowers and peace. . . . The world is a nasty horrible place because it didn't give us everything we cried for.' Right? Crying for it wasn't enough.

"The thing the sixties did was show us the possibility and the responsibility that we all had. It wasn't the answer. It just gave us a glimpse of the possibility."

This interview was his last. Six hours later he was killed.

===

John was a dreamer, but he was also a fighter; he was a working-class wit and a proud father. In an age of cynical superstars, he struggled against becoming a commodity. He worked to tell the truth not only about his wish for peace and love but also about his anger and misery.

Double Fantasy represented a great achievement for John, but it should not be regarded as the culmination of his life's work. Nothing in John's life was ever definitive. That was part of his appeal. He was a person who was always in the process of becoming.

"Your way of life," he once said, "is a political statement." Politically, he was important because he made himself part of the movements seeking an end to the Vietnam war and freedom and equality for blacks and women. He shared the movements' hopes, arguments, confusions, and occasional triumphs. He joined in.

"I know you," he sang; "you know me." We knew him as an artist, and we also knew something about him as a person. The best of his work as an artist coincided with the biggest risks he took as a person. From "Working Class Hero" to "Watching the Wheels," he struggled to make the personal and the political come together.

Epilogue: The Struggle
of Mark David Chapman

 Mark David Chapman's tie to John Lennon was not random. John had a special significance for many people who grew up in the sixties, and Chapman was one of them. In his healthier moods Chapman was a fan. But when his paranoia overwhelmed him, Lennon took on a terrible significance.

Chapman's feelings about Lennon were shaped by the media culture that permeates American society. Beyond the daily life of family, work, and friends, the media create a second reality: the world of stars and celebrities —people who seem as familiar as friends and neighbors. Fans are given richly detailed accounts of their idols' lives and loves. As a result, fans may feel they know more about their idols than they do about friends and neighbors.

This sense of familiarity with stars is seductive even to those who are emotionally strong and healthy. For those who have no intimate relations with real people in their lives, or whose relations with family and friends are disturbed, the imagined intimacy with stars can become an absorbing substitute for an empty or frightening daily life.

The emotional power of stardom comes not just from information about celebrities; stars become personifications of people's fantasies and wishes.

Stars have beauty, talent, energy, luck; they devote their lives to play and to passionate love affairs. They are at ease in the world. For people whose own wishes seem unattainable, the stars who represent those wishes can become figures of great significance.

Stardom creates more for fans than personifications of their wishes; it creates expectations. The Hollywood beauty must remain beautiful, the fighter must not give up the fight. When these expectations are not met, most fans are simply disappointed. But those with a tenuous hold on reality find it especially threatening when the stars who personify their dreams turn them into nightmares.

John Lennon did brilliant things with his status as a celebrity. He didn't give fans the clichés of a rock star's life and loves; instead he revealed, or at least seemed to reveal, his real feelings. He showed that he was not like other stars—he was not at ease in the world, he had fears and weaknesses he was struggling to overcome. At a time when young people's relations with parents had become much more problematic than in previous decades, John suggested the importance of shared intimacy among youth. And he provided them with an example of self-revelation.

Lennon personified some of his fans' deepest and most powerful wishes, and in strikingly direct ways—not just a wish for good looks or an exciting life, but to be a truthful person, to achieve intimate relationships. For most of his fans John's struggles provided confirmation for their own. He was important not as a source of new values, but rather as an exemplar of values that were already widely shared in sixties culture.

As a result, John bore an especially heavy burden of expectations. The intensity of these feelings about him gave rise to what can be called a literature of betrayal—books, articles, memoirs, attempting to prove that he was a false god, that he lied, cheated, sold out.

Mark David Chapman felt a sense of intimacy with John, and John personified his wishes, in ways that were distorted by his psychosis. The court psychiatrist testified, "He idolized and adored this man." But intimacy is deeply threatening for paranoids, and Chapman was a true paranoid. He became convinced John was a "phony." He decided the man who represented his special wishes had betrayed him. He bought a gun and headed for the Dakota.

=====

Chapman was born on May 10, 1955, and grew up outside Atlanta. In 1965, while Beatlemania was reaching its high point, ten-year-old Chapman began to withdraw from the world. He told his court-appointed psychiatrist that he had created an imaginary world of "little people" who populated the walls of his living room. He controlled their lives and they "worshipped him like a king." To prove he was a good king, "he would stage concerts for his people. . . . The performers in these imaginary concerts were the Beatles." Already the Beatles were associated in his mind with goodness.

Chapman argued that Lennon was the most talented of the Beatles, a ninth-grade classmate recalled; Chapman ended letters to friends with quotes from Lennon. Chapman also learned to play the guitar. The year before, John's LSD use had been publicized; Chapman now took lots of LSD and other hallucinogens, and according to friends "had real bad experiences."

When he was fifteen or sixteen, Chapman had a religious conversion and became a Jesus freak. He sold his Beatles records, cut his long hair, and denounced Lennon for having said the Beatles were more popular than Jesus. His high school prayer group sang "Imagine John Lennon dead." Friends remember that Chapman became intensely preoccupied with the struggle between good and evil. "He wanted to prove that he was a good person, that there was no bad person inside of him."

Here Chapman was entering his own paranoid world, remote from sixties culture. He defined goodness in terms of purity, self-sacrifice, and saintliness. Lennon exemplified a completely different view. For him, the world was not divided into saints and sinners; as he said more than once, "We are all in this together." He suggested that we all have possibilities for goodness as well as for destruction, we all have to work to make ourselves better, we have responsibilities to each other.

The YMCA offered Chapman a way to do good as he defined it. He became an active member, and in 1975, twenty years old, he went to Lebanon to work at the Beirut YMCA, but was forced to leave two weeks later when war broke out. Then he took a job helping Vietnamese refugees at the Fort Chaffee, Arkansas, resettlement center. He did "outstanding" work, his supervisor said, worked long hours, and was "very concerned about the refugees."

During this period people noticed that he was extremely dependent on others for his identity and for the organization of his daily life. At Fort Chaffee he fell in love with a girl named Jessica. "Everything Mark did he did because of Jessica," a friend recalled: "his whole involvement with religion, even what he ate and drank." When his old friend Dana arrived at the end of the Fort Chaffee project, Chapman demonstrated the same dependency: "He cleaned his nails for Dana, he put on clean clothes for Dana, he made telephone calls for [him]." He would later become dependent on Lennon for his identity, but in his own distorted way, struggling to fulfill his concept of purity.

When the refugee project ended in December 1975, Chapman went into a deep depression. He dropped out of college, broke up with his girlfriend, quit the Y, and got interested in guns. During the next year "he became engrossed in political and philosophical thoughts," according to his psychiatrist, "and concluded that the world was run by a small group of selfish men." He needed to blame his depression on something, so he blamed it on them. "He found himself anguishing over some things, like Vietnamese children dying from napalm bombs," and "continued to be obsessed with what he considered to be the phoniness and corruptness of the world."

In 1977 Chapman moved to Hawaii, where his mother had moved after divorcing his father. Here he apparently concluded his problem was the phoniness and evil not of the world, but rather inside himself. He made an unsuccessful suicide attempt and was hospitalized for psychiatric treatment.

Chapman got better in 1978, and got a job in the same hospital where he had received psychiatric care. Again he fulfilled his dream of being a good person. His supervisor remembered that "he was so sympathetic to the old people. He would . . . pay attention to them when no one would. Some of them hadn't spoken to anybody in years, but they started again when Mark showed them some attention."

In June 1979 he married a Japanese-American woman, Gloria Abe, who was four years older than he was. (Yoko was six years older than John.) He started feeling bad again. He changed jobs, becoming a security guard, returning to his interest in guns. He was seen at work with the name "John Lennon" taped over his own nametag. Sometimes he knew what was happening to him: on September 10, 1980, he wrote to a friend, "I'm going nuts." His wife liked her job and made enough for both of them to live on; Chapman decided to retire and let his Japanese wife make the money—like Lennon. On October 23, the day he "retired," he signed himself out as John Lennon.

Of course staying home while his wife went to work failed to bring Chapman any relief. It only deepened his depression and gave him more time for his paranoid thinking. It was then, apparently, that Chapman read the cover story in the November 1980 *Esquire*, part of that literature of betrayal which sought to destroy Lennon's persona. The piece was a disturbingly effective one. The author, Lawrence Shames, wrote that he had gone looking for Lennon, "the conscience of an age," but all he found was "a 40-year-old businessman" with "lawyers to squeeze him through tax loopholes." He described the four mansions Lennon owned, his herd of cattle, his swimming pools, his yacht, his "millions of dollars' worth of deeds and mortgages." John had turned down a request for an interview; Shames wrote that he had only one question to ask: "Is it true, John? Have you really given up?"

In the *Esquire* article, Chapman found the explanation he needed for his torment: John, he said, was a "phony." The problem was not in himself; it was in his idol. He didn't need to kill himself, as he had tried before; he needed to kill the source of his problem. The language of the article spoke directly to Chapman, particularly the statement that Lennon had been a "conscience" and the moralistic condemnation of the corrupt life Lennon was supposedly living. Chapman bought a gun on October 27 and left for New York the next day.

Even when Chapman was staying a half block from the Dakota, with his gun at his side, he had deep doubts about his decision. He later told a minister that during this period he was wrestling with good and evil spirits. He told the court psychiatrist he could feel Satan's demons around him: "I can feel their thoughts. I hear their thoughts. I can hear them talking, but not from the outside, from the inside." This marks Chapman as a classic paranoid schizophrenic.

He won this early November struggle with his demons. Instead of trying to kill Lennon at this point, he left New York and traveled to Atlanta, his home town, visiting the sites of many of his past failures. Then he returned to New York.

After the murder, Chapman told the police they could find the explanation for his act in J. D. Salinger's *The Catcher in the Rye.* He had the book with him at the time of the murder, and was reading it when the police arrived. For the young protagonist in the book, Holden Caulfield, the worst thing a person can be is a "phony." Caulfield's world is full of phonies—fakes, frauds, hypocrites, people who pretend to be good and virtuous when they know they are not.

When the judge at Chapman's sentencing hearing asked if he had anything to say, he read the passage from *The Catcher in the Rye* that explains the book's title. Holden Caulfield has a fantasy: little kids are playing in a field of rye, running around, and he catches them before they fall over a "crazy cliff." Chapman wanted to save helpless people from falling into craziness. Most of all, he wanted to save himself.

Chapman said he wanted to be Holden Caulfield. That was a healthy wish: Caulfield was lonely and troubled, but wonderfully sane. Chapman had a moment like that, when he returned to New York from Atlanta at the end of November. He called his wife and told her, "I've won a great victory. I'm coming home." And he made an appointment at a Honolulu mental health clinic for November 26. He was right: that decision was a great victory, a victory of sanity over the internal forces that tormented him. But it was only temporary. He never went back to Hawaii, and a week later he started hanging around in front of the Dakota. Mark David Chapman had lost his struggle; now he would put an end to Lennon's.

An Interview with Yoko Ono

Jon Wiener: You moved from Japan to the U.S. with your family in 1954, attended Sarah Lawrence College, and returned to Japan as an avant-garde artist in 1960. Kate Millett, who was there at the same time, told me, "Yoko was utterly fearless in the face of Japan's tedious Victorian conventions. She had an enormous amount of strength, unconventionality, and scintillating mental power."

Yoko Ono: Yes, I was like that, but it caused a lot of heartache for me. A group concert was canceled when the concert hall discovered that I was one of the participants. The reviews of my concerts were written with venom, shall we say. A Norman Mailer of Japan wrote about "women wearing pants coming back from abroad who think they know something." At dinners some would make a point of not speaking to me or not sitting near me. People would say, "If Yoko is coming, I'm not," to the host, who then had a choice of having a very, very small dinner party with me or a big one without. In those days I went through hell about these things. I paid the price with my heart.

Q. In 1961 you joined the New York avant-garde art group Fluxus, headed by George Maciunas. That was different.

A. I could talk about George Maciunas for hours. In 1959 I was doing the first loft concerts in Manhattan. By the end, two hundred people were coming. Then I was told that everybody was going to perform at a gallery on Madison Avenue instead. I was a bit hurt; I asked who was doing it. "George Maciunas, he was at your concert the other day, don't you remember?" Something to that effect. The bastard, he stole my idea, I thought.

Then I got a call from George asking if I would do a one-woman show in his gallery. That was the start of a great friendship, but I didn't know it yet. I went to his gallery as I was asked to. It was a beautiful space, and an exceptionally handsome man was talking with an elegant woman in candle-light. There was a new IBM typewriter on a Bauhaus-type table. It looked terribly romantic.

It turned out the handsome man was Maciunas, the elegant woman was his mother, the candlelight was because they couldn't pay the electric bill, the gallery had been leased by someone else, and the typewriter was rented. George Maciunas always said he was just a graphic designer, not an artist; he was getting artists to do things. But Fluxus was his art. He was too shy to declare that he was an artist.

Q. You left New York in 1966 and went to London. What was your first impression of John Lennon?

A. To me he looked like a sensitive person. A clean-cut man with his own elegance. After we got together, I told him that, and we had a big argument about it. "No," he said, "I was funky! 'Clean-cut' . . . you make me sound like a public school boy!"

Q. John said in an interview, "At first, we were not going to be lovers."

A. That's true. For many reasons we both hesitated becoming lovers. I treasured any freedom I had and dreaded another involvement. John, though he was a young man then, in reality had to weigh everything very carefully because of the position he had achieved in the world. So he became a patron of my artwork and sponsored my Half-A-Wind Show at Lisson Gallery in London in 1967.

There was something sad about making John Lennon be an art patron, when he was such a brilliant artist himself. So I suggested that he might think of an art piece himself to put in the gallery show. That's the least I could do. John looked up at the ceiling and immediately said, "How about putting the other halves in bottles?" Just like that. It was beautiful. So his bottles with labels like "the other half of a chair," et cetera, were exhibited on a shelf in the gallery where I had my half objects. His were the invisible halves.

Q. In interviews early in your relationship, John often explained that he was attracted to you because "she's me in drag." Did you have that feeling, that the two of you were identical?

A. Well, he was definitely the other half, my mirror image, strangely, in the body of a man. I didn't have much respect for men until then, because they are so limited in their way of thinking, as you know. Women tend to be more versatile. But John had versatility. He also knew that his way of thinking was right, but he didn't have the mirror image to confirm it.

I remember when he did the "erotic lithographs." The materials had been left for him to try out, by the art book people. One afternoon, when we were on a nice mescaline high, overlooking the English garden from our bedroom, he did the whole thing in an hour or two. I thought the lines were exquisite. He thought they weren't good enough to give to the book people. I was starting to get angry that he didn't realize how good they were. I compared them with Haiku, Leonardo da Vinci, and Goya. He laughed and said, "If you say so," or something to that effect, and released them.

I was only thinking about the lines and the artistic merits of the drawings when I encouraged him to release them. I totally forgot about the subject matter of the drawings . . . I mean, that angle . . . how it would be taken. There was a tremendous furor when they were released. So now we were terribly embarrassed. Friends nervously asked us if we were part of a sexual threesome, et cetera., because of one of the lithographs. Of course, we weren't. We were pretty conservative as lovers. But then, aren't most couples when they're in love? John and I were too involved in each other to think of diversions.

=====

Q. Many people interpreted your songs on your 1973 album *Approximately Infinite Universe* as describing your relationship with John shortly before the breakup. Especially your song "What a Bastard the World Is." You sing to an unnamed man, "What a bastard you are, leaving me all night missing you." You call him a jerk, a pig, the scum of the earth; then you say, "Please don't go, I didn't mean it." You conclude that women's liberation is "nice for Joan of Arc but it's a long way for Terry and Jill."

A. That wasn't about John. It was inspired by the wife of one of the men in Elephant's Memory, the band we were working with. One day she was waiting, and her husband never showed up, and she was crying. I tuned in to her pain. She was the Terry in the song.

I wrote the song at Bank Street early one morning while John was asleep. We had an electric piano in the front room. I turned the volume down as low as it would go. When he woke up, I said, "Wait till you hear this one." He said, "It's a great song, but let's not record it because it sounds like I am that husband, and I'm not that way at all." I said, "You're not going to kill this one, because it's too good to kill." He agreed with me in the end. So we put it out. People thought it was about John. So he was right, poor John.

The pain that I had at that time I would have had even if I hadn't met John. The pain was always there. I tuned in to some of it in that song.

Q. "I Want My Love to Rest Tonight" is a very different song: "Sisters don't blame my man too much."

A. John loved that one—no surprise! When I thought of that song, we were in the car; he was sleeping in my lap.

———

Q. John said, "Heroin was not too much fun. We took it because of the pain." You recently said in *Rolling Stone* that you took heroin in celebration of yourselves as artists.

A. That was a rebellious remark I made intentionally. There are many dangerous drugs. Alcohol is a dangerous drug. It damages the brain. But people who take heroin are persecuted and made into criminals, regardless of the amount. The amounts we took were very small. We never injected, for instance. But it was made into a big thing by the media. I would never want to take heroin again because of the painful withdrawal. But the same society that defines certain drug-taking as a crime is full of legalized drugs that are harmful to human and animal lives. What we did was not *that* sinister. It did not take anybody's life except ours in a small way.

The pain of life is great. We have different ways of coping. Some take alcohol, some take Valium. Hopefully all of us would cope with life in ways that would not threaten others'. When you look at John's and my life, there were more times when we were peaceful health-food "addicts" than when we were on drugs. But that fact was ignored and we were punished for telling the truth. The persecution that followed took many forms; as a weapon to intimidate us in our political stands, to attack us in business, and to condemn us as unfit parents, long after we had anything to do with drugs. It was heartbreaking for us two.

Q. What do you mean, "condemn us as unfit parents"?

A. When I was pregnant with Sean, John especially was superstitious about the birth. I had had many miscarriages, and many abortions before that. John was so sweet. He thought preparing the crib and the baby's room before the birth would be bad luck . . . so nothing was prepared. We had no crib, no baby clothes, we didn't buy any baby things, in fact. We were afraid that if we had another miscarriage, we would be heartbroken to come home to a room full of baby things.

Most people think we scheduled the Cesarean birth to coincide with John's birthday. But that wasn't how it happened. We had prepared for a natural childbirth, Lamaze and all that. Early the morning of October 9, the contractions were starting. We went to the hospital. At that point the doctor decided to take precautions and deliver the baby by Cesarean.

They injected me with a partial anesthetic and then realized they didn't have my blood type, which was rare. So they called around to other hospitals to get it. That threw the timing of the anesthetic off. When the blood arrived, they had to give me a second injection. Then they delivered the baby. Cesarean birth is painful, and usually they give you another injection afterwards. I was in agony, saying, "Please give me something." But they said they couldn't give me anything because I'd already had two heavy shots.

The baby was taken to intensive care. John kept checking and reporting back to me, "He's fine, he's fine." But the baby was having problems—muscle spasms. The doctors thought he might have something wrong. John was so choked up, but he was hiding it from me.

They decided to test my urine, and they came and told me and John that they had found evidence of drugs in my urine and that the baby might have been damaged by this. John shouted, "We weren't taking drugs! We were on a health-food diet!" He said, "We're taking our baby and getting out of here!" The doctor said, "If you take that baby, we'll get a search warrant to search your residence, and we could get a court order to take your baby away from you for being unfit parents." We were terrified. But we knew we hadn't taken any drugs.

Our private physician tried to help us, and he did what he could, but once the baby was in intensive care, the intensive care doctor had the power to make decisions.

We had planned that I would nurse the baby, and I kept asking to. But for three days they didn't allow me to see the baby. Finally they let me go down to intensive care. When I saw our baby for the first time, I cried. The baby was all strung up with tubes and wires. Then they told me I couldn't nurse the baby ever, because I hadn't started to nurse him in the first three days and that it was too late. Well, why didn't they warn us about it? (I did successfully breastfeed the baby for two months, though the milk stopped after that.)

John said, "I didn't tell you: to test the baby, they took fluid from his spinal cord." It was a very difficult thing for the doctor, and if the needle had been just a little bit off, the baby would have been paralyzed for life. They were doing this just for a test. It turned out there was no reason to do it. But the doctor was proud and excited that he had done it without paralyzing the baby.

Finally, they decided there was nothing wrong with the baby. Just nerves, maybe! Then they admitted that what the urine tests had picked up was the extra anesthetic they had given me because they had had to wait for the right blood. John and I actually ran out of the hospital carrying the baby. A nurse ran after us saying, "We need to do one more blood test and we have to cut his toe and take some blood." John shouted, "Not another test! Poor kid! Have some pity, please!"

When we got home, the baby's spasm was still there. John and I took turns staying up at night and rubbed Chinese herbal medicine on Sean every two hours. We prayed. The spasms stopped after several months of this. Since then Sean has been a very healthy boy. John was always afraid to tell this story, about the hospital. . . . He was afraid they could still take Sean away from us.

I can tell you many horror stories like this. People attacked us for mainly three reasons: one, to cover themselves and what they have done; two, to discredit us for some business gain; and three, just to be mean. John and I had become closer to each other because of the pain we shared. Most of the time we couldn't tell half the story to anyone in the fear that it would backlash.

======

Q. John often said he learned about the oppression of women from you.

A. John felt that Paul's "Get Back" was addressed to me, saying I wasn't acting like a woman was supposed to.

When people first encounter me, they see I'm small and seem unthreatening. But then they learn I'm not a wimp. They say, "She's no woman." Men who are sexually strong are supposed to be admired, but if a woman is sexually strong, for instance, they call her a bitch or a nymphomaniac.

John believed my work as an artist wasn't accepted in part because I was a woman. He got angry when people said about me, "She's not a woman, she's a female impersonator." John said, "If I had been gay and gotten together with a guy who was talented like you, after ten years that guy would have become famous as an artist in his own right. Maybe we should come out and say, 'Actually Yoko is a guy.' Maybe that will do it!" That made him laugh a lot.

John learned about women's oppression from me, but I learned a lot about men's vulnerability from him. He expressed his vulnerability, unlike a lot of other men. I learned that it's not just men oppressing women. Men also suffer, they feel fear and guilt.

For example, I thought the fact that men buy prostitutes was terrible. It filled me with indignation. But John explained it differently. "It's humiliating for a guy to buy a whore," he told me. "It's proof he's rejected, he's desperate." I had never thought of that: for men who go to prostitutes, sex is connected to being rejected and humiliated.

I always hated people who committed sex crimes, but through John I tuned in to their pain. John told me that it was unfortunate for the poor guy whose sexual preference was a crime and something to be feared. John's perspective was "I'm *lucky* I'm normal."

=====

Q. What has it been like for you as a Japanese person living in the U.S., and before that in England?

A. People say to me, "Surely you're not subject to racism. Your case is different." My naïve New York friends think that. They don't realize that the fact that I was an Oriental was a large factor in the attacks people made on me. If John had left his ex to marry a woman from English high society, that would not have been controversial. People would have said that John married up. But the world looked on me as the opportunist Oriental. They felt he was marrying down, though in his mind he was the pauper, a Liverpool boy, and I was the princess, a New York sophisticate.

The attacks on me continued for ten years. In 1974, when we were separated, I did a benefit for WBAI. One of the big three New York newspapers wrote in their review something like "shaking her boobs, with her slanted eyes, thinking she's sexy or something, but it doesn't impress the writer. . . ." A London newspaper recently ('81) referred to "sloe-eyed songstress Yoko Ono." It's always "slanted-eyed" this and that. Few women are described in the press, as John said, using the word "ugly." But I was Oriental, so they felt free to call me ugly. When John and I were first together he got lots of threatening letters: "That Oriental will slit your throat while you're sleeping." The Western hero had been seized by an Eastern demon.

At the Grammies, it occurred to me that I was probably the first Oriental to receive the award. But that was only because I was receiving it *for* John. In hindsight, I thought, they applauded my sorrow, which was different from applauding my joy.

Q. Sean is half Japanese.

A. Friends tell me, "Sean looks like you." They mean it as a compliment. But, as an Oriental who suffered very much in the Western world, that compliment makes me worry for Sean. I don't want him to have to go through anything like what I have gone through. John and I worried before he was born that our half-Oriental child would be the victim of prejudice. Because of that John said, "We'll have to really look after him. Just in case there is too much prejudice in the West, we have to make sure that Sean has a foot in Japan, that he is accepted in Japan." It was sad. I knew that Sean would never be accepted as Japanese in Japan. So we had that loneliness.

Q. You were an active opponent of the war in Vietnam. Do you think your Asian background made you more sensitive to the Vietnamese, and thus more committed to peace?

A. No. Everybody is interested in peace. The Japanese have no special commitments. Orientals can be extremely insensitive to the sufferings of fellow Orientals.

Q. What was it like when you and John made your first trip to Japan together?

A. For a long time John had been a sensitive Westerner interested in Oriental culture as an alternative society. Opposites attract, you know. It was a sixties thing, as well. He had spent time in India. He found Oriental culture inspiring. When we got to Japan, he was just totally overjoyed to be there. He was happy every day. Whereas for me, it was less exciting. It was only exciting when I saw my country through John's or Sean's eyes.

The first time John met my family was before Sean was born. We went on a slow boat from Los Angeles. Arriving in Yokohama port, we looked scrubby as hell. Nobody noticed us. We went directly to my parents. John was an unshaven, funky guy. My parents are conservative tweedy people. They got the shock of their lives. But they were polite.

John had thought all Orientals were short. He had always told me, "My daddy is short, but at least he is taller than your daddy." I said, "Well, he's taller than you." My father looked like a tall American Indian chief—he stood straight, he was elegant and proud. When they met, John got his "I'm from Liverpool" attitude. He whispered to me, "You're right! He's really tall!"

After that meeting John said, "This was totally the wrong approach." So the next time, when we went with Sean, John said, "Let's show your family I'm not just a scrubby rocker. Let's show 'em we're cultured. Let's invite all your relatives to a great party. Let's do it right, for Sean's sake."

Q. How did you "do it right"?

A. We sent handwritten invitations to a hundred of my relatives. John did an elegant sumi-e Japanese traditional drawing of the three of us on each invitation. I wrote the words in Japanese flowing-style writing. We used beautiful Japanese paper. We had special rooms for the children to play in and watch cartoons. Two of my great-uncles didn't come. They thought *we* should be visiting them instead of the other way around, since we were the younger generation of the family. But everybody else came.

John dressed in a dark navy suit with a pink carnation. When we arrived, everyone stood up. John went around the tables and shook hands with each person and thanked each for coming. The garden party was a great success. He was delighted. Afterwards he said, "We did it!"

=====

Q. Tell me about the photos in your book *Summer of '80* of the two of you naked in bed.

A. John said, "They think that the king and queen after ten years aren't doing it anymore. Let's show that a couple like us still do." So we set up a bedroom in a gallery, and shot the "Walking on Thin Ice" video there as well as these still photos. We didn't actually make love, though. And if you could see the outtakes, you would see that we were very modest. John carefully covers me so you don't really see anything.

First I couldn't go through the pictures; it was too painful for me. So the art director and the photographers chose the photos before I checked them. I wrote the introduction, found the publisher, and made the deal for the photographers. The photographers divide the royalties, except for ten percent which goes to the Spirit Foundation. I wouldn't have picked that last picture [of John lying on top of Yoko, sleeping peacefully]. It reminds me too much of what happened.

=====

Q. In 1960 your Chambers Street loft cost you $50.50 a month. Now you control something like $150 million. What was it like changing from a starving artist into a wealthy businessperson?

A. My life has gone through so many changes. In fact, that wasn't the biggest one. When I was eight or nine, during World War II, we were evacuated from Tokyo to the countryside. The farm folks hated the city folks, saying that they had fun all their lives in the city and now they're crawling to the farmers for food. Our money couldn't buy food. It all depended on the farmers' whim. Sometimes you would give expensive jewelry in exchange for a bowl of rice, and still they would skip on the deal. It was jealousy. But knowing what it was didn't make it any easier for us. The farm boys threw stones at me and wrote me strange letters at the same time. My mother said, "You can write about all this one day when it's over." That was my one hope amidst the terrible days of war. "One day I'll write about all this." By saying that, I felt better.

But then almost every year was a big turnaround. We moved to the U.S.A. I went to college. I became an artist. Every year could have been a book and a half.

Learning to deal with money was like learning anything else. John and I had to learn to deal with managers, lawyers, then politicians in the immigration case. I had to learn the rock music world as opposed to the classical and the avant-garde. The world of money wasn't so different from any other world as a learning process in life.

Q. Do you think the rich are different from everyone else?

A. They say the true sign of being rich is that you don't know what you have. I guess that makes me one of the true rich! But I have some of the same problems that we all have: my tax money goes to build weapons. That's on my conscience. I'm a guilty partner. But rebellion for rebellion's sake will not bring us the desired result. It would just cause friction and harm to us. I have to be realistic and comply with the tax laws.

The difference between the privileged class and the people is that the privileged have put on blinkers. They don't look on themselves as part of the whole. I don't have blinkers on. I'm aware that I am only part of the whole and what happens to others affects my life directly and very fast. I try to do my best to help others because I know that that is the only logical thing to do if one wishes to survive. We have to survive together or we'll all fall.

Every day people write me, asking for help. Help, help, help. Sometimes I can't sleep because I hear a tremendous chorus of pained voices. But even if I gave everything up, it seems like it would be just a drop in the ocean of suffering. In fact, I have very little power, but I'd like to maintain it, to use it for good.

I got a letter from a woman in Ireland. She said Jackie Onassis and I were rich widows flying around in private jets, when the rest of us widows are so poor we can't even take a weekend vacation. She was bitter and angry.

I thought about that letter all day. I understand the sentiment. To that Irish woman, I'd like to say, "We're both widows. You're on a small boat, I'm on a big ship. But we're both on the same ocean, and we have the same problem: we're both trying not to sink. To keep a large ship from sinking, you need incredible energy. John and I did it together, but now he's gone. I'm keeping this boat floating alone, and it's hard."

Acknowledgments

This work began as a documentary broadcast by KPFK-FM and the Pacifica Radio Network, produced by Claire Spark. Her encouragement was crucial. Elaine Markson agreed to work as my agent on the basis of a two-page letter I sent her. The confidence that she showed in my project carried me a long way. She and her wonderful associates Raymond Bongiovanni and Geri Thoma provided unflagging support.

The earliest proposal was read by Bruce Dancis, Jimm Cushing, and Ted Koditcheck; their enthusiasm and comments were essential. The friends who read the first draft had the hardest job: conveying the appropriate mixture of encouragement and the advice that a lot more work needed to be done. I couldn't have done without Perry Anderson, Grace Barnes, Bob Edelman, Greil Marcus, Ted Rosengarten, and Paul Thomas.

I imposed on a few close friends to read more than one draft: Judy Fiskin, Bill Hackman, Mickey Morgan. I'm especially grateful to each of them for their extraordinary willingness to help.

Danny Schechter told me to sue the FBI, put me on my first network TV show, gave me a tape of his own 1973 interview with John and Yoko, and went wild with excitement when we made the front page of the New York *Post*. Working with him recalled our sixties plans to launch a syndicated news program, *The Schechter-Wiener Report*. In a way, that's what this book is.

Robert Christgau generously let me make copies of clippings from his massive files, as did A. J. Weberman. I found indispensable archives and reference services in the fan magazines. Marsha Ewing of *Instant Karma!* was a real help and source of enthusiasm. Two other fan magazine editors provided assistance and support: Barb Fenick of *The Write Thing* and Bill King of *Beatlefan.*

I'm especially grateful to Lennon's old friends who consented to interviews. A list of their names appears in the Note on Sources. Their recollections and insights were invaluable. Several people also provided crucial audio or video tapes: Steve Gebhardt, Elliot Mintz, Edward Hume, and Kathie Stream.

Phil Pochoda kept up with the project from the beginning, and Fred Jordan provided excellent suggestions for revision, as did Jeanie Attie. I'm grateful to each of them.

I'm indebted also to the ACLU of Southern California, whose attorneys have been fighting the Reagan administration to win the release of the withheld portions of Lennon's FBI file. Mark Rosenbaum has been a model of commitment and energy, as have Paul Hoffman and Dan Marmalevsky.

Narda Zacchino got the Lennon–FBI files story on the front page of newspapers around the country, just like she said she would. Bob Scheer got Jason Epstein interested in the project. Beverly Haviland, my editor, understood what I was trying to do, even when I didn't; she handled countless problems with impressive calm, she was always a pleasure to work with, she made the book better in hundreds of ways. And copy editor Laurie Stearns did a masterful job.

Yoko Ono always respected the independence of my project. I am grateful to her for providing indispensable documentary material, as well as for the interview with which the book concludes.

Chronology

October 9, 1940: John Winston Lennon born in Liverpool, England.

Early 1956: John forms the Quarrymen, a skiffle group, while at Quarry Bank Grammar School; meets Paul McCartney on June 15, invites him to join band.

Fall 1957: John enters Liverpool Art College.

July 15, 1958: Julia Lennon killed in car accident.

1959: John leaves art college to work full-time with band, which now includes George Harrison.

early 1960: John names group the Beatles, after Buddy Holly's Crickets.

August 1960: Beatles begin performing in Hamburg.

November 9, 1961: Brian Epstein sees Beatles perform at the Cavern Club in Liverpool; signs contract on December 13.

Summer 1962: Cynthia Powell, John's girlfriend, discovers she is pregnant; they marry on August 23.

December 1962: "Love Me Do," first Beatles hit, peaks on British charts at Number Seventeen.

April 8, 1963: Julian Lennon born in Liverpool.

October 1963: Beatlemania begins in Britain.

Early 1964: Beatles leave Liverpool, move to London.

January 1964: "I Want to Hold Your Hand" tops U.S. charts.

February 7, 1964: Beatles arrive in United States and hold first U.S. press conference; John says "all our songs are antiwar."

March 1964: *John Lennon in His Own Write* published.

July 1964: *A Hard Day's Night* released.

April 4, 1965: John and Paul write "Help!."

June 12, 1965: Beatles awarded MBEs.

August 1965: *Help!* film released; single tops charts.

January 1966: *Rubber Soul* released.

June 15, 1966: *"Yesterday"* . . . *and Today* album with the "butcher cover" released in the United States and then recalled; John terms cover "as relevant as Vietnam."

August 1966: *Revolver* released.

August 1966: "More popular than Jesus" controversy; Beatles record–burnings; John apologizes at Chicago press conference on August 12; Ku Klux Klan pickets Beatles in Memphis on August 19.

August 22, 1966: At New York press conference Beatles come out against Vietnam war.

September–October 1966: *How I Won the War* filmed.

November 1966: John meets Yoko Ono at Indica Gallery, London, preview of her show.

February 1967: "Strawberry Fields Forever" released.

June 2, 1967: *Sgt. Pepper's Lonely Hearts Club Band* released.

August 24–25, 1967: John first studies meditation with Maharishi Mahesh Yogi.

August 27, 1967: Brian Epstein dies of accidental drug overdose.

October 1967: *How I Won the War* released.

February 16–April 20, 1968: In India with the Maharishi.

May 1968: John and Yoko spend their first night together, are henceforth inseparable.

June 1968: Beatles record "Revolution"; released in August.

October 18, 1968: John and Yoko arrested, charged with possession of cannabis.

November 1968: *Two Virgins,* with nude cover, released.

November 1968: White Album released.

January 1969: *Black Dwarf* exchange of letters.

March 20, 1969: John and Yoko marry in Gibraltar.

March 26, 1969: Amsterdam bed event begins.

May 26–June 3, 1969: Montreal bed event; "Give Peace a Chance" recorded on June 1, released on July 7 in United States.

May 30, 1969: "The Ballad of John and Yoko" released.

August 1969: John and Yoko move to Tittenhurst Park, Ascot.

September 13, 1969: *Live Peace in Toronto* recorded; released in December.

September 1969: John and Yoko join Save Biafra campaign.

October 1969: *Abbey Road* released in United States.

October 1969: "Cold Turkey" released.

November 26, 1969: John returns MBE.

December 9, 1969: Altamont.

December 9, 1969: John and Yoko announce their support of Hanratty inquiry.

December 15, 1969: John and Yoko launch "War Is Over" campaign with UNICEF benefit concert at Lyceum in London.

December 17, 1969: John and Yoko announce plans for Toronto Peace Festival, to be held July 3–5, 1970. Cancelled in February.

February 4, 1970: John and Yoko announce their support for black power spokesman Michael X.

February 6, 1970: "Instant Karma!" released.

February 26, 1970: *Hey Jude* released.

March 1970: John and Yoko begin primal therapy with Arthur and Vivian Janov in London; continue in Los Angeles until August.

December 11, 1970: *Plastic Ono Band* released.

January 7 and February 4, 1971: *Lennon Remembers* interview published in *Rolling Stone.*

March 8, 1971: *Red Mole* interview published.

March 22, 1971: "Power to the People" released in United States.

July 7, 1971: "God Save Us"/"Do the Oz" released as part of *OZ* defense campaign.

August 11, 1971: John and Yoko join *OZ*/IRA demonstration in London.

August 12, 1971: John and Yoko announce support for striking shipbuilders.

August 1971: John and Yoko leave England and move to New York City.

September 9, 1971: *Imagine* released in United States.

October 1971: John and Yoko demonstrate with Onondaga Indians, Syracuse, New York.

November 1971: John and Yoko move into Bank Street apartment in Greenwich Village.

December 1, 1971: "Happy Xmas (War Is Over)" released in United States.

December 10, 1971: John Sinclair benefit concert, Ann Arbor, Michigan.

December 17, 1971: Attica families benefit concert, Apollo Theatre, New York City.

February 4, 1972: Senator Strom Thurmond suggests in secret memo to Attorney General John Mitchell that Lennon be deported.

February 7, 1972: John and Yoko demonstrate in New York against British policy in Northern Ireland.

February 14–18, 1972: John and Yoko co-host *Mike Douglas Show.*

March 6, 1972: INS refuses to renew John's visa; hearings on deportation proceedings held March 16, April 18, May 12, May 17.

April 24, 1972: "Woman Is the Nigger of the World" released.

April 29, 1972: John claims deportation action based on his antiwar stand.

May 13, 1972: John and Yoko participate in antiwar demonstrations in New York City.

June 12, 1972: *Some Time in New York City* released.

August 30, 1972: One to One concert held at Madison Square Garden.

November 7, 1972: Nixon reelected.

March 23, 1973: INS orders John to leave country within sixty days or face deportation; Yoko granted permanent residency. On April 2, appeal filed.

June 1973: John and Yoko attend International Feminist Planning Conference at Harvard Divinity School, Cambridge, Massachusetts.

June 28, 1973: John and Yoko demonstrate at South Vietnamese embassy, Washington, D.C.

June 29, 1973: John and Yoko attend Watergate hearings.

October 1973: John and Yoko separate; John travels to Los Angeles with May Pang.

October 17, 1973: John sues INS under Freedom of Information Act, seeking evidence of prejudgment and wiretapping.

October 31, 1973: INS appeal hearing held.

November 2, 1973: *Mind Games* released in United States.

March 1, 1974: John moves in U.S. district court for temporary restraining order of INS appeal ruling.

March 12, 1974: Troubadour incident in Los Angeles.

May 1, 1974: U.S. district court denies stay of INS appeal ruling.

July 17, 1974: INS board denies John's appeal, orders him to leave country within sixty days.

August 8, 1974: Nixon resigns.

September 23, 1974: "Whatever Gets You thru the Night" released in United States.

September 26, 1974: *Walls and Bridges* released.

November 2, 1974: John sues INS, claiming he was victim of political vendetta.

November 28, 1974: John appears onstage at Elton John concert at Madison Square Garden; last live concert appearance.

December 5, 1974: *Rolling Stone* reveals political origins of deportation case, prints copy of Thurmond memo.

January 2, 1975: U.S. district court grants John right to question INS officials and inspect files to seek evidence that he was victim of political vendetta.

January 1975: John and Yoko reunited.

February 17, 1975: *Rock 'n' Roll* released in United States.

March 1975: "Fame" with David Bowie released.

June 16, 1975: John sues former Attorneys General John Mitchell and Richard Kleindienst, and other INS officials, claiming that their actions against him were improper.

October 7, 1975: U.S. court of appeals overturns INS deportation order.

October 9, 1975: Sean Ono Lennon born in New York City; John becomes househusband.

October 24, 1975: *Shaved Fish* released.

July 27, 1976: INS grants John permanent residency.

November 12, 1980: "(Just Like) Starting Over" released.

November 15, 1980: *Double Fantasy* released.

December 8, 1980: Mark David Chapman kills John Lennon outside Dakota.

A Note on Sources

Government Files

Twenty-six pounds of FBI and Immigration and Naturalization Service (INS) files on John Lennon were obtained under the Freedom of Information Act.

The FBI files are composed of the main Washington, D.C., office file and field office files from New York City (the office of origin), Detroit, Los Angeles, Washington, and Dallas. They include some CIA and State Department documents. Two thirds of the main file has been withheld on the claim that it concerns national security matters; this claim is currently being challenged in U.S. district court.

The INS files comprise transcripts of deportation proceedings; the A-file, containing documents that pertain to Lennon's alien status; correspondence; and clippings.

Interviews

Stew Albert, Oakland, California, May 8, 1982.
Tariq Ali, London, June 26, 1981.
Peter Andrews, Los Angeles, February 14, 1981.
Robin Blackburn, London, June 15, 1981.
Peter Brown, Laguna Beach, California, May 18, 1981.
Joe Butler, New York City, June 6, 1981.
Dick Cavett, telephone, October 21, 1983.
Steve Gebhardt, Los Angeles, February 17, 1981.
Allen Ginsberg, telephone, July 20, 1983.
Dick Gregory, Irvine, California, February 8, 1984.

Stuart Hall, Urbana, Illinois, July 2, 1983.
Jon Hendricks, New York City, December 12, 1982.
Eric Hobsbawm, Los Angeles, March 29, 1981.
Abbie Hoffman, telephone, February 20, 1981.
Arthur and Vivian Janov, Los Angeles, June 3, 1983.
Paul Krassner, telephone, October 6, 1983.
Nobu Kurasako, translated by Rex Jones, Los Angeles, December 4, 1983.
Kate Millett, Poughkeepsie, New York, October 23, 1982.
Elliot Mintz, Los Angeles, September 8 and 16, 1983.
Yoko Ono, New York City, November 14 and 16, 1983.
David Peel, New York City, June 16, 1981.
Craig Pyes, telephone, August 13, 1983.
Dan Richter, New York City, June 7, 1981.
Geraldo Rivera, New York City, October 21, 1982.
Jerry Rubin, New York City, June 19, 1982.
Danny Schechter, Los Angeles, February 1, 1981.
Bobby Seale, Los Angeles, February 3, 1982.
Pete Seeger, telephone, February 15, 1981.
Judy Sims, Los Angeles, November 24, 1981.
John Sinclair, telephone, July 19, 1983.
A. J. Weberman, New York City, June 1981.
Stu Werbin, New York City, April 3, 1982.
Leon Wildes, New York City, June 21, 1983.

Television Sources

Shindig!, January 20, 1965.
News coverage of anti-Beatle protests, August 1966.
Tonight show, May 15, 1968.
News coverage of bed-ins, March 26–30 and May 26–June 3, 1969.
"John Lennon: A Tribute," Canadian Broadcasting Company special, November 26, 1969.
BBC "Man of the Decade" special, December 31, 1969.
Dick Cavett Show, September 23, 1971.
David Frost Show, January 13, 1972.
Mike Douglas Show, February 14–18, 1972.
NBC coverage of New York antiwar demonstrations, May 1972.
Geraldo Rivera interview, May 1972.
Dick Cavett Show, May 11, 1972.
Jerry Lewis Labor Day Telethon, September 6, 1972.
One to One concert, ABC, December 14, 1972.
Old Grey Whistle Test, BBC, 1975.
Tomorrow show, April 28, 1975.
Today show, April 29, 1975.
Salute to the Beatles with David Frost, May 21, 1975.

Radio Sources

Mersey Beat interview, October 9, 1963.

Beatles' first American press conference, New York City, February 7, 1964.

Carroll James–WWDC (Washington, D.C.) documentary on Beatles' visit to Washington, D.C., February 1964.

Murray the K interview, WINS (New York City), April 27, 1964.

WINS (New York City) interview, August 28, 1964.

Art Schreiber interview, KFWB (Los Angeles), 1965.

Jerry Gee documentary on Beatles' American tour, WKYC (Cleveland), August 1965.

Beatles' Chicago press conference, August 12, 1966.

Beatles' New York City press conference, August 22, 1966.

Ken Douglas documentary on Beatles' 1966 American tour.

"Newsfront" interview, WNET (New York City), May 22, 1968.

Dan Chandler interview, WQAM (Miami), 1969.

Radio Luxembourg interview, June 22, 1969.

"John and Yoko's 1970 Peace Message" (syndicated), December 1969.

Lennon Remembers, published in *Rolling Stone* on January 7 and February 4, 1971, excerpts broadcast on KSAN (San Francisco), 1971.

Interview on WIXY (Cleveland), May 1971.

Alex Bennett interview, WPLJ (New York City), June 1971.

Scott Muni interview, WNEW-FM (New York City), late 1971.

Danny Schechter interview, WBCN (Boston), June 3, 1973.

John as disc jockey, WNEW-FM (New York City), September 28, 1974.

Kenny Everett interview, Capital Radio (England), December 1974.

Earth News Radio interview (syndicated), December 1975.

"An Evening with John Lennon," Capital Radio (England), 1975.

"From Liverpool to Legend" documentary, RKO Radio, 1978.

BBC interview, December 6, 1980.

RKO interview, December 8, 1980. RKO asked that the following statement be included in this note: "The interview, conducted on behalf of RKO Radio Network, Inc., by Dave Sholin, Laurie Kaye, Ron Hummel, and Bert Keane, took place in New York City at the Dakota apartment of John Lennon and Yoko Ono on Monday, December 8, 1980, from 1:00 P.M. to 4:30 P.M. Eastern Standard Time. Upon conclusion of the interview, only one person knew it would be Lennon's last . . . his name was Mark David Chapman. A few hours later the whole world knew."

Bibliography

Allen, Gary. "More Subversion Than Meets the Ear." *American Opinion*, Vol. 12 (February 1969), pp. 49–62.

Alterman, Loraine. "John Lennon Talks about Music, Money, Marriage, and Fame." *Viva*, March 1975.

Anderson, Jack. Columns on Lennon immigration case. *Washington Post*, August 29, 1974; June 14, 1975; October 4, 1975.

Anderson, Perry. *Arguments within English Marxism*. London: New Left Books, 1980.

Anson, Robert Sam. *Gone Crazy and Back Again: The Rise and Fall of the Rolling Stone Generation*. New York: Doubleday, 1981.

Attie, Jeanie, and Josh Brown. "John Lennon." *Radical History Review*, No. 24 (fall 1980), pp. 188–90.

Bacon, David, and Norman Maslov. *The Beatles' England*. San Francisco: 910 Press, 1982.

Baker, Glenn A. "Rock's Angry Voice." *Goldmine*, July 1982.

Ballaster, Barry. "Who and What Killed the Toronto Peace Festival?" *Rolling Stone*, December 24, 1970.

Bangs, Lester. "Thinking the Unthinkable about John Lennon." Los Angeles *Times*, December 14, 1981.

Barrett, Jane. "John Sinclair: The Rally and the Release." *Village Voice*, December 16, 1971, p. 93.

"The Beatles—Those Lucky Lads from Liverpool." *Insurgent*, Vol. 1, No. 1 (March–April 1965), p. 12.

Beckett, Alan. "Stones." *New Left Review*, No. 47 (January–February 1968), pp. 24–29.

Berman, Marshall. *All That Is Solid Melts into Air.* New York: Simon & Schuster, 1982.

———. *The Politics of Authenticity: Radical Individualism and the Emergence of Modern Society.* New York: Atheneum, 1970.

———. "Sympathy for the Devil." *New American Review,* No. 19 (1974), pp. 23–76.

Blackburn, Robin, and Tariq Ali. "Lennon: The Working-Class Hero Turns Red." *Ramparts,* July 1971, pp. 43–49.

———. " 'Power to the People!' John Lennon & Yoko Ono Talk to Robin Blackburn and Tariq Ali." *Red Mole,* March 22, 1971, pp. 1–3.

Blake, John. "John: Giving His All to His Family." Liverpool *Echo,* April 27, 1979.

Braun, Michael. *Love Me Do: The Beatles' Progress.* London: Penguin, 1964.

Brown, Peter, and Steven Gaines. *The Love You Make: An Insider's Story of the Beatles.* New York: McGraw-Hill, 1983.

Brussell, Mae. "Why Was Martha Mitchell Kidnapped?" *The Realist,* No. 93 (August 1972).

Buhle, Paul, ed. "Fifteen Years of Radical America." *Radical America,* Vol. 16, No. 3 (May–June 1982).

Cannon, Geoffrey. "The Age of Aquarius." *Partisan Review,* No. 36 (1969), pp. 282–87.

Carr, Roy, and Tony Tyler. *The Beatles: An Illustrated Record.* 2nd. ed. New York: Crown, 1978.

Carson, Claybourne. *In Struggle: SNCC and the Black Awakening of the 1960s.* Cambridge: Harvard University Press, 1981.

"The Case for Michael X." *New Statesman,* June 22, 1973, p. 1.

Castleman, Harry, and Walter J. Podrazik. *All Together Now: The First Complete Beatles Discography 1961–1975.* New York: Ballantine, 1975.

Charlesworth, Chris. "Lennon Today." *Melody Maker,* November 3, 1973, pp. 36–37.

Chester, Andrew. "For a Rock Esthetic." *New Left Review,* No. 59 (January–February 1970), pp. 83–87.

Christgau, Robert. *Any Old Way You Choose It: Rock and Other Pop Music, 1967–1973.* Baltimore: Penguin, 1973.

———. *Christgau's Record Guide: Rock Albums of the '70s.* New Haven and New York: Ticknor & Fields, 1981.

———. "Defending the Beatles." *Cheetah,* May 1968, p. 37.

———. "Double Fantasy: Portrait of a Relationship." In *The Ballad of John and Yoko,* edited by Jonathan Cott and Christine Doudna. New York: Doubleday/Rolling Stone, 1982.

———. "John Lennon, 1940–1980." *Village Voice,* December 10, 1980, p. 1.

———. "Now That We Can't Be Beatle Fans Anymore." *Village Voice,* September 30, 1971.

———. "The Political Power of Rock and Roll." *Newsday,* July 9, 1972.

———. "The Rolling Stones." In *The Rolling Stone Illustrated History of Rock & Roll,* edited by Jim Miller. 2nd ed. New York: Random House/Rolling Stone, 1980.

———. "Symbolic Comrades." *Village Voice,* January 14, 1981, pp. 31–32.

———, and John Piccarella. "Portrait of the Artist as a Rock & Roll Star." In *The Ballad of John and Yoko,* edited by Jonathan Cott and Christine Doudna. New York: Doubleday/Rolling Stone, 1982.

Cleave, Maureen. "Old Beatles, a Study in Paradox." *New York Times Magazine,* July 3, 1966.

Cleaver, Eldridge. *Soul on Ice.* New York: Random House, 1968.

Cockburn, Claud. Column on *OZ* trial. *Private Eye*, August 13, 1971, p. 15.

Coleman, Ray. "Lennon on Elections." *Disc Weekly*, April 2, 1966, p. 10.

———. "Lennon: A Night in the Life." *Melody Maker*, September 9, 1974, pp. 15–16.

Connolly, Ray. *John Lennon 1940–1980: A Biography*. London: Fontana, 1981.

———. "Crippled Inside: An Interview with John Lennon." *Circus*, December 1971.

Corrigan, Paul, and Simon Frith. "The Politics of Youth Culture." In *Resistance through Rituals: Youth Subcultures in Post-war Britain*, Stuart Hall and Tony Jefferson, eds. London: Hutchinson, 1976.

Cott, Jonathan. "The Last *Rolling Stone* Interview." In *The Ballad of John and Yoko*, edited by Jonathan Cott and Christine Doudna. New York: Doubleday/Rolling Stone, 1982.

———. "Rolling Stone Interview: Jean-Luc Godard." *Rolling Stone*, June 14, 1969, pp. 19–24.

———. "Rolling Stone Interview: John Lennon." *Rolling Stone*, November 23, 1968, pp. 1–4.

———, and Christine Doudna, eds. *The Ballad of John and Yoko*. New York: Doubleday/Rolling Stone, 1982.

Dalton, David. *The Rolling Stones: The First Twenty Years*. New York: Knopf, 1981.

Dancis, Bruce. "For the Love of Lennon." *In These Times*, December 24, 1980, pp. 8–9.

Davies, E. "Psychological Characteristics of Beatle Mania." *Journal of the History of Ideas*, No. 30 (April 1969), pp. 273–80.

Davies, Hunter. *The Beatles: The Authorized Biography*. 2nd ed. New York: McGraw-Hill, 1978.

Davies, Russell. "Lennon's Confessions." *London Review of Books*, February 5, 1981, pp. 17–18.

De'Ath, Wilfred. "An American Exile." *Observer Magazine*, December 8, 1974, p. 56.

Demoraine, Hermine. "Jean-Luc Godard Talks to Hermine Demoraine." *I.T.*, September 6, 1968, p. 4.

Denisoff, R. Serge. *Solid Gold: The Popular Record Industry*. New Brunswick, New Jersey: Transaction, 1975.

Denisoff, R. Serge, and Richard A. Peterson, eds. *The Sounds of Social Change*. Chicago: Rand McNally, 1972.

Dickstein, Morris. *Gates of Eden: American Culture in the Sixties*. New York: Basic, 1977.

DiFranco, J. Philip, ed. *The Beatles in Richard Lester's "A Hard Day's Night": A Complete Pictorial Record of the Movie*. New York: Chelsea House, 1977.

Donner, Frank. *The Age of Surveillance: The Aims and Methods of America's Political Intelligence System*. New York: Knopf, 1980.

Eagleton, Terry. "New Bearings: The Beatles." *Blackfriars*, Vol. 45 (April 1964), pp. 175–78.

Edwards, Henry. "Yoko Ono (and John)." *Crawdaddy*, August 19, 1971, pp. 25–35.

Eisen, Jonathan, ed. *The Age of Rock*. New York: Vintage, 1969.

———. *The Age of Rock 2*. New York: Vintage, 1970.

———. *Altamont: Death of Innocence in the Woodstock Nation*. New York: Avon, 1970.

Elbert, Joan. "Growing Up with Lennon." *Christian Century*, December 24, 1980, pp. 1260–61.

Eliot, Marc. *Death of a Rebel*. New York: Anchor, 1979.

"Elliot Mintz Interviews John Lennon." Los Angeles *Free Press*, October 15, 1971, p. 2.

Epstein, Brian. *A Cellarful of Noise*. New York: Pyramid, 1964.

Evans, Sara. *Personal Politics: The Roots of Women's Liberation in the Civil Rights Movement and the New Left.* New York: Knopf, 1979.

"Everywhere's Somewhere." *The New Yorker,* January 8, 1982, p. 29.

"Ex-Beatle Told to 'Love It or Leave It.'" *Black Panther,* May 20, 1972, p. 5.

Fawcett, Anthony. *John Lennon: One Day at a Time.* 2nd. ed. New York: Grove, 1980.

Flippo, Chet. "Lennon's Lawsuit: Memo from Thurmond." *Rolling Stone,* July 31, 1975, p. 16.

————. "The Private Years." In *The Ballad of John and Yoko,* edited by Jonathan Cott and Christine Doudna. New York: Doubleday/Rolling Stone, 1982.

Foot, Paul. *The Rise of Enoch Powell.* London: Penguin, 1969.

————. *Who Killed Hanratty?* London: Cape, 1971.

Frith, Simon. "Beggars Banquet." In *Stranded: Rock and Roll for a Desert Island,* edited by Greil Marcus. New York: Knopf, 1979.

————. "John Lennon." *Marxism Today,* January 1981, pp. 23–25.

————. "Rock and Popular Culture." *Socialist Revolution,* No. 31 (January–February 1977), pp. 97–112.

————. *Sound Effects: Youth, Leisure, and the Politics of Rock and Roll.* New York: Pantheon, 1982.

————, and Angela McRobbie. "Rock and Sexuality." *Screen Education,* No. 24 (winter 1978/79), pp. 3–19.

Frost, David. "John's Gospel." *Spectator,* August 12, 1966, pp. 12–13.

Garbarini, Vic, and Brian Cullman. *Strawberry Fields Forever: John Lennon Remembered.* New York: Bantam, 1980.

Gillett, Charlie. *Sound of the City: The Rise of Rock 'n' Roll.* New York: Dell, 1970.

Gitlin, Todd. "John Lennon Speaking." *Commonweal,* September 22, 1972, p. 502.

————. "The Underground and Its Cave-In." In *The Campaign against the Underground Press,* by Geoffrey Rips. San Francisco: City Lights, 1981.

————. *The Whole World Is Watching: Mass Media in the Making and Unmaking of the New Left.* Berkeley: University of California Press, 1980.

————. "Working Class Hero." *Soho News,* December 10, 1980, p. 10.

————, ed. *Campfires of the Resistance: Poetry from the Movement.* Indianapolis: Bobbs-Merrill, 1971.

Giuliano, Geoffrey. "Yoko Ono." *Playgirl,* July 1983, pp. 114–15.

Gleason, Ralph J. "Aquarius Wept." *Esquire,* August 1970, pp. 84–92.

————. "Have You Seen Your Critic, Baby?" In *Altamont: Death of Innocence in the Woodstock Nation,* edited by Jonathan Eisen. New York: Avon, 1970.

————. "Perspectives: Fair Play for John and Yoko." *Rolling Stone,* June 22, 1972, p. 34.

Goldman, Albert. ". . . Or 'A Whitewash of Jagger'?" (Review of *Gimme Shelter* film.) New York *Times,* January 3, 1971, section 2, p. 9.

Goldstein, Richard. *Goldstein's Greatest Hits: A Book Mostly about Rock 'n' Roll.* New York: Prentice-Hall, 1970.

Greenfield, Jeff. *No Peace, No Place: Excavations along the Generational Fault.* New York: Doubleday, 1973.

Greenfield, Robert. "Keith Richards." In *The Rolling Stone Interviews: Talking with the Legends of Rock & Roll, 1967–1980,* by the Editors of Rolling Stone. New York: St. Martin's/Rolling Stone, 1981.

Gross, Leonard. "John Lennon: Beatle on His Own." *Look,* December 13, 1966, pp. 58–60.

Guggenheim, Peggy. *Out of This Century: Confessions of an Art Addict.* New York: Universe, 1979.

Guralnick, Peter. *Feel Like Going Home: Portraits in Blues & Rock 'n' Roll.* New York: Vintage, 1971.

Hall, Stuart. "The Hippies: An American 'Moment.' " In *Student Power,* edited by Julian Nagel. London: Merlin Press, 1969.

————, Dorothy Hobston, Andrew Lowe, and Paul Willis, eds. *Culture, Media, Language: Working Papers in Cultural Studies, 1972–79.* London: Hutchinson, 1980.

————. and Tony Jefferson, eds. *Resistance through Rituals: Youth Subcultures in Postwar Britain.* London: Hutchinson, 1976.

Hamill, Pete. "Long Night's Journey into Day: A Conversation with John Lennon." *Rolling Stone,* June 5, 1975.

Hardy, Phil, and Dave Laing, eds. *Encyclopedia of Rock: Volume 2, From Liverpool to San Francisco.* Frogmore, St. Albans, Herts, England: Panther Books, 1976.

Harry, Bill, ed. *Mersey Beat: The Beginnings of the Beatles.* London: Omnibus Press, 1977.

Hentoff, Nat. "The Crackin', Shakin', Breakin' Sounds." *The New Yorker,* October 24, 1964.

Hilburn, Robert. "Lennon Exorcises the Beatles' Ghost." Los Angeles *Times,* October 14, 1980, part VI, p. 1.

————. "Lennon: He Doesn't Believe in Magic or the Beatles." Los Angeles *Times,* November 16, 1980, part VI, p. 1.

Hoffman, Abbie (Free, pseud.). *Revolution for the Hell of It.* New York: Dial, 1968.

————. *Woodstock Nation: A Talk-Rock Album.* New York: Pocket, 1971.

Hoggart, Richard. *The Uses of Literacy.* London: Pelican, 1958.

Holden, Stephen. "Gimme Some Truth: The Songs of John Lennon." In *The Ballad of John and Yoko,* edited by Jonathan Cott and Christine Doudna. New York: Doubleday/Rolling Stone, 1982.

Howard, Mel, and the Reverend Thomas King Forcade, eds. *The Underground Reader.* New York: New American Library, 1972.

Hoyland, John. "An Open Letter to John Lennon." *Black Dwarf,* October 27, 1968, n.p.

Illustrated Encyclopedia of Rock. By the editors of *New Musical Express.* London: Harmony, 1977.

Janov, Arthur. *The Primal Scream.* New York: Coward-McCann, 1970.

Kempton, Murray. "Mark Chapman's Family." *New York Review of Books,* October 22, 1981, p. 28.

————. "The Sad Secrets of an Assassin's Mind: Mark David Chapman." *Rolling Stone,* October 15, 1981, pp. 13–15.

Kopkind, Andrew. "I Wanna Hold Your Head: John Lennon after the Fall." *Ramparts,* April 1971, p. 56.

————. "Lennon without Tears." *Soho News,* December 17, 1980, p. 10.

Kurtz, Irma. "In the Bag: Yoko Ono." *Nova,* March 1969, pp. 53–57.

Laing, Dave. *The Sound of Our Time.* New York: Quadrangle, 1969.

Landau, Jon. *It's Too Late to Stop Now: A Rock and Roll Journal.* San Francisco: Straight Arrow, 1972.

Lasch, Christopher. *The Culture of Narcissism.* New York: Pantheon, 1979.

Leamer, Laurence. *The Paper Revolutionaries: The Rise of the Underground Press.* New York: Simon & Schuster, 1972.

Leary, Timothy. *Flashbacks: An Autobiography.* Los Angeles: Tarcher, 1983.

Lennon Remembers. Edited by Jann Wenner. New York: Fawcett, 1972.

Lennon '69: Search for Liberation. Featuring a conversation between John Lennon and Swami Bhaktivedanta. Los Angeles: Bhaktivedanta Book Trust, 1981.

The Lennon Tapes: John Lennon and Yoko Ono in Conversation with Andy Peebles 6 December 1980. London: BBC, 1981.

Lennon, Cynthia. *A Twist of Lennon.* New York: Avon, 1978.

Lennon, John. " 'Have We All Forgotten What Vibes Are?' " *Rolling Stone,* April 16, 1970, p. 1.

————. *In His Own Write & A Spaniard in the Works.* New York: Signet, 1964, 1965.

————. "Interview/Interview with by/on John Lennon and/or Dr. Winston O'Boogie." *Andy Warhol's Interview,* November 1974, pp. 11–12.

————. Review of *The Goon Show Scripts. New York Times Book Review,* September 30, 1973, p. 11.

————. "A Very Open Letter to John Hoyland from John Lennon." *Black Dwarf,* January 10, 1969, n.p.

————. "Why Make It Sad to Be Gay?" In *The Gay Liberation Book,* edited by Len Richmond and Gary Noguera. San Francisco: Ramparts Press, 1973.

————, and Yoko Ono. "Imagine." *SunDance,* August–September 1972, p. 68.

————. "It's Never Too Late to Start from the Start." *SunDance,* No. 1 (April–May 1972), pp. 67–69.

————. Letter to the Editor. *Village Voice,* October 7, 1971, p. 4.

Lewis, David L. *King: A Biography.* Urbana: University of Illinois Press, 1978.

Lydon, Michael. "Rock for Sale." *Ramparts,* 1969. Reprinted in *The Age of Rock 2,* edited by Jonathan Eisen. New York: Vintage, 1970.

Lydon, Susan. "Would You Want Your Sister to Marry a Beatle?" *Ramparts,* November 17, 1968, pp. 65–68.

MacDonald, Dwight. *On Movies.* Englewood Cliffs, New Jersey: Prentice-Hall, 1969.

Magruder, Jeb Stuart. *An American Life: One Man's Road to Watergate.* New York: Atheneum, 1974.

Marcus, Greil. "Amazing Chutzpah." (Review of Dylan's *Slow Train Coming* LP.) *New West,* September 24, 1979, pp. 95–96.

————. "The Apocalypse at Altamont." In *The Sixties,* edited by Lynda Rosen Obst. New York: Random House/Rolling Stone, 1977.

————. "The Beatles." In *The Rolling Stone Illustrated History of Rock & Roll,* edited by Jim Miller. 2nd ed. New York: Random House/Rolling Stone, 1980.

————. "Lies about Elvis, Lies about Us." (Review of *Elvis,* by Albert Goldman.) *Village Voice Literary Supplement,* December 1981, pp. 16–17.

————. *Mystery Train: Images of America in Rock 'n' Roll Music.* New York: Dutton, 1975.

————. "Recollections of an Amnesiac." *Creem,* June 1975, p. 69.

————. "Self-Portrait No. 25." *Rolling Stone,* July 23, 1970, pp. 17–18.

————, ed. *Rock and Roll Will Stand.* Boston: Beacon, 1969.

————. *Stranded: Rock and Roll for a Desert Island.* New York: Knopf, 1979.

"Marcuse Defines His New Left Line." (Translation of interview with the editors of *L'Express.*) *New York Times Magazine,* October 27, 1968.

Marsh, Dave, and John Swenson, eds. *The Rolling Stone Record Guide.* New York: Random House/Rolling Stone, 1979.

Maslin, Janet. "Bob Dylan." In *The Rolling Stone Illustrated History of Rock & Roll,* edited by Jim Miller. 2nd ed. New York: Random House/Rolling Stone, 1980.

Mellers, Wilfrid. *Twilight of the Gods: The Music of the Beatles.* New York: Macmillan, 1973.

Merton, Richard. "Comment." *New Left Review,* No. 47 (January–February 1968), pp. 29–31.

———. "Comment." *New Left Review,* No. 59 (January–February 1970), pp. 88–96.

Miles, comp. *The Beatles in Their Own Words.* New York: Quick Fox, 1978.

———. *John Lennon in His Own Words.* New York: Quick Fox, 1981.

Miles, Michael W. *The Radical Probe: The Logic of Student Rebellion.* New York: Atheneum, 1973.

Miller, Jim. "The Beach Boys." In *The Rolling Stone Illustrated History of Rock & Roll,* edited by Jim Miller. 2nd ed. New York: Random House/Rolling Stone, 1980.

———, ed. *The Rolling Stone Illustrated History of Rock & Roll.* 2nd ed. New York: Random House/Rolling Stone, 1980.

Muldoon, Roland. "Subculture: The Street-Fighting Pop Group." *Black Dwarf,* October 15, 1968, n.p.

Naipaul, V. S. "Michael X and the Black Power Killings in Trinidad." In Naipaul, *The Return of Eva Perón.* New York: Vintage, 1981.

Nairn, Tom. "Enoch Powell: The New Right." *New Left Review,* No. 61 (May–June 1970), pp. 3–27.

Naison, Mark. "Youth Culture: A Critical View." *Radical America,* September–October 1970, pp. 14–23.

Neville, Richard. *Play Power.* London: Paladin, 1971.

Ney, Jutta. "John and Yoko Interview." *Jazz and Pop,* March 1970, pp. 31–33.

Nixon, Richard M. *RN: The Memoirs of Richard Nixon.* New York: Grosset & Dunlap, 1976.

Noebel, David A. *The Legacy of John Lennon: Charming or Harming a Generation?* Nashville: Thomas Nelson, 1982.

———. *The Marxist Minstrels: A Handbook on Communist Subversion of Music.* Tulsa: American Christian College Press, 1974.

Norman, Philip. *Shout! The Beatles in Their Generation.* New York: Simon & Schuster, 1981.

Ono, Yoko. "Yoko Ononism." *I.T.,* July 23, 1967, p. 9.

Palmer, Robert. "John Lennon: Must an Artist Self-Destruct?" New York *Times,* November 9, 1980.

Palmer, Tony. *The Trials of OZ.* London: Blond & Briggs, 1971.

Pang, May, and Henry Edwards. *Loving John: The Untold Story.* New York: Warner, 1983.

Parsons, Michael. "Rolling Stones." *New Left Review,* No. 49 (May–June 1968), pp. 85–86.

"Playboy Interview: The Beatles." *Playboy,* February 1965.

"Playboy Interview: John Lennon and Yoko Ono." *Playboy,* January 1981.

The Playboy Interviews with John Lennon and Yoko Ono. Conducted by David Sheff. Edited by G. Barry Golson. New York: Playboy Press, 1981.

Poirier, Richard. "Learning from the Beatles." *Partisan Review,* No. 34 (fall 1967), pp. 526–46.

Poster, Mark. *Existential Marxism in Postwar France: From Sartre to Althusser.* Princeton: Princeton University Press, 1975.

Pyes, Craig. "Rolling Stone Gathers No Politix." In *Counterculture and Revolution,* edited by David Horowitz, Michael P. Lerner, and Craig Pyes. New York: Random House, 1973.

"The Real John Lennon." *Newsweek,* September 29, 1980, p. 77.

Rips, Geoffrey. *The Campaign against the Underground Press: PEN American Center Report.* San Francisco: City Lights, 1981.

Robertson, Geoff. "Michael X on Death Row." *New Statesman,* January 11, 1974, pp. 40–41.

Robinson, Lisa. "A Day in the Life of a Permanent Resident." *Hit Parader,* January 1977, pp. 48–50.

———. "John Didn't Want to Be 'Shot Like Gandhi.' " *Rocky Mountain News,* December 21, 1980.

The Rolling Stone Interviews: Talking with the Legends of Rock & Roll, 1967–1980. New York: St. Martin's/Rolling Stone, 1981.

Rolling Stones. *Our Own Story.* As told to Pete Goodman. New York: Bantam, 1965.

Roxton, Lillian. "What Did John Winston Lennon and James Paul McCartney Really Do in Those 101 Hours They Spent in New York?" *Eye,* September 1968.

Rubin, Jerry. "Ann Arbor." *East Village Other,* December 16, 1971, p. 3.

———. *Growing (Up) at 37.* New York: Warner, 1976.

Sabin, Jon. "Back in the U.S.A." *The First Issue* (Cornell SDS), December 1968, n.p.

Salewicz, Chris. "Pete Townshend: True Confessions." *Time Out* (London), June 4, 1982, pp. 15–17.

Sanchez, Tony. *Up and Down with the Rolling Stones.* New York: Morrow, 1979.

Sander, Ellen. "John and Yoko Ono Lennon: Give Peace a Chance." *Saturday Review,* June 28, 1969, pp. 46–47.

Scaduto, Anthony. *Bob Dylan.* New York: Grosset & Dunlap, 1971. (Updated with a new afterword by Steven Gaines: Signet, 1979.)

———. "Won't You Listen to the Lambs, Bob Dylan?" *New York Times Magazine,* November 28, 1971.

Schaffner, Nicholas. *The Beatles Forever.* New York: McGraw-Hill, 1977.

Schaumburg, Ron. *Growing Up with the Beatles.* New York: Pyramid, 1976.

Schjeldahl, Peter. Review of *Gimme Shelter.* New York *Times,* January 3, 1971.

Schultheiss, Tom. *The Beatles: A Day in the Life.* New York: Quick Fox, 1981.

Shames, Laurence. "John Lennon, Where Are You?" *Esquire,* November 1980.

Sinclair, John. Excerpts from prison notebooks. Ann Arbor *Sun,* Supplement, October 29, 1971 (entire).

———. *Guitar Army: Street Writings/Prison Writings.* New York: Douglas, 1972.

———. *Music and Politics.* New York: World, 1971.

Skoler, Ron. "An Interview with John & Yoko." *Rock,* August 14, 1972.

Spence, Tom. "Beat City! The Home of the 'Mersey Sound.' " *Daily Worker* (London), November 2, 1963.

Spitz, Robert Stephen. *Barefoot in Babylon: The Creation of the Woodstock Music Festival, 1969.* New York: Viking, 1979.

Tomkins, Calvin. *The Bride and the Bachelors: Five Masters of the Avant Garde.* New York: Viking, 1965.

U.S. Congress. House. Select Committee on Crime. *Crime in America—Illicit and Dangerous Drugs,* October 23–25, 27, 1969. Testimony of Art Linkletter.

————. Senate. Internal Security Subcommittee of the Committee on the Judiciary. *Report for Fiscal Year Ending February 29, 1972.* 92nd Congress, 2nd Session, 1972.

————. Senate. Internal Security Subcommittee of the Committee on the Judiciary. *Hearings: Extent of Subversion in the New Left, Pt. 8.* 92nd Congress, 2nd Session, 1972. Testimony of Clifford A. Murray.

————. Senate. Select Committee to Study Governmental Operations with Respect to Intelligence Activities ("Church Committee"). *Final Report. Book II: Intelligence Activities and the Rights of Americans. Book VI: Supplementary Reports on Intelligence Activities.* 94th Congress, 2nd Session, 1976.

Unger, Craig. "John Lennon's Killer: The Nowhere Man." *New York,* June 22, 1981, pp. 30–42.

Vishner, Mayer. "Whining through the Apocalypse." *Oui,* May 1973, pp. 87–88.

Vogel, Amos. " 'I Made a Glass Hammer': John and Yoko at Cannes." *Village Voice,* June 24, 1971.

Wain, John. "In the Echo Chamber." (Review of *A Spaniard in the Works,* by John Lennon.) *New Republic,* Vol. 153 (August 7, 1965), pp. 20–22.

Wallechinsky, David, and Irving Wallace. *The People's Almanac.* Garden City, New York: Doubleday, 1975.

Wenner, Jann. "Man of the Year." *Rolling Stone,* February 7, 1970, p. 1.

Werbin, Stu. "John & Jerry & David & John & Leni & Yoko." *Rolling Stone,* February 17, 1972, p. 1.

————. "John & Yoko & Chuck: Just Wanna Rock & Roll." Boston *Phoenix,* February 9, 1972, pp. 24–25.

White, Theodore H. *The Making of the President 1968.* New York: Atheneum, 1968.

Wiener, Jon. "Woodstock Revisited." In *The Age of Rock 2,* edited by Jonathan Eisen. New York: Vintage, 1970.

Willis, Ellen. *Beginning to See the Light: Pieces of a Decade.* New York: Knopf, 1981.

Wittner, Lawrence A. *Cold War America: From Hiroshima to Watergate.* Expanded edition. New York: Holt, Rinehart and Winston, 1978.

"Women, Sex, and the Abolition of the Family." *Black Dwarf,* January 10, 1969, n.p.

Wood, Michael. "Four Beatles, Five Stones." *Commonweal,* December 27, 1968, pp. 439–40.

————. "John Lennon's Schooldays." *New Society,* June 27, 1968, pp. 948–49.

Yorke, Ritchie. "John, Yoko, & Year One." *Rolling Stone,* February 7, 1970, pp. 18–22.

Young, Israel G. "Frets and Frails." *Sing Out!,* January 1964, p. 77.

Notes

Introduction: FBI Rock Criticism

p. xiii: "Lennon [was] formerly with group": FBI airtel (an official communication sent by air), special agent in charge (SAC), Detroit, to director, December 27, 1971; enclosed LHM ("Letterhead Memo"), p. 3.

p. xiv: lyrics to "John Sinclair": Ibid., p. 5.

p. xiv: "can't even remain on key": Detroit FBI file, document DE-3.

p. xv: "We came here to show": *Ten for Two* (unreleased film of Free John Sinclair concert).

1. "The Dream Is Over"

p. 3: "not just a particular form": Robert Sam Anson, *Gone Crazy and Back Again*, p. 129.

p. 4: "Rock for Sale": Michael Lydon, *Ramparts*, 1969, reprinted in Jonathan Eisen, ed., *The Age of Rock 2*, pp. 51–62. See also Craig Pyes, "Rolling Stone Gathers No Politix."

p. 4: "several large establishment-oriented": Lydon, op. cit., p. 61.

p. 4: "If you are": Ibid.

p. 4: "10 Student Rebels": *Eye*, September 1968.

p. 4: the FBI and the downfall of radical newspapers: Geoffrey Rips, *The Campaign against the Underground Press.*

p. 5: rock's contradictory politics: Simon Frith, *Sound Effects.*

p. 5: "a contradictory and doomed": Todd Gitlin, "John Lennon Speaking," p. 502.

p. 6: "God": see also Greil Marcus, "The Beatles," p. 187.

p. 6: "Long before Tom Wolfe": Andrew Kopkind, "Lennon without Tears," p. 10.

p. 6: "What's so startling": Andrew Kopkind, "I Wanna Hold Your Head: John Lennon after the Fall," p. 56.

p. 7: "To make private pains": Gitlin, op. cit., p. 502.

p. 7: "a song for the revolution": *Lennon Remembers,* p. 110.

p. 7: politics of authenticity: Marshall Berman, *The Politics of Authenticity.*

p. 8: Through self-disclosure: See also Christopher Lasch, *The Culture of Narcissism,* p. 48.

p. 8: "The workers are dreaming": Robin Blackburn and Tariq Ali, "Lennon: The Working-Class Hero Turns Red," p. 45.

p. 8: "The people who are in control": *Lennon Remembers,* pp. 11–12.

p. 9: "I lost her twice": *The Playboy Interviews with John Lennon and Yoko Ono,* p. 137.

p. 9: "I put 'Whole Lotta Shakin' ' on": Scott Muni radio interview, WNEW-FM.

p. 10: "Don't get therapy confused": *Lennon Remembers,* pp. 36–37.

p. 10: "People think": One to One concert video.

p. 10: "It's all right now": Wilfrid Mellers, *Twilight of the Gods,* p. 160.

p. 10: "trying to shave off": *The Lennon Tapes,* p. 82.

p. 10: "It's terribly uncommercial": *Lennon Remembers,* p. 140.

p. 10: "It's the best thing": Ibid., p. 29.

2. First Steps toward Radical Politics: The 1966 Tour

p. 11: "more popular than Jesus": Interview with Maureen Cleave, London *Evening Standard,* March 4, 1966; quoted in *Datebook,* August 1966.

p. 11: "give the youth": Memphis *Commercial Appeal,* August 11, 1966.

p. 12: "What have the Beatles said": David A. Noebel, *The Marxist Minstrels,* p. 96.

p. 12: "Father, Sock, and Mickey Most": Ibid., pp. 101–102, quoting Lennon, *A Spaniard in the Works,* p. 173.

p. 12: "The Beatles are not welcome": Memphis *Commercial Appeal,* August 10, 1966.

p. 12: "wished to assure": Memphis *Commercial Appeal,* August 11, 1966.

p. 12: "I do not care": Ibid.

p. 12: A Methodist pastor quoted: Ibid.

p. 12: "for once in their lives": Ibid.

p. 13: "John, please don't go": "Blues for the Beatles," *Newsweek,* August 15, 1966, p. 94.

p. 13: "I didn't want to tour": interview on "From Liverpool to Legend" radio documentary, author's collection.

p. 13: "a horror of being shot": Peter Brown, interview with author.

p. 13: "We should be wearing targets": Judy Sims, editor of *Teen Set,* traveling with the Beatles; interview with author.

p. 13: "keep a lookout": Peter Brown and Steven Gaines, *The Love You Make,* p. 213.

p. 13: "outside the Ku Klux Klan": Philip Norman, *Shout!,* p. 267.

p. 13: "Every one of us": interview on "From Liverpool to Legend" radio documentary, author's collection.

p. 13: "shown the whole world": Memphis *Commercial Appeal,* August 20, 1966.

p. 13: "decoyed" by promises: Ibid.

p. 14: "to a modified 'twist' ": Ibid.

p. 14: New York *Times* report: April 10, 1956.

p. 14: "a means of pulling the white man down": Ibid.

p. 14: attack on Nat "King" Cole: New York *Times*, April 11, 1956.

p. 14: "but I think": David Frost Beatles TV special, January 13, 1972.

p. 14: WABC banned the Beatles: Al Sussman, *Beatlefan*, Vol. 4, No. 5, August–September 1982, p. 14.

p. 15: Spain and South Africa banned the Beatles: Tom Schultheiss, *The Beatles: A Day in the Life*, p. 164.

p. 15: "some subjects": Nicholas Schaffner, *The Beatles Forever*, p. 58.

p. 15: "I have seen many demonstrations": David L. Lewis, *King*, p. 339.

p. 15: John's apology: The Beatles' Chicago press conference, August 12, 1966, audio; Brown and Gaines, op. cit., p. 212.

p. 16: "What He Meant Was . . .": New York *Times*, August 16, 1966.

p. 17: "a serious lapse": *Time*, June 20, 1966, p. 67.

p. 17: "attempt at pop satire": Schaffner, op. cit., p. 55.

p. 17: "as relevant as Vietnam": Philip Norman, op. cit., p. 265.

p. 17: "reads all the daily newspapers": Maureen Cleave, "Old Beatles, a Study in Paradox," p. 10.

p. 17: "Reds gun down": Memphis *Commercial Appeal*, August 20, 1966.

p. 17: "We don't like war": New York *Times*, August 23, 1966.

p. 17: "We think of it every day": Miles, *The Beatles in Their Own Words*, p. 123.

p. 17: "Most British people": Eric Hobsbawm, interview with author.

p. 18: "tired and pale": New York *Times*, August 23, 1966.

p. 18: "obstruction of the Vietnam war": Ibid.

p. 18: "We must form our own": Ibid.

p. 18: "Lennon forgiven": "Blues for the Beatles," *Newsweek*, August 15, 1966, p. 94.

p. 19: "Their enjoyment of life": Israel G. Young, "Frets and Frails," p. 77.

p. 19: "on the same Carnegie Hall stage": Noebel, op. cit., p. 106.

p. 19: "It was widely believed": Robin Blackburn, interview with author.

p. 19: "more than most pop-singers": Terry Eagleton, "New Bearings: The Beatles," p. 175.

p. 20: "I hope when they get older": Michael Braun, *Love Me Do*, p. 115.

p. 20: "Don't you feel?": Ibid., p. 124.

p. 20: "The Beatles apparently could not carry": Ibid., p. 110.

p. 20: "a fine mass placebo": Ibid.

p. 20: "A lot of people want": Ibid., p. 108.

p. 20: "They wear their hair": Ibid., p. 12.

p. 20: "It's about time": Ibid., p. 100.

p. 20: "The Beatles display": Ibid., p. 113.

p. 20: "They are male and yet": Ibid., p. 138.

p. 20: embassy reception: Ibid., p. 112.

p. 21: "a pretty radical thing": Miles, op. cit., p. 123.

p. 21: "The trouble with government": Ray Coleman, "Lennon on Elections," p. 10.

p. 21: "just too much": Miles, op. cit., p. 123.

p. 21: "Everybody can go around": Leonard Gross, "John Lennon: Beatle on His Own," p. 63.

p. 21: "The class system": *Lennon Remembers,* p. 11.

p. 21: "We weren't as open": Gross, op. cit., p. 63.

p. 21: "Brian put us in suits": *Lennon Remembers,* p. 46.

3. Private Gripweed and Yoko Ono

p. 25: "We can't go on holding hands": Cleave, "Old Beatles," p. 10.

p. 27: "tasteless": "New Movies: Vaudeville of the Absurd," *Time,* November 17, 1967, p. 71.

p. 27: "reminds one": Richard Schickel, *Life,* November 17, 1967, p. 8.

p. 27: other critics on *How I Won the War:* see Robert Hatch, the *Nation,* November 13, 1967, p. 206: Richard Gilman, the *New Republic,* November 27, 1967, p. 8; Wilfrid Sheed, *Esquire,* January 1968, p. 29; Brendan Gill, *The New Yorker,* November 18, 1967, p. 43; Penelope Mortimer, the *Observer Review,* October 22, 1967, p. 7.

p. 27: "We want a low-budget comedy": J. Philip DiFranco, ed., *The Beatles in Richard Lester's "A Hard Day's Night,"* p. 7.

p. 27: "an exploitation film": Ibid.

p. 28: "overtakes a company director's Rolls": Ibid., p. 61.

p. 29: "We were trying": Ibid., p. 11.

p. 29: "the Marx Brothers' characters": Ibid., p. 12.

p. 29: "the true and unique voice": "The Beatles—Those Lucky Lads from Liverpool," p. 12.

p. 30: "witless orgy of expensive production": Dwight MacDonald, *Esquire,* June 1966; reprinted in MacDonald, *On Movies,* pp. 403–406.

p. 30: "They had to be passive": DiFranco, op. cit., p. 13.

p. 30: "The first thing": Ray Connolly, *John Lennon,* p. 94.

p. 31: Yoko in Japan with Cage: Peggy Guggenheim, *Out of This Century,* pp. 365–66.

p. 31: "Yoko was utterly fearless": Kate Millett, interview with author.

p. 31: "orchestra is banded together": "Fluxorchestra Circular Letter No. 2," *Fluxus Etc.: The Gilbert and Lila Silverman Collection* (Bloomfield Hills, Michigan: Cranbrook Academy of Art Museum, 1981), p. 359.

p. 31: "It's quite harmless": Yoko Ono, "Yoko Ononism," p. 9.

p. 31: "Our minds met": *Mike Douglas Show,* February 14, 1972, video.

p. 31: "we weren't going to be lovers": Charles McCarry, "John Rennon's Excrusive Gloupie," *Esquire,* December 1970, p. 248.

p. 32: "Yoko's art was like a big open door": Dan Richter, interview with author.

p. 32: "I just didn't have the guts": Vic Garbarini and Brian Cullman, *Strawberry Fields Forever,* p. 101.

4. Sgt. Pepper and Flower Power

p. 33: "time to think": *The Playboy Interviews,* p. 40.

p. 33: grim orphanage: photos appear in David Bacon and Norman Maslov, *The Beatles' England,* pp. 101–103. That Strawberry Fields was an orphanage has been concealed in the Beatles literature. Even as late as 1980, John's description of it as an orphanage was cut from a *Playboy* interview. Compare the complete text—*The Playboy Interviews,* p. 132—with the version published in the magazine in the December 1980 issue.

p. 34: "You mean this thing": Greil Marcus, ed., *Rock and Roll Will Stand,* p. 68.

p. 35: "A Day in the Life": see also Richard Goldstein, "I Blew My Cool through the New York *Times,*" in *Goldstein's Greatest Hits,* pp. 150–52; Richard Poirier, "Learning from the Beatles."

p. 36: "went with the flow": Robert Christgau and John Piccarella, "Portrait of the Artist as a Rock & Roll Star," p. 252.

p. 36: "I got the wrong . . . message": *Lennon Remembers,* p. 77.

p. 36: flower power: see also Stuart Hall, "The Hippies: An American 'Moment' "; Marshall Berman, "Sympathy for the Devil."

p. 38: first underground papers: Laurence Leamer, *The Paper Revolutionaries,* pp. 27–43.

p. 38: "the best rock album": Robert Christgau, "Defending the Beatles," p. 37; but see also Christgau, *Any Old Way You Choose It,* p. 41.

p. 38: right-wing critics: Noebel, op. cit., p. 105.

p. 38: "an underground Eucharist service": Joan Elbert, "Growing Up with Lennon," pp. 1260–61.

p. 38: *Time* cover story: October 6, 1967, pp. 31–34.

p. 38: "For the first time": Goldstein, *Goldstein's Greatest Hits,* p. 152.

p. 39: "We must combine": Lewis, op. cit., p. 358.

p. 39: "excessive and unjustified force": David Wallechinsky and Irving Wallace, *The People's Almanac,* p. 252.

p. 40: "There was enormous pressure": Peter Brown, interview with author.

p. 41: "gentleness combined with strength": Jon Sabin, "Back in the U.S.A."

p. 41: Walrus as a symbol of socialism: *The Playboy Interviews,* p. 156.

p. 42: "Who Breaks a Butterfly": *Times* of London, July 1, 1967.

p. 42: ad calling for legalization of marijuana: *Times* of London, July 24, 1967.

p. 42: "The way things are run": Tony Sanchez, *Up and Down with the Rolling Stones,* p. 82.

p. 42: Brian Jones had opposed it: Ibid., p. 65.

p. 42: "salutary" and "mature": Christgau, *Any Old Way You Choose It,* pp. 53, 55.

p. 42: *John Wesley Harding:* see also Jon Landau, *It's Too Late to Stop Now,* pp. 54–56; Anthony Scaduto, *Bob Dylan,* pp. 248–49; Morris Dickstein, *Gates of Eden,* p. 199.

p. 43: "The last time I went to London": Scaduto, *Bob Dylan,* p. 238.

p. 43: "His business was the revitalization of myths": Jim Miller, "The Beach Boys," p. 164.

p. 44: "I knew we were in trouble": *Lennon Remembers,* p. 52.

5. From Brian Epstein to the Maharishi

p. 45: victim of anti-Semitism: Norman, op. cit., pp. 127–28; for a different view see Brown and Gaines, op. cit., p. 59.

p. 45: *A Cellarful of Goys: The Rutles* (1978 Warner Brothers album that satirizes the Beatles), booklet included with LP.

p. 46: "We'd been meek and mild": Hunter Davies, *The Beatles,* p. 77.

p. 46: "used to shout": Ibid., p. 78.

p. 46: "After a few drinks": Ibid., p. 80.

p. 46: "full of experience": *The Rutles,* op. cit.

p. 46: "When we got back": Radio interview with Dan Chandler, WQAM (Miami), 1969.

p. 47: "Rowe must be kicking": Connolly, op. cit., p. 49.

p. 47: "make it very, very big": *Lennon Remembers*, p. 46.

p. 47: rock as a form of sexual control: Simon Frith and Angela McRobbie, "Rock and Sexuality."

p. 48: "neither boys-together aggression": Ibid., p. 11.

p. 49: "Their chords were outrageous": Scaduto, op. cit., p. 175.

p. 50: "Man, those Beatles": Alan Smith, "London Beat," *Mersey Beat*, November 15, 1962.

p. 50: "Someone with the Negro sound": Greil Marcus, "Lies about Elvis, Lies about Us," p. 16.

p. 50: Early Beatles music: see also Greil Marcus, "The Beatles"; Charlie Gillett, *Sound of the City*, pp. 281–87; Phil Hardy and Dave Laing, eds., *Encyclopedia of Rock: Volume 2*, pp. 38–43; Robert Christgau and John Piccarella, "Portrait of the Artist as a Rock & Roll Star."

p. 50: Beatles under Epstein "sold out": Connolly, op. cit., p. 52.

p. 51: "It was a week": Cynthia Lennon, *A Twist of Lennon*, p. 94.

p. 51: "It was almost a love affair": "Playboy Interview: John Lennon and Yoko Ono," p. 107.

p. 51: "I smashed him up": Davies, op. cit., p. 177.

p. 52: "I'm no good with women": Norman, op. cit., p. 287.

p. 52: John contributed to *The Gay Liberation Book:* edited by Len Richmond and Gary Noguera. San Francisco: Ramparts Press, 1973, pp. 94–95.

p. 52: "Through meditation I've learned": interview on *David Frost Show*, September 30, 1967, with George and the Maharishi; transcript in Tony Barrow, "Harrison & Lennon Discuss Religion," *Beat*, November 4, 1967.

p. 52: "Somebody had a place": Garbarini and Cullman, op. cit., p. 118.

p. 53: " 'Why?' I said, 'If you're so cosmic' ": *Lennon Remembers*, pp. 55–56.

p. 53: "bloody old con man": Sanchez, op. cit., p. 84.

p. 53: "I did write": Ray Connolly, "Crippled Inside: An Interview with John Lennon," p. 20.

p. 53: "I hate war": Connolly, *John Lennon*, p. 87.

p. 54: "original, mature, serious": Alan Beckett, "Stones," pp. 24–29.

p. 54: Beatles "have never strayed": Richard Merton, "Comment," *New Left Review*, No. 47.

p. 54: "Who does the denouncing?": Michael Parsons, "Rolling Stones."

p. 54: "an artist's private purpose": Richard Merton, "Comment," *New Left Review*, No. 59.

p. 55: "Both of us came out": interview with Robert Hilburn, Los Angeles *Times*, October 4, 1981.

p. 55: "Art students have had this sort of haircut": David Dalton, *The Rolling Stones*, p. 36.

p. 55: "Would You Let Your Daughter": Ibid.

p. 55: "dirtier, streakier": Associated Press article reproduced in ibid., p. 38.

p. 56: "an atmosphere of middle class 'gentility' ": The Rolling Stones, *Our Own Story*, p. 6.

p. 56: "Mick seemed destined": "Quints—by their Mums," *Everybody's* magazine, reproduced in Dalton, op. cit., p. 11.

p. 56: "He sometimes talked of becoming a dentist": Ibid., p. 12.

p. 56: "quite different from the Beatles": Ibid., p. 38.

p. 56: Early Rolling Stones: see also Jon Landau, *It's Too Late to Stop Now,* pp. 64–76; Charlie Gillett, *Sound of the City,* pp. 288–89; Peter Guralnick, *Feel Like Going Home,* pp. 27–28.

6. May '68: Rock against Revolution

p. 58: "it had something to do": Norman, op. cit., p. 330.

p. 58: "We were very shy": Connolly, *John Lennon,* p. 96.

p. 58: "Then we just made love": Ibid.

p. 59: "She's me in drag": *The Beatles Tapes,* 1976 Polydor LP. David Wigg interviewed Lennon in July 1969.

p. 59: "The monstrous spectacle": Mark Poster, *Existential Marxism in Postwar France,* pp. 372–73.

p. 59: war as "insanity": Radio interview on WNET (New York City), May 22, 1968.

p. 59: "had this, you know, 'God will save us' ": *Lennon Remembers,* p. 131.

p. 60: "nominated in a sea of blood": Theodore H. White, *The Making of the President 1968.*

p. 60: " 'Revolution' sounds like the hawk plank": Berkeley *Barb,* August 1968, quoted in Richard Neville, *Play Power,* p. 133.

p. 60: "Hubert Humphrey couldn't have said": Jon Landau, "Rock 'n' Radical?," Liberation News Service dispatch, in *Daily World,* February 22, 1969.

p. 60: a "betrayal": Susan Lydon, "Would You Want Your Sister to Marry a Beatle?"

p. 60: "a lamentable petty bourgeois cry": Richard Merton, "Comment," *New Left Review,* No. 59, p. 93.

p. 60: "It is puritanical to expect": Christgau, *Any Old Way You Choose It,* p. 100.

p. 60: "Well, it isn't": Susan Lydon, op. cit., p. 67.

p. 61: "the words of a message song": Greil Marcus, *Rock and Roll Will Stand,* p. 97.

p. 61: criticized "radical activists": "Apples for the Beatles," *Time,* September 6, 1968, p. 59.

p. 61: "I put in both": Blackburn and Ali, op. cit., p. 44.

p. 62: "pacifist idealism": Jon Sabin, "Back in the U.S.A.," n.p.

p. 62: "they mean that statements": Michael Wood, "Four Beatles, Five Stones," pp. 439–40.

p. 62: "That's why I did": Jonathan Cott, "Rolling Stone Interview: John Lennon," p. 4.

p. 62: "painting in sound": Blackburn and Ali, op. cit., p. 44.

p. 62: "for eight minutes": Christgau and Piccarella, op. cit., p. 254.

p. 63: "enjoyed somebody who reacted": *Lennon Remembers,* p. 123.

p. 63: "calls for a reevaluation": WIXY (Cleveland), following a telephone interview with John at the Montreal bed-in.

p. 63: "The Beatles are simply telling the Maoists": Gary Allen, "More Subversion Than Meets the Ear," p. 49.

p. 63: "The stuff you're writing": Scaduto, op. cit., p. 176.

p. 64: "struck a responsive chord": Jon Landau, op. cit., p. 214.

p. 64: *Another Side of Bob Dylan:* see also Janet Maslin, "Bob Dylan," p. 222.

p. 64: White Album as post-LSD music: Christgau and Piccarella, op. cit., pp. 254–55.

p. 64: "Oh, I love it": *Lennon Remembers*, p. 136.

p. 65: "The Beatles were always nice kids": Susan Lydon, op. cit., p. 67.

p. 65: "The Beatles satirize": Jon Landau, "Rock 'n' Radical?," Liberation News Service dispatch, in *Daily World*, February 22, 1969.

p. 65: "The Beatles have used parody": Ibid.

p. 65: "The radicalism of the initial revolt": Merton, "Comment," *New Left Review*, No. 59, p. 91.

p. 66: "The first flush of mastery": Marcus, *Rock and Roll Will Stand*, p. 103.

p. 66: "The Stones strike for realism": Jon Landau, "Rock 'n' Radical?," Liberation News Service dispatch, in *Daily World*, February 22, 1969.

p. 66: "violence, certainty, and repetition": Ibid.

p. 66: "relentless, inescapable": Geoffrey Cannon, "The Age of Aquarius," pp. 282–87.

p. 66: Jagger became "a committed revolutionary": Sanchez, op. cit., p. 122.

p. 66: "Nobody would get me in uniform": Ibid.

p. 66: Jagger "leaped at the chance": Ibid.

p. 67: Keith Richards sings the first: see Richards in *The Rolling Stone Interviews*, p. 172.

p. 67: "emptily patronizing phrases": Merton, *New Left Review*, No. 59, p. 94; see also Simon Frith, "Beggars Banquet," pp. 36–37.

p. 68: "change the world": Berman, "Sympathy for the Devil," p. 33.

p. 68: "on one level": Ibid.

p. 68: "Decca's involvement": Sanchez, op. cit., p. 123.

p. 68: "the most important philosopher": "Marcuse Defines His New Left Line," pp. 29, 97.

p. 69: "the most interesting aspect": Ibid.

7. Two Virgins

p. 73: "Western communism": Paul's comment on the *Tonight* show, May 15, 1968.

p. 73: interviews at the St. Regis: Lillian Roxton, "What Did John Winston Lennon and James Paul McCartney Really Do in Those 101 Hours They Spent in New York?," p. 81.

p. 73: full-page photo of Beatle wives: *Rolling Stone*, No. 1, November 9, 1967, p. 3.

p. 74: "It's another piece of insanity": "Newsfront," WNET (New York City), May 22, 1968.

p. 74: " 'It bites,' as Bob Dylan says": actually Dylan said "it swears" on "It's All Right Ma."

p. 75: "Replies came in": Anthony Fawcett, *John Lennon*, p. 38.

p. 75: "The idea of John Lennon": Dan Richter, interview with author.

p. 75: "It seemed to be all khaki": Norman, op. cit., p. 64.

p. 75: rock stars who went to art college: Frith, *Sound Effects*, pp. 75–76.

p. 76: "In England, if you're lucky": *The Rolling Stone Interviews*, p. 158.

p. 76: "John's effort was always hopeless": Norman, op. cit., p. 49.

p. 76: "A piece of pure rustic wackiness": Bill Harry, *Mersey Beat: The Beginnings of the Beatles*, p. 6.

p. 76: "Tomorrow will be muggy": Ibid.

p. 76: "Looking at it now": John Lennon, review of *The Goon Show Scripts*, p. 11.

p. 77: "guide" to the local clubs: *Mersey Beat*, September 14, 1961.

p. 77: "Wanted urgently by ex-rock group": *Mersey Beat*, August 17, 1961.

p. 77: "worth the attention of anyone": Davies, op. cit., p. 200.

p. 77: "a rich plumcake": Braun, op. cit., p. 68.

p. 77: Michael Wood: "John Lennon's Schooldays."

p. 77: "Harassed Wilsod": John Lennon, *In His Own Write & A Spaniard in the Works*, pp. 122–23.

p. 77: "The first thing": John Wain, "In the Echo Chamber," pp. 20–22.

p. 78: "backward oral area": Marshall McLuhan, quoted in ibid., p. 21.

p. 78: "the formal controlled use": Ibid., p. 22.

p. 78: "nothing personal to communicate": Ibid.

p. 78: "The place for this": Michael Wood, "John Lennon's Schooldays," p. 949.

p. 78: "the jew with a view": John Lennon, *In His Own Write & A Spaniard in the Works*, p. 153; "an abnorman fat growth," p. 26; "all fat on her thirtysecond birthday," p. 21.

p. 79: "We don't know": Cott, "Rolling Stone Interview: John Lennon," p. 22.

p. 79: *Newsweek* on *Sympathy for the Devil:* March 30, 1970, p. 83; see also Penelope Gilliatt in *The New Yorker*, May 20, 1970, pp. 104–109.

p. 79: "It's good here": Hermine Demoraine, "Jean-Luc Godard Talks to Hermine Demoraine," p. 39.

p. 79: "That's sour grapes": Cott, "Rolling Stone Interview: John Lennon," p. 4.

p. 80: "the basic ingredient": Eldridge Cleaver, *Soul on Ice*, p. 73.

p. 80: "It's something like that": Cott, "Rolling Stone Interview: John Lennon," p. 100.

p. 80: "The thing was set up": *Tomorrow* show, April 28, 1975.

p. 80: "you're the loudmouth": *Today* show, April 29, 1975.

p. 80: "headhunting cop . . . no skin off my nose": *Tomorrow* show, April 28, 1975.

p. 81: "No bed for Beatle John:" News photo caption John and Yoko used as the title for a track on their 1969 LP *Unfinished Music No. 2: Life with the Lions*, in which they read aloud newspaper clippings about their situation.

p. 81: Yoko's miscarriage: Brown and Gaines, op. cit., pp. 319–20. The *Life with the Lions* LP cover shows Yoko in bed at the maternity hospital and John lying on the floor at her side; John and Yoko included "Baby's Heartbeat" on the album.

p. 81: "classics of our time": Roland Muldoon, "Subculture: The Street-Fighting Pop Group," n.p.

p. 82: "Marx/Engels/Mick Jagger": *Black Dwarf*, October 27, 1968, p. 1.

p. 82: "What we're up against": John Hoyland, "An Open Letter to John Lennon," n.p.

p. 82: "It's John Lennon here": Tariq Ali, interview with author.

p. 83: "Where's the women?": *The Lennon Tapes*, p. 62.

p. 83: "the loosening of traditional ties": "Women, Sex, and the Abolition of the Family," n.p.

p. 83: "I don't worry": Lennon, "A Very Open Letter to John Hoyland from John Lennon," n.p.

p. 83: "We don't blame people": Hoyland, "John Hoyland Replies," *Black Dwarf*, January 10, 1969, n.p.

p. 84: "It just seemed natural": Cott, "The Rolling Stone Interview: John Lennon," p. 4.

p. 84: nakedness had signified becoming real: Marshall Berman, *All That Is Solid Melts into Air,* pp. 105–10.

p. 84: "Look, it's two people": Cott, "Rolling Stone Interview: John Lennon," p. 4.

p. 85: "Hey, Chink": Norman, op. cit., p. 334.

p. 85: "scurrilous and depraved nature": Frank Donner, *The Age of Surveillance,* p. 233.

p. 85: "mounting evidence of moral depravity": Ibid.

p. 85: "nude photographs": FBI airtel, January 11, 1969, SAC, New Haven, to director.

p. 85: "does not meet the existing criteria": letter, J. Edgar Hoover to Honorable Ancher Nelsen, March 10, 1969; memo, Will R. Wilson, assistant attorney general, to director, FBI, March 11, 1969.

p. 85: "a substantial number of criminals": FBI memo, M. A. Jones to Mr. Bishop, March 20, 1969; main FBI file.

p. 85: "I think he wanted to believe it": Peter Brown, interview with author.

p. 86: life on tour was like Fellini's *Satyricon: Lennon Remembers,* p. 84.

p. 86: "All I could think of": Cynthia Lennon, op. cit., p. 186.

p. 86: "After the huge orchestras": Jon Wiener, "On the Tube," *Old Mole* (Cambridge, Mass.), December 12, 1968, p. 9. The underground newspaper took its name from Marx's sentence "Our old friend, our old mole, who knows so well how to burrow underground, suddenly to appear: the revolution!"

p. 86: "They didn't realize": *The Lennon Tapes,* pp. 20–21.

p. 86: "the first time I appeared": Cott, "The Last *Rolling Stone* Interview," p. 188.

p. 87: "a very strong sound": Radio Luxembourg interview, June 22, 1969.

p. 87: "there's as much": Ibid. Part of the concert can be heard on John and Yoko's album *Life with the Lions.*

8. Avant-Garde Peacenik

p. 88: "If people are invited": Schaffner, op. cit., p. 120.

p. 88: "These guys were sweating": *The Lennon Tapes,* p. 22.

p. 88: "I hope it's not": Schaffner, op. cit., p. 120.

p. 88: "our protest": Ibid.

p. 88: "We're sending out a message": Montreal bed-in statement, on *Wedding Album* LP.

p. 89: "All revolutions are unpleasant": Christgau, *Any Old Way You Choose It,* p. 98.

p. 89: "This must rank": Schaffner, op. cit., p. 120.

p. 89: John "seems to have come perilously near": Ibid.

p. 89: "We can't go out": Anthony Fawcett, op. cit., p. 45.

p. 90: "Every night we play": *Los Angeles Weekly,* February 8, 1982, p. 9.

p. 90: "Successful enough": Radio Luxembourg interview, June 22, 1969.

p. 90: "Because people kept saying": "John and Yoko's 1970 Peace Message," syndicated radio, December 1969.

p. 90: "Some guy wrote": *The Beatles Tapes,* 1976 Polydor LP, David Wigg interview, July 1969.

p. 90: "Imagine if the American army": Ibid.

p. 91: "Very hard": Peter Brown, interview with author.

p. 92: "It's easier to get into Russia": Charleston (West Virginia) *Gazette*, September 13, 1969.

p. 92: "I don't believe there's any park": John and Yoko's *Give Peace a Chance* film.

p. 93: "The students are being conned": Ellen Sander, "John and Yoko Ono Lennon: Give Peace a Chance," pp. 46–47.

p. 93: "Lennon's call": Christgau, *Any Old Way You Choose It*, p. 99.

p. 93: "Sit-ins are okay": Metromedia TV news interview, May 1969.

p. 94: "We were told by the system": Ibid.

p. 94: Al Capp episode: audio tape, author's collection.

p. 97: "The organizers of the marches": "The Peace Anthem," *Newsweek*, December 1, 1969, p. 102.

p. 97: "I guess I faced": Pete Seeger, interview with author.

p. 97: "I saw pictures": Amos Vogel, " 'I Made a Glass Hammer': John and Yoko at Cannes," p. 65.

p. 97: "I'm shy and aggressive": *Lennon Remembers*, p. 110.

p. 97: "Now it will serve": "The Peace Anthem," *Newsweek*, December 1, 1969, p. 102.

p. 98: "Come on, come on": John and Yoko's *Give Peace a Chance* film.

p. 98: "Undoubtedly some people wanted": Pete Seeger, interview with author.

9.   The "Renunciation of What the Beatles Had Stood For"

p. 100: "We were both . . . I'd love to": *Lennon Remembers*, pp. 188–89.

p. 100: "Dylan's *McCartney*": Landau, *It's Too Late to Stop Now*, p. 57.

p. 100: "some sort of Kafkaesque brain-washing": Scaduto, op. cit., p. 260.

p. 101: Nixon invited Johnny Cash: "President Nixon's Fave Raves," *Rolling Stone*, April 16, 1970, p. 9.

p. 101: "Dylan was becoming interested": Scaduto, op. cit., pp. 260–61.

p. 101: "How do you know?": Christgau, *Any Old Way You Choose It*, p. 202.

p. 101: "peace and prosperity": *Lennon '69: Search for Liberation*, pp. 42, 19, 34, 35.

p. 102: "Come Together" as a political song: Timothy Leary, *Flashbacks*, pp. 280–81, 388.

p. 102: " 'Come Together' is *me* ": *The Playboy Interviews*, p. 169.

p. 102: "a nice little song": "Beatles Splitting? Maybe, Says John," *Rolling Stone*, January 21, 1970, p. 3.

p. 102: "Opinion has shifted": Christgau, *Any Old Way You Choose It*, p. 109.

p. 102: "they would gather": Elbert, op. cit., p. 1261.

p. 103: "the largest, most peaceful gathering": Robert Stephen Spitz, *Barefoot in Babylon*, p. vii.

p. 103: "The limits have changed": Greil Marcus, *Rolling Stone*, quoted in Anson, op. cit., p. 128.

p. 103: "Nightmare in the Catskills": New York *Times*, August 18, 1969.

p. 103: "Remember Woodstock?": Jon Wiener, "Woodstock Revisited," p. 170.

p. 104: "The real thing": Los Angeles *Times*, September 6, 1982.

p. 104: Country Joe at Woodstock: Spitz, op. cit., p. 414; Glenn A. Baker, "Rock's Angry Voice," p. 11.

p. 104: "aristocrats of the rock empire": Abbie Hoffman, *Woodstock Nation,* pp. 5, 142–43.

p. 104: "All those hippies": Chris Salewicz, "Pete Townshend: True Confessions," p. 16.

p. 104: Rock "can be": Ellen Willis, *The New Yorker,* quoted in Anson, op. cit., p. 129.

p. 104: rejection of John's offer to perform at Woodstock: Spitz, op. cit., p. 104.

p. 105: "I just threw up": Connolly, *John Lennon,* p. 119.

p. 105: "I don't care": Ibid.

p. 106: "he was so disgusted": Brown and Gaines, op. cit., p. 182.

p. 106: "After breakfast": Fawcett, op. cit., p. 57.

p. 106: "Whenever I remember it": "John Lennon: A Tribute," Canadian TV special, November 26, 1969.

p. 106: "A few snobs": Fawcett, op. cit., p. 58.

p. 106: "Whatever abuse": Ibid.

p. 106: "at the spearhead": *Times* of London, December 9, 1980.

p. 107: "the bizarre treat": *Times* of London, October 25, 1969.

p. 107: Save Biafra Campaign: *Times* of London, December 12, 1969.

p. 107: "Do you care?": Neville, op. cit., p. 81.

p. 107: "the left in Britain": Tariq Ali, interview with author.

p. 107: school for gypsy children: London *Daily Mirror,* December 1, 1969.

p. 107: Irish island: New York *Times,* November 14, 1969; *Times* of London, November 14, 1969.

p. 108: John "showed the crowd": "Random Notes," *Rolling Stone,* February 7, 1970, p. 11. The concert can be heard on side three of *Some Time in New York City.*

p. 108: "We're not used to seeing": Dick Gregory, interview with author.

p. 108: "You are going to sound": Abe Peck, "Communies," *Chicago Seed,* reprinted in Mel Howard and the Reverend Thomas King Forcade, eds., *The Underground Reader,* p. 232.

p. 108: "You've got the power": "John and Yoko's 1970 Peace Message," December 1969, audio tape, author's collection.

p. 108: Phil Ochs's "War Is Over" campaign: Marc Eliot, *Death of a Rebel,* pp. 129–33, 143–44.

p. 109: "Not many people are noticing": BBC "Man of the Decade" TV special, December 31, 1969.

10. Hanratty and Michael X

p. 110: "I am taking up the case": London *Daily Mirror,* December 11, 1969.

p. 110: unfurled a banner: *Times* of London, December 12, 1969.

p. 110: bag event: London *Daily Mirror,* December 15, 1969.

p. 110: "Britain! You killed Hanratty": the performance can be heard on side three of *Some Time in New York City.*

p. 110: Hanratty case: Paul Foot, *Who Killed Hanratty?*

p. 112: "spent many hours": *The Beatles Tapes,* 1976 Polydor LP, David Wigg interview, July 1969.

p. 113: campaign to abolish the death penalty: London *Daily Mirror,* December 11, 17, and 19, 1969.

p. 113: "The Beatles are treated": *The Beatles Tapes,* 1976 Polydor LP, David Wigg interview, July 1969.

p. 113: "unfortunate image": *Times* of London, December 21, 1969.

p. 113: "Clown of the Year": London *Daily Mirror,* December 18, 1969.

p. 113: "The Establishment reminds me": Jutta Ney, "John and Yoko Interview," p. 33.

p. 114: first three notes of "Instant Karma!": John as disc jockey on WNEW-FM radio, September 28, 1974.

p. 114: "promoting peace": *Times* of London, January 5, 1970.

p. 114: protests against the South African rugby team: *Times* of London, February 12, 1970.

p. 114: "and if we are going to have a baby": *Times* of London, March 30, 1970.

p. 114: "Winter Carnival for Peace": "One Hundred Grand for Moratorium," *Rolling Stone,* March 7, 1970, p. 5.

p. 114: "In an ass-backwards way": Christgau, *Any Old Way You Choose It,* pp. 235–6.

p. 115: hair auctioned: London *Daily Mirror,* February 5, 1970.

p. 115: "destroyed his last shred": Brown and Gaines, op. cit., pp. 366–67.

p. 115: Naipaul: "Michael X and the Black Power Killings in Trinidad."

p. 115: "I didn't have much confidence": Robin Blackburn, interview with author.

p. 115: "Michael X was a hustler": Tariq Ali, interview with author.

p. 116: "in this country": Paul Foot, *The Rise of Enoch Powell,* p. 59.

p. 116: "a much more conscious": Tom Nairn, "Enoch Powell: The New Right," p. 1.

p. 116: "We spent hours with Michael": *The Beatles Tapes,* 1976 Polydor LP, David Wigg interview, July 1969.

p. 116: "Direct communication:" Jonathan Steele, "Michael X, His Story," Manchester *Guardian,* May 17, 1968.

p. 116: "arrogant and confused": Ibid.

p. 116: "essential reading": Colin MacInnes, "Rough Black Diamond," *New Statesman,* May 17, 1968, p. 655.

p. 117: "Aside from Michael": Stuart Hall, interview with author.

p. 118: "We have to do something": Jon Hendricks, interview with author.

p. 118: " 'Do you think' ": Kate Millett, interview with author.

p. 119: "revolutionary pamphlets appeared": Naipaul, op. cit., pp. 41, 43.

p. 119: "He was a fantastic": Dick Gregory, interview with author.

p. 119: "flimsy, questionable evidence": "The Case for Michael X," p. 1.

p. 120: "recovered just as mysteriously": Geoff Robertson, "Michael X on Death Row," pp. 40–41.

p. 120: "I think it's possible": Stuart Hall, interview with author.

p. 120: "John and Yoko came up here": Kate Millett, interview with author.

p. 121: "I met with the lawyer:" Dick Gregory, interview with author.

p. 121: "Do you realize": John Lennon and Yoko Ono, "To Whom It May Concern," July 16, 1973, Jon Hendricks collection.

p. 122: "appears to have been framed": Kate Millett statement, defense committee fact sheet.

p. 122: PEN American Center to H.R.H. Elizabeth of England, August 29, 1973; on defense committee fact sheet.

p. 122: "I have known Michael": "Statement of William Burroughs on Behalf of Michael X, London, September 1973," on defense committee fact sheet.

p. 122: "a fellow traveller": Dick Gregory, June 16, 1973, on defense committee fact sheet.

p. 122: "Michael Abdul Malik, free spirit": John Lennon and Yoko Ono, telegram to Erica Williams, December 6, 1973; Jon Hendricks collection.

p. 123: "If the plea succeeds": *Sunday Times* of London, February 3, 1974.

p. 123: "frivolous and vexatious": quoted in Robertson, op. cit., p. 40.

p. 123: "We got the word": Jon Hendricks, interview with author.

p. 123: "The dead man": Robertson, op. cit., p. 40.

p. 123: "The execution of Michael X": Kate Millett, interview with author.

p. 123: On Michael X, I have also benefitted from a conversation with Professor Robert A. Hill of UCLA and from correspondence with Professor Andrew Salkey of Hampshire College.

11. Altamont and Toronto

p. 124: "An Angel grabbed Hunter's head": John Burks, "In the Aftermath of Altamont," *Rolling Stone*, February 7, 1970, p. 8.

p. 125: "Brothers and sisters": *Gimme Shelter* film.

p. 125: "The Hell's Angels were as helpful": Sam Cutler on KSAN radio, quoted in "Let It Bleed," *Rolling Stone*, January 21, 1970.

p. 126: "could have taken up a collection": "Let It Bleed," *Rolling Stone*, January 21, 1970, p. 9. On Woodstock security, see Spitz, op. cit., p. 171.

p. 126: " 'The Stones Have Not Acted Honorably' ": *Rolling Stone*, April 3, 1970.

p. 126: "lassitude" of the authorities: Donovan Bess, "The Altamont Trial," *Rolling Stone*, April 1, 1971, p. 13.

p. 126: "the state of California": Ibid.

p. 126: "I didn't know": *The Rolling Stone Interviews*, pp. 174–76.

p. 127: "When the fighting was going on": Ibid., p. 201.

p. 127: "People are responsible": Ralph J. Gleason, "Have You Seen Your Critic, Baby?," p. 252.

p. 127: "totally irresponsible": Gleason, "Aquarius Wept," pp. 84–92. See also Greil Marcus, "The Apocalypse at Altamont."

p. 127: "It was pitiful": Gleason, "Perspectives: Altamont Revisited on Film," *Rolling Stone*, April 1, 1971, p. 31.

p. 127: "a whitewash of Jagger": Albert Goldman, ". . . Or 'A Whitewash of Jagger'?"

p. 128: "thrilling, disturbing, shocking": Peter Schjeldahl, Review of *Gimme Shelter*, New York *Times*, January 3, 1971.

p. 128: "We aim to make it": Ritchie Yorke, "John, Yoko & Year One," p. 18.

p. 128: "the image and the mood": Ibid., p. 19.

p. 128: "we would like to take": *Village Voice*, December 23, 1969.

p. 128: "We're asking everyone": quoted in Yorke, op. cit., p. 19.

p. 129: "John enthusiastically outlined": Fawcett, op. cit., p. 67.

p. 129: "If there were more leaders": Ibid.

p. 129: "A five-hour private meeting": Jann Wenner, "Man of the Year," p. 1.

p. 129: "Peace Network": Jon Carroll, "John Brower Wants Your Shit," *Rolling Stone*, April 16, 1970, p. 7.

p. 129: "New Left—Foreign Influence": FBI airtel via courier, Legat ("legal attaché"), Ottawa, to director, June 24, 1970.

p. 129: "everywhere we went": Barry Ballaster, "Who and What Killed the Toronto Peace Festival?," p. 17.

p. 130: "Year One" declaration: audio tape, author's collection.

p. 130: "Do we still need a Festival?": John Lennon, " 'Have We All Forgotten What Vibes Are?,' " p. 1.

p. 130: "We've got to keep hope alive": Yorke, "A Private Talk with John," *Rolling Stone*, February 7, 1970, p. 14.

12. Primal Therapy and the Breakup

p. 134: "All we are saying": Jeff Greenfield, *No Peace, No Place*, p. 252.

p. 134: Kent State and the national student strike: see Michael W. Miles, *The Radical Probe*, p. 258.

p. 134: "the worst type of people": Lawrence A. Wittner, *Cold War America*, pp. 355–56.

p. 135: "a peaceful assembly": Ibid.

p. 135: "these bums": Richard M. Nixon, *RN: The Memoirs of Richard Nixon*, Vol. 1, p. 562.

p. 135: "My child was not a bum": Ibid., p. 566.

p. 135: "predictable," given the "traitors and thieves": Wittner, op. cit., p. 356.

p. 135: "on the edge": Henry Kissinger, *White House Years*, quoted in ibid.

p. 135: "completely unwarranted": Ibid., p. 357.

p. 135: "While Lennon has shown": Director, FBI, to SACs, New York and Los Angeles, April 23, 1970.

p. 136: "somebody at the publishing house": Arthur Janov, interview with author.

p. 136: "the suppression of feeling": Arthur Janov, *The Primal Scream*, p. 28.

p. 136: "That's me": *The Playboy Interviews*, p. 103.

p. 136: Julia "met another man": Davies, op. cit., p. 7.

p. 136: "I would never have gone": *The Playboy Interviews*, p. 105.

p. 136: not "improved functioning": Janov, *The Primal Scream*, p. 99.

p. 136: "stimulates intense real feelings": Ibid., p. 352.

p. 137: "When we arrived": Arthur Janov, interview with author.

p. 137: "Lennon had a lot": Dick Gregory, interview with author.

p. 137: "It's excruciating": Blackburn and Ali, op. cit., p. 44.

p. 137: "John was really taken": Arthur Janov, interview with author.

p. 138: "having conferred the greatest benefits": Scaduto, op. cit., p. 267.

p. 138: "home of Amerika's wealthy": Ibid.

p. 139: "What is this shit?": Greil Marcus, "Self-Portrait No. 25," p. 17.

p. 139: "It speaks to us": Landau, *It's Too Late to Stop Now*, p. 58.

p. 139: "I told them": Scaduto, op. cit., p. 269.

p. 139: "a love song to life": Ibid., pp. 270–71.

p. 139: Christgau gave it an A: Christgau, *Christgau's Record Guide*, p. 116.

p. 139: "We've got Dylan back": Scaduto, op. cit., p. 270.

p. 139: *New Morning* "wasn't much": *Lennon Remembers*, p. 44.

p. 139: "brainwashed" by rock music: James M. Naughton, "Agnew Assails Songs That Promote Drug Culture," New York *Times*, September 15, 1970.

p. 140: "It's only a rock group": *The Beatles Tapes*, 1976 Polydor LP, David Wigg interview, July 1969.

13. Working-Class Hero

p. 142: "It's no game": Connolly, *John Lennon*, p. 135.

p. 142: "John was always writing": Dan Richter, interview with author.

p. 142: "a new kind of populist art song": Stephen Holden, *Rolling Stone*, July 20, 1972, p. 42.

p. 142: "the crushing, exhilarating": Landau, *It's Too Late to Stop Now*, p. 122.

p. 143: "Lennon refuses": Robin Blackburn, *Red Mole*, March 8, 1971, p. 10.

p. 143: "Even when he is fervidly shedding personas": Christgau, *Any Old Way You Choose It*, pp. 241–43.

p. 143: " 'Like all seminal rock' ": *The Lennon Tapes*, p. 35. Andy Peebles, interviewing John for the BBC in 1980 two days before his death, quoted an unnamed critic writing about "God": "Some of the finest of all rock-singing on the last verse." John said, "Who is this wonderful . . . Where is he when we need him? You know, who is he? I want to send him a card." (*The Lennon Tapes*, p. 37.) Peebles didn't answer his question; the quote came from Greil Marcus. Actually Marcus wrote, "John's singing on the last verse of 'God's Song' may be the finest in all of rock." (Dave Marsh and John Swenson, eds., *The Rolling Stone Record Guide*, p. 219.)

p. 143: inappropriate pop-star grin: see the *Shindig!* broadcast, January 20, 1965, on video.

p. 144: "We love every minute": "Playboy Interview: The Beatles," p. 83.

p. 144: "The real feeling": Connolly, "Crippled Inside," p. 21.

p. 144: Tina Turner's "Help!": See the ABC *20/20* Emmy Award–winning profile of her, produced by Danny Schechter in 1981.

p. 144: "fat Elvis period": *The Playboy Interviews*, p. 112.

p. 144: "junked-up middle-class bitches": *Lennon Remembers*, p. 20.

p. 144: "the first song": *The Playboy Interviews*, p. 129.

p. 144: "In My Life" a favorite: "John Hoyland Replies," *Black Dwarf*, January 10, 1969, n.p.; Bruce Dancis, "For the Love of Lennon."

p. 144: "Fuckin' big bastards": *Lennon Remembers*, p. 87.

p. 145: "just not too much fun": Ibid., p. 38.

p. 145: "There isn't a person": Henry Edwards, "Yoko Ono (and John)," p. 25.

p. 145: "ugly race": *Lennon Remembers*, p. 14.

p. 145: "torture . . . just sucking us to death": Ibid., p. 11.

p. 145: "Look at me": Ibid., p. 166.

p. 145: "But now I'm wearing": Ibid., p. 132.

p. 146: "Not necessarily . . . do what the blacks are doing": Ibid.

p. 146: "fuckin' Duchamp": Ibid., p. 169.

p. 146: "a cool and seemingly effortless confidence": Calvin Tomkins, *The Bride and the Bachelors*, p. 9.

p. 146: "Working class?": *Daily Worker* (London), September 7, 1963.

p. 146: "I get terribly annoyed": London *Sunday Express*, March 30, 1969.

p. 147: "Before the Beatles": Peter Brown, interview with author.

p. 147: "That was the end": Dan Chandler interview on WQAM (Miami), 1969.

p. 147: "When I heard it": Connolly, *John Lennon*, p. 32.

p. 148: "the worst Teddy boy": Norman, op. cit., p. 33.

p. 148: "People say we're loaded": Braun, op. cit., p. 13.

p. 148: "I'll just ask them": Ibid., p. 47.

p. 148: "still warmly 'alright' ": Richard Hoggart, *The Uses of Literacy*, p. 73.

p. 148: "the first thing we did": Blackburn and Ali, op. cit., p. 44.

p. 148: "In London, the Liverpool accent": Peter Brown, interview with author.

p. 148: "gave themselves airs": Hoggart, op. cit., p. 73.

p. 148: "The Liverpool fans": Peter Brown, interview with author.

p. 148: "instinctive socialist": RKO radio interview, December 8, 1980.

p. 148: "The world of 'them' ": Hoggart, op. cit., pp. 62–63.

p. 149: "The real working-class hero": Ibid., p. 113.

p. 149: "When I worked": Peter Brown, interview with author.

p. 150: "master of his own house": Hoggart, op. cit., p. 38.

14. The Red Mole

p. 151: "Once a month": Tariq Ali, interview with author.

p. 151: Ali was denied permission to enter the United States: London *Daily Mirror*, December 3, 1969.

p. 152: "John was anti-establishment": Dan Richter, interview with author.

p. 152: "I said I wished": Tariq Ali, interview with author.

p. 152: "John was absolutely undogmatic": Robin Blackburn, interview with author.

p. 152: "I still remember": Tariq Ali, interview with author.

p. 152: "I've always been politically minded": Blackburn and Ali, op. cit., p. 43.

p. 154: "In retrospect": Robin Blackburn, interview with author.

p. 154: "The acid dream is over": London *Observer*, March 7, 1971, p. 9.

p. 154: "The song 'Power to the People' ": Tariq Ali, interview with author.

p. 155: "hire Teamsters": Seymour Hersh, New York *Times*, September 24, 1981.

p. 156: "the dreadful curse": Roy Carr and Tony Tyler, *The Beatles: An Illustrated Record*, p. 94.

p. 156: "parroting the well-worn clichés": Schaffner, op. cit., p. 146.

p. 156: "the best movement song": *Great Speckled Bird*, reprinted in *Outlaw* (St. Louis), October 22, 1971, p. 7.

p. 156: "a nervy 45": Dave Marsh and John Swenson, eds., *The Rolling Stone Record Guide*, p. 219.

p. 156: "Rubbish": Blackburn and Ali, op. cit., p. 44.

p. 156: "was at the Yippie end": Robin Blackburn, interview with author.

p. 157: "in London": Neville, op. cit., pp. 172–73.

p. 157: "sexist and raunchy": Robin Blackburn, interview with author.

p. 157: "The trial": Tariq Ali, interview with author.

p. 157: "lust without love": Tony Palmer, *The Trials of OZ*, p. 74.

p. 157: "would not convert people": Ibid., p. 81.

p. 157: "The media's tactic": *OZ*, February 12, 1970, p. 8.

p. 157: "Why the Ferocious Sentences?": *I.T.*, August 26, 1971, p. 21.

p. 157: "MPs Condemn OZ Gaolings": Ibid.

p. 157: "disgusting fascism": Ibid.

p. 158: "It is obvious enough": Claud Cockburn, column on *OZ* trial, p. 15.

p. 158: "unmask the realities": "Repression," *Red Mole*, September 1, 1971, p. 7.

p. 158: "Every major country": *I.T.*, July 26, 1971, back page.

p. 158: "the best of rock": Greil Marcus, *Stranded*, p. 268.

p. 158: "Spiggy Topes" and "Len Trott": "The Young Idea," *Private Eye*, August 27, 1971, p. 13.

p. 159: "Yes, it's hilarious": Tariq Ali, interview with author.

p. 159: "are integral matters": *Times* of London, August 12, 1981. See also *I.T.*, August 26, 1971; *Red Mole*, September 1, 1971. John and Yoko included footage of the demonstration in their *Imagine* film.

15.   "We Hope Some Day You'll Join Us"

p. 160: "irrational yet beautiful": *Rolling Stone*, January 22, 1981, p. 66.

p. 160: an "altruistic" song: Ron Schaumburg, *Growing Up with the Beatles*, p. 130.

p. 160: a song of "optimism": Don Heckman, New York *Times*, May 19, 1971, section 2, p. 27.

p. 161: "Imagine *one* religion": *The Playboy Interviews*, p. 179.

p. 161: "didn't understand it": Ibid.

p. 161: "I like . . . 'Imagine' ": Schaffner, op. cit., p. 148.

p. 161: "So you think": Ibid.

p. 161: "carries the presumption": Ron Whitehorne, "The Beatles, John Lennon and the Youth Rebellion," Philadelphia Workers' Organizing Committee, *The Organizer*, January 1980 *(sic.: 1981)*, p. 13.

p. 161: "undistinguished" and "methodical": Ben Gerson, *Rolling Stone*, October 28, 1971, p. 67.

p. 161: John's fundamentalist critics: Noebel, op. cit., p. 99.

p. 163: "simplistic ranting": Stephen Holden, *Rolling Stone*, July 20, 1972, p. 42.

p. 163: " 'Imagine' is Lennon's vision": Tom Harper, *Great Speckled Bird*, reprinted in *Outlaw* (St. Louis), October 22, 1971, p. 5.

p. 163: "Gimme Some Truth": the song was first recorded at the *Let It Be* sessions in January 1969; it can be heard on the bootleg record album *Sweet Apple Trax v. 3*, where John sings "no freaked-out yellow-bellied son of Gary Cooper" instead of "Richard Nixon."

p. 163: "the kind that makes you": Blackburn and Ali, op. cit., p. 44.

p. 163: "horrifying and indefensible": Gerson, op. cit., p. 67.

p. 163: "I think he's capable": *Lennon Remembers*, p. 122.

p. 163: *Imagine* album: see also Wilfrid Mellers, *Twilight of the Gods*, pp. 175–76; Robert Christgau, *Christgau's Record Guide*, p. 224.

p. 164: "John succeeded": Dan Richter, interview with author.

p. 164: "He needs continual reminders": Christgau, *Any Old Way You Choose It*, pp. 243–46.

p. 164: "John Lennon has really grown": Tom Harper, op. cit., p. 5.

p. 164: "uncompromisingly commercial": Connolly, "Crippled Inside," p. 20.

p. 165: "Everybody has this guilt": Scott Muni radio interview, WNEW-FM (New York City), 1971.

p. 165: "this guy called Claudio": Alex Bennett radio interview, WPLJ (New York City), June 1971. May Pang reports that the confrontation was filmed: *Loving John*, pp. 38–39.

p. 165: "We appreciate Zappa": Ibid.

p. 165: "This is WFBI": Miles, *John Lennon in His Own Words*, p. 99.

p. 166: "We asked Debray": Tariq Ali, interview with author.

p. 166: "Debray had heard": Robin Blackburn, interview with author.

p. 167: "political collaboration": Ibid.

p. 167: "I said, 'Look' ": Tariq Ali, interview with author.

p. 167: "That's an amazing": Ibid.

p. 167: "A factory occupation": Special Clydeside Supplement, *Red Mole*, July 1971, p. 5.

p. 168: "shop stewards' fighting fund": *Times* of London, August 13, 1971.

p. 168: "He suddenly packed": Tariq Ali, interview with author.

p. 168: Tony Cox and Kyoko: Brown and Gaines, op. cit., pp. 407–408.

p. 168: "The miners would have radicalized": Robin Blackburn, interview with author.

p. 169: "We're really grateful": "Working Class Heroes," *I.T.*, September 1, 1971, p. 7.

p. 169: "I don't want to say": Robin Blackburn, interview with author.

p. 170: "The Beatles are treated": *The Beatles Tapes*, 1976 Polydor LP, David Wigg interview, July 1969.

16.   Life on Bank Street

p. 173: "It has more Jews": "Everywhere's Somewhere," *The New Yorker*, January 8, 1982, p. 29.

p. 173: "It's really inspiring": Ron Skoler, "An Interview with John & Yoko," p. 24.

p. 174: "I was a very depressed": Stu Werbin, "John & Jerry & David & John & Leni & Yoko," p. 6.

p. 174: "John was very playful": Jerry Rubin, interview with author.

p. 174: "How the Yippies": Ibid.

p. 174: "All we can do": Abbie Hoffman, interview with Tom Forcade in *Georgia Straight*, reprinted in Howard and Forcade, eds., op. cit., p. 71.

p. 175: "Everybody knows your people": audio tape, author's collection.

p. 175: "Yoko says": Jerry Rubin, interview with author.

p. 175: "Now That We Can't Be Beatle Fans Anymore": Robert Christgau, *Village Voice*, September 30, 1971; reprinted as "Living without the Beatles" in Christgau, *Any Old Way You Choose It*, pp. 235–255.

p. 175: "We have never read": John Lennon and Yoko Ono, Letter to the Editor.

p. 175: "On Avenue B": Christgau, "John Lennon, 1940–1980," p. 1.

p. 175: "I said, 'You guys' ": Joe Butler, interview with author.

p. 176: "They were always": Ibid.

p. 176: "It was pretty frantic": Kate Millett, interview with author.

p. 177: "The use of dope laws": Allen Ginsberg, interview with author.

p. 177: "a guy I had evicted": Joe Butler, interview with author.

p. 178: "We heard that some dudes": Bobby Seale, interview with author.

p. 178: "This was John's 'Imagine' period": Jerry Rubin, interview with author.

p. 178: "I saw them go cold turkey": Stew Albert, interview with author.

p. 179: "I was shook up": David Peel, interview with author.

p. 179: "I'm standing in back": *The John Lennon/Yoko Ono Interview by Ron Skoler, Summer 1972*, Orange Records cassette tape (released by David Peel).

p. 179: "because I knew something": David Peel, interview with author.

p. 179: "We got moved on": *The John Lennon/Yoko Ono Interview by Ron Skoler, Summer 1972*, Orange Records cassette tape (released by David Peel).

p. 179: "I told Jerry": David Peel, interview with author.

p. 179: "At Apple": Ibid.

p. 180: "We loved his music": *The John Lennon/Yoko Ono Interview by Ron Skoler, Summer 1972*, Orange Records cassette tape (released by David Peel).

p. 180: "Lennon always said": Stew Albert, interview with author.

p. 180: "I went to Bank Street": Bobby Seale, interview with author.

p. 181: "He agreed": Elliot Mintz, interview with author.

p. 181: "They hit it off": Stew Albert, interview with author.

p. 181: "Free Bob Dylan" button: photo in New York *Post,* June 9, 1971.

p. 181: "Pakistanis starve": Liberation News Service dispatch, in *Great Speckled Bird,* December 20, 1971, p. 9.

p. 181: "Capitol-ist stop": Ibid.

p. 181: "Capitol is trying": Ibid.

p. 181: "John and Yoko are the newest members": Ibid.

p. 181: "publicly apologize": *Village Voice,* December 2, 1971, p. 59.

p. 182: John contributed "thousands": A. J. Weberman, interview with author.

p. 182: "Klein the Swine": *Village Voice,* March 9, 1972; *Variety,* March 1, 1972.

p. 182: "convinced John and Yoko": A. J. Weberman, interview with author.

p. 182: John was among the "artist-auctioneers": Howard Smith, "Scenes," *Village Voice,* December 16, 1971, p. 82.

p. 182: "Jerry took me": Craig Pyes, interview with author.

p. 183: "an alternative": Craig Pyes and Ken Kelley, editorial statement, *SunDance,* No. 1 (April–May 1972), p. 3.

p. 183: "It's Never Too Late": *SunDance,* No. 1, pp. 67–69.

p. 184: "To us, it is a direct descendant": "Imagine," *SunDance,* No. 2 (August 1972), p. 68.

p. 184: "One has oneself": Scott Muni radio interview, WNEW-FM, 1971.

p. 185: "leading missionaries": Art Linkletter, testimony in U.S. Congress, House Select Committee on Crime, *Crime in America—Illicit and Dangerous Drugs,* p. 152.

p. 186: "Celebrities feel a void": Dick Gregory, interview with author.

p. 186: "You wonder": Stew Albert, interview with author.

17. "It Ain't Fair, John Sinclair"

p. 187: "Guerrillas wanted!": *Guerrilla: A Monthly Newspaper of Contemporary Kulchur,* February 1967. Presumably this was an invitation to work on the newspaper.

p. 188: "hippies will not be": *Guerrilla,* June 1967.

p. 188: the MC5: see Ben Fong-Torres, "Shattered Dreams," *Rolling Stone,* June 8, 1972, p. 30; Dave Marsh and Kevin Stein, *Rolling Stone,* October 1, 1981; Phil Hardy and Dave Laing, eds., *Encyclopedia of Rock: Volume 2,* p. 229.

p. 188: "With our music": Neville, op. cit., pp. 107–08.

p. 188: "Music means nothing": John Sinclair, *Music and Politics,* p. 25.

p. 188: "We will fuck": John Sinclair, "Free!," from the White Panther Community News Service, reprinted in Howard, and Forcade, eds., op. cit., p. 117.

p. 188: Sinclair "espouses": Ellen Willis, *Beginning to See the Light,* p. 57.

p. 188: "put the cultural revolution": John Sinclair, *Guitar Army: Street Writings/Prison Writings,* p. 67.

p. 188: "The White Panthers": Stu Werbin, interview with author.

p. 188: "What drugs should it encourage": Mark Naison, "Youth Culture: A Critical View," in Paul Buhle, ed., "Fifteen Years of Radical America," pp. 74–76.

p. 189: "I know who you are": Werbin, "John & Jerry & David & John & Leni & Yoko," p. 6.

p. 189: "I would like to say": Testimony of Clifford A. Murray, in U.S. Congress, Senate Internal Security Subcommittee of the Committee on the Judiciary, *Hearings: Extent of Subversion in the New Left, Pt. 8.* Distributed by Liberation News Service, reprinted in *Space City* (Houston), December 23, 1971, p. 11.

p. 189: "Our political ideas": Ben Fong-Torres, "Shattered Dreams," *Rolling Stone,* June 8, 1972, p. 30.

p. 189: "Young people know": John Sinclair, statement to the Michigan Senate, distributed by Liberation News Service, reprinted in *Sweet Fire* (Albany, New York), December 1, 1971, p. 7.

p. 190: "When we planned": John Sinclair, interview with author.

p. 190: "Stevie Wonder on the line": Peter Andrews, interview with author.

p. 191: "I was thrilled": Allen Ginsberg, interview with author.

p. 191: "I got to speaking": Bobby Seale, interview with author.

p. 191: "We've got to": Dave Dellinger, quoted in Liberation News Service dispatch in *Space City* (Houston), December 23, 1971, p. 10.

p. 191: "You can teach": Elsie Sinclair, quoted in David Fenton and John Collins, "John Sinclair: The Rally," Ann Arbor *Sun,* December 17, 1971, p. 14.

p. 191: "What we are doing here": Jerry Rubin, quoted in Liberation News Service, op. cit.

p. 192: "a fresh breath": Jane Barrett, "John Sinclair: The Rally and the Release," p. 93.

p. 192: "The place is screaming": David Peel, interview with author.

p. 192: "The room was so high": Jerry Rubin, "Ann Arbor," p. 3.

p. 192: "John was terrified": Stu Werbin, interview with author.

p. 193: "What went down here": Lenox Rafael, "Ann Arbor," *East Village Other,* December 23, 1971, p. 3.

p. 193: "We were there": Rubin, "Ann Arbor," p. 3.

p. 193: "One couldn't distinguish": *Michigan Daily,* quoted in Liberation News Service dispatch, reprinted in *Space City* (Houston), December 30, 1971, p. 11.

p. 193: "a cavalcade of stars": *Outlaw* (St. Louis), December 24, 1971.

p. 193: "the least offensive": Rubin, "Ann Arbor," p. 3.

p. 193: "urged political activism": Barrett, op. cit., p. 93.

p. 193: "not a rock concert": Rubin, "Ann Arbor," p. 3.

p. 193: "rock festivals turned": Ibid.

p. 194: "I had already served": John Sinclair, interview with author.

p. 194: "an incredible tribute": Rubin, "Ann Arbor," p. 3.

p. 194: "Jerry was in ecstasy": Werbin, "John & Jerry & David & John & Leni & Yoko," p. 1.

p. 194: "Lennon was very groovy": John Sinclair, interview with author.

p. 194: "Sinclair talks": Werbin, "John & Jerry & David & John & Leni & Yoko," p. 1.

p. 195: "how the Ann Arbor event": John Sinclair, interview with author.

p. 195: " 'This is gonna be' ": Werbin, "John & Jerry & David & John & Leni & Yoko," p. 1.

p. 195: "one-shot affair": "Sinclair Rally," *Outlaw* (St. Louis), December 24, 1971, p. 9.

p. 195: "It seemed to me": Allen Ginsberg, interview with author.

p. 195: "The main thing": radio interview, source unknown.

p. 196: "John and Yoko talked": Jerry Rubin, interview with author.

p. 196: "We talked to Lennon": Allen Ginsberg, interview with author.

p. 196: "Dylan came to my house": Jerry Rubin, interview with author.

p. 196: "There was this guy": Stew Albert, interview with author.

18. The Apollo Theatre and the *Mike Douglas Show*

p. 198: "prisoners slashed the throats": New York *Times*, September 14, 1971.

p. 198: "The Black community": *Urban League News*, February 1, 1972, p. 3.

p. 198: "John and Yoko Lennon": audio tape, author's collection.

p. 198: news or reviews: "Attica Dead Honored, Families Aided at Apollo," *Amsterdam News* (New York), December 25, 1971; Liberation News Service, in *Space City* (Houston), December 30, 1971, p. 7.

p. 199: "You're making it sound": *David Frost Show*, January 13, 1972.

p. 200: "there was a guy": Stew Albert, interview with author.

p. 200: "Racism is a hard thing": New York *Times*, January 12, 1972, p. 33.

p. 200: "Okay, group": Stu Werbin, "John & Yoko & Chuck: Just Wanna Rock & Roll," pp. 24–25.

p. 201: "The song I just sang": *Mike Douglas Show*, February 14–18, 1972.

p. 204: FBI transcript: Memo from special agent [name deleted] to SAC, New York, February 22, 1972, requesting taping; airtel from SAC, New York, to director, February 25, 1982, enclosing transcript of Rubin comments.

p. 207: "The central committee": Bobby Seale, interview with author.

p. 207: "The limousine's at the curb": Stu Werbin, interview with author.

19. Front-Page Songs

p. 208 "Today at Forty-fourth": audio tape, author's collection.

p. 210: page one of the *Times* of London: February 7, 1972.

p. 210: "I don't know": Skoler, "An Interview with John and Yoko," p. 24.

p. 210: "Of course we sympathize": Letter distributed by Liberation News Service, in *Georgia Straight* (Vancouver), March 24, 1972, n.p.

p. 211: "It takes being there": Kate Millett, interview with author.

p. 212: "We got a request": Skoler, "An Interview with John and Yoko," p. 25.

p. 212: "coming around": Liberation News Service dispatch in *Great Speckled Bird* (Atlanta), December 20, 1971, n.p.

p. 212: L.A. *Free Press* cover: December 13, 1971.

p. 212: "felt strongly": Scaduto, *Bob Dylan*, 1979 ed., p. 337.

p. 212: "This is ugly nonsense": Christgau, *Any Old Way You Choose It*, p. 210.

p. 212: "It works": Scaduto, op. cit., p. 339.

p. 212: Dylan's "George Jackson": see also Dave Marsh, who called it his "best topical song," better than any of John's political music, in his review of Lennon's LP *Shaved Fish*, *Rolling Stone*, December 18, 1975, p. 68.

p. 213: "It was endlessly argued": Kate Millett, interview with author.

p. 213: Sara Evans: *Personal Politics*, pp. 212–13.

p. 214: *Broadcasting* magazine: Cited in *Rolling Stone*, June 8, 1972, p. 4.

p. 214: "I think it will offend people": Ibid.

p. 214: "Dick Gregory helped us": *The Lennon Tapes*, p. 50.

p. 214: "Every show is run": Dick Cavett, interview with author.

p. 214: "If you define 'nigger' ": Quoted by John on the *Dick Cavett Show*, May 11, 1972.

p. 215: "I believe in reincarnation": Irma Kurtz, "In the Bag: Yoko Ono," p. 54.

p. 215: "directly inspired by life": *The Lennon Tapes*, p. 49; see also Henry Edwards, "Yoko Ono (and John)," pp. 25–35.

p. 215: "simply a list": Stephen Holden, review of *Some Time in New York City, Rolling Stone*, July 20, 1972, p. 48.

p. 215: the first women's liberation song: *The Lennon Tapes*, p. 49.

p. 217: "They wanted Phil": Stew Albert, interview with author.

p. 217: "Lennon was optimistic": Ibid.

p. 217: "horrendous . . . protest epics": Dave Marsh and John Swenson, eds., op. cit., p. 219.

p. 217: "glib politicizing": *Illustrated Encyclopedia of Rock*, pp. 139–40.

p. 217: "mindless overkill": Carr and Tyler, op. cit., p. 102.

p. 217: "so embarrassingly puerile": review of *Some Time in New York City, Rolling Stone*, July 20, 1972, p. 48; see also Holden, "Lennon's Music: A Range of Genius," *Rolling Stone*, January 22, 1981, p. 66.

p. 217: "It's good": Craig Pyes, *SunDance*, No. 3 (August–September 1972), p. 79. For another enthusiastic review, see Peter Nickol in *Gramophone*, January 1973, p. 1387.

p. 217: "The time is right": Robert Christgau, "The Political Power of Rock and Roll," *Newsday*, July 9, 1972.

p. 218: "Front-page songs": Dan Richter, interview with author.

p. 218: "The songs we wrote": *SunDance*, No. 2 (August–September 1972), p. 68.

p. 218: "I don't think they are the best": "An Evening with John Lennon," Capital Radio (England), 1975.

p. 218: "Yoko said, 'Well, you know' ": RKO radio interview.

p. 218: "Every newspaper headline": Eliot, op. cit., p. 59.

p. 218: "From New York's": Ibid., p. 84.

p. 218: "I used to love": *Lennon Remembers*, p. 188.

p. 218: Suze and CORE: Scaduto, op. cit., pp. 111–12.

p. 219: "I think it's the best": Ibid., p. 112.

p. 219: "civil rights": Ibid., p. 117.

p. 219: "It means a lot": Ibid., p. 118.

p. 219: "A Hard Rain": see Morris Dickstein, op. cit., p. 195.

p. 219: "During the Cuban thing": Scaduto, op. cit., p. 127.

p. 220: "Bobby Dillon": "Northern Folk Singers Help Out at Negro Festival in Mississippi," *New York Times*, July 7, 1963. Dylan's trip is documented in the D. A. Pennebaker film *Don't Look Back*.

p. 220: The Greenwood project: Claybourne Carson, *In Struggle*, pp. 77–81.

p. 220: "I've been in Mississippi, man": Nat Hentoff, "The Crackin', Shakin', Breakin' Sounds," p. 88.

p. 220: "He wasn't a song writer": Scaduto, op. cit., pp. 137–38.

20. Deportation: "A Strategic Counter-Measure"

p. 225: "This group has been strong advocates": the text was first released in Chet Flippo, "Lennon's Lawsuit: Memo from Thurmond," p. 16.

p. 226: "We can use the available political machinery": the "enemies list" memo was revealed in the New York *Times,* June 29, 1973.

p. 226: "Ray, . . . When is he coming?": Richard Kleindienst to Raymond Farrell, February 14, 1972; document reproduced in Chet Flippo, "Lennon's Lawsuit: Memo from Thurmond," p. 16.

p. 226: "not quite what I had in mind": quoted in Jeb Stuart Magruder, *An American Life: One Man's Road to Watergate,* p. 89.

p. 227: "When they first came to me": Leon Wildes, interview with author.

p. 227: "Crazy Annie": Stew Albert, interview with author.

p. 227: "Recipients are reminded": FBI airtel, director to SACs, New York, Los Angeles, San Diego, Washington Field Office, February 15, 1972.

p. 227: "The public will soon become aware": FBI teletype, SAC, New York, to director, January 28, 1972.

p. 227: "obviously being heavily influenced": FBI cable, director to legal attaché, London, February 11, 1972.

p. 228: "The organization ceased to exist": FBI LHM, March 29, 1972, "Election Year Strategy Information Center (Formerly Known as the Allamuchy Tribe)."

p. 228: "Subject continues to plan": FBI airtel, director to SAC, New York, April 10, 1972.

p. 228: PL "was founded in 1962": FBI LHM, February 28, 1972, "Election Year Strategy Information Center (Formerly Known as the Allamuchy Tribe)," p. 2.

p. 228: "a youthful indiscretion": Stew Albert, interview with author.

p. 228: "temporary residence": FBI cable, urgent and coded, New York to director, February 2, 1972; information repeated in FBI LHM, March 16, 1972, "John Winston Lennon," p. 3.

p. 228: "promptly initiate discreet efforts": FBI airtel, director to SAC, New York, April 10, 1972.

p. 228: "We reviewed carefully": Leon Wildes, interview with author.

p. 228: "We announce the birth": the "Declaration of Nutopia" appears on the *Mind Games* record jacket.

p. 229: "Yoko apologized later": Leon Wildes, interview with author.

p. 229: "They were very nervous": Ibid.

p. 229: "to keep child hidden": FBI teletype, coded, New York to acting director, May 16, 1972.

p. 229: "I'd open the door": "An Evening with John Lennon," Capital Radio (England), 1975.

p. 229: "It will enhance the paranoia": FBI memo, SAC, Philadelphia, "New Left Notes," quoted in Donner, op. cit., p. 178.

p. 229: "We knew we were being wiretapped": Lisa Robinson, "A Conversation with John Lennon," *Hit Parader,* December 1975, p. 34.

p. 229: "I was so paranoid": "An Evening with John Lennon," Capital Radio (England), 1975.

p. 230: "Over drinks Lennon gave Hoffman": Fred Sparkes, St. Louis *Globe-Democrat,* September 30, 1971.

p. 230: "Money is such a sensitive issue," "especially cooperative": Donner, op. cit., p. 238, quoting Senate Select Committee to Study Governmental Operations with Respect to Intelligence Activities ("Church Committee"), *Final Report,* Book 6, pp. 762, 812–15, 817.

p. 230: "especially cooperative": Ibid.

p. 230: "I received information": Leon Wildes, interview with author.

p. 230: John "considered the possibility": Jerry Rubin, *Growing (Up) at 37*, p. 20.

p. 230: "putting a snitch jacket": Donner, op. cit., pp. 190–94.

p. 230: "the creating of impressions": FBI letter, director to SAC, Albany, July 5, 1968; reproduced in Rips, op. cit., p. 61.

p. 230: "attach the stigma": FBI document reproduced in Rips, op. cit., p. 68.

p. 230: "Lennon is allegedly in U.S.": FBI airtel, director to SAC, New York, April 10, 1972.

p. 231: "yesterday they were appointed": INS Deportation Proceedings, transcript of hearing, April 18, 1972.

p. 231: "New York Office confirmed": FBI memo, R. L. Shackelford to E. S. Miller, April 21, 1972, p. 2.

p. 231: "appointed by an executive assistant": INS Deportation Proceedings, transcript of hearing, April 18, 1972.

p. 231: "Observations: Irony of subject": FBI memo, Shackelford to Miller, op. cit.

p. 231: "Inquiry developed no information": FBI teletype, urgent and coded, Washington Field Office to director, April 21, 1972.

p. 232: "Dear Mr. Haldeman": letter, sender's name deleted, April 25, 1972; FBI file. Haldeman stated that he could not remember the letter or the case (Cable News Network, March 22, 1983); John D. Ehrlichman made a similar statement (letter to author, August 25, 1983).

p. 232: "It seems to me": Leon Wildes, interview with author.

p. 232: "Lennon was observed": FBI teletype, New York to director, April 18, 1972.

p. 233: "Mayor Lindsay Deplores": New York *Times*, April 29, 1972.

p. 233: "unconventional views": "Love It and Leave It," New York *Times*, May 2, 1972.

p. 233: "their antiwar stand": New York *Times*, April 29, 1972. For another newspaper that supported John and Yoko editorially at this point, see "Let John Lennon Stay," Chicago *Sun-Times*, May 22, 1972.

p. 233: "very sedate behavior": Sally Quinn, "Party of Parties," Washington *Post*, May 10, 1972.

p. 233: "Why are you being deported?": Geraldo Rivera television interview, May 1972, video.

p. 233: "Revolutionary Activities": FBI teletype, urgent, coded, New York to director, May 3, 1972.

p. 234: "We ain't used to speakin' ": NBC-TV news clip, May 12, 1972.

p. 234: "told the 30,000": Unidentified news clipping in INS file, document C-694.

p. 234: John announced his support: New York *Post*, May 19, 1972, p. 5; in FBI files.

p. 235: "FBI agents testifying": FBI teletype, coded, acting director to SACs, New York and Houston, May 24, 1972.

p. 235: "I was sharing": Dick Cavett, interview with author.

p. 235: "The issue resolves itself": INS Deportation Proceedings, transcript of hearing, May 12, 1972.

p. 236: "a number of major corporations": Ibid.

p. 236: "When I arrived": Dick Cavett, interview with author.

p. 236: "By their constant restless activity": INS Deportation Proceedings, transcript of hearing, May 12, 1972.

p. 236: "Do I understand": Ibid.

p. 237: "the documentation is immaterial": Ibid.

p. 237: FBI memo on International Committee for John and Yoko: FBI airtel, SAC, New York, to acting director, December 8, 1972.

p. 237: National Committee for John and Yoko statement and letters: INS proceedings file, documents P725–P918.

p. 238: "has received information that the LENNONS": FBI airtel, SAC, Miami, to acting director, June 5, 1972.

p. 238: "restrict their travel": FBI Memo, special agent [name deleted] to SAC, Houston, June 8, 1972.

p. 238: "Lennon is reportedly planning": Mike Jahn, Baltimore *Evening Sun*, February 27, 1972.

p. 239: "The pigs probably REALLY freak": Ann Arbor *Sun*, April 27, 1972, p. 3.

p. 239: "I think in his subconscious": Dick Gregory, interview with author.

p. 239: "They think we're going": *Dick Cavett Show*, May 11, 1972.

p. 239: "The only thing": Skoler, "An Interview with John and Yoko," p. 14.

p. 239: "We're not going": Stew Albert, interview with author.

p. 239: "I constantly advised them": Leon Wildes, interview with author.

p. 239: "headed for trouble": John Sinclair, interview with author.

21. From Madison Square Garden to Election Night

p. 241: letters concerning deportation case: INS correspondence file.

p. 244: "Ex-Beatle Told": *Black Panther*, May 20, 1972, p. 5.

p. 244: "Where the hell is everybody?": Ralph J. Gleason, "Perspectives: Fair Play for John and Yoko," p. 34.

p. 244: "dirty-mouthed wife": *Rolling Stone*, June 22, 1972, p. 5.

p. 245: "The day we met": Elliot Mintz, interview with author.

p. 245: " 'By the way' ": Craig Pyes, interview with author.

p. 246: black market in methadone: "Survey Finds Increase in Methadone Black Market," New York *Times*, January 2, 1972.

p. 247: "The most amazing thing": Craig Pyes, interview with author.

p. 247: "but I didn't have the money": Paul Krassner, interview with author.

p. 247: "no one in the White House staff": Wittner, op. cit., p. 376.

p. 248: a "political coup d'état": Mae Brussell, "Why Was Martha Mitchell Kidnapped?," p. 30.

p. 248: Louis Tackwood: Ibid., pp. 30–31.

p. 248: a "collection of absurdities": Wittner, op. cit., pp. 376–77.

p. 248: "We were all in a very paranoid state": Paul Krassner, interview with author.

p. 248: his "theory that, with all the political assassinations": Ibid.

p. 248: "The whole idea": Geraldo Rivera, interview with author.

p. 249: One to One concert: ABC-TV special, December 14, 1972, video. *Crawdaddy*, April 1973, called it "the best network televised rock to date" (p. 39). For a concert review, see Don Heckman, New York *Times*, August 31, 1972.

p. 250: "Miami should note": FBI airtel, SAC, New York, to acting director, July 27, 1972.

p. 250: "descriptive data and photograph" FBI LHM, "John Winston Lennon," New York, July 27, 1972.

p. 251: "Does he look": *Rolling Stone,* February 17, 1972, p. 6.

p. 251: "To the hard-hats": *SunDance,* No. 2 (August–September 1972), p. 68.

p. 251: "as a member . . . previously planned": FBI memo, SAC, New York, to acting director, August 30, 1972.

p. 252: "failed to reflect": FBI memo, SAC, Miami, to acting director, October 24, 1972.

p. 252: "John and I love this country": Jerry Lewis Telethon, September 6, 1972, audio tape.

p. 252: American Coalition for Citizens with Disabilities: Los Angeles *Times,* August 25, 1981.

p. 253: "He came into the house screaming": Jerry Rubin, interview with author.

p. 253: "This is it?": Mayer Vishner, "Whining through the Apocalypse," p. 88.

p. 253: "There were about six people left": Jerry Rubin, interview with author. May Pang refers to the same incident in *Loving John,* p. 56.

p. 255: "They could have been": Kate Millett, interview with author.

22. "Lennon Forgets"

p. 256: "In view of subject's inactivity": FBI airtel, SAC, New York, to acting director, December 8, 1972.

p. 256: "conspiracy to pervert": *Times* of London, November 8, 1972.

p. 257: bill introduced in Congress: *Congressional Record,* April 30, 1973, p. E 2685.

p. 257: "as they began to see": Jon Hendricks, interview with author.

p. 257: "You might think it's trivial": Danny Schechter radio interview, WBCN (Boston), June 3, 1973, audio tape.

p. 260: attended Senate Watergate Committee hearings: ". . . And Faces in the Crowd," Washington *Post,* June 29, 1973.

p. 260: "I thought it was better on TV": Chris Charlesworth, "Lennon Today," p. 36.

p. 260: picketing the South Vietnamese embassy: photo in Washington *Post,* June 28, 1973.

p. 261: "The Supervision of the Activities": Joel Siegel, "Lennon: Back in the U.S.S.R.," *Rolling Stone,* October 10, 1974, p. 11.

p. 261: "Review failed to indicate": FBI memo, SAC, Miami, to acting director, October 24, 1972.

p. 262: "It was originally called": *The Playboy Interviews,* pp. 179–80.

p. 262: "rejection of the mindless militancy": Carr and Tyler, op. cit., p. 108.

p. 262: Ron Schaumburg: *Growing Up with the Beatles,* p. 132.

p. 262: Nicholas Schaffner: *The Beatles Forever,* p. 163.

p. 263: "This ain't Frantz Fanon": Lester Bangs, *Creem,* February 1974. Also in *Creem,* Robert Christgau gave it a B: March 1974.

p. 263: "managing to submerge": Noe Goldwasser, Review of *Mind Games, Crawdaddy,* February 1974, p. 66.

p. 263: "lost in the changing . . . environment": Jon Landau, Review of *Mind Games, Rolling Stone,* January 3, 1974, p. 61.

p. 263: "Lennon Forgets": Patrick Snyder-Scumpy, *Crawdaddy,* March 1974, p. 47.

p. 264: "You're not angry": May Pang and Henry Edwards, *Loving John,* p. 87.

p. 264: "Tell me about the new album": Chris Charlesworth, op. cit., pp. 36–37.

p. 264: "basically a reggae middle-eight": *The Lennon Tapes*, p. 54.

p. 264: "It was as if": Elliot Mintz, interview with author.

p. 264: "Having just celebrated": "John & Yoko Fight Deportation Decision," *Rolling Stone*, April 26, 1973, p. 10.

p. 265: "he was affecting his eligibility": Leon Wildes, interview with author.

23. "No More '74"

p. 266: "Whoopee! Bachelor life!": *The Playboy Interviews*, p. 20.

p. 266: "I picked them up": Elliot Mintz, interview with author.

p. 267: "lost weekend . . . when the feminist side died": *The Lennon Tapes*, p. 56.

p. 267: "With John": Pang and Edwards, op. cit., p. 216.

p. 267: "How could I stay?": Ibid., pp. 201–02.

p. 268: Troubadour incident: John's fullest account is in *The Playboy Interviews*, p. 23. See also "Notes on People," New York *Times*, March 16, 1974; "Call It John Lennon's Hard Day's Night," Washington *Post*, March 15, 1974; INS file, documents A-429, C-658.

p. 268: "suicidal . . . I didn't want to see": Robert Hilburn, "Lennon: He Doesn't Believe in Magic or the Beatles," p. 1.

p. 268: "I thought, what can I do": 1982 Beatlefest video, unidentified.

p. 269: "Now that seems": Ray Coleman, "Lennon: A Night in the Life," p. 15.

p. 269: "intolerable": *Wall Street Journal*, March 28, 1973.

p. 269: "less than zealous": "The Lennon Case," New York *Post*, July 22, 1974.

p. 270: "Lennon now has political lobbyists": San Francisco *Examiner*, August 11, 1974.

p. 270: "It was kind of odd": Leon Wildes, interview with author.

p. 270: "one of the Senate's most secretive": John H. Averill, "Senate Cools on Security Panel's Spending," Washington *Post*, March 9, 1973.

p. 270: "more effectively handicapped": Donner, op. cit., p. 413.

p. 270: "a lot of ex-McCarthyites": Averill, op. cit.

p. 271: "scorn for legal niceties": Donner, op. cit., p. 409.

p. 271: SISS annual report: U.S. Congress, Senate Internal Security Subcommittee of the Committee on the Judiciary, *Report for Fiscal Year Ending February 29, 1972*.

p. 271: Jack Anderson column: Washington *Post*, August 29, 1974; see also Joel Siegel, op. cit., p. 11.

p. 271: John filed a new lawsuit: New York *Times*, November 2, 1974, p. 35.

p. 271: his first real victory: Joe Treen, "Lennon Wins Right to Quiz Justice Dept.," *Rolling Stone*, February 13, 1975, p. 12.

p. 272: "afraid with your heart pounding": Blackburn and Ali, op. cit., p. 44.

p. 272: "one of my least favorites": Pang and Edwards, op. cit., p. 239.

p. 273: "Q. Were you drunk?": John Lennon, "Interview/Interview with by/on John Lennon and/or Dr. Winston O'Boogie," p. 11.

p. 273: "The only thing new": interview with Kenny Everett, Capital Radio (England), 1974.

p. 273: "I'm not ashamed": Hilburn, op. cit., p. 1.

p. 273: "There's craftsmanship": Garbarini and Cullman, op. cit., pp. 121–22.

p. 273: "Yoko and I were apart": Hilburn, op. cit., p. 1.

p. 273: "Politics?": Wilfred De'Ath, "An American Exile," p. 58.

p. 274: "I was always": French radio interview, 1974, author's collection.

p. 275: John's search for his past: Jon Landau, "Lennon Gets Lost in His Rock & Roll," *Rolling Stone*, May 22, 1975, p. 66; see also Greil Marcus, "Recollections of an Amnesiac," *Creem*, June 1975, p. 69.

p. 275: "I couldn't stand to listen": "An Evening with John Lennon," Capital Radio (England), 1975.

p. 275: "Something flashed through me mind": *The Lennon Tapes*, pp. 69–70.

p. 275: "It was a great high": Pete Hamill, "Long Night's Journey into Day: A Conversation with John Lennon," p. 46.

p. 275: "The separation didn't work out": Ibid., p. 48.

p. 276: "A friend called me": Conversation with John Lennon, recorded January 1, 1976, by Elliot Mintz; used with permission.

p. 276: "There was a time": *Tomorrow* show, April 28, 1975; video.

p. 276: " 'If you want to be quoted' ": Leon Wildes, interview with author.

p. 276: "I am not in the group": Loraine Alterman, "John Lennon Talks about Music, Money, Marriage, and Fame," p. 96.

p. 277: "jumpy" and "nervous": Pete Hamill, op. cit., p. 46.

p. 278: "We were part of the peace movement": "An Evening with John Lennon," Capital Radio (England), 1975.

p. 279: "We'd done Leboyer": Conversation with John Lennon, recorded January 1, 1976, by Elliot Mintz; used with permission.

p. 279: "not too good in England": interview on Earth News Radio, December 1975.

p. 279: "The baby things": conversation with John Lennon, recorded January 1, 1976, by Elliot Mintz; used with permission.

p. 279: "Wasn't I the greatest": Hilburn, op. cit., p. 1.

p. 279: "Walking away is much harder": *The Playboy Interviews*, p. 8.

p. 279: "It was more important": Hilburn, "Lennon Exorcizes the Beatles' Ghosts," p. 1.

24. Watching the Wheels

p. 283: "My life was built around Sean's": Garbarini and Cullman, op. cit., pp. 97–98.

p. 283: "coughed a little": RKO radio interview.

p. 283: "got fed up": Ibid.

p. 283: "You hardly have time": *The Lennon Tapes*, p. 75.

p. 284: "stay in, go out": RKO radio interview.

p. 284: "usually Yoko's still down": Ibid.

p. 284: "The nanny probably reads": Ibid.

p. 284: "What the hell you doin'?": Ibid.

p. 284: "He really seems": John Blake, "John: Giving His All to His Family," Liverpool *Echo*, April 27, 1979.

p. 284: "He was fantastic": Ibid.

p. 284: "Where's the friction": Garbarini and Cullman, op. cit., p. 123.

p. 284: "If I'm feeling depressed": RKO radio interview.

p. 285: "He'd see me": Ibid.

p. 285: "I needn't feel guilty": Ibid.

p. 285: "idealized the nuclear family ideal": Andrew Kopkind, "Lennon without Tears," p. 10.

p. 286: "I'll say to all housewives": Garbarini and Cullman, op. cit., p. 118.

p. 286: "You feed them": *The Lennon Tapes*, p. 74.

p. 286: "How is *she?*": Garbarini and Cullman, op. cit., p. 118.

p. 287: "I've learned to make bread": *The Lennon Tapes*, p. 75.

p. 287: "I'm a rich housewife": Garbarini and Cullman, op. cit., p. 119.

p. 287: "In the first 18 months": Robinson, "John Didn't Want to Be 'Shot Like Gandhi.' "

p. 287: "John was prone to exaggeration": Elliot Mintz, interview with author.

p. 288: "he must have written": Ibid.

p. 288: "I'm interested in history": Garbarini and Cullman, op. cit., p. 111.

p. 288: "where he could do": Elliot Mintz, interview with author.

p. 288: "I'm an avid reader": Garbarini and Cullman, op. cit., p. 111.

p. 288: "One of the books": Elliot Mintz, interview with author.

p. 289: "property is the best thing": Garbarini and Cullman, op. cit., p. 103.

p. 290: Palm Beach house: Laurence Shames, "John Lennon, Where Are You?," p. 40.

p. 290: "I found that I spent": Alterman, op. cit., p. 96.

p. 290: "They're all male": *The Playboy Interviews*, p. 10.

p. 290: "I enjoy the security": Alterman, op. cit., p. 96.

p. 290: policy of tithing: "Playboy Interview: John Lennon and Yoko Ono," p. 88.

p. 291: "various disarmament groups": Los Angeles *Times*, December 7, 1981; her statement is reproduced in *Rolling Stone*, January 21, 1982, p. 84.

p. 292: " 'She will say things' ": Flippo, "The Private Years," p. 168.

p. 292: "shocking secrets": headline in *Star*, December 8, 1981.

p. 292: "Evening with Salvador Allende": Eliot, op. cit., p. 237.

p. 292: "War Is Over" rally: Ibid., pp. 244–45.

p. 292: No European left movement: Perry Anderson, *Arguments within English Marxism*, p. 152.

p. 293: "For eighteen months": Stuart Hall, interview with author; see also "Rock against Racism," *Rolling Stone*, December 14, 1980, p. 40.

p. 293: Dylan's song "Hurricane": see Christgau, *Christgau's Record Guide*, p. 118.

p. 293: "Night of the Hurricane": Chet Flippo, "Hurricane's Night: Thunder in the Garden," *Rolling Stone*, January 15, 1976; Les Ledbetter, "Knockin' on Hurricane's Door," *Rolling Stone*, January 15, 1976; Joe Nick Patoski, "Hurricane II: Thunder in the Heart of Texas," *Rolling Stone*, February 26, 1976.

p. 294: massive waste and internal dissension: Selwyn Rabb, "Dissension Splits Rubin Carter Camp," New York *Times*, June 20, 1976, p. 1.

p. 294: "No. . . . I'd like to publicly thank": Robinson, "A Day in the Life of a Permanent Resident," p. 48.

p. 295: "one of the greatest" and subsequent quotations in the same paragraph: Ibid.

p. 295: "I said to him": Peter Brown, interview with author.

p. 295: "Looks like the boys": postcard to Barbara Graustark, 1980.

p. 295: John and Yoko's "love letter": New York *Times*, May 27, 1979.

p. 296: "Why should the Beatles give more?": *The Playboy Interviews*, p. 61.

p. 296: "What about the charge": Ibid., pp. 42–44.

25. Starting Over

p. 297: "In the last ten years": *The Lennon Tapes*, p. 91.

p. 297: "new sounds, new forms": Frith, *Sound Effects*, p. 158.

p. 297: "I thought, oh": *The Lennon Tapes*, pp. 90–91.

p. 298: "That was a heavy show": Ibid., p. 33.

p. 298: "The whole time I was growing up": Bruce Springsteen, comment to author, 1982.

p. 298: "I think it's a great record": RKO radio interview.

p. 298: Dylan had a lot to say: see Greil Marcus, "Amazing Chutzpah," pp. 95–96.

p. 298: "The king is always killed": Garbarini and Cullman, op. cit., p. 101.

p. 299: "the culture he came out of": Marcus, *Mystery Train*, p. 173.

p. 299: "Get the axe . . . like diarrhea": *The Lennon Tapes*, p. 93.

p. 300: "basically misogynist": Geoffrey Stokes, Review of *Double Fantasy*, *Village Voice*, January 7, 1981, p. 31.

p. 300: "basically sexist": Christgau, "Symbolic Comrades," p. 32.

p. 301: "so all-fired powerful": Stokes, review of *Double Fantasy*, op. cit., p. 31.

p. 301: "comfortable and happy": Frith, "John Lennon," p. 25.

p. 301: "unrelenting sentimentality": Kopkind, "Lennon without Tears," p. 10.

p. 301: a "pop fairy tale": Stephen Holden, "Gimme Some Truth: The Songs of John Lennon," p. 283.

p. 302: "We're not the first": Cott, "The Last *Rolling Stone* Interview," p. 190.

p. 302: "This album doesn't say": RKO radio interview.

p. 302: "I have great hopes": *Lennon Remembers*, p. 110.

p. 303: "That radicalism was phony": "The Real John Lennon," p. 77. This quotation does not appear in the forty-nine-page "full" version of this interview in Garbarini and Cullman, *Strawberry Fields Forever*. The interviewer, Barbara Graustark, did not reply to an inquiry about the discrepancy.

p. 303: "All the rock critics": Robinson, "John Didn't Want to Be 'Shot Like Gandhi.' "

p. 303: "The only thing that would have been bigger": David Peel, interview with author.

p. 303: "It didn't really come off": *The Playboy Interviews*, p. 182.

p. 303: "Man, it's nice": Ibid., p. 185.

p. 303: "In England, there are only": Ibid., pp. 79–80.

p. 303: "Zen Marxist": Garbarini and Cullman, op. cit., p. 103.

p. 304: "a kind of Japanese-American Woody Guthrie": Nobu Kurasako, interview with author (translated by Rex Jones).

p. 304: "She had sympathy": Ibid.

p. 304: "We are with you": Copies of statement provided by Nobu Kurasako and Yoko Ono, author's collection.

p. 305: "If so," they told him: Nobu Kurasako, interview with author.

p. 305: "John was very happy to do this": Geoffrey Giuliano, "Yoko Ono," pp. 114–15.

p. 305: "In retrospect": RKO radio interview.

p. 305: "I'm more feminist now": Ibid.

p. 305: "the opening up of the sixties": Ibid.

p. 306: "Your way of life": "Elliot Mintz Interviews John Lennon," p. 2.

Epilogue: The Struggle of Mark David Chapman

p. 307: Chapman's life: the fullest account is Craig Unger, "John Lennon's Killer: The Nowhere Man." The best interpretive essay is Murray Kempton, "The Sad Secrets of an Assassin's Mind: Mark David Chapman." All quoted material in the Epilogue has been taken from these two articles.

Index

Latin American Classical Composers

A Biographical Dictionary

Compiled and Edited by

MIGUEL FICHER

MARTHA FURMAN SCHLEIFER

JOHN M. FURMAN

The Scarecrow Press, Inc.
Lanham, Md., & London
1996

SCARECROW PRESS, INC.

Published in the United States of America
by Scarecrow Press, Inc.
4720 Boston Way
Lanham, Maryland 20706

4 Pleydell Gardens, Folkestone
Kent CT20 2DN, England

British Cataloguing-in-Publication Information Available

Library of Congress Cataloging-in-Publication Data

Ficher, Miguel.
 Latin American classical composers : a biographical dictionary / compiled and
edited by Miguel Ficher, Martha Furman Schleifer, John M. Furman.
 p. cm.
 Includes bibliographical references and index.
 1. Music—Latim America—Bio-bibliography—Dictionaries. 2. Composers—
Latin America—Biography. I. Schleifer, Martha Furman. II. Furman, John M.
III. Title.
 ML105.F53 1996
 780'.92'28—dc20   96-7711
 [B]   CIP
                                                                        MN

ISBN 0–8108–3185-6 (cloth : alk.paper)

⊖™ The paper used in this publication meets the minimum requirements of
American National Standard for Information Sciences—Permanence of
Paper for Printed Library Materials, ANSI Z39.48–1984.
Manufactured in the United States of America.

Miguel Ficher

To the memory of my father, Jacobo Ficher,
a towering figure in the history of Argentine music in the
twentieth century and
to my wife, Ilda, who has supported and encouraged the
realization of this book.

Martha Furman Schleifer

To my supportive, loving, and tolerant family,
my husband, Charles,
and my sons Marc, David, and Daniel, the latter of whom
is also my extraordinary assistant.

John M. Furman

To Klara, a caring wife and mother of our talented
children.

CONTENTS

FOREWORD

There are compelling reasons why a volume such as this is needed, foremost of which is the huge gap in our knowledge about Latin American composers of the past as well as the present. Reference works in English have tended to neglect large numbers of serious Latin American composers while informing the public of only those who could not be ignored.

Gilbert Chase, who served as Latin American specialist in the Library of Congress from 1940 to 1943, was a major factor in bringing Hispanic music to the attention of North Americans. His book, *The Music of Spain* (1941) and his efforts to gather the music of South American composers for The Edwin A. Fleisher Collection of Orchestral Music, cast what he called "the spell of Spanish music" over multitudes of musicians and their audiences in the United States.

A decade later, the Pan-American Union of the Organization of American States began a series of volumes entitled *Composers of the Americas*, which up to now had presented biographical and bibliographical information on some two hundred Latin American composers. Still later specialists in the music of their own countries, presented studies that greatly enhanced our knowledge of Latin American music.

Despite all these worthy efforts, however, no comprehensive research was done to bring the information together into one volume. Dr. Miguel Ficher, in the late eighties, recognized the need for a biographical dictionary that would present the latest data available and, at the same time, correct as many of the errors of the past as possible. This volume presents a new generation of composers, and revives interest in those of the past who may have been deleted from earlier reference works or may have appeared only in studies of the music of their own countries. With editorial assistance from Dr. Martha Furman Schleifer and John Furman, Dr. Ficher has made a monumental contribution to our understanding of Latin American music.

Sam Dennison, Curator Emeritus
The Edwin A. Fleisher Collection of Orchestral Music, The Free
Library of Philadelphia, Philadelphia, Pennsylvania

PREFACE

The *Latin American Classical Composers: A Biographical Dictionary* brings to light an unprecedented number of Latin American composers. The composers included in the *Dictionary* are restricted to those who have written in the classical or cultivated tradition. The goal of this volume is to introduce Latin American composers, past and present, recognized and unknown, to the widest possible audience. Each one deserves recognition for his or her contributions to the enrichment of the musical world. The heightened awareness of these composers will hopefully stimulate publication and performance of their music.

The *Dictionary* presents important biographical data and list of works for each composer. In order to produce this *Dictionary* we solicited information from the composers, their families and colleagues, musicologists, and musical organizations, and schools. In addition, we made a thorough search of available materials in Spanish and English.

We invite you to join us in our continued effort to gather additional information about Latin American composers and their works. Please contact us trough The Scarecrow Press.

ACKNOWLEDGMENTS

We are very grateful to the following people whose contributions have been of great help in making this project possible (in alphabetical order):

Enrique A. Arias, musicologist, Chicago, Illinois;
Susan Berdahl, musicologist, Kingsville, Texas;
Eduardo Cáceres, composer, Agrupación Musical ANACRUSA, Santiago de Chile, Chile;
Daisy Coll, SACVEN, Caracas, Venezuela;
Cecília Conde, director, Conservatório Brasileiro de Música, Rio de Janeiro, Brazil;
Daniel A. Cozzi, secretario de extensión cultural, Facultad de Humanidades y Artes, Universidad Nacional de Rosario, Rosario, Province of Santa Fe, Argentina;
Ricardo Dal Farra, composer, Buenos Aires, Argentina;
Manuel de Elías, national coordinator for music and opera, Instituto Nacional de Bellas Artes, Mexico D.F., Mexico;
Igor De Gandarias, Dirección General de Promoción Cultural, Guatemala City, Guatemala;
Kerlinda Degláns, musicologist, Río Piedras, Puerto Rico;
Gerardo Dirié, coordinator, Latin American Music Center, Indiana University at Bloomington, Indiana;
Marta R. de Fahsen, minister of culture and sports, Guatemala;
Alvaro González Otero, cultural attaché, Embassy of Uruguay, Washington, D.C.;
Grüb Geschwindt, Laura, composer, Voorhees, New Jersey;
Dante Grela, composer, Instituto Superior de Música, Universidad Nacional del Litoral, Santa Fe, Province of Santa Fe, Argentina;
Nancy L. Harper, musicologist, Universidade do Minho, Braga, Portugal;
Stephen F. Henner, cataloguer, The Edwin A. Fleisher Collection of Orchestral Music, The Free Library of Philadelphia, Pennsylvania;
Malena Kuss, director, Center Latin American Music Bibliography, North Texas State University, Denton, Texas;
María Landis, Embassy of Guatemala, Washington, D.C.;
Eva I. Lopszyc, composer and conductor, Municipal Conservatory of Music Manuel de Falla, Buenos Aires, Argentina;
Cristina Magaldi Rocha, musicologist, Los Angeles, California;
Pablo Marentes, cultural attaché, Embassy of Mexico, Washington, D.C.;
Maritza H.F. Mascarenhas, musicologist, Houston, Texas;

Michael Meckna, associate professor of music, Texas Christian University, Forth Worth, Texas;

Emilio Mendoza, State University of New York, Potsdam, New York;

Nancy Paddleford, musicologist, St.Olaf College, Northfield, Minnesota;

Efraín Paesky, general secretary, CIDEM, Organization of American States, Washington, D.C;

Mirtha V. de Perea, cultural attaché, Embassy of Costa Rica, Washington, D.C.;

Joâo G. Ripper, composer, Washington, D.C.;

James Ryon, assistant professor of music, The University of Akron, Akron, Ohio;

Susana Salgado, musicologist, Alexandria, Virginia;

Jorge Sarmientos, composer and conductor, Guatemala City, Guatemala;

Kile Smith, curator, The Edwin A. Fleisher Collection of Orchestral Music, The Free Library of Philadelphia, Pennsylvania;

Juan María Solare, High School of Music, Cologne, Germany;

Frederico Lemos de Souza, assistant executive, UBC, Rio de Janeiro, Brazil;

Darío Suro, plenipotentiary minister of cultural affairs, Embassy of the Dominican Republic, Washington, D.C.;

Carmen Helena Tellez, director, Latin American Music Center, Indiana University at Bloomington, Indiana;

René Teseo, composer, Asociación Argentina de Compositores, Buenos Aires, Argentina;

Donald Thompson, musicologist, Río Piedras, Puerto Rico;

Aurelio de la Vega, composer, California State University, Northridge, California;

Werner Wagner, composer, Buenos Aires, Argentina;

Arlene B. Woehl, professor of music, Holy Names College, Oakland, California;

Benjamín Yepez, director, Centro Documentación Musical, Colcultura, Bogotá, Colombia;

GUIDELINES FOR USE

Bibl. (bibliography): Books in general that contain substantial information concerning individual composers. Some entries contain a specific bibliography concerning the individual composer.

Sources: Reference works such as dictionaries, encyclopedias, and books with lists of composers and countries in which specific information concerning individual composers has been located.

Composers with multiple last names are listed by their initial last name, i.e.: Mario Kuri Aldana is listed as Kuri Aldana, Mario.

Surnames are alphabetized as though continuous in spelling, i.e.:
D'Agnillo, Corradino
Dal Farra, Ricardo L.
Dallo y Lana, Miguel Mateo de
Daluisio, Rodolfo
D'Astoli, Bruno

Musical works usually appear in the following order: stage (opera and ballet), choral-symphonic music, symphonic music, chamber music, piano pieces, songs.

Specific works are written with first letter of work capitalized, i.e.: Concerto for orchestra; multiple works of the same type are written with ordinal numbers and small first letter, i.e.: 3 symphonies, 2 trios.

Orch. (orchestra). When *Orch.* is used as a subtitle in the sections entitled *Works*, listings are for orchestra and soloist and/or group mentioned, i.e.: Concerto for violin means concerto for violin and orchestra; Los Niños Héros, cantata for chorus, means cantata for chorus and orchestra.

When dates of birth and death differ according to various sources, we present each date with the corresponding source.

GENERAL ABBREVIATIONS

ADEMA	Asociación de Músicos de Argentina
AGMA	Agrupación Gremial de Músicos de la Argentina
ANPPOM	Associaçâo Nacional de Pesquisa e Pos-Graduaçâo em Música (Brazil)
APO	Asociación del Profesorado Orquestal (Argentina)
b.	born
BBC	British Broadcasting Corporation
bibl.	bibliography
BM	Bachelor of Music
c.	circa
CBS	Columbia Broadcasting System
CENIDIM	Centro Nacional de Investigación, Documentación e Información Musical (Mexico)
CICMAT	Centro de Investigación y Comunicación Masiva, Arte y Tecnología (Argentina)
CIDEM	Consejo Interamericano de Música, Washington, D.C.
CIDEMP	Centro de Investigaciones y Desarrollo de la Música Peruana (Peru)
CIM	Consejo Internacional de la Música (United Nations)
CONAC	Consejo Nacional de la Cultura (Venezuela)
cons.	conservatory, conservatorio
CUDA	Compositores Unidos de la Argentina
d.	died
dept.	department
DMA	Doctor of Musical Arts
ENA	Escuela Nacional de Arte (Cuba)
FAC	Federación Argentina de Compositores
fl.	flourished
FUNARTE	Fundación Nacional de Arte (Brazil)
IMS	International Musicological Society
INBA	Instituto Nacional de Bellas Artes (Mexico)
inst.	institute, instituto, institution, institución
ISA	Instituto Superior de Arte (Cuba)
ISCM	International Society of Contemporary Music
IUDEM	Instituto Universitario de Estudios Musicales (Venezuela)

MEC	Ministerio de Educaçâo e Cultura (Brazil)
MM	Master of Music

Months of the year

Jan	January
Feb	February
Mar	March
Apr	April
May	May
Jun	June
Jul	July
Aug	August
Sep	September
Oct	October
Nov	November
Dec	December

ODILA	Orchestra of Latin American Instruments (Venezuela)
orch.	orchestra, orchestras, orchestral
OSSODRE	Orquesta Sinfónica de SODRE (Uruguay)
Presb.	Presbyterian, presbyter
prov.	province, provincial
Rev.	Reverend
SACVEN	Sociedad de Autores y Compositores de Venezuela
SADAIC	Sociedad Argentina de Autores y Compositores (Argentina)
SCIUM	Society of Composers of the University of Miami
SODRE	Servicio Oficial de Difusión Radio Eléctrica (Uruguay)
UBC	Uniâo Brasileira de Compositores (Brazil)
UFRJ	Universidade Federal do Rio de Janeiro (Brazil)
UNAM	Universidad Nacional Autónoma Mexicana (Mexico)
UNESCO	United Nations Educational, Scientific, and Cultural Organization (United Nations)
UNIRIO	Universidade do Rio de Janeiro (Brazil)
USA	United States of America

SOURCES

ADBM   Barbacci, Rodolfo. *Apuntes para un Diccionario Biográfico Musical Peruano*. Lima: Fénix, Revista de la Biblioteca Nacional, Vol. VI, 1949.

BB   Slonimsky, Nicolas, ed. *Baker's Biographical Dictionary of Musicians*. New York: Schirmer Books, 7th and 8th editions, 1984, 1992.

BHMCU   Salgado, Susana. *Breve Historia de la Música Culta en el Uruguay*. Montevideo: A. Monteverde y Cia, S.A., 1980.

CA   Senillosa, Mabel. *Compositores Argentinos*. Buenos Aires: Casa Lottermoser, S.R.L., 1956.

CAMR   *100 Años de Música Rosarina*. Rosario, Argentina: Universidad Nacional de Rosario, 1991.

CB   Vázquez Messmer, Peter. *Compositores Bolivianos*. La Paz: Talleres Escuela de Artes Gráficas Don Bosco, 1975.

CMC   Alvarez Coral, Juan. *Compositores Mexicanos*. Mexico D.F.: Editores Asociados, S.R.L., 1971.

CPR   Deglâns, Kerlinda and Luis E. Pabón Roca. *Catálogo de Música Clásica Contemporánea de Puerto Rico*. Río Piedras, Puerto Rico: Pro-Arte Contemporáneo, 1989.

CTA   *Composers of the Americas*. Washington, D.C.: The Organization of American States, 19 Vols., 1955-1983 [CTA1 = Vol. 1, etc.].

DCM   Vinton. John, ed. *Dictionary of Contemporary Music*. New York: E.P. Dutton & Co., Inc., 1971.

DEW   Information supplied by the Dominican Republic Embassy in Washington, D.C. Santo Domingo: Revista de Educación, Vol.29, 1959.

DM   Della Corte, Andrea and Guido M. Gatti.
            Diccionario de la Música, with an appendix, *Música
            y Músicos de América*, by Néstor R. Ortíz Oderigo.
            Buenos Aires: Ricordi Americana, 1950.

DMC   Orovio, Helio, ed. *Diccionario de la Música
            Cubana.* Havana: Editorial Letras Cubanas, 1981.

EMA   Arizaga, Rodolfo. *Enciclopedia de la Música
            Argentina.* Buenos Aires: Fondo Nacional de las
            Artes, 1971.

EMB   Marcondes, Marcos Antônio, ed. *Enciclopedia da
            Música Brasileira: Erudita, Folclórica, Popular.*
            Sâo Paulo: Art Editora, 1977.

GDM   Sadie, Stanley, ed. *The New Grove Dictionary of
            Music and Musicians.* London: Macmillan
            Publishers Limited, 20 Vols., 1980.

GMM   Moncada García, Francisco. *Pequeñas Biografías de
            Grandes Músicos Mexicanos.* Ediciones Framong,
            Mexico D.F., 1966.

GMP   Raygada, Carlos. *Guía Musical del Perú.* Lima:
            Fénix, Revista de la Biblioteca Nacional, Vol. XII,
            1955-57; Vol. XIV, 1964.

HMB   Mariz, Vasco. *História da Música no Brasil.*
            Brasília: Civilizaçâo Brasileira, 1a ediçâo, 1981,
            2a ediçâo, 1983.

HMC   Claro Valdés, Samuel and Jorge Urrutia Blondel.
            Historia de la Música en Chile. Santiago de Chile:
            Editorial Orbe, 1973.

HMG   Anleu Díaz, Enrique. *Historia de la Música en
            Guatemala.* Guatemala City: Tipografía Nacional,
            1986.

IBCC   Bull, Storm. *Index to Biographies of Contemporary
            Composers.* Lanham, Maryland, The Scarecrow
            Press, Vol. III, 1987.

IEW   Cohen, Aaron I. *International Encyclopedia of Women Composers*. New York and London: R.R. Bowker Co., 1981.

ISC   Information supplied by the composer, a relative, and/or an interested party.

KTL   Frank, Paul and Wilhelm Altmann. *Kurzgefasstes Tonkünstler-Lexikon,* Burchard Bulling, Florian Noetzel, and Helmut Rösner, eds., Wilhelmshaven, Germany: Heinrichschofen's Verlag, Vol. I, 1974, Vol. II, 1978.

MLA   Slonimsky, Nicolas. *Music of Latin America*. New York: Thomas Y. Crowell Co., 1945.

MMLA   Mayer-Serra, Otto. *Música y Músicos de Latinoamérica*. Mexico D.F.: Editorial Atlante, 1947.

MMPA   Boettner, Juan Max. *Música y Músicos del Paraguay*. Asunción: Edición de autores paraguayos, 1956.

MMPR   Callejo, Fernando. *Música y Músicos Puertorriqueños*. San Juan, Puerto Rico: Editorial Coquí, 1971.

MU   Lagarmilla, Roberto. *Músicos Uruguayos*. Montevideo: Editorial Medina, 1970.

NGDWC   Sadie, Julie Anne and Rhian Samuel, eds. *The New Grove Dictionary of Women Composers*. London: Macmillan Publishers Limited, 1994.

NH   Information supplied by Dr. Nancy Lee Harper, professor of music, Universidade do Minho, Braga, Portugal.

NP   Information supplied by Dr. Nancy Paddleford, professor of music, St.Olaf College, Northfield, Minnesota.

NWC   Magaldi Rocha, Cristina, musicologist,
Los Angeles, California.

PEFCM   Program of the *First Ecuadorian Festival of
Contemporary Music*, 1987.

UEW   Information provided by the Uruguayan Embassy in
Washington, D.C.

VMA   Kuricz, Ladislao. *Vademecum Musical Argentino*.
Buenos Aires, 1983.

ZCCC   Zapata Cuencar, Heriberto. *Compositores
Colombianos*. Medellín, Colombia: Editorial
Carpel, 1962.

A

Aberle, Juan, Salvadoran composer of Italian origin; b.19th century, Italy. He settled first in Guatemala and later in El Salvador. *Works: Salvadoran National Anthem.*
Sources: DM, MLA

Abreu, José Antonio, Venezuelan composer; b.17 May 1939, Valera, Venezuela. He studied with local teachers in Valera, then he moved to Caracas, Venezuela, where he studied with Vicente Emilio Sojo.
Works (selective list): *Sinfonietta Neoclásica*; 2 symphonies; *Sancta et Immaculata Virginitas*, symphonic poem; *Tríptico*, for 11 instruments; Quintet for wind instruments; string quartets; choruses.
Sources: BB, CTA14

Acevedo Gajardo, Remigio, Chilean composer, organist, and conductor; b.1863, Santiago de Chile, Chile; d.29 May 1911, Chile. He studied organ and composition at the National Cons. of Chile; in 1902, he was granted a scholarship to continue studying in Milan, Italy. Organist in several churches in Santiago de Chile.
Works (selective list): *Caupolicán,* opera (1902); abundant production of religious music.
Sources: HMC, MMLA

Acevedo Raposo, Remigio, Chilean composer; b.16 Dec 1896, Santiago de Chile, Chile; d.1951, Chile. He started music studies with Francisco Avendaño, and then studied composition with Federico Stöber. Member of the Sociedad de Compositores de Chile. Director and professor of piano and composition at the School Remigio Acevedo Gajardo of Santiago de Chile.
Works (selective list): *Stage: Thamar*, biblical opera; *El Corvo*, creole opera; *Rapa Nui*, ballet. *Sinfonía de América*; *Suite Araucana*; *Choapinos*; *Las Tres Pascualas*; *La Diosa de la Montaña*; Concerto for cello and piano; *Libertad*, concerto for 2 pianos; String quartet; *Leyenda Mexicana*, suite for piano; songs; piano pieces.
Sources: HMC, MMLA

Acosta de Barón, Josefina, Colombian composer, pianist, and teacher; b.12 Jun 1897, Bogotá, Colombia; d.? In 1905, she studied theory, solfeggio, and harmony with Santos Cifuentes, and piano with María de Cifuentes, at the Beethoven Academy of Bogotá. From 1909 to 1912, she took piano lessons with Eliseo Hernández and Honorio Alarcón, and harmony with Guillermo Uribe Holguín. In

1931, she went to Barcelona, Spain, to study at the Marshall Academy with Mass y Serracán and Manuel Burges. In 1917, she founded the Centro Musical de Chapinero of Bogotá, which she directed until 1929. Professor of music at the Inst. Pedagógico Nacional and the National Cons., both in Bogotá; professor at the Cons. of Ibagué, Tolima, Colombia, from 1936 to 1945.

Works (selective list): *Las Estaciones*, suite for piano; *Valses, Nocturnos e Impromptu, in Chopin's style*; *Preludio y Fuga, in Bach's style*; religious music; piano pieces.

Source: MMLA

Adalid y Gamero, Manuel de, Honduran composer; b.8 Feb 1872, Danlí, Honduras; d.? Studied music with his mother, and then at the Cons. of Guatemala, solfeggio and voice with Leopoldo Cantilena, and piano with Peralta. He also studied harmony and composition with Axel C.F. Holm, and counterpoint with Deliponti. Director of the Banda Marcial of Tegucigalpa, Honduras, in 1915. He organized the Banda de los Supremos Poderes, which he conducted until 1924. Founder of the Escuela de Músicos Mayores of Tegucigalpa where he taught theory, harmony, and conducting.

Works (selective list): From 1925 to 1929: *Remembranzas Hondureñas,* concert waltz; *Suite Tropical; La Novia del Torero,* Spanish march; *Voces de la Tarde,* waltz; *Rosas de Otoño,* waltz; *Una Noche en Honduras,* symphonic intermezzo. *Mañana de Primavera en Washington*, march (1934); *Funerales de un Conejito*, symphonic poem (1936). **Books:** *Arte de Dirigir*, 1921.

Sources: DM, MLA, MMLA

Adame, Rafael G., Mexican composer and cellist; b.11 Sep 1906, Mexico City, Mexico. He studied cello and guitar. Principal cellist of the Mexico Symphony Orch., Mexico City.

Works: *Sinfonía Folklórica,* for military band; Concertino for guitar and orch.

Sources: DM, MLA

Adomián, Lan, Mexican composer of Russian origin; b.29 Apr 1905, Mogilev, Belarus, formerly part of Russia; d.9 May 1979, Mexico City, Mexico. He started to study music in Russia. In 1923, he moved to the United States and studied at the Peabody Cons. of Music in Baltimore, Maryland, and at the Curtis Inst. of Music in Philadelphia, Pennsylvania. In 1952, he moved to Mexico and became a Mexican citizen.

Works (selective list): *La Macherata,* opera (1969-72); *Auschwitz,* dramatic scene for baritone and instruments (1970); 8 symphonies; choruses, songs.

Source: BB

Adrianza, Alfredo Marcano, Venezuelan composer and percussionist: b.13 Nov 1953, Maracaibo, State of Zulia, Venezuela. He studied music history and percussion at the Juan José Landaeta Cons. in Caracas, Venezuela, and composition with Yannis Ioannidis from 1973 to 1976. From 1976 to 1978, with a scholarship from CONAC, he studied at the CICMAT in Buenos Aires, Argentina. He completed his composition studies at the Robert Schumann Inst. of Düsseldorf, Germany, under Gunther Becker. As a percussionist he played in the Chamber Orch. of the Radio Nacional de Caracas, the Symphony Orch. of Venezuela, and the Youth Symphony Orch. Simón Bolívar. Member of the Sociedad Venezolana de Música Contemporánea.
Works (selective list): *Coincidencias,* for percussion (1975); *Opresión,* for piano and gong (1976); *Cidencias,* for 10 instruments (1976); *Dencias,* for magnetic tape (1977); *Sur,* for symphony orch. (1981); *Urano,* for small orch. (1981); *Sinfonietta del Avila,* for chamber orch. (1987); chamber music; electronic music.
Source: ISC

Advis, Luis, Chilean composer, pianist, and art historian; b.10 Feb 1935, Iquique, Chile. He studied at the Cons. of Santiago de Chile, Chile. Professor at the Univ. of Chile, Santiago de Chile.
Works (selective list): *Popular Symphony,* for orch.; *Canción,* for ancient instruments; chamber music; incidental music for the theater and television.
Source: KTL

Agudelo Murguía, Graciela, Mexican pianist, singer, teacher, and composer; b.7 Dec 1945, Mexico City, Mexico. She studied piano with Homero Valle at the Escuela Nacional de Música and composition with Héctor Quintanar and Mario Lavista at the National Cons. of Music, both of Mexico City.
Works (selective list): *Navegantes del Crepúsculo,* for clarinet, bassoon, and piano (1993); chamber music; electronic music; piano pieces; songs.
Sources: IBCC, IEW, NGDWC

Agüero y Barreras, Gaspar, Cuban composer, musicologist, and teacher; b.15 Feb 1873, Camagüey, Cuba; d.18 May 1951, Havana, Cuba. He studied at the Univ. of Havana. Professor at the Cons. of Music of Havana.
Works (selective list): Symphonies; 10 zarzuelas; Piano concerto; masses.
Source: KTL

Aguila, Miguel del, Uruguayan composer and pianist; b.15 Sep 1957, Montevideo, Uruguay. He studied piano with Santiago Baranda Reyes and composition with Vicente Ascone in Uruguay. In 1979, he entered the San Francisco Cons., California, USA, where he studied piano with Paul Hersh, and later he continued at the Hochschule für Musik in Vienna, Austria, with Erich Urbanner.
Works (selective list): *Cuauhtemoc,* opera (1992); *Symphonic Scenes,* for chamber orch.; *Prisons,* for orch.; *The Naked King,* for orch.; *Toccata,* for orch.; Concerto for clarinet and orch.; *A Conga Line in Hell,* for chamber ensemble (1993); chamber music; piano pieces; songs; choruses.
Source: ISC

Aguilar Ahumada, Miguel, Chilean composer, pianist, and teacher; b.12 Apr 1931, Huara, Chile. He studied in Santiago de Chile, Chile, with Domingo Santa Cruz and Juan Orrego Salas, and later took courses in conducting in Cologne, Germany. Professor at the Escuela Moderna de Música of Santiago de Chile and the Cons. of the Symphony Orch. and Escuela de Música of the Univ. of Concepción, Chile.
Works (selective list): *Obertura al Teatro Integral,* for orch. (1954); Septet for wind instruments and double bass (1954); *Sonatina Concertante,* for clarinet and piano (1956); *Simetrías,* for piano (1958); *Música Aleatoria,* for orch. (1969); vocal works to texts by the Chilean poet Vicente Huidobro.
Sources: BB, CTA14, DCM, HMC

Aguirre, Avelino, Argentine composer and conductor of Spanish origin; b.1841, Bilbao, Spain; d.1901. He settled in Buenos Aires, Argentina, in 1876. He conducted the orch. of the Teatro de la Opera of Buenos Aires and taught at the Prov. School of Music, Prov. of Buenos Aires, Argentina.
Works (selective list): *Lo que Puede el Mate,* zarzuela (1877); *Nicolasita,* zarzuela (1885); *Misa de Gloria* (1877); Symphony for chorus and orch. *Books: Nuevo Método Teórico-Práctico de Lectura Musical,* 1877.
Source: EMA

Aguirre, Julián, Argentine composer, b.28 Jan 1868, Buenos Aires, Argentina; d.13 Aug 1924, Buenos Aires. He studied piano with Dámaso Izabalza and Carlos Beck, composition with Emilio Arrieta and Aranguren, and fugue with Cató at the National Cons. of Music of Madrid, Spain. Member of the Academia Nacional de Bellas Artes of Buenos Aires. Secretary and professor of solfeggio and piano at the National Cons. of Music Carlos López Buchardo of Buenos Aires.

Works (selective list): More than 60 compositions for piano and songs. *Music for piano: Tres Aires Criollos; Aires Nacionales Argentinos; Gato; Zamba; Huella; Dos Intimas; La Danza de Belkiss. Songs: El Nido Ausente; Serenata Campera; Caminito; Rosas Orientales; Las Mañanitas.* Sonata for violin and piano. *Gato y Huella* (op. 49), most popular piece, orchestrated by Ernest Ansermet.
Bibl.: J.F. Giacobbe, *Julián Aguirre*, Buenos Aires, 1945. C. García Muñoz, *Julián Aguirre*, Buenos Aires, 1970.
Sources: BB, CA, DM, EMA, GDM, MLA, MMLA

Aguirre, Manuel, Peruvian composer; b.1 Aug 1863, Arequipa, Peru; d.6 Feb 1951, Arequipa. He was self-taught in music. In 1945, he was appointed lifetime honorary director of the Southern Regional School of Music of Peru.
Works: Mainly compositions for piano and songs.
Source: CTA13

Aizaga, Claudio, Ecuadorian composer and pianist; b.1928, Quito, Ecuador. He studied at the National Cons. of Music of Quito with Julia Espinosa and Françoise Lambert.
Works (selective list): *Ballets: Cumandá; Daquilema; Niño Agua; Abolorios; Navidad Montubia; Acuarelas Cero. Misa Popular Ecuatoriana,* for soloists, chorus, and orch.; 3 suites for orch.; Concerto for piano and orch.; music for solo instruments; piano pieces.
Source: ISC

Ajubita, Marcelo, Argentine composer and violist; b.19 Nov 1958, Venado Tuerto, Prov. of Santa Fe, Argentina. He studied viola with Mary Barg and Tomás Tichauer, and composition with Dante Grela. Member of the *Agrupación de Música Contemporánea Klank* and *Agrupación Nueva Música,* both of Rosario, Prov. of Santa Fe. Founding member of the *Grupo de Avant Rock Fritz the Cat.* Violist in several orch. and of the *Quinteto Barroco.*
Works (selective list): *Talking Talking Dreams,* for string orch., electric guitar, and synthesizer; *Idiot Performance,* monodrama for strings, tenor saxophone, electric guitar, prepared piano, and mezzo-soprano; *La Caja de Pandora,* for strings, percussion, 3 electric guitars, and rhythmic box; chamber music.
Source: CAMR

Alais, Juan, Argentine composer and guitar player; b.1838, Buenos Aires, Argentina; d.1914, Argentina. He was self-taught in music. Famous as a guitar player of his time.

Works: More than 80 pieces for guitar, including *La Perezosa*, mazurka; *Estilo en La; Un Momento*, waltz.
Source: EMA

Alamo, Lázaro del, Mexican composer of Spanish origin; b.c.1530, El Espinar, near Segovia, Spain; d.between 17 Mar and 19 May 1570, Mexico City, Mexico. He studied with Gerónimo de Espinar and Bartolomé de Olaso, *maestro de capilla* (chapelmaster) at the Cathedral of Segovia, Spain. Singer at the Mexico City Cathedral, and in 1556, after being ordained, he was appointed *maestro de capilla* (chapelmaster) at the same Cathedral.
Works: Alternatim Psalm, composed for the commemoration services for Charles V, held in Mexico City on 29 November 1559; motets; villancicos; chansonnettes for Corpus Christi and Christmas.
Bibl: R. Stevenson, *Lázaro del Alamo, Primer Compositor Europeo en México, Heterofonía: Revista Musical Bimestral,* 1970 .
Source: GDM

Alas, Ciriaco Jesús, Salvadoran composer and conductor; b.7 Apr 1866, Santa Tecla, El Salvador; d.? After taking music lessons at the Liceo de San Luis, El Salvador, under Juan Daniel Alas, he studied violin with Rafael Oledo and composition with Juan Aberle and José Kessels. Voice teacher at the Central Inst. of El Salvador in 1886. Director of the Banda de los Supremos Poderes from 1888 to 1890, and of the Banda Regimental de Sonsonate from 1901 to 1944, both in El Salvador.
Works (selective list): *Orch: Fantasy* on themes from *Cavalleria Rusticana; Rosita; Fantasy* on themes from *Il Trovatore; El Maestro Hiram; Neo Cadina; La Coronación,* overture on themes from the *Salvadoran National Anthem; Marden,* intermezzo. Music for violin; music for band; religious works.
Sources: DM, MLA, MMLA

Albano, Enrique, Argentine composer; b.1910, Coronel Suárez, Prov. of Buenos Aires, Argentina. He studied under Alfredo L. Schiuma. He collaborated in the formation of the Inst. de Cultura Musical of the School of Architecture, National Univ. of Buenos Aires, Argentina, and was its first director.
Works (selective list): *Misa de Gloria; Cantata A la Virgen de Luján,* for soloists, choir, and orch.; *Dos Series Argentinas,* for orch.; Trio for piano, violin, and cello; 2 sonatas for violin and piano; songs.
Sources: EMA

Alberdi, Father Francisco María, Ecuadorian composer and chorus conductor of Spanish origin; b.5 Jan 1878, Durango, Vizcaya, Spain;

Quito, Ecuador. He settled in Ecuador in 1890. He was a self-taught musician. Priest, ordained in 1891.
Works (selective list): 5 misas de Requiem for 3 voices and organ; *Misa de Requiem,* for 2 voices; *Misa de Pastorela Jesu Redemptor,* for 3 voices and organ; *Las Siete Palabras,* oratorio for 3 voices and organ; large number of religious compositions; *El Capricho Quiteño,* suite based on Inca themes.
Source: MMLA

Alberdi, Juan Bautista, Argentine philosopher, jurist, statesman, poet, diplomat, and composer; b.29 Aug 1810, Tucumán, Prov. of Tucumán, Argentina; d.18 Jun 1884, Paris, France. He studied music under Cambeses in Buenos Aires, Argentina. One of the most eminent personalities of the Latin American liberalism.
Works: Brief and elegant collection of minuets, waltzes, and songs.
Books: Las Bases, which established the basis for the writing of the Argentine Constitution in 1853; *El Espíritu de la Música a la Capacidad de todo el Mundo; Ensayo sobre un Método Nuevo para Aprender a Tocar el Piano con la Mayor Facilidad.*
Sources: DM, EMA, MLA, MMLA

Alberti, Luis Felipe, Dominican composer; b.19 Apr 1906, La Vega, Dominican Republic. He studied under Emilio Arté and Juan Francisco García. Professor of choral singing at public schools of Santiago and San Cristóbal, Dominican Republic. *Maestro de capilla* (chapelmaster) at the Iglesia Parroquial Mayor of Santiago.
Works: *Compadre Pedro Juan,* merengue; *Potpourri Albertiano,* serenata.
Sources: DM, MMLA

Albornoz, Pedro, Argentine composer and conductor; b.1808, Buenos Aires, Argentina; d.1880, Buenos Aires. He studied with Father Picassarri and Juan Pedro Esnaola. He conducted opera at the old Teatro Colón of Buenos Aires. In 1860, he was appointed ball director of the Club Progreso, leading social inst. of the day in Buenos Aires.
Works: Popular dances: series of *Lanceros* (for Club Progreso). Arrangement of the *Argentine National Anthem*; salon music.
Source: EMA

Albuquerque, Armando, Brazilian composer; b.29 Jun 1901, Rio Grande do Sul, Brazil; d.?
Works: *Trip,* quintet for piano and strings (1947); *Suite Breve,* for orch. (1954); *Evocaçâo,* for orch.; *Caleidoscopio,* for string orch.
Source: HMB

Alcedo (Alzedo), José Bernardo, Peruvian composer; b.11 Aug 1798, DM (1788, ADBM), Lima, Peru; d.28 Dec 1878, Lima. He studied at the Convento de los Agustinos with the *maestro de capilla* (chapelmaster) Fray Cipriano Aguilar. He lived in Chile from 1823 to 1863, where he taught music at public schools and conducted military bands. On his return to Peru in 1864, he was appointed general director of the army bands.
Works (selective list): *Peruvian National Anthem*, 1821. *Religious music: Miserere; Pasión para el Domingo de Ramos; Pasión para el Viernes Santo;* 3 misas solemnes; several motets; hymns; patriotic songs; music for band. **Books:** *Filosofía Elemental de la Música.*
Bibl.: E. Pereira Salas, *Los Orígenes del Arte Musical en Chile,* Santiago de Chile, 1941.
Sources: ADBM, DM, GMP, MMLA

Alchourron, Rodolfo, Argentine guitarist and composer; b.1934, Buenos Aires, Argentina. He studied with Alberto Ginastera, Julián Bautista, Jacobo Ficher, and Francisco Kröpfl.
Works (selective list): *Música,* for guitar and sextet (1959); *Preludio,* for piano (1960); Sonata for piano (1961); *Aldeana,* for choir a cappella (1962); *Microhombre,* pantomime for bandonion and guitar (1962); *Tres Piezas,* for guitar and percussion (1963); Quartet for strings (1967).
Source: EMA

Alcorta, Amancio, Argentine economist and composer; b.16 Aug 1805, Santiago del Estero, Prov. of Santiago del Estero, Argentina; d.3 May 1862, Buenos Aires, Argentina. He studied harmony, flute, and violin at the Colegio de Monserrat, Córdoba, Prov. of Córdoba, Argentina, under professor Cambeses.
Works (selective list): *Lamentaciones,* for contralto, tenor, bass, and organ; *Gradual para el Día de San Martín,* for baritone, flute, and piano or organ; Trio in E flat for piano, flute, and violin; Trio in G for piano, flute, and violin; Quartet for piano, flute, violin, and cello; *Gran Fantasía,* for flute and piano; many romances for voice and piano; piano pieces.
Bibl.: A. Williams, *Antología de Compositores Argentinos,* Comisión Nacional de Cultura, Buenos Aires.
Sources: DM, EMA, GDM, MLA, MMLA

Aldana, José Manuel, Mexican composer and violinist; b.1758, Mexico City, Mexico; d.7 Feb 1810, Mexico City. He studied violin with Nicolás Gil de la Torre at the Mexico City Cathedral Colegio de Infantes.
Works: *Te Deum; Misa in D major;* religious music.

Bibl.: G. Saldívar, *Historia de la Música en México*, Mexico City, 1934. O. Mayer-Serra, *Panorama de la Música Mexicana*, Mexico City, 1941. R. Stevenson, *Music in Mexico*, New York, 1952.
Sources: GDM, MLA, MMLA

Alejandro, Esther, Puerto Rican composer; b.10 Mar 1947, New York City, New York, USA. She studied languages at the Univ. of Puerto Rico and music education and composition at the Cons. of Music of Puerto Rico under Luis Antonio Ramírez. In 1972, she studied with Nadia Boulanger at the American School of the Arts in Fontainebleau, France. Later she entered graduate school at the Univ. of California at Los Angeles to study composition and conducting.
Works (selective list): *Autobiografía de Trapo*, for orch. (1978); *Hecatombe*, tape (1978); *Suite de Danzas Antiguas*, for chamber orch. (1978); *Lares 1868,* for soloists, chorus, and orch. (1979); *El Zapatero Prodigioso*, for orch. (1980); *Gloria*, for chorus and orch. (1982); *Quietud*, for synthesizer (1985); *Choteo*, for female or male voices and synthesizer (1986); *Sonseis*, for orch. (1987); chamber music; piano pieces; songs; choruses.
Source: CPR

Alemann, Eduardo Armando, Argentine composer and music critic; b.12 Jan 1922, Buenos Aires, Argentina. He studied harmony and counterpoint with Erwin Leuchter, composition with Guillermo Graetzer and Carlos H. Veerhoff, and piano with Tila Montés. Member of the Asociación Argentina de Compositores. Founding member of the Asociación Jóvenes Compositores de la Argentina. Director and music critic of the newspaper *Argentinisches Tageblatt* of Buenos Aires.
Works (selective list): ***Orch.:*** *Sinfonietta Concertante*, for flute, oboe, clarinet, bassoon, and string orch. (1955); *Bahiana Nova*, for string orch. (1971); *Encuentro*, for clarinet and string orch. (1971); *Ensayo*, for string orch. (1974); *Cuatro Caminos*, for chamber orch. (1976); *Episodios*, for percussion and chamber orch. (1979); *Curriculum Vitae* (1982); *Balada*, for electric guitar and string orch. (1988); *Odisea* (1991). Chamber music; music for solo instruments; songs.
Sources: ISC, VMA

Alencar Pinto, Aloisio de, Brazilian pianist and composer; b.3 Feb 1912, Fortaleza, Ceará, Brazil. He studied in his native town and then in Rio de Janeiro, Brazil, at the National School of Music. Later he went to France where he studied at the Fontainebleau Cons. with Robert Casadesus and Jean Batalla and in Paris with Nadia Boulanger and Marguerite Long.
Works: Music for piano: *Romance Antigo; Calsa-Capricho; Nocturno; Folha de Album.* Songs.

Sources: HMB, MMLA

Alexander, Leni, Chilean composer of German origin; b.8 Jun, 1924, Breslau, Germany. She settled in Chile in 1939, where she studied with Free Focke, and later she studied in Paris, France, with Olivier Messiaen at the Paris Cons., and privately with René Leibowitz. She also took lessons from Bruno Maderna and Luigi Nono. She returned to Chile in 1955. Professor at the State Univ. and at the Goethe Inst., both of Santiago de Chile. From 1969 to 1970, she worked in the electronic studio of Columbia Univ., New York City, New York.
Works (selective list): *Stage: Música para el Teatro de Niños,* pantomime (1955); *Divertimento Rítmico,* incidental music for the theater (1956); *Las Tres Faces de la Luna,* ballet (1966). *Orch.: Música para Orquesta* (1951); *Cinco Epigramas* (1952); *Sinfonía Tríptica* (1954); *Divertimento Rítmico* (1956); *De la Muerte a la Mañana,* cantata for baritone and women chorus (1958); *Equinoccios* (1962); *Tessimenti,* cantata for soprano, contralto, and chamber orch. (1964); *Aconteceres* (1965); *Aulicio* (1968). Chamber music; piano pieces; music for percussion; songs.
Sources: HMC, IBCC, IEW, NGDWC

Alfonseca de Baris, Juan Bautista, Dominican composer; b.1810, Dominican Republic; d.1875, Dominican Republic. He is considered the father of Dominican national music. Instructor in the band of the national army.
Works: First Dominican patriotic song, *Himno de la Independencia* (1844), which became the first *Dominican National Anthem.*
Sources: DM, MLA, MMLA

Allende, Juan José, Argentine violinist and composer; b.1814; d.1880? He resided in Chile, Peru, and Ecuador.
Works: First *Ecuadorian National Anthem* (1865).
Source: EMA

Allende Blin, Juan, Chilean composer and teacher; b.24 Feb 1928, Santiago de Chile, Chile. He studied in Santiago de Chile with his uncle, Humberto Pedro Allende, and with Free Focke, and then composition with René Amengual and oboe with Pizzi at the National Cons. of Chile. In 1951, he went to Germany where he studied with Günter Bialas and Kurt Thomas at the Detmold Musikakademie, with Kaufmann in Hamburg, and with Olivier Messiaen in Darmstadt. In 1954, he returned to Chile and was appointed professor at the National Cons. of Chile. He returned to live permanently in Germany in 1957, and worked for radio stations in Hamburg and Frankfurt.

Works (selective list): *Sequence,* ballet (1961); *Profils,* ballet (1964); *Open Air and Water Music,* for an outdoor instrument, orgelwiese, which uses water-filled cylinders to produce aural and visual effects; chamber music; music for the organ; songs.
Sources: GDM, HMC

Allende Sarón, Adolfo, Chilean composer and music critic; b.29 Aug 1892, HMC (1890, DM), Santiago de Chile, Chile; d.1966, Santiago de Chile. Brother of Humberto Pedro Allende Sarón. He studied with Enrique Soro at the National Cons. of Music of Santiago de Chile.
Works (selective list): *Nocturno Chileno; Talagante,* set of 6 songs; *Cantos Populares Chilenos; Canciones Araucanas; Canciones y Rondas Infantiles;* music for orch.; chamber music; choruses.
Sources: DM, HMC, MLA

Allende Sarón, Humberto Pedro, Chilean composer; b.29 Jun 1885, Santiago de Chile, Chile; d.16 Aug 1959, Santiago de Chile. Brother of Adolfo Allende Sarón. He studied violin, music theory, harmony, and composition at the National Cons. of Chile of Santiago de Chile. Professor of violin at the Escuela Normal de Preceptores No.1, and of music at the Escuela Normal José A. Nuñez, both in Santiago de Chile. He taught harmony and composition at the National Cons. of Chile.
Works (selective list): *La Cenicienta,* chamber opera for children (1948). *Orch.:* Overture in G major (1904); Symphony in B flat (1910); *Escenas Campesinas Chilenas,* for orch. (1913); Cello concerto (1915); *La Voz de las Calles,* symphonic poem (1920); *Tres Tonadas,* (1925); *La Despedida,* for 2 sopranos and contralto (1934); Violin concerto (1942); Piano concerto (1945). String quartet (1945); 3 piano sonatas (1906-15); *12 Tonadas de Carácter Popular Chileno,* for piano (1918-22); chamber music; choral music; songs; piano pieces. *Books: Método Original de Iniciación Musical,* Santiago de Chile, 1937.
Bibl.: Special issue of Revista Musical Chilena, Sept. 1945. N. Slonimsky, *Humberto Allende, First Modernist of Chile, Musical America,* Aug. 1942. V. Salas Viú, *La Creación Musical en Chile,* Santiago, 1952.
Sources: BB, CTA2, DCM, DM, GDM, HMC, MLA, MMLA

Allica, Alfredo, Argentine composer and pianist; b.1945, Rosario, Prov. of Santa Fe, Argentina. He studied piano and composition at the Cons. Rivera of Rosario. In 1976, he graduated from the Escuela de Música de la Facultad de Humanidades y Artes of the National

Univ. of Rosario, where he studied piano with Ricardo Vidal, Antonio de Raco, and Aldo Antognazzi, and composition with Virtú Maragno. He also took composition lessons with Dante Grela. Professor of history of music and musical analysis at the Escuela de Música of the National Univ. of Rosario. Founding member of the Asociación Santafesina de Compositores.
Works: Music for orch.; chamber music; choruses; piano pieces.
Sources: CAMR

Almeida, Laurindo, Brazilian guitarist and composer; b.2 Sep 1917, Prainha, Sâo Paulo, Brazil; d.26 Jul 1995, Los Angeles, California, USA. In 1933, he settled in Rio de Janeiro, Brazil, and began piano studies with his mother. Later he entered the Escola Nacional do Música in Rio de Janeiro where he studied composition with Mario Castelnuovo Tedesco. In 1947, he moved to California, USA.
Works: More than 500 compositions, mainly for the guitar. Complete database of all his works is available at the Univ. of California Northridge Music Library.
Source: ISC

Almeida, Waldemar de, Brazilian composer; b.24 Aug 1904, Macau, Brazil; d.26 May 1975, Sâo Paulo, Brazil. He studied solfeggio and music theory with Lima Coutinho, piano with Luciano Gallet, and harmony with Agnelo França at the National Inst. of Music of Rio de Janeiro, Brazil. Later he studied piano with Rudolf Hauschild and harmony with Wilhelm Marx in Berlin, Germany, and piano with Vlado Perlemutter in Paris, France. Professor of *canto orfeónico* (male choral singing) and religious music at Colegio San Antonio and founder and director of the Musical Inst., both of Rio Grande del Norte, Natal, Brazil.
Works (selective list): *Paisagens de Leque,* for piano; *Danza de Indios,* for piano and orch.; *Cuatro Divertimentos,* for piano; *Danza de Mamulengos,* for piano (1940); religious music; piano pieces.
Sources: DM, MMLA

Almeida Prado, José Antonio de, Brazilian composer; b.8 Feb 1943, Santos, Brazil. He started music studies with his brother. At the age of eight he studied piano with Dinorah de Carvalho and at age fourteen he studied harmony with Osvaldo Lacerda and composition with Camargo Guarnieri. He studied in Darmstadt, Germany, with Györgi Ligeti and Lukas Foss, and later in Paris, France, he took some lessons with Nadia Boulanger and Olivier Messiaen. Director of the Municipal Cons. of Cubatâo, Sâo Paulo, Brazil, from 1973 to 1974. Professor of composition at the State Univ. of Campinas, Brazil, in 1974.

Works (selective list): *A Missa da Paz,* for chorus a cappella (1965); *Os Pequenos Funerais Cantantes,* for soloists, chorus, and orch. (1969); Sinfonía No.1 (1970); *Villegagnon* or *Les Isles Fortunées,* for soprano and orch. (1973); *Exoflora,* for piano and orch. (1974); *Aurora,* for piano and small chamber ensemble (1975); *Thérèse* or *O Amor de Deus,* oratorio (1975); Concerto for violin and orch. (1976); chamber music; piano pieces; choruses; songs.
Sources: GDM, HMB

Almouhian, Jean, Argentine composer and choral conductor of Greek origin. He settled in Argentina in 1947. He studied with Emilio Sampietro, Carlos Tuxen-Bang, Pedro Valenti Costa, Alberto Ginastera, and Roberto Kinsky. In 1960, he traveled to Armenia to study and research Armenian ethnic music.
Works (selective list): Sonata for clarinet and piano; Trio for wind instruments; Quintet for clarinet and strings; *Movimiento Sinfónico,* for orch.; piano pieces; songs; choruses.
Source: VMA

Alomía Robles, Daniel, Peruvian composer and ethnomusicologist; b.3 Jan 1871, Huánaco, Peru; d.17 Jul 1942, Lima, Peru. He studied in Lima with Claudio Rebagliati and in Buenos Aires, Argentina, with Felipe Pedrell. Chief of the Fine Arts Section of the Ministry of Public Education.
Works (selective list): *Illa-Cori,* opera; *El Amanecer Andino,* symphonic poem; *El Indio,* symphonic poem; *El Resurgimiento de los Andes,* symphonic poem; *Evocación en el Templo del Sol,* symphonic poem; folkloric music. He spent most of his life collecting indigenous songs of Peru, Ecuador, and Bolivia.
Bibl.: R. Holzmann, *Daniel Alomía Robles* and *La Obra Musical de Alomía Robles, Eco Musical,* Buenos Aires, July 1943. *Catálogo de las Obras de D. Alomía Robles, Boletín Bibliográfico de la Biblioteca Central de la Univ. Mayor de San Marcos,* Lima, July 1943.
Sources: BB, DM, GDM, MLA, MMLA

Alonso, Julia, Mexican composer, organist, pianist, and teacher; b.1889, Oaxaca, Mexico; d.? She studied at the National Cons. of Music of Mexico City, where she also taught organ, piano, and composition after graduating.
Works: Tonantzin, opera; 2 symphonies; 2 suites for chamber orch.; 2 string quartets.
Source: IEW

Alsina, Carlos Roqué, Argentine composer; b.19 Feb 1941, Buenos Aires, Argentina. He studied music with Teodoro Fuchs and electronic physics with Francisco Kröpfl in Buenos Aires. From 1964 to 1966, he lived in Berlin, Germany, where he studied with Luciano Berio. In 1951, he joined the *Agrupación Nueva Música* of Buenos Aires. From 1966 to 1968, he taught at the New York State Univ. at Buffalo, New York. In 1969, he founded the improvisatory group *New Phonic Art*, together with Vinko Globokar, Jean Pierre Drouet, and Michel Portal. He spent several years in Berlin and finally settled in Paris, France.

Works (selective list): *Stage: Texts 1967,* for soprano, flute, trombone, violin, cello, double bass, percussion, and piano (1967); *Fusión*, choreographic music for dancer, 2 pianos, and 2 percussionists (1974); *Encore,* musical spectacle (1976); *La Muraille,* opera (1981); *Del Tango,* azione scenica (1982). *Orch.: Three Pieces,* for strings (1964); *Symptom* (1969); *Dispersión* (1969); *Conquest,* for 4 instrumental soloists (1970); *Omnipotenz,* for chamber orch. (1971); *Schichten I and II* (1971, 1972); *Aproach,* for piano and percussion (1972); *Thema II,* for percussion and strings (1974-75); *Stücke* (1977); *Señales,* for piano and chamber orch. (1977); *Decisions,* for chamber orch. (1977); *Etudes,* for tape (1979); *Prima Sinforian,* for soprano, flute, and cello (1983); Piano concerto (1985). Chamber music; choral music.

Sources: BB, DCM, EMA

Alvarado López, Alberto M., Mexican violinist, conductor, and composer; b.10 Dec 1864, Durango, State of Durango, Mexico; d.18 Jun 1939, Durango. He began to study music very early in life with Pedro H. Ceniceros, and later he continued with Manuel Herrera. Conductor of the State Band of Durango.

Works (selective list): Overtures; fantasias; operas; operettas; symphonic pieces including *El Príncipe de Asturias* and *Cuauhtémoc.* Two waltzes, *Río Rosa* and *Recuerdo,* became internationally famous. *Angel Mujer; Almas Destrozadas; La Fiesta Encantadora; Suite Tropical; Corazón Latino.*

Sources: BB, GMM

Alvares Pinto, Luiz, Brazilian composer, teacher, and poet; b.1719, Recife, Brazil; d.1789?, Recife. He started music studies in his native town, and then he went to Portugal where he studied theory and composition with Henrique da Silva Esteves Negrão. He taught in Lisbon, Portugal, and was a cellist in the royal chapel ensemble. In 1762, he returned to Brazil and became a member of the Irmandade de Nossa Senhora do Livramento. In 1782, he was appointed *maestro de capilla* (chapelmaster) of San Pedro dos Clérigos in Recife, and in 1787, he founded the Irmandade de Santa Cecilia dos Músicos.

Works: Religious music: hymns; masses; Passion music; *Te Deum*; *Salve Regina. Amor Mal Correspondido*, musical comedy.

Bibl.: J.C. Diniz, *Revelaçâo de um Compositor Brasileiro do Século XVIII, Yearbook,* Inter-American Institute for Musical Research, Vol.4, 1968.
Source: GDM

Alvarez, Calixto, Cuban composer, pianist, and organist; b.15 Mar 1938, Santa Isabel de las Lajas, Cuba. He studied first in Santa Clara, Cuba, and then moved to the USA to continue his musical education. From 1967 to 1970, he studied in Poland with Andrzej Dobrowolski. In Cuba he also studied with Federico Smith and Leo Brouwer.
Works (selective list): Sonatina; Wind quintet; *Torus; Pocker; Stripofumios,* for chamber orch.; *Varsiflorius,* for chamber orch.; Trio.
Source: DMC

Alvarez, Ignacio, Argentine composer; b.1837, Mendoza, Prov. of Mendoza, Argentina; d.1888, Argentina. He studied under Ledesma in Santiago de Chile, Chile. Professor at the María Monastery and the High School of Mendoza.
Works: More than 100 works, in general suited for the salon repertoire: mazurkas; polkas; waltzes.
Source: DM

Alvarez, Luis Manuel, Puerto Rican composer and guitarist; b.31 Mar 1939, Humacao, Puerto Rico. He studied guitar with Moisés Cordero. He received Master's degrees in composition and ethnomusicology from the Univ. of Indiana at Bloomington, Indiana, where he studied with Héctor Tosar, Roque Cordero, Juan Orrego Salas, Bernard Hayden, Iannis Xenaquis, and John Eaton. Professor of guitar and composition at the Univ. of Puerto Rico.
Works (selective list): *La Creación,* for narrator and orch. (1974); *La Calle Poemario de Dalia Nieves,* for narrator, synthesizer, guitar, cuatro, and percussion (1975); *Ay, Ay, Ay, de mi Tierra,* ballet (1978); chamber music; music for solo instruments; piano pieces; songs.
Source: CPR

Alvarez, Rafael, Guatemalan composer; b.24 Oct 1858, Comalapa, Dept. of Chimaltenango, Guatemala; d.? He studied music theory with his father, Rosendo Alvarez, and later he studied harmony, orchestration, and composition with Emilio Dresner. Director of the Music School of Comalapa.
Works: Guatemalan National Anthem, 1887.
Sources: DM, MMLA

Alvarez Ríos, María, Cuban composer; b.5 Jun 1919, Tuinicú, Cuba. She began music studies very early in life, then attended the Univ. of Havana, Cuba, and the Univ. of Michigan, Ann Arbor, Michigan, where she received her doctorate in music.
Works (selective list): *Songs: Abrázame Amor; Anda Dí, Corazón; Ya no me Llamas; La Rosa y el Ruiseñor; Como se Duele;* poems by Nicolás Guillén. Music for the stage.
Source: DMC

Alvarez Sanabria, Carlos, Cuban composer; b.2 Mar 1945, Havana, Cuba. He studied flute, composition, and conducting at the National School of Art with Roberto Ondina, Emigdio Mayo, Federico Smith, and Roberto Valdés Arnau.
Works (selective list): *Orch.: M-267; Ser; Pueblo Invisible,* for chamber orch.; *Sobre Piedras; Grabados. Despedida a un Guerrillero,* for voice and piano. Incidental music for the theater and movies; music for voice soloists and chorus.
Source: DMC

Alves Lobo, Elías, Brazilian composer; b.1834, Itu, Prov. of Sâo Paulo, Brazil; d.1901, Brazil.
Works (selective list): *Missa de Sâo Pedro de Alcántara* (1858); *Noite de Sâo Joâo, opera* (1860); *A Louca,* opera; religious music; songs.
Source: MMLA

Alves Pinto, Luiz, Brazilian *maestro de capilla* (chapelmaster) and composer; b.1719, Brazil; d.1780, Brazil. Founder of the musical school of Pernambuco, Brazil.
Works: Te Deum; hymns; masses; sonatas; almost all of his works have been lost.
Sources: MMLA

Amat, José, Argentine composer, pianist, singer, and conductor of Spanish origin; b.Spain, settled in Buenos Aires, Argentina, in 1854; d.? Director of the Philharmonic Society of Buenos Aires until 1856. In 1854, he founded the musical journal *La Lira Argentina.*
Works: L'Autre Waterloo, opera; *Il Gondoliero,* opera; songs; piano pieces. *Books: Gramática Musical,* 1855.
Source: EMA

Amat, José, Brazilian composer of Spanish origin; b.Spain. Settled in Brazil in 1848. He founded the National Opera of Brazil and the Imperial Academy of Music in Rio de Janeiro.
Works: Mélodies Brésiliennes and *Les Nuits Brésiliennes,* songs (modinhas) written on poems by Gonçalves Días.
Sources: MLA, MMLA

Amelong, Juan Enrique, Argentine composer of German origin; b.1814, Hamburg, Germany; d.1906, Buenos Aires, Argentina. He settled in Argentina in 1838. Teacher of Manuelita Rosas, daughter of Juan Manuel de Rosas. He conducted choirs and promoted chamber music.
Works: Gran Fantasía y Variaciones, for piano; *El Carnaval de Buenos Aires,* for piano
Source: EMA

Amenábar Ruíz, Juan, Chilean composer; b.22 Jun 1922, Santiago de Chile, Chile. He started music studies with his father, Alfredo Amenábar Ossa, a cellist, and later he entered the Catholic Cons. of Santiago de Chile where he studied music theory and piano. From 1948 to 1952, he studied composition with Jorge Urrutia Blondel at the National Cons. of Music of Santiago de Chile. He was interested in electronic music and, in 1956, he created the Experimental Sound Workshop at the Catholic Univ. In 1958, he studied electronic music with Werner Meyer Eppler at the Univ. of Bonn, Germany. Board member and president of the National Association of Composers of Chile.
Works (selective list): *Electronic music: Los Peces* (1957); *Klesis (Invitación)* (1968); *El Vigía del Personal* (1968); *Música Contínua* (1969); *High Key* (1970); *Sueño de un Niño* (1970); *Amacata* (1972); *Ludus Vocalis* (1972). *Misa Litúrgica,* for male chorus and ensemble (1964); *Sol de Septiembre,* for male chorus, ensemble, and percussion (1964); instrumental music.
Bibl.: R. Escobar, *Instituto Chileno-Alemán de Cultura, Revista Musical Chilena,* 1970.
Sources: CTA17, DCM, GDM, HMC

Amengual Astaburuaga, René, Chilean composer; b.2 Sep 1911, Santiago de Chile, Chile; d.2 Aug 1954, Santiago de Chile. He studied piano with Alberto Spikin and Rosita Renard, 1923-34, and composition with Humberto Allende, 1929-39, at the National Cons. of Music of Santiago de Chile. He studied musical aesthetics and pedagogy at the Teachers College of Columbia Univ. of New York. Secretary of the Inst. de Extensión Musical of Chile, director of the Chamber Music Section at the same Inst., and professor of piano and composition at the National Cons. of Music of the Univ. of Chile.
Works (selective list): *Preludio,* for orch. (1934); Sonatina for piano (1938); *Introducción y Allegro,* for 2 pianos (1939); Concerto for piano and orch. (1942); *El Vaso,* for voice and chamber orch. (1944); 2 string quartets (1941, 1942); Sonata for violin and piano (1943); Concerto for harp and orch. (1943); choral music; piano pieces; songs.

18 - Amicola

Bibl.: M. Aguilar, *La Evolución Estilística en la Obra de René Amengual, Revista Musical Chilena,* 1954. V. Salas Viú, *La Obra de René Amengual del Neoclasicismo al Expresionismo, Revista Musical Chilena,* 1964.
Sources: BB, DCM, DM, HMC, MLA, MMLA

Amicola, Víctor Juan Carlos, Argentine composer; b.20 Oct 1931, Buenos Aires, Argentina. He studied violin with Eduardo Acedo and composition with Carlos Suffern. Vice president of the Asociación de Jóvenes Compositores de la Argentina. Consultant for SADAIC.
Works (selective list): *Una Luz en los Espejos,* opera (1989); *Temperamentos,* for string orch. (1963); *Diálogos,* for string orch. (1964); *Oda a García Lorca,* for speaker, female chorus, and orch. (1965); *Impromptu,* for orch. (1968); *Odas sin Destino,* for orch. (1982); *Sueños Recurrentes,* for orch. (1984); *Juegos,* for orch. (1985); chamber music; piano pieces; songs; music for solo instruments.
Sources: ISC, VMA

Anckermann, Carlos, Cuban clarinetist, violinist, and composer of Spanish origin; b.10 Mar 1829, Palma de Mallorca, Spain; d.17 Feb 1909, Havana, Cuba. He settled in Cuba in 1847. First violin at the orch. of the Teatro de Tacón and professor at the Cons. Hubert de Blanck, both in Havana.
Works: Gran Misa, for 4 voices, known as the *Misa de los Asturianos*; several zarzuelas.
Sources: DMC, MMLA

André, José, Argentine composer, teacher, and music critic; b.17 Jan 1881, Buenos Aires, Argentina; d.13 Jul 1944, Buenos Aires. He studied in Buenos Aires with Alberto Williams. He received an official scholarship to study at the Schola Cantorum of Paris, France, with Vincent D'Indy, Florent Schmidt, and Albert Roussel. Founding member of the Sociedad Nacional de Música, renamed in 1915 Asociación Argentina de Compositores. Music critic for the daily newspaper *La Nación* of Buenos Aires. Professor of composition at the National Cons. of Music Carlos López Buchardo of Buenos Aires.
Works (selective list): *Santa Rosa de Lima,* cantata for soloists, choir, and orch. (1930); *Impresiones Porteñas,* for orch. (1929); Quintet for strings and piano (1923); series of songs on French poems by Paul Verlaine, Alfred de Musset, and Tristan Klingsor.
Sources: CA, EMA, MLA, MMLA

Andrés, Alfredo, Argentine composer and pianist; b.25 Aug 1934, Buenos Aires, Argentina. He studied at the Cons. Williams in 1941, then he entered the National Cons. of Music Carlos López Buchardo, both of Buenos Aires, where he studied piano and graduated in 1950. He also studied piano with Jorge de Lalewicz, harmony with Julián Bautista, counterpoint and fugue with José Torre Bertucci, and rhythm with Athos Palma. Professor at the Provincial Cons., Prov. of Buenos Aires, and at the National Cons. of Music Carlos López Buchardo.

Works (selective list): *Dos Canciones,* on poems by Rafael Alberti (1950); *Momentos Musicales,* for piano (1950); *Coral de los Angeles,* text by González Lanuza, for voice and piano (1951); Sonata for piano (1951); *Movimiento Sinfónico,* for orch. (1951); *El Ciervo Herido,* text by Leopoldo Marechal, for voice and string orch. (1953); Quintet for violin, viola, cello, oboe, and clarinet (1954); *Dos Coros Populares,* for 4 female voices; *El Espantapájaros,* farce for 2 pianos, trumpet, trombone, and percussion.

Source: CA

Andrino, José Escolástico, Guatemalan organist and composer; b.1837, Guatemala; d.14 Jul 1862. He settled in El Salvador where he spent most of his life. He studied music with his brother, Máximo Andrino. In 1845, he established a school of music in El Salvador and, as a result, is considered the founder of musical art in that country.

Works (selective list): *La Mora Generosa,* opera; *Lejos de la Patria; Brisas Guatemaltecas; Recuerdos del Hogar;* religious vocal music.

Bibl.: V. Miguel Díaz, *Las Bellas Artes en Guatemala,* Guatemala, 1934. R. González Sol, *Historia del Arte de la Música en El Salvador,* San Salvador, 1940.

Sources: MLA, MMLA

Angelis, Arturo de, Argentine composer and conductor of Italian origin; b.1879, Perusa, Italy; d.1916, Buenos Aires, Argentina. He studied in Bologna, Italy.

Works: Beatrice, lyric comedy.

Source: MMLA

Angulo, Héctor, Cuban composer; b.3 Sep 1932, Santa Clara, Cuba. He started music studies in Santa Clara and later he continued them in Havana, Cuba. He also entered architecture school but did not finish. In 1959, he obtained a scholarship to study at the Manhattan School of Music in New York City. He returned to Cuba in 1964 and continued studies with Leo Brouwer. Musical consultant for the Teatro de Guiñol of Havana.

Works (selective list): *Ibeyi Ana,* chamber opera for puppets; Trio for flute, violin, and piano; Sonata for 11 instruments; String quartet;

Variations for string orch.; *Poema,* for 6 instruments; *Sonera,* for piano; *Son,* for piano; Sonata for piano; *Dos Canciones,* on poems by Nicolás Guillén; *Poemas Africanos.*
Source: DMC

Anido, María Luisa, Argentine guitarist and composer; b.1908, Morón, Prov. of Buenos Aires, Argentina. She studied guitar with Domingo Prat and Miguel Llobet.
Works (selective list): *Music for guitar: Pericones; Aires Norteños; De mi Tierra; Gato; Canciones de Yucatán; Barcarola; Preludio; Canción de Cuna; Estudio; Triste; Aire de Vidalita; Estilo; Tres Preludios; Camperos; Vidala; Danza; Variaciones de Gato; Chacarera; Preludio Criollo; Preludio Pampeano; Canto de la Llanura; Boceto Indígena; Catamarqueña; Misachico; Santiagueña; Variaciones Camperas.* She transcribed works by Mendelssohn, Debussy, McDowell, Grieg, Bach, Scharwenka, Mozart, Händel, and Scarlatti for the guitar.
Sources: CA, EMA

Anleu Díaz, Enrique, Guatemalan composer and violinist; b.1940, Guatemala City, Guatemala. He studied solfeggio, harmony, counterpoint, composition, violin, history of music, and orch. conducting with Augusto Ardenois, José Castañeda, Enrique Raudales, Humberto Ayestas, and José Luis Abelar at the National Cons. of Music in Guatemala City. He played the violin at the Cons. Orch. and the Guatemala Symphony Orch. Founding member of the *Ernest Bloch Quartet.*
Works (selective list): *Orch: Adagio,* for strings (1960); *Obertura para el Siglo XX* (1963); *Homenaje a Debussy* (1963); 3 symphonies (1967, 1968, 1970); *Ciudades Mayas,* suite (1967); *La Fundación de Guatemala* (1968); *Dos Parábolas Sinfónicas* (1969); Sinfonietta (1969); *Tres Espacios* (1970); Concerto for viola (1968); Concerto Grosso for violin, viola, cello, and strings (1971). Chamber music; piano pieces; songs.
Source: CTA18

Anton, Susana, Argentine composer and teacher; b.19 Aug 1947, Guaymallén, Prov. of Mendoza, Argentina. She studied at the Music School of the National Univ. of Cuyo in Mendoza, Prov. of Mendoza, with Miguel Francese and Elifio Rosaenz. She took classes with Jorge Fontenla and Eduardo Tejeda. She also studied electronic music with Francisco Kröpfl. Professor at the Music Schools of the National Univ. of San Juan, Prov. of San Juan, and Cuyo.
Works (selective list): *El Cíclope,* for narrators, chorus, and orch. (1972-73); *Paradigma,* for orch. (1973); *Carnaval,* for orch. (1976);

Vanidad, for mixed chorus and chamber ensemble (1979-80); chamber music; piano pieces; choruses.
Source: ISC

Antunes, Jorge, Brazilian composer; b.23 Apr 1942, Rio de Janeiro, State of Guanabara, Brazil. He studied violin, composition, and conducting at the Federal Univ. of Rio de Janiero, Brazil, with Henrique Morelembaum, José Siqueira, and Eleazar de Carvalho. From 1969 to 1970, he studied electronic music at the Inst. Di Tella of Buenos Aires, Argentina, under Alberto Ginastera, Luis de Pablo, and Gerardo Gandini. From 1970 to 1973, he continued his electronic studies at the Univ. of Utrecht, Netherlands, and at the *Groupe de Recherches Musicales* in Paris, France. Professor of composition and director of the Electronic Music Dept. at the Univ. of Brasilia, Brazil.
Works (selective list): *Contato,* chamber opera (1966-68); *Sarau No.1 and No.2,* for orch. (1962-63); *Dissoluçâo,* for chamber orch., percussion, and magnetic tape (1966); *Tres Eventos da Luz Branca,* for chamber orch. and magnetic tape (1967); *Cromoplastofonía,* for orch., tape, and moving object (1967-68); *Acusmorfose,* for chamber orch. (1968); *Isomerism,* for chamber orch. (1970); *Tartinia MCMLXX,* for violin and orch. (1970); choruses; chamber music; music for magnetic tape; integral art (use of sounds, colors, odors, and flavors).
Sources: CTA16, GDM

Aponte Ledée, Rafael, Puerto Rican composer; b.15 Oct 1938, Guayama, Puerto Rico. He studied composition with Cristóbal Halffter at the Madrid Cons., Spain, 1957-64, and with Alberto Ginastera at the Latin American Center of Advanced Musical Studies at the Di Tella Inst. of Buenos Aires, Argentina. In 1967, in San Juan, Puerto Rico, he founded the *Fluxus Group* for the promotion of new music, with Francis Schwartz. From 1968 to 1974, he taught composition and theory at the Univ. of Puerto Rico and at the Music Cons. of Puerto Rico.
Works (selective list): *Tema y Seis Diferencias,* for piano (1963); *Dialogantes 1,* for flute and violin (1965); *Elegía,* for 13 strings (1965); *Presagio de Pájaros Muertos,* for narrator and tape (1966); *Epithasis,* for 3 oboes, 2 trombones, double bass, and 3 percussionists (1967); *Dialogantes 2,* for 3 flutes, 3 trombones, and 3 clarinets (1968); *La Ventana Abierta,* for 3 mezzo-sopranos, 3 flutes, clarinet, trumpet, 2 percussionists, celesta, piano, violin, cello, and double bass (1968); *Streptomicyne,* for soprano, flute, clarinet, trumpet, and piano (1970); *SSSSS,* for double bass solo, 3 flutes, trumpet, and percussion (1971); *Volúmenes,* for piano (1971); *Elvira en Sombras,* for piano and orch. (1973); *Estravagario, In Memoriam Salvador*

Allende, for orch. and tape (1973); *Cuídese de los Angeles que Caen,* musique concrète (1974); *Los Huevos de Pandora,* for clarinet and tape (1974); *El Palacio en Sombras,* for orch. without violins and cellos (1977); *La Ventana Abierta,* for orch. (1986); Cantata for soloists and orch. (1986); *Dos Cuentos Para Orquesta* (1986); *A Flor de Piel,* for soprano, mezzo-soprano, flute, clarinet, horn, violin, cello, and double bass (1986); chamber music; piano pieces.
Sources: BB, CPR, CTA17, DCM

Arandia Navarro, Jorge, Argentine composer; b.1929, Buenos Aires, Argentina. He studied with Alejandro Szenkar, Roberto García Morillo, Roberto Kinsky, Alberto Ginastera, Bruno Maderna, and Olivier Messiaen.
Works (selective list): *Intemperancias,* for soprano and chamber ensemble (1962); *Playas Rítmicas No.1,* for piano (1963); *Combinatoria,* for piano and woodwind quartet (1964); *Forma Sonora de Ondina,* for soprano, children's choir, magnetic tape, and orch. (1964); *El Martes Fantástico,* ballet (1964-65); String quartet (1965); Concerto for piano and orch. (1965); *Espacios de Tiempo,* for two pianos (1965); *Playas Rítmicas No.2,* for piano (1966).
Source: EMA

Araujo, Gina de (Araujo Regis d'Oliveira), Brazilian singer and composer; b.3 Apr 1890, Rio de Janeiro, Brazil; d.1960, Rio de Janeiro. She studied voice in Paris, France, with Jules Massenet, André Gédalge, and Jean de Reszke.
Works (selective list): *Evocaçâo,* symphonic poem; *Cega Rega,* for orch. (1943); sacred music; piano pieces; songs.
Source: IEW

Araújo Porto Alegre, Ignacio Francisco de, Brazilian composer; b.1854, Brazil; d.1900, Brazil. He studied music in Portugal with Daddi and Monteiro de Almeida, and in Florence, Italy, with Teódulo Mabellini and Tocchinardi. Professor of solfeggio and choral singing at the National Inst. of Music of Brazil. Music critic for *Diario de Noticias.*
Works: Fariboles, series of pieces for piano; choruses.
Source: MMLA

Arce Revilla, Luis Felipe, Bolivian composer and teacher; b. 25 Aug 1900, Potosí, Bolivia; d.1 Sep 1966, La Paz, Bolivia. He studied at the National School for Teachers Mariscal Sucre of Chuquisaca, Bolivia. Later he studied at the National Cons. of Music Carlos López Buchardo of Buenos Aires, Argentina. Director of the Dirección Nacional de Educación Musical of Bolivia for 30 years, a position

that he had to relinquish due to an accident that damaged his spine. After his recovery he was appointed director of the National Cons. of Music, a position kept for four years until his death in 1966. Founder of music schools in Tarija and Oruro, Bolivia.
Works: *Canto a Eduardo Avaroa*; *Canto a los Próceres*; *Canción a Murillo*; *Evocación al Maestro*.
Source: CB

Ardévol, José, Cuban composer of Spanish origin; b.13 Mar 1911, Barcelona, Spain; d.7 Jan 1981, Havana, Cuba. Settled in Cuba in 1930. He studied with his father, Fernando Ardévol, director of the Chamber Orch. of Barcelona. He studied conducting with Hermann Scherchen. Director of the Chamber Orch. of Havana, which he founded in 1934. Editor-in-chief of the journal *Musicalia*. Music critic for the newspaper *Acción*. Professor at the Municipal Cons. of Havana. National Director for Music until 1965. Dean of the Dept. of Music of the Inst. Superior de Arte of Havana.
Works (selective list): Concerto for three pianos and orch. (1938); 3 symphonies (1943, 1945, 1946); *Variaciones Sinfónicas,* for cello and orch. (1951); *El Son,* for violin and orch. (1952); *Tríptico de Santiago,* for orch. (1953); *Música,* for chamber orch. (1957); *Música para Pequeña Orquesta* (1958); *Cantos de la Revolución* (1962); *Por Viet-Nam,* words by Fidel Castro (1966); *Música,* for guitar and chamber orch. (1967); *Movimientos Sinfónicos Nos.1-2* (1967, 1969); *Cantata Che Comandante* (1968); *Cantata Lenin* (1970); *Tríptico Sinfónico de Pinar del Río*; *La Victoria de Playa Girón,* cantata; chamber music; piano pieces; songs.
Sources: BB, CTA1, DCM, DM, DMC, GDM, MLA, MMLA

Arena, José, Argentine composer of Italian origin; b.1869, Palmi, Calabria, Italy; d.1954, Buenos Aires, Argentina. He settled in Argentina at the end of the 19th century. Director of military bands.
Works: *Military Marches: Curu-Malal; Suipacha; General Belgrano.*
Source: EMA

Aretz de Ramón y Rivera, Isabel, Argentine composer and ethnomusicologist; b.13 Apr 1909, Buenos Aires, Argentina. She studied piano with Rafael González, harmony, counterpoint, and composition with Athos Palma, and orchestration with Heitor Villa-Lobos in Buenos Aires. She received a Ph.D. in musicology in 1967 from the Catholic Univ. of Buenos Aires. She also studied anthropology, folklore, and musicology with José Imbellone, Enrique Palavecino, and Carlos Vega at the Argentine Museum of Natural Sciences of Buenos Aires. In 1933, she entered the Musicology Section of the Argentine Museum of Natural Sciences, under the

direction of Carlos Vega. She devoted most of her time to research Hispanic American music and its sources. She served as an associate member of the Argentine Inst. of Musicology, 1938-50. First professor of ethnomusicology at the National Dance Inst. of Argentina, 1950-52. In 1953, she settled in Caracas, Venezuela, and was appointed research fellow in ethnomusicology and folklore at the National Folklore Inst. of Venezuela. In 1965, she became director of the Folklore Dept. of the Inst. Nacional de Cultura y Bellas Artes in Caracas. In 1970, she was appointed director of the Inter-American Inst. of Ethnomusicology and Folklore.
Works (selective list): *Ballets: El Llamado de la Tierra* (1954); *Tocuyana* (1957); *Ahonaya* (1958); *Movimientos de Percusión* (1960); *Páramo* (1961). *Simiente,* cantata for narrator, choir, and orch. (1964). *Orch.: Puneñas* (1937); *Dos Acuarelas* (1939); *Serie Criolla* (1949); *Soneto de la Fe en Cristo* (1956); *Chimiterias* (1959). *Chamber music: Altipampa* (1936); *Tres en Sonata* (1965); Suite (1966). Piano pieces; songs. *Books: Música Tradicional Argentina: Tucumán, Historia y Folklore,* Buenos Aires, 1946; *El Folklore Musical Argentino,* Buenos Aires, 1953; *Manual de Folklore Venezolano,* Caracas, 1952; *Cantos Navideños en el Folklore Venezolano,* Caracas, 1962; *Instrumentos Musicales en Venezuela,* Caracas, 1967; *La Artesanía en Venezuela,* Caracas, 1967; *El Traje en Venezuela,* Caracas, 1972; *El Tamunangue,* Barquisimeto, 1976.
Sources: BB, CTA17, DM, EMA, GDM, MLA, NGDWC

Argüello Montero, Antonio, Costa Rican composer, pianist, and lecturer; b.31 Aug 1906, San José, Costa Rica. He studied piano with Alvise Castegnaro, David Sequeira, and Guillermo Aguilar Machado. Pianist of the Orquesta de Músicos Profesionales, society of which he was president in 1936, and secretary, 1940-43.
Works: *Viuda Desnuda,* musical comedy (1942); *Los Refugiados,* zarzuela (1943); *Mariposa Trágica,* ballet piece (1943).
Source: MMLA

Arias, Luis, Argentine composer; b.16 Jul 1940, Buenos Aires, Argentina. He studied with Alberto Ginastera, Gerardo Gandini, and Roberto Caamaño at the Facultad de Artes y Ciencias Musicales of the Argentine Catholic Univ., 1962- 66, and also at the Centro Latinoamericano de Altos Estudios Musicales of the Inst. Di Tella, both in Buenos Aires. Professor at the Provincial Cons. of Buenos Aires and at the Graduate School of Fine Arts of the National Univ. of La Plata, both in the Prov. of Buenos Aires, Argentina.

Works (selective list): *Orch: Introducción y Cortejo* (1960); *Isofonías* (1965); *Fonosíntesis II* (1966); *Polarizaciones* (1972); *Transiciones IV* (1973); *Ricercare's Blues* (1976); *Contactos II* (1980); *Equisonancias III,* for mixed chorus (1982); *Introducción y Passacaglia* (1986). *Chamber orch.: Tres Movimientos* (1962); *Elegía* (1963); *Variaciones* (1964); *Contactos IV* (1981). Chamber music; music for solo instruments; choruses.
Sources: EMA, ISC

Arias, Luis Felipe, Guatemalan composer and teacher; b.23 Aug 1870, Guatemala de la Asunción, Guatemala; d.24 Mar 1908, assasinated in Guatemala City, Guatemala. He studied piano, violin, and harmony at the Royal Cons. of Naples, Italy. When he returned to Guatemala in 1901, he was appointed director of the National Cons. of Guatemala, a position held for ten years.
Works: Danse Mauresque, for orch.; *Himno a Minerva,* for chorus; piano pieces.
Sources: HMG, MLA

Arias Quintero, Carlos Efraín, Panamanian composer; b.2 Feb 1903, Ciudad de David, Panama. He studied at the Colegio La Salle of Panama, Panama City, and graduated from the Real Academia de Santa Cecilia of Rome, Italy, in 1932. Professor of music in several schools in Panama. Professor of piano and deputy director of a cons. in Ecuador.
Works: Religious compositions; preludes; waltzes.
Source: MMLA

Arizaga, José Tomás, Argentine composer of Spanish origin; b.Guipúzcoa, Spain; d.? In the early 19th century he settled in Argentina.
Works: Grand Minuet and Valse (1830), dedicated to Juan Manuel de Rosas. Songs published in the *Cancionero Argentino* (1838): *La Niña Enferma; El Recuerdo; La Ultima Tarde; A los Lechuginos Enamorados; Vidalita; A una Lágrima.*
Source: EMA

Arizaga, Rodolfo, Argentine composer and music critic; b.11 Jul 1926, Buenos Aires, Argentina; d.12 May 1985, Buenos Aires. He studied with Alberto Williams, José Gil, Luis Gianneo, and Teodoro Fuchs in Buenos Aires. In Paris, France, he studied with Nadia Boulanger, Olivier Messiaen, and Ginette Martenot. He also studied law and philosophy. Music critic for the daily newspaper *El Clarín* and the weekly magazine *Primera Plana.* Founding member of Asociación de Conciertos de Cámara, Seminario de Jóvenes Músicos

Argentinos, Unión de Compositores de la Argentina, and Consejo Argentino de Música. Professor at the Graduate Inst. of Music of the National Univ. of Rosario, Prov. of Santa Fe, and at the Univ. del Salvador of Buenos Aires.

Works (selective list): *Stage: Jacquinot,* ballet (1945); *Prometeo,* dramatic poem (1948); *Prometeo 45,* opera (1958); *El Ombligo de los Limbos, la Momia y una Encuesta* (1969); *Paralaxi* (1971). **Orch.:** 2 chorals (1945); *Pequeño Vals en Tono Gris* (1948); *Sonada de la Anunciación* (1949-51); *Tango* (1951); *Serenata* (1953); *Passacaglia* (1953); *Scherzo de Juguete* (1954); *Delires,* cantata (1957); *Serranillas del Jaque*
(1958); Concerto for piano (1963); *Tientos para Santa María)* (1965); *Música para Cristóbal Colón* (1966); *Hymnus,* string (1970). Chamber music; choruses; songs; piano pieces; music for solo instruments; incidental music for 20 theatrical works and 5 movies.
Sources: BB, CA, CTA5, DCM, EMA

Arizti Sobrino, Cecilia, Cuban composer, pianist, and teacher; b.28 Oct 1856, Havana, Cuba; d.30 Jun 1930, Havana. She studied music with her father, Fernando Arizti, and with Francisco Fuente and Nicolás Ruíz Escudero. Professor at the Peyrellade Cons. of Music of Havana.
Works (selective list): Trio; *Impromptu in F minor; Vals Lento, Romanza, Nocturno, and Capricho,* for piano; chamber music; piano pieces; songs.
Sources: DMC, NGDWC

Arredondo, José María, Dominican composer and organist; b.1840, Dominican Republic; d.1924, Dominican Republic. Director of the Military Band and chorus master at the Cathedral of Santo Domingo (Ciudad Trujillo), Dominican Republic.
Works (selective list): *Dominican National Anthem. El Calambanche,* zarzuela; overtures; zarzuelas; marches; popular pieces.
Sources: DM, MLA, MMLA

Arredondo Miura, Clodomiro, Dominican composer; b.1864, Dominican Republic; d.1935, Dominican Republic.
Works: Religious music; marches; waltzes; indigenous barcarollas.
Source: MLA

Arto, Francisco Rodrigo, Venezuelan composer of Spanish origin; b.17 May 1938, Valtierra, Navarra, Spain. He began music studies at the Victoria Eugenia Cons. in Granada, Spain. In Caracas, Venezuela, he continued to study harmony, counterpoint, and fugue with Vicente Emilio Sojo, and later he studied with Evencio Castellanos at the

Escuela Superior de Música José Angel Lamas. Professor at the José Angel Lamas Cons., the Lino Gallardo Music Academy, and the Univ. Inst. for Musical Studies, all in Caracas.
Works (selective list): *Orch.: Hoy nos Ha Nacido un Salvador,* cantata for soloists and chorus (1977); *Lamentación en el Mar,* cantata for chorus (1977); *Tres Antífonas de Santa Cecilia,* for soprano and double chorus (1977); *La Epopeya de la Espiga,* choral-symphonic poem (1979); *Churum-Meru,* symphonic poem (1981); *Itinerario Místico de Santa Teresa de Avila,* symphonic poem (1982); *Doliente Amada,* for voice and chamber orch. (1983); *Himno al Santísimo Sacramento,* choral-symphonic poem (1983); Mandolin concerto (1984); *Escorzos Sonoros* (1987); *Eguara,* symphonic poem (1989); Harp concerto (1990); *Cantiga de la Pasión,* for soprano and chorus (1991); *Isabel La Católica, Reina de España,* symphonic poem for soprano (1991); Clarinet concerto (1993); Piano concerto (1993). Chamber music; religious hymns; piano pieces; music for solo instruments; sacred songs; choral music, a cappella and accompanied by organ; songs.
Source: ISC

Ascone, Vicente, Uruguayan composer of Italian origin; b.16 Aug 1897, Siderno, Calabria; d.5 Mar 1979, Montevideo, Uruguay. He studied trumpet with Aquiles Gubitosi at the Cons. La Lira, and harmony and composition with Luis Sambucetti at the Verdi Inst., both in Montevideo. Director of the Municipal Band and director of the Municipal School of Music, both in Montevideo. First trumpet of the orch. of the SODRE. Professor of harmony and composition at the Verdi Inst.
Works (selective list): 5 operas, including *Paraná Guazú* (1931); 3 symphonies (1945, 1955, 1959); *Preludio y Marcha de los Brahamines* (1924); *Suite Uruguaya* (1926); *Farsa Sentimental y Grotesca* (1927); *Salmo de David,* for soloist, female chorus, wind instruments, and percussion (1931); *Cantos del Atardecer,* for orch. (1933); *Nocturno Nativo,* ballet (1934); *Acentos de América,* symphonic poem (1941); *Sobre el Río Uruguay,* symphonic poem (1946); *Politonal,* for piano and orch. (1967); Trumpet concerto (1969); Violin concerto (1970); songs; piano pieces.
Sources: BB, BHMCU, CTA16, DCM, DM, MLA, MMLA, MU

Astuni, Silvia, Argentine composer; b.1959, Rosario, Prov. of Santa Fe, Argentina. She studied composition with Dante Grela at the Escuela de Música de la Facultad de Humanidades y Artes of the National Univ. of Rosario. She also took some courses with Mariano Etkin, Carmelo Saitta, and Alcides Lanza. Founding member of the Asociación Santafesina de Compositores and member of the

Agrupación de Música Contemporánea Klank of Rosario. Teacher at the Escuela Municipal de Música Juan Bautista Massa, the Escuela de Música of the National Univ., and the Escuela Nacional de Música, all of Rosario.
Works (selective list): *Tres Piezas,* for 2 percussionists (1982); *Diáfana Latencia,* for orch. (1987); *Tinku,* for mixed chorus (1989); chamber music; music for solo instruments; piano pieces.
Sources: CAMR

Asuar, José Vicente, Chilean composer; b.20 Jul 1933, Santiago de Chile, Chile. He studied composition with Jorge Urrutia Blondel at the National Cons. of Santiago de Chile and in Germany, with Boris Blacher at the Hochschule für Musik of Berlin, and with Jacques Wildberger at the Karlsruhe Hochschule für Musik. He also studied engineering in Chile and in Germany. From 1963 to 1965, he was professor of acoustics and contemporary music at the National Cons. of Santiago de Chile. From 1965 to 1968, he directed a studio for electronic music in Caracas, Venezuela. From 1968 to 1972, he taught a course in sound technology at the Univ. of Chile.
Works (selective list): *Estudio Aleatorio,* for electronic tape (1962); *Heterophonías,* for orch. (1965); Octet for 4 flutes and 4 percussionists (1966); *Guararia Repano,* for indigenous indian instruments (1968); *Formas I-II,* for computer and orch. (1971, 1972).
Sources: BB, DCM, GDM, HMC

Atehortúa, Blas Emilio, Colombian composer, conductor, and teacher; b.3 Oct 1933, Medellín, Colombia. He studied at the Cons. of the National Univ. of Colombia in Bogotá, Colombia, with Olav Roots, Andrés Pardo Tovar, Fabio González Zuleta, and José Rozo Contreras. Later he studied at the Inst. Torcuato Di Tella of Buenos Aires, Argentina, with Alberto Ginastera, Iannis Xenakis, and Luigi Nono. Professor at the Univ. Pedagógica y Tecnológica of Tunja and director of the Bogotá Cons., both in Colombia.
Works (selective list): *Concertante,* for timpani and chamber orch. (1968); *Estudios Sinfónicos,* for orch. (1968); Concerto for string orch. (1970); *Divertimento,* for string orch. (1970); *Diagramas,* for orch. (1971); *Partita 72,* for strings (1972); *Dos Pastiches a la Manera de Vivaldi y Haydn,* for strings (1974); *Sh'ma Deuteronomio 6-4,* for orch. (1976); *Soggetto da Vivaldi,* for orch. (1977); *Suite Colombiana,* for orch. (1977); choruses; chamber music; piano pieces; electronic music.
Sources: CA19, GDM

Atienza y Pineda, Francisco de, Mexican composer probably of Spanish origin; b.c.1657, Spain?; d.Mar 1726, Puebla, Mexico. He was ordained a priest. In 1703, he left Mexico City and settled in Puebla where he was appointed *maestro de capilla* (chapelmaster), a position he held until his death in 1726.
Works: *Religious music:* masses; motets; vesper psalms; hymns; villancicos.
Bibl.: R. Stevenson, *Mexico City Cathedral Music: 1600-1750, The Americas,* 1964. A.R. Catalyne, *Music of the 16th through the 18th Centuries in the Cathedral of Puebla, Yearbook,* Inter-American Institute for Musical Research, 1966.
Source: GDM

Auza León, Atiliano, Bolivian composer and violinist; b.5 Oct 1928, Sucre, Bolivia. He studied at the Escuela Normal of Sucre and graduated as music teacher in 1950. In La Paz, Bolivia, he studied violin with Maldonado and counterpoint with Eisner, and later, upon returning to Sucre, he studied piano with Thorrez and composition with Hochman. In Buenos Aires, Argentina, he studied with Alberto Ginastera, Roger Sessions, Maurice Le Roux, and Mario Davidovsky at the Inst. Torcuato Di Tella.
Works (selective list): *Trío Breve* (1964); *Madrigal y Cueca,* choral (1965); *Anfiblástula; Cinco Epigramas Griegos; Tránsito; Preludio, Invención, Passacaglia y Postludio,* on a 12-note series of Dallapiccola. **Books:** *Dinámica Musical en Bolivia,* La Paz, 1967.
Source: GDM

Avilés, Danilo, Cuban composer and clarinetist; b.5 May 1948, Holguín, Cuba. He began to study composition with Argeliers León, and later he entered the Escuela Superior de Arte of Havana, Cuba, where he studied with José Ardévol and José Loyola.
Works (selective list): *Mujer Nueva* and *Tres Poemas Mínimos,* for voice and piano; *Dibujos* and *Variaciones,* for string quartet; *Esa Sangre en las Calles de Santiago,* for soprano and orch.; *Siento un Bombo Mamita,* for symphony orch.; music for children; songs; incidental music.
Sources: DMC

Axenfeld, Salvador, Argentine composer; b.30 Nov 1913, Buenos Aires, Argentina. He studied under Leopoldina Julia Roller, and later with Miguel Mastroggiani and Athos Palma at the National Cons. of Music Carlos López Buchardo of Buenos Aires.
Sources: DM, EMA

Ayala Pérez, Daniel, Mexican violinist, composer, and conductor; b.21 Jul 1906, Abala, State of Yucatán, Mexico; d.20 Jun 1975, Veracruz, Mexico. He studied at the Music School of Mérida, Mexico. Later he studied violin with Silvestre Revueltas and Ezequiel Sierra and composition with Manuel Ponce, Candelario Huízar, and Julián Carrillo at the National Cons. of Music of Mexico City, Mexico. Violinist with the Mexico Symphony Orch. in 1931, and professor of music at the Dept. of Fine Arts, both in Mexico City. In 1934, he formed the *Grupo de los Cuatro* (Group of the Four), together with José Moncayo García, Salvador Contreras Sánchez, and Blas Galindo Dimas. Director of the Musical Band of the State of Yucatán and the Police Band of Mérida in 1940. Director of the Cons. of Music of the State of Yucatán. In 1942, he founded the Symphony Orch. of Yucatán.

Works (selective list): **Ballets:** *El Hombre Maya* (1940); *La Gruta Diabólica* (1940). **Symphonic poems:** *Tribu* (1935); *Paisaje* (1935); *Panoramas de México* (1936); *Mi Viaje a Norte América* (1947). *Uchben x' Coholte,* for soprano and chamber orch. (1931); *U Kayil Chaac,* for soprano, chamber orch., and indigenous percussion (1934); Piano concertino (1974). Chamber music; songs.

Sources: BB, DCM, DM, GDM, MLA, MMLA

Azpurúa, Manuel F., Venezuelan composer and pianist; he lived during the second half of the 19th century. He studied cello with Bernardino Montero and piano with his sister, Concepción Azpurúa de Ponce de León. Director of music at the Colegio Vargas of Curaçao. He returned to Caracas, Venezuela, and devoted his time to teaching piano and performing.

Works: Trio for piano, violin, and cello; songs; pieces for violin and piano.

Source: MMLA

B

Baca Elorriaga, Luis, Mexican composer; b.15 Dec 1826, Durango, State of Durango, Mexico; d.1855, Mexico City, Mexico. He studied in Durango with Vicente Guardado and in Mexico City with José Antonio Gómez. In 1844, he went to France, and in 1846, he entered the Paris Cons. where he studied harmony, counterpoint, composition, and orchestration with Edmundo Jouvin.
Works (selective list): *Operas: Leonor; Juana de Castilla. Ave Maria,* for voice and organ. *Polkas: La Linda; Josefina; Julieta; Jenny; Delfina; La Amada.*
Bibl.: F. Sosa, *Biografías de Mexicanos Distinguidos,* Mexico, 1884. A. Leduc and L. Lara y Pardo, *Diccionario de Geografía, Historia, y Biografías Mexicanas,* Paris-Mexico, 1910. J.C. Romero, *Luis Baca, Estudio Bibliográfico, Revista Musical Mexicana,* 1944.
Sources: GMM, MMLA

Bal y Gay, Jesús, Mexican composer and pianist of Spanish origin; b.23 Jun 1905, Lugo, Spain; d.3 Mar 1993, Madrid, Spain. He studied piano at the Royal Cons. of Music in Madrid. He lived in Madrid until 1935, in Cambridge, England, from 1935 to 1938, in Mexico City, Mexico, from 1938 to 1957, when he returned to Madrid.
Works (selective list): *Hojas de Album,* for piano (1946-48); *Cuatro Piezas,* for voice and piano (1946); *Divertimento,* for flute, oboe, clarinet, and bassoon (1946); Sonata for clarinet and piano (1947); *Serenata,* for string orch. (1947); *Concierto Barroco* (1951); *Leñador, no Tales el Pino,* for chorus a cappella; Concerto grosso for symphony orch. (1965).
Source: ISC

Bal y Gay, Rosa de, Mexican composer and pianist of Spanish origin; b.8 Apr 1902, Madrid, Spain. She studied with her mother, Mrs. García Obispo. Later she took lessons from Felipe Pedrell and Enrique Granados, 1914-16, Manuel de Falla, 1916-35, and Nadia Boulanger, 1938. Only woman member of the *Grupo de los Ocho* (Group of the Eight) in Madrid. She lived in Madrid until 1935, in Cambridge, England, from 1935 to 1938, in Mexico City, Mexico, from 1939 to 1965, when she returned to Madrid.
Works (selective list): Suite for orch.; Concerto for piano and orch.; *Preludio,* for piano (1947); chamber music; piano pieces.
Source: ISC

Ballivian, Adolfo, Bolivian statesman, writer, and composer; b.1831, La Paz, Bolivia; d.14 Feb 1874, Sucre, Bolivia. Very little is known about his musical background. He became President of Bolivia in 1873.
Works: Atahualpa, opera; *Sueño de Rosas,* waltz.
Source: CB

Balzanelli, Alberto, Argentine composer and choral and orch. conductor; b.7 Jun 1941, Buenos Aires, Argentina. He studied piano with Alfredo Pinto, harmony, counterpoint, and composition with Jacobo Ficher, choral conducting with Robert Shaw and Pedro Valenti Costa, and orch. conducting with Enrique Sivieri. He also took courses in renaissance and baroque music with Sergio Siminovich in Rome, Italy, and composition with Alberto Ginastera in Geneva, Switzerland. Professor of choral music and vocal ensemble at the Inst. Superior de Arte of the Teatro Colón of Buenos Aires. Professor of choral conducting at the Facultad de Artes y Ciencias Musicales of the Argentine Catholic Univ. of Buenos Aires. Director of the Inst. Superior de Arte of the Teatro Colón.
Works (selective list): *El Mago de los Sueños,* opera (1972); *El Patito Feo,* ballet (1972); *Credo,* for chorus and orch. (1980); *Soneto a Jesús Crucificado,* for chorus and orch. (1982); *Que Pena me Da Mirarte,* for chorus and orch. (1991); piano pieces; songs; choruses a cappella.
Source: ISC

Bandoni, Alfredo, Argentine composer; b.1946, Buenos Aires, Argentina. He studied with Virtú Maragno and Roberto García Morillo in Buenos Aires. Member of the Asociación Argentina de Compositores.
Works (selective list): *El Dragoncillo,* comic opera; *El Gran Dragón,* comic opera; *El Jardín de las Delicias,* for orch.; Concerto grosso for string orch.; *Sinfonía Madrigalesca,* for chorus and orch.; *Bing,* for chorus and percussion; *Misa,* for chorus and 5 instruments; *Magnificat,* for soloists, chorus, and orch.; *Laudate Domine,* for soloists, chorus, and orch.; *Sinfonía Malabar,* for orch.; chamber music; songs; choruses.
Source: VMA

Baptista, Raphael, Brazilian composer and teacher; b.17 Nov 1909, Petrópolis, State of Rio de Janeiro, Brazil. He studied piano, composition, and conducting at the Federal Univ. Music School of Rio de Janeiro, Brazil, 1937-38. He also took conducting lessons from Eugen Szenkar in Brazil, and composition lessons with Jean Rivier in Paris, France. Professor at the Federal Univ. School of Music of Rio de Janeiro since 1945. Member of the Brazilian and

National Music Academies. Founder of the orch. of the Univ. Club of Rio de Janeiro in 1934, the orch. of Suplemento Juvenil do Jornal A Noite in 1942, and the Univ. Orch. in 1946.
Works (selective list): *A Conquista do Sertâo,* symphonic poem for orch. and chorus; *Terenzhina,* ballet; *Lincoln; Dansa da India Enamorada; Papai Noel,* for orch. and chorus; *Valsa; Instantáneos Folclóricos Nos 1 y 2,* for wind quintet; songs.
Source: ISC

Baqueiro Foster, Gerónimo, Mexican composer and musicologist; b.7 Jan 1898, Hopelchén, Mexico; d.29 May 1967, Mexico City, Mexico. He studied composition with Julián Carrillo at the National Cons. of Music of Mexico in Mexico City. Founder of the Unión Mexicana de Cronistas de Teatro y Música in 1938, and of the *Revista Musical Mexicana* in 1942. Professor of solfeggio, music history, and acoustics at the National Cons. of Music of Mexico.
Works: Huapangos, orch. suite; dances; songs. *Books and articles:* about Mexican folk music and music history.
Sources: DM, GDM, MLA

Baranda Reyes, Santiago, Uruguayan composer, teacher, and pianist; b.5 May 1910, Salto, Uruguay; d.17 May 1982, Montevideo, Uruguay. He studied piano with Angelita Riffaud and Romualdo Moro, and solfeggio, harmony, and composition with Francisco de Peñalosa, Manuel Fernández Espiro, Guido Santórsola, Enrique Casal Chapí, and Carlos Estrada in Montevideo. Founder of the Cons. of Music Johann Sebastian Bach in Montevideo. Professor at the National Cons. of Music in Montevideo, and director and professor of the Cons. Oficial Departamental of the city of San José, Uruguay.
Works: La Sombra de un Crimen, incidental music for a film (1952-53); chamber music; piano pieces; songs.
Sources: BHMCU, DM, MU

Baratta, María M. de, Salvadoran composer; b.27 Feb 1894, San Salvador, El Salvador; d.? She studied piano with her mother and solfeggio with Agustín Solórzano. Later she studied with María Zimmermann and Antonio Gianoli at the National Cons. of Music in San Salvador. She furthered her musical knowledge with Agustín Roig and Vicente de Arrillaga. Founder of the Asociación de Amigos del Arte. President of the Research Committee on National Folklore and Native Art of the Ministry of Public Education.
Works (selective list): *Nahualismo,* ballet; *Ofrenda de la Elegida* and *Danza del Incienso,* dances for piano, later orchestrated. *Songs: La Campana Llora; Los Tecomatillos; Can-Calagui-Tunal.*
Sources: DM, MLA, MMLA

Barbacci, Rodolfo, Peruvian composer, pianist, and musicologist of Argentine origin; b.28 Feb 1911, Buenos Aires, Argentina. He studied piano and harmony with Antonio Toro Chacón and Cayetano Troiani. In Milan, Italy, he studied piano and composition with Héctor Pozzoli, Moscarola, and Ferrari, and violoncello with Berti. In Argentina he studied harp with Augusto Sebastiani. Founder of the journals *América Musical, Clave, Revista Musical Argentina,* in Argentina; and *Revista Musical Peruana,* in Peru. He settled in Peru in 1937. Professor of harp at the National Academy of Music Alcedo in Lima, Peru. First harpist at the National Symphony Orch. of Lima.
Books: *La Nerviosidad de los Músicos,* 1939; *Educación de la Memoria Musical,* 1940; *Anécdotas Musicales,* 1942.
Works: Fugues; sonatas; fantasias; variations; suites; other compositions for the harp, piano, voice, and chamber ensembles.
Sources: DM, MLA

Barbosa, Cacilda Campos Borges, Brazilian pianist, choir conductor, and composer; b.18 May 1914, Rio de Janeiro, Brazil. She studied piano with P. Cháves, theory with Lima Coutinho, harmony with Oscar Lorenzo Fernández, counterpoint and fugue with Paulo Silva, composition with Francisco Braga, and conducting with Francisco Mignone at the National Inst. of Music of Rio de Janeiro. She also studied voice with M. Figuero Bezerra and Vera Janacopulos. Director of the Inst. Villa-Lobos of Rio de Janeiro.
Works (selective list): *Uirapiranga,* dance for orch. (1955); *Chibraseando,* for orch. (1973); chamber music; sacred music; songs.
Source: IEW

Barletta, Alejandro, Argentine bandonion player and composer; b.1925, Buenos Aires, Argentina. He studied with Julián Bautista, Athos Palma, and Alberto Ginastera in Buenos Aires, and with Daniel Lesur in Paris, France.
Works (selective list): *Dos Aires de Danza,* for bandonion (1954); *Tres Intimas,* for bandonion (1954); chamber music; music for bandonion and orch.
Source: EMA

Barón Superville, Susana, Argentine composer; b.1910, Buenos Aires, Argentina. She studied with Nadia Boulanger and Vera Vaurabourg in Paris, France, with Furio Francheschini and Hans Koellreuter in Sâo Paulo, Brazil, and with Gilardo Gilardi and Juan Carlos Paz in Buenos Aires. Member of the *Agrupación Nueva Música.*
Works (selective list): **Chamber music:** String quartet (1947); *Divertissement Sériel,* for string quartet, woodwind quartet, and

trumpet (1952); *Composición 57,* for 10 instruments and percussion (1957); *Sonnet,* for voice and 6 instruments (1960); *Poème,* for voice and 8 instruments (1962); *Un Homme Va et Vient,* for voice and 8 instruments (1962). *Tres Pequeños Coros,* for mixed chorus and piano (1932); songs; piano pieces.
Source: EMA

Barradas, Carmen (María del Carmen Pérez Giménez), Uruguayan composer and teacher; b.18 Mar 1888, Montevideo, Uruguay; d.10 May 1963, Montevideo. She studied with Antonio Franck, Aurora and Vicente Pablo, and Martín López at the Musical Cons. La Lira of Montevideo. In 1914, she settled in Spain where she began to develop a new musical notation system. In 1928, she returned to Montevideo and began teaching at the Inst. Normal.
Works (selective list): *Music for piano: Fabricación* (1924); *Taller Mecánico* (1926); *Aserradero* (1928); *Estudios Tonales* (1930); *Fabricación,* new version for 2 pianos (1932); *Mar-Tragedia-Misterio,* triptych. Many children's songs.
Sources: BHMCU, DM, MMLA, MU, NGDWC

Barraquero, Carlos Washington, Argentine composer and choral and orch. conductor; b.in the first half of the 20th century, Mendoza, Prov. of Mendoza, Argentina. He studied at the Escuela Superior de Música, today known as Facultad de Artes of the National Univ. of Cuyo, Mendoza. He continued his music studies with Emilio Dublanc, Alejandro Derevitzky, Pedro Valenti Costa, Robert Shaw, and Clyton Kriebhel. Assistant director and conductor of the chamber chorus of the Facultad de Artes of the National Univ. of Cuyo. Also at the same inst. he was professor of harmony, choral conducting, musical form, and orchestration.
Works (selective list): *Choral-symphonic: Tripticum Sacrum; Memento, Homo; Libera me Domine; Tríptico Navideño; Cantos para mi Tierra; Nostalgias del Suelo Amado; Cantata Antártica. Por mis Valles y Montañas,* poem for strings; Concerto for violin and orch.; chamber music; choruses; songs.
Source: VMA

Barreto, Homero, Brazilian teacher and composer; b.1854, Brazil; d.1924, Brazil. Professor of voice at the Inst. Nacional de Música of Rio de Janeiro, Brazil.
Works: Jati, opera that he never orchestrated.
Source: MMLA

Barrios, Agustín Pío, Paraguayan composer and guitarist; b. 23 May 1885, San Juan Bautista de las Misiones, Paraguay; d.7 Aug 1944,

36 - Barros Marcarián

San Salvador. He studied guitar with Gustavo Sosa Escalada in Paraguay, and with Antonio Giménez Manjón in Uruguay.
Works: More than 100 compositions for the guitar, including *Danza Paraguaya* and *El Catedral.*
Bibl.: P. Sensier, *Agustín Barrios, Guitar,* Vol.2, 1974.
Source: GDM

Barros Marcarián, Nadile de, Brazilian pianist and composer; b.1914, Brazil.
Works (selective list): *Toada e Dansa,* for cello; *Lamento e Dansa,* for orch.; Trio for piano, violin, and cello; *Poema,* for orch. and piano; Cantata for soloists, chorus, and orch.; *Cantiga de Roda,* for piano.
Source: MMLA

Barroso, Sergio, Cuban composer and teacher; b.3 Mar 1946, Havana, Cuba. He settled in Canada in 1980 and became a citizen of that country. He studied piano, theory, and composition at the National Cons. of Havana, from 1950 to 1966. Also studied at the Prague Superior Academy of Music, Czechoslovakia, from 1966 to 1968. He took classes in computer music at Stanford Univ., California. Professor at the National Cons. of Havana, 1968-73 and 1978-80, the National School of Music of Havana, 1968-76, the Inst. Superior de Artes of the Univ. of Havana, 1976-80, the Trent Univ. of Ontario, Canada, 1981, the Univ. of Victoria, Canada, 1981-82, and the Simon Fraser Univ., Canada, 1988 and 1991.
Works (selective list): ***Orch.:*** *La Fiesta Grande,* for solo synthesizer (1990); *Yantra VII* (1977); Oboe concerto (1967-68); *Oda al Soldado Muerto* (1967). ***Ballets:*** *La Casa de Bernarda Alba* (1969); *Plasmasis* (1970). Electroacoustic music; chamber music; piano pieces.
Sources: ISC, DCM

Barroso Neto, Joaquím Antônio, Brazilian composer, teacher, and pianist; b.30 Jan 1881, Rio de Janeiro, Brazil; d.1 Sep 1941, Rio de Janeiro. He studied first with Francisco Malio, and later he entered the Inst. Nacional de Música of Rio de Janeiro, where he studied with Henrique Braga, I.F. Araújo Porto Alegre, Frederico Nascimento, Alberto Nepomuceno, and Alfredo Bevilacqua. Professor of piano at the Inst. Nacional de Música. Artistic director of the Sociedade de Cultura Musical of Rio de Janeiro.
Works (selective list): ***Music for piano:*** *Coriscos; Tarantela; Valsa Lenta; Galhofeira; Pastoral; Ite Missa Est; Rapsodia Guerreira. Minha Terra,* for piano and orch.; songs; choruses; pieces for violin and for cello.
Bibl.: T. Gomes, *Barroso Neto,* Rio de Janeiro, 1939.
Sources: BB, DM, GDM, MLA, MMLA

Bassi, Nicolás, Argentine violinist, conductor, and composer of Italian origin; b.19th century, Italy. Conductor of the orch. of the Teatro Colón of Buenos Aires between 1874 and 1888. Founding member of the *Sociedad del Cuarteto.* Director and professor of harmony at the Escuela de Música de la Provincia, Prov. of Buenos Aires, Argentina. He conducted the orch. of the Teatro Alla Scala of Milan and of the Teatro San Carlo of Naples, both in Italy.
Works: *Gran Sinfonía Dramática* (1875); *Himno,* for orch. (1877); *Gran Marcha Rivadavia* (1880); *Europa* (1880); *Fantasía* (1883).
Source: EMA

Bautista, Julián, Argentine composer of Spanish origin; b. 21 Apr 1901, Madrid, Spain; d.8 Jul 1961, Buenos Aires, Argentina. He settled in Argentina in 1940. He studied violin with Julio Francés, piano under Pilar Fernández de la Mora, and composition under Conrado del Campo at the Madrid Cons. Professor of harmony at the National Cons. of Music of Madrid and the National Cons. of Music Carlos López Buchardo of Buenos Aires.
Works (selective list): *Juerga,* ballet (1921); *Colores,* 6 piano pieces (1922); Sonatina for string trio (1924); *Obertura para una Opera Grotesca,* for orch. (1932); *Suite all'Antica,* for orch. (1932); *Tres Ciudades,* for voice and orch. (1937); *Cuatro Poemas Gallegos,* for voice, flute, oboe, clarinet, viola, cello, and harp (1946); *Sinfonía Breve* (1956); Symphony No.2 (1957); 3 string quartets (1922-23, 1926, 1958); chamber music; piano pieces; songs.
Sources: BB, DCM, DM, EMA, GDM, MLA

Becerra Schmidt, Gustavo, Chilean composer; b.26 Aug 1925, Temuco, Chile. He studied composition with Pedro Humberto Allende and Domingo Santa Cruz, conducting with Armando Carvajal, and musicology with Vicente Salas Viú at the National Cons. of Music of Santiago de Chile, Chile. He graduated from the Univ. of Chile, Santiago de Chile, in 1949, where he became professor of musical analysis and composition in 1952. From 1968 to 1970, he served as cultural attaché to the Chilean embassy in Bonn, Germany.
Works (selective list): *La Muerte de Don Rodrigo,* opera (1958); 3 symphonies (1955, 1958, 1960); 2 oratorios: *La Araucana* (1965) and *Lord Cochrane in Chile* (1967); Violin concerto (1950); Flute concerto (1957); Piano concerto (1958); 4 guitar concertos (1964-1970); Concerto for oboe, clarinet, bassoon, and string orch. (1970); 7 string quartets; Saxophone quartet; 3 violin sonatas; Viola sonata; 3 cello sonatas; Sonata for double bass and piano; *Provocación,* mini-drama (1972); *Parsifae,* opera (1973); chamber music; music for solo instruments; choral music.

Bibl.: Special issue of *Revista Musical Chilena* dedicated to *Becerra Schmidt,* 1972.
Sources: BB, CTA8, DCM, GDM, HMC

Bello Montero, Atanasio, Venezuelan composer and teacher; b.late 18th century, Caracas, Venezuela; d.after 1847. He studied with Pedro Palacios y Sojo. He founded a music academy in Caracas with composer Luis Jumel, and with composer José María Izaza he established a philharmonic society. Director of the Free Music School of the Sociedad Económica de Amigos del País in Caracas.
Works: Religious music: Pange Lingua (1825); *Lamentación a Nuestra Señora de los Dolores* (1826); *Vigilia y Misa para los Muertos* (1842); *Miserere; Te Deum; Stabat Mater; Lamentación para el Miércoles de Semana Santa. Los Pepitos,* lyric plaything; *Canción Nacional para el 9 de Febrero de 1843; Canción Nacional para el 5 de Julio de 1845.*
Bibl.: Boletín del Archivo General de la Nación, Caracas, 1970.
Source: GDM

Belloc, Enrique, Argentine composer and conductor; b.1936, Buenos Aires, Argentina. He studied piano with Oreste Castronuovo and composition with Francisco Kröpfl. He also studied philosophy between 1955 and 1960 at the National Univ. of Buenos Aires. With a scholarship granted by the Ford Foundation he went to Germany to study with Gilbert Amy and Lorin Maazel. He also participated in the International Courses on New Music in Darmstadt, Germany, and at the Research Center Pierre Bourdan in France. He returned to Buenos Aires in 1969 and created the *Cuarteto Contemporáneo,* instrumental ensemble dedicated to the promotion of 20th century music. In 1970, he was appointed director of the Municipal Cons. of Music Manuel de Falla of Buenos Aires.
Works: Incidental music for *La Poudre d'Intelligence* by Khateb Yacine and for *8,600,000 Litres d'Eau par Seconde* by Michel Butor; *Movimientos,* for flute, oboe, clarinete, and piano (1965).
Source: EMA

Bemberg, Hermann, Argentine composer who lived most of his life in France; b.1861, Buenos Aires, Argentina; d.1931, Bern, Switzerland. He studied in Paris, France, with Jules Massenet, Georges Bizet, Henri Maréchal, Théodore Dubois, and Charles Gounod.
Works (selective list): *Le Baisier de Suzan,* opera (1888); *Elaine,* opera (1892); *La Mort de Jeanne d'Arc,* cantata for soprano, chorus, and orch. (1886); *Les Djinns,* fantastic legend for soloists, chorus, and orch. (1881); *La Ballade du Désesperé,* for voice and orch.

(1889); *Heurs de Camps,* for orch. (1879); songs; salon music, including the waltzes *Manolo* and *La Florida.*
Source: EMA

Benavente, Manuel José, Bolivian composer and pianist; b.1 Jan 1901, Sucre, Bolivia; d.13 Apr 1987, Buenos Aires, Argentina. He settled in Buenos Aires in 1921. He studied piano with his mother and with Prudencio Bustillo, and also harmony and composition in his native town. Later he studied piano with Edouard Risler and music pedagogy with Faría de Vasconcellos at the Paris Cons., France. Interested in Inca folklore.
Works (selective list): *Music for piano:* Suite No.1 (1923); *Procesión,* passacaglia (1928); *Noches en el Altiplano* (1930); *La Luna sobre las Ruinas del Tiahuanaco* (1935); Sonata. *Pala-Pala,* ballet (1939); songs; choruses; music for flute or oboe and piano.
Sources: DM, ISC

Benavente, Regina, Argentine composer; b.21 Jan 1932, Buenos Aires, Argentina. She began music studies with her father, Manuel J. Benavente, and later she entered the National Cons. of Music Carlos López Buchardo of Buenos Aires, where she studied harmony, counterpoint, fugue, piano, and music history with Abraham Jurafsky, Roberto García Morillo, Pedro Sáenz, Gilardo Gilardi, and Rafael González. She also studied composition with Alberto Ginastera and took courses at the Centro Latinoamericano de Altos Estudios Musicales of the Inst. Di Tella of Buenos Aires, in 1967 and 1968. Professor of harmony and counterpoint at the National Cons. of Music Carlos López Buchardo and the Inst. Santa Ana, both of Buenos Aires.
Works (selective list): *Orch.: Pastoral y Danza; Sinfonía de Primavera;* Sinfonietta; *Kronos; Galaxias; Imágenes; Secuencias; Toccata,* for piano. Music for chamber and string orch.; chamber music; piano pieces; choruses; electronic music.
Source: ISC

Benzaquén Bencomo, Jorge Isaac, Venezuelan composer and teacher; b.17 Mar 1949, Caracas, Venezuela. He studied music theory and solfeggio with Antonio Ochoa and Raimundo Pereyra, music history and aesthetics with Rhazes Hernández López, guitar with Antonio Lauro, flute with Simón Alvarez, harmony and composition with Yannis Ioannidis, music appreciation with Abraham Abreu, and modern music and musical analysis with Kryzstof Penderecki. Founding member of the Sociedad Venezolana de Música Contemporánea, the Sociedad Orquesta Típica Nacional, the Sociedad Venezolana de Autores y Compositores, and the Sociedad Cultural Leonardo da Vinci.

Works (selective list): *Phases,* for string orch.; *Onomatopeya,* for mixed chorus; *Amanecer en Moguer,* for chamber orch.; *Un Industrioso Insecto y la Dulzura de los Otros,* for chamber orch.; *Fonocromía,* for orch.; chamber music; music for the guitar; choruses; piano pieces.
Source: ISC

Bermudes (Bermúdez), Pedro, Composer of Spanish origin, resided in colonial Peru and Mexico; b.Granada, Spain, fl.1592-1606; d.? He settled in Peru in 1597. *Maestro de capilla* (chapelmaster) at the Cathedral of Cuzco, Peru, and the Cathedral of Puebla, Mexico. Later he became *maestro de capilla* (chapelmaster) at the Cathedral of Guatemala City.
Works (selective list): *Misa de Bomba;* 3 antífonas; 2 invitatorios; Salmo; 20 himnos; 4 Salve Regina.
Bibl.: R. Stevenson, *Renaissance and Baroque Musical Sources in the Americas,* Washington, D.C., 1970.
Source: GDM

Bermúdez Silva, Jesús, Colombian composer; b.24 Dec 1884, Bogotá, Colombia; d.25 Oct 1969, Bogotá. He studied with Luis Figueroa, José María Prado, and Guillermo Uribe Holguín at the National Cons. of Colombia of Bogotá. In 1929, he traveled to Madrid, Spain, where he studied at the Royal Cons. with Conrado del Campo. In 1935, he was appointed professor of counterpoint and composition at the Cons. of Bogotá. From 1928 to 1940, he was music instructor at the Escuela Normal of Tunja, Dept. of Boyacá, Colombia. From 1942, he was director of the Cons. of Tolima in Ibagué, Colombia. Professor of harmony and counterpoint at the Cons. of Music of the National Univ. of Colombia of Bogotá.
Works (selective list): *Cuento de Hadas,* for violas, flutes, and orch. (1930); *Torbellino,* symphonic poem (1931); Symphony in C major (1933); Concerto for piano and orch. (1947); *Orgía Campesina,* symphonic poem (1959); *Estampa Criolla,* symphonic impression (1959); *Leyenda de Oro,* for 4 voices (1938); *Canción Arrullo de María Isabel,* for 3 voices (1938); chamber music; piano pieces; songs.
Sources: CMC, CTA8, DM, GDM, MLA, MMLA, ZCCC

Bernal Jiménez, Miguel, Mexican composer and organist; b.16 Feb 1910, Morelia, State of Michoacán, Mexico; d.26 Jul 1956, León, State of Guanajato, Mexico. He studied with Felipe Aguilera Ruíz and Ignacio Mier y Arriaga. In Italy he studied organ with Rafael Manari, counterpoint and fugue with César Dobici, musicology and composition with Rafael Casimiri, harmony and orchestration with Licinio Refice, and Gregorian chant with the Benedictine abbot Paolo

M. Ferretti at the Istituto Pontificio di Música Sacra of Rome. Director of the Escuela Superior de Música Sagrada and the Cons. Las Rosas, both of Morelia. Professor at the Music Department of Loyola Univ. of New Orleans, Louisiana.

Works (selective list): *Tata Vasco,* opera (1941); *Timgambato,* ballet (1943); *Los Tres Galanes de Juana,* ballet (1952); *Noche en Morelia,* symphonic poem (1941); *Michoacán,* suite for orch.; *Cuarteto Virreinal,* for string quartet (1951); 2 masses; *Te Deum;* sacred music; music for the organ.

Bibl.: O. Mayer-Serra, *Tata Vasco, A Mexican Opera Based on the Life of a Great Religious Hero, The Commonwealt,* New York, 1941.

Sources: DCM, DM, GDM, GMM, MLA, MMLA

Bernasconi, Luis José, Argentine composer and pianist; b.1845, Buenos Aires, Argentina; d.1885. Teacher at the Provincial School of Music, Prov. of Buenos Aires, Argentina. Music critic for the weekly *La Lira* and *Mefistófeles;* also wrote for the *La Gaceta Musical.*

Works (selective list): Music for the copofon (18th century instrument that consists of a series of tuned crystal glasses containing different amounts of water, introduced into Buenos Aires in 1865 by the Italian Cominjeo Gagliano). Quartet for glasses (1869); *Llora, Llora, Urutaú,* for orch. (1875); *Flores y Mariposas,* for 4 hand-copofon (1879); *La Plata,* march for orch. (1882); *Capricho de Concierto,* for piano (1882); songs; piano pieces.

Source: EMA

Berón, Saturnino Filomeno, Argentine band conductor, performer on 16 different instruments, and composer; b. 1847, Paraná, Prov. of Entre Ríos, Argentina; d.1898. He studied at the traditional Colegio de Concepción del Uruguay, Prov. of Entre Ríos. He entered the military school and became a lieutenant colonel. Director of the School of Instrumentalists of the Army. He organized numerous military bands.

Works (selective list): *Buenos Aires,* symphony (1878); *La Pampa,* symphonic poem (1878); *Entre Ríos,* symphony (1878); *Himno a Rivadavia* (1880); music for band. *Books: Tratado Completo de la Música Moderna,* 1889.

Source: EMA

Berrini, José Francisco, Argentine composer, conductor, and teacher; b.30 Mar 1897, Rosario, Prov. of Santa Fe, Argentina; d.1963, Argentina. He studied piano with Clemente Sismondo and harmony and composition with Constantino Gaito. Conductor of the orch. of the Profesorado Orquestal and the Sociedad Cultural Alemana

Argentina, both in Rosario. Artistic director of the Asociación Sinfónica of Rosario since its creation in 1932.

Works (selective list): *Egogla con Lluvia y Sol,* symphonic poem; *Visiones del Paraná,* symphonic poem; songs; piano pieces; choruses.

Sources: CAMR, DM, MLA

Berroa, Catalina, Cuban pianist, guitarist, harpist, organist, violinist, choral conductor, composer, and teacher; b.28 Feb 1849, Trinidad, Cuba; d.23 Nov 1911, Trinidad. She organized and directed the choruses and was also the organist at the San Francisco de Asís and Santísima Trinidad churches, both in Trinidad, where she also founded a music school.

Works: Sacred music: La Trinitaria, mass; hymns; masses; *Salve Regina.*

Sources: DMC, IEW, NGDWC

Berroa, Jorge, Cuban composer; b.13 Dec 1938, Havana, Cuba. He studied music at the Cons. Amadeo Roldán of Havana. Director of music of the Comisión de Extensión Cultural of the Univ. of Havana. He worked at the Empresa de Grabaciones y Ediciones Musicales of Cuba.

Works (selective list): *Un Hombre ha Pasado,* for soprano and piano; *Miguel Matamoros, In Memoriam,* for soprano, orch., and magnetic tape; *Décimas Contemporáneas,* for soprano; *Lamento,* for actor, soprano, and orch.; *Lo Antiguo y lo Moderno,* for soprano and magnetic tape; Concerto for piano and orch.; *Proposiciones para Explicar la Muerte de Ana,* on a poem by Nicolás Guillén, for baritone; *El Son de la Discusión,* children's opera.

Source: DMC

Bértola, Eduardo, Argentine composer; b.14 Jul 1939, Córdoba, Prov. of Córdoba, Argentina. He studied at the National Cons. of Music Carlos López Buchardo of Buenos Aires, Argentina, and the Paris Cons., France.

Works (selective list): *Electronic music: Dynamus; Pexoa; Penetraciones; Signals,* for 21 instruments; *Hertz,* for 14 instruments.

Source: KTL

Berutti, Arturo, Argentine composer; b. 27 Mar 1862, San Juan, Prov. of San Juan, Argentina; d.3 Jan 1938, Buenos Aires, Argentina. Brother of Pablo Berutti. He studied with his father, Antonio L. Berutti, and Ignacio Alvarez, and later, in Buenos Aires, with Nicolás Bassi. In 1884, with a fellowship, he entered the Cons. of Leipzig, Germany, where he studied with Carl Reinecke and Salomon Jadassohn.

Works (selective list): *Operas: La Vendetta* (1892); *Evangelina* (1893); *Taras Bulba* (1895); *Pampa* (1897); *Yupanki* (1899); *Khrise* (1902); *Horrida Nox* (1908); *Los Héroes* (1919). *Orch.: Andes*, overture (1886); *Rivadavia*, symphony (1888); *Colombiana*, symphony (1888); *Sinfonía Argentina* (1890).
Bibl.: E.M. Navarro, *San Juan en la Historia de la Música*, San Juan, Argentina, 1964.
Sources: BB, DM, EMA, GDM, MLA, MMLA

Berutti, Pablo, Argentine composer; b.24 Sep 1866, San Juan, Prov. of San Juan, Argentina; d.17 Jun 1914, Buenos Aires, Argentina. Brother of Arturo Berutti. He started music studies in Mendoza, Prov. of Mendoza, Argentina, and later he continued them at the Cons. of Leipzig, Germany, where he graduated with a Doctor of Music degree. When he returned to Argentina, he founded a cons. and worked there as a teacher.
Works (selective list): *Cochabamba,* opera (1890); *Misa Solemne* (1891); *Gran Sinfonía* (1891); *Te Deum; Ofertorio; Ave Maria;* a volume of 60 piano pieces under the title *Hojas Caídas.*
Sources: DM, EMA, GDM, MLA

Bevilacqua, Francisco Alfredo, Brazilian composer and pianist; b.1846, Brazil; d.1927, Brazil. He started music studies with his mother, and later continued in Europe. In Italy, he studied piano, composition, and orchestration, and in Paris, France, he studied piano with Georges Mathias. He taught piano to the Brazilian imperial princesses. The government of the Brazilian Republic requested him, together with Leopoldo Miguéz and José Rodrígues Barboza, to reorganize the old cons., which later became the Inst. Nacional de Música of Brazil in Rio de Janeiro. He was the first piano teacher at the new inst.
Works: Grande Missa, for choruses and orch. *Music for piano: Nocturnes; Romances; Barcarolas.*
Sources: HMB, MMLA

Biase Bidart, Lycia de, Brazilian pianist, violinist, conductor, teacher, and composer; b.18 Feb 1910, Vitoria, Espírito Santo, Brazil. She studied piano with Neusa França and harmony, counterpoint, fugue, and composition with Giovanni Gianetti in Rio de Janeiro, Brazil, and later she studied piano with Magdalena Tagliaferro.
Works (selective list): *Stage: A Noiva do Mar,* opera; *Som e Cor,* ballet (1971); *Simbolismo e Vivência do Jardim Botánico do Rio de Janeiro,* ballet (1976). *Orch.: Anchieta,* symphonic poem (1934); *Angelus,* symphonic episodes (1934); *Andante e Allegro Cantabile,* for piano (1969); *Concerto Rio 70,* for piano (1970); *Interludio,* for

piano (1969); *Adagio Improviso* (1971); *Symphonic Fantasy on Dance Rhythms* (1976); *Serie Germánica,* (1977). Chamber music; piano pieces; songs; sacred music.
Sources: IEW, NGDWC

Bimboni, Oreste, Argentine conductor and composer of Italian origin; b.1840, Florence, Italy; d.1904, Argentina. He settled in Buenos Aires, Argentina, in 1870.
Works: María Stuart, opera; *Modella,* opera; *Plegaria,* for soprano, chorus, and orch.
Source: EMA

Biondo, Juan Carlos, Argentine composer; b.14 Aug 1933, Buenos Aires, Argentina.
Works (selective list): *Poema,* for orch. (1958); Symphony No.1 (1972); Concerto No.1 for piano and orch. (1964); Concerto for clarinet and orch. (1965); 2 piano concertos for the left hand; music for solo instruments; piano pieces; songs.
Sources: CTA18, VMA

Biriotti, León, Uruguayan composer, conductor, and oboist; b.1 Dec 1929, Montevideo, Uruguay. He studied violin with Antonio Maiques and Juan Fabbri, and at the Municipal Music School of Montevideo he studied oboe with Cardoso, harmony with Vicente Ascone, and musicology with Lauro Ayestarán. Later he continued oboe studies with Jean Louis Le Roux and composition with Enrique Casal Chapí. He founded a string orch. Conductor of the instrumental group Juventudes Musicales of Uruguay. Cultural and press director for the Embassy of Israel in Montevideo.
Works (selective list): 6 symphonies (1964, 1965, 1968, 1969, 1982, 1991); *Los Extasis de la Montaña,* for voice and instrumental group (1952); *Suite Concertante,* for violin and orch. (1953); *El Paseo de Buster Keaton,* cantata for voices and orch. (1955); Concertino for trumpet and strings (1963); *Permutaciones,* for orch. (1970); *Hamlet,* incidental music (1979); *Sefarad,* symphony concertante (1982); Concerto for oboe and orch. (1983); *Concerto Brandenburlesque,* for piano and 13 instruments (1985); chamber music; piano pieces; music for different solo instruments; choral music.
Sources: BB, BHMCU, CTA13, GDM, MU

Bisquertt Prado, Próspero, Chilean composer; b.8 Jun 1881, Santiago de Chile, Chile; d.2 Aug 1959, Santiago de Chile. He was a self-taught musician. Director of the Inst. de Extensión Musical of the Facultad de Bellas Artes of Santiago de Chile.
Works (selective list): *Sayeda,* opera (1930); *Taberna al Amanecer,* symphonic poem (1922); *Procesión del Cristo de Mayo,* symphonic

poem (1930); *Destino,* symphonic poem (1934); *Nochebuena,* symphonic triptych (1935); *Misceláneas,* suite (1936); *Dos Emocionales,* for orch. (1940); *Metrópolis,* symphonic poem (1940); *Juguetería,* suite for orch. (1943); *1945,* symphonic poem (1945); *Preludio Lírico,* for orch.; *Poema Pastoril,* for orch.; chamber music; songs; piano pieces.
Sources: DM, GDM, HMC, MLA, MMLA

Blamey Lafone, Ricardo Q., Argentine composer, lawyer, diplomat, and teacher; b.1878, Andalgala, Prov. of Catamarca, Argentina; d.1946 in an airplane accident. Doctor of Jurisprudence. Teacher at the Colegio Nacional de Buenos Aires, Buenos Aires, Argentina. He entered diplomatic service and worked at the Argentine Embassy in London.
Works (selective list): *Andalgala,* symphonic rhapsody (1932); *Escenas Catamarqueñas,* 5 sketches for orch. (1934); *Juvenilia,* symphonic series (1936); *El Ombú,* symphonic poem (1938); ballet music.
Source: EMA

Blanck, Hubert de, Cuban pianist and composer of Dutch origin; b.11 Jun 1856, Utrecht, Netherlands; d.28 Nov 1932, Havana, Cuba. He settled in Havana in 1883. He studied at the Cons. of Liege, Belgium. He gave many concerts in Europe and South and North America. In 1885, he founded a cons. bearing his name, which later became the Cons. Municipal de Música of Havana.
Works (selective list): *Operas: Actea; Patria; Icoana. Hymn to Martí; Habanera; Capricho Cubano; Allegro de Concierto; Marcha Heróica*; Quintet for piano and strings; zarzuelas; piano pieces; songs.
Sources: DMC, MMLA

Blanck, Olga de, Cuban composer and teacher; b.11 Mar 1916, Havana, Cuba. She studied with her father, Hubert de Blanck. She also studied with Amadeo Roldán and Pedro Sanjuán in Cuba, with Walter Burle Marx in New York, and with Julián Carrillo and Carlos Jiménez Mabarak in Mexico. Deputy director of the Cons. Nacional de Música of Havana in 1945.
Works (selective list): *Cuento de Navidad,* opera (1950); *Bohío,* suite for orch. (1964); *Cantata Guajira,* for soloists, chorus, and orch. (1967); music for the theater; chamber music; choruses; songs.
Sources: DMC, IBCC, IEW

Blanco, Juan, Cuban composer; b.29 Jun 1920, BB (1919, DMC), Havana, Cuba. He studied composition with José Ardévol at the Cons. Municipal de Música of Havana.

Works (selective list): *Texturas*, for orch. and tape (1964); Four sets of *Contrapunto Espacial*, for different groups distributed through the area of performance (1965-70); *Vietnam*, soundlike composition (1968); *Tríptico Coral; Cantata de la Paz; Elegía;* Quintet for woodwinds and cello; *Divertimento*; *Música de Danza; Ensemble V; Estudios*, for magnetic tape; *Episodio; Erotofonías;* music for movies and ballet.
Sources: BB, DCM, DMC

Blarduni, Jorge, Argentine composer; b.1930, La Plata, Prov. of Buenos Aires, Argentina. He studied with Luis Gianneo. Fellow at the Inst. Di Tella of Buenos Aires, Argentina, from 1969 to 1970.
Works (selective list): *Toccata*, for piano (1960); Suite for piano (1960); Sonata for clarinete and piano (1962); *Nocturnos de la Ventana*, for voice and instrumental ensemble (1963); *Evocación*, for narrator, voice, and instrumental ensemble (1965); *Variaciones*, for orch. (1965); Quintet (1967); *Poemas de Sandra*, for voice and instrumental ensemble (1968); *Cantata de la Guerra Civil Española*, for baritone, chorus, and orch. (1968); *De Murmullos el Silencio*, for chamber ensemble (1969).
Source: EMA

Blauth, Brenno, Brazilian composer; b.1931, Pôrto Alegre, Brazil. He studied in his native city with Enio de Freitas e Castro, and in Rio de Janeiro, Brazil, with Paulo Silva and Newton Padua. In 1963, he moved to Sâo Paulo, Brazil, where he studied with Camargo Guarnieri. He did research in Brazilian folklore and utilized some of it in his music.
Works (selective list): 2 symphonic suites; 2 symphonies; *Elegía*, for orch.; *No Cimo das Copas*, for soprano and wind quintet (1975); chamber music; piano pieces.
Source: HMB

Bocchino, Alceu, Brazilian composer and teacher; b.30 Nov 1918, Curitiba, Paraná, Brazil. He studied with Rosa Lubrano, Antônio Melilo, and Joâo Poeck. He also studied law at the Faculdade de Direito in Curitiba. In 1944, he settled in Sâo Paulo, Brazil, where he continued his music studies with Camargo Guarnieri and Dinorah de Carvalho. Professor at the Escola de Música e Belas Artes of Curitiba and the Cons. of Santos, Brazil. Music director of radio Mayrink-Veiga e Mundial. Conductor of the orch. of radio stations Sâo Paulo, Tupi, Difusora e Record in Sâo Paulo, and the National Symphony Orch. of Rio de Janeiro, Brazil. Professor at the Academia de Música Oscar Lorenzo Fernández of Rio de Janeiro.

Works (selective list): *Suíte Brasileira,* for cello and piano (1948-50); *Suíte Miniatura,* for orch. (1952); Sinfonía; chamber music; over 30 songs; piano pieces.
Sources: HMB

Boero, Felipe, Argentine composer; b.1 May 1884, Buenos Aires, Argentina; d.9 Aug 1958, Buenos Aires. He studied with Pablo Berutti in Buenos Aires and with Paul Vidal and Gabriel Fauré at the National Cons. of Paris, France. Professor of musical culture at the Escuela Normal de Profesores, and of choral singing at the National Inst. of Physical Education, both in Buenos Aires. He founded the Sociedad Nacional de Música, which became the Asociación de Compositores Argentinos.
Works (selective list): *Operas: Tucumán* (1914); *Ariana y Dionisio* (1916); *Raquela* (1918); *El Matrero* (1925); *Siripo* (1937); *Zincali* (1954). *Orch.: Madrugada en la Pampa* (1920-30); *Suite de Danzas Argentinas* (1920-30); *Suite Argentina* (1940). *Misa* (1918); piano pieces; songs.
Sources: CA, CTA15, DM, EMA, GDM, MLA, MMLA

Boettner, Juan Max, Paraguayan composer, musicologist, and physician; b.1899, Asunción, Paraguay; d.?
Works (selective list): *Suite Guaraní,* for orch.; *El Sueño de Renée,* ballet for soloists, chorus, and orch.; *El Alma del Inca,* for orch.; Sinfonía en Mi; piano pieces; guaranias; songs and children songs.
Source: MMPA

Bolaños, César, Peruvian composer and electronic technician; b.4 Jun 1931, Lima, Peru. He studied music theory and composition in Lima, and later studied at the RCA Inst. of Electronic Technology in New York. In 1963, he obtained a fellowship to study in Buenos Aires, Argentina, at the Latin American Center for Advanced Musical Studies of the Inst. Di Tella, where he later was appointed professor.
Works (selective list): *Cantata Solar,* for voices, chorus, orch., and tape (1963); *Variaciones,* for contralto and chamber ensemble (1963); *Intensidad y Altura,* tape (1964); *Divertimento I,* for instrumental ensemble (1966); *Divertimento II,* for chorus, flute, clarinet, piano, and electric guitar (1966); *Interpolaciones,* for electric guitar and tape (1966); *Divertimento III,* for instrumental ensemble (1967); *Alfa-Omega,* for 2 narrators, chorus, electric guitar, percussion, double bass, tape, 2 dancers, and lighting (1967); *1-10-AIFG-Rbt-1,* for ensemble (1968); *Flexum,* for orch. and tape (1969); *Ñacahuasu,* for narrator and 21 instruments (1970).
Sources: CTA17, GDM

Bolet, Alberto, Cuban composer; b.10 Sep 1905, Havana, Cuba. He started music studies at the Cons. Falcón of Havana, furthering his violin studies with Casimiro Zertuche, 1917-21, and Fermín Touche, 1923-25, and his composition studies with Silvain Noack, 1930-33. Founder of the *Trío de la Habana,* the Sociedad de Conciertos, and the Official Radio C.M.2. Director of the National Symphony Orch., 1939-43, and of the Police Band, 1942-44, both of Havana.
Works (selective list): 2 string quartets (1937); Quartet with piano (1938); Trio (1938); Sonata for violin and piano (1939); *Solitude,* symphonic poem (1941); *El Vendedor de Sueños,* symphonic poem (1942); *Sinfonía Romántica* (1943); *Variaciones Satíricas,* for string orch. (1944); *Ballet Cubano.*
Source: MMLA

Bologna, Nora, Argentine composer and teacher; b.5 Jul 1946, Rosario, Prov. of Santa Fe, Argentina. She studied at the Facultad de Artes y Ciencias Musicales of the Argentine Catholic Univ. of Buenos Aires, Argentina, from which she graduated in 1973. She studied composition with Francisco Kröpfl, 1980-82, Paul Mefano, 1983, and Helmut Lachemann, 1984. She furthered her studies with Carmelo Saita and Erwin Leuchter. Professor of harmony, counterpoint, and musical form at the Cons. of Banfield and Morón, both in the Prov. of Buenos Aires, Argentina. Member of *Grupo de Creación Musical* and of Asociación Argentina de Compositores.
Works (selective list): *Tres Poemas,* for orch.; *Los Vikingos,* symphonic poem; *Improviso II,* for orch.; String quartet; chamber music; piano pieces; songs.
Source: ISC

Bonilla Chavarría, Jesús, Costa Rican flutist and composer; b.15 Nov 1912, Santa Cruz, Prov. of Guanacaste, Costa Rica. Self-taught in harmony, counterpoint, composition, and instrumentation. First flutist at the Military Band of Alajuela, Costa Rica, in 1929. Director of the Military Band of Liberia, Africa, in 1932. In 1933, he returned to Costa Rica where he taught in several schools and organized an orch. in San José.
Works: Music for band: Nocturno No.1; Elegía; Atardecer Guanacasteco; Preludio No.1; Nocturno No.2. Serenata, for flute and piano.
Source: MMLA

Borbolla Téllez, Carlo (Carlos), Cuban composer and teacher; b.1 Feb 1902, Manzanillo, Cuba. He studied harmony and composition with Louis F.M. Aubert in Paris, France, from 1927 to 1931.
Works (selective list): *Music for piano:* 25 Cuban studies; 20 habaneras; 25 rumbas; 35 sones; 5 suites; *Variaciones sobre Ma-*

Teodora; Variaciones sobre La Bayamesa. Music for violin and piano; songs.
Source: GDM

Botet, Maria Emma, Cuban teacher and composer; b.1903, Matanzas, Cuba.
Works: Suite Cubana; Cajita de Música que Toca una Cubana; piano pieces; songs.
Sources: DMC, IEW

Bottiroli, José Antonio, Argentine composer, teacher, and poet; b.1 Jan 1920, Rosario, Prov. of Santa Fe, Argentina; d.15 Mar 1990, Rosario. He studied in Barcelona, Spain, with the musicologist José M. Llorens. Director of the female vocal sextet *Juan María Gutiérrez.*
Works: 13 for orch.; 5 for choral ensembles; 17 for different instrumental ensembles; 56 for piano.
Source: CAMR

Botto Vallarino, Carlos, Chilean composer; b.4 Nov 1923, Viña del Mar, Chile. He studied in Valparaiso, Chile, and later at the Santiago de Chile Cons. with Domingo Santa Cruz and Juan Orrego Salas. He continued composition studies with Luigi Dallapiccola in New York, USA. In 1952, he was appointed to the faculty of the Chilean National Cons. of Music, and in 1969, he became instructor of composition at the Catholic Univ. of Chile, both in Santiago de Chile.
Works (selective list): String quartet (1954); *Diez Preludios*, for piano (1955); *Caprichos*, for piano (1958); *Fantasía*, for viola and piano (1962); piano pieces; songs.
Sources: BB, CTA14, DCM, HMC

Boudet, Pedro, Cuban organist and composer; b.beginning of 19th century, Santiago de Cuba, Cuba; d.1880, Santiago de Cuba. Organist at the Cathedral of Santiago de Cuba. From 1878 he was *maestro de capilla* (chapelmaster) at the same Cathedral.
Works: Mass for voice and orch.
Source: DMC

Boudet, Silvano, Cuban violinist, pianist, and composer; b.27 Nov 1828, Santiago de Cuba, Cuba; d.9 Mar 1863, Santiago de Cuba. Conductor of the orch. at the Cathedral of Santiago de Cuba.
Works: *Religious music:* masses; lections. *Music for violin:* El canto del Canario; Recuerdo a mi Madre; El Ave entre las Flores. *Music for piano:* Pensamientos Melancólicos; La retozona, contradance.
Source: DMC

Bracesco, Renzo, Peruvian composer and teacher; b.22 Oct 1888, Lima, Peru; d.? He studied piano with Claudio Rebagliati in Lima. In Italy he studied harmony and counterpoint with Simplicio Gualco and piano with Alberto Bersani, and later, at the Cons. of Milan, he studied composition with Vincenzo Ferroni and piano with Giuseppe Frugatta. Professor of music theory at the Cons. of Milan, 1923-28, and director of the Monteverdi School of Music, also of Milan, 1928-33. When he returned to Lima after World War II, he was appointed director of the Regional School of Music of the North in Trujillo, Peru.
Works (selective list): *Misa en Fa,* for voices and organ (1918); *De Profundis e Requiem,* for chorus (1920); *O Salutaris Hostia,* for voices and organ (1923); *Ave Maria,* for chorus (1942); *Laudate Dominum,* for voices and organ (1943); *Canto Incaico,* for chorus (1953); *La Rosa y el Clavel,* for chorus (1955); chamber music.
Sources: CTA1, GDM

Braga, Ernani, Brazilian composer, pianist, teacher, and music critic; b.1898, Rio de Janeiro, Brazil; d.1948, São Paulo, Brazil. He studied at the National Inst. of Music of Rio de Janeiro with Alfredo Bevilacqua. He founded the Cons. of Pernambuco, Brazil, in 1930.
Works (selective list): *Prenda Minha,* based on Gaucho folklore; *Cantigas Praianas; Jacaré,* string quartet; Trio for piano, violin, and piano; *Homenagem a Carlos Gómes,* symphonic poem for large orch. and choruses; songs; piano pieces.
Sources: DM, HMB, MMLA

Braga, Francisco Antonio, Brazilian composer and conductor; b.15 Apr 1868, Rio de Janeiro, Brazil; d.14 Mar 1945, Rio de Janeiro. He studied clarinet at the Cons. of Music of Rio de Janeiro under Luiz Antonio de Moura, and harmony under Carlos de Mesquita. He studied harmony with Antoine Taudou and counterpoint with Jules Massenet in Paris, France.
Works (selective list): *Jupira,* opera (1899); *Insomnia, Cauchemar, Paysage,* programmatic pieces for orch.; *Marabá,* symphonic poem; Trio in G minor for piano, violin, and cello; *Tango Caprichoso,* for violin and piano; *Toada,* for cello and piano or orch.; *Variaçôes sobre un Tema Brasileiro;* piano pieces, songs. Once the Brazilian Republic had been established, the government commissioned him to write an official patriotic song, a hymn entitled *Hino à Bandeira.*
Bibl.: T. Gómes, *Biography of Francisco Braga,* Rio de Janeiro, 1937. *Exposiçâo Comemorativa do Centenario do Nascimento de Francisco Braga,* Rio de Janeiro, 1968.
Sources: BB, DM, HMB, MLA, MMLA

Braga, Henrique, Brazilian composer; b.1845, Campos, Brazil; d.1917, Brazil. He studied in Paris, France, with François E.J. Bazin. Professor of piano in Campos, and in Macaé, Brazil. Professor of solfeggio in the Inst. Nacional de Musica of Rio de Janeiro, Brazil.
Source: MMLA

Brncic, Gabriel Oliverio, Chilean composer; b.16 Feb 1942, Santiago de Chile, Chile. He studied viola with Zoltan Fisher, oboe with Gaetano Girardello, and composition with Gustavo Becerra Schmidt at the National Cons.of Music in Santiago de Chile. He studied composition with Alberto Ginastera, music analysis with Gerardo Gandini, and electronic music with Francisco Kröpfl at the Inst. Torcuato Di Tella of Buenos Aires, Argentina, 1965-66. From 1967 he assisted Kröpfl and taught electronic music at that Inst. He also studied engineering at the Univ. of Chile, 1960-64.
Works (selective list): *Oda a la Energía,* for orch. (1963); Octet for brasses (1966); *Dialexis,* for 9 percussionists (1966); *Momento, Mortus Est!,* for violin, clarinet, and electronic sounds on tape (1967); Concerto for viola and orch. (1967); *Puerto Montt,* for female voice, chorus, chamber orch., piano, and electronic sounds on tape (1969); chamber music; electronic music.
Sources: DCM, GDM, HMC

Brooks, Alfredo, Cuban conductor and composer; b.13 Dec 1884, Santiago de Cuba, Cuba; d.? He studied with several teachers, including María Mitchell. Also studied at the Academy Victor Herbert in the USA.
Works (selective list): *Ave Maria,* for voice and piano; *Angelus,* for voice and orch.; 3 quartets; piano pieces; songs.
Source: DMC

Broqua, Alfonso, Uruguayan composer; b.11 Sep 1876, Montevideo, Uruguay; d. 24 Nov 1946, Paris, France. He studied with Vincent d'Indy at the Schola Cantorum in Paris.
Works (selective list): *La Cruz del Sur,* opera (1918); *Telen y Nagüey,* Inca ballet (1934); *Isabelle,* romantic ballet (1936); *Tabaré,* poetic cycle for soloists, female chorus, and piano or orch. (1908); *Poema de las Lomas,* triptych for piano (1912); Piano quintet (1914); *Tres Cantos del Uruguay,* for voice, flute, and 2 guitars (1925); *Cantos de Paraná,* for voice and guitar (1929); *Evocaciones Criollas,* 7 pieces for guitar (1929); piano pieces; music for the guitar; songs.
Sources: BB, BHMCU, CTA16, DM, MLA, MU

Brouwer, Leo, Cuban composer and guitarist; b.1 Mar 1939, Havana, Cuba. He studied in the USA with Vincent Persichetti and Stefan Wolpe at The Juilliard School of Music in New York, and with

Isadore Freed at Hartt College in Hartford, Connecticut. He occupied various administrative posts in Radio Havana. Professor of harmony and counterpoint in 1961 and of composition in 1963 at the Cons. Amadeo Roldán of Havana.
Works (selective list): *Sonograma,* for prepared piano (1963); *Dos Conceptos del Tiempo,* for 10 players (1965); *Conmutaciones,* for prepared piano and 2 percussionists (1966); *Tropos,* for orch. (1967); *Hexahedron,* for 6 players (1969); Flute concerto (1972); *Ludus Metallicus,* for saxophone quartet (1972); *Basso Continuo I,* for bass clarinet and magnetic tape (1972); *Per Suonare a Due,* for guitar and magnetic tape (1972); Concerto for guitar and chamber orch. (1972); *El Gran Zoo,* on text by Nicolás Guillén, for narrator, soloists, chorus, and orch. (1972); *Controversias,* for 2 orch. and 2 conductors (1972); *Esteban Salas Ha Venido,* for 11 string instruments (1973); *Cantata de Chile,* on text by Patricio Manns, for male chorus and orch. (1974); Concerto for violin and orch. (1976); *La Región Más Transparente,* symphony for orch. (1976-77).
Sources: BB, DCM, DMC

Buligovich de Ventura, Rita, Argentine composer and pianist of Bulgarian origin.
Works: El Gráfico de la Petenera, for orch.; *Siete Cancioncillas,* for soprano, flute, piano, and percussion; *Variaciones,* for wind quintet.
Source: VMA

Burger, Carlos Reinaldo, Argentine conductor and composer of German origin; b.20 Apr 1946, Nievenheim, Germany. He studied at the Staatliche Musik Hochschule in Cologne, Germany, and at the National Cons. of Music Carlos López Buchardo and the Teatro Colón, both of Buenos Aires, Argentina.
Works (selective list): *Requiem Breve,* for soloists, chorus, orch., and organ; String quartet; Suite for orch.; Trio for bandonion, clarinet, and cello; *Nada te Turbe,* cantata; songs; music for the organ.
Source: VMA

Bustillos, Freddy, Bolivian teacher and composer; b.1 Jun 1945, Tarija, Bolivia. He studied at the Escuela Nacional de Maestros Mariscal Sucre of Chuquisaca, Bolivia, from which he graduated in 1966. Music teacher at various public and private schools in La Paz, Bolivia. Conductor of the chorus San Pedro of La Paz.
Works (selective list): 2 piano concertos; Concerto for violin and orch.; 4 sonatas for piano; *Una Cantata de la Pasión; Surinama,* choral poem; *La Pachamama; Nostalgias,* for piano; marches; hymns.
Source: CB

Busto, Angel de, Puerto Rican bassoonist and composer; b.22 Feb 1897, Ponce, Puerto Rico; d.? He started music studies in Santurce, Puerto Rico. In 1915, he moved to the USA and during WWI he was sent to France where he studied at the Paris Cons. and at the Escuela de Chaumont. In 1919, he returned to the USA and continued studying in the Governor's Island and at the Band Masters School in New York City. In 1922, he graduated as bassoonist from the New York Inst. for Musical Art. He became instructor at the American Orch. Society in 1923, and in 1924, was appointed professor at the New York Inst. for Musical Art. He received a DM degree at the Soellner Cons. of Hollywood, California. Principal bassoonist at the Symphony Orch., the Metropolitan Opera Orch., both of New York City, and the Detroit Symphony Orch., Detroit, Michigan. Instructor of music at the Univ. of Wayne, Detroit.

Works (selective list): ***Orch.:*** *Homenaje a Bach,* double fugue; Suite in D minor; *Malagueña,* flamenco march; *Doce Danzas Caribes. Cuatro danzas,* for 2 pianos.

Source: MMLA

C

Caamaño, Roberto, Argentine composer and concert pianist: b.7 Jul 1923, Buenos Aires, Argentina; d.8 Jun 1993, Buenos Aires. He studied composition with Athos Palma at the National Cons. of Music Carlos López Buchardo of Buenos Aires, 1939-46. He also studied piano with Amelia Cocq de Weingand and Fritz Masbach. Artistic director of the Teatro Colón of Buenos Aires, 1961-64. Professor at the Univ. Nacional del Litoral, Rosario, Prov. of Santa Fe, Argentina, 1949-52. In 1964, he was appointed professor at the Univ. Católica Argentina of Buenos Aires, where he became dean of the Facultad de Artes y Ciencias Musicales in 1966. In 1969, he became a member of the Academia Nacional de Bellas Artes.
Works (selective list): *Choral-symphonic music: Psalmus CXLIX* (1948); *Magníficat* (1954); *Cantata para la Paz* (1966). *Orch.:* Suite for strings (1949); *Variaciones Americanas* (1953); Concerto for bandonion (1954); *Preludio, Adagio y Fuga* (1954); *Música para Cuerdas* (1957); 2 piano concertos (1957, 1971); Harp concerto (1973); Guitar concerto (1974). *Balada*, for soprano, clarinet, Yamaha WX7, and tape (1991); 2 string quartets; Quintet for piano and strings; choral works; songs; piano pieces. *Books: Historia del Teatro Colón,* Buenos Aires, 1969; *Apuntes para la Formación del Pianista Profesional,* Buenos Aires, 1979.
Bibl.: N. Cenal, *Roberto Caamaño (1923), Revista del Inst. de Investigación Musicológica Carlos Vega,* No.7, Buenos Aires, 1986.
Sources: BB, CA, CTA8, DCM, DM, EMA

Caba, Eduardo, Bolivian composer; b.12 or 13 Oct 1890, Potosí, Bolivia; d.3 Mar 1953, La Paz, Bolivia. He studied first with his mother, Adelina Balsalia, and later, in Buenos Aires, Argentina, he studied harmony with Eduardo Melgar and counterpoint with Felipe Boero. In Spain, he studied with Joaquín Turina and Bartolomé Pérez Casas. In 1942, he was appointed director of the Cons. Nacional de Música y Declamación of La Paz.
Works (selective list): *Doce Aires Indios,* for piano; *Once Canciones de Cámara; Kollana,* ballet; *Potosí,* pantomime; *El Poema de la Quena,* for piano, oboe, and flute; *El Poema del Charango,* for piano and orch.; *Leyenda Quechua,* for piano; *Himno al Sol;* sonatas for piano.
Sources: CB, DM, EMA, MLA

Caballero, Policarpo, Peruvian composer and musicologist; b.26 Jan 1901, Pomacanchi, Prov. of Acomayo, Cuzco, Peru. He studied music in Cuzco and Lima, Peru, in La Paz, Bolivia, and in Tucumán, Prov. of Tucumán, and Buenos Aires, Argentina. He also studied

Peruvian musical folklore and collected about 5,000 traditional melodies.
Works: Several pieces inspired by indigenous folklore. *Books: La Música Incaica; Los Instrumentos Musicales Peruanos.*
Sources: DM, MLA, MMLA

Cabero, Telésforo, Argentine composer and pianist: b.1830, Mendoza, Prov. of Mendoza, Argentina; d.1871, Mendoza. He started his musical studies in Mendoza and completed them in Chile with Fernando Guzmán.
Works: Most compositions lost, only three surviving: *Recuerdos del Challao*; *El Terremoto de Mendoza*; *Tempestad en el Cabo de Hornos.*
Sources: DM, EMA

Cabrera, Ana S. de, Argentine composer, guitarist, and folklorist; b.1897, Simoca, Prov. of Tucumán, Argentina; d.1970, Argentina. She began her first musical lessons at the Simoca Church. In Córdoba, Prov. of Córdoba, Argentina, she studied music and took guitar lessons from Andrés Segovia. She studied northern Argentine folklore.
Works: Serie de Cantos Nativos and *Danzas y Canciones Argentinas,* collection of northern Argentine folk music.
Sources: DM, EMA

Cabrera, Silvia María Pires, Brazilian pianist, choir conductor, teacher and composer; b.4 Apr 1958, Sâo Paulo, Brazil. She studied piano with Amílcar Zanni, composition with Willy Correa de Oliveira, and conducting with Ronaldo Bologna at the Univ. of Sâo Paulo.
Works: chamber music; piano pieces; music for solo instruments; songs.
Source: IEW

Cáceres, Germán Gustavo, Salvadoran composer and conductor; b.9 Jul 1954, San Salvador, El Salvador. He studied harmony, counterpoint, and musical form with Ion Cubicec and Esteban Servellón in San Salvador. He studied oboe and chamber music with Ronald Roseman and composition with Stanley Wolfe at The Juilliard School of Music of New York, 1977-78. While in New York, he also studied composition with Julián Orbón and orch. conducting with José Serebrier. In 1989, he earned a Doctor of Musical Arts degree from the Univ. of Cincinnati, Ohio, where he studied composition with Jonathan Kramer. Director of the Dept. of Music of the National Center for the Arts, San Salvador. Principal conductor of El Salvador

Chamber Orch., 1979-84, and principal conductor and music director of El Salvador Symphony Orch., 1985.
Works (selective list): *Orch.: Yulcuicat,* suite (1973); Harp concerto (1977); *Estancias,* for soprano (1979); Piano concerto (1981); Symphony (1983); *Diferencias* (1988); Violin concerto (1989); *En mi Muerte Conjurada,* for soprano (1990). Chamber music; piano pieces; songs; music for solo instruments.
Source: ISC

Calabró, Domingo S., Argentine composer of Italian origin; b.19 Nov 1910, Messina, Sicily, Italy. He settled in Buenos Aires, Argentina, and, in 1927, he entered the National Cons. of Music Carlos López Buchardo of Buenos Aires where he studied under Edmundo Weingand, Constantino Gaito, Ricardo Rodríguez, and José Gil. Director of the Music School of the National Penitentiary. Conductor of the Municipal Band of Buenos Aires.
Works (selective list): Sinfonietta; *Bufón,* overture; *Misa de Cámara; Cuarteto Breve;* piano pieces; songs.
Sources: DM, EMA

Calcagno, Elsa, Argentine composer; b.19 Oct 1910, Buenos Aires, Argentina. She studied privately with Eduardo Melgar and then at the National Cons. of Music Carlos López Buchardo of Buenos Aires under Pascual de Rogatis, Floro Ugarte, José Gil, Ricardo Rodríguez, and Constantino Gaito. Professor of music in the school system of the National Board of Education of Buenos Aires.
Works (selective list): *Stage: El Rosal de las Ruinas* (1935-36); *Postreras Visiones,* symphonic-choreographic poem (1938-39); *Boda en el Jardín,* children's comedy (1939); *El Arroyo de las Tres Hermanas,* ballet (1942-43). *Orch.:* Piano concerto (1935); *Plenilunio en un Balneario del Río de la Plata* (1938); *Siete Bocetos Sinfónicos de Expresión* (1940); Fantasía for piano (1941); *Sinfonía Dramática a una Mujer,* for chorus (1953); *Suite Sinfónica* (1954); *Tema con Variaciones* (1955). Chamber music; piano pieces; songs.
Sources: CA, DM, EMA

Calcaño, José Antonio, Venezuelan composer and musicologist; b.23 Mar 1900, Caracas, Venezuela; d.11 Sep 1980, Caracas. He started his musical education with his father and later he studied piano, theory, composition, and music history at the Escuela Superior de Música in Caracas, 1911-19, and at the Bern Cons., Switzerland, 1936. He was appointed to the faculty of the Univ. of Caracas. He organized an indigenous chorus, *Coro Creole,* and was conductor of the *Orfeón Lamas* (male singing society) and the Coral Polifónica de Caracas. Director and professor of the Escuela de Música Padre Sojo,

Caracas. Founder and director of the Cons. Teresa Carreño, and professor at the Univ. Central de Venezuela, both in Caracas.
Works (selective list): *Mirando en Rusia,* ballet; Symphony; 2 string quartets; choruses. *Books: Cuatrocientos Años de Música Caraqueña,* Caracas 1967; *La Ciudad y su Música: Crónica Musical de Caracas,* Caracas 1958.
Sources: BB, CTA14, GDM, MLA

Calcavecchia, Benone, Uruguayan composer of Italian origin; b.27 Jun 1886, Messina, Sicily, Italy; d.15 Jan 1953, Montevideo, Uruguay. He settled in Uruguay in 1907. He studied trumpet with Ignacio Colloriti in Italy. In Montevideo, he studied harmony and counterpoint with José Tomás Mujica. Director of the Municipal Band of Montevideo. Founder of the Escuela Municipal de Música of Montevideo. He promoted the creation of the symphony orch. of the SODRE.
Works (selective list): *Pastorale* (1926); *Hymn to the Uruguayan Soccer Game* (1927); Overture (1929); *Visiones del Ganges* (1930); *Marcha del Centenario* (1930); *Suite Uruguay* (1931); *Impresiones Nocturnas,* overture; marches; waltzes; dances.
Sources: BHMCU, DM, MLA, MMLA, MU

Calderón, Vidal, Venezuelan composer; b. 16 Nov 1877, Egido, State of Mérida, Venezuela; d.? At age eight he went to Maracaibo, Venezuela, where he studied piano with Juan Delgado, violin with Julio Añez Puchi, and composition with Carbonell. Assistant conductor of the Band of the State of Zulia, Venezuela, in 1916. Conductor of the Municipal Band of Maracaibo.
Works (selective list): *Ensueño de Amor,* operetta (1915); *Un Viejo Prudente,* zarzuela (1910); *Las Siete Palabras* (1917); Mass for 4 voices (1928); Requiem for 4 voices and chorus (1930); religious music; waltzes; patriotic marches.
Source: MMLA

Calligaris, Sergio, Argentine pianist, teacher, and composer; b.22 Jan 1941, Rosario, Prov. of Santa Fe, Argentina. He began to study piano with Domingo Scarafia. Then he studied with Arthur Loesser at the Cleveland Inst. of Music, Ohio, 1964-66, and later with Guido Agosti at the Accademia di Santa Cecilia in Rome, Italy. He taught at the Cleveland Inst. of Music, the California State Univ. at Los Angeles, the Cons. San Pietro a Majella in Naples, and the Cons. Alfredo Casella in L'Aquila, the last two in Italy. In 1974, he settled in Italy and became an Italian citizen.
Works (selective list): Concerto for string orch. (1989); chamber music; piano pieces; choral works.
Source: BB

Calzadilla, Santiago, Argentine music critic, writer, pianist, and composer; b.1806, Buenos Aires, Argentina; d.1896, Buenos Aires. He studied with Juan Pedro Esnaola. He wrote regularly in *El Mundo Artístico*. Music critic for *El Correo del Domingo* between 1864 and 1867.
Works: Salon music. He published a piano version of the *Argentine National Anthem* and a compilation of works by Esnaola.
Source: EMA

Cámara, Juan Antonio, Cuban composer; b.28 Sep 1917, Havana, Cuba. He studied with Benjamín Orbón. At the Municipal Cons. of Music of Havana he studied harmony with Amadeo Roldán, 1937-39, and counterpoint and composition with José Ardévol in 1939. Secretary of the *Grupo Renovación*. In 1940, he was appointed assistant professor of harmony and history of music at the Municipal Cons. of Music of Havana.
Works (selective list): Suite for 3 wind instruments (1942); Sonata in Doric D for piano (1942); piano pieces; songs; choral works.
Sources: DM, MLA, MMLA

Cameu, Helza (Helza Cameu de Cordoville), Brazilian composer, pianist, musicologist, and teacher; b.28 Mar 1903, Rio de Janeiro, Brazil. She studied with Alberto Nepomuceno, Alfredo Richard, and Joâo Nunes at the Inst. Nacional de Música in Rio de Janeiro. Later she studied harmony with Agnelo França, counterpoint and fugue with Assis Republicano and Franscisco Braga, and composition with Oscar Lorenzo Fernández. In 1936, she studied *canto orfeónico* (male choral singing) with Heitor Villa-Lobos. She was a pioneer investigator of indigenous music in Brazil.
Works (selective list): Suite for string trio (1935); Suite for string quartet (1934); Concerto for piano and orch. (1936); String quartet (1937); *Modinha,* for voice and orch. (1937); *Quadro Sinfónico* (1939); *Líricas,* for voice and orch. (1941); *Seresta No.1* and *No.2,* for chamber orch. (1942, 1942); *Terra de Solo,* symphonic poem for soloists and orch.; chamber music; piano pieces; songs. *Books: Introduçâo ao Estudo da Música Indígena Brasileira,* Rio de Janeiro, 1977.
Sources: EMB, ISC, MMLA, NGDWC

Campa, Gustavo E., Mexican composer and teacher; b.8 Sep 1863, Mexico City, Mexico; d.29 Oct 1934, Mexico City. He studied with Julio Ituarte and Felipe Larios. At the National Cons. of Music of Mexico City, he studied under Melesio Morales. Professor of composition at the National Cons. of Music and director from 1907 to 1913. Director of the journal *Gaceta Musical.* In 1886, he founded

the Musical Inst. Campa-Hernández-Acevedo, together with other composers, intended to promote modern musical education.
Works: *El Rey Poeta*, opera (1901); *Misa Solemne; Berceuse, Lamento,* and *Marcha Antigua,* for orch.; *En Mayo* and *Rêve,* for violin and orch.; *Himno Sinfónico* (1884).
Bibl.: A. Herrera y Ogazón, *El Arte Musical en México,* Mexico City, 1917.
Sources: DM, GMM, MLA, MMLA

Campbell Batista, Ramón, Chilean composer, music researcher, and physician; b.1911, Chile. He studied with Humberto Allende and Luigi Giarda at the National Cons. of Music of Chile in Santiago de Chile.
Works: *Nocturno Sinfónico,* for orch. (1948); Concerto grosso; *Sinfonía Hotu-Matua; Sonata Romántica,* for violin and piano; *Sonata Clásica,* for cello and piano; piano pieces; songs. **Books:** *La Música de la Isla de Pascua.*
Source: HMC

Campmany, Montserrat, Argentine composer and teacher of Spanish origin; b.1901, Barcelona, Spain. She settled in Buenos Aires, Argentina, in 1907. She studied piano with Julián Aguirre, composition with Constantino Gaito, cello with Alfredo Schiuma, and voice with G. Capocci in Buenos Aires. From 1929 to 1940, she taught music in Barcelona. In 1943, she graduated from the Cons. Nacional de Música Carlos López Buchardo of Buenos Aires.
Works (selective list): *La Perí,* symphonic poem (1923); *Danza India,* for wind orch., piano and percussion (1927); *Visión Sinfónica,* for orch. (1929); chamber music; choral music; piano pieces; songs.
Sources: DM, EMA

Campos, Meneleu, Brazilian composer; b.1872, Pará, Brazil; d.1927. He studied at the Milan Cons., Italy, with Vincenzo Ferroni.
Works (selective list): *Os Heróis,* opera; Concerto for piano and orch.; Concerto for violin and orch.; Symphony in A minor; 2 string quartets; chamber music; songs; piano pieces.
Source: MMLA

Campos Araujo, Joaquina de, Brazilian pianist, teacher, and composer; b.1 Nov 1906, Rio de Janeiro, Brazil. She studied piano with Francisco A. Bevilacqua and Lois Amabile, and composition with Paulo Silva and Francisco Braga at the Music School of the Univ. of Brazil. Professor at the Federal Univ. and the Oscar Lorenzo Fernández Music Academy, both of Rio de Janeiro.
Works: chamber music; piano pieces; songs.
Source: IEW

Campos Parsi, Héctor, Puerto Rican composer, poet, journalist, music critic, educator, television commentator, and concert manager; b.10 Oct 1922, Ponce, Puerto Rico. He studied with Francis Judd Cooke and Carl McKinley at the New England Cons. of Music, Boston, Massachusetts. He also took classes at Berkshire Music Center in Tanglewood, Massachusetts, with Irving Fine in 1948, Olivier Messiaen in 1949, and Aaron Copland in 1950 and 1956. From 1950 to 1954, he studied harmony, counterpoint, composition, and orchestration with Nadia Boulanger in Paris, France. Professor at the Cons. of Puerto Rico, 1960-73, and associate professor at the Dept. of Humanities of the Colegio Universitario of Cayey, Puerto Rico, since 1983.

Works (selective list): *Incidente,* ballet (1948); *Música,* for 3 violins (1949); *Psalm 121,* for voice and orch. (1949); String quartet (1950); *Versículos,* for viola (1950); *Melos,* ballet (1952); *Divertimento del Sur,* for flute, clarinet, and strings (1953); Sonatina for violin and piano (1953); Piano sonata (1953); *Annunciation,* cantata (1954); *Juan Bobo,* ballet (1957); *Urayoán,* ballet (1958); *Madrigales,* for contralto and strings (1959); *Rapsodia Elegíaca, in memoriam Villa-Lobos,* for strings (1960); *Dúo Trágico,* for piano and orch. (1965); *Petroglifos,* for piano trio (1966); *Ubao Moín,* for narrator, narrating chorus, singing chorus, and orch. (1968); *El Casorio,* incidental music for the theater (1970); *La Bella Durmiente,* incidental music for flute, harp, cello, and 2 pianos (1978); *Fanfarria para un Festival,* for 3 trumpets, 3 trombones, and percussion (1982); *Las Troyanas,* incidental music, for indigenous ensemble and tape (1984); *Tureyareito,* for orch. (1984); *Variation V on a theme by Mozart,* for orch. (1991); piano pieces; music for solo instruments; songs; choruses.

Bibl.: F. Caso, *Héctor Campos Parsi,* in the *History of 20th Century Music in Puerto Rico,* Indiana University, 1972.
Sources: BB, CPR, ISC

Campoverde, Juan, Ecuadorian composer and musicologist; b.1964, Cuenca, Ecuador. He studied at the Cons. José María Rodríguez and at the School of Musicology of the Catholic Univ., both of Cuenca.
Works: *Tientos,* for orch.
Source: PEFCM

Camps, Pompeyo, Argentine composer and music critic; b.27 Oct 1924, Paraná, Prov. of Entre Ríos, Argentina. In 1947, he settled in Buenos Aires, Argentina, where he studied with Jaime Pahissa. Staff member of the Argentine Catholic Univ. and the Asociación de Jóvenes Compositores de la Argentina. Music critic for the daily newspaper *Noticias Gráficas,* 1957-1962, and *La Opinión* since 1971.

Works (selective list): *Stage: La Pendiente,* opera (1959); *Balada de la Cárcel de Reading,* choreographic drama (1964); *Después de la Mañana,* ballet (1966). *Orch.: Homenaje a Roberto Arlt* (1958); *Viñetas Porteñas* (1960); *Fantasía,* for strings (1961); *Romance de la Ciudad de San Juan de la Frontera,* for contralto and chorus (1962); *Sinfonía para un Poeta,* for baritone (1967). *Chamber music:* 2 string quartets (1957, 1974); *Tres Canciones,* for contralto, viola, and piano (1960); *Pieza Concertante,* for violin and piano (1960); *Pas de Quatre,* for 2 trumpets and 2 trombones (1961); *Tríptico Arcáico,* for flute, viola, cello, and guitar (1961); *Blues para una Muchacha Muerta,* for voice and 4 instruments (1963); *Danzas,* for percussion (1966); *Reflejos,* for 13 brasses and percussion (1966); *Ciudad sin Tregua,* for string quartet (1974). Piano pieces; songs.
Sources: BB, EMA

Canales Pizarro, Marta, Chilean violinist, choral conductor, and composer; b.1895, Chile; d.? She studied with Luigi Esteban Giarda. She founded several women choral groups.
Works (selective list): *Marta y María,* oratorio for soloists, chorus, organ, and chamber orch. (1929); *Misa de Navidad,* for mixed chorus and chamber orch. (1930); *Misa Eucarística,* for soloists, mixed chorus, and chamber orch. (1930); *Madrigales Teresianos,* for chorus a cappella (1933); *Misa Gregoriana,* for chorus a cappella (1937); *Elevación,* for organ, harp, and chamber orch. (1946). Chamber music; sacred music; songs.
Sources: HMC, IBCC, IEW, NGDWC

Cancián, Germán, Argentine composer; b.Resistencia, Prov. El Chaco, Argentina. He studied with Alfredo Perduca in Resistencia. In 1985, he moved to Rosario, Prov. of Santa Fe, Argentina, where he studied at the Escuela de Música of the National Univ. of Rosario with Jorge Molina. He also studied harmony and musical analysis with Dante Grela and composition with Jorge Horst, and took courses with Mariano Etkin, Gerardo Gandini, Francisco Kröpfl, Carmelo Saitta, Vieira, Federico Monjeau, M.C. Aguilar, Jorge Rapp, and Guillermo Pozzati.
Works: Cíclope, for female voice, violin, and viola; *Hasta Ptolomeo, y Después del Tercer Viaje,* for bass clarinet, horn, cello, double bass, and percussion; *Puzzle,* for flute, clarinet, bass clarinet, violin, viola, and cello.
Source: CAMR

Cancino de Cuevas, Sofía, Mexican pianist and composer; b.29 Jul 1898, Mexico City, Mexico. She studied piano with Luis Ogazón and composition at the Facultad de Música of the UNAM.

Works (selective list): *Operas: Gil González de Avil* (1937); *Anette* (1945); *Michoacna* (1950); *Promessa d'Artista e Parole di Re* (1952). Symphony in G for orch.; *Gallo en Patzcuaro,* symphonic poem; chamber music; piano pieces; songs.
Sources: IBCC, IEW, KTL

Candiani Herrera, Salvador, Chilean composer, conductor, and physician; b.3 Jan 1917, Santiago de Chile, Chile; d.24 Jul 1969, Santiago de Chile. He studied with Domingo Santa Cruz.
Works (selective list): *Nuco y Tralana,* opera; *La Noche de San Juan,* ballet (1952); 3 symphonies; 5 sonatas for piano; incidental music for films.
Source: HMC

Cantillano, Roberto, Costa Rican composer and band conductor; b.2 Mar 1887, Santo Domingo de Heredia, Costa Rica; d.? He studied with Rubén Lizano, Moisés Salvatierra, Lucio de Avendaño, and Juan Loots. Conductor of the military band of Costa Rica and general director of bands of Costa Rica.
Works: Ausencia and *Odilie,* mazurkas for flute and piano; *Idilio Eterno* and *Hanya,* waltzes; *Noche de Luna,* serenade for flute and piano; *Amanecer Guanacasteco,* symphonic poem.
Sources: DM, MLA, MMLA

Cantú, Agostino, Brazilian composer and pianist of Italian origin; b.24 Apr 1880, Milan, Italy; d.? He studied at the Cons. of Milan. Professor of piano at the Musical Cons. of Sâo Paulo, Brazil.
Works: Il Poeta, opera (1902). *Music for piano: Tres Rapsodias Brasileiras; Tres Lendas Brasileiras; Impressôes Brasileiras.*
Sources: DM, HMB, MLA

Cárdona, Ismael, Costa Rican violinist and composer; b.5 Dec 1877, San Ramón, Costa Rica; d.? He studied in San José, Costa Rica, and in New York. After returning to Costa Rica from New York, he continued studying harmony and instrumentation with Alvise Castegnaro. Violinist at the National Symphony Orch. and professor of music and violin at the Escuela Normal, both in San José.
Works (selective list): Masses for voices and orch.; String quartet in A minor; *Suite Miniatura,* for orch.(1928); *Suite Ballet,* for orch.; *La Novia de Tilarán,* zarzuela; Serenata for violin and piano (1909); *Canción de Cuna,* for violin and piano (1910); music for the stage; children's comedies.
Sources: DM, MLA, MMLA

Cardoso, Daniel Carlos, Argentine composer and teacher; b.Rosario, Prov. of Santa Fe, Argentina. He studied with Roberto Caamaño,

Licia B. de Parodi, and Juan Carlos Zorzi at the Escuela de Música de la Facultad de Humanidades y Artes of the National Univ. of Rosario. He attended courses taught by Edgar Willems, Juan Carlos Paz, Ernesto Epstein, Kurt Pahlen, Manuel Rego, Francisco Kröpfl, Mariano Etkin, Carmelo Saitta, and Alcides Lanza. Professor at various cultural institutions. Founding director of the National School of Music of Rosario. Founder and first president of the Inst. Nacional del Profesorado de Música of Rosario, branch of the National Ministry of Education and Justice. Founding member of the Asociación Santafesina de Compositores.

Works (selective list): *Ensayos,* for soloist and orch.; *Espacios Finitos,* for electronic sounds; chamber music; songs.

Source: CAMR

Cardoso, Lindembergue Rocha, Brazilian composer; b.30 Jun 1939, Livramento, Bahia, Brazil. He studied composition with Ernst Widmer, and bassoon at the Univ. of Bahia. After graduating, he was appointed professor at the Univ. of Bahia and the Catholic Univ. of Salvador, Brazil. Conductor of the madrigal group and the univ. choir. Founder and member of the *Grupo de Compositores de Bahia.*

Works (selective list): *A Lenda do Bicho Turuna,* opera (1974). *Orch.:* *A Festa da Canabrava* (1966); *Minisuite* (1967); *Viasacra* (1968); *Extrême* (1970); *Abertura* (1970); *Serestachorofrevo* (1970); *Influência,* string orch. (1971); *Pleorama* (1971). *Choral music*: *Procissão das Carpideiras,* for 8 sopranos, contralto, and orch. (1969); *Captações,* for 4 voices and orch. (1969); *Aleluia,* for chorus and percussion (1970); *Kyrie Christe,* for soprano, chorus, trombone, and string quartet (1971); *Oratório Cênico,* for 3 voices, chorus, and orch. (1972); *Requiem in Memory of Milton Gomes (1974).* Chamber music.

Bibl.: L. Biriotti, *El Grupo de Compositores de Bahía,* Montevideo, 1971.

Sources: DCM, GDM, HMB

Carnicer, Fernando, Cuban teacher and composer of Spanish origin; b.1865, Madrid, Spain; d.1936, Havana, Cuba. He studied music in Spain. Professor at various music schools. Founder of the Carnicer Music Schools. In 1917, he was appointed professor of harmony and counterpoint at the Municipal Cons. of Music of Havana.

Works: 3 symphonic compositions; 2 operas; religious music; piano pieces.

Source: DMC

Carnicer, Ramón, Chilean composer of Spanish origin; b.1789, Lérida, Spain; d.1855, Chile. Studied with organist Buenaventura

64 - Caro de Boesi

Feliú and Bruno Paquera. Member of the choir of the Cathedral of Seo de Urgel, Spain.
Works: Chilean National Anthem (1828). *Operas: Adela de Lusignan*; *Cristóforo Colombo*.
Sources: DM, HMC, MLA

Caro de Boesi, José Antonio, Venezuelan composer; b.c.1750, Chacao, near Caracas, Venezuela; d.16 Oct 1814, Cumaná?, Venezuela. Very little is known about his life.
Works: Requiem (1779); 4 masses; 6 motets; *Oficio de Difuntos* (1793).
Bibl.: J.B. Plaza, *Music in Caracas during the Colonial Period (1770-1811)*, *MQ*, Vol.29, 1943. J.A. Calcaño, *La Ciudad y su Música*, Caracas, 1958.
Sources: GDM, MLA, MMLA

Carpio Valdés, Roberto, Peruvian composer; b.23 Feb 1900, Arequipa, Peru; d.? He studied piano with his father and with Luis Duncker Lavalle and Francisco Ibáñez. Self-taught in composition. Professor of piano at the Bach Musical Inst. of Lima, Peru.
Works (selective list): Music for the movie *Petróleo del Sur,* for orch. (1941); *Aire de Vals,* for violin and piano (1938). *Music for piano*: *Nocturno y Preludio* (1921); *Tres Estampas de Arequipa* (1927); *Hospital,* suite (1928); *Triste* (1928); *Dos Piezas* (1930); *Tríptico* (1932); *Payaso* (1933); *Cuatro Preludios* (1933); *Tres Miniaturas* (1934); *Preludio* (1937); *Dos Preludios* (1939); *Nocturno y Pastoral* (1940). Songs.
Sources: CTA13, DM, MLA, MMLA

Carrasco Candil, Alfredo, Mexican organist and composer; b.4 May 1875, Culiacán, State of Sinaloa, Mexico; d.31 Dec 1945, Mexico City, Mexico. He studied music with the flutist Andrés Tenorio and then with organist Francisco Godínez in Guadalajara, Mexico. Organist at the Cathedral of Guadalajara and later conductor of the children's chorus at the same Cathedral.
Works (selective list): *El Bufón,* opera; *Motete Eucarístico,* for soloists, mixed choir, and orch. (1915); *Gran Misa de Requiem* (1933); *Preludio, Scherzo Sinfónico y Leyendas,* and *Dos Aires de Ballet,* for orch.; *Marcha Nacional de las Reservas,* for military band (1943); *Adiós,* dance-song, also known as *El Adiós de Carrasco*; religious music; piano pieces; music for violin and piano; choral music.
Sources: GMM, MMLA

Carreño, Cayetano José, Venezuelan composer; b.7 Aug 1772, Caracas, Venezuela; d.4 Mar 1836, Caracas. He studied music at

Father Sojo Music School in Caracas. Choirmaster and organist at the Metropolitan Church of Caracas.

Works (selective list): 2 masses; 10 motets for chorus and orch. or organ; *Pésame a la Virgen,* sacred piece; patriotic songs.

Bibl.: J.B. Plaza, *Music in Caracas during the Colonial Period (1770-1811), MQ,* Vol.29, 1943.

Sources: DM, GDM, MLA, MMLA

Carreño, Inocente, Venezuelan composer and chorus conductor; b.28 Dec 1919, Porlamar, Margarita, Venezuela. He studied French horn, clarinet, piano, and theory in Caracas, Venezuela, and composition with Vicente Sojo at the National School of Music in Caracas, where he graduated with a degree in composition in 1946. Choirmaster and French horn player in the Venezuelan Symphony Orch. Professor of music theory at the José Angel Lamas School of Music in Caracas.

Works (selective list): *El Pozo,* symphonic poem (1946); *Suite Breve,* for string orch. (1947); *Margariteña,* suite for orch. (1954); Concerto for horn and strings (1958); *Sinfonieta Satírica,* for 11 instruments (1965); *Diálogo,* for flute and chamber orch. (1965); chamber music; choruses.

Sources: BB, CTA14, GDM

Carreño, María Teresa, Venezuelan pianist, singer, conductor, and composer; b.22 Dec 1853, Caracas, Venezuela; d.12 Jun 1917, New York, USA. She started music studies with her father, Manuel Antonio Carreño. At the age of eight she was taken to New York where she studied with Louis Moreau Gottschalk. Later she studied with Georges Mathias and Anton Rubinstein in Paris, France.

Works: Himno a Bolívar, for chorus and orch. (1883); *Himno a El Ilustre Americano,* for chorus and orch. (1886); *Serenata,* for string orch. (1895); *Petite Danse Tsigane,* for orch.; String quartet in B; piano pieces.

Bibl.: J.B. Plaza, *Teresa Carreño,* Caracas, 1938. I. Peña, *Teresa Carreño,* Caracas, 1953.

Sources: BB, GDM, IBCC, IEW, MLA, MMLA, NGDWC

Carrillo Trujillo, Julián Antonio, Mexican composer and teacher; b.28 Jan 1875, Ahualulco, State of San Luis de Potosí, Mexico; d.9 Sep 1965, Mexico City, Mexico. He studied harmony with Melesio Morales and violin with Pedro Manzano at the National Cons. of Mexico, Mexico City, from which he graduated in 1899. He also studied composition with Salomón Jadassohn and orch. conducting with Hans Sitt at the Leipzig Cons., Germany. He created a new

theoretical music system based on the division of the sound in 16 equidistant intervals named *Sonido 13* (Sound 13). In 1905, he returned to Mexico and was appointed general supervisor of music and director of the National Cons. of Mexico, 1913-14 and 1920-24.
Works (selective list): *Operas: Ossian* (1903)*; Matilda* (1909); *Zultil* (1922). *Orch.:* 3 symphonies (1901, 1905, 1948); 3 symphonies for fractional tones (1926); Triple concerto for flute, violin, and cello (1918); Concertino for violin, guitar, cello, piccolo, and harp in fractional tones, with orch. in normal tuning (1926); *Horizontes*, for violin, cello, and harp in fractional tones (1947); Concertino, *Metamorfoseador Carrillo,* for piano in third tones (1950); Concerto for cello (1954); *Balbuceos*, for piano and chamber orch. (1960); 2 concertos for violin in quarter tones (1963, 1964). *Chamber music:* String sextet (1902); Piano quintet (1918); Four atonal quartets (1928-48); *Preludio a Cristóbal Colón,* for soprano and 5 instruments in fractional tones (1925); Sonata for guitar in quarter tones (1925); sonatas for string instruments in quarter tones, with piano. *Mass for Pope John XXIII*, for chorus a cappella (1962).
Bibl.: A. Pike, *The Discoveries and Theories of Julián Carrillo, 1875- 1965, Inter-American Music Bulletin,* IV (1966).
Sources: BB, DCM, DM, GDM, MLA, MMLA

Carrique, Ana, Argentine composer; b.1886, Buenos Aires, Argentina; d.? She studied piano with Julián Aguirre and harmony, counterpoint, fugue, and composition with Athos Palma at the National Cons. of Music Carlos López Buchardo of Buenos Aires.
Works (selective list): *Music for piano:* Sonatina in E flat; sonatas; *Preludio Criollo; Preludio Pampeano; Suite Campera;* Suite; Gato; Mazurca; Impromptu. Songs; school songs; hymns; choruses.
Sources: DM, EMA, MMLA

Carvajal Quirós, Armando, Chilean conductor, violinist, and composer; b.7 Jun 1893, Santiago de Chile, Chile; d.1972, Santiago de Chile. He studied piano, violin, and composition at the National Cons. of Santiago de Chile with Varalla, Luigi S. Giarda, and Enrique Soro Barriga. Concertmaster at the Municipal Theater Orch. of Santiago de Chile. Professor at the National Cons. of Santiago de Chile. In 1921, he was appointed conductor of the Symphony Orch. of Chile, Santiago de Chile.
Works: Mainly compositions for children, including *Tres Piezas para Niños: Canon a la 5a.; Canción de Cuna; Tonada Triste.*
Sources: DM, GDM, HMC, MLA

Carvalho, Dinorah de, Brazilian composer and pianist; b.1 Jun 1905, Uberala, Minas Gerais, Brazil; d.28 Feb 1980, Sâo Paulo, Brazil. She studied piano at the Municipal Cons. of Sâo Paulo, and then in Paris, France, with Isidor Philipp. In Sâo Paulo she finished her studies of harmony, counterpoint, and composition with Lamberto Baldi and Martín Braunwieser, and conducting with Ernst Mehlich. She founded and directed the *Orquesta Femenina* of Sâo Paulo, the first all-women orch. in South America. Member of the Academia Brasileira de Música.

Works (selective list): *Fantasía*, for piano and orch.; *Tres Dansas Brasileiras*, for string orch. and percussion; *Jogos no Jardim*, 5 pieces for piano; *E Bambo-Bambue*, for voice, string orch., and percussion; *Pau Piá*, for voice and orch.; *Boi Tungao*, for 4 mixed voices; *Festa na Vila*, for orch.; *Serenata da Saudade*, for orch.; *Procissao do Senhor Morto*, for orch.; 2 concertos for piano and orch.; piano pieces.

Sources: DM, GDM, HMB, MLA, MMLA, NGDWC

Carvalho, Eleazar de, Brazilian composer and conductor; b.28 Jul 1912, Iguatú, Ceará, Brazil. He studied composition at the National School of Music of Rio de Janeiro, Brazil. In 1941, he was assistant conductor of the Brazilian Symphony Orch. of Rio de Janeiro. In 1946, he studied conducting with Serge Koussevitzky at the Berkshire Music Center, Massachusetts. Guest conductor in USA and Europe. From 1963 to 1968, he was conductor of the Saint Louis Symphony Orch., Saint Louis, Missouri. From 1969 to 1973, he was conductor of the Hofstra Univ. Orch., Hempstead, New York.

Works (selective list): **Operas:** *A Descoberta do Brasil* (1939); *Tiradentes* (1941). **Symphonic poems:** *A Traiçao* (1941); *Batalha Naval de Riachuelo* (1943); *Guararapes* (1945). *Sinfonía Branca* (1943); 3 overtures; 2 trios; 2 string quartets; Violin sonata; songs.

Sources: BB, DM, HMB, MLA, MMLA

Casa, Luis, Cuban band conductor and composer; b.24 May 1882, Camagüey, Cuba; d.? Flutist in orch. of several Italian lyric opera companies. Professor at the National Cons. Hubert de Blanck of Havana, Cuba.

Works (selective list): *Martí*, overture; *La Vida*, symphonic poem; marches; zarzuelas; suites; potpourris; dances; criollas.

Source: MMLA

Casabona, Francisco, Brazilian composer and teacher; b.16 Oct 1894, Sâo Paulo, Brazil; d.? He studied piano with Alessandro Longo, music theory with Camillo de Nardis, and composition with Giovanni Barbieri at the Cons. of Naples, Italy. Director of the Musical Cons. of Sâo Paulo.

Works (selective list): **Comic operas:** *Godiamo la Vita* (1917); *Principessa dell'Atelier* (1918). **Symphonic poems:** *Nero* (1915); *Crepúsculo Sertanejo* (1926); *Noite de Sâo Joâo* (1934). 2

symphonies (1937, 1940); *La Fable d'Einstein,* for orch. (1946); *Maracatú,* Afro-Brazilian dance (1946); Violin sonata; piano pieces; choruses; songs.
Sources: BB, DM, MLA, MMLA

Casal Chapí, Enrique, Dominican composer of Spanish origin; b.15 Feb 1909, Madrid, Spain. In 1940, he settled in the Dominican Republic. He studied at the Cons. of Madrid with Conrado del Campo. In 1941, he was appointed conductor of the National Symphony Orch. of Ciudad Trujillo, Dominican Republic.
Works (selective list): *Preludio y Rondó,* for orch.; Overture for orch.; ballets; piano pieces; songs.
Sources: DM, MLA, MMLA

Casamitjana, Juan, Cuban flutist and composer of Spanish origin; b.c.1800, Barcelona, Spain; d.1880 in Paris, France. Between 1832 and 1850, he lived in Santiago de Cuba, Cuba. In 1850, he settled in Paris. He studied flute at the Paris Cons. He founded a music school in Santiago de Cuba and later he moved to Havana, Cuba, where he taught and conducted orch. and bands.
Works: Very little is known about his musical production. He wrote an opera that was premiered in Paris.
Source: MMLA

Casanova Vicuña, Juan, Chilean conductor and composer; b.27 Dec 1894, Santiago de Chile, Chile; d.? He studied with Humberto Pedro Allende and Enrique Soro Barriga.
Works: Cuatro Bosquejos, suite for orch. (1931); *El Indio y el Huaso,* symphonic poem (1934); *Alegre la Tristeza y Triste el Vino,* symphonic poem.
Sources: HMC, MLA

Casella, Enrique Mario, Uruguayan composer and teacher; b.1 Aug 1891, Montevideo, Uruguay; d.10 Dec 1948, Tucumán, Prov. of Tucumán, Argentina. He studied in Buenos Aires, Argentina, with Ferruccio Cattelani and Edmundo Pallemaerts. He continued his studies in Bologna, Italy, with Enrico Bossi and in Brussels, Belgium, with César Thomson and Maurice Estaminet. He also studied with Paul Vidal and Foucher in Paris, France. In 1921, he settled in Tucumán where he founded the Musical Inst. and the Asociación Sinfónica. He devoted most of his time to teaching. Conductor of the Band of Music of Tucumán.
Works (selective list): **Operas:** *Corimayo; La Vidala; La Tapera; Las Vírgenes del Sol; El Maleficio de la Luna; El País del Ensueño.* **Symphonic poems:** *Brujerías; Nauhel Huapí; En la Puna; Don Quijote; Faetón; El Rey Midas. Tavantisuyo,* symphonic suite;

Quintet for violin, viola, cello, piano, and French horn; 2 string quartets; Sonata for violin and piano.
Sources: CA, DM, EMA, MLA, MMLA

Castañeda, José, Guatemalan composer; b.24 May 1898, Guatemala City, Guatemala; d.1983, Guatemala City. He developed a notation system of twelve chromatic tones eliminating the use of sharps and flats. Founder of the National Cons. of Music of Guatemala, Guatemala City. Conductor of the orch. *Ars Nova* of Guatemala City.
Sources: DM, HMG, MLA

Castegnaro, Lola, Costa Rican conductor and composer; b.17 May 1905, San José, Costa Rica. She studied with her father, Alvise Castegnaro. Later she went to Italy where she studied at the Verdi Cons. of Milan, and then at the Academia Filarmónica of Bologna. In 1940, she returned to Costa Rica. In 1945, she settled in Mexico where she taught at the Academia de Canto de Fanny Anitúa.
Works: Suite for orch.; *Mirka,* operetta; about 70 songs; religious compositions.
Source: MMLA

Castellanos, Evencio, Venezuelan, composer, organist, and conductor; b.3 May 1915, Cúa, Miranda, Venezuela; d.1984. He started music studies with his father, Pablo Castellanos. In 1944, he graduated from the Escuela Superior de Música of Caracas, Venezuela. Later he studied in the USA. Professor at the Escuela Superior de Música. Organist at the Cathedral of Caracas.
Works (selective list): Concerto for piano and orch. (1944); *El Río de las Siete Estrellas,* for orch. (1946); *Suite Avileña,* for orch. (1947); *Mass Ave Maris Stella,* for chorus (1953); *Santa Cruz de Pacairigua,* for orch. (1963); *El Tirano Aguirre*, oratorio for soloists, chorus, and orch. (1967); madrigals; chamber music; songs.
Sources: CTA14, GDM

Castellanos Yumar, Gonzalo, Venezuelan composer and conductor; b.3 June 1926, Canoabo, Carabobo, Venezuela. He started music studies with his father, Pablo Castellanos, and later studied with Vicente Sojo at the Escuela Superior de Música of Caracas, Venezuela. He also studied orchestration with Daniel Lesur and Pierre Wissmer at the Schola Cantorum in Paris, France, and conducting with Sergiu Celibidache in Siena, Italy. *Maestro de capilla* (chapelmaster) of the Church San José, and director of the Escuela de Música Juan Manuel Olivares, the Venezuelan Symphony Orch., and the Collegium Musicum, all in Caracas.
Works (selective list): *Suite Sinfónica Caraqueña,* for orch. (1947); *Fantasía Cromática,* for orch. (1952); *Antelación e Imitación Fugaz,*

for piano and orch. (1954); *Fantasía Sinfónica,* for piano and orch. (1954); chamber music; choruses; songs.
Sources: CTA14, GDM

Castilla, Alberto, Colombian composer; b.9 Apr 1883, BB (Jul 1878, CMC), Bogotá, Colombia; d.10 Jun 1937, Ibagué, Colombia. He studied at the National Academy of Music in Bogotá with Julio Quevedo Arvelo. He also studied engineering. In 1898, he settled in Tolima, Colombia, where he founded a music school.
Works (selective list): *Bunde Tolimense; Guabina Ibaguereña;* many songs.
Sources: BB, CMC, ZCCC

Castillo, Fructos del, Mexican composer of Spanish origin from the 16th century; b.Segovia?, Spain; fl.1600. Active in Puebla, Mexico.
Works (selective list): *Monstra te Esse Matrem,* second strophe of the hymn *Ave Maris Stella,* his only surviving composition found to date and preserved in an appendix to *Libro de Coro 2b* at the archives of the Cathedral of Puebla.
Bibl.: R. Stevenson, *Renaissance and Baroque Musical Sources in the Americas,* Washington, D.C., 1970.
Source: GDM

Castillo, Gabriel del, Dominican composer; b.18 Mar 1874, Higüey, Dominican Republic; d.? He studied with José Galván. Conductor of the Municipal Band of San Pedro de Macorís, Dominican Republic, until 1946. Founder of the Music Academy Patria.
Works (selective list): *Macorís,* overture for band; *La Fiesta de San Pedro,* lyric comedy; *Guachupino,* aire campestre (rural air); *Reminiscencia Higüeyana,* fantasia; *El Día de los Ayuntamientos,* fantasia; music for wind instruments; waltzes; dances; mazurkas; polkas; marches; hymns.
Sources: DM, MMLA

Castillo, Jesús, Guatemalan composer and folklorist; b.9 Oct 1877, San Juan Ostuncalco, Dept. of Quetzaltenango, Guatemala; d.23 Apr 1946, Quetzaltenango. He is half brother of Ricardo Castillo. He studied with Alejandro and Miguel Espinosa, Fernando Soria, and Rafael Guzmán. He devoted himself to research the musical folklore of Guatemala.
Works (selective list): 5 indigenous overtures (1897-1910); 2 indigenous suites (1912-32); 3 indigenous potpourris (1922-26); *Quiché Vinák,* opera (1919-24); *Tecúm Umán,* symphonic poem (1936); *Nicté,* opera (1936); *Guatema,* ballet (1938); *Vartizanic,* symphonic poem (1941). *Books: La Música Maya-Quiché,* Quetzaltenango, 1941.

Sources: DM, GDM, MLA, MMLA

Castillo, Ricardo, Guatemalan composer; b.1 Oct 1894, Quetzaltenango, Guatemala; d.1967. Half brother of Jesús Castillo. Studied violin with A. Lefort, 1912-17 and harmony with Paul Vidal, 1919-21, in Paris, France. Professor of music history, harmony, and counterpoint at the Cons. of Guatemala, Guatemala City. *Works*: *La Doncella Ixquic,* ballet (1942). *Orch.*: *Guatemala,* symphonic movements (1934); *La Procesión* (1935); *Primavera,* acuarela sinfónica (1935); *Homenaje a Ravel,* symphonic minuet; Symphony (1943); *Xibalba,* symphonic poem (1944). *Music for piano:* *L'Eau qui Court; Barcarola; Nocturno; Poema Pastoral; Scène Pastorale; Guatemala,* suite (1933-34).
Sources: CTA1, DM, MLA, MMLA

Castillo Olivari, Arcángel, Venezuelan composer, and choral and orch. conductor; b.3 Oct 1959, Mérida, Venezuela. He studied at the IUDEM in Caracas, Venezuela. Choral director at several educational inst. Director of the audiovisual archive at the Music Dept. of the Venezuelan National Library, Caracas. Conductor of the Mérida State Symphonic Band and the National Youth Orch. of Mérida since 1992. *Works* (selective list): Trio for oboe, clarinet, and bassoon (1985); String trio (1986); *Elegía,* for strings (1987); *Passacaglia y Fuga Modal,* for string trio (1990); *Aforismos,* for symphony orch. (1991); *Postludio,* for harp (1992); songs.
Source: ISC

Castro, Aloysio de, Brazilian writer, professor of medicine, and composer; b.14 Jun 1881, Rio de Janeiro, Brazil; d.7 Oct 1959, Rio de Janeiro, Brazil.
Works: Many songs on French poems, including: *Chant d'Amour et de la Tristesse; Coeur Battant; Enchantement.*
Source: MMLA

Castro, José María, Argentine composer, conductor, and cellist; b.15 Dec 1892, Avellaneda, Prov. of Buenos Aires, Argentina; d.2 Aug 1964, Buenos Aires. Brother of Juan José and Washington Castro. He studied cello with Humberto Ferrari and José García, harmony with Constantino Gaito, and composition with Eduardo Fornarini. He played in several chamber ensembles. Founder of the *Sociedad del Cuarteto* and the Chamber Orch. *Renacimiento,* conductor of the Chamber Orch. and the Philharmonic Orch. of APO, and conductor of the Municipal Band, all of Buenos Aires. Founder, with other leading avant-garde composers, of the *Grupo Renovación,* in 1929, and of the *Liga de Compositores de la Argentina,* in 1947.

Works (selective list): *Ballets: Georgia* (1937); *El Sueño de la Botella* (1948); *Falarka* (1951). *Orch.:* Concerto grosso (1932); *Obertura para una Opera Cómica* (1934); Piano concerto (1941-56); Concerto (1944); *Tres Pastorales* (1945); Concerto for cello and 17 instruments (1945); *El Libro de los Sonetos,* for voice (1947); *Preludio y Toccata,* for strings (1949); *Tema Coral con Variaciones* (1952); Concerto for violin and 18 instruments (1953); *Diez Improvisaciones Breves* (1957); *Cinco Líricas,* for voice (1958); *Preludio, Tema con Variaciones y Final* (1959); *Sinfonía de Buenos Aires* (1963); *Con la Patria Adentro,* for tenor (1964). *Chamber music:* Concerto for violin and piano (1917); 2 sonatas for violin and piano (1918, 1957); 3 string quartets (1932, 1944, 1956); Sonata for cello and piano (1933); Sonata for 2 cellos (1938); 6 sonatas for piano (1919, 1924, 1927, 1931, 1939, 1934). Piano pieces; many songs.
Sources: BB, CA, CTA11, DM, EMA, GDM, MLA, MMLA

Castro, Juan José, Argentine composer and conductor; b.7 Mar 1895, Avellaneda, Prov. of Buenos Aires, Argentina; d.3 Sep 1968, Buenos Aires, Argentina. Brother of José María and Washington Castro. He studied piano and violin with Manuel Posadas, harmony with Constantino Gaito, and counterpoint, fugue, and composition with Eduardo Fornarini. In Paris, France, he studied with Vincent d'Indy at the Schola Cantorum, and piano with Eduardo Risler. Founder of the *Sociedad del Cuarteto* and of the Chamber Orch. *Renacimiento,* where he started his career as a conductor. He conducted the orch. of the Teatro Colón, the symphony orch. of APO, and the Asociación Filarmónica, all of Buenos Aires. From 1947 to 1951, he conducted in Cuba and Uruguay; from 1952 to 1953, he was principal conductor of the Victorian Symphony Orch. of Melbourne, Australia. In 1955, he returned to Argentina and, from 1956 to 1960, was the conductor of the National Symphony Orch. of Buenos Aires. From 1959 to 1964, he was director of the Cons. of San Juan, Puerto Rico.
Works (selective list): *Operas: La Zapatera Prodigiosa* (1943); *Proserpina y el Extranjero* (1951); *Bodas de Sangre* (1952); *Cosecha Negra* (1959-61). *Ballets: Mekhano* (1934); *Offenbachiana* (1940). *Symphonic-choral music: Sinfonía Bíblica,* for chorus and orch. (1932); *Martín Fierro,* for baritone, chorus, and orch. (1944); *Elegía a la Muerte de García Lorca,* for soprano, chorus, and orch. (1945); *De Tierra Gallega,* for chorus and orch. (1946); *Epitafio en Ritmos y Sonidos,* for chorus and orch. (1961). *Orch.: En el Jardín de los Muertos* (1923); *A una Madre* (1925); *La Chellah* (1927); 4 symphonies (1931, 1934, 1939, 1956); *Suite Infantil* (1928); *Suite Breve* (1929); *Allegro, Lento y Vivace* (1930); *Música del Bosque* (1946); *El Llanto de las Sierras* (1947); *Corales Criollos No 3*

(1953); *Fanfare for the Queen* (1953); *Adiós a Villa Lobos* (1962).
Chamber music: Sonata for violin and piano (1914); *Canción y Danza,* for clarinet and piano (1914); Sonata for cello and piano (1916); *Serenata,* for cello and piano (1918); String quartet (1942); *Intrata y Danza Rústica,* for violin and piano (1946); 2 piano sonatas (1917, 1939); *Corales criollos No.1* and *No.2,* for piano (1947, 1947). Piano pieces; many songs.
Bibl.: R. Arizaga, *Juan José Castro,* Buenos Aires, 1963.
Sources: BB, CA, CTA4, DCM, DM, GDM, MLA, MMLA

Castro, Sergio de, Argentine composer; b.15 Sep 1922, Buenos Aires, Argentina. He started his musical studies in Lausanne, Switzerland, and studied harmony and counterpoint with Guido Santórsola in Montevideo, Uruguay, and instrumentation at the SODRE. Self-taught in composition. Also a painter.
Works (selective list): *Títeres,* choreographic suite for winds, piano, percussion, and strings (1939-42); Ballet for two pianos and chamber orch. (1942-45); Quintet for flute, clarinet, bassoon, violin, and cello (1943-48); 2 symphonies; *Homenaje a Falla.*
Sources: DM, EMA, MLA

Castro, Washington, Argentine composer and cellist; b.13 Jul 1909, Buenos Aires, Argentina. Brother of José María and Juan José Castro. He studied with Alberto Schiuma, José María Castro, and Honorio Siccardi in Buenos Aires, and with Maurice Marechal in Paris, France. Professor at the Municipal Cons. of Music Manuel de Falla of Buenos Aires. Founder of the *Haydn Quartet.* Conductor of the Chamber Orch. of APO. Appointed assistant conductor and first cellist of the National Symphony Orch. of Buenos Aires in 1947. Member of the *Grupo Renovación* and *Liga de Compositores de la Argentina,* both in Buenos Aires.
Works (selective list): *Orch.: Salmo XXIII,* for chorus and chamber orch. (1962); *Obertura Festiva* (1941); *Belén* (1943); *Obertura Trágica* (1946); *El Concierto Campestre,* symphonic suite (1946); *Variaciones y Fuga* (1947); *Obertura para Niños* (1951); *Música,* for chamber orch. (1951); Symphonic suite (1952); 2 symphonies (1956, 1959); Concerto for orch. (1963); *Symphonic Music for Joan d'Arc* (1968); *Three Pieces* (1970); *Variaciones sobre un Tema de Händel* (1970); *Concierto Elegíaco,* for viola (1950); Piano concerto (1960); *Rapsodia,* for cello (1965). *Chamber music:* 3 string quartets (1945, 1950, 1965); Sonata for cello and piano (1943); *Divertimento,* for flute, oboe, clarinet, bassoon, and string quartet (1944); 2 wind quintets (1952, 1969); 3 tangos for cello and piano (1969); piano pieces; songs.
Sources: CA, CTA4, DM, EMA, GDM, MLA

Castro Herrera, Ricardo, Mexican pianist and composer; b.7 Feb 1864, Durango, Mexico; d.28 Nov 1907, Mexico City, Mexico. He studied harmony with Melesio Morales and piano with Juan Salvatierra at the National Cons. of Music of Mexico City. Director of the National Cons. of Music of Mexico City.
Works (selective list): *Operas: La Leyenda de Rudel* (1906); *Atzimba* (1900); *Satán Vencido; Rousalka.* 2 symphonies (1883, 1887); Concerto for piano and orch. (1904); piano pieces.
Sources: BB, CM, DM, GDM, GMM, MMLA

Cattelani, Ferruccio, Argentine conductor, violinist, and composer of Italian origin; b.1867, Parma, Italy; d.1932. He settled in Buenos Aires, Argentina, in 1897, where he lived until 1927. He founded the *Sociedad Orquestal Bonaerense* and the *Cuarteto Cattelani.*
Works: *Atahualpa,* opera (1900); *Hymn Commemorating the Centenary of the May Revolution,* written for an orch. of 400 players (1910).
Source: EMA

Cerón, José Dolores, Dominican composer and physician; b.29 Jun 1897, Santo Domingo, Dominican Republic; d.2 Mar 1969, Santo Domingo. He graduated from the Dominican Republic Medical School. He studied music with José de Jesús Ravelo and Esteban Peña Morell. In 1930, he became conductor of the band of the First Regiment in Santo Domingo.
Works: *Enriquillo,* symphonic poem; *Las Vírgenes de Galindo,* symphonic poem; Symphony; *Tres Preludios,* for orch.
Sources: DEW, DM, MLA, MMLA

Ceruti, Roque, Peruvian composer of Italian origin; b.c.1683, Milan, Italy; d.6 Dec 1760, Lima, Peru. He settled in Peru in 1708. He studied violin and composition in Milan. Composer and conductor at the Peru Viceroy's Palace in Lima from 1708 to 1717. In 1720, he moved to Trujillo, Peru, where he was appointed *maestro de capilla* (chapelmaster) at the Cathedral, 1721 to 1728. On August 1728, he returned to Lima to become *maestro de capilla* (chapelmaster) at the Cathedral of Lima.
Works (selective list): *El Mejor Escudo de Perseo,* mythological opera; 24-line Latin carmen panegyricum; 15 Spanish-text festival pieces for vocal duet, trio, or quartet accompanied by violins and continuo.
Bibl.: R. Stevenson, *The Music of Peru,* Washington, D.C., 1960. A. Sas, *La Música en la Catedral de Lima durante el Virreinato: Diccionario Biográfico,* Vol.1, Lima, 1972.
Source: GDM

Cervantes, María, Cuban pianist and composer; b.1889, Havana, Cuba; d.? Daughter of the Cuban composer Ignacio Cervantes Kawanag, with whom she started her music education. She continued her studies with González Nuñes and Enriqueta García de Pujol. *Works*: Piano pieces and songs. *Source:* IEW

Cervantes Kawanag, Ignacio, Cuban composer; b.31 Jul 1847, Havana, Cuba; d.29 Apr 1905, Havana. Father of Cuban composer María Cervantes. He studied with Nicolás Ruíz Espadero and Louis Moreau Gottschalk. In 1865, he went to Paris, France, and studied at the Paris Cons. with Antoine François Marmontel and Charles Valentín Alkan. He was one of the pioneers of native Cuban music. *Works* (selective list): *Operas: El Submarino Peral* (1889); *Maledetto* (1895); *Los Saltimbanquis* (1899). Symphony in C minor (1879); *Scherzo Caprichoso* (1886); many Cuban dances for piano; piano pieces; songs. *Bibl.:* E. Sánchez de Fuentes, *Ignacio Cervantes Kawanag,* Havana, 1963. A. Carpenter, *La Música en Cuba,* Mexico, 1946. *Sources:* BB, DM, DMC, GDM, MLA, MMLA

Cervetti, Sergio, Uruguayan composer; b.9 Nov 1941, Dolores, Uruguay. He studied piano with Hugo Balzo, José María Martino Rodas, and Reynaldo Reyes, and composition with Carlos Estrada and Guido Santórsola at the National Cons. of Music of Montevideo, Uruguay. In 1963, he went to the USA and attended classes of Ernst Krenek and Stefan Grové at the Peabody Cons. of Music in Baltimore, Maryland, 1963-67. He studied electronic music with Mario Davidovsky and Vladimir Ussachevsky at the Columbia-Princeton Electronic Music Center, and conducting with Lázsló Halász in New York. In 1970, he was appointed professor at the New York Univ. School of the Arts. Composer in residence at the Deutscher Akademisher Kunstler Program, West Berlin, Germany, 1969-70. Associate professor at McGill Univ., Montreal, Canada, 1978. *Works* (selective list): *Orbitas*, for orch. (1967); *El Carro de Heno*, for small chorus and orch. (1967); *Dies Tenebrarum*, for electric organ, 3 percussionists, male chorus, and strings (1968); *Pulsar*, for brass sextet (1969); *Prisons No.1*, for singers, dancers, pantomime, 2 trombones, electric organ, electric guitar, double bass, and percussion (1969); *Prisons No.2*, for speaking chorus, orch., and tape (1970-71); *Peripetia*, for 20 to 100 singers and instrumentalists (1970); *Cocktail Party* (1970); *Plexus,* for small orch. (1971); *Cuatro Fragmentos de Pablo Neruda,* for soprano, oboe, guitar, cello, and percussion (1970); *Raga I*, for ensemble, *Raga II*, for trombone and tape (both 1971); *Graffiti*, for speaking chorus, orch., and tape (1971); ...*from*

The Earth..., for ensemble (1972); *Madrigal 3,* for 2 sopranos and chamber ensemble (1976); *Inés de Castro,* ballet (1988); Concerto for harpsichord and 11 instruments (1990); *Leyenda,* for soprano and orch. (1991); chamber music; piano pieces; songs.
Sources: BB, BHMCU, CTA17, DCM, GDM

Charpentier de Castro, Eduardo, Panamanian composer and conductor; b.12 Mar 1927, Panama City, Panama. He started music studies at the Cons. of Music of Panama City. Later he continued his education at Roosevelt Univ. of Chicago, Illinois, where he studied composition with Karel B. Jirák, and at the Paris Cons., France, where he studied orch. conducting with Eugène Bigot. In 1957, he took advanced studies at the Eastman School of Music in Rochester, New York. Conductor of the Symphony Orch. of Panama. Director and adviser of the National Cons. of Panama.
Works (selective list): ***Orch.:*** *Fuga in A minor* (1950); *Ensayo Típico* (1950); *Siesta y Fiesta* (1961); *Tres Estampas* (1968). Chamber music; piano pieces; songs; music for band.
Source: CTA17

Chavarri, Norberto, Argentine teacher and composer; b.1940, Buenos Aires, Argentina. Self-taught musician. He also studied at the Municipal Cons. of Music Manuel de Falla of Buenos Aires and at the Inst. Di Tella. Music critic for *Tribuna Musical.*
Works: *Homenaje a Webern,* for piano (1963); *Y Emergieron Músculos y Huesos,* for cello and piano (1964); *Espacio 67,* music with electronic and concrete means (1967); *Fablada Escénica,* for string quartet, percussion, narrator, six women, and audience (1969); *Visiones,* for string quartet and 2 videocameras (1969); *Música para el Lobo Estepario,* for alto saxophone, chorus, and instrumental ensemble (1970).
Source: EMA

Chávez Aguilar, Pablo, Peruvian composer and priest; b.3 Mar 1899, Lima, Peru; d.? He studied solfeggio, music theory, harmony, Gregorian chant, piano, oboe, organ, and composition with the Reverend José Coll. In Rome, Italy, he studied organ with Manari, composition and Gregorian chant with Licinio Refice, and choir conducting with Raffaele Casimiri at the Escuela Pontificia Superior de Música. He continued composition studies with Angelo de Santi in Rome. Organist and *maestro de capilla* (chapelmaster) at the Cathedral of Lima and professor of harmony at the National Cons. of Music of Lima.
Works: *Preludios Incaicos,* for piano; *Variaciones sobre un Tema Incaico*; religious compositions.
Sources: ADBM, DM, GMP, MLA, MMLA

Chávez y Ramírez, Carlos Antonio de Pádua, Mexican composer and conductor; b.13 Jun 1899, Calzada de Catube, near Mexico City, Mexico; d.2 Aug 1978, Mexico City. He started music studies with his brother Manuel; later he studied piano with Pedro Luis Ogazón and harmony with Juan B. Fuentes and Manuel Ponce. Director of the National Cons. of Mexico, 1928-34, and general director of the Inst. Nacional de Bellas Artes, 1946-52, both of Mexico City. He founded the Symphony Orch. of Mexico in 1928, and remained its conductor until 1949.
Works (selective list): *Operas: Pánfilo y Lauretta (1953),* later revised as *El Amor Propiciado* (1959), and later retitled *The Visitors. Ballets: El Fuego Nuevo* (1921); *Los Cuatro Soles* (1925); *Caballos de Vapor* (1926); *Antígona* (1940); *La Hija de Colquide* (1943); *Pirámide* (1968). *Orch.:* Sinfonía (1915); *Cantos de México* (1933); *Sinfonía de Antígona,* Sinfonía No.1 (1933); *Obertura Republicana* (1935); *Sinfonía India,* No.2 (1935); Concerto for 4 horns (1937); Piano concerto (1938-40); *Cuatro Nocturnos,* for soprano and contralto (1939); *Toccata* (1947); Violin concerto (1948); Symphony No.3 (1951); *Sinfonía Romántica,* No.4 (1952); Symphony No.5 for strings (1953); Symphony No.6 (1961); Symphony N.7 (1960); *Resonancias* (1964); *Elatio* (1967); *Discovery* (1969); *Clio,* symphonic ode (1970); *Initium* (1972); *Mañanas Mexicanas* (1974); *Sonante,* for string orch. (1974); Trombone concerto (1975-76). *Choral works: Tierra Mojada,* for chorus, oboe, and English horn (1932); *El Sol,* for chorus and orch. (1934); *Sinfonía Proletaria,* for chorus and orch. (1934); *La Paloma Azul,* for chorus and orch. (1940); *Prometheus Bound,* cantata (1956). *Chamber music:* Piano and string sextet (1919); 3 string quartets (1921, 1932, 1944); *Three Pieces,* for guitar (1923); Violin sonatina (1924); Cello sonatina (1924); *Energía,* for 9 instruments (1925); *Tres Espirales,* for violin and piano (1934); *Xochipilli Macuilxochitl,* for 4 wind instruments and 6 percussionists (1940); *Toccata,* for 6 percussionists (1942); *Inventions* (1965, 1967); Variations for violin and piano (1969). *Music for piano:* 6 sonatas (1917, 1919, 1928, 1941, 1960, 1961); *Siete Madrigales* (1921-22); *Polígonos* (1923); Sonatina (1924); *Diez Preludios* (1937); *Fugas* (1942); *Cuatro Estudios* (1949); *Cinco Caprichos* (1975-76). Many songs.
Bibl.: H. Weinstock, *Carlos Chávez, Musical Quarterly* (1936). R. García Morillo, *Carlos Chávez, Vida y Obra,* Buenos Aires, 1960. R. Halffter, compiler, *Carlos Chávez, Catálogo Completo de sus Obras,* Mexico City, 1971.
Sources: BB, CTA3, DCM, DM, GDM, MLA, MMLA

Chimenti, Armando, Argentine pianist and composer; b.1881, Buenos Aires, Argentina; d.12 Jul 1927, Buenos Aires. Self-taught in music.

Works: *Marcha Triunfal,* for orch.; *Aires Montañeses,* for orch.; *Tres Impromptus,* for piano; *Las rosas,* waltz-intermezzo for piano; *Serenata Española,* for piano; *Suite argentina,* for piano.
Sources: DM, MMLA

Cifuentes, Santos, Colombian composer; b.1 Nov 1870, Bogotá, Colombia; d.1 Sep 1932, Buenos Aires, Argentina. He studied at the National Academy of Music of Bogotá with Julio Quevedo Arvelo, Augusto Azzali, and Diego Fallón, and also studied fugue and counterpoint with Honorio Alarcón. In 1910, he founded the Academy Beethoven in Bogotá and in 1911, he founded a similar academy in Cartagena, Colombia. In 1913, he settled in Buenos Aires where he taught at the Cons. Fontova and the National Cons. of Music Carlos López Buchardo, both of Buenos Aires.
Works (selective list): *Sinfonía sobre Aires Tropicales;* Concerto for piano and orch.; *Balada,* for flute and piano; Sonata for violin and piano; Variations for guitar; Overture in two movements; *Albores Musicales,* symphony; *La Soledad,* for orch.; *La Balada del Zipa;* chamber music; songs.
Bibl.: J.I. Perdomo Escobar, *Historia de la Música Colombiana,* Bogotá, 1945.
Sources: CMC, CTA18, DM, ZCCC

Cimaglia Espinosa, Lía, Argentine pianist and composer; b.1906, Buenos Aires, Argentina. She studied at the National Cons. of Music Carlos López Buchardo of Buenos Aires under Alberto Williams and Celestino Piaggio. She completed her piano studies with Jorge de Lalewicz. In Paris, France, she studied with Isidor Philipp, Ives Nat, and Alfred Cortot. Professor at the National Cons. of Music Carlos López Buchardo.
Works (selective list): **Stage:** *Egloga de Nochebuena* (1934); *El Carnaval del Diablo* (1943); *El Trigo es de Dios* (1949). **Music for piano:** *Improvisación* (1911); *Cajita de Música* (1912); *Tres Preludios en Homenaje a Debussy* (1936); *Suite Argentina* (1936-37); *Recuerdos de mi Tierra,* suite (1939); *Triste y Danza* (1939-40). *Leyendas,* for cello and piano (1920-28); *Serenata,* for violin and piano (1920-28); *Poema,* for violin and piano (1939-40); *Nocturno,* for violin and piano (1939-40). Many songs.
Sources: CA, DCM, DM, EMA, MMLA

Claro Valdés, Samuel, Chilean composer and musicologist; b.31 Jul 1934, Santiago de Chile, Chile. He studied at the National Cons. of Music of Santiago de Chile, and at Columbia Univ., New York. Since 1964, he devoted himself to research Chilean and Latin American music.
Works: Choral music; chamber music; electronic music.

Source: HMC

Claudio, Pablo, Dominican clarinetist and composer; b.1855, Azua, Dominican Republic; d.1899, Dominican Republic.
Works: Musical dramas: América; María de Cuellar. More than 700 other compositions.
Sources: DM, MLA, MMLA

Clemente, Joaquín, Argentine composer and conductor of Portuguese origin; b.22 Oct 1901, Lisbon, Portugal; d.1950, Buenos Aires, Argentina. He started music studies with his father, Luis Clemente. Then he studied piano with Joaquín Pedro López and harmony with Laurentino Serra e Moura. In 1919, he entered the Lisbon National Cons. where he studied composition with Rocha Pires. He settled in Argentina in 1928. Director of the Municipal Cons. of San Francisco, Prov. of Córdoba, Argentina. Director of the Municipal Band in 1932, and of the Police Symphonic Band in 1941, both of Buenos Aires. From 1934 to 1937, he was conductor of the Women's Symphony Orch. of Buenos Aires.
Works (selective list): *Themis,* symphonic poem (1937); *Coimbra, Portuguese Symphonic Suite* (1937); *Portuguese Eucharistic Hymn* (1934); many transcriptions and orchestrations for band and orchestra.
Books: Método de Trompeta.
Sources: EMA, MMLA

Clérice, Justino, Argentine composer; b.1863, Buenos Aires, Argentina; d.1908, Toulouse, France. At age eighteen he went to France to complete his music studies that he began in Buenos Aires. In Paris, France, he studied with Leo Delibes and Emile Pessard.
Works (selective list): *Vercingetorix,* opera (1901). *Comic operas: Le Meunier d'Alcalá* (1887); *Figarelle* (1889); *Le Deuxième Hussard* (1894); *Pavie* (1897); *Flagrant Délit* (1901); *La Fille Jackson*; *La Fiancée de Salamanque. Operettas: Viperine* (1881); *Margarred* (1900); *La Petite Vénus* (1900); *L'Ordre de l'Empereur* (1903). *Ballets: Au Temps Jadis,* ballet-opera (1905); *Au Pays Noir* (1891); *Colibrí* (1896); *Dame de Coeur* (1900); *Mimosa* (1905); *Timbre d'Or* (1906). Pantomimes; lyric comedies; vaudevilles; piano pieces; songs.
Sources: DM, EMA

Cleto, Marcelino, Brazilian composer; b.1842, Pernambuco, Brazil; d.1922, Brazil.
Works: (selective list): *Symphonies: Evoluçao; Porvir. Sacred dramas and pastorals: N.S. da Aparecida; San Benedito; Santa Clotilde.*

Source: MMLA

Cluzeau Mortet, Luis, Uruguayan composer, violist, and pianist; b.16 Nov 1889, Montevideo, Uruguay; d.28 Sep 1957, Montevideo. He studied piano with his grandfather, Pierre Paul Faget, and violin with María Visca. He was self-taught in composition. First violist in OSSODRE. Professor of music history at the Inst. Normal of Montevideo.
Works (selective list): *Stage: La Patria en Armas,* incidental music (1950); *Cédulas de San Juan,* incidental music (1950). *Orch.: Fantasía Concierto,* for piano and chamber orch. (1927-38); *Poema Nativo* (1931); *Llanuras* (1932); *Soledad Campestre* (1936); *Rancherío* (1940); *Artigas* (1951); *Sinfonía del Este* (1951). *Cuatro Ritmos Criollos,* for string quartet; *Bagatelas Criollas,* for 4 flutes; choruses; piano pieces; songs.
Sources: BB, BHMCU, CTA14, DM, GDM, MLA, MMLA, MU

Codina, Genaro, Mexican composer; b.10 Sep 1852, Zacatecas, Mexico; d.22 Nov 1901, Zacatecas. Very little is known about the life of this composer, only that he played the harp.
Works: Zacatecas, march that became so popular it was considered the second *Mexican National Anthem.*
Source: GMM

Coelho Neto, Marcos, Brazilian composer, conductor, and French horn player; b.c.1750, Vila Rica (today Ouro Prêto), Brazil; d.22 Oct 1823, Vila Rica. His father, also Marcos Coelho Neto, was a composer, conductor, and French horn player. Both were members of the Vila Rica Brotherhood of Sâo José dos Homens Pardos.
Works: Maria Mater Gratiae, hymn for mixed chorus, strings, and French horns (1787); *Credo*; 3 ladainhas (litanies); 3 masses.
Bibl.: F.C. Lange, *La Música en Vila Rica, Minas Gerais, siglo XVIII, Revista Musical Chilena,* Vol.22, 1967. G. Béhague, *Música "Barroca" Mineira: Problemas de Fontes e Estilística, Universitas,* Vol.2, Salvador, Bahia, 1969.
Source: GDM

Colabella, Angel Victorino, Argentine composer; b.1911, Pergamino, Prov. of Buenos Aires, Argentina. He was ordained a Catholic priest in 1936. Organist at the Seminario Mayor San José of La Plata, Prov. of Buenos Aires. He dedicated most of his time to choral conducting in different schools in the Prov. of Buenos Aires.
Works (selective list): *Capricho Criollo,* for string quartet; *Tres Danzas Argentinas,* for piano; motets for organ; songs.
Source: EMA

Comellas, José, Cuban pianist and composer; b.21 Feb 1842, Matanzas, Cuba; d.9 Feb 1888, Havana, Cuba. He studied music in Leipzig, Germany. Professor at the Peabody Cons. of Music in Baltimore, Maryland.
Works: Sonata Brillante, for piano.
Source: DMC

Contreras Sánchez, Salvador, Mexican composer; b.10 Nov 1912, Cuerámaro, Mexico. He studied violin and orch. conducting with Silvestre Revueltas, harmony, counterpoint, and musical form with Candelario Huízar, and composition with Carlos Chávez at the National Cons. of Mexico, Mexico City. Violinist at the Symphony Orch. of Mexico. In 1935, together with Daniel Ayala Pérez, José Moncayo García, and Blas Galindo Dimas, he formed the *Grupo de Jóvenes Compositores* (Group of Young Composers), which later became the *Grupo de los Cuatro* (Group of the Four). Professor at the New England Cons. of Music, Boston, and at Harvard Univ., Cambridge, both in Massachusetts. Professor of violin, harmony, and orch. conducting at the National Cons. of Mexico.
Works (selective list): *Ballets: Provincianas* (1948); *La Paloma* (1949); *Titeresca* (1951). *Orch.: Tres Poemas,* for soprano and chamber orch. (1936); *Música para Orquesta Sinfónica* (1940); *Corridos,* for chorus (1941); *Obertura en Tiempo de Danza* (1942); 4 symphonies (1944, 1945, 1957, 1967). Chamber music; piano pieces.
Sources: DM, GDM, GMM, MLA, MMLA

Cordero, Ernesto, Puerto Rican composer and guitarist; b.9 Aug 1946, New York City, New York. In 1963, he started to study music at the Cons. of Music of Puerto Rico with Alfredo Romero and Amaury Veray. In 1971, he graduated from the Cons. of Music of Madrid, Spain, and later he studied in Italy and in New York. Professor at the Philharmonic Academy of Rome, Italy, and the New York Community College. Professor of guitar and composition at the Univ. of Puerto Rico.
Works (selective list): *Tres Canciones,* for soprano and orch. (1973); *Fantasía sobre Tres Cuadros de José Campeche,* for guitar and orch. (1974); *Concierto Evocativo,* for guitar and orch. (1977); *Concierto Antillano,* for guitar and orch. (1983); *Cállate Silencio Mío,* for soprano and orch. (1986); *Concierto Criollo,* for cuatro and orch. (1986); *Dice la Fuente,* for soprano and orch. (1986); *Era mi Dolor Tan Alto,* for soprano and orch. (1986); *La Hija del Viejo Pancho,* for orch. (1986); chamber music; music for solo instruments; songs.
Source: CPR

Cordero, Roque, Panamanian composer, conductor, and teacher; b.16 Aug 1917, Panama City, Panama. He first studied in Panama;

then he went to the USA in 1943, and studied counterpoint and composition with Ernest Krenek in Minneapolis, Minnesota, and conducting with Stanley Chapple at the Berkshire Music Center in Tanglewood, Massachusetts. Professor at the National Inst. of Music in Panama, 1950-66, and its director, 1953-64. He taught at Indiana Univ. in Bloomington, Indiana, 1966-69, and at Illinois State Univ., Chicago, from 1972. Conductor of the National Orch. of Panama, Panama City, 1964-66.

Works (selective list): ***Ballets:*** *Setatule; Sensemaya. Capriccio Interiorano,* for band (1939); *Obertura Panameña No.2* (1944); Piano concerto (1944); 3 symphonies (1947, 1956, 1965); *Eight Miniatures,* for orch. (1948); *Rapsodia Campesina,* for orch. (1949); Quintet for flute, clarinet, violin, cello, and piano (1949); *Cinco Mensajes Breves,* for orch. (1959); Cello sonata (1962); Violin concerto (1962); *Sonata Breve,* for piano (1966); *Circunvoluciones y Móviles,* for 57 players (1967); *Permutaciones 7,* for 7 instrumentalists (1967); 2 string quartets (1968, 1969); *Paz, Paix, Peace,* for 4 trios and harp (1969); *Variations and Theme for 5,* for woodwind quartet and horn (1975); *Music,* for 5 brass (1980); *Petite Mobiles,* for bassoon and trios (1983); *Three Permutations 3,* for violin, cello, and string bass (1984); *Serenatas,* for flute, clarinet, viola, and harp (1987); *Dodecaconcerto,* for 12 instruments (1990). ***Books:*** *Curso de Solfeo,* Panama City, 1956; *Actualidad Musical en Panama, Buenos Aires Musical,* Vol.12, 1957; *¿Nacionalismo versus Dodecafonismo?, Revista Musical Chilena,* No.67, 1959.

Bibl.: G. Chase, *Composed by Cordero, Americas,* Vol.10, 1958.
Sources: BB, CTA8, DCM, DM, GDM, MLA

Correa Luna, María Celia, Uruguayan composer, pianist, and choral conductor; b.28 Feb 1908, Montevideo, Uruguay; d.? She studied music in Paris, France, with Clementina Montal and Paul Brand, and continued in Montevideo, where she studied harmony, counterpoint, and composition under José Tomás Mujica and Angel Turriziani. Professor of music at various high schools.

Works (selective list): *Siete Momentos Infantiles,* ballet for children; *Divertimento,* for piano and orch.; *Artigas,* choral-symphonic poem; chamber music; piano pieces; songs.
Sources: BHMCU, MU

Corretjer, Leopoldo, Argentine composer and orch. and choral conductor of Spanish origin; b.1862, Barcelona, Spain; d.1941, Argentina. He settled in Buenos Aires, Argentina, in 1887. He studied at the Royal Cons. Isabel II of Barcelona.

Works (selective list): *El Saludo a la Bandera,* patriotic song; patriotic songs for student choruses.
Source: EMA

Cortés, Francisco Pedro, Puerto Rican conductor and composer; b.31 Jan 1873, Ponce, Puerto Rico; d.? He studied in Ponce with Oriol Pasarell, Manuel Tavárez, and Font. In 1893, he went to Barcelona, Spain, where he studied with Vicente Costa Noguera at the Cons. of Music. In the same year, he entered the National Cons. of Music of Paris, France, where he was a student of Charles de Bériot until July 1896.

Works: *L'Echanson du Roy d'Yvetot,* comic opera; *Porto Rico,* concert waltz-capriccio; *Plainte Amoureuse,* waltz for piano and orch.; *Bock-Marche,* for piano and orch.; *Une Féte à Cuba,* suite for orch.; *Sangre Mora,* operetta; *Nuit de Noël*, mimodrama.
Source: MMLA

Cortés López, Joaquín, Argentine composer; b.10 Apr 1884, Buenos Aires, Argentina; d.1948, Buenos Aires. He studied with Constantino Gaito and Eduardo Fornarini.
Works (selective list): Trío; Sonata for violin and piano; *Fantasía,* for violin and piano; Sonata for piano; Suite for piano; choral works.
Sources: DM, EMA

Cortinas, César, Uruguayan composer; b.9 Aug 1890, San José, Uruguay; d.23 Mar 1918, Córdoba, Argentina. He studied piano with Camilo Giucci. In 1909, with a scholarship from the Uruguayan government, he went to Berlin, Germany, to study at the Royal Academy of Music with Max Bruch, Donnay, and Engelbert Humperdinck.
Works (selective list): *La Ultima Gaviota,* opera (1916). *Incidental music: Idilio,* for tenor and orch. (1912); *La Sulamita,* lyric poem for narrators, chorus, and orch. (1917). Concerto in D for piano and orch.; *Samson*, for narrator and orch.; choral music; chamber music; religious music; songs; piano pieces.
Sources: BHMCU, CTA16, GDM, MU

Cosentino, Iván René, Argentine composer; b.1935, Rosario, Prov. of Santa Fe, Argentina. He studied piano with Roberto Locatelli, composition with Erwin Leuchter, and Argentine folklore with Carlos Vega. He also studied new techniques concerning phonoelectric recording. Music critic for the daily newspaper *Clarín.* Professor at the National Cons. of Music Carlos López Buchardo of Buenos Aires, 1962-68. Professor of musicology at the National School of Dance in Buenos Aires. Professor at the Music School of SADAIC. From 1983 to 1989, he was national director of music and national director of artistic education.
Works: Popular and classical music. *Canción del Centauro,* song; Incidental music for the movie *La Conquista de la Pampa; Cantata para una Dinastía,* for double chorus, soloists, and chamber orch.

84 - Cosme

Sources: CAMR, EMA

Cosme, Luiz, Brazilian composer, violinist, and teacher; b.9 Mar 1908, Pôrto Alegre, Brazil; d.17 Jul 1965, Rio de Janeiro, Brazil. He studied violin with a relative and harmony at the Pôrto Alegre Cons. with Assuero Garritano. In 1927, he went to the USA where he studied violin with Robert Perutz and composition with Wladimir Bakaleinikoff at the Cincinnati Cons., Cincinnati, Ohio. He taught at the Inst. Musical and at the Colegio Americano, both of Pôrto Alegre. Consultant in music librarianship at the National Library of Brazil. Member of the Academia Brasileira de Música.
Works (selective list): *Salamanca do Jaráu,* ballet (1935); *O Lambe Lambe,* ballet (1946); *O Menino Atrasado,* puppet drama (1946); *Antígona,* incidental music for chorus and orch. (1948); *Nau Catarineta,* puppet drama (1948); *Novena á Senhora da Graça,* for narrator, female dancer, piano, and string quartet (1950); chamber music; piano pieces; songs.
Bibl. L.H.C. de Azevedo, *Luiz Cosme, Música Viva,* 1940. G. Béhague, *Luiz Cosme (1908-65): Impulso Creador versus Conciencia Formal, Yearbook, Inter-American Institute for Musical Research,* Vol.5, 1969. V. Mariz, *Figuras da Música Brasileira Contemporânea,* Brasilia, 1970.
Sources: CTA2, DM, GDM, HMB, MLA, MMLA

Costa, Alberto, Brazilian composer; b.1879, Brazil; d.1923, Brazil.
Works: *Soror Madalena,* opera; piano pieces; songs.
Source: MMLA

Costa, Dalmiro, Argentine pianist, organist, and composer of Uruguayan origin; b.7 May 1836, Montevideo, Uruguay; d.9 Aug 1901, Buenos Aires, Argentina. He spent most of his life in Buenos Aires. He studied with Remigio Navarro and Roque Rivero and took a few lessons with Sigismund Thalberg in Buenos Aires. Organist at the church San Ponciano of La Plata, Prov. of Buenos Aires, Argentina.
Works: *Fantasía,* for piano (1855); *Polonia y México,* polka (1863); *Funeral March* (1861); *El 10 de Noviembre,* military polka (1860); *Los Diamantes de la Corona,* mazurka for orch. (1863); *Nubes que Pasan,* waltz (1880); *Sobre el Río Negro,* mazurka (1881); *Cielito* (1882); *La Pecadora,* habanera for piano (1872).
Sources: BHMCU, EMA

Costa Horts, Narciso, Mexican conductor and composer of Spanish origin; b.1907, Gerona, Spain. He studied violin and solfeggio with his father, piano with José Cantó, and theory and composition with José Baró Güell in Spain. He settled in Mexico in 1940 where he

reorganized the mixed choir *Orfeó Catalá* (Catalonian choral singing society).
Works (selective list): String quartet (1936); Symphony in D (1944); songs; choral works.
Source: MMLA

Costanzo, Miguel Angel, Argentine composer and choral conductor; b.1937, Las Parejas, Prov. of Santa Fe, Argentina. He studied at the Escuela de Música de la Facultad de Humanidades y Artes of the National Univ. of Rosario, Prov. of Santa Fe, Argentina. He organized and directed several choral groups in the Prov. of Santa Fe and other regions of Argentina. Founding director of the Music Cons. of San Pedro, Prov. of Buenos Aires, in 1985.
Works: *Bienaventuranzas,* for chorus and chamber orch. (1965); *Palmera*, for narrator, chorus, and orch. (1968); *Objetos I; Sustractos; La Tijera del Buzo; Los Ojos del Cielo; Abstracción; Orbitas.*
Source: CAMR

Cotapos Baeza, Acario, Chilean composer; b.30 Apr 1889, Valdivia, Chile; d.22 Nov 1969, Santiago de Chile, Chile. He studied piano and composition in Santiago de Chile, and continued studying composition in New York under Ernest Bloch. He adopted an advanced quasi-serial technique of monothematic mottoes of 8 or more notes. Founding member of the International Composers' Guild and the League of Composers.
Works (selective list): *La Rebelión del Hombre*, ballet; *Voces de Gesta,* music drama (1933); *El Pájaro Burlón*, opera (1939); *Four Symphonic Preludes* (1923); *Voces de Gesta,* suite for orch. (1934); *Imaginación de mi País* (1950); chamber music; piano pieces.
Bibl.: Revista Musical Chilena, No.76, 1961.
Sources: BB, DCM, DM, HMC, GDM, MLA

Cozzella, Damiano, Brazilian composer; b.1930, Sâo Paulo, Brazil. He was self-taught in composition until 1950, when he began to study with Hans Joachim Koellreutter. In 1961, he attended the Darmstadt, Germany, summer courses. Member of the *Música Nova Group* of Sâo Paulo. Professor at the Escola Livre de Música of Sâo Paulo, and the Univ. of Brasília, Brazil.
Works: *Musica I-IV,* for various instrumental ensembles (1954-62); *Catálogo*, for piano (1962); *Discontínuo,* for piano (1963).
Source: GDM

Cozzi, Daniel Alberto, Argentine composer; b.1949, Cañada de Gómez, Prov. of Santa Fe, Argentina. He studied at the Escuela de Música de la Facultad de Humanidades y Artes of the National Univ.

of Rosario, Prov. of Santa Fe, with Virtú Maragno. He also studied with Dante Grela and attended classes by Alcides Lanza, Carlos Rauch, Mariano Etkin, Luis María Serra, Ruffo Herrera, Isabel Aretz Thiele, Luis Felipe Ramón y Rivera, Francisco Kröpfl, Carmelo Saitta, and Enrique Gerardi. Professor at the Escuela de Música de la Facultad de Humanidades y Artes of the National Univ. of Rosario. Founding member and president of the Asociación Santafesina de Compositores. Secretary of the Extensión Cultural de la Escuela de Música de la Facultad de Humanidades y Artes and member of the Board of Directors of the same Facultad.
Works: Dos Miniaturas, for string quintet; Trio for flute, clarinet, and prepared piano; *Etnográficas I,* for viola, double bass, percussion, and magnetic tape; *Introspección,* for orch.; *La Cripta de Chopin,* for piano and musical theater; *Espacios,* for piano; *A Olivero,* for voice, flute, oboe, clarinet, percussion, and piano.
Source: CAMR

Cubano, Miguel, Puerto Rican composer; fl.second half of the 20th century. He studied guitar at the Cons. of Music of Puerto Rico and graduated from the Univ. of Puerto Rico. Later he moved to France where he studied with Alberto Ponce at the National Cons. of Aubervilliers. In Paris, France, he received a degree in composition from the Schola Cantorum where he studied with Alan Kremsky.
Works (selective list): *Cantos del Sol,* for soprano, flute, oboe, guitar, and percussion (1983); Trio for violin, viola, and cello (1984); music for the guitar.
Source: CPR

Curiel Barba, Gonzalo, Mexican composer, pianist. and conductor; b.10 Jan 1904, Guadalajara, Mexico; d.4 Jun 1958, Mexico City, Mexico. He studied music and medicine.
Works (selective list): Piano concerto; Concerto for orch.; Opera; songs.
Source: KTL

Curubeto Godoy, María Isabel, Argentine composer and pianist; b.1898, San Juan, Argentina; d.1959. She studied piano in Vienna, Austria, with Theodor Leschetizky and at the Royal Cons. of Milan, Italy, and composition with Giovanni Sgambati at the Royal Cons. of Rome, Italy. Professor of piano at the Univ. of La Plata, Prov. of Buenos Aires, Argentina.
Works (selective list): *Fedra,* incidental music for the Greek tragedy by Eurípides; *Pablo y Virginia,* opera; *Oración Fúnebre,* for string orch.; *Evocando a Beethoven,* for orch.; chamber music; piano pieces; choruses; songs.
Sources: CA, DM, EMA

D

D'Agnillo, Corradino, Argentine composer and teacher of Italian origin; b.1868, Agnone, Campobasso, Italy; d.1948, Buenos Aires, Argentina. He settled in Buenos Aires in 1888. Founding member of the Asociación Wagneriana of Buenos Aires.
Works: *Il Leone di Venezia*, opera (1892); *La Zíngara*, opera (1895).
Sources: DM, EMA

Dal Farra, Ricardo L., Argentine electroacoustic music performer and composer; b.29 Nov 1957, Buenos Aires, Argentina. Professor of electroacoustic composition at the Municipal Cons. of Music Manuel de Falla of Buenos Aires; codirector of the Electronic Music Laboratory of the Argentine Society for Musical Education; director of the radio program Música Electroacústica y por Computadora of the Radio Municipal de Buenos Aires, LS1.
Works: *Estudio sobre Ritmo y Espacio,* tape piece (1982); *Karma,* tape piece (1986); *Ancestros,* for aerophones and electroacoustic processors (1986). *Music for guitar and electroacoustic processors: Integrados* (1986); *Double* (1986); *Clones* (1986); *EGT* (1989); *Disolución IV* (1991). *GI, Gravitacional,* and *GII, Inercial,* for MIDI guitar and a DX7 digital synthesizer (1987); *Uhuru,* for 4 computer resynthesized voices (1988); *Xastock,* for tenor sax and live electroacoustic processings (1989); *Tramas,* for small orch. and live electroacoustic processings (1990); *Ashram,* for Mukha Veena and tape (1991); *Teragón,* for computer and electronic musical instruments controlled in real time (1992); *Homotecia,* for bandonion and tape (1992); *Memorias,* for computer-generated sounds (1992).
Sources: BB, ISC

Dallo y Lana, Miguel Mateo de, Mexican composer of Spanish origin; b.c.1650, Spain; d.1 Sep 1705, Puebla, Mexico. He settled in Mexico in 1688. *Maestro de capilla* (chapelmaster) at the Cathedral of Puebla.
Works: Religious compositions: 7 vesper psalms; 2 Magnificat; Beatus vir; Credidi propter; 3 Dixit Dominus; 3 Lauda Jerusalem; 2 Laudate Dominum; villancicos.
Bibl.: R. Stevenson, *Renaissance and Baroque Musical Sources in the Americas,* Washington, D.C., 1970.
Source: GDM

Daluisio, Rodolfo, Argentine composer, bandonionist, and teacher; b.31 Jan 1952, Chacabuco, Prov. of Buenos Aires, Argentina. He started music studies, theory, solfeggio, and bandonion in 1958. In 1968, he started to study piano, harmony, and instrumentation. In

1971, he entered the Municipal Cons. of Music Manuel de Falla of Buenos Aires. Since 1977, he studied composition and some other musical disciplines with Juan Francisco Giacobbe. Professor of theory, harmony and bandonion at the Municipal Cons. of Music Manuel de Falla. Professor of organ at the Escuela Superior de Música of Concepción del Uruguay, Prov. of Entre Ríos, Argentina.

Works (selective list): *Máscaras,* choreographic suite for orch.; *La Guitarrita,* choreographic drama for bandonion and orch.; *Los Misterios Dolorosos,* oratorium for soprano, baritone, chorus, and orch.; Concerto for bandonion and orch.; numerous works for bandonion solo and with other instruments; chamber music; music for the organ; songs; choruses.

Source: ISC

D'Astoli, Bruno, Argentine conductor and composer of Italian origin; b.1934, Terni, Italy. He studied at the Academia Santa Cecilia of Rome, Italy. He settled in Argentina in 1950. In 1956, he was appointed assistant conductor at the Teatro Colón of Buenos Aires.

Works: *Canto a la Noche,* for orch. (1965); *Espectros*, for chamber ensemble (1966); *Rondas,* for chamber ensemble (1967); *Imágenes,* for chamber ensemble (1967); *Rituali,* for brass ensemble (1968); *Spiritu tuo*, choreographic drama (1969).

Source: EMA

Davidovsky (Davidowsky), Mario, Argentine composer; b.4 Mar 1934, Médanos, Prov. de Buenos Aires, Argentina. In Buenos Aires, Argentina, he studied with Guillermo Graetzer, Teodoro Fuchs, Erwin Leuchter, and Ernesto Epstein. He continued his studies in the USA with Milton Babbitt at the Berkshire Music Center, Tanglewood, Massachusetts. In 1960, with a fellowship from the Guggenheim Foundation, he worked in the USA with Edgar Varese, Milton Babbitt, Vladimir Ussachevsky, Otto Luening, and Roger Sessions, and then at the Electronic Music Centers of Columbia Univ., New York, and Princeton Univ., New Jersey. He taught at the Univ. of Michigan, Ann Arbor, Michigan, in 1964, the Di Tella Inst. of Buenos Aires in 1965, the Manhattan School of Music in New York, 1969-70, the City College of New York, 1968-80, and Columbia Univ., where he was appointed director of the Columbia-Princeton Electronic Music Center, in 1981.

Works (selective list): Concertino for percussion and strings (1954); 4 string quartets (1954, 1958, 1976, 1980); *El Payaso*, symphonic suite (1955); Quintet for clarinet and strings (1955); *Three Pieces*, for woodwind quintet (1956); Noneto (1956); *Serie Sinfónica* (1959); *Contrastes No.1*, for strings and electronics (1960); *Pianos,* for orch. (1961); *Three Studies*, for tape (1961, 1962, 1965); Trio for clarinet, trumpet, and viola (1962); *Synchronisms,* eight pieces for different

instrumental combinations (1963-74); *Inflexions,* for chamber ensemble (1965); *Junctures,* for flute, clarinet, and violin (1966); *Music,* for violin (1968); *Chacona,* for violin, cello, and piano (1971); *Transientes,* for orch. (1972); *Shir-ha-Shirim,* scenes for soprano, 2 tenors, baritone, and chamber orch. (1975); *Pennplay,* for 16 players (1978); *Consorts,* for symphonic band (1980); String trio (1982); *Romancero,* for soprano, flute, clarinet, violin, and cello (1983); *Divertimento,* for cello and orch. (1984); *Capriccio,* for 2 pianos (1985).
Sources: BB, EMA, GDM

Debali, Francisco José, Uruguayan composer, conductor, and instrumentalist (he played several wind instruments) of Hungarian origin; b.26 Jul 1791, Hungary; d.1859, Montevideo, Uruguay. *Maestro de capilla* (chapelmaster) in Ovada y Finale Marina, Italy. *Músico Mayor* of the regiments in Savona, Casal, and Piamonte, Italy. First clarinetist and *Segundo Músico Mayor* of the King's guard in Sardinia, Italy. As soon as he settled in Uruguay in 1838, he was appointed *Músico Mayor* of the presidential escort of President Rivera. From 1841 to 1848, he conducted the orch. of the Casa de Comedias, and in 1852, he was appointed *Músico Mayor* of the Batallón de Cazadores.
Works (selective list): *Uruguayan National Anthem.* Wrote 143 compositions, which are mostly divertimenti in Mozart's style; 10 symphonies (overtures); several concertos; Trio for violin, clarinet in C, and guitar; *La Batalla de Cagancha,* symphonic poem; religious music; waltzes; polkas; and all kinds of salon music of that time.
Source: BHMCU

De Carvalho, Delgado, Brazilian composer; b.1872, Rio de Janeiro, Brazil; d.1921, Rio de Janeiro.
Works (selective list): *Operas: Moema; Hostia.* Sonata for piano; piano pieces.
Source: MMLA

De Elías, Manuel Jorge, Mexican composer, conductor, pianist, and teacher; b.5 Jun 1939, Mexico City, Mexico. He studied with his father, Alfonso de Elías. He entered the UNAM and the National Cons. of Music in Mexico City where he studied piano, organ, flute, violin, and cello, 1959-62. He also attended courses in Mexico City on musique concrète with Jean-Etienne Marie, 1967, on new music with Karlheinz Stockhausen, 1968, and in conducting with Luis Herrera de la Fuente, 1968-72. He attended a class on electronic music at Columbia Univ. in New York, 1974, and enrolled in a workshop in opera and ballet conducting with Edgar Doneux in

Brussels, Belgium, 1974-75. In 1975, he created and organized the Inst. of Music of the Univ. of Veracruz, Mexico, and in 1980, he founded and conducted the Symphony Orch. of Veracruz. He was appointed conductor of the Symphony Orch. of Guadalajara in 1987, and in 1988, he founded the Symphony Orch. of Jalisco, both of Mexico. He became director of music of the National Inst. of Fine Arts and was appointed permanent member of the Academy of Fine Arts in 1991.

Works (selective list): *Pequeños Corales*, for chorus a cappella (1954-57); *Estampas Infantiles*, suite for strings (1959); Sinfonietta (1958-61); *Vitral No.1*, for chamber orch. (1962), *No.2*, for chamber orch. and tape (1967), and *No.3*, for orch. (1969); *Jahel*, ballet for 2 pianos (1964); *Aforismo No.1, Pájaros Perdidos*, for chorus a capella (1963); *Aforismo No.2*, for flute and tape (1968); *Guanajuato*, overture-divertimento for orch. (1964); *Impresiones sobre una Estampa Colonial*, divertimento for orch. (1965); *Elegía Heróica*, symphonic poem (1967); *Memento*, for recorder, chorus, strings, and narrator (1967); *Musica Nupcial*, for contralto and brass or strings (1967); *Tres Kaleidoscopios*, for organ (1969, 1973, 1974); *Sonante No.1*, for piano (1971), *No.2*, for solo clarinet (1970), *No.3*, for trumpet, trombone, and horn (1970), *No.4*, for orch. ((1971), *No.5*, for orch. (1972), No.6, *Homenaje a Neruda,* for string orch. (1973), *No.7*, for orch. (1974); *Parámetros I*, for synthesizer (1971); *Ludus,* for 3 choruses (1972-73); Concertante No.1 for violin and orch. (1973); *Música Doméstica*, for recorder and percussion (1973); *Sine Nomine*, for string quartet and piano (1975); *Jeux*, for horn, trumpet, and bassoon (1975); *Obertura-Poema*, for soloists, chorus, organ, and wind orch. (1975); *Adagio para Cuerdas*, for string orch. (1983); *A Voces,* for mixed chorus a cappella (1983); *Sonante No.10,* for mixed chorus and orch. (1984); *Mictlan Tlatelolco,* for string orch. (1985-86); *Cartas de Primavera*, for string orch. (1986); *Poema,* for string orch. (1988); Concerto for cello and orch. (1990); chamber music; music for solo instruments; piano pieces; songs.
Sources: BB, CTA15, ISC

Delano, Jack, Puerto Rican composer of Ukrainian origin; b.1 Aug 1914, Kiev, Ukraine. He settled in the USA in 1923 and moved to Puerto Rico in 1946. He started to study music with his father in Kiev and continued at the Settlement Music School in Philadelphia, Pennsylvania. Between 1923 and 1937, he was granted a scholarship to study art at the Pennsylvania Academy of Fine Arts in Philadelphia. When he moved to Puerto Rico in 1946, he founded and directed the Cinematography Section of the Division for the Education of the Community within the Dept. of Education. Administrator of the Radio and Television System of the Government of Puerto Rico.

Works (selective list): *Ofrenda Musical,* for viola, French horn, and string orch. (1959); *Laura y Georgina,* for orch. (1960); *La Incógnita,* for orch. (1960); *Esta Luna es Mía,* for soprano, female chorus, and piano (1962); *Le Marche de Giboros,* for orch. (1965); *La Reina Tembamdumba,* overture-fantasia (1966); *La Bruja de Loíza,* ballet (1984); *Los Aguinaldos del Infante,* for narrator, boys chorus, and orch. (1984); Sinfonietta for strings (1984); *Burundanga,* cantata for soloists, chorus, and orch. (1988).
Source: CPR

Del Cioppo, Crisanto, Argentine band conductor and composer of Italian origin; b.1830, Italy; d.1915, Argentina. He settled in Argentina in 1882.
Works: 24 sonatas for piano; several military marches.
Source: EMA

Delgadillo, Luis Abraham, Nicaraguan composer and band conductor; b.26 Aug 1887, Managua, Nicaragua; d.20 Dec 1961, Managua. He studied with Manuel Silva Guerrero, María Teresa Muñoz de Campari, and Alberto Selva. In Italy, he furthered his studies at the Royal Cons. of Milan under Pablo Delachi, Miguel Saladino, Héctor Pozzoli, and Vincenzo Appiani, 1906-12. General director of Musical Culture of Nicaragua. Between 1921 and 1925, he lived in Mexico City, Mexico, where he was professor of music theory at the National Cons. of Music and director of the *Orfeón Popular No.5* (male choral singing group).
Works (selective list): **Operas:** *El Final de Norma; Mavaltayan.* **Orch.**: *Sinfonía Indígena* (1921)*; Sinfonía Mexicana* (1924); *Teotihuacan* (1925); *Sinfonía Incaica* (1926); *Sinfonía Serrana* (1928); 12 short symphonies (1953); *Obertura Debussyana y Obertura Schoenbergiana* (1955). *La Cabeza del Rawi,* ballet; 7 string quartets; church music; piano pieces.
Sources: BB, CTA2, DM, GDM, MLA, MMLA

Del Giúdice, Rafael, Argentine conductor and composer; b.1911, Rosario, Prov. of Santa Fe, Argentina. He studied with Franco Alfano at the Cons. of Turin, Italy, 1921-28. Conductor of the Municipal Band of Buenos Aires, 1953-56.
Works: Wrote several orch. works.
Source: EMA

Del Hoyo, Faustino, Argentine double bass player and composer; b.1909, Buenos Aires, Argentina. Principal double bass at the orch. of the Teatro Colón of Buenos Aires, 1928-1967. He taught double bass at the National Cons. of Music Carlos López Buchardo of Buenos Aires.

Works (selective list): *En los Mares Australes,* symphonic poem; Concerto grosso for chamber orch.; *Nocturno y Burlesca,* for chamber orch.; Quintet for 4 double basses and piano; chamber music; choral music; piano pieces.
Source: EMA

Delli Quadri, Juan Carlos, Argentine composer and professor of music; b.18 Feb 1931, Buenos Aires, Argentina. Member of Jóvenes Compositores de Argentina and Asociación Argentina de Compositores.
Works (selective list): *Tres Corales,* for mixed chorus and 4 voices; Suite for wind octet (1961); Quintet (1963); Trio (1963); *Tres Movimientos,* for chamber orch. (1964); Septet (1965); *Cantos a mi Tierra* (1970); *Salmo 127,* choral-symphonic suite for mixed chorus and organ (1976); *Tema con Variaciones y Moto Perpetuo,* for violin (1979); *Tres Corales,* for string orch. (1981); songs and school songs; choruses.
Source: VMA

Del Mónaco, Alfredo, Venezuelan composer; b.29 Apr 1938, Caracas, Venezuela. He studied piano and composition with Moisés Moleiro and Primo Casale in Venezuela, and later at Columbia Univ., New York, where he received a Doctor of Musical Arts degree in 1974. He studied electronic and computer music at the Columbia-Princeton Electronic Music Center, New York. He also studied law at the Catholic Univ. in Caracas. He pioneered electronic music in Venezuela at the Estudio de Fonología Musical. In 1968, he founded the Venezuelan branch of the ISCM.
Works (selective list): *Dos Fugas Académicas,* for string orch. (1964); *Cromofonías I,* electronic music (1967); *Cromofonías II,* for orch. (1968); *Tres Ambientes Coreográficos para Sonia Sanoja,* electroacoustic music (1970); *Synus 17/251271,* electronic music for computers (1972); *Tupac-Amarú,* for orch. (1977); *Cuarteto II,* conceptual music (1978); *Tientos de la Noche Imaginada,* for guitar and orch. (1991); chamber music; electronic music; piano pieces; music for solo instruments.
Sources: CTA17, ISC

Delorenzi, Jorge Ricardo, Argentine composer and chorus conductor; b.24 Jul 1945, Buenos Aires, Argentina. He studied at the Municipal Cons. of Music Manuel de Falla of Buenos Aires, then he continued studies of harmony, counterpoint, and musical analysis with Juan Francisco Giacobbe, Carlos Guastavino, and Emilio Dublanc. Director of the Coro Polifónico of the Prov. of Corrientes, Argentina. Professor at the Municipal Cons. of Music Manuel de Falla.

Works (selective list): *Himnos a la Noche,* symphonic poem for piano and orch. (1990); *Paráfrasis,* 5 songs for soprano and orch. (1992); *Sinfonía del Lago,* symphonic poem for orch. (1993); chamber music; songs; piano pieces.
Source: ISC

Del Ponte, Clementino, Argentine pianist and composer of Italian origin; b.1858, Turin, Italy; d.1914, Buenos Aires, Argentina. He settled in Argentina sometime between 1878 and 1880.
Works: *Poema de Mayo,* song cycle; piano pieces; songs.
Sources: DM, EMA

De Nito, Humberto, Argentine teacher, pianist, and composer; b.1 Jan 1891, Rosario, Prov. of Santa Fe, Argentina; d.1957, Rosario. Brother of José De Nito. He studied piano with Alessandro Longo and composition with Camillo De Nardis at the Royal Cons. of Naples, Italy.
Works: *Pequeña Suite,* for orch. *Piano pieces for children: Minué de la Muñeca; Berceuse; Cajita de Música; Baby Vals; Página de Album; La Ronde qui Passe. Himno al Presidente Avellaneda,* on the 50th anniversary of his death.
Sources: CA, EMA

De Nito, José, Argentine pianist, music critic, and composer; b.12 Nov 1887, Rosario, Prov. of Santa Fe, Argentina; d.26 Aug 1945, Rosario. Brother of Humberto De Nito. He studied first in Rosario with José Caiano, and in 1901, he went to Italy where he studied piano, composition, instrumentation, and conducting with Giuseppe Martucci, Paolo Serrao, Camillo De Nardis, and Alessandro Longo at the Cons. San Pietro a Majella of Naples. He graduated in 1909, and returned to Argentina. He created the Cons. Beethoven in Rosario, which he directed together with his brother Humberto.
Works (selective list): String quartet; Sonata for piano; *Bocetos Líricos,* 10 pieces for piano; songs.
Sources: CA, EMA

Dente, Domingo, Uruguayan choral conductor and composer; b.10 Jul 1896, Montevideo, Uruguay; d.? He studied in Uruguay with Stampanoni, then in Italy, piano, voice, and composition at the Cons. of Naples. In Uruguay, he founded the *Asociación Coral Palestrina.* Choral conductor at SODRE.
Works (selective list): *Poema del Alba,* symphonic poem; Sonata for violin and piano; songs; piano pieces.
Sources: DM, MMLA

De Pedro, Roque, Argentine teacher, music critic, musicologist, and composer; b.1935, Comodoro Rivadavia, Prov. of Chubut, Argentina. He studied at the National Cons. of Music Carlos López Buchardo and at the Inst. Di Tella, both of Buenos Aires. He also studied drawing at the Escuela Nacional de Bellas Artes Manuel Belgrano of Buenos Aires. In Buenos Aires, he taught at the National Cons. of Music Carlos López Buchardo and the Municipal Cons. of Music Manuel de Falla. Music critic for the daily newspaper *Clarín*.
Works (selective list): *Tres Piezas Mágicas,* for piano (1935); *Orbitas,* for wind sextet (1966); *Aleaciones,* for 2 pianos, dice, and percussion (1966); Concerto for piano and orch. (1968); incidental music for the theater; audiovisual works.
Source: EMA

De Rogatis, Pascual, Argentine composer of Italian origin; b.17 May 1880, Teora, Italy; d.2 Apr 1980, Buenos Aires, Argentina. At a very young age, he settled in Argentina. He studied at the Cons. of Music of Buenos Aires under Pietro Melani, Rafael Díaz Albertini, and Alberto Williams. Professor of chamber music at the National Cons. of Music Carlos López Buchardo of Buenos Aires. Member of the Comisión Nacional de Bellas Artes.
Works (selective list): **Stage:** *Anfión y Zeto,* incidental music for the theater (1915); *Huemac,* lyric drama (1916); *La Novia del Hereje,* opera (1935). **Symphonic-choral music:** *Oratorio Laico* (1928). **Orch.**: *Suite Arabe* (1902); *Danza de las Driadas* (1902); *Preludio* (1903); *Marcha Heróica* (1904); *Paisaje Otoñal* (1905); *Marko y el Hada* (1905); *Belkiss en la Selva* (1906); *Elegía,* for cello (1907); *Zupay* (1910); *Suite Americana* (1924); *Atipac* (1931); *La Fiesta de Chiqui* (1935); *Estampas Argentinas* (1923); *Evocaciones Indígenas* (1945). Piano pieces; songs; school songs.
Bibl.: C. Muñoz, *Pascual De Rogatis (1880-1980), Revista del Inst. de Investigación Musicológica Vega,* No.7, Buenos Aires, 1986.
Sources: BB, CA, DM, EMA

De Rubertis, Víctor, Argentine teacher, music critic, and composer of Italian origin; b.1893, Lucito, Prov. of Campobasso, Italy; d.1961, Buenos Aires, Argentina. He graduated from the Royal Cons. of Naples, Italy. In Buenos Aires, in 1933, he founded a musical bulletin *La Silurante Musicale.*
Works: Music for piano and for voice and piano. **Books**: *Pequeño Diccionario Musical Tecnológico y Biográfico.*
Source: EMA

D'Espósito, Arnaldo, Argentine composer and conductor; b.30 Aug 1907, Buenos Aires, Argentina; d.1945, Buenos Aires. He studied at the National Cons. of Music Carlos López Buchardo of Buenos Aires

with Jorge de Lalewicz, Athos Palma, and Floro Ugarte. Conductor at the Teatro Colón of Buenos Aires. Professor at the National Cons. of Music Carlos López Buchardo.
Works (selective list): *Lin Calel,* opera; *Cuento de Abril,* ballet (1940); *Ajedrez,* ballet; Concerto for piano and orch.; *Rapsodia del Tango,* for orch.; Sonata for violin and piano; Quartet for strings and piano; Quintet; piano pieces; songs.
Sources: CA, DM, EMA, MMLA

Devoto, Alberto, Argentine composer and recorder player; b.12 Dec 1945, Buenos Aires, Argentina. He studied at the National Cons. of Music Carlos López Buchardo of Buenos Aires. Professor at the National Cons. of Music Carlos López Buchardo and at the Municipal Cons. of Music Manuel de Falla, both in Buenos Aires. Founder and director of the Escuela Superior Municipal de Música de Concepción del Uruguay, Prov. of Entre Rios, Argentina.
Works: *Tres Preludios*, for recorder and orch.; *Cuatro Miniaturas,* for recorder and narrator; *Suite Infantil,* for chamber ensemble; *Silencios,* for voice and piano; *Soliloquio,* for solo flute; *Preludiando en Amarillo,* for chamber ensemble.
Source: ISC

Devoto, Daniel, Argentine composer; b.25 Dec 1916, Buenos Aires, Argentina. He studied with Julio Perceval, Juan Carlos Paz, and Jacqueline Ibels. He also studied with René Leibowitz and Jane Bathori. He graduated with a doctorate in literature from the Nacional Univ. of Buenos Aires and La Sorbonne in Paris, France. Professor of music history and aesthetics at the National Cons. of Music Carlos López Buchardo of Buenos Aires and the Academy of Fine Arts of the National Univ. of Cuyo, Mendoza, Prov. of Mendoza, Argentina. Founding member of the *Agrupación Nueva Música.* In 1954, he settled in France and devoted all his time to literature.
Works: *Diferencias del Primer Tono,* for solo flute (1946); *Libro de Cantos* (1947). *Books*: *Dos Clases Públicas de Historia de la Música* (1945); *Las Marchas Paralelas* (1945); *Bibliografía Razonada de Historia de la Música* (1947); *Las Hojas* (1950); *Sobre Paremiología Musical Porteña* (1950); *La Fama Europea de Josquin Des Prez y un Romance de Góngora* (1954).
Bibl.: R. Chalupi, *Un Poète Musicien d'Argentine, Ronsard,* Vol.2, Paris, 1947. J.C. Paz, *A Panorama of Argentine Music, Listen,* Vol.9, New York, 1947.
Sources: DM, EMA, GDM

Dianda, Hilda, Argentine composer; b.13 Apr 1925, Córdoba, Prov. of Córdoba, Argentina. She studied in Buenos Aires with Honorio Siccardi and in Europe with Gian Francesco Malipiero and Hermann

Scherchen. From 1958 to 1962, she worked at Radiodiffusion Française in Paris, France. She also worked at the Inst. of Phonology of Milan, Italy, and attended international courses in new music in Darmstadt, Germany. From 1967 to 1971, she was professor at the Escuela de Artes of the National Univ. of Córdoba. Conductor of the chamber orch. of the same Escuela de Artes.

Works (selective list): *Poemas de Amor Desesperado,* for voice and 6 instruments (1942); 3 string quartets (1947, 1960, 1962); Concertante for cello and chamber orch. (1952); Wind quintet (1957); *Díptico,* for 16 instruments (1962); *Canciones,* for soprano, guitar, vibraphon, and 3 percussionists (1962); *Percusión 11,* for 11 percussionists (1963); *Núcleos,* for string orch., 2 pianos, and percussion (1964); *Resonancias 1,* for 5 horns (1964); *Resonancias 3,* for cello and orch. (1965); *Ludus 1,* for orch. (1966); *a-7,* for cello and magnetic tape (1966); *Resonancias 5,* for chorus a cappella (1967-68); *Ludus 2,* for 11 instruments (1969), *Idá-ndá's,* for 3 percussionists (1969); *Ludus 3,* for organ (1969); *Impromptu,* for string orch. (1970); *Canto,* for orch. (1972); Requiem for bass, chorus, and orch. (1984); Concerto for viola and orch. (1988); *Cántico,* for mixed chorus and string orch. (1988); *Juegos,* for solo percussion and string orch. (1993); chamber music.
Sources: BB, CTA9, DCM, EMA, NGDWC

Díaz, Ramón, Dominican composer and bassonist; b.1901, Puerto Plata, Dominican Republic. He studied in Santiago de los Caballeros, Dominican Republic, at the Municipal Music Academy with José Ovidio García. Conductor of the Band and director of the Municipal Academy of Salcedo and conductor of the Band of San Cristóbal, both of the Dominican Republic. Professor of theory and music history at the Escuela Normal of San Cristóbal. First bassoonist at the National Symphony Orch. of Ciudad Trujillo, Dominican Republic.
Works: *Escenas Bíblicas,* for soloists, chorus, and orch.; *Hispaniola,* overture for band; *Evocación,* symphonic poem; *Elegía, Marcha Heróica y Minué,* for orch.
Sources: DM, MMLA

Díaz Gainza, José, Bolivian teacher and composer of Spanish origin; b.1908, Trujillo, Spain; d.1966, Potosí, Bolivia. He studied music in Spain. Dean of the Academy of Fine Arts of the Univ. of Potosí, Bolivia.
Works (selective list): *Capricho Sinfónico; Camino del Inca; Himno a Potosí;* several cuecas in which he used his own musical system based on Inca tunes. *Books:* *Teoría Analítica,* 3 volumes; *Pedagogía Musical; Historia de la Música en Bolivia.*
Source: CB

Díaz Zelaya, Francisco R., Honduran composer; b.4 Oct 1900, Ojojona, Honduras; d.? He studied solfeggio, theory, harmony, counterpoint, fugue, musical form, and music history with Carlos Haertling, Manuel de Adalid y Gamero, and Wenceslao Lefrank at the Escuela de Músicos Mayores, from 1918 to 1928. General conductor of the Band of the Republic of Honduras, of the Banda de los Supremos Poderes, and of the National Symphony Orch., all of Tegucigalpa, Honduras. He taught music theory, harmony, and voice in several schools.
Works (selective list): 2 symphonies; 35 waltzes; 12 romances; 20 hymns; 6 nocturnes; 46 military marches; 12 religious works.
Sources: DM, MLA, MMLA

Dimas de Melo Pimenta, Emanuel, Brazilian composer and architect; b.3 Jun 1957, Sâo Paulo, Brazil. He studied at the Braz Cubas Univ. in Sâo Paulo, from which he received a degree in architecture and urban studies in 1985. He studied music with Hans Joachim Koellreutter.
Works (selective list): *Spheres,* for large ensemble (1981); *Cantos,* for ensemble (1982); *Spheres III,* for ensemble and tape (1981-82); *Frankenstern,* minimal opera for 20 TV sets, videos, soprano, 2 mezzo-sopranos, baritone, piano, and tape (1984); *A Bao a Qu,* for ensemble, synthesizers, video score, and tape (1985); *Factory,* for 2 tenors and tape (1986-87); chamber music; magnetic tape music; digital tape music.
Source: BB

Dirié, Gerardo Enrique, Argentine composer, conductor, performer, and arranger; b.20 Sep 1958, Córdoba, Prov. of Córdoba, Argentina. He studied at the National Univ. of Córdoba with Atilio Argüello, Oscar Bazán, and César Franchisena. In 1987, he was granted a scholarship from the Fulbright Foundation to study composition at Indiana Univ., Bloomington, Indiana, with Eugene O'Brien and John Eaton, and then he entered a doctoral program in composition at the same univ. Coordinator at the Latin American Music Center of Indiana Univ.
Works (selective list): *Romance para Lorca Solo,* for narrator, oboe, bassoon, and bells (1986); *Canto Adverso,* for alto flute, French horn, and strings (1987); *Música para una Ventana*, for flute, bassoon, and percussion (1988); *Dirección del Fuego,* for chorus and orch. (1984); *Puerto de Cántaros,* for orch. (1989); *Story Board,* for soprano saxophone, brass, and percussion (1983); *Los Ocho Puentes,* for 4 recorders, mandolin, and percussion (1985); *Preludio a Bernoulli,* for 6 recorders and percussion (1985); *Cinco Canciones debajo del Ladrillo,* for alto recorder, violin, clarinet, and percussion (1988); *El Sueño de la Mula Negra,* for tape and variable number of performers

(1990); *Balada*, for soprano, clarinet, Yamaha WX7, and tape (1991); *Chuang Tzu* or *A Butterfly in New York,* for 4 recorders (1991); *Terra,* for electric viola, 2 pianos, and marimba (1991); *Iquitos-Manaus,* for soprano, jazz-rock band, Brazilian percussion, aerophones, and live electronics (1991); *Orpheus Turns his Head,* for voice, viola, Yamaha WX7, and Norwegian flute (1992); chamber music; songs; choruses; music for solo instruments.
Source: ISC

Di Tada Paz, Herberto, Argentine composer; b.1903, Juárez, Prov. of Buenos Aires, Argentina. He studied with Ernesto Drangosch and Constantino Gaito.
Works: Sonata in A minor for piano (1921); *Epigramas y epitafios,* for piano (1924); Suite for piano and orch. (1930); *Caperucita Roja,* ballet (1930); *Imágenes Americanas,* symphonic poem (1934).
Source: EMA

Domínguez, Alberto, Mexican composer; b.21 Apr 1913, Chiapas, Mexico; d.2 Sep 1975, Mexico City, Mexico. He studied piano with Julián Carrillo and Joaquín Amparón, solfeggio with José R. Vázquez, composition with José Rolón and Blas Galindo Dimas, and orch. conducting with Silvestre Revueltas. Founding member of the Sociedad de Autores y Compositores de Mexico.
Works (selective list): Sonatina for chamber orch.; Concerto for piano and orch. Many popular songs, including: *Frenesí; Eternamente; Perfidia; Por la Cruz; Di Que no Es Verdad; Bayadera; Al Son de la Marimba.*
Bibl.: J. Alvarez Coral, *Alberto Domínguez, Autor de Perfidia y Frenesí,* Mexico, 1977.
Source: NH

D'Pool, Adolfo, Venezuelan composer; b.11 Jan 1882, Maracaibo, Venezuela; d.? He studied first with his brother, Arturo D'Pool, and later he studied trumpet, piano, and mandolin. He also studied harmony and composition with Diego Carborell. Member of the Municipal Band of Maracaibo. Professor of music at the Music School Rafael María Baralt and director of the Escuela de Música y Declamación of the Atheneum of Maracaibo.
Works: Many waltzes; hymns; popular songs; marches; religious music.
Source: MMLA

Drangosch, Ernesto, Argentine pianist, conductor, and composer; b.22 Jan 1882, Buenos Aires, Argentina; d.26 Jun 1925, Buenos Aires. He studied with Homeyer and Collin, and later with Julián Aguirre and Alberto Williams. In Berlin, Germany, he continued his studies with Karl Heinrich Barth, Max Bruch, and Joseph Joachim, and later with Conrad Ansorge and Engelbert Humperdinck. He returned to Argentina in 1905 and was one of the first conductors of the Philharmonic Orch. of APO. Professor at the Williams Cons. of Buenos Aires and, in 1924, he was appointed professor at the newly organized National Cons. of Music of Buenos Aires, today the National Cons. of Music Carlos López Buchardo.

Works (selective list): *Carnaval,* opera; *La Gruta de los Milagros,* operetta; *El Sátiro y la Ninfa,* symphonic poem; *Obertura Criolla; Sueño de un Baile,* symphonic suite; Concerto for piano and orch.; *Sinfonía Argentina;* chamber music; songs; piano pieces.

Sources: BB, CA, DM, EMA, MLA, MMLA

Dublanc, Emilio Antonio, Argentine composer; b.15 Jul 1911, La Plata, Prov. of Buenos Aires, Argentina. He studied with Sister Leonor Maturana and Josefina Abella de Rossi, and then piano with Esperanza Lothringer, harmony with Constantino Gaito, counterpoint with José Gil, and composition with Ricardo Rodríguez at the National Cons. of Music Carlos López Buchardo of Buenos Aires, Argentina. He also studied composition with Athos Palma. Professor at the Cons. of Cuyo, Mendoza, Prov. of Mendoza, Argentina.

Works (selective list): Sonata for viola and piano (1946); songs.

Sources: CTA12, DM, EMA, MLA

Dueño Colón, Braulio, Puerto Rican composer; b.1854, Puerto Rico; d.1934, Puerto Rico.

Works: Music for piano; music for orch.; many songs and school songs.

Source: MMLA

Duncker Lavalle, Luis, Peruvian violinist, pianist, composer, mathematician, and astronomer; b.15 Jul 1874, Arequipa, Peru; d.29 Oct 1922, Arequipa. He studied with his father.

Works: *Lágrimas,* for voice and piano; *Marcha Nupcial,* for orch. *Music for piano: Leyenda Apasionada; Minuetto in E minor; Minuetto in A flat; Picaflor,* concert fantasy; *Quenas, Llanto y Risa, Mariposas, Margarita, Luz y Sombra, Cholita,* waltzes.

Sources: ADBM, DM, MMLA

Duprat, Rogerio, Brazilian composer; b.1932, Rio de Janeiro, Brazil. He studied cello at the Villa-Lobos Cons. in Sâo Paulo, and later studied music theory and composition with Olivier Toni and Claudio Santoro. In 1962, he attended courses in Darmstadt, Germany, and studied electronic music in Cologne and Karlsruhe, Germany, and in Paris, France. When he returned to Brazil, he founded the Symphony Orch. and the Chamber Orch., both of Sâo Paulo. With other Brazilian composers he organized the *Grupo Música Nova* of Sâo Paulo in 1963.

Works (selective list): *Noturno,* for flutes, clarinet, and strings (1956); *Suite para Crianças,* for strings (1956); *Variaçôes sobre um Copo d'Agua,* for strings (1956); Concertino for oboe, horn, and strings (1958); *Variaçôes,* for 12 instruments and percussion (1959); *Organismo,* for 5 solo voices, 11 instruments, and percussion (1960); *Mbaepre I,* for 17 instruments (1961); *Antinomies I,* for chamber orch. (1963); *Antinomies II,* for piano and strings (1963).

Sources: DCM, GDM

E

Eggers, Roberto, Brazilian composer; b.18 Dec 1899, Pôrto Alegre, Brazil; d.?
Works: Farrapos, opera; *A Noite de Natal,* symphonic poem; *A Mulher que eu Sonhei,* musical comedy; *Preço de un Capricho,* musical comedy; *Missões,* lyric drama.
Source: MMLA

Eisenstein, Silvia, Argentine pianist and composer; b.1917, Buenos Aires, Argentina. She studied with Ernesto Drangosch, Esperanza Lothringer, and Jorge de Lalewicz. In 1937, she entered the laboratory of musicology at the Museo Argentino de Ciencias Naturales in Buenos Aires under the direction of Carlos Vega, where she worked on folkloric research. She settled in Caracas, Venezuela.
Works (selective list): *Supay el Diablo,* ballet based on an indigenous legend (1950); choruses; songs.
Sources: DM, EMA

Eitler, Esteban, Argentine composer and flutist of Italian origin; b.25 Jun 1913, Bolzano, Tirol, Italy; d.25 Jun 1960, Sâo Paulo, Brazil. He studied piano, cello, and flute at the Royal Univ. of Budapest, Hungary. In 1936, he moved to Buenos Aires, Argentina, and in 1945, he settled in Santiago de Chile, Chile. Flutist with the Symphony Orch. of Budapest. Flutist with the Philharmonic Orch. of Buenos Aires and the Symphony Orch. of AGMA. He was a member of the *Agrupación Nueva Música* of Buenos Aires. In Chile, he founded the *Asociación de Música Contemporánea Tonus.*
Works (selective list): *Serie Boliviana,* for flute and string orch. (1941); *Microsinfonía Politonal,* for orch. (1943); Concertino for piano and 11 instruments (1947); Concertino for horn and 11 instruments (1949); *Policromía,* for string orch. (1950); *Microsinfonía Atonal,* for orch. (1956); chamber music.
Sources: BB, DM, EMA

Elías, Alfonso de, Mexican pianist and composer; b.30 Aug 1902, Cuernavaca, Mexico; d.19 Aug 1984, Mexico City, Mexico. Father of the Mexican composer Manuel De Elías. He studied orchestration and composition with Gustavo Campa and Rafael Tello at the National Cons. of Mexico, Mexico City, 1915-27. Studied piano with José Velázquez. Professor at the UNAM from 1958, and the National Cons. of Mexico from 1963.
Works (selective list): *Las Biniguendas de Plata,* ballet (1933); *El Jardín Encantado,* symphonic triptych (1924); 3 symphonies (1926, 1934, 1968); *Variaciones sobre un Tema Mexicano,* for orch. (1927);

Leyenda Mística del Callejón del Ave María, symphonic poem (1930); *Tlalmanalco,* suite for clarinet, bassoon, trumpet, piano, and strings (1936); *Cacahuamilpa,* symphonic poem (1940); chamber music; commemorative masses for soloists, organ, and strings; motets.
Sources: BB, CTA18, DM, MLA

Elías, Graciela Morales de, Mexican composer and violinist; b.28 Oct 1944, Mexico City, Mexico. She studied violin with H. Novelo, L. Samuel Saloma, and J.R. Vasca, and at the Escuela Nacional de Música of UNAM. She took classes with Jean Etienne Marie and Karlheinz Stockhausen. Founding member of the *Univ. Group of Composition X-1.* Professor at the Inst. Mexicano de Música.
Works (selective list): *Tangente,* for 3 soloists and orch. (1973); chamber music; choruses; songs.
Sources: IBCC, IEW

Elie, Justin, Haitian composer; b.1 Sep 1883, Cap Haïtien, Haiti; d.3 Dec 1931, New York, USA. He studied in Haiti and at the Paris Cons., France. When he returned to Haiti, he became interested in the music of the voodoo cult. In 1922, he settled in New York.
Works (selective list): *Suite Aborigen,* for piano, later orchestrated; piano pieces; music for violin; songs.
Sources: DM, MLA, MMLA

Elisio, Flavio (Alfredo d'Escragnello-Taunay, Viscount of Taunay), Brazilian music critic and composer; b.1843, Brazil; d.1889, Brazil. Music critic for the *Revista Brasileira* and the *Jornal do Comércio.*
Works (selective list): *Chopinianas,* series of waltzes; Sonata in E flat for piano; *Dois Capriches,* for violin and piano; piano pieces; songs.
Source: MMLA

Elízaga Prado, José Mariano, Mexican organist, *maestro de capilla* (chapelmaster), and composer; b.27 Sep 1786, Valladolid (today Morelia), State of Michoacán, Mexico; d.2 Oct 1842, Morelia. He studied with José María Carrasco, organist of the cathedral of Valladolid, and later with Soto Carrillo. He founded the first Symphony Orch. of Mexico, the first Mexican Philharmonic Society, the first Mexican and American Cons. of Music, and the first Mexican publishing company of music.
Works: *Miserere for the Holy Wednesday;* lamentaciones; responsorio; maitines de la transfiguración; oficios y misas for the Cathedrals of Guadalajara and Morelia. **Books:** *Elementos de Música, Ordenados por Don Mariano Elízaga,* Mexico, 1823, first Mexican

book on music didactics; *Principios de la Harmonía y de la Melodía,*
Mexico, 1835.
Bibl.: R. Stevenson, *Music in Mexico,* New York, 1952. J.C.
Romero, *José Mariano Elízaga,* Mexico City, 1934.
Sources: GDM, GMM

Elorduy Medina, Ernesto, Mexican pianist and composer; b.11 Dec
1855, Zacatecas, State of Zacatecas, Mexico; d.6 Jan 1913, San
Angel (today Villa Obregón), Mexico. He studied harmony with
Husprug and piano with Clara Schumann at the Cons. of Hamburg,
Germany, and took some lessons with Anton Rubinstein. After
several years, he continued his studies in Paris, France, with Georges
Mathias, director of the Paris Cons. Professor at the National Cons.
of Music of Mexico City.
Works (selective list): *Zulema,* operetta. *Music for piano:* waltzes;
mazurkas; nocturnes; capriccios; dances.
Source: GMM

Engelbrecht, Richard, Argentine conductor and composer of German
origin; b.1907, Munich, Germany. He settled in Rosario, Prov. of
Santa Fe, Argentina. He studied at the Music Academy of Munich.
Director of the Argentine Cons. of Rosario. Conductor of the
Philharmonic Orch. of Rosario.
Works (selective list): Symphony; *Canonic Variations,* for orch.;
Wind quintet; Cantata for choir; Composition for solo violin.
Source: MMLA

Enríquez Salazar, Manuel, Mexican composer and violinist; b.17
Jun 1926, Ocotlán, Jalisco, Mexico; d.26 Apr 1994, Mexico. He
studied violin with Ignacio Camarena and composition with Miguel
Bernal Jiménez at the Guadalajara Cons., Mexico, 1942-50. In New
York City, he studied composition with Peter Mennin and violin with
Ivan Galamian at The Juilliard School of Music, 1955-57. Also
studied theory with Stefan Wolpe and attended the Columbia-
Princeton Electronic Music Center, New York City, in 1971.
Concertmaster of the Guadalajara Symphony Orch. He supervised
music courses at the Inst. of Fine Arts in Mexico City. He founded
the group *Nueva Música de México* together with other composers.
Works (selective list): 2 violin concertos (1955, 1966); Symphony
No.1 (1957); *Preámbulo,* for orch. (1961); *Obertura Lírica,* for orch.
(1963); *Transición,* for orch. (1965); *Poema,* for cello and string
orch. (1966); *Ego,* for female voice, flute, cello, piano, and
percussion (1966); *Trayectorias,* for orch. (1967); *Si Libet,* for orch.
(1968); *Five Plus Two,* for flute, viola, trombone, piano, and
percussion, with actress and director (1969); *Concierto para 8* (1969);
Ixamatl, for orch. (1969); Piano concerto (1971); *El y Ellos,* for

violin and orch. (1973); *Ritual,* for orch. (1973); *Corriente Alterna,* for orch. (1977); *Raíces,* for orch. (1977); *Fases,* for orch. (1978); Sonatina for orch. (1980); Cantata for baritone, chorus, and orch. (1983); *Vivencias Líricas,* for orch. (1986); *Rapsodia Latinoamericana,* for orch. (1987); *Obertura sobre Temas de Juventino Rosas,* for orch. (1989); *Un Mundo Mejor,* for children's chorus and orch. (1990); Cello concerto (1985); chamber music; piano pieces; songs; music for the theater and for movies.
Sources: BB, CTA15, DCM, GDM, ISC

Escobar, Luis Antonio, Colombian composer; b.14 Jul 1925, Villapinzón, near Bogotá, Colombia. He studied music at the Bogotá Cons. and then took courses with Nicolás Nabokov at the Peabody Cons. of Music in Baltimore, Maryland, and with Boris Blacher in Berlin, Germany. Professor at the Bogotá Cons., 1953-62.
Works (selective list): *Stage: Avirama,* ballet (1955); *La Princesa y la Arveja,* children's opera (1957); *Los Hampones,* opera (1961). *Orch.:* Concertino for flute (1951); *Scherzo* (1952); *Sinfonía Cero* (1955); *Sinfonía X* (1955); Harpsichord concertino (1958); Piano concerto (1959); *Pequeña Sinfonía* (1960); *Epitafio a la Memoria de Jorge Gaitán Durán* (1962); *Juramento a Bolívar,* symphonic poem (1964). Chamber music; choral works; piano pieces; songs.
Sources: BB, CTA8, GDM, MLA, ZCCC

Escobar, María Luisa, Venezuelan pianist and composer; b.5 Dec 1903, Valencia, Venezuela. She started her music studies in Curaçao, Lesser Antilles, and then continued them in Paris, France, with Roger Ducasse. Founder of the Atheneum of Caracas, Venezuela, and the Asociación Venezolana de Autores y Compositores. Founder and President of the Asociación Venezolana de Compositores.
Works (selective list): *Operas: Blanca Nieves; Cuento Musical; El Rey Cuaicaipuro. Ballets: Las Cinco Aguilas Blancas; Kanaime; Murachi; Orinoco; Ruptura de Relaciones; Orquídeas Azules,* symphony-ballet. *Vals Sentimental,* concerto for piano and orch.; piano pieces; songs; school songs; hymns; religious music.
Sources: DM, IBCC, IEW, MLA, MMLA

Escobar Budge, Roberto, Chilean composer and music critic; b.11 May 1926, Santiago de Chile, Chile. He studied composition with René Amengual and Alfonso Letelier. He taught at the Catholic Univ. of Chile in Santiago de Chile.
Works (selective list): Wind quintet (1957); *Diferencias Sinfónicas,* for orch. (1962); *Los Bisontes,* symphonic suite (1964); Nonet (1965); *Cuarteto Estructural,* for strings (1965); *Sinfonía Valparaíso* (1967); *Incógnita,* for harpsichord, trumpet, bassoon, cello, and percussion (1967); choruses; piano pieces. *Books: Música Compuesta*

en Chile 1900-1968, Santiago de Chile; *Música sin Pasado,* Santiago de Chile, 1971.
Sources: BB, CTA14, HMC

Escobar Larrazábal, Gustavo, Colombian composer; b.1890, Colombia; d.? Director of the National Cons. of Music and the Academy of Music that bears his name, both in Colombia.
Works: Music for piano: Bambuco en Rondó; Bambuco Característico; Estudios de Pasillo; Escena Popular.
Source: MMLA

Escola, Héctor Jorge, Argentine composer; b.1928, Buenos Aires, Argentina. He studied at the National Cons. of Music Carlos López Buchardo of Buenos Aires, graduating in 1941. He also studied law at the Law School of the National Univ. of Buenos Aires, graduating in 1950.
Works: Seis Pequeñas Piezas, for orch. (1944); *Canciones del Peregrino,* for voice and piano (1945); *Dos Piezas Folklóricas,* for string orch. (1945); String trio (1944); Sonata for cello and piano (1945); *El Rey Burgués,* symphonic poem (1953).
Source: EMA

Escot Pozzi, Olga, Peruvian composer; b.1 Oct 1931, Lima, Peru. She settled in the USA in 1953. She studied with Andrés Sás at the Sás-Rosay Academy of Music in Lima, 1949-53, with William Bergsma at The Juilliard School of Music in New York, 1956-57, and with Philipp Jarnach at the Hamburg Hochschule für Musik, Germany, 1957-61. Professor at the New England Cons. of Music in Boston, 1964-67 and 1980-81, and at the Wheaton College in Norton from 1972, both in Massachusetts.
Works (selective list): *Metamorfosis,* ballet (1951); 3 symphonies (1952-53, 1955, 1957); *Three Poems of Rilke,* for narrator and string quartet (1959); *Three Trilogies: Lamentus, Christos, and Visione,* for voice and different instruments (1962-64); *Sands,* for 5 saxophones, electric guitar, 17 violins, 9 double basses, and percussion (1965); *Interra I,* for piano, tape, lights, and film (1968); *Ainu,* for 4 ensembles of 5 voices (1970); *Neyrac Lux,* for 2 guitars and electric guitars (1978); *Interra II,* for piano and tape (1980); *Missa Triste,* for 3 women's choruses and 3 optional treble instruments (1981); *Pluies,* for alto saxophone and tape (1981); Concerto for piano and chamber orch. (1982); *Visione* (1987); *Your Kindled Valors Bend* (1989); chamber music; piano pieces; songs.
Sources: BB, CTA17, NGDWC

Esnaola, Juan Pedro, Argentine composer and pianist; b.18 Aug 1808, Buenos Aires, Argentina; d.8 Jul 1878, Buenos Aires. He first studied music with his uncle, Father José Antonio Picasarri, and then he continued in Paris, France, in Madrid, Spain, in Vienna, Austria, and in Naples, Italy. When he returned to Buenos Aires in 1822, he became active at the Escuela de Música y Canto founded by his uncle. Founder of the Academia de Música and president of the *Sociedad del Cuarteto*.

Works (selective list): Revised and rearranged the *Argentinian National Anthem*, composed by Blas Parera. *Gran Sinfonía* (1824); *Misa*, for 3 voices (1824); Requiem for orch. (1825); *Misa*, for 4 voices (1825); *Misa Sinfónica* (1825); *Marcha Fúnebre* (1827); *Cánticos para Semana Santa* (1832); *Vals,* for large orch. (1837); *Pasodoble*, for band (1837); *Rondó a la Española* (1840); piano pieces; songs; hymns.

Sources: DM, EMA, MLA, MMLA

Espoile, Raúl H., Argentine composer; b.25 Jan 1888, Mercedes, Prov. of Buenos Aires, Argentina; d.1958, Buenos Aires, Argentina. Studied with Adolfo Rinaldi, Corradino D'Agnillo, Pavanelli, Josefina Avella, and Edmundo Pallemaerts. He also studied with Vincent D'Indy at the Schola Cantorum of Paris, France. Professor of medieval and modern history at the Escuela Normal de Profesores of La Plata, Prov. of Buenos Aires, and of Argentine history at the National School Bernardino Rivadavia of Buenos Aires. Supervisor of music at the schools of the National Board of Education. Director of the Municipal Cons. of Music Manuel de Falla of Buenos Aires.

Works: *Operas: Frenos* (1928); *La Ciudad Roja* (1936). *Symphonic poems: En la Cuesta del Totoral; El Centinela de los Andes; En la Paz de los Campos; Kuntur.*

Sources: CA, DM, EMA, MLA

Estévez, Antonio, Venezuelan composer, oboist, and clarinetist; b.3 Jan 1916, Calabozo, State of Guárico, Venezuela; d.26 Nov 1988, Caracas, Venezuela. He studied composition with Vicente Emilio Sojo in Caracas. Played oboe in the Caracas Symphony Orch. At the age of fifty he became interested in electronic music and obtained a fellowship from the Venezuelan National Inst. of Culture and Fine Arts to study electronic techniques in Paris, France. Professor of harmony at the National School of Music of Caracas. Director of the choirs at the Liceo Andrés Bello and of the *Orfeón Universitario* (male singing ensemble).

Works (selective list): *Suite llanera,* for orch. (1942); Concerto for orch. (1949-50); *Cantata Criolla,* for voices and orch. (1954); a group of electronic works under the titles of *Cosmovibrafonía* (1968) and *Cromofonía* (1968); choruses; piano pieces.

Sources: BB, CTA14, GDM, MMLA

Estévez, Milton, Ecuadorian composer, architect, and socioeconomist. He studied at the National Cons. of Music of Quito, Ecuador, with Carlos Bonilla and Hilda Olgiesser. He studied composition, electroacoustic composition, and musical information through computers in France, with Max Deutsch, Yoshihisa Taira, Michel Reverdy, Mesías Maiguashca, and François Pinot, between 1980 and 1985. Director of the Research Dept. at the National Cons. of Music of Quito.
Works: *Introducción,* for wind instruments and percussion (1983-84); *Cinco Desencuentros con Episodio Cualquiera,* for orch. and magnetic tape (1986); *Patch 13,* for magnetic tape and percussion (1984); *Guitarra...Guitarra,* for electric guitar (1984); *El Bricolage de Gyor,* for 2 flutes, 2 clarinets, piano, and strings (1984); *Apuntes con Refrán,* for orch. and electroacoustic sounds.
Source: PEFCM

Estrada, Carlos, Uruguayan composer; b.15 Sep 1909, Montevideo, Uruguay; d.7 May 1970, Montevideo. He studied in Montevideo with Manuel Estrada Espiro, and later at the Cons. of Paris, France, composition with Roger Ducasse and Henri Busser, counterpoint and fugue with Noel Gallo, and orch. conducting with Philippe Gaubert. Founder and conductor of the Chamber Orch. of Montevideo. Associated with the State Radio, 1940-54. Director of the National Cons. of Montevideo, 1954-68.
Works (selective list): *Daniel,* oratorium (1942). *Stage: L'Annonce Faite à Marie* (1943); *Scene Pastorale,* ballet (1947); *Les Uns et les Autres* (1950); *L'Illiade,* ballet (1957); *Artigas* (1958). *Orch.*: *Preludio, Minué y Final* (1936); 2 suites (1937, 1942); *Tema con Variaciones* (1938); *Danza elegíaca* (1944); Concertino for piano (1944); *Robaiyat,* for soprano (1955); 2 symphonies (1951, 1967). Chamber music; piano pieces; choral music; songs.
Sources: BB, BHMCU, CTA16, DM, GDM, MLA, MMLA

Estrada, José Jesús, Mexican composer, organist, and pianist; b.1 Dec 1898, Teocaltiche, Mexico; d.? He studied music in Guadalajara, Mexico, in Rome, Italy, in Paris, France, and in Vienna, Austria. Professor at the National Cons. of Music and at the Univ. of Mexico, both in Mexico City.
Works: Oratorios; masses; motets; music for the organ; songs.
Source: KTL

Estrada, Julio, Mexican musicologist, music historian, teacher, and composer; b.10 Apr 1943, Mexico City, Mexico. He studied with del Castillo, Alfonso de Elías, de Tercero, and Julián Orbón in Mexico, 1955-63, with Gerhard Muench in Germany, 1963-65, and with Nadia Boulanger, Esla Barraine, Raffi Ourgandjian, Olivier

Messiaen, Jean E. Marie, Henri Pousseur, and Iannis Xenakis in Paris, France. Later he studied with Karlheinz Stockhausen and György Ligeti in Germany. He returned to Mexico in 1970 and worked at the Radio Univ. Professor at the Escuela Nacional de Musica of the UNAM since 1973. Researcher at the Inst. de Investigaciones Estéticas from 1976 and at the Mexican Ministry of Education, Mexico City, 1984-90.

Works: Persona (1969); *Solo* (1970); *Memorias,* para piano (1971); *Melódica* (1973); *Canto Mnémico,* fugue in 4 dimensions (1973); *Canto Tejido,* for piano (1974); *Canto Naciente,* for 3 trumpets, 2 cornets, 2 trombones, and tuba (1975-78); *Canto Oculto,* for violin (1977); *Canto Alterno,* for cello (1978); *Diario,* for 15 stringed instruments (1980); *eua'on I,* for tape (1981); *eolo'oolin,* for 6 percussionists (1981-82); *eoa'on II,* for orch. (1983); *yuunohui'yei,* for cello (1983); *ishini'ioni,* for string quartet (1984-90); *yuunohui'nahui,* for double bass (1985); *yuunohui'ce,* for violin (1990); *yuunohui'ome,* for viola (1990). *Books:* General editor of *La Música de Mexico,* 10 volumes, Mexico, 1984.
Source: BB

Estrella de Mescoli, Blanca, Venezuelan composer, pianist, and teacher; b.5 Sep 1915, San Felipe, Venezuela; d.1986, Venezuela. She studied piano with Elena Arrarte and Moisés Moleiro, and composition with Vicente Emilio Sojo, at the Escuela Nacional de Música y Declamación in Caracas, Venezuela. Later she continued her studies with Primo Casale and Yannis Ioannidis. In 1962, she founded the Escuela Experimental de Música Blanca Estrella.
Works (selective list): *María Leonza,* symphonic poem (1950); *Imagen de Barquisimeto Romántico,* for orch.; *Symphonic Ballet* (1968); chamber music; piano pieces; songs.
Sources: IBCC, IEW

Etkin, Mariano, Argentine composer and teacher; b.5 Nov 1943, Buenos Aires, Argentina. He studied piano, theory, solfeggio, and harmony at the National Cons. of Music Carlos López Buchardo in Buenos Aires, 1955-58. He also studied piano and music analysis with Ernesto Epstein, composition with Guillermo Graetzer, and later continued composition studies at the Centro Latinoamericano de Altos Estudios Musicales of the Inst. Torcuato Di Tella of Buenos Aires with Alberto Ginastera, Earle Brown, Mario Davidovsky, Gerardo Gandini, Maurice Le Roux, Roger Sessions, and Iannis Xenakis. From 1968 to 1970, he studied electronic music with Gottfried M. Koenig and orch. conducting with Paul Hupperts at the Univ. of Utrecht, Netherlands, orch. conducting with Pierre Boulez in Basil, Switzerland, and with Franco Ferrara in Siena, Italy, and composition with Luciano Berio at The Juilliard School of Music in New York

City. Professor at the National Univ. of Tucumán, Prov. of Tucumán, the National Univ. of Litoral, Rosario, Prov. of Santa Fe, the Facultad de Bellas Artes of the National Univ. of La Plata, Prov. of Buenos Aires, and the National Univ. of Buenos Aires, all in Argentina, and from 1982 to 1985, at the Music Department of the Wilfried Laurier Univ. in Ontario, Canada.

Works (selective list): *Tres Parábolas,* for chamber ensemble (1963-64); *Elipses,* for string orch. (1964); *Música Ritual,* for orch. (1971-74); *Otros Tiempos,* for quintet or string orch. (1978-81); *Paisaje,* for string orch. (1979-80); *Resplandores Sombras,* for orch. (1986); chamber music; piano pieces; music for solo instruments.

Source: ISC

F

Fabini, Eduardo Félix, Uruguayan violinist, teacher, and composer; b.18 May 1882, Solís de Mataojo, Uruguay; d.17 May 1950, Montevideo, Uruguay. He studied violin with his older brother, Santiago, and then with Romeo Massi, Italo Casella, Virgilio Scarabelli, and Miguel Ferroni at the Cons. La Lira of Montevideo. In 1900, he entered the Cons. of Brussels, Belgium, where he studied violin with Deloc and César Thompson, and harmony and composition with Augusto de Boeck. Founder of the Cons. of Music of Uruguay and the Uruguayan Association of Chamber Music.
Works (selective list): *Mburucuyá,* ballet (1933); *Mañana de Reyes,* ballet (1937); *Campo,* symphonic poem (1922); *La Isla de los Ceibos,* overture (1926); *Melga Sinfónica,* symphonic movement (1931); *Patria Vieja,* symphonic overture for soloists, chorus, and orch. (1931); *Fantasía,* for violin and orch. (1929); chamber music; choral works; piano pieces; songs.
Bibl.: R. Lagarmilla, *Eduardo Fabini,* Montevideo, 1954.
Sources: BB, BHMCU, CTA2, DCM, DM, GDM, MLA, MMLA, MU

Falabella Correa, Roberto, Chilean composer; b.13 Feb 1926, Santiago de Chile, Chile; d.15 Dec 1958, Santiago de Chile. Paralized by polio since childhood, Falabella was educated privately at home by Lucila Césped, 1945-46, Alfonso Letelier, 1949-50, Gustavo Becerra, 1952, Miguel Aguilar, and Esteban Eitler, 1956-57.
Works (selective list): *Epitafios Fúnebres,* chamber opera (1952); *Del Diario Morir,* miniature opera (1954); *El Peine de Oro,* ballet (1954); *Palimpsestos,* for contralto, bassoon, horn, and percussion (1954); Symphony No.1 (1955); *Two Divertimenti,* for strings (1955); *Andacollo,* ballet for voices, piano, and percussion (1957); *La Lámpara en la Tierra,* cantata for baritone and orch. (1958); chamber music.
Sources: BB, HMC

Faleni, Arturo, Argentine composer and teacher of Italian origin; b.15 Nov 1877, Chieti, Italy; d.24 Sep 1942, Buenos Aires, Argentina. He moved to Buenos Aires in 1880. He studied with Jenusky in Genoa, Italy, and in Argentina, he furthered his studies with Juan Panizza, Aromatori, and Juan Gutiérrez. In 1901, he founded the Inst. Verdi in Buenos Aires, which later was renamed Cons. Faleni.
Works: Composed a large number of works that are not well known.
Books: *Teoría de la Música,* 4 volumes (1904); *Compendio de Historia de la Música* (1910); *Tratado de Armonía,* 2 volumes.

Sources: DM, EMA, MMLA

Fariñas Cantero, Carlos, Cuban composer; b.28 Nov 1934, Cienfuegos, Cuba. He studied at the Havana Cons., Havana, Cuba, with José Ardévol and Harold Gramatges. In 1956, he went to the USA to take courses at the Berkshire Music Center in Tanglewood, Massachusetts, where he studied composition with Aaron Copland and conducting with Eleazar de Carvalho. From 1961 to 1963 he studied at the Moscow Cons., Russia, with Alexander Pirumov. He returned to Cuba in 1963 and was active as a composer for television. Director of the Cons. Alejandro García Caturla, the Council for National Culture in the Dept. of Music Education, and the Music Section of the National Library, all in Havana.
Works (selective list): *Pregón y Variaciones,* for flute and string quartet (1955); *Despertar,* ballet (1960); *Tiento I,* for clarinet, guitar, piano, and percussion (1966); *Oda a Camila,* for orch. (1966); *Tiento II,* for 2 pianos and percussion (1969); *Relieves,* for 5 instrumental groups with audience participation (1969); *Muros, Rejas y Vitrales,* for orch. and various objects (1972); Concerto for violin and percussion (1975); *El Bosque ha Echado a Andar,* for orch. (1976).
Sources: BB, GDM

Fasetti, Gustavo Enrique, Argentine composer and professor of music; b.18 Dec 1953, La Plata, Prov. of Buenos Aires, Argentina. He studied at the Facultad de Bellas Artes of the National Univ. of La Plata. Professor of harmony, counterpoint, orchestration, and musical form at the Facultad de Bellas Artes of the National Univ. of La Plata.
Source: VMA

Faulhaber, Manuel Porto Alegre, Brazilian composer and pianist; b.25 May 1867, Rio de Janeiro, Brazil; d.7 Feb 1922, Rio de Janeiro. He started music studies with his father, Paul Faulhaber, continuing later with Alfredo Bevilacqua. Librarian and honorary member of the National Inst. of Music of Rio de Janeiro.
Works (selective list): *Music for piano: Ballade; Caprice; Valse; Diálogo; Noturno; Prelúdio; Romance; Scherzo; Trois Morceaux.*
Source: EMB

Fava Ninci, Enrique, Peruvian composer of Italian origin; b.4 Oct 1883, Spezia, Italy; d.5 Dec 1948, Lima, Peru. He started his music studies in his native town and then in Pesaro, Italy, he studied violin with Fenucci, flute with Filiberti Peri, piano with Alejandro Ferrari, composition with Pietro Mascagni and Amilcare Zanella, and history of music with L. A. Villanis. Director of the Academia de Música Alcedo of Lima.

Works (selective list): *La Cadena de Huáscar,* ballet; *La Visión de Viracocha,* ballet; *Navidad,* lyric scene for soloists, chorus, and orch.; *Visiones,* suite for orch.; *Ayacucho,* hymn for orch.; chamber music; piano pieces.
Sources: ADBM, DM

Febo Ortíz, Félix, Puerto Rican composer; b.31 Mar 1950, Río Piedras, Puerto Rico. He studied at the Univ. of Puerto Rico and at the Cons. of Music of Puerto Rico. He also attended the State Univ. of Michigan, East Lansing, Michigan, where he studied bassoon. Professor of harmony and solfeggio at the Univ. of Puerto Rico. Director of the Collegium Musicum of that univ.
Works (selective list): *Isabel Viendo Llover en Macondo,* for flute, clarinet, and bassoon (1972); *Prolongaciones,* for clarinet, bassoon, and piano (1974); Sextet for flute, oboe, clarinet, bassoon, violin, and viola (1976); *Naika,* for flute, oboe, clarinet, bassoon, piano, and violin (1978); *Improvisaciones,* for 10 violins and percussion (1980); music for solo instruments; piano pieces.
Source: CPR

Fernandes (Fernández), Gaspar, Mexican composer and organist of Portuguese origin; b.c.1570, Portugal; d.before 18 Sep 1629, Puebla, Mexico. Singer and organist at the Cathedral of Evora, Portugal. In 1599, he moved to Central America and became organist and *maestro de capilla* (chapelmaster) at the Cathedral of Guatemala. In 1606, he was appointed *maestro de capilla* (chapelmaster) at the Cathedral of Puebla, Mexico.
Works: 2 masses for 3 and 5 voices; *Magníficat,* for 4 voices; 8 *Benedicamus Domino,* for 4 voices; hymns; festal chansonnettes and villancicos; organ tientos; *Elegit eum Dominus*, Latin secular work for 5 voices.
Bibl.: R. Stevenson, *Renaissance and Baroque Musical Sources in the Americas,* Washington, D.C., 1970.
Source: GDM

Fernández, Guillermo Juan, Argentine composer and choral conductor; b.23 Jun 1953, Rosario, Prov. of Santa Fe, Argentina. He studied piano with Antonio de Raco, Ricardo Vidal, and Aldo Antognazzi, choral conducting with Cristián H. Larguía and Carlos Gantus, and composition with Virtú Maragno at the National Univ. of Rosario. Conductor of choirs in various cities of the Prov. of Santa Fe and the Prov. of Buenos Aires, Argentina.
Works (selective list): *Cuatro Piezas*, for flute; *Antigua*, for flute and guitar; *Algama*, for flute, clarinet, and percussion; *Gestatio-Omnis,* for clarinet and French horn; *Superposiciones,* for guitar quartet; music for solo instruments; piano pieces.

Sources: CAMR, VMA

Fernández, Juan de Jesús, Guatemalan violinist, singer, and composer; b.3 Nov 1846, Guatemala; d.?
Works: *Misa de Nuestra Señora de los Dolores;* many secular and religious compositions.
Source: MMLA

Fernández, Oscar Lorenzo, Brazilian composer; b.4 Nov 1897, Rio de Janeiro, Brazil; d.26 Aug 1948, Rio de Janeiro. He started piano and music theory lessons with Joâo Otaviano and later he studied piano, harmony, counterpoint, and fugue at the National Inst. of Music of Rio de Janeiro with Francisco Braga, Federico Nascimento, and Henrique Oswald. Professor of harmony at the National Inst. of Music. In 1929, he founded the journal *Ilustraçâo Musical* and the choir of the National Inst. of Music. In 1935, he was appointed professor at the Art Inst. of the Federal District, and in 1936, director of the Brazilian Cons. of Music of Rio de Janeiro.
Works (selective list): *Suite Sinfónica sôbre 3 Temas Populares Brasileiros* (1925); *Imbapara,* symphonic suite (1929); *Reisado do Pastoreio,* suite for orch. (1930); *Amaya,* ballet (1939); *Malazarte,* opera (1941); Violin concerto (1942); 2 symphonies (1945, 1947); *Variaçôes Sinfónicas,* for piano and orch. (1948); chamber music; piano pieces; songs.
Sources: BB, CTA15, DCM, DM, GDM, HMB MLA, MMLA

Fernández Barroso, Sergio, Cuban composer; b.4 Mar 1946, Havana, Cuba. He studied piano with César Pérez Sentenat in Havana and composition with Václav Dobiás and Karel Janecek in Prague, Czechoslovakia. Professor of counterpoint, fugue, and musical form at ENA and the Cons. Amadeo Roldán, both in Havana. Director of the Music Dept. of the National Library José Martí and the Univ. of Havana.
Works (selective list): *Ballets: Oda a los Soldados Muertos*; *La Casa de Bernarda Alba* (1969); *Plásmasis* (1970); *Dinámica* (1971). Oboe concerto; Concerto for piano, percussion, and audience (1968); Electric guitar concerto; chamber music; piano pieces; songs.
Sources: HMC, KTL

Fernández Esperón, Ignacio, Mexican composer; b.14 Feb 1894, Mexico City, Mexico; d.? He studied solfeggio with his mother, Piedad Esperón, and Macedonia Alcalá, and piano with Salvador Ordoñez Ochoa. He studied harmony and composition with Edgar Varese in New York from 1923 to 1924, and with Paul de Flem in Paris, France, from 1931 to 1936. He furthered his studies in

orchestration with Edgar Varèse during his stay in Paris. Director of several popular orch. in various Mexican radio stations.
Works (selective list): *Diez Romanzas en Estilo Clasicista;* String quartet (1934); 3 trios (1935-37); *El Zihuateco,* fantasia for piano and orch. (1939); music for the stage.
Source: MMLA

Fernández Goes, Custodio, Brazilian composer and teacher; b.1886, Brazil; d.? Professor of piano at the Escuela Nacional de Música of Rio de Janeiro, Brazil.
Works: Several pieces for piano, violin, and cello; songs; hymns.
Source: MMLA

Fernández Hidalgo, Gutierre, Peruvian composer and *maestro de capilla* (chapelmaster) of Spanish origin; b.1553, Andalusia, Spain; d.not before 1620, Cuzco?, Peru. In 1584, he came to Bogotá, Colombia, to conduct music at the Cathedral and to teach at the Conciliar Seminary of San Luis. In 1585, he was appointed rector of the Seminary. He was appointed *maestro de capilla* (chapelmaster) in 1588 at the Cathedral of Quito, Ecuador, in 1591 at the Cathedral of Cuzco, Peru, and from 1597 to 1620 at the Cathedral of La Plata (today Sucre), Bolivia.
Works: Masses; *Magnificat,* settings for 4 to 6 voices; *Magnificat Quarti Toni;* psalms for 4 voices; hymns; *Music of the Office for Holy Week*; motets; *Salve Regina,* settings for 4 and 5 voices.
Bibl.: R. Stevenson, *The Music of Peru,* Washington, D.C., 1950. R. Stevenson, *Renaissance and Baroque Musical Sources in the Americas,* Washington, D.C., 1970.
Source: GDM

Fernández Naranjo, Nicolás, Bolivian composer; b.6 Dec 1905, Sud Yungas, Dept. of La Paz, Bolivia; d.1972, Bolivia. He dedicated his life to music after abandoning studies for the priesthood. Professor in various public schools. Choir conductor at the Sucre Seminary, Sucre, Bolivia, and professor of solfeggio and harmony at the Inst. de Bellas Artes in La Paz.
Works: *Tantum Ergo,* sacred music for 8 mixed voices; *Te Deum,* for orch. and mixed chorus.
Source: CB

Ferrari, Claudio A., Argentine composer; b.19 Dec 1962, Rosario, Prov. of Santa Fe, Argentina. He studied musical analysis and composition with Dante Grela, and furthered his music studies with Mariano Etkin, Luis M. Serra, Alcides Lanza, Carmelo Saitta, Francisco Kröpfl, Marta Lambertini, and Federico Monjeau.

Works: Misceláneas I, for clarinet and clarone (1986); *Cinco Miniaturas,* for flute and piano (1986); *Dos Piezas,* for clarinet, violin, and piano (1987); *Quantum,* for flute, clarinet, violin, and viola (1987); Octeto for instrumental ensemble (1989); *Inflexiones I-IV,* for flute, violin, and piano (1989); *Con Ruido Secreto,* for flute, clarone, viola, double bass, piano, and percussion.
Source: CAMR

Ferrari, Jorge Luis, Argentine composer, singer, and choral conductor; b.26 Jun 1954, Rosario, Prov. of Santa Fe, Argentina. He studied composition with Virtú Maragno, voice with Julio Somaschini, Angel Matiello, and Noemí Souza, and choral conducting with Néstor Andrenacci at the Escuela de Música de la Facultad de Humanidades y Artes of the National Univ. of Rosario.
Works: Mainly for the voice and choruses: *Sueño,* for mixed chorus; *La Ciudad de Urk,* children's opera.
Source: CAMR

Ferreira, Domingo José, Brazilian composer; b.1837, Brazil; d.1916, Brazil. He studied at the Cons. of Rio de Janeiro, Brazil.
Works (selective list): *Corte de Mónaco,* opera; *O Descobrimento de América,* opera; religious music.
Source: MMLA

Ferrer Otero, Monsita Monserrate, Puerto Rican pianist and composer; b.1882, San Juan, Puerto Rico; d.1966, San Juan. She started piano studies with Rosa Sicardo and Ana Otero, and harmony with Julio Carlos de Arteaga and Arístides Chavier Arévalo. She continued her piano studies with Gonzalo Nuñes in New York, and Jesús María Sanromá at the Cons. of Music of Puerto Rico.
Works: Chamber music; sacred music; piano pieces; songs.
Sources: IBCC, IEW

Ferreyra, Beatriz, Argentine composer, pianist, violinist, and electronic instrumentalist; b.21 Jun 1937, Córdoba, Prov. of Córdoba, Argentina. She started her music education in Córdoba, studying piano and violin, and later she studied piano in Buenos Aires, Argentina, with Celia Bronstein. She also studied harmony and musical analysis with Nadia Boulanger in Paris, France, from 1962 to 1963, and electroacoustic and electronic music in Paris and Milan, Italy, with Edgardo Cantón. She joined the Groupe de Recherches Musicales of French Radio in 1963, under the direction of Pierre Schaeffer, and in 1968, she attended a composition course in Darmstadt, Germany, with György Ligeti, Karlheinz Stockhausen, and Earl Brown.

Works: Tape: Médisances (1968); *L'Orvietan* (1970); *Siesta Blanca* (1972); *Canto del Loco* (1974); *Tierra Quebrada*, for violin (1976); *Echo* (1978); *Bruissements*, for oboe (1982); *The UFO Forest* (1985); *Mirage Contemplatif* (1992). Electronic music; incidental music for television.
Sources: IEW, NGDWC

Ficher, Jacobo L., Argentine composer, conductor, violinist, and teacher of Russian origin; b.15 Jan 1896, Odessa, Ukraine, formerly part of Russia; d.9 Sep 1978, Buenos Aires, Argentina. He studied violin in Odessa with Piotr Stoliarsky and M. Hait. In 1912, he entered the Imperial Cons. of Saint Petersburg, Russia, where he studied violin with S. Korguieff and Leopold Auer, and harmony, counterpoint, fugue, composition, and orchestration with Vasili Kalafati, Maximilian Steinberg, Nikolai Tcherepnin, and Nicolai Socoloff. He graduated in 1917. Concertmaster at the State Opera of Leningrad, USSR. He settled in Buenos Aires in 1923. Conductor of the Symphony Orch. of ADEMA. Professor of composition at the Escuela Superior de Música of the Univ. of la Plata, Prov. of Buenos Aires, Argentina. Professor at the National Cons. of Music Carlos López Lopez Buchardo, the Municipal Cons. of Music Manuel de Falla, and the Inst. Superior de Arte of the Teatro Colón, all of Buenos Aires. Founding member of the *Grupo Renovación* in 1929, and of the *Liga de Compositores de la Argentina* in 1947. Full member of the National Academy of Fine Arts.
Works (selective list): *Chamber operas: El Oso* (1952); *Pedido de Mano* (1956). *Ballets*: *Colombina de Hoy* (1933); *Los Invitados* (1933); *Melchor* (1939); *Golondrina* (1942). *Choral-symphonic music: Salmo de Alegría,* cantata for soloists, choir, and orch. (1949); *Mi Aldea,* for soprano, contralto, tenor, and chamber orch.; *Kadish,* cantata for soloists, choir, and orch. (1969). *Orch.:* 10 symphonies (1932, 1933, 1938-40, 1946, 1947, 1956, 1958-59, 1965, 1973, 1976-77); 2 symphonic suites (1924-66, 1926-62); *Poema Heróico,* symphonic poem (1928); *Sulamita,* symphonic poem (1927-60); *Obertura Patética Exodus* (1928-60); *Tres Bocetos Inspirados en el Talmud* (1930); Violin concerto (1942); 3 piano concertos (1945, 1954, 1964); *Hamlet,* 4 symphonic movements (1948); *Don Segundo Sombra,* overture (1954); Harp concerto (1955); *Oda a la Libertad,* for narrator and orch. (1957); *Variaciones y Fuga sobre un Tema de Mozart* (1961); *Obertura Festiva* (1962); Flute concerto (1968); *Capricho Argentino* (1972); Cello concerto (1974): *Obertura Dramática* (1975). *Chamber orch.: Dos Poemas* from *The Gardener by R. Tagore* (1926); *Gaucho,* suite (1944); *Preludio, Coral y Fuga* (1945); *Seis Fábulas,* second series (1951); *Serenata,* for string orch. (1947); Suite (1953). *Chamber music:* 4 string quartets (1927-47, 1936, 1943, 1952); *Suite en Estilo Antiguo,*

for woodwind quartet, horn, and trumpet (1930); Trio for piano, violin, and cello (1935); Piano quintet (1961); Wind quintet (1969); *Tres Piezas,* for brass and percussion (1971); *Introducción y Allegro,* for piano, violin, viola, flute, oboe, and bassoon (1971); sonatas for 2, 3, and 4 woodwind instruments (1949, 1949, 1959); Saxophone quartet (1957). Many sonatas for string and wind instruments with piano; piano pieces; music for solo instruments; songs; choruses.
Bibl.: B. Zipman, *Jacobo Ficher,* Buenos Aires, 1966.
Sources: BB, CA, CTA2, DCM, DM, EMA, GDM, MLA, MMLA

Fidemraizer, Sergio Oscar, Argentine composer and teacher; b.1958, Rosario, Prov. of Santa Fe, Argentina. He studied composition with Dante Grela and Francisco Kröpfl and conducting with Mario Benzecry. Founding member of several musical institutions in Rosario, including *Agrupación Nueva Música, Agrupación de Jóvenes Compositores Rosarinos,* and *Grupo Klank.* He worked at the Laboratorio PHONOS, Fundación Miró of Barcelona, Spain.
Works: Pieza, for flute (1980); *Aulofonías,* for flute quartet (1980); *Tres Preludios,* for violin and piano (1981); Sonata for flute and guitar (1981); *Basod,* for female voice, clarinet, clarone, piano, cello, and percussion (1981); *Cinco Bagatelas,* for guitar (1982); Trio for violin, clarinet, and piano (1982); *Cadencias,* for chamber ensemble (1983); *Música para un Encuentro Imaginario* (1987); *Cantos del Alba,* for electronic sounds (1988).
Source: CAMR

Figueredo, Carlos, Venezuelan composer; b.15 Aug 1910, Valencia, Venezuela; d.1986, Venezuela. He studied at the Caracas School of Music with Vicente Emilio Sojo. In 1948, he entered the diplomatic service as cultural attaché at the Venezuelan Embassy in Paris, France, and consul in Copenhagen, Denmark, and Madrid, Spain.
Works (selective list): 4 symphonies; chamber music; choruses.
Sources: BB, CTA14

Figueredo Cisneros, Pedro, Cuban composer, lawyer, and farmer; b.1819, Cuba; d.17 Aug 1870, Santiago de Cuba, Cuba. On October 18, 1868, he entered the Cuban Army of Liberation where he became general. The Spanish troops took him prisoner and executed him.
Works: Wrote the lyrics and music of the *Cuban National Anthem,* originally titled *Himno Bayamés.*
Sources: DM, MMLA

Figueroa, Víctor M., Guatemalan oboist and composer; b.1870, Guatemala City, Guatemala; d.1929, Guatemala City. He studied at

the Music Cons. of Guatemala City. Taught oboe in Guatemala. He resided in Naples, Italy, where he studied composition.
Works: Masses; marches; dancing music.
Source: MMLA

Figueroa Morales, Ramón, Cuban violinist and composer; b.4 May 1928, Santiago de Cuba, Cuba. Cofounder and vice director of the Academia Municipal de Bellas Artes of Oriente, Cuba.
Works: Patriotic hymns; Masonic hymn; songs; waltzes.
Source: MMLA

Filomeno, Bartolomé, Peruvian composer and *maestro de capilla* (chapelmaster). He resided in Chile from 1822 to 1843, when he returned to Peru where he was professor of solfeggio, voice, piano, violin, and guitar. In 1846, he was appointed professor of music at the Colegio de la Señora María Estevanes de Cot in Peru.
Works (selective list): *Misa a Dúo; Copla a Nuestro Amo; Misa a 3 Voces;* villancicos.
Sources: ADBM, MMLA

Fleites, Virginia, Cuban composer; b.10 Jul 1916, Melena del Sur, Havana, Cuba. She studied piano with Fernando Carnicer, and harmony, composition, music history, and aesthetics with Amadeo Roldán and José Ardévol. Professor at the Municipal and the National Cons. of Music of Havana. Secretary in charge of public concerts and radio programs of *Grupo Renovación Musical* of Havana.
Works: *Soneto de Dante,* for soprano and tenor (1940); *Soneto de Petrarca,* for soprano, contralto, tenor, and bass (1941). *Music for piano:* Sonatina (1941); *Invención* (1941); Sonata in D (1942); *Tres Pequeñas Piezas* (1942); *Preludio y Fuga* (1942). *Chamber music:* Sonata de cámara in D for 2 violins and cello (1942); *Ricercare,* for string quartet (1943); Suite for flute, oboe, and bassoon (1943).
Sources: DM, MLA, MMLA

Flores, Bernal, Costa Rican composer and researcher in ethnomusicology and music history of Costa Rica; b.28 Jul 1937, San José, Costa Rica. He studied in Costa Rica, and then went to the USA where he studied at the Eastman School of Music in Rochester, New York, with Bernard Rogers, Wayne Barlow, and Howard Hanson; received a Master's degree in 1962 and a Ph.D. in 1964. Professor at the Cons. of San José.
Works (selective list): *The Land of Heart's Desire,* opera (1964); Symphony No.1, for strings (1965); Symphony No.2 (1966); *William:* Concerto for piano, percussion, and orch. (1963); Clarinet concerto (1968); chamber music; piano pieces; songs.

Sources: BB, CTA15, NP

Flores, José Asunción, Paraguayan composer; b.27 Aug 1904, Asunción, Paraguay. He studied at the Police Music School in Asunción, and then furthered his studies in Buenos Aires, Argentina, where he settled in 1934. Interested in Paraguayan folklore, he created the *guarania,* a song in 6/8 rhythm.
Works: Guaranias: India; Kerasy; Panambí-Verá; Nde Rendapeayú; Jejui, for piano and violin, or for piano, violin, and cello, all written in 1929. *Mburica'o,* symphonic poem (1932); *Buenos Aires, Salud!,* for chorus and orch. (1932); *Pyjharé-Pyté,* symphonic poem for soloist, double chorus, and orch.; *Nanderuvusu,* ballet.
Sources: DM, EMA, MLA, MMLA

Flores Barrientos, Víctor, Bolivian composer; b.1915, Oruro, Bolivia. He was self-taught in music. Legal counsel of the Sociedad Boliviana de Autores y Compositores de Música of Oruro. President of the committee on Bolivian Ethnography and Folklore.
Works: Lamento de mi Tarka; Fantasía Incaica; Romance Chuquisaqueño; Orurenita Gentil; En mi Soledad; Eres mi Delirio.
Source: CB

Floriani, Carlos, Argentine composer and physician; b.29 Feb 1911, DM (1901, EMA), Buenos Aires, Argentina; d.1958, Buenos Aires. He studied piano with his father, Juan Bautista Floriani, harmony with Ernesto Suner, and counterpoint with Pascual Grisolía. He was self-taught in composition. Graduated from the Medical School of the National Univ. of Buenos Aires. Founder and conductor of the Physicians' Orch. of Buenos Aires. President of the Artistic Association of Buenos Aires.
Works: Tríptico, for cello and piano (1943). *Books: La Soprano del Colón,* novel; *Ráfagas,* dramatic comedy.
Sources: DM, EMA

Fonseca, Euclides Aquino da, Brazilian composer; b.1854, Recife, Brazil; d.1929, Brazil.
Works (selective list): *Operas: Leonor; As Damas d'Honor; Il Maleditta; A Princeza de Catete. Sinfonía Republicana; Te Deum;* music for orch.; piano pieces; songs.
Source: MMLA

Fonseca, Julio, Costa Rican teacher, church organist, and composer; b.22 May 1885, San José, Costa Rica; d.22 Jun 1950, San José. He started his studies at the National School of Music of San José, and later he studied with Alvise Castegnaro. He continued his studies at the Cons. of Milan, Italy, and then in Brussels, Belgium, with Edgar

Tinel and Louis Van Dam. In 1927, he was appointed professor of music at the Colegio Superior de Señoritas, and in 1942, he took the chair of theory and harmony at the National School of Music. He was appointed principal instrumentalist of the bands of the Republic and *maestro de capilla* (chapelmaster) at the Church of La Merced. Founder and director of the Academia de Música Euterpe.

Works (selective list): *Money Is not All,* operetta; *Caperucita Roja,* children's opera. **Orch.**: *Leda,* waltz intermezzo (1914); *Ecce Homo,* funeral march (1920); *Suite Tropical sobre Temas Costarricenses* (1934); *Himno del Centenario de la Aparición de la Virgen de los Angeles,* for chorus (1934); *Himno-Cantata a la Música,* for chorus (1935); *Marcha Festiva de la Orden Mercedaria,* for chorus (1937); *Gran Fantasía Sinfónica sobre Motivos Folklóricos* (1937); *Las Ruinas de Ujarras,* overture (1938). Chamber music; salon pieces for piano; religious music.

Sources: BB, DCM, DM, GDM, MLA

Fontenla, Jorge, Argentine composer, pianist, and composer; b.1927, Buenos Aires, Argentina. He studied piano with Raúl Spivak, harmony with Alberto Ginastera, harmony, and counterpoint with José Torre Bertucci at the National Cons. of Music Carlos López Buchardo of Buenos Aires. He furthered his studies with Suzanne Bauthian and Jorge Fanelli in piano, and with Carlos Suffern in composition. He was appointed permanent conductor of the Symphony Orch. of the Univ. of Cuyo, Mendoza, Prov. of Mendoza, Argentina, in 1968. Professor at the National Cons. of Music Carlos López Buchardo, the Municipal Cons. of Music Manuel de Falla, the Inst. de Arte del Teatro Colón, the Argentine Catholic Univ., all in Buenos Aires, as well as at the Inst. Superior de Música of the National Univ. of Litoral, Rosario, Prov. of Santa Fe, Argentina. Director of the Liceo Municipal of Santa Fe, Prov. of Santa Fe, and the Municipal Cons. of Music Manuel de Falla of Buenos Aires.

Works (selective list): **Orch.**: *Tres Piezas* (1950); *Suite Sinfónica de Cui-Ping-Sing* (1952); Concerto for bassoon and orch. (1955); *Ofrenda,* variations for clarinet on a theme by Fauré (1965); *Ofrenda,* for clarinet (1966); *Cantata de la Danza y la Muerte,* for narrator and mixed chorus (1972); *Cántico de Santa Teresa,* for chorus (1979); *Cantata Jubilar,* for narrator, double chorus, and organ (1981); *Lamento,* for cello and chamber orch. (1980); *Adagio* (1980); *Mass Spiritus Domini,* for soprano, mixed chorus, and organ (1981); *La Orquesta,* series of symphonic microforms in 4 movements (1981-83); *Mass Signum Magnum,* for soprano and female chorus (1983). *Dos Canciones,* for female chorus a cappella (1962); *Divertimento,* for flute, oboe, clarinet, bassoon, harp, violin, and cello (1954); String quartet (1960); *Resonancias,* variations on a Gregorian theme for piano and wind quintet (1969); songs; piano pieces.

Sources: CA, EMA, VMA

Forte, Vicente, Argentine composer and musicologist; b.1888, Buenos Aires, Argentina; d.1966, Buenos Aires. He studied in Paris, France, and in the USA. He thoroughly researched Spanish music and its influence on Argentine songs. Consultant in the Folklore Section of the Inst. of Argentine Literature, School of Philosophy and Literature of the Univ. of Buenos Aires. Professor of Hispanic-American literature at the Univ. of Leipzig, Germany.
Works: *Cantos Montañeses Vascos;* piano pieces; songs.
Sources: DM, EMA

Forti, Hermeş, Argentine composer of Italian origin; b.21 Sep 1906, Trieste, Italy; d.1972, Buenos Aires, Argentina. He studied at the Royal Cons. Santa Cecilia of Rome, Italy, with Alfredo Casella, Renzi, Fernando Germani, and Ottorino Respighi. Professor of piano at the Casa de España and assistant conductor at the School of Voice of the Royal Theatre of Opera, both in Rome. Professor of organ and composition at the Royal Cons. Arrigo Boito of Parma, Italy. He settled in Buenos Aires and was appointed assistant conductor at the Teatro Colón for the 1940 season. Professor of organ and organist at the Colegio Nacional de Buenos Aires.
Works: *Assetta,* opera; incidental music; songs.
Sources: DM, EMA

Fossati, Florencio D., Argentine pianist and composer; b.8 Jun 1907, Buenos Aires, Argentina. He studied with Elmérico Fracassi, Gabriel Monteaux, Alberto Zanardini, and Felipe Montigny. In 1942, he founded the Fossati Cons.
Works (selective list): *Operas: Elena; El Indio. Zenzontle,* symphonic poem; *Recuerdo de Viaje,* suite; *Alla Antica,* suite; songs.
Sources: DM, EMA

Fracassi, Américo, Argentine composer of Italian origin; b.29 Feb 1880, Lucito, Campobasso, Italy; d.15 Aug 1936, Goya, Prov. of Corrientes, Argentina. Brother of Elmérico Fracassi.
Works: Piano pieces; songs.
Sources: BB, EMA

Fracassi, Elmérico, Argentine composer and teacher of Italian origin; b.19 Dec 1874, BB (1878, EMA), Lucito, Campobasso, Italy; d.12 Oct 1930, Buenos Aires, Argentina. Brother of Américo Fracassi. Early in life he was brought to Buenos Aires, and in 1890, he returned to Italy where he studied music at the Naples Cons. with Rossomandi and D'Arienzo. In 1904, he was appointed director of the

Almagro Cons. and in 1900, he founded the Fracassi Cons., both of Buenos Aires.
Works (selective list): *Operas: Finlandia* (1914); *Merletti di Burano.* Piano concerto; Violin sonata; piano studies; songs; 4 Argentine anthems, one of which, *Himno al Centenario,* won a prize from the Argentine government.
Sources: BB, EMA

França, Agnelo, Brazilian teacher and composer; b.14 Dec 1875, Valença, Brazil; d.12 Jul 1964, Rio de Janeiro, Brazil Professor of harmony at the Escuela Nacional de Música of Rio de Janeiro.
Works (selective list): *As Parasitas,* opera; piano pieces; songs; religious music.
Source: MMLA

Franceschini, Furio, Brazilian composer and organist of Italian origin; b.1880, Rome, Italy; d.1976, Sâo Paulo, Brazil. He studied at the Academy Santa Cecilia of Rome, Italy, and later in Paris, France, with Charles Widor and Vincent D'Indy. *Maestro de capilla* (chapelmaster) and organist at the Metropolitan Cathedral of Sâo Paulo for 60 years.
Works: More than 600 compositions, mainly religious music and music for the organ.
Source: HMB

Franchisena, César Mario, Argentine composer; b.1923, General Pinedo, Prov. of Chaco, Argentina. Professor at the School of Fine Arts of the National Univ. of Córdoba, Córdoba, Prov. of Córdoba, Argentina. He experimented with different technical musical advances, including electroacoustics and dodecaphonic system, and also studied the relationship between mathematics and music.
Works (selective list): Concerto for piano and orch. (1954); *Variaciones Tímbricas,* for orch. (1963); Suite for flute and piano (1948); String quartet (1953); *Treno,* for quintet (1953); *Variaciones,* for violin and piano (1957); Trio for violin, bassoon, and piano (1957); *Rhythmus,* for string quartet (1965); *Psalmus Fidel,* for 9 instruments (1967); choruses; piano pieces; percussion pieces; songs.
Source: EMA

Franze, Juan Pedro, Argentine musicologist, music critic, and composer; b.10 Jul 1922, Buenos Aires, Argentina. He studied with Ivi Herczegh, Emma Jaenicke, William von Sadler, Georg Runschke, and Dimitri Macridimas. He also studied at the School of Philosophy and Literature of the National Univ. of Buenos Aires and took history and musicology lessons with his father, Johannes Franze. Founding member of the Argentine Catholic Univ., consultant at the Municipal

Theater, 1945-47, organizer and first administrative director of the Philharmonic Orch., administrator of the Mozarteum Argentino, 1952-56, secretary of the Inst. de Musicología, 1953-56, professor at the National Cons. of Music Carlos López Buchardo, 1966-69, and the Univ. of El Salvador, all in Buenos Aires. He also was professor at the National Univ. of Cuyo, Mendoza, Prov. of Mendoza, 1947-52, and director of the Inst. Superior de Música de Santa Fe, Prov. of Santa Fe, 1956-64, both of Argentina.
Works (selective list): *Pequeña Suite de Cámara*, for orch. (1940-43); *Kio Fong,* music for the stage (1942-43); *La Danza de la Muerte,* choreographic poem (1951); *Lamento Quechua,* for orch. (1952); *Berceuse Trágica*, for soprano and orch. (1954-64); *Juana, Cordura y Locura de Amor,* music for the stage (1972); piano pieces; songs.
Sources: EMA, VMA

Fraser, Norman, Chilean composer; b.26 Nov 1904, Valparaiso, Chile. He studied at the Cons. of Valparaiso, at the Cons. of Lausanne, Switzerland, and at the Royal Academy of Music in London, England, with Carlo Albanesi. He also studied with Isidor Philipp in Paris, France, Tobias Matthay in London, and Leonie Gombrich in Vienna, Austria. He took some lessons with Ignacy Paderewski in piano, and with Maurice Ravel in composition. Director of music at Charta Theatre in 1932, and of George Pharlane Concert Management in 1933, both in London. Professor and librarian at the National Cons. of Music of the Univ. of Santiago de Chile, Chile, 1934-35. Director of the Technical Section of the Dept. of Music of the BBC of London, 1936-39, and director of music of the Latin American Dept. of BBC, 1939-43. In 1943, he was appointed director of music for Latin America at the British Council in Buenos Aires, Argentina. He settled in England in 1973.
Works (selective list): *Four Chilean Dances,* for chamber orch. (1937); *Cueca,* for 2 violins and piano (1926); *En el Tiempo de la Chicha,* for cello and piano (1932); piano pieces; songs; choruses.
Sources: BB, MMLA

Frega, Ana Lucía, Argentine composer and teacher; b.25 Nov 1935, Buenos Aires, Argentina. She studied at the National Cons. of Music Carlos López Buchardo of Buenos Aires. Director of the Inst. de Altos Estudios of the Teatro Colón of Buenos Aires, and professor at the National Cons. of Music Carlos López Buchardo.
Works: Mainly songs. *Books*: On music education.
Source: IEW

Freitas Antunes, Jorge de, Brazilian composer; b.23 Apr 1942, Rio de Janeiro, Brazil. He started music studies in 1958 and later entered the Escola de Música of the UFRJ. He also studied composition and

orch. conducting with César Guerra Peixe, José Siqueira, Henrique Morelembaum, and Eleazar de Carvalho. He continued his music studies at the Inst. Di Tella of Buenos Aires, Argentina, 1969-70. With a scholarship from the Netherlands' government, he went to the Inst. de Sonología at the Univ. of Utrecht where he studied with Gottfried Koenig. With another scholarship from the French government, he studied in Paris with Pierre Schaeffer, François Bayle, Guy Reibel, and Luiz Heitor. In 1967, he organized the Center of Music Research of the Inst. Villa-Lobos of Rio de Janeiro. Professor of composition and acoustics at the Music Dept. of the Univ. of Brasilia, Brazil.
Works (selective list): *Isomerism,* for orch. (1970); *Catástrofe Ultra-Violeta,* for orch., male chorus, and 3 magnetic tapes; *Intervertige,* for string quartet, 2 percussionists, and wind quintet (1974); *Concerto para un Mês de Sol,* for cello and orch. (1974); *Vivaldía, Scriabinía, Bartokollagía, Proudhonnía, Tartinia,* all homage works where he utilized many experimental instruments (gasoline drums, metal pipes, paper pipes, zinc plates, etc.) and audience participation, magnetic tapes, lights combination, and chamber orch.; piano pieces; songs; choruses.
Source: HMB

Freitas Castro, Enio de, Brazilian composer; b.1911, Pôrto Alegre, Brazil; d.1975, Brazil. He started music studies at the Inst. de Bellas Artes of Pôrto Alegre, and continued them with Guilherme Fontainha and Francisco Braga at the National School of Music in Rio de Janeiro, Brazil.
Works: Sonata for violin; *Pequeña Suite,* for string instruments; Trio for piano, violin, and cello; String quartet; Symphony.
Sources: HMB, MMLA

Frick, Guillermo, Chilean lawyer, engineer, teacher of physics and chemistry, and composer of German origin; b.15 Jul 1813, Berlin, Germany; d.12 Aug 1905, HMC (1896, MMLA), Chile. He settled in Valdivia, Chile, in 1840, where he founded a musical club and organized the musical activities of the city.
Works: *La Gran Polonesa; Himno a los Vencedores de Maipú; Las Cosechas Alemanas en Valdivia; La Esperanza de los Polacos,* written for Ignacio Domeyko and performed by Ignacy Paderewski in Poland in 1919, the day of the establishment of the Polish Republic.
Bibl.: E. Pereira Salas, *Los Orígenes del Arte Musical en Chile,* Santiago de Chile, 1941.
Sources: HMC, MMLA

Frôes, Sylvio Deolindo, Brazilian composer; b.28 Oct 1865, Salvador, Brazil; d.3 Dec 1948, Salvador. He studied music with his mother. Later he continued studying in Paris, France, and in Leipzig and Karlsruhe, Germany.
Works: Symphonic poem; Symphony; Sonata for piano; Sonata for violin and piano; *A Lenda de D. Sanches,* ballad for voice and orch.
Sources: EMB, MMLA

Fuchs, Arno, Mexican composer, writer, and music critic of German origin; b.1 Aug 1909, Dresden, Germany. He studied music in Dresden, Erlangen, and Leipzig, all in Germany. Received a degree in music in Erlangen. Music critic in Leipzig and Stuttgart. He lived in Mexico City, Mexico, from 1936 to 1956, and in 1957, went back to Germany.
Works (selective list): Sonata in B minor for piano; *Moderne Bilder Tonmalereien,* in 2 volumes, music for piano; choral works; music for the organ; arrangements of Mexican folksongs. *Books: The ABC of Music,* Mexico, 1947.
Source: NH

Fuentes, Juan Bautista, Mexican teacher and composer; b.15 Mar 1869, Guadalajara, Jalisco, Mexico; d.11 Feb, 1955, León, Guanajuato, Mexico. He studied in Mexico City, Mexico. Taught music in various music schools.
Works: Sinfonía Mexicana, for orch.; piano pieces. *Books: Teoría de la Música* (1899); *Tratado de Intervalos y Trasposición* (1909); *Método de Armonía* (1920).
Source: BB

Fuentes Matons, Laureano, Cuban composer and violinist; b.3 Jul 1825, Santiago de Cuba, Cuba; d.30 Sep 1898, Santiago de Cuba. Father of Laureano Fuentes Pérez. He started musical studies with his sister Baldomera. Later he studied with Carlos Miyares Hierrezuelo, Juan París, and Juan Casamitjana. First violin at the Cathedral of Santiago de Cuba. Founder of the musical journal *La Lira Cubana.* Professor at the College of Santiago de Cuba.
Works (selective list): *Seila,* opera; *Recuerdos de Sívori, El Rocío,* and *El Arpa del Poeta,* romantic fantasias for orch.; *Misa de Difuntos,* for 3 voices and orch. (1856); *Stabat Mater; América,* symphonic poem; *Galatea,* overture (1868); 2 Requiem; 6 sonatas for 2 violins, viola, and cello; *Colón,* marche; *Marcha Solemne;* zarzuelas; chamber music; religious music; piano pieces; songs.
Book: Las Artes en Santiago de Cuba, Santiago de Cuba, 1893.
Bibl.: O. Martínez, *Program of the Philharmonic Orchestra of Havana,* Nov 18, 1946.

Sources: DM, DMC, MMLA

Fuentes Pérez, Laureano, Cuban pianist and composer; b.14 Sep 1854, Santiago de Cuba, Cuba; d.27 Dec 1927, Havana, Cuba. Son of Laureano Fuentes Matons.
Works (selective list): *Rapsodia Cubana; Elegía; Marcha Triunfal; Idilio; Oriente* and *Brulé,* fantasias; *La Mocita* and *Galimatías,* capriccios; *Alina,* waltz; dances.
Sources: DMC, MMLA

Furtado, Murilo, Brazilian composer; b.11 Feb 1873, Pôrto Alegre, Brazil; d.2 May 1958, Rio de Janeiro. He started music studies in Pôrto Alegre, and later continued them at the Verdi Cons. in Milan, Italy, where he studied harmony, counterpoint, fugue, and violin.
Works: Sandro, opera; *Selisk,* operetta. He wrote more than 150 compositions for violin, cello, piano, flute, and voice.
Source: MMLA

G

Gaito, Constantino, Argentine composer; b.3 Aug 1878, Buenos Aires, Argentina; d.14 Dec 1945, Buenos Aires. He studied with his father, Cayetano Gaito, and then continued his studies at the Cons. of San Pietro a Majella of Naples, Italy, with Pietro Platania. He conducted the orch. of the Cons. of Milan, Italy. When he returned to Buenos Aires, in 1900, he conducted several seasons of opera at the Teatro Argentino of La Plata, Prov. of Buenos Aires, Argentina. Board member of the Teatro Colón of Buenos Aires. Professor of harmony, counterpoint, orchestration, and choir and opera repertoire at the National Cons. of Music Carlos López Buchardo of Buenos Aires.
Works (selective list): *Operas: Shafras* (1907); *I Doria* (1915); *I Paggi di sua Maesta* (1918); *Caio Petronio* (1919); *Flor de Nieve* (1922); *Ollantay* (1926); *Lázaro* (1929); *La Sangre de las Guitarras* (1932). *El Ombú,* symphonic poem (1924); *La Flor del Irupé,* ballet (1929); *Antígona,* music for the stage (1930); *San Francisco Solano,* oratorio (1940); *La Ciudad de Puertas,* ballet (1947); overtures; piano pieces; songs.
Sources: BB, CA, CTA12, DCM, DM, EMA, MLA, MMLA

Galimany, Alberto, Panamanian composer of Spanish origin; b.31 Dec 1889, Villafranca, Catalonia, Spain; d.? He studied solfeggio with Juan Lamothe de Grignon, harmony with Antonio Nicolau, piano with Juan Pellicer, and cello with José Soler at the Municipal Cons. of Music in Barcelona, Spain. Director of the Band of the Republic of Panama. Professor at the National Cons., the National Inst., and the Colegio de Señoritas, all of Panama City, Panama.
Works: *Marcha Panama,* considered the second *Panamanian National Anthem; Capricho Típico Panameño* (1928); *Vasco Nuñez de Balboa,* symphonic suite (1941).
Sources: MLA, MMLA

Galindo Dimas, Blas, Mexican composer; b.3 Feb 1910, San Gabriel, State of Jalisco, Mexico; d.19 Apr 1993, Mexico City, Mexico. He studied harmony, counterpoint, and fugue with José Rolón, music analysis with Candelario Huízar, composition with Carlos Chávez, and piano with Manuel Rodríguez Vizcarra at the National Cons. of Mexico, Mexico City, from 1931 to 1942. He had composition lessons with Aaron Copland at the Berkshire Music Center in Tanglewood, Massachusetts, 1941-42. In 1935, together with Daniel Ayala Pérez, Salvador Contreras Sánchez, and José P. Moncayo García, he founded and organized the *Grupo de los Cuatro* (Group of the Four) for the promotion of modern music. Professor of

music and director of the National Cons. of Mexico from 1942 to 1961. In 1955, he became conductor of the orch. of the Mexican Inst. of Social Security, Mexico City.
Works (selective list): **Ballets:** *Entre Sombras Anda el Fuego* (1940); *Danza de las Fuerzas Nuevas* (1940); *El Zanate* (1947); *La Manda* (1951); *El Sueño y la Presencia* (1951); *La Hija del Yori* (1952); *El Maleficio* (1954). **Orch.:** *Sones de Mariachi* (1940); 2 piano concertos (1942, 1962); *Nocturno* (1945); *Don Quijote* (1947); *Homenaje a Cervantes,* suite (1947); *Astucia* (1948); *Poema de Neruda,* for string orch.(1948); *Pequeñas Variaciones* (1951); *Los Signos del Zodíaco* (1951); 3 symphonies (1952, 1957, 1961); *Obertura Mexicana* (1953); Flute concerto (1960); *Four Pieces* (1961); *Edipo Rey* (1961); Violin concerto (1962); *Tres Piezas,* for clarinet (1962); Overture for organ and strings (1963); *Tres Piezas,* for horn and orch. (1963); Concertino for electric guitar and orch. (1973); *En Busca de un Muro* (1973); *Tríptico* (1974); Concertino for violin and string orch. (1978); *Oberturas Mexicanas Nos.2 y 3* (1981, 1982). *Jicarita,* for voice (1939); *Primavera,* cantata (1944); *Arrullo,* for voice and small orch. or piano (1945); *La Montaña,* for chorus a cappella (1945); *A la Patria,* cantata (1946); *Tres Canciones de la Revolución,* for chorus and orch. (1953); *Homenaje a Juárez,* cantata (1957); *A la Independencia,* cantata (1960); *Quetzalcoatl,* for orch. and narrator (1963); *Tríptico Teotihuacán* (1964); *Letanía Erótica para la Paz* (1963-65); *La Ciudad de los Dioses* (1965); *Homenaje a Rubén Darío* (1966); chamber music; choruses; music for solo instruments; music for organ; piano pieces; songs.
Bibl.: C. Chávez, *Blas Galindo, Nuestra Música,* Vol.1, 1946. F. Agea, *Blas Galindo, Mexico en el Arte 1948,* 1948.
Sources: BB, CTA11, DCM, DM, GDM, GMM, ISC, MLA, MMLA

Gallac, Héctor I., Argentine musicologist, composer, and physician; b.3 Jun 1896, Rosario, Prov. of Santa Fe, Argentina; d.? He studied with Patricio Legarra and Gaspar Chiaffredo.
Works (selective list): *Impresiones Camperas,* suite for piano (1934); *Humahuaqueña,* for flute, oboe, and bassoon (1939); *Pastoral Calchaquí,* for flute and piano (1945); songs. **Books:** *Ensayos Musicológicos,* Buenos Aires, 1939.
Sources: DM, MLA

Gallardo, José León, Argentine theologian, linguist, and composer; b.1871, Buenos Aires, Argentina; d.1924. He graduated as a lawyer in 1894, then studied music with Vincent D'Indy at the Schola Cantorum of Paris, France. He was ordained a priest in 1908 and devoted his life to religion working in a small chapel in a town close to Rome, Italy.

Works (selective list): *Sonata Pascual,* for organ; *Suite argentina,* for piano; religious compositions; piano pieces; songs.
Source: EMA

Gallet, Luciano, Brazilian composer and ethnomusicologist; b.28 Jun 1893, Rio de Janeiro, Brazil; d.29 Oct 1931, Rio de Janeiro. He studied with Henrique Oswald and Glauco Velásquez at the National Inst. of Music in Rio de Janeiro, where he later became director. Founder of the *Pró Art Society* in 1924 and the *Associaçâo Brasileira de Música* in 1930.
Works: *Caxinguelé,* tango for piano; *Tango-Batuque,* for piano (1922); *Dois Cadernos de Melodias Populares,* for piano (1924); *Doze Exercicios Brasileiros,* for four-hand piano; Suite for flute, oboe, clarinet, and bassoon; *Nho Chico,* triptych; *Turuna,* for violin, viola, clarinet, and percussion (1926); *Suite sobre Temas Negro-Brasileiros,* for piano, flute, oboe, clarinet, and bassoon (1929).
Books: Monographs on Brazilian folkloric music: *O Indio na Música Brasileira; O Negro na Música Brasileira; Estudos de Folclore.*
Bibl.: L.H. Correa de Azevedo, *150 Anos de Música no Brasil (1800-1950),* Rio de Janeiro, 1956.
Sources: DM, GDM, MLA, MMLA

Gandini, Gerardo, Argentine composer; b.16 Oct 1936, Buenos Aires, Argentina. He studied in Buenos Aires with Pía Sebastiani, Roberto Caamaño, and Alberto Ginastera, 1956-59, and in Rome, Italy, with Goffredo Petrassi, 1966-67. Professor at the Catholic Univ. and the Centro Latinoamericano de Altos Estudios Musicales of the Inst. Di Tella, both in Buenos Aires. In 1970, he was appointed to the faculty of the American Opera Center at The Juilliard School of Music in New York City. He founded the *Grupo de Experimentación Musical* in Buenos Aires for the promotion of avant-garde music.
Works (selective list): Piano concerto (1960); Variations for orch. (1962); Concertino I for clarinet, string trio, and percussion; II for flute and instruments; III for harpsichord and instruments (1962-63); *Por Mauricio Rinaldi,* for chamber orch. (1963); *Música Nocturna I,* for flute, piano, and string trio (1964); *Música Nocturna II,* for chamber orch. (1965); *Hecha Sombra y Altura,* for chamber ensemble (1965); *Mutantes I,* for chamber orch. (1966); *Cadencias I,* for violin and chamber orch. (1966); *Cadencias II,* for chamber orch. (1967); *Fuggevole,* for chamber orch. (1967); *A Cow in a Mondrian Painting,* for flute, and instruments (1967); *Soria Moria,* for variable instrumental ensemble (1968); *Contrastes,* for 2 pianos and orch. (1968); *Fases,* for clarinet and orch. (1969); *Fantasie-Impromptu, An Imaginary Portrait of Chopin,* for piano and orch. (1970); Guitar concerto (1975).
Sources: BB, DCM, EMA, GDM

Garay, Narciso, Panamanian composer and diplomat; b.12 Jun 1876, Panama City, Panama; d.27 Mar 1953, Panama City. He began music studies at the Musical Inst. of Cartagena, Colombia. In 1897, he studied at the Royal Cons. of Brussels, Belgium, and after that, in Paris, France, at the Cons. with Martin Marsick and at the Schola Cantorum with Gabriel Fauré. Minister of Foreign Affairs and Ambassador of Panama in Costa Rica. Director of the National School of Music of Panama, Panama City, from 1904 to 1918.
Works (selective list): Sonata for violin and piano; Fugue for string quartet; songs. *Books: Tradiciones y Cantares de Panamá,* treatise on Panamanian folk music, 1930.
Sources: BB, DM, GDM, MLA

García, Juan Francisco, Dominican composer; b.16 Jun 1892, Santiago de los Caballeros, Dominican Republic; d.1974, Dominican Republic. He studied with José Ovidio García at the Municipal Academy of Music in his native city. Conductor of the bands of Santiago de los Caballeros and Puerto Plata, Dominican Republic. Director of the Cons. Nacional de Música y Declamación of Ciudad Trujillo, Dominican Republic.
Works (selective list): 5 symphonies, the first named *Sinfonía Quisqueyana; Scherzo Clásico,* for orch.; *Sambumbia,* Dominican rhapsody; piano pieces; dances.
Sources: CTA2, DM, MLA, MMLA

García, Miguel, Cuban choral conductor and composer; b.8 Sep 1927, Havana, Cuba. He studied at the Municipal Cons. of Havana. In Santiago de Cuba, Cuba, together with Pablo Hernández Balaguer, he founded the Dept. of Music of the Univ. of Oriente. Conductor of the *Coro de Madrigalistas.* Professor and director of the Cons. Esteban Salas and director of music of the National Cultural Council, both of Havana.
Works: Several orch. and choral works, as well as incidental music for the theater.
Source: DMC

García, Orlando Jacinto, Cuban composer and teacher; b.13 Feb 1954, Havana, Cuba. He moved to the USA in 1961. He studied theory and composition with Joseph Rohm and jazz guitar and music arrangement with Cal Wilson at the Florida International Univ. of Miami, Florida, where he received a BM degree in 1980. Later, he studied composition with Dennis Kam and electronic music with Don Wilson at the Univ. of Miami, where he received an MM in 1982 and a DMA in 1984. He took additional composition studies with John Corigliano, David Del Tredici, Donald Erb, Earle Brown, Morton Feldman, Bernard Rands, and Harvey Sollberger. Assistant professor

and director of music theory and composition at the Florida International Univ. of Miami. Adjunct lecturer at the Univ. of Miami. *Works* (selective list): *Spheres,* for chamber ensemble (1987); *Sonic Islands in a Sea of Solitude,* for wind quartet (1987); *Music for Chamber Ensemble,* for chamber group (1988); *Treno para las Americas,* for soprano and orch. (1988); *In Deference to the King,* for percussion and chamber ensemble (1990); *Possession,* for solo tape and dancers (1990); *Improvisations with Metallic Materials,* for WX7 synthesizer (1990); *Sitio sin Nombre,* for voice and tape (1991); *Music for the Opus* and *Collage,* for tape (1990); *Metallic Images,* for tape and percussion (1991); *Momentos Congelados,* for viola and piano (1992); music for solo and different combination of instruments.
Source: ISC

García Acevedo, Mario, Argentine teacher, musicologist, and composer; b.28 Apr 1926, Buenos Aires, Argentina. He studied with José Román Erquicia, Vicente Scaramuzza, Juan Agustín' García Estrada, Alexander Szenkar, Carlos Vega, Isabel Aretz, and Lauro Ayestarán. Graduated from the Facultad de Filosofía y Letras of the National Univ. of Buenos Aires. Professor at the National Cons. of Music Carlos López Buchardo and the Municipal Cons. of Music Manuel de Falla, both of Buenos Aires. Professor at the Facultad de Filosofía y Letras of the National Univ. of Buenos Aires.
Works (selective list): *Orch.*: *Suite Argentina* (1950); *Adagio,* for string orch. (1951); *Preludio, Fuga y Toccata* (1952-53); *Poema Coral en Re* (1955); *Exedra* (1986); *Wayra-Jirka* (1986); *Poema Himno* (1987); *Reflexión Lisztiana* (1987); *Transmutación Bruckneriana* (1987); *Symposion* (1987); *Saga* (1988); *Poema Concertante* (1987) and *Rapsodia* (1988) for bandonion and string orch. Chamber music; music for organ; music for solo instruments; choruses; songs. *Books: La Música Argentina durante el Período de la Organización Nacional,* 1961; *La Música Argentina Contemporánea,* 1963.
Sources: EMA, ISC

García Arancibia, Fernando, Chilean composer, teacher, and trombonist; b.4 Jul 1930, Santiago de Chile, Chile. He studied trombone at the National Cons. of Santiago de Chile and composition privately with Juan Orrego Salas, Carlos Botto, and Gustavo Becerra Schmidt. Professor at the Cons. Nuñoa and Cons. Independencia, the Escuela Moderna de Música, and the Univ. of Chile, all in Santiago de Chile.
Works (selective list): *Orch.*: *Estáticas* (1963); *Urania* (1965); *La Tierra Combatiente,* for 3 narrators (1965); *Sebastián Vásquez,* for 2 narrators and soprano (1966); *La Arena Traicionada* (1967);

Firmamento Sumergido (1968); *Los Héroes Caídos Hablan,* for 3 narrators and speaking chorus (1968). Chamber music; songs.
Sources: DCM, HMC

García Cánepa, Julio César, Argentine composer and teacher; b.14 Aug 1940, Buenos Aires, Argentina. He studied piano with Perla Brúgola and Jorge Fontenla, composition with Roberto García Morillo, Virtú Maragno, and Valdo Sciammarella, and orch. conducting with Roberto Castro at the National Cons. of Music Carlos López Buchardo of Buenos Aires. Professor at the Municipal Cons. of Music Manuel de Falla of Buenos Aires and the National Cons. of Music Carlos López Buchardo.
Works: *Tres Miniaturas,* for solo flute; *In Memoriam ASdT,* for piano; *Momentos,* for piano; *Canto de Alabanza,* for mixed chorus; *Movimiento Sinfónico; Tres Piezas,* for string quartet; *Nexo,* for violin and piano; *Microtemas,* for piano.
Source: ISC

García Caturla, Alejandro, Cuban composer and lawyer; b.7 Mar 1906, Remedios, Prov. of Las Villas, Cuba; d.12 Nov 1940, assassinated in Remedios. He studied in his native town with Fernando Estrems and María Montalvan. When he moved to Havana, Cuba, he studied harmony, counterpoint, and fugue with Pedro Sanjuán. In 1928, he went to Paris, France, where he studied with Nadia Boulanger. Founder and first conductor of the chamber orch. of Caibarién, Cuba, in 1932. District judge in Remedios.
Works (selective list): *Tres Danzas Cubanas,* for orch. (1927); *Bembé,* for 14 instruments (1929); *Dos Poemas Afro-Cubanos,* for voice and piano (1929); *Primera Suite Cubana,* for piano and 8 wind instruments (1930); *Yamba-O,* Afro-Cuban oratorio (1931); *Rumba,* for orch. (1931); *Manita en el Suelo,* Afro-Cuban comic mythology for narrator, marionettes, and chamber orch. (1934); *El Caballo Blanco y Canto de los Cafetales,* for mixed chorus a cappella (1937); Suite for orch. (1938); *Cuban Overture* (1938); *Sabas,* for violin, piano, and 5 wind instruments; piano pieces; choruses; chamber music; music for band.
Bibl.: A. Salazar, *La Obra Musical de Alejandro Caturla, Revista Cubana,* 1938. N. Slonimsky, *Caturla of Cuba, Modern Music,* 1940. A. Carpenter, *La Música en Cuba,* Havana, 1946. R. Nodal Consuegra, *La Figura de A. García Caturla en la Música Cubana, Exilo,* 1971.
Sources: BB, CTA3, DCM, DM, DMC, GDM, MLA, MMLA

García Estrada, Juan Agustín, Argentine composer and lawyer; b.8 Nov 1895, Buenos Aires, Argentina; d.27 Sep 1961, Buenos Aires.

He studied with José Gil in Buenos Aires, then took composition lessons with Jacques Ibert in Paris, France.
Works (selective list): *Tres Aires Argentinos,* for orch. (1929); *La Cuarterona,* opera (1951); *Ruralia Argentina,* symphonic suite for orch.; chamber music; songs.
Sources: BB, DM, EMA

García Mansilla, Eduardo, Argentine composer and diplomat; b.7 Mar 1870, Argentine Embassy, Washington, D.C., USA; d.9 May 1930, Paris, France. Studied in Paris with Jules Massenet, Camille Saint-Saëns, André Gédalge, and Vincent D'Indy, and at the Imperial Cons. of Vienna, Austria. He also studied with Nikolai Rimsky-Korsakov and Spasky in Saint Petersburg, Russia.
Works (selective list): *Operas: Ivan* (1905); *La Angelical Manuelita* (1917). Religious music; choruses.
Bibl.: J.M. Veniard: *Los García, los Mansilla y la Música,* Buenos Aires, 1986.
Sources: BB, DM, EMA, MMLA

García Morillo, Roberto, Argentine composer and music critic; b.22 Jan 1911, Buenos Aires, Argentina. He studied piano with Julián Aguirre, Rafael González, and Juan José Castro, and solfeggio with Ricardo Rodríguez at the Argentine School of Music, and harmony with Floro Ugarte, counterpoint with José Gil, composition with José André, and orchestration with Constantino Gaito at the National Cons. of Music Carlos López Buchardo of Buenos Aires. Music critic for the newspaper *La Nación* of Buenos Aires in 1938. Professor at the National Cons. of Music Carlos López Buchardo and the Municipal Cons. of Music Manuel de Falla, both of Buenos Aires.
Works (selective list): *Stage: Usher,* mimodrama (1940-41); *Harrild,* ballet (1941); *Moriana,* choreographic cantata for soloists, chorus, and orch. (1957-58); *La Máscara y el Rostro,* choreographic concerto for piano and orch. (1963); *Tungasuka,* incidental music (1963); *El Caso Maillard,* opera (1972-75); *Arkady, el Mexicano,* opera (1980-81). *Symphonic-choral music: Marín,* cantata for tenor, chorus, and orch. (1948-50); *El Tamarit,* cantata for soprano, baritone, and orch. (1953); *Romances del Amor y la Muerte,* for bass and orch. (1959); *Cantata de los Caballeros,* for soprano and orch. (1965). *Orch.:* Concerto for piano (1937-39); *Música,* for violin and strings (1967); *Poema* (1932); *Berseker,* symphonic movement (1933); *Tres Pinturas de Paul Klee* (1944); *Symphonic movement* (1946); 3 symphonies (1946-48, 1954-55, 1961); *Overture for a Romantic Drama* (1954); *Variaciones Olímpicas* (1958); *Tres Pinturas de Piet Mondrian* (1960); *Divertimento sobre Temas de Paul Klee* (1967-70); *Ciclo de Dante Alighieri* (1970); *Dionysos* (1971); *Sexta Cantata* (1976); *Séptima Cantata* (1981). Chamber music; piano pieces; songs;

choruses. *Books: Mussorgsky*, Buenos Aires, 1943; *Rimsky-Korsakov*, Buenos Aires, 1945; *Estudios sobre Danza*, Buenos Aires, 1948; *Siete Músicos Europeos*, Buenos Aires, 1949; *Carlos Chávez*, Buenos Aires, 1960.
Sources: BB, CA, CTA8, DM, EMA, GDM, MLA, MMLA

García Muñoz, Carmen, Argentine pianist and composer; b.3 Mar 1929, Buenos Aires, Argentina. She started to study piano at the age of eight with Cecilia B. de Más, continuing later with Rafael González. She graduated from the National Cons. of Music Carlos López Buchardo of Buenos Aires in 1949, where she studied harmony with Abraham Jurafsky and Lita Spena, counterpoint with Héctor Iglesias Villoud, fugue with Gilardo Gilardi, and composition and orchestration with Floro Ugarte and Juan F. Giacobbe. She also studied organ with Julio Perceval. Professor at the National Cons. of Music Carlos López Buchardo.
Works (selective list): *El Ruiseñor,* symphonic poem; Concerto in A minor for piano and orch.; *La Noche Encantada,* ballet; *Sinfonietta Poemática,* for 29 instruments; *Catedral,* for 2 sopranos and chamber orch.; *Danza Criolla,* for orch.; *Serie Argentina,* for orch.; Suite for string orch.; *Un Sueño en el Camino,* ballet; *Elegía Porteña,* for clarinet and piano; piano pieces; songs.
Sources: CA, EMA

Garciaporruá, Jorge, Cuban professor of music and composer; b.9 Jun 1938, Havana, Cuba. He studied at the Cons. Castillo, the Cons. Amadeo Roldán, and the National School for the Arts (ENA), all in Havana.
Works (selective list): Requiem for orch.; *Viet Nam,* for orch.; *Tres Preludios,* for piano; *Tema con Variaciones y Fuga,* for piano; String quartet; songs; choral music; chamber music.
Source: DMC

García Robson, Magdalena, Argentine composer and pianist; b.28 Jan 1916, Buenos Aires, Argentina. She studied with Ricardo Rodríguez, Athos Palma, José Gil, Arturo Luzzatti, and Constantino Gaito at the National Cons. of Music Carlos López Buchardo of Buenos Aires. She studied piano with Corina H. de Lima and Guillermo Kolischer. Professor at the National Cons. of Music Carlos López Buchardo.
Works (selective list): *La Cenicienta,* symphonic suite (1939); *Coplas de Soledad,* for mezzo-soprano, oboe, bassoon, percussion, celesta, and string quintet (1948); *Variaciones Breves,* for flute, oboe, clarinet, bassoon, horn, and piano (1948); *Tres Bocetos Sinfónicos,* for orch. (1951); chamber music; songs.
Sources: CA, DM, EMA

Garrido Lecca Seminario, Celso, Peruvian composer; b.9 Mar 1926, Piura, Peru. He studied music theory with Andrés Sas and Rodolfo Holzmann in Lima, Peru. Then, he went to Santiago de Chile, Chile, to take courses in composition with Domingo Santa Cruz and Free Focke at the Univ. of Chile. In 1964, he received a Guggenheim fellowship. In 1967, he was appointed to the faculty of the Univ. of Chile.
Works (selective list): Sinfonía (1961); *Laudes,* for orch. (1963); *Elegía a Machu Picchu* (1965); *Música,* for 6 instruments and percussion (1957); *Divertimento,* for wind quintet (1965); String quartet (1963); *Antaras,* for string nonet (1969); *Apu Inca Atahualpaman,* for reciter, 3 choruses, and orch. (1971); *El Movimiento y el Sueño,* for 2 reciters, chorus, chamber orch., and tape (1972); choruses; piano pieces; songs.
Sources: BB, DCM, GDM

Garrido Vargas, Pablo, Chilean composer and folklorist; b.26 Mar 1905, Valparaiso, Chile; d.14 Sep 1982, Santiago de Chile, Chile. He was self-taught in music; then, he studied composition with Giuseppe Quintano and Eduardo Van Dooren. President of the Orchestral Union of Santiago de Chile. Founder of the journals *Vida Musical* and *Nueva Música.* Founder and director of the symphony orch. of Antofagasta, Chile. Music critic for the newspapers *La Nación* and *El Mercurio.*
Works (selective list): *Cowboys,* ballet (1926); *Fantasía Militar,* for orch. (1932); *Ballet Mecánico,* for orch. (1934); *Fantasía Submarina,* for piano and orch. (1934); *Rapsodia Chilena,* for piano and orch. (1938); Piano concerto (1950); *Fantasía Antillana,* for cello and orch. (1950); *Adán y Eva,* ballet (1952); *La Sugestión,* opera (1961); *El Guerrillero,* ballet (1963); chamber music; piano pieces; songs based on Chilean folklore.
Sources: BB, CTA9, DM, GDM, HMC, MLA, MMLA

Gavira, Joaquín, Cuban violinist, professor, and composer; b.1780, Havana, Cuba; d.1880, Havana. In 1802, he played violin and cello at the Chapel of the Cathedral of Havana. He was very much involved in the development of the art of music in Cuba. In 1852, he was appointed *maestro de capilla* (chapelmaster) of the Cathedral of Havana.
Works: Mainly religious music.
Source: DMC

Gennero, Segundo, Argentine contemporary composer; b.first half of the 20th century, La Banda, Prov. of Santiago del Estero, Argentina. He studied in Santiago del Estero with Alfredo Grandi, and then, in Buenos Aires, Argentina, with Floro Ugarte and Jorge de Lalewicz.

He was self-taught in composition. Professor of harmony at the Provincial Cons. of Music, Prov. of Buenos Aires, Argentina. **Works:** *El Pala Pala,* ballet; *Al Alba Florecen los Ceibos,* for orch.; Concerto for piano and orch.; *Yaraví,* for harp and string quartet; *Preludio y Fuga a 3 Voces en el Estilo de J.S. Bach.*
Source: DM

Gerardi, Enrique, Argentine composer; b.1926, Buenos Aires, Argentina. He studied with Luis Gianneo, Alberto Ginastera, and Gilardo Gilardi at the Escuela Superior de Bellas Artes of La Plata, Prov. of Buenos Aires, Argentina. He also studied engineering and land surveying at the National Univ. of La Plata. Professor at the Facultad de Artes y Ciencias Musicales of the Argentine Catholic Univ. of Buenos Aires.
Works: Music for chamber ensembles and various vocal and instrumental combinations; music for the theater and movies. He uses avant-garde techniques of the 1960s.
Source: EMA

Gerdes, Federico, Peruvian composer; b.19 May 1873, Tacna, Peru; d.18 Oct 1953, Lima, Peru. He studied at the Cons. of Heinrich Spangenberg in Wiesbaden and then piano with Carl Reinecke and harmony and counterpoint with Salomon Jadassohn at the Royal Cons. of Leipzig, both in Germany. He also studied conducting with Carl Panzner. He played frequently in Europe as a soloist and accompanist. Director of the Schola Cantorum at the Imperial Opera of Berlin, Germany, deputy director of choirs, musical assistant, and choral conductor of the Wagner festivals in Bayreuth, Germany, under Hugo Rüdel. In 1908, he returned to Peru and was director of the *Philharmonic Society* and founder of the Academia Nacional de Música y Declamación, both in Lima.
Works (selective list): *Music for piano: El Rotario,* marche; *Danza del Siglo XVIII*; *Gavota Homenaje a Watteau* (1917); *Berceuse Homenaje a Becquer* (1919); *Habanera* (1942). *Marcha Festiva,* for orch.; *Impresiones de la Tarde,* for violin and piano; songs; choruses; music for string quartet.
Bibl.: R. Barbacci, *Revista Musical Peruana,* Lima, July 1939.
Sources: DM, GDM, GMP, MLA

Giacobbe, Juan Francisco, Argentine composer; b.27 Mar 1907, Buenos Aires, Argentina; d.31 Jan 1990, Buenos Aires. He graduated from the National Cons. of Music Carlos López Buchardo of Buenos Aires in 1929, where he studied with Floro Ugarte. He also studied in Italy and France. He studied religious polyphony with Licinio Refice at the Capilla Liberiana of the Church Santa María Maggiore of

Rome, and Gregorian chant and Byzantine hymnography at the Monastery Santa María del Monte of Cesena, both in Italy. Director of the *Argentine Polyphonic Association* and musical consultant at the *National Comedy Theater*. Director of the National Cons. of Music Carlos López Buchardo, chief of Extensión Universitaria of the National Univ., professor at the Municipal Cons. of Music Manuel de Falla, all in Buenos Aires. Professor at the National Univ. of Córdoba and director of their Escuela Superior de Bellas Artes, Prov. of Córdoba, Argentina. Music critic for the journal *Histonium*.

Works (selective list): **Operas:** *Martín Fierro* (1929); *Natividad* (1934-36); *Juventas* (1935-41); *Il Re Nascosto* (1959-70). *Missa Brevis* (1931); *Nuestra Señora de Luján,* mistery for soloists, chorus, and orch. (1931-34); *Ella y el Angel,* 4 choreographic poems (1943-45); *Pampa,* choreographic sinfonietta; *Chaqueña,* ballet (1948); *El Angel y Yo,* ballet (1953-54); *El Diálogo Secreto,* for speaking voices and orch. (1959); *Tema Perpetuo,* choreographic symphony (1960); 2 Te Deum for chorus and orch. (1976, 1976-77); *Concerti da Chiesa,* for orch. (1977); chamber music; choruses; music for solo instruments; piano pieces; religious music; songs. **Books:** *Julián Aguirre; Gioachino Rossini; Frederic Chopin.*
Sources: CA, DM, EMA, GDM, MMLA

Gianneo, Luis, Argentine composer, conductor, pianist, and teacher; b.9 Jan 1897, Buenos Aires, Argentina; d.15 Aug 1968, Buenos Aires. He studied piano with Luis Romaniello and Ernesto Drangosch, harmony with Constantino Gaito, and counterpoint with Eduardo Fornarini. Conducted the orch. of the Royal Cons. of Turin, Italy, in 1938, the orch. of the APO of Buenos Aires, and the Philharmonic of Rosario, Prov. of Santa Fe, Argentina. From 1923 to 1943, he taught at the Musical Inst. of Tucumán, Prov. of Tucumán, Argentina. Member of the *Grupo Renovación.* Professor at various schools in Buenos Aires. In 1945, he organized and conducted the Orquesta Sinfónica Juvenil. From 1955 to 1960, he was director of the National Cons. of Music Carlos López Buchardo of Buenos Aires. Professor at the Provincial Cons. of La Plata, Prov. of Buenos Aires, and at the Argentine Catholic Univ. of Buenos Aires. Full member of the National Academy of Fine Arts.

Works (selective list): *Blanca Nieves,* ballet (1939). **Orch.:** *Two Minuets,* for string orch. (1917); *Turay-Turay,* symphonic poem (1930); *Canción y Danza* (1932); 3 symphonies (1938, 1945, 1963); *Obertura para una Comedia Infantil* (1939); Sinfonietta (1940); Concerto for piano (1941); *Concierto Aymará,* for violin (1942); *Transfiguración,* for baritone (1946); *Preludio y Fuga* (1946); *Pericón* (1948); *Preludio, Nocturno y Danza Orgiástica* (1949); *Cantica Dianae,* for soloists and chorus (1949); *Pastoral* (1950); *Variaciones sobre un Tema de Tango* (1953); *Angor Dei,* cantata for

soprano (1962); *Obertura del Sesquicentenario* (1965); *Poema de la Saeta,* for soprano (1966). *Chamber music: Tres Piezas Criollas,* for string quartet (1923); *Cuatro Cantos Incáicos,* for string quartet (1924); 2 piano trios (1925, 1943); *Divertimento,* for flute, clarinet, and bassoon (1934); Sonata for cello and piano (1934); Sonata for violin and piano (1935-52); 4 string quartets (1936, 1944, 1952, 1958); Trio for violin, viola, and cello (1938-39); *Concertino Serenata,* for wind and string quintets (1938-40); *Divertimento,* for flute, oboe, and clarinet (1943); Sonatina for harp (1946); *Preámbulo, Fuga y Epílogo,* for two pianos (1953); *Tres Piezas,* for violin (1963). Piano pieces; songs; choral pieces.
Sources: BB, CA, CTA4, DM, EMA, MLA, MMLA

Giarda, Luigi Stephano, Chilean composer, cellist, and teacher of Italian origin; b.19 Mar 1868, Cassolnovo, Italy; d.3 Jan 1952, Viña del Mar, Chile. He taught many Chilean composers.
Works (selective list): *Symphonic poems: La Vida* (1916); *Loreley* (1918); *Más allá de la Muerte* (1923). 2 operas; chamber music; music for solo instruments; songs.
Source: HMC

Gil, José, Argentine composer, teacher, and music critic of Spanish origin; b.29 May 1886, Haro, Spain; d.12 May 1947, Buenos Aires, Argentina. He settled in Argentina in 1889. He studied violin with Augusto Maurage and harmony and counterpoint with Alberto Williams. He devoted most of his time to teaching. Teacher in the school system of the National Board of Education from 1919 to 1935. Professor at the National Cons. of Music Carlos López Buchardo, the Municipal Cons. of Music Manuel de Falla, and the High School Mariano Moreno, all of Buenos Aires. Music critic for the newspaper *El Mundo* and for the journal *Nosotros.*
Works: *Obertura,* for orch.; Trio in A major for piano, violin, and cello; Quartet in B flat major for piano, violin, cello, and piano; Sonata in A major for cello and piano; Sonata in D minor for violin and piano; *Introducción y Allegro,* for cello and piano; *Danzas Argentinas,* for piano and string quartet; *Madrigales,* for baritone and piano or string orch. and harp; Sonatina for piano; *Tres Piezas,* for piano; the official anthem for the International Eucharistic Congress held in Buenos Aires in 1934.
Sources: CA, DM, EMA, MLA, MMLA

Gilardi, Gilardo, Argentine composer; b.25 May 1889, San Fernando, Prov. of Buenos Aires, Argentina; d.16 Jan 1963, Buenos Aires. He studied with his father and then with Pablo M. Berutti. Charter member of the *Grupo Renovación.* Conductor of the chamber

orch. of the APO of Buenos Aires. Professor of counterpoint and composition at the School of Fine Arts of the National Univ. of La Plata, Prov. of Buenos Aires, Argentina.
Works (selective list): *Operas: Ilse* (1923); *La Leyenda del Urutaú* (1932). *Choral-symphonic music*: *Misa de Requiem,* for soloists, chorus, and orch. (1914-18); *Te Deum Laudamus,* for chorus, organ, and orch. (1936); *Misa de Gloria,* for chorus, organ, and orch. (1936); *El Libertador,* cantata for tenor, speaker, chorus, and orch. (1948); *Stabat Mater,* for soloists, chorus, and orch. (1952). *Orch.*: *Serie Argentina* (1928-29); *El Gaucho con Botas Nuevas* (1936); *Piruca y Yo* (1936); *Triste Estaba mi Alma Hasta la Muerte* (1942); *Poema Fluvial* (1943); *Obertura Tritemática* (1952); *Sinfonía Cíclica* (1961). *Stage: Ollantay* (1936). Chamber music; piano pieces; songs; choral pieces.
Sources: CA, CTA12, DM, EMA, MLA, MMLA

Gilardoni, Eduardo, Uruguayan composer and pianist; b.9 Nov 1935, Conchillas, Dept. of Colonia, Uruguay. He studied piano with Esther Giucci, and harmony and composition with Carlos Giucci and Héctor Tosar, then later studied with Hugo Balzo and Armando Bascans. In 1964, with a scholarship from the Inst. de Cultura Hispánica, he traveled to Europe, visiting Italy, France, and Spain. In Barcelona, Spain, he studied piano with Alicia de Larrocha and voice with Conchita Badía. He also took some lessons in composition with Joaquín Nin Culmell.
Works (selective list): *Music for piano:* 2 sonatinas (1958, 1961); *Dos Nocturnos* (1963); *Tres Nocturnos* (1965); *Suite Muntaner 401* (1965); *Historia del Señor Don Gato* (1967). Songs.
Sources: BHMCU, MU

Gil Marchex, Henri, Argentine composer of French origin; b.16 Dec 1894, St. Georges d'Espérance, France; d.1971, Buenos Aires, Argentina. He settled in Argentina in 1940. He studied with Ferruccio Busoni, Alfred Cortot, Xavier Leroux, Paul Vidal, Maurice Ravel, and Albert Roussel at the National Cons. of Paris, France. Professor of piano at the Escuela Normal de Música of Paris. Professor of music aesthetics at the National Cons. of Music Carlos López Buchardo of Buenos Aires.
Works: Balada Porteña, for piano (1937); *Suite Francesa in D major,* for violin and piano (1939); *Dos Imágines del Viejo Japón,* for piano (1943); *Himno a los Muertos de la Francia Desdichada,* for orch.
Books: Tres Músicos Franceses, Buenos Aires, 1945.
Works: DM, EMA

Giménez, Herminio, Paraguayan composer; b.20 Feb 1905, Caballeros, Paraguay. He started his music education at the Music

Band of the 2nd. Military Zone under conductor Emil Laskozky. He continued his studies at the Music Inst. of Asunción, Paraguay, the Cons. Williams of Buenos Aires, Argentina, and with Oscar Lorenzo Fernández in Rio de Janeiro, Brazil. President of the *Agrupación Tradicional Guaraní* and the *Asociación de Artistas Paraguayos* in Buenos Aires.
Works (selective list): *Orch.*: *El Canto de mi Selva,* Paraguayan air #1 (1937); *Che Trompo Arazá,* for strings (1938); *Rabelero,* symphonic poem for violin (1943); *Neny,* Paraguayan air #2 (1953); *La Epopeya,* overture (1954); *El Pájaro,* suite #1 (1956); *Viejo Tala,* symphonic ballet (1958); *Juan José,* suite #3 (1962); *Yasi Yatere,* ballet for strings (1963). Choral-symphonic compositions.
Source: CTA15

Giménez, Remberto, Paraguayan composer; b.4 Feb 1889, Coronel Oviedo, Paraguay; d.? He studied in Buenos Aires, Argentina, with Alberto Williams and in Paris, France, at the Schola Cantorum. Director of the Escuela Normal de Música and conductor of the Symphony Orch. of Asunción, Paraguay.
Works: Official version of the *Paraguayan National Anthem. Rapsodia Paraguaya,* for orch.
Sources: DM, MLA, MMLA, MMPA

Giménez Noble, Javier, Argentine composer and teacher; b.25 Aug 1953, Buenos Aires, Argentina. He studied at the Municipal Cons. of Music Manuel de Falla in Buenos Aires with Roberto García Morillo. In 1985, he traveled to Italy with a scholarship from the Fondo Nacional de la Artes of Buenos Aires, where he studied with Giacomo Manzoni in Milan, and Franco Donatoni in Siena. From 1988 to 1991, he studied in Boston, Massachusetts, and graduated with an MM degree in composition from the New England Cons. of Music, Boston. Professor at the Municipal Cons. of Music Manuel de Falla and the Argentine Catholic Univ., both in Buenos Aires, and at the Provincial Cons. Julián Aguirre and the Escuela de Bellas Artes of the National Univ. of La Plata, both in the Prov. of Buenos Aires, Argentina.
Works (selective list): *El Monte Análogo,* for orch. (1980); *Música para Pequeña Orquesta,* for orch. (1980); *Tríptico Coral,* for mixed chorus a cappella (1983); *Variaciones sobre un Número Pitagórico,* for orch. (1984); chamber music; piano pieces; music for solo instruments; songs.
Source: ISC

Ginastera, Alberto Evaristo, Argentine composer; b.11 Apr 1916, Buenos Aires, Argentina; d.25 Jun 1983, Geneva, Switzerland. He began music studies with T. Rodríguez, C. Argenziani, and C.

Piaggio, and later entered the National Cons. of Music Carlos López Buchardo of Buenos Aires, where he studied with Athos Palma, José Gil, and José André. Professor of solfeggio, theory, and harmony at the National Cons. of Music Carlos López Buchardo and the Liceo Militar de la Nación of Buenos Aires. He helped to create the Cons. of the Prov. of Buenos Aires in 1948, and was professor at the Univ. of La Plata, Prov. of Buenos Aires, Argentina. In 1958, he founded the School of Musical Science and Art at the Catholic Univ. of Buenos Aires. In 1963, he created the Latin American Center for Musical Studies of the Inst. Di Tella in Buenos Aires. Full member of the National Academy of Fine Arts.
Works (selective list): *Operas: Don Rodrigo* (1964); *Bomarzo* (1967); *Beatrix Cenci* (1971). *Ballets: Panambí* (1935); *Estancia* (1952). *Orch.*: *Concierto Argentino,* for piano (1935); *Salmo CL,* for chorus and boys' chorus (1938); *Sinfonía Porteña* (1942); *Obertura para el Fausto Criollo* (1943); *Sinfonía Elegíaca* (1944); *Ollantay,* symphonic triptych (1947); *Variaciones Concertantes* (1953); *Pampena No.3* (1954); Concerto for harp (1956); *Cantata para América Mágica,* for soprano and percussion orch. (1960); 2 concertos for piano (1961, 1972); Concerto for violin (1963); *Sinfonía Don Rodrigo,* for soprano (1964); *Bomarzo,* cantata for speaker, male voice, and chamber orch. (1964); Concerto for strings (1965); *Estudios Sinfónicos* (1969); 2 concertos for cello (1970, 1981); *Milena,* cantata for soprano (1973); *Serenata,* for cello, baritone, and chamber ensemble (1973); *Turbae ad Passionem Gregorianam,* for tenor, baritone, bass, boys' chorus, and mixed chorus (1975); *Glosses sobre Temes de Pau Casals,* for string orch. and string quintet in lontano (1976); *Iubilum* (1979-80). *Chamber music: Impresiones de la Puna,* for flute and string quartet (1942); Dúo for flute and oboe (1945); *Pampeana No.1,* for violin and piano (1947); 4 string quartets (1948, 1958, 1973, 1974); *Pampeana No.2,* for cello and piano (1950); Piano quintet (1963); *Puneña No.2,* for cello solo (1976); Guitar sonata (1976); Cello sonata (1979); *Fanfare,* for 4 trumpets (1980); *Serenata,* for cello, flute, oboe, clarinet, bassoon, horn, double bass, harp, and percussion (1980). *Choruses: Hieremiae Prophetae Lamentationes,* a cappella (1946). Piano pieces; music for organ; songs.
Bibl.: P. Suárez Uturbey, *Alberto Ginastera,* Buenos Aires, 1967. D. Ewen, *Composers since 1900,* New York, 1969.
Sources: BB, CA, CTA1, DCM, DM, EMA, GDM, MLA, MMLA

Giribaldi, Tomás, Uruguayan composer; b.18 Oct 1847, Montevideo, Uruguay; d.11 Apr 1930, Montevideo. He studied with Strigelli, Battesini, Carmelo Calvo, and José Giuffra. Supervisor of Municipal Theaters. In 1907, he organized the first Municipal Band,

and later, together with his nephew Luis Sambucetti, he organized the first National Symphony Orch. in Montevideo.

Works (selective list): ***Operas:*** *La Parisina* (1878), first opera written by an Uruguayan composer; *Manfredi di Svevia* (1882); *Inés de Castro* (1884); *Magda* (1905). ***Orch.***: *Fantasía sobre Aires Criollos; Scenes Militaires,* suite; *Scherzando,* symphony; *Pequeña Melodía Religiosa.* Music for band; piano pieces.
Sources: BHMCU, MU

Giucci, Carlos, Uruguayan composer; b.4 Nov 1906, Montevideo, Uruguay; d.7 May 1958, Montevideo. He studied with his mother, pianist Luisa Gallo de Giucci, and later with Manuel García de la Lera and Ignacio Friedmann. Professor of music culture at high schools and at the Inst. Normal de Señoritas. Staff member of the Musicology Section of the National History Museum of Montevideo.
Works (selective list): ***Ballets:*** *Yuka-Tatu* (1926); *Fiesta de la Selva.* ***Orch.***: *Madrugada* (1930); *Dos Visiones Criollas* (1933); *Pequeña Suite* (1933); *Noches,* symphonic impressions; *Poema de los Ranchos,* prelude to the ballet Yuka-Tatu (1936); *Toccata in A minor,* for piano; *Tierra Adentro,* for piano (1938). Chamber music; piano pieces; songs.
Sources: BHMCU, CTA16, MU

Giudice, Alberto Oscar Toscano, Argentine orch. and choral conductor, and composer; b.1906, Buenos Aires, Argentina. He shared his musical education with a religious vocation. After being ordained a priest, he studied composition with Gilardo Gilardi and Gregorian chant with the Benedictines. Choral conductor and organist at the Church El Salvador and at the Metropolitan Cathedral of Buenos Aires. Professor at the Pontificial Seminary from 1926 to 1946. He decided to devote all his time to music and left the priesthood. Director of studies and conductor of the orch. of the Teatro Argentino de La Plata, Prov. of Buenos Aires, and professor at the National Univ. of Litoral, Rosario, Prov. of Santa Fe, both of Argentina. In 1954, he was appointed conductor of the Symphony Orch. of Paraná, Prov. of Entre Rios, Argentina.
Works: Compositions with a religious flavor, including the hymn *Oremos Pro Pontífice,* for 3-voice chorus a cappella.
Source: EMA

Gnattali, Radamés, Brazilian composer, pianist, conductor, and violinist; b.27 Jan 1906, Pôrto Alegre, Brazil; d.3 Feb 1988, Rio de Janeiro, Brazil. He started his music education with his mother, and then, he studied piano, violin, composition, and conducting at the Cons. of Pôrto Alegre and at the National School of Music in Rio de

Janeiro, Brazil. Viola player in the *Henrique Oswald Quartet.* Conductor of the National Radio orch. of Rio de Janeiro.
Works (selective list): *Orch.: Poema,* for violin (1934); 4 piano concertos (1934, 1936, 1960, 1967); Cello concerto (1941); *Brasilianas No.1-3* (1945, 1948, 1948); *No.6,* for piano (1960); *No.9-10* (1962); *No.12,* for 2 pianos and string orch. (1968); 3 violin concertos (1947, 1962, 1969); *2 Concêrtos Românticos,* for piano (1949, 1964); *3 Concêrtos Cariocas,* for various instrumental soloists (1950-70); 4 guitar concertinos (1952, 1953, 1955, 1968); *3 Sinfonías Populares* (1955, 1962, 1969); Harp concerto (1958); 2 harmonica concertos (1958, 1968). Chamber music; music for solo instruments; songs.
Bibl.: L.H. Corrêa de Azevedo, *150 Anos de Música no Brasil (1800-1950),* Rio de Janeiro, 1956. V. Mariz, *Figuras da Música Brasileira Contemporânea,* Brasilia,1970.
Sources: BB, CTA16, DM, GDM, MLA, MMLA

Goldberg, Lucio, Argentine composer; b.23 Jun 1907, Buenos Aires, Argentina. He studied harmony, counterpoint, fugue, and instrumentation with Constantino Gaito in Buenos Aires.
Works (selective list): *El Rosal de las Ruinas,* opera; *Zara,* ballet; *Quinteto Criollo* (1937); String quartet (1946); Sonata for violin and piano; piano pieces; music for violin and piano; songs.
Sources: DM, EMA

Golijov, Osvaldo, Argentine composer; b.5 Dec 1960, La Plata, Prov. of Buenos Aires, Argentina. He settled in the USA in 1986. He studied piano with his mother and composition with Gerardo Gandini. Later he studied at the Rubin Academy of Jerusalem, Israel, and with Franco Donatoni at the Accademia Chigiana in Siena, Italy. He also participated for two years in Luciano Berio's masterclasses at the Jerusalem Music Center, and Pierre Boulez's conducting seminar at Carnegie Hall in New York City. In the USA, he studied with George Crumb at the Univ. of Pennsylvania, Philadelphia, where he received his Ph.D., and with Lukas Foss and Oliver Knussen at Tanglewood, Massachusetts.
Works (selective list): *Mournes,* ballet for 8 voices, clarinet, 2 horns, and 3 cellos; *The Distance to the Moon,* chamber opera; *Hypertango,* pantomime with dancers, puppets, and instruments; *Crónicas,* for string orch.; *Botteghe Oscure,* for chamber orch.; *Deaths of the Angel,* for chamber orch.; *Yiddish Rwakh,* for clarinet, 2 horns, and 3 string ensembles; *Amor que Mueve el Sol,* for strings; *Amor Americano,* for 2 string ensembles and poet; chamber music; music for solo instruments; songs; choruses.
Source: ISC

Gomes, André da Silva, Brazilian composer of Portuguese origin; b.Dec 1752, Lisbon, Portugal; d.17 Jun 1844, Sâo Paulo, Brazil. He studied music in Lisbon. He came to Sâo Paulo in 1773, together with the new bishop of the Cathedral of Sâo Paulo, and was appointed *mestre de capela* (chapelmaster) of the Cathedral.
Bibl.: C. de Oliveira, *André da Silva Gomes (1752-1844),* Sâo Paulo, 1954.
Works: Mass for double chorus and orch.; many religious compositions.
Source: GDM

Gomes, Carlos Antônio, Brazilian composer; b.11 Jul 1836, Campinas, Brazil; d.16 Sep 1896, Pará, Belém, Brazil. He began music studies with his father, Manuel José Gomes, and then entered the Imperial Cons. of Music of Rio de Janeiro, Brazil, where he studied with Joaquim Giannini. Emperor Don Pedro II granted him an official scholarship, and he went to Milan, Italy, where he studied with Lauro Rossi. In 1895, he was appointed director of the newly founded Cons. of Pará, but he died soon after arriving there.
Works (selective list): *Operas: Il Guarany (O Guarany)* (1870); *Fosca* (1873); *Salvator Rosa* (1874); *María Tudor* (1879); *Lo Schiavo (O Escravo)* (1889); *Cóndor* (1891). *Musicals: Se sa Minga* (1867); *Nella Luna* (1868). *Il Saluto del Brasile,* hymn written for the centenary of the American independence (1876); *Colombo,* oratorio written for the Columbus festival in 1892; choruses; piano pieces; songs.
Bibl.: S. Boccanera Jr., *Um Artista Brasileiro: In Memoriam,* Bahia, 1904. H.P. Vieira, *Carlos Gomes, Sua Arte e sua Obra,* Sâo Paulo, 1934. R. Seidl, *Carlos Gomes, Brasileiro e Patriota,* Rio de Janeiro, 1935. L.F. Vieira Souto, *Antônio Carlos Gomes,* Rio de Janeiro, 1935. Centenary issue of *Revista Brasileira de Música* 1936. J. Brito, *Carlos Gomes,* Sâo Paulo, 1936. R. Almeida, *Carlos Gomes,* Rio de Janiero, 1937. I. Gomes Vaz de Carvalho, *A Vida de Carlos Gomes,* Rio de Janeiro, 1937. M. de Andrade, *Carlos Gomes,* Rio de Janeiro, 1939. P. Cerquera, *Carlos Gomes,* Sâo Paulo, 1944.
Sources: BB, DM, GDM, HMB, MLA, MMLA

Gomes, José Pedro de Santana, Brazilian composer; b.1834, Brazil; d.1908, Brazil. Brother of Carlos Antônio Gomes. He studied with his father, Manuel José Gomes.
Works (selective list): *Operas: Alda; Semira.* Orch. compositions; chamber music.
Source: MMLA

Gomes da Rocha, Francisco, Brazilian composer, conductor, and singer; b.?; d.9 Feb 1808, Vila Rica, Brazil. Active in Minas Gerais,

Brazil, during colonial times. He entered the Brotherhood of Saint
Joseph of Coloured Men in 1768. In 1800, he succeeded Lôbo de
Mesquita as conductor for the Brotherhood of the Third Order of
Carmo.
Works: Novena de Nossa Senhora do Pilar a 4 (1789); *Spiritus
Domini a 8* (1795); *Popule Meus a Quatro Vozes; Cum
Descendentibus in Lacum para Sexta Feira da Paixâo.*
Bibl.: F.C. Lange, *La Música en Vila Rica, Minas Gerais, siglo
XVIII, Revista Musical Chilena,* No.102, 1967, No.103, 1968. G.
Behague, *Música "Barrôca" Mineira; Problemas de Fontes e
Estilística, Universitas, Revista de Cultura da Universidade Federal
da Bahia,* Vol.2, 1969.
Source: GDM

Gomes de Araújo, Joâo, Brazilian composer; b.5 Aug 1846, BB
(1849, MMLA), Pindamonhangaba, Brazil; d.8 Sep 1942, BB (1943,
HMB), Sâo Paulo, Brazil. Father of Joâo Gomes Junior. He studied
in Sâo Paulo and Milan, Italy. In 1905, he became a teacher at the
Sâo Paulo Cons., and remained there almost to the end of his life.
Works (selective list): *Operas: Edmea; Carmosina* (1888); *María
Petrowna* (1904); *Helena* (1910). 6 symphonies; 6 masses; vocal and
instrumental works.
Sources: BB, HMB, MLA, MMLA

Gomes Junior, Joâo, Brazilian composer; b.1872, Sâo Paulo, Brazil;
d.1963, Brazil. Son of Joâo Gomes de Araújo.
*Works: Operas: Foscarina; La Buscaiuola; Dom Casmurro;
Yugomar; Severo Toreli; Anita Garibaldi.*
Sources: HMB, MMLA

Gómez, José Antonio, Mexican organist, conductor, and composer;
b.21 April 1805, Mexico City, Mexico; d.between 1868 and 1870,
Tulancingo, State of Hidalgo, Mexico. He started music studies with
his father, José Santos Gómez. Later he studied composition with
Manuel Izquierdo, Magín Ginesta, and Manuel Corral. *Maestro de
capilla* (chapelmaster) at the Cathedral of Mexico. Conductor of the
orch. of the Colegio San Gregorio. Founder of the Gran Sociedad
Filarmónica.
Works (selective list): *Cantata a la Consumación de la
Independencia; La Independencia,* for piano, flute, and cello; masses
for full orch.; *Miserere,* for 8 voices and orch.; *Salmos para
Vísperas; Responsorios para Maitines;* piano pieces.
Sources: GMM, MMLA

Gomezanda, Antonio, Mexican composer; b.3 Sep 1894, Lagos,
Jalisco, Mexico; d.26 Mar 1961, Mexico City, Mexico. He studied

piano with Manuel Ponce, and later he went to Germany where he studied composition and conducting in Berlin. Professor at the National Cons., 1921-29, and at the Univ. of Mexico, 1929-32, both in Mexico City.
Works (selective list): *Xiuhzitzquilo,* Aztec ballet (1928); *Fantasía Mexicana,* for piano and orch. (1923); piano pieces; songs.
Source: BB

Gómez Cardiel, José María, Venezuelan teacher and composer; b.beginning of the 19th century, Cumaná, Venezuela; d.1872, Cumaná. He taught in Cumaná and Margarita, Venezuela, in Barcelona, Spain, and in Trinidad-Tobago Island.
Works (selective list): *Misa Solemne; Misa Fúnebre; Miserere,* for 4 voices; *Las Trenodias;* hymns; popular songs.
Source: MMLA

Gómez Carrillo, Manuel, Argentine composer; b.8 Mar 1883, Santiago del Estero, Argentina; d.1968, Argentina. Father of María Inés Gómez Carrillo. He was educated at the Seminaries of Salta, Prov. of Salta, and Catamarca, Prov. of Catamarca, both in Argentina, because his parents wanted him to become a priest. He later studied at the Thibaud-Piazzini Cons. of Music of Buenos Aires, Argentina, and later, with Alfredo Grandi in Santiago del Estero, and with José Rodoreda in Buenos Aires. Since 1908, he dedicated himself to full-time teaching in Santiago del Estero and other Argentine cities. In 1916, he was invited by the National Univ. of Tucumán, Prov. of Tucumán, Argentina, to conduct research on northern folklore and he compiled more than 400 Inca-Calchaquí themes. In 1944, he settled in Buenos Aires where he continued with his teaching duties and choral conducting.
Works (selective list): *Rapsodia Santiagueña,* for orch. (1922); *La Telesita,* choreographic-lyric piece; *La Salamanca,* ballet; *Danza de la Huaca,* symphonic poem; *Fiesta Criolla,* symphonic suite; piano pieces; songs.
Sources: CA, DM, EMA, MMLA

Gómez Carrillo, María Inés, Argentine pianist and composer; b.1918, Santiago del Estero, Argentina. Daughter of Manuel Gómez Carrillo. She studied piano with Rafael González and composition with Athos Palma at the National Cons. of Music Carlos López Buchardo of Buenos Aires, Argentina. She also studied piano with Edward Steurmann and composition with Jerzy Fitelberg in the USA.
Works: String quartet; piano pieces; songs.
Source: IEW

Gonçalves, Joâo Octaviano, Brazilian pianist and composer; b.22 Apr 1892, Pôrto Alegre, Brazil; d.19 Feb 1962, Rio de Janeiro, Brazil. He studied at the National School of Music of Rio de Janeiro with Francisco Braga.
Works (selective list): *Operas: Iracema; Poema da Vida; Sonho de una Noite de Luar; Fernao Dias.* Symphonies; ballets; chamber music; piano pieces; choruses; songs.
Sources: KTL, MMLA

Gonzaga, Francisca Edwiges Neves, Brazilian composer, conductor, and pianist; b.17 Oct 1847, Rio de Janeiro, Brazil; d.28 Feb 1935, Rio de Janeiro. She studied piano with José de Sousa Lobo and Arthur Napoleâo dos Santos in Rio de Janeiro. Piano teacher. She conducted the Band of the Military Police of Rio de Janeiro.
Works (selective list): *Operettas: A Corte na Roca* (1885); *Forrobodo* (1912); she wrote 77 stage works. *O Gaúcho,* tango (1897); *O Abre-Alas,* march (1899). Published 310 works: waltzes; polkas; tangos; maxixes; lundus; mazurkas; quadrilles; gavottes; habaneras; barcarolles; serenatas; fados; modinhas; marchas; choros.
Bibl.: M. Lira, *Chiquinha Gonzaga: Grande Compositora Brasileira,* Rio de Janeiro, 1939. V. Mariz, *A Cançao Brasileira,* 3rd edition, Rio de Janeiro, 1977.
Sources: EMB, NGDWC, NWC

González, José Antonio, Chilean *maestro de capilla* (chapelmaster) and composer; b.?, fl. first third of the 19th century; d.1840? *Maestro de capilla* (chapelmaster) at the Cathedral of Santiago de Chile, Chile, from 1802 to 1840.
Works: Tres Villancicos de Navidad; Himno a la Victoria de Yerbas Buenas; Himno del Instituto Nacional. Several works in the Archive of the Cathedral still remain uncatalogued.
Sources: HMC, MMLA

González, José Luis, Mexican pianist and composer; b.21 May 1937, Guadalajara, Mexico. He studied music at the Guadalajara Music School. Member of the *Mexican Association for New Music.*
Works: Orch. music; chamber music; piano pieces; electronic music.
Source: KTL

González, Julián, Guatemalan composer; b.1870, Guatemala; d.1898, Guatemala. He studied piano and composition at the Guatemala Cons. in Guatemala City, and then, with a scholarship, he went to study in Naples, Italy. When he returned to Guatemala in 1891, he taught piano and was appointed director of the Guatemala Cons.
Works: Large amount of dance music.

Source: MMLA

González, Manuel B. Puerto Rican composer and pianist; b.3 Jan 1930, Arecibo, Puerto Rico. He studied piano with Juanita Iguina Dávila and Luis Varona, Jr.
Works (selective list): *Operas: Nela,* (1972); *El Jíbaro* (1980); *Los Jíbaros Progresistas* (1981); *Una Jíbara* (1983). *El Juramento,* zarzuela (1976); *Cantata a Puerto Rico,* for baritone, chorus, and orch. (1979); *Misa en Do mayor,* for soloists, chorus, and orch. (1986); chamber music; piano pieces.
Source: CPR

González Avila, Jorge, Mexican composer; b.10 Dec 1925, Mérida, Yucatán, Mexico. In 1949, he moved to Mexico City, Mexico, where he studied composition with Rodolfo Halffter, harmony with Blas Galindo, piano with Francisco Agea Hermosa, and theory with Eduardo Hernández Moncada at the National Cons. of Mexico, Mexico City, 1949-53. He took courses in composition with Jesús Bal y Gay in 1952, and with Carlos Chávez in 1953, at the National College of Mexico City. In 1972, he was appointed director of the Autotranscription Division at CENIDIM of the National Inst. of Fine Arts in Mexico City.
Works (selective list): *Invention,* for soprano, piano, and orch. (1964); *Invention Concertante No.1,* for piano and orch. (1973); *Invention Interpolar,* for piano and orch. (1974); *Invention,* for English horn, piano and orch. (1975); *Prelude and Invention,* for string orch. (1976); chamber music; piano pieces; music for solo instruments.
Source: BB

González Bravo, Antonio, Bolivian composer and teacher; b.2 Sep 1885, La Paz, Bolivia; d.1961, La Paz. He studied at the Cons. Nacional de Música of La Paz. He introduced the Dalcroze method into Bolivian schools. He conducted research on indigenous music. Three times director of the Cons. Nacional de Música of La Paz.
Works: Trova a la Virgen de Copacabana, for female chorus and orch.; *Preludio,* for piano; *Preludio,* for chorus and orch.; *Fiesta en los Andes.*
Sources: CB, DM, MLA

González Casellas, Fernando, Argentine composer; b.1925, Buenos Aires, Argentina. He studied with Jaime Pahissa. He also studied classic languages at the Facultad de Filosofía y Letras of the National Univ. of Buenos Aires.
Works: 3 string quartets; *Tres Piezas,* for organ; Sonata for cello and piano; *Siete Invenciones,* for orch. (1966).

Source: EMA

González Castro, J. Francisco, Costa Rican professor of music and composer; b.29 Jul 1897, Heredia, Costa Rica; d.? He began music studies in Heredia, from 1907 to 1910, and from 1924 to 1929, he studied with Vicente Stea in Lima, Peru. From 1923 to 1929, he was professor at the Cons. Stea and conductor of the salon orch. of the Sala San Martín in Lima. Professor of music at the Liceo of Costa Rica, director of the *Orfeón* (male singing chorus) at the same inst., and *maestro de capilla* (chapelmaster) at the Church San Pedro de Montes de Oca. **Books:** *Resumen de la Historia de la Música.*
Works: *Misa de Requiem* (1927); songs written for the *Orfeón.*
Source: MMLA

González Gamarra, Francisco, Peruvian composer and painter; b.4 Jun 1890, Cuzco, Peru; d.? He studied piano and violin.
Works: *Music for piano:* *Noche de Luna en el Cuzco; Homenaje a Garcilaso de la Vega; Dos Canciones; Suite Chopiniana; Suite Cuzqueña.*
Sources: MLA, MMLA

González Iñíguez, Hilario, Cuban pianist, researcher, teacher, and composer; b. 24 Jan 1920, Havana, Cuba. He studied piano with Jascha Fischermann and harmony with José Ardévol in Cuba, and with Vicente Emilio Sojo and Anthony de Blois Carreño in Venezuela, as well as counterpoint and fugue with the latter. He also took conducting lessons with Sergiu Celibidache and Angel Sauce. From 1947 to 1960, he taught piano at the Preparatory School of Music of Caracas, Venezuela. In 1960, he returned to Cuba where he was appointed professor at the Cons. Amadeo Roldán and the Seminary of Popular Music, both of Havana. Founding member of the *Grupo de Renovación Musical.* Researcher at the National Museum of Music of Havana. Music critic for the newspapers *El Mundo* and *Acción,* and the journal *Ahora.*
Works (selective list): *Tres Preludios en Conga* (1933); *Dos Danzas* (1938); Sonata in A minor (1942); *Suite de Canciones Cubanas,* for voice and orch. (1943); Concerto in D for piano and orch. (1946); Symphony; *Antes del Alba,* ballet (1947); *Las Puertas Abiertas* (1964); *Los Zapaticos de Rosa,* miniopera a cappella; many songs.
Sources: DM, DMC, MLA, MMLA

González Mantici, Enrique, Cuban conductor, violinist, and composer; b.4 Nov 1912, Sagua La Grande, Las Villas, Cuba; d.29 Dec 1974, Havana, Cuba. He started music studies with his mother, and later studied violin with José Valls. He studied composition with Rafael Pastor and Emilio Grenet, and orch. conducting with Erich

Kleiber. At the Tchaicovsky Cons. of Moscow, Russia, he took classes with Nikolai Anosov, Alexander Gauk, and G.Lev Ginsburg. First violin of the *Havana String Quartet* and of the Havana Symphony Orch. Founder of the National Inst. of Music of Havana. *Works*: 2 violin concertos (1953, 1957); *Pregón y Danza,* for orch. (1954); *Tres Piezas,* para piano; *Cimarrón,* ballet; *Tríptico Vocal,* for soprano and piano; Sinfonía concertante for cello and orch.; *Tríptico,* for string orch.; Trio for oboe, clarinet, and bassoon; *El Circo,* ballet (1966); *Mestiza,* ballet (1966); *Cuba,* overture.
Source: DMC

González Zuleta, Fabio, Colombian composer; b.2 Nov 1920, Bogotá, Colombia. He studied organ and composition at the Bogotá Cons. with Egisto Giovanetti and Demetrio Haralambis. Professor at the Bogotá Cons., and from 1957 to 1972, its director.
Works (selective list): 8 symphonies (1956-1971); Suite for orch. (1953); *Estampa Heróica,* for orch. (1955); Concerto for violin and orch. (1958); *Bíptico,* for string orch. (1960); *Dos Poemas del Niño y del Amor,* for string orch. and percussion (1960); Concerto grosso for harpsichord and string orch. (1968); *Introducción y Bambuco sobre un Tema de Campoverde,* for orch. (1971); *Música de Ballet* (1972); choruses; religious music; chamber music; piano pieces; songs.
Sources: BB, GDM, ZCCC

Goyarrola, Aitor, Venezuelan composer; b.29 Sep 1972, Caracas, Venezuela. He started music studies in London, England, with Winston Ingram in piano and organ, then moved to the USA where he studied piano with Robert Chumbley. At the age of seven, he entered the Miami School of Musical Arts, Miami, Florida, where he studied solfeggio, theory, and composition with William Banchs. In 1983, he returned to Venezuela to begin studies at the Cons. of the Philharmonic of Caracas with Aldemaro Romero, Harriet Serr, Miguel Angel Noya, and Eduardo Marturet. He continued his music education in Cambridge, England. In 1990, he entered the Univ. of Miami, Florida, where he received a BM in theory and composition before attending the Univ. of Iowa, Iowa. Teacher at the Miami School of Musical Arts and lecturer at the Univ. of Miami. Member of SACVEN, of South Alliance of Composers of Florida, and of SCIUM.
Works (selective list): **Orch.**: *Creación del Mundo* (1985); *Port de la Selva* (1986); *Collage Mundo Actual* (1988); *Ocaso del Mundo,* for piano (1989) *Shadows of my Nature,* for double bass (1990); *Zigma,* for string orch. (1990); *The Holy Word of God,* for chorus (1991); *Enigma,* for 2 orch. (1991); *I'm Old and Putrefying,* for chorus (1991); *Mozartiana,* for piano (1992); *Vivendi,* for double bass (1992). Chamber music; piano pieces.

Source: ISC

Graetzer, Guillermo, Argentine composer of Austrian origin; b.5 Sep 1914, Vienna, Austria; d.1993, Buenos Aires, Argentina. He settled in Buenos Aires in 1939. He studied in Berlin, Germany, with E.L. von Knorr and Paul Hindemith, and in Vienna with Paul Pisk. In 1946, he founded the Collegium Musicum of Buenos Aires, and was its director and professor as well. He taught composition, instrumentation, and choral conducting at the Escuela Superior de Música of the National Univ. of La Plata, Prov. of Buenos Aires, Argentina. He is a member of the *Liga de Compositores de la Argentina.*
Works (selective list): *Stage: Siete Princesas muy Desdichadas,* ballet (1940); *Jacobo en la Fuente,* ballet (1940); *Pequeña Leyenda de Danza,* ballet (1941); *Jerusalem Eterna,* incidental music (1942); *Bar Cojbah,* incidental music (1944). *Orch.:* Concerto (1939); *Variaciones sobre un Tema de Salomone Rossi* (1941-51); *Rapsodia,* for violin (1941-43); *Danza de la Muerte y la Niña* (1942); *La Parábola* (1946-47); Sinfonietta for strings (1947); *Sinfonía Brevis* (1951); Concerto for bassoon (1952); Chamber concerto (1953); *Los Burgueses de Calais,* for male chorus (1954-55); Cello concerto (1955-57). *Chamber music:* Sonatina for recorder and piano (1937); String quartet (1941); *Divertimento,* for wind quintet (1934-35); *Grave,* for solo violin (1945); Dúo for flute and clarinet (1956). Choruses; piano pieces; songs.
Sources: BB, CTA4, DM, EMA, MLA, MMLA

Gramatges, Harold, Cuban composer; b.26 Sep 1918, BB (26 Nov 1918, DMC), Santiago de Cuba, Cuba. He started his musical education at the Provincial Cons. of Oriente, Cuba, in 1928. Later he entered the Granados Cons. in Havana, Cuba, where he studied with Flora Mora in 1937. He studied harmony, music history, music aesthetics, and composition at the Havana Municipal Cons. with José Ardévol and Amadeo Roldán. In 1942, he went to the USA and took a course in composition with Aaron Copland at the Berkshire Music Center in Tanglewood, Massachusetts. With other Cuban composers, he founded the *Grupo de Renovación Musical* in 1943. He organized the Music Dept. of the Casa de las Américas in Havana. In 1945, he founded and directed the orch. of the Municipal Cons. of Havana, where he also was a professor. From 1961 to 1964, he was a member of the Cuban Embassy in Paris, France.
Works (selective list): *Soneto,* for mixed choir (1940); *Canción,* for mixed choir (1940); *Invenciones,* for chamber orch. (1941); *Icaro,* ballet (1943); *Mensaje al Futuro,* for wind orch. (1944); Symphony (1945); Concertino for piano and wind instruments (1945); Sinfonietta for orch. (1955); Wind quintet (1957); *Móvil,* for 7

instruments (1969); *La Muerte del Guerrillero,* for speaker and orch. (1969); *Móvil II,* for flute, French horn, piano-celesta, vibraphone, xylophone, and percussion (1970); *Cantata para Abel* (1973); Concerto for guitar and orch. (1974); *Diseños* (1976); chamber music.
Sources: BB, DM, DMC, MLA, MMLA

Granda, Juan Manuel, Argentine composer and recorder player; b.16 Dec 1964, Rosario, Prov. of Santa Fe, Argentina. He studied piano, recorder, percussion, and composition with Gustavo Puccini, Jorge Horst, Mariano Etkin, Gerardo Gandini, and Francisco Kröpfl. He also took courses in music history, aesthetics, musical analysis, orchestration, and electroacoustic music.
Works: Solo, for flute and piano (1989); *La Espuma de los Días,* for flute, oboe, bass clarinet, and piano (1990); *Dieciseis Cuerdas,* violin, viola, cello, and double bass (1990).
Source: CAMR

Grande Castelli, Santiago, Argentine composer and teacher; b.Rosario, Prov. of Santa Fe, Argentina. He studied harmony, counterpoint, composition, and orchestration with Teodoro Fuchs. Professor at the Escuela Municipal de Música Juan Bautista Massa of Rosario.
Works (selective list): *Ballets: El Angel Negro; Lil; El Sueño de Polichinela.* Concerto for guitar and chamber orch.; Symphony in E flat major; *Tres Preludios,* for guitar and wind quintet; piano pieces.
Source: CAMR

Grasso, Gerardo, Uruguayan composer, band conductor, flutist, and teacher of Italian origin; b.1864, Capocele, near Naples, Italy; d.18 Jun 1937, Montevideo, Uruguay. Conductor of the band of the Escuela de Artes y Oficios of Montevideo.
Works: *Pericón Nacional* (1887); *Auras Criollas,* fantasia for piano, later orchestrated for band; military marches. In 1934, by an ordinance of the Uruguayan National Government, he arranged the *Uruguayan National Anthem* for voice and piano.
Sources: BHMCU, MU

Grau, Alberto, Venezuelan composer, conductor and teacher of Spanish origin; b.7 Nov 1937, Barcelona, Spain. He studied theory and solfeggio with Angel Sauce, piano with Cristina V. de Pereira, composition with Vicente E. Sojo, music history and aesthetics with Juan B. Plaza, conducting with Gonzalo Castellanos, ethnomusicology with Luis F. Ramón y Rivera, and voice with Carmen T. de Hurtado at the Music Schools José Angel Lamas and Juan Manuel Olivares of

Caracas, Venezuela. He continued his music studies at the Music Cons. of Geneva, Switzerland, with Edgar Willems, and in Bologna, Italy, with Sergiu Celibidache. Professor of artistic education at various municipal schools in Caracas, professor of piano at the Music School Juan Manuel Olivares, director of the Music School José Lorenzo Llamozas, professor of conducting at the Inst. Venezolano de Música Simón Bolívar, all in Caracas. Founder, director, and professor of choral conducting of the Schola Cantorum of Caracas.
Works (selective list): *Ballet La Doncella,* for mixed chorus and chamber orch. (1978); *Tríptico,* for mezzo-soprano and orch. (1984); *Epílogo,* for magnetic tape (1981); choral music; piano pieces; songs.
Source: ISC

Gregori, Nininha, Brazilian composer; b.20 Jan 1925, Sâo Paulo, Brazil. She studied music with Hans Koellreutter.
Works: chamber music; songs.
Sources: IBCC, IEW

Grela Herrera, Dante Gerardo, Argentine composer, pianist, and teacher; b.13 Aug 1941, Rosario, Prov. of Santa Fe, Argentina. He studied with Efraín Paesky, Luis Angel Machado, Virtú Maragno, Francisco Kröpfl, and Washington Castro at the Inst. Superior de Música of the National Univ. of Litoral of Rosario, from which he graduated in 1964. Director of the Creativity Dept. and professor of composition at the School of Music of the National Univ. of Rosario. Professor and researcher at the Inst. Superior de Música of the National Univ. of Litoral. Professor at the Art Dept. of the National Univ. of Tucumán, Prov. of Tucumán, Argentina.
Works (selective list): Trio for piano, violin, and cello (1963); *Música para Ocho Instrumentos* (1966); *Música Concreta para una Exposición de Pop-Art* (1966); *Música para Teatro* (1966); *Cuatro Piezas,* for solo flute (1966); *Composición,* for mezzo-soprano, chorus, and instruments (1967); *Espacios,* for septet (1968); *Combinaciones,* for chorus, percussion, and magnetic tape (1968); *Ejercicio I,* for electronic sounds (1969); *Superficies,* for orch. (1969); *Estatismos,* for orch. (1970) *Nueve Estudios,* for orch. (1973); *Interpretaciones,* for chamber ensemble (1976); *Paisaje Imaginario,* for chamber ensemble (1980); *Oráculo,* for contralto and chamber ensemble (1982); *Colores,* for orch. (1983); *Crepuscular,* for orch. (1986); *Encantamientos,* for chamber ensemble (1987); chamber music; piano pieces; songs.
Sources: EMA, ISC

Greppi, Clemente, Argentine composer of Italian origin; b.1858, Lucca, Italy; d. 1938, Buenos Aires, Argentina. He settled in Buenos

Aires in 1893. Conducted children's choruses at the Teatro Colón and Teatro de la Opera, both of Buenos Aires. He devoted his life to music teaching, and in this capacity he worked at the Argentine National Board of Education from 1907 to 1932.
Works: School songs, including the classic *A mi Bandera.*
Source: EMA

Grever, María, Mexican composer; b.14 Sep 1885, León, Guanajato, Mexico; d.15 Dec 1951, New York, USA. She studied music with Claude Debussy in Paris, France.
Works: The Gypsy, one-act song drama (1928); *El Cantarito,* opera (1939); piano pieces; 850 songs.
Sources: IBCC, IEW, NGDWC

Grippa, Jorge, Argentine composer; b.28 Mar 1900, Buenos Aires, Argentina; d.? He studied with Antonio Eduardo D'Agostino and Athos Palma.
Works (selective list): *Dos Danzas Argentinas,* for orch. (1945); Two fugues for piano; Trio; *Los Gnomos,* symphonic suite; chamber music; piano pieces; songs.
Sources: DM, EMA

Grisolía, Pascual, Argentine composer and band conductor; b.4 Feb 1904, Chivilcoy, Prov. of Buenos Aires, Argentina. He studied harmony with Athos Palma, counterpoint with José Gil, composition with José André, and piano with Vicente Scaramuzza at the National Cons. of Music Carlos López Buchardo of Buenos Aires, Argentina. For more than 20 years, he was associate conductor of the Municipal Symphonic Band of Buenos Aires. He founded and conducted the Symphonic Band of the *Patronato Nacional de Ciegos* (National Association for the Blind).
Works (selective list): *Preludio Sinfónico,* for orch. (1930); *Boceto Sinfónico,* for orch. (1931); *La Tarde,* symphonic poem (1938); *Recuerdos de la Infancia,* suite for piano (1940); *Alamo bajo el Rocío,* for voice and orch. (1948); *Obertura Clásica,* for orch. (1954); Wind quartet (1955); Trio for oboe, clarinet, and bassoon (1961); *Ricercare,* for string orch. (1971); chamber music; piano pieces; songs.
Sources: CA, DM, EMA, MLA, MMLA, VMA

Grüb Geschwindt, Laura, Mexican composer and synthesist; b.29 Jan 1958, Mexico City, Mexico. She started early in her life to study music. At age eight she entered the Escuela Nacional de Música of the UNAM, Mexico City, where she studied composition with Juan Antonio Rosado, and cello. In 1980, she received a scholarship to

study composition and music theory at the Tchaikovsky Cons. in Moscow, Russia, with Mikhail Chulaki and Mikhail Leman. In 1984, she entered the Berklee College of Music in Boston, Massachusetts, where she graduated in composition, film scoring, music synthesis, and music production and engineering. Lecturer at the Massachusetts Inst. of Technology, Cambridge, Massachusetts.
Works (selective list): *Symphonic Poem,* for orch., chorus, and synthesizers; *Introduction,* for orch. and synthesizers; *On the Mountains,* for marimba, Aztec caracol, and specific designed sounds; *Variation on a Poulenc's Theme,* for Tx-816 synthesizer with specific designed sounds, harp, oboe, clarinet, and flute; chamber music; electronic music; ballet piece; jazz piece; music for movies.
Source: ISC

Guarín, José Joaquín, Colombian composer and pianist; b.1825, Bogotá, Colombia; d.4 Dec 1854, Bogotá. Professor at several schools in Bogotá. In 1848, he founded the *Sociedad Lírica,* an organization whose main goal was the study of religious music and its performance in churches.
Works: Series of contradances, waltzes, and polkas. *Canción Nacional,* for 4 voices and orch.; *Oficio de Difuntos*; hymns; sacred music.
Bibl.: J.I. Perdomo Escobar, *Esbozo Histórico sobre la Música Colombiana.*
Sources: MLA, MMLA

Guaritano, Assuero, Brazilian composer and teacher; b.1889, Sâo Paulo, Brazil; d.? He started to study music in Sâo Paulo, and continued at the National School of Music in Rio de Janeiro, Brazil. Professor at the Inst. de Bellas Artes in Pôrto Alegre, Brazil, and at the National School of Music in Rio de Janeiro.
Works (selective list): Symphony in F sharp minor; *Cántico del Sole,* for soloists, chorus, and orch.; Quintet for piano and string instruments; piano pieces; songs.
Source: MMLA

Guarnieri, Camargo Mozart, Brazilian composer; b.1 Feb 1907, Tieté, State of Sâo Paulo, Brazil; d.13 Jan 1993, Sâo Paulo, Brazil. He studied with his parents. Later he studied piano with Antonio de Sá Pareira and Ernani Braga, and composition with Lamberto Baldi and Mario de Andrade. In 1938, he went to Paris, France, where he studied composition with Charles Koechlin and conducting with François Ruhlmann. Professor at the Dramatic and Musical Cons. of Sâo Paulo. Conductor of the choir of the Municipal Dept. of Culture of Sâo Paulo and the Symphony Orch. of Sâo Paulo.

Works (selective list): *Operas: Pedro Malazarte* (1931); *Um Homem Só* (1960). *Orch.:* 5 piano concertos (1936, 1946, 1964, 1967, 1970); 2 violin concertos (1940, 1953); *Dansa Brasileira* (1941); *Overture Concertante* (1943); 4 symphonies (1944, 1946, 1952, 1963); *Dansa Negra* (1947); *Chôro,* for violin (1951); *Variations on a Northeast Brazilian Theme,* for piano (1953); *Suite IV Centenario* (1954); *Chôro,* for clarinet (1956); *Chôro,* for piano (1957); *Sêca,* cantata (1957); *Suite Vila Rica* (1958); *Chôro,* for cello (1961); Piano concertino (1961); *Seresta,* for piano and chamber orch. (1965); *Guaná Bará,* cantata (1965); *Homage to Villa-Lobos,* for wind orch. (1966); *Següencia, Coral e Ricercare,* for chamber orch. (1966). 3 string quartets (1932, 1944, 1962); chamber music; piano pieces; songs.
Sources: BB, CTA4, DCM, DM, GDM, MLA

Guastavino, Carlos, Argentine composer; b.4 Apr 1914, Santa Fe, Prov. of Santa Fe, Argentina. He studied piano with Esperanza Lothringer and Dominga Iaffei Guastavino in Santa Fe. At the National Cons. of Music Carlos López Buchardo of Buenos Aires, Argentina, he studied harmony and composition with Athos Palma, and continued piano studies with Rafael González. Professor at the Municipal Cons. of Music Manuel de Falla of Buenos Aires.
Works (selective list): *Fue una Vez,* ballet (1942); *Sonetos del Ruiseñor,* for soprano, flute, clarinet, cello, and piano (1951); *Romance de Santa Fe,* for piano and orch. (1952); Sonata for violin and piano (1952); choruses; piano pieces; many songs.
Sources: BB, CA, CTA1, DM, EMA, MLA, MMLA

Guerra Peixe, César, Brazilian composer, violinist, and conductor; b.18 Mar 1914, Petrópolis, Brazil; d.23 Nov 1993, Rio de Janeiro. He studied violin with Gáo Omacht at the Escola de Música Santa Cecilia in Petrópolis. In 1931, he entered the National School of Music of Rio de Janeiro where he studied violin and piano with Paulino d'Ambrosio, harmony with Arnaud Gouveia, and chamber ensemble with Orlando Federico. In 1938, he entered the Cons. Brasileiro de Música of Rio de Janeiro where he continued harmony studies with Newton Pádua, with whom he also studied counterpoint, fugue, and composition. In 1944, he studied composition with Hans Joachim Koellreutter. He played violin in theater orch. and arranged music for radio. Member of the group *Música Viva*.
Works (selective list): 2 symphonies (1946, 1960); Nonet (1945); 2 string quartets (1947, 1958); Violin sonata (1950); Piano trio (1960); Guitar sonata (1969); Dúo for clarinet and bassoon (1970); *Roda de Amigos,* for chamber orch.; *Sumidouro,* cantata for voice, piano, cello, and piano (1980); chamber music; piano pieces; songs.
Sources: BB, CTA16, DCM, DM, GDM, HMB

Guerrero Díaz, Félix, Cuban conductor and composer; b.13 Jan 1917, Havana, Cuba. He studied music with his father, and later studied piano, harmony, and composition with César Pérez Sentenat, Pedro Sanjuán, and Amadeo Roldán. In New York, he studied at The Juilliard School of Music, and in 1952, he went to Paris, France, where he studied with Eugène Bigot and Nadia Boulanger. Professor at the Cons. García Caturla of Havana. Conductor of the orch. of the Cuban National Theater for Ballet and Opera, and of the National Symphony Orch., both in Havana.
Works: Concerto for clarinet and orch.; *Tríptico Campesino,* for voice and orch.; *Cuadros Sonoros,* for French horn and orch.; *Suite Cubana; Homenaje al Songoro Cosongo.*
Sources: DMC, GDM

Guevara, Gerardo, Ecuadorian composer and conductor; b.1930, Quito, Ecuador. He studied harmony, counterpoint, fugue, composition, piano, violin, and oboe at the Quito Cons. In 1959, through a scholarship granted by UNESCO, he studied in Paris, France, with Nadia Boulanger. Director of the chorus of the Central Univ. of Quito. Founding member of the Sociedad de Autores y Compositores Ecuatorianos and its first president. In 1972, he reorganized and directed the National Symphony Orch. of Quito.
Works: *La Tunda,* ballet (1954); *Yaguar Shungo,* ballet for reciters, chorus, and orch. (1958); *Cantata de la Paz* (1963-64); String quartet (1964); *Cuadernos de la Tierra,* for reciters, chorus, and orch. (1971); *Suite Ecuador* (1972); *Et in Terra Pax Hominibus,* for baritone and orch. (1986); *Historia,* for orch. and magnetic tape (1990).
Source: ISC

Guidi Drei, Claudio, Argentine composer; b.17 Aug 1927, Buenos Aires, Argentina. He studied at the National Cons. of Music Carlos López Bucardo of Buenos Aires, and at the Rossini Cons. of Pessaro, Italy. He also studied composition in Italy with Guido Turchi, and orch. conducting with Paul van Kempe. Director of studies at the Teatro Argentino of La Plata, Prov. of Buenos Aires, Argentina, and assistant conductor and director of studies at the Teatro Colón of Buenos Aires. Professor of theory, solfeggio, and harmony at National Cons. of Music Carlos López Bucardo.
Works: *Nocturno y Scherzo,* for string orch. (1953); String quartet (1961); *Miniaturas,* for orch. (1966); *Lupapag,* chamber ballet (1969); *Medea,* opera; *Ottonata,* for orch.; *Requiem sin Palabras.*
Sources: EMA, VMA

Guiliani, Juan José, Argentine composer and teacher; b.2 Jul 1927,Corrientes, Prov. of Corrientes, Argentina. He studied with Luis Gianneo, Pedro Sáenz, Carlos Suffern, Valdo Sciamarella, Jorge Fontenla, Gerardo Gandini, and Roberto Caamaño at the Facultad de Artes y Ciencias Musicales of the Argentine Catholic Univ. of Buenos Aires, Argentina. Professor at the Provincial Cons. of Music of Bahía Blanca, Prov. of Buenos Aires, Argentina. Professor at the Escuela del Cuerpo Profesional del Ejército.
Works (selective list): *Orch.: Seis Piezas on Tankas,* by Jorge L. Borges; *Contrastes y Similitudes; Retrospección,* for flute, clarinet, piano, and string orch.; *Impulsos,* for string orch. *Chamber operas: Juicio por no Pago de Expensas; Opus Unum.* Chamber music; music for military band; choruses.
Source: ISC

Guraieb Kuri, Rosa, Mexican composer, pianist, and teacher; b.20 May 1931, Matías Romero, Mexico. She studied piano, theory, and harmony with Michel Chesnikoff at the National Cons. of Beirut, Lebanon. Later she studied harmony with José Pablo Moncayo, piano with Salvador Ordoñes Ochoa, and attended composition workshops with Carlos Chávez at the National Cons. of Mexico, Mexico City, Mexico. She also studied piano and composition with Gerhart Muench, Alfonso de Elías, Mario Lavista, and Daniel Catán at the National Cons. of Mexico.
Works: Piano concerto; 2 string quartets; Trio for oboe, bassoon, and piano; piano pieces; songs.
Sources: IEW, NGDWC

Gurjao, Henrique Eulalio, Brazilian composer; b.1834, Pará, Belém, Brazil; d.1884, Brazil. He was a student of Carlos Gomes.
Works (selective list): *Idaliam,* lyric drama; music for the theater; marches; hymns; romances; sacred music.
Source: MMLA

Gutiérrez, Benjamín, Costa Rican composer, pianist, and conductor; b.3 Jan 1937, Guadalupe, Costa Rica. He studied at the National Univ. of Costa Rica. Later, he studied piano and composition with Augusto Ardenois at the National Cons. of Guatemala, Guatemala City, Guatemala. He was granted a scholarship by the Costa Rican government and by the International Inst. of Education to continue his studies at the New England Cons. of Music of Boston, Massachusetts, where he graduated with an MM degree. He also studied in Aspen, Colorado, with Darius Milhaud, in Ann Arbor, Michigan, with Ross Lee Finney, and in 1964, with Alberto Ginastera at the Inst. Torcuato Di Tella of Buenos Aires, Argentina. Director of the string orch. and choir of the Univ. of Costa Rica.

Works (selective list): *Ofrenda Musical,* for viola, French horn, and string orch. (1959); *Concertino Clásico,* for trumpet in C and small orch. (1965); *Dos Danzas de Juan Morel Campos,* arrangement for symphony orch. (1960); *La Reina Tembandumba,* overture-fantasia for orch. (1966); chamber music.
Source: ISC

Gutiérrez, Hipólito Felipe, Argentine composer; b.4 Feb 1931, Buenos Aires, Argentina. He studied at the Municipal Cons. of Music Manuel de Falla of Buenos Aires. He studied harmony, counterpoint, fugue, instrumentation, and composition with Jacobo Ficher, and piano with Elsa Piaggio de Tarelli. President of the Asociación de Jóvenes Compositores de la Argentina. Board member of the Compositores Unidos de la Argentina and of the Consejo Argentino de la Música.
Works (selective list): *Música para Arcos,* for string orch.; *Unamuniana,* overture; *Tres Eternidades,* for mezzo-soprano and orch.; *Oda II,* for orch.; *Nocturno y Scherzoso,* for orch.; chamber music; piano pieces; songs.
Source: ISC

Gutiérrez, Juan, Argentine composer; b.1840?, Buenos Aires, Argentina; d.1906?, Buenos Aires. He studied music in Spain with Hilarión Eslava. When he returned to Buenos Aires in 1877, he presented a dramatic work at the old Teatro Colón, and because of this event, he was given a scholarship to study in Europe, the first Argentine musician to win that award. When he returned to Argentina, he worked toward the creation of the National Cons. of Music in Buenos Aires.
Works: *La Sombra de los Muertos,* dramatic scene for baritone, chorus, and orch. (1877); *La Vuelta al Hogar,* cantata for tenor, chorus, and orch. (1877). *Books: Arte del Solfeo*, 1891-92, written for the newly created National Cons. of Music.
Source: EMA

Gutiérrez, Manuel María, Costa Rican composer; b.1 Sep 1829, Heredia, Costa Rica; d.25 Dec 1887, Costa Rica. General director of bands of Costa Rica.
Works: Costa Rican National Anthem. El Palacio, waltz (1855); *Santa Fe,* march (1856); *Regina,* mazurka; *Memorias de un Amigo,* march.
Bibl.: C. Jinesta, *Manuel María Gutiérrez,* Cartago, Costa Rica, 1929.
Sources: DM, MMLA

Gutiérrez Heras, Joaquín, Mexican composer; b.28 Sep 1927, Tehuacán, Mexico. He studied architecture at the National Univ. of Mexico, Mexico City. He studied composition with Blas Galindo and Rodolfo Halffter at the National Cons. of Mexico, Mexico City, 1950-52. In Paris, France, he studied with Olivier Messiaen, Jean Rivier, and Georges Dandelot at the Paris Cons., 1952-53. He also studied composition with William Bergsma and Vincent Persichetti at The Juilliard School of Music in New York City, 1960-61. Radio lecturer and music theory teacher.
Works (selective list): *Divertimento,* for piano and orch. (1949); *El Deportista,* satirical ballet (1957); *Chamber Cantata on Poems by Emilio Prado,* for soprano, 2 flutes, harp, and 4 strings (1961); *The Hunters,* symphonic scene (1962); *Night and Day Music,* for wind orch. (1973); *De Profundis,* for a cappella chorus (1977); chamber music; piano pieces; scores for theater and films.
Sources: BB, DCM

Gutiérrez Illanes, Emilio, Bolivian teacher and composer; b.20 Jul 1925, Cochabamba, Bolivia. He studied at the Academy Man Césped of Cochabamba. Later, he studied at the National Cons. of Music of La Paz, Bolivia. Founder and director of the *Centro Coral Melodramático Boliviano.* Director of the Dirección Nacional de Educación Musical of La Paz from 1966 to 1969.
Works (selective list): **Choral music and songs: *Quejas; Evocación a mi Tierra; Brisas del Lago.* Bolivian dances: *Cuecas: Orgullo de Cochala; Lily; Cariñito Mío; Viva La Paz; Linda Capinota.* Taquiraris: *Helahí Benianinga; Cochalita Primorosa; Olvídate de Mi.*** Several sonatas for piano; music for school; marches.
Source: CB

Gutiérrez y Espinosa, Felipe, Puerto Rican composer; b.26 May 1825, San Juan, Puerto Rico; d.27 Nov 1899, San Juan. He started music lessons with his father, Julián Gutiérrez. In 1845, he was appointed *músico* (musician) at the Iberia battalion, and in 1855 he was appointed *maestro de capilla* (chapelmaster) at the Cathedral of San Juan. Conductor of the orch. of the Teatro Tapia, San Juan, during opera seasons.
Works (selective list): **Operas: *Guarionex; El Bearnés; Macías; El Amor de un Pescador.*** Large number of religious compositions: 5 masses; 2 Requiem masses; 8 Salve Regina; Passions; Letanías.
Bibl.: R. Stevenson, *A Guide to Caribbean Music History,* Lima 1975. B. Dueño Colón, *Felipe Gutiérrez y Espinosa, Revista del Café, Suplemento,* Vol.31, Ponce, 1976.
Source: GDM

Guzmán Frías, Federico, Chilean pianist and composer; b.1837, EMA (1827, HMC), Santiago de Chile, Chile; d.18 Aug 1885, Paris, France. He studied piano with Louis Moreau Gottschalk in Costa Rica, and later in Europe with Alexandre Biffet and Adolphe de Groot.

Works (selective list): Over 200 compositions for the piano, including *Gran Mazurka; Tristesse de l'Ame; Prantos; Señorita.*

Bibl.: E. Pereira Salas, *Los Orígenes del Arte Musical en Chile,* Santiago de Chile, 1941.

Sources: EMA, MMLA

H

Haertling, Carlos, Honduran composer of German origin; b.second half of the 19th century; d.? Husband of Guadalupe Haertling. He studied at the Royal Academy of Munich, Germany. When he moved to Honduras, he was appointed conductor of the National Band and director of the School of Music, both of Tegucigalpa, Honduras.
Works: Honduran National Anthem.
Source: DM

Haertling, Guadalupe, Honduran teacher and composer; b.1 Feb 1871, Tegucigalpa, Honduras; d.? She studied with Laureano Campos and other teachers in Honduras. Associate director of the Cons. Mariana Ugarte. Professor of music at various private and public schools in Tegucigalpa. Director of her own school for piano in San Pedro Sula, Honduras. Collaborator with her husband, composer Carlos Haertling.
Works (selective list): *Elena,* polka for piano; *General Francisco Morazán,* march for piano; piano pieces.
Source: MMLA

Halac, José Eduardo, Argentine composer; b.18 Feb 1962, Córdoba, Prov. of Córdoba, Argentina. He studied with César Franchisena at the National Univ. of Córdoba, Córdoba, and with Charles Dodge at the Brooklyn College Cons. of Music of the City Univ. of New York. He also took classes with Francisco Kröpfl in Buenos Aires, Argentina. Teacher of music at the British School and at the National Univ., both of Córdoba. He settled in New York in Sep 1990.
Works (selective list): *Cachalote,* for orch. (1986); *La Caída del Angel,* for orch. (1987); chamber music, some including magnetic tape; music for the theater and films.
Source: ISC

Halffter, Rodolfo, Mexican composer of Spanish origin; b.30 Oct 1900, Madrid, Spain; d.14 Oct 1987, Mexico City, Mexico. He was a self-taught musician who learned composition by studying classical works. In 1929, he received some instruction and advice from Manuel de Falla in Granada, Spain. He was a member of the *Grupo de los Ocho,* devoted to the promotion of Spanish modern music. From 1934 to 1936, he was a music critic for *La Voz.* He was chief of the Music Section of the Ministry of Propaganda in 1936, and member of the Central Music Council of the Spanish Republic in 1937. After the Loyalist defeat, he fled to France and then to Mexico, where he settled in 1939. In 1940, he founded the first Mexican company for contemporary ballet *La Paloma Azul*. Professor at the National Cons. of Mexico in Mexico City, and founder-editor of the journal *Nuestra Música*. In 1946, he founded Ediciones Mexicanas de Música. In 1959, he was appointed secretary at the Music Dept. of the National Inst. of Fine Arts of Mexico City. In 1961, he was appointed board member of the National Symphony Orch. of Mexico, Mexico City.

Works (selective list): **Ballets:** *Don Lindo de Almería* (1935); *La Madrugada del Panadero* (1940); *Elena la Traicionera* (1945). **Orch.**: Suite (1924-28); *Obertura Concertante,* for piano (1932); *Divertimento,* for 9 instruments (1935); Violin concerto (1939-40); *Tres Sonatas de Antonio Soler* (1951); *Obertura Festiva* (1953); *Tres Piezas,* for string orch. (1955); *Tripartita* (1960); *Diferencias* (1970); *Alborada* (1976). **Chamber music:** *Tres Piezas Breves,* for solo harp (1944); String quartet (1957-58); Cello sonata (1960); *Tres Movimientos,* for string quartet (1962); *Ocho Tientos (Fantasías),* for string quartet (1973). Piano pieces; choruses; songs.
Sources: BB, CTA2, DCM, DM, GDM, MLA, MMLA

Hargreaves, Francisco A., Argentine pianist and composer; b.1849, Buenos Aires, Argentina; d.1900, Buenos Aires. He is considered the most prominent Argentine composer of the 19th century because he was the first to compose operas and was also a pioneer of Argentine musical nationalism. He studied with Maglione in Florence, Italy.
Works (selective list): **Operas:** *La Gatta Bianca* (1875), probably the first opera composed by an Argentine composer; *El Vampiro* (1876); *L'Assedio di Livorno; Una Noche de Loreto* (1890); *Los Estudiantes de Bolonia* (1897); *Psyché.* **Orch.**: *La Danza de las Culebras*, waltz (1877); *Idilio* (1878); *La Danza de los Alfes,* Scandinavian capriccio (1879); *Gran Marcha* (1880); *Tutto Muore,* romance for tenor (1880); *Fantasía y Capricho sobre el Gato y el Cielito* (1880); *Marcha Nupcial* (1882); *Lanceros Porteños,* for piano (1887); *Elena y Clota,* waltz (1888). *Salve Maria,* for soprano, harp, cello, and organ (1882); piano pieces; songs.
Sources: DM, EMA

Haro y Tamariz, Jesús, Mexican composer; b.25 Feb 1892, Mexico City, Mexico; d.? He studied at the National Cons. of Music and at the Escuela Superior de Música of the UNAM, both in Mexico City. Among his professors were Ignacio del Castillo, Carlos J. Meneses, Estanislao Mejía, Juan B. Fuentes, Manuel Ponce, Julián Carrillo, and José Rocabruna.
Works: Sonata for piano; *Seis Sonatinas Mexicanas,* for piano; *Canción Mexicana,* for 4 voices; *Suite Coral*; Symphony in C (1934).
Source: MMLA

Henrique, Waldemar, Brazilian composer and pianist; b.15 Feb 1905, Belém do Pará, Brazil. In 1930, he entered the Cons. of Belém and later, he studied in Rio de Janeiro, Brazil, with Joaquím Barroso Neto, Oscar Lorenzo Fernández, Newton Pádua, and Artur Bosmans. *Works* (selective list): *Valsinha de Marajó,* for piano; *Muiraquitâ,* overture for orch. *Songs: Foi Boto; Sinhá; Cobra Grande; Tambatajá; Matimtaperêra; Uirapuru; Curupira; Mânha Ningâra; Boi Bumbá; Coco Peneruê; Farinhada; Senhora Dona Sancha; Rolinha; Violeiro da Estrada; Trem de Alagoas; Essa Nega Fulô;* more than 120 compositions for voice and some pieces for piano. *Source:* HMB

Heredia, Juan, Argentine composer and conductor; b.17 Feb 1898, General Villegas, Prov. of Buenos Aires, Argentina; d.? He studied with Arturo Berutti, Floro Ugarte, Ernesto de la Guardia, Jorge Cabral, José Gil, and José André. Assistant conductor at the Teatro Colón of Buenos Aires, Argentina. Professor at the National Cons. of Music Carlos López Buchardo of Buenos Aires, and at the Escuela Superior de Bellas Artes of the National Univ. of La Plata, Prov. of Buenos Aires. *Works* (selective list): *El Uturunco,* opera; *Preludio Sinfónico,* for orch.; Overture for orch.; songs; piano pieces. *Books: Teoría Musical,* Buenos Aires, 1935. *Sources:* DM, EMA

Hernández, Hermilio, Mexican composer; b.2 Feb 1931, Autlán, Jalisco, Mexico. He studied with José Valadez and Domingo Lobato at the Escuela Superior Diocesana de Música Sagrada in Guadalajara, Mexico, and graduated in 1956. He continued studying in Italy and Paris, France. *Works* (selective list): *Cantata Adviento* (1953); *Five Pieces,* for orch. (1955); Violin concerto (1960); Sonata for chamber orch. (1964); String quartet (1954); Piano trio (1955); Wind quintet (1965); chamber music; music for solo instruments; songs. *Source:* BB

Hernández, José, Cuban professor of music and composer born in Trinidad Island who settled in Cienfuegos, Cuba, at a very young age; d.1918, Cienfuegos. *Works* (selective list): *Eureka,* zarzuela (1897); danzones (Cuban slow dance); waltzes. *Source:* MMLA

Hernández, Julio Alberto, Dominican composer; b.27 Sep 1900, Santiago de los Caballeros, Dominican Republic; d.? He studied with Ramón E. Peralta, José O. García Vila, Juan Francisco García, and

Pedro Sanjuán, with the latter in Havana, Cuba. Conductor of the Orch. of the Symphonic Society of Ciudad Trujillo, the Municipal Band of Bani, and the Municipal Band of Santiago de los Caballeros, all in the Dominican Republic. Director of the Musical Inst. Juan Francisco García.
Works (selective list): *Orch.: Suite Romántica; Danza Oriental; Vals Triste; Romanza sin Palabras. Zarzuelas: El Sí que las Pierde; La Ilusion que Pasa; La Bruja de la Luna.* Piano pieces; music for band; songs.
Sources: DM, MLA, MMLA

Hernández, Rodolfo, Cuban composer, organist, and teacher; b.30 Sep 1856, Santiago de Cuba, Cuba; d.21 Mar 1937, Santiago de Cuba. He studied flute, piano, and violin with Laureano Fuentes Matons, and harmony, composition, and organ with Juan Cardona. At the age of sixteen, he became organist and *maestro de capilla* (chapelmaster) of the Capilla del Asilo San José, and later, of the Cathedral of Santiago de Cuba. Conductor of the orch. of the *Sociedad Haydn.*
Works (selective list): *Zarzuelas: El Asalto; Geografía Física. Orch.: Intermezzo; Gavota; Caprichosa.* Mass in C major; piano pieces.
Books: On music theory and harmony.
Source: DMC

Hernández Acevedo, Juan, Mexican composer and flutist: b.23 Jun 1859 or 1862, Mexico City, Mexico; d.6 Apr 1894, Mexico City. He studied harmony and composition with Melesio Morales, and flute with Mariano Jiménez in Mexico. In 1881, he went to Paris, France, where he continued his flute studies with Joseph Henri Altès. In 1889, he returned to Mexico and, together with Ricardo Castro, Felipe Villanueva, and Gustavo E. Campa, he founded a musical inst. He also organized a symphony orch. in Mexico City, and later, one in San Luis de Potosí, Mexico, where he settled and devoted most of his time to teaching.
Works (selective list): 2 symphonies; *Misa de Requiem; Misa Solemne; Wedding March;* music for the flute.
Source: MMLA

Hernández Balaguer, Pablo, Cuban musicologist and composer; b.13 Jul 1928, Havana, Cuba; d.1966, Havana. Professor at the Univ. of Santiago de Cuba, Cuba. Founder of the Musical Archives of the Univ. de Oriente, Cuba.
Works: Orch. music; songs.
Source: KTL

Hernández Gonzalo, Gisela, Cuban composer and choral conductor; b.15 Sep 1912, DCM (1910, MMLA), Cárdenas, Matanzas, Cuba; d.23 Aug 1971, Havana, Cuba. She studied harmony, music history, and aesthetics with María Muñoz de Quevedo at the Bach Cons., Havana, 1930-35, and composition with José Ardévol at the Havana Municipal Cons., 1940-44. She also studied with Gustav Strube and Theodore Chandler at the Peabody Inst. of Music, Baltimore, Maryland, 1944-47. Director of the Dept. of Music of Ariel College. Member of the *Grupo Renovación Musical.* Director of the *Havana Chorale.* Professor at the Cons. Hubert de Blanck in Havana.
Works (selective list): *Music for piano:* Sonata (1942); *Prelude and Gigue* (1943); *Zapateo Cubano* (1954); *Cuatro Cubanas* (1957); *Seis Preludios* (1961-69). *Choral music: Suite Coral* (1942); *Tres Canciones* (1943); *Dos Villancicos* (1944); *Soneto* (1943); *Romance* (1942); *Aleluya* (1944); *La Muchacha de Quang-Nam* (1969). Chamber music; incidental music for the theater; songs.
Sources: DCM, DM, DMC, GDM, MLA, MMLA, NGDWC

Hernández López, Rhazés, Venezuelan composer and musicologist; b.30 Jun 1918, Petare, Venezuela. He studied with Vicente Emilio Sojo and Juan Bautista Plaza in Caracas, Venezuela.
Works (selective list): *Las Torres Desprevenidas,* symphonic poem (1951); *Sonorritmo,* for orch. (1953); *Mérida, Geografía Celeste,* symphonic suite (1958); *Expansión Tres,* for orch. (1965); *Tres Dimensiones,* for strings (1967); *Cuadros,* for flute, violin, viola, cello, and harp (1950); *Horizontal,* for flute and strings (1966); chamber music; piano pieces; songs.
Source: BB

Hernández Moncada, Eduardo, Mexican composer; b.24 Sep 1899, Jalapa, Veracruz, Mexico; d.? He studied solfeggio with Joaquín Beristain and Rafael Tello and piano and composition with Aurelio Barrios y Morales at the National Cons. of Music of Mexico City, Mexico. Assistant conductor at the Symphony Orch. of Mexico, Mexico City, in 1936. He taught at various official inst. of Mexico. Director of the choir of the National Opera of Mexico, Mexico City. Secretary of the National Cons. of Music.
Works (selective list): *Elena,* opera; *Ballets: Procesional* (1940); *Ixtepec* (1945). *Poemontaje,* cantata (1933); *Seis poemas del Rubayat,* for voice and chamber orch. (1931); 2 symphonies; *Album del Corazón,* for piano.
Sources: BB, DM, GDM, MMLA

Herra, Luis Diego, Costa Rican composer; b.23 Feb 1952, San José de Costa Rica, Costa Rica. He studied composition with Benjamín Gutiérrez and conducting with Agustín Cullell in Costa Rica. He also

studied composition with Ivo Malec and Betsy Jolas, and conducting with J.S. Bereau, León Barzin, and Pierre Derveaux at the Cons. of Strasbourg, France.
Works (selective list): *Canción,* for clarinet and orch. (1974); *Preludio,* for orch. (1976); *Adagio,* for strings (1976); *Cuadros,* for orch. (1978); *De la Piedra,* ballet (1981); *Triforme,* for symphonic band (1987); Sinfonía No.1 (1990); *Morazán Vive,* overture for orch. (1992); *Llegas a mis Sueños,* love songs for voice quartet, chorus, and orch. (1993); chamber music; choruses; piano pieces; music for solo instruments; incidental music; songs.
Source: NP

Herrarte, Manuel, Guatemalan pianist and composer; b.Guatemala; fl.first half of the 20th century. He studied in Guatemala with Georgette Contoux de Castillo and Ricardo Castillo. With a scholarship from the US government, he studied composition with Howard Hanson and conducting with Paul White at the Eastman School of Music of the Univ. of Rochester, New York. He studied briefly with Igor Stravinsky, and took piano lessons from Robert Casadesus.
Works: Sinfonietta for piano and orch.; *Seis Bocetos,* for piano; Suite for piano; *Scherzo,* for piano.
Sources: HMG, MMLA

Herrera, Florentino, Cuban flutist and composer; b.6 Feb 1895, Havana, Cuba; d.3 Dec 1929, Switzerland. He studied in Havana, and later, in New York City and in Paris, France, where he took composition lessons from Vincent D'Indy at the Schola Cantorum.
Works (selective list): *Capricho Cubano,* for orch.; *Danzas Cubanas,* for piano; piano pieces; songs.
Source: DMC

Herrera, Mariano, Costa Rican organist, band musician, and composer; b.22 Nov 1902, Guadalupe de Goicoechea, Prov. of San José, Costa Rica. He began music studies in his native town. He moved to San José, Costa Rica, where he studied harmony with Alvise Castegnaro, composition with Julio Fonseca, orchestration with Juan Loots, and piano with César Nieto. Member of the Band of San José.
Works (selective list): **Music for band:** *Marcha Solemne* (1931); *Marcha Festiva* (1932); *Suite en Cinco Números* (1935); *Melodías Pintorescas* (1941); *Suite Sinfónica e Intermezzo* (1942). **Religious music:** *Misa de Requiem* (1929); *Misa de Gloria* (1943). Songs.
Source: MMLA

Herrera, Tomás de, Peruvian composer and organist; fl.1611-20, Cuzco, Peru; d.before 25 Feb 1682, Cuzco. In 1611, he was appointed organist at the Cathedral of Cuzco.
Works: *Hijos de Eva Tributarios,* 3-part chansonnette.
Bibl.: R. Stevenson, *The Music of Peru,* Washington, D.C., 1960. R. Stevenson, *Renaissance and Baroque Musical Sources in the Americas,* Washington, D.C., 1970.
Source: GDM

Herrera de la Fuente, Luis, Mexican composer and conductor; b.26 Apr 1916, Mexico City, Mexico. He studied piano and violin, and took composition lessons with Rodolfo Halffter. Principal conductor of the National Symphony Orch. of Mexico, Mexico City, from 1954 to 1972. Conductor of the National Symphony Orch. of Peru, Lima, from 1965 to 1971. In 1978, he was appointed music director of the Oklahoma Symphony Orch., Oklahoma City.
Works (selective list): *Cuauhtemoc,* opera; *La Estrella y la Sirena,* ballet; *Fronteras,* ballet; chamber music.
Source: BB

Herrera y Chumacero, Juan de, Colombian composer; b.c.1665, Bogotá, Colombia; d.before 18 Mar 1738, Bogotá. He studied music at the Seminario Conciliar of San Luis, Colombia. Choirmaster at the Cathedral of Bogotá.
Works: *Misa de Requiem* (1704); *Toquen los Clarines y Suenen las Cajas,* villancico (1707); *Que Sacra, Eterna Palabra,* villancico (1712); *Lamentaciones de las Tinieblas,* for 4 voices (1719); *Misa Ferial* (1748); *Misa de Befagni y Misa en Cordis* (1749); *Salmos de Vísperas,* for 5 voices (1764); *Lecciones y Salmos de Exequias* (1794).
Bibl.: J.I. Perdomo Escobar, *Esbozo Histórico sobre la Música Colombiana, Bol.Lat.Am.Mus,* IV, 1938. J.I. Perdomo Escobar, *Historia de la Música en Colombia,* Bogotá, 1963. R. Stevenson, *Renaissance and Baroque Musical Sources in the Americas,* Washington, D.C., 1970.
Sources: DM, GDM, MMLA

Herzfeld, Conrado, Argentine pianist and composer of German origin; b.1845, Berlin, Germany; d.1914, Buenos Aires, Argentina. He settled in Buenos Aires in 1868. Director of the choral society *Germania.* He founded the Cons. La Capital in Buenos Aires.
Works (selective list): Requiem for soloists, chorus, and orch. (1877); *Te Deum,* for soloists, chorus, and orch. (1886); *Gran Fantasía,* for orch. (1870); piano pieces; songs.
Source: EMA

Hobert, Egon, Argentine composer; b.21 Jun 1905, Buenos Aires, Argentina. He studied with Ernesto Drangosch, Athos Palma, and Héctor Belucci. In 1926, he was appointed assistant conductor and assistant to the director of studies of the Teatro Colón of Buenos Aires. In 1927, he was appointed professor at the National Cons. of Music Carlos López Buchardo of Buenos Aires.
Works: Africa, symphonic poem; *Dos Danzas Españolas,* for trio; *Dos Canciones Eslavas,* for baritone and orch.; songs.
Sources: DM, EMA

Holzmann, Rodolfo, Peruvian composer and ethnomusicologist of German origin; b.27 Nov 1910, Breslau, Germany; d.4 Apr 1992, Lima, Peru. He settled in Peru in 1944. He studied piano with Winfried Wolf, composition with Vladimir Vogel, and orch. conducting with Robert Robitschek at the Klindworth-Scharwenka Cons. of Berlin, Germany. In 1933, he studied with Nadia Boulanger in Paris, France. Professor of composition at the National Cons. of Music of Lima, where he also was the director of the Library and Archives. Professor of composition at the National Academy of Music Alzedo of Lima.
Works (selective list): *Orch.*: *Suite Radiofónica* (1932); *Divertimento Concertante* (1941); *Dos Movimientos Obstinados* (1945); *Suite Arequipeña* (1946); First symphony (1946); *Pequeña Suite Peruana* (1948); Piano concerto (1949); *Partita,* for string orch. (1951); Suite sinfónica (1954); *La Pasión del que Mora en la Tierra,* cantata for chorus (1959); *Dodedicata* (1966). Choruses; chamber music; piano pieces; songs. *Books*: *Panorama de la Música Tradicional del Perú,* Lima, 1966.
Sources: DM, GDM, MLA, MMLA

Horst, Jorge, Argentine composer and teacher; b.26 Apr 1963, Rosario, Prov. of Santa Fe, Argentina. He studied composition with Dante Grela, Francisco Kröpfl, Jorge Molina, Mariano Etkin, Carmelo Saitta, and Gerardo Gandini. Founding member of *Grupo Klank* for contemporary music and the Asociación Santafesina de Compositores. Professor at the Cultural and Educational Center of San Lorenzo, at the Escuela Nacional de Música of Rosario, and at the Inst. Nacional del Profesorado of Rosario, all in Prov. of Santa Fe, and at the Facultad de Bellas Artes of the National Univ. of La Plata, Prov. of Buenos Aires, Argentina.
Works: *Paramos Humanos,* for male voice, clarinet, viola, piano, and percussion (1984); *Canciones al Tiempo,* for female voice, flute, clarinet, double bass, and percussion (1985); *Axos (A y B),* for clarinet (1986); *Madrigale a Gesualdo,* for string quintet (1990); *Corales,* for bass clarinet, bassoon, tenor saxophone, trombone, and 2 double basses (1988); *Fresco,* for orch. (1989); *Piante,* for 2

bandonions and 2 double basses (1989); ...*Sobre la Nieve Negra,* for bass clarinet, double bass, and piano (1990); *Van Gogh,* for flute, oboe, viola, piano, and percussion (1990).
Source: CAMR

Huízar García de la Cadena, Candelario, Mexican composer; b.2 Feb 1888, DM (1883, BB), Jérez, State of Zacatecas, Mexico; d.3 May 1970, Mexico City, Mexico. He studied violin and composition. In 1917, he settled in Mexico City where he continued his studies with Gustavo Campa at the National Cons. of Mexico. Copyist in various music schools, 1920-25. Librarian and professor of musical analysis and composition at the National Cons. of Music of Mexico. Horn player with the Mexico Symphony Orch., Mexico City, 1929-37.
Works (selective list): 4 symphonies (1930, 1936, 1938, 1942); *Imágenes,* symphonic poem (1929); *Pueblerinas,* symphonic poem (1931); Sonata for clarinet and bassoon (1931); *Surco,* symphonic poem (1935); String quartet (1938); choral works; songs.
Bibl.: O. Mayer-Serra, *Panorama de la Música Mexicana,* Mexico 1941. J.C. Romero, *Candelario Huízar, Nuestra Música,* January 1951.
Sources: BB, DM, GDM, MLA, MMLA

I

Ibarra Groth, Federico, Mexican composer and pianist; b.25 Jul
1946, Mexico City, Mexico. He studied composition at the National
School of Music of the UNAM in Mexico City. In 1971, he went to
France to continue his studies through a scholarship granted by the
Radio Universidad and Radio Televisión Francesa, and in 1975, with
another scholarship, he attended a course in composition in Santiago
de Compostela, Spain.
Works (selective list): *Operas: Leoncio y Lena* (1980-81); *Orestes
Parte* (1981); *Madre Juana* (1986); *El Pequeño Príncipe* (1988);
Alicia (1989-90). *Cantata I Paseo sin Pie,* for narrator, soloists,
mixed chorus, piano, harmonium, celesta, and percussion (1967);
Cantata II Nocturno Sueño, for tenor, male chorus, flute, and piano
(1969); *Cantata III Nocturno de la Estatua,* for narrator, 2 mixed
choruses, 2 trumpets, trombone, 4-hand piano, percussion, and
electric generator (1969); *El Proceso de la Metamórfosis,* for narrator
and orch. (1970); *Cinco Misterios Eléusicos,* for orch. (1979);
Imágenes del Quinto Sol, ballet (1980); Concerto for cello and orch.
(1988-89); Sinfonía I for orch. (1991); *Tres Piezas para Orquesta,*
for orch. (1991); chamber music; piano pieces; choruses; songs.
Source: ISC

Iberê de Lemos, Artur, Brazilian composer; b.9 Jun 1901, Belém de
Pará, Brazil; d.13 Feb 1967, Rio de Janeiro. He studied cello with
John Barbirolli and harmony at the Royal Academy of Music in
London, England, and continued his music studies in Berlin,
Germany, and Milan, Italy.
Works (selective list): *A Ceia dos Cardeais,* opera; *Momentos Líricos;
Canção Arabe; Ave,* symphonic poem; *Patria,* symphonic poem.
Sources: DM, HMB

Iglesias Villoud, Héctor, Argentine composer; b.31 Jan 1913, San
Nicolás, Prov.of Buenos Aires, Argentina. He studied in Buenos
Aires, Argentina, at the Cons. Fracassi and Thibaud-Piazzini, and in
1926, he entered the Cons. Gaito where he studied harmony,
counterpoint, fugue, composition, and instrumentation with
Constantino Gaito, graduating in 1933. Professor at the National
Cons. of Music Carlos López Buchardo of Buenos Aires, the Escuela
Superior de Bellas Artes of the Univ. of La Plata, Prov. of Buenos
Aires, and the National Univ. of Litoral, Rosario, Prov. of Santa Fe,
Argentina. Director of the Teatro Argentino of La Plata.
Works (selective list): *Operas: El Oro del Inca* (1953); *Redención*
(1955). *Ballets: Amancay* (1937); *El Malón* (1943). *Orch.: Dos
Danzas Argentinas* (1937); *Escenas Indoamericanas* (1949); *Embrujo*

Pampeano, for piano (1952); *Sinfonía Independencia* (1967). Piano pieces; choruses.
Sources: CA, DM, EMA, GDM, MLA

Ignacio, Rafael, Dominican composer; b.15 Jun 1897, San Francisco de Macorís, Dominican Republic; d.1984, Santo Domingo, Dominican Republic. He studied with Father Andrés Requena and Oguís Negrette. He played trumpet, flute, and double bass in military bands, and later conducted a dance orch. called *Amores y Amoríos.* In 1941, he was appointed assistant conductor of the military band in Santiago de los Caballeros, Dominican Republic.
Works: *Quisqueya Lírica,* suite; Symphony in C minor; *Suite Folklórica.*
Sources: DM, MLA

Imbroisi, Juan, Argentine composer of Italian origin; b.1866, Paola, Italy; d.1942, Buenos Aires, Argentina. He settled in Argentina at the end of the 19th century.
Worsk: Marches and school songs, including *A mi Bandera,* sung for the first time in 1906, still in the repertoire.
Source: EMA

Inzaurraga, Alejandro, Argentine composer and lawyer; b.16 Apr 1882, Buenos Aires, Argentina; d.1956, Buenos Aires. He studied in Buenos Aires with Alberto Williams. He also became a lawyer and worked at the Argentine Justice Dept. He taught music in various inst. and also was a music critic.
Works (selective list): Sonata in F for piano; Trio in F for piano, violin, and cello; String quartet; *Por Sierras de Córdoba; Serie Sentimental; Matinal,* for voice and piano; music for choir; piano pieces; songs.
Sources: DM, EMA

Iporre Salinas, Humberto, Bolivian pianist, teacher, and composer; b.28 Dec 1915, Potosí, Bolivia. He was self-taught in music. Professor of piano at the Academy of Fine Arts of the Univ. Tomás Frías of Potosí. Conductor of the Symphony Orch. of the Univ. of Potosí.
Works: *Suites Indias, 1 and 2; La Oración del Mitayo; Koya Raimi; Sueño de la Nusta; Fantasía India; El Pututo; Tu Orgullo; Potosino Soy.*
Source: CB

Ippisch, Franz, Guatemalan composer of Austrian origin; b.18 Jul 1883, Vienna, Austria; d.20 Feb 1958, Guatemala City, Guatemala. He settled in Guatemala in 1938. In 1939, he was appointed general

director of Músicas Marciales in Guatemala City, Guatemala. Professor and conductor of the ensemble class at the National Cons. of Guatemala City.
Works (selective list): *Sinfonía Guatemalteca;* 2 symphonies; *Pastorale,* for cello and chamber orch.; Violin concerto; Overture; Suite for string orch.; chamber music.
Sources: DM, MLA

Ipuche Riva, Pedro, Uruguayan composer, music critic, lecturer, teacher, and radio commentator; b.26 Oct 1924, Montevideo, Uruguay. He studied at the Cons. of Montevideo with Carlos Estrada, and later, with a scholarship from the French government, he studied in Paris, France, with Jean Rivier and Noel Gallon. Artistic director of SODRE and director of the *Revista del SODRE* of Montevideo. Professor at the National Cons. and the Inst. de Profesores Artigas, both in Montevideo.
Works (selective list): *El Arbol Solo,* symphonic poem (1961); *La Prueba de Abraham,* oratorio for soloists, chorus, and orch. (1961); *Homenaje a Tchaicovsky,* ballet (1961-64); *La Discreta Enamorada,* overture (1961); 3 symphonies (1962, 1965, 1968); Cello concerto (1962); *Fantasía Concertante,* for trumpet and string orch. (1963); *Cantata a Artigas,* for baritone, chorus, and orch. (1964); Concerto for small orch. (1966); *Sinfonietta-Concertino,* for piano and orch. (1967); *Animales Ilustres,* suite for wind quintet (1967); chamber music; piano pieces; choruses; songs.
Sources: BB, BHMCU, CTA12, MU

Isamitt Alarcón, Carlos, Chilean composer and painter; b.13 Mar 1887, Rengo, Colchagua, Chile; d.2 Jul 1974, Santiago de Chile, Chile. He studied violin with Sante Lo Priore and composition with Domingo Brescia and Humberto P. Allende at the National Cons. of Music of Chile in Santiago de Chile. He studied painting and drawing at the School of Fine Arts of Santiago de Chile. He also studied in Spain, Italy, France, and the Netherlands. He became interested in the folk music of the Araucanian Indians. In 1927, he was appointed director of the School of Fine Arts, the School of Applied Arts, and the Museum of Fine Arts, all in Santiago de Chile. In 1928, he was appointed general director of art education of the Ministry of Public Education of Chile. President of the Asociación de Compositores de Chile. Professor of musical pedagogy at the National Cons. of Music. Permanent member of the Chilean Academy of Fine Arts.
Works (selective list): *Friso Araucano,* for soprano, tenor, and orch. (1931); Suite sinfónica (1932); *Mito Araucano,* for orch. (1935); *Gato con Botas,* children's play (1941); *El Pozo de Oro,* ballet (1942); Suite for cello and chamber orch. (1950); *Cuatro Movimientos Sinfónicos* (1960); Concerto for harp and chamber orch.

(1962); Concerto for violin and orch. (1966); *Evocaciones Huiliches,* for soprano, baritone, and orch. (1966); *Grito de la Sangre,* ballet (1968-69); *Lautaro,* symphonic poem (1970); chamber music; piano pieces; songs.
Sources: BB, CTA13, DCM, DM, GDM, HMC, MLA, MMLA

Itiberê, Brasílio da Cunha Luz, Brazilian composer; b.17 May 1896, Curitiba, State of Paraná, Brazil; d.10 Dec 1967, Rio de Janeiro, Brazil. Nephew of Brasílio da Cuhna Iteberê. At first, he studied civil engineering, but under the influence of Ernesto Nazareth, he decided to study music. He studied piano with Corradi and Leonhard Kessler. He was appointed by Heitor Villa-Lobos to teach folk music at the National Cons. of *Canto Orfeónico* (male choral singing) in 1942, and was appointed to the same position at the Univ. do Distrito Federal, Rio de Janeiro, in 1938.
Works (selective list): *A Infinita Vigilia,* for soprano and chorus (1941); *Contemplaçâo,* for female chorus and chamber orch. (1942); *Oraçâo da Noite,* for mezzo-soprano and chorus (1945); *O Canto Absoluto,* cantata for mixed chorus and orch. (1947); *Estancias,* choral poem for mezzo-soprano and chorus (1947); *Epigrama,* for chorus a cappella (1948); *Preludio Vivaz,* for orch. (1951); *Momento Eufórico,* for orch. (1951); *O Salmo 150,* for chorus and orch. (1954); chamber music; piano pieces; choruses; songs.
Sources: CTA16, DM, GDM, HMB, MLA, MMLA

Itiberê da Cunha, Brasílio, Brazilian composer, pianist, and diplomat; b.1 Aug 1846, Paranaguá, Brazil; d.11 Aug 1913, Berlin, Germany. Brother of Joâo Itiberê da Cunha. He was self-taught in music.
Works: *Music for piano:* A Sertaneja, Brazilian rhapsody; *Poème d'Amour; Nuits Orientales; Sous les Tropiques; Sérénade; Gavotte; Etude de Concert; Soirées à Venise; Rhapsodies Brésiliennes.*
Sources: GDM, HMB, MMLA

Itiberê da Cunha, Joâo, Brazilian composer, poet, and music and art critic; b.8 Aug 1869, Curitiba, State of Paraná, Brazil; d.25 Feb 1953, Rio de Janeiro, Brazil. Brother of Brasílio Itiberê da Cunha. He studied music and law in Brussels, Belgium. He used the pen name: Iwan d'Hunac. Music critic for the Rio de Janeiro newspaper *Correio da Manhâ* for more than 40 years.
Works: *Série Brasileira: Despertar de Matuto, Acalanto Ingenuo, Cançâo Ritual de Macumba,* for orch.. *Music for piano:* Etude (Printemps que chante); Prelúdio e Fuga; Prelúdio e Fugato; Marcha Humorística; Danse Plaisante et Sentimentale; Fête Villageoise; Quatre Portraits du Vieux Carnaval.

Sources: DM, GDM, MMLA

Ituarte, Julio, Mexican pianist and composer; b.15 May 1845, Mexico City, Mexico; d.15 May 1905, Mexico City. He started music studies with José M. Oviedo and Agustín Balderas, and later continued piano with Tomás León and harmony and counterpoint with Melesio Morales. Professor at the Cons. Nacional de Música y Declamación of Mexico City.
Works (selective list): *Zarzuelas: Sustos y Gustos; Gato por Liebre. Fantasía Dramática on Themes from Carmen,* for piano; *Pensamientos Musicales; Minuetto; En los Bosques,* mazurka; *El Ultimo Pensamiento de Weber,* lyric-dramatic composition; transcriptions for piano of operas and operettas; piano pieces.
Bibl.: O. Mayer-Serra, *Panorama de la Música Mexicana,* Mexico, 1941. L. Castillo Ledón, *Los Mexicanos Autores de Opera,* 1910.
Source: MMLA

Iturri Gonzáles, Wálter, Bolivian conductor and composer; b.21 Sep 1934, La Paz, Bolivia. He studied at the Military School of Music of La Paz. In 1965, he studied at the National Cons. of Music of La Paz, then in 1966, with a scholarship, he studied orch. conducting in Zagreb, Yugoslavia. In 1970, he conducted the Bolivian National Symphony Orch. and the Band of the Military Engineering School, both in La Paz.
Works: *Campanas de Triunfo,* overture for orch.; compositions based on Bolivian popular rhythms: *Cuecas: Mi Madre...; Canturreando. Kullawuas: Rasputín; Enchoro; Saleroso. Taquirari: Besad y...,.*
Source: CB

Iturriaga, Enrique, Peruvian composer and teacher; b.3 Apr 1918, Lima, Peru. He studied piano, theory, and harmony at the Sas-Rosay Academy of Lima, and later, he continued studies of theory and composition with Rodolfo Holzmann at the National Cons. of Music of Lima. In 1950, he went to Paris, France, where he studied with Arthur Honegger. Professor of theory and composition at the National Cons. of Music and the Univ. Nacional Mayor de San Marcos. Director of the Escuela Nacional de Música, previously the National Cons. of Music of Lima. Music critic for the newspaper *El Comercio* of Lima.
Works (selective list): *Orch.: Canción y Muerte de Rolando,* for soprano (1947); *Preludio y Danza* (1954); *Tres Canciones,* for 4 violins (1957); Suite (1957); *Obertura para una Comedia* (1964); *Vivencias* (1965); *Homenaje a Stravinsky* (1971). Chamber music; songs.
Source: GDM

Iturribery, Juan José, Uruguayan composer; b.24 Oct 1936, Pando, Prov. of Canelones, Uruguay. He studied piano with Genoveva F. de Parga and Numen Vilariño, and composition with Carlos Estrada, Héctor Tossar, and Angel Turriziani. He also took classes in electroacoustical techniques with Mauricio Maidanik at the Facultad de Humanidades of Montevideo, Uruguay.
Works (selective list): *Dúo Sacro,* for 2 flutes; *Elegía,* for cello and piano; Variations for piano; *Meditation in F* (1975).
Sources: BB, BHMCU

Izarra, Adina Margarita, Venezuelan composer; b.27 Aug 1959, Caracas, Venezuela. She studied piano with Guiomar Narvaez in Caracas and with Marta Clare and Dorothea Law in London and York, England, and composition with Alfredo del Mónaco in Caracas and Vic Hoyland in York. She received a Ph.D. in composition from the Univ. of York.
Works (selective list): *Orch.: Oshunmare,* violin concerto (1982); *Mujer con Telar* (1986); *Tejedora de Arpilleras Mágicas* (1986); *Pitangus Sulphuratus*, concerto for flute and string orch. (1987); *Luna de Aves,* for chamber orch. (1988); *Homenaje* (1991). Chamber music; music for solo instruments; songs.
Source: ISC

J

Jabor, Najla (Najla Jabor Maia de Carvalho), Brazilian conductor and composer; b.25 Sep 1915, IEW (1914, IBCC), Rio de Janeiro, Brazil. She studied piano with Henrique Oswald, and fugue, composition, and orchestration with Francisco Braga at the Escola Nacional de Música of the Univ. of Rio de Janeiro.
Works: Orch.: Piano concerto (1953); *Prelúdio Sinfônico* (1957); *Y Juca Pirama* (1957); *Américas,* symphonic triptych (1958); *A Dança do Paje,* symphonic poem; *Tango Brasileiro,* symphonic poem (1960); *Batuquinho Clássico* (1966). Piano pieces; songs.
Sources: IBCC, IEW, NGDWC

Jatobá, Pedro Ireneo, Brazilian composer and organist; b.15 Dec 1895, Salvador, Brazil; d.12 Dec 1948, Salvador. He started music studies with his father, Pedro Orlando Jatobá. Later he studied organ with Father Mouton, from the Cons. of Brussels, Belgium, harmony and composition with Carlos Werbeck and Alberto Muylaert, and music aesthetics with Basilio Ettel, from the Univ. Marl Laach in Germany. Professor at the Music Inst. of Bahía. Founder of the Escuela Normal de Música of Bahía.
Works: Impressôes de Bahía; Meditaçâo, Ofertorio y Canto, for organ. *Books: Fraseología Musical.*
Source: MMLA

Jeanty, Occide, Haitian composer and band conductor; b.1860, Port-au-Prince, Haiti; d.1936, Port-au-Prince. The Haitian government sent him to study music in Paris, France. He returned to Haiti in 1886 and was appointed musical director of the Republic of Haiti.
Works: Large number of marches.
Source: MLA

Jerusalem, Ignacio, Mexican composer and violinist of Italian origin; b.c.1710, Lecce, Italy; d.1769, Mexico. He settled in Mexico in 1742. In 1746, he was appointed interim *maestro de capilla* (chapelmaster) at the Cathedral of Mexico, a position made permanent in 1750, and one he held until his death.
Works: 6 masses; 5 Magnificat; 2 Te Deum; 15 Miserere; 4 Lamentations; 18 vesper psalms; 25 motets and psalms; 12 hymns; 9 invitatories; 89 responsories; Christmas pastoral; villancicos.
Bibl.: R. Stevenson, *Renaissance and Baroque Musical Sources in the Americas,* Washington, D.C., 1970. R. Stevenson, *Christmas Music from Baroque Mexico,* Berkeley and Los Angeles, 1974.
Source: GDM

Jiménez, José Manuel, Cuban pianist and composer; b.7 Dec 1851, Trinidad; d.1917, Hamburg, Germany. He studied with his father, José Julián Jiménez, and then he went to Europe where he studied with Carl Reinecke and Ignaz Moscheles at the Cons. of Leipzig, Germany, and with Antoine François Marmontel in Paris, France. In 1879, he returned to Cuba and settled in Cienfuegos where he taught piano. In 1890, he was appointed professor at the Cons. of Hamburg, Germany.
Works (selective list): *Estudio Sinfónico; Elegía; Solitude; Murmullo del Céfiro; Rapsodia Cubana; Vals Capricho;* piano pieces; songs.
Source: DMC

Jiménez Mabarak, Carlos, Mexican composer; b.31 Jun 1916, Tacuba, Mexico. He studied piano with Jesús Castillo in Guatemala, attended classes in humanities in Santiago de Chile, Chile, 1930-33, and studied musicology and music history with Charles Van den Borren and harmony and analysis with Marguerite Wouters at the Royal Cons. in Brussels, Belgium, 1933-36. In Paris, France, he studied dodecaphonic techniques with René Leibowitz. In 1937, he returned to Mexico and studied conducting with Silvestre Revueltas. Professor of music theory and harmony at the National Cons. of Music of Mexico City, 1942-65, and at the School of Arts in Villahermosa, Mexico, 1965-68.
Works (selective list): *Calígula,* incidental music (1947); *Misa de Seis,* opera (1962). *Ballets: Perifonema* (1940); *El Amor del Agua* (1950); *El Ratón Pérez* (1955). *Orch.:* Piano concerto (1944); *Balada del Pájaro y las Doncellas* (1947); *Los Niños Héroes,* cantata for chorus (1947); *Balada del Venado y la Luna* (1948); 2 symphonies (1945, 1962); *Balada Mágica* (1951); *Balada de los Quetzales* (1953); Sinfonía concertante for piano (1966). *Concierto del Abuelo,* for piano and string quartet (1938); Concerto for timpani, bells, xylophone, and percussion (1961); *Pitágoras Dijo...,* for small ensemble (1966); cantatas; chamber music; piano pieces; songs.
Sources: BB, CTA8, MLA

Jolles, Henry (Heinz), Brazilian composer and pianist of German origin; b.28 Nov 1902, Berlin, Germany; d.16 Jul 1965, Sâo Paulo, Brazil. He studied at the Univ. of Berlin, Germany, and was a student of Edwin Fischer, Artur Schnabel, and Kurt Weill. Professor at the Klindworth-Scharwenka Cons. in Berlin and the Music School of Cologne, Germany. In 1940, he emigrated to Brazil where he was appointed professor at the Music School of Sâo Paulo.
Works: Ballets; chamber music; piano pieces; songs.
Source: KTL

Jorge, Santos, Panamanian composer of Spanish origin; b.1 Nov 1870, Peralta, Navarra, Spain; d.22 Dec 1941, Panama City, Panama. He studied at the Cons. of Madrid, Spain. Conductor of the Banda del Batallón Colombia and the Banda de la República, both in Panama City. Voice teacher and inspector of music in the schools of Panama City.
Works: Himno Istmeño (1897), which was proclaimed the *Panamanian National Anthem* when Panama became independent from Colombia, and the Panamanian Republic was established in 1903; *Himno al Trabajo; Himno al Maestro.*
Sources: DM, MLA, MMLA

Juanas, Antonio, Mexican composer, probably of Spanish origin; b.Spain?; d.after 1819, Spain? Active as composer by 1789. *Maestro de capilla* (chapelmaster) at the Cathedral of Mexico City, Mexico, from 1790 to 1816. In 1819, he returned to Spain.
Works: Religious music: 18 masses with instruments; 10 masses a cappella; 11 Te Deum; 45 vesper psalms; 100 responsories; 22 Salve; 3 Lamentations; motets; hymns; villancicos.
Bibl.: G. Saldívar, *Historia de la Música en México (Epocas Precortesiana y Colonial),* Mexico City, 1943. R. Stevenson, *Renaissance and Baroque Musical Sources in the Americas,* Washington, D.C., 1970.
Source: GDM

Juárez, Manuel, Argentine composer; b.22 Apr 1937, Córdoba, Prov. of Córdoba, Argentina. He studied composition with Guillermo Graetzer and piano with Ruwin Erlich in Buenos Aires, Argentina. Founder and president of the Asociación Argentina de Compositores. Professor at the National Univ. of Buenos Aires, Buenos Aires.
Works: Ballets; chamber music; piano pieces; choruses; songs.
Source: KTL

Juliâo, Joâo Batista, Brazilian composer and teacher; b.19 Sep 1886, Silveiras, Brazil; d.20 May 1961, Sâo Paulo, Brazil.
Works: Choral music; educational pieces for schools; piano pieces.
Source: MLA

Jurafsky, Abraham, Argentine composer; b.26 Aug 1906, Buenos Aires, Argentina. He studied at the National Cons. of Music Carlos López Buchardo of Buenos Aires, where later he was appointed professor of harmony. Artistic director of the Asociación Wagneriana of Buenos Aires.
Works (selective list): *Preludio Sinfónico,* for orch.; 2 sonatas for violin and piano; piano pieces; songs.
Sources: CA, DM, EMA

K

Kagel, Mauricio Raúl, Argentine composer; b.24 Dec 1931, Buenos Aires, Argentina. He studied in Buenos Aires with Juan Carlos Paz and Alfredo Schiuma and also attended courses in philosophy and literature at the National Univ. of Buenos Aires, Buenos Aires. In 1949, he became associated with the *Agrupación Nueva Música* of Buenos Aires. From 1949 to 1956, he was choral director at the Teatro Colón of Buenos Aires and music adviser to the National Univ. of Buenos Aires. In 1957, he settled in Cologne, Germany, where he worked at the laboratories of the Westdeutscher Rundfunk. Guest lecturer at the International Festival Courses for New Music at Darmstadt, Germany, from 1960 to 1966. In 1965, he was professor of composition at the State Univ. of New York in Buffalo, New York. In 1969, he was director of the Inst. of New Music at the Rheinische Musikschule of Cologne. In 1974, he was appointed professor at the Cologne Hochschule für Musik.

Works (selective list): *Palimsestos,* for chorus a cappella (1950); String sextet (1953); *Traummusik,* for instruments and musique concrète (1954); *Anagrama,* for speaking chorus, 4 vocalists, and chamber ensemble (1958); *Transición I,* for electronic sounds (1958); *Transición II,* for piano, percussion, and 2 magnetic tapes (1959); *Pandora's Box,* for magnetic tape (1961); *Sonant,* for electric guitar, harp, double bass, and 20 instruments (1961); *Sur Scène,* for 6 participants in mixed media (1959-60); *Heterophonie,* for 42 solo instruments (1959-61); *Phonophonie,* instrumental theater (1963-64); *Composition and Decomposition,* a reading piece (1963); *Diaphonie I,* for chorus, orch., and slide projections (1962); *Diaphonie II,* for orch. and slide projectors (1962-64); *Diaphonie III,* for chorus and slide projectors (1962-64); *Music for Renaissance Instruments,* for 23 performers (1966); String quartet (1967); *Montage,* for different sound sources (1967); *Ornithologica Multiplicata,* for exotic birds (1968); *Ludwig van,* for piano, flute, trumpet, trombone, balalaika, harmonium, double bass, and 2 percussionists (1970); *Staatstheater,* a scenic composition (1971); *Variations ohne Fuge,* for orch. (1972); *Con Voce,* for 3 mute actors (1972); *Mare Nostrum,* scenic play (1975); *Country Music,* for voice and instruments (1975); *Variété,* concert-spectacle for artists and musicians (1977); *Die Erschöpfung der Welt,* opera (1980); chamber music; songs.

Bibl.: D. Schnebel, *Mauricio Kagel: Musik, Theater, Film,* Cologne, 1970. K.H. Zrius, *Staatstheater von Mauricio Kagel,* Vienna, 1977. **Sources:** BB, DCM, EMA, GDM

Katunda, Eunice (Eunice Catunda do Monte Lima), Brazilian composer and pianist; b.14 Mar 1915, Rio de Janeiro, Brazil. She studied piano with Branca Bilhar, Marieta Lion, and Oscar Guanabarino, composition with Furio Franceschini, Camargo Guarnieri, Hans Joachim Koellreutter, and Bruno Maderna, and conducting with Hermann Scherchen. In 1946, she joined the modernistic group *Música Viva*, started by Hans Joachim Koellreutter in 1939. In 1948, she was appointed lecturer at the Univ. of Brasília, Brazil. In 1956, she went to Salvador, Bahía, Brazil, to study the music of Afro-Brazilian cults.

Works (selective list): *O Negrinho do Pastoreio,* cantata for female voices, flute, guitar, and percussion (1946); *Quatro Cantos à Morte,* for orch. (1948); *Homenagem a Schoenberg,* for clarinet, bass clarinet, viola, cello, and piano (1949); *A Negrinha e Iemanja,* for voice and orch. (1955); Concerto for piano and orch. (1955); *Seresta,* for 4 saxophones (1956); *A Moça Fantasma de Belo Horizonte,* ballet (1959); *Ode à Brasília,* for chorus and orch. (1960); *Cantata dos Marinheiros,* for chorus, soloists, and orch. (1975); *Cinco Líricas Gregas,* for soloists, chorus, and percussion (1977); *Cantata do Soldado Morto,* for soloists, chorus, and percussion (1977); chamber music; piano pieces; songs.

Sources: BB, EMB, HMB, NCM, NGDWC

Kellner, Hiltrud, Uruguayan composer of Romanian origin; b.1913, Transylvania, Romania. She lived many years in Uruguay where she studied with her husband, Mexican composer Carlos Zozaya, and with Enrique Casal Chapí and Héctor Tosar.

Works: *Tres Movimientos,* for string orch. (1950); *Cuatro Movimientos,* for symphony orch. (1952); Concerto for orch. with piano concertante.

Source: UEW

Kersenbaum, Sylvia Haydée, Argentine pianist and composer; b.27 Dec 1941, Buenos Aires, Argentina. She studied piano with Esperanza Lothringer and Vicente Scaramuzza, and composition with Gilardo Gilardi, Julián Bautista, and Roberto García Morillo. She also studied at the Accademia Musicale Chigiana in Siena, Italy, at the Accademia Nationale di Santa Cecilia in Rome, Italy, and in Geneva, Switzerland, with Nikita Magaloff and Hans Graff.

Works: *La Máscara Roja,* ballet; songs.

Source: IEW

Kiefer, Bruno, Brazilian composer of German origin; b.9 Apr 1923, Baden-Baden, Germany. He settled in Pôrto Alegre, Brazil in 1934. He studied with Enio de Freitas e Castro and Hans Joachim Koellreutter. Director of the Music Division of the Secretary of Education of the State of Rio Grande do Sul, Brazil.

Works (selective list): *Diálogo,* for piano and orch. (1966); *Electra, Convertimento e Poema Telúrico,* 3 pieces for orch.; *Linhas Contorcidas,* for flute, clarinet, bassoon, 2 violins, cello, and double bass; piano pieces; chamber music; songs; choruses a cappella.
Source: HMB

Kinsman, Benjamín Roberto J., Brazilian violinist, music critic, and composer; b.1853, Rio de Janeiro, Brazil; d.1934, Brazil.
Works: *Himno Republicano do Brasil,* for chorus, orch., and band. Many pieces for violin.
Source: MMLA

Koc, Marcelo, Argentine composer of Russian origin; b.4 Jun 1918, Vitebsk, U.S.S.R., currently Belarus. He settled in Argentina in 1938. He studied harmony, counterpoint, fugue, and composition with Jacobo Ficher, and piano with Elene Larrieu and Oreste Castronuovo. He also studied composition with Guillermo Graetzer and Juan Carlos Paz. Founding member of the Asociación de Jóvenes Compositores de la Argentina and of the Unión de Compositores Argentinos.
Works (selective list): *Orch.*: *Invención,* for strings (1948); *Preludio, Intermezzo y Fuga,* for strings (1951); *Tres Piezas* (1958); *Divertimento,* for strings (1957); *Estructuras Líricas* (1964); *Núcleos* (1968); Violin concerto (1974); *Amor y Amar,* for mezzo-soprano (1978); *Canto a San Martín,* for narrator, mezzo-soprano, chorus (1979); Viola concerto (1983); Piano concerto (1988); Cello concerto (1989); *Sonoridades* (1989); *Poemas Americanos,* for voice (1990); Harpsichord concerto (1991); Recorder concerto (1991). Chamber music; music for solo instruments; piano pieces; songs; choruses.
Sources: CA, CTA14, EMA, ISC

Koellreutter, Hans Joachim, Brazilian composer of German origin; b.2 Sep 1915, Freiburg, Germany. He settled in Brazil in 1937. He studied composition and choral conducting with Kurt Thomas, orch. conducting with Hermann Scherchen, and piano with C.A. Martienssen in Berlin, Germany. In Geneva, Switzerland, he studied flute with Marcel Moyse. In 1935, he founded the *Circle of Contemporary Music* in Berlin, and the *Group Música Viva* in Brasil. In 1938, he was appointed professor at the Cons. Brasileiro de Música of Rio de Janeiro, Brazil. Professor of composition at the Musical Inst. of Sâo Paulo, Brazil. Founder of the *Sâo Paulo Instrumental Quintet* in 1942.
Works (selective list): *Orch.:* *Música* (1947); *Sinfonía de Cámara,* for 11 instruments (1948); *Concretion* (1960); *Construction ad Synesin* (1962); *Advaita,* for sitar (1968); *Sunyata,* for flute, chamber orch. of Western and Indian instruments, and tape (1968). *8 Hai-kais*

de Pedro Xisto, for baritone and 8 instruments (1963); *Cantos de Kulka,* for soprano and piano or orch. (1964); *Mu-Dai,* for any voice without accompaniment; *Isei,* for voice and instruments; *Cidadezinha Qualquer,* for chorus a cappella.
Sources: BB, DM, HMB, MLA, MMLA

Kohan de Scher, Celina, Argentine composer and pianist; b.31 Jan 1931, Buenos Aires, Argentina. She studied piano with Ana Litovsky de Grünwald and Aldo Romaniello, and harmony, counterpoint, fugue, composition, and orchestration with Abraham Jurafsky, Pedro Sáenz, Juan Francisco Giacobbe, Héctor Iglesias Villoud, Floro Ugarte, and Alberto Ginastera at the National Cons. of Music Carlos López Buchardo of Buenos Aires. She continued piano studies with Raúl Spivak and composition with Gilardo Gilardi. Teacher at elementary schools of the National Board of Education from 1950 to 1983. Board member of the Asociación Argentina de Compositores.
Works (selective list): *Mariquita Sánchez,* opera. *Orch.: Fantasía y Fuga,* for string orch. (1954); Concertino for viola (1955); 2 symphonies (1955, 1983); *Rondo,* for string orch. (1960); Suite sinfónica (1967); *Tríptico Porteño,* for soprano and chamber orch. (1978); *Adiós a Mahatma Gandhi,* cantata for mixed chorus, soprano, and baritone narrator (1978); *Había una Vez...,* suite for children chorus (1982); Concerto for alto recorder or oboe (1987); Concerto for cello and string orch. (1990). Chamber music; piano pieces; guitar pieces; songs.
Sources: EMA, ISC

Kostakowsky, Jacobo, Mexican composer and violinist of Russian origin; b.5 Feb 1893, Odessa, Ukraine, formerly part of Russia; d.17 Aug 1953, Mexico City, Mexico. Settled in Mexico in 1925. Studied violin with Max Fiedelman in Odessa, Otakar Sevcik in Vienna, Austria, Kilian in Munich, Germany, and with Hans Sitt and Hans Becker in Leipzig, Germany. Studied harmony with Arnold Schoenberg in Vienna, composition with Vincent D'Indy at the Schola Cantorum in Paris, France, and orch. conducting with Max Reger in Leipzig.
Works (selective list): *Ballets: Clarín,* (1935); *Creación del Hombre* (1937). *Orch.: Taxco,* symphonic poem (1936); Piano Concerto (1937); *El Romancero Gitano,* suite (1937); *Triángulo,* suite (1937); *Escenas Callejeras,* for chamber orch. (1937); *Suite Lírica* (1938); *La Serenata* (1941); *Marimba,* capriccio for piano (1940); 2 violin concertos (1942, 1942). Chamber music; songs.
Sources: DM, MLA, MMLA

Kotzarew, Oleg, Argentine composer of Russian origin; b.1932, Pialigorek, Russia. He settled in Argentina in 1949 and until 1964 he lived in the city of Tucumán, Prov. of Tucumán, Argentina, where he was very active as a chamber musician and at the Univ. of Tucumán Symphony Orch. He also taught at the local cons. In 1964, he joined the Philharmonic Orch. of Buenos Aires, and in 1965, the Camerata Bariloche, both in Argentina.

Works (selective list): *Pujillay,* ballet (1965); *Heterodoxia,* for string orch. (1964); *Ocasional Música para un Concierto,* for orch.; 3 string quartets; Sonata for cello and piano; chamber music; piano pieces.

Source: EMA

Krieger, Armando, Argentine composer and conductor; b.7 May 1940, Buenos Aires, Argentina. He studied piano with John Montés, composition with Alberto Ginastera, and orch. conducting with Roberto Kinsky. He is one of the first graduates from the Centro Latino Americano de Altos Estudios Musicales of the Inst. Di Tella of Buenos Aires. Assistant conductor at the Teatro Colón of Buenos Aires. Professor at the Argentine Catholic Univ. and the National Univ., both of Buenos Aires.

Works (selective list): *Cantata II,* for soprano, female chorus, and orch. (1963); Concerto for 2 pianos and orch. (1963); *Metamorfosis d'après une Lecture de Kafka,* for piano and orch. (1968); *Elegía I,* for clarinet and piano (1960); *Elegía II,* for voice and instrumental ensemble (1962); *Sonatina 2,* for violin and piano (1961); *Cinco Nocturnales,* for chamber ensemble (1964); *Tensiones III,* for voice and ensemble (1967); *De Muertes y Resurrecciones,* for voice and 5 instruments (1969); piano pieces; songs.

Source: EMA

Krieger, Edino, Brazilian composer; b.17 Mar 1928, Brusque, Santa Catarina, Brazil. He studied music with his father, Aldo Krieger, director of the local cons., and later with Hans Joachim Koellreutter at the Cons. Brasileiro de Música de Rio de Janeiro, Brazil. In 1948, he studied with Aaron Copland at the Berkshire Music Center in Tanglewood, Massachusetts, then at The Juilliard School of Music in New York City with Peter Mennin. He also studied with Ernest Krenek in Brazil, in 1952, and with Lennox Berkeley in London, England. In 1947, he became member of the *Grupo Música Viva* organized by Hans Joachim Koellreutter. Director of the Art and Music Dept. of the Radio Jornal do Brasil in Rio de Janeiro, 1963-73; president of the Brazilian Society of Contemporary Music.

Works (selective list): *Convergencias,* ballet with chorus. *Orch.:* *Movimiento Misto* (1947); *Chôro,* for flute and strings (1955); *Abertura Sinfónica* (1955); *Concertante,* for piano (1955); *Divertimento,* for strings (1959); *Brasiliana,* for viola or alto saxophone (1960); *Variaçôes Elementares,* for chamber orch. (1964);

Ludus Symphonicus (1966); *Canticum Naturale,* for soprano (1972); *Estro Armónico.* Choral music; chamber music; piano pieces; songs.
Sources: BB, CTA13, DM, HMB

Kröpfl, Francisco, Argentine composer of Hungarian origin; b.26 Feb 1931, Szeged, Hungary. He settled in Buenos Aires, Argentina, in 1932. Studied with Juan Carlos Paz. In 1950, he joined the *Agrupación Nueva Música.* In 1959, he organized the Dept. of Musical Phonology at the National Univ. of Buenos Aires, Buenos Aires. Director of the Electronic Laboratory of the Inst. Di Tella of Buenos Aires, where he also taught. In 1962, he was appointed musical consultant at the National Museum of Fine Arts of Buenos Aires.
Works (selective list): *Tres Piezas,* for piano (1948); *Música,* for flute and clarinet (1951); *Cuatro Canciones de Aldo,* for soprano, flute, and clarinet (1952); *Variaciones,* for piano (1953); *Dos Estudios,* for piano (1953); *Tres Canciones de Mario Porro,* for soprano and instruments (1954-56); *Música 1958,* for piano; *Música,* for 25 instruments (1959); *Ejercicio de Texturas,* electronic music (1960); *Ejercicio con Impulsos,* electronic (1961); *Música,* for 3 percussionists and electronic sounds (1962); *Móvil II,* for piano (1962); *Ejercicio en Movimientos,* electronic music (1962); *Acciones,* for piano (1962-66); *Diálogos I, II and III,* electronic music (1964-65, 1965, 1968); *Música 1966,* for piano.
Sources: EMA, GDM

Kubik, Rodolfo, Argentine composer of Italian origin; b.24 Jan 1901, Pola, Istria, Italy. He studied at the Royal Cons. Tartini in Trieste, Italy, with Illersberg. In 1927, he settled in Argentina where he organized the chorus of the National Univ. of La Plata, Prov. of Buenos Aires, and other choral groups.
Works (selective list): *La Beffa,* opera (1925); *Tupac,* symphonic-choral poem; *Temas Mesopotámicos,* suite for orch. and chorus; *Fuga,* for quartet; *Nocturno,* for violin and piano; piano pieces; songs.
Sources: DM, EMA

Kumok, Jorge, Argentine composer, pianist, and teacher; b.21 May 1931, Buenos Aires, Argentina. He studied at the National Univ. of La Plata, Prov. of Buenos Aires, Argentina.
Works (selective list): *Triptychon,* symphony; *Música,* for piano and orch.; orch. music; piano pieces; songs.
Source: KTL

186 - Kuri Aldana

Kuri Aldana, Mario, Mexican composer and teacher; b.15 Aug 1931, Tampico, Tamaulipas, Mexico. He studied piano with Carlos del Castillo at the Academia Juan Sebastián Bach in Mexico City, Mexico, 1948-51, and theory with Juan Tercero at the National School of Music of the UNAM in Mexico City, 1952-60. He also studied conducting with Igor Markevitch and Jean Giardino at the Inst. Nacional de Bellas Artes in Mexico City, 1957-58, and advanced techniques of composition with Rodolfo Halffter and Luis Herrera de la Fuente, 1961-62. He took lessons with Alberto Ginastera in Buenos Aires, Argentina. Professor of composition at the Academia Juan Sebastián Bach, and of theory, harmony, and counterpoint at the UNAM. Professor of music at the Academia de la Danza of the INBA of Mexico, Mexico City.

Works (selective list): 3 symphonies (1959, 1966, 1976); *Los Cuatro Bacabs,* suite for double wind orch. and optional narrator (1960); *Máscaras,* concerto for marimba and wind orch. (1962); *Pasos,* for piano and orch. (1963); *Bacab de las Plegarias,* for 2 flutes, 2 clarinets, trumpet, harp, and strings (1966); *Formas de Otros Tiempos,* for string orch. and harp (1971); *Concierto de Santiago,* for flute, string orch., and 2 percussion players (1973); *Concertino Mexicano,* for violin and string orch. (1974); chamber music; piano pieces; songs.

Bibl.: S. Kahan, *El Compositor Kuri Aldana, Carnet Musical de X.E.L.A.,* Mexico City, 1963.

Sources: BB, DCM, GDM

L

Lacerda, Osvaldo Costa de, Brazilian composer and teacher; b.23 Mar 1927, Sâo Paulo, Brazil. He studied composition with Ernesto Kierski and Camargo Guarnieri. In 1963, through a scholarship from the Guggenheim Foundation, he went to the USA where he studied composition with Vittorio Giannini in New York and with Aaron Copland in Tanglewood, Massachusetts. He founded the *Coral da Sociedade Paulista de Arte* and the *Sociedade Pro-Música Brasileira*. Professor at the Escola Municipal de Música of Sâo Paulo. President of the Comissâo Estadual de Música de Sâo Paulo, in 1967, and of the *Sociedade Pró-Música Brasileira,* from 1961 to 1966. Member of the Academia Brasileira de Música.
Works (selective list): *Suite Piratininga,* for orch. (1962); Concerto for string orch. (1964); *Abertura No.1,* for orch. (1972); *Quatro Pecas Modais,* for string orch. (1975); *Quatro Movimentos,* for string orch. (1976); *Missa a Duas Vozes,* for chorus and organ (1966); *Missa Ferial,* for mixed chorus a cappella (1966); *Missa Santa Cruz,* for mixed chorus and organ (1967); *Missa a Tres Vozes Iguais,* for chorus and organ (1971); chamber music; music for wind ensembles; music for brass ensembles; music for percussion instruments; piano pieces; more than 50 songs for voice and piano or other instruments.
Sources: CTA15, DCM, GDM, HMB

Lado, Norma, Argentine composer and pianist; b.8 Oct 1934, Lanús, Prov. of Buenos Aires, Argentina. She studied piano with Haydée Loustaunau and harmony, counterpoint, fugue, and composition with Jacobo Ficher. President of the Asociación de Jóvenes Compositores de la Argentina.
Works (selective list): *Music for piano: Tres Preludios* (1957); *Preludio y Fuga* (1959); *Variaciones sobre un Tema de Mozart* (1960); *Sonata* (1961); *Cuatro Imágenes Infantiles* (1963); *Tres Piezas* (1981). *Dos Piezas,* for string orch.(1968); *Adagio* (1982). Chamber music; songs.
Sources: ISC, VMA

Lafinur, Juan Crisóstomo, Argentine composer; b.27 Jan 1797, Prov. of San Luis, Argentina; d.13 Aug 1824, Chile. He studied at the Colegio Monserrat of Córdoba, Prov. of Córdoba, Argentina. Director of the chorus at the Cathedral of Córdoba. He participated in many historical events of those times, and in the war of independence against the Spaniards. Professor of philosophy at the National Univ. of Buenos Aires; he resigned because of his extremely liberal ideas, and then he moved to the Prov. of Mendoza, where he taught at the Colegio de la Santísima Trinidad.

Works: Clarisa y Betsy, musical melodrama (1821); *Himno Patriótico,* homage to San Martin's South American campaign of liberation and independence.
Sources: EMA, MMLA

Lafuente, Valentín, Guatemalan composer; fl.first half of the 20th century.
Works: 2 masses, for orch.; *La Danza Negra,* overture; *Miserere,* for 4 voices and orch.; *Tota Pulcra,* for 3 voices and orch.; *Miserere,* for orch.; *Gradual de Viernes de Dolores,* for orch.; *Gloria Patri,* for orch.; *Regina,* for 3 voices and orch.
Source: MMLA

Lagarmilla, Roberto Eugenio, Uruguayan music critic and composer; b.25 May 1913, Montevideo, Uruguay; d.13 Mar 1992, Montevideo. He studied at the Musical Inst. Falleri, and later took classes in harmony, counterpoint, and composition with Benone Calcavecchia in Montevideo. Music critic for the newspapers *La Mañana, El Plata, Mundo Uruguayo,* and *El Día.*
Works (selective list): *Queguay,* ballet (1935); *Impresiones Bravías,* for piano (1936); *Dos Preludios,* for guitar (1942); Concertino in A for piano and orch. (1936); Concerto for piano and orch. (1943); *Variaciones Tangueadas,* for orch. (1950-52); piano pieces; songs.
Books: Eduardo Fabini, Montevideo, 1954; *Músicos Uruguayos,* Montevideo, 1970.
Sources: BHMCU, MMLA

Lamarque Pons, Jaurés, Uruguayan composer and pianist; b.6 May 1917, Salto, Uruguay; d.11 Jun 1982, Montevideo. He started music studies very early in life; studied piano with María Victoria Varela. In 1935, he moved to Montevideo, Uruguay, where he studied piano with Guillermo Kolischer and harmony, counterpoint, and instrumentation with José Tomás Mujica, Guido Santórsola, and Enrique Casal Chapí.
Works (selective list): *Marta Gruni,* opera (1965). *Ballets: Sortilegio* (1951); *Suite de Ballet según Figari* (1952); *Suite Rioplatense* (1954); *El Encargado* (1956); *Un Tal Sombrero* (1963); *Contrarritmo* (1965). *Tres Danzas Pintorescas,* for orch. (1947); *Tríptico Montevideano,* for orch. (1956); Concerto for piano, strings, and percussion; incidental music for movies and theater; chamber music; piano pieces.
Sources: BHMCU, CTA16, MU

Lamas, José Angel, Venezuelan composer; b.2 Aug 1775, Caracas, Venezuela; d 9 Dec 1814, Caracas. He studied with Juan Manuel

Olivares at the Padre Sojo's Music School in Caracas. Bassoonist at the Cathedral of Caracas, a position that he held until his death.
Works: Popule Meus, for 3 voices, 2 violins, 2 oboes, 2 French horns, viola, and bass (1801); Mass in D (1810); *Miserere; Ave Maris Stella* (1808); 30 motets.
Bibl.: R. de la Plaza, *Ensayos sobre el Arte en Venezuela,* Caracas, 1883. J.B. Plaza, *Music in Caracas during the Colonial Period 1770-1811, The Musical Quaterly,* New York, April 1943.
Sources: MMLA, GDM

Lambertini, Marta, Argentine composer; b.13 Nov 1937, San Isidro, Prov. of Buenos Aires, Argentina. She studied with Luis Gianneo, Roberto Caamaño, and Gerardo Gandini at the Facultad de Artes y Ciencias Musicales of the Argentine Catholic Univ. of Buenos Aires, 1965-72. She studied new disciplines in music with Francisco Kröpfl, Gerardo Gandini, Gabriel Brncic, and José Maranzano through a scholarship granted by CICMAT, 1973-74. Member of the *Asociación Argentina de Musicología* and board member of the *Agrupación Nueva Música.* Professor at the Facultad de Artes y Ciencias Musicales of the Argentine Catholic Univ. of Buenos Aires. Professor at the National Cons. of Music Carlos López Buchardo of Buenos Aires and the Facultad de Bellas Artes of the National Univ. of La Plata, Prov. of Buenos Aires.
Works (selective list): *Choral-symphonic music: Odas* (1972); *Proverbios* (1972). *Orch.: Concertino-Serenata,* for flute, clarinet, harp, piano, percussion, and string orch. (1981); *Misa de Pájaros* (1983); *Galileo Descubre las Cuatro Lunas de Júpiter* (1985). 2 string quartets (1971, 1978); *Enroque a 7,* for flute, clarinet, piano, and string quartet (1970); *Serenata,* for flute, clarinet, cello, piano, and percussion (1973); *La Espada de Orión,* for wind quintet, string quartet, harp, and piano (1981); *Ewigkeitt..! (homage to J.S. Bach),* for baritone, string quartet, piano, and percussion (1985); *Lo Stivale,* cycle of popular Italian songs, for baritone, piccolo, flute, flute in G, clarinet, bass clarinet, violin, cello, bass, piano, and percussion (1986); *Antígona,* for solo viola, clarinet, bass clarinet, mandolin, guitar, and piano (1987); choruses; piano pieces; incidental music for the stage; songs.
Sources: ISC, NGDWC

Lamego, Carlinda J., Brazilian pianist, teacher, and composer; b.20 May 1910. She studied piano with de Vasconcellos, theory with Oscar Lorenzo Fernández, and harmony, counterpoint, and fugue with Paulo Silva in Brazil.
Works: Chamber music; sacred music; piano pieces; songs.
Source: IEW

Lamothe, Ludovic, Haitian composer; b.12 May 1882, Port-au-Prince, Haiti; d.? He studied in his country and at the Paris Cons., France. Chief of music of the Republic of Haiti.
Works: *Music for piano: Nibo (Meringue de Carnaval); La Dangereuse (Meringue Haitienne); Fleur d'Haiti.* Songs.
Sources: DM, MLA

Lamuraglia, Nicolás J., Argentine composer; b.19 Feb 1896, Buenos Aires, Argentina; d.? He studied harmony, counterpoint, and composition with Athos Palma. President of SADAIC. Taught at the Univ. of Cuyo, Mendoza, Prov. of Mendoza, Argentina.
Works (selective list): *Poema Sinfónico,* for tenor and orch. (1938); *Cuatro Impresiones Sinfónicas,* for orch.; *Obertura para una Farsa Trágica,* for orch.; Suite for piano and string orch.; *Figuras,* for violin and chamber orch.; Sinfonietta for chamber orch.; String quartet; Sonatina for piano; piano pieces; choruses; songs.
Sources: CA, DM, EMA, MLA, MMLA

Landaeta, Juan José, Venezuelan composer; b.10 Mar 1780, Caracas; d.16 Oct 1814, Cumaná, Venezuela. Studied at the Padre Sojo's Music School in Caracas. Musician at various Venezuelan churches. Director of the first French opera company in Caracas.
Works: *Venezuelan National Anthem,* adapted from his song *Gloria al Bravo Pueblo*; *Sincamisa,* song written with his uncle, violinist José Luis Landaeta. **Religious music:** *Pésame a la Virgen,* cantata for voice and orch.; *Salve Regina,* for 4 voices and orch.; *Ave Maria Stella,* for 3 voices; 5 motets.
Bibl: R. de la Plaza, *Ensayos sobre el Arte en Venezuela,* Caracas 1883. J.B. Plaza, *Music in Caracas during the Colonial Period (1770-1811), The Musical Quarterly,* New York, April 1943.
Sources: DM, GDM, MLA, MMLA

Lanza, Alcides, Argentine composer; b.2 Jun 1929, Rosario, Prov. of Santa Fe, Argentina. He studied with Julián Bautista, Alberto Ginastera, Ruwin Erlich, and Roberto Kinsky in Buenos Aires, Argentina. Later he took courses with Olivier Messiaen, Riccardo Malipiero, Aaron Copland, Bruno Maderna, and Vladimir Ussachevsky at the Di Tella Inst. of Buenos Aires. Assistant conductor and artistic coordinator at the Teatro Colón of Buenos Aires, from 1959 to 1965. In 1965, he was awarded a scholarship from the Guggenheim Foundation and moved to the USA, where he dedicated his time to teaching and composing at the Columbia-Princeton Center for Electronic Music, New York. In 1971, he moved to Canada and became professor of composition at McGill Univ. in Montreal. From 1972 to 1973, he was composer-in-residence at the Deutscher Akademischer Austauschdienst in Berlin, Germany.

Works (selective list): *Plectros I,* for 1 or 2 pianos (1962); *Eidesis Sinfónica,* for orch. (1963); Concerto for piano and orch. (1964); *Exercise I,* electronic music (1965); *Plectros II,* for piano and magnetic tape (1966); *Interferencias I,* for 2 wind ensembles, piano, and electronic sounds (1966); *Plectros II,* for piano and tape (1966); *Acúfenos,* for trombone and 4 percussionists (1966); *Eidesis II,* for 13 instruments (1967); *Interferencias II,* for percussion and electronic sounds (1967); *Ekphonesis,* for piano, winds, strings, and magnetic tape (1968); *Espontaneidad,* audiovisual spectacle (1970); *Penetrations V,* mixed media (1971); *Acúfenos II,* for 4 instruments and tape ((1971); *Eidesis III,* for 1/2 orch. and tape (1971); *Mantis I* (1972); *Hip'nes I* (1973); *Kron'ikelz 75* (1975).
Sources: CAMR, CTA17, DCM, EMA, GDM

Lapeiretta de Brower, Ninón, Dominican pianist and composer; b.4 Jan 1907, Ciudad Trujillo, Dominican Republic; d.1989, Ciudad Trujillo. She started music lessons, solfeggio, theory, and piano at the Liceo Musical of Ciudad Trujillo, and then studied piano with Blanca Mieses and Manuel Polanco, and composition with Enrique Casal Chapí. Founder and president of the Círculo de Bellas Artes of Ciudad Trujillo. General secretary of the Asociación de Autores y Compositores Dominicanos.
Works (selective list): *El Nacimiento de Venus,* ballet; *Abominación de la Espera,* for voice and orch. (1943); *Preludio Pastoral,* for small orch.; *Obertura Jocosa,* for large orch.; *Suite Arcaica,* for string quartet; *Dos Caprichos,* for wind instruments (1942); chamber music; piano pieces.
Sources: DEW, MMLA

Lara Bareiro, Carlos, Paraguayan composer, violinist, and conductor; b.6 Mar 1914, Capiatá, Paraguay. He started to study violin in Asunción, Paraguay, and continued violin studies, together with composition and conducting, with Newton Pádua, Virginia Fiuzza, José Paulo Silva, J. Otaviano, and Francisco Mignone at the National School of Music of the Univ. of Brazil, Rio de Janeiro, Brazil. In 1951, he returned to Paraguay and organized the Symphony Orch. of the Asociación de Músicos de Paraguay in Asunción. Later, he settled in Buenos Aires, Argentina.
Works (selective list): *Suite Paraguaya,* for orch.; Concerto in D minor for piano and orch.; *Co-é Yú Mba'é Apojhara Rapa-Ne,* symphonic poem. *Guaranias: Lustrabotas; Ñasaindy yavé.*
Sources: BB, CTA15, MMPA

Larios, Felipe, Mexican composer and teacher; b.1817, Mexico City, Mexico; d.1875, Mexico City. He started music studies with Eduardo Campuzano, Mariano Malpica, and Mateo Velasco. He continued his

studies of harmony, counterpoint, and orchestration with José Antonio Gómez. He was one of the founders and professor of harmony of the National Cons. of Music of Mexico, Mexico City. *Works*: Overtures; piano pieces; religious music. *Books: Método de Armonía Teórico-Práctico.*
Sources: GMM, MMLA

Larrazábal, Felipe, Venezuelan lawyer, historian, composer, and violinist; b.31 Jul 1816, Caracas, Venezuela; d.23 Nov 1873, Caracas. He studied music with José María Montero. He received a doctorate in law in 1842. Professor of law at the Univ. of Caracas. *Works* (selective list): *Gran Trío in A,* for piano, violin, and cello; *Nocturno Sentimental; Gran Fantasía Dramática;* songs.
Sources: MLA, MMLA

Lasala, Angel E. Argentine pianist and composer; b.9 May 1914, Buenos Aires, Argentina. He studied with Athos Palma, José Gil, and Ernesto de la Guardia at the National Cons. of Music Carlos López Buchardo of Buenos Aires. Vice provost and professor of harmony at the National Cons. of Music Carlos López Buchardo. Director and professor of chamber music at the Municipal Cons. of Music Manuel de Falla of Buenos Aires. Member and president of the Asociación Argentina de Compositores.
Works (selective list): *Chasca Ñahuí,* ballet (1944); *Amancay,* ballet (1955); *Cuatro Impresiones Corales* (1938); *Movimientos Orquestales,* for piano and orch.; *Cantata a San Martín de Porres,* for soloists, narrator, mixed chorus, and orch.; *Quebrada,* symphonic poem; *Santa María de los Buenos Aires,* cantata for narrator, mixed chorus, and orch.; Concerto for 2 guitars and orch.; *Suite en Compás Ternario,* for orch.; 3 string quartets; chamber music; music for solo instruments; piano pieces; songs; choruses.
Sources: CA, DM, EMA, VMA

La Salvia, Antonio Santos, Argentine composer and teacher; b.1877, Buenos Aires, Argentina; d.1933, Buenos Aires. He studied in Buenos Aires with Santo Discépolo, and then at the Cons. of Milan, Italy. Professor at the National Cons. of Music of Buenos Aires, founded by Juan Gutiérrez.
Works: *Rapsodia Criolla,* for orch.; *A los Andes,* march. *Books: Teoría de la Música.*
Source: EMA

Lauro, Antonio, Venezuelan guitarist and composer; b.3 Aug 1917, Ciudad Bolívar, Venezuela; d.1986, Venezuela. He studied in Caracas, Venezuela.

Works (selective list): *Cantacharo*, symphonic poem; Concerto for guitar and orch.; several symphonies; suites; choruses; many pieces for guitar; songs.
Sources: BB, CTA14

Lavalle García, Armando, Mexican composer; b.23 Nov 1924, Ocotlán, Jalisco, Mexico. He studied violin at the National Cons. of Music of Mexico City, Mexico. Studied composition with Miguel Bernal Jiménez, Silvestre Revueltas, and Rodolfo Halffter. He played viola at the National Symphony Orch. of Mexico City. Conducted the Xalapa Symphony Orch., Mexico.
Works: *Ballets*: *La Canción de los Buenos Principios* (1957); *Tres Tiempos de Amor* (1958); *Corrido* (1959). *Mi Viaje,* symphonic poem (1950); *Obertura Colonial,* for orch. (1954); *Estructuras Geométricas,* for string orch. and percussion (1960); Concerto for viola and string orch. (1965); Concerto for violin, string orch., and percussion (1966); *Ipalnemohuani,* for chorus and orch. (1966); chamber music.
Sources: BB, CTA15

Lavín Acevedo, Carlos, Chilean composer and ethnomusicologist; b.10 Aug 1883, Santiago de Chile, Chile; d.27 Aug 1962, Barcelona, Spain. He studied in Paris, France, with André Caplet and Roger Pénau in 1923, and with M. Mauss at the Inst. of Ethnology of La Sorbonne, and in 1931, with Erich M. von Hornbostel at the Univ. of Berlin, Germany. Involved in folklore research and comparative musicology. Collaborator in the *Musical Dictionary* by Hugo Riemann. He returned to Chile in 1943. Member of the research staff of the Inst. of Folklore at the Univ. of Chile, 1945-48, and director of the Folk-Music Archive of the Inst. for Musical Research, 1948-60, both in Santiago de Chile.
Works (selective list): *Ballets: La Encantada* (1925); *Automnales* (1928); *Quiray* (1930); *Danza Blanca* (1936). *Fiesta Araucana,* for orch. (1926); *Lamentaciones Huiliches,* for orch. (1928); chamber music; piano pieces; incidental music for films.
Bibl.: J. Urrutia Blondel, *Carlos Lavín Compositor, Revista Musical Chilena,* 1967.
Sources: CTA4, DM, GDM, MLA

Lavista, Mario, Mexican composer; b.3 Apr 1943, Mexico City, Mexico. He studied piano with Francisco Gyves, and harmony, counterpoint, and composition with Rodolfo Halffter and Héctor Quintanar. He attended classes and seminars of Karlheinz Stockhausen, Henri Pousseur, Gyorgy Ligeti, and Iannis Xenakis in Darmstadt and Cologne, Germany. When he returned to Mexico in

1970, he founded *Quanta,* an improvisational music group. From 1964 until 1967, he taught music appreciation, music initiation, and music of the 20th century at the UNAM in Mexico City. In 1971, he joined the Laboratory of Electronic Music of Mexico, Mexico City. Professor at the National Cons. of Music of Mexico, Mexico City.
Works (selective list): *Orch.*: *Sinfonía Modal* (1965); *Ondina* (1966); *Six Pieces,* for string orch. (1967); *Contínuo,* for brass, percussion, 2 prepared pianos, and strings (1970); *Lyhannh* (1976); *Nocturnos,* for mezzo-soprano (1986). *Monologue,* for baritone, flute, vibraphone, and double bass (1966); *Five Pieces,* for string quartet (1967); *Divertimento,* for wind quintet, 5 woodblocks, and 3 shortwave radios (1968); *Homage to Samuel Beckett,* for 3 amplified choruses (1968); *Jaula,* for any number of prepared pianos (1976); chamber music; choruses; piano pieces; music for tape.
Sources: BB, CTA15

Lavista Peimbert, Raúl, Mexican composer and conductor; b.1913, Mexico City, Mexico; d.1980, Mexico City. He studied first with María Vázquez, Pedro Luis Ogazón, and Manuel Barajas, and later he entered the School of Music of the National Univ. of Mexico, Mexico City, where he studied with José Rolón, Manuel M. Ponce, and Silvestre Revueltas.
Works (selective list): *Estampas* (1933); *Tríptico Pianístico;* Concerto for 2 pianos and orch.; *Tuna Muerta; Veracruzana;* music for about 500 films.
Source: ISC

Laya, José Clemente, Venezuelan composer and violist; b.20 Oct 1913, Caracas, Venezuela. He studied violin, first with Pedro Antonio Silva and later with Espinel. He studied harmony with Andrés Delgado Pardo and composition with Vicente Emilio Sojo at the Escuela Superior de Música José Angel Lamas of Caracas. Violist at the Venezuela Symphony Orch., Caracas. Professor at the Escuela Preparatoria de Música Juan Manuel Olivares, Caracas. Director of the School of Music of San Cristóbal and School of Music of Aragua State, both in Venezuela.
Works (selective list): *Sinfonietta sobre Temas Taurepanes,* for orch. (1948); *Obertura Infantil sobre Temas de Canciones Escolares,* for orch. (1954); *Suite Venezolana,* for orch. (1956); *Rapsodia,* for orch. (1957); chamber music; piano pieces; songs; choruses.
Source: CTA14

Lébano, Félix, Argentine harpist and composer of Italian origin; b.1856, Palermo, Sicily, Italy; d.1915, Argentina. He was chamber harpist for Queen Elizabeth II of Spain, and for King Edward VII of England.

Works: *Triumphal March*, for orch., dedicated to the President Juárez Celman of Argentina; incidental music for the *sainete* (one-act farce) *Los Consejos de Don Javier*, by Manuel Argerich; salon pieces.
Source: EMA

Le Bellot, Luis, Argentine composer; b.1888, La Rioja, Argentina. d.1948, Argentina. He studied with Alberto Williams and Edmundo Pallemaerts. In 1924, he entered the diplomatic service of Argentina.
Works: *Catequil,* ballet for soloists, chorus, and orch.; *Dafne y Like*, ballet; *La Máscara de la Muerte*, mimodrama; *La Salamanca,* tone poem; *Recuerdos de Provincia,* suite for piano (1919-23).
Source: EMA

Lecuna, Juan Vicente, Venezuelan composer; b.20 Nov 1898, DM (1891, BB; 1899, MMLA), Valencia, Venezuela; d.15 Apr 1954, Rome, Italy. He graduated from the Escuela Normal of his native town in 1906, and then he moved to Caracas, Venezuela, where he studied music theory with Juan Vicente and piano with Salvador Llamozas at the Cons. of Music of Caracas. He also studied orchestration with Gustav Strube in Baltimore, Maryland, and composition with Alexander Savine and Elisabeth Kuyper in New York. In 1937, he went to Buenos Aires, Argentina, where he took composition lessons with Jaime Pahissa. He then returned to Caracas where he entered the diplomatic service. In 1943, he was sent by the Venezuelan Dept. of Education to study musical education in Brazil, Uruguay, Argentina, and Chile. Secretary of the Venezuelan Legation in Rome and member of the Venezuelan Legation at the Vatican, Italy.
Works: Piano concerto; *Suite Venezolana,* for 4 guitars; String quartet; *Suite of 4 Venezuelan Dances,* for piano; *Dos Danzas Venezolanas*, for piano; *Dos Preludios*, for piano; *Cuatro Canciones sin Palabras,* for piano; *Quatre Pièces pour Piano;* Sonata for harp; *El Canto de la Sangre,* suite for orch.
Bibl.: W. Guido, *Ficha Biográfica y Catálogo de la Obra Musical de Juan Vicente Lecuna, Revista Musical de Venezuela,* Jan-Apr, 1981.
Sources: BB, CTA14, DM, MLA, MMLA

Lecuona, Ernesto, Cuban composer and pianist; b.7 Aug 1896, Guanabacoa, Cuba; d.29 Nov 1963, Santa Cruz de Tenerife, Canary Islands, Spain. Brother of Ernestina Lecuona Casado. He studied at the National Cons. of Music in Havana, Cuba, in 1913, and later he took courses with Joaquín Nin. Leader of a dance band, *Lecuona's Cuban Boys,* which became internationally known.
Works (selective list): **Stage:** *El Cafetal,* zarzuela; *Lola Cruz,* zarzuela; *El Sombrero de Yarey; Rosa la China; María la O; El*

Batey; La Tierra de Venus; Niña Rita. Rapsodia Negra, for piano and orch. (1943); Suite for orch. **Songs:** *La Comparsa; Danza Negra; Palomita Blanca; Siboney; Malagueña; Mariposa*; and many more. 70 dances for piano.
Sources: BB, GDM, MLA, MMLA

Lecuona Casado, Ernestina, Cuban composer, pianist, and teacher; b.16 Jan 1882, Matanzas, Cuba; d.3 Sep 1951, Havana, Cuba. Sister of Ernesto Lecuona and grandmother of Leo Brouwer. She studied at the Academia del Centro Asturiano and the School of Music Amadeo Roldán, both in Havana. Later she continued her studies at the Paris Cons., France. Founder of the *Orquesta Femenina de Concierto* (Female Concert Orch.).
Works: Latin American dances; hymns; waltzes; songs.
Source: NGDWC

Legrand, Diego, Uruguayan composer; b.20 Sep 1928, Montevideo, Uruguay. He studied piano with Adela Taborda and Sarah Bourdillón, harmony with Nydia Pereyra, and counterpoint, fugue, instrumentation, and composition with Guido Santórsola.
Works: *Danza Criolla; Tema y Variaciones*, for flute, oboe, and bassoon; Wind quintet; *Música*, for strings; Sinfonietta; *Cuadros Sinfónico-Corales*, for narrator, chorus, and orch.; *Halos*, for orch.; *Equivalencias*, for orch.; *Espacios*, for orch.
Sources: BHMCU, MU

Leite, Vânia Dantas, Brazilian composer, pianist, and composer; b.13 Aug 1945, Rio de Janeiro, Brazil. She studied piano with Zilá de M. Brito and composition with Frederico Egger at the Escola Nacional de Música of the Univ. of Rio de Janeiro. Later she studied electronic music with Per Hartmann in London, England, in 1974, and composition with Esther Scliar in Brazil. Professor at the Cons. Brasileiro de Música in Rio de Janeiro.
Works (selective list): Symphony No.1 (1971); *Abertura 1822*, for orch. (1972); *Entre Vidas*, for orch. (1974); *Réquiem para um Poeta*, for chorus and orch; chamber music; electronic music.
Source: NGDWC

Leite Dias Batista, Clarisse, Brazilian pianist, teacher, and composer; b.11 Jan 1917, São Paulo, Brazil. She studied piano with Zilda Leite Rizzo and José Kliass, harmony with João Sepe, composition with J. Wancolle and Teodoro Nogueira, and orchestration with O. Farinello at the Cons. Dramático e Musical of São Paulo. She also studied in France in 1930. Professor at the Academia Internacional de Música do Rio de Janeiro, Brazil.

Works (selective list): 2 piano concertos (1972, 1975). *Music for piano: Impressôes de Vienna; Ciclo do Jazz; Quilombo dos Palmares.* Songs.
Sources: IBCC, IEW

Leng Haygus, Alfonso, Chilean composer and dentist; b.11 Feb 1884, Santiago de Chile, Chile; d.7 Nov 1974, Santiago de Chile. He studied dentistry in Santiago de Chile, and music with Enrique Soro at the National Cons. of Music of Santiago de Chile. He joined other prominent composers to form the *Grupo Los Diez* (Group of the Ten).
Works (selective list): *Cinco Dolores,* for orch. (1920); *La Muerte de Alsino,* symphonic poem (1920); *Canto de Invierno,* for orch. (1932); *Fantasía,* for piano and orch. (1936); *Psalm 77,* for soloists, chorus, and orch. (1941); chamber music; piano pieces; songs.
Bibl.: A special issue of the *Revista Musical Chilena* (Aug/Sept 1957) was published in his honor.
Sources: BB, CTA15, DCM, DM, GDM, HMC, MLA, MMLA

León, Argeliers, Cuban composer, teacher, and ethnomusicologist; b.7 May 1918, Havana (Pinar del Río, GDM), Cuba. In 1943, he graduated in music pedagogy from the Univ. of Havana, and in 1945, he graduated from the Municipal Cons. of Havana, where he studied with Mompó, Luaces, and César Pérez Sentenat. He studied composition, first with José Ardévol in Havana, and later with Nadia Boulanger in Paris, France. In 1951, he received a scholarship to study folklore and musical didactics at the Univ. of Chile, Santiago de Chile, Chile. Professor at the Municipal Cons., professor of musicology at the Inst. Superior de Arte, and director of the Music Dept. of the Casa de las Américas, all in Havana. Editor of the journal *Conservatorio.*
Works (selective list): Symphony for string orch. (1946); *Suite Cubana,* for string orch. (1946); Symphony No.1 (1946); Concertino for flute, piano, and string orch. (1948); *Cánticos de Homenaje,* for orch. (1958); Symphony No.2 (1962); *Sonatas para la Virgen de Cobre,* for piano and string orch.; *Creador del Hombre Nuevo,* cantata for narrator, voices, chorus, woodwind instruments, and percussion; choruses; chamber music; piano pieces; songs. *Books: Influencias Africanas en la Música de Cuba,* 1959; *Música Folklórica Cubana,* 1964; *Del Canto y del Tiempo,* 1974.
Sources: DM, DMC, GDM, MMLA

León, Tania Justina, Cuban composer and conductor; b.14 May 1943, Havana, Cuba. She started to study piano at the age of four, and later graduated with a BA in music in 1963 and an MA in music education in 1964 from the Peyrellade Cons. of Music in Havana. She settled in New York in June 1967 and studied composition with Ursula Mamlok at the Univ. of New York. Music director of the Brooklyn College Orch., New York, in 1991. Board member of the New York Foundation for the Arts and the American Composers Orch. Composer-in-residence at Yale Univ., New Haven, Connecticut, in 1993.

Works: *Stage: The Beloved,* ballet (1972); *Tones,* ballet (1972); *Dougla,* ballet (1974); *La Ramera de la Cuena,* musical (1974); *Belé,* ballet (1981); *Scourge of Hyacinths,* opera (1994). *Concerto Criollo,* for timpani and orch. (1980); *Ascend,* for brass and percussion (1983); *Bata,* for orch. (1985); *Kabiosile,* for piano and orch. (1988); *Indígena,* for chamber orch. (1991); *Ritual,* for piano (1991); *Parajota Delate,* for mixed quintet (1992); *Carabalí,* for orch. (1992); commissioned new works for different instrumental ensembles (1992-94).

Sources: ISC, NGDWC

León, Tomás, Mexican pianist and composer; b.21 Dec 1828, Mexico City, Mexico; d.28 Mar 1893, Mexico City. He studied with Felipe Larios. Together with other prominent musicians he founded and organized the Sociedad Filarmónica Mexicana in 1866, from which emerged the Cons. de Música six months later. This cons. became the National Cons. of Music of Mexico, Mexico City, at which León was appointed professor of piano.

Works: Jarabe Nacional, for piano; *Cuatro Danzas Habaneras; Sara,* mazurka; *Una Flor para Ti,* mazurka; *Pensamiento Poético,* melodic capriccio; nocturnes; songs.

Source: GMM

Leonardo, Luisa, Brazilian pianist, actress, writer, teacher, and composer; b.22 Oct 1859, Rio de Janeiro, Brazil; d.12 Jun 1926, Salvador, Brazil. She started to study piano with Isidoro Bevilacqua and later with Antoine François Marmontel, and harmony and composition with Albert Lavignac and Anton Rubinstein at the Paris Cons., Paris, France.

Works (selective list): *Marcha Fúnebre,* march (1892); *Hino a Carlos Gómez,* for orch. (1903); chamber music; piano pieces; songs.

Sources: IEW, NGDWC

Letelier Llona, Alfonso, Chilean composer and agronomic engineer; b.4 Oct 1912, Santiago de Chile, Chile; d.27 Aug 1994, Santiago de Chile. He studied composition with Pedro Humberto Allende and piano with Raúl Hügel at the Cons. of Music of the Univ. of Chile, Santiago de Chile. Founder, together with René Amengual, Juan Orrego Salas, and Elena Waiss, and director of the Escuela Moderna de Música of Santiago de Chile. From 1946, professor of harmony at the Cons. of Music, and from 1952 to 1962, dean of the Faculty of Fine Arts, both of the Univ. of Chile. Vice provost of the Univ. of Chile from 1958 to 1962. Member of the Academia de Bellas Artes of the Inst. de Chile. Director of the Dept. of Musical Education of the Secretary of Education. In 1986, he was appointed dean of the Facultad de Artes y Educación Física of the Univ. Metropolitana de Ciencias de la Educación, Santiago de Chile. Director of the *Revista Musical Chilena.*

Works (selective list): *Stage: La Magdalena,* opera (1930); *La Historia de Tobías y Sara,* opera-oratorio (1955). *Orch.: Pequeña Suite* (1928-29); *Misa Solemne,* for soloists, harp, organ, and strings (1930); *Balada y Canción,* for voice (1936); *Vida del Campo,* for piano (1937); *Canciones de Cuna,* for female voice (1939); *Suite Grotesca* (1946); *Sonetos de la Muerte,* for female voice (1943-48); *Vitrales de la Anunciación,* for soprano, female chorus, and chamber orch. (1950); *Divertimento* (1955); *Aculeu,* suite (1955-56); Guitar concerto (1960); *Preludios Vegetales* (1967-68); *Tres Canciones,* for female voice and 16 instruments (1974). Choruses; chamber music; piano pieces; songs.

Sources: BB, CTA2, DCM, DM, HMC, ISC, MLA, MMLA

Letelier Valdés, Miguel Francisco, Chilean composer and organist; b.29 Sep 1939, Santiago de Chile, Chile. He studied harmony, counterpoint, and organ with Julio Perceval at the National Cons. of the Univ. of Chile, Santiago de Chile, and composition with Alberto Ginastera at the Latin American Center for Advanced Musical Studies of Buenos Aires, Argentina. He also studied with Maurice Le Roux and Iannis Xenakis in Buenos Aires, with Max Deutsch in Paris, France, and with Diether de la Motte in Hamburg, Germany.

Works (selective list): *Instantes,* 5 pieces for orch. (1966); Concerto for 2 pianos, percussion, and string orch. (1970); music for solo instruments; chamber music; choruses.

Source: DCM

Levy, Alexandre, Brazilian composer; b.10 Nov 1864, Sâo Paulo, Brazil; d.17 Jan 1892, Sâo Paulo. Brother of Luis Henrique Levy. He studied with Luiz Maurice and Gabriel Giraudon, and later took classes in harmony with Georg von Mandeweiss and Gustavo Wertheimer. In France, he studied with Emil Durand and Vicenzo Ferroni. Founder of the *Haydn Club* in Sâo Paulo in 1883.

Works (selective list): Symphony in E; *Comala,* symphonic poem; *Hymne au 14 Juillet,* for orch.; *Suite Brasileira,* for orch.; *Variaçôes sobre un Tema Brasileiro* for orch.; *Fantasía sôbre Motivos do Guaraní,* for piano; *Schumannianas,* for piano; *Tango Brasileiro,* for piano; *Samba,* for piano; chamber music; piano pieces; songs.

Bibl.: G. Pimenta, *Alexandre Lévy,* Sâo Paulo, 1911. R. Almeida, *Compendio de História da Música Brasileira,* Rio de Janeiro, 1947. G. Béhague, *The Beginning of Musical Nationalism in Brazil,* Detroit, 1971.
Sources: BB, DM, GDM, HMB, MLA, MMLA

Levy, Luis Henrique, Brazilian composer and pianist; b.8 Aug 1861, Sâo Paulo, Brazil; d.8 Aug 1935, Rio de Janeiro, Brazil. Brother of Alexandre Levy. He studied piano with Gabriel Giraudon. Founding member of the *Haydn Club* in Sâo Paulo in 1883.
Works: Many compositions for the piano.
Source: EMB

Ley, Salvador, Guatemalan composer and pianist; b.2 Jan 1907, Guatemala City, Guatemala. He studied in Guatemala with Herculano Alvarado and Louis Roche. At the age of fifteen he went to Berlin, Germany, where he studied piano with Georg Bertram and theory and other music disciplines with Hugo Leichentritt, Wilhelm Klatte, and Oscar Guttmann at the Hochschule für Musik. In Poland, he furthered his piano studies with Egon Petri. He returned to Guatemala in 1934, and was appointed director of the National Cons. of Guatemala, Guatemala City, a position he occupied until 1937. In 1938, he became teacher of piano at the same cons., where in 1944, he was again appointed director. In 1953, he settled in the USA and became professor at the Westchester Cons. in New York.
Works (selective list): *Lera,* opera (1959); *Serenade,* for strings (1949); *Obertura Jocosa,* for orch. (1950); Concertante for viola and string orch. (1962); Concerto for piano and chamber orch.; piano pieces; songs.
Sources: BB, CTA12, DCM, DM, GDM, MLA, MMLA

Lichius, Father Santiago, Argentine composer and lecturer of German origin; b.4 Feb 1877, Eitorf, Prov. of the Rhine, Germany; d.? He settled in Argentina in 1900. He studied music in Vienna, Austria, where he also was ordained a priest in 1900. He occupied many ecclesiastic positions in religious schools and seminaries.
Works (selective list): *Sacred music:* 24 masses with organ; 19 Eucharistic motets; 22 Ave Marias; 2 Magnificat; 8 Stabat Mater; 9 Te Deum; 10 Requiem masses. *Los Enanos,* melodrama; 176 school songs; pieces for violin and piano. *Books:* 20 on music.
Sources: CA, EMA

Lienas, Juan de, Mexican composer of Spanish origin?; b.c.1550 Spain?; fl.in Mexico between 1620 and 1650.

Works: Mass for 5 voices and bass; *Magnificat Primi Toni*, for 8 voices; *Magnificat Tertii Toni*, for 5 voices and bass; Requiem for 5 voices and bass; 2 Lamentaciones.
Bibl.: R. Stevenson, *Renaissance and Baroque Musical Sources in the Americas*, Washington, D.C., 1970.
Source: GDM

Lifchitz, Max, Mexican composer, conductor, and pianist; b.11 Nov 1948, Mexico City, Mexico. He settled in the USA in 1974. He studied composition with Luciano Berio and conducting with Dennis Russell Davies at The Juilliard School of Music in New York City. He received a BM in composition in 1970, and an MS in composition in 1971. He also studied composition with Darius Milhaud and Charles Jones at Aspen Music School, Colorado, from 1967 to 1968, and with Jacob Druckman, Bruno Maderna, Elliot Carter, and Earl Kim at Tanglewood/Berkshire Music Center, Massachusetts, in 1972. From 1971 to 1974, he completed course work leading toward the Ph.D. in composition at Harvard Univ., Cambridge, Massachusetts, under Leon Kirchner, Earl Kim, and Arthur Berger. Teacher at The Juilliard School of Music, the Manhattan School of Music, the Columbia Univ. Dept. of Music, all in New York City, and at Harvard Univ. Dept. of Music. Associate professor at the State Univ. of New York at Albany since 1986.
Works (selective list): **Orch.**: *Intervención* (1976); *Yellow Ribbons No.8 and No.9* (1982); *Yellow Ribbons No.17 and No.18* (1983); Piano concerto (1989). **Chamber orch.**: *Tiempos* (1969); *Globos* (1971); *Roberta* (1972); *Sueños* (1974); *Exploitations* (1975); *Yellow Ribbons No.11 and No.12* (1982); *Night Voices No.5* (1984), *No.6* (1985), *and No.10* (1989). Chamber music; music for percussion; piano pieces; music for solo instruments; vocal music; music for band.
Source: ISC

Lima, Emirto de, Colombian composer; b.25 Jan 1893, Barranquilla, Colombia; d.? He studied violin with Mario Castellani, piano with Angelo Gasparini, harmony and counterpoint with Giuseppe Pietri, and composition with Lorenzo Parodi at the Liceo Musicale Amilcare Zanella of Genoa, Italy. Later, he studied harmony with Achille Philip, counterpoint with Triconi, composition with Vincent D'Indy, organ with Pineau, and violin with Claveau and Armand Parent at the Schola Cantorum of Paris, France. He taught at various private and public music schools. Music critic for various Colombian publications, including the newspaper *El Heraldo* of Barranquilla. He was also in the diplomatic service.

Works: *El Club de los Solteros,* operetta; *Sonatina,* fantasia-ballet; Concerto for piano and orch.; *Poema Indio,* for orch.; String quartet; *Danzas Colombianas,* for violin and piano. **Books:** *El Arte Musical en Colombia,* 1916; *La Fiesta de la Música Catalana,* 1918; *Crónicas Musicales,* 1924; *Folklore Colombiano,* 1942.
Sources: DM, MLA, MMLA

Lins de Vasconcelos Chaves, Paulino, Brazilian pianist and composer; b. 26 Jun 1883, Natal, Brazil; d.31 Jul 1948, Rio de Janeiro, Brazil. Professor at the Escuela Nacional de Música of Rio de Janeiro.
Works (selective list): Symphony in E minor; *Ave Maria; Preludio e Fuga in D minor*; songs.
Source: MMLA

Llamozas, Salvador N., Venezuelan pianist, composer, and music critic; b.29 Oct 1854, Cumaná, Venezuela; d.? Studied piano with José Antonio Gómez Cardiel. In 1874, he published a music journal *Album Lírico.* Editor of the art journal *La Lira Venezolana.* Member of the Academia del Inst. de Bellas Artes in Caracas, Venezuela.
Works: *Noches de Cumaná,* for piano; *Himno a la Caridad,* for piano; *Dos Romanzas,* for voice and piano; piano pieces.
Source: MMLA

Lluán, Claudio, Argentine composer and double bass player; b.1957, Rosario, Prov. of Santa Fe, Argentina. Studied composition with Virtú Maragno and Marta Varela, and double bass with Norberto Nofri at the Escuela de Música de la Facultad de Humanidades y Artes of the National Univ. of Rosario. He continued his music studies with Dante Grela and Francisco Kröpfl. Professor at the Escuela de Música of the National Univ., the Escuela Nacional de Música, and the Inst. Nacional del Profesorado de Música, all of Rosario. Vice president of the Asociación Santafesina de Compositores and member of the *Agrupación Nueva Música* of Rosario.
Works: *Cinco Naditas,* for string quartet (1979); *Vidala de los Tiempos Muertos* (1980); *Música,* for double bass and piano (1984); *Estudio Cinético No.1,* for electronic sounds (1987); *Vestigios,* electroacoustic music (1991).
Source: CAMR

Lôbo, Elías Alvares, Brazilian composer; b.9 Aug 1834, Itu, Sâo Paulo, Brazil; d.15 Dec 1901, Sâo Paulo. Self-taught in music. Professor of music at the Escola Normal de Sâo Paulo.

Works (selective list): *Missa de Sâo Pedro de Alcântara* (1858); *A Noite de Sâo Joâo,* opera (1860); *A Louca,* opera; church music; salon pieces (modinhas and lundus).
Sources: GDM, HMB

Lombardi, Enrique, Argentine composer, chorus conductor, organist, and musicologist; b.5 Aug 1922, Ensenada, Prov. of Buenos Aires, Argentina. He studied at the Facultad de Bellas Artes of the National Univ. of La Plata, Prov. of Buenos Aires, from which he graduated in 1953. Ordained a priest in 1948. Professor of Gregorian chant in the courses of Catholic culture of the Escuela Superior de Bellas Artes of La Plata. Editor of the publication *Psallite,* devoted exclusively to sacred music. Founder and director of several choirs.
Works (selective list): *Música Incidental para Cada Uno; Misa Pascual; Misa Natalicia; Misa de Requiem;* Concerto in E major for organ and orch.; *Tríptico,* for organ and orch.; *Breve Fantasía,* for orch.; choral music. **Books:** *Jubilate Deo; Manual de Canto Gregoriano; Cultura Musical; La Música Sagrada.*
Source: VMA

López Buchardo, Carlos, Argentine composer; b.12 Oct 1881, Buenos Aires, Argentina; d.21 Apr 1948, Buenos Aires. Brother of Próspero López Buchardo. He began studies of piano and violin with Héctor Bellucci, and later he continued with Alfonso Thibaud. He studied harmony with Constantino Gaito and Luis Forino in Buenos Aires, and composition with Albert Roussel in Paris, France. In 1916, he was appointed president of the Asociación Wagneriana of Buenos Aires, a position that he held for 32 years. Director of the Art Inst. of the Teatro Colón of Buenos Aires. In 1923, he was appointed the first director of the Escuela Superior de Bellas Artes of the National Univ. of La Plata, Prov. of Buenos Aires, Argentina. In 1924, he created the National Cons. of Music of Buenos Aires, which, after his death, was named after him. Member of the Board of Directors of the Teatro Colón.
Works (selective list): **Stage:** *Il Sogno di Alma,* opera (1914); *Madama Lynch,* lyric comedy (1932); *La Perichona,* lyric comedy (1933); *Romeo y Julieta,* incidental music (1934); *Amalia,* musical comedy (1935). *Escenas Argentinas,* symphonic poem (1920); choruses; sacred music; piano pieces; songs.
Bibl.: A. Jurafsky, *Carlos López Buchardo,* Buenos Aires, 1966.
Sources: BB, CA, CTA12, DM, EMA, GDM, MLA, MMLA

López Buchardo, Próspero, Argentine composer and painter; b.2 Jul 1883, Buenos Aires, Argentina; d.1964, Buenos Aires. Brother of Carlos López Buchardo. He studied music with Luis Forino and Carlos Marchal. He also studied painting in Paris, France.

Works (selective list): String quartet (1934); *Evocaciones,* musical triptych for orch. and chorus (1935); *Plenilunio,* poem for orch. (1936); *Alí Babá,* ballet pantomime (1937); Sonatina for piano (1938); *Nidos,* suite for piano and orch. (1939); Sonata for cello and piano (1943); piano pieces; songs.
Sources: DM, EMA

López Capillas, Francisco, Mexican composer and organist of Spanish origin?; b.c.1615, Andalusia?, Spain; d.18 Jan or 7 Feb, 1673, Mexico City, Mexico. He studied with Juan de Riscos, who was *maestro de capilla* (chapelmaster) in Jaén, Spain. He settled in Mexico in 1641 and was hired as organist and bassoonist at the choir of the Cathedral of Puebla, under Juan Gutiérrez de Padilla, and in 1647, he was appointed principal organist. In 1654, he was appointed *maestro de capilla* (chapelmaster) and organist at the Cathedral of Mexico City.
Works: 8 masses; 8 Magnificat; 15 motets; hymns.
Bibl.: R. Stevenson, *Renaissance and Baroque Musical Sources in the Americas,* Washington, D.C., 1970. R. Stevenson, *Francisco López Capillas, Heterofonía,* Vol.6, 1973. L. Brothers, *A New World Hexachord Mass by Francisco López Capillas, Yearbook for Inter-American Musical Research,* Vol.9, 1973.
Source: GDM

López de la Rosa, Horacio, Argentine composer; b.26 Oct 1933, Buenos Aires, Argentina. He studied piano with Oreste Castronuovo and composition with Julián Bautista. He also studied at the National Cons. of Music Carlos López Buchardo of Buenos Aires. Founding member of the Asociación de Jóvenes Compositores de la Argentina and the Unión de Compositores de la Argentina. Professor of composition at the National Cons. of Music Carlos López Buchardo and at the Prov. Cons. Juan José Castro, Prov. of Buenos Aires, Argentina.
Works (selective list): *Tempi,* for orch. (1960); *Salmo CXXVII,* for female chorus and chamber orch. (1961); *Tres Cantos de Dios,* for 2 narrators and orch. (1963); *Tempi,* for orch. (1963); *Tercer Surrealismo,* for orch. (1964); *Camaruco,* ballet (1964-65); *Cantata para mi País,* for narrator, soprano, chorus, and chamber orch. (1966); chamber music; choruses; piano pieces; organ pieces; songs.
Sources: EMA, VMA

López Mindreau, Ernesto, Peruvian composer; b.17 Jun 1890, Chiclayo, Peru; d.1971, Peru. He studied with Federico Gerdes at the Academy of Music of Lima, Peru. Later, he went to New York where he took some piano lessons with Sergei Rachmaninoff and Sigismund

Stojowsky at the Inst. of Musical Art. In 1920, with a subsidy from the Peruvian government, he went to Germany to the Hochschule für Musik in Berlin, where he studied piano with Xaver Scharwenka, and composition and orchestration with Hugo Leichtentritt. In Panama City, he founded the Panama Cons. of Music where he also taught piano, and the Saint Mary Academy in the Canal Zone, both in Panama. In 1929, he was appointed director of music of the Peruvian Army. Professor of music at the National Univ. of Peru, Lima, Peru. In 1940, he founded the Academia de Música Scharwenka in Trujillo, Peru.

Works (selective list): *Nueva Castilla,* opera (1926), later titled *Cajamarca; Francisco Pizarro,* opera (1943); *Tema y Variaciones*, for piano and orch. (1936); *La Misa al Señor de la Caña de Chiclín* (1945); chamber music; piano pieces; popular and indigenous pieces; songs; school songs.

Sources: ADBM, DM, MLA, MMLA

López Rovirosa, María Isabel, Cuban composer; b.8 Jul 1912, Havana, Cuba. She studied harmony and composition with José Ardévol, whom she later married.

Works: Dos Canciones Corales (1934); *Fanfarria,* for small orch.; *Preludio y Allegro,* for string orch. (1935); Suite for flute, oboe, bassoon, violin, viola, cello, and piano (1938).

Sources: IEW, MMLA

Lopszyc, Eva Irene, Argentine composer, conductor, and pianist; b.1 Oct 1956, Buenos Aires, Argentina. She studied composition with Jacobo Ficher and Augusto Rattenbach, and also with Roberto García Morillo at the Municipal Cons. of Music Manuel de Falla of Buenos Aires, where she also studied orch. conducting with Adela Marshall, Alfonso Stagno, and Miguel Angel Gilardi; she continued conducting lessons with Mario Benzecry at the National Cons. of Music Carlos López Buchardo of Buenos Aires. She also studied piano, first with her mother, Tatiana V. de Lopszyc, and later with Elsa Piaggio de Tarelli. In 1985, she was appointed assistant professor in orch. conducting and conductor of the orch. of the Municipal Cons. of Music Manuel de Falla. Conductor of the vocational chamber orch. of the Escuela Municipal de Bellas Artes Carlos Morel of Quilmes, Prov. of Buenos Aires, Argentina. Since 1989 she has been director of the *Grupo de Música Contemporánea* of the Municipal Cons. of Music Manuel de Falla.

Works (selective list): Sinfonietta for chamber orch. (1983-84); *Dramáticas,* for tenor and chamber ensemble (1984); *Obertura*, for orch. (1984); *En Esta Tierra Oscura*, for soprano, mixed chorus, and orch. (1984-85); *Alfa Libre,* for instrumental ensemble (1989);

Aphéticos, for soprano, clarinet, cello, piano, and crotales (1990-91); chamber music; music for solo instruments; piano pieces; choruses; songs.
Source: ISC

Loyola, José, Cuban flutist and composer; b.12 Feb 1941, Cienfuegos, Cuba. He studied flute with Roberto Ondina and Emigdio Mayo at the National School for the Arts of Havana, Cuba, and later he studied composition at the Escuela Superior de Música of Warsaw, Poland, with Witold Rufzinski. Vice provost of education and professor of composition and musical analysis at the Inst. Superior de Arte of Havana.
Works: *Música*, for flute and strings (1970); *Música Viva No.1*, for percussion instruments (1972); *Tres Imágenes Poéticas*, for baritone and piano (1972); *Música Viva No.2*, for orch.; *Monzón y el Rey de Koré*, opera (1973); *Cantata a los Mártires del 5 de Septiembre*, for narrator, chorus, and orch. (1974); *Poética del Guerrillero*, for voice and orch., dedicated to Ernesto (Che) Guevara (1976); *Homenaje a Brindis de Salas*, for solo violin (1975).
Source: DMC

Luc, María Eugenia, Argentine composer; b.6 Dec 1958, Rosario, Prov. of Santa Fe, Argentina. She began music studies in 1976 at the Escuela de Música de la Facultad de Humanidades y Artes of the National Univ. of Rosario. Later she continued her studies with Dante Grela, Francisco Kröpfl, Daniel Sueiro, Julio Viera, and María del Carmen Aguilar. Professor at the Municipal Cons. of Music Manuel de Falla, the Univ. del Salvador, the National Univ., and the Collegium Musicum, all of Buenos Aires. Founding member of the Asociación Santafesina de Compositores, and member of the *Grupo Otras Músicas* and the *Grupo Ars Contemporánea*.
Source: CAMR

Luengo, María Teresa, Argentine composer and musicologist; b.25 Nov 1940, Quilmes, Prov. of Buenos Aires, Argentina. She studied at the Facultad de Artes y Ciencias Musicales of the Argentine Catholic Univ., Buenos Aires, Argentina, from which she graduated with a Licenciate degree in musicology, music criticism, and composition. She studied composition with Alberto Ginastera, Luis Gianneo, Roberto Caamaño, and Gerardo Gandini, and musicology with Carlos Vega and Lauro Ayestarán. She taught various music disciplines at the Escuela Municipal de Bellas Artes of Quilmes, the Escuela de Musicoterapia of the Medical School of the Univ. of El Salvador of Buenos Aires, the Facultad de Artes y Ciencias Musicales of the Argentine Catholic Univ., and Facultad de Bellas Artes of the

National Univ. of La Plata, Prov. of Buenos Aires. Director of the Music Dept. of the Escuela Municipal de Bellas Artes of Quilmes. *Works* (selective list): *Cuatro Soles,* for flute, oboe, cello, piano, and percussion (1973); *Del Museo Imaginario,* for violin, viola, cello, piano, and percussion (1975); *El Libro de los Espejos,* for 2 flutes, clarinet, violin, viola, cello, piano, and percussion (1976); *Seis Imágenes Mágicas,* for flute, clarinet, cello, and percussion (1978); Music for the film *Taumanía* (1987); chamber music; piano pieces. *Sources:* ISC, NGDWC

Luna, Adolfo V., Argentine guitarist, teacher, and composer; b.24 Mar 1889, La Rioja, Prov. of La Rioja, Argentina; d.1970, Argentina. He studied music with Armando Schiuma and guitar with Domingo Prat. He taught guitar for many years to many students. *Works* (selective list): 3 sonatinas for guitar; Sonata for guitar and string quintet; *El Milagro del Agua,* ballet; *Serie Argentina,* for violin and piano; *Escenas Norteñas,* for piano; songs; piano pieces; many pieces for the guitar and for voice and guitar, as well as transcriptions for this instrument. *Sources:* CA, EMA

Luna de Espaillat, Margarita, Dominican composer, pianist, and organist; b.31 Jul 1921, Santiago, Dominican Republic. She began her music studies with Juan Francisco García, and later she continued studying piano with Manuel Rueda G., organ with Juan Urteaga, and harmony, counterpoint, and fugue with Manuel Simó. From 1964 to 1967, she studied composition in New York with Hal Overton at The Juilliard School of Music. Director of the Liceo de Música and the chorus of the Catholic Univ., both in Santiago. Professor at the National Cons. of Santo Domingo, Dominican Republic. *Works* (selective list): *Tres Preludios*, for string orch. (1964); *Cambiantes*, for cello and chamber orch. (1967); *Vigilia Eterna*, oratorio for narrator, soloists, mixed chorus, male chorus, and orch. (1967); *Epitafio en el Aire,* elegy for narrator, mixed chorus, and orch. (1970); *Cantata al Padre de la Patria,* for narrator, chorus, and orch. (1976); chamber music; piano pieces; songs. *Sources:* CTA19, IBCC, IEW

Luzuriaga, Diego, Ecuadorian composer and architect; b.1955, Loja, Ecuador. He studied at the National Cons. of Music and the Cons. Superior de Música, both of Quito, Ecuador, and at the Escuela Normal de Música of Paris, France. *Works:* *Felipillo,* for percussion and orch. *Source:* PEFCM

Luzzatti, Arturo, Argentine composer, pianist, conductor, and teacher of Italian origin; b.24 May 1875, Turin, Italy; d.25 Jun 1959, Buenos Aires, Argentina. He studied at the Verdi Cons. in Milan, Italy. From 1912 to 1913, he conducted the orch. of the Opera of Boston, Massachusetts. From 1925 to 1926, he conducted the orch. of the Teatro Colón of Buenos Aires. Pianist of the *Trío Buenos Aires*. Professor of counterpoint and fugue at the National Cons. of Music Carlos López Buchardo of Buenos Aires.

Works (selective list): *Afrodita,* opera (1928); *Judith,* ballet (1938); *Salomón,* oratorio (1942); 2 symphonies; *El Jardín Voluptuoso,* symphonic poem; *Noche Veneciana,* symphonic poem; Concerto for piano and orch.; Concerto for violin and orch.; chamber music; songs; pieces for piano.

Sources:. CA, DM, EMA, MLA

M

Macedo, Manuel Joaquín, Brazilian composer and violinist; b.1847, Cantagalo, Prov. of Rio de Janeiro, Brazil; d.3 Dec 1925, Cataguases, Brazil. He studied violin with Hubert Léonard and Henri Vieuxtemps, and harmony with Adolphe Fétis in Brussels, Belgium. In 1871, he went back to Brazil where he was offered a position at the Royal Chapel.
Works: More than 300 compositions, rarely performed, mostly unkown, including the opera *Tiradentes.*
Source: MMLA

Machado, Alberto José, Argentine composer and music critic; b.1881, DM (1882, EMA), Buenos Aires, Argentina; d.1929, Buenos Aires. He studied with Alberto Williams and Julián Aguirre. In Paris, France, he furthered his studies with Nicola D'Arienzo and Giovanni Sgambati.
Works (selective list): *El Nilo,* symphonic poem; *Suite Antigua,* for string orch.; *Ananke,* lyric interlude; 2 masses for 3 and 6 mixed voices; Sonata for piano; Sonata for viola and piano; Sonata for violin and piano; Sonata for cello and piano; piano pieces; songs.
Sources: DM, EMA

Machado, Luis Angel, Argentine organist, composer, and teacher; b.1922, Correa, Prov. of Santa Fe, Argentina. He received his education at the Seminaries of Santa Fe, Prov. of Santa Fe, and La Plata, Prov. of Buenos Aires, Argentina, where he was ordained a Catholic priest. He furthered his musical studies with Juan Carlos Paz and Teodoro Fuchs. Professor of Gregorian chant at the Seminary San José of La Plata, the Seminary of Rosario, Prov. of Santa Fe, and at the National Univ. of Litoral, Rosario. Professor of harmony and composition at the *Asociación Amigos del Arte* of Rosario. In 1970, he settled in Buenos Aires, Argentina.
Works: Gozos de Santa María, for voice and piano; Sonata for piano; *Madrigales de Navidad,* for chorus a cappella; *Toccata and Fugue,* for 2 guitars.
Source: EMA

Mackenna Subercaseaux, Carmela, Chilean pianist and composer; b.1879, Santiago de Chile, Chile; d.31 Jan 1962, Santiago de Chile. She studied music theory with Bindo Paoli in Santiago de Chile, and piano with Konrade Ansorge and composition with Hans Mersmann in Berlin, Germany.

Works: Piano concerto (1934); *Dos Movimientos Sinfónicos,* for orch. (1935); Mass for chorus and string orch.; chamber music; sacred music; piano pieces; songs.
Sources: HMC, IBCC, IEW, MLA, NGDWC

Macridimas, Dimitri, Argentine composer and doctor in jurisprudence of Greek and Italian origin; b.1900, Trieste, Italy; d.1956, Buenos Aires, Argentina. He settled in Buenos Aires in 1939. He studied in Vienna, Austria, with Félix Weingartner.
Works (selective list): *Operas: Agamemnon*; *Mogreb*; *Los Amores de don Perimplín y Belisa en su Jardín*; 3 string quartets; *Cantatas de Primavera*, for chorus a cappella; songs.
Source: EMA

Madina, Francisco de, Argentine composer and Lateran priest of Spanish origin; b.1907, Oñate, Spain. He settled in Buenos Aires, Argentina. He studied in Burgos, Spain, with José de Beobide, and in Buenos Aires with Gilardo Gilardi.
Works (selective list): *Flor de Durazno,* lyric poem; *La Cadena de Oro,* mystery for organ, chorus, and orch.; *Cantata Pascual,* for soloists, female chorus, and orch.; *Salmo XCV,* for organ and chorus; *Tríptico de Navidad,* for organ and orch.; 4 masses for 3 voices and organ; *Misa de Requiem,* for organ and orch.; 2 string quartets; Trio; Sonata for violin and piano; Sonata for organ; songs; school songs.
Source: EMA

Mahle, Ernest, Brazilian composer, conductor, and teacher of German origin; b.3 Jan 1929, Stuttgart, Germany. He settled in Brazil in 1951. He studied in Stuttgart with Nepomuk David and in Sâo Paulo, Brazil, with Hans Joachim Koellreutter. He also took some post graduate courses in Europe with Olivier Messiaen, Ernst Krenek, and Rafael Kubelik.
Works (selective list): *Maroquinhas Fru Fru,* opera; Sinfonietta (1957); *Sinfonía em un Movimento* (1974); 4 trios; 3 string quartets; Brass quintet (1975); chamber music; songs.
Source: HMB

Maiguashca, Mesías, Ecuadorian composer; b.1938, Quito, Ecuador. He studied at the National Cons. of Music of Quito. Later he studied at the Eastman School of Music, Rochester, New York, where he received a Master's degree in piano and composition in 1963. Also took courses in composition at the Latin American Center of Advanced Music Studies of the Inst. Di Tella of Buenos Aires, Argentina, with Olivier Messiaen and Alberto Ginastera, and in electronic music at the Hochschule für Musik in Cologne, Germany,

with Herbert Eimert and Karlheinz Stockhausen. Professor of composition at the National Cons. of Music of Quito.
Works (selective list): Concertino for clarinet and chamber orch. (1962); *Huacayñán,*.for orch. (1962); *Quiet Music,*.for orch. (1963); *...Y Ahora Vamos por Aquí,* for magnetic tape and 8 instruments; *Intensidad y Altura,* for percussion and electroacoustic sounds; choruses; chamber music; piano pieces; concrete and electronic music; songs.
Sources: CTA17, PEFCM

Maiztegui, Isidro, Argentine composer; b.14 Jul 1905, Gualeguay, Prov. of Entre Ríos, Argentina. He started to study music at the Beethoven Cons. of Gualeguay, and continued to study harmony, counterpoint, and composition with Athos Palma and José André at the National Cons. of Music Carlos López Buchardo of Buenos Aires, Argentina. Assistant conductor at the Teatro Colón of Buenos Aires, 1931-39. Professor and subdirector of the Music Cons. of the National Univ. of Cuyo, Mendoza, Prov. of Mendoza, Argentina, 1940-43. Chorus director at the National Board of Education and the *Galician Society Terra Nosa,* both in Buenos Aires.
Works (selective list): *Levana y las Tres Tristezas,* ballet (1947); *Romance de la Niña Negra,* ballet; *Mazias o Namorado,* staged cantata for soprano, tenor, chorus, and orch. (1956); *Danza Exótica,* for orch. (1936); *Media Caña,* for orch. (1936); *Gran Vals,* for orch. (1937); *Homenaje a Cuatro Vihuelistas Españoles del Siglo XVI,* for guitar and strings (1967); chamber music; piano pieces; songs; incidental music for many movies.
Sources: CA, DM, EMA

Malcher, José Cándido da Gama, Brazilian composer and teacher; b.1853, Pará, Belém, Brazil; d.1921, Brazil. He studied in Milan, Italy. Professor at the Cons. and the Escuela Normal, both of Pará.
Works: *Bug Jargal,* opera (1890); *Iara,* opera (1895); *Idilio* and *Seminarista,* unfinished operas.
Source: MMLA

Malcolm, Carlos, Cuban composer; b.24 Nov 1945, Guanabacoa, Cuba. He studied piano with Juan M. Quiñones and Sonia Montalvo, and composition with Federico Smith. He also studied at the Cons. Amadeo Roldán of Havana, Cuba.
Works: Montaje Contornos, for narrator, chorus, and orch.; *Estudios,* for piano; *Marionetas; Allegro en Son,* for wind quintet; *Tonos de Orquesta; Fragmentos,* for piano; *Oposiciones-Cambios,* for 3 pianos and percussion.
Source: DMC

Malsio, José, Peruvian composer and conductor; b.2 Sep 1924, Bellavista, Peru. He studied in Lima, Peru, and in the USA: Eastman School of Music, Rochester, New York, Yale Univ., New Haven, Connecticut, and Harvard Univ., Cambridge, Massachusetts; he was a student of Paul Hindemith and Arnold Schoenberg. Professor and director of the Cons. of Music of Lima.
Works (selective list): *Rondo Concertante,* for orch.; Concerto grosso; chamber music; piano pieces.
Source: KTL

Mambretti, Mabel, Argentine composer and musicologist; b.29 Nov 1942, Buenos Aires, Argentina She began to study piano, solfeggio, and music theory with Helvecia Braga and Elizabeth Bagnes. She studied at the National Cons. of Music Carlos López Buchardo of Buenos Aires and at the Argentine Catholic Univ. of Buenos Aires, from which she graduated in 1968 with a Licenciate degree in music. In addition, she studied with Alberto Ginastera, Luis Gianneo, Roberto Caamaño, Juan Carlos Paz, Gerardo Gandini, Yannis Ioannidis, and Antonio Estévez, and with several musicologists from Argentina, Venezuela, and Uruguay, and took classes with Robert Stevenson and Francisco Curt Lange. From 1969 to 1983, she resided in Caracas, Venezuela, where she was the director of the Dept. of Music of the Inter-American Inst. of Ethnomusicology and professor at the National Inst. of Folklore of Venezuela. Since 1990, she has been professor at the National Cons. of Music Carlos López Buchardo.
Works (selective list): *String orch.:* Concertino (1967); *Secuencias Libres* (1976); *Secuencias Integradas* (1978); *Divertimento* (1989). Choral music; chamber music; piano pieces; songs.
Source: ISC

Mancilla, Mauricio, Bolivian conductor of military bands and composer; b.1846, La Paz, Bolivia; d.1879, La Paz.
Works: Many marches including *Colorados de Bolivia.*
Source: CB

Mansilla de García, Eduarda, Argentine singer, music critic, and composer; b.1835, Buenos Aires, Argentina; d.1892, Buenos Aires. Music critic for *La Gaceta Musical* of Buenos Aires.
Works: *Brunette,* ballad for piano; *October,* romance for voice and piano; *Se Alquila,* bolero; *Yo no Se si te Quiero,* song; *Cantares.*
Source: EMA

Maragno, Virtú, Argentine composer, choral conductor, and teacher; b.18 Mar 1928, Santa Fe, Prov. of Santa Fe, Argentina. He began music studies in Santa Fe, piano with Angélica Mora de Paraván and

composition with Emilio Piselli. In Buenos Aires, Argentina, he studied piano with Vicente Scaramuzza and Antonio De Raco, and composition with Luis Gianneo. In 1959, he studied in Italy, composition with Goffredo Petrassi in Rome, choral conducting with Santa Zanon in Venice, and electronic music with Bruno Maderna at the Inst. de Fonología in Milan. Professor at the National Univ. of Litoral, Rosario, and the National Univ. of Rosario, Prov. of Santa Fe, and at the National Univ. of La Plata, Prov. of Buenos Aires, Argentina. President of Juventudes Musicales de la Argentina.
Works (selective list): **Orch:** *Cantata de la Vida Nueva,* for soloists, chorus (1951-52); Concertino for piano (1954); *Laudes Creaturarum,* for chorus (1968); *Composición No.1,* for voice, instruments, and magnetic tape (1962); *Crónica de los que Van a Morir,* for narrator and string orch. (1966); *Diálogos sin Voz,* for piano (1968); *Triste y Danza* (1947); *Tres Piezas,* for string orch. (1952); *Scherzo Sinfónico* (1952); *Movimiento Sinfónico* (1960); *Combinaciones y Diferencias* (1960); *Expresión* (1962); *Intensidad y Espacio* (1962); *Ricercare Fantasía* (1968); *Ecce Homo* (1969); Symphony (1970). *Divertimento,* for wind quintet (1952); *Baladas Amarillas,* for soprano and 5 instruments (1952); 2 string quartets (1959, 1961); *Asénticas,* for 11 instruments (1960); *Synapsis,* for violin and percussion (1966); chamber music; choruses; piano pieces; songs.
Sources: BB, CA, CTA8, EMA

Maranzano, José Ramón, Argentine composer; b.1940, Santiago del Estero, Prov. of Santiago del Estero, Argentina. He studied composition with Alberto Ginastera, Gerardo Gandini, Francisco Kröpfl, and Roberto Caamaño at the School of Musical Arts and Sciences of the Argentine Catholic Univ. of Buenos Aires, Argentina. He was awarded a scholarship at the Centro Latino Americano de Altos Estudios Musicales of the Inst. Di Tella of Buenos Aires, from 1969 to 1970.
Works: String quartet I; *Pequeño Tríptico,* for 2 pianos and percussion.
Source: EMA

Marcelli, Nino, Chilean composer; b.21 Jan 1890, Santiago de Chile, Chile; d.16 Aug 1967, San Diego, California, USA. He studied at the National Cons. of Santiago de Chile. In 1920, he went to the USA and played cello at the San Francisco Symphony Orch., California. In 1927, he organized the San Diego Symphony Orch., which he conducted until 1937.
Works: *Suite Araucana,* based on Chilean Indian folklore; marches; overtures.
Source: BB

Marchal, Carlos, Argentine composer of Belgian origin; b.1867, Brussels, Belgium; d.1946, Buenos Aires, Argentina. He studied at the Royal Cons. of Music of Brussels with the cellist Jacobs, and later with Joseph Servais and Jenö Hubay. In 1888, he was hired by the Argentine government to teach cello and chamber music at the National Cons. of Córdoba, Prov. of Córdoba, Argentina. In 1891, he moved to Buenos Aires to work as *maestro de capilla* (chapelmaster) at the Lacordaire College. Professor at the National Cons. of Music Carlos López Buchardo of Buenos Aires.
Works (selective list): 2 rhapsodies for cello, violin, and piano; *Seis Piezas Melódicas*, for cello, violin, and piano; *La Muerte del Payador,* on a poem by Rafael Obligado, for voice, piano, and string quartet; *Berceuse, Elégie, Nostalgie et Méditation,* for orch.; songs; religious pieces.
Sources: DM, EMA

Marchena Dujarric, Enrique de, Dominican composer and diplomat; b.13 Oct 1908, Ciudad Trujillo, Santo Domingo, Dominican Republic; d.1988, Ciudad Trujillo. He studied at the Dominican Republic National Univ. graduating in 1929 with a degree of Licenciate in law and political sciences. At the same time, he studied music at the Liceo Musical of Ciudad Trujillo, piano with Flérida de Nolasco and harmony and composition with Enrique Casal Chapí and Esteban Peña Morell. One of the founders of the Symphonic Society of Ciudad Trujillo. Music critic for *Listín Diario* and correspondent for *Musical America* of New York. President of the Sociedad de Autores y Compositores de la República Dominicana. In 1945 he was appointed general director of Fine Arts and vice provost at the Univ. of Ciudad Trujillo.
Works (selective list): Concerto for violin and orch. (1940); *Suite de Imágenes: Amanecer, Scherzo de Luz, Crepúsculo,* for orch. (1942); *Arco Iris,* symphonic poem (1943); Concertino for flute and orch. (1944); Concerto for piano and orch.; chamber music; piano pieces.
Sources: DM, MLA, MMLA

Marín Varona, José, Cuban composer; b.1859, Camagüey, Prov. of Camagüey, Cuba; d.1912, Havana, Cuba. Self-taught in music. Conductor of the orch. of the Teatro Alhambra in Havana. Organized and conducted the Band of the Artillery Division. Founder of the Music Section of the National Academy of Arts and Literature of Havana. Founder and editor of the journal *Cuba Musical.*
Works (selective list): *Tropicales,* Cuban concert dances for piano; several zarzuelas including *El Brujo;* songs. *Books: Tratado Completo de Teoría.*

Bibl.: O. Martínez, *Program of the Philharmonic Orchestra of Havana.*
Source: DM

Mariscal Canseco, Juan León, Mexican composer; b.10 Aug 1899, Oaxaca, Mexico; d.21 Sep 1972, Mexico. He studied at the National Cons. of Music of Mexico, Mexico City, with Julián Carrillo. In 1923, he received a Mexican government fellowship to study in Germany. Professor at the National Cons. of Music of Mexico.
Works (selective list): 2 symphonies; *Fantasía Mexicana,* for orch.; *Tres Estampas Oaxaqueñas,* orch. suite; *Guelaguetza,* suite for orch.; Sinfonietta; Septet; String quartet.
Sources: DM, MLA, MMLA

Marotta, Alejandro, Argentine composer and orch. conductor of Italian origin; b.1830?, Italy; d.?. Persecuted by the Austrians, he escaped to Switzerland in 1848. In 1851, he was in Montevideo, Uruguay, and the following year he conducted the orch. of the Sociedad Filarmónica of Buenos Aires, Argentina. Conductor of the orch. of the Teatro Victoria, Teatro Argentino, and Teatro Colón, all of Buenos Aires.
Works: *Gismonda,* opera; *Edita di Lorno,* opera; *Himno a la Libertad,* on a poem by Bartolomé Mitre, for chorus and orch.
Source: EMA

Márquez Sacasa, Juan, Cuban composer; b.8 Feb 1945, Havana, Cuba. Assistant conductor of the orch. of the Cuban National Ballet of Havana. Musical consultant for the Cuban Inst. of Cinematographic Art and Industry of Havana.
Works: Suite for piano; *Rimas,* for voice and piano; Trio for trumpet, French horn, and trombone; *Pequeña Toccata,* for violin, viola, and cello; *Sexta Primera,* for string instruments.
Source: DMC

Martí Llorca, José, Argentine violist and composer of Spanish origin: b.8 Oct 1903, Valencia, Spain. He settled in Argentina when he was a child and became an Argentine citizen in 1936. He studied with Celestino Piaggio, Pascual De Rogatis, Edmundo Weingand, and Torcuato Rodríguez Castro. Member of the orch. of the Teatro Colón of Buenos Aires from 1926 until 1954. Professor at the Municipal Cons. of Music Manuel de Falla of Buenos Aires.
Works (selective list): *Tres Piezas,* for string orch. (1933); *Dos Piezas Líricas,* for string orch. (1934); *Siete Piezas,* for orch. (1936); *Evocaciones Valencianas,* for orch. (1945); *Variaciones,* for orch. (1954); Concertino for oboe and orch. (1956); Symphony No.1 for

orch. (1960); *Tres Canciones,* for voice and orch. (1965-66); Concertino for guitar and orch. (1968-69); chamber music.
Sources: EMA, VMA

Martín, Edgardo, Cuban composer, music critic, and teacher; b.6 Oct 1915, Cienfuegos, Cuba. He began to study with his maternal grandmother, pianist Aurea Suárez. Later, he studied piano with Jascha Fischerman and César Pérez Sentenat, and composition with José Ardévol at the Municipal Cons. of Havana, Cuba. He has a doctorate in pedagogy from the Univ. of Havana. Professor of music history at the Municipal Cons. of Havana, 1945-68, and of music analysis at the National School for the Arts of Havana, 1969-73. Music critic for the newspaper *Acción.* Member of the *Grupo Renovación Musical* of Havana. From 1962 to 1971, he served as executive secretary for the National Committee of Music of UNESCO.
Works (selective list): Concerto for 9 wind instruments (1944); 2 symphonies (1947, 1948); *Los Dos Abuelos,* for chorus and instrumental ensemble (1949); *El Caballo de Coral,* ballet (1960); *Canto de Héroes,* for voices and orch. (1967); *La Carta del Soldado,* for narrator, tenor, chorus, speaking chorus, and orch. (1970); *Granma,* for chorus and instruments (1976); chamber music; piano pieces; guitar pieces; songs. *Books: Catálogo Biográfico de Compositores de Cuba*, Havana, 1970. *Panorama Histórico de la Música en Cuba,* Havana, 1971.
Sources: BB, CTA7, DM, DMC, MLA, MMLA

Martínez, José Daniel, Puerto Rican composer of American origin; b.8 Sep 1956, Bethesda, Maryland, USA. He studied at the Cons. of Puerto Rico with Luis Antonio Ramírez and Luz N. Hutchinson. In 1977, he received a Bachelor's degree in composition, and in 1980, a Master's degree in piano, both from the Eastman School of Music, Rochester, New York. Professor of piano and theory at the Hochstein School of Music in Rochester, 1977-80. Professor at the Cons. of Music, 1981-82, and the Metropolitan Univ. College, 1982, both of Puerto Rico. From 1982 to 1983, he resided in New York City where he worked as accompanying pianist. Professor of piano at the Inter-American Univ. of Puerto Rico in San Germán, Puerto Rico, since 1985.
Works (selective list): *Tiempo Sinfónico,* for orch. (1976); *Arreglos de Aguinaldos Típicos de Puerto Rico,* for orch. (1980); *Fanfarria Preámbulo,* for brass and percussion (1981); *Música para la Interamericana,* for baroque orch. (1984). *Dances for orch.: Margarita* (1985); *Mis Amores* (1985); *Violeta* (1985); *Linda Mayagüezana* (1985). *Concierto para Aulos...Reflexiones sobre el*

Retorno de un Cometa, for wind instruments and piano (1986); chamber music; piano pieces; songs.
Source: CPR

Martínez, Luis María, Argentine composer; b.21 Sep 1897, La Plata, Prov. of Buenos Aires, Argentina; d.1938, Buenos Aires, Argentina. He studied harmony with Athos Palma, counterpoint with José Gil, and composition with José André at the National Cons. of Music Carlos López Buchardo of Buenos Aires. Music critic for the daily newspaper *La Nación.*
Works (selective list): *Preludio,* for orch.; Sonata for violin and piano; String quartet; *Dos Preludios,* for piano; motets; madrigals; songs.
Sources: DM, EMA, MMLA

Martínez, Orlando, Cuban composer and musicologist; b.17 Oct 1916, Havana, Cuba. He studied at the Cons. Hubert de Blanck of Havana, from which he graduated as piano professor in 1936. Editor and commentator in programs of the Philharmonic Orch. of Havana. Music critic for the musical journals *Cubamena* and *Conservatorio.*
Works (selective list): *María Merced,* zarzuela; *Berceuse,* for piano; *Nocturno,* for the left hand; *Four Cuban Dances,* for piano; songs.
Books: Eduardo Sánchez de Fuentes, Havana 1944; *La Interpretación Musical,* Havana 1945; *Recuerdos de Arte,* Havana 1945; *Vigencia de Chopin,* Havana 1946. He collaborated in the writing of the *Diccionario Enciclopédico de la Música,* Barcelona, 1946.
Sources: DM, DMC, MMLA

Martínez Corres, Cristóbal, Cuban composer and pianist; b.Jun 1822, Havana, Cuba; d.21 Jan 1842, Genoa, Italy. He studied in Bourdeaux and Paris, France.
Works (selective list): *El Diablo Contrabandista,* comic opera; *Don Papanero,* opera; *Misa Solemne*; *Gran Morceau para una Opera Seria;* Septuor; piano pieces.
Bibl.: O. Martínez, *Program of the Philharmonic Orchestra of Havana.*
Sources: DM, DMC

Martínez de la Torre y Shelton, Emma, Cuban pianist and composer; b.15 Jan 1889, Havana, Cuba; d.? She studied with Rafael Toniasi Requena at the Academia de Santa Cecilia in Rome, Italy. She settled in Tenerife, Canary Islands, Spain, where she continued her music studies with Santiago Sabina Corona.
Works (selective list): *Stage: Danzas Gitanas,* dances; *Mañana de Abril,* incidental music; *Tenerife 1942,* children's play. *Orch.: Estampas de Siglo XVIII; Marionetas.* Chamber music; songs.

218 - Martínez Oyanguren

Sources: IBCC, IEW

Martínez Oyanguren, Julio, Uruguayan guitarist and composer; b.3 Jul 1901, Durazno, Uruguay; d.? He studied with Alfredo Hargain. *Works: Arabia* (1933); *Aires Andaluces; Oriente,* triptych: *Preludio, Danza y Leyenda; Fantasía Gaucha; Preludio y Fuga,* for guitar.
Source: DM

Martini, Juan Emilio, Argentine opera and ballet conductor and composer; b.19 Jul 1910, Buenos Aires, Argentina. He studied piano with Cayetano Troiani, and harmony, counterpoint, and composition with Athos Palma. Since 1934, he has been a staff member of the Teatro Colón of Buenos Aires. He taught opera repertoire at the Inst. Superior de Arte del Teatro Colón. Professor at the School of Musical Science and Art of the Argentine Catholic Univ. of Buenos Aires. Artistic director of the Teatro Colón in 1955.
Works: Sonata for cello and piano (1935); *Cinco Líricas,* for voice and piano (1937); Concertino for piano and orch. (1939).
Sources: DM, EMA

Martinoli, Carlos, Argentine composer, conductor, and pianist of Italian origin; b.1863, Busto Arsizu, near Milan, Italy; d.1942, Rosario, Prov. of Santa Fe, Argentina. He studied piano, violin, harp, organ, harmony, composition, and pedagogy at the Reggio Cons. of Milan, Italy. He settled in Rosario in 1887. Founder of several music cons. in Rosario.
Works (selective list): *El Viejo Castillo,* suite for piano; *Resurrección*; Operetta; sacred music; songs.
Source: CAMR

Marturet, Eduardo, Venezuelan composer and conductor; b.1953 Caracas, Venezuela. He graduated from the Anglia Polytechnic Univ., Cambridge, England, in 1978. He studied orch. conducting with Franco Ferrara in Italy, at the Accademia Chigianna, Siena, 1976, and in Rome, 1981-83. Conducted several European orch. He performed research in music therapy. Artistic director of the Sinfonietta Caracas, 1986. Music director of the Teatro Teresa Carreño of Caracas, 1984-87. Permanent conductor of the Venezuela Symphony Orch. of Caracas, 1987.
Works (selective list): *Notturno,* for orch. (1981); *Sol por Occidente,* for orch. (1982); *Secretos*, ballet (1986); *XXXIII Variaciones sobre un Tema Alemán,* for orch. (1989); chamber music; incidental music for films; piano pieces.
Source: ISC

Marx, Walter Burle, Brazilian composer and conductor; b.23 Jul 1902, Sâo Paulo, Brazil; d.28 Dec 1990, Akron, Ohio, USA. He studied first with his mother and then with Henrique Oswald and Agnelo França. Later he went to Germany where he studied piano with James Kwast, counterpoint, fugue, and composition with Friedrich Ernst Koch and Emil Nikolaus von Reznicek, and orch. conducting with Félix Weingartner. Founder of the Philharmonic Orch. of Rio de Janeiro, Brazil. He settled in the USA where he promoted Brazilian symphonic music. Professor at the Univ. of Rio de Janeiro, 1932-33. Artistic director of the Opera of Rio de Janeiro, 1947. Professor of piano and composition at the Settlement Music School, Philadelphia, Pennsylvania, 1952-77.
Works (selective list): Four symphonies (1945, 1950, 1956, 1973); *Ave Maria,* for soprano, women's chorus, boys' chorus, and orch. (1938); *Pater Noster,* cantata for baritone, mixed chorus, boys' chorus, and orch. (1940); *Lincoln's Gettysburg Address,* for bass and orch. (1957); *Samba Concertante,* for orch. (1960); *The Witch-Kids,* musical play with ballet (1964); 2 concertinos for piano and orch. (1980, 1984); Concerto for cello and orch. (1982-84); chamber music; music for the guitar.
Bibl.: R. Almeida, *Historia da Música Brasileira,* Rio de Janeiro, 1942.
Sources: BB, DM, MLA, MMLA

Massa, Juan Bautista, Argentine conductor, teacher, and composer; b.29 Oct 1885, Buenos Aires, Argentina; d.7 Mar 1938, Rosario, Prov. of Santa Fe, Argentina. In Buenos Aires, he studied with Casazza, Melani, Sartori, and Aromatari, then he settled in Rosario where he studied with Alfredo Donizetti. Conductor of the *Argentine Choral Society* in Rosario.
Works (selective list): *Operas: Zoraide* (1909); *L'Evaso* (1922); *La Magdalena* (1929). *Operettas: Esmeralda* (1903); *Triunfo del Corazón* (1910); *La Eterna Historia* (1911). *El Cometa,* ballet (1932); *La Muerte del Inca,* symphonic poem (1932); *Charito,* symphonic prelude; 2 Argentine suites for orch.; *Tres Canciones Indígenas,* for voice and 5 instruments (1935); Quartet for four violins (1923); piano pieces; songs.
Bibl.: F.C. Lange, *Juan Bautista Massa, Boletín Latino Americano de Música,* Washington, D.C., 1938.
Sources: BB, DM, EMA, MLA

Massini, Esteban, Argentine composer and teacher of Italian origin; b.1788, Genoa, Italy; d. 1838, Argentina. He settled in Buenos Aires, Argentina, in 1822. Teacher of flute, clarinet, and guitar. Flutist at the Teatro Coliseo Provisional of Buenos Aires.

Works: *Himno a los Restauradores,* after a text of José Rivera Indarte; *Canción Fúnebre a la Memoria del General Juan Facundo Quiroga,* dedicated to Manuelita Rosas, daughter of Juan Manuel de Rosas; *Himno a la Libertad; El 25 de Mayo,* patriotic song.
Source: EMA

Mastrogiovanni, Antonio, Uruguayan composer; b.26 Jul 1936, Montevideo, Uruguay. He studied with Nieves Varacchi and Héctor Tosar. Later, he entered the National Cons. of Music of Montevideo where he studied composition with Carlos Estrada. During 1969 and 1970, he lived in Buenos Aires, Argentina, and studied electronic music and avant-garde musical form under Alberto Ginastera, Gerardo Gandini, and Francisco Kröpfl at the Centro Latinoamericano de Altos Estudios Musicales of the Inst. Di Tella.
Works (selective list): *Auqui Paukar,* ballet (1960); *Introducción, Passacaglia y Danza,* for orch. (1963); *Larghetto,* for oboe and string orch. (1964); Concerto for piano and orch. (1964); Chamber symphony for orch. (1965); *Contrarritmos,* for 2 string orch. and percussion (1967-68); *Reflejos,* for instrumental ensemble (1970); *Secuencial I,* for large orch. (1970); *Secuencial II,* for tape (1970); *Maderas,* for ensemble (1974); chamber music; music for the organ; electronic music; piano pieces; songs.
Sources: BHMCU, CTA17, DCM, GDM, MU

Mata, Eduardo, Mexican conductor and composer; b.5 Sep 1942, Mexico City, Mexico; d.4 Jan 1995 in a plane accident near Mexico City. He began music studies with Rodolfo Halffter at the National Cons. of Music of Mexico, Mexico City, 1954-60, and then he took lessons in composition and conducting with Carlos Chávez, 1960-65, and Julián Orbón, 1960-63. In 1964, he went to the Berkshire Center in Tanglewood, Massachusetts, where he attended conducting classes with Max Rudolph, Gunther Schuller, and Erich Leinsdorf. Conductor of the Symphony Orch. of Guadalajara, Mexico, 1964-66, the Symphony Orch. of Phoenix, Arizona, 1970-78, and the Symphony Orch. of Dallas, Texas, 1977-94. Head of the Concert Dept. of the Univ. of Mexico in Mexico City and conductor of its orch.
Works (selective list): 3 symphonies (1962, 1963, 1966-67); *Débora,* ballet music (1963); *La Venganza del Pescador,* suite for 2 flutes, trombone, violin, guitar, and percussion (1964); *Aires Sobre un Tema del Siglo XVI,* for mezzo-soprano, 2 flutes, oboe, bassoon, 2 violas, cello, and double bass (1964); Cello sonata (1966); chamber music; piano pieces.
Sources: BB, DCM

Mata, Julio, Costa Rican composer and cellist; b.9 Dec 1899, San José, Costa Rica; d.? He studied harmony, composition, and cello at the Musical Academy of Brooklyn, New York, 1921-26. He returned to Costa Rica in 1930, and in 1940 was appointed conductor of the Military Band of San José. First cello at the National Symphony Orch. of Costa Rica.

Works (selective list): *Tupuyán,* opera; *Rosas de Norgaria,* operetta; *Piedras Preciosas (Diamante, Amatista, Zafiro, Rubí y Esmeralda),* symphonic suite; *Suite Abstracta,* for orch.; marches; songs; chorus pieces.

Sources: DM, MLA, MMLA

Matamoros, Gustavo, Venezuelan composer; b.8 Apr 1957, Caracas, Venezuela. He settled in Miami, Florida, in 1979 and became a permanent resident of the USA. He studied composition with Barry Brosh, Dennis Kam, and John Van Der Slice at the Univ. of Miami, where he received a BM degree in 1983. In 1987, he attended master classes in composition with Earle Brown, Donald Erb, Bernard Rands, Steve Reich, and Roger Reynolds in Buffalo, New York. Appointed artistic and executive director of the South Florida Composers Alliance in Miami in 1989.

Works (selective list): *Cervatana Music,* for flute and live processing (1982); *Threnody and Passacaglia,* for prepared piano and orch. (1982); *142857,* for live electronics and tape (1986); *Entropy Etude,* for string orch. (1987); *Fanfarria for X Number of Instruments* and *Fanfarria I,* both for any number of instruments (1988); *In Memory of Gentle Giant,* for percussion or live electronics and tape (1989); *Portrait: Bob Gregory,* for poet and tape (1990); *Portrait: Joseph Celli,* for wind controller and tape (1990); *Retrato: Flores Chaviano,* for guitar and tape (1990); *Retrato: Ricardo Dal Farra,* for tape and real-time processing (1992); *RCA Victor's True Story,* for piano, live electronics, and mid-sized dog (1993); *Dreamcatcher,* for string quartet and tape (1993).

Source: ISC

Matos Priolli, María Luisa de, Brazilian pianist and composer; b.24 May 1915, Rio de Janeiro, Brazil. She started her music education with her mother, and later entered the Inst. Nacional de Música of Rio de Janeiro, where she studied piano with M.A. Rumley, harmony with Agnelo França, counterpoint and fugue with Paulo Silva, composition with Joâo Otaviano, and conducting with Francisco Mignone. She also studied piano and music analysis with W. Bantock and composition with W. Chatermann at the Trinity College of Music in London, England. Member of the National Academy of Music of Brazil.

Works: Concerto in C minor for piano (1940); chamber music; sacred music; piano pieces; songs.
Sources: IBCC, IEW

Maturana, Eduardo, Chilean composer and violist; b.14 Apr 1920, Valparaiso, Chile. He started to study music in Valparaiso, and then at the National Cons. of Music of Santiago de Chile, Chile, viola with Luis Mutschler, composition with Humberto P. Allende and Samuel Negrete, and chamber music with Armando Carvajal. Secretary of the Musicians' Union. Founder of the *Agrupación Tonus.* Violist with the Municipal Philharmonic Orch. of Santiago de Chile. Secretary-general of the Asociación Nacional de Compositores Chilenos. Coordinator of the Municipal Theatre Chamber Opera.
Works (selective list): *Regreso a la Muerte,* opera (1963); *Gamma I,* for orch. (1962); *Introducción y Allegro,* for chamber orch. (1963); *Tres Piezas,* for orch. (1965); Concertante for horn and orch. (1967); *Cinco Móviles,* for string orch. (1968); *Responso para el Che Guevara,* for orch. and tape (1968); *Elegías,* for cello and orch. (1970); chamber music; piano pieces; songs.
Sources: DCM, GDM

Maurage, Augusto, Argentine violinist and composer of Belgian origin; b.1875, Brussels, Belgium; d.1925, Buenos Aires, Argentina. He settled in Buenos Aires in 1904. He studied violin with Eugène Ysaÿe in Brussels in 1894. In 1912, after touring extensively in Europe and the USA as a violin virtuoso, he founded a cons. in Buenos Aires.
Works: Tupá, opera (1919); *Les Noces d'Or,* lyric idyl (1924).
Source: EMA

Mauri, José, Cuban composer of Spanish origin; b.12 Feb 1855, Valencia, Spain; d.11 Jul 1937, Havana, Cuba. He studied first with his father, and then continued to study violin with Reinaldo Revagliatti and Anselmo López, and piano, harmony, counterpoint, composition, fugue, and instrumentation with Manuel Ubeda. Director of the National Band of Music in Colombia. Artistic director of the Teatro Albisu in Havana. Conductor of the Band of the Reformatory of Guanajay in Cuba. Founding member of the Musical Section of the Academia Nacional de Artes y Letras of Havana.
Works (selective list): *La Esclava,* opera; Symphony in A major. *Symphonic poems: Grandeza y Locura de Don Quijote; Serenata de Dulcinea; Los Gnomos del Moncayo.* Adagio for orch.; zarzuelas; songs.
Bibl.: O. Martínez: *Program of the Philharmonic Orchestra of Havana.*

Sources: DM, DMC

Maurício, José, Brazilian composer, *maestro de capilla* (chapelmaster), and music teacher; b.22 Sep 1767, Rio de Janeiro, Brazil; d.18 Apr 1830, Rio de Janeiro. He studied music with Salvador José. He also pursued religious instruction and was ordained a priest at age twenty five.
Works (selective list): *Le Due Gemelle,* opera; *Zemira,* overture; *Missa in B-flat; Missa de Réquiem; Missa Mimosa; Missa de Santa Cecilia; Missa Festiva; Missa Pastoril para a Noite de Natal; Te Deum; Tantum Ergo;* large number of religious compositions.
Source: HMB

Mejía, Adolfo, Colombian composer; 5 Feb 1909, Cartagena, Colombia; d.1970?, Colombia. He studied with Juan de Sanctis, Jesús Bermúdez Silva, and Gustavo Escobar Larrázabal at the National Cons. of Music of Bogotá, Colombia. With a scholarship, he went to Paris, France, where he studied with Nadia Boulanger at the Ecole Normal de Musique, and with Henri Koechlin. Librarian at the Cons. of Music and the National Symphony Orch., instructor and director of the orch. and band of the Colombian Navy at the Naval Base of Cartagena, and professor at the Escuela Departamental de Música and the Inst. de Música of Cartagena.
Works: Pequeña Suite, for string orch. (1938); *Preludio para la Tercera Salida de Don Quijote; Improvisación y Bachianas,* for string orch.; *Música para una Película; Juguetes Infantiles,* for piano; *Capricho Español; Intima Primera; Suite de Danzas Españolas; Danza Ritual Africana; Luminosidad de Aguas; Hymn to Cartagena; Hymn to the Navy;* Concerto in D minor for piano and orch.
Sources: CMC, DM, MLA, MMLA, ZCCC

Mejía Arredondo, Enrique, Dominican composer; b.24 Dec 1901, Ciudad Trujillo (Santo Domingo), Dominican Republic; d.1951, Dominican Republic. He began to study music with his grandfather, José María Arredondo, and later studied piano with Américo Lugo Romero and composition with Enrique Casal Chapí. Director of the Symphony Society of Santo Domingo and conductor of the first Dominican Symphony Orch. created in 1932. Music critic for the newspaper *La Opinión.* President of the Sociedad de Compositores y Autores Dominicanos.
Works (selective list): 2 symphonies; *Renacimiento,* symphonic poem; Concerto for piano and orch.; *Evocaciones,* suite for orch.; *Reverie,* for violin and orch.; *Cuento Nocturno,* based on an indigenous legend; *Danzas Quisqueyanas,* for orch.; Quintet for wind instruments; chamber music; piano pieces; songs.
Sources: DM, MLA, MMLA

Mejía Castro, Estanislao, Mexican composer and teacher; b.13 Nov 1882, San Idelfonso Hueyotlipan, Tlaxcala, Mexico; d.15 Jun 1967, Mexico. He studied with José de Jesús León, Arturo Aguirre, Gabriel Unda, and José Rivas at the National Cons. of Music, Mexico City, Mexico. In 1911, he studied harmony with Rafael J. Tello, counterpoint, fugue, and instrumentation with Gustavo E. Campa, and organ with Father José Guadalupe Velázquez. Professor at the National Cons. of Music of Mexico, director of the Dept. of Music of the UNAM, and professor at the Escuela Univ. de Música, all in Mexico City. Organized the National Symphony Orch. of Mexico, Mexico City.
Works (selective list): *Edith,* opera; Suite for strings; *Sinfonía en Estilo Romántico* (1920); *Suite Mexicana,* for orch.; *Shadani,* sympho-choreographic poem (1933); chamber music; piano pieces; songs. **Books:** *Composición Musical,* Mexico, 1941-42.
Sources: DM, GMM, MLA, MMLA

Mell, Eidylia Rosa Lía, Argentine composer; b.29 May 1927, Prov. of Buenos Aires, Argentina. She studied with Gilardo Gilardi, Luis Gianneo, Floro Ugarte, Juan F. Giaccobe, Abraham Jurafsky, Pedro Valenti Costa, Carlos Pessina, Amelia C. de Weigand, Angel Mangiamarchi, Rosalinda Crocco, Roberto Castro, Juan Emilio Martini, and Bruno Bandini. She also studied guitar with Narciso Yepes, voice with Jacqueline Ibels, and orchestration with Alexander Szenkar. Professor at the National Cons. of Music Carlos López Buchardo, and at the Municipal Cons. of Music Manuel de Falla, both of Buenos Aires.
Works (selective list): *La Farsa,* opera (1991); *Vida de una Cortesana,* ballet; *Radan,* for mixed chorus and orch.; *Andante y Alegro Sinfónico,* for orch.; *Tiempo de Baguala y Tiempo de Milonga,* for orch.; *Homenaje a Gilardo Gilardi,* for symphonic band; *Armonías Vespertinas,* for orch.; Concerto for clarinet and orch.; Concertino for piano and string orch.; chamber music; piano pieces; choruses.
Source: ISC

Melo Cruz, Carlos, Chilean composer, pianist, and conductor; b.5 Apr 1897, Concepción, Chile; d.? He studied piano, music theory, and harmony with Luigi S. Giarda and Federico Stöber at the National Cons. of Music, Santiago de Chile, Chile, from 1912 to 1919. At the same time, he studied at the Law School of the Univ. of Chile, Santiago de Chile. Professor at the National Cons. of Music until 1925. Director of the *Orfeón Obrero Nacional* (male singing chorus) and artistic director of the Municipal Theater. Secretary of the Society of Chilean Composers.

Works (selective list): *Mauricio,* opera (1939); several symphonic poems and preludes for large orch.; chamber music; choruses; songs.
Sources: HMC, MMLA

Melo Gorigoytía, Héctor, Chilean composer; b.30 Oct 1899, Santiago de Chile, Chile; d.? He studied theory and solfeggio with Aníbal Aracena, harmony with José Salinas, violin with Aurelio Silva, instrumental ensemble with Enrique Soro, and composition with Carlos Lavín at the National Cons. of Music of Chile, Santiago de Chile, 1916-23. At the same time, he studied mine engineering. Director of the Univ. Orch. and the *Choral Ensemble of Engineers* of Chile, Santiago de Chile. Member of the Faculty of Fine Arts of the Univ. of Chile, Santiago de Chile.
Works (selective list): *Alucinaciones de Primavera,* ballet for voices, chorus, and orch. (1916); *Manchas de Color,* for string instruments and piano; *Leie,* for violin, French horn, oboe, and harp; *Medieval,* for voices, piano, and string orch.; *Chañarcillo,* for chorus and orch.; *Lebe,* symphomic poem; *La Mina Abandonada,* symphonic poem; *Poema Anacrónico,* for orch.; chamber music; piano pieces; songs.
Sources: DM, HMC, MLA, MMLA

Mena, Luis E., Dominican composer; b.12 Nov 1895, Ciudad Trujillo, Dominican Republic; d.1964, Dominican Republic. He studied with José de Jesús Ravelo at the Liceo Musical of Ciudad Trujillo. Later, he became professor at that inst. and at the National Cons. of Music of Ciudad Trujillo. Conductor of the Orch. of the Official Radio Station.
Works (selective list): *Sinfonía Giocosa; Sinfonía de Juguetes; Recuerdos de Infancia,* suite in 13 sections for orch.; *Intermedio Andaluz y Zapateado,* for orch.; Suite for flute and string orch.; *Homage to the Dominican National Anthems,* for orch.; Overture for orch.; *El Camino del Cielo,* for orch.; *Ecos de Libertad,* for orch; *Marcha Fúnebre,* for orch.; chamber music; music for organ; piano pieces.
Sources: DEW, DM, MLA, MMLA

Mendes, Gilberto Ambrósio García, Brazilian composer; b.13 Oct 1922, Santos, Brazil. He studied harmony with Savino de Benedictis and piano with Antonieta Rudge at the Musical Cons. of Santos. Later, he studied with Claudio Santoro and Olivier Toni, and attended the Darmstadt, Germany, summer courses in 1962 and 1968, taking classes with Pierre Boulez, Henri Pousseur, and Karlheinz Stockhausen. In 1962, he founded the *Festival Música Nova de Santos,* the oldest festival of contemporary music held in all Latin America, of which he is the program and artistic director. Visiting

professor at the Univ. of Wisconsin, Milwaukee, Wisconsin, and the Univ. of Texas at Austin, Texas. Professor at the Univ. of Sâo Paulo, Brazil, and at the Faculty of Music of Santos.
Works (selective list): **Orch.**: *Santos Football Music,* (1969); Concerto for piano (1981); *Partitura* (1985); *The Last Tango in Vila Parisi* (1987). **Small ensembles:** *Rotationis* (1962); *Qualquer Música* (1980); *Ulysses em Copacabana Surfing with James Joyce and Dorothy Lamour* (1988); *Il Samba del Soldato* (1991). Chamber music; piano pieces; choruses; music for the theater.
Sources: DCM, GDM, ISC

Mendoza, Emilio, Venezuelan composer; b.8 Aug 1953, Caracas, Venezuela. He settled in Potsdam, New York, in 1991. He studied classical guitar with Flaminia de Desola at the Juan Manuel Olivares Music School and composition with Yannis Ioannidis at the Metropolitan Univ., both in Caracas. He received a Doctor of musical arts degree from The Catholic Univ. of America in Washington, D.C., in 1990. He founded, conducted, and directed the orch. of ODILA in Caracas, 1982-87. Assistant professor at the IUDEM in Caracas, 1982-84. Chief of the Music Division of the Venezuelan National Library, Caracas, 1985-87. In 1991, he was appointed assistant professor at the Crane School of Music, Potsdam College of the New York State Univ., Potsdam, New York.
Works (selective list): *Pasaje,* for string orch. (1976); *Contienda,* for orch. (1982); *Tregua,* for orch. (1981); *El Ultimo Canto,* for Latin American instruments (1984); *Transonar,* for Latin American instruments (1985); *Virtual Suicide,* for tape (1991); *Survival of the Indigenous*, for tape (1992); chamber music; piano pieces; music for solo instruments.
Sources: BB, ISC

Mendoza, José Alberto, Guatemalan pianist and composer; b.30 Mar 1889, Guatemala City, Guatemala; d.2 Jul 1960, Guatemala. He studied with Luis Felipe Arias, Germán Alcántara, Eduardo Lebegotti, and Herculano Alvarado. In 1925, he was appointed director of the National Cons. of Guatemala, Guatemala City, a position he held until 1931. Director of the oldest Guatemalan music organization, *Sociedad Filarmónica-Religiosa*, founded in 1813.
Works (selective list): *Gloria al General García Granados,* triumphal march; *Improvisación Sinfónica; Quezalcoatl;* piano pieces; songs.
Sources: DM, HMG, MMLA

Mendoza Gutiérrez, Vicente Teódulo, Mexican composer, musicologist, and folklorist; b.27 Jan 1894, Cholula, State of Puebla, Mexico; d.27 Oct 1964, Mexico City, Mexico. He started music studies with his father, Vicente M. Mendoza, in his native town. He

moved to Mexico City where he entered the Academia de Bellas Artes, and later the National Cons. of Music where he studied piano with Lauro Beristáin and Herminia R. de Cruz, and harmony and composition with Gabrielli. From 1913 to 1925, he studied harmony, counterpoint, fugue, and the theory and practice of *Sonido 13* (Sound 13) with Julián Carrillo. In 1937, he was appointed folklore researcher at the Inst. de Investigaciones Estéticas of the UNAM in Mexico City. Founder and president of the Sociedad Folklórica de Mexico. In 1955, he received a Master's degree in music from the Univ. of Mexico. Taught at the UNAM, the National Cons. of Music, and in public schools of Mexico City.
Works (selective list): ***Orch.***: *Tríptico de los Mendigos* (1927); *Escena de Ballet (Danza Tarahumara),* for small ensemble (1931); *No.V,* from the *Ballet de la Revolución (Maquinismo)* (1932); *Tierras Solares,* suite michoacana (1936); *Suite Estival* (1941); *Danza Ritual* (1941); *Danza Negra* (1942). Choral music; chamber music; piano pieces; songs. **Books:** with D. Castañeda, *Instrumental Precortesiano,* Mexico, 1933-39; *Panorama de la Música Tradicional de México,* Mexico, 1956.
Sources: GDM, MLA, NH

Mendoza Nava, Jaime , Bolivian composer and conductor; b.1 Dec 1925, La Paz, Bolivia. He settled in Los Angeles, California, in 1953. He studied at The Juilliard School of Music in New York City. Later, he studied at the Cons. of Music of Madrid, Spain, and in Paris, France, with Nadia Boulanger and Arthur Honneger. In 1952, he was appointed conductor of the National Symphony Orch. of Bolivia in La Paz.
Works (selective list): *Don Alvaro,* for orch.; *Preludio Sinfónico*, for orch.; *Suite Andina,* for wind trio; *Estampas y Estampillas,* for cello ensemble; Sonata for horn and piano; music for films.
Source: GDM

Meneses, Miguel, Mexican composer; b.Mexico; d.Bombay, India. He studied with Cenobio Paniagua.
Works: Operas: *Agorante, Rey de la Nubia; El Hada del Lago; Judith; Luisa de Lavalliere. Atala,* lyric drama.
Source: MMLA

Meserón, Juan, Venezuelan composer and flutist; b.Venezuela; he lived during the first half of the 19th century.
Works: 3 masses; *Miserere; Himno al Santísimo Sacramento.*
Source: MMLA

Mesquita, Carlos de, Brazilian composer; b.23 May 1864, Rio de Janeiro, Brazil; d.27 Nov 1953, Paris, France. He studied in Rio de

Janeiro, and later in Paris, with César Franck, Jules Massenet, Emil Durand, and Antoine F. Marmontel. First professor of harmony at the Escuela Nacional de Música in Rio de Janeiro. *Works* (selective list): *Operas: Esmeralda; Souvent l'Homme Varie.* Piano pieces; violin pieces; orch. works.
Sources: DM, MMLA

Mesquita, Henrique Alves de, Brazilian composer and teacher; b.15 Mar 1836, Rio de Janeiro, Brazil; d.12 Jul 1906, Rio de Janeiro. He studied at the Cons. of Music in Rio de Janeiro, and later, with a scholarship, in Paris, France, with François E.J. Bazin. Professor of solfeggio at the Cons. of Music, and of brass instruments at the National Inst. of Music, both in Rio de Janeiro. Permanent conductor of the orch. of the Teatro Fénix Dramática of Rio de Janeiro. *Works* (selective list): *Operas: Noivado em Paquetá; O Vagabundo. Operettas: Triunfo ás Avessas; Gata Borralheira; Noite no Castelo; Alí Babá; Loteria do Diabo; Coroa de Carlos Magno. L'Etoile du Brésil,* symphonic overture; salon music.
Sources: GDM, HMB, MMLA

Mesquita, José Joaquím Emérico Lôbo de, Brazilian composer and organist; b.between 1740 and 1750, Vila do Príncipe do Serro do Frío, Brazil; d.1805, Rio de Janeiro, Brazil. Active in the prov. of Minas Gerais, Brazil, at the end of the 18th century. Entered the Brotherhood of Nossa Senhora das Merces dos Homens Crioulos in Arraial do Tejuco (now Diamantina), Brazil. Organist at the Irmandade do Santísimo Sacramento in the same city. Later, he moved to Vila Rica (Ouro Prêto), Brazil, and worked as composer, conductor, and organist of the Irmandade da Ordem Terceira do Carmo.
Works: Antífona Regina Coeli Laetare; Antífona Zelus Domus tuae; Missa em Mi bemol; Missa em Fa; Te Deum; Antífona de Nossa Senhora (Salve Regina), for chorus, strings, and organ (1787); *Ladainha in Honorem Beatae Mariae Virginis; Ofertorio de Nossa Senhora (Benedicta et Venerabilis Es).*
Bibl.: F.C. Lange, *La Música de Vila Rica, Minas Gerais, Siglo XVIII, Revista Musical Chilena,* No.102, 1967; No.103, 1968.
Sources: HMB, GDM

Meza, Miguel C., Mexican choral conductor, teacher, and composer; b.29 Sep 1903, San Luis Potosí, Mexico. He studied piano and composition at the National Cons. of Music of Mexico City where he graduated in 1932.
Works: Sinfonía en Estilo Mexicano; Revolución, symphonic poem; *Las Biniguendas de Plata,* ballet; *Impresiones,* orch. suite.
Sources: MLA, MMLA

Miceli, Antonino, Argentine composer of Italian origin; b.1 Dec 1890, San Vito lo Capo, Italy; d.? He lived in Argentina since childhood. He started music studies with Father Francisco Zaninetti at Colegio Salesiano San Juan Bautista of Buenos Aires, Argentina. Later, he studied solfeggio with Jaime Bustamante, piano with Celestino Piaggio, and harmony and composition with Alberto Williams at the National Cons. of Music Carlos López Buchardo of Buenos Aires. He also studied voice with Storges Graziani, Arnoldo Bottaro, and Luis Benvenuto. Professor at the National Cons. of Music Carlos López Buchardo. Professor in the school system of the National Board of Education, the Colegio Nacional La Salle, and the Inst. Normal Santa Catalina, all in Buenos Aires.
Works (selective list): *Gran Misa,* for male chorus, string orch., and organ; piano pieces; songs.
Sources: DM, EMA

Michaca Valenzuela, Pedro, Mexican composer and teacher; b.26 Nov 1897, Canatlán, State of Durango, Mexico; d.16 Jul 1976, Mexico City, Mexico. He studied music in his native town, and in 1919, he moved to Mexico City where he entered the National Cons. of Music to study solfeggio and harmony with Estanislao Mejía, counterpoint, fugue, composition, and musical analysis with Gustavo E. Campa and Rafael J. Tello, piano with Manuel M. Ponce, and organ with Aurelio Barrios y Morales. Professor at the National Cons. of Music and the Music School of the UNAM in Mexico City. Founding member and president of the *Ateneo Musical Mexicano.*
Works: El Zarco, symphonic poem; religious music; piano pieces; songs. *Books: El Nacionalismo Musical Mexicano; La Evolución de la Armonía a través del Principio Cíclico Musical.*
Sources: GMM, MLA

Michans, Carlos Eduardo, Argentine composer, chorus conductor, and teacher; b.18 Aug 1950, Buenos Aires, Argentina. He studied with Almah Melgar, Carlos Larrimbe, Pedro Valenti Costa, Bruno D'Astoli, and Roberto García Morillo. He graduated from Escuela de Coro of the Univ. del Museo Social Argentino and from the Inst. Superior del Teatro Colón, both of Buenos Aires. Member of the Asociación Argentina de Compositores.
Works (selective list): *Tres Piezas,* for chamber orch. (1980); *Divertimento,* for piano, clarinet, and 7 string instruments (1981); *Tres Piezas Breves,* for wind quartet (1976); choral religious music; chamber music.
Source: VMA

Migliori, Gabriel, Brazilian composer; b.9 Nov 1909, Sâo Paulo, Brazil; d.2 Jan 1975, Sâo Paulo.

230 - Mignone

Works: Variações Sinfónicas, on a popular theme, for orch.; Concerto for violin and orch.; *Impressiões Brasileiras,* for string instruments; *Pirapora,* for 15 instruments.
Source: MMLA

Mignone, Francisco Paulo, Brazilian composer and conductor; b.3 Sep 1897, Sâo Paulo, Brazil; d.18 Feb 1986, Rio de Janeiro, Brazil. He started music studies with his father, and then took courses in piano, flute, and composition with Silvio Motto, Savino de Benedictis, and Agostinho Cantú at the Sâo Paulo Cons. Later, in 1920, he studied with Vincenzo Ferroni at the Milan Cons., Italy. Professor of piano and harmony at the Sâo Paulo Cons., from 1914 to 1920 and from 1929 to 1932. In 1933, he was appointed to the faculty of the Escola Nacional de Música of the Univ. of Brazil in Rio de Janeiro and taught there until 1967.
Works (selective list): *Operas: O Contratador de Diamantes* (1924); *L'Innocente* (1928); *O Chalaça* (1972). *Ballets: Maracatú de Chico-Rei* (1934); *Leilâo* (1941); *O Espantalhao* (1941); *Quadros Amazónicos* (1949); *O Guarda Chuva* (1954). *Orch.: Suite Campestre* (1918); *Congada,* from the opera *O Contratador de Diamantes* (1922); *Scenas da Roda,* symphonic dance (1923); *Festa Dionisíaca* (1923); *Intermezzo Lírico* (1925); *Momus,* symphonic poem (1933); *Suite Brasileira* (1933); *Sonho de un Menino Travesso* (1937); *Cuatro Fantasías Brasileiras,* for piano (1931-37); *Seresta,* for cello (1939); *Miudinho,* symphonic dance (1941); *Festa das Igrejas* (1942); *Sinfonía Tropical* (1958); Piano concerto (1958); Violin concerto (1961); Concerto for violin and piano (1966); Concertino for clarinet and small orch. (1957); Bassoon concertino (1957); Concerto for violin and chamber orch. (1975). *Chamber music:* 2 sextets (1935,1968); String octet (1956); 2 wind quintets (1960,1962); 2 string quartets (1956,1957); Sonata for 4 bassoons (1966); 2 wind trios (1967,1968). Choruses; several works for different combinations of wind instruments; piano pieces; songs.
Bibl.: L.H. Correa de Azevedo, *Francisco Mignone, Música Brasileña Contemporánea,* Rosario, Argentina, 1952.
Sources: BB, CTA4, DM, GDM, MLA, MMLA

Míguez, Leopoldo Américo, Brazilian composer; b.9 Sep 1850, Niterói, Rio de Janeiro, Brazil; d.6 Jul 1902, Rio de Janeiro. He studied with Nicolau Ribas in Oporto, Portugal. In 1890, he was appointed director of the Inst. Nacional de Música in Rio de Janeiro, where he remained until his death.
Works (selective list): *Pelo Amor,* opera (1897); *Os Saldunes,* opera (1901); Symphony in B flat (1882); *Parisina,* symphonic poem (1888); *Ave, Libertas,* symphonic poem (1890); *Hino à Proclamaçâo da República* (1890); *Prometeo,* symphonic poem (1892); *Ode a*

Victor Hugo, for orch.; *Suite a l'Antique,* for orch.; overtures; piano pieces; songs; marches.
Bibl.: O. Bevilacqua, *Leopoldo Míguez e o Instituto Nacional de Música, Revista Brasileira de Música,* Vol.7, 1940.
Sources: BB, DM, GDM, HMB, MLA

Mihovilcevic, Luis, Argentine composer; b.24 Oct 1958, Rosario, Prov. of Santa Fe, Argentina. He studied piano with Enrique Graino and Jorge Sala, theory and solfeggio with Pedro Crapanzano and Carlos Goldberg, harmony with Jacobo Ficher, counterpoint and composition with Salvador Ranieri, musical analysis with Milko Kelemen, and electronic music with Enrique Belloc. Board member of *Ars Contemporánea,* CUDA, and FAC.
Works (selective list): Concerto for string orch. and timpani (1986); *El Jardín (Grito de Auschwitz),* for children's chorus (1979); *Intermezzo,* for narrator and amplified piano (1984-85); *Dos Imagénes,* for mixed chorus (1984); *El Jinete Acuático,* for 2 actors, piano, percussion, objects, and other circumstantial instruments (1986-87); chamber music; choruses; piano pieces.
Source: ISC

Milici, Luis, Argentine composer and conductor; b.23 Nov 1910, Rosario, Prov. of Santa Fe, Argentina. He started his music studies with Antonio Boreto and Alfonso Ingo, and later continued studying composition and instrumentation with Juan Bautista Massa. He conducted the Philharmonic Orch. of Rosario and the Symphony Orch. of the APO of Buenos Aires, Argentina. Professor of choral singing at the Escuela Profesional de Mujeres de la Nación and director of the Inst. de Educación Musical of the Univ. of Litoral, both in Rosario.
Works (selective list): *Anyaay,* symphonic poem (1940); *El Inca Triste,* poem for soprano, chorus and orch. (1942); *Danza Guerrera,* for orch. (1943); *Impresiones Norteñas,* symphonic suite (1946); *Malambo,* for orch. (1948); *Sinfonía in Memoriam,* for soloists, chorus and orch. (1953); *Aire de Gato,* for orch.; *Aire de Bailecito,* for string quartet; choruses a cappella; piano pieces; songs.
Sources: CA, DM, EMA

Mindlin, Adolfo, Argentine pianist and composer; b.1922, Carlos Casares, Prov. of Buenos Aires, Argentina. He settled in Paris, France, in 1952. He studied piano with Raúl Spivak, and harmony, counterpoint, fugue, composition, and instrumentation with Jacobo Ficher in Buenos Aires, Argentina.
Works: *Juan Cristóbal,* overture for orch.; chamber music; piano pieces; songs.
Source: EMA

Miniño, Manuel Martino, Dominican composer; b.2 Jan 1930, Baní, Dominican Republic. He studied harmony, counterpoint, and composition with Roberto Caggiano and Alfredo de Migno in Rome, Italy, and later he studied in Paris, France.
Works: Symphonies; Concerto Grosso; Piano concerto; Cantata.
Sources: DEW, KTL

Miramontes, Arnulfo, Mexican composer and pianist; b.18 Jul 1882, Tala, State of Talisco, Mexico; d.1960, Mexico. He started his music studies in Mexico, and then he studied piano with Martín Krause, composition with Philippe Rueffer, and orch. conducting with Alexander von Fielitz at the Sternsches Konservatorium of Berlin, Germany, in 1908. He returned to Mexico in 1911 and dedicated himself to piano playing and teaching, and to conducting.
Works (selective list): *Anáhuac,* opera; *Cihuatl,* opera; *Iris,* symphonic ballet; 3 symphonies; *Primavera,* overture; *Suite Sinfónica Mexicana; Poema Sinfónico de la Revolución; Baile Mexicano;* chamber music; piano pieces; music for organ; choruses; religious music; songs.
Sources: DM, MLA, MMLA

Miranda, Ronaldo, Brazilian composer and music critic; b.1948, Rio de Janeiro, Brazil. He studied piano with Dulce de Saules and composition with Henrique Morelenbaum at the Music School of the Federal Univ. of Rio de Janeiro. Music critic for the newspaper *Jornal do Brasil.* Professor of composition at the Music School of the Federal Univ. of Rio de Janeiro.
Works: Trajetória (1978); *Variaçôes Sinfônicas,* for orch. (1981); *Oriens III,* for 3 flutes (1983); *Prólogo, Discurso e Reflexâo,* for piano (1985); *Imagens,* for clarinet and percussion (1986); *Três Momentos,* for solo cello (1987).
Source: ISC

Miyara, Federico, Argentine composer and pianist: b.4 Sep 1958, Rosario, Prov. of Santa Fe, Argentina. He was self-taught in music. After graduating as an electronic engineer, he studied piano with Alicia Correas and composition with Dante Grela. Founding member of the Asociación Santafesina de Compositores and of the *Grupo Klank-Música Contemporánea* of Rosario.
Works (selective list): *Malvinas,* for chorus; *Elegía y Fanfarra,* for trumpet; *Fantasía,* for clarinet, violin, and piano; *Culpas,* for flute, piano, and percussion; *Impromptu y Kinesis I,* for clarinet and piano; *Rapsodia, Kinesis II y Azeuxis,* for flute and piano; piano pieces.
Source: CAMR

Moleiro, Moisés, Venezuelan composer; b.28 Mar 1905, Zaraza, Venezuela; d.1972, Venezuela. He studied with Vicente Sojo in Caracas, Venezuela. Professor of piano at the Caracas School of Music.
Works: Toccata for piano; Sonatina for piano; choruses; songs.
Sources: CTA14, DM, MLA, MMLA

Molina, Francisco J., Bolivian instrumentalist and composer; b.3 Dec 1863, La Paz, Bolivia; d.2 Apr 1925, La Paz. He started music studies with his uncle, Issac Palacios. He studied clarinet with Mancilla. He spent some years in the army during the war with Chile. After the war he studied several instruments, including clarinet, trumpet, piano, and violin with Donaire. Professor of music at the Seminario de La Paz and in the main municipal schools.
Works: Te Deum Anime, mass; *El Obligado de Violín; La Noche fue un Día; San Francisco Javier,* meditation; *Recuerdo a mi Madre; Amor de Madre.* **Books**: *Elementos de Música y Canto,* became the official textbook in schools and colleges.
Source: CB

Molina, José Antonio, Dominican composer and conductor; b.4 Jun 1960, Santo Domingo, Dominican Republic. He started music studies at the National Cons. of Music of Santo Domingo, and continued them in the USA, at the Manhattan School of Music and The Juilliard School of Music, both in New York City, under Paulo Bracalli and Vincent La Selva.
Works: Merengue Fantasía, for orch. (1989).
Source: DEW

Molina Pinillo, José, Guatemalan composer; b.28 Aug 1889, Guatemala City, Guatemala; d.? He studied with Julián Carrillo in Mexico City, Mexico, and with Xaver Scharwenka in Berlin, Germany.
Worls: Rapsodias Guatemaltecas; Miniatura; Cromos Nacionales.
Sources: DM, MLA, MMLA

Moncayo García, José Pablo, Mexican composer; b.29 Jun 1912, Guadalajara, State of Jalisco, Mexico; d.16 Jun 1958, Mexico City, Mexico. He studied composition with Candelario Huízar and Carlos Chávez, and piano with Eduardo Hernández Moncada. Member of the *Grupo de los Cuatro* (Group of the Four), together with Daniel Ayala Pérez, Salvador Contreras Sánchez, and Blas Galindo Dimas. In 1932, he joined the percussion section of the Mexican Symphony Orch., Mexico City. In 1944, he was appointed artistic director of the National Symphony Orch. of Mexico City, which he conducted from 1949 to 1952.

Works (selective list): *La Mulata de Córdoba,* opera (1948); *Zapata,* ballet (1953); *Huapango,* for orch. (1941); Sinfonía No.1 (1942); Sinfonietta (1944); *Homenaje a Cervantes,* for 2 oboes and strings (1947); *Cumbres,* for orch. (1954); *Huepayan,* symphonic dance; chamber music; piano pieces; songs.
Sources: BB, DCM, DM, GMM, MLA, MMLA

Moncho, Vicente, Argentine composer, violinist, and teacher; b.10 Jul 1939, San Juan, Prov. of San Juan, Argentina. He studied violin in San Juan and in Mendoza, Prov. of Mendoza, Argentina, from 1956 to 1962. From 1962 to 1965, he studied violin and viola with Humberto Carfi and harmony with Teodoro Fuchs, in Buenos Aires, Argentina. In 1965, he entered the Escuela de Bellas Artes of the National Univ. of La Plata, Prov. of Buenos Aires, Argentina, where he studied harmony and counterpoint with Jacobo Ficher, and orch. conducting with Mariano Drago. He also studied at the Escuela de Bellas Artes of the National Univ. of Córdoba, Prov. of Córdoba, Argentina. Professor at the Escuela de Bellas Artes of the National Univ. of Córdoba.
Works (selective list): *Orch.*: *Tres Estructuras* (1969); *Transmutaciones* (1973); *Introspección* (1975); *Crecientes* (1990); *El Don del Aguila,* for band (1991). *El Regreso de Anaconda,* ballet (1982); *En Honor a la Verdad,* operatic farce for soloists, chorus, orch., and actors (1988); chamber music; choruses.
Source: ISC

Mondino, Luis Pedro, Uruguayan composer; b.19 Nov 1903, DM (1904, BHMCU), Montevideo, Uruguay; d.1974, Europe. He studied piano with Luisa Gallo and Camilo Giucci and harmony with Felipe Larrimbe in Montevideo. In 1927, he went to Europe where he studied composition with Léon Jongen, Raymond Moulaert, and Nadia Boulanger.
Works: *Fiesta Vasca,* for lute quartet. *Songs: La Vidalita; Diálogo Campero; La Liebre Arisca; Señora Loba, Señora Luna; Se Enojó la Luna; Señor jardinero.*
Sources: BHMCU, DM, MLA, MMLA

Monestel, Alejandro, Costa Rican composer and organist; b.26 Apr 1865, San José, Costa Rica; d.3 Nov 1950, San José. He studied first in Costa Rica, and then at the Cons. of Brussels, Belgium, piano, organ, and harmony. In 1884, he returned to Costa Rica and became organist and *maestro de capilla* (chapelmaster) at the Cathedral of San José. Director of the Philharmonic Society and the National School of Music of Costa Rica. Professor at the National Cons. of San José. He lived in New York from 1902 to 1937, where he was active as a church organist and composer.

Works: 14 masses; 4 requiem; 5 cantatas on the life of Jesus; *Rapsodia Costarricense,* for orch. (1935); *Dos Rapsodias Guanacastecas,* for band.
Sources: BB, DM, MLA, MMLA

Montalvo, José A., Puerto Rican composer; b.2 Feb 1951, Mayagüez, Puerto Rico. He began music studies with Alfredo Romero at the Cons. of Music of Puerto Rico. Later, he moved to Indiana Univ. at Bloomington, Indiana, where he received a Bachelor's degree and a Master's degree in music as a student of Fred Fox. He continued music studies at New York Univ. under Dinu Ghezzo.
Works (selective list): *Canto para la América Sufrida,* for timpani and strings (1979); *Afirmación,* for cello and chamber ensemble (1980); *Antillana,* for orch. (1983); *Espejos,* for orch. (1985); chamber music; music for solo instruments; piano pieces; songs.
Source: CPR

Montecino Montalva, Alfonso, Chilean composer and pianist; b.28 Oct 1924, Osorno, Chile. He studied piano with Alberto Spikin and composition with Domingo Santa Cruz and Jorge Urrutia Blondel at the Cons. of Music of the Univ. of Chile, Santiago de Chile, Chile. In 1947, he went to the USA where he studied composition with Randall Thompson, Edgar Varèse, Bohuslav Martinu, and Roger Sessions. At the same time, he continued his piano studies with Claudio Arrau and Rafael de Silva. Professor of piano at the School of Music of Indiana Univ. at Bloomington, Indiana.
Works (selective list): *Obertura Concertante,* for orch. (1948); *Concertino de Cámara,* for orch. (1965); choral works; chamber music; piano pieces; songs.
Source: CTA19

Montero, José Angel, Venezuelan composer; b.1839, Caracas, Venezuela; d.1881, Caracas. He started music studies with his father, José María Montero. He studied several instruments, including the flute, for which he had a predilection. *Maestro de capilla* (chapelmaster) at the Iglesia Metropolitana and member of the Academy of Music, branch of the National Inst. of Fine Arts in Caracas.
Works (selective list): *Virginia,* opera; 15 zarzuelas; 16 overtures; 5 marches; 30 oficios de difuntos; salon music.
Sources: MLA, MMLA

Montiel Olvera, Armando, Mexican composer and pianist; b.14 Oct 1917, San Juan Teotihuacán, Mexico. He studied with Manuel M. Ponce, José Rolón, Candelario Huízar, Joaquín Amparán, José

Rocabruna, and Luis G. Saloma at the National Cons. of Music of Mexico, Mexico City, Mexico, from which he graduated in piano in 1940, and in composition in 1941. He took a master class with Claudio Arrau. Professor of piano at the National Cons. of Music of Mexico.
Works (selective list): *Semblanza Morisca,* for piano and orch. (1939); *Concertino Mexicano,* for piano and orch. (1943); *Asombro,* cantata for baritone, chorus, and orch. (1945); *Conga,* for chamber orch. (1947); *Dos Movimientos Sinfónicos* (1950); *Tienda de Sueños,* ballet (1956); music for the organ; chamber music; piano pieces; songs.
Source: ISC

Moraga, Manuel E., Guatemalan composer and teacher; b.middle of 19th century, Guatemala; d.beginning of 20th century, Guatemala City, Guatemala.
Works (selective list)*: Te Deum,* for 4 voices; *Religiosa,* march; *Una Lágrima,* funeral march; *Salve,* for solo tenor; *Salve Regina,* for solo tenor; waltzes; mazurkas; polkas; dances; marches.
Source: MMLA

Morales, Carlos O., Puerto Rican composer and guitarist; b.17 Jun 1953, San Juan, Puerto Rico. He studied at the Cons. of Music of Puerto Rico where he obtained two Bachelor degrees, one in guitar and the other in music education. He also studied at the Chigiana Academy of Music in Siena, Italy. In 1979, he went to California where he obtained a Master's degree in musical arts in 1981. Professor of guitar at the Cons. of Music of Puerto Rico and of music history at the Inter-American Univ. at the Metropolitan Campus in San Juan.
Works (selective list): *Guanina,* symphonic poem (1981); *La Campana del Ingenio,* symphonic poem (1984); chamber music; music for the guitar; music for solo instruments; children songs; hymns.
Source: CPR

Morales, Lorenzo, Guatemalan composer; b.10 Aug 1833, Zacapa, Guatemala; d.17 Oct 1896, Guatemala City, Guatemala. He studied with Francisco Isaac Sáenz. Professor at the National Cons. of Music of Guatemala City and several private inst.
Works (selective list): *Los Solterones,* zarzuela; *Miserere;* 5 overtures; piano pieces.
Source: MMLA

Morales, Melesio, Mexican composer and teacher; b.4 Dec 1838, Mexico City, Mexico; d.12 May 1908, San Pedro de los Pinos,

Mexico. He studied with Jesús Rivera, Agustín Caballero, Felipe Larios, Antonio Valle, and Cenobio Paniagua. He studied composition in France, and with Teódulo Mabellini in Florence, Italy. Professor of composition at the National Cons. of Music of Mexico, Mexico City.

Works (selective list): *Operas*: *Romeo y Julieta* (1863); *Ildegonda* (1866); *Gino Corsini* (1877); *Cleopatra* (1891); *Carlomagno; El Judío Errante*. *Misa Solemne; Dios Salve a la Patria,* hymn-symphony; symphonic works; chamber music; piano pieces.

Bibl.: I.M. Altamirano, *Don Melesio Morales, El Renacimiento,* Mexico, 1869. A. Herrera y Ogazón, *El Arte Musical en México,* Mexico, 1917. O. Mayer-Serra, *Panorama de la Música Mexicana, Fondo de Cultura,* Mexico, 1941. J. Romero, *Melesio Morales, Revista Musical Mexicana,* Mexico, 1943.

Sources: BB, DM, GDM, MLA, MMLA

Morales Nieva, Ignacio, Puerto Rican composer, conductor, and music critic of Spanish origin; b.18 Dec 1928, Valdepeñas (Ciudad Real) in the region of La Mancha, Spain. He studied with Enrique Masso, Joaquín Turina, and Conrado del Campo at the Royal Cons. of Music of Madrid, Spain. He also studied orch. conducting at the Manhattan School of Music of New York City. In 1954, he moved to Puerto Rico and became professor at the Univ. of Turabo, Puerto Rico, and the Cons. of Music of Puerto Rico. In 1978, he founded and conducted the Padre Antonio Soler Chamber Orch.

Works (selective list): *La Luz Lejana,* lyric drama (1957); *El Primer Angelus,* cantata for soloists and orch. (1958); *Pilar María de los Dolores,* lyric novel (1958); *El Dorado,* lyric drama (1962); *Maese Tomé,* comic opera (1964); *La Dama Duende,* suite for strings (1966); *El Grito de Lares,* for string orch. (1970); *Música para Arcos,* for string orch. (1970); *Soltero Setenta y Dos,* musical comedy (1971); 4 symphonies (1974, 1974, 1985, 1986); Concerto Grosso for orch. (1972); *La Enamorada del Rey,* musical comedy (1972); *La Tragedia del Santo Domingo,* lyric drama (1976); *Obertura al Gusto Teatral Italiano,* for orch. (1978); *Oda a Héctor Berlioz,* symphonic poem (1980); *Salmo XI,* for soprano and orch. (1982); *La Maja y el Dragón*, overture (1983); *Las Siete Palabras de Nuestro Señor Jesucristo,* cantata for orch. (1984); *Ebed Jahave,* for narrator and orch. (1987); *El Espectro Insaciable,* lyric drama (1988); *Reconquista,* for orch. (1988); chamber music; piano pieces; music for organ.

Source: CPR

Morales Pino, Pedro, Colombian composer; b.1862, Cartago, Dept. of Valle del Cauca, Colombia; d.1926, Bogotá, Colombia. He studied with Julio Quevedo Arvelo. He founded *La Lira Colombiana,*

chamber ensemble devoted to promote Colombian music, in Colombia and abroad.
Works: *Las Cuatro Preguntas,* based on the classic traditional rhythm bambuco; *Fantasía sobre Motivos Colombianos,* for orch.
Source: MMLA

Morel Campos, Juan, Puerto Rican composer, organist, flutist, double bass player, and orch. and band conductor; b.12 May 1857, Ponce, Puerto Rico; d.12 May 1896, Ponce.
Works (selective list): *Puerto Rico,* symphony; *Un Día de Elecciones,* zarzuela; *Un Viaje por América,* zarzuela; *Amor es Triunfo,* zarzuela; Overture; *Marcha Procesional;* sacred music; waltzes; marches; mazurkas; polkas; more than 200 Puerto Rican dances.
Sources: MMLA, MMPR

Morel (Morell) Guzmán, Antonio, Dominican composer; b.20 Dec 1920, Tamboril, Peña, Dominican Republic. He studied with Federico Camejo and Enrique Casal Chapí. Director of the Academy of Music of the Reformatory Presidente Trujillo in San Cristóbal, Dominican Republic.
Works: Sonata for string quartet; Concerto for strings; several dances in ancient style.
Sources: DM, MMLA

Moreno, Alberto, Ecuadorian composer, poet, and journalist; b.1889, Cotacachi, Ecuador; d.1980, Ecuador. He studied at the National Cons. of Music of Quito, Ecuador.
Works: *Solar Nativo,* suite for orch.
Source: EFCMP

Moreno, Hilarión, Argentine composer, marine, and diplomat; b.1863, Buenos Aires; d.1931, Portugal.
Works: *El Príncipe Luzbel,* zarzuela (1894); *Sulamita,* opereta. Famous for his Boston waltzes, very popular in Europe.
Source: EMA

Moreno Andrade, Segundo Luis, Ecuadorian composer and musicologist; b.3 Aug 1882, Cotacachi, Imbabura, Ecuador; d.18 Nov 1972, Quito, Ecuador. He studied at the National Cons. of Music of Quito with Domínico Brescia. Director-founder of the Music Cons. of Cuenca, and director of the Cons. of Guayaquil, both in Ecuador. Organizer and director of the First Festival of Indigenous Dances, under a project of the Unión Nacional de Periodistas.
Works (selective list): *Mostly for military band*: *Preludio Sinfónico* (1910); *Diez de Agosto,* overture; *La Coronación* (1918); *La Emancipación,* cantata (1920); *Nueve de Julio,* overture (1925); 3

suites ecuatorianas for orch. (1921, 1944, 1945); songs. *Books: Música en el Ecuador, El Ecuador en Cien Años de Independencia,* Quito, 1930; *Música y Danzas Autóctonas del Ecuador,* Quito, 1949; *La Música de los Incas,* Quito, 1957; *Historia de la Música en el Ecuador,* Quito, 1972.
Bibl.: C. Sigmund, *Segundo Luis Moreno: his Contributions in Ecuadorian Musicology,* University of Minnesota, 1971.
Sources: BB, DM, GDM, MLA, MMLA

Moreno González, Juan Carlos, Paraguayan composer and pianist; b.9 Feb 1912, Asunción, Paraguay. At the beginning, he was self-taught in music, and later, in 1938, he went to Sâo Paulo, Brazil, to study piano and composition. Director of the Cons. del Ateneo of Asunción.
Works (selective list): Violin concerto in G; Piano concerto in A; *Symphonic Suite on Folkloric Themes; El Amanecer,* for orch.; *Primavera,* for orch.; Trio for piano, violin, and cello; String quartet; piano pieces; guaranias; tangos.
Sources: DM, KTL, MLA, MMPA

Moreno Manzano, Salvador, Mexican composer, poet, and painter; b.3 Dec 1916, Orizaba, State of Veracruz, Mexico. In 1936, he entered the National Cons. of Music in Mexico City, Mexico, where he studied solfeggio with Teodoro Campos Arce, harmony with José Rolón, piano with Francisco Agea, and composition with Carlos Chávez. He also studied composition in Barcelona, Spain, where he settled in 1955.
Works: Severino, opera (1961); children's choruses; songs. *Books: Carnet Musical; Los Angeles Músicos.*
Source: GMM

Moretto, Nelly, Argentine composer; b.1925, Rosario, Prov. of Santa Fe, Argentina; d.1976, Buenos Aires, Argentina. She studied at the National Cons. of Music Carlos López Buchardo of Buenos Aires. Later, she continued studies at the Univ. of Illinois in Chicago, Illinois, and in Buenos Aires with Juan Carlos Paz. Member of the *Agrupación Nueva Música.*
Works: Trio for oboe, violin, and cello (1956); *Composición No.7,* for flute, viola, bass clarinet, and guitar (1959); *Composición No.8,* for instrumental ensemble (1962); *Composición No.9,* for 2 instrumental ensembles, magnetic tape, dance, and lights show (1966); *Collage y Música para un Espectáculo de Danza* (1967); *Coeri Battenti,* for string quartet and magnetic tape (1968).
Sources: CAMR, EMA

Mucillo, Luis, Argentine composer and pianist: b.1956, Rosario, Prov. of Buenos Aires, Argentina. He studied piano with Aldo Antognazzi and Gerardo Gandini and composition with Jorge Rotter and Francisco Kröpfl. He also studied in Germany under Hans Ulrich Humpert at the Dept. of Electronic Music of the Univ. of Cologne. Director of the *Núcleo de Música Contemporánea* of Brasília, Brazil. *Works*: *Dos Poemas Chinos,* for voice and piano (1974); *Dos Poemas de Li Po,* for voice and piano (1974); *Composición,* for clarinet (1976); *Música,* for winds, piano, and percussion (1976); *Nocturno V,* for chamber orch. (1978); *Sonetos de Petrarca,* for voice and instrumental ensemble (1978); *Tres Preludios,* for harpsichord (1981); *Impromptu in Memoriam of Berg,* for flute, piccolo, harpsichord, and celesta (1985); *Isla de Cristal,* electroacoustic music (1982); *Au Delá des Portes D'Ivoiré,* electroacoustic music (1984); *Imágenes,* for harpsichord and orch. (1987).
Source: CAMR

Muench, Gerhart, Mexican composer and pianist of German origin; b.23 Mar 1907, Dresden, Germany; d.9 Nov 1988, Tacámbaro, Mexico. He studied piano with his father, a professor at the Dresden Cons. In 1947, he emigrated to America, and settled in Mexico in 1953. Taught at the National Univ. of Mexico, Mexico City, Mexico. *Works* (selective list): *Tumulus Veneris,* opera (1950); *Concerto da Camara,* for piano and chamber orch. (1926); *Capriccio Variato,* for piano and orch. (1941); *Vocaciones,* for piano and chamber orch. (1951); Bassoon concerto (1956); *Muerte sin Fin,* for orch. (1957); Concerto for piano and strings (1957); Violin concerto (1959); *Labyrinthus Orphei,* for orch. (1965); *Oxymora,* for orch. (1967); *Epitomae Tacambarensiae,* for orch. (1974); chamber music; sacred music; choruses; songs.
Source: BB

Mujica, José Tomás, Uruguayan composer of Spanish origin; b.10 Feb 1883, Tolosa, Prov. of Guipúzcoa, Spain; d.28 Feb 1963, Tacuarembó, Uruguay. He studied in his native city with Felipe Gorriti and Eduardo Mocoroa. In Madrid, Spain, he studied at the Royal Cons. Later he studied with E. Morera in Barcelona, Spain, and with Paul Gilson in Brussels, Belgium. He settled in Uruguay in 1913. Director of the Municipal Cons. of Tacuarembó. *Works* (selective list): String quartet; *Tema con Variaciones,* for cello; Concerto for flute and piano; *Ayacucho,* symphonic poem; several orch. works; school songs; chamber music.
Sources: BHMCU, DMD, MU

Muñoz, José Luis, Venezuelan composer; b.1928, Caracas, Venezuela. He started his music studies at the Salesian Fathers

Boarding School. In 1947, he entered the Escuela Superior de Música of Caracas, where he studied solfeggio and music theory with Inocente Carreño, piano with Moisés Moleiro and Emma Stopello, harmony with Primo Moschini, music history and aesthetics with Juan Bautista Plaza, and composition with Vicente Emilio Sojo. Later, he went to the USA to complete advanced music studies.

Works (selective list): *Preludio*, for orch. (1959); *Fantasía de Bolsillo*, for orch. (1964); *Móbiles, Partitura Aleatoria*, for orch. (1967); chamber music; piano pieces; songs.
Sources: CTA14

Mussolino, Rodolfo Rubens, Argentine composer and physician; b.1917, Buenos Aires, Argentina. He studied with Constantino Gaito and Rafael González. He graduated from the School of Medicine of the National Univ. of Buenos Aires.
Works: *Music for piano:* El Relato del Arpa; Romance de la Niña Mora; Arrullo; Balada del Mar.
Source: EMA

N

Napoleón, Alfredo, Argentine pianist and composer of Portuguese origin; b.1852, Oporto, Portugal; d.1917, Oporto. He settled in Buenos Aires, Argentina, in 1870. In 1875, he was appointed professor at the Provincial Music School of the Prov. of Buenos Aires, Argentina.
Works: 3 concertos for piano and orch.; *Obertura Sinfónica, Andante, y Polonesa,* for piano and orch.; Sonata in G for piano; Gran sonata in C minor for piano.
Source: EMA

Napolitano, Emilio Angel, Argentine composer and violinist; b.12 Nov 1907, Buenos Aires, Argentina. He studied violin with Edmundo Weingand, piano with Arturo Luzzatti, harmony with Floro M. Ugarte, counterpoint with José Gil, and fugue and instrumentation with Constantino Gaito. Artistic director of the Teatro Colón of Buenos Aires in 1948. First violin at the orch. of the Teatro Colón. Founder of the quartet of the Sociedad Nacional de Música, today Asociación Argentina de Compositores. Professor of violin and chamber music at the National Cons. of Music Carlos López Buchardo of Buenos Aires.
Works (selective list): *Apurimac,* sympho-choreographic poem; Sonata for violin and piano (1936); *Suite Argentina,* for string quartet; Quartet for flute, clarinet, bassoon, and piano; piano pieces; songs.
Sources: CA, DM, EMA, MLA, MMLA

Nascimento, Adelmo Francisco de, Brazilian composer and violinist; b.1848, Bahia, Brazil; d.1898. *Maestro de capilla* (chapelmaster) at the Metropolitan Cathedral of the city of Salvador, Brazil.
Works: Missa a N.S. da Boa Esperança.
Source: MMLA

Nascimento, Elviro do, Brazilian composer; b.12 Dec 1890, Uberaba, Minas Gerais, Brazil; d.? Conductor of the police band of Minas Gerais. Professor at the Cons. of Music of Minas Gerais.
Works (selective list): *Iara,* opera; several symphonies; sacred music.
Source: MMLA

Navarre Viscarra, Gustavo, Bolivian pianist and composer; b.17 Jul 1931, La Paz, Bolivia. He started music lessons with his mother. In 1947, he studied piano with Egon Carl Schilf. In 1948, he entered the National Cons. of Music in La Paz where he studied piano with Mario Estensoro and Alicia Eguino Justiniano, theory and solfeggio with

Teófilo Molina, and harmony and counterpoint with Erich Eisner. In 1957, he was appointed professor of harmony, counterpoint, and composition at the National Cons. of Music in La Paz. In 1968, in a competition held in Geneva, Switzerland, he received a scholarship to study music in Paris, France; he studied orchestration, composition, and musical analysis with Henry Ortilleux, Marcel Mihalovici, and Pierre Petit. In 1970, he became director of the same cons., a position held until 1974.
Works: 3 piano sonatas; Quintet; Trio; 2 symphonies; 2 quartets.
Source: CB

Navarro, Juan, Mexican composer, chorus singer, and Franciscan priest of Spanish origin; b.c.1550, Cádiz, Spain; d.c.1610, Mexico? He worked in the Mexican prov. of Michoacán as a Franciscan priest, confessor, and chorus singer.
Works: Liber in quo Quatuor Passiones Christi Domini Continentur; Octo Lamentationes; Oratioque Hieremie Prophete.
Bibl.: G. Chase, *Juan Navarro Hispalensis and Juan Navarro Gaditanus, MQ,* Vol.31, 1945. R. Stevenson, *Music in Mexico,* New York, 1952.
Source: GDM

Nazareth (Nazaré), Ernesto Júlio de, Brazilian composer and pianist; b.20 Mar 1863, Rio de Janeiro, Brazil; d.4 Feb 1934, GDM (1937, MLA), Rio de Janeiro. He started to study piano with his mother, and then continued with Eduardo Madeira and Lucien Lambert, but he was mainly a self-taught musician.
Works (selective list): *Music for piano:* more than 200 compositions: tangos brasileiros; polkas; waltzes; marches; dances in the rhythms of samba and chôro.
Bibl.: M. de Andrade, *Ernesto Nazareth,* Estado de Sâo Paulo, 1940. R. Almeida, *História da Música Brasileira,* Rio de Janeiro, 1942. B. Itiberê, *Ernesto Nazareth na Música Brasileira, Boletín Latinoamericano de Música,* Vol.6, 1946.
Sources: BB, CTA10, GDM, HMB, MLA, MMLA

Negrete Woolcock, Samuel, Chilean composer and teacher; b.18 Dec 1893, Santiago de Chile, Chile; d.? He studied music at the National Cons. of Music of Santiago de Chile, where he later became professor and director, 1944-46. He also studied architecture, and at one time he taught mathematics.
Works (selective list): *Escenas Sinfónicas,* for orch. (1933); *La Fiesta del Camino,* symphonic poem; 3 string quartets; Wind septet; pieces for piano; choruses; songs.
Sources: DM, HMB, MLA, MMLA

Nepomuceno, Alberto, Brazilian composer, conductor, pianist, and organist; b.6 Jul 1864, Fortaleza, Brazil; d.16 Oct 1920, Rio de Janeiro, Brazil. He began to study music with his father, Vitor Nepomuceno, in Pernambuco, Brazil. Later he went to Europe where he studied in Rome, Italy, with Eugenio Terziani and De Sanctis at the Academia Santa Cecilia; in Berlin, Germany, he studied composition with Heinrich von Herzogenberg, composition for the organ with Arne Kleffel, and piano with Heinrich Ehrlich at the Akademische Meister-Schule; in Paris, France, he studied organ with Alexandre Guilmant. In 1895, he returned to Brazil, and in 1902, he was appointed director and professor of organ at the Inst. Nacional de Música in Rio de Janeiro.
Works (selective list): *Operas: Artemis* (1898); *O Garatuja* (1904); *Abul* (1913). *Orch.: Prière* (1887); *Rapsodie Brésilienne* (1887); *Série Brasileira* (1892); *Scherzo Vivace* (1893); *Sinfonía* (1894); *Seis Valsas Humorísticas,* for piano (1903); *O Garatuja,* prelude (1904); *Romance e Tarantella,* for cello (1908). Chamber music; piano pieces; songs.
Bibl.: J.R. Barbosa, *Alberto Nepomuceno, Revista Brasileira de Música,* Vol.7, 1940. L.H. Corrêa de Acevedo, *150 Anos de Música no Brasil (1800-1950),* Rio de Janeiro, 1956. G. Béhague, *The Beginnings of Musical Nationalism in Brazil,* Detroit, 1971.
Sources: BB, CTA10, DM, GDM, HMB, MLA, MMLA

Neumane, Antonio, Ecuadorian composer of German origin; fl.second half of 19th century. First director of the National Cons. of Music of Quito, Ecuador, in 1870.
Works: *Ecuadorian National Anthem.*
Sources: DM, MLA

Nieto, César, Costa Rican composer of Spanish origin; b.1892, Barcelona, Spain; d.? He settled in Costa Rica in 1899, and became a Costa Rican citizen in 1936. Conductor of a choral society in San José, Costa Rica.
Works: *La Piedra del Toxil,* ballet; salon music; waltzes; marches.
Source: MLA

Nin Culmell, Joaquín María, Cuban composer and pianist of German origin; b.5 Sep 1908, Berlin, Germany. Son of Joaquín Nin y Castellanos. He settled in the USA, and became an American citizen in 1951. He started his music education in Barcelona, Spain, where he studied solfeggio with Conchita Badia, 1913-14. In 1924, he went to Paris, France, where he studied at the Schola Cantorum and at the National Cons. of Music, piano with Paul Brand, Alfred Cortot, and Ricardo Viñes, and composition with Paul Dukas. He also took some lessons with Manuel de Falla in Granada, Spain. Pianist at the Escuela

Española of Middleburg, Vermont, professor at the Williams College of Williamstown, Massachusetts and the Univ. of California at Berkeley, California, and visiting professor at the Association of American Colleges, all in the USA.
Works (selective list): *Stage: Yerma,* incidental music (1956); *El Burlador de Sevilla,* ballet (1957-65); *La Celestina,* opera (1965-85); *Le Rêve de Cyrano,* ballet (1978); *Cybelline,* incidental music (1981). *Orch.: Homenaje a Falla* (1933-90); Concerto for piano (1946); *Tres Piezas Antiguas Españolas* (1959-61); *Diferencias* (1962); Concerto for cello or guitar (1962-63); *Cantata del Padre Pradas,* for voice, harpsichord, and strings (1965-66); *Seis Canciones Populares Sefardíes,* for voice (1982). Chamber music; piano pieces; songs; choruses. *Books: The Music of Cuba,* Washington, 1943; *Latin American Composers and the I.S.M.C., Music Between the Wars,* Oxford Univ. Press.
Sources: BB, DCM, DM, ISC, MMLA

Nin y Castellanos, Joaquín, Cuban composer, teacher, and pianist; b.29 Sep 1879, Havana, Cuba; d.24 Oct 1949, Havana. Father of Joaquín Nin Culmell. He studied music theory with Felipe Pedrell and piano with Carlos Vidiella in Barcelona, Spain, and composition with Vincent D'Indy and piano with Moritz Moszkowski at the Schola Cantorum in Paris, France. Honorary professor at the Schola Cantorum and at the New Univ. of Brussels, Belgium. From 1910 to 1939, he gave concert tours throughout Europe, North Africa, Cuba, and South America. In 1939, he returned to Cuba and settled in Havana as a piano teacher at the Municipal Cons. of Music; he also organized a musical society and was the editor of a musical bulletin.
Works (selective list): *20 Cantos Populares Españoles,* for voice and piano (1923); *16 Sonates Anciennes d'Auteurs Espagnols,* for piano (1925); *7 Chants Lyriques and 7 Chansons Picaresques Espagnoles Anciennes,* for voice and piano (1926); *Mensaje a Claude Debussy,* for piano (1929); *10 Noëls Espagnols,* for voice and piano (1932); *Canto de Cuna para los Huérfanos de España,* for piano (1939); 3 symphonies; Ballet; Mimodrama; chamber music; piano pieces; songs. *Books: Pro Arte,* 1909; *Idées et Commentaires,* 1912.
Sources: BB, DMC, ISC, MLA

Nito, Humberto de, Argentine composer, teacher, and pianist; b.1 Jan 1891, Rosario, Prov. of Santa Fe, Argentina; d.? Brother of José de Nito. Studied with Alejandro Longo and Camillo De Nardis at the Royal Cons. of Music San Pietro a Majella of Naples, Italy. Director, together with his brother, of the Cons. Beethoven of Rosario.
Works (selective list): *Pequeña Suite,* for orch.; children's music for piano; choral music.
Sources: DM, MMLA

Nito, José de, Argentine composer, conductor, teacher, and pianist; b.1887, Rosario, Prov. of Santa Fe, Argentina; d.1945, Rosario. Brother of Humberto de Nito. He studied in Rosario with José Cayano. In 1901, he entered the Royal Cons. of Music San Pietro a Majella of Naples, Italy, where he studied with Giuseppe Martucci, Pablo Serrano, Camillo De Nardis, and Alejandro Longo. He founded, together with his brother, the Cons. Beethoven of Rosario. *Works* (selective list): Sonata for piano; Symphonic poem; String quartet; piano pieces; songs.
Sources: DM, MLA, MMLA

Nobre, Marlos, Brazilian composer; b.18 Feb 1939, Recife, Brazil. He studied piano and theory at the Pernambuco Cons. of Music, Brazil, 1948-59. In 1960, he went to Rio de Janeiro, Brazil, where he studied with Hans Joachim Koellreutter and later he studied with Camargo Guarnieri at the Sâo Paulo Cons., Brazil, 1963-64, and with Alberto Ginastera in Buenos Aires, Argentina, 1963-64; he took a course in electronic music with Vladimir Ussachevsky at Columbia Univ., New York, in 1969. Music director of the National Symphony Orch. of Brazil, 1971-76, and of Radio MEC. First director of the National Inst. of Music at the Funarte, 1976-1979. Composer-in-residence at the Brahms-Haus in Baden-Baden, Germany, 1980-81. President of the Brazilian Academy of Music. Coordinator of contemporary music programs at Radio MEC. President of the National Music Committee of UNESCO. General director of Brazilian Jeunesses Musicales.
Works (selective list): Concertino for piano and strings (1959); *Divertimento,* for piano and orch. (1965); *Ukrinmakrinkrin,* for soprano, wind instruments, and piano (1964); *Rhythmetron,* for 32 percussion instruments (1968); *Convergencias,* for orch. (1968); *Desafío I,* for viola and string orch. (1968); *Desafío II,* for cello and string orch. (1968); *Desafío III,* for violin and string orch. (1968); *Desafío IV,* for double bass and string orch. (1977); *Desafío V,* for 6 cellos (1977); *Desafío VI,* for string orch. (1979); *Desafío VII,* for piano and string orch. (1980); *Concerto Breve,* for piano and orch. (1969); *Ludus Instrumentalis,* for chamber orch. (1969); *Mosáico,* for orch. (1970); *Biósfera,* for string orch. (1970); *O Canto Multiplicado,* for voice and string orch. (1972); *In Memoriam,* for orch. (1976); Concerto No.1 for string orch. (1975-76); Concerto No.2 for string orch. (1981); *Cantata do Chimborazo,* for soloists, chorus, and orch. (1982); *Abertura Festiva,* for orch. (1982); Concerto for piano and string orch. (1984); *Quatro Danças Latinoamericanas,* for chamber orch. (1989); Concerto for trumpet and string orch. (1989); *Concertante do Imaginario,* for piano and string orch. (1989); *Xingu,* for orch. (1989); *Columbus,* for soloists, chorus, and orch. (1990); *O Café,* opera (1991); *Cantata do Café,* for

soloists, chorus, and orch. (1991); Sinfonía No.1 for orch. (1992); chamber music; piano pieces; choruses.
Bibl.: G. Béhague, *Music in Latin America: An Introduction,* New Jersey, 1979. D.P. Appleby, *The Music in Brazil,* Austin, Texas, 1983.
Sources: BB, CTA17, GDM, ISC

Nobre Olivares, Ramón, Mexican composer and choral conductor; b.25 Sep 1920, Pachuca, Mexico. He studied at the National Cons. of Music of Mexico, Mexico City, where later he became its director.
Works: Orch. compositions; choral music; music for the guitar.
Source: KTL

Nogueira, Ilza, Brazilian composer and teacher; b.12 Dec 1948, Salvador, Bahia, Brazil. She studied piano with Fritz Pierre Klose and composition with Ernst Widmer at the Universidade Federal da Bahia. In 1972, she received a fellowship from the German government to study composition with Mauricio Kagel at the Rheinische Musikschule in Cologne. She was appointed to teach music at the State Univ. of Paraíba, Brazil, in 1977. From 1982 to 1985, she studied for a Doctorate degree in composition under Lejaren Hiller at the State Univ. of New York at Buffalo, New York, and in 1990 she was a post doctoral fellow at Yale Univ., New Haven, Connecticut, under the supervision of Janet Schmalfeldt. Member and first president of the board of directors of ANPPOM.
Works (selective list): *Metástase,* for chorus and magnetic tape (1971); *Idiossincrasia,* for 7 violins, ronda, percussion, magnetic tape, voices (soprano, chorus, with audience participation), and synthesizer, requiring staging and dance (1972); *Triloquia,* for violin, horn, bassoon, piano, and percussion, and tape with piccolo, trumpet, and cello (1977); *Cromossons,* for 3 orch. prerecorded (1977); *Kaleidoscope,* for brass ensemble (1984); *Transforms,* for quartet of saxophones and tape (1985); *Urtext,* for soprano, baritone, woodwinds, string quartet, and percussion (1985); *In Memoriam,* for soprano and percussion (1988).
Sources: NGDWC, NWC

Nogueira, Teodoro Ascendino, Brazilian composer and violinist; b.9 Oct 1913, Santa Rita de Passa Quatro, Brazil. He studied in his native town and later in Araraquara, Brazil. He completed his violin studies with Torquato Amore in Sâo Paulo, Brazil.
Works (selective list): 5 symphonies; 2 quartets; 12 valsas-choro; 10 serestas; 6 brasilianas; Concertino for string orch.; *Senzala,* suite of dances; *Missa de N.S. dos Navegantes;* piano pieces; songs.
Source: HMB

Nolasco Colón, Pedro, Venezuelan composer; he lived around 1800.
Works: La Llorona; Motete a la Inmaculada Concepción; Pésame a la Virgen.
Source: MMLA

Nova Sondag, Jacqueline, Colombian composer of Belgian origin; b.6 Jan 1935, Ghent, Belgium; d.13 June 1975, Bogotá, Colombia. She studied with Fabio González Zuleta, Luis Antonio Escobar, Olav Roots, and Blas Emilio Atehortúa at the Facultad de Artes of the National Univ. of Colombia in Bogotá. In 1967, she received a scholarship to attend the Inst. Torcuato Di Tella in Buenos Aires, Argentina, where she studied with Alberto Ginastera, Luigi Nono, Francisco Kröpfl, Vladimir Ussachevsky, Roman Haubenstock Ramati, F. von Reichenback, and Gerardo Gandini. She worked with Francisco Kröpfl at the Laboratorio de Acústica, Estudio de Fonología Musical in Buenos Aires. She formed the *Agrupación Nueva Música* in Bogotá.
Works (selective list): *Music for the theater: Julius Caesar; Macbeth. Orch.: Metamórfosis III* (1966); *Móviles 12,* for piano and strings (1967); *Ensayos,* for strings (1968); *Segmentos,* for oboe (1979). Chamber music; electronic music; sacred music; choruses; piano pieces; songs.
Sources: IBCC, IEW, NGDWC

Nunes, Francisco, Brazilian composer; b. 1875, Minas Gerais, Brazil; d.1934, Brazil. He studied first with his father, Francisco Nunes Neto Leâo. Later he studied at the National Inst. of Music of Rio de Janeiro, Brazil, where he became professor of clarinet. Founder and director of the Cons. of Music of Minas Gerais. He was one of the organizers of the Sociedade de Conciertos Sinfónicos and one of the conductors of its orch.
Works: Preludio, Coral y Fuga, for orch.; *Grande Marcha Sinfónica; Grande Valsa de Concerto;* music for the play *Bodas de Lía.*
Source: MMLA

Nunes, Joâo, Brazilian composer; b.20 Jan 1877, Sâo Luiz, State of Maranhâo, Brazil; d.18 Aug 1951, Rio de Janeiro, Brazil. He studied at the National Inst. of Music in Rio de Janeiro, and later, with a scholarship from the State of Maranhâo, in Europe.
Works: Music for piano: Pièces Drôles; La Vie des Abeilles; Les Harmonies de la Cathédrale; As Peças Infantis; Os Tres Meninos.
Source: MMLA

Nunes García, José Mauricio, Brazilian composer; b.22 Sep 1767, Rio de Janeiro, Brazil; d.18 Apr 1830, Rio de Janeiro. He started his music education with his mother and an aunt. Later he studied music

theory with a local teacher, Salvador José, and also philosophy, languages, and theology. He was ordained a priest in 1792. He played in bands and orch. and also performed as a singer. *Maestro de capilla* (chapelmaster) at the old Cathedral of Rio de Janeiro, today Church of the Rosario.
Works (selective list): *Religious music: Missa en Si bemol* (1801); *Missa de Defuntos* (1809); *Tantum Ergo; Missa de Requiem* (1816); masses; graduals; sequences; offertories; funeral music; music for Holy Week; matins; vespers; antiphons; hymns; litanies; novenas; motets; canticles; psalms. *Secular music: Sinfonía Fúnebre* (1790); *Zemira,* overture (1803); *Sinfonía Tempestade;* choruses; chamber music; piano pieces; songs.
Sources: DM, GDM

Nunó, Jaime, Mexican composer of Spanish origin; b.8 Sep 1824, San Juan de las Abadesas, Catalonia, Spain; d.18 Jul 1908, Buffalo, New York, USA.
Works: Mexican National Anthem.
Sources: DM, MLA, MMLA

Nuñez, José G., Venezuelan composer; b.7 Jul 1834, Maturín, Venezuela; d.? He studied flute, piano, and organ in Trinidad, and later he studied harmony and counterpoint in Ciudad Bolívar, Venezuela. He lived and taught in Bogotá, Colombia, until 1863, when he returned to Venezuela.
Works: Canto de un Proscripto, zarzuela; *Fantasía,* for flute and piano; *Oficio de Difuntos.*
Source: MMLA

Nuñez Navarrete, Pedro, Chilean composer; b.3 Aug 1906, Constitución, Prov. of Maule, Chile. He studied theory and solfeggio with Ferruccio Pizzi, history of music with Domingo Santa Cruz, piano with Norman Fraser, Juan Reyes, and Rosita Renard, chorus and orch. conducting with Armando Carvajal, and harmony, counterpoint, fugue, and composition with Humberto Allende at the National Cons. of Music of Santiago de Chile, Chile. Professor at various schools in Santiago de Chile. Together with a group of young musicians, he founded the Sociedad Chilena de Música in 1942, and was its first president.
Works (selective list): String quartet (1939); *Adoremus,* motet (1939); *Sinfonía de los Andes* (1941); Quartet for cellos (1942); *El Poeta Jacob,* cantata for tenor and orch. (1962); *Los Guanayes,* for orch. (1968); Wind quintet (1969); piano pieces; songs.
Sources: DM, HMC, MMLA

O

Ogando, Eduardo, Argentine composer; b.1933, La Plata, Prov. of Buenos Aires, Argentina. He studied piano with Rafael González. He studied composition with Gilardo Gilardi and orch. conducting with Mariano Drago at the Escuela Superior de Bellas Artes of the National Univ. of La Plata. In 1954, he settled in Rome, Italy, where he worked with Goffredo Petrassi and Guido Turchi.
Works: Concertino for piano and orch.; *Oda*, for baritone on a text by Ronsard; *Variaciones*, for orch. (1953); Concerto for violin and orch.; *Líricas de Safo*.
Source: EMA

Olazábal, Tirso de, Argentine composer; b.24 May 1924, Buenos Aires, Argentina; d.5 May 1960, Buenos Aires. He studied at the National Cons. of Music Carlos López Buchardo of Buenos Aires with Lita Spena, Athos Palma, Oreste Castronuovo, and Jorge de Lalewicz. In 1951, he received a scholarship to study in France with Arthur Honegger, Roland Manuel, and Pierre Fournier. In 1957, he received a scholarship from the British Council to study in London, England, with Matyas Seiber, Lennox Berkeley, and Norman del Mar. Professor at the Cons. of the Prov. of Buenos Aires, Argentina, where he taught acoustics, and at the Municipal Cons. of Music Manuel de Falla of Buenos Aires.
Works (selective list); Trio for clarinet, cello, and piano (1946); *Scherzo,* for 9 instruments (1946); *Dos Canciones Castellanas* on poems by Garcilaso de la Vega, for soprano or organ and strings (1946); Sonata for 5 wind instruments (1948); *Divertimento No.1,* for flute, oboe, and clarinet (1953); *Introducción y Tema Variado,* for clarinet, piano, and string quartet (1954); *Divertimento No.2,* for oboe, clarinet, and bassoon (1955); *Bayaceto,* music for the stage (1958); *Macbeth,* music for the stage (1959); piano pieces; songs.
Sources: EMA, ISC

Olivares, Carlos, Argentine composer and conductor; b.11 Aug 1890, Tigre, Prov. of Buenos Aires, Argentina; d.? He studied cello at the Williams Conservatory of Buenos Aires. In 1911, he received a scholarship to attend the Schola Cantorum of Paris, France, where he studied cello with François Dressen, harmony with León Saint-Requier, chamber music with Louis de Serres, and composition with Vincent d'Indy. In Germany, he studied orch. conducting with Arthur Nikish. One of the founders of the Philharmonic Orch. of Tucumán, Prov. of Tucumán, Argentina, in 1929, which he conducted for several years. In 1934, he founded and conducted the orch. of the Asociación Argentina de Conciertos of Buenos Aires. Professor of

artistic culture at the Colegio Nacional de Buenos Aires and the National Univ. of Buenos Aires.
Works: Sinfonía en Mi bemol for orch.; *Primera Suite Argentina,* for orch.; *Segunda Suite Argentina,* for orch.; 2 string quartets; *Serie Argentina,* for piano, violin, and cello; Sonata for cello and piano; *Impromptu,* for piano; *Elegía,* for cello and piano.
Sources: DM, EMA

Olivares, Juan Manuel, Venezuelan composer, violinist, organist, pianist, and teacher; b.12 Apr 1760, Venezuela; d.1 Mar 1797, Venezuela. Nothing is known about his musical education. He belonged to a group of artists that followed Padre Sojo. One of the first Venezuelan musicians of the colonial period.
Works: Sacred music for the Cathedral of Caracas. Most of his works have been destroyed. Masses; Lessons of the Dead; Lamentations for Good Friday; Miserere; Salve; Stabat Mater; villancicos.
Bibl.: R. de la Plaza, *Ensayos sobre el Arte en Venezuela,* Caracas, 1883. J.B. Plaza, *Music in Caracas during the Colonial Period (1770-1811), The Musical Quarterly,* New York, 1943. C.F. Duarte, *Los Olivares en la Cultura de Venezuela,* Caracas, 1967.
Sources: GDM, MMLA

Oliveira, Alda de Jesús, Brazilian composer and teacher; b.3 Mar 1945, Bahia, Brazil. She studied at the Univ. Federal da Bahia from which she received two BA degrees, one in performance in 1968, and the other in music education in 1971. She also received an MA degree from Tufts Univ., Medford, Massachusetts, in 1979 under the auspices of Thomas Jefferson Anderson, and a Ph.D. in music education from the Univ. of Texas at Austin, Texas, in 1986, under the supervision of Judith Jellison. In 1992, she became head of the School of Music of the Univ. Federal da Bahia.
Works (selective list): *Songs for Music Initiation* (1967); Quartet for recorders and 3 porcelain plates (1969); *O Foguete,* for ensemble and children's chorus (1969); *Tubala,* for ensemble (1970); *Fundo do Mar,* functional music for children's play (1972); *Acento no Assento,* ballet (1979); *Boneco de Cêra,* for chorus (1980); *In Memoriam,* for small ensemble (1989); *Tecendo a Manhâ,* for ensemble (1990); piano pieces; songs.
Source: NWC

Oliveira, Jamary, Brazilian composer; b.21 Mar 1944, Saúde, Bahia, Brazil. She studied composition with Ernst Widmer, as well as flute, viola, and tuba at the Univ. Federal da Bahia. Member of the *Grupo Experimental de Percusión* and founding member of the *Grupo de Compositores da Bahia.* Professor of literature, theory of music, and composition at the Univ. of Bahia.

Works (selective list): *Ponteio*, for string orch. (1963); *O Sertão*, for orch. (1964); *Grocerto*, for orch. (1967); *Preambulu*, for orch. (1968); *Tonal-a-Tonal*, for orch. (1969); *Pseudopodes*, for orch. (1971); vocal music; chamber music; piano pieces.
Bibl.: L. Biriotti, *El Grupo de Compositores de Bahia*, Montevideo, 1971.
Source: GDM

Oliveira, Jocy de, Brazilian composer and pianist; b.11 Apr 1936, Curitiba, Paraná, Brazil. She studied with José Kliass in Sâo Paulo, Brazil, from 1946 to 1953. From 1953 to 1960, she lived in Paris, France, where she took lessons from Marguerite Long. In 1968, she received a Master's degree in music from Washington Univ. in Saint Louis, Missouri, where, from 1963 to 1968, her husband Eleazar de Carvalho was the conductor of the Saint Louis Symphony Orch. While at the univ. she studied composition with Robert Wykes. Assistant professor at the Univ. of Florida in Tampa, Florida. In 1977, she taught at the New Music School in New York City.
Works: *Estória II,* for voice, percussion, and tape (1967); *Polinterações I, II, and III* (1970); *Dimensôes,* for amplified piano, amplified harpsichord, electric organ, and electric piano (1976); *Wave Song,* for piano and tape (1977); *Estória IV,* for voice, electric violin, bass, and percussion (1978); *Música no Espaço,* multimedia (1982); *Fata Morgana,* opera.
Sources: EMB, HMB, NGDWC, NWC

Oliveira, Sophie Marcondes de Mello, Brazilian pianist, musicologist, teacher, and composer; b. 23 Aug 1897, Guaratingueta, Brazil; d.16 Dec 1980, Sâo Paulo, Brazil. She studied piano with Victoria Pinto Serva Pimenta at the Luigi Chiafarelli School in Sâo Paulo, and harmony, counterpoint, and composition with Arthur Pereira.
Works: Chamber music; sacred music; piano pieces; songs.
Source: IEW

Oliveira, Willy Corrêa de, Brazilian composer; b.11 Feb 1938, Recife, Brazil. He started to study music with teachers in his native town and later studied music theory and composition in Sâo Paulo, Brazil, with Olivier Toni. Under a scholarship from the Brazilian and German governments, he went to Germany to study at the Darmstadt summer courses with Pierre Boulez, Hans Werner Henze, and Karlheinz Stockhausen. Later he continued studying with Luciano Berio and Henri Pousseur. Professor at the Cons. Lavignac of Santos, Brazil, the Univ. of Sâo Paulo, and the Escola Superior de Propaganda in Sâo Paulo.

Works (selective list): *Preludio e Fuga,* for orch. (1959); *Ouviver a Música,* for piano and string orch. (1965); *Divertimento,* for orch. (1967); *Signus,* symphony for orch. (1968); choral music; chamber music; piano pieces; songs.
Sources: DCM, GDM, HMB

Orbón de Soto, Julián, Cuban composer of Spanish origin; b.7 Aug 1925, BB (1926, DM), Avilés, Spain; d.20 May 1991, Miami Beach, Florida, USA. He settled in Cuba at the end of the Spanish Civil War. He studied at the Cons. Musical de Oviedo, Spain, with his father, Benjamín Orbón, and with Oscar Lorié. In Cuba, he studied composition, and music aesthetics and history with José Ardévol. He completed his music studies with Aaron Copland at the Berkshire Music Center in Tanglewood, Massachusetts, in 1946. Member of the *Grupo de Renovación Musical,* 1942-49. Director of his father's Orbón Cons. in Havana, Cuba, 1946-60. Music critic for the newspaper *Alerta.* After the Cuban revolution of 1959, he went to Mexico and taught at the National Cons. of Music of Mexico City, 1960-63. In 1964, he settled in New York City, New York.
Works (selective list): *Cantar a Nuestra Señora,* on a poem by Fray Luis de León (1943); *Capricho Concertante,* for chamber orch. (1943); *Pregón,* on a poem by Nicolás Guillén, for violin, flute, oboe, bassoon, French horn, and piano, (1943); *Romance de Fontefrida,* for four mixed voices (1944); Symphony in C, for orch. (1945); *Danzas Sinfónicas,* for orch. (1955); Concerto grosso for orch. (1958); *Oficios de Tres Días,* for chorus and orch. (1970); *Partita No.4,* for piano and orch. (1983); chamber music; piano pieces; choruses; songs.
Sources: BB, CTA6, DCM, DM, MLA, MMLA

Orejón y Aparicio, José de, Peruvian composer and organist; b.1706, Huacho, Peru; d.between 7 and 21 May 1765, Lima, Peru. He studied music with Tomás de Torrejón y Velasco, and organ with Juan de Peralta, both of the Cathedral of Lima. He received a Licentiate degree from the Univ. of San Marcos in Lima. He was appointed *maestro de capilla* (chapelmaster) at the Cathedral of Lima in 1760, while continuing as organist.
Works: Religious music: masses; motets; hymns; litanies.
Bibl.: R. Stevenson, *The Music of Peru,* Washington, 1960. A. Sas, *Notas sobre José de Orejón y Aparicio, Músico Peruano del Siglo XVIII, Revista Peruana de Cultura,* Vol.5, 1965. R. Stevenson, *Renaissance and Baroque Musical Sources in the Americas,* Washington, 1970.
Sources: ADBM, GDM

Orozco Alemán, Keyla María, Cuban composer and pianist; b.22 Sep 1969, Santiago de Cuba, Cuba. She studied piano with Esteban Salas at the Cons. of Santiago de Cuba and with Ileana Bautista at the National School of Music of Havana, Cuba. In 1988, she entered the Music School of the ISA, where she studied composition with Harold Gramatges.

Works (selective list): *Baroque Concerto,* symphonic variations on a theme by Corelli (1991); *Southern Chant,* for clarinet and string orch. (1992); Concerto for violin and orch. (1993); chamber music; piano pieces; choruses.

Source: ISC

Orrego Salas, Juan Antonio, Chilean composer; b.18 Jan 1919, Santiago de Chile, Chile. He studied with Alberto Spikin, Julio Z. Guerra, Humberto Allende, Armando Carvajal, and Domingo Santa Cruz at the National Cons. of Music of Santiago de Chile, 1936-43. With grants from the Rockefeller and Guggenheim Foundations he went to the USA and attended classes in musicology with Paul Henry Lang and George Herzog at Columbia Univ. in New York, 1944-45. Later he studied composition with Randall Thompson at Princeton Univ., Princeton, New Jersey, 1945-46, and with Aaron Copland at Tanglewood, Massachusetts in 1946. In 1953, he received a diploma as Profesor Extraordinario de Composición from the Univ. of Chile, and was awarded the honorary degree of Doctor Scientiae by the Catholic Univ. of Chile in 1971, both in Santiago de Chile. From 1942 to 1961, he taught at the Univ. of Chile. In 1961, he was appointed professor of composition and Latin American music history and director of the Latin American Music Center at Indiana Univ. in Bloomington, Indiana.

Works (selective list): *Stage: El Retablo del Rey Pobre,* opera-oratorio (1950-52); *Juventud,* ballet (1948); *Umbral del Sueño,* ballet (1951); *El Saltimbanqui,* ballet (1960). *Orch.: Escenas de Cortes y Pastores,* 7 symphonic scenes (1946); *Obertura Festiva* (1948); 4 symphonies (1949, 1954, 1961, 1966); 2 piano concertos (1950, 1985); *Concierto de Cámara,* for flute, oboe, clarinet, bassoon, 2 horns, harp, and string orch. (1952); *Serenata Concertante* (1954); *Jubileaus Musicus* (1956); *Psalms,* for wind orch. (1962); *Concerto a Tre,* for violin, cello, and piano (1962); Concerto for wind orch. (1964); *Volte,* for chamber ensemble (1971); *Variaciones Serenas,* for string orch. (1971); Concerto for oboe and string orch. (1980); Violin concerto (1983); *Riley's Merriment,* scherzo (1986); *Fantasía,* for piano and wind orch. (1987). Chamber music; cantatas; oratorios; piano pieces; songs.

Bibl.: V. Salas Viú, *La Creación Musical en Chile (1900-1951),* Santiago, 1951. J. Merino, *Visión del Compositor Orrego Salas, Revista Musical Chilena,* 1978.

Sources: BB, CTA1, DCM, DM, GDM, HMC, MMLA

Ortega Alvarado, Sergio, Chilean composer; b.2 Feb 1938, Antofagasta, Chile. He studied composition with Roberto Falabella Correa and Gustavo Becerra Schmidt at the National Cons. of Chile, Santiago de Chile, Chile.
Works (selective list): *Recabarren,* opera; *La Dama del Canasto,* musical comedy; *Asunto Sofisticado,* musical comedy; *Joaquín Murieta,* cantata; Violin concerto (1962); chamber music.
Source: HMC

Ortega del Villar, Aniceto, Mexican composer, pianist, and physician; b.17 Apr, 1825, Tulancingo, Hidalgo, Mexico; d.17 Nov 1875, Mexico City, Mexico. He entered the Seminario Conciliar of Mexico City in 1837, San Idelfonso Seminary in 1840, and the School of Medicine in 1841. Founding member of the Sociedad Filarmónica Mexicana.
Works (selective list): *Guatimotzin,* opera; *Viola Tricolor; Invocación a Beethoven; Republicana,* march; *Potosina,* march; *Zaragoza,* march, considered the second *Mexican National Anthem* (1863); salon music; piano pieces.
Bibl.: A. Herrera y Ogazón, *El Arte Musical en México,* Mexico, 1917. O. Mayer-Serra, *Panorama de la Música Mexicana,* Mexico, 1941. G. Baqueiro Fóster, *Historia de la Música en México,* Mexico City, 1964.
Sources: DM, GDM, GMM, MMLA

Ortíz, José Antonio (Cristóbal Pirioby), Argentine composer; b.1764, Misión de San Carlos, Alto Paraná, Argentina; d.1794, Buenos Aires, Argentina. He taught music and voice to prominent families in Buenos Aires.
Works: Salon dances and songs.
Source: EMA

Ortíz Alvarado, William, Puerto Rican composer; b.30 Mar 1947, Salinas, Puerto Rico. He started music studies at the Cons. of Puerto Rico. He received a Master's degree in composition from the State Univ. of New York at Stony Brook, New York, and a Ph.D. in composition from the State Univ. of New York at Buffalo, New York.
Works (selective list): *Kantuta, Ritual para Orquesta* (1976); *Elegía a los Inocentes Caídos,* for orch. (1978); *Antillas,* for orch. (1981); *Resonancia Esférica,* for orch. (1982); *Llegó la Banda,* for orch. (1984); *Rican,* opera (1986); *Pasacalle,* for orch. (1988); chamber music; music for solo instruments; piano pieces; songs.
Source: CPR

Ortíz de Zárate, Eliodoro, Chilean composer; b.29 Dec 1865, Valparaiso, Chile; d.27 Jun 1953, Santiago de Chile, Chile. He studied in Valparaiso and at the Cons. of Milan, Italy.
Works: La Fioraia di Lugano (1895), probably the first Chilean opera to be produced in Santiago de Chile.
Source: BB

Ortíz y San Pelayo, Félix, Argentine conductor, teacher, and composer of Spanish origin; b.1857, Azpeitía, Guipúzcoa, Spain; d.1940, Buenos Aires, Argentina. He settled in Buenos Aires in 1879. He studied at the Royal Cons. of Madrid, Spain, and later at the Cons. of Milan, Italy. Professor at the Escuela de Música de la Provincia, Prov. of Buenos Aires, Argentina.
Works (selective list): *Artzay Mutilla,* opera; *Obertura en La*; *El Medallón,* zarzuela (1882); *De Rusia a Valladolid,* zarzuela (1882); *Misa* (1882); *Cantata Vasca* (1885); *Scherzo,* for orch.; piano pieces.
Source: EMA

Oswald (Ochswald), Henrique, Brazilian composer; b.14 Apr 1852, Rio de Janeiro, Brazil; d.10 Jun 1931, Rio de Janeiro. He started music studies in Sâo Paulo, Brazil, with Gabriel Guiraudon. At sixteen years of age, he was sent to Florence, Italy, where he studied harmony, counterpoint, and composition with Grazzini and Maglioni, and piano with Giuseppe Buonamici. Director of the National Inst. of Music of Rio de Janeiro, 1903-06. Brazilian vice consul in The Hague, Netherlands, and Genoa, Italy.
Works (selective list): *Operas: La Croce d'Oro* (1872); *Il Neo* (1900); *Le Fate* (1902). Suite for orch. (1884); Concerto for piano and orch. (1888); Concerto for violin and orch. (1888); Symphony in C for orch. (1910); *Andante e Variaçôes,* for piano and orch.; *Missa,* for 4 mixed voices, organ, and orch.; Requiem; chamber music; piano pieces.
Bibl.: R. Almeida, *História da Música Brasileira,* Rio de Janeiro, 1942.
Sources: DM, GDM, HMB, MLA, MMLA

Ovalle (Ovale), Jaime, Brazilian composer, violinist, and guitarist; b.5 Aug 1894, Pará, Belém, Brazil; d.1955, Rio de Janeiro, Brazil. Self-taught in music. In 1933, he was appointed cultural attaché to the Brazilian embassy in London, England. Founding member of the Brazilian Academy of Music.
Works (selective list): *Descobrimento do Brasil,* suite for orch.; *Pedro Alvares Cabral,* symphonic poem; *Legendas,* for piano; *Dois Tangos,* for piano; *Desafío,* for piano; *Azulâo,* for voice and piano; *Tres Cantos Nativos,* for violin and piano; *Mondinha,* for voice and piano; chamber music; piano pieces; songs.

Sources: DM, HMB, MLA, MMLA

P

Pacheco, Assis, Brazilian composer; b.1865, Itú, Brazil; d.1937, Brazil. He studied music in Europe.
Works: Operas: Dor; Cleopatra. Brasil, cantata; operettas; musical shows.
Source: MMLA

Pacheco de Céspedes, Luis, Peruvian violinist, conductor, and composer; b.25 Nov 1895, Lima, Peru; d.? He studied harmony with Father Villalba Muñoz and violin with Claudio Rebagliati. In France he continued his music studies, piano with Victor A. Duvernoy, violin with Jacques Thibaud, harmony, counterpoint, and fugue with Reynaldo Hahn and Gabriel Fauré, and voice with Hattich. He conducted opera in Cannes, France, and Monte Carlo. He returned to Lima in 1940 and was appointed conductor of the National Symphony Orch. of Lima.
Works: La Masque et la Rose, comic opera; *La Conquista,* opera; *La Mariscala,* operetta; *Navidad en la Trinchera,* symphonic poem; *El Himno al Sol,* symphonic poem; *Danza sobre un Tema Indio,* for orch.; *La Selva,* symphonic poem; *La Procesión del Señor de los Milagros,* symphonic poem; *Suite Limeña,* symphonic poem; 3 sonatas for violin and piano.
Bibl.: R. Barbacci, *Revista Musical Peruana,* Lima, October 1940.
Sources: DM, MLA, MMLA

Pádua, Newton de Menezes, Brazilian composer and cellist; b.1894, KTL (1896, MMLA), Brazil; d.? He studied composition with Francisco Braga at the Music School of the Univ. of Rio de Janeiro, Brazil, and later went to Rome, Italy, to study cello and church music. Professor at the National Cons. of Music and Univ. of Mexico, both in Mexico City.
Works (selective list): *Branca Dias,* opera (1931); *Anchieta,* symphonic poem; *Preludios, Suite Sinfónica, Cançao e Dansa,* for cello and orch.; symphonies; chamber music; piano pieces; music for the organ; masses; motets.
Sources: KTL, MMLA

Pahissa, Jaime, Argentine composer, conductor, teacher, and musicologist of Spanish origin; b.6 Oct 1880, Barcelona, Spain; d.27 Oct 1969, Buenos Aires, Argentina. He settled in Argentina in 1937. He studied with Francisco Laporta and Enrique Morera in Barcelona. Director of the Escuela Municipal de Música and professor of musical aesthetics and culture at the Cons. of the Liceo, both in Barcelona, 1933-36.

Works (selective list): *Operas: La Presó de Lleida* (1906); *Gala Placidia* (1913); *La Morisca* (1919); *Marianela* (1923); *La Princesa Margarita* (1928); *Cantata a la Tumba de García Lorca* (1937); *Angélica* (1938); *Bodas en Montaña* (1946); *Don Gil de las Calzas Verdes* (1955); *Tragicomedia de Calixto y Melibea* (1956). *Orch.: El Combat,* overture (1900); 2 symphonies (1900, 1921); *En las Costas Mediterráneas,* overture (1904); *El Camí,* symphonic poem (1909); *El Rabadá,* overture (1917); *Nit de Somnis,* symphonic poem (1921); *Monodía* (1925); *Canto y Cortejo Nupcial* (1926); *Suite Intertonal* (1926); *Dos Danzas Catalanas* (1939); *Somni d'Infant,* for piano (1949). Chamber music; choral works; piano pieces; songs. *Books: Cultura General,* Barcelona, 1935; *Los Grandes Problemas de la Música,* Buenos Aires, 1945; *Espíritu y Cuerpo de la Música,* Buenos Aires, 1946; *Vida y Obra de Manuel de Falla,* Buenos Aires, 1946. *Sources:* DM, EMA, GDM, MLA, MMLA

Palacios, Rafael, Mexican composer. Fl.mid-19th century.
Works: La Vendetta, opera; *Stabat Mater;* Mass.
Source: MMLA

Palacios y Sojo, Father Pedro, called El Padre Sojo, Venezuelan composer; he lived in the second half of the 18th century. In spite of never having a formal music education, he was a pioneer and promoter of Venezuelan music. He finished his priesthood studies at the Seminary of Caracas, Venezuela, and then traveled to Madrid, Spain, and Rome, Italy, to collect music and instruments.
Works: El Paria, for voices and piano; *La Vivandera,* overture; *Te Deum; Misa Solemne; Responsorio,* for 3 voices and organ; 70 masses; waltzes; salon pieces for piano.
Bibl.: O. Mayer-Serra, *Panorama de la Música Mexicana,* Mexico, 1941.
Sources: MLA, MMLA

Palazuelo, José María, Argentine teacher and composer; b.1840, Buenos Aires, Argentina; d.1893, Buenos Aires. Organist at the Cathedral of Buenos Aires.
Works: Misa de Requiem; Agnus Dei; motets; salon music.
Source: EMA

Palazuelo, Jr., José María, Argentine violinist and composer; b.1867, Buenos Aires, Argentina; d.1910, Buenos Aires. He studied with his father, José María Palazuelo. Violinist with the orch. of the Teatro de la Opera of Buenos Aires.
Works: L'Ucellino, for violin and piano; marches.
Source: EMA

Pallemaerts, Edmundo, Argentine composer and pianist of Belgian origin; b.1867, Malinas, Belgium; d.1945, Buenos Aires, Argentina. He studied at the Royal Cons. of Brussels, Belgium, with Hubert Kufferath, Arthur de Greef, and François A. Gevaert. He settled in Buenos Aires in 1889, and devoted his efforts to education, first at the cons. founded by Juan Gutiérrez, and later at his own Cons. Argentino.
Works (selective list): *Bodnoguat,* oratorio; *Suite Flamenca,* for orch.; Symphony in C minor; *Fantasía Argentina,* for orch.; piano pieces.
Sources: DM, EMA

Palma, Athos, Argentine composer and teacher; b.7 Jun 1891, Buenos Aires, Argentina; d.10 Jan 1951, Miramar, Prov. of Buenos Aires, Argentina. He studied piano with Cayetano Troiani, solfeggio with A. Cattáneo, and violin with José García Jacot in Buenos Aires. He spent ten years in Europe and when he returned to Buenos Aires, he studied composition with Cayetano Troiani. He also graduated from the Facultad de Filosofía y Letras of the Univ. of Buenos Aires, and studied for six years at the Medical School of the Univ. of Buenos Aires. Professor at the National Cons. of Music Carlos López Buchardo of Buenos Aires. General director and member of the board of the Teatro Colón of Buenos Aires. Supervisor of music at the school system of the National Board of Education.
Works (selective list): **Operas:** *Nazdah* (1924); *Los Hijos del Sol* (1928). *Cantares de mi Tierra,* suite for strings (1914); *Los Hijos del Sol,* symphonic poem (1929); *Jardines* (1930); chamber music; songs and school songs. **Books:** *Teoría Razonada de la Música*; *Tratado Completo de Armonía.*
Bibl.: N. Lamuraglia, *Athos Palma: Vida, Arte, Educación,* Buenos Aires, 1954.
Sources: BB, CA, DM, EMA, GDM, MLA

Palmero Nava, Armando, Bolivian cellist, pianist, teacher, and composer; b.1900, Potosí, Bolivia; d.1968, Tunari, Bolivia. Founder of the string quartet *Cochabamba,* director of the Music Academy Man Césped, and conductor of the Philharmonic Orch. of Cochabamba, Bolivia.
Works: La Rueda; Poema Indio; piano pieces.
Source: CB

Paniagua, Raúl, Guatemalan pianist and composer; b.17 Feb 1898, DM (1897, MMLA), Guatemala City, Guatemala; d.? He started music studies with his father, Miguel A. Paniagua, and later he enrolled at the National Cons. of Guatemala City where he studied with Herculano Alvarado. He also studied composition in New York.

Professor at the National Cons. of Panama, Panama City, in 1916, and the National Cons. of Guatemala, 1931-39, and director of the National Cons. of San Salvador, El Salvador, 1939-42. Music critic for the *Diario Oficial* of Guatemala.

Works (selective list): *Leyenda Maya,* for orch.; Mass for mixed voices; *Tres Canciones Originales,* for voice and orch.; several religious hymns for voice and orch.

Sources: DM, MLA, MMLA

Paniagua y Vásques, Cenobio, Mexican composer, organist, violinist, and conductor; b.30 Oct 1821, Tlalpujahua, Mexico; d.2 Nov 1882, Córdoba, Veracruz, Mexico. He studied violin with Eusebio Vázquez in Tlalpujahua, and at the Academy of Agustín Caballero and Joaquín Beristáin in Mexico City. He worked as a violinist in the orch. of several cathedrals. He is considered the first Mexican opera composer. In 1859, he founded the *Academia de Armonía y Composición* in Portal de Tejada, Mexico.

Works (selective list): *Catalina de Guisa,* opera (1845); *Pietro d'Abano,* opera (1863); *Siete Palabras,* cantata (1869); *Tobías,* oratorio (1970); Requiem (1882); about 70 masses; dances; marches; salon pieces for the piano.

Bibl.: M.G. Revilla, *Cenobio Paniagua, Revista Musical Mexicana,* Vol.2, 1942. R. Stevenson, *Music in Mexico,* New York, 1952.

Sources: GDM, GMM, MLA

Panizza, Héctor (Ettore), Argentine conductor and composer; b.12 Aug 1875, Buenos Aires, Argentina; d.27 Nov 1967, Milan, Italy. He started music studies with his father, Juan Grazioso Panizza, in Italy. He graduated from the Verdi Cons. of Milan where he studied composition with Amintore Galli, Michele Saladino, and Vincenzo Ferroni, and piano with Giuseppe Frugatta. He began his career as an opera conductor in Italy in 1899, and continued successfully for more than fifty years.

Works (selective list): *Operas: Il Fidanzato del Mare* (1897); *Medioevo Latino* (1900); *Aurora* (1908); *Bizancio* (1939). *El Rey de la Floresta,* for soloists, chorus, and orch.; *Tema con Variaciones,* for orch.; *Bodas Campestres,* symphonic suite; Sonata for violin and piano; Sonata for cello and piano; String quartet; Trio for piano and strings; piano pieces; songs. *Books: Medio Siglo de Vida Musical,* an autobiography, Buenos Aires, 1952.

Sources: BB, CA, DM, EMA, GDM, MLA, MMLA

Panizza, Juan Grazioso, Argentine cellist and composer; b.1851, Gazzuolo, Cremona, Italy; d.1898, Buenos Aires, Argentina. Father of Héctor Panizza. He settled in Buenos Aires in 1875, and was hired as a cellist at the orch. of the Teatro Colón of Buenos Aires. Director

of the musical society *La Lira* and of the concerts of *Jardín Florida,* both of Buenos Aires.
Works: *Cecilia,* opera; *Clara,* opera; *Capitán Bastogge,* operetta; *Sinfonía Pastoral,* for orch.; *El Paraíso Perdido,* symphonic poem; Gran trío for piano, violin, and cello; *La Argentina,* march.
Source: EMA

Paolantonio, Franco, Argentine conductor and composer; b.1884, Buenos Aires, Argentina; d.1934, Brazil. He studied with Jaime Bustamante, Julián Aguirre, and Alberto Williams at the Music Cons. of Buenos Aires. With a scholarship from the Comisión Nacional de Bellas Artes of Argentina, he went to Naples, Italy, where he studied at the Cons. San Pietro a Majella with Paolo Serrao and Giuseppe Martucci.
Works (selective list): *Serenata Oriental; Nocturno in B minor; Preludio Sinfónico in D major; Hymn to Justo José de Urquiza;* piano pieces; songs.
Sources: DM, EMA

Paredes, Hilda, Mexican composer; b.22 Sep 1959, Puebla, Mexico. She began musical studies in Mexico City, Mexico, and then moved to London, England, in 1979, where she studied flute and composition at the Guildhall School of Music and Drama. She also took classes with Maxwell Davies and Harrison Birtwistle at Dartington Summer School of London. She returned to Mexico and was appointed professor at the National Univ. of Mexico in Mexico City.
Works (selective list): *La Séptima Semilla,* chamber opera (1989); *Ikal,* for solo recorder; orch. music; chamber music; choral music; dances.
Source: NGDWC

Parera, Blas, Argentine organist, teacher, and composer of Spanish origin; b.1777, Barcelona, Spain; d.183?, Barcelona. Organist at the Cathedral, and at the churches La Merced and San Ignacio, all of Buenos Aires, Argentina. In 1893, he was hired by the management of Coliseo Provisional de Buenos Aires as *primer músico, maestro, compositor y director de orquesta* (first musician, teacher, composer, and orch. conductor).
Works: During the May Revolution of 1810, he composed several patriotic songs, and in 1813, he was commissioned by the Asamblea General Constituyente to put music to the *Argentine National Anthem,* based on a poem written by Vicente López y Planes.
Sources: DM, EMA, MLA

París, Juan, Cuban pianist and composer of Spanish origin; b.1759, Barcelona, Spain; d.10 Jul 1845, Santiago de Cuba, Cuba. In 1805, he was appointed *maestro de capilla* (chapelmaster) at the Cathedral of Santiago de Cuba. He continued the musical work of Esteban Salas in Santiago de Cuba.
Works (selective list): Three-part mass; *Introito; Salmo; Lección Primera de Difuntos; Oficio de difuntos;* Christmas carols; motets; villancicos.
Sources: DMC, GDM

Parpart, Gunter, Argentine composer, choral conductor, and music critic of German origin; b.10 May 1928, Duisburg, Rhineland, Germany. He settled in Buenos Aires, Argentina, in 1952. He studied with Roberto García Morillo, Carlos Guastavino, and Juan F. Giacobbe at the Municipal Cons. of Music Manuel de Falla of Buenos Aires. Board member of the Asociación Argentina de Compositores and of the Editoral Argentina de Compositores.
Works (selective list): 4 symphonies; *Ascención,* symphonic sketch; *Cantos de Soledad,* cantata for soprano and instrumental ensemble; Mass for soloists, chorus, and orch.; *Tres Movimientos Sinfónicos,* for orch.; *Salón de Baile Porteño,* for instrumental sextet; Wind quintet; chamber music; piano pieces; songs.
Sources: ISC, VMA

Parreiras Neves, Ignacio, Brazilian composer, conductor, and singer; b.c.1730, Vila Rica, Brazil; d.c.1793, Vila Rica. His activity was centered mainly in the Prov. of Minas Gerais, Brazil. Singer at the Brotherhood of Our Lady of Mercy, and in 1752, he entered the Brotherhood of Saint Joseph of Coloured Men where he became involved in its musical affairs.
Works: *Credo,* for mixed chorus and small orch. (1780-85); *Oratoria ao Menino Deos para a Noite de Natal,* Christmas oratorio.
Bibl.: G. Béhague, *Música Mineira Colonial à Luz de Novos Manuscritos, Barroco,* Vol.3, 1971.
Source: GDM

Pascual Navas, María E., Argentine composer. She studied at the National Cons. of Music Carlos López Buchardo of Buenos Aires.
Works (selective list): *Poema,* for guitar; *La Ñusta Kori-Huanca (La Virgen Efigie de Oro),* for oboe, viola, female voice, percussion, and guitar; songs.
Source: DM

Pasqués, Víctor A., Argentine lawyer and composer; b.23 Mar 1896, Baradero, Prov. of Buenos Aires, Argentina; d.? He studied music with Josefina Abella. In 1920, he graduated with a doctorate in

jurisprudence from the National Univ. of Buenos Aires, Argentina. Music teacher at various schools.
Works: *Preludio*, for orch.; *Incendio*, for female chorus; *Six Lieder*, on poems by Leopoldo Lugones; *Tres Canciones Argentinas* and *Dos Laúdes*, on text by Alfredo Bufano.
Sources: DM, EMA

Patiño Andrade, Gabriela, Argentine composer; b.7 Feb 1920, Buenos Aires, Argentina. She studied with Jorge C. Fanelli, Jorge de Lalewicz, Athos Palma, José Torre Bertucci, and Arturo Luzzatti at the Williams Cons. and at the National Cons. of Music Carlos López Buchardo, both of Buenos Aires. She also studied with Julián Bautista.
Works (selective list): Symphony for piano and orch.; *Dos Bocetos Sinfónicos;* Suite for piano; Sonata for violin and piano; *Tema con Variaciones,* for violin and piano; String quartet; piano pieces; songs.
Sources: DM, EMA

Pavia, Marcela, Argentine composer; b.Rosario, Prov. of Santa Fe, Argentina. She graduated from the Escuela de Música de la Facultad de Humanidades y Artes of the National Univ. of Rosario with a degree in composition. Later she continued music studies with Dante Grela, Francisco Kröpfl, and Daniel Sueiro. Professor at the Collegium Musicum, the Univ. of the Argentine Social Museum, and the Municipal Cons. of Music Manuel de Falla, all of Buenos Aires, Argentina. Member of the Agrupación Santafesina de Compositores and of the *Agrupación Nueva Música*, both of Rosario.
Works: *Eccos,* for 2 flutes; *Hardyal,* for clarinet; Requiem for symphony orch.; Octet for flute, oboe, clarinet, French horn, and string quartet; *Pieza,* for flute; Dúo for flute and clarinet; *Pieza,* for chamber orch.
Source: CAMR

Paz, Juan Carlos, Argentine composer, musicologist, and music critic; b.5 Aug 1901, Buenos Aires, Argentina; d.25 Aug 1972, Buenos Aires. He studied composition with Constantino Gaito and Eduardo Fornarini in Argentina, and later with Vincent D'Indy at the Schola Cantorum in Paris, France. He studied piano and organ with Roberto Nery and Jules Beyer. Founding member of the *Grupo Renovación* in 1929, and the *Agrupación Nueva Música* in 1936, both of Buenos Aires.
Works (selective list): **Orch.**: *Canto de Navidad* (1927); *Movimiento Sinfónico* (1930); *Suite for Ibsen's Juliano Emperador* (1931); *Tres Piezas* (1931); *Passacaglia* (1936); *Música: Preludio y Fuga* (1940); *Passacaglia,* for string orch. (1944-49); *Rítmica Constante* (1952); *Seis Superposiciones* (1954); *Transformaciones Canónicas* (1955-56);

Música, for bassoon, strings, and percussion (1955-56); *Continuidad 1960* (1960-61); *Estructuras 1962,* for chamber orch. (1962); *Música,* for piano (1964). **Chamber music:** *Tema y Transformaciones,* for 11 winds (1929); Wind octet (1930); Three sonatinas: No.1 for clarinet and piano (1930); No.2 for flute and clarinet (1932); No.3 for oboe and bassoon (1933); Concierto No.1 for flute, oboe, clarinet, bassoon, trumpet, and piano (1932); Concierto No.2 for oboe, trumpet, 2 trombones, bassoon, and piano (1935); *Cuatro Composiciones Dodecafónicas:* No.1 for flute, English horn, and cello (1934); No.2 for flute and piano (1935); No.3 for clarinet and piano (1937); No.4 for solo violin (1938); *Overture,* for 12 instruments (1936); *Cuatro Piezas,* for solo clarinet (1936); *Tres Composiciones en Trío:* No.1 for flute, clarinet, and bassoon (1937); No.2 for clarinet, trumpet, and alto saxophone (1938); No.3 for flute, oboe, and bass clarinet or bassoon (1940-45); 2 string quartets (1938, 1940-43); *Música,* for flute, saxophone, and piano (1943); *Dedalus 1950,* for flute, clarinet, violin, cello, and piano (1950-51); *Continuidad 1953,* for piano and percussion (1953-54); *Tres Contrapuntos,* for clarinet, electric guitar, celesta, trumpet, trombone, and cello (1955); *Invención,* for string quartet (1961); *Concreción,* for flute, clarinet, bassoon, horn, trumpet, trombone, and tuba (1964). Chamber music; piano pieces; music for organ. **Books:** *Introducción a la Música de Nuestro Tiempo,* Buenos Aires, 1952; *La Música en los Estados Unidos,* Buenos Aires, 1952; *Arnold Schoenberg, o el Fin de la Era Tonal,* Buenos Aires, 1954; *Alturas, Tensiones, Ataques, Intensidades,* Buenos Aires, 1970.
Bibl.: J.C. Bechinsky, *Juan Carlos Paz,* Buenos Aires, 1964. J. Romano, *Juan Carlos Paz, Tribulaciones de un Músico,* Buenos Aires, 1970.
Sources: BB, CA, CTA2, DCM, DM, GDM, MLA, MMLA

Peacan del Sar, Rafael, Argentine composer; b.6 Jun 1884, Buenos Aires, Argentina; d.1960, Buenos Aires. He studied harmony, counterpoint, composition, and orchestration with Carlos Pedrell and Eduardo Torrens Boqué. Artistic director of the International Exhibition of Art at the Centenary of the Argentine Revolution in 1910. Professor at the National Cons. of Music Carlos López Buchardo of Buenos Aires and the Escuela Superior de Bellas Artes of the National Univ. of La Plata, Prov. of Buenos Aires, Argentina.
Works (selective list): *Chrysanthème,* opera (1927); *Las Rosas,* ballet (1915); *Misa de Requiem*; *La Conversión de Longino,* oratorium; chamber music; songs.
Sources: CA, DM, EMA, MMLA

Pedreira, José Enrique, Puerto Rican composer and pianist; b.2 Feb 1904, San Juan, Puerto Rico; d.Dec 1959, Puerto Rico. He started his

music studies at the Piano Academy of Rosa and Ana Sicardó of Puerto Rico. In 1928, he went to New York to study piano with Sigismund Stojowsky. When he returned to Puerto Rico in 1932, he opened his piano studio, and formed a piano and organ duo with his student, José Raúl Ramírez.
Works (selective list): Concerto in D for piano and orch. (1924); music for the piano, some compositions later orchestrated by his student, José Raúl Ramírez; chamber music; songs.
Source: CPR

Pedrell, Carlos, Uruguayan composer; b.16 Oct 1878, Minas, Uruguay; d.3 Mar 1941, Montrouge, near Paris, France. He studied with his uncle Felipe Pedrell in Madrid and Barcelona, Spain, and later with Vincent D'Indy and Pierre Bréville at the Schola Cantorum in Paris, France. Supervisor of music at the school system of the National Board of Education in Buenos Aires, Argentina. Professor at the Univ. of Tucumán, Prov. of Tucumán, Argentina. In 1921, he went to Paris where he remained for the rest of his life.
Works (selective list): *Operas: Ardid de Amor* (1917); *Cuento de Abril* (1924); *La Guitarra* (1924). *Ballets: La Rose et le Gitan* (1930); *Alleluia* (1936). *Orch.: Une Nuit de Schéhérazade* (1908); *Danza y Canción de Aixa* (1910); *En el Estrado de Beatriz* (1910); *Fantasía Argentina* (1910); *Ouverture Catalane* (1912); *Pastorales,* for voice and orch. (1928). Choruses; songs.
Bibl.: A. Suáres, *Carlos Pedrell, Revue Musicale,* June 1931.
Sources: BB, BHMCU, DM, EMA, GDM, MLA, MMLA

Pedrolini, Aquiles, Argentine composer and priest; b.1872, Buenos Aires, Argentina; d.1930, Buenos Aires.
Works: Masses; hymns; psalms; music for children.
Source: EMA

Pelaia, Emilio, Argentine teacher, music critic, and composer of Italian origin; b.21 Jan 1894, Limbadi, Italy; d.? He studied violin with Hércules Galvani at the Cons. Santa Cecilia of Buenos Aires, and harmony and composition with the priest Josué Macrí. Professor at various high schools of the National Board of Education in Buenos Aires.
Works (selective list): *De los Apeninos a los Andes,* children's comedy; *Un Viaje a la Luna,* children's comedy; *Primera Suite Argentina* and *Segunda Suite Argentina,* for orch.; *Danza India,* for orch.; *Quena en el Valle,* for orch.; *Suite Clásica,* for chamber orch.; *Plegaria Profana,* for chamber orch.; piano pieces; songs.
Sources: DM, EMA

Pelazza, Juan Bautista, Argentine organist and composer of Italian origin; b.1848, Turin, Italy; d.1936, Argentina. He settled in Argentina in 1898.
Works: Cristóforo Colombo, oratorio.
Source: EMA

Pemberton, Carlos, Argentine composer; b.1932, Buenos Aires, Argentina. He studied with Julián Bautista and Roberto García Morillo. Member of the Asociación de Jóvenes Compositores of Buenos Aires.
Works (selective list): *Tres Paisajes de Antonio Machado,* for mezzo-soprano, flute, violin, and cello (1957); *Concertino de Cámara,* for piano and ensemble (1962); *Variaciones Fugitivas,* for piano (1962, orchestrated in 1966); *Perseo,* ballet (1965-67); *Malleus Maleficarum,* for orch. (1968); songs.
Source: EMA

Peña Hen, Jorge, Chilean composer and conductor; b.1928, Santiago de Chile, Chile; d.1973, Chile. He studied with Pedro Humberto Allende, René Amengual, and Domingo Santa Cruz. Director of the Regional Cons. of La Serena, Chile.
Works: La Cenicienta, opera; *Coronación,* ballet; Concertino for piano and children's orch.; Piano concerto; String quartet; incidental music for movies.
Source: HMC

Peña Morel, Esteban, Dominican folklorist and composer; b.1897, DM (1894, MMLA), Santo Domingo (Ciudad Trujillo), Dominican Republic; d.6 Mar 1938, DM (1939, MMLA), Barcelona, Spain. He studied with Alfredo Soler. Bassoonist at the Havana Philharmonic Orch., Havana, Cuba He performed important studies in folklore research.
Works: Anacoana, symphonic poem; *Sinfonía Bárbara,* for military band; *Embrujo Antillano; Alma Criolla.* **Books:** *La Folklo-Música Dominicana,* unpublished.
Sources: DM, MLA, MMLA

Peña Ponce, Belisario, Ecuadorian composer and pianist; b.1902, Quito, Ecuador. He studied piano with Ettore Pozzoli and composition with Julio César Pasibini and Ildebrando Pizzetti at the Verdi Cons. in Milan, Italy, from 1922 to 1929. When he returned to Ecuador in 1930, he was appointed subdirector of the National Cons. of Music in Quito, and later he became director.
Works (selective list): Mass in D minor; motets; hymns; piano pieces.
Source: MMLA

Peñin, José, Venezuelan composer of Spanish origin; b.14 Oct 1942, Pereda de Ancares, León, Spain. He studied music at the Facultad de Artes y Ciencias Musicales of the Catholic Univ. of Buenos Aires, Argentina, and graduated with a Licentiate degree in musical education, musicology, and composition, in 1974. He also studied at the Inter-American Inst. of Ethnomusicology and Folklore of Caracas, Venezuela, where he later became a researcher. Director of the Academy of Music San Agustín in Buenos Aires, 1969-72, and researcher at the Inst. Latino Americano de Investigaciones y Estudios Musicales Vicente E. Sojo of Caracas, in 1978.
Works: *Ainapsih,* symphonic poem for chorus, orch., and non-conventional instruments; *Espejo,* for string quartet; Sonata for organ; *Música para Sonar con Corno y Maderas; Requiem para un Coro Muerto,* choral-symphonic composition; *Cinco Estampas a Petare,* for 4 mixed choruses.
Source: ISC

Perales, Stella, Argentine composer; b.1944, Rosario, Prov. of Santa Fe, Argentina. She graduated from the Escuela de Música de la Facultad de Humanidades y Artes of the National Univ. of Rosario with degrees in composition and music education. She studied later with Dante Grela and Francisco Kröpfl. Director of the Escuela National de Música of the National Univ. of Rosario.
Works: *Gestación I,* for trio and dance (1975); *Divertimento,* for 11 instruments (1976); String quartet (1977); *Contraste,* for piano (1981); *Conflicto en el Tiempo,* electroacoustic music (1985); *Semejanzas,* for cello (1985); *Gestación II,* electroacoustic music (1985).
Source: CAMR

Peralta Castera, Angela, Mexican pianist, singer, and composer; b.6 Jul 1845, Puebla, Mexico; d.30 Aug 1883, Mazatlán, Sinaloa, Mexico. She studied voice with Agustín Balderas, solfeggio with Manuel Barragán, and composition with Cenobio Paniagua in Mexico. In Italy she studied voice with Francesco Lamperti.
Works: Nineteen salon pieces for piano (1875).
Source: IEW

Perceval, Julio Miguel Adolfo, Argentine organist and composer of Belgian origin; b.17 Jul 1903, Brussels, Belgium; d.7 Sep 1963, Santiago de Chile, Chile, in a car accident. He studied organ with Paul de Maleingrau at the Brussels Royal Cons., and later with Marcel Dupré in Paris, France. He settled in Argentina, in 1926. Organist at the Metropolitan Cathedral of Buenos Aires, the Colegio Nacional de Buenos Aires, a high school affiliated to the National Univ. of Buenos Aires, and at the Teatro Colón of Buenos Aires. He had a strong relationship with the founding members of the *Grupo Renovación*, and later he became a member of the *Agrupación Nueva Música*. In 1939, he organized and directed the Cons. of Music of the Univ. Nacional de Cuyo, Mendoza, Prov. of Mendoza, Argentina. In 1959, he settled in Chile, where he was professor of organ, composition, and counterpoint at the Facultad de Ciencias Musicales of the National Univ. of Chile, Santiago de Chile.

Works (selective list): *Cantata para la Primera Fundación de Buenos Aires,* for soloists, chorus, and orch. (1935); *Te Deum,* for soloists, organ, chorus, and orch. (1944-45); *Poema Criollo,* for piano and orch. (1945); *Canto a San Martín,* cantata for soloists, chorus; children's chorus, military band, and orch. (1950); *Salve,* hymn for voices a cappella (1956); chamber music; piano pieces; music for organ.

Sources: BB, CA, DM, EMA, MLA, MMLA

Percuoco, Carlos, Argentine trumpeter and composer of Italian origin; b.27 Oct 1888, Naples, Italy; d.? He settled in Buenos Aires, Argentina, in 1908. He studied with Vicente Scaramuzza, Eduardo Fornarini, and Constantino Gaito in Buenos Aires. Principal trumpet of the Municipal Band of Buenos Aires, 1910-26, and later its associate conductor, 1926-33.

Works: *Obertura en La menor,* for orch. (1944); *Norteñas,* symphonic poem (1946).

Sources: CA, EMA

Pereira, Antonio de Sá, Brazilian composer; b.Aug 1888, Salvador, Brazil; d.21 Feb 1966, Rio de Janeiro, Brazil. He was the founder of the Cons. of Pelotas, Brazil.

Works (selective list): *Tango Brasileiro,* for piano; *Berceuse,* for piano; harmonization of the *Brazilian National Anthem,* for 4-voice chorus; piano pieces; songs; choruses.

Source: MMLA

Pereira, Arthur, Brazilian composer; b.12 Sep 1894, Sâo Paulo, Brazil; d.3 Aug 1946, Sâo Paulo. He studied at the Cons. of Naples, Italy. Professor at the Cons. of Music of Sâo Paulo.

Works: *Atala,* opera; *L'Intrusa,* opera; *Cabocla Bonita,* for mixed chorus; *Capim da Lagoa,* for mixed chorus; *Seis Peças Monotonais sobre Temas do Folklore Brasileiro,* for piano; *O Poema da Negra,* for voice and orch., on a poem by Mario de Andrade; *Missa da Glória; Canções Populares Brasileiras,* for chorus and orch.

Sources: DM, MLA, MMLA

Pereira, Elpidio, Brazilian composer; b.16 Oct 1872, Caxias, Brazil; d.13 Apr 1961, Rio de Janeiro, Brazil. At sixteen years of age he went to Paris, France, where he studied harmony with Antoine Taudou. He returned to Brazil and started to teach violin and music theory in Pará and Manaus. In 1913, he went back to Paris where he furthered his composition studies with Paul Vidal.
Works (selective list): *Orch.: Preludio; Fantasía Pastoral; Sol Poente; Scherzo.* Sacred music; operas; symphonies; piano pieces; songs.
Source: MMLA

Pereira da Silva, Adelaide, Brazilian pianist and composer; b.5 Jul 1928, Sâo Paulo, Brazil. She studied piano with Nair de Sousa, Hans Bruch, and Dinorá de Carvalho, and harmony and counterpoint with Osvaldo Lacerda, and composition with Camargo Guarnieri. She taught at the Faculdade de Música Marcelo Tupinamba, the Escola Superior de Música Santa Marcelina, and the Faculdade Santa Cecilia, all in Sâo Paulo, Brazil.
Works (selective list): *Music for piano:* 2 suites (1965); Sonatina (1975). *Choral music: Ele Nasceu lá na Loanda* (1964); *Reza de Umbanda* (1971); *Coros Infantis Brasileiros* (1977); *Canto da Terra* (1980). Chamber music; songs.
Sources: IBCC, IEW, NGDWC

Pereira Lecaros, Celerino, Chilean composer and teacher; b.1874, Santiago de Chile, Chile; d.1942, Santiago de Chile. He studied with Ceradelli in Santiago de Chile. Professor and director of the National Cons. of Music of Chile, Santiago de Chile.
Works (selective list): *Mirando al Mar,* symphonic sketch (1903); *Capricho y Danza Fantástica,* for orch. (1904); *Elegía,* for orch. (1904); Mass (1971); chamber music; choruses; piano pieces; songs.
Source: HMC

Pereyra Lizaso, Nydia, Uruguayan composer, pianist, and teacher; b.12 May 1916, Rocha, Uruguay. She started music studies with Dolores Bell and Carmen Barrera at the Cons. Teresiano of Rocha. Later she settled in Montevideo, Uruguay, where she studied piano with Guillermo Kolischer, harmony, counterpoint, and fugue with José Tomás Mujica, and composition with Enrique Casal Chapí. Professor at the Kolischer Cons. and at the Inst. de Enseñanza Musical, both in Montevideo.
Works (selective list): *Cantata de Navidad;* Symphony; String quartet; Sonatina for piano; Duo for clarinet and piano; *Cuatro Miniaturas,* for violin and viola; music for the stage; piano pieces; chamber music; choral music; songs.
Sources: BHMCU, MU, NGDWC

Pérez Sentenat, César, Cuban teacher, pianist, and composer; b.18 Nov 1896, Havana, Cuba; d.4 May 1973, Havana. He studied music theory and solfeggio with José Molina, and piano with Antonio Saavedra, Rafael Serrano, and Hubert de Blanck. From 1913 to 1922, he studied in Paris, France, with Joaquín Nin Castellanos and Léon Saint-Requier at the Schola Cantorum. In 1922, he returned to Cuba and became professor of piano and harmony at the National Cons. of Havana. He helped to organize the Havana Symphony Orch., together with Gonzalo Roig and Ernesto Lecuona, and in 1924, he joined Amadeo Roldán to create the Havana Philharmonic Orch. Professor of piano at the Havana Municipal Cons., where he became director in 1931. He held several official posts in musical inst. before and after the 1961 revolution. In 1965, he was appointed general director of the National Culture Council of Cuba.
Works: *Music for piano: Suite Cubana in G minor; Preludios en Todos los Tonos; Cuatro Estampas para un Pionero.* *Songs*: *Martianas; Tres Canciones Campesinas; Tríptico de Villancicos Cubanos.*
Source: DMC

Perusso, Mario, Argentine composer; b.16 Sep 1936, Buenos Aires, Argentina. He studied at the Inst. Di Tella of Buenos Aires. He began his music career singing in the opera chorus at the Teatro Colón of Buenos Aires. In 1967, he was appointed opera conductor at the Teatro Argentino in La Plata, Prov. of Buenos Aires, Argentina, activity that he later expanded to other Argentine cities, Tucumán, Prov. of Tucumán, Bahía Blanca, Prov. of Buenos Aires, and Buenos Aires. Member of the Asociación de Jóvenes Compositores de la Argentina.
Works: *La Voz del Silencio,* opera (1969); *Tres Movimientos Sinfónicos,* for orch. (1956); *Elegía,* for orch. (1964); *Cantos de Guerra,* for soprano and orch. (1965); *Partita,* for cello solo (1967); *Invenzioni,* for string quartet (1967); *La Eternidad y el Viento,* for orch. (1968).
Sources: BB, EMA

Pey Casado, Diana, Chilean composer of Spanish origin; b.8 Mar 1922, Madrid, Spain. She started music studies in Madrid and continued them at the National Cons. of Music of Chile, Santiago de Chile, Chile, where she studied composition with René Amengual, Juan Orrego Salas, and Alfonso Letelier.
Works: Sonatina for flute and piano (1954); *El Cantar de los Cantares,* cantata (1961); Sonata for 2 pianos (1961).
Source: HMC

Peyrellade, Carlos Alfredo, Cuban composer and pianist; b.1840, Santa María de Puerto Príncipe, Camagüey, Cuba; d.9 Dec 1908, Havana, Cuba. He studied piano with Nicolás Ruíz Espadero in Havana. Since 1871, he has lived in Havana where he founded a cons. that bears his name.
Works: *Ecos Tropicales,* Cuban capriccio (1866); *Gran Scherzo.*
Source: MMLA

Piaggio, Celestino, Argentine composer and conductor; b.20 Dec 1886, Concordia, Prov. of Entre Ríos, Argentina; d.28 Oct 1931, Buenos Aires, Argentina. He started music studies with his father, and then studied harmony with Alberto Williams, piano and composition with Julián Aguirre, violin with Andrés Gaos, and orch. ensemble with Carlos Marchal. In the Schola Cantorum of Paris, France, he studied harmony with Léon Saint-Requier, counterpoint with Groz, organ with Cinand and Abel Decaux, Gregorian chant with Amédée Gastoué, and composition with Vincent D'Indy. He returned to Buenos Aires in 1921, and was appointed professor of composition at the Williams Cons. of Buenos Aires.
Works: Overture in C minor for orch. (1914); Sonata in C sharp minor for piano; *Homenaje a Julián Aguirre,* for piano; songs.
Sources: CA, DM, EMA, MLA, MMLA

Piantino, Eduardo, Argentine contemporary composer; b.Rosario, Prov. of Santa Fe, Argentina. He graduated from the Escuela de Música de la Facultad de Humanidades y Artes of the National Univ. of Rosario with a degree in composition. He continued music studies with Dante Grela and Francisco Kröpfl. Professor at the Escuela de Música of the National Univ. of Rosario, the Escuela Nacional de Música of Rosario, and the Inst. Nacional del Profesorado de Música of Rosario.
Works: Vocal and instrumental compositions; music for the stage.
Source: CAMR

Piazzini, Edmundo, Argentine composer, pianist, and teacher of Italian origin; b.1857, Missaglia, Milan, Italy; d.1927, Castelar, Prov. of Buenos Aires, Argentina. He settled in Buenos Aires, Argentina, in 1878. In 1904, he founded, together with Alfonso Thibaud, the Thibaud-Piazzini Cons. of Music of Buenos Aires.
Works: Piano pieces.
Source: EMA

Piazzolla, Astor, Argentine composer and bandonion player; b.11 Mar 1921, Mar del Plata, Prov. of Buenos Aires, Argentina; d. 5 Jul 1992, Buenos Aires, Argentina. He started music studies in New

York City, New York, with Bela Wilde. In 1940, he returned to Buenos Aires and studied composition with Alberto Ginastera and piano with Raúl Spivak. Later he took lessons from Nadia Boulanger in Paris, France.
Works (selective list): Suite for harp and strings (1943); *Rapsodia Porteña,* for orch. (1948); Suite for oboe and string orch. (1949); *Contemplación y Danza,* for clarinet and string orch. (1950); *Buenos Aires,* three symphonic movements (1951); *Tango Dramático,* for 13 instruments (1953); Sinfonietta for chamber orch. (1953); *Tres Minutos con la Realidad,* for bandonion, celesta, and string orch. (1955); *Tango Ballet,* for octet (1956); *Hombre de la Esquina Rosada,* for narrator, voice, and 12 instruments (1960); *Tango para una Ciudad,* for quintet (1961); *Serie del Diablo,* for quintet (1962); *Serie de Tangos,* for orch. (1963); *Oda Intima a Buenos Aires,* for narrator, voice, and orch. (1965); *María de Buenos Aires,* chamber opera for narrator, soloists, and 11 instruments (1968); *Tangata,* for orch. (1969).
Sources: CA, EMA

Picchi, Silvano, Argentine composer and music critic of Italian origin; b.15 Jan 1922, Pisa, Italy. He settled in Córdoba, Prov. of Córdoba, Argentina, in 1926, and then moved to Buenos Aires, Argentina, in 1938. He studied with Arnaldo D'Espósito, Constantino Gaito, José Torre Bertucci, Gilardo Gilardi, Carlos Suffern, Roberto García Morillo, Alberto Ginastera, Floro Ugarte, Arturo Luzzatti, and Erwin Leuchter. Music critic for the newspaper *La Prensa* in Buenos Aires, since 1962. Professor at the Municipal Cons. of Music Manuel de Falla of Buenos Aires.
Works (selective list): *Orch.: Suite Irreverente* (1949); *Divertimento,* for 2 guitars and chamber orch. (1951); *Música para Caballos* (1952); *Cuatro Poemas Cordobeses,* for mixed choir (1958); *Nocturnales,* for soprano (1958); *Ruth,* biblical cantata for soloists and mixed chorus (1963); Concerto for violin (1965); Concierto for piano (1965); *Contrapunto all'Antica,* for strings (1968); *Eue, Funeral Song on an African Theme,* for strings (1968); *Homenajes* (1969); 4 symphonies (1970, 1977, 1979, 1986). *Tríptico,* for chorus a cappella (1963); *Pequeños Corales de Amor,* for chorus a cappella (1967); *Invención Copernicana* (1984); *Magnificat* (1985); chamber music; piano pieces; music for organ; music for guitar; songs.
Sources: BB, CTA15, EMA

Pickenhayn, Jorge Oscar, Argentine composer, musicologist, and music critic; b.1921, Buenos Aires, Argentina. He graduated from the National Cons. of Music Carlos López Buchardo of Buenos Aires. He also received his doctorate at the Facultad de Filosofía y Letras of the

National Univ. of Buenos Aires. Music critic for the newspaper *El Pueblo* of Buenos Aires. He founded the musical magazine *Polifonía* in 1944. Director of the Inst. Superior de Arte of the Teatro Colón of Buenos Aires. Professor at the National Cons. of Music Carlos López Buchardo and the Municipal Cons. of Music Manuel de Falla, both of Buenos Aires.
Works: Sonatina for piano (1939); *Diez Corales Breves,* four parts (1939); 30 songs for voice and piano (1956).
Source: EMA

Pineda Duque, Roberto, Colombian composer; b.29 Aug 1910, Santuario, Antioquía, Colombia; d.1977, Colombia. He started music studies at the Inst. de Bellas Artes in Medellín, Colombia, and later he studied piano with Joaquín Fuster and harmony with Carlos Posada Amador. In 1942, he went to Cali, Colombia, to study choral singing with Antonio María Valencia. In the early fifties, he studied counterpoint, fugue, orchestration, 12-tone technique, and composition with Carlo Jachino. Professor of harmony and composition at the National Cons. of Music, and *maestro de capilla* (chapelmaster) at the Church Nuestra Señora de las Nieves, both in Bogotá, Colombia.
Works (selective list): *Orch.: Fantasía y Tema con Variaciones* (1953); *Serenata,* for strings (1954); *Fantasía Coral,* for chorus (1958); *Edipo Rey,* cantata for 2 narrators, talking chorus, and mixed chorus (1959); *Andante y Presto,* for strings (1959); *Preludio Sinfónico* (1960); Concerto for piano (1960); Concerto for violin (1960); Sinfonía (1961). Chamber music; sacred music.
Source: CTA7

Pinilla, Enrique, Peruvian composer; b.3 Aug 1927, Lima, Peru. He studied at the Bach Inst. with Carlos Sánchez Málaga, at the Sas-Rosay Academy of Music with Andres Sas, and at the National Cons. of Music with Rodolfo Holzmann, all in Lima. In 1947, he went to Spain and then to Paris, France, where he studied with Charles Koechlin. Later he lived for several years in Madrid, Spain, where he studied at the Royal Cons. With a scholarship awarded him by the Deutscher Akademischer Auslandsdienst, he spent two years in Berlin, Germany, studying with Boris Blacher. He also studied electronic music with Vladimir Ussachevsky at Columbia Univ., New York, 1966-67. He returned to Lima in 1961, and was appointed professor at the National Cons. of Music where he taught music history and ethnomusicology.
Works (selective list): *Orch.: Four Pieces* (1960-61); *Festejo* (1965); *Evoluciones* (1967); *Song* (1968); Piano concerto (1970); *Peruvian Suite* (1972). Chamber music; piano pieces; ballets; film scores; incidental music.

Sources: CTA11, DCM, GDM

Pinto, Alejandro, Argentine composer of Polish origin; b.30 Aug 1922, Nieswiez, Nowogrodek, Poland. He settled in Argentina in 1935. He studied with Guillermo Graetzer. Member of the Asociación de Jóvenes Compositores de la Argentina. Founding member of the Editorial Argentina de Compositores.

Works (selective list): *Los Raptores,* chamber opera (1951); *Tiempo de Alejandra,* for voice and orch. (1968); Requiem for 4-voice mixed chorus; *Requiem para Alejandra,* for orch.; *Dybbuk,* suite for orch.; *Tempo di Marcia,* for orch.; *Canto a San Martín,* cantata for narrator, baritone, mixed chorus, and orch.; *Adonias,* opera; chamber music; more than 120 songs for voice and piano.

Sources: EMA, ISC, VMA

Pinto, Alfredo A., Argentine composer and pianist of Italian origin; b.22 Oct 1891, Mantua, Italy; d.26 May 1968, Buenos Aires, Argentina. He settled in Argentina in 1915. He studied piano with Alessandro Longo and composition with Camillo de Nardis at the Cons. San Pietro a Majella in Naples, Italy.

Works (selective list): *Operas: La Ultima Esposa* or *Sheherazade; Gualicho* (1940). *Nostalgias,* symphonic prelude (1929); *Eros,* symphonic poem (1930); *Contrastes,* for orch. (1932); *Comentario a un Canto d'Annunziano,* for orch. (1934); *Serie Popular Italiana,* for orch. (1936); *Rebelión,* symphonic poem (1939); *La Esposa de Cadi,* lyric drama, (1939); *El Pillán,* ballet (1947); piano pieces; choruses; songs.

Sources: BB, CA, CTA14, EMA, MLA

Pinto, Octavio, Brazilian composer; b.3 Nov 1890, Sâo Paulo, Brazil; d.31 Oct 1950, Sâo Paulo. He was trained as an architect. He studied piano with Isidor Philipp in Paris, France.

Works: Scenas Infantis, for piano (1932); *Children's Festival,* for piano (1939); many piano pieces.

Source: BB

Pinzón Urrea, Jesús, Colombian composer, conductor, pianist, and ethnomusicologist; b.10 Aug 1928, Bucaramanga, Colombia. He began his music studies in Bucaramanga, and later entered the Cons. of Music of the National Univ. of Colombia, Bogotá, where he studied with Olav Roots, Tatjana Gontscharowa de Espinosa, Roberto Pineda Duque, Fabio González, Andrés Pardo, and José Rozo. Founding member and first conductor of the Philharmonic Orch. and professor at the Cons. of Music, both in Bogotá. President of the Sociedad de Autores y Compositores of Colombia.

Works (selective list): *Orch.:* Sinfonía No.1 (1966); *Estudio* (1970); *Estructuras* (1971); Sinfonía No.2 for soloists and chorus (1971); Concertante for trumpet (1964); Concerto for viola (1971); *Contrastes*, for strings (1963). Chamber music; choral music; piano pieces.
Source: CTA17

Pires dos Reis, Hilda, Brazilian pianist, conductor, teacher, and composer; b.10 Oct 1919, Rio de Janeiro, Brazil. She studied piano and orch. conducting at the Federal Univ. Music School of Rio de Janeiro. She later taught at the Federal Univ. and at the Cons. of Brazil, both in Rio de Janeiro.
Works: Spanish Fantasy, for orch. (1945); *Revery,* for orch. (1963); chamber music; piano pieces; songs.
Sources: IBCC, IEW

Planchart, Alejandro Enrique, Venezuelan composer and musicologist; b.29 Jul 1935, Caracas, Venezuela. He studied composition at Yale Univ., New Haven, Connecticut, with H.L. Baumgartner, Quincy Porter, and Richard Donovan, and musicology at Harvard Univ., Cambridge, Massachusetts. Professor at Yale Univ.
Works: Tropes, for orch. (1968); chamber music; piano pieces; songs.
Source: DCM

Plaza Alfonzo, Eduardo, Venezuelan composer, diplomat, and political scientist; b.11 Nov 1911, Caracas, Venezuela. He studied music with his brother, Juan Bautista Plaza Alfonzo. Professor at the Escuela Superior de Música José Angel Lamas and the Preparatory School of Music Juan Manuel Olivares, both of Caracas. Director of the Escuela Superior de Música and of the Preparatory School of Music.
Works (selective list): *Elegía Arcaica*, for orch. (1965); *Himno de Pro Venezuela*, for 4 voices and orch. (1959); *Himno del Cuerpo Técnico de la Policía Judicial*, for chorus and orch. (1966); chamber music; religious music; piano pieces; music for organ; songs.
Source: CTA14

Plaza Alfonzo, Juan Bautista, Venezuelan composer and musicologist; b.19 Jul 1898, Caracas, Venezuela; d.1 Jan 1965, Caracas. Brother of Eduardo Plaza Alfonzo. He studied piano and solfeggio with Jesús María Suárez in Caracas. In 1920, he went to Rome, Italy, where he studied at the Pontifical Inst. of Sacred Music with Licinio Refice, Césare Dobici, Raffaele Casimiri, Raffaele Manari, Paolo M. Ferretti, and Edoardo Dagnino. He returned to

Venezuela in 1923, and became *maestro de capilla* (chapelmaster) and organist at the Cathedral of Caracas. Professor at the National School of Music and supervisor of artistic education at the Centro de Extensión Cultural of the National Secretary of Education, both of Caracas.
Works (selective list): *Symphonic poems: El Picacho Abrupto* (1926); *Vigilia* (1928); *Campanas de Pascua* (1930); *Las Horas* (1930). *Misa in E minor*, for 2 voices and organ (1924); *Misa in D major* for 3 mixed voices and organ (1926); *Fuga Criolla*, for string quartet (1931); *Sonatina Venezolana*, for piano; chamber music; sacred music; piano pieces; songs. *Books: Music in Caracas during the Colonial Period (1770-1811), MQ*, Vol.29, 1943. *Música Colonial Venezolana, Letras Venezolanas,* Caracas, 1958.
Sources: BB, CTA9, DM, GDM, MLA, MMLA

Ponce, Manuel María, Mexican composer and pianist; b.8 Dec 1882, Fresnillo, State of Zacatecas, Mexico; d.24 Apr 1948, Mexico City, Mexico. He started music studies with his older sister, Josefina, and with Cipriano Avila. Later he studied at the National Cons. of Music of Mexico City. In 1904 he went to Europe where he took lessons in composition and orchestration with Enrico Bossi and Luigi Torchi in Bologna, Italy, and studied piano with Martin Krause, in Berlin, Germany. After WWI he went to Paris, France, where he took lessons with Paul Dukas. When he returned to Mexico he was appointed professor of piano at the National Cons. of Music of Mexico City. Conductor of the Mexican Symphony Orch. of Mexico City. Co-director, together with Ruben M. Campos, of the *Revista Musical Mexicana.* Editor of the monthly musical magazine *Cultura Musical.*
Works (selective list): *Estampas Nocturnas,* for orch. (1923); *Canto y Danza de los Antiguos Mexicanos,* for orch. (1933); *Chapultepec,* symphonic triptych (1929); *Suite en Estilo Antiguo,* for orch. (1935); *Poema Elegíaco,* for orch. (1935); *Ferial,* for orch. (1940); *Concierto del Sur,* for guitar and orch. (1941); Violin concerto (1943); chamber music; piano pieces; songs, including *Estrellita* which became internationally famous.
Bibl.: D. López Alonso, *Manuel María Ponce: Ensayo Biográfico,* Mexico City, 1950. J. Romero, *Efemérides de Manuel Ponce, Nuestra Música,* 1950.
Sources: BB, CTA1, DCM, DM, GDM, MLA, MMLA

Ponce de León, José María, Colombian composer; b.1846, Bogotá, Colombia; d.21 Sep 1882, Bogotá. He studied music first with Juan Crisóstomo Osorio in Colombia, and then, in 1867, he went to Paris, France, where he studied under Charles Gounod and Ambroise

Thomas at the Cons. of Music. In 1871, he returned to Bogotá and became conductor of the Bogotá Band.
Works: Operas: *Los Diez; Ester; El Castillo Misterioso; Florinda. Sinfonía sobre Temas Colombianos,* for orch.; *El Himno a los Andes; Apoteosis de Bolívar; Misa de Gloria; La Voz Humana,* cantata; *Salve Regina; Misa de Requiem.*
Sources: MLA, MMLA

Portugal, Marcos, Brazilian composer of Portuguese origin; b.1762, Lisbon, Portugal; d.Feb 1830, Brazil. He settled in Brazil in 1811. He studied in Naples, Italy.
Works: Operas: *Damofoonte; Merope; L'Oro no Compra Amore; A Saloia Namorada; Augúrio de Félicitá.* These operas established the beginning of the lyric theater in Brazil.
Source: MMLA

Posada Amador, Carlos, Colombian composer; b.25 Apr 1908, Medellín, Colombia. He started music studies at the School of Santa Cecilia of his native town, and in 1931, he went to Paris, France, to study at the National School of Music with Nadia Boulanger and George Dandelot. Later he studied Gregorian chant and conducting with Vincent D'Indy and Paul Dukas. Director of the Cons. of Medellín. Since 1943, he has lived in Mexico where he taught at the Music School of the UNAM and the National Cons. of Music, both in Mexico City.
Works (selective list): *Marinas,* for orch. (1934); *Obertura,* for orch. (1937); *La Coronación del Zipa en Guatavita,* symphonic poem (1939); chamber music; music for solo instruments; choruses; piano pieces; songs.
Sources: CTA8, DM, MLA, ZCCC

Posada Saldarriaga, Andrés, Colombian composer; b.24 Feb 1954, Medellín, Colombia. He received a Bachelor's and a Master's degrees in composition from The Mannes College of Music in New York City, where he studied with Leo Edwards and Peter P. Stearns. Founder and director of the Laboratorio Colombiano de Música Electrónica Jaqueline Nova in the Univ. Autónoma of Manizales, Colombia. Music teacher at the Facultad de las Artes of the Univ. of Antioquía, Colombia.
Works (selective list): *Poema para una Catedral Invisible,* for orch. (1984); *Obertura para un Concierto* (1987); *Los Colores,* for orch. (1988); *Eventos Móviles,* for 20 players (1991); *Danza para Orquesta* (1992); chamber music; choral music; electroacoustic music; songs.
Source: ISC

Posadas, Florencio, Bolivian violinist, percussionist, and composer; b.7 Nov 1939, Potosí, Bolivia; d.6 Dec 1968, Bolivia. He studied music in Potosí with Father José Díaz Gainza and José Sandi. Later he studied at the National Cons. of Music Carlos López Buchardo of Buenos Aires, Argentina.
Works: Piano pieces; songs; music for percussion.
Source: CB

Prado Quesada, Alcides, Costa Rican composer; b.5 Nov 1900, San Ramón, Costa Rica; d.? He started music studies with his father, conductor of the Municipal Band of San Ramón, who taught him to play the viola and the clarinet. Later he entered the Colegio de Salesianos in Cartago, Costa Rica, where he studied piano with Eduardo Peralta and Manuel J. Freer, with whom he also studied music theory and harmony. He also studied harmony and counterpoint with Julio Fonseca. Clarinetist and conductor of several bands in Costa Rica. Conductor of the Military Band of Alajuela, Costa Rica, in 1932. In 1940, he was appointed Technical Director of Music at the schools of the Republic of Zone I in Panama.
Works: *La Casa del Diablo,* opera; *Amor Campestre,* zarzuela; String quartet; *Misa de Requiem,* for 3 voices, organ, and orch.; *Dolorosa,* funeral march; *Plegaria a la Virgen de la Soledad,* for tenor and organ.
Source: MMLA

Prieto y Fernández de la Llana, María Teresa, Mexican composer of Spanish origin; b.22 Apr 1908, NH (1896, NGDWC), Oviedo, Spain; d.24 Jan 1982, Mexico City, Mexico. She studied piano and composition with Saturnino del Fresno at the Escuela de Bellas Artes of Oviedo. Later she studied piano with José Antonio Cubiles and harmony and composition with Benito García de la Parra at the Cons. de Música y Declamación of Madrid, Spain. In 1936, when the Spanish Civil War started, she moved to Mexico and studied composition and orchestration with Manuel M. Ponce, Carlos Chávez, and Rodolfo Halffter. She took lessons from Darius Milhaud at Mills College, Oakland, California, in 1946 and 1947.
Works (selective list): *Orch.:* *Impresión Sinfónica,* for piano (1940); *Excelsitud,* symphonic poem for chorus (1941); *Sinfonía Asturiana* (1942); *Chichen Itza,* symphonic poem (1944); *Sinfonía Breve* (1945); *Variaciones y Fuga* (1946); *Adagio y Fuga,* for cello (1948); *Oración de Quietud,* symphonic poem for voice (1949); *Sinfonía de la Danza Prima* (1955); *Sinfonía Cantabile* (1956); Symphonic suite from the ballet *El Palo Verde* (1967); *Cuadro de la Naturaleza* (1967); *Tema Variado y Fuga (dodecafónico)* (1968); *Sonata Modal en Tres Movimientos,* for voice (1971). Chamber music; songs.
Sources: MMLA, NH

Pro, Serafín, Cuban composer; b.30 Jul 1906, Havana, Cuba. He studied piano with María Luisa Chartrand and harmony, counterpoint, and music history and aesthetics with José Ardévol at the Municipal Cons. of Music in Havana. Professor at the Municipal Cons. of Music Amadeo Roldán and the García Caturla Cons., both of Havana. Director of the bulletin of the *Grupo de Renovación Musical.*
Works (selective list): *La Tarde,* for chorus (1940); *Estar Así,* for chorus (1940); *Las Siete Doncellas,* for chorus (1940); *Canción,* for chorus (1940); Sonata for orch. (1951); *Chorale and Fugue,* for string orch. (1951); piano pieces; songs.
Sources: DM, GDM, MMLA

Prudencio B., Cergio, Bolivian composer; b.3 Nov 1955, La Paz, Bolivia. He studied guitar and flute, and later composition and conducting at the Bolivian Catholic Univ. of La Paz. Professor of harmony, composition, and musical analysis at the National Cons. of Music of La Paz.
Works (selective list): *Perpetuidad,* ballet (1978); *La Ciudad,* for native instruments orch. (1980); *Juegos Imaginados,* ballet (1985-87); *AWASQA,* electroacoustics (1985); *Cantos de Piedra,* for native instruments orch. (1989); *Cantos de Tierra,* for native instruments orch.; chamber music; incidental music for film and theater.
Source: ISC

Puelma Francini, Roberto, Chilean composer and conductor; b.24 Mar 1893, Santiago de Chile, Chile; d.? He studied with Nino Marcelli and Enrique Soro at the National Cons. of Music of Chile, Santiago de Chile, and later he studied in Europe and the USA.
Works (selective list): **Operas:** *Lihuén* (1945); *Ardid de Amor (1951).* Violin concerto (1935); *El Reino de las Almas,* symphonic poem (1939); *Sinfonía Abajeña* (1940); chamber music; songs.
Source: HMC

Pulgar Vidal, Francisco Bernardo, Peruvian composer; b.12 Mar 1929, Huánaco, Peru. He studied piano with Gustavo Leguía and violin with Mariano Béjar Pacheco, and later studied harmony, counterpoint, and orchestration with Andrés Sas, and fugue and composition with Roberto Pineda Duque in Bogotá, Colombia. He received a degree in music from the National Cons. of Lima, Peru, and a law degree from the Univ. Mayor de San Marcos of Lima. Professor of humanities at the Univ. Jorge Tadeo Lozano of Bogotá.
Works (selective list): *Suite Mística (Danzas Mestizas),* for string orch. (1956); *Taki No.1,* for orch. (1960); *Chulpas,* 7 estructuras sinfónicas (1968); *Apu Inqa,* for soprano, reciter, chorus, and orch. (1970); piano pieces; choruses; songs.
Sources: CTA16, GDM

Q

Quaratino, Pascual, Argentine composer; b.13 Jun 1904, Buenos Aires, Argentina. He studied first in Buenos Aires, and later at the Royal Cons. San Pietro a Majella of Naples, Italy; he studied piano with Juan Barbieri, organ with José Cotrufo, harmony with Genaro Nápoli, counterpoint, fugue, and composition with Camillo de Nardis, orchestration with Rafael Caravallis, and organ composition with Juan Tebaldini. Professor at the National Cons. of Music Carlos López Buchardo and director of the Municipal Cons. of Music Manuel de Falla, both of Buenos Aires. Assistant conductor at the Teatro Colón of Buenos Aires, Teatro Municipal of Rio de Janeiro, Brazil, Teatro Municipal of Sâo Paulo, Brazil, Teatro San Carlos of Naples, and Teatro Real de Opera of Rome, Italy.
Works (selective list): *Tríptico,* for orch.; *Voces de la Tierra,* for orch. Quartet in D major; choruses; piano pieces; songs.
Sources: CA, DM, EMA, MLA

Quesada, José, Costa Rican composer; b.6 Oct 1894, San Rafael, Costa Rica; d.? He studied music in San José, Costa Rica. Conductor of a military band in San José.
Works: El Son de la Luna, for orch. (1930); *Costa Rican Dances,* for band.
Source: MLA

Quevedo Arvelo, Julio, Colombian composer, and orch., band, and chorus conductor; b.16 Mar 1829, Quesada, Colombia; d.26 Mar 1896, Zipa, Colombia. He started to study music very early in life. At age fifteen he was playing piano, violin, and cello, and was already composing school songs. He founded the *Sexteto de la Armonía,* society dedicated to promote chamber music.
Works: *Religious works: Salve Pastoral; Te Deum,* for 4 voices; *Lamentaciones de la Semana Santa*; *Misa de Santo Tomás; Misa Negra; Misa in D minor; Oración de Jeremías. Fantasías Concertantes,* for violin and orch.
Bibl.: J.I. Perdomo Escobar, *Historia de la Música Colombiana,* Bogotá, 1945.
Source: MMLA

Quintanar, Héctor, Mexican composer; b.15 Apr 1936, Mexico City, Mexico. He studied with Carlos Chávez, Rodolfo Halffter, and Blas Galindo at the National Cons. of Mexico City, 1959-64. He also studied electronic music with Andrés Lewin Richter at Columbia Univ. in New York, 1964, and with Jean Etienne Marie in Paris, France, 1967, and in Mexico City, 1968. He supervised the

construction of the country's first Electronic Laboratory at the National Univ. of Mexico, Mexico City, in 1968. Director of the Music Dept. of the Secretaría Técnica del Inst. Nacional de Bellas Artes, Mexico City, 1965-70. Founder and director of the Electronic Music Studio of the Cons. of Mexico City and subdirector of the Orch. of the Mexico City Opera.
Works (selective list): 3 symphonies (1961, 1962, 1964); *Sinfonía Modal* (1961-62); *El Viejo y el Mar,* symphonic poem (1963); *Fábulas,* for chorus and orch. (1964); Double quartet for string and wind quartets (1964-65); String trio (1965-66); Violin sonata (1967); *Aclamaciones,* for chorus, tape, and orch. (1967); Sonata for 3 trumpets (1967); *Galaxias,* for orch. (1968); *Sideral I,* for tape (1968); *Sideral II,* for orch. (1969); *Solutio?,* for soprano and piano (1969); *Símbolos,* for violin, clarinet, saxophone, horn, trumpet, trombone, piano, tape, optical slides, and lights (1969); *Ilapso,* for clarinet, bassoon, trumpet, trombone, percussion, violin, and double bass (1970); *Sideral III,* for tape (1971); *Voz,* for soprano and tape (1971); Quintet for piano, violin, double bass, flute, and trumpet (1973); *Diálogos,* for piano and tape (1973).
Sources: BB, CTA15, DCM, GDM

Quintanilla, Alba, Venezuelan composer, harpist, harpsichordist, pianist, and conductor; b.11 Jul 1944, Mérida, Venezuela. She started her music education with her parents and later she studied piano, harp, harpsichord, composition, and conducting with Vicente Emilio Sojo, R. Pereira, Juan Bautista Plaza, Gonzalo and Evencio Castellanos, C. de Majo, E. Taborda, L. Butterini, and P. Manelski at the Escuela Superior de Música José Angel Lamas in Caracas, Venezuela. Teacher of music in various cons. and music schools.
Works (selective list): *La Llanura,* cantata for mixed chorus and string orch. (1969); *Tres Canciones,* for mezzo-soprano and orch. (1967); Brass quintet; piano pieces; choruses; songs.
Source: IEW

Quinteros Figueroa, Abelardo, Chilean composer; b.10 Dec 1923, Valparaiso, Chile. He studied industrial design at the Univ. Santa María of Valparaiso, and composition with Humberto Allende and Free Focke in Santiago de Chile, Chile. With a scholarship from the Austrian government, he went to Vienna to study serial techniques and voice at the Othmar Steinbauer Academy.
Works (selective list): *Tres Arabescos Concertantes,* for clarinet and orch.; *Sinfonema,* for violin and orch.; *Obertura Austral,* for orch.; Concerto for soprano and chamber orch.; *Misa de Navidad,* for voice and organ; chamber music; music for the organ; songs.
Sources: GDM, HMC

Quintón, José Ignacio, Puerto Rican composer and pianist; b.1 Feb 1881, Caguas, Puerto Rico; d.19 Dec 1925, Coamo, Puerto Rico. He studied harmony, counterpoint, composition, and piano with his father, Juan Bautista Quintón. Organist at the Parroquia San Blas.
Works (selective list): *El Coquí,* dance for orch. (1901); *Misa de Requiem*, for orch. (1903); *Obertura de Concierto*; *Una Página de mi Vida,* for orch. (1920); chamber music; piano pieces; religious music.
Sources: CPR, MMLA

R

Radamés, Apóstol, Argentine composer, pianist, and teacher; b.18 Dec 1929, San Fernando, Prov. of Buenos Aires, Argentina. He studied piano with Dvieta de Castro and harmony with Amelia Oses. *Works: Tritemática,* for orch.; Suite for orch.
Source: VMA

Raffelin, Antonio, Cuban composer and teacher; b.1796, Havana, Cuba, DM (Catalonia, Spain, DMC); d.1882, Marianao, Cuba. He studied cello and double bass with Gregorio Velázquez, counterpoint and fugue with Manuel Cocco, and violin with Thomas Tlown. Founder of the Academia Filarmónica de Cristina. He lived for some time in Philadelphia, Pennsylvania, where he edited the musical journal *La Lira Católica.*
Works (selective list): *Religious music:* hymns; motets; masses; passion books. 3 symphonies; String quartet.
Bibl.: A. Carpenter, *La Música en Cuba,* Mexico, 1946.
Sources: DM, DMC

Rafols, Félix, Cuban teacher and composer of Spanish origin; b.1894, Barcelona, Spain; d.1961, Camagüey, Cuba. He studied in Spain with Enrique Granados. When he arrived in Cuba, he settled in Camagüey, where he founded the *Orfeón Catalán* (Catalan male singing society) and later the Rafols Cons. He conducted several choral groups.
Works: Music for orch.; piano pieces; choruses.
Source: DMC

Rago, Alexis, Venezuelan composer and pianist; b.25 May 1930, Caracas, Venezuela. He began to study music in Caracas and continued at the Peabody Cons. of Music in Baltimore, Maryland. He also studied piano with Aldo Mantía and composition with Franco Margola and Armando Renzi in Vienna, Austria, and in Rome, Italy. Director of the Music Cons. of the State of Aragua, Venezuela.
Works (selective list): *Orch.: Antantepuy,* symphonic poem (1962); *Milles Gärten,* symphonic poem (1963); *Una Sinfonía para los Niños* (1965); *Hambre,* dramatic cantata for mezzo-soprano, mixed chorus, and children's chorus (1966); *Cinco Instantes para Orquesta* (1968); *Guri,* Indian symphonic poem (1968); *Sincronismos Audio-Sonorrítmicos* (1969); *Coro de Espectros,* for mixed chorus (1969). Chamber music; piano pieces; songs.
Sources: BB, CTA14

Ramírez, Luis Antonio, Puerto Rican composer; b.10 Feb 1923, San Juan, Puerto Rico. He studied piano and harmony with Alfredo Romero in San Juan, 1954-57. Then he went to Spain, where he studied composition with Cristóbal Halffter and Daniel Bravo, and piano with Juan Molinari at the Cons. of Music of Madrid, Spain, 1957-60. Professor of harmony and composition at the Cons. of Music of Puerto Rico since 1968.
Works (selective list): *Orch.:* Sinfonietta for string orch. (1963); *La Buena Herencia,* documental music for flute, oboe, clarinet, horn, timpani, piano, and strings (1965); *Tres Homenajes,* for string orch. (1962-65); Suite for small orch. (1966); *Balada Concierto,* for violin (1967); *Fantasía sobre un Mito Antillano,* for guitar horn, timpani, double bass, and strings (1969); *Fragmentos,* three pieces (1973); *Nueve Cantos Antillanos* (1975); *Rasgos y Perfiles,* symphonic poem (1977); *Figuraciones,* symphonic poem (1974); *Aire y Tierra,* symphonic poem (1978); *Ciclos,* symphonic poem (1979); *El Cuarto Rey Mago,* symphonic poem (1983); *La Tierra Escuchó tu Voz,* symphonic poem (1984); *2 Suites para la Navidad* (1982, 1983); *Días sin Alborada* (1986); *Siete Episodios Históricos,* for flute, cello, horn, timpani, and strings (1986). Chamber music; songs.
Sources: BB, CPR

Ramírez Avila, Hernán, Chilean composer and physician; b.10 Jun 1941, Santiago de Chile, Chile. He started music studies with L. Vilches and Lucila Césped, and then he studied composition with Carlos Botto and Gustavo Becerra.
Works (selective list): *En Viet Nam* (1970); String quartet (1971); Piano concerto (1970); *Cuatro Trozos Aleatorios,* for orch. (1970); chamber music; songs.
Source: HMC

Ramírez Sierra, Alvaro, Colombian composer and teacher; b.6 Jun 1932, Cali, Colombia. He studied at the Cons. of Cali and the Cons. of Boston, Massachusetts. Professor at the Cons. of Cali.
Works: Orch. works; Piano concerto; Violin concerto; Guitar concerto; Concerto for 2 violins and orch.; chamber music; piano pieces; choruses.
Source: KTL

Ramos, Juan José, Argentine composer and pianist; b.17 Jul 1930, Córdoba, Prov. of Córdoba, Argentina. He studied with Clara Moltini, Jaime Pahissa, and Alicia de Larrocha. Founder of the chamber octet *Tango Ensemble.*

Works (selective list): *Rapsodia Popular de Buenos Aires*, for orch.; *Siete Variaciones de Tango*, for bandonion and orch.; *Suite Porteña*, for guitar and piano; *Momento de Tango*, for piano; *Suite Pampeana*, for guitar and orch.; piano pieces.
Source: VMA

Ramos Junior, Ezequiel, Brazilian composer; b.1874, Sâo Paulo, Brazil; d.19 Dec 1928, Jundiaí, Brazil. He studied at the Cons. of Geneva, Switzerland, with Henri Ruegger and Jacques Dalcroze. *Works* (selective list): Quintet in C minor; Quartet in A minor; *Angelus*, for orch.; *Adagio*, for orch.; chamber music; piano pieces.
Source: MMLA

Ranieri, Salvador, Argentine composer and clarinetist of Italian origin; b.1930, Arena, Prov. of Catanzaro, Italy. He settled in Argentina in 1947.
Works: Autos, for flute and piano; *Tres Invenciones*, for piano; *Organum*, for organ; *Cantiche Strane*, for voice and wind quintet; *Sinfonietta Syntónica*, for string orch.; *I Semi Dei*, for baritone and piano.
Source: EMA

Rattenbach, Augusto Benjamín, Argentine composer; b.5 Feb 1927, Buenos Aires, Argentina. He studied composition with Teodoro Fuchs in Buenos Aires, 1947-58. Later he studied in Germany at the Hochschule für Musik in Hamburg, with Ernest G. Klussman and Philip Jarnach, 1959-60. In 1974 and 1975, he studied electronic music with Francisco Kröpfl and José Maranzano, and also took composition lessons from Juan F. Giacobbe. Director of the Municipal Cons. of Music Manuel de Falla of Buenos Aires, 1973-74 and 1986-89, and director of Artistic and Special Education at the Municipality of Buenos Aires, in 1975 and in 1989. Regional secretary for Latin America of the Consejo Internacional de la Música (CIM-UNESCO).
Works (selective list): **Operas:** *Jettatore* (1972); *La Planta* (1981); *El Brujo de la Cortada* (1984); *Edipo en San Telmo* (1985); *El Tigre Enamorado* (1987); *Los Amantes de la Calle Corrientes* (1987); *La Piedra Azul* (1990). **Ballets:** *Un Episodio Vulgar* (1961); *El Tiempo y el Fuego* (1970); *Martina* (1987). **Orch.:** Suite sinfónica (1955); *Passacaglia* (1956); *Concertino Pastoral*, for oboe and string orch. (1958); *Variaciones Sinfónicas* (1959); *Cuatro Piezas* (1960); *Microvariaciones I*, for strings and timpani (1961); Cantata for soprano, baritone, and mixed choir (1962); *Cinco Piezas*, for oboe and strings (1963); Sinfonietta for chamber orch. (1962); *Cinco Momentos Líricos* (1963); *Ficción*, for flute (1963); *Cuatro Tristes*, for baritone (1964); *Microvariaciones Concertantes*, for clarinet and

French horn (1964); *Obstinaciones* (1965); Sonatina for wind orch. and percussion (1966); Piano concerto (1966); *Divertimento*, for brass and percussion (1968); *Doble Concierto*, for clarinet and English horn (1969); *Díptico*, for strings (1970); *Recuperación de la Memoria*, for voice (1970); *Serenata*, for chamber orch. (1971); *Interpolaciones* (1973); *Variaciones y Fuga sobre un Tema Infantil*, for string orch. (1973); *Tríptico Lídico* (1973-75); Concerto for organ and strings (1974); Double bass concerto (1975); French horn concerto (1977-78); Concerto for recorder and string orch. (1978); *Obertura Festiva para el Día de la Música* (1978); Sonatina for chamber orch. (1980); *Variaciones Buenos Aires* (1982); *Sinfonietta Bucólica*, for chamber orch. (1984); *Alberdiana*, for chamber orch. (1984); *Movimiento Concertante*, for horn and chamber orch. (1984); *Cinco Variantes Elegíacas*, for string orch. (1985); Chamber concerto for cello and instrumental ensemble (1987); *Introducción y Tango*, chamber ensemble (1988); *Sinfonía de Otoño*, (1989); *Tango de Cámara*, for chamber ensemble (1989); *Variaciones Concertantes*, for chamber orch. (1990); *Concierto Breve*, for piano (1990). Chamber music; piano pieces; songs.
Sources: BB, CTA12, EMA

Ravelo, José de Jesús, Dominican composer; b.21 Mar 1876, Ciudad Trujillo (Santo Domingo), Dominican Republic; d.12 Feb 1951, Ciudad Trujillo. He studied music with Juan Francisco Pereyra in 1890. Conductor of the Banda Pacificador. Founder of the *Octeto del Casino de la Juventud*, which later became the Orch. of the Sociedad de Conciertos of the Dominican Republic. Founder and first director of the Liceo Musical and the School Children's Band, both of the Dominican Republic.
Works (selective list): *Marcha Fúnebre*, for band (1900); *Himno Masónico*, for voice and orch. (1903); String quartet (1929); *La Muerte de Cristo*, oratorium (1939); *Misa de Requiem*, for 4 voices and orch. (1940); *La Resurrección de Cristo*, oratorium (1942); *Las Siete Palabras*, for 3 voices and orch. (1943); religious music; music for the organ; piano pieces; choruses; songs.
Sources: DEW, DM, MLA, MMLA

Rebagliati, Claudio, Peruvian pianist, violinist, conductor, composer, and teacher of Italian origin; b.6 Oct 1843, Noli, near Savona, Italy; d.23 Dec 1909, Lima, Peru. He settled in Lima in 1863. First violinist at the Orch. of the Teatro Principal of Lima. In 1868, he was appointed conductor of the orch. of the Sociedad Filarmónica of Lima. President of the Music Section of the Sociedad de Bellas Artes of Lima and founding member and first president of the Sociedad Musical de Aficionados of Lima, both in 1879.

Works (selective list): *Obertura a Gran Orquesta,* for orch. (1867); *Un 28 de Julio en Lima,* Peruvian rhapsody for orch.; *Canción Nacional de Bolivia,* for orch. (1873); *Primicias,* overture for orch. (1896); *Misa Solemne,* for soloists, chorus, and orch.; *Misa de Requiem,* for soloists, chorus, and orch.; *Invitatorium,* for soloists, chorus, and orch. Restored *the Peruvian National Anthem,* written by José Bernardo Alcedo, to its original version, and orchestrated it.
Bibl.: R. Barbacci, *Revista Musical Peruana,* Lima, 1940.
Sources: DM, GMP, MLA

Rebolledo, Pedro, Panamanian composer and band conductor; b.27 Apr 1895, Panama City, Panama; d.? He studied with Rufino Sainz Alvarez, and later at the Cons. Nacional de Música y Declamación of Panama, Panama City, and at the National Cons. of Music of Mexico, Mexico City, under Julián Carrillo. Conductor of the Republican Band and president of the Musical Union, both of Panama.
Works: *Obertura 1903;* Suite in B minor; *Fugue,* for orch.; String quartet; *Fantasía sobre Motivos Panameños;* 2 movements of a symphony; 2 triumphal marches.
Sources: DM, MMLA

Reboucas, José, Brazilian composer; b.1789, Brazil; d.1843, Brazil. He studied violin in Paris, France, and harmony, counterpoint, and composition in Bologna, Italy.
Works: Magnificat.
Source: MMLA

Reis, Julio, Brazilian composer and pianist; b.1863, Brazil; d.1933, Brazil.
Works: Operas: Heliofar; Soror Mariana. He left over one hundred compositions.
Source: MMLA

Rengifo, Javier, Chilean composer, conductor, and pianist; b.17 Mar 1879, MMLA (1884, HMC), Santiago de Chile, Chile; d.1958, Chile. He started music studies, piano, and violin with Juan Agustín Reyes. Later he entered the National Cons. of Chile in Santiago de Chile, where he studied theory and solfeggio with Zubicueta, harmony with Federico Stöber, and counterpoint with Domingo Brescia. In 1904, he went to Europe where he studied piano with Théophile Ysaÿe, and counterpoint, fugue, composition, and musical form with Désiré Pâque in Brussels, Belgium. Later he studied with Auguste De Boeck and Paul Gilson, and briefly with Jules Massenet in Paris, France. He also took lessons in orchestration and orch. conducting from Lecail. Music critic for the newspaper *La Nación.*

Director of the Academia Musical del Club de La Unión, from 1926 to 1941, and of the Academia Musical de los Colegios de los Padres Franceses, both in Santiago de Chile.
Works (selective list): *Amor Plebeyo,* zarzuela; *Himno a León XIII,* for soloists, chorus, and orch.; *Himno a la Ciencia,* for 4 voices; *Juan José,* opera; *Intermedios,* for string quartet; *Oda Heróica;* hymns; piano pieces; songs.
Sources: HMC, MMLA

Renta, Beatriz, Argentine composer, musicologist, and teacher; b.Buenos Aires, Argentina. She graduated from the Argentine Catholic Univ. of Buenos Aires.
Works (selective list): Sonata for cello and piano; Quintet for piano and string quartet; *Serranilla,* for bass, flute, harp, viola, and cello; piano pieces; songs.
Source: VMA

Repetto Espinosa, Amelia, Uruguayan contemporary composer and teacher; b.Montevideo, Uruguay; fl.mid-20th century. She studied piano with Julieta Bizzozero and harmony, counterpoint, and orchestration with Guido Santórsola. Professor of music appreciation in the high school system, and teacher in elementary schools.
Works (selective list): *Dualisme,* vocal distich (1961); String quartet; *Poema Crepuscular,* for voice and string quartet; chamber music; choral music; piano pieces; songs.
Sources: BHMCU, MU

Republicano, Antonio de Assis, Brazilian composer; b.15 Nov 1897, Pôrto Alegre, Brazil; d.26 May 1960, Rio de Janeiro, Brazil. He studied bassoon at the Inst. of Pôrto Alegre, and then studied with Francisco Braga and Agnello França at the National School of Music of Rio de Janeiro.
Works: Operas: O Bandeirante; A Natividade de Jesús; Amazonas; O Ermitâo da Gloria. Sinfonía de las Multitudes, for orch., chorus, and military band; *Improviso,* for cello and orch.
Sources: DM, MLA, MMLA

Restano, Antonio, Argentine composer; b.1860, Buenos Aires, Argentina; d.1928, Buenos Aires. He studied at the Royal Cons. of Milan, Italy, with Amilcare Ponchielli. After residing in Europe for 27 years, he returned to Buenos Aires where he founded a cons.
Works (selective list): *Operas: Un Milioncino* (1885); *Moroveldo* (1886); *Margherita d'Orleans* (1887). *Cantata al Calvario,* for chorus and orch.; *Himno al Centenario,* for chorus and orch.; Overture in B flat for orch.; piano pieces.
Source: EMA

Revueltas, Silvestre, Mexican composer, conductor, and violinist; b.31 Dec 1899, Santiago Papasquiaro, State of Durango, Mexico; d.5 Oct 1940, Mexico City, Mexico. He began violin studies at age eight in Colima, Mexico, and entered the Juárez Inst. in Durango at age twelve. Later he studied composition with Rafael J. Tello and violin with José Rocabruna in Mexico City, 1913-16, and took courses at St. Edward College in Austin, Texas, 1916-18. Then he went to the Chicago Musical College, Chicago, Illinois, to study violin with León Sametini and composition with Félix Borowsky, 1918-20. Later he studied violin with Paul Kochansky and Otakar Sevcik, 1922-26, also in Chicago. Assistant conductor of the Symphony Orch. of Mexico, Mexico City, 1929-35, and later he was appointed permanent conductor. Professor of violin at the National Cons. of Music of Mexico, Mexico City.
Works (selective list): **Ballets:** *El Renacuajo Paseador* (1933); *La Coronela,* left unfinished at his death and completed by Blas Galindo and Candelario Huízar (1941). **Orch.:** *Cuauhnahuac* (1931-32); *Esquinas* (1931); *Ventanas* (1931); *Alcancías* (1932); *Colorines* (1932); *Ocho por Radio* (1933); *Janitzio* (1933); *Caminos* (1934); *Planos,"Geometric Dance"* (1934); *Redes* (1935); *Homenaje a García Lorca* (1935); *Sensemaya,* for voice (1937); *Música para Charlar,* concert suite (1938); *Hora de Junio,* for narrator (1938); *La Noche de los Mayas,* concert suite (1939); *Itinerarios* (1939); *Paisajes* (1940); *Parias,* for soprano and chorus (1940); *Troka* (1940). 3 string quartets (1930, 1931, 1931); *Toccata sin Fuga,* for violin and 7 winds (1933); *Canto de Guerra de los Frentes Leales,* for 3 trumpets, 3 trombones, 2 tubas, percussion, and piano (1938); *Tres Sonatas,* for chamber ensemble (1940); *Three Little Serious Pieces,* for piccolo, oboe, trumpet, clarinet, and saxophone (1940); piano pieces; songs.
Bibl.: O. Mayer-Serra, *Silvestre Revueltas and Musical Nationalism in Mexico, Musical Quarterly,* Vol.27, 1941. G. Contreras, *Silvestre Revueltas: Genio Atormentado,* Mexico City, 1954.
Sources: BB, CTA1, DCM, DM, GDM, MLA, MMLA

Reyes, José, Dominican composer; b.1835, Dominican Republic; d.1905, Dominican Republic. He studied with Juan Bautista Alfonseca.
Works: *Dominican Republic National Anthem.*
Sources: DM, MLA

Reyes, José Trinidad, Honduran composer; b.11 Jun 1797, Tegucigalpa, Honduras; d.29 Sep 1855, Tegucigalpa. He studied music with his father, Felipe Santiago Reyes. He became a priest in 1822 at the Convento de Recoletos.
Works: Masses; villancicos; songs; zarzuelas. Most of his music has been lost.

Sources: MLA, MMLA

Reyes Camejo, Angel, Cuban teacher and composer; b.1889?, Matanzas, Cuba; d.? He studied in Cienfuegos, Cuba, with César Bonafú, and in Havana, Cuba, with Pedro Sanjuán. In Mexico, he studied with Julián Carrillo.
Works: Symphonic poem; Suite for orch.; Concerto for violin and orch.; *Tambó,* for quintet; *Yemayá,* for violin and piano; *Fantasía,* for harp.
Source: DMC

Reynoso, Antonio, Argentine violinist, conductor, and composer of Spanish origin; b.1869, Bilbao, Spain; d.1912, Buenos Aires, Argentina. He settled in Buenos Aires in 1890.
Works: Sainetes (one-act farce) and zarzuelas: Guardia Nacional; Una Heroína; Libertad de Sufragio; Las Aves Negras; La Esquila; El Embargo Preventivo; Justicia Criolla. Music for 11 chapters of the *Passion of Jesus Christ. El Chiripá Rojo,* lyric drama on a book by Enrique García Velloso.
Source: EMA

Ribeiro, León Julio Alfredo, Uruguayan composer and teacher; b.11 Apr 1854, Montevideo, Uruguay; d.12 Mar 1931, Montevideo. He studied with Carmelo Calvo and Luis Sambucetti. In 1885, he was appointed professor of harmony at the Cons. of Music La Lira in Montevideo, where he became professor of piano, and then, in 1889, technical director, and two years later, director, a position that he occupied until his death in 1931.
Words (selective list): *Operas: Liropeya* (1881); *Don Ramiro; Nidia; Nora; Yole; Harpago y Helena.* 4 symphonies; *Misa Solemne,* for 4 voices; *Misa,* for 2 voices; *Salve Regina,* for 2 voices and harmonium; String quartet (1897); Sextet for piano, flute, oboe, clarinet, bassoon, and French horn; chamber music; piano pieces; songs.
Sources: BHMCU, MLA, MU

Ribeiro Neves, Víctor, Brazilian composer; b.14 Sep 1900, Santa Victoria do Palmar, Brazil; d.? Professor of history of music at the Inst. de Bellas Artes of Pôrto Alegre, Brazil.
Works (selective list): *Ponaím,* opera; *Agonia da Tarde,* prelude for voice, chorus, and piano; symphonic pieces.
Source: MMLA

Richter, Frederico, Brazilian composer of German origin; b.1932, Hamburg, Germany. He received a doctorate in music in Pôrto Alegre, Brazil. He did his post graduate studies in electronic music at

McGill Univ. in Montreal, Canada. Professor of composition, orch. conducting, and chamber music in Pelotas, Santa María, and in Pôrto Alegre, Brazil. Director and acting dean of the Dept. of Music of the Univ. of Santa María, Brazil.

Works (selective list): *Dom Quixote de Portinari,* opera; *Concentratas No.1, 2 e 3,* for orch.; *Três Contos Poéticos,* for orch.; chamber music; music for solo instruments; choruses; songs.

Source: HMB

Ried, Aquinas, Chilean composer and physician of German origin; b.between 1810 and 1813, Bavaria, Germany; d.17 May 1869, Chile.

Works (selective list): *Operas: La Telésfora; Il Grenatiere; Walhalla; Diana; Ismenilda; Idona; Ondega; Atacama. Misa Solemne;* many songs.

Sources: HMC, MLA, MMLA

Riesco Grez, Carlos, Chilean composer; b.23 Dec 1925, Santiago de Chile, Chile. He studied composition with Humberto Allende in Chile, and then studied abroad with Aaron Copland, Olivier Messiaen, and Nadia Boulanger. In 1966, he was appointed director of the Inst. de Extensión Musical of the Univ. of Chile in Santiago de Chile.

Works: *Semblanzas Chilenas,* for piano (1946); *Canzona e Rondo,* for violin and piano (1948); Violin concerto (1951); *Passacaglia y Fuga,* for string orch. (1952); *Cuatro Danzas,* for orch. (1952-53); *Candelaria,* ballet (1954-55); Sonata for piano (1959); Piano concerto (1961-63).

Source: HMC

Ripper, Joâo Guilherme, Brazilian composer and conductor; b.1959, Rio de Janeiro, Brazil. He studied with Henrique Morelenbaum, Ronaldo Miranda, Garth M. Drozin, and Roberto Duarte. In 1987, he inaugurated in Rio de Janeiro the *Bank of Orchestral Scores* of the National Music Inst. and organized the catalogue *Brazilian Music for Orchestra,* published by the same Inst. Professor of composition at the Music College of the Federal Univ. of Rio de Janeiro.

Works: *Musica Sacra, uma Nova Proposta; Rio Sâo Francisco, Imagem Sinfônica.*

Source: ISC

Rivera, Luis, Dominican composer and violinist; d.22 Jun 1901, Monte Cristi, Dominican Republic; d.1986, Dominican Republic. He studied music with Father José de Jesús Rivera, and violin with García Vila. In Cuba, he studied harmony and composition with Amadeo Roldán. Artistic director of *La Voz Dominicana.* Professor of

solfeggio and harmony at the National Cons. of Music and conductor of the Band of the National Police, both in the Dominican Republic.
Works (selective list): *Rapsodia Dominicana,* for piano and orch.; *Rapsodia Dominicana,* for orch.; *Poema Indio,* for narrator, baritone, and orch.; piano pieces; songs.
Sources: DEW, MLA, MMLA

Rivera Bonizovich, Enrique, Chilean composer; b.28 Dec 1941, Santiago de Chile, Chile. He studied composition with Juan Orrego Salas and Gustavo Becerra, and later he continued at the Inst. Di Tella of Buenos Aires, Argentina.
Works: Suite Sine Nomine, for piano (1962); *La Ausencia,* song cycle (1962); 2 sonatas for piano (1963, 1965); *El Hombre Acecha,* 2 songs and 1 interlude for voice and piano (1966); *Los Lectores,* for 2 narrators, guitars, and percussion (1966).
Source: HMC

Robles, Manuel, Chilean composer; b.6 Nov 1780, Renca, Chile; d.27 Aug 1837. He started music studies with his father, Marcos Matías Robles.
Works: First *Chilean National Anthem* (1819). (The second and definitive *Chilean National Anthem* was written by Ramón Carnicer in 1828.)
Sources: HMC, MLA, MMLA

Rocha Mussurunga, Domingos da, Brazilian composer and teacher; b.1807, Brazil; d.1856, Brazil. In 1833, he was appointed professor of music.
Works (selective list): *Te Deum for the Coronation of Don Pedro II*; 9 missas festivas for grand orch.; religious music; hymns; waltzes.
Source: MMLA

Rodas, Arturo, Ecuadorian contemporary composer; b.Quito, Ecuador. He studied at the National Cons. of Music of Quito. Later he studied composition, electroacoustic composition, and musical information through computers in France, with Yoshihisa Taira, Michéle Reverdy, Mesías Maiguashca, and François Pinot. Founder and member of the board of directors of the musical association *Denosjours* of Paris, France. Editor and coordinator of the journal *Opus,* published by the Music Division of the Central Bank of Ecuador.
Works: Arcaica, for orch.; *Fibris,* for orch.; *Espacios Invertidos,* for percussion; *Entropía,* for orch.; *Andino III,* for solo flute; *Ramificaciones Temporales,* for solo clarinet.
Source: PEFCM

Rodríguez, Esther, Cuban composer; b.29 Nov 1920, Manzanillo, Cuba. She studied piano and solfeggio at the Orbón Cons. of Havana, Cuba, with Berta Momoyito and Julián Orbón, and later entered the Municipal Cons. of Havana where she studied harmony, counterpoint, and history of music with José Ardévol and Amadeo Roldán. Member of the *Grupo de Renovación Musical* of Cuba.
Works: String quartet in A major; *Preludio*, for piano; Sonata for cello and piano; *Invenciones y Preludio*, for piano; choral music.
Sources: DM, MLA, MMLA

Rodríguez, José Napoleón, Salvadoran composer; b.24 Jul 1901, San Lorenzo, Dept. of San Vicente, El Salvador. He studied in his native town with Carlos Martínez and Francisco C. Cañadas. Conductor of the Banda Regimental de Usulután, El Salvador. Professor of voice at official schools and *maestro de capilla* (chapelmaster) at parochial schools. In 1932, he was appointed conductor of the Banda Regimental of Zacatecoluca, Dept. of La Paz, El Salvador.
Works: *Libertad y Paz,* overture; *Salve, Insigne Patriota,* overture; *Sueño y Realidad,* fantasia; piano pieces; songs; military marches; boleros; religious music.
Source: MMLA

Rodríguez, Laureano, Argentine composer, pianist, and organist; b.1905, Tucumán, Prov. of Tucumán, Argentina. He studied at the Academy of Fine Arts of Tucumán. In 1929, he settled in Jujuy, Prov. of Jujuy, Argentina, where he worked as an organist at the San Francisco Church. Professor of music at the Jujuy High School and director of the Inst. Musical Jujuy.
Works (selective list): *Preludio y Tema Fugado,* for piano; *Dos Nocturnos,* for violin and piano; *Scherzo*, for organ; *Ausencia,* for 5-voice a cappella choir; chamber music; songs.
Sources: DM, EMA

Rodríguez, Marcela, Mexican composer and guitarist; b.18 Apr 1951, Mexico City, Mexico. She studied composition with María Antonieta Lozano and Leo Brouwer and attended composition seminars at Brown Univ., Providence, Rhode Island, and the Hochschule für Musik in Freiburg, Germany.
Works (selective list): *La Sunamita,* opera (1991); Concerto for recorders and orch. (1993); *Religiosos Incendioa,* for orch.; *La Fábula de las Regiones,* for string orch.; music for the theater; chamber music.
Source: NGDWC

Rodríguez, Ricardo, Argentine composer; b.15 Apr 1879, EMA (1877, MMLA), Concordia, Prov. of Entre Ríos, Argentina; d.1 Oct

1951, Buenos Aires, Argentina. He began music studies in Concordia, and then continued violin with Pietro Melani and composition with Alberto Williams in Buenos Aires. After winning the Grand Prix Europa in 1904, he went to Paris, France, where he entered the Schola Cantorum and studied harmony with Victor Vreuls and León Saint-Requier, counterpoint with Albert Roussel, organ with Abel Decaux and Alexandre Guilmant, Gregorian chant with Amédée Gastoué, chamber music with Louis Serres, and composition with Auguste Sérieyx and Vincent d'Indy. Professor of composition at the National Cons. of Music Carlos López Buchardo of Buenos Aires. Director of the Escuela Argentina de Música Julián Aguirre. Member of the Board of Directors of the Teatro Colón and member of the National Academy of Fine Arts, both of Buenos Aires.
Works (selective list): *Symphonic poems: El Palmar; Atardecer en la Tablada; El Yuquerí.* Overture for orch.; Sonata in G for violin and piano; Quartet for piano, clarinet, viola, and bassoon; *San Ignacio,* cantata for soloists, chorus, and orch.; piano pieces; songs.
Sources: CA, DM, EMA, MMLA

Rodríguez Alvira, José, Puerto Rican composer and guitarist; b.3 Jan 1954, Havana, Cuba. He started his music studies with Alfredo Romero and Leonardo Egúrbida in Cuba. Between 1972 and 1976, he studied at the Cons. of Music of Puerto Rico with Héctor Tosar, Luis A. Ramírez, Amaury Veray, and N. Justicia. In 1976, he went to Paris, France, where he studied with Alberto Ponce, Roberto Aussel, Antonio Ruíz Pipó, and Narcis Bonet. In 1981, he graduated in guitar from the National Cons. of Aubervilliers, France, and in music aesthetics from the Ecole Normale of Paris. Professor at the Cons. of Music of Puerto Rico.
Works (selective list): *Fantasía,* for string orch. (1986); *Suite de Canciones Puertorriqueñas,* for soprano, flute, clarinet, violin, cello, and guitar (1987); chamber music; music for solo instruments; piano pieces.
Source: CPR

Rodríguez Amador, Augusto Alejandro, Puerto Rican composer and conductor; b.9 Feb 1904, San Juan, Puerto Rico. He studied literature at the Univ. of Puerto Rico, and music at Harvard Univ., Cambridge, Massachusetts, with Edward B. Hill, Walter Piston, and Hugo Leichtentritt, 1933-34. Appointed professor at the Univ. of Puerto Rico in 1934.
Works: Choruses; dance suites; piano pieces; songs.
Sources: BB, MMLA

Rodríguez Arresón, José María, Puerto Rican composer and conductor; b.24 Sep 1870, Añasco, Puerto Rico; d.1947. He started music studies, violin and solfeggio, with his father. At age twelve he went to Mayagüez, Puerto Rico, where he studied violin with Marcelina Medina and Mariano Casanova. He graduated from the Inst: Provincial de San Juan, Puerto Rico, with a BA degree. He continued studying harmony and composition in Barcelona, Spain. For 40 years he lived in the Dominican Republic where he was conductor of the Municipal Band, director of the Municipal Academy, the Musical Center, and the Escuela Normal Superior, all of Puerto Plata, Dominican Republic.

Works (selective list): *Sinfonía quasi una Fantasía 30 de Marzo,* for orch.; *16 de Agosto,* military fantasia; *Ave Maria Stella,* cantata for soloists, chorus, and orch.; *Himno a Santa Cecilia,* for chorus and orch.; hymns; marches; waltzes. **Books:** *El Clasicismo en Música; El Arte Musical y el Estado.*
Sources: DM, MMLA

Rodríguez Cubillos, José Antonio, Colombian composer and pianist; b.12 Oct 1897, Bogotá, Colombia; d.? In 1912, he entered the National Cons. of Bogotá where he studied piano with Pedro Villa and Lucía Gutiérrez de Uribe Holguín, and composition with Guillermo Uribe Holguín. Later, in Brussels, Belgium, he studied musical pedagogy with Henry Joos, then at the Schola Cantorum of Paris, France, he studied with Paul Braud and Vincent D'Indy, 1925-28. He also studied piano with Pierre Lucas and composition with Louis Aubert and Joaquín Nin y Castellanos, 1929-31. Professor of piano and music theory at the National Cons. of Bogotá from 1919 to 1923.

Works: *Habanera,* for piano; *Twelve Impromptus,* for piano; *Suite Santafereña.*
Source: MMLA

Rodríguez Ferrer, Antonio, Cuban composer and teacher; b.23 Aug 1864, Havana, Cuba; d.? He studied with Felipe Palau. Director of several singing societies. Professor of solfeggio and music theory at the Hubert Blanck National Cons. of Havana.

Works: **Music for band:** *Marcha de Concierto*; *Gran Marcha Triunfal*; *Martí,* military march; *Maceo,* solemn march; *La Marcha Presidencial*; *Suite Elegíaca,* for orch. and band. *Preludio Temático,* for orch.; *Gran Cantata a Colón,* for tenor, bass, chorus, and orch.; *Danzas de Concierto Cubanas.*
Source: MMLA

Rodríguez Socas, Ramón, Uruguayan composer and teacher; b.31 Aug 1890, MMLA (1886, BHMCU), Montevideo, Uruguay; d.28 Nov 1957, Montevideo. He studied with Francisco Baldomir and León Ribeiro at the Cons. La Lira of Montevideo, where later he was

appointed director. He continued studies at the Verdi Cons. in Milan, Italy, with Ettore Pozzoli, Giacomo Orefice, and Michele Saladino. *Works*: *Operas*: *Alda* (1908); *Yeba* (1908); *Amor Marinero* (1909); *Morte di Amore* (1912); *Antony* (1923); *Urunday* (1940). *Afrodita*, triptych for orch.; *Ondinas*, symphonic sketch; *Himno al Centenario del Uruguay; Grito de Asencio*, symphonic poem; *Zulul*, choreographic poem (1937); *Obertura Andina* (1938); Concerto for piano and orch. (1943); *Kishuar*, choreographic poem (1944); *Sinfonía Artigas*, for chorus, organ, and orch. (1948).
Sources: BHMCU, DM, MLA, MMLA, MU

Roig, Gonzalo, Cuban composer and conductor; b.20 Jul 1890, Havana, Cuba; d.13 Jun 1970, Havana. He studied solfeggio, piano, and violin with several teachers, and later he graduated from the Hubert Blanck National Cons. of Havana. He played violin in theater orch. In 1922, he organized the Havana Symphony Orch. Conductor of the Municipal Band and the orch. of Teatro Martí, both of Havana. *Works: Cecilia Valdés,* zarzuela. In 1912, he wrote the bolero *Quiéreme Mucho,* which became a popular hit.
Sources: BB, DM

Rojas, Miguel, Argentine composer; b.1845, San Nicolás de los Arroyos, Prov. of Buenos Aires, Argentina; d.1904, Argentina. Active at the society *Los Negros* where he participated as orch. and chorus conductor.
Works (selective list): **Zarzuelas:** *Los Dos Padres* (1867); *El Pasaporte* (1869); *Amor y Orgullo* (1882). *La Gatta Bianca,* operetta; *Recuerdos del Carnaval,* grand waltz for orch. (1868); *Cos'e Amore,* romance for voice and orch. (1878); *Himno Oficial a Rivadavia* (1880); *Tres Marchas Fúnebres,* for orch.; *Ave Maria,* for violin, cello, piano, and harmonium (1895); *Chaquira Liew,* incidental music (1903); songs.
Source: EMA

Rojas Enríquez, Gilberto, Bolivian teacher and composer; b.10 Mar 1910, Oruro, Bolivia. He studied piano with Samsó and Arana in Bolivia. Later he went to Buenos Aires, Argentina, to study harmony, composition, and orchestration. Professor in many private and public schools. Music supervisor at the Dirección Nacional de Educación Musical in La Paz, Bolivia.
Works: Bolivian popular dances: Tiqui Miniqui, taquirari; *Hay que Trabajar,* huayno; *Flor de Chuquisaca,* cueca; *Palmeras,* polka. *El Valle de los Sueños*, zarzuela (first Bolivian zarzuela ever written).
Source: CB

Roldán, Amadeo, Cuban composer, conductor, and violinist; b.12 Jul 1900, Paris, France (of Cuban parents); d.2 Mar 1939, Havana, Cuba. He studied at the Royal Cons. of Music of Madrid, Spain, with Pablo Hernández, Agustín Soler, and Antonio Fernández Bordas, graduating in 1916. Later he studied harmony and composition with Conrado del Campo and Pedro Sanjuán in Madrid. He settled in Cuba in 1921. Concertmaster at the Philharmonic Orch. of Havana. Founder of the *Havana Quartet.* Assistant conductor and later, conductor and music director of the Philharmonic Orch. of Havana, 1925, 1932. Founder of the Escuela Normal de Música of Havana. Professor at the Municipal Cons. of Havana.
Works (selective list): *Obertura sobre Temas Cubanos* (1925); *La Rebambaramba,* ballet (1928); *El Milagro de Anaquillé,* religious choreographic play (1929); *Danza Negra,* for voice and 7 instruments (1929); *Motivos de Son,* for voice and 9 instruments (1930); *Tres Toques,* for chamber orch. (1931); *Seis Rítmicas,* Nos. 1-4 for piano and wind quintet, Nos. 5-6 for percussion ensemble; *Tres Pequeños Poemas: Oriental, Pregón, Fiesta Negra,* for orch.; *Curujey,* for chorus, 2 pianos, and percussion; chamber music; piano pieces; songs.
Sources: BB, CTA1, DCM, DM, DMC, GDM, MLA

Rolón, José, Mexican composer; b.22 Jun 1883, Ciudad Guzmán, Jalisco, Mexico; d.3 Feb 1945, Mexico City, Mexico. He studied piano with Moritz Moszkowski, and later harmony and counterpoint with Nadia Boulanger, fugue with André Gédalge, and orchestration with Paul Dukas at the Ecole Normale in Paris, France. In Mexico, he founded a music school in Guadalajara. Director of the National Cons. of Music of Mexico, and chief of the Music Section of the Secretary of Education of Mexico, both in Mexico City.
Works (selective list): *Obertura de Concierto,* for orch. (1920); Symphony in E minor (1923); *El Festín de los Enanos,* ballet (1925); *Cuauhtémoc,* symphonic poem (1930); *Zapotlán,* symphonic suite (1932); Piano concerto (1942); 2 string quartets; Piano quintet; piano pieces; songs.
Sources: BB, DCM, DM, GDM, MLA, MMLA

Rolón, Zenón, Argentine teacher and composer; b.1856, Buenos Aires, Argentina; d.1902, Argentina. He studied first in Buenos Aires, and later in Italy.
Works (selective list): *Operas: Fides; Solanel; Le Prove.* *Operettas: Le Chateau du Pic Tordu* (1885); *Chink-Yonk* (1886); *El Castillo Hechizado* (1887); *La Torre degli Spiriti* (1888); *Los Dos Veteranos* (1889). *Gran Marcha La Argentina* (1880); *Himno al Sol de Julio* (1891); *Una Noche de Farra,* zarzuela (1900); *Salve Coral* (1900); *Himno a Sarmiento; Himno a Falucho; Himno a Francia; Himno al*

Saber; Stella d'Italia, cantata; *Oda Sinfónica; Obertura,* for orch.; *Misa del Carmen* (1901); *Kyrie* (1903); piano pieces.
Source: EMA

Romaniello, Luis, Argentine composer and pianist of Italian origin; b.1858, DM (1862, EMA), Naples, Italy; d.1917, Buenos Aires, Argentina. He studied at the Cons. San Pietro a Majella of Naples, Italy, with Beniamino Cesi. He settled in Buenos Aires in 1896, and founded a music cons. Music critic for Argentine and Italian publications.
Works: *Alda,* opera; *El Corsario,* symphonic poem; *Manfredo,* symphonic poem; *Bug Jargal,* symphonic suite; Concerto for piano and orch.; 2 symphonies; 2 string quartets; chamber music; songs.
Books: Several musical textbooks.
Sources: DM, EMA

Roncal, Simeón, Bolivian composer and pianist; b.20 Apr 1870, Sucre, Bolivia; d.12 Jan 1953, La Paz, Bolivia. Choirboy at the Cathedral of Sucre. Teacher at the Colegio Pichincha in 1910. In 1917, he founded the Círculo de Bellas Artes of Potosí, Bolivia.
Works (selective list): *Tres de Febrero,* funeral march; *Las Campanas de la Catedral,* funeral march; *Música Nacional Boliviana,* piano pieces based on Bolivian popular dances: *cueca; bailecito; tonada; burro katina.* Hymns; marches.
Bibl.: A. Alba, *Don Simeón Roncal,* Potosí, 1970.
Sources: CB, GDM, MLA, MMLA

Ronchi, Apolo, Uruguayan composer of Romanian origin: b.8 Mar 1896, Galatz, Romania; d.? He studied with Gerardo Metallo in Montevideo, Uruguay, with Falcetti, in Turin, Italy, and at the Official Cons. of Argel, Romania. Later he furthered his training in harmony and counterpoint with Bruno Goyeneche in Paysandú, Uruguay. Professor of choral singing and musicology at the Liceo Departamental, and of music history at the Inst. Normal, both of Uruguay.
Works: *Siete Canciones para los Niños de América* (1934); *El Tiempo Pasa,* choreographic fantasia (1936); *Tormenta de Verano,* ballet with choir (1940); *El Reino de las Ideas,* fantasia with chorus, dialogues, and ballet (1941).
Source: DM

Rosaenz, Elifio Eduardo, Argentine composer; b.13 Oct 1916, Junín, Province of Buenos Aires, Argentina. He studied with José André, Constantino Gaito, Athos Palma, José Torre Bertucci, and José Gil at the National Cons. of Music Carlos López Buchardo of Buenos Aires. He also studied piano with Jorge Fanelli. Professor at

the National Cons. of Music Carlos López Buchardo in 1941, and in 1942, professor at the Escuela Superior de Música of the Univ. of Cuyo, Mendoza, Prov. of Mendoza, Argentina, where in 1958, he was appointed director.
Works (selective list): Quartet in E flat, for piano, violin, viola, and cello (1951); *Tres Movimientos Sinfónicos,* for orch. (1961); *Tríptico,* for string orch. (1965); *Música,* for orch. (1969); *Homenaje,* for orch. (1973); chamber music; choral music
Sources: EMA, VMA

Rosas, Juventino, Mexican composer and violinist; b.23 Jan 1868, Santa Cruz de Galeana, Mexico; d.13 Jul 1894, Batabanó, Cuba. He played the violin in various churches and at the Angela Peralta's touring opera orch.
Works: Salon pieces: waltzes; polkas; mazurkas; schottisches. A cycle of waltzes, titled *Sobre las Olas,* gained international popularity.
Bibl: R. Stevenson, *Music in Mexico,* New York, 1952.
Sources: GDM, MLA, MMLA

Rosas Fernandes, María Helena, Brazilian composer, conductor, and pianist; b.8 Jul 1933, Brazópolis, Minas Gerais, Brazil. She studied with Liddy Mignone and Joâo de Souza Lima at the Brazilian Cons. of Rio de Janeiro, Brazil. In 1977, she enrolled at the Santa Marcelina Music College of Sâo Paulo, Brazil, where she studied composition and orch. conducting with Oswaldo Lacerda and José Antonio de Almeida Prado. In 1992, she held a teaching appointment at Campinas Univ., Sâo Paulo.
Works: Maráwawa, for chorus and chamber ensemble (1978); *Ciclos,* for piano (1979); *Dawawa Tsawidi,* for soprano and percussion (1979); *Território e Ocas,* for string quartet and percussion (1979); *Nakutuak,* for chamber ensemble (1980); *In Memoriam,* for oboe, clarinet, and strings (1980); *Daprava,* for mixed voices chorus (1980).
Sources: HMB, NGDWC, NWC

Rosato, Clorinda, Brazilian composer; b.1914, Sâo Paulo, Brazil.
Works: String quartet; *Quatro Corais,* for chorus; piano pieces; choral music.
Source: MMLA

Rosquellas, Mariano Pablo, Argentine violinist, composer, and singer of Spanish origin; b.1790, Madrid, Spain; d.1859, Sucre, Bolivia. He settled in Buenos Aires, Argentina, in 1823. He was the first organizer of opera seasons in Argentina. Between 1825 and

1830, he presented most of Rossini's operas and some of Mozart's operas in Buenos Aires. He founded the *Sociedad Filarmónica Dramática* in Sucre.
Works (selective list): *Variaciones,* for violin and orch. (1823); *El Califa de Bagdad,* opera (1826); *Gran Cantata,* with choruses (1827); *El Pampero,* overture (1828); *La Batalla de Ayacucho,* symphony (1832); songs.
Source: EMA

Rosseger, Mario, Argentine composer, violinist, and teacher of Italian origin; b.12 Sep 1877, Trieste, Italy; d.1945, Argentina. He studied in Fiume, Yugoslavia, with Giovanni Baldini and at the Cons. of Milan, Italy, with Giovanni Rampazzini. First violin at the orch. of the Teatro Real de San Carlos, Lisbon, Portugal. Conductor of several orch. in Switzerland. Concertmaster with the first symphony orch. created in Buenos Aires, the Sociedad Orquestal Bonaerense, Prov. of Buenos Aires, Argentina. Professor at the Provincial Cons., Prov. of Buenos Aires, at the Thibaud-Piazzini Cons. of Buenos Aires, and at the Rosseger Cons., founded in 1914 in Buenos Aires.
Works: Music for violin and piano: A la Bourrée; *Canción de Cuna*; *Polacca*; *Vuelo de Abejas*. *Primavera Itálica,* for voice and piano.
Sources: DM, EMA

Rossi, Rinaldo, Brazilian composer, conductor, and teacher; b.9 Jul 1945, Recife, Brazil. He started to study music privately at five years of age, and later he continued at the Escola da Música da Bahia, Brazil. At the Universidade Federal da Bahia he studied piano, percussion, composition, and orch. conducting. Professor at the Universidade Federal da Bahia and at the Universidade da Brasília, Brazil. Conductor of the National Symphony Orch., in 1970, and of the Brazilian Symphony Orch., in 1971, both in Rio de Janeiro, Brazil.
Works (selective list): *Paisagem Antagónica No.2,* for orch. (1967); *Réquiem para o Velho Mundo,* for orch. (1970); *Epifanías,* for string quartet (1973).
Source: EMB

Rotter, Jorge, Argentine composer and conductor; b.1942, Buenos Aires, Argentina. He graduated from the Escuela Superior de Bellas Artes of the Univ. of La Plata, Prov. of Buenos Aires, Argentina, where he studied with Mariano Drago, Guillermo Graetzer, Teodoro Fuchs, and Francisco Kröpfl. He studied conducting with Hermann Scherchen in Berlin, Germany. Assistant conductor of the Philharmonic Orch. of La Plata, 1961-62. Assistant conductor of the Symphony Orch. of the Univ. of Tucumán, Prov. of Tucumán,

Argentina, 1963-64. Assistant conductor at the Teatro Colón of Buenos Aires, 1964-65. Member of the *Agrupación Nueva Música.* Conductor of the Provincial Orch. of Rosario, Prov. of Santa Fe, Argentina.
Works: Canto, for French horn, viola, and percussion.
Source: EMA

Rozo Contreras, José, Colombian composer; b.7 Jan 1894, Bochalema, Dept. of Santander, Colombia; d.1974, Bogotá, Colombia. He studied in Vienna, Austria, with Eugene Zádor and Rudolf Nilius, from 1929 to 1931. Conductor of the National Band of Bogotá, and the Dept. Band of Norte de Santander. Professor of orchestration and band conducting at the Cons. of Music of the National Univ. of Colombia in Bogotá.
Works (selective list): *Orch.: Tierra Colombiana,* suite (1930); *Obertura No.2* (1932); *Scherzo sobre un Aire de Bambuco* (1932); *Burlesca,* symphonic scherzo (1940). Choruses; transcriptions for symphony orch. and band; songs.
Sources: CTA18, DM, MLA, ZCCC

Ruano, Marcelo, Ecuadorian composer; b.1962, Tulcán, Ecuador. He studied at the National Cons. of Music of Quito, Ecuador.
Works: Imágenes, for narrator and orch.; *Movimientos Sonoros,* for orch.
Source: PEFCM

Rubin, Marcel, Mexican composer of Austrian origin; b.7 Jul 1907, Vienna, Austria. He studied music theory and composition at the Musikakademie of Vienna with Franz Schmidt, and in 1925 he furthered his music studies with Darius Milhaud in Paris, France. He settled in Mexico in 1942. Guest conductor of the Univ. of Mexico Symphony Orch. in Mexico City.
Sources (selective list): *La Princesa Brambila,* opera; *La Ciudad Espera,* ballet; *Tierra,* symphony; *Guerra y Paz,* symphony; Concerto for violin and orch.; 2 string quartets; String trio; *Serenata,* for solo violin; 3 sonatas for piano; Sonata for cello and piano.
Source: MMLA

Rud, Diana, Argentine composer and pianist; b.Rosario, Prov. of Santa Fe, Argentina; fl.mid-20th century. She studied with Antonio de Raco, Virtú Maragno, and Dante Grela at the Escuela de Música of the National Univ. of Rosario. She also studied with Francisco Kröpfl. Founding member of the Asociación Santafesina de Compositores and member of the *Agrupación Nueva Música* of Rosario, and Asociación Argentina de Compositores. Professor at the

Escuela de Música de la Facultad de Humanidades y Artes of the National Univ. of Rosario, and the Escuela Nacional de Música and the Inst. Nacional del Profesorado de Música, both of Rosario.
Works: Palabras al Hijo por Nacer, for soprano and instrumental ensemble; *Música,* for piano; *Tres Piezas,* for clarinet; *Amor con Lluvia y Palomas,* for mixed chorus; *Tema, Variaciones y Final,* for orch.; *Tres Melancolías,* for flute and piano; *Cuatro Vertientes,* for string quartet.
Source: CAMR

Rugeles, Ana Mercedes de, Venezuelan composer and teacher; b.8 Aug 1915, Barquisimeto, State of Lara, Venezuela. She organized programs for Radio Nacional de Venezuela, from 1953 to 1964. In 1970, she was appointed director of the Escuela Preparatoria de Música J.M. Olivares of Venezuela.
Works: Serenata Barquisimetana, for double quintet and piano (1967); sacred music; piano pieces; songs.
Source: IEW

Ruíz, Federico, Venezuelan composer; b.8 Feb 1948, Caracas, Venezuela. He graduated from the Escuela Superior de Música José Angel Lamas in Caracas in 1974, where he studied composition with Primo Casale, Vicente Emilio Sojo, and Evencio Castellanos. He also studied 20th century's composition techniques with Yannis Ioannidis, electroacoustics techniques with Eduardo Kusnir, and orch. and choral conducting with Silvia Eisenstein and Gonzalo Castellanos. Professor at the Escuela Superior de Música José Angel Lamas and the National Cons. of Music Juan José Landaeta of Caracas.
Works (selective list): *Orch.: Evocación,* for baritone and mixed chorus (1974); *Pieza para Orquesta* (1977); Piano concerto (1979); *Lauda* (1980); *Viaje,* for narrator, quintet of mixed voices, and organ (1981); *Elegía* (1982); Trumpet concerto (1993). *La Pastora,* musical comedy (1975); *Los Martirios de Colón,* opera (1982-93); music for band; choral music; chamber music; electroacoustic music; music for the stage; songs.
Source: ISC

Ruíz Armengol, Mario, Mexican composer and pianist; b.17 Mar 1911, Veracruz, Mexico. He studied at the National Cons. of Music of Mexico in Mexico City.
Works: Las Frías Montañas, for piano. *Songs: Ausencia; Tengo Miedo; Estoy Enamorado; ¿Porqué Llorar?; Aunque; Cuando tu no me Quieras; Muchachita.*
Source: NH

Ruíz Espadero, Nicolás, Cuban composer and pianist; b.15 Feb 1832, Havana, Cuba; d.30 Aug 1890, Havana. He started music studies with his mother and continued with José Miró, and later with Fernando Arizti.
Works (selective list): 2 sonatas for piano; *Inocencia,* poetic capriccio for piano; *Pureza y Calma,* for piano; *Two Romances,* for piano; *Preludio,* for piano; *Barcarola,* for piano; *Grand Trio*; *Rondó Brillante,* for 2 violins, viola, and cello; *Scherzo,* for 2 violins, viola, cello, and piano; *Serenata Cubana,* for voice and piano; *Romance,* for voice and piano; *Grand Symphony,* for orch.; *El Canto del Esclavo,* for violin and piano; *Canto del Guajiro,* for piano.
Bibl.: J.L. Vidaurreta, *El Compositor y Pianista Nicolás Ruíz Espadero,* Havana, 1937. O. Martínez, *Nicolás Ruíz Espadero, Program of the Philharmonic Orchestra of Havana,* 12 Dec 1946. A. Carpenter, *La Música en Cuba,* Mexico, 1946.
Sources: DM, DMC, MMLA

Ruíz Lastres, Magaly, Cuban composer; b.2 Oct 1941, Santa Clara, Cuba. She studied piano with César Pérez Sentenat at the Guillermo Tomás Cons. of Havana, Cuba, and later she studied composition with Roberto Valera at the Inst. Superior de Arte, Havana, from which she received a degree in music in 1981. Member of the Faculty of Artistic Education of the Inst. Superior Pedagógico Enrique José Varona of Havana.
Works: Oboe concerto (1979); *Tres Ambientes Sonoros,* for orch. (1981); *Variaciones en Habanera,* for oboe and orch. (1983); choruses; chamber music; piano pieces; songs.
Source: NGDWC

S

Saccaggio, Adelina Luisa Nicasia, Argentine teacher and composer; b.29 Oct 1918, Buenos Aires, Argentina. She studied at the National Cons. of Music Carlos López Buchardo, at the Municipal Cons. of Music Manuel de Falla, and at the Inst. de Música Sagrada, all of Buenos Aires. Professor at the National Cons. of Music Carlos López Buchardo and in the school system of the National Board of Education of Buenos Aires.
Works: Chamber music; sacred music; songs.
Source: IEW

Sáenz, Benedicto, Guatemalan composer; b.1815, Guatemala; d.1857, Guatemala. He studied medicine, graduating with a licenciate degree from the Univ. of San Carlos, Guatemala. Later he studied music, especially organ and piano. *Maestro de capilla* (chapelmaster) at the Cathedral of Guatemala City, Guatemala. Because of his contribution to music in Guatemala he was named *Prince of Music of Guatemala.*
Works: *Sacred music: Misa Grande; Invitatorio al Sagrado Corazón de Jesús; Duetto a la Santísima Virgen;* 8 hymns for orch.; *Parce Mihi*, for tenor and orch.; *Responso,* for 4 voices; *Salmo de Difuntos,* for 3 voices and orch; *Domine Salvam fac Republicam; Regina sine Labe Concepta; Te Deum.* Patriotic songs and hymns.
Sources: HMG, MMLA

Sáenz, Francisco Isaac, Guatemalan composer, conductor, pianist, and teacher; b.1816, Guatemala; d.1 Jan 1880, Guatemala. Professor of voice at the Colegio Seminario and *maestro de capilla* (chapelmaster) at the Cathedral, both of Guatemala City, Guatemala.
Works: Misa in E flat, for 4 voices; *Lamentación in F minor.*
Source: MMLA

Sáenz, Pedro A., Argentine teacher and composer; b.4 May 1915, Buenos Aires, Argentina. He studied with Carlos Pellicer, Alberto Williams, and José Gil at the Williams Cons. of Buenos Aires. He graduated from the National Cons. of Music Carlos López Buchardo of Buenos Aires, where he studied composition, fugue, and counterpoint with José Gil, harmony with Athos Palma, and piano with Jorge de Lalewicz. In Paris, France, he continued his training with Darius Milhaud, Arthur Honegger, and Jean Rivier. Professor at the National Cons. of Music Carlos López Buchardo. Director of the Municipal Cons. of Music Manuel de Falla, 1955-63, and dean of the Faculty of Musical Arts and Sciences of the Argentine Catholic Univ., 1963-65, both of Buenos Aires.

Works (selective list): *Orch.*: *Dos Piezas* (1934); Suite for strings (1936); *Salmo CL,* for choir (1938); *Vals Brillante* (1959); *Movimientos Sinfónicos* (1963); *Música para los Jardines de Versailles* (1968). Chamber music; music for harpsichord; piano pieces; songs.
Sources: BB, CA, CTA12, DM, EMA, VMA

Sagreras, Julio S., Argentine guitarist and composer; b.22 Nov 1879, Buenos Aires, Argentina; d.20 Jul 1942, Buenos Aires. He started music studies with his father, Gaspar Sagreras, and Carlos Marchal. He graduated as professor of guitar from the Academy of Fine Arts of Buenos Aires. Professor of guitar and solfeggio at the Academy of Fine Arts. Founding member and first president of the Asociación Guitarrística Argentina.
Works: Music for guitar (more than 200 compositions): *Sonatinas; Mercedes; Dulces Cadenas; Rapsodia sobre Motivos Criollos; El Colibrí; Flor de Pasión; Cajita de Música. Books: Lecciones de Guitarra,* Buenos Aires; *Técnica Superior de Guitarra,* Buenos Aires.
Sources: DM, MMLA

Salas y Castro, Esteban, Cuban composer, conductor, and priest; b.25 Dec 1725, Havana, Cuba; d.14 Jul 1803, Santiago de Cuba, Cuba. He studied organ and theology. *Maestro de capilla* (chapelmaster) at the Cathedral of Santiago de Cuba and conductor of a chamber ensemble. He became a priest in 1790, and began teaching philosophy, theology, and ethics.
Works: Sacred music: Las Siete Ultimas Palabras, for voices and orch; *Stabat Mater,* for soloists, chorus, organ, and instruments (1790); 5 masses; 3 requiem; 5 hymns; 12 Salve; 2 litanies; 3 canticles; 12 anthems; 3 Passions; 29 alleluias; 7 sequences; 12 antiphonies; 5 psalms; 2 motets; 8 lessons; many Christmas carols and villancicos.
Bibl.: P. Hernández Balaguer, *Obras de Esteban Salas,* Santiago de Cuba, 1960. P. Hernández Balaguer, *La Capilla de Música de la Catedral de Santiago de Cuba, Revista Musical Chilena,* 1964.
Sources: BB, DM, DMC, GDM, MMLA

Salazar, Adolfo, Mexican musicologist and composer of Spanish origin; b.6 Mar 1890, Madrid, Spain; d.27 Sep 1958, Mexico City, Mexico. He studied in Madrid with Manuel de Falla and Bartolomé Pérez Casas, and then went to Paris, France, where he completed his training with Maurice Ravel. Editor-in-chief of the *Revista Musical Hispano-Americana,* 1914-18, and music critic for Madrid's *El Sol,* 1918-36. Founder and later secretary of Sociedad Nacional de Música of Spain, 1915-22. He settled in Mexico in 1938, after the Spanish Civil War. Professor at the Colegio de México and the National Cons of Mexico, both in Mexico City. Corresponding member of the Sociedad Hispánica de América and the Inst. Español de Musicología of Spain.

Works: *Paisajes,* for orch.; *Estampas,* for orch.; *Don Juan de los Infiernos,* for orch.; *Tres Preludios,* for piano; *Trois Poèmes de Paul Verlaine,* for voice and piano; *Rubaiyat,* for string quartet; *Romancillo,* for guitar. **Books:** More than 30 books on music history and aesthetics, and about 20 important essays, including *La Música en la Sociedad Europea,* Mexico, 1942-46.

Sources: BB, DM, GDM, MLA, MMLA

Salazar (Zalazar), Antonio de, Mexican composer of Spanish origin; b.c.1650, Spain; d.before 27 May 1715, Mexico City, Mexico. *Maestro de capilla* (chapelmaster) at the Cathedral of Puebla, Mexico, in 1679. Later he was appointed *maestro de capilla* (chapelmaster) at the Cathedral of Mexico City.

Works: Sacred music: *Missa sine Nomine,* for 5 voices; *Oficio de Defuntos,* for 4 voices; 2 Magnificat for 5 and 12 voices; *Litaniae Lauretanae; Salve Regina,* for 8 voices; 11 hymns; *Motet,* for 8 voices; 6 responsories for 8 voices; many villancicos and chansonnettes.

Bibl.: R. Stevenson, *Music in Mexico,* New York, 1952. A.R. Catalyne, *Music of the Sixteenth through the Eighteenth Centuries in the Cathedral of Puebla, Mexico, Yearbook, Inter-American Institute for Musical Research,* Vol.2, 1966. R. Stevenson, *Renaissance and Baroque Musical Sources in the Americas,* Washington, D.C., 1970.

Sources: GDM, MMLA

Salcedo de las Cuevas, Rafael Pascual, Cuban pianist and composer; b.23 Oct 1844, Santiago de Cuba, Cuba; d.15 Apr 1917, Santiago de Cuba. He started music studies with his father, and subsequently with Juan Casamitjana and Isidro Matón, organist at the Cathedral of Santiago de Cuba. In 1856, he went to Paris, France, where he studied harmony, counterpoint, composition, piano, and orch. conducting with Félix Le Couppey. He returned to Cuba in 1865, and some years later founded a cons. and the *Beethoven Musical Society.*

Works: Symphony in F; *Lumen,* symphonic poem; *Arma Virumque Cano,* symphonic poem dedicated to the memory of the martyrs that fought for the freedom of Cuba; *Sinfonía sobre Himnos de los Aliados* (1915); religious music; piano pieces.

Sources: DMC, MMLA

Salgado, Luis Humberto, Ecuadorian composer, pianist, and teacher; b.10 Dec 1903, Cayambe, Ecuador; d.1977, Ecuador. He studied with his father, and later entered the Cons. of Quito, Ecuador,

from which he graduated as pianist in 1928. Professor at the National Cons. of Music of Quito.
Works: *Atahualpa*, symphonic suite; *Pasillo-Intermezzo*, orch. dance; Symphony No.6 for strings and timpani (1968).
Sources: CTA4, DM, DMC, MLA, MMLA

Salgado Fiuza, Virginia, Brazilian conductor and composer; b.5 Aug 1897, Fortaleza, Brazil; d.? She studied at the National Inst. of Music of Rio de Janeiro, Brazil, with Nicia Silva, Alfredo Richard, Arnaud Gouveia, and Agnelo França. She continued her music education with Paulo Silva, with whom she studied harmony, counterpoint, and fugue. She also studied folklore with Luis Heitor, composition and orchestration with Joâo Otaviano, and conducting with Francisco Mignone. Deputy director of the Cons. of Music of Brazil in Rio de Janeiro.
Works: Chamber music; piano pieces; songs.
Source: IEW

Salgado Torres, Gustavo Enrique, Ecuadorian composer; b.5 Sep 1905, Cayambe, Ecuador. He started music lessons at the National Cons. of Quito, Ecuador, under Francisco Tipán and his father, Francisco Salgado, who taught him piano, harmony, counterpoint, and fugue, 1915-25. Later he furthered his piano training with Jan Javorski at the Moscow Cons., Russia, 1929-30. When he returned to Ecuador, he was appointed honorary professor of history of music at the National Cons. of Quito, 1938-39. In 1943, he was appointed professor at the Central Univ. of Quito.
Works: *Music for piano: A Orillas del Lago Leman,* prelude; *El Expreso Paris-La Rochelle,* poem; *Crepúsculo Andino,* poem; *Erranzas Bajo la Luna,* nocturne; *Fantasía Lunar,* poem.
Source: MMLA

Salvatti, Renzo, Venezuelan composer of Italian origin; b.13 Aug 1906, Trento, Italy. Venezuelan citizen. He studied at the Cons. of Pesaro and Parma, Italy. Founder and director of the Music Academy in Acarigua, Venezuela.
Works: Symphonies; orch. compositions; requiem; masses; chamber music; songs.
Source: KTL

Sambucetti, Luis, Uruguayan composer and violinist; b.29 Jul 1860, Montevideo, Uruguay; d.7 Sep 1926, Montevideo. He studied in Montevideo with Luis Preti and José Strigelli. In 1885, he traveled to Paris, France, where he studied violin with Hubert Leonard, harmony with Théodore Dubois, and composition with Jules Massenet, Ernst Guiraud, and Leo Delibes at the National Cons. of Paris. Founder of

the Cons. Verdi in Montevideo in 1890. He also organized the National Orch. of Uruguay in Montevideo, which he conducted from 1908 to 1914.
Works (selective list): *Colombinson,* operetta (1893); *El Diablo Rojo, zarzuela* (1893); *El Fantasma,* operetta (1894); *San Francesco D'Assisi,* mystic poem (1910); *Invocación,* prelude for orch. (1889); *Leyenda Patria,* prelude for orch. (1889); *Indiana,* instrumental capriccio (1897); Suite for orch. (1899); chamber music; choral music; piano pieces; songs.
Sources: BHMCU, CTA14, MLA, MU

Sammartino, Luis R.D., Argentine composer and pianist; b.8 Apr 1890, Buenos Aires, Argentina; d.31 Aug 1973, Buenos Aires. He studied piano with Corradino d'Agnillo and Elmérico Fracassi, and composition with Constantino Gaito. Professor of music in several high schools. Supervisor of music at the school system of the National Board of Education of Buenos Aires.
Works: *Suite Orquestal*; *Obertura en Re,* for orch.; Suite for piano and string orch.; Sonata for cello and piano; Sonatina for piano; *Acuarelas,* for piano (1929); *Zamba,* for piano (1930); *Pericón,* for piano (1946); *Canción,* for piano (1948); Sonata for violin and piano (1935); songs.
Sources: CA, DM, EMA

Samper, Baltasar, Mexican composer, pianist, and musicologist of Spanish origin; b.3 May 1888, Palma de Mallorca, Spain; d.18 Feb 1966, Mexico City, Mexico. In 1942, he emigrated to Mexico and became a Mexican citizen. He studied in Spain with Enrique Granados and Felipe Pedrell.
Works: Orch. suite; cantatas; chamber music; choruses.
Source: KTL

Sánchez, Manuela Cornejo de, Argentine teacher and composer; b.1854, Salta, Prov. of Salta, Argentina; d.1902, Argentina. Professor at the Escuela Normal of Salta.
Works: School songs: El Sol de Mayo; Himno a Rivadavia; Himno a Colón; El Sol de Julio; A mi Patria; Canto a Güemes; Canto Patriótico; La Escuela. Sacred music.
Source: EMA

Sánchez de Fuentes, Eduardo, Cuban musicologist and composer; b.3 Apr 1874, Havana, Cuba; d.7 Sep 1944, Havana. He studied with Sancho and Arturo Quiñones at the Cons. of Music Hubert de Blanck of Havana. Later he studied with Carlos Anckermann and Ignacio Cervantes. Music critic for the newspaper *El Mundo* of Havana. President of the Academia Nacional de Artes y Letras of Cuba and founding member of the National Corporation of Authors, both in Havana.

Works (selective list): *Operas: Yumurí* (1898); *El Náufrago* (1901); *La Dolorosa* (1910); *Doreya* (1918); *El Caminante* (1921); *Kabelia* (1942). *Tríptico Cubano,* for orch. (1916); *Bocetos Cubanos,* for soprano, women's chorus, and orch. (1922); *Anacoana,* symphonic poem (1928); *Dioné,* ballet (1940); *Temas del Patio,* symphonic prelude; *Navidad,* oratorio; String quartet; piano pieces; songs. *Books: El Folklore en la Música Cubana,* 1923; *Folklorismo,* 1928; *Viejos Ritmos Cubanos,* 1937.
Bibl.: O. Martínez, *Eduardo Sánchez de Fuentes: In Memoriam,* Havana 1944. M. Guiral, *Un Gran Musicógrafo y Compositor Cubano: Eduardo Sánchez de Fuentes,* Havana, 1944. A. Carpenter, *La Música en Cuba,* Mexico, 1946.
Sources: BB, DM, DMC, GDM, MLA, MMLA

Sánchez Málaga, Carlos, Peruvian composer, choral conductor, and teacher; b.8 Sep 1904, Arequipa, Peru. He studied at the San Francisco School of Arequipa with Father Francisco de María Palomino. Professor of solfeggio and choral singing at the National Cons. of Music of La Paz, Bolivia. After his return to Peru in 1929, he was appointed professor and later, in 1932, director of the National Cons. of Music Alcedo of Lima, Peru. Professor of piano and director of the Inst. de Música Bach of Lima. President of the Peruvian Society of Authors and Composers.
Works (selective list): *Music for piano: Cayma* (1925); *Yanahuara* (1925); *Crepúsculo* (1928); *Vísperas* (1933); *Suite Acuarelas Infantiles* (1938). Choruses; hymns; songs.
Sources: CTA15, DM, GDM, GMP, MLA, MMLA

Sandi, Marvin, Bolivian composer; b.17 May 1938, Potosí, Bolivia; d.30 Apr 1968, Madrid, Spain. He studied first with his father, José Sandi, and later he went to Buenos Aires, Argentina, where he studied with Jacobo Ficher, Alberto Ginastera, and Roberto Locatelli.
Works: Cantata Siciliana, for piano; *In Memoriam de Eduardo Caba.*
Source: CB

Sandi Meneses, Luis, Mexican composer and conductor; b.22 Feb 1905, Mexico City, Mexico. He studied violin with José Rocabruna, 1923-30, and composition with Gustavo Campa and Estanislao Mejía, 1925-31, at the National Cons. of Music of Mexico City. Conductor of the chorus of the National Cons., 1922-35; in 1937, he founded the *Coro de Madrigalistas,* which he conducted until 1965. Professor of music in primary schools, 1924-32, and chief of the Music Section of the Ministry of Public Education, 1933-65.

Works (selective list): *Operas: Carlota* (1948); *La Señora en su Balcón* (1964). *Ballets: Día de Difuntos* (1938); *Bonampak* (1948); *Coatlicue* (1949). *Orch.: El Venado* (1932); *Sonora* (1933); *Suite Banal* (1936); *Norte* (1941); Concertino for flute (1944); *Tema y Variaciones* (1944); *Esbozos Sinfónicos* (1951); *Cuatro Miniaturas* (1952); *América*, symphonic poem (1965). *Las Troyanas*, for chorus and instruments (1936); *Gloria a los Héroes*, cantata (1940); *La Suave Patria*, cantata (1951); chamber music; choruses; piano pieces; songs.
Bibl.: C. Chávez, *Luis Sandi, Nuestra Música,* Vol.4, July 1949.
Sources: BB, CTA14, DM, GDM, GMM, MLA, MMLA

Sandoval, Andrés, Venezuelan composer, violinist, and conductor; b.3 Aug 1924, Caracas, Venezuela. He studied violin in Caracas with Ricardo Odnoposoff. Director of the Music School of San Cristóbal, Venezuela.
Works: Symphonies; chamber music; choruses; masses.
Source: KTL

Sandoval Cabrera, Miguel Angel, Guatemalan composer and conductor; b.22 Nov 1903, Gazacapán, Guatemala; d.23 Aug 1953, New York City, New York, USA. He lived in New York City from 1919 until 1953. He studied piano with Hersilia D. de Tronchi and Humberto Paniagua in Guatemala City, Guatemala, 1912-17, and continued to study piano with Edoardo Trucco and theory and composition with Vicente Mañas, 1919-20. In 1922, he entered the Santini School of Music in New York City. Director of the Guatemalan National Broadcasting Station.
Works: Recuerdos en un Paseo, symphonic poem; voluminous output of music, both classical and popular; film scores; commercial music; orch. pieces; choruses; piano pieces; songs.
Sources: BB, ISC

Sanguesa, Iris, Chilean composer, pianist, conductor, and percussionist; b.1938, Chile. She studied with Herminia Raccagni, Flora Guerra, and Germán Berner at the National Cons. of Music in Santiago de Chile, Chile. She also studied percussion with Jorge Canelo, conducting with Agustín Cullel, and composition with Gustavo Becerra and Alberto Ginastera.
Works (selective list): *Ballets: Copahue,* based on an Araucanian legend (1963); *Los Trabajos del Bailarín. Orch.: Síncresis* (1963); *Abstractas* (1965); *Aforismos del Bhagavad Gita* (1965); *Estudios Orquestales* (1966); *Transiciones* (1967). Chamber music; piano pieces; sacred music.
Sources: IBCC, IEW

Sanjuán, Pedro, Cuban conductor, teacher, and composer of Spanish origin; b.15 Nov 1887, DMC (1886, BB), San Sebastián, Spain; d.18 Oct 1976, Washington, D.C., USA. He studied in Madrid, Spain, with Joaquín Turina, and also in Paris, France. In 1924, he moved to Cuba where he founded the Philharmonic Orch. of Havana. He settled in the USA in 1942, when he was appointed professor of composition at Converse College in Spartanburg, South Carolina.
Works (selective list): *Rondó Fantástico,* for orch. (1926); *Castilla,* suite for orch. (1927); *Liturgia Negra* (1930); *Invocación a Ogún* (1942); *Canción Yorubá* (1942); *La Macumba,* ritual symphony (1945); *Poema Antillano,* for band (1945); *Sketch Caribe* (1946); *Symphonic Suite*; choruses; piano pieces.
Sources: BB, DMC

Santa Cruz Wilson, Domingo, Chilean composer, teacher, and music administrator; b.5 Jul 1899, La Cruz, Prov. of Valparaiso, Chile; d.6 Jan 1987, Santiago de Chile, Chile. He studied jurisprudence at the Univ. of Chile in Santiago de Chile and graduated with a law degree in 1921. Then he entered the diplomatic service. He studied music with Enrique Soro in Santiago de Chile, and with Conrado del Campo in Madrid, Spain. Professor at the National Cons. of Santiago de Chile, and dean of the Faculty of Fine Arts at the Univ. of Chile, 1933-51 and 1962-68. Director of the Inst. de Extensión Musical of the Univ. of Chile.
Works (selective list): *Cinco Piezas Breves,* for string orch. (1937); *Cantata de los Ríos de Chile,* for chorus and orch. (1942); *Variaciones,* for piano and orch. (1943); *Sinfonía Concertante,* for flute, piano and strings (1945); 4 symphonies (1948, 1948, 1965, 1968); *Egloga,* for soprano, chorus, and orch. (1950); *Cantares de la Pascua,* for chorus a cappella (1950); 3 string quartets; *Oratorio Ieremieae Prophetae* (1969); chamber music; choruses; piano pieces; songs.
Bibl.: V. Salas Viú, *La Creación Musical en Chile 1900-1951,* Santiago de Chile, 1951. *Revista Musical Chilena,* Vol.8, 1952. R. Stevenson, *Chilean Music in the Santa Cruz Epoch, Inter-American Music Bulletin,* 1968.
Sources: BB, CTA2, DCM, DM, GDM, HMC, MLA, MMLA

Santoro, Cláudio, Brazilian composer, violinist, and conductor; b.23 Nov 1919, Manaus, State of Amazonas, Brazil; d.27 Mar 1989, Brasília, Brazil. He studied violin with Edgard Guerra, harmony with Nadile Barros, and musicology with Augusto Lopes Gonçalves at the Cons. of Rio de Janeiro, Brazil. He also studied composition with Hans Joachim Koellreutter and, in Paris, France, with Nadia Boulanger. Music teacher at various schools. He conducted extensively in South America, Europe, and Russia. In 1970, he went

to Germany and became professor of composition at the Hochschule für Musik in Heidelberg. He returned to Brazil in 1978.
Works (selective list): *Ballets: A Fábrica* (1947); *Anticocos* (1951); *O Café* (1953); *Icamiabas* (1959); *Zuimaaluti* (1960); *Prelúdios* (1962). 9 symphonies (1940, 1945, 1945, 1949, 1956, 1960, 1963, 1963, 1982); *Variations on a 12-tone Row,* for orch. (1945); *Ponteio,* for string orch. (1945); *Ode to Stalingrad,* for chorus and orch. (1947); *Choro,* for saxophone and orch. (1952); *Abertura Trágica,* for orch. (1958); 2 violin concertos (1951, 1958); 3 piano concertos (1953, 1959, 1960); Cello concerto (1961); 7 string quartets (1943-1965); *Cantata Elegíaca,* for narrator, 2 choruses, and orch. (1970); *Aus den Sonnetten an Orpheus,* cantata for tenor, chorus, and string orch. (1979); chamber music; piano pieces; songs.
Sources: BB, CTA9, DCM, DM, HMB, MLA, MMLA

Santórsola, Guido, Uruguayan composer, violinist, violist, and conductor of Italian origin; b.18 Nov 1904, Canosa di Puglia, Italy. He settled in Sâo Paulo, Brazil, in 1909, where he started to study music with his father. Later he entered the Cons. Dramático y Musical of Sâo Paulo, where he studied violin with Zacarías Autori, and harmony, counterpoint, and composition with Agostinho Cantú and Lamberto Baldi. He also studied violin in Italy with Gaetano Fusella and in London, England, with Alfred Mitowsky. Founder of the Brazilian Music Inst. Professor of violin, viola, and harmony at the Cons. Dramático y Musical of Sâo Paulo. In 1931, he settled in Montevideo, Uruguay, and became violist of the Symphony Orch. of the SODRE in Montevideo. Professor of harmony and music aesthetics at the Inst. de Estudios Superiores de la Escuela Normal de Música of Montevideo. He founded and conducted the orch. of the Uruguayan Cultural Association and formed the *Kleiber Quartet*, both in Montevideo.
Works (selective list): *Orch.: Canción Brasileña* (1930); *Saudade* (1931); Concerto for viola (1932); *Preludio No.1,* for string orch. (1936); *Tres Estados Psicológicos,* for violin (1936); *Preludio y Fuga a la Manera Clásica,* for double string orch. (1937); Concerto for piano (1938-39); Concertino for guitar (1942); *Vida de Artigas* (1951); Symphony No.1 (1957); *Rapsodia Criolla* (1960); Concerto for violin (1962); Concerto (1964); *Cantata a Artigas,* for narrator and chorus (1965); Concerto for 4 violins (1969). Chamber music; music for the guitar; choruses; piano pieces.
Sources: BHMCU, CTA8, DCM, DM, GDM, MLA, MMLA, MU

Santos, Domingo, Salvadoran composer; b.4 Aug 1892, San Esteban, El Salvador; d.? He studied harmony, counterpoint, fugue, musical form, and orchestration with Ricardo Storti, and violin and piano with Monteli, Neglia, Alicandri, and Antonio d'Illía at the

National Inst. of Music of Rome, Italy. When he returned to El Salvador, he was appointed conductor of the 5th regiment's Military Band and director of the Escuela Nacional de Música Rafael Olmedo in San Salvador.

Works: *Martita*, overture for orch.; *Dorita*, overture for orch.; 3 piano sonatas; *Marcha Heróica; Requiem V*, for 2 male voices, orch., and organ; *Requiem VI*, for 3 voices and orch.; 6 funeral marches; 2 fantasias for violin and piano; *Salve*, for mixed voices; *Salve Regina*, for baritone and mixed voices.

Sources: DM, MLA, MMLA

Sanz, Rocío (Carmen Rocío Sanz Quirós), Costa Rican composer and teacher; b.28 Jan 1934, San José, Costa Rica. She started to study music with her mother, Rosita Quirós, and then she entered the National Cons. of Music of Costa Rica in San José and the Los Angeles City College, Los Angeles, California. She also studied at the National Cons. of Music of Mexico, in Mexico City, with Carlos Jiménez Mabarak, Blas Galindo Dimas, and Rodolfo Halftter. She was awarded a scholarship to study at the Tchaikovsky Cons. in Moscow, Russia, with Vladimir Fere in 1965 and 1966. Professor at the Escuela de Danza y Arte Dramático of the Inst. de Bellas Artes and at the Theater Centre of the Univ. of Costa Rica, both in San José.

Works (selective list): *Ballets: El Forastero* (1973); *Letanía Erótica para la Paz* (1973). *Orch.: Ballet Suite* (1959); *Suite Hilos; Cantata de la Independencia,* for baritone, chorus, and symphonic band (1971); *Canciones de la Muerte,* for soprano and strings. Music for the theater and films; chamber music; choruses; songs.

Sources: IBCC, IEW, NGDWC

Sanz Guerrero, Fernando, Bolivian pianist, conductor, and composer; b.6 Nov 1936, La Paz, Bolivia. He studied piano in Buenos Aires, Argentina, and graduated as professor of piano in 1951. In 1960, he moved to the USA where he studied at the Peabody Inst. in Baltimore, Maryland, and at Columbia Univ. in New York City. He received Masters' degrees in composition and conducting. Among his teachers were Leonard Bernstein, Peter Mennin, Lázsló Halász, Ifor Jones, Howard Mitchell, and Max Rudolph. Founder and director of the choir of Johns Hopkins Univ. and of the chamber orch. of the Peabody Inst., both of Baltimore. He also founded the *Chamber Ensemble* and the *Panamerican Musical Society*, both of Buenos Aires. In 1973, he was appointed director of the Bolivian Opera, and in 1974, director of the National Cons. of Music, both of La Paz. In 1974, he became National Supervisor of Musical Education of Bolivia in La Paz.

Works: *Ritmo de Cueca; Scherzo,* for wind instruments; string quartet.
Source: CB

Sarmientos de León, Jorge Alvaro, Guatemalan composer and conductor; b.19 Feb 1931, San Antonio Suchitepequez, Guatemala. He studied at the Cons. Nacional de Música y Declamación of Guatemala City, Guatemala. In 1955, he went to Paris, France, to study piano with Blanche B. de Geraldi and Lucile Geraldi Bascourret, composition with Tony Aubin, and orch. conducting with Jean Fournet at the Ecole Normale Superieur de Musique. In 1965, he received a scholarship to study for two years at the Centro Latinoamericano de Altos Estudios Musicales of the Inst. Di Tella in Buenos Aires, Argentina, with Alberto Ginastera, Maurice Le Roux, Iannis Xenakis, Roger Sessions, Mario Davidovsky, and Fernando von Reishenbach. In 1972, he was appointed music and artistic director of the National Symphony Orch. of Guatemala, Guatemala City.
Works (selective list): *Orch.*: *Cinco Estampas Cakchiqueles Descriptivas* (1953); *David y Betzabé,* symphonic poem (1954-55); *Viola concerto* (1954-55); *Marimba concerto* (1957); *3 piano concertos* (1959, 1960, 1968-69); *Obertura Popular* (1962); *Coropoema Sinfónico Bolívar,* for narrator, chorus, and dance (1962-63); *Oda a la Libertad* (1963); *Sinfonía Coreográfica* (1965); *Preludio y Danza Orgiástica* (1965); *Planetarium* (1969); *Violin concerto* (1971); *Ofrenda y Gratitud* (1976); *Clarinet concerto* (1981); *Tres Cuadros Corales Sinfónicos,* for narrator and chorus (1982). Chamber music; choruses; piano pieces.
Source: ISC

Sas Orchassal, Andrés, Peruvian composer, musicologist, and folklorist of French origin; b.6 Apr 1900, Paris, France; d.25 Jul 1967, Lima, Peru. He studied in Belgium at the Music Academy of Anderlecht-Brussels, and later theory and solfeggio with Fernand Bauvias, violin with Alfred Marchot, history of music with Ernest Closson, and chamber music with Paul Miry at the Royal Cons. of Brussels. He continued his musical training in violin with Johan Schmitt, and harmony, counterpoint, and fugue with Maurice Imbert. Concertmaster of the orch. of the National Society of Belgian Composers. Professor of violin at the Forest Music School in Brussels. In 1924, the Peruvian government engaged him to teach violin and conduct the orch. of the National Academy of Music of Lima. In 1929, he founded the Sas-Rosay Academy of Music, together with his wife, pianist Lily Rosay.
Works (selective list): *Le Malade Imaginaire,* incidental music to Moliere's play (1943). *Ballets: La Señora del Pueblo* (1946); *El Hijo*

Pródigo (1948). *Orch.: Canción India* (1927); *Rapsodia Peruana,* for violin (1928); *Tres Estampas del Perú* (1936); *Poema Indio* (1941); *Sueño de Zamba* (1943); *Danza Gitana* (1944); *La Patrona del Pueblo* (1945); *La Parihuana* (1946); *Las Seis Edades de la Tía Conchita* (1947); *La Leyenda de la Isla de San Lorenzo* (1949); *Fantasía Romántica,* for trumpet (1950). Chamber music; piano pieces; choruses; songs.
Sources: BB, CTA2, DM, GDM, MLA, MMLA

Satalía, Agustín, Argentine cellist, music critic, and composer; b.28 Nov 1904, Concordia, Prov. of Entre Ríos, Argentina. He studied cello with Ramón Vilaclara.
Works (selective list): *Music for piano: En el Ocaso; Preludio en Sol menor; Momento Musical; Minué. Melodía,* for cello; songs.
Source: DM

Sauce, Angel, Venezuelan composer and conductor; b.2 Aug 1911, Caracas, Venezuela. He studied music composition at the National School of Music of Caracas and then took a course with Vicente E. Sojo in 1944. Conductor of the Concert Orch. of the Radio Caracas. Founder and director of the *Orfeón* (male singing society) *Obrero Juan Manuel Olivares.* Organizer and conductor of the Banda Obrera of Caracas.
Works: Sonata for violin and piano; Symphony; choral music; piano pieces; songs.
Sources: CTA14, MMLA

Saumell Robredo, Manuel, Cuban composer and pianist; b.1817, Havana, Cuba; d.14 Aug 1870, Havana. At first he was self-taught in music but later studied piano with Juan Federico Edelmann and harmony, counterpoint, and orchestration with Mauricio Pyke. He initiated Cuban musical nationalism, and is considered the father of the Cuban contredanse.
Works: Plegaria, for soprano and organ; *Melopea,* for orch.; Concerto for cello and piano; *Idilio,* for piano, violin, and cello; *Ave Maria,* for soprano and orch. Creator of several native dances: *contredanse; habanera; danzón; guajira; clave; criolla.*
Bibl.: O. Martínez, *Program of the Philharmonic Orchestra of Havana,* Nov 4, 1946. A. Carpenter, *Saumell y el Nacionalismo, La Música en Cuba,* Mexico City, 1946.
Sources: DM, DMC, GDM, MLA, MMLA

Savin, Francisco, Mexican conductor and composer; b.18 Nov 1929, Mexico City, Mexico. He studied piano with José Velásquez, 1944-53, orch. conducting with Hermann Scherchen, and composition with Rodolfo Halffter, 1955-56, in Mexico City. Then he went to Europe

where he studied composition with Karel Janecek at the Music Academy in Prague, Czechoslovakia, 1957-59. Assistant conductor of the Mexican National Symphony Orch., Mexico City, 1959-62, and principal conductor of the Xalapa Symphony Orch., Xalapa, Mexico, 1963-67. Director of the National Cons. of Music in Mexico City, 1967-70. Professor of music aesthetics and art history at the Univ. of Veracruz, Mexico, and at the National Cons. of Music. In 1972, he was appointed head of the Music Dept. of the National Inst. of Fine Arts of Mexico in Mexico City.
Works (selective list): *Quetzalcoatl,* symphonic poem for 2 narrators and orch. (1957); *Metamórfosis,* for orch. (1962); *Concreción,* for electronic organ and orch. (1969); *Monología de las Delicias,* for 4 female voices and orch. (1969); *Quasar 1,* for electronic organ, tape, and percussion (1970).
Sources: BB, DCM

Scheller Zembrano, María, Argentine composer; b.1917, Buenos Aires, Argentina; d.1944, Buenos Aires. She graduated from the National Cons. of Music Carlos López Buchardo of Buenos Aires in 1937, where she studied with Rafael González, Ricardo Rodríguez, and José André.
Works: String quartet in F major (1936); Suite for piano (1937); Sonata in E flat for piano (1938); Sonata for violin and piano (1939); Concerto in A minor for piano and orch. (1939); 4 sonatas for piano.
Sources: EMA, IEW

Schemper, Raúl, Argentine composer; b.27 May 1921, Buenos Aires, Argentina. He studied composition with Jacobo Ficher, piano with Oreste Castronuovo, trumpet with Salomón Flechter, contemporary techniques of composition with Eduardo Tejeda, and electronic music with Francisco Kröpfl.
Works (selective list): Suite for orch.; *Variaciones,* for orch.; *Elegía,* for trumpet, French horn, trombone, timpani, and strings; *Variante,* for orch.; chamber music; piano pieces.
Source: VMA

Schianca, Arturo C., Argentine pianist, musicologist, and composer; b.26 Dec 1889, Mercedes, Prov. of Buenos Aires, Argentina; d.?
Works: Dances and songs inspired on the Argentine folklore. *Books: Historia de la Música Argentina,* Buenos Aires, 1933.
Sources: DM, MLA, MMLA

Schidlowsky Gaete, León, Chilean composer; b.21 Jul 1931, Santiago de Chile, Chile. He studied philosophy and psychology at the Univ. of Chile, 1948-52, composition with Free Focke and harmony with Juan Allende Blín at the National Cons. of Music of

Chile, both in Santiago de Chile. He went to Germany for further music studies at the Detmold Music Academy and with Hanns Jelinek in Barsbüttel, 1952-55. When he returned to Chile in 1955, he became a member of the *Agrupación Tonus*. Music teacher at the Hebrew Institute in Santiago de Chile, 1955-61. Director of the Music Archives of the Inst. de Extensión Musical of the Univ. of Chile, 1961-65, and later director of the Inst. and a member of the Faculty of the National Cons. of Music, 1965-69. In 1969, he emigrated to Israel where he was appointed to the Faculty of the Rubin Academy in Tel Aviv.

Works (selective list): *Die Menschen,* opera (1970); *Requiem,* for soprano and chamber orch. (1954); *Caupolicán,* epic narrative for narrator, chorus, 2 pianos, celesta, and percussion orch. (1958); *Tríptico,* for orch. (1959); *Oda a la Tierra,* for 2 narrators and orch. (1958-60); *La Noche de Cristal,* symphony for tenor, male chorus, and orch. (1961); *Erostrato,* for percussion orch. (1963); *Invocación,* for soprano, narrator, percussion, and string orch. (1964); *Nueva York,* for orch. (1965); *Jeremías,* for 8 mixed voices and string orch. (1966); *Kadish,* for cello and orch. (1967); *Epitaph for Hermann Scherchen,* for orch. (1967); *Babi Yar,* for string orch., piano, and percussion (1970); *Serenata,* for chamber orch. (1970); *Arcanas,* for orch. (1971); *Constellation II,* for string orch. (1971); *Rabbi Akiba,* scenic fantasy for narrator, 3 soloists, children's and mixed chorus, and orch. (1972); *Amereida,* for narrator and orch. (1965-72); *Prelude to a Drama,* for orch. (1976); *Images,* for string orch. (1976); *Lux in Tenebris,* for orch. (1977); *Tel Aviv,* for orch. (1978-83); *Ballade,* for violin and orch. (1986); *Elegy,* for orch. (1988); *Laudatio,* for orch. (1988); chamber music; piano pieces; songs.

Bibl.: M.E. Grebe, *León Schidlowsky, Síntesis de su Trayectoria Creativa, Revista Musical Chilena,* 1968. W. Elías, *León Schidlowsky,* Tel Aviv, 1978.

Sources: BB, CTA10, DCM, HMC, GDM

Schiuma, Alfredo Luis, Argentine composer, conductor, and violinist of Italian origin; b.25 Jun 1885, Spinazzola, Italy; d.24 Jul 1963, Buenos Aires, Argentina. Brother of Armando Schiuma. He settled in Argentina in 1889. He studied violin with his father, Rafael Schiuma, and David Bolia, and composition with Luis Romaniello. First violin at the orch. of the Teatro Colón of Buenos Aires. Founder of the chamber orch. of the Asociación Argentina de Música de Cámara of Buenos Aires.

Works (selective list): *Operas: Biancafiore* (1913); *Amy Robsart* (1920); *Litigio de Amor* (1922); *La Sirocchia* (1922); *Tabaré* (1925); *Las Vírgenes del Sol* (1939). *La Pampa,* symphonic poem (1920); *La Vida de un Hombre,* symphonic poem (1922); *Chacayaleras,* symphonic suite (1927); 4 symphonies (1928-57); *Pitunga,*

symphonic poem (1929); *Los Incas,* symphonic poem (1930); *La Infanta,* ballet (1941); choruses; chamber music; songs.
Sources: BB, CA, DM, EMA, MLA, MMLA

Schiuma, Armando, Argentine conductor and composer of Italian origin; b.23 Feb 1891, Spinazzola, Italy; d.1955, Buenos Aires, Argentina. Brother of Alfredo Luis Schiuma. He studied in Buenos Aires with Luis Romaniello, Ernesto Drangosch, and Eduardo Fornarini. Assistant conductor at the Teatro Colón of Buenos Aires. Teacher in various schools.
Works (selective list): Overture for orch.; *Música de Escena,* for orch.; *Passacaglia,* for orch.; *Impresiones de mi Tierra,* for orch.; String quartet; Sextet for piano and strings; chamber music; children's songs.
Sources: DM, EMA

Schiuma, Rafael, Argentine music teacher and composer; b.1844, Spinazzola, Italy; d.1940, Buenos Aires, Argentina. Father of Alfredo Luis and Armando Schiuma. He settled in Argentina in 1889.
Works: Salon music; hymns for Garibaldi and Humberto I.
Source: EMA

Schreiber, Jacky, Venezuelan composer; b.26 Jan 1951, Caracas, Venezuela. He studied guitar with Antonio Ochoa and electroacoustic composition with Eduardo Kusnir at the Conservatory J.J. Landaeta of Caracas.
Works (selective list): *Preguntas a mi Mismo y a Alguien Más,* electroacoustic sounds on a magnetic tape (1985); *El Ojo del Golem,* for orch. (1985-86); *La Paz de los Mundos,* electroacoustic sounds on a magnetic tape (1986); *Adagio,* for string orch. (1986); *Cuando Lleguen los Bomberos...Todo Habrá Pasado,* for flute, baritone saxophone, and electroacoustic sounds on a magnetic tape (1988); *La Meditación del Loro Moro,* for chamber orch. (1991); *Animalia,* for orch. (1990-91); music for the stage; music for solo instruments; chamber music; choral music; piano pieces.
Source: ISC

Schwartz, Francis, Puerto Rican composer of American origin; b.10 Mar 1940, Altoona, Pennsylvania, USA. He settled in Puerto Rico in 1965. He studied piano in Texas with Patricio Gutiérrez, and later he entered The Juilliard School of Music in New York City where he studied with Lonny Epstein, Vittorio Giannini, and Louis Persinger. He received Bachelor, and Master, degrees from The Juilliard School of Music, and a Ph.D. in music aesthetics from the Univ. of Paris, France, under the supervision of Daniel Charles. Professor, and later also chairman from 1971 to 1980, of the Music Dept. at the Univ. of

Puerto Rico. From 1977 to 1979, he was a visiting professor at the Univ. of Paris. Director of Cultural Affairs at the Univ. of Puerto Rico from 1981 to 1986. He established the first Electronic Music Laboratory and New Music Workshop in the Caribbean. Music critic for the newspaper *San Juan Star* of Puerto Rico.

Works (selective list): *Auschwitz*, for tape, aromas, lights, and corporal movements (1968); *Homenaje a una Obscenidad*, for free ensemble (1970); *El Zoológico de Cristal*, incidental music (1970); *Las Bacantes*, incidental music (1970); *Plegaria*, for voice and orch.(1973); *Suicida y Requiescit*, for soprano, instruments, and tape (1973); *GEO-FLUX*, electric ballet and tape (1974); *Yo Protesto*, for orch. and tape (1974); *Caníbal-Calibán*, for voice and free ensemble (1975); *The Tropical Trek of Tristán Trimble*, for orch. (1975); *Time, Sound, and the Hooded Man*, for actors, tape, and video (1975); *Is There Sex in Heaven?*, chamber opera (1976); *Hommage a K...*, musical theater (1978); *Amistad III*, for guitar and orch.(1979); *Mon Oeuf*, polyartistic work, for tape, video, aromas, and sculpture (1979); *L'Oncle de Baudelaire*, instrumental theater (1980); *Un Sourire Festif*, instrumental theater (1981); *Gestos*, for orch. (1983); *Grimaces*, for voice and instruments (1983); *The Night of the Fiery Angels*, for instruments and participating audience (1987); *El Sueño de Bolívar*, for soprano, clarinet, violin, and piano (1988); chamber music; music for solo instruments; electronic music; songs.
Sources: CPR, ISC

Sciammarella, Valdo, Argentine choral conductor, teacher, and composer; b.20 Jan 1924, Buenos Aires, Argentina. He graduated from the National Cons. of Music Carlos López Buchardo of Buenos Aires. He also studied piano with Vicente Scaramuzza and Antonio De Raco, and composition with Julián Bautista. From 1958 to 1969, he was associated with the Teatro Colón of Buenos Aires, first as an assistant conductor and later as director of the children's chorus and associate director of the permanent adult chorus. Professor at the National Cons. of Music Carlos López Buchardo, the School of Fine Arts of the Univ. of La Plata, Prov. of Buenos Aires, Argentina, and the Argentine Catholic Univ. of Buenos Aires. Founding director of the chorus *Los Pequeños Virtuosos del Mozarteum Argentino*.
Works (selective list): *Variaciones Concertantes*, for piano and orch. (1952); *Díptico*, for orch. (1953); *Canzona*, for soprano and orch. (1954); *Rondas*, for orch. (1955); *Cantata para la Fundación de Buenos Aires*, for bass, chorus, brass orch., and percussion (1956); *Marianita Limeña*, lyric comedy (1957); *Salmo I*, for soloists and orch. (1958); *Recordad el Amor*, ballet (1962); *Galería Humana*, ballet (1962); *Credo*, ballet (1964); chamber music; piano pieces; songs.
Sources: BB, CA, CTA12, EMA

Scliar Cabral, Esther, Brazilian composer, pianist, conductor, and teacher; b.28 Sep 1926, Pôrto Alegre, Brazil; d.1978, Rio de Janeiro, Brazil. She studied piano in Pôrto Alegre with Judite Pacheco and Demófilo Xavier. In 1948, she studied with Hans Joachim Koellreutter in Rio de Janeiro. Also in 1948, she went to Venice, Italy, to study orch. conducting with Hermann Scherchen. In 1949, she returned to Rio de Janeiro, and studied composition with Claudio Santoro and Edino Krieger. In 1952, she formed the chorus of the Associaçâo Juvenil Musical. From 1962 to 1975, she taught musical analysis and form at the Villa-Lobos Inst. and the Pró Arte Music School, both of Rio de Janeiro.
Works: Sonata for piano (1961); *O Auto da Barca do Inferno,* prelude for orch. (1962); Sonata for flute and piano (1962); *Desenho Leve,* for chorus (1962); *O Menino Ruivo,* for chorus (1962); String quartet (1963); *Canto Menor com Final Heróico,* for chorus (1964); *A Busca da Identidade entre o Homen e o Río,* for chorus (1971); *Entre o Ser e as Coisas,* for voice and piano (1973). *Books: Fraseología Musical,* Pôrto Alegre, 1882; *Elementos de Teoría Musical,* Sâo Paulo, 1985-87.
Sources: EMB, HMB, NGDWC, NWC

Sebastiani, Pía, Argentine pianist and composer; b.27 Feb 1925, Buenos Aires, Argentina. She studied piano with Jorge de Lalewicz and composition with Gilardo Gilardi. In 1947, she received a scholarship from the French government to further her studies with Darius Milhaud and Olivier Messiaen in Paris, France, and in Boston, Massachusetts. Member of the Seminario de Jóvenes Músicos Argentinos and of the Liga de Compositores de la Argentina.
Works (selective list): Concerto for piano and orch. (1941); *Coral, Fuga, y Final,* for orch. (1945); *Estampas,* for orch. (1946); Sonatina for 2 violins (1948); *Cuatro Preludios,* for piano (1944-47); *Canción de Cuna para Bibí,* for piano (1947); songs.
Sources: CA, DM, EMA, IEW

Sepe, Joâo, Brazilian composer and teacher; b.21 Apr 1889, Tatuí, State of Sâo Paulo, Brazil; d.27 Aug 1961, Sâo Paulo, Brazil. Professor of harmony and counterpoint at the Cons. Dramático y Musical of Sâo Paulo.
Works: Carnaval Carioca, fantasia for orch.; *Cascata; Preludio e Elegía. Books: Tratado de Harmonía.*
Source: MMLA

Sepúlveda Maira, María Luisa, Chilean composer, pianist, and teacher; b.14 Aug 1898, MMLA (1896, NGDWC), Chillán, Chile;

d.5 Apr 1959, HMC (1958, NGDWC), Santiago de Chile, Chile. She studied with Luigi Giarda and Domingo Brescia at the National Cons. of Music of Santiago de Chile. First woman composer to graduate in Chile. She was a pioneer in the compilation and research of Chilean folk music. Professor at the National Cons. of Music and the Escuela de Cultura Artística, both of Santiago de Chile.
Works: Estudio Sinfónico, for orch. (1932); *Greca,* for orch. (1932); *Canción de las Corhuillas,* for orch. (1940); *Trutruka,* for orch. (1940); Suite for piano and chamber orch. (1940); *Cancionero Chileno,* collection of 16 Chilean songs for voice and piano; school songs; music for children; music for piano; music for guitar.
Sources: HMC, MMLA, NGDWC

Serebrier, José, Uruguayan conductor and composer; b.3 Dec 1938, Montevideo, Uruguay. He started music studies in Montevideo at the Municipal School of Music, violin with Juan Fabbri and Miguel Pritsch, and composition with Vicente Ascone. Later he studied piano with Sarah Bourdillon and counterpoint, fugue, composition, and conducting with Guido Santórsola, and also took lessons in composition with Carlos Estrada. In 1950, he went to the USA and studied composition with Vittorio Giannini at the Curtis Inst. in Philadelphia, Pennsylvania, and orch. conducting with Antal Dorati in Minneapolis, Minnesota. He also took conducting lessons with Pierre Monteaux in Maine. Composer-in-residence with the Cleveland Symphony Orch., Cleveland, Ohio, 1968-70, and conductor of the Cleveland Philharmonic, 1968-71.
Works (selective list): Quartet for saxophones (1955); *Pequeña Música,* for wind quintet (1955); Symphony No.1 (1956); *Momento Psicológico,* for string orch. (1957); *Suite Canina,* for wind trio (1957); Symphony for percussion (1960); *The Star Wagon,* for chamber orch. (1967); *Nueve,* for double bass and orch. (1970); *Colores Mágicos,* variations for harp and chamber orch. with "Synchrona" images (1971); *Nueve-Ritual,* for speakers, choruses, double bass, orch., and lights (1971); chamber music; choral pieces; band music; songs.
Sources: BB, BHMCU, DCM, GDM, MU

Serendero Proust, David, Chilean composer, conductor, musicologist, and violinist; b.28 Jul 1934, Santiago de Chile, Chile. He studied violin and composition at the National Cons. of Music in Santiago de Chile with Juan Orrego Salas, Alfonso Letelier, and Gustavo Becerra. Then he went to Germany, where he studied orch. conducting in Stuttgart. From 1967 to 1972, he was conductor of the Symphony Orch. of Chile in Santiago de Chile. In 1972, he moved to Germany, where he became active as conductor in Wiesbaden.

Works: String trio (1952); *Dúo Heterogéneo,* for flute and clarinet (1953); *Suite Barroca,* for violin and piano (1956); *Interludio Orquestal* (1959); *La Leyenda de la Creación,* cantata (1959); *El Ensayo,* melodrama for soprano and 14 instruments (1962); *A la Nueva Eva,* magnificat for voices and orch. (1963-64); *Estratos,* for orch. (1969).
Sources: BB, CTA15, HMC

Serpentini, Juan, Argentine organist and composer of Italian origin; b.1864, Recanati, Italy; d.1937, Buenos Aires, Argentina. He studied in Recanati with José Guardabassi, Tabellini and Carlo Pedrotti. He settled in Argentina in 1886, and studied counterpoint and composition with Juan Bautista Montano in La Plata, Prov. of Buenos Aires, Argentina. Director of music education in the La Plata school system. Professor at the Escuela Normal de Profesores Mariano Acosta in Buenos Aires. Organist at the Church San Ponciano of Buenos Aires.
Works: Dos Preludios, for orch.; *La Platense,* for orch.; *Caridad,* cantata for soloists, chorus, and orch.
Source: DM

Serra, Luis María, Argentine composer, lecturer, and choral and orch. conductor; b.18 Apr 1942, Lanús, Prov. of Buenos Aires, Argentina. He studied privately with Roberto Locatelli and Lita Spena, and with Alberto Ginastera, Roberto Caamaño, Gerardo Gandini, and Francisco Kröpfl at the Argentine Catholic Univ. of Buenos Aires, Argentina.
Works: *Tres Piezas,* for piano (1964); *Vitraux I,* for piano and percussion (1965); *Ave Maria,* for mixed chorus (1965); *Adagio,* for strings (1965); *Elegía y Toccata,* for orch. (1965); *Tres Poemas,* for mezzo-soprano, flute, violin, viola, harp, and percussion (1966); *Nocturno,* for mezzo-soprano and ensemble (1967); *Trígono,* for 2 flutes and harpsichord (1967); *Inocentes,* for mixed chorus (1968); *Momento,* for string quartet (1968); Cantata for soloists, chorus, and orch. (1968); *Tenebrae Factae Sunt,* for magnetic tape (1968).
Source: EMA

Serrallach, Lorenzo, Argentine composer; b.18 Jul 1893, Córdoba, Prov. of Córdoba, Argentina; d.? He studied violin with A. Ruta, piano with A. Vasconsellos, harmony, counterpoint, and fugue with Toro Chacón and Goula. He continued his studies in Spain with Sánchez. Professor at the Municipal Cons. of Music Manuel de Falla and teacher at the School of Opera of the Teatro Colón, both of Buenos Aires, Argentina.

Works: Chamber music; piano pieces; choruses; songs. *Books: Pedagogía Musical; Método de Lectura Musical en Clave de Fa en Cuarta Línea; Nueva Pedagogía Musical.*
Source: DM

Serrano Redonnet, Ana, Argentine guitarist, conductor, music critic, and composer; b.30 Dec 1914, Buenos Aires, Argentina. She studied guitar with Antonio Sinópoli and composition with Gilardo Gilardi and Jaime Pahissa. She devoted herself to research the sources of Argentine popular song. Music critic for the newspaper *Tribuna* of Buenos Aires.
Works (selective list): *Stage: El Niño Alcalde* (1943); *La Chaya* (1944); *Tierra* (1945); *Vidala* (1946). *Indianas,* for soprano, flute, and Indian drum; *Quebradeñas,* for voice, flute, oboe, clarinet, bassoon, guitar, and Indian drum; *La Soledad,* poem for voice, chorus, and chamber orch.; *Canción del Guagua* (1936); *Seis Aires Argentinos* (1939); *Coplas Tuyas* (1941); *Escenas de Navidad Norteña* (1946); *Rapsodia del Paraná;* guitar pieces; songs.
Sources: DM, EMA

Setti, Kilza (Kilza Setti de Castro Lima), Brazilian ethnomusicologist, composer, and pianist; b.26 Jan 1932, Sâo Paulo, Brazil. She graduated from the Cons. Dramático y Musical of Sâo Paulo in 1953, where she studied composition with Camargo Guarnieri, and then she went to Buenos Aires, Argentina, to study with Alberto Ginastera at the Inst. Torcuato Di Tella. Later she went to Lisbon, Portugal, where she investigated Portuguese folklore under the supervision of Michel Giacometti and Fernando Lopes-Graça. She devoted herself to research Brazilian folklore. In 1977, she became a founding member of the Brazilian Folklore Association while she was teaching at the Santa Marcelina Musical College in Sâo Paulo.
Works: Obialá Korô and *Iemanjá Otô,* both for chorus a cappella (1958); *Balada do Reis das Sereias,* cantata; *Lenda do Céu,* cantata; *Folgança,* suite for chamber orch.; Suite for flute, clarinet, and strings; *Trova de Muito Amor,* for voice; *Cantorias Paulistas,* for voice; *Oito Variações on a Popular Theme,* for piano (1972); *Dois Momentos I,* for recorder (1972); *Dois Momentos II,* for recorder (1975).
Sources: EMB, NGDWC, NWC

Siccardi, Honorio, Argentine composer and teacher; b.13 Sep 1897, Buenos Aires, Argentina; d.10 Sep 1963, Buenos Aires. He studied with Felipe Boero, Pablo Berutti, Ernesto Drangosch, and Gilardo Gilardi. In Italy, he studied at the Cons. of Parma with Gian Francesco Malipiero. Member of the *Grupo Renovación* of Buenos Aires.

Works (selective list): *Stage: Buenos Aires,* ballet (1935); *Títeres,* ballet (1936); *Flechas y Arcabuces,* opera (1940). *Orch.*: *Variaciones sobre un Tema de Haendel* (1921); *Dos Poemas sobre Martín Fierro* (1925); *Pasa la Tropa* (1926); *Crescendo* (1926); *Gandhi,* symphonic poem (1936); Concerto for violin (1939); Symphony (1950); Concerto for piano (1951). *Tres Cantatas,* on Prometheus by Aeschilus (1923); *Odas Seculares,* cantata (1948); *Las Nueve Musas,* cantata (1952); chamber music; choruses; piano pieces; songs.
Sources: CA, CTA2,DM, EMA, MLA

Siciliani, José, Argentine pianist, choral conductor, and composer; b.20 Apr 1910, Buenos Aires, Argentina. He studied with Athos Palma, José Gil, Arturo Luzzati, and Constantino Gaito at the National Cons. of Music Carlos López Buchardo of Buenos Aires. Music teacher at various elementary and high schools and at the National Cons. of Music Carlos López Buchardo. President of the cultural association *El Unísono.*
Works (selective list): *Tres Series Argentinas,* for orch.; *Atardecer,* symphonic poem; *Tres Preludios Sinfónicos,* for orch.; Sonata for piano; Sonatina for piano; *Doce Preludios,* for piano; Sonata for violin and piano; Trio for piano, violin, and cello; String quartet; choral pieces; songs.
Sources: CA, ISC

Sierra, Roberto, Puerto Rican composer; b.9 Oct 1953, Vega Baja, Puerto Rico. He studied at the Cons. of Music and the Univ. of Puerto Rico. After graduation, he went to Europe to continue his musical education, first at the Royal College of Music and the Univ. of London, England, from 1976 to 1978, and later, in 1978, at the Inst. of Sonology in Utrecht, Netherlands. Between 1979 and 1982, he took advanced studies in composition at the Hochschule für Musik in Hamburg, Germany, under György Ligeti. When he returned to Puerto Rico in 1982, he occupied various positions in arts administration and higher education, first at the Univ. of Puerto Rico and later as chancellor of the Cons. of Music of Puerto Rico. In 1989, he settled in the USA and became composer-in-residence of the Milwaukee Symphony Orch., Milwaukee, Wisconsin.
Works (selective list): *Polarizaciones,* for 2 orch. groups (1979); *El Mensajero de Plata,* opera (1985); *Júbilo,* for orch. (1985); *Cuatro Ensayos Orquestales,* for orch. (1986); *El Contemplado,* ballet (1987); *Glosas,* for piano and orch. (1987); *Descarga,* for orch. (1988); *Concierto Nocturnal,* for harpsichord and chamber ensemble; *Preámbulo,* for orch.; *SASIMA,* for orch.; *Concierto Evocativo,* for French horn and string orch.; chamber music; music for solo instruments; piano pieces; songs.
Sources: CPR, ISC

Siliézar, Felipe, Guatemalan composer; b.1 May 1903, Guatemala City, Guatemala. He studied in Guatemala City and in New York, where he resided for five years. Conductor of bands in various cities of Guatemala.
Works: Doña Beatriz la Sinventura, opera; *Hechicería Maya,* for orch.
Sources: DM, HMG, MLA

Silva, Alfonso de, Peruvian composer; b.22 Dec 1903, Callao, Peru; d.7 May 1937, Lima, Peru. He studied at the Academy of Music of Lima with Federico Gerdes, completing his training at the Cons. of Madrid, Spain, with Conrado del Campo.
Works (selective list): *Instantes (Extasis, Jardines Antiguos, Elegía Ingenua, Vísperas y Consolación),* symphonic suite; *Cuento de Hadas,* symphonic sketch for orch.; *Canción Amarilla,* for orch.; chamber music; piano pieces; choruses; songs.
Sources: ADBM, DM, GMP, MMLA

Silva, Alipio César Pinto da, Brazilian composer and teacher; b.1871, Pará, Belém, Brazil; d.1923, Brazil. He studied first in Belém, and later in Milan, Italy. Founder of the *Centro Musical Paraense* of Pará.
Works: (selective list): *Nette Bizarra,* opera; *Brasilea,* march; symphonic music; piano pieces.
Source: MMLA

Silva, Antonio Jesús, Venezuelan composer; b.13 Jun 1833, Caracas, Venezuela; d.? Professor of music theory and solfeggio at the National Inst. of Fine Arts of Caracas. Active member of the Academy of Music of Caracas.
Works: Misa de Requiem; Stabat Mater; Motete a la Virgen; Motete al Santísimo Sacramento; La Esperanza, symphonic overture; *La Regeneración,* patriotic hymn.
Source: MMLA

Silva, Cayetano Alberto, Argentine composer of Uruguayan origin; b.1868, San Carlos, Dept. of Maldonado, Uruguay; d.1920, Rosario, Prov. of Santa Fe, Argentina. He studied solfeggio, violin, trumpet, and French horn at the Escuela de Artes y Oficios with Estanislao Grasso and started his music career by playing trumpet in the band of his native town. After settling in Argentina, he founded the Band of the Firemen Corp of Mendoza, Prov. of Mendoza. In Rosario, he founded the Band of Rosario and a cons., where he taught until his death.

Works: Two military marches adopted by the Argentine Army: *San Lorenzo* (1902) and *Curupaytí* (1905). *La Aurora de la Vida,* hymn for soloists, chorus, and orch. (1887); incidental music for the play *Canillita* by Florencio Sánchez.
Sources: BHMCU, EMA

Silva, Eloísa d'Herbil de, Argentine composer of Cuban origin; b.1842, Cuba; d.1944, Buenos Aires, Argentina. She studied piano with Louis Moreau Gottschalk in Cuba. She settled in Argentina in 1870. Very active as a pianist, in Europe and in Argentina.
Works: Music for piano: Minuet con Variaciones; Scherzo; Saltarello; A Orillas del Mar, waltz; *Remember; La Caridad; Serenata.* Songs.
Source: EMA

Silva, Francisco Manuel da, Brazilian music teacher, choral conductor, and composer; b.21 Feb 1795, Rio de Janeiro, Brazil; d.18 Dec 1865, Rio de Janeiro. He studied with Marcos Portugal, José Mauricio Nunes García, and Segismundo Neukomm. In 1833, he founded the Sociedade Beneficente Musical. He also founded the Cons. of Rio de Janeiro in 1847. He participated in the creation of the Imperial Academy of Music and the National Opera in 1857, Rio de Janeiro.
Works: *Hino ao 7 de Abril, Brazilian National Anthem* (1831); *Hino â Coroaçâo* (1841); *Hino das Artes* (1854); *Missa dos Mortos,* for 4 voices and orch.; *Tedeum Laudamus,* for 4 voices and orch.; *O Prestigio da Lei,* opera; many religious and profane pieces; hymns; romances; modinhas; waltzes. *Books: Compêndio de Música Prática,* Rio de Janeiro, 1832; *Compêndio de Música,* Rio de Janeiro, 1838; *Compêndio do Principios Elementares de Música,* Rio de Janeiro, 1848.
Bibl.: A. de Albuquerque, *Ouviram di Ypiranga, Vida de Francisco Manuel da Silva,* Rio de Janeiro, 1959. A. de Andrade, *Francisco Manuel da Silva e seu Tempo, 1808-65. Uma Fase do Passado Musical do Rio de Janeiro a Luz de Novos Documentos,* Rio de Janeiro, 1967.
Sources: BB, DM, GDM, HMB, MLA, MMLA

Silveira, Guillermo, Argentine composer and conductor; b.1959, Buenos Aires, Argentina. He studied piano with Marta B. de Levín, Héctor Moreno, Marisa L. de Maranca, and Lucía Maranca, chamber music with Ljerko Spiller, composition with Gerardo Gandini, Francisco Kröpfl, and Roberto Caamaño, and orch. conducting with Mario Benzecry, Pedro Calderón, Bruno D'Astoli, and Alberto Balzanelli in Buenos Aires. He received Master's and Ph.D. degrees in music composition from the Benjamin T. Rome School of Music of the Catholic Univ. of America, Washington, D.C., in 1985 and 1988, respectively. Professor at the Santa Ana Cons. of Buenos Aires.

Works (selective list): *Obacaesnas,* for voices, four-hand piano, and tape (1979); *DROB,* for voices, instruments, piano, and tape (1980); *Concierto Porteño,* for piano and instruments (1983); *Ten Mad Songs for the End of the World,* musical (1983); *Latelaraña,* chamber opera (1984); *Varieté,* musical (1984); *Más Allá del Río Grande,* for voice, clarinet, cello, and percussion orch. (1987); *In Memory of Jorge Luis Borges,* for voice, clarinet, guitar, piano, and synthesizer (1987); *Concrete Unconsciousness,* madrigal dramático for voices and instruments (1987); *La Ronda del Angelito,* for voices and electronic sounds (1989); *Suite Standard,* for voices, instruments, and electronic sounds (1989); *Morning,* cantata for voice and electronic sounds (1991); *Sur 2,* rhapsody for piano and electronic sounds (1991); *Ladies and Gentlemen...,* for baritone, voices, and electronic sounds (1992); music for voices and/or different instruments with electronic sounds; chamber music; music for solo instruments.
Source: ISC

Simó, Manuel, Dominican composer; b.30 Jun 1916, Los Cacaos, Dominican Republic; d.1988, Dominican Republic. He started music studies at the Municipal Academy of his native town. Later he moved to Ciudad Trujillo, Dominican Republic, where he studied composition with Enrique Casal Chapí, 1941-45. He received a scholarship to continue his music studies at the Kolisher Cons. of Montevideo, Uruguay. He graduated as composer and professor of composition. Founding member and director of the National Symphony Orch. of the Dominican Republic, Ciudad Trujillo. Director of the National Cons. of Music in Ciudad Trujillo from 1955 to 1959, and later again, until he retired in 1979.
Works (selective list): *Concertante,* for wind quintet; Overture for orch.; *Pastoral,* for orch.; Symphony in D major for orch.; *A la Patria,* cantata; Sonata for piano; *Toccata,* for 2 pianos; chamber music; piano pieces; songs.
Sources: DEW, DM, MLA, MMLA

Simoniello, Juan Pablo, Argentine composer and guitarist; b.8 Jul 1969, Rosario, Prov. of Santa Fe, Argentina. He studied guitar with Víctor Rodríguez in 1983. He studied at the Escuela Nacional de Música and the Inst. Nacional del Profesorado de Música, both of Rosario, following a career as a guitar player. From 1988 to 1989, he studied composition with Jorge Horst, and later with Mariano Etkin and Gerardo Gandini.

Works: Contornos, for oboe, viola, guitar, and double bass (1990); *Solo para Decir,* for flute, clarinet, piano, and double bass (1990); *A Tempo Nuevo,* for flute, oboe, clarinet, French horn, trombone, and violin (1990); *A Ella le Gusta Mucho,* for flute, English horn, bass clarinet, guitar, piano, percussion, violin, viola, and cello (1991).
Source: CAMR

Sindici, Oreste, Colombian singer and composer of Italian origin; b.1837, Italy; d.1904, Colombia. He studied music with Julio Quevedo Arvelo.
Works: Colombian National Anthem.
Sources: DM, MLA, ZCCC

Sinópoli, Antonio, Argentine guitarist, music teacher, and composer; b.14 Oct 1878, San Isidro, Prov. of Buenos Aires, Argentina; d.? He studied guitar with Julio S. Sagreras, and harmony with Constantino Gaito and Morera.
Works: Music for guitar: Vidalita con Variaciones; Canción Indígena; Canción de los Alpes; Saudades do Brazil. Many transcriptions for guitar of works by Bach, Beethoven, and other composers. *Books: Gran Método Aguado-Sinópoli,* for the Guitar.
Source: DM

Siqueira, Baptista, Brazilian musicologist and composer; b.8 Jul 1906, Princesa, Brazil. Brother of Joâo de Lima Siqueira. He studied at the Univ. of Rio de Janeiro, Brazil.
Works: Operas; ballets; 3 symphonies; symphonic and orch. compositions; Piano concerto; chamber music; piano pieces; sacred music.
Source: KTL

Siqueira, Joâo de Lima, Brazilian conductor and composer; b.24 Jun 1907, Conceiçâo, State of Paraíba, Brazil. Brother of Baptista Siqueira. He studied saxophone and trumpet with his father, and then he entered the National School of Music in Rio de Janeiro, Brazil, where he studied music theory with Paulo Silva, orch. conducting with Walter Burle Marx, composition with Francisco Braga, and piano with Luis Amabile. In 1940, he founded the Brazilian Symphony Orch. of Rio de Janeiro, which he conducted until 1948. In 1949, he organized the Symphony Orch. of Rio de Janeiro. Professor of harmony at the National School of Music of Rio de Janeiro. In 1951, he went to Europe for further studies with Olivier Messiaen, Tony Aubin, Eugène Bigot, and Jacques Chailly at the Cons. of Paris, France. Member of the Brazilian Academy of Music.

Works (selective list): *Stage: Uma Festa na Roça,* ballet (1943); *O Carnaval do Recife,* ballet (1947); *A Compadecida,* opera (1959); *Gimba,* lyric drama (1960); *O Carnaval Carioca,* festive theater piece (1965). *Orch.:* Os Pescadores, symphonic poem; *Alvorada Brasileira,* symphonic poem (1936); *O Despertar de Ariel,* symphonic poem; *Cuatro Poemas Indígenos* (1944); 4 symphonies (1933, 1951, 1954, 1956); Cello concerto (1952); Piano concerto (1955); *Seis Danças Brasileiras;* 5 symphonic suites on Brazilian themes (1955-70); *Candomblé,* oratorium (1957); *Encantamento da Magia Negra,* motet on native themes (1957); Violin concerto (1957). Chamber music; piano pieces; songs.
Bibl.: E. Nogueira Franca, *Festival José Siqueira, Revista Brasileira de Música,* Vol.2, 1963.
Sources: BB, CTA16, DM, GDM, MLA

Smith, Federico, Cuban composer of American origin; b.2 Mar 1929, New York. Cuban citizen. He studied in Boston, Massachusetts, and at the National Cons. of Music of Mexico, Mexico City, Mexico. He lived in Mexico from 1950 to 1962, and then settled in Cuba.
Works: Ballets; orch. works; chamber music; piano pieces; choruses; music for films and for television.
Source: KTL

Soares, Hostilio, Brazilian composer; b.1896, Minas Gerais, Brazil; d.? Professor at the Cons. Mineiro de Música of Minas Gerais.
Works: A Vida, opera; *Príncipes Románticos,* operetta; *Annie Besante,* symphony; *Cavaleiros da Tavola Redonda,* overture; *Suite Brasileira,* for band.
Source: MMLA

Soares Gómes dos Santos, Milton, Brazilian composer and physician; b.26 Aug 1916, Salvador, Brazil.
Works: Orch. music; chamber music; piano pieces; choral music.
Source: KTL

Soderini, Domingo, Argentine composer of Italian origin; b.28 Feb 1887, Sersale, Italy; d.? He settled in Argentina and studied in Buenos Aires at the Beethoven Cons. with Adolfo Rinaldi and Lorenzo Scalese, and in Bologna, Italy, with Giuseppe Martucci. Since 1936, professor at the Escuela Normal Nacional of Junín, Prov. of Buenos Aires, Argentina.
Works: Music for piano: Tres Preludios (1925); *Suite Argentina* (1926); Sonata in C sharp minor (1927); *Vidala* (1927); *Suite Moderna* (1937); Concerto in C major (1938); *Suite Mecánica: En*

Avión, En Automovil, En Ferrocarril (1948). *Orch.:* Overture in F minor; Overture in F sharp minor.
Source: DM

Sodré, Joanídia Núñez, Brazilian composer; b.22 Dec 1903, Pôrto Alegre, Rio Grande do Sul, Brazil; d.7 Sep 1975, Rio de Janeiro, Brazil. She began to study piano with Alberto Nepomuceno and later went to the National Inst. of Music of Rio de Janeiro, Brazil, where she studied piano with João Nunes and composition with Francisco Braga. In 1925, she was appointed professor of harmony and musical form at the National Inst. of Music of Rio de Janeiro. In 1927, she went to Germany where she studied composition with Paul Juon and orch. conducting with Ignaz Waghalter in Berlin. When she returned to Brazil, she founded and conducted the *Coral Femenino*, 1930, and the Orquesta Sinfónica Infantil and the Orquesta da Juventude, both in 1939. From 1946 to 1967, she was director of the National School of Music of the Univ. of Brazil in Rio de Janeiro.
Works: Casa Forte, opera (1927); *A Cheía do Paraíba,* incidental music for the stage (1927); *Girassol,* for chorus and orch.; *Incêndio em Roma,* for chorus and orch.
Source: NGDWC

Sofía, Pedro, Argentine composer; b.1 Jan 1890, Buenos Aires, Argentina; d.? He studied at the Wagner Cons. and at the Massún Cons., both in Buenos Aires. Founding member and first president of the Argentine Association of Chamber Music. Professor at various public schools.
Works: Ironías del Destino, lyric comedy; *Reyma,* lyric comedy (1910); *Intillay,* for chorus; *Vendimiadores,* for chorus; *Virgen del Sol,* for chorus; songs. *Books: Method for Guitar.*
Sources: DM, EMA

Sojo, Vicente Emilio, Venezuelan composer, conductor, teacher, and ethnomusicologist; b.8 Dec 1887, Guatire, Venezuela; d.11 Aug 1974, Caracas, Venezuela. He studied first with Régulo Rico in his native town, and then with Andrés Delgado Pardo and Primo Moschini at the Academia de Bellas Artes in Caracas. Director of the *Orfeón Lamas* (male singing society) and professor of music theory, and later director, at the Escuela Superior de Música, both in Caracas. In 1937, he founded the Venezuelan Symphony Orch. in Caracas. Very active in national ethnomusicology.
Works (selective list): String quartet (1913); masses; *Requiem a la Memoria del Libertador Bolívar; Te Deum;* motets; cantatas; hymns; liturgic psalms.
Bibl.: R. Fernández, *Vicente E. Sojo,* Caracas, 1968.
Sources: BB, CTA14, DM, GDM, MLA, MMLA

Solare, Juan María, Argentine composer and pianist; b.11 Aug 1966, Buenos Aires, Argentina. He studied piano with María Teresa Criscuolo and Perla Brúgola, orch. conducting with Mario Benzecry, and composition with Fermina Casanova, Valdo Sciammarella, and Juan Carlos Zorzi. He received degrees from the National Cons. of Music Carlos López Buchardo in Buenos Aires, as professor of piano in 1989, and as professor of composition in 1993. He also studied music analysis with Francisco Kröpfl. Professor of harmony, counterpoint, musical form, history of music, acoustics, and chamber music at the Cons. of Tandil, Prov. of Buenos Aires, Argentina.
Works (selective list): *Veinticinco de Agosto 1983,* chamber opera (1992-93); *Orchestral Variations,* for orch. (1991); chamber music; piano pieces; music for solo instruments; choruses; songs.
Source: ISC

Solares Echeverría, Enrique, Guatemalan composer and pianist; b.11 Jul 1910, Guatemala City, Guatemala. He studied piano with Salvador Ley and Raúl Paniagua in Guatemala, and with Ernest Bacon and Misha Pelz in San Francisco, California, and composition with Raymond Moulaert and Joseph Jongen in Brussels, Belgium, with Jaroslav Kricka in Prague, Czechoslovakia, 1936-39, and with Alfredo Casella in Rome, Italy, 1939-42. In 1943, he returned to Guatemala and taught piano. Later he entered the diplomatic service.
Works: *Ricercare sobre el Nombre de Bach,* for string orch. (1941); *Toccatina,* for guitar (1946); *Partita,* for string orch. (1947); Sonata for solo violin (1958); *Fantasía,* for guitar (1959); *Idea con 15 Deformaciones,* for piano (1962); *Siete Travesuras,* for piano (1969); *Doce Microtransparencias,* for piano (1970).
Sources: BB, CTA4, DCM, MMLA

Solomonoff, Natalia, Argentine composer and recorder player; b.1968, Rosario, Prov. of Santa Fe, Argentina. She studied composition with Jorge Horst, Mariano Etkin, and Gerardo Gandini and was a student at the Escuela Superior de Música and at the Inst. Nacional del Profesorado de Música, both of Rosario.
Works: *Rocal,* for violin, viola, cello, and oboe; *Azathots,* for flute, trombone, violin, and double bass; *Epitafios Rasgados,* for string trio; *"...de Nada",* for flute, oboe, clarinet, and bassoon.
Source: CAMR

Somellera, Josefa, Argentine pianist and composer; b.1810, Buenos Aires, Argentina; d.1885, Argentina. Niece of Candelaria Somellera de Espinosa. She studied with Juan Antonio Picasarri and Juan Pedro Esnaola at the Escuela de Música y Canto in Buenos Aires.
Works: Mainly salon music. Song *La Muerte de Corina* on words by Juan Cruz Varela, published in *El Cancionero Argentino* in 1837.

Source: EMA

Somellera de Espinosa, Candelaria, Argentine composer from the 19th century. Aunt of Josefa Somellera.
Works: Minuet for piano.
Source: IEW

Soriano, Alberto, Argentine composer and ethnomusicologist; b.5 Feb 1915, Santiago del Estero, Prov. of Santiago del Estero, Argentina; d.16 Oct 1981, Concepción del Uruguay, Prov. of Entre Ríos, Argentina. He studied violin with Dante Souza, and harmony and counterpoint with Silvio Deolindo Roes in Bahia, Brazil. He lived mostly in Brazil and Uruguay; many considered him an Uruguayan composer, but he never relinquished his Argentine citizenship. From 1953 to 1969, he was professor of ethnomusicology at the Univ. of Montevideo, Uruguay.
Works (selective list): *Orch.:* Guitar concerto No.1 (1952); Sinfonietta for guitar and strings (1952); Piano concerto (1954); Suite for ballet (1954); *Divertimento,* for bassoon and strings (1955); *Cuatro Rituales Sinfónicos* (1957); Violin concerto (1957); Guitar concerto No.2 (1958); *Cantos Sinfónicos, Series I y II* (1962); *Tres Canciones,* for soprano (1962); *Tres Esquemas Sinfónicos sobre la Vida de Artigas* (1964); *Tiempo Sinfónico para los Caídos en Buchenwald* (1964); Cello concerto (1964); *Pastoral,* for flute (1965); *Tríptico de Praga* (1966); Suite sinfónica (1967); *Homenaje a Dresden,* for viola, (1967); *Baladillas de Buenos Aires,* piano (1970). Chamber music; piano pieces.
Sources: BB, BHMCU, CTA16, EMA

Soro Barriga, Enrique, Chilean composer, conductor, and pianist; b.15 Jul 1884, Concepción, Chile; d.3 Dec 1954, Santiago de Chile, Chile. Son of the Italian composer José Soro Sforza, with whom he started his music education. He graduated from the Cons. of Milan, Italy, in 1904, where he studied with Luis Mapelli and Gellio Coronaro. Returning to Chile in 1905, he was appointed supervisor of musical education in primary schools. He joined the Faculty of the Cons. of Santiago de Chile in 1906, and from 1919 to 1928, he was its director. In 1942, he was appointed director of the Inst. de Extensión Musical in Santiago de Chile, a position held until his death.
Works (selective list): *Orch.:* *Andante Appassionato* (1915); *Danza Fantástica* (1916); *Suites Sinfónicas No.1 and No.2* (1918, 1919); Piano concerto (1919); *Sinfonía Romántica* (1920); *Tres Preludios Sinfónicos* (1936); *Aires Chilenos* (1942); *Suite en Estilo Antiguo* (1943). *Chamber music:* String quartet (1904); Piano quintet (1919);

Piano trio (1926); Violin sonata; Cello sonata; 3 piano sonatas (1920, 1923, 1942); piano pieces; songs.
Bibl.: V. Salas Viú, *La Creación Musical en Chile 1900-1951,* Santiago de Chile, 1953.
Sources: BB, CTA1, DCM, DM, GDM, HMC, MLA, MMLA

Sosaya, José Roberto, Peruvian composer; b.8 Jun 1956, Trujillo, Peru. He studied piano at the Escuela Regional de Música of Trujillo. Later he studied composition at the National Cons. of Music in Lima, Peru, with Edgar Valcárcel. He also studied composition with Yoshihisa Taira at the Ecole Normale de Musique, and electroacoustic music with Philippe Mion and Jacques Lejeune at the Groupe de Recherche Musicale, both in Paris, France. He furthered his music studies with Alain Louvier, Michel Zbar, and Sergio Ortega. Professor and later chairman of the Dept. of Composition at the National Cons. of Music in Lima. Founder and artistic director of the CIDEMP.
Works (selective list): *Orch.:* *Coral* (1984); *Miniature* (1986); *Texturas* (1990-91). Chamber music; electronic music; piano pieces; choral works.
Source: ISC

Soublette, Sylvia (Sylvia Soublette de Valdés), Chilean composer, choral conductor, and singer; b.5 Feb 1924, Antofagasta, Chile. She studied voice with Clara Oyuela and composition with Domingo Santa Cruz and Federico Heinlein at the National Cons. of Music in Santiago de Chile, Chile. In 1951, through a scholarship from the French government, she studied composition and choral conducting at the Paris Cons., France, with Darius Milhaud and Olivier Messiaen. Professor at the Catholic Univ. of Valparaiso, Chile. She founded several choral groups.
Works (selective list): *Stage: Alicia in the Country of Mirrors; Le Sicilien. Preludio y Fuga,* for orch. (1949); *Te Deum,* for soloists, chorus, and orch.; chamber music; choruses; sacred music; songs.
Sources: HMC, IBCC, IEW

Souza, Antonio Miguel de, Brazilian composer, band conductor, and clarinetist; b.1868, Minas Gerais, Brazil; d.1915, Brazil.
Works: Hino do Bi-Centenario de Mariana; sacred music; dance music.
Source: MMLA

Souza Coutinho, Joâo Francisco de, Brazilian composer; b.1804 or 1808, Santa Catarina, Brazil; d.1869, Brazil.
Works: Large number of sacred compositions.
Source: MMLA

Souza Lima, Joâo de, Brazilian composer and pianist; b.21 Mar 1898, Sâo Paulo, Brazil; d.1982, Sâo Paulo. He studied piano with Luigi Chiaffarelli and harmony and composition with Agostinho Cantú in his native city, and then went to Paris, France, where he studied piano with Isidor Philipp and Marguerite Long, music history with Maurice Emmanuel, and chamber music with Camille Chevillard and Paul Paray at the Paris Cons. He also studied harmony and composition with E. Cools, organ with Eugène Gigout, and piano with Alexander Brailowsky. Member of the Academia Brasileira de Música.
Works: *O Rei Mameluco,* symphonic poem; *Andrea del Sarto,* opera; Concerto for piano and orch.; *Danças Brasileiras,* for piano and orch.; *Improvisaciones sobre Temas Populares,* for piano; *Suite Infantil,* for piano. **Books:** *Técnica Moderna; Nociones de Música.*
Sources: DM, HMB, MLA, MMLA

Spena, Lita, Argentine composer; b.4 Oct 1904, Buenos Aires, Argentina. She studied at the National Cons. of Music Carlos López Buchardo of Buenos Aires.
Works: More than 30 children's songs; Sonata for piano (1937); *Cuatro Preludios Impresionistas,* for piano (1938); *Coplas Jujeñas,* for voice and piano (1939); *Kildina,* ballet.
Sources: DM, EMA

Spena, Lorenzo, Argentine composer of Italian origin; b.29 Apr 1874, Naples, Italy; d.? He studied in Naples with Luis Porro and Constantino de Crescenzo. In 1901, he settled in Buenos Aires, Argentina, and in 1907, he founded the Clementi Cons.
Works: 6 operas; symphonic music; chamber music; many compositions for the piano. **Books:** *Tratado Analítico de la Teoría Musical.*
Sources: DM, MLA

Spies Heilbronn, Claudio, Chilean composer, musicologist, and conductor; b.26 Mar 1925, Santiago de Chile, Chile. He settled in the USA in 1942, and entered the New England Cons. of Music in Boston, Massachusetts, where he studied piano, bassoon, cello, orch. conducting, and analysis of musical form. In 1943, he enrolled at the Longy School of Music in Cambridge, Massachusetts, where he attended classes in counterpoint, composition, and analysis with Nadia Boulanger. Later he took courses with Irving Fine, Walter Piston, Paul Hindemith, Tillman Merritt, and Randall Thompson at Harvard Univ., Cambridge, Massachusetts. Instructor at Harvard Univ., lecturer at Vassar College, Poughkeepsie, New York, and professor at Swarthmore College, Swarthmore, Pennsylvania, and

Princeton Univ., Princeton, New Jersey. Conductor of the Swarthmore College orch.
Works (selective list): *In Paradisum,* for voice soloists (1950); *Music for a Ballet,* for orch. (1955); *Il Cantico di Frate Sole,* for baritone and orch. (1958); *Tempi,* for 14 instruments (1962); *Five Orchestral Songs,* for soprano and orch. (1966); chamber music; choruses; songs.
Bibl.: P. Lansky, *The Music of Claudio Spies, Tempo,* 1972.
Sources: BB, CTA15, GDM, HMC

Spreafico, Juan Carlos, Argentine conductor and composer; b.1 Nov 1890, Concepción del Uruguay, Prov. of Entre Ríos, Argentina; d.? He studied in Santa Fe, Prov. of Santa Fe, Argentina, with Martín Hardin, and in Buenos Aires, Argentina, with Eduardo Fornarini. Between 1927 and 1932, he taught in several schools of the National Board of Education of Buenos Aires. In 1931, he settled in Santa Fe and was a founding member of the Asociación Filarmónica. He also helped to create the Provincial Cons. in 1937, and was appointed professor at the Liceo Municipal in 1939, both in Santa Fe.
Works (selective list): *S.O.S.,* symphonic poem (1931); *Suite Antigua,* for orch.; *Norteña,* for orch.; *Obertura Dramática,* for orch.; children's songs; hymns.
Sources: DM, EMA

Stea, Vicente, Peruvian pianist, band and orch. conductor, and composer of Italian origin; b.19 Apr 1884, Gioia del Colle, Prov. of Bari, Italy; d.10 Jun 1943, Lima, Peru. He studied first with his father and later entered the Cons. San Pietro a Majella in Naples, Italy, where he studied flute with Italo Piazza, harmony with Camillo de Nardis, and piano with Alessandro Longo. He also studied counterpoint with Paolo Serrao. He settled in Peru in 1917. Director of the National Academy of Music Alcedo in Lima.
Works (selective list): Symphony in G; *Sinfonía Autóctona; Meditación,* for cello and orch.; *Páginas de Album,* for piano; *Nocturnos,* for piano; *Romanzas sin Palabras,* for piano; *Burlesca,* for piano; *Plegaria del Canto 33 del Paraíso del Dante,* for voice and piano.
Bibl.: R. Barbacci, *Revista Musical Peruana,* Lima, Feb.1939.
Sources: ADBM, DM, MLA, MMLA

Steiger, María Susana, Argentine composer; b.3 Nov 1953, Rosario, Prov. of Santa Fe, Argentina. She graduated from the Escuela de Música de la Facultad de Humanidades y Artes of the National Univ. of Rosario, with a degree in composition. She also studied composition with Dante Grela. Founding

member of the Asociación Santafesina de Compositores and member of the *Agrupación Nueva Música* of Rosario.
Works: *Estudio,* for piano with 2 performers; *Transparencias,* for flute, clarinet, piano with 2 performers, and percussion; *Dos Preludios,* for amplified guitar; *"1983",* for piccolo, flute, oboe, clarinet, bass clarinet, double bass, and percussion; *Ideas,* for flute and clarinet.
Source: CAMR

Stiattesi, César Alberto, Argentine violinist, conductor, and composer of French origin; b.1881, Nice, France; d.1934, Buenos Aires, Argentina. He studied violin in France with Amadeo Magri. He settled in Argentina in 1889, and continued to study piano with Hércules Galvani and Coumerme, and composition with Cayetano Troiani. Teacher at the school system of the National Board of Education and at the National Cons. of Music Carlos López Buchardo, both of Buenos Aires. Conductor of the orch. and chorus of the Teatro Colón of Buenos Aires.
Works: *Blanca de Beaulieu,* opera; songs.
Sources: DM, EMA, MMLA

Storm, Ricardo, Uruguayan composer; b.14 Mar 1930, Montevideo, Uruguay. He studied piano with Cora Abal, Guillermo Kolischer, and Maria A. Piola, and harmony, counterpoint, and composition with Enrique Casal Chapí.
Works (selective list): *El Regreso,* opera (1958); *Introducción y Allegro,* for orch. (1954); *Música,* for strings, piano, and timpani (1959); Sonata for strings (1968); *Tres Canciones,* for mezzo-soprano and orch. (1963); choral music; chamber music; piano pieces; songs.
Sources: BHMCU, MU

Strigelli, José, Argentine conductor and composer of Italian origin; b.1844, Vigévano, Milan, Italy; d.1916, Buenos Aires, Argentina. He studied with Amilcare Ponchielli in Milan. He settled in Argentina in 1875. Professor of composition at the Escuela de Música de la Provincia, Prov. of Buenos Aires, Argentina. Conductor of the orch. of the Teatro de la Opera of Buenos Aires from 1875 to 1879. He resided in Mendoza, Prov. of Mendoza, Argentina, from 1886 to 1890. In 1893, he became blind.
Works (selective list): **Operas:** *I Figli di Borgia; Inés de Castro; Los Contrabandistas. La Presa di Troia,* operetta; *Una Scena nel Olimpo,* operetta; *Tres de Febrero,* march commissioned by President Sarmiento; *El Pronunciamiento de Mayo,* zarzuela; *Sinfonía Original,* for orch.; *Gran Valzer Sinfónico; Corona sulla Tomba di Vittorio Emanuele,* march; marches.

Source: EMA

Stubbs du Perron, Eduardo Walter, Peruvian composer and conductor; b.31 Dec 1891, Lima, Peru; d.? In 1909, he went to Buenos Aires, Argentina, where he studied music with Alberto Williams and Carlos Pedrell. Later he continued his music studies in Paris, France, under Vincent D'Indy. In 1940, he returned to Peru and started to work for the Radio Nacional.
Works: Fille Indienne, opera; *Elegie in Memoriam; Atahualpa,* ballet; Symphony in 3 movements; *Flamenca,* symphonic suite; *Six Amabilités,* for orch.; *Pancho,* operetta; String quartet; Piano trio; *Suite Incáica.*
Sources: GMP, MLA, MMLA

Sudupe, Estanislao de, Cuban composer and organist of Spanish origin; b.9 Jun 1915, Azcoitía, Guipúzcoa, Spain. He studied piano with Father José María Arregui and harmony with Father Celaya in Spain. He settled in Havana, Cuba, where he studied counterpoint, fugue, and orchestration with José Luis Vidaurreta. He finished his studies of composition and organ at the Yon Music Studios of Carnegie Hall, New York, under Pietro A. Yon. In 1938, he was appointed organist and *maestro de capilla* (chapelmaster) at the Church San Francisco in Havana.
Works (selective list): *Cautivo del Corsario,* zarzuela (1930); *Variaciones sobre un Tema Vasco,* for organ (1942); *Preludio y Fuga,* for orch. (1940); choral music; piano pieces.
Source: MMLA

Suffern, Carlos, Argentine pianist, music administrator, and composer; b.25 Sep 1905, Luján, Prov. of Buenos Aires, Argentina. He studied with César Stiattesi, Athos Palma, and Constantino Gaito at the National Cons. of Music Carlos López Buchardo of Buenos Aires, Argentina. He was artistic director of the Teatro Colón of Buenos Aires twice, in 1949 and in 1970. In 1970, he was appointed to the board of directors of SADAIC, the first classical musician to hold this position. Member of the Comisión Nacional de Cultura, now Subsecretaría de Cultura of Argentina. Music critic for the newspaper *La Razón* of Buenos Aires. Founding member of the Mozarteum Argentino of Buenos Aires. Professor of music at the National Cons. of Music Carlos López Buchardo, the National Univ. of Rosario, Prov. of Santa Fe, Argentina, the Escuela Superior de Bellas Artes of La Plata, Prov. of Buenos Aires, and the Argentine Catholic Univ. in Buenos Aires.
Works (selective list): *Tierna Historia del Príncipe Jazmín y la Princesa Almendra,* ballet (1934); *Dos Bocetos Sinfónicos,* for orch.

(1932); *Aire con Diferencias,* for string orch. (1938); *La Noche,* symphonic poem (1944); *Las Orientales,* for mezzo-soprano, bass, chorus, and orch. (1946); *Rey Lear,* overture for orch. (1961); *Belkiss,* for soloists, narrator, chorus, and orch.; chamber music; choruses; piano pieces; songs. **Books:** *Biography of Gluck.*
Sources: DM, EMA, MLA, MMLA

Sumaya (Zumaya), Manuel de, Mexican composer and *maestro de capilla* (chapelmaster); b.c.1678, Mexico; d.between 12 Mar and 6 May 1756, Oaxaca, Mexico. He studied with Antonio Salazar, *maestro de capilla* (chapelmaster) at the Cathedral of Mexico City, and later he studied with Joseph Ydíaquez, principal organist of the Cathedral. In about 1700, he was ordained a priest. *Maestro de capilla* (chapelmaster) and organist at the Cathedral of Mexico City.
Works: *Partenope,* the first opera written in Mexico; *El Rodrigo,* incidental music. **Religious compositions:** Lamentation; 3 motets; 13 hymns; villancicos; 3 Magnificat; 2 psalms; Mass.
Bibl.: R. Stevenson, *Music in Mexico,* New York, 1952. R. Stevenson, *Renaissance and Baroque Musical Sources in the Americas,* Washington, D.C., 1970.
Sources: GDM, MMLA

T

Tacuchian, Ricardo, Brazilian composer, conductor, lecturer, and teacher; b.1939, Rio de Janeiro, Brazil. He took his undergraduate and graduate music courses at the Univ. Federal do Rio de Janeiro, and studied composition with José Siqueira, Francisco Mignone, and Claudio Santoro. He attended the Univ. of Southern California at Los Angeles, California, on a Fulbright scholarship, and studied composition with Stephen Hartke; received a doctorate in music. Member of the Brazilian Academy of Music. He has joined the Faculty of UFRJ and UNIRIO.
Works (selective list): Concertino for piano and orch.; Concertino for flute and orch.; Sinfonietta for strings; *Nuclei,* for chamber orch.; *Hayastan,* ballet; *Estruturas Sincréticas,* for winds, percussion, projected slides, and electronic resources (1970); *Estruturas Simbólicas* (1973); *Estruturas Primitivas* (1975); *Estruturas Sinfónicas,* for orch. (1976); *Estruturas Verdes* (1976); *Estruturas Divergentes,* for flute, oboe, and piano (1977); *Estruturas Gêmeas,* for piano (1979); 4 cantatas; chamber music; piano pieces; tape music.
Sources: HMB, ISC

Tada Paz, Herberto di, Argentine composer; b.25 Dec 1903, Juárez, Prov. of Buenos Aires, Argentina. He studied piano and composition with Ernesto Drangosch and Constantino Gaito. Professor of music at several high schools in Buenos Aires.
Works: Sonata in A minor for piano (1921); *Epigramas y Epitafios,* for piano (1924); *Caperucita Roja,* ballet (1930); *Le Regret,* for voice and piano (1931); Suite for piano and orch. (1931); *Imágenes Americanas,* symphonic poem (1943).
Sources: DM, MMLA

Talavera, Mario, Mexican composer, singer, and conductor; b.13 Dec 1885, Jalapa, Mexico; d.27 Mar 1960, Mexico. He studied at the National Cons. of Music of Mexico in Mexico City. Member of the Mexican Fine Arts Academy.
Works: Mater Nostra; Los Muertos Hablan; La Cruz y la Espada; orch. music; songs.
Source: KTL

Tapia Colmán, Simón, Mexican composer, violinist, and conductor; b.24 Mar 1906, Aguarón, Mexico. He studied at the Cons. of Madrid, Spain, and also took lessons from Paul Hindemith. Professor at the Cons. of Mexico City.

Works: Ballet; symphonic music; Symphony for strings; Violin concerto; 2 guitar concertos; chamber music.
Source: KTL

Tauriello, Antonio, Argentine conductor and composer; b.20 Mar 1930, Buenos Aires, Argentina. He studied piano with Walter Gieseking, and composition with Alberto Ginastera. He conducted the orch. of the Teatro Colón of Buenos Aires, the Lyric Opera of Chicago, Illinois, the Opera Society of Washington, D.C., and the New York City Opera, New York.
Works (selective list): *Obertura Sinfónica,* for orch. (1951); *Serenata,* for orch. (1957); *Ricercare I-VI,* for orch. (1963); *Transparencias,* for 6 instrumental groups (1964); *Música III,* for piano and orch. (1965); *Serenata II,* for 7 instruments (1966); *Escorial,* opera (1966); *Canti,* for violin and orch. (1967); Piano concerto (1968); *Mansión de Tlaloc,* for piano, percussion, and strings (1969); *Impromptus,* for violin, piano, double bass, and 11 string soloists (1980); *Impromptus IV,* for 2 pianos and marimba (1982); Concerto for guitar and small orch. (1982); *Les Guerres Picorocholines,* chamber opera; chamber music; piano pieces.
Sources: BB, CA, DCM, DM, EMA, VMA

Tavares, Hekel (Heckel), Brazilian composer; b.1896, Satuba, Brazil; d.Aug 1969, Rio de Janeiro, Brazil. He was mostly self-taught in music, but in 1921, he studied orchestration with Joâo Otaviano in Rio de Janeiro.
Works: Concerto for piano and orch.; *André de Leâo e o Demônio de Cabelo Encarnado,* symphonic suite; *Canções Brasileiras,* for voice and piano; *Cantiga dos Sertanejos Cuibanos,* for chorus; Concerto for violin and orch.; *Anhangüera,* symphonic poem for soloists, chorus, children's chorus, and orch. He revised and harmonized many Brazilian folk songs.
Bibl.: C. Torres Pastorino, *Pequeña Historia da Música,* Rio de Janeiro, 1938.
Sources: DM, MLA, MMLA

Tavares, Mário, Brazilian composer, conductor, and cellist; b.18 Apr 1928, Natal, State of Rio Grande do Norte, Brazil. At age seven he started to study cello with Tommaso Babini. In 1947, he settled in Rio de Janeiro, Brazil, where he studied at the Escola Nacional de Música. Cellist at the Brazilian Symphony Orch. Founder and conductor of the Orquestra de Cámara da Rádio Ministério da Educação in 1957.

Works: *Ballets: Praiana* (1963); *Dualismo* (1963). *Moda e Ponteio,* for harp, celesta, and strings (1955); *Abertura Folclórica,* for mixed chorus and orch. (1955); *Potiguara, Segunda Dança Brasileira,* for string orch. (1957); *Ganguzama,* symphonic poem (1959); *Concertino,* for flute, bassoon, and strings (1959); *Divertimento,* for cello and orch.; *Rio, a Epopéia do Morro,* cantata (1965); Symphony No.1 for orch.; *Suite Copihue,* for orch. (1975); Concerto for cello and orch. (1981).
Sources: CTA16, HMB

Tavares de Lacerda, Lucas, Brazilian composer; b.1888, Minas Gerais, Brazil; d.? He studied at the National Inst. of Music in Rio de Janeiro, Brazil.
Works: *Sonho de Oiro,* operetta; music for orch.; 2 symphonies; Lyric poem.
Source: MMLA

Tavárez, Manuel Gregorio, Puerto Rican composer, conductor, and teacher; b.1843, San Juan, Puerto Rico; d.1 Jul 1883, Ponce, Puerto Rico. He started music studies with pianist José Cabrizas and organist Domingo Delgado. In 1858, with a scholarship from Sociedad Económica de Amigos del País, he entered the Paris Cons., France, where he studied piano with Eugène d'Albert, and harmony and composition with Daniel François Auber.
Works (selective list): *Gran Fantasía de Concierto,* for orch.; *A Campeche,* funeral march for orch.; *Vals de Concierto; Redención,* triumphal march for orch.; dances; piano pieces; songs.
Sources: MMLA, MMPR

Tejeda, Eduardo, Argentine composer; b.1923, Buenos Aires, Argentina. He studied piano with Oreste Castronuovo, and harmony, counterpoint, fugue, orchestration, and composition with Gilardo Gilardi, Luis Gianneo, and Jacobo Ficher. In 1962, he began to study and use avant-garde techniques under the supervision of Carlos Roqué Alsina and Francisco Kröpfl. Founding member of the Asociación de Jóvenes Compositores de la Argentina and the Unión de Compositores de la Argentina. Member of the *Agrupación Nueva Música.*
Works: *Espartaco,* overture; *Serenata,* for orch.; Symphony in three movements for orch.; Wind quintet; *Canciones del Paraná*; Sonata 1958 for piano; *Tres Piezas,* for voice and 5 instruments; *Tres Movimientos,* for 5 instruments and percussion; *Estructura,* for 5 wind instruments; *Protestatio,* for orch.; *Once Estructuras,* for piano; *Secuencias Móviles I,* for voice and 8 instruments; *Secuencias Móviles II,* for quintet; *Música Electrónica 1969; Estudio Electrónico II; Antakarana,* for chamber ensemble; *Senzar,* for electroacoustic

devices; *At-Ocso,* for orch. and magnetic tape; *Mantram IV,* for violin, piano, and clarinet.
Sources: EMA, VMA

Tejera, Francisco M., Venezuelan composer, teacher, and pianist; b.1840, Caracas, Venezuela; d.1878, Caracas.
Works: Romances; salon waltzes; variations on operatic themes.
Books: Gramática Musical.
Source: MMLA

Tello Rojas, Rafael J., Mexican composer, teacher, and pianist; b.5 Sep 1872, Mexico City, Mexico; d.17 Dec 1946, Mexico City. He started his musical education with his mother, Julia Rojas Caso. Later he studied piano with Carlos J. Meneses and Julio Ituarte, and composition with Ricardo Castro. Director of the Cons. Libre de México. Professor at the National Cons. of Music and at the Faculty of Music of UNAM, both in Mexico City. Music critic for several Mexico City newspapers.
Works (selective list): *Operas: Juno* (1896); *Nicolás Bravo* (1910); *Dos Amores* (1916); *El Oidor* (1942). *Sonata Trágica,* for violin and chamber orch. (1928); *Patria Heróica,* symphonic poem (1929); *Tríptico Mexicano,* for orch. (1939); Sextet for piano and wind instruments; *Drama en Música,* for string quartet; *Fantasía,* for 2 pianos and orch. (1943); chamber music; sacred music.
Sources: DM, GMM, MLA, MMLA

Teppa, Carlos, Venezuelan cellist and composer; b.4 Jun 1923, Caracas, Venezuela. He studied in Caracas, in New York City, New York, and in Siena, Italy.
Works: 5 symphonic compositions; 3 violin concertos; 2 cello concertos; music for voice and orch.; chamber music.
Source: KTL

Terraza, Emilio, Brazilian composer, conductor, teacher, and pianist of Argentine origin; b.1929, Bahía Blanca, Prov. of Buenos Aires, Argentina. He studied piano with Ruwin Erlich, and composition with Jacobo Ficher in Buenos Aires, Argentina. He continued his music studies with Leon Barzin in Paris, France, then settled in Brazil in 1958. Assistant conductor of the Symphony Orch. of the Univ. of Rio de Janeiro, Brazil, 1959-64. Professor of music at various Brazilian univ.
Works (selective list): *La Farra de la Búsqueda,* ballet (1956); *Preludio e Fuga,* for string orch. (1961); chamber music; piano pieces; songs.
Source: HMB

Terzián, Alicia, Argentine composer; b.1 Jul 1934, Córdoba, Prov. of Córdoba, Argentina. She studied at the Prov. Cons. of Córdoba, and graduated from the National Cons. of Music Carlos López Buchardo of Buenos Aires, Argentina, in 1958. She studied piano with Rafael González and Celia Bronstein, harmony and composition with Alberto Ginastera, fugue with Gilardo Gilardi, counterpoint with Floro Ugarte, and orchestration with Roberto García Morillo. In 1962, under Father Leoncio Daian at the National Mekitarist Congregation in Venice, Italy, she was involved in a research project concerning religious Armenian music, neumes, and microtones. Secretary of the Board of Directors of the IMS. Faculty member of the Argentine Catholic Univ., Consejo Argentino de la Música, Asociación Argentina de Compositores, and Asociación Argentina de Musicología, all of Buenos Aires. She was appointed professor at the National Cons. of Music Carlos López Buchardo in 1960, at the Escuela Superior de Bellas Artes of the National Univ. of La Plata, Prov. of Buenos Aires, Argentina, in 1967, and at the Inst. Superior de Arte of the Teatro Colón of Buenos Aires in 1968. Director of the Society for the Promotion of New Music in the Three Americas and executive secretary of the Latin American and Caribbean divisions of the International Music Council of UNESCO.
Works (selective list): **Orch.:** *Cantata de la Tarde,* for narrator and chorus (1958-59); *Introducción y Cántico de Primavera,* based on Solomon's Song of Songs, for chorus (1958-59); *Movimiento Sinfónico* (1956); *Recitativo Dramático del Mensajero,* for bass (1957); *Oración de Jimena,* for soprano (1957); *Escena Lírica,* for soprano and tenor (1957); First symphony (1957); Violin concerto (1959); *Movimientos Contrastantes* (1964); *Atmósferas II* (1969-70); *Gris de la Noche* (1969-70); *Imágenes Cósmicas II* (1970); *Proagon,* for violin and strings (1970); *Sinfonía Apocalíptica,* for tape (1978-80); *Achtamar,* ballet (1979); *Narek,* for voice, chamber orch., and tape (1979); *Y la Luz Se Oirá,* for chamber orch. (1982); *Amores,* for various instruments, soloists, and ensembles (1984-87); *Buenos Aires, me Vas a Matar,* for piano, actors, and tape (1990); *Yagua-ya Yuca,* for percussion (1992); *Off the Edge,* for baritone, string orch., and tam-tam (1992-93). Chamber music; choruses; music for the theater; piano pieces; songs.
Sources: EMA, ISC, NGDWC

Teseo, René, Argentine composer; b.5 Jan 1926, Rio Cuarto, Prov. of Córdoba, Argentina. He graduated from the Music School of the Univ. of Litoral, Rosario, Prov. of Santa Fe, Argentina. In Buenos Aires, Argentina, he studied piano with Domingo Scarafia, Ruwin Erlich, Josefina Preli, and Moisés Makaroff, harmony, counterpoint, composition, and orchestration with Teodoro Fuchs, Jacobo Ficher, and Roberto Garcia Morillo. He taught music theory and harmony at

the D'Elía y Balmoral Music School of the Univ. of la Plata, Prov. of Buenos Aires, Argentina. Professor of music at the Coro Nacional de Niños. President of Juventudes Musicales de Argentina and the Asociación Argentina de Compositores.
Works (selective list): *El Ser,* cantata for mixed chorus and orch.; *Balada de la Placeta,* for baritone, children chorus, and orch.; *Obertura para una Quimera,* for orch.; *Suite para la Juventud,* for orch.; *Movimiento Sinfónico,* for orch.; *Movimiento de Tango,* for orch.; *Dos Tangos,* for string ensemble; chamber music; piano pieces; choral music; songs.
Source: ISC

Thibaud, Alfonso, Argentine pianist and composer of French origin; b.1861, Paris, France; d.1937, Buenos Aires, Argentina. He studied piano with Antoine Marmontel at the Paris Cons. He founded, the Thibaud-Piazzini Cons. in Buenos Aires in 1904, with Edmundo Piazzini.
Works: Suite for orch.; Sonata for violin and piano; String quartet in E major; *Ave Maria,* for organ, chorus, and orch.
Source: EMA

Thompson, Casildo, Argentine composer; b.1826, Buenos Aires, Argentina; d.1873, Buenos Aires.
Works: Music for voice and piano: El Tipógrafo, waltz (1862); *La Locomotiva* (1857); *Recuerdos del Campamento* (1865); *Las Ilusiones,* romance (1870); *Una Lágrima de Amor.*
Source: EMA

Tollis (Tolis) de la Roca, Matheo, Mexican composer and harpsichordist of Spanish origin?; b.c.1710, Spain?; d.between 5 and 18 Sep 1781, Mexico City, Mexico. He settled in Mexico City in 1756. In 1757, he was appointed assistant *maestro de capilla* (chapelmaster) and organist of the Mexico City Cathedral.
Works: 4 orch. masses; 3 requiems; 14 liturgical compositions accompanied by orch.
Bibl.: R. Stevenson, *Renaissance and Baroque Musical Sources in the Americas,* Washington, D.C., 1970.
Source: GDM

Tomás, Guillermo M., Cuban orch. and band conductor, musicologist, teacher, and composer; b.10 Oct 1868, Cienfuegos, Cuba; d.30 Oct 1933, Cienfuegos. He began music studies with his father, then in 1888, went to New York to continue his musical education and received a doctorate in music. In 1899, he returned to Cuba and founded the Aguado-Tomás Vocal Inst., and later the band of the National Police, which became the Municipal

Band of Havana. In 1903, he founded the O'Farrell School of Music which later became the Municipal Music School of Havana, and in 1908, he founded and directed the journal *Bellas Artes*. He created the Havana Symphony Orch. in 1910, and in 1911, he organized the Municipal Cons. of Music Félix Alpizar in Havana.

Works (selective list): *Sakuntala,* opera; *La Oración del Creyente,* cantata for tenor, chorus, and wind orch.; *Canto de Guerra,* for voices (1896); *Veilée de Fête,* symphonic poem; *Ronde Interrompue,* symphonic poem; *Escenas de un Ballet Imaginario,* for orch.; *Coral y Fuga,* for orch.; *Danzas Intimas,* for wind band; *Esbozos de mi Tierra,* for piano and orch.; piano pieces.
Sources: DMC, GDM

Toni, Olivier George, Brazilian composer and conductor; b.27 May 1926, Sâo Paulo, Brazil. He began his music education with piano and bassoon lessons, and later studied music theory, composition, and conducting with Martín Braunwieser, Hans Joachim Koellreutter, Camargo Guarnieri, and Mario Rossini. Founded several music groups and orch. in Sâo Paulo.
Works (selective list): *Preludios,* for chamber orch. (1946); *Anunciaçâo,* for voice and orch. (1959); *Três Variaçôes,* for orch. (1959); chamber music; choruses; piano pieces; songs.
Source: CTA19

Torrá, Celia, Argentine violinist and composer; b.18 Sep 1889, Concepción del Uruguay, Prov. of Entre Rios, Argentina; d.1962, Buenos Aires, Argentina. She studied harmony, counterpoint, fugue, and composition with Alberto Williams and Athos Palma in Buenos Aires, with Paul Le Flem, and Vincent d'Indy in Paris, France, and with Zoltan Kodaly in Budapest, Hungary. She also studied violin with Américo Montenegro and Andrés Gaos in Buenos Aires, with César Thompson in Brussels, Belgium, and with Jeno Hubay in Budapest. Artistic director of the *Asociación Sinfónica Femenina* and *Asociación Coral Argentina*.
Works (selective list): *Rapsodia Entrerriana,* for orch. (1931); *Suite Incaica,* for orch. (1938); *Himno a la Paz,* for chorus and orch.; *Atardecer,* for chorus and orch.; *El Arroyo,* for chorus and orch.; *Crepuscular,* for chorus and orch.; choral music; piano pieces; songs.
Sources: CA, DM, EMA, MLA, MMLA

Torre Bertucci, José, Argentine composer; b.8 Jul 1888, Buenos Aires, Argentina; d.1970, Buenos Aires. He studied with Alberto Williams and Eduardo Fornarini. Professor of counterpoint and acoustics at the National Cons. of Music Carlos López Buchardo of Buenos Aires.

Works: Sonata in C sharp minor for piano (1924); Suite in A for piano; *Choral in C minor,* for piano; *Choral in A minor,* for piano; *Duettino,* for violin and piano; *Tres Poemas (Soledad, Canción Ingenua,* and *El retorno),* for voice and piano. *Books: Tratado de Contrapunto,* Buenos Aires, 1947.
Sources: CA, DM, EMA, MLA, MMLA

Torrens Boqué, Eduardo, Argentine pianist and composer of Spanish origin; b.Tarragona,Spain; fl.second half of the 20th century. After an extensive tour through various American countries with violinist Agustín Robbio, he settled in Argentina in 1878. He performed at the *Sociedad del Cuarteto.*
Works: Operas: Gualterio (1883); *El Secreto* (1900); *Marangoré.* Piano pieces, including a fantasia on the Argentinian dance *El Cielito.*
Source: EMA

Torres, José de, Mexican composer; he lived at the beginning of the 18th century. Succesor to Manuel de Sumaya as *maestro de capilla* (chapelmaster) at the Cathedral of Mexico.
Works: Misa sobre los Ocho Tonos, for voices, violins, and double bass; *Letatus Sum,* for 5 voices, violins, oboes, French horns, double basses, and organ; *Magnificat,* for 8 voices, violins, and double bass.
Source: MMLA

Torres Santos, Raymond, Puerto Rican composer, pianist, arranger, and director for TV and movie industries in Hollywood; b.19 Jun 1958, Río Piedras, Puerto Rico. He began to study music with his father, Ramón Torres Olivo, and then continued at the Escuela Libre de Música with Jaime Meléndez. In 1976, he entered the Cons. of Music of Puerto Rico where he studied piano with Narciso Figueroa, and composition with Amaury Veray. In 1980, he settled in Los Angeles, California, and studied composition with Henry Lazarof and Paul Reale, conducting with Samuel Kralmanick, and film music with David Raskin at the Univ. of California at Los Angeles, where he received a Master's degree and a doctorate in music. In 1982, he studied at the Inst. of New Music in Darmstadt, Germany, with Brian Ferneyhough and Clarence Brown, and in 1985, he studied computer research in music and acoustics at Stanford Univ., Stanford, California. Assistant professor at the California State Univ. at San Bernardino. Professor at the Dept. of Music of the Univ. of Puerto Rico.
Works (selective list): *Ballets: Movements* (1980); *Monchín del Alma* (1988). *Orch.: Sinfonietta Concertante* (1980); *Esta Es Toda mi Historia: Sol, Avidez, Cansancio,* cantata for mixed chorus (1980); *Elegía de Reyes,* cantata for narrator, soloist, rondalla, and chamber orch. (1981); *Exploraciones,* for string orch. (1982); *La Canción de*

las Antillas; *Areytos*, symphonic picture (1986); *El País de Cuatro Pisos* (1988); *Danza* (1991). Chamber music; music for films; choral music; music for tape; piano pieces.
Sources: BB, CPR, ISC

Tort, César, Mexican composer; b.4 Sep 1929, Puebla, Mexico. He studied piano with Ramón Serratos in 1946 in Mexico, and composition with Conrado del Campo at the Cons. of Madrid, Spain, 1950-53. When he returned to Mexico, he became very involved in changing and organizing music education for children.
Works: Impresiones, for piano (1954); *El Orador*, for piano (1955); *Estirpes*, symphonic poem (1958); *La Espada*, cantata (1966); *El Piano Mágico*, for piano (1972).
Source: BB

Tosar Errecart, Héctor, Uruguayan composer, conductor, and pianist; b.18 Jul 1923, Montevideo, Uruguay. He studied piano with Guillermo Kolischer, harmony with José Tomás Mujica, and composition and instrumentation with Lamberto Baldi. In 1946, with a scholarship from the Guggenheim Foundation, he went to the USA and studied composition with Aaron Copland, and orch. conducting with Serge Koussevitzky. Later, on a scholarship awarded by the French government, he studied composition with Darius Milhaud and Jean Rivier at the Paris Cons., and composition with Arthur Honegger, and orch. conducting with Pierre Fournet and Eugène Bigot at the Ecole Normale de Musique of Paris, France. He taught at the Montevideo Cons. and the Montevideo Univ. In 1974, he was appointed chairman of the Composition Dept. of the Puerto Rico Cons.
Works (selective list): *Orch.:* 3 symphonies (1949, 1959, 1973); Concertino for piano (1941); *Oda a Artigas*, for speaker (1951); *Serie Sinfónica* (1952); *Salmo CII*, for soprano and mixed chorus (1955); Sinfonía concertante for piano (1957); *Te Deum*, for bass and mixed chorus (1960); *Recitativo y Variaciones* (1967). *Aves Errantes*, for baritone and 11 instruments (1964); chamber music; madrigals; sacred choruses; piano pieces; songs.
Sources: BB, BHMCU, CTA6, DCM, DM, GDM, MLA, MMLA, MU

Traversari, Pedro Pablo, Ecuadorian composer; b.28 Jul 1874, Quito, Ecuador; d.? He studied flute with Federico Lucares, cello and double bass with Giuseppe Marangoni, and harmony and composition with Federico Stöber at the National Cons. of Music of Santiago de Chile, Chile. Professor of voice at the National Inst., of music theory, solfeggio, and music history at the National Cons. of Music, and director of the Academia Musical, all in Santiago de Chile. Director of the Cons. Nacional de Música y Declamación of Quito, professor at the Academy of Fine Arts of Rio Bamba, Ecuador, and professor of musicology and folklore at the Univ. Central of Quito.

Works: *Melodramas: Cumandá o La Virgen de las Selvas; La Profecía de Huiracocha; Kizkiz o El Ultimo Exponente del Alma Incaica; Los Hijos del Sol; La Araucana. Glorias Andinas,* symphonic poem; *Meditación,* for orch.; dances; hymns. **Books:** *Tratado Práctico de Teoría General de la Música; Método Ilustrado de Caligrafía Musical; Sinopsis de las Relaciones de la Escala General Temperada; Historia General Ilustrada de la Música Indígena y Popular de los Paises Americanos; Tratado de Musicología; Tratado de Folklore Ecuatoriano.*
Sources: DM, MLA, MMLA

Trespuentes, José, Cuban teacher and composer of Spanish origin; b.1798, Logroño, Spain; d.1862, Havana, Cuba. In 1823, he settled in Havana to teach music, algebra, and geometry at the San Cristóbal School. Organist at the Cathedral of Havana. In 1844, he became director of the Music Dept. of the Liceo de Havana. Editor of the journal *Revista Musical.* In 1823 and 1842, he founded several music schools for the teaching of harmony, counterpoint, and composition.
Works (selective list): **Operas:** *Gonzalo de Córdoba*; *Le Baccanale di Roma*; *Stabat Mater;* Mass; chamber music; songs.
Source: DMC

Troiani, Cayetano, Argentine pianist, teacher, and composer of Italian origin; b.20 Oct 1873, Chieti, Italy; d.30 Sep, 1942, Buenos Aires, Argentina. He studied piano with Achille Simonetti, composition with Paolo Serrao, and harmony with Camillo De Nardis at the Royal Cons. of Naples, Italy. Codirector and later director of the Inst. Musical Santa Cecilia of Buenos Aires. Professor of harmony at the National Cons. of Music Carlos López Buchardo of Buenos Aires.
Works (selective list): *Scene Infantili,* suite for orch.; *Estilo y Cueca,* for string orch.; *Ettincelles,* 15 pieces for piano; *Rêves et Fantaisies,* 20 pieces for piano; *Evocaciones,* 3 pieces for piano; *Ritmos Argentinos,* 7 folkloric pieces for piano; *Motivos de la Sierra y la Llanura,* 12 folkloric pieces for piano; Overture for orch.
Sources: CA, DM, EMA, MLA

Tsilicas, Jorge, Argentine composer; b.16 Oct 1930, Buenos Aires, Argentina; d.Jan 1995, Buenos Aires. He studied harmony, counterpoint, fugue, instrumentation, and composition with Jacobo Ficher, and musical form with Enrique Belloc and Francisco Kröpfl. With a scholarship granted by the Italian government and the Fondo Nacional de las Artes of Argentina, he attended workshops with

Franco Donatoni at the Verdi Cons. in Milan, and with Boris Porena at the Santa Cecilia Academy in Rome, both in Italy. He taught courses on contemporary music at the Teatro General San Martín of Buenos Aires, organized by ISCM.

Works (selective list): *Tres Piezas,* for string orch. (1968); *Homenaje,* for narrator and orch. (1971); *Texturas,* for chamber orch. (1972); *De Thanatos a Eros,* for orch. (1974); *Serenata,* for guitar and string orch. (1977); *Microformas,* for chamber ensemble (1979); *Oda a Picasso,* for narrator and chamber ensemble (1985); *Secuencias Concertantes,* for guitar and orch. (1986); *Tres Poemas,* for voice and chamber ensemble (1987); *Latinoamericano,* for voice, chamber chorus, and instrumental ensemble (1991); chamber music; choruses; songs.

Source: ISC

Tuxen-Bang, Carlos, Argentine composer and pianist; b.24 May 1933, Santiago del Estero, Prov. of Santiago del Estero, Argentina. He started music studies at the Cons. Manuel Gómez Carrillo of Santiago del Estero. In 1950, he entered the National Cons. of Music Carlos López Buchardo of Buenos Aires, where he studied piano with Rafael González, counterpoint and orchestration with José Torre Bertucci and Floro Ugarte, and composition with Athos Palma and Alberto Ginastera. He graduated in 1953. In 1958, with a scholarship from the French government, he studied in Paris, France, with René Leibowitz, Eugène Bigot, and Olivier Messiaen. In 1955, he was appointed professor at the National Cons. of Music Carlos López Buchardo and substitute conductor at the Teatro Colón, both of Buenos Aires. In 1958, he settled in France where he worked as a piano accompanist.

Works: 2 string quartets (1951, 1958); *Tres Motetes,* for chorus a cappella (1951); *Balada Sinfónica,* for orch. (1952); *Variaciones Lauda Sion Salvatorem,* for piano (1952); Concerto for trumpet and strings (1955); *Coral, Interludio y Fuga,* for piano (1957); *Canciones de San Juan de la Cruz,* for chorus a cappella (1957); *Nocturnos,* for voice and piano (1957); *Variaciones,* for orch. (1959); *Quince Robaiyat de Omar Khayam,* for baritone and piano (1959-64); *Abyssus,* 4 pieces for orch. (1966).

Sources: CA, EMA

U

Ubeda, Friar Manuel, Uruguayan composer of Spanish origin; b.c.1760, Valencia, Spain; d.4 May 1823, Porongos, Uruguay. He went to Rio de Janeiro, Brazil, in 1800, and settled in Montevideo, Uruguay, in 1801.
Works: Misa para el Día de los Difuntos, for 4 voices and some instruments (1802).
Sources: BHMCU, MU

Ugarte, Floro M., Argentine composer; b.15 Sep 1884, Buenos Aires, Argentina; d.11 Jun 1975, Buenos Aires. He studied violin with Hércules Galvani, and harmony with Cayetano Troiani in Buenos Aires. Later studied harmony with Emil Pesard and Albert Lavignac, and counterpoint, composition, and instrumentation with Félix Fourdrain at the National Cons. of Paris, France. He returned to Argentina in 1913. Professor and director of the National Cons. of Music Carlos López Buchardo, at various times music director of the Teatro Colón, and director of the Municipal Cons. of Music Manuel de Falla, all of Buenos Aires. Also professor at the Escuela Superior de Bellas Artes of the Univ. of La Plata, Prov. of Buenos Aires, Argentina. President of the Sociedad Nacional de Música and member of the Comisión Nacional de Cultura.
Works (selective list): *Saika,* operatic fairy tale (1920); *El Junco,* ballet (1955). *Orch.: Paisaje de Estío* (1912); *Cortejo Chino* (1913); *Escenas Infantiles* (1915); *Entre las Montañas,* symphonic poem (1922); *De mi Tierra,* 2 symphonic suites (1923, 1934); *La Barca,* poem for voice and orch. (1925); *La Rebelión del Agua,* symphonic poem (1931); Symphony in A (1947); *Tango* (1951); Violin concerto (1964); chamber music; piano pieces; music for bandonion; songs.
Books: Manual de Armonía.
Sources: BB, CA, CTA1, DM, EMA, GDM, MLA, MMLA

Umaña Santamaría, Carlos, Colombian composer; b.1862, Bogotá, Colombia; d.1917, Bogotá. He began to study piano in Colombia, and completed his studies in Rome, Italy, where he was also ordained a priest at the Colegio Pío Latino. *Maestro de capilla* (chapelmaster) at the Cathedral of Bogotá.
Works: Himno Latino, for chorus, organ, and orch.; Mass; *Cuento Arabe,* for piano; *Estudios y Valses,* for piano.
Source: MMLA

Uribe Holguín, Guillermo, Colombian composer and violinist; b.17 Mar 1880, Bogotá, Colombia; d.26 Jun 1971, Bogotá. He studied violin with Ricardo Figueroa, harmony with Santos Cifuentes, and counterpoint with Augusto Azzali at the National Academy of Music of Bogotá. He also studied violin with Narciso Garay. In 1907, he went to Paris, France, where he studied violin with Armand Parent, and composition with Vincent d'Indy at the Schola Cantorum. Later he took violin lessons with César Thompson and Emile Chaumont in Brussels, Belgium. In 1910, he returned to Colombia and became director of the newly reorganized National Cons. of Bogotá, known previously as the National Academy of Music of Bogotá. He resigned in 1935, but was reappointed director in 1942, a position he held until 1947.

Works (selective list): *Stage: Furatena,* opera; *Prometheus Vinctus,* incidental music. *Orch.: Sinfonía del Terruño* (1924); *Tres Danzas* (1927); *Marcha Festiva* (1928); *Serenata* (1928); *Carnavalesca* (1929); *Cantares* (1929); *Villanesca* (1930); *Bajo su Ventana* (1930); *Suite Típica* (1932); *Concierto a la Manera Antigua,* for piano (1939); *Bochica* (1940); 11 symphonies (1910-1950); *Conquistadores* (1959); 2 violin concertos; Viola concerto. 10 string quartets; 2 piano trios; 7 violin sonatas; Cello sonata; Viola sonata; Piano quartet; 2 piano quintets; choruses; sacred works; songs. *Books: Vida de un Músico Colombiano,* Bogotá, 1941 (autobiography).
Bibl.: F.C. Lange, *Guillermo Uribe Holguín, Boletín Latino-Americano de Música,* Vol.4, Bogotá, 1938. L.A. Escobar, *El Maestro Guillermo Uribe Holguín: Un Precursor de la Música en Colombia, Lámpara,* Vol.4., 1957. G.G. Randón, *Maestros de la Música: Guillermo Uribe Holguín (1880-1971), Música,* Havana, 1971.
Sources: BB, CTA1, DM, GDM, MLA, MMLA

Urreta (Urrueta) Arroyo, Alicia, Mexican pianist, teacher, and composer; b.12 Oct 1935, Veracruz, Mexico; d.20 Dec 1987, Mexico City, Mexico. She studied piano with Joaquín Amparán, and harmony with Rodolfo Halffter in Mexico City, 1948-54. She also studied with Eduardo Hernández Moncada, León Mariscal, and Sandor Roth. She studied piano privately with Alfred Brendel and Alicia de Larrocha. Instructor in acoustics at the Inst. Politécnico Nacional of Mexico City.
Works (selective list): *Romance de Doña Balada,* radio opera (1972); *Canto, Homage to Falla,* for voice, actor, and dancers; *Tributo,* ballet; *De Natura Mortis,* for voice, instruments, and tape (1972); several scores of concrete music.
Sources: BB, NGDWC

Urrutia Blondel, Jorge, Chilean composer and musicologist; b.17 Sep 1905, La Serena, Chile; d.1981, Chile. He studied piano with Raúl Hügel, and composition with Pedro Humberto Allende and Domingo Santa Cruz in Chile. In 1928, he traveled to Europe where he studied with Charles Koechlin, Paul Dukas, and Nadia Boulanger in Paris, France, and with Paul Hindemith and Hans Mersmann in Berlin, Germany. When he returned to Chile, he was appointed professor of theory, harmony, and composition at the National Cons. of Chile in Santiago de Chile. Secretary and acting dean of the Facultad de Ciencias y Artes Musicales of the Univ. of Chile and research member of the Inst. de Investigaciones Musicales, both in Santiago de Chile.

Works (selective list): *La guitarra del Diablo,* ballet (1942), from which he extracted 2 symphonic suites; *Música para un Cuento de Antaño,* for orch. (1948); Piano concerto (1950); Piano trio (1933); Concertino, for harp and guitar (1943); String quartet (1944); Violin sonata (1954); choruses; piano pieces; songs.

Bibl.: V. Salas Viú, *La Creación Musical en Chile, 1900-1951,* Santiago, 1952.

Sources: BB, CTA14, DM, GDM, HMC, MLA, MMLA

Urteaga, Irma Graciela, Argentine composer and choral and orch. conductor; b.7 Mar 1929, San Nicolás, Prov. of Buenos Aires, Argentina. She started music studies in Paraná, Prov. of Entre Ríos, Argentina. Later she studied in Buenos Aires, Argentina, first at the National Cons. of Music Carlos López Buchardo with Roberto Caamaño, Valdo Sciamarella, Roberto García Morillo, Carlos Suffern, and Alicia Terzian, and then at the Inst. Superior de Arte del Teatro Colón of Buenos Aires with Jacobo Ficher, Enrique Sivieri, Jorge Fontenla, Carlos Malloyer, Isaac Weinstein, and Roberto Kinsky. She also studied piano with María L.M. de Gilardi, Josefa Hernandorena, and Jorge Fanelli, and harmony with Beatriz Hernandorena and Gilardo Gilardi. Professor at the National Cons. of Music Carlos López Buchardo and the Inst. Superior de Arte del Teatro Colón. Assistant conductor at the Teatro Colón from 1974 to 1977.

Works (selective list): *Ambitos,* for orch. (1970); *Paolo y Francesca,* for soprano, tenor, percussion, and chamber orch. (1971); *L'Inferno,* for mixed chorus and orch. (1971); *La Maldolida,* opera (1987); *El Mundo del Ser,* for mezzo-soprano and orch. (1989); chamber music; piano pieces; songs.

Sources: ISC, NGDWC, VMA

Urzúa, Armando, Chilean composer; b.1903, Curicó, Chile; d.1941, Panama City, Panama.

Works: Ave Maria, for chorus and string orch. (1931); *Motetes,* for mixed voices (1931-32); *Miniaturas,* for piano (1934).

Source: HMC

V

Vaggione, Horacio, Argentine composer; b.1940, Moldes, Prov. of Córdoba, Argentina. He studied at the Escuela de Artes of the National Univ. of Córdoba, Córdoba, Prov. of Córdoba. He received scholarships from the Inst. de Cultura Hispánica de Madrid, Spain, in 1964, and the US government in 1966. Founding member of the Centro de Música Experimental de la Escuela de Artes and director of its Laboratory of Electronic Music.
Works: *Música Electrónica I* (1960); Sonata for piano (1960); *Cantata,* electronic music (1961); *Cálimo 0,* for voices and piano (1962); *Hierro y Espacio,* electronic music (1963); *Diafonía,* for orch. (1963); *Secuencias,* for piano and 5 instruments (1963); *Música Ceremonial,* electronic music (1963); *Ananke,* electronic music (1963-64); *Cálimo I,* spatial music, instrumental, and electronic tape (1963-64); *Salmo,* electronic music (1964); *Espacios Transformables,* for any sound source (1964); *Proposiciones I,* for orch. (1964); Sonata II for piano and electronic sounds (1965); Sonata III for piano, flute, oboe, trumpet, and cello (1965); Sonata IV for piano and electronic sounds (1965); *Proposiciones II,* for string orch.; *Untitled,* musical theater, actions, and lights (1965); *Verticales I,* for 4 flutes, piano, and percussion (1965); *Verticales II,* for 4 flutes, mandolin, banjo, guitar, piano, and percussion (1965); *Faust,* incidental music for orch. and electronic tape (1966); *Sonata de Weston,* for nylon baloons (1966); *Piano Total,* for 4-hand piano (1966); *Cuatro Expresiones,* figurative graphics without sound (1966); *Tierra-Tierra,* electronic music (1966); *Tres Piezas Electrónicas* (1966); *Cálimo II,* electronic music (1966); *Pieza para el Osciloscopio,* film (1967); *Música para Cromoplásticos,* electronic music (1967); Suite for magnetic tape (1967); Sonata V for piano and string orch. (1967); *Electrata,* for life electronic sounds (1967); *Ceremonia para Dos Pianistas* (1967); *Página de Album,* score with pictures of any instrument (1967); Quartet for 4 cellos (1967-68); *Serenata,* for orch. (1968).
Source: EMA

Valcárcel, Edgar, Peruvian composer and pianist; b.4 Dec 1932, Puno, Peru. Nephew of Teodoro Valcárcel. He studied composition with Andrés Sas at the National Cons. of Lima, Peru, and with Donald Lybbert at Hunter College, New York. Later he went to Buenos Aires, Argentina, where he took composition lessons with Alberto Ginastera. He then studied with Olivier Messiaen in Paris, France, and with Riccardo Malipiero, Bruno Maderna, and Luigi Dallapiccola in Italy. He also joined the Electronic Music Center of Columbia-Princeton Univ., New York, and worked with Vladimir

Ussachevsky. Teacher of piano and harmony at the National Cons. of Lima.
Works (selective list): *Orch.*: Sinfonietta (1956); Concerto for clarinet and strings (1966); *Queña* (1965); *Aleaciones* (1967); Piano concerto (1968); *Checán II* (1970); *Ma'karabotasaq Hachana* (1971); *Sajra* (1974). *Chamber music:* 2 string quartets (1962, 1963); *Espectros I,* for flute, viola, and piano (1964); *Espectros II,* for French horn, cello, and piano (1968); *Dicotomías III,* for 12 instruments (1966); *Fisiones,* for 10 instruments (1967); *Hiwana Uru,* for 11 instruments (1967); Trio for amplified violin, trombone, and clarinet (1968); *Poema,* for amplified violin, voice, piano, and percussion (1969); *Checan I,* for 6 instruments (1969); *Checán III,* for 19 instruments (1971); *Montage 59,* for string quartet, clarinet, piano, and lights (1971); *Checán V,* for strings (1974). Music for piano; electronic works; various multimedia pieces with chorus, electronic sounds, and lights; choruses a cappella.
Sources: BB, CTA17, DCM, GDM

Valcárcel, Theodoro, Peruvian composer and pianist; b.17 Oct 1900, Puno, Peru; d.20 Mar 1942, Lima, Peru. Uncle of Edgar Valcárcel. He studied first with his mother. At age fourteen he was sent to Europe where he studied with Vincenzo Appiani and Schieppatti at the Cons. of Milan, Italy, and with Felipe Pedrell in Barcelona, Spain. In 1920, he settled in Lima, and in 1928, he was awarded a gold medal from the municipality of Lima for his studies of Peruvian folk music. Researcher and promoter of Peruvian folklore. In 1934, he was appointed director and conservator of musical folklore of Peru.
Works: *K'Antuta,* opera; *Suray-Surita,* singing ballet; *Ckori Kancha,* ballet; *Concierto Indio,* concerto for violin and orch. (1939); 2 symphonic suites (1939); *En las Ruinas del Templo del Sol,* symphonic poem (1940); *Tres Ensayos,* for an ensemble of native instruments; *Fiestas Andinas,* for piano; *Suite Autóctona,* for violin and piano; *30 Cantos de Alma Vernacular; 4 Canciones Incaicas; 25 Romances de Costa y Sierra Peruana; 180 Melodías del Folklore.*
Bibl.: R. Holzmann, *Catálogo de las Obras de Theodoro Valcárcel, Boletín Bibliográfico de la Universidad Nacional Mayor de San Marcos,* Vol.12, Lima, 1942. R. Holzmann, *Ensayo Analítico de la Obra Musical del Compositor Peruano Theodoro Valcárcel, Revista Eco Musical,* Buenos Aires, 1943.
Sources: ADBM, BB, DM, GDM, GMP, MLA, MMLA

Valderrama, Carlos, Peruvian composer and pianist; b.4 Sep 1887, Trujillo, Peru; d.1 Aug 1950, Lima, Peru. He studied piano with Ricardo Tejada, and composition with Daniel Hoyle in Trujillo. Later he received a degree in electrical engineering from Cornell Univ., New York, then he decided to devote himself to music and attended the Musical Inst. Frank Damrosch of New York, where he studied with Pietro Albini and Rudolph Ganz.

Works: *Inty Raymi (La Fiesta del Sol),* opera (1935); *In Memoriam,* symphonic poem; *La Campana de María Angola,* fantasia; *Los Funerales del Inca,* funeral march; many pieces on old Inca themes in a light popular vein.

Sources: BB, GMP, MLA, MMLA

Valdés, Gilberto, Cuban composer and conductor; b.21 May 1905, Matanzas, Cuba. He studied in Havana, Cuba, with Pedro Sanjuán. Guest conductor at the Havana Symphony Orch. and the CBS orch. in New York.

Works: *Danza de los Braceros (Estampas Coloniales),* for orch.; *Rumba Abierta,* for orch.; *Oggere,* for orch.; *Rapsodia de Pregones,* for orch.; *Liko Ta Tumbe,* for orch.

Source: DM

Valdés, Mario, Cuban composer and violinist; b.1901, Sagua la Grande, Cuba. He studied violin with Buenaventura Costa and Joaquín Molina in Cuba, and with Eduardo Trucco in New York.

Works: *Preludio Sinfónico;* String quartet; *Mirian,* Cuban capriccio; *Rapsodia Cubana,* for violin and piano.

Source: MMLA

Valdés, Marta, Cuban composer and guitarist; b.6 Jul 1934, Havana, Cuba. She studied harmony and composition with Harold Gramatges, Francisqueta Vallalta, and Leopoldina Nuñez. Vice president of the Sociedad Cubana de Compositores.

Works: Incidental music for several plays; many songs.

Source: IEW

Vale, Francisco, Brazilian composer; b.20 Mar 1869, Pôrto das Flores, Brazil; d.10 Oct 1906, Brazil. He studied in Paris, France, with César Franck.

Works: *Depois da Guerra,* symphonic poem; Suite for sextet; Octet minuet; Sonata in C minor for piano.

Source: MMLA

Valencia, Antonio María, Colombian composer and pianist; b.10 Nov 1902, Cali, Colombia; d.22 Jul 1952, Cali. He started his music studies with his father, Julio Valencia Belmonte, and then he entered the Cons. of Music of Bogotá, Colombia, where he took piano lessons with Alarcón. In 1923, he studied piano with Paul Braud, harmony with Leon Saint-Requier, counterpoint with Paul Le Flem, chamber music with Gabriel Pierné, orchestration with Manuel de Falla, and composition and orch. conducting with Vincent d'Indy at the Schola Cantorum in Paris, France. In 1930, he returned to Colombia and founded the Cali Cons. of Music, where he was director until his death. He also was director of the Cons. of Music of Bogotá.

Works (selective list): *Chirimia y Bambuco Sotareño,* for orch. (1942); *Egloga Incaica,* for flute, oboe, clarinet, and bassoon (1935); *Emociones Caucanas,* for piano, violin, and cello (1938); Requiem (1943); piano pieces; church music; choruses; songs.

Bibl.: A.P. Tovar, *Antonio María Valencia, Artista Integral,* Cali, 1958.

Sources: BB, CTA17, GDM, ZCCC

Valencia Courbis, Pedro, Chilean composer, pianist, and *maestro de capilla* (chapelmaster); b.6 Feb 1892, San Felipe, Prov. of Aconcagua, Chile; d.1961, Santiago de Chile, Chile. He started his music studies under Enrique Soro at the National Cons. of Chile, Santiago de Chile, and at the same time studied humanities and religion at the Seminario Pontificio of Santiago de Chile. After his ecclesiastic studies, he was ordained a priest. He then studied harmony and organ with Mattoni, Remigio Renzi, and Lorenzo Perosi, and Gregorian chant with Monsignor Rella and Giulio Bas in Rome, Italy, and later at the School for Sacred Music, Ratisbon, Germany, with Fran Xaver Haberl, Michael Haller, Josef Renner, and Peter Griesbacher. In 1916, he studied at the Schola Cantorum of Paris, France, under Vincent D'Indy. In 1921, he founded the Catholic Cons. of Santiago de Chile, and was its first director.

Works: *Colección Selecta de Cánticos Sagrados Populares; Pregiera Religiosa,* for soloist, chorus, and orch.; piano pieces; songs. *Books:* *La Música, su Origen, Base, y Elementos Constitutivos; Beethoven,* biography; *Lecciones de Cultura Musical.*

Source: MMLA

Valenti Costa, Pedro, Argentine composer and choral conductor; b.13 Nov 1905, Buenos Aires, Argentina; d.1975, Buenos Aires. He studied in Buenos Aires with Francisco Corbani, P. Tabanelli, Raúl Espoile, Julio Perceval, and Gilardo Gilardi. With a scholarship from the Comisión Nacional de Cultura in 1938, he went to Europe to further his studies in organ with Leonce de Saint Martin, in Gregorian chant with Amédée de Vallambrosa, and in orchestration with Roland Manuel. In Buenos Aires, he was conductor of the choirs of the National Cons. of Music Carlos López Buchardo, 1942-54, the Philharmonic Association, 1944-47, Asociación Wagneriana, 1944 -48, and the National Radio, 1954-55. Organist at the Church La

Piedad, 1930-37, and at the Basílica Nuestra Señora de la Merced, 1937-39, both in Buenos Aires. In 1940, he became associated with the Teatro Colón of Buenos Aires, as assistant conductor, director of the choir school, director of the opera school, artistic director, and general director. Professor at the Escuela de Bellas Artes of the National Univ. of La Plata, Prov. of Buenos Aires, Argentina, 1947-54.

Works (selective list): *Orch.: San Agustín*, oratorium for soloists and chorus; *Campo*, poem for tenor (1936); *Preludio y Fuga* in F minor (1937); *Coral y Fuga* in A minor (1937); *Misa de Gloria*, for organ and chorus (1939); *Estampas*, dyptic for strings (1949); *Canto Elegíaco, Psalm VI*, for baritone (1958); *Las Horas de Bómbolo*, symphonic suite (1959); *Movimiento Sinfónico* (1959). Choruses; chamber music; piano pieces; songs.
Sources: CA, DM, EMA

Valera, Roberto, Cuban composer; b.21 Dec 1938, Havana, Cuba. He studied at the Municipal Cons. of Havana (today Cons. Amadeo Roldán) with Leo Brouwer, José Ardévol, and Edgardo Martín. He graduated from the Univ. of Havana with a doctorate in pedagogy. In 1952, he went to Poland to study at the Escuela Superior de Música of Warsaw. When he returned to Cuba, he was appointed deputy director at the Cons. García Caturla in Havana. In 1968, he became professor of harmony and contemporary techniques at the National School for the Arts in Havana.
Works: Dances for symphony orch. and chamber ensembles; choral music including *Devenir, Conjuro, Jitanjafora.*
Source: DMC

Valle, Antonio, Mexican composer and violinist; b.1825, Mexico City, Mexico; d.1876, Mexico City. Brother of Octaviano Valle. He studied violin with Manuel Covarrubias, and harmony and composition with Cenobio Paniagua and Saberio Sanelli. He played the violin in several opera company orch.
Works (selective list): *Zarzuelas: Tribulaciones*; *De Ceuta a Marruecos*. *Religious compositions:* large and small masses; responses; motets; responsories; Te Deums; matins.
Bibl.: M.G. Revilla, *Obras*, Vol.I: *Biografías de Artistas*, Mexico, 1908.
Source: MMLA

Valle, Octaviano, Mexican composer. b.Mexico; d.Mexico; fl.in the 2nd. half of the 19th century. Brother of Antonio Valle. He studied music with Cenobio Paniagua.
Works: Clotilde de Cosenza, opera; *Fantasía*, for 2 pianos.

Bibl.: M.G. Revilla, *Obras,* Vol.I: *Biografías de Artistas,* Mexico, 1908.
Source: MMLA

Valle Riestra, José María, Peruvian composer; b.9 Nov 1859, Lima, Peru; d.25 Jan 1925, Lima. As a child, he studied in London, England, and from 1895 to 1897, he studied harmony, counterpoint, and orchestration with André Gédalge in Paris, France. Professor at the National Academy of Music in Lima.
Works (selective list): *Operas: Ollanta* (1900); *Las Rosas de Jamaica; Atahualpa. Misa de Requiem,* for chorus and orch. (1913); *En Oriente,* for orch.; *Elegía,* for string orch.; choruses a cappella; piano pieces; songs. *Books: Compendio de Teoría Musical.*
Bibl.: R. Barbacci, *Revista Musical Peruana,* Lima, 1940.
Sources: ADBM, BB, DM, MLA, MMLA

Vallejo, Oscar, Bolivian composer; b.1930, Potosí, Bolivia. He studied string instruments with José Sandi, and harmony and composition with Father José Díaz Gáinza in Potosí. He finished his musical education at the Academia de Bellas Artes of Potosí, where he conducted the chorus. He also conducted the orch. and chorus of the Univ. of Sucre, Bolivia. He created the *Sistema Décimo Tonal* (Tonal Decaphonic System) based on old pentatonic scales.
Works (selective list): *El Hijo Pródigo,* oratorium; 2 concertos for violin and orch.; 2 symphonies; preludes for piano; String trio; sonatas for various instruments; choral-symphonic works.
Source: CB

Varela, Marta Inés, Argentine composer, teacher, and pianist; b. first half of the 20th century, Rosario, Prov. of Santa Fe, Argentina. She studied piano with Antonio de Raco, chamber music with Simón Blech, and composition and orchestration with Virtú Maragno and Francisco Kröpfl. She graduated from the Escuela de Música de la Facultad de Humanidades y Artes of the National Univ. of Rosario with a degree of professor of harmony and composition. Director and professor at the same Escuela de Música.
Works: Sonata for piano; *Ensayo,* for percussion instruments; *Cuatro Piezas,* for piano; *Variaciones,* for clarinet, cello, and piano; *Fantasía,* for piano; *Los Nueve Monstruos,* cantata for soloists, chorus, orch., and percussion; *Proyecciones,* concertino for 2 pianos, orch., and percussion; songs.
Source: CAMR

Varela Borjas, Fernando, Honduran composer and double bass player; b.31 May 1895, Tegucigalpa, Honduras; d.? Self-taught in music theory and several instruments, including double bass. In 1912, he organized several orch. ensembles, and in 1914, his own named Rossini. Professor of solfeggio and school songs at the Escuela Normal de Varones in 1916. Conductor of the military band of San Pedro Sula, Mexico.

Works: *Himno a la Exposición Nacional,* written in 1921, for the celebration of the centenary of the Honduran independence; tangos; waltzes; hymns; school songs; fox-trots.
Source: MMLA

Vargas, Carlos Enrique, Costa Rican composer, teacher, and pianist; b.25 Jul 1919, San José, Costa Rica. He started music studies with his father, José Joaquín Vargas. He also studied science and literature at the Liceo de Costa Rica. In Rome, Italy, from 1938 to 1939, he studied piano with Carlo Zecchi, harmony and composition with Cesare Dobici, and organ and Gregorian chant with Rev. A. Santini at the Inst. Pontificio de Música Sacra and the Royal Cons. of Music Santa Cecilia. When he returned to Costa Rica, he devoted most of his time to teaching music and playing piano.

Works (selective list): Concerto for piano and orch. (1944); Symphony (1943); piano pieces; choruses; songs.
Source: MMLA

Vargas Candia, Teófilo, Bolivian composer and folklorist; b.3 Nov 1868, DM (1886, CB), Cochabamba, Bolivia; d.1961, Bolivia. Self-taught in music. Chorus master at the Cathedral of Cochabamba from 1892 to 1938.

Works: *Niño Dios,* mass for chorus and orch.; *La Coronilla,* symphonic overture; *El Huérfano; Suspiros; Idilio; Ecos del Litoral; Aires Nacionales de Bolivia,* a series of Bolivian folkloric songs (1940).
Sources: CB, DM, MLA

Vargas Wallis, Darwin Horacio, Chilean composer and choral conductor; b.8 Mar 1925, Talagante, Chile. He studied with Domingo Santa Cruz, Jorge Urrutia Blondel, and Juan Orrego Salas at the Cons. of Music of Santiago de Chile, Chile. Assistant conductor of the choir of the Catholic Univ. in Santiago de Chile. Music teacher at the Talagante Seminary, the González Academy in Santiago de Chile, the Naval School in Valparaiso, Chile, and the Catholic Univ. in Santiago de Chile.

Works (selective list): *Chamber Cantata,* for soloists and orch. (1954); *Obertura para los Tiempos de Adviento* (1958); *Cantos del Hombre,* for baritone and orch. (1959- 60); *Rapsodia para Días de*

Duelo y Esperanza, for guitar and orch. (1961-62); *Responso para un Músico,* for soloists, chorus, and orch. (1965); *Meditation,* symphony (1965); chamber music; religious compositions; piano pieces; choral music; songs.
Sources: CTA17, GDM, HMC

Vásquez Cano, José Francisco, Mexican conductor and composer; b.4 Oct 1895, Guadalajara, State of Jalisco, Mexico; d.20 Dec 1961, Mexico City, Mexico. He studied piano with Ignacio and César del Castillo, cello with Horacio Avila, and composition with Rafael J. Tello and Julián Carrillo at the National Cons. of Music in Mexico City. Director of the Univ. Radio. Professor at the National Cons. of Music and the Faculty of Music of the National Univ. in Mexico City, where he also was the conductor of the symphony orch.
Works (selective list): *Operas: Los Mineros; El Mandarín; El Rajah; Citlali; Ultimo Sueño; Nuñez de Balboa. Tríptico Sinfónico; Misa de Requiem*; 3 symphonies; 4 piano concertos; Violin concerto; 2 symphonic poems; chamber music; piano pieces; songs.
Sources: DM, GMM, MLA, MMLA

Vázquez, Carlos, Puerto Rican composer; b.9 Mar 1952, Mayagüez, Puerto Rico. He studied music at the Univ. of Puerto Rico and obtained a Master's degree in composition from the Univ. of Pittsburgh, Pennsylvania. He also studied at New York Univ. and the Sorbonne Univ. in Paris, France. He studied composition with Rafael Aponte Ledée, Frank McCarty, and Bruce Saylor. Professor at the Music Dept. and director of the Laboratory of Electroacoustic Music of the Univ. of Puerto Rico. Founding member and first president of the Asociación Nacional de Compositores of Puerto Rico.
Works (selective list): *Flamboyán,* for orch. (1982); *Brisas del Caribe,* symphonic suite (1986); *Ecua-Jey,* concerto for piano and orch. (1986); chamber music; electronic music; piano pieces; music for solo instruments; songs.
Source: CPR

Vázquez Grille, Isidoro, Chilean lawyer and composer; b.21 Jun 1864, Talca, Chile; d.18 Sep 1926, Santiago de Chile, Chile. He graduated from law school in 1887.
Works: Don Cleto, zarzuela.
Source: HMC

Veerhoff, Carlos, Argentine composer; b.3 Jun 1926, Buenos Aires, Argentina. He studied with Hermann Grabner, 1943-44, and Boris Blacher, 1952, at the Hochschule für Musik in Berlin, Germany. He taught in the city of Tucumán, Prov. of Tucumán, Argentina. He moved to Germany permanently in 1951, was assistant to Ferenc Fricsay in Berlin, 1951-52, and then settled in Munich. *Works* (selective list): *Operas: Targusis* (1958); *Die Goldene Maske* (1968); *Der Grune* (1972); *Es Gibt doch Zebrastreifen* (1972). *Ballets: Pavane Royale* (1953); *El Porquerizo del Rey* (1963). *Prólogo Sinfónico,* for orch. (1951); *Symphonic Movement* (1952); 4 symphonies (1953, 1956, 1966, 1974); *Mirages,* for orch. (1961); *Gesänge auf dem Wege,* for baritone and orch. (1964); *Akróasis,* for 24 wind instruments and percussion (1966); *Ut Omnes Unum Sint,* chamber cantata (1967); *Textur,* for string orch. (1969); *Sinotrauc,* for orch. (1973); *Torso,* for orch. (1974); chamber music. *Sources:* BB, EMA

Vega, Augusto, Dominican composer; b.10 Oct 1885, Puerto Plata, Dominican Republic; d.? He studied in Mérida, Mexico, with José María Rodríguez Arresón, and later with Arturo Cosgaya y Caballero. *Works: Indígena,* opera; *Folklore Sinfónico,* orch. suite; *Duarte,* overture. *Source:* DM

Vega, Aurelio de la, Cuban composer; b.28 Nov 1925, Havana, Cuba. He studied law at the Univ. of Havana, and music with Frederick Kramer, 1942-46. In 1947, he went to the USA and took composition lessons with Ernest Toch. Returning to Cuba, he studied composition with Harold Gramatges at the Inst. Musical Ada Iglesias in Havana, 1950-55, and was appointed dean of the Music School of the Univ. of Oriente in Santiago de Cuba, Cuba, 1953-59. In 1959, he settled in California and taught at the San Fernando Valley State College. As the distinguished professor of music, he served as the director of the Electronic Music Studio and composer-in-residence at the California State Univ. at Northridge. *Works* (selective list): *Débora y Traulio,* ballet (1951). *Orch.: Obertura a una Farsa Seria* (1950); *Introducción y Episodio* (1952); *Elegía,* for strings (1954); *Divertimento,* for violin, cello, piano, and strings (1956); *Cantata,* for 2 sopranos, contralto, and 21 instruments (1958); *Sinfonía en 4 Partes* (1961); *Analigus* (1966); *Intrata* (1972); *Adiós* (1978). *Structures,* for piano and string quartet (1962); *Coordinates,* for magnetic tape (1963); *Olep ed Arudamot,* in different versions (1974); *Septicilium,* for clarinet and instrumental ensemble (1975); *Inflorescence,* for soprano, bass clarinet, and tape (1976); *The Infinite Square,* for any combination of any instruments and/or voices (1977); *Undici Colori,* for bassoon, stamping right foot, and slide projections (1981); *Galandiacoa,* for clarinet and guitar (1982); chamber music; piano pieces; songs. *Books: Arnold Schoenberg and the Atonalists,* Havana, 1947; *The Negative Emotion,* Havana, 1950; *The New Romanticism,* Havana, 1951.

Bibl.: J.R. Schortt, *Aurelio de la Vega, un Compositor de las Américas, Revista Musical Chilena,* 1963.
Sources: BB, CTA7, DCM, GDM

Vega Caso, Rafael, Cuban composer and teacher; b.1901, Gibara, Cuba. He studied in Madrid, Spain, with Conrado del Campo.
Works: Symphonic poems; Cantata; Cuban traditional music.
Source: DMC

Vega Matus, Alejandro, Nicaraguan composer and orch. conductor; b.17 Aug 1875, Masaya, Nicaragua; d.26 Nov 1937, Masaya. He started music studies with Don Carmen in Nicaragua, and continued them in Guatemala under Giovanni Aberle, with whom he studied harmony, counterpoint, and fugue. When he returned to Nicaragua, he founded his own orch., which he conducted until his death.
Works (selective list): *Fuga;* 4 symphonic poems; 2 string quintets; 3 operettas; 10 zarzuelas; 5 overtures; 107 funeral marches; 9 intermezzos; religious music; waltzes; marches; songs.
Source: MMLA

Velasco Llanos, Santiago, Colombian composer; b.28 Jan 1915, Cali, Colombia. He studied with Antonio María Valencia in Cali, and later with Domingo Santa Cruz and Pedro Humberto Allende in Santiago de Chile, Chile. Director of the Cali Cons.
Works (selective list): *Sinfonía Breve* (1947); *Sinfonietta* (1966); *Bambuco Jocoso,* for orch. (1967); 2 string quartets; piano pieces; choruses; songs.
Source: BB

Velasco Maidana, José María, Bolivian composer and conductor; b.4 Jul 1899, BB (1901, GDM), Sucre, Bolivia. He studied in Buenos Aires, Argentina, with José María Vásquez and Domingo García Silva at the Cons. Fontova. Founder of the National Symphony Orch. of Bolivia, which he conducted for several seasons. Professor at the National Cons. of Music in La Paz, Bolivia.
Works (selective list): *Amerindia,* ballet (1938); *Incario,* ballet (1938); *Los Mineros,* ballet (1942); *Cuento Brujo,* symphonic poem (1935); *Los Khuzillos,* symphonic poem (1936); *Danza del Viento,* symphonic poem (1936); *Los Hijos del Sol,* symphonic overture (1938); *Estampas de mi Tierra,* symphonic suite (1939); *Vida de Cóndores,* for orch. (1942); *Los Huacos,* for orch. (1942); *Altiplano,* symphonic poem (1942); chamber music; choruses; songs.
Sources: BB, CTA11, DM, GDM, MLA, MMLA

Velásquez, Glauco, Brazilian composer of Italian origin; b.23 Mar 1884, Naples, Italy; d.21 Jun 1913, Rio de Janeiro, Brazil. He began studying music in Italy, and in 1892, at the age of eight, he moved to Brazil where he studied harmony with Federico Nascimento, and counterpoint with Francisco Braga, at the Inst. Profesional Masculino of Rio de Janeiro.
Works: *Soeur Beatrix,* unfinished opera; 4 trios; String quartet; Sonata for violin and piano; chamber music; piano pieces; songs.
Sources: GDM, HMB, MLA, MMLA

Velásquez (Velásques, Velázquez), José Francisco, Venezuelan composer; he lived and was active at the beginning of the 19th century. He held positions in various churches in Caracas, Venezuela.
Works: Tonos; Stabat Mater; Oficio de Difuntos; 4 masses; *Te Deum; Salve*; 3 Lamentations; several graduals and offertories.
Sources: GDM, MLA, MMLA

Velázquez, Father José Guadalupe, Mexican religious composer and *maestro de capilla* (chapelmaster); b.12 Dec 1856, Pueblito, Querétaro, Mexico; d.18 Feb 1920, Mexico City, Mexico. He followed an ecclesiastic career at the Colegio Apostólico de la Santa Cruz and the Seminario Conciliar, both in Querétaro; he was ordained a priest in 1886. He then went to Europe to specialize in ecclesiastic music, which he studied at the School of Sacred Music in Ratisbon, Germany. When he returned to Mexico, he became director of the School of Sacred Music of Querétaro in 1890. In Mexico City, he taught at the Seminario Colegial and at the National Cons. of Music, and also was *maestro de capilla* (chapelmaster) at several churches.
Works: Religious music.
Bibl.: Presb. E. de la Isla, *El Padre J. Guadalupe Velázquez, Revista Musical Mexicana, Mexico,* February 21, 1942.
Source: MMLA

Velázquez, Higinio, Mexican violinist and composer; b.11 Jan 1926, Guadalajara, Mexico. He studied composition with Bernal Jiménez and Rodolfo Halffter. Violinist at the National Symphony Orch. in Mexico City, Mexico. In 1969, he joined the string quartet of the National Inst. of Fine Arts in Mexico City.
Works: Vivencias, for orch. (1958); *Cacique,* overture (1958); *Juárez,* brief symphony (1961); *Revolución,* symphonic poem (1963); *Elegía,* for oboe and piano (1969); *Estructuras,* for piano (1969); Sonatina for cello (1970); String quartet (1970); *Andante Atonal,* for strings (1971).
Source: BB

Velázquez, Leonardo, Mexican composer; b.6 Nov 1935, Oaxaca, Mexico. He studied at the National Cons. of Mexico, Mexico City. *Works: Cuauhtémoc,* for wind orch.; orch. compositions.
Source: KTL

Veloz, Julián, Argentine pianist, organist, and composer; b.unknown date and place of birth; d.1868, Argentina. He studied with Juan Pedro Esnaola.
Works: Songs: El Deseo, published in *El Cancionero Argentino* of 1838; *El Desconsuelo; Mi Sueño; La Súplica Zilia.* Piano pieces.
Source: EMA

Veray, Amaury, Puerto Rican composer; b.14 Jun 1922, Yauco, Puerto Rico. He began his musical studies with Olimpia Morel Campos, and later he studied piano with Emilio Baco Pasarell. He graduated from the Univ. of Puerto Rico and the New England Cons. of Music, Boston, Massachusetts. He continued postgraduate studies at the Accademia di Santa Cecilia in Rome, Italy, under Ildebrando Pizzetti, and at the Manhattan School of Music in New York City. Director of the Dept. of Theory and Composition and professor at the Cons. of Music of Puerto Rico. Musical adviser for the Puerto Rican Inst. of Culture. Member of the Academy of Arts and Sciences of Puerto Rico.
Works (selective list): *Film music for orch.: El Puente,* (1953); *Doña Julia,* (1954); *El de los Cabos Blancos,* (1955); *La Sombra de una Huella,* (1982). *La Encantada,* ballet (1958); *Canto a Fili-Mele,* for orch. (1959); *Cuando las Mujeres...,.*scenes of ballet for orch. (1964); *Fantasía para Orquesta* (1965); *Jolgorio en la Jacana,* estampas yaucanas, for orch. (1965); *Oda Seráfica a San Francisco de Asís,* for orch. (1972); *Díptico,* for 17 percussion instruments and piano (1973); chamber music; incidental music for the stage; piano pieces; songs.
Source: CPR

Verneuil, Raoul de, Peruvian composer; b.9 Apr 1899, Lima, Peru; d.? He studied with Father Villalba Muñoz, furthering his studies in Paris, France, with André Bloch and Henri Dallier. He lived in Paris and Madrid, Spain, for many years. In 1940, he returned to Lima.
Works: Las Llamas, ballet (1936); Quartet (1930); Trio; Wind quintet; *Danza Peruana,* for orch.; *Inca Legend,* for voice and 8 instruments; *Ritmos del Sol,* for 12-part chorus; piano pieces.
Sources: BB, DM

Vianna (Viana), Fructuoso (Frutuoso) de Lima, Brazilian composer and pianist; b.6 Oct 1896, BB (6 Sep 1896, GDM), Itajubá, Minas Gerais, Brazil; d.22 Apr, 1976, Rio de Janeiro, Brazil. He studied music first with his father, and in 1912, he began to study piano with Henrique Oswald, and harmony and composition with Agnelo França and Arnaud de Gouveia. In 1923, he went to Europe where he continued studying piano with Hanschild in Berlin, Germany, Arthur de Greef in Brussels, Belgium, and Blanche Selva in Paris, France. He also studied the Dalcroze method of eurhythmics. When he returned to Brazil, he was appointed professor at the Belo Horizonte Cons. and the Sâo Paulo Cons., both in Brazil, and director of the *Coral Paulistano* of the Sâo Paulo Cons. Professor of choral singing at the National Technical School, and of piano at Bennet College, both in Rio de Janeiro.
Works (selective list): *Music for piano: Serenata Espanhola* (1923); *Variaçôes sôbre un Tema Popular* (1923); *Dança dos Negros* (1924); *Sete Miniaturas* (1924); *Acalanto* (1924); *Valsas* (waltzes with Brazilian flavor); *Toadas* (melodic romances); *Tanguinhos* (little Brazilian tangos). Chamber music; choruses; songs.
Sources: BB, CTA4, DM, GDM, MLA, MMLA

Vidal, Pedro, Argentine composer, teacher, and violinist of Spanish origin; b.1893, Spain; d.1971, Rosario, Prov. of Santa Fe, Argentina. He studied at the Escuela Municipal of Barcelona, Spain, and at the Royal Cons. of Brussels, Belgium. He settled in Rosario in 1914. Inspector of music at the Prov. of Santa Fe education system.
Works: Gran Misa; Canción de Cuna; music for violin and piano.
Source: CAMR

Vidal Pacheco, Gonzalo, Colombian composer; b.23 Nov 1863, Popayán, Colombia; d.? Self-taught in music. Professor at the School of Music Santa Cecilia, Medellín, Colombia. In 1901, he founded the journal *Revista Musical.*
Works (selective list): *Missa pro Defunctis,* in memory of his daughter María. *Music for piano:* Sonata in E minor; Sonata in E major; *Suite: Preludio Fugado, Romanza sin Palabras, Serenata, Soliloquio, Miniatura, Súplica de Amor,* and *Ensoñación.*
Source: MMLA

Vidaurreta, José Luis, Cuban musicologist and composer; b.25 May 1912, Havana, Cuba. He studied violin and viola with Fernando Gómez Aday, and composition, music aesthetics, and conducting with Fernando Carnicer at the Municipal School of Music and the Cons. Carnicer, both of Havana. Professor of theory, solfeggio, harmony, and composition at the Municipal School of Music and the

National Cons. of Music, both of Havana. Associate conductor of the Havana Symphony Orch. Since 1940, full member of the National Academy of Arts and Literature.

Works (selective list): *Preludio y Fuga,* for orch.; *Plenitud del Héroe,* symphonic poem; *Música,* for string orch.; *Boceto Sinfónico,* for orch.; *Veni Domine,* for male chorus and orch.; *Tres Contrapuntos,* essays of atonalism and polytonalism; *Amor,* incidental music; *Himno.* Chamber music; songs. *Books: El Compositor y el Pianista Nicolás Ruíz Espadero; Ensayo sobre la Música Cubana; Música Popular del Continente; Panorama de la Cultura Musical Cubana.*
Sources: DM, MMLA

Vieira Brandâo, José, Brazilian composer, pianist, and choral conductor; b.26 Sep 1911, Cambuquira, Minas Gerais, Brazil. In 1924, he entered the National Inst. of Music of Rio de Janeiro where he studied with Paulo Silva and furthered his piano studies with Marguérite Long in 1932. In 1933, he finished a course on *Canto Orfeónico* (male singing ensemble) and founded *Madrigal Vox,* a chorus ensemble that he conducted for ten years. Professor at the National Cons. of *Canto Orfeónico* and professor of piano at the National School of Music, both in Rio de Janeiro. Artistic adviser at the Secretary of Education and Culture of Rio de Janeiro.
Works (selective list): *Máscaras,* opera (1956-59); 2 string quartets (1944, 1960); Piano trio (1962-63); Wind quintet (1968); chamber music; songs.
Sources: HMB, MMLA

Vila, Cirilo, Chilean pianist and composer; b.1937, Santiago de Chile, Chile. He studied composition at the National Cons. of Music of Santiago de Chile with Alfonso Letelier and Gustavo Becerra, and later he continued studying in France.
Works: Sonata for piano; *Cantata de Cámara*; *Fantasía,* for piano; *Secuencia,* for string quartet; *Tres Canciones Corales.*
Source: HMC

Villalba Muñoz, Alberto, Argentine pianist, organist, choral conductor, and composer of Spanish origin; b.10 Nov 1878, Valladolid, Spain; d.? He studied piano and voice with his father, Alvaro Villalba, and harmony and composition with Felipe Pedrell in Spain. Conductor of the Symphony Orch. of Lima, Peru. Professor of music at the Colegio Nacional San Luis in Tarija, Bolivia. Director of the Cons. Clementi in the city of Jujuy, Prov. of Jujuy, Argentina.
Works: *Misa de Requiem,* for chorus and organ; *Yaraví,* for chorus ; *Los Andes,* symphonic poem. **Music for piano:** *Seis Caprichos; Inspiradas; El Poema del Sol; La Leyenda del Zorro del Río Xingu; Scherzetto.*

Sources: DM, MLA, MMLA

Villa-Lobos, Heitor, Brazilian composer; b.5 Mar 1887, Rio de Janeiro, Brazil; d.17 Nov 1959, Rio de Janeiro. Studied cello with his father, Raúl Villa-Lobos, and later with Benno Niederberger. In 1907, he entered the National Inst. of Music in Rio de Janeiro, where he studied with Frederico Nascimento, Agnelo França, and Francisco Braga. He was active in music education in Sâo Paulo, Brazil, and Rio de Janeiro. In 1942, he founded a cons. under the auspices of the Ministry of Education, and introduced many important innovations into the national program in music education, with emphasis on the cultural resources of Brazil. In 1945, he established the Brazilian Academy of Music in Rio de Janeiro, and was its president until his death.
Works (selective list): *Operas: Izaht* (1912-14); *Magdalena* (1947); *Yerma* (1953-56); *A Menina das Nuvens* (1957-58). *Ballets: Uirapuru* (1917); *Possessâo* (1929); *Pedra Bonita* (1933); *Dança da Terra* (1939); *Rudá* (1951); *Génesis* (1954); *Emperor Jones* (1955). *Orch.*: 12 symphonies (1916-57); *Dansas Africanas* (1914); 2 cello concertos (1915, 1953); 2 sinfoniettas (1916, 1947); *Amazonas* (1917); *Fantasy of Mixed Movements,* for violin (1922); *Momoprecoce,* for piano (1929); *Caixinha de Boâs Festas* (1932); *Ciranda das Sete Notes,* for bassoon and string orch. (1933); 3 suites entitled *Descobrimento do Brasil* (1937); *The New York Skyline* (1939); *Rudepoema* (1942); *Madona,* tone poem (1945); 5 piano concertos (1945-54); *Fantasía,* for cello (1945); *Fantasía,* for soprano, saxophone, two horns, and string orch. (1948); *Erosion, or The Origin of the Amazon River* (1951); Guitar concerto (1951); Harp concerto (1953); *Odyssey of a Race,* symphonic poem (1953); *Dawn in a Tropical Forest* (1953); Harmonica concerto (1955); *Izi,* symphonic poem (1957). 9 bachianas brasileiras (1932-44); 15 chôros (1920-29); 18 symphonic poems; 16 string quartets; chamber music; choruses; piano pieces; songs. He composed a total of 727 works.
Bibl.: F.C. Lange, *Villa-Lobos, un Pedagogo Creador, Boletín Latino-Americano de Música,* Vol.1, 1935. A. Muricy, *Villa-Lobos, Bulletin of the Pan American Union,* 1945. C. Sprague Smith, *H. Villa-Lobos (1889-1959), Inter-American Musical Bulletin,* 1960. J. Orrego Salas, *Heitor Villa-Lobos: Man, Work, and Style, Inter-American Musical Bulletin,* 1966.
Sources: BB, CTA3, DCM, DM, GDM, HMB, MLA, MMLA

Villalpando, Alberto, Bolivian composer; b.21 Nov 1940, La Paz, Bolivia. He started music studies with Santiago Velázquez and Rev. José Díaz Gáinza. In 1957, he went to Buenos Aires, Argentina, to study at the National Cons. of Music Carlos López Buchardo with

Abraham Jurafsky, Ricardo Rodríguez, Roberto Castro, and Roberto García Morillo. In 1963, he obtained a scholarship from the Inst. Di Tella of Buenos Aires where he studied with Alberto Ginastera, Aaron Copland, Riccardo Malipiero, José Vicente Asuar, Bruno Maderna, Olivier Messiaen, and Luigi Dallapiccola. When he returned to Bolivia, he was appointed national director of music at the Ministry of Culture and Education until 1973. Professor at the Bolivian Catholic Univ. and the National Cons. of Music, both of La Paz.
Works (selective list): *Cuatro Juegos Fantásticos,* for clarinet, cello, piano, and percussion; String quartet; *Cantata Solar,* for soloists, chorus, and chamber orch. (1964); *Liturgias Fantásticas,* for piano and orch.; *Concertino Semplice,* for flute and orch. (1965); *Del Amor, del Miedo y del Silencio,* for piano and chamber orch. (1967); *Danzas para una Imagen Perdida,* ballet (1970).
Sources: CB, DCM, GDM

Villalpando, Fernando, Mexican composer and violinist; b.30 May 1844, Zacatecas, Mexico; d.21 Dec 1902, Zacatecas. Conductor of the bands of Zacatecas and Aguascalientes, Mexico.
Works (selective list): *México,* overture for orch.; several masses; marches; dances; mazurkas.
Source: MMLA

Villanueva, Cecilia, Argentine composer and pianist; b.4 Sep 1964, La Plata, Prov. of Buenos Aires, Argentina. She studied piano with Leticia Corral and Elizabeth Westerkamp, and composition with Mariano Etkin at the Facultad de Bellas Artes of the Univ. of La Plata, Prov. of Buenos Aires, Argentina. Teacher at the Dept. of Instrumentation and Orchestration of the Facultad de Bellas Artes of the Univ. of La Plata.
Works (selective list): *Erosiones,* for orch. (1987-88); *Birlibirloque,* for flute, clarinet, trumpet, trombone, piano, 2 violins, viola, cello, and double bass (1988); *Escenario,* for piano and orch. (1989); *Música Descalza,* for flute, oboe, clarinet, percussion, piano, violin, viola, and cello (1989); chamber music.
Source: ISC

Villanueva Galeano, Ignacio, Honduran composer; b.1 Feb 1885, Esperanza, Dept. of Intibucá, Honduras; d.? He studied solfeggio and music theory with Ladislao López, and clarinet with Camilo Rivera at the Escuela de Música of his native town. In 1907, he was appointed conductor of the Military Band of Valladolid, today Comayagua, Honduras, and later he occupied a similar position in military bands of other towns in Honduras, El Salvador, and Bolivia.

Works (selective list): *La Isla del Tigre,* overture for orch.; *Primer Centenario,* symphonic poem; concert waltzes; marches; polkas; tangos; gavottes; intermezzos; capriccios.
Sources: MLA, MMLA

Villanueva Gutiérrez, Felipe, Mexican pianist and composer; b.5 Feb 1862, Santa Cruz Tecamac, Mexico; d.28 May 1893, Mexico City, Mexico. He started to study violin with his brother, Luis, and piano with his cousin, Carmen Villanueva, and later went to Mexico City, where he studied piano at the National Cons. of Music, and privately with Antonio Valle and Julio Ituarte. He was self-taught in composition. Professor of piano and music at various schools. In 1887, he founded a Musical Inst. with other Mexican composers, Ricardo Castro, Gustavo E. Campa, and Juan Hernández Acevedo, and in 1892, together with Gustavo E. Campa and Carlos J. Meneses, he founded the *Sociedad Anónima de Conciertos.*
Works (selective list): *Keofar,* comic opera; *La Casa de Locos,* zarzuela. **Dances:** *Seis Danzas Humorísticas; Cupido; Venus; La Pedrada.* **Waltzes:** *Vals Poético; Idolina.* Mazurkas; nocturnes. He created the *danza mexicana,* based on the contradanza habanera of Manuel Saumell and Ignacio Cervantes.
Sources: DM, GMM, MMLA

Villarini, Awilda, Puerto Rican composer, pianist, and musicologist; b.6 Feb 1940, Patillas, Puerto Rico. She was the first known Puerto Rican woman to write a work for orch.
Works (selective list): Concerto for piano and orch.; *La Muerte no Entrará en Palacio,* incidental music; *Plena,* for orch.; chamber music; piano pieces.
Source: CPR

Villate, Gaspar, Cuban composer; b.27 Jan 1851, Havana, Cuba; d.9 Oct 1891, Paris, France. He studied in Cuba with Nicolás Ruiz Espadero. In 1868, he moved to the USA, and from there he went to Paris, where he studied with François E.J. Bazin, Adolphe L. Danhauser, and Victorin de Joncières at the Paris Cons.
Works: **Operas:** *Angelo, Tirano de Padua* (1867); *Las Primeras Armas de Richelieu* (1871); *Zilia* (1877); *La Czarine* (1879); *Baltazar* (1885); *Cristóforo Colombo* (1884-86); *Lucifer* (1887-89). *Marche des Petites Pompiers,* for orch. (1878); *Contradanzas,* for piano (1873); Eight waltzes for piano; *Soirées Cubaines,* for piano; *Adiós a Cuba,* for piano (1876); *Serenade Havanaise* (1876), for soprano y piano; *Misa Solemne,* for soloists, chorus, and orch.; *Serenata Cubana,* for orch.

Bibl.: O. Martínez, *Program of the Philharmonic Orchestra of Havana,* 10 February, 1946. A. Carpentier, *La Música en Cuba,* Mexico City, 1946.
Sources: DM, GDM, MMLA

Villena, Federico, Venezuelan composer, *maestro de capilla* (chapelmaster), organist, and conductor; b.May 1835, Turmero, Venezuela; d.1900, Venezuela. Self-taught in music. *Maestro de capilla* (chapelmaster) at the Turmero Church, and in 1865, he settled in Ciudad Bolívar, and was appointed *maestro de capilla* (chapelmaster) and organist at the Cathedral, conductor of the military band, and professor at the Music School.
Works (selective list): *Ave Maria,* for 3 voices and instrumental sextet; *Misa in E flat,* for soprano, contralto, tenor, bass, chorus, and orch.; zarzuelas; hymns; romances; overtures; misas de requiem; fantasias for violin; elegies for cello; songs.
Source: MMLA

Viloni, José, Argentine composer of Italian origin; b.4 Sep 1895, Catanzaro, Italy; d.? He settled in Argentina and studied in Buenos Aires, violin with Darío Grassi, and harmony and composition with Gilardo Gilardi. President of the Asociación Coral Bonaerense, Prov. of Buenos Aires, Argentina.
Works (selective list): *Preludio y Danza,* for orch.; *Soledad en la Puna,* for orch.; *Fiesta en la Pampa,* for orch.; *Serie Argentina,* for strings. *Music for violin and piano: Moto Perpetuo* (1926); *Gitana* (1927); *Orientale* (1931); *Andante religioso* (1931). Piano pieces; songs. *Books: Moderna Teoría de la Música,* Buenos Aires, 1925.
Source: DM

Vincenti, Benedetto de, Bolivian composer of Italian origin.
Works: Bolivian National Anthem.
Source: DM

Viscarra Monje, Humberto, Bolivian composer; b.30 Mar 1898, Sorata, Dept. of La Paz, Bolivia; d.2 Sep 1971, La Paz. He studied at the National Cons. of Bolivia in La Paz with Pietro Bruno, and then he went to Europe, where he studied piano and composition with Giovanini, in Italy, and with Camille Decreus, in Paris, France. He returned to Bolivia and served as director of the Cons. of La Paz, 1930-32, and 1950-68. Director of the Academy of Fine Arts in Cochabamba, Bolivia.
Works: Music for piano based on Bolivian themes: Andante; Canción; Minueto Romántico; Rondino.
Sources: BB, DM, MMLA

Vivado Orsini, Ida, Chilean composer and pianist; b.Aug 1916, Tacna, Chile. She studied piano with E. Castrillón and A. Spikin Howard, and composition with Domingo Santa Cruz and Free Focke. President of the Asociación Nacional de Compositores from 1981 to 1987.

Works (selective list): *Tres Poemas y una Canción,* for voice and piano (1952); *Ay Huasa,* divertimento for voice and orch. (1972); *Picaresca,* for contralto and orch. (1977); piano pieces; songs.

Sources: IBCC, IEW, NGDWC

W

Wagner, Werner, Argentine composer and *impresario* (music manager) of German origin; b.3 Dec 1927, Cologne, Germany. He settled in Buenos Aires, Argentina, in 1937. He studied piano with Berta Sujovolsky, and harmony, counterpoint, fugue, orchestration, and composition with Jacobo Ficher in Buenos Aires. President of the Asociación de Jóvenes Compositores, 1965-66; member of the Unión de Compositores de la Argentina and of the Consejo Argentino de la Música. Cofounder and president of the Editorial Argentina de Compositores.
Works (selective list): *Orch.*: Suite No.1 for string orch. (1953); *Poema,* for violin (1953); Suite No.2 (1954); *Obertura de Concierto* (1961); *Rapsodia Argentina* (1962); Piano concerto (1965); *Concierto de Cámara* (1968); *Lamentaciones* (1968); *Música a 12* (1968); *Suite para Niños,* for string orch. (1970); *Improvisación Sinfónica* (1970); *Rapsodia,* for cello (1972-73); *Música Concertante,* for French horn and strings (1974); *Capricho* (1984); *La Tierra es Mía,* for chorus (1985); *Cánticos,* for soprano. Chamber music; choral music; piano pieces; songs.
Sources: CTA15, EMA, ISC, VMA

White, José Silvestre, Cuban violinist and composer; b.17 Jan 1836, Matanzas, Cuba; d.15 Mar 1918, Paris, France. He started music studies with his father, and then studied with José M. Román and Pedro Lecerf. He went to Paris where he furthered his violin studies with Jean D. Alard at the Paris Cons. In 1875, he returned to Havana, Cuba, and from there he went to Brazil where he served as a court musician for the Emperor Pedro II, and as director of the Imperial Cons. In 1889, he settled in Paris.
Works (selective list): Mass for two voices and orch.; Violin concerto; Quintet for flute, 2 violins, viola, and double bass; String quartet; Duo for 2 violins and piano; *Seis Estudios Brillantes,* for violin; *Bolero,* for violin and orch.; *Marcha Cubana; Danzas,* for piano; *Variaciones sobre un Tema Original,* for harpsichord and orch.; *La Bella Cubana;* church music; chamber music.
Bibl.: J.M. Troter, *Music and Some Highly Musical People,* Boston, 1880.
Sources: BB, DM, DMC

Widmer, Ernst, Brazilian composer and teacher of Swiss origin; b.25 Apr 1927, Aurau, Switzerland; d.? He studied at the Cons. of Zurich, Switzerland, with Willy Burkhard, Walter Frey, and Hoerler and graduated in 1950. He settled in Salvador, Bahia, Brazil, in 1956, at

the invitation of Hans Joachim Koellreutter. Professor at the Escola de Música da Univ. da Bahia, Brazil, where he also conducted the *Madrigal Group*, and in 1963, was appointed chief composition professor.
Works (selective list): *Hommages à Stravinsky, Frank Martin, and Bela Bartok,* for oboe and orch. (1960); *Quasars,* for orch. (1970); *Prismas,* for piano and orch. (1971); *ENTROncamentos SONoros,* for piano, 5 trombones, strings, and tape (1972); *Convergencias,* for string quartet (1973); *Trilema,* for vocal sextet; *Catalise,* for chamber orch.; *Concerto de Cámara,* for violin and string orch.; *Opus 127,* for violin and piano; *Opus 129,* for 2 flutes and chamber orch.; *Opus 130,* for string quartet; choral music; chamber music; songs.
Bibl.: L. Biriotti, *Grupo de Compositores de Bahia,* Montevideo, 1971.
Sources: GDM, HMB

Wilde, Eduardo Guillermo, Argentine composer and teacher; b.30 Nov 1942, Remedios de Escalada, Prov. of Buenos Aires, Argentina. He studied with Roberto Caamaño, Gerardo Gandini, Pedro Sáenz, Carlos Suffern, Juan F. Giacobbe, and Juan E. Martini at the Facultad de Música of the Argentine Catholic Univ. of Buenos Aires. Professor at the Facultad de Música of the Argentine Catholic Univ., the Provincial Cons. of Banfield, Prov. of Buenos Aires, Argentina, and the Facultad de Bellas Artes of the National Univ. of La Plata, Prov. of Buenos Aires.
Works (selective list): *Tres Movimientos,* for piano and orch. (1974); Concerto for 2 pianos and orch. (1975); *Esquemas,* for string orch. (1980); *Sectores*, for orch. (1983); chamber music; piano pieces; choral music; songs.
Sources: ISC, VMA

Wilensky, Osías, Argentine pianist, photographer, and composer; b.1933, Buenos Aires, Argentina. He studied piano with Vicente Scaramuzza in Buenos Aires. With a scholarship from the Williams Foundation, he went to the USA to study piano with Simon Barer at The Juilliard School of Music in New York City.
Works: Concerto for piano and orch.
Source: EMA

Wilkes, Josué Teófilo, Argentine musicologist and composer; b.8 Jan 1883, Buenos Aires, Argentina; d.10 Jan 1968, Buenos Aires. He studied harmony and composition with Alberto Williams and cello with Carlos Marchal at the National Cons. of Music in Carlos López Buchardo of Buenos Aires. Later he went to Europe and studied with Sergei Liapunov in Saint Petersburg, Russia, and with Vincent d'Indy at the Schola Cantorum in Paris, France. He returned to Buenos Aires in 1914, and for many years taught music in elementary schools. Later he taught music at a school in Quilmes, Prov. of Buenos Aires, Argentina, and at the Univ. of Litoral, Rosario, Prov. of Santa Fe, Argentina. He was particularly interested in Gregorian chant, colonial and indigenous music.

Works (selective list): *Operas: Noche Persa* (1916-20); *Por el Cetro y la Corona* (1924); *El Horóscopo* (1926-27). *La Cautiva,* secular oratorium (1930); *Humahuaca,* symphonic trilogy (1911-14); String octet; chamber music; songs. *Cincuenta Canciones Populares Cuyanas,* arranged and harmonized; *Cancionero Musical Rioplatense,* Argentine dances. *Books: Danzas Patrióticas Anónimas,* Buenos Aires, 1945; *Formas Musicales Rioplatenses,* Buenos Aires 1946; *Génesis Hispánica del Cancionero Musical Rioplatense,* Buenos Aires, 1947; *Los Senderos Sonoros de la Música Argentina, Popular y Culta,* Barcelona, 1948.
Sources: BB, DM, EMA, GDM

Williams, Alberto, Argentine composer, conductor, pianist, and teacher; b.23 Nov 1862, Buenos Aires, Argentina; d.17 Jun 1952, Buenos Aires. Father of Irma Williams. He started to study piano with Pedro Beck, and then entered the Music School of the Prov. of Buenos Aires, Argentina, where he studied harmony with Nicolás Bassi and piano with Luis Bernasconi. He went to Paris, France, with a scholarship from the Argentine government where he studied piano with Georges Mathías, harmony with Auguste Durand, counterpoint and ensemble with Benjamin Godard and Ernest Guiraud, and composition with César Franck and Charles de Bériot at the Paris Cons. He returned to Buenos Aires in 1889, and founded the Williams Cons. in 1893. President and vice president of the Comisión Nacional de Bellas Artes, president of the Asociación Argentina de Conciertos, and member of the National Academy of Fine Arts, all in Buenos Aires. He founded a music publishing company, *La Quena,* and also a magazine of that name.

Works (selective list): 9 symphonies (1907-1939); 2 concerto overtures (1889, 1892); *Poema de las Campanas,* symphonic poem (1913); *Poema de los Mares Australes,* symphonic poem (1933); *Las Milongas de la Orquesta* (1938); *Poema del Iguazú,* symphonic poem (1942); chamber music; piano pieces; choruses; songs. *Books: Teoría de la Música,* Buenos Aires.
Bibl.: Z.R. Lacoigne, *Alberto Williams: Músico Argentino,* Buenos Aires, 1942. *Homenajes a A. Williams, Containing Messages and Opinions of Musicians on his 80th birthday,* Buenos Aires, 1942. N. Slonimsky, *Alberto Williams: Father of Argentinian Music, Musical America,* 1942. V.A. Risolía, *A. Williams, Curriculum Vitae,* Buenos Aires, 1944.

Sources: BB, CA, CTA2, DM, EMA, GDM, MLA, MMLA

Williams, Irma, Argentine pianist and composer; b.Buenos Aires, Argentina; fl. first half of the 20th century. She studied at the Music Cons. of Buenos Aires with her father, Alberto Williams. Professor at the Music Cons. of Buenos Aires.
Works: Music for piano and for violin.
Source: DM

X

Xarau, Jaime, Argentine organist, bassoonist, and composer of Spanish origin; b.1843, Caldas de Montbúy, Catalonia, Spain; d.1918, Buenos Aires, Argentina. He studied at the Monastery of Montserrat, Spain. He settled in Buenos Aires in 1865, and in 1873, he was appointed organist at the Metropolitan Cathedral of Buenos Aires.
Works: Te Deum (1887); several salon pieces, such as *Lanceros del Club Social de Córdoba;* habaneras; tangos.
Source: EMA

Y

Yampolschi, Roseane, Brazilian pianist, singer, and composer; b.18 Jul 1956, Rio de Janeiro, Brazil. She studied stage direction and composition at the Federal Univ. of Rio de Janeiro, and voice privately with Ghyta Taghy.
Works: chamber music; songs.
Source: IEW

Z

Zamudio, Daniel, Colombian composer, organist, conductor, and folklorist; b.28 Aug 1887, Bogotá, Colombia; d.3 Jul 1952, Bogotá, Colombia. He started music studies with his father, Daniel Zamudio Torres, and later studied piano with Honorario Alarcón, and theory with Santos Cifuentes. Organist at the Iglesia de la Candelaria in Bogotá in 1920. He founded the Inst. Musical in Cartagena, Colombia, in 1926, and the *Orfeón* (male choral ensemble) *del Centro de Cultura Social* in Bogotá in 1936. Director of the Cons. of Tolima in Ibagué, Colombia, in 1936.
Works (selective list): *Marcha Triunfal,* for orch.; *Danza Oriental,* for orch.; *Canción de Cuna,* for cello and piano; *Romanza,* for violin and piano; *Vesperal,* for 8 mixed voices; *Stabat Mater,* for 4 mixed voices; *Misa de Nuestra Señora de la Candelaria* (1941); *Impresiones en Zipaquirá,* for piano; salon pieces; songs.
Bibl.: A. Pardo Tovar, *La Vida Ignorada y Fecunda de Daniel Zamudio, Micro,* Medellín, January 1944.
Sources: GDM, MMLA

Zanni, Rodolfo, Argentine conductor, music critic, and composer; b.1906, Buenos Aires, Argentina; d.1927, Buenos Aires. Self-taught musician. Music critic for the daily newspapers *Crítica* of Buenos Aires, and *El Orden* of Tucumán, Prov. of Tucumán, Argentina.
Works (selective list): *Rosmunda,* opera; *A la Aurora,* symphonic poem; *L'Uragano,* symphonic poem; *En la Selva,* symphonic poem; *Las Ninfas,* ballet; *Obertura Dramática,* for orch.; *Nerón,* overture for orch.; *Cleopatra,* overture for orch.; *Julio César,* overture for orch.; chamber music.
Source: EMA

Zapiola, José, Chilean musicologist and composer; b.beginning of the 19th century, 1807?, Chile; d.1885, Chile. He studied cello with Carlos Drewetche. In 1852, he founded the *El Semanario Musical,* the first weekly paper dealing with the development and dissemination of Chile's musical culture, together with Isidora Zegers and Francisco Oliva. Professor, vice director, and director of the Cons. Nacional de Música of Chile in Santiago de Chile.
Works: *Himno a San Martin; Christus,* oratorium; Mass for 3 voices; Requiem; *Domine ad Adjuvandum me; Himno a Yungay; Canción a la Bandera de Chile.*
Sources: DM, MMLA

Zavalía, Salustiano, Argentine composer, lawyer, and statesman; b.8 Jun 1808, Tucumán, Prov. of Tucumán, Argentina; d.16 Jan 1873, Tucumán. He studied with Cambeses.
Works: Salon pieces for piano, guitar, and flute, inspired in Argentine popular themes.
Sources: EMA, MMLA

Zegers y Montenegro, Isidora, Chilean composer of Spanish origin; b.1 Jan 1803, Madrid, Spain; d.14 Jul 1869, Santiago de Chile, Chile. She studied voice with Federico Massimino in Paris, France, as well as piano, harp, guitar, harmony, and composition. Founder of the Sociedad Filarmónica, center of the artistic movement in Chile. Honorary director of the Cons. Nacional de Música of Chile in Santiago de Chile. Together with José Zapiola and Francisco Oliva, she founded *El Semanario Musical,* a weekly paper and the first to deal with the development and dissemination of Chile's musical culture.
Works: Minuets and contredanses: La Flora; La Capricieuse; La Mercedes; La Penélope; La Badlam; La Pomone; La Madeleinette; La Clochette; La Adraste; La Tancreda; La Camille; Le Calife de Bagdad. Romances: La Coquette Fixée; Les Regrets d'une Bergère; L'Absence; Les Tombeaux Violés; Canción. Books: El Origen de la Opera en Francia.
Bibl.: E. Pereira Salas, *Los Orígenes del Arte Musical en Chile,* Santiago, 1941.
Sources: HMC, MMLA, NGDWC

Zimbaldo, Daniel, Argentine composer; b.Rosario, Prov. of Santa Fe, Argentina. He graduated from the Escuela de Música de la Facultad de Humanidades y Artes of the National Univ. of Rosario with a degree in composition. He also studied electronic music with Dante Grela. He worked in France at the Groupe de Musique Electroacustique in Bourges, and in Austria at the Inst. für Elektroakustik and Experimentalle Musik, in Vienna. Professor of counterpoint and musical form at the Cons. de Música de la Comunidad Autónoma of Madrid, Spain.
Works (selective list): *Tres Composiciones,* for 2 performers and flute (1975); *Dos Canciones,* for tenor, piano, and magnetic tape (1976); *A los que Llaman,* for flute, oboe, clarinet, bassoon, french horn, violin, viola, cello, organ, and synthesizer; *El Casamiento de la Esponja,* for flute (1978); *La Isla de los Muertos,* for violin, flute, piano, percussion, and magnetic tape (1980); *Composición en Desnudo,* for flute, cello, piano, and synthesizer (1981); *Variaciones sobre dos Personajes de Aldous B. Peil,* for orch. (1983); *La Incertidumbre del Silencio,* for guitar and piano (1983); *Naturaleza*

Muerta, electroacoustic music (1985); *Introspección,* for magnetic tape and instrumental group (1985); *Silencios y Densidades,* for piano and percussion (1987); *Omaggio a L. Dallapiccola,* for chamber orch. (1988); *La Llave de Cristal,* for piano and electronic sounds (1989); *Vietnam, el País del Sur,* music for a documentary series (1989).
Source: CMR

Zipoli, Domenico, Argentine organist and composer of Italian origin; b.15 Oct 1688, Prato da Toscana, Italy; d.2 Jan 1725, EAM (1726, DM), Córdoba, Prov. of Córdoba, Argentina. Organist at the Jesuit Church of Rome, Italy, in 1716. In the same year, he entered the Compañía de Jesús in Seville, Spain. He came to Buenos Aires in 1717, then went to Córdoba to become *maestro de capilla* (chapelmaster) at the Jesuit Church.
Works (selective list): Mass for 3-voice chorus, soloists, 2 violins, organ, and basso continuo; *Delle Offese a Vendicarmi,* cantata for soprano and basso continuo; *Credo,* for chorus; *Sonate d'Involatura per Organo o Cimbalo* (1716); *Sant'Antonio,* oratorium; *Santa Caterina Vergine e Martire,* oratorium; choruses; sacred music. *Books: Principia seu Elementa ad Bene Pulsandum Organum et Cimbalum* (1716).
Bibl.: L. Ayestarán, *Domenico Zipoli, el Gran Compositor y Organista Romano del 1700 en el Río de la Plata,* Montevideo 1941.
Sources: DM, EMA, MMLA

Zorzi, Juan Carlos, Argentine conductor and composer; b.1936, Buenos Aires, Argentina. He studied with Gilardo Gilardi and Mariano Drago at the National Cons. of Music Carlos López Buchardo of Buenos Aires. He went to Italy where he studied with Goffredo Petrassi and Franco Ferrara at the Academia Santa Cecilia of Rome, and the Academia Chigiana of Siena. He conducted major symphony orch. in different Argentine cities. He taught orch. conducting at the Inst. Superior de Arte of the Teatro Colón of Buenos Aires in 1970, until he was appointed permanent conductor of the Symphony Orch. of Chile in Santiago de Chile.
Works: (selective list): *Danza para Ahuyentar la Pena,* ballet (1956); *El Timbre,* opera (1970); *Requiem,* for soloists, chorus, and orch. (1957); *Adagio Elegíaco,* for strings (1964); *Variaciones Enigmáticas,* for orch. (1965); *Ludus,* for 6 instrumental groups (1966); Quintet for piano and strings; Concerto for orch.; *Fantasía,* for cello and orch.; chamber music; piano pieces; songs.
Sources: EMA, VMA

Zorzoli, Miguel Angel, Argentine composer; b.1959, Rosario, Province of Santa Fe, Argentina. He graduated from the Escuela de Música de la Facultad de Humanidades y Artes of the National Univ. of Rosario with a degree in composition. He studied with Dante Grela, Mariano Etkin, Alcides Lanza, and Carmelo Saitta. Founding member of the Asociación Santafesina de Compositores and member of the *Grupo Klank-Música Contemporánea* of Rosario. Professor at the Escuela Nacional de Música of Rosario, and in the Prov. of Buenos Aires, Argentina, at the Cons. Provincial de Música of Lincoln, and at the Cons. Provincial de Música of Junín.

Works: A-Tema y Variaciones, for piano (1983); *Artificios,* for clarinet, viola, synthesizer, and percussion (1984); *La Naranja Mecánica,* for flute (1985); *Delirios Celestes,* for flute and viola (1986); *Laberinto de Espejos,* for tenor saxophone, French horn, viola, electric guitar or violin, vibraphone, and piano (1988); *Lejanía de Niveles*, for symphony orch. (1988); *Destemple para un Músico y una Guitarra* (1990).
Source: CMR

Zozaya, Carlos, Mexican pianist, conductor, and composer; b.28 Jul 1893, San Luis de Potosí, Mexico; d.Buenos Aires, Argentina. He started music studies with his mother, and then continued to study piano with Joaquín Villalobos. In 1909, he entered the Cons. Nacional de Música de Mexico in Mexico City, where he studied piano with Carlos Meneses, harmony with Gustavo Campa, and counterpoint with Rafael J. Tello. In 1912, he traveled to Europe; in Paris, France, he studied harmony with Emile Pessard, counterpoint and fugue with Goupil, and piano with Isidor Philipp, and in Brussels, Belgium, he studied composition with Joseph Jongen. He later settled in Buenos Aires, and devoted himself to teaching piano, harmony, counterpoint, and composition.

Works (selective list): *Divertimento,* for flute, oboe, clarinet, horn, and bassoon (1935); 2 sonatas for piano (1936); Concerto for piano and orch. (1937); String quartet No.1 (1938); *Niobe,* ballet (1943); *Prometheus,* symphonic poem; Symphony.
Sources: DM, MMLA

Zubillaga, Luis, Argentine composer; b.1928, Buenos Aires, Argentina. He studied with Juan Carlos Paz. Since 1960 he has taught at the Inst. Pedagógico Experimental de Formación Docente and the Inst. de Arte Contemporáneo in Caracas, Venezuela, at the Escuela Superior de Música of the National Univ. of Tucumán, Prov. of Tucumán, Argentina, 1964-68, and at various public inst. of the Prov. of Buenos Aires. In 1969, he was granted a scholarship from the Centro de Altos Estudios Latinoamericanos of Buenos Aires.

Works (selective list): *Música para Elda,* for orch. (1966); *Ongilash,* for orch. (1968); *Nadas Vacías,* for voice, piano and percussion (1962); *Music for 10 Instruments* (1963); *Tres Piezas,* for 2 pianos (1965); *Direccionales,* for string quartet (1966); *Unidades II,* for 11 instruments (1966); *Noches,* for 6 instruments and an improvising ensemble (1970); chamber music; piano pieces.
Source: EMA

Zumaque Gómez, Francisco, Colombian composer; b.18 Jul 1945, Montería, Córdoba, Colombia. He studied instrumentation, band and orch. conducting, counterpoint, fugue, and composition with José Rozo Contreras, Olav Roots, and Fabio González Zuleta at the National Cons. of Music of Bogotá, Colombia. With a scholarship from the Colombian government, he studied in Paris, France, composition with Nadia Boulanger, Annette Dieudonné, and Michel Philippot.
Works (selective list): *Danza Sinfónica,* for orch. (1971); *Zynuth,* suite for orch. (1972); *Le Grand Diseur,* ballet (1973); chamber music; piano pieces; songs.
Source: CTA19

Zúñiga, Julián, Mexican composer and organist; b.19 Jun 1893, Querétaro, Mexico; d.? He studied organ and composition at the Escuela de Música Sagrada of Querétaro with Agustín González. Then he went to the USA, and continued his studies with Lucius Lescale. In 1906, he was *maestro de capilla* (chapelmaster) at the Church La Merced of Querétaro, and in 1921, he was appointed organist of the Basílica de Guadalupe in Mexico.
Works: Misa en Honor de Nuestra Señora de Guadalupe (1931); *Motet,* for 3 voices (1931); Sonata for organ (1931); *31 Misterios de la Virgen,* 2 collections (1931, 1937); *30 Misterios al Sagrado Corazón* (1931); *12 Cánticos para la Navidad* (1933); *Guadalupana,* poem for organ (1934); *Missa pro Defunctis,* for 2 voices and organ (1940); *Missa Beataes,* for 4 mixed voices (1943); *30 Preludios,* for organ or harmonium (1943).
Sources: DM, MMLA

COMPOSERS BY COUNTRY

ARGENTINA

Aguirre, Avelino
Aguirre, Julián
Ajubita, Marcelo
Alais, Juan
Albano, Enrique
Alberdi, Juan
Albornoz, Pedro
Alchourron, Rodolfo
Alcorta, Amancio
Alemann, Eduardo Armando
Allende, Juan José
Allica, Alfredo
Almouhian, Jean
Alsina, Carlos Roqué
Alvarez, Ignacio
Amat, José
Amelong, Juan Enrique
Amicola, Víctor Juan Carlos
André, José
Andrés, Alfredo
Angelis, Arturo de
Anido, María Luisa
Anton, Susana
Arandia Navarro, Jorge
Arena, José
Aretz de Ramón y Rivera, Isabel
Arias, Luis
Arizaga, José Tomás
Arizaga, Rodolfo
Astuni, Silvia
Axenfeld, Salvador

Balzanelli, Alberto
Bandoni, Alfredo
Barletta, Alejandro
Barón Superville, Susana
Barraquero, Carlos Washington

Bassi, Nicolás
Bautista, Julián
Belloc, Enrique
Bemberg, Hermann
Benavente, Regina
Bernasconi, Luis José
Berón, Saturnino Filomeno
Berrini, José Francisco
Bértola, Eduardo
Berutti, Arturo
Berutti, Pablo
Bimboni, Oreste
Biondo, Juan Carlos
Blamey Lafone, Ricardo Q.
Blarduni, Jorge
Boero, Felipe
Bologna, Nora
Bottiroli, José
Buligovich de Ventura, Rita
Burger, Carlos Reinaldo

Caamaño, Roberto
Cabero, Telésforo
Cabrera, Ana S. de
Calabró, Domingo
Calcagno, Elsa
Calligaris, Sergio
Calzadilla, Santiago
Campmany, Montserrat
Camps, Pompeyo
Cancián, Germán
Cardoso, Daniel Carlos
Carrique, Ana
Castro, José María
Castro, Juan José
Castro, Sergio de
Castro, Washington